A
PRONOUNCING
DICTIONARY

OF

AMERICAN ENGLISH

BY

JOHN SAMUEL KENYON, Ph.D.

Professor of the English Language in Hiram College;
Consulting Editor and Author of the Guide to Pronunciation,
Webster's New International Dictionary, Second Edition

AND

THOMAS ALBERT KNOTT, Ph.D.

Professor of English in the University of Michigan;
Editor of the Middle English Dictionary; General Editor,
Webster's New International Dictionary, Second Edition

MERRIAM-WEBSTER INC., PUBLISHERS
SPRINGFIELD, MASS., U.S.A.

To
Myra Pow Kenyon
and
Myra Powers Knott

This publication was in large part made possible by funds granted by Carnegie Corporation of New York. That Corporation is not, however, the author, owner, publisher, or proprietor of this publication, and is not to be understood as approving by virtue of its grant any of the statements made or views expressed herein.

PREFACE

More than ten years ago several scholars especially interested in American English suggested to one of the present editors the making of a phonetic pronouncing dictionary of the speech of the United States that might serve, both in the United States and elsewhere, the purposes served for Southern British English by Professor Daniel Jones's *English Pronouncing Dictionary.* About six years ago the editors became associated in this work.

Although as a pioneer in the field great credit must go to Professor Jones, who has placed all later lexicographers under inescapable obligation to him, our task is much different from his. He records the pronunciation of a limited and nearly homogeneous class of people in England in a type of speech identical with that of the editor himself. Our problem has been to record without prejudice or preference several different types of speech used by large bodies of educated and cultivated Americans in widely separated areas and with markedly different backgrounds of tradition and culture. Here let it be emphasized once for all that we have no prejudice whatever either for or against any of these varieties of American speech.

As the book is completed, we are keenly aware that only a beginning has been made, subject to later supplementation by other students of the field. On the whole, Southern speech has in the past received least attention. If we have failed to do it the full justice that was our intention, our failure must be laid in part to conflicting testimony, but mainly to the fact that this field has still largely to be investigated.

It was originally intended to include Canadian speech as one of the main regional divisions. A number of questionnaires were sent to Canada, and some correspondents took pains to send us excellent material (see acknowledgments below). The material was not, however, extensive enough to warrant full record of Canadian pronunciation, so that we have had to content ourselves with occasional references thereto. See mention of some Canadian variants (§118).

The scope of this work is limited. It is not intended as a source book for the study of American dialects. That work is being done by the *Linguistic Atlas of the United States and Canada.* It is our aim to record only what is rather vaguely called standard speech (see further, Introduction, §§1–2, 57–58, 76, 90). It is not our purpose even to try to exhaust that field. Almost certainly we have omitted many "good" pronunciations. Many of these are provided for in the Introduction by the lists of variants not fully recorded in the vocabulary (§§90 ff.). Recent studies and records of American speech have made it clear that there exists far greater variety than was formerly supposed in the speech of Americans of unquestioned cultivation and importance. Considering the actual facts of contemporary American pronunciation, the editors feel that on the whole they have been conservative in the variety recorded.

The vocabulary is intended to include the great body of common words in use in America. Besides, it includes a great many somewhat unusual words, inserted for a variety of reasons. Especial attention has been given to American proper names, though an exhaustive treatment of these is far beyond the scope of this work. The editors have had in mind the needs of college and university students, and have therefore included many names of history and literature likely to be encountered by them, as well as a large number of notes on various aspects of the English language. While foreign names are, strictly, outside the scope of a dictionary of American English, it is impossible to avoid including many often heard and used by Americans. The field of British place and personal names, tempting to one interested in pronunciation, has been little entered. A few of general interest must be included, and a considerable number of names of places in England whose pronunciation was verified locally by one of the editors have been inserted. Many of these names are of historical and traditional interest to Americans, and a great number have been transferred to America.

As in all trustworthy dictionaries, the editors have endeavored to base the pronunciations on actual cultivated usage. No other standard has, in point of fact, ever finally settled pronunciation. This book can be taken as a safe guide to pronunciation only insofar as we have succeeded in doing this. According to this standard, no words are, as often said, "almost universally mispronounced," for that is self-contradictory. For an editor the temptation is often strong to prefer what he thinks "ought to be" the right pronunciation; but it has to be resisted. For example, on etymological grounds the word *dahlia* "ought to be" ˈdɑljə; by traditional Anglicizing habits of English it should be ˈdeljə (as it is in England and often in Canada); as a fact, in America it is prevailingly ˈdæljə. In this case the variants are current enough to allow free choice; but in many cases the theoretically "right" pronunciation of a word is not even current.

In a work of this sort it is unavoidable to adopt certain devices to save space. These are explained in the Introduction (§§59 ff.). If the reader is now and then annoyed by these, he is asked to reflect that this makes possible the inclusion of far more material than would otherwise be possible, and on the whole makes this material easier for the reader to find.

A question naturally arises as to the relation of this work to the other dictionaries published by G. & C. Merriam Company. This book is published on a different basis from their other publications. For this book they act only as publishers and distributors, without editorial supervision. The Merriam Company is in no way responsible for any statements made in this book. That responsibility rests solely on the two authors.

The purpose of this dictionary is quite new in America. First, it deals solely with pronunciation. Even the entries are determined to a considerable extent by that purpose; for example, certain proper names of persons or places are selected, not for their intrinsic importance, but for some interest or problem in their pronunciation.

But the chief difference between this and the other Merriam dictionaries is that this is a dictionary of colloquial English, of the everyday unconscious speech of cultivated people—of those in every community who carry on the affairs and set the social and educational standards of those communities. *Webster's New International Dictionary, Second Edition* (Introduction, p. xii) thus defines its purpose in regard to pronunciation:

"In this edition, the style adopted for representation is that of formal platform speech—and this must be clearly remembered by consultants of the pronunciations here given. The omission of less precise pronunciations of familiar words does not, of course, indicate either that those pronunciations do not exist or that the editors of the dictionary refuse to recognize them. They do exist, and very naturally so when the occasion suits. . . . The recording of all such colloquial pronunciations of every separate word is not, however, possible in such a Dictionary as the *New International*. . . . The pronunciations contained in this Dictionary are not theoretical. They represent actual speech—the speech of cultivated users of English, speaking formally with a view to being completely understood by their hearers."

On the other hand, the pronunciation which the present editors intend to represent in this book is what has been called "easy English," "the speech of well-bred ease"—not slovenly or careless speech, nor, on the other hand, formal platform speech. Of course the great majority of English words are pronounced alike in colloquial and in formal speech, and much the largest part of the vocabulary will be found to have the same pronunciations in both books, and a large part of the differences will be the differences between colloquial and formal pronunciation. (For fuller discussion of the term *colloquial*, see Introduction, §§1–2.)

The *New International* does not attempt to represent the pronunciation of words as they occur in connected speech. The editors state, "It would be impossible, even were it desirable, to attempt to record the pronunciation of 'running speech,' that is, of words as elements in connected spoken discourse. . . . " The present book does not attempt to do this completely, could not, in fact, but in many instances does show modified pronunciations brought about by the phonetic effect of words on one another. Still more often the pronunciation of words as here indicated has been influenced, not so much by preceding or following sounds, as by rhythm, tempo, intonation, sense stress, etc. This will account for a goodly number of differences between the two books.

Another difference of aim lies in the scope of the two works. The *New*

International avowedly includes the pronunciation "of all parts of the English-speaking world" (p. xii), and puts little emphasis on regional differences within America. This book only occasionally and incidentally represents British or other non-American pronunciation of English, and represents as fully as practicable the main regional differences in America.

In some cases there are differences of accentuation that do not represent real inconsistencies. In the Guide to Pronunciation in the *New International* (p. xxxvi, col. 1) it is pointed out that a great many English words have no fixed accentuation, and that the accent shown in the vocabulary is merely one possible accentuation among others that may be equally correct. In this book, in some instances, the accentuation may depend on the colloquial character of the pronunciation. In some cases, too, differences of accentuation are due merely to a difference of practical policy. For instance, the *New International*, like many dictionaries, usually places no accent mark on a final third syllable though it may have secondary stress; thus the word *calabash* has only the first syllable marked, whereas in this book the mark of secondary accent is regularly placed on such words (ˈkælə͵bæʃ). This represents no difference of accentuation in the two books but merely a difference of practice, both methods being quite defensible.

The editors believe that this book is a natural complement to *Webster's New International Dictionary, Second Edition*. The *New International* fully recognizes the validity and importance of colloquial English speech. In its Guide to Pronunciation, §8, it states: "The most important of these different styles [of spoken English] is what may be called the cultivated colloquial, which has aptly been termed the style of well-bred ease. This is the most used of the standard styles, it is acceptable to every class of society, whether used by them or not. . . . " The *New International* provides for colloquial pronunciation by means of certain flexible symbols. Thus the Webster symbol ā̆ ('italic short *a*') "is used to suggest a variable sound... tending..., especially in familiar speech, to the neutral vowel [ə]" (Guide, §91). The symbol ĕ ('italic short *e*') serves a similar purpose: "In the great majority of everyday words, unaccented *e* before *n* or *l*, and in many words in other unaccented position, as in *quiĕt, propriĕty*, is obscured to the neutral vowel [ə] in colloquial speech" (Guide, §127). Thus our book gives chief emphasis to colloquial speech, while the *New International*, though fully recognizing it, treats it only as one among many features of the English language.

The *New International* has also given a table of the International Phonetic Alphabet for English with full illustration of its use: see especially Guide, pp. xxii–xxv, and thereafter throughout the Guide. The G. & C. Merriam Co. would therefore seem to be in a logical position to publish a dictionary of colloquial American speech in the symbols of the International Phonetic Alphabet. In the upshot, we believe that the actual differences in pronunciation between the Merriam-Webster dictionaries and this one are comparatively few.

The eager and extensive co-operation which the editors have received in the prosecution of this work has gone far beyond our expectation, and has placed us under great obligation to all who have shown interest and given help. First of all we wish to express our thanks to the Carnegie Corporation for a grant-in-aid through the University of Wisconsin to one of the editors, and to that University for inviting him to spend the year 1940–41 in residence to prosecute the work; to the Carnegie Corporation, on recommendation of the American Council of Learned Societies, for extending the grant-in-aid to supply this editor with an instructor at Hiram College in 1941–42 to enable him to give more time to the dictionary; to Dr. Margaret Waterman for competently fulfilling this appointment; and to Hiram College for granting him leave of absence in 1940–41.

We are under very particular obligations to Professor Miles L. Hanley, of the University of Wisconsin, for his hearty encouragement of the dictionary from its beginning, for placing at our disposal his great collection of rimes and spellings at the University of Wisconsin, and for many valuable suggestions; and to Mrs. Louise Hanley for much help in the utilization of the above-mentioned collections, and for many items of expert editorial advice.

We have profited greatly from the material thus far published by the *Linguistic Atlas of the United States and Canada*, and in addition we wish to thank the Directors for placing at our disposal a considerable amount of unpublished material from the collections covering parts of the Central West and of the South.

We thankfully acknowledge our great indebtedness, in common with all students of the English language, to the great *Oxford English Dictionary*.

Intimately associated as the editors have been with *Webster's New International Dictionary, Second Edition*, it is inevitable that we should be influenced by its standards and indebted to its materials in many ways. We gladly acknowledge the deepest obligations to it.

We are indebted to many individuals who have supplied us with details of information in their respective fields; among them, Professors Myles Dillon (Celtic), William Ellery Leonard (English), J. Homer Herriott (Spanish), Joseph L. Russo (Italian), Alexander A. Vasiliev (Russian), R-M. S. Heffner (German and Phonetics), Einar Haugen (Scandinavian), Casimir Zdanowicz (French), Dr. Karl G. Bottke (French and Italian), Mr. Charles E. Condray (Southern speech),—all at the University of Wisconsin; to Mr. Edward Artin, G. & C. Merriam Co., Springfield, Mass. (Eastern speech), Professor J. D. M. Ford, Harvard University (Italian), Professor Bernard Bloch, Brown University (Eastern speech), Dr. George L. Trager, Yale University (Linguistics), Dr. Ruth E. Mulhauser, Hiram

College (Romance Languages), Professor R. H. Stetson, Oberlin College (Syllabics).

To scholars and other competent observers in various parts of the United States and Canada we are under special obligation for material which they have collected on the speech of their regions, with valuable comment and in many instances with phonograph records: to Professors Katherine Wheatley, University of Texas; William A. Read, Louisiana State University; George P. Wilson, Woman's College, University of North Carolina; C. K. Thomas, Cornell University; C. M. Wise, Louisiana State University; Lee S. Hultzén, University of California at Los Angeles; W. Norwood Brigance, Wabash College; Mr. John Kepke, New York City; Mr. L. Sprague de Camp, New York City; Dr. Raven I. McDavid, Jr., South Carolina; Dr. Martin Joos, University of Toronto, Can.

We also wish to thank a number of scholars and teachers who responded to our request for advice on the editing (published in *American Speech*, XI, Oct. 1936, pp. 227–31), replying either in the columns of that journal or by private correspondence. Their suggestions were all carefully considered, and many of them were adopted.

To Mr. Donald A. Bird, Mr. Philip M. Davies, and Mrs. Wayne Caygill of the University of Wisconsin we are indebted for valuable assistance in preparing the manuscript.

In addition to those mentioned above, the editors also have to express lasting obligations to many more scholars, teachers, and others, who made transcriptions of their own and others' speech, and often supplied supplementary notes; in several instances also they sent phonograph records. To those whose names follow and a few that we had no means of identifying we extend our sincere thanks. Titles are omitted; and since it could not be significant without detailed explanation, address and locality are omitted. Suffice it to say that the informants were well distributed over the United States. Those from Canada are so marked.

Virgil A. Anderson, Phyllis B. Arlt, A. M. Barnes, L. L. Barrett, A. C. Baugh, J. F. Bender, C. L. Bennet (Can.), E. B. Birney (Can.), Morton W. Bloomfield (Can.), Hilda Brannon, Alexander Brede, Jr., Christine Broome, William F. Bryan, Donald C. Bryant, C. H. Carruthers (Can.), Philip H. Churchman, Roy B. Clark, T. F. Cummings, Edwin B. Davis, J. de Angulo, L. R. Dingus, Sarah Dodson, Julia Duncan, Norman E. Eliason, Bert Emsley, E. E. Ericson, Paul H. Flint, Frances A. Foster, Elizabeth F. Gardner, James Geddes, Jr., Erma M. Gill, W. Cabell Greet, Louis A. Guerriero, Harold F. Harding, Harry W. Hastings, Grace E. Ingledue, Annie S. Irvine, Cary F. Jacob, Joseph Jones, W. Powell Jones, Claude E. Kantner, Clifford Anne King, C. A. Knudson, C. A. Lloyd, C. M. Lotspeich, William F. Luebke, Klonda Lynn, T. O. Mabbott, John C. McCloskey, Cassa L. McDonald, James B. McMillan, Kemp Malone, Edward W. Mammen, Albert H. Marckwardt, E. K. Maxfield, R. J. Menner,

Alice W. Mills, George Neely, T. Earl Pardoe, Gordon E. Peterson, Holland Peterson (Can.), Louise Pound, E. G. Proudman, Robert L. Ramsay, W. Charles Redding, Loren D. Reid, Stuart Robertson, J. C. Ruppenthal, I. Willis Russell, C. Richard Sanders, Edwin F. Shewmake, Loretta Skelly, Gordon W. Smith, Paul L. Stayner, J. M. Steadman, Jr., W. J. Stevens (Can.), Everett F. Strong, Morris Swadesh, C. H. Thomas, Argus Tresidder, E. H. Tuttle, W. Freeman Twaddell, Charles H. Voelker, Chad Walsh, Lois P. Ware, Raymond Weeks, Walter H. Wilke, Rudolph Willard, A. M. Withers, Robert Withington.

The typesetting and electrotyping of this book were done by the George Banta Publishing Company, of Menasha, Wisconsin. To all members of its staff who were concerned in any way with its making, the editors express their grateful appreciation.

The editors feel that the making of the dictionary has been a co-operative enterprise, and if it has value, this is in large measure due to expert help from many voluntary contributors; for its defects the editors hold themselves solely responsible.

Vachel Lindsay Room, Hiram College   John S. Kenyon
          September, 1943   Thomas A. Knott

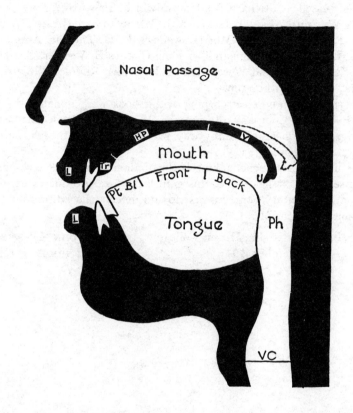

CONVENTIONALIZED DIAGRAM OF THE SPEECH ORGANS

(Reprinted by permission from Kenyon's *American Pronunciation*, 8th ed.)

LL=Lips. Pt=Tongue Point. Bl=Tongue Blade. Tr=Teethridge. HP=Hard Palate. V=Velum (soft palate): black: lowered, or open; dotted: raised, or closed. U=Uvula. Ph=Pharynx. VC=Vocal Cords.

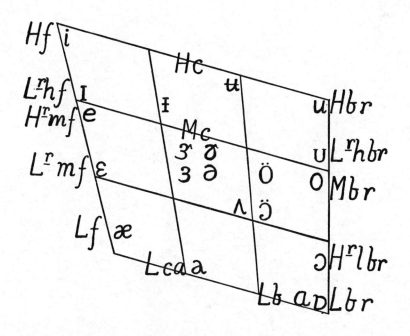

CHART OF THE TONGUE POSITIONS OF THE VOWELS

(Reproduced, with slight changes, from Kenyon's *American Pronunciation*, 8th edition, by permission.)

The left of the figure represents the front of the mouth

Hf = High-front	Hc = High-central	Hbr = High-back round
L^{r}hf = Lower high-front		L^{r}hbr = Lower high-back round
H^{r}mf = Higher mid-front	Mc = Mid-central	Mbr = Mid-back round
L^{r}mf = Lower mid-front		H^{r}lbr = Higher low-back round
Lf = Low-front	Lca = Low-central advanced	Lbr = Low-back round
		Lb = Low-back

INTRODUCTION

THE STYLE OF SPEECH REPRESENTED

§1. It is the purpose of this dictionary to show the pronunciation of cultivated colloquial English in the United States. The meaning of the word *colloquial* is sometimes misunderstood. A common misunderstanding is that in dictionaries the label *Colloq.* attached to a word or pronunciation brands it as inferior, and therefore to be avoided.

Webster's New International Dictionary, Second Edition, thus defines *colloquial:* "Pertaining to, or used in, conversation, esp. common and familiar conversation; conversational; hence, unstudied; informal; as, *colloquial* phrases or pronunciations; specif., of a word or a sense or use of a word or expression, acceptable and appropriate in ordinary conversational context, as in intimate speech among cultivated people, in familiar letters, in informal speeches or writings, but not in formal written discourse (*flabbergast; go slow; harum-scarum*). Colloquial speech may be as correct as formal speech. 'Every educated person speaks his mother tongue in at least two ways, and the difference between the dignified and the *colloquial* style is considerable.' —G. L. Kittredge." It should be noted that the illustrative words do not refer to pronunciation but to diction, though the definition includes pronunciation.

The definition in the *Oxford Dictionary* is concise and also adequate. Though it does not mention pronunciation, "etc." may safely be taken to include it: "Of words, phrases, etc.: Belonging to common speech; characteristic of or proper to ordinary conversation, as distinguished from formal or elevated language. (The usual sense.)".

Definitions of *colloquial* that only concern choice of words and give as examples only oaths or slang are perhaps in part responsible for some of the popular misunderstanding of the term.

A less frequent, but still not uncommon error is the confusion of *colloquial* with *local*, the assumption that a *colloquialism* is a *localism*, and so to be avoided.

Another not uncommon confusion is to regard *colloquial* English as the opposite of *standard* English (*standard* being confused with *formal* or *literary*). There is standard colloquial English and standard formal or literary English, as there is nonstandard colloquial and nonstandard formal English. As regards pronunciation, one kind of nonstandard formal English is the artificial type in which vowels that are normally unaccented are pronounced with their accented sounds, in which articles (*a, an, the*), prepositions (*to, from, of*), and other normally unstressed particles are pronounced with their emphatic forms instead, in which the tempo and intonation are not those of traditional living speech, in which abnormal accentuation and loudness are practiced, together with similar distortions that detract from unostentatious sincerity.

The accepted meaning of *colloquial* is to be found in the work of such linguistic scholars as Professor Henry Cecil Wyld, of Oxford, whose *History of Modern Colloquial English* deals with the unstudied speech and familiar correspondence of the cultivated classes, and reminds us of the importance both to literature and to general culture of this central core of the English language. Says Professor Wyld, "The style of literary prose is alive and expressive, chiefly insofar as it is rooted in that of colloquial utterance.... The style of Literature is rooted in the life and conversation of the age."[1] Similarly, the American scholar and poet William Ellery

---

[1] *History of Modern Colloquial English,* London 1925, pp. 157, 188.

Leonard: "In general every good colloquialism is possible in good prose (or verse), for quite rightly good prose (or verse) is becoming more and more a skillful adaptation of the vigorous, compact, racy idiom of the best spoken speech."[2]

§2. Colloquial pronunciation is here treated as the conversational and familiar utterance of cultivated speakers when speaking in the normal contacts of life and concerned with what they are saying, not how they are saying it. There are, of course, different styles of colloquial, from that of the everyday contacts of family life to the somewhat less familiar contacts of social and business or professional life. The variant pronunciations of the same word frequently shown will often reflect the different styles of the colloquial. In all cases of words that are not formal per se, unstudied everyday speech is the basis. It is of course true that the majority of words in general use are the same for colloquial as for formal language, and are pronounced alike in both styles.

The editors are aware that the attempt to represent in fairly accurate symbols the everyday speech of the cultivated is likely now and then to cause surprise and to tempt criticism. The average observer has not been trained to observe speech on the wing, and is too apt to be influenced by unconscious habitual association with spelling forms. No experience is commoner with trained observers than to hear certain pronunciations in the very statements in which the critic is denying them.

It must also be remembered that not all words are of a colloquial nature. Words not in colloquial use have, properly speaking, no colloquial pronunciation. Thus the word *exorcise* does not often occur in conversation. Its pronunciation is therefore what it would be in formal context, with the -*or*- fully sounded. If it should become a popular word, it would sound just like *exercise*. So the word *adhibit*, not being colloquial, receives the full sound of the first vowel as in *add*, while in the more popular word *advise* the first vowel is normally obscured.

THE PHONETIC ALPHABET

§3. Pronunciation in this dictionary is indicated by the alphabet of the International Phonetic Association (IPA). These symbols and the pronunciations represented by them invariably appear in **boldface type.** More than half of these are the ordinary letters of the English alphabet or familiar variations of them.

Each symbol stands for only one speech sound, and each speech sound has only one symbol to represent it. In accord with the practice of many British and American users of this alphabet the accented sounds ʌ, ɜ, ɝ are considered to be separate speech sounds from the unaccented sounds ə and ɚ. Diphthongs are regarded as single sounds and their symbols (aɪ, aʊ, ɔɪ, etc.) as single symbols. The same is true of tʃ, dʒ.

In using the phonetic alphabet the reader must be careful to give only the one designated sound to those letters which in ordinary spelling represent more than one sound. Thus the symbol g has only the sound in *get* gɛt, never that in *gem* dʒɛm; s has only the sound in *gas* gæs, never that in *wise* waɪz or that in *vision* ˈvɪʒən. The dotted i has only the sound in *machine* məˈʃin, never that in *shin* ʃɪn; ordinary e always has the sound in *gate* get, never that in *met* mɛt. Below is the list of symbols with key words. The notes after the table give fuller information and additional symbols. The accent mark (ˈ) always precedes the syllable accented.

VOWELS

Symbol	Spelling	Spoken Form	Symbol	Spelling	Spoken Form
i	bee	**bi**	ʊ	full	**fʊl**
ɪ	pity	**ˈpɪtɪ**	u	tooth	**tuθ**
e	rate	**ret**	ɝ	further	**ˈfɝˑðɚ** *accented syllable only, r's sounded*
ɛ	yet	**jɛt**			
æ	sang	**sæŋ**	ɜ	further	**ˈfɜðə** *accented syllable only, r's silent*
a	bath	**baθ** *as heard in the East, between æ (sang) and ɑ (ah)*	ɚ	further	**ˈfɝˑðə** *unaccented syllable only, r's sounded*
ɑ	ah	**ɑ**	ə	further	**ˈfɜðə** *unaccented syllable only, r's silent*
	far	**fɑr**		custom above	**ˈkʌstəm** *unaccented syllable* **əˈbʌv**
ɒ	watch	**wɒtʃ** *between ɑ (ah) and ɔ (jaw)*			
ɔ	jaw	**dʒɔ**	ʌ	custom above	**ˈkʌstəm** *accented syllable* **əˈbʌv**
	gorge	**gɔrdʒ**			
o	go	**go**			

DIPHTHONGS

aɪ	while	**hwaɪl**	ju	using	**ˈjuzɪŋ**
aʊ	how	**haʊ**		fuse	**fjuz**
ɔɪ	toy	**tɔɪ**	ɪu	fuse	**fɪuz**

CONSONANTS

Symbol	Spelling	Spoken Form	Symbol	Spelling	Spoken Form
p	pity	**ˈpɪtɪ**	dʒ	jaw	**dʒɔ**
b	bee	**bi**		edge	**ɛdʒ**
t	tooth	**tuθ**	m	custom	**ˈkʌstəm**
d	dish	**dɪʃ**	m̩	keep 'em	**ˈkipm̩**
k	custom	**ˈkʌstəm**	n	vision	**ˈvɪʒən**
g	go	**go**	n̩	Eden	**ˈidn̩**
f	full	**fʊl**	ŋ	sang	**sæŋ**
v	vision	**ˈvɪʒən**		angry	**ˈæŋˑgrɪ**
θ	tooth	**tuθ**	l	full	**fʊl**
ð	further	**ˈfɝˑðɚ**	l̩	cradle	**ˈkredl̩**
s	sang	**sæŋ**	w	watch	**wɒtʃ**
z	using	**ˈjuzɪŋ**	hw	while	**hwaɪl**
ʃ	dish	**dɪʃ**	j	yet	**jɛt**
ʒ	vision	**ˈvɪʒən**	r	rate	**ret**
h	how	**haʊ**		very	**ˈvɛrɪ**
tʃ	watch	**wɒtʃ**		far	**fɑr**
	chest	**tʃɛst**		gorge	**gɔrdʒ**

ACCENT MARKS

§4. The mark ' above the line and before a syllable indicates that that syllable has the principal accent, as in *action* 'ækʃən. The corresponding mark ˌ below the line and before a syllable indicates that that syllable has an accentuation somewhat weaker than the main one, as in *acrobat* 'ækrəˌbæt, *Aberdeen* ˌæbɚ'din, *shoemaker* 'ʃuˌmekɚ. For discussion of accent, see §§48–54.

LENGTH MARK

§5. The colon (:) after a vowel or a consonant symbol indicates that its sound is prolonged. Thus the form sæːnd beside sæt means that the æ sound in *sand* is longer than in *sat;* and the form dʒɔɪs: means that in one pronunciation of the plural *joists* (with omitted t) the s is longer than it is in *rejoice* rɪ'dʒɔɪs. In the vocabulary the length sign is used only occasionally or in certain classes of words. See fuller discussion of length at §55.

NOTES ON THE SYMBOLS

§6. **ɪ.** The symbol ɪ is used for accented or unaccented syllables. Though the accented and unaccented vowels in *pity* 'pɪtɪ, *sitting* 'sɪtɪŋ, *visit* 'vɪzɪt, etc., are sometimes different in quality, the differences are here ignored, since they vary with different speakers and with the different sounds that precede or follow. This accords with common practice in transcription.

When final, the unaccented vowel in *pity* 'pɪtɪ and similar words varies with different speakers in America from a sound like the ɪ in *bit* bɪt, or like the first ɪ in 'pɪtɪ, to a sound that approaches the i in *bee* bi. See the ending *-y* in the vocabulary.

§7. **e.** The vowel in *rate* ret and other words with "long *a*" is very often (but by no means always) a diphthong (gliding from one vowel to another in the same syllable) eɪ, ɛɪ, ɛe, or the like. On linguistic principles the one symbol e properly stands for all varieties of the sound (whether diphthong or not). The variants never distinguish words otherwise alike.

§8. **ɛ.** The symbol ɛ is used not only for words like *yet* jɛt, *send* sɛnd, but also for one type of pronunciation of the vowel sound in *there* ðɛr, *swear* swɛr, *air* ɛr, as pronounced by many. When thus followed by r, the ɛ sound is usually a little more like the æ in *sang* sæŋ than is the ɛ in *yet* jɛt, *send* sɛnd. Many speakers pronounce æ in such words in both America and England. Both pronunciations are given in the vocabulary (*there* ðɛr, ðær).

§9. **æ.** This ligature is a unit symbol (not two letters) standing for a single simple vowel sound. It was the letter used in Anglo-Saxon times for the same sound in Old English as in present English *sat* (OE *sæt*). Originally combined from the Latin letters *a* and *e* (since its sound lay between the two Latin sounds), its present value in the IPA alphabet is the same as in its oldest use in English.

§10. **a.** This vowel sound, not in general use in America as a whole, is about midway between the vowel of *sang* sæŋ and the vowel of *ah* ɑ, *father* 'fɑðɚ. It is often heard in New England and New York City in such words as *ask* ask, *chaff* tʃaf, *bath* baθ (which are also there pronounced æsk, tʃæf, bæθ or ɑsk, tʃɑf, bɑθ). It commonly begins the diphthongs in *while* and *how*. The vowel a is an important sound in French, Spanish, and other foreign languages, and is common in cultivated Northern British, Scottish, Anglo-Irish, and Canadian. The symbol a must always be carefully distinguished from ɑ. For the use of a in Eastern American, see §§102 f.

§11. ɑ. This is the "broad *a*" sound in *ah* ɑ, *far* fɑr, *father* ˈfɑðɚ in most of America. It is also used by the majority of Americans in "short *o*" words such as *top* tɑp, *got* gɑt, *fodder* ˈfɑdɚ, in which some speakers pronounce ɒ.

§12. ɒ. The symbol ɒ represents a vowel not in universal American use. It is the historical "short *o*" now generally used in England in words like *top* tɒp, *got* gɒt, *fodder* ˈfɒdə, by many Easterners and Southerners, and in certain kinds of words by many speakers in all parts of the country. It is a sound about midway between ɑ in *ah* and ɔ in *wall*. It may be approximated by trying to sound ɑ in *ah* while (without moving the tongue) rounding the lips for ɔ in *wall*. As with a, so with ɒ, there is no key word that will convey to all Americans its exact sound. The key word *watch*, here used, frequently is spoken with ɒ in all parts of America, but it is also often pronounced wɑtʃ, with ɑ as in *ah*, and wɔtʃ, with ɔ as in *wall*.

§13. o. Like e, the symbol o represents either a simple vowel or a diphthong (oʊ, öʊ, ɔʊ, etc.). For the same reason stated at e (§7 above) the symbol o is used for both the simple vowel and the diphthong. For ö see *-ow* in the vocabulary.

§14. ʊ, u. The small capital ʊ (*full* fʊl) and the lower-case u (*tooth* tuθ) are to be carefully distinguished from each other.

§15. ɝ. The symbol ɝ represents the accented form of the so-called "*r*-colored" vowel used in the first syllable of *further* ˈfɝðɚ by those who do not "drop their *r*'s." In current spelling it is spelt with a vowel letter followed by the letter *r* (*word, fur, term, firm, earn*). But in sound this vowel ɝ is not followed by r; it is a vowel made while the tongue is at the same time holding the position for r. Such vowels are common in many types of English. The consonantal r sound that formerly followed the vowel (hence the present spelling) long ago merged with the preceding vowel and disappeared as a separate sound, though its effect is still heard in the *r*-coloring of the vowel. The simple proof of the nature of the present sound is that the vowel cannot be pronounced separately from the r without producing a quite different sound, whereas this can easily be done with, say, the ɑ and r of *farm*.

§16. з. The symbol з represents the corresponding vowel in the word *further* of those who "drop their *r*'s," the tongue for this vowel з being in the same general central position in the mouth as for ɝ, but without the simultaneous adjustment of the tongue for the *r*-coloring (usually the elevation of the tip). For those accustomed to pronounce ɝ a fairly good з can be made by trying to pronounce ɝ in *bird* with the point of the tongue placed against the backs of the lower teeth, and with the jaw a trifle more closed than for the vowel ʌ in *sun*. This з is often followed by r, as in *furry* ˈfɜ·rɪ, from *fur* fз. While the majority of Americans pronounce *fur* fɝ, and *furry* ˈfɝ·ɪ, most British and many eastern and southern Americans pronounce *fur* fз, and *furry* ˈfɜ·rɪ. But in words like *hurry*, which is not derived from a simple form *hur* as *furry* is from *fur*, three American pronunciations are common,—ˈhɝ·ɪ, ˈhɜ·rɪ, ˈhʌ·rɪ, the last being least frequent and tending to become ˈhɜ·rɪ or ˈhɝ·rɪ.

§17. ɚ. The symbol ɚ is the unaccented *r*-colored vowel, like ɝ inseparable from its *r* quality, as pronounced by those who do not "drop their *r*'s." The two symbols ɝ and ɚ are formed from the IPA symbols з and ə (as used, e.g., in the word *Herbert* ˈhзbət in Ida C. Ward's *Phonetics of English*, Cambridge, Engd. 1939, p. 108), by attaching the hook of retroflexion (*r*-coloring) used by the IPA on the consonants s, z, t, d, etc. (*Le Maître Phonétique*, Jan.–Mar. 1942, inside front cover). This makes easy the comparison of such words as *Herbert* as pronounced by those who "drop their *r's*" (ˈhɜbət) and by those who sound them (ˈhɜ˞bɚt), showing at a glance the phonetic relation between such words in the two types of speech (*further* ˈfɜðɚ—ˈfɜ˞ðɚ, *perverse* pəˈvɜs—pɚˈvɜ˞s, *bird* bɜd—bɜ˞d, *over* ˈovə—ˈovɚ), all four sounds ɜ, ɜ˞, ə, ɚ being vowels, none of them here followed by r.

§18. ə. The symbol ə represents the "neutral vowel," or "schwa" ʃwɑ, heard in the un-accented syllable of *custom* ˈkʌstəm, or, as just shown above, in that of *further* from those who "drop their *r's*" (ˈfɜðə). With many such speakers the ə of ˈfɜðə is not exactly like the ə of ˈkʌstəm, but is commonly regarded as the same speech sound.

§19. ʌ. This represents the accented vowel of *custom* ˈkʌstəm, *above* əˈbʌv, *undone* ʌnˈdʌn. In ʌnˈdʌn the first syllable is not quite without accent, but has sufficient accent (though not marked) to make it audibly more prominent than the *un-* of *unless* (spoken colloquially) ənˈlɛs. Compare *unlace* ʌnˈles with *unless* ənˈlɛs, or *undone* ʌnˈdʌn with *and done* in the phrase *over and done with* ˈovɚ ənˈdʌn wɪð, or *untilled* with *until* in *This land was untilled until now* ʌnˈtɪld ənˈtɪl nau. The prefix *un-* is commonly pronounced ʌn- with more or less subordinate accent. See *un-* in the vocabulary.

§20. ai, au. For regional varieties of these diphthongs see *Variants* §§105–108.

§21. ju. This is a rising diphthong—the last part being stressed more than the first. It begins with the glide consonant j (as in *yet* jɛt) and ends with the vowel u (as in *tooth* tuθ). ju would not be separately listed as a vowel symbol, being a consonant plus vowel, except for comparison with the diphthong ɪu (see below), with which it often alternates, for ju is of the same nature as other combinations of consonantal j plus a vowel (as in *ye* ji, *yea* je, *yaw* jɔ, *yet* jɛt, etc.) or of consonantal w plus a vowel (*we* wi, *way* we, *woe* wo, etc.).

§22. ɪu. This is either a falling diphthong (first element stressed, as in the diphthongs ai, au, ɔi), or a level-stress diphthong, both elements being about equally prominent. If the last element becomes more prominent, then ɪu becomes ju, as it did historically in such words as *use* juz. The form ɪu is heard from many speakers in such words as *fuse* fɪuz, where others pronounce ju (fjuz). For the occurrence of ɪu in America, see *Variants* §109.

ɪu is a modified form of ɪu, occurring chiefly as an alternative to u or ju that has been re-duced from u or ju by lack of stress (*superb* suˈpɝb, sɪuˈpɝb, sjuˈpɝb) or before r (*curious* ˈkjurɪəs, ˈkɪurɪəs). The phonetic surroundings lead without effort to the modified ɪu and ju.

§23. ŋ. It should be noted that this sound is a simple, single sound, which cannot be di-vided. It is made by contact of the tongue back with the velum, as the simple sound n is made by contact of the tongue point with the upper teethridge. The usual spelling with two letters (*ng*) has sometimes led to an impression that ŋ is a combination sound. It is also spelt with *n* only (*angry* ˈæŋ·grɪ, *ink* ɪŋk). When speakers "drop their *g's*" (as in *runnin'* for *running*), they drop no sound, but they replace the tongue-back nasal ŋ (ˈrʌnɪŋ) with the tongue-point nasal n (ˈrʌnɪn).

§24. m̩, n̩, l̩. These are called syllabic consonants because they form syllables without any vowel whatever, either alone (*stop 'em* ˈstɑp·m̩, *button* ˈbʌt·n̩, *saddle* ˈsæd·l̩) or with other con-sonants (*opened* ˈop·m̩d, *buttoned* ˈbʌt·n̩d, *saddled* ˈsæd·l̩d). These and such forms as *keep 'em* ˈkipm̩, *Eden* ˈidn̩, *cradle* ˈkredl̩ have no vowel in the unaccented syllable because, for m̩, the lips continue closed throughout pm̩, and, for n̩ and l̩, the tongue point remains in contact with the teethridge throughout tn̩ and dl̩. Between some other consonants, as sn̩ (*lessen*

ˈlɛsn̩), zn̩ (*reason* ˈrizn̩), pl̩ (*apple* ˈæpl̩) the transition to the second consonant is so quick, or the opening of the speech organs is so slight, that no vowel intervenes.

All of the foregoing forms can also be uttered with the schwa vowel ə plus a nonsyllabic consonant (ˈkipəm, ˈidən, ˈbʌtən, ˈkredəl, ˈlɛsən, ˈrizən, ˈæpəl), but in some of these and many others the pronunciation with ə is either not accepted in good use, or is a mark of formal, noncolloquial pronunciation. On this point see further, *Variants* §114.

The remaining nasal consonant ŋ can also be syllabic, as in the colloquial *I can go* ˌaɪkŋ̩ˈgo. Here the tongue back remains in contact with the velum throughout the k and the ŋ. The syllabic marker is sometimes placed over the symbol ŋ, but is here not deemed necessary, since syllabic ŋ is not frequent, and ŋ is never syllabic in the same position in which it is nonsyllabic. It is always syllabic after a consonant (ˌaɪkŋ̩ˈgo, ˈbægŋ̩ˈbægɪdʒ, ˈmekŋ̩) and never syllabic after a vowel (sɪŋ, ˈbægɪŋ, ˈmekɪŋ).

As ˈæpl̩ and ˈæpəl show the alternation between a syllabic consonant (l̩) and schwa plus the same consonant (əl), so syllabic consonants may alternate with nonsyllabic consonants, but here sometimes with a difference of meaning: *help 'em eat* ˈhɛlpm̩ ˈit (3 syllables)—*helpmeet* ˈhɛlpˌmit (2 syls.); *ordinance* ˈɔrdn̩əns (3 syls.)—*ordnance* ˈɔrdnəns (2 syls.); *double it* ˈdʌbl̩ ɪt (3 syls.)—*doublet* ˈdʌblɪt (2 syls.). Such alternation is often shown in the vocabulary in connection with the ending *-ing;* thus *blazoning* is pronounced either ˈblez·n̩·ɪŋ or ˈblez·nɪŋ; *handling* is either ˈhæn·dlɪŋ or ˈhæn·dl̩·ɪŋ. The one deemed most usual in colloquial speech is given first; but often there is little choice, the form depending on style of speech.

§25. **hw.** Linguists are disagreed whether **hw** should be regarded as a single speech sound or as two—**h** followed by **w.** When regarded as a single phoneme it is often transcribed with inverted w (ʍ). Here the symbol **hw** is used for the sound spelt *wh* in words like *while* **hwaɪl.** For variation in pronunciation of words spelt with *wh* see *Variants* §113.

§26. **r.** In this book the symbol **r** is used for the consonant, as in *rate* **ret,** *cradle* ˈkredl̩, where it is parallel in phonetic structure to **w** in *wait* **wet,** *twain* **twen,** and to **j** in *Yale* **jel,** *cue* **kju,** that is, a glide consonant or semivowel before a vowel in the same syllable. In addition, the symbol **r** is here used for the sound in *very* ˈvɛrɪ, *far* **fɑr,** *gorge* **gɔrdʒ,** which some regard as a nonsyllabic vowel forming a diphthong with the preceding vowel. This is sometimes expressed by the vowel symbol ɚ (ˈvɛɚɪ, fɑɚ, gɔɚdʒ), which is defensible on laboratory evidence. But the ends of simplicity seem better served to confine the use of ɚ to representing the *syllabic* vowel, so that whenever ɚ occurs in this book it always represents a syllable, either alone, as in *better* ˈbɛt·ɚ, or with a consonant, as in *perceive* pɚˈsiv. Thus the word *flower*, which is pronounced either with two syllables or with one, can be transcribed with two (ˈflauɚ) or with one (flaur). In the speech of those who "drop their *r*'s" the two-syllable pronunciation is shown by separating the syllables with a centered period (ˈflau·ə) and the one-syllable pronunciation without it (flauə). Here the accent mark also implies more than one syllable, but would not help to distinguish three-syllable *cornflower* ES ˈkɔənˌflau·ə from two-syllable *corn flour* ˈkɔənˌflauə, or three-syllable *flower cup* ˈflau·əˌkʌp from two-syllable *flour cup* ˈflauəˌkʌp. In current speech (and often in poetry) all such words as *flower, flour, higher, hire* have either two syllables or one. In this dictionary, as a rule the number of syllables indicated follows the conventional spelling form.

The symbol **r** is also used between ə and a vowel in such a position as in *flattery* ˈflætərɪ, which might (less conveniently) be regarded as *flatter* ˈflætɚ plus -*y*-ɪ, or by those who "drop their *r*'s" as ˈflætə plus -rɪ. The slight difference in sound between ˈflætɚ·ɪ and ˈflætə·rɪ depends on where the last syllable begins, and is here disregarded.

In a few cases ɚ is used to represent the speech of those who "drop their *r*'s," as in *overact* ˌovɚˈækt, where all speakers would normally sound the *r* before a vowel.

Besides the usual American sounds of **r,** the symbol **r** indicates certain different sounds in some varieties of English and in foreign languages; as (1) the tongue-point trill (vibration against the upper teethridge) in Scottish, Anglo-Irish, Italian, Spanish, and sometimes German and French; (2) the uvular trill (vibration of the uvula against the back of the tongue) found in French and German; and (3) the uvular fricative, or "scrape," found in French and German. These varieties of **r** have special IPA symbols not needed in this book, where they are all represented by **r.**

ADDITIONAL PHONETIC SYMBOLS

In addition to the symbols given above, a number of symbols are used to express less common English sounds and the sounds of foreign languages recorded in the dictionary. The descriptions of the foreign sounds are only approximate, and are intended for those not familiar with the foreign sounds. The symbols not here described, when used to express foreign pronunciations, have approximately the same sounds as in English words.

§27. **x.** This stands for the consonant in German *ich* ɪx, *ach* ɑx, Scottish *loch* lɒx, Spanish *junto* ˈxunto, an "open" **k** sound made by forcing voiceless breath through a loose contact of the back of the tongue with the soft palate (velum) at the same point where a firm contact would stop the breath and make the **k** sound. A separate symbol (ç) is sometimes used to express the more forward variety of the sound heard in *ich*. But, as Bloomfield has shown, one symbol is sufficient for both varieties.

§28. **ɡ.** This is the fricative *g* sound (we here use the older and better IPA symbol), pronounced like **x** except with voiced breath (vocal cords vibrating), and related to the English stop **ɡ** just as **x** is related to stop **k.**

§29. **ɬ.** The so-called Welsh fricative *l*, expressed in current Welsh spelling by *ll*, is a kind of *l* sound made by forcible expulsion of voiceless breath at one side of the tongue near the back teeth, the tongue being in contact near the teethridge in front and at the other side. In Anglicized pronunciation of Welsh names ɬ is sometimes replaced by English **fl** (*Fluellen* for *Llewelyn*, *Floyd* for *Lloyd*) or by English θl (θlænˈbɛrɪs for *Llanberis*).

§30. **ḷ.** This is ordinary English **l** except that it is voiceless. Its chief use is in the French pronunciation of such words as *debacle* deˈbɑːkḷ, where the ḷ is final after a voiceless consonant. It is almost inaudible to an English ear, and is sometimes actually lost in French conversation. (Voiceless **m** (m̥) occurs in a word or two; cf *umph.*)

§31. **ṛ.** Voiceless **r** is used in some French words when final after a voiceless consonant (*Joffre* ʒɔ̃fṛ). Like ḷ, it is sometimes lost in French speech.

§32. **ʎ.** This is the palatal lateral, or palatal *l* (not the same as palatalized *l*, occasionally represented by **lj** in the vocabulary). It may be approximated by keeping the tongue pressed against the backs of the lower teeth while trying to sound **l.** In the vocabulary ʎ is used chiefly in Spanish and Italian words.

§33. **ɲ.** This is palatal *n* (different from palatalized *n*, expressed in the vocabulary, when needed, by **nj**). Like **ʎ**, it can be approximated by keeping the tongue pressed against the backs of the lower teeth while trying to sound **n**. In the vocabulary **ɲ** is used chiefly in French, Spanish, and Italian words.

§34. **ʍ.** Inverted w, see **hw**.

§35. **ʔ.** The glottal stop. Not a distinctive speech sound in English (it never distinguishes words otherwise alike). It often occurs before a vowel in English in clear, emphatic utterance. It is formed by closing the glottis as in holding the breath with open mouth. The glottal stop followed by its explosive release is heard in coughing.

§36. **β.** This is the voiced bilabial fricative. It sounds, and is made, somewhat like **v**, but in **β** the upper lip replaces the upper teeth, the voiced breath passing out with friction between the slightly separated lips, instead of (as in **v**) between the lower lip and the upper teeth. In the vocabulary **β** occurs chiefly in Spanish words (*Habana* a'**βana**).

§37. **Φ.** This, the "candle-blowing" sound, is the voiceless counterpart of **β**, and bears the same relation to **f** that **β** does to **v**. For an example, see *whew* in the vocabulary.

§38. **ɥ.** This sound is used only in French words. It is nearly equivalent to **j** pronounced with rounded lips, being the glide, or semivowel, corresponding to the front rounded vowel **y** (§42 below). It is made by a quick glide (with rounded lips) from the position for **y** to a following vowel, just as the glide semivowel **j** is made by a quick glide (with unrounded lips) from the position of **i** to a following vowel, or as the glide **w** is made by a quick glide from the position for **u** to a following vowel. An example of **ɥ** is seen in French *nuance* **nɥɑ̃:s**.

§39. **ɨ.** This represents a vowel sound about midway between (front) **i** and (back) **u**. It is common in Welsh (*Llandudno* **ɬanˈdɨdno**).

§40. **ɪ.** This represents a vowel made with the tongue retracted somewhat from the lower high-front position for ordinary **ɪ** (*bid*). It is regularly heard as the first element of the common American diphthong **ɪu**, in this book written **ɪu** (*fuse* **fɪuz**). The sound **ɪ** is also common in the endings -*ed* (*stated*), -*es* (*glasses*) if they are not pronounced either -**ɪd**, -**ɪz**, or -**əd**, -**əz**. See the ending -*ed* in the vocabulary. This symbol is not often used in the vocabulary.

§41. **ʊ.** This is commonly heard as the final element of the American diphthong **ɪu** (*fuse* **fɪuz**). It represents a vowel resembling **u** but with the tongue advanced from the position for **u**. Like **ɪ**, the symbol **ʊ** is not regularly used in the vocabulary, the diphthong **ɪu** being regularly written **ɪu**, and the advanced **ʊ** not being distinguished from **u**. The advanced sound denoted by **ʊ** is also heard by itself in the speech of many who do not use **ɪu**, but who distinguish, for example, *brewed* **brʊd** from *brood* **brud**. See *Variants* **ju, ɪu, u**, §109.

§42. **y.** This is the high-front rounded vowel of German *hübsch* **hypʃ**, *kühn* **ky:n**, or of French *lune* **lyn**, *dur* **dy:r**. It may be approximated by trying to pronounce **ɪ** (*bid*) or **i** (*bee*) with lips rounded as for **u** (*too*).

§43. **ø.** This is the mid-front rounded vowel of German *schön* **ʃø:n** or French *peu* **pø**. It may be approximated by trying to sound **e** (*rate*) with lips rounded as for **o** (*go*).

§44. **œ.** This is the low-front or lower mid-front rounded vowel of German *können* **ˈkœnən** or French *heure* **œ:r**, and may be approximated by trying to pronounce **ɛ** or **æ** of *there* **ðɛr**, **ðær** with lips rounded as for **ɔ** (*wall*).

§45. **ǫ** This is the symbol for an *o* sound intermediate between **o** (*go*) and **ɔ** (*wall*). Cf. §98.

§46. ɔ̆. This is a kind of ɔ sound with the tongue pushed farther forward than in *wall*. It may be approximated by sounding ʌ (*sun*) with lips rounded as for ɔ (*wall*). It is nearly the sound of French "short *o*" in *cotte* kɔ̆t, this symbol being regularly used in the vocabulary to denote this French vowel. The symbol ɔ̆ is also used to denote the so-called "New England short *o*," shown in the vocabulary for certain words that usually have the vowel o (*go*), but which, according to Grandgent, are also pronounced with ɔ̆ by many cultivated speakers in New England.

§47. The French nasalized vowels æ̃, ɑ̃, õ, œ̃ are, respectively, the vowel sounds æ, ɑ, o, œ pronounced with the nasal passage open to the throat, the velum being lowered as when breathing through nose and mouth together. In works on French phonetics, for reasons incident to practical transcription, æ̃ is usually written ɛ̃, and õ written ɔ̃, but they are described as æ̃ and õ sounds, and are here so represented.

STRESS, ACCENT, SENSE STRESS

§48. *Stress* is the general term for prominence of a sound or syllable, whether that prominence is produced by force of utterance, by pitch, by duration of sound, or (as usually) by some combination of these elements. *Accent* is the specific term for the prominence of one syllable over others in a plurisyllable (word of more than one syllable), as *practice* ˈpræktɪs, *remain* rɪˈmen, *element* ˈɛləmənt. Monosyllables therefore have no accent in this sense.

§49. *Sense stress*, or *sentence stress*, is the prominence of certain words among others in a group that makes sense—phrase, clause, or sentence; as *The* ˈ*farmer dis*ˈ*posed of his* ˈ*holdings.* Here the marked words have more sense stress than the unmarked *the, of, his.* The same marks can show sense stress of monosyllables (*The* ˈ*man has* ˈ*gone to his* ˈ*house*). The sense stress of plurisyllables always falls on their accented syllables.

In the vocabulary every word of more than one syllable has a primary accent mark in the pronunciation (*clothing* ˈkloðɪŋ, *amiss* əˈmɪs, *variant* ˈvɛrɪənt, *preceding* prɪˈsidɪŋ, *inflected* ɪnˈflɛktɪd). Some words have two, when two syllables are nearly or quite equal (*redheaded* ˈrɛdˈhɛdɪd).

§50. Syllables more prominent than one or more others in a word, but less prominent than the strongest one in the word, have some degree of subordinate accent, which may or may not be indicated by the secondary accent mark (ˌ), as *hesitate* ˈhɛzəˌtet, *hesitation* ˌhɛzəˈteʃən. Since subordinate accent varies from nearly the weakest to nearly the strongest in words where it can occur, and varies moreover with innumerable styles of speech, no dictionary can accurately mark all instances. Hence the use of secondary accent marks here is largely conventional. Secondary accent is usually marked in words with a clear rhythmical alternation of accents (*satisfy* ˈsætɪsˌfaɪ, *satisfaction* ˌsætɪsˈfækʃən), or when it is adjacent to the chief accent in compound words whose parts are also well known as separate words (*horseplay* ˈhɔrsˌple), and wherever needed to make the whole accentuation clearer (*Winchester* ˈwɪnˌtʃɛstɚ; cf also *Gambia* and *Gambier* in the vocabulary). Cf §19.

§51. In the vocabulary certain monosyllables that have varying sense stress are marked with primary and secondary accents beside forms without accent, to show how they would be stressed in connected speech. Thus *his* in its stressed forms is marked ˈhɪz, ˌhɪz, as they might occur in *This is his* ˌðɪs ɪz ˈhɪz or *His friend was gone* ˌhɪz ˈfrɛnd wəz ˈgɔn, by the side of its un-stressed form, as in *I met his father* aɪ ˈmɛt ɪz ˈfɑðɚ.

§52. In words where a syllabic l or n is followed by an accented syllable beginning with a vowel (*ventilation* ˌvɛntl̩ˈeʃən, *ventilate* ˈvɛntl̩ˌet, *ordination* ˌɔrdn̩ˈeʃən, *ordinary* ˈɔrdn̩ˌɛrɪ), the accent mark is placed after the l or n̩, for if placed before (ˌvɛntˈl̩eʃən, ˌɔrdˈn̩eʃən), this would imply that l or n̩ is accented, which is impossible in English. Stetson's laboratory findings indicate that part of the l or n̩ may be carried over to the following syllable, but without being so markedly doubled or lengthened as it would be in *a little late* ˈlɪtl̩ˈlet or *a sudden need* ˈsʌdn̩ˈnid. Hence the accentuation must be shown as ˌvɛntl̩ˈeʃən, ˌɔrdn̩ˈeʃən, but with the understanding that the syllable division may be within the l or n̩, which is, nevertheless, not so long as l̩l or n̩n. The problem may be evaded in such words by ignoring the l or n̩ and transcribing ˌvɛntɪ-ˈleʃən, ˌvɛntəˈleʃən, ˌɔrdɪˈneʃən, ˌɔrdəˈneʃən, but to assume that such pronunciations are more usual in cultivated colloquial speech is merely to shut our eyes to the facts. (Syllabic m or ŋ seldom if ever occurs in such situations.)

§53. Shifting accent is often seen in such compound adjectives as *high-strung* ˈhaɪˈstrʌŋ, thus marked with the normal accentuation of the word when spoken alone or when used predi-catively as in *He's rather high-strung.* When this is immediately followed by a strong stress (*high-strung nerves*), the second accent is reduced (ˈhigh-ˌstrung ˈnerves). For fuller discussion, see *Webster's New International*, pp. xxxv f., §66. The rhythmic factor involved sometimes brings about permanent changes of accent. Certain adjectives (as *cold-blooded*) occurring often in the attributive position (ˈcold-ˌblooded ˈman) may become generalized with the accent of the attributive use, so that some speakers always say ˈcold-ˌblooded (ˈcold-ˌblooded ˈman, He's ˈcold-ˌblooded), where others would say ˈcold-ˌblooded ˈman, but He's ˈcold-ˈblooded. For the method of showing this in the vocabulary see §54(2). Other words than compound adjectives are subject to the same shift when followed by a strong accent, as *Shaw'nee* but ˈShawˌnee ˈtribes. Many examples of these shifts are given in the vocabulary.

Another type of shift in accent is brought about by emphasis. When such adverbs as ˈabsoˌlutely, ˈnecesˌsarily, ˈordiˌnarily are made emphatic, they are likely to be accented ˌabsoˈlutely, ˌnecesˈsarily, ˌordiˈnarily. Most adverbs of this type show this tendency in Ameri-can English, and in some cases this accentuation has become generalized; i.e., many speakers say ˌordiˈnarily, ˌnecesˈsarily under all circumstances, even when these are not emphatic. The shifted accentuation is usually shown in the vocabulary thus: "*esp. if emphatic* ˌnecesˈsarily," which means that this accentuation may occur at any time, and is especially apt to occur under emphasis.

Shifting or variable secondary accent often occurs in such words as aˌcadeˈmician, ˌanastig-ˈmatic, ˌimpeccaˈbility, ˌimpenetraˈbility, ˌincompreˈhensible, ˌincorpoˈreity, inˌferiˈority, where in longer words the secondary accent precedes the primary. Here, in actual speech, such alterna-tive accentuations as aˌcadeˈmician or ˌacadeˈmician, ˌimpenetraˈbility or imˌpenetraˈbility, inˌferiˈority or ˌinferiˈority are very common, and do not represent more and less desirable pronunciations, but chiefly show the effect of varying sense stress, emphasis, speech rhythm, semantic distinctions, and other constantly varying factors of connected speech, so that in many such instances the question which accentuation is preferable is irrelevant. See also §57.

§54. In the vocabulary, accent marks are sometimes used on words in ordinary spelling (lightface roman type) when it is desired to show only the accentuation, after a pronunciation already given. This occurs chiefly in two ways:—

(1) As at the entry *heartsore*, where, after the pronunciation and accent in phonetic symbols, there is added "*acct* + ˈheartˈsore," which means, "Besides the accentuation just given, the following different accentuation is also current."

(2) As at the entry *cloven-footed*, a form in ordinary spelling with accent marks is added in parentheses to show a different accentuation from that already given, especially a shifted accentuation (§53). Thus the basic accentuation is shown in the pronunciation ˈklovənˈfʊtɪd, but in the attributive construction the accent on -ˈfʊtɪd is reduced before a following stressed syllable, and this is shown by the phrase in parentheses (ˈcloven-ˌfooted ˈox). Less usually the same device is used to illustrate or confirm the accentuation just given. Thus after the entry and pronunciation *week-end*, adj, ˈwikˈɛnd, the first example in parentheses by its speech rhythm confirms the accentuation just given (ˈweek-ˈend ˌparty), and the second example illustrates the shift in accent due to a different speech rhythm (ˈweek-ˌend ˈtrip). The reader can usually confirm the instances of level-stress accentuation by putting the entry word into a phrase with predicate construction, as *The ox is* ˈcloven-ˈfooted.

Since it is impossible in the vocabulary to give such examples of variant accentuation at every entry where it would be appropriate, it is to be understood from the occasional examples given that it can occur in all similar cases.

In all cases where accent marks are used with lightface roman type, only accentuation, and no other feature of pronunciation, is referred to.

LENGTH OF VOWELS

§55. As a rule the length of English vowels is not indicated in the vocabulary. In few cases in American English as a whole is time length, or duration, of vowels significant—that is, used to distinguish from each other words otherwise alike. Instances are found here and there, some speakers distinguishing *halve* **hæːv** from *have* **hæv** by a longer **æ**, or *vary* **vɛːrɪ** from *very* **vɛrɪ** by a longer **ɛ**.

In the E and S, however, some speakers distinguish certain classes of words by vowel length; e.g., *cart* **kɑːt** from *cot* **kɑt** by a longer **ɑ**, and this is therefore a convenient way of marking words in which **r** has been dropped after **ɑ** or **a** with a resultant lengthening of the vowel sound, as *farm* **fɑrm**; ES **fɑːm**, E + **fɑːm**. The length sign is sometimes omitted in longer words of this kind when **ɑ** or **a** is noticeably shorter, as in *impartiality* ˌɪmpɑrˈʃælətɪ; ES ˌɪmpɑˈʃælətɪ.

Since the other vowels before a silent *r* in ES are followed by **ə** (**iə, ɪə, ɛə, æə, ɔə, oə, ʊə, uə**), there the length mark is not needed; as *fear* **fɪr**; ES **fɪə(r**, and the length colon is therefore only used with **ɑ** and **a**. On the use of **ɔə** in such words see *Variants* §96.

When the length sign is used, it invariably indicates time length, or duration, not vowel quality, or tamber, and therefore has nothing to do with such distinctions as between so-called "short *i*" (**ɪ**) and "long *i*" (**aɪ**), or between "short *u*" (**ʌ**) and "long *u*" (**ju** or **ɪu**), or between "short *a*" (**æ**) and "long *a*" (**e**), etc.

In cases like *Aachen* ˈɑkən, ˈɑxən (*Ger* ˈɑːxən), in which the vowel **ɑ** is marked long in the foreign pronunciation (where length is significant) but left unmarked in the English, this does not necessarily mean that the English vowel is shorter than the foreign one, but merely that its length is of no importance, and hence is not indicated.

SINGLE AND DOUBLE CONSONANTS

§56. In reading the pronunciations the consultant should give particular attention to single and double consonants. In ordinary spelling, doubled letters in English words commonly represent only single sounds (*happy* **'hæpɪ**, *manner* **'mænɚ**, *goodness* **'gʊdnɪs**). Only in compounds (*coattail*) or when suffixes are added (*thinness*) are the sounds really doubled (**'kot,tel**, **'θɪnnɪs**), and not always then (*laterally* **'lætərəlɪ**). Strict heed must be paid to the rule—one symbol, one sound; two symbols, two sounds. See §3, 2d paragraph.

In some foreign pronunciations added to compare with the English (esp. Italian) this must be watched; thus in English, *Monticello* has but one **l** sound (**,mɑntə'sɛlo**), but in Italian it has two (**,monti'tʃɛl·lo**). In Italian when **tʃ, dʒ, ts, dz** are doubled, **tʃ** becomes **ttʃ** (*Puccini* Eng **pu-'tʃɪnɪ**, but It **put'tʃiːni**), **dʒ** becomes **ddʒ** (*Maggiore* Eng **mə'dʒorɪ**, but It **mɑd'dʒoːre**), **ts** becomes **tts** (*Tetrazzini* Eng **,tɛtrə'zinɪ**, but It **,tetrɑt'tsiːni**), **dz** becomes **ddz** (*mezzo* Eng **'mɛdzo**, but It **'mɛddzo**).

THE ORDER OF VARIANT PRONUNCIATIONS

§57. For words that are in general colloquial use it is intended to give first what is believed to be the most usual colloquial pronunciation. But it must be emphasized that not too much importance should be given to the order. For it is our purpose to give (unless otherwise indicated) only pronunciations that are in general cultivated use—to give none that need be avoided as incorrect or substandard. In a very large number of instances the different pronunciations of a word are of approximately equal frequency and validity, and yet they can be printed only in successive order. In numerous cases it is impossible to maintain on any solid grounds that one pronunciation given is "better" than another, as, for example, that one pronunciation of *swamp* is better than the others given; that **kɛr** for *care* is either better or worse than **kær**; that **'kɑŋkwɛst** is better or worse than **'kɑnkwɛst**, **lɔg** than **lɑg** or **lɒg**, **'lɛvɚ** than **'livɚ**, and so on. Often, too, the variants given represent only differences of colloquial style, depending on occasion, speed, degree of informality, etc., and having no bearing on the question of correctness.

§58. Where statistics indicate relative frequency, this has been recorded; but fuller collections might change the order. Statistics at present available are often based on the assumption that all words of a given phonetic or historical class (as the "*ask*" words) will be pronounced consistently. But that is not always true. A proof of this is found in the records of the *Linguistic Atlas of New England*, which show that some words that might be expected to have the vowel sound **a** or **ɑ** (where British prevailingly has **ɑ**) are seldom heard with **a** or **ɑ** (as *answer*), while others of the same group often or prevailingly have **a** or **ɑ** (as *calf, half, aunt*).

DIRECTIONS FOR USE

READING THE ENTRIES AND PRONUNCIATIONS

§59. Each entry, or article, in the vocabulary begins with a head word in lightface roman type, followed without punctuation by the pronunciation in **boldface**.[3] The simplest form of entry is

bequest br'kwɛst

with no derivatives and no variant pronunciations. If the word with the same spelling and pronunciation is also found as a proper name (whether or not it is the same word), it is usually thus indicated:—

clarion, C- 'klærɪən

which means that *clarion* and *Clarion* are pronounced alike. The proper name may be entered first:—

Cologne, c- kə'lon

which means that *Cologne* and *cologne* are pronounced alike.

If the entry has a current variant spelling, that is entered in its alphabetical order, unless it would be very near, or has a bearing on the pronunciation, in which case it is given at the same entry. Words alternatively spelt *-tre* are, however, always found with those in *-ter* (*center*).

In the large group of words like *travel(l)ed*, the optional second *l* is disregarded.

WORDS LISTED UNDER HEAD WORDS

§60. If a word is not found in alphabetical order, it is to be looked for under some obviously related head word. Thus many adverbs will be found with the corresponding adjectives; as,

holy 'holɪ |holily 'holəlɪ, -lɪlɪ

This method permits the inclusion of far more words than would otherwise be possible.

§61. If a word has variant pronunciations not dependent on locality, they are separated by commas:—

every 'ɛvrɪ, 'ɛvərɪ

defect dɪ'fɛkt, 'difɛkt

§62. Commonly, to show such variants only the part that varies is repeated. In representing such fragments of spelling or pronunciation the hyphen shows which part of the word is intended. Thus *de-* is the first part, *-min-* a middle part, and *-ant* a final part. For example,

logwood 'lɔg,wʊd, 'lɑg-, 'lɒg-

By adding the omitted part (here shown in parentheses) to each fragment we get 'lɑg(,wʊd), 'lɒg(,wʊd) as the 2d and 3d variants.

midday 'mɪd,de, -'de

By adding the omitted part, with its accent, to the fragment, we get ('mɪd)'de for the 2d variant.

Lofthouse 'lɔftəs, 'lɒft-, -,haʊs

---

[3] In the vocabulary all spelling forms (except catchwords) are printed in light roman type, all pronunciations in **boldface**, and explanatory matter in *italic* (except the regional labels E, S, N, etc.). In the solid print of the Introduction, italic has to be used for spelling forms (as in general usage); but there also, when spelling forms with their pronunciations are set off by themselves, these follow the typography of the vocabulary.

Adding the omitted part to each fragment, we get ˈlɒft(əs), (ˈlɔft)ˌhaʊs, (ˈlɒft)ˌhaʊs as the 2d, 3d, and 4th variants.

Naomi ˈneəˌmaɪ, neˈomaɪ, -mɪ, -mə

Adding the omitted parts in turn to the two fragments, we get (ˈneə)mɪ, (ˈneə)mə, (neˈo)mɪ, (neˈo)mə, six variants in all.

Nazareth ˈnæzərəθ, -rɪθ, ˈnæzr-

Adding the omitted parts, we get, besides the first full pronunciation, (ˈnæzə)rɪθ, ˈnæzr(əθ), ˈnæzr(ɪθ).

ONE ENTRY INCLUDING DIFFERENT WORDS

§63. When more than one spelling appears at the same entry with the same pronunciation, these spellings are not necessarily of the same word or part of speech, especially in proper names. Likewise a single entry may represent two or more words spelt and sounded alike. Thus the word *angle* includes all the words—nouns, verbs, etc., with their different meanings but all with the same pronunciation. When derivative or inflectional endings are added, they are to be fitted only to the appropriate meanings or parts of speech, but this does not affect the pronunciation, and usually need not concern the reader. Thus under *angle* the form *angled* can be the adjective formed from the noun (*wide-angled*) or the past or past participle of the verb (*it angled off*), and the form *angling* can be the adjective (*an angling path*), the participle (*he is angling with flies*), or the noun (*the angling was good*). At the entry *instance* the ending *-es* may be that of the plural of the noun or the 3 sg of the verb. At *intelligence* the entry may be noun or verb, the ending *-es* the plural or 3 sg, the ending *-ed* may be that of the past participle or of the "apparent participle," the adjective formed from the noun. The entry *slew* may be a noun, a verb in the present tense, or the past of the verb *slay*.

LABELS FOR PARTS OF SPEECH

§64. Only when it concerns the pronunciation are these labels added, or in a few cases where there might be doubt whether the various uses of the word had the same pronunciation.

DEFINITIONS

§65. Instead of labels for parts of speech, frequently definitions are appended. These are never full, and are used only to identify the word. Definitions are in quotation marks. Explanatory identification that does not define is without quotation marks.

GEOGRAPHICAL AND LINGUISTIC LABELS

§66. Geographical labels are often appended to place names to indicate the location, or to personal names to indicate residence or nationality. The linguistic abbreviations *Fr, Sp, Ger*, etc., refer to the pronunciation; thus

Lodi *US* ˈloˌdaɪ; *Italy* ˈlodi (*It* ˈlɔːdi)

means that the various Lodi's in the US are pronounced ˈloˌdaɪ; that Lodi in Italy is pronounced in American English ˈlodi; and that the Italian pronunciation is ˈlɔːdi.

When the linguistic labels *It, Fr*, etc., precede the first pronunciation, this means that only the foreign pronunciation is given; as,

voyageur *Fr* vwajaˈʒœːr

THE VERTICAL BAR AND THE ADDITION OF INFLECTIONAL AND DERIVATIVE ENDINGS

§67. The following examples show the uses of the vertical bar:—

press prɛs |presses 'prɛsɪz |pressed prɛst

Here the bar, in its simplest use, is followed in each case by a new spelling form in roman type, with corresponding pronunciation in boldface.

finish 'fɪnɪʃ |-es -ɪz |-ed -t

Here, after the first bar, follows a spelling fragment (-es) with its corresponding pronunciation fragment (**-ɪz**). The simple rule for combining is, Add the spelling fragment (-es) to the first spelling form (finish-es) and the pronunciation fragment (**-ɪz**) to the first pronunciation form (**'fɪnɪʃ-ɪz**); and so after the next bar (finish-ed **'fɪnɪʃ-t**). Add to the head forms before the first bar, *and add* roman *to* roman, **boldface** *to* **boldface**.

It is important to add each fragment (spelling to spelling, and pronunciation to pronunciation) to the forms before the first bar. The sole exception to this is the adverb ending *-bly* **-blɪ** when the first entry does not end in *-ble* **-b|**. In that case *-bly* **-blɪ** are fitted to the immediately preceding forms in *-ble* **-b|**. See *-bly* in the vocabulary.

Hyphenated words are never thus divided after a bar, but are separately entered as head words, to avoid confusing the compounding hyphen with that which separates the fragments.

§68. When the first word in a vocabulary entry is a monosyllable, no accent mark is used (with the exception noted in §51), as *set* **sɛt**. But when one or more syllables are added after the bar (|) thus, *set* **sɛt** |*-back* **-ˌbæk** |*-ting* **-ɪŋ**, then primary accent must be assumed on the plurisyllables, and the entries must be read thus: *set* **sɛt** |*setback* **'sɛtˌbæk** |*setting* **'sɛtɪŋ**.

§69. There is no significance in the fact that sometimes full forms of the derivatives are given, as in the first example, and sometimes fragments, as in the second. The editors have not sought mere mechanical uniformity, owing to considerations of time, of space, and of other disturbing factors. They have sought only to make each article clear in itself. The occasional full forms may help to make the abbreviated ones clearer.

§70. It should be noted that a pronunciation fragment need not correspond letter for letter with its spelling fragment:—

inflate ɪn'flet |-d -ɪd

Here, adding spelling *-d* to spelling *inflate* gives *inflated,* and adding pronunciation **-ɪd** to pronunciation **ɪn'flet** gives **ɪn'fletɪd**. See next example also.

Often, for greater clearness, more than a minimum fragment of pronunciation is given:—

flatten 'flætn̩ |-ed -d |-ing 'flætn̩ɪŋ, -tnɪŋ

This is to show that *flattening* is pronounced either **'flæt·n̩·ɪŋ** (3 syls.) or **'flæt·nɪŋ** (2 syls.). Likewise the frequent adverb ending *-ically* is thus shown:—

symmetric sɪ'mɛtrɪk |-al -| |-ally -|ɪ, -ɪklɪ

Here the last two pronunciations are **sɪ'mɛtrɪk·|·ɪ, sɪ'mɛtrɪk·lɪ,** the last being made a little clearer by **-ɪklɪ** than by **-lɪ** alone, though **-lɪ** would be strictly correct.

Some added letters may be silent, as in *bar* **bɑr** |*-red* **-d**, where *-re-* are silent; or letters silent in the first entry may represent sounds in the addition, as *rogue* **rog** |*-ry* **-ərɪ**, where the silent *e* of *rogue* represents ə in *roguery* **'rogərɪ**.

§71. Observe cases like

abut ə'bʌt |-ted -ɪd

where addition of -*ted* doubles the letter *t* (abutted) but not the sound t (ə'bʌtɪd); or like

total 'totḷ |-ed -d |-ly -ɪ

where addition of -*ly* doubles the letter *l* (totally) but not the sound l ('totḷɪ).

Thus when the final letter of the spelling entry is the same as the first letter of the spelling fragment (total |-ly), it is to be doubled (i.e., the fragment is added regularly). So, too, when the first pronunciation ends with the same sound that begins the pronunciation fragment, this sound also is to be doubled; as,

foreign 'fɔrɪn, 'far-, 'fɒr-, -ən |-ness -nɪs

This is to be expanded into 'fɔrɪnnɪs, 'farɪnnɪs, 'fɒrɪnnɪs, 'fɔrənnɪs, 'farənnɪs, 'fɒrənnɪs, in all cases with double **n.** Whenever space allows, such doubled sounds are shown by doubled symbols; as,

thin θɪn |thinned θɪnd |-ness 'θɪnnɪs

The few exceptions to this rule for doubling are such as to give no trouble. The most usual one consists of words ending in -*th*; as,

truth truθ |-'s -θs |-ths -ðz, -θs

in which the expanded forms are obviously not truθθs and truθðz or truθθs, but truθs and truðz or truθs, since the combinations θθs and θðz do not occur in English.

CUTTING BACK

§72. There are, however, a great many words in which the fragments cannot be added directly to the head words:—

suspicion sə'spɪʃən |-cious -ʃəs

Here, in order to make the proper junction of the spelling fragment, we must take in some letter near the end of the head word to begin the fragment. This we call "cutting back." Thus we cut off the spelling -*cion* and replace it with -*cious* (suspi-cious); and likewise cut off from the head pronunciation the corresponding sounds -ʃən, and replace them with -ʃəs (sə'spɪ-ʃəs).

Cutting back and direct addition are often used in the same word:—

prude **prud** |-dish -ɪʃ

Since -*ish* cannot be added to *prude*, we take in the *d* and add -*dish* (pru-dish); then, since to add the pronunciation -dɪʃ to **prud** would wrongly give 'pruddɪʃ, we simply add -ɪʃ directly to **prud** ('prudɪʃ). Similarly, in

negative 'nɛgətɪv |-d -d |-vism -ˌɪzəm

where -*d* and -**d** are added directly, -*vism* has to be cut back (negati-vism), and -ˌɪzəm (not -ˌvɪzəm) is directly added to 'nɛgətɪv ('nɛgətɪvˌɪzəm).

A "cutback" must always take in more than the final letter of the entry form, for otherwise it would be taken as a direct addition with doubling of the final letter or sound (see the exception above at *truth*, at the end of §71).

§73. In adding suffixes certain familiar changes are made, as of -*y* to -*i*; as,

quarry 'kwɔrɪ |-ied -d, *i.e.*, quarried 'kwɔrɪd

or of *f* to *v*; as in

housewife 'haʊsˌwaɪf |-ves -vz, *i.e.*, housewives 'haʊsˌwaɪvz

where -*ves* and -**vz** are not directly added, but replace -*fe* and **f.**

LISTING OF VERB FORMS

§74. When the past tense and the past participle of strong ("irregular") verbs are given, the past regularly follows the first bar, and the past participle the second bar, usually without labels:—

drive draɪv |drove drov |driven 'drɪvən

sing sɪŋ |sang sæŋ or sung sʌŋ |sung sʌŋ

When such verbs end in sibilants, the 3 sg pres precedes the past and pptc:—

choose tʃuz |-s -ɪz |chose tʃoz |chosen 'tʃozn̩

If the past and pptc are alike, they are given but once:—

shine ʃaɪn |shone ʃon

stand stænd |stood stʊd

fight faɪt |fought fɔt

§75. The bar, not followed by a spelling form, is sometimes used at the end of an article to separate an added item from the immediately preceding one, and to imply its application to the whole article:—

road rod |-ed -ɪd; | NEngd+rɔ̈d

THE MAIN REGIONAL DIVISIONS

§76. For indicating American regional pronunciations the well-known division into three regions is followed, the East (E), the South (S), and, for want of a better term, the North (N). Geographically the East includes New York City (NYC) and environs, and New England east of the Connecticut River. The South includes Virginia, North Carolina, South Carolina, Tennessee, Florida, Georgia, Alabama, Mississippi, Arkansas, Louisiana, Texas, and parts of Maryland, West Virginia, Kentucky, and Oklahoma. The North includes the rest of the US.

In the use of the terms E, S, N, certain modifications must be kept in mind. The speech of the S differs markedly in the more northerly parts from that in the more southerly ones, and (partly coinciding with this) in the more inland regions from that in the coastal ones. Certain features labeled S are therefore not equally applicable to all of the S.

Owing to movements of population, and probably also to the schools, innumerable individuals and often considerable groups in the S speak a type virtually identical with that of the N. The same is true in the E, especially NYC. In NEngd also, and in the southeastern coastal regions, are certain "speech islands" having a similar type, perhaps preserved, by isolation, from a time when it was more general. Allowance must also be made for mixed types of speech in all the border areas between the main regions. The irregular use of the *r* sound is especially noticeable in the border areas.

It is not the function of this dictionary to deal with these more irregular and exceptional features,—to make a dialect map of the country. That work is being done by the *L.A.* Our concern is only with the main types of cultivated American English—something of a fiction, if you will, as all "standard" speech is.

It should be noted that the pronunciations assigned to particular regions are regarded only as the ones prevailing there. It is unsafe to deny the existence of any pronunciation in any region. Thus, when it is indicated that in the S the word *glory* is pronounced **'glorɪ**, while in the E and N it is either **'glorɪ** or **'glɔrɪ**, it is not meant that **'glɔrɪ** does not exist in the S, but that according to the evidence we have, ˈglɒrɪ is not sufficiently frequent in the S to be recorded as a characteristic S pronunciation. The same may be said of the ɛ sound in such words as *air*, *there*, etc. Evidence does not show that the vowel ɛ in such words is widespread in the S. The same principle is to be applied to all regional pronunciations.

§77. Linguistically the most generally observed characteristic of the three regions is the treatment of the *r* sound, the E and the S being in the main alike in this respect in contrast with the N. The S is separated from the E by a number of features, such as the character of the aʊ and aɪ diphthongs, the prevalence of "flat *a*" (æ) in certain groups of words, the "long *e*" sound before **r**, the tendency to diphthongize many vowels, and many features of intonation and tempo—none of them equally distributed over the S—features that enable the ordinary observer to distinguish a Southerner from an Easterner, but not all of them conveniently or profitably recorded in a work with the scope and purpose of this.

INDICATION OF REGIONAL PRONUNCIATIONS

§78. In the vocabulary, the Eastern (E) and Southern (S) pronunciations are separated from the Northern (N) by semicolons. The pronunciations in entries that contain no regional labels (E, ES, S, N, EN, etc.) are valid for all the US, as *delicious* dɪˈlɪʃəs. When an entry contains a regional label, the unlabeled pronunciations are valid everywhere in the US except in the regions designated; thus

glory ˈglorɪ, ˈglɔrɪ; S ˈglorɪ

means that the first two pronunciations are both valid everywhere except in the S; there only ˈglorɪ prevails; or, stated otherwise, ˈglorɪ and ˈglɔrɪ are characteristic of the E and the N; only ˈglorɪ is so of the S.

perform pɚˈfɔrm; ES pəˈfɔəm

This means that in the US except the E and the S the pronunciation is pɚˈfɔrm; in the E and the S it is pəˈfɔəm.

aircraft ˈɛrˌkræft, ˈær-; E ˈɛə-, ˈæə-, -ˌkraft, -ˌkrɑft; S ˈæəˌkræft

Combining regularly, for the N, besides ˈɛrˌkræft, we get ˈærˌkræft; for the E, ˈɛəˌkræft, ˈæəˌkræft, ˈɛəˌkraft, ˈæəˌkraft, ˈɛəˌkrɑft, ˈæəˌkrɑft; for the S, ˈæəˌkræft.

Very often two regions (usually E and S) have one or more variants in common. They are then usually separated only by commas:—

scarce skɛrs, skærs; E skɛəs, ES skæəs

This means that in the N *scarce* is pronounced skɛrs or skærs; in the E it is pronounced skɛəs, and in both E and S it is pronounced skæəs; or, stated otherwise, in the E it is pronounced skɛəs or skæəs, while in the S only skæəs prevails. See also *board, ear, premonitory* (§80).

ACCENT AS A FACTOR IN COMBINING THE FORMS

§79. Only the forms that agree in accent are to be combined:—

Carew kəˈru, -ˈrɪu, ˈkɛru, ˈke-, -rɪu, -rɪ

For the first accentuation, besides kəˈru we have (kə)ˈrɪu; for the second accentuation, besides ˈkɛru and ˈke(ru) we have (ˈkɛ)rɪu, (ˈke)rɪu, (ˈkɛ)rɪ, (ˈke)rɪ.

empyreal ɛmˈpɪrɪəl, ˌɛmpəˈriəl, -paɪ-

Here the first form cannot be combined with -paɪ- because this is not accented, as is the corresponding -ˈpɪ-. Hence only the second form can combine with -paɪ-, thus: (ˌɛm)paɪ(ˈriəl), the unaccented -paɪ- replacing the unaccented -pə-.

bifurcate *v* ˈbaɪfɚˌket, baɪˈfɝ·ket; ES ˈbaɪfə-, -ˈfɜket, -ˈfɝ·ket

Here the Eastern and Southern fragment ˈbaɪfə- can combine only with the omitted part found in ˈbaɪfɚˌket, with the same accent, thus: ˈbaɪfə(ˌket). The last two fragments must be combined with the omitted part of baɪˈfɝ·ket, having the same accent, thus: (baɪ)ˈfɜket, (baɪ)ˈfɝ·ket. (For regional pronunciations see §§76-78.)

discourse *n* ˈdɪskors, dɪˈskors, -ɔrs; ES -oəs, E + -ɔəs

Here the fragment -ors, which does not include the accent mark, will fit both of the first two forms without disturbing their accents, thus: (ˈdɪsk)ors, (dɪˈsk)ors; and likewise the Eastern and Southern fragments: ES (ˈdɪsk)oəs, (dɪˈsk)oəs, Eastern also (ˈdɪsk)ɔəs, (dɪˈsk)ɔəs.

THE PLUS SIGN (+)

§80. The sign (+) is invariably to be read "also." It means that in addition to pronunciations already given, other designated pronunciations are to be heard from cultivated speakers. This sign does not imply that these additional pronunciations have inferior standing, or necessarily are less frequent, though we have not placed it before pronunciations known to be markedly in the majority. The following examples indicate the use of the plus sign:—

hot **hɑt**; ES + **hɒt**

This means that the word spelt *hot* is, in all regions of the US, pronounced **hɑt**; but that there are also many cultivated speakers in the East and the South who usually pronounce it **hɒt**.

fast **fæst**; E + **fast, fɑst**

This means that the word *fast* in all parts of the US is pronounced **fæst**; but that there are also many cultivated speakers in the East who usually pronounce it **fast** or **fɑst**.

board **bord, bɔrd**; ES **boəd, E +** **bɔəd**

This means that *board* is pronounced **bord** or **bɔrd** in the North, but in the East and the South it is pronounced **boəd,** and in the East, in addition to **boəd,** it is also pronounced **bɔəd.**

ear **ɪr**; ES **ɪə(r, S + ɛə(r**

This means that *ear* is pronounced **ɪr** in the North, but in the East and the South it is pronounced **ɪə(r,** and in the South, in addition to **ɪə(r,** it is also pronounced **ɛə(r.**

premonitory **prɪˈmɑnəˌtorɪ, -ˌtɔrɪ; S -ˌtorɪ, ES + -ˈmɒn-**

Where, as here, the pronunciation after + is a fragment, it is to be taken as a pronunciation additional to that of the corresponding parts of the preceding forms. In this example, Eastern has, besides the pronunciations **prɪˈmɑnəˌtorɪ** and **-ˌtɔrɪ**, which it shares with the North, also **prɪˈmɒnəˌtorɪ** and **-ˌtɔrɪ**; while Southern has, besides **prɪˈmɑnəˌtorɪ** (but not **-ˌtɔrɪ**), also **prɪˈmɒnəˌtorɪ.**

It is believed that any other uses of the sign +, if it is merely read "also," will be clear to the reader as they occur. It should be noted that a pronunciation with + prefixed is never the sole pronunciation of the word.

JOINING REGIONAL FRAGMENTS TO FIRST FORMS

§81. In fitting fragments to forms before the first bar, the regional fragments are to be fitted to the corresponding regional forms before the first bar; as,

woodwork **ˈwʊdˌwɝk; ES ˈwʊdˌwɜk, -ˌwɝk; |-er -ɚ; ES -ə(r**

Expanding the fragments after the bar, we get

woodworker ˈwʊdˌwɝ˞kɚ; ES ˈwʊdˌwɝkə(r, ˈwʊdˌwɝkə(r

in which the unlabeled N fragment -ɚ is fitted to the first unlabeled (N) pronunciation, and the ES fragment -ə(r is fitted to the first two ES pronunciations.

For the meaning of (r see §82.

LINKING r—THE MEANING OF -ɜ(r, -ɑ:(r, -ə(r

§82. When pronunciations are thus indicated,—*fur* fɜ(r, *far* fɑ:(r, *bitter* ˈbɪtə(r, *here* hɪə(r, *there* ðɛə(r, ðæə(r, *war* wɔə(r, *more* mɔə(r, *poor* pʊə(r,—this means that (in the E and S) r is not sounded and these words are pronounced fɜ, fɑ:, ˈbɪtə, hɪə, ðɛə, ðæə, wɔə, mɔə, pʊə unless a vowel sound follows, either in the same word (by addition of an ending, as *furry* ˈfɜrɪ, *bitterest* ˈbɪtərɪst) or in a word that follows without pause (*the fur is wet* ðə fɜr ɪz wɛt, *far away* fɑr əˈwe, *bitter end* ˈbɪtər ɛnd). The effect of pause on linking r is seen in the following utterance of a distinguished American: *over, and over, and over again* ˈovə, ən ˈovə, ənd ˈovər əˈgɛn.

When -ə(r follows a vowel in the same syllable, as in *here* hɪə(r, *there* ðæə(r, *more* mɔə(r, and a vowel sound is added, then r either replaces ə (*herein* hɪrˈɪn, *here it is* hɪr ɪt ɪz, *therein* ðærˈɪn, *there it goes* ðær ɪt goz, *moreover* morˈovə, *more ice* mor aɪs, *poorest* ˈpʊrɪst, *poor and needy* pʊr ən ˈnidɪ), or, less usually, the r is added to ə (hɪərˈɪn, hɪər ɪt ɪz, moərˈovə, ˈpʊərɪst, etc.). This alternative is to be understood in all similar cases.

In such words as *adjure* əˈdʒʊr, əˈdʒɪʊr; ES -ə(r, the -ə(r is to be understood as replacing the final r of the N pronunciation.

Some speakers, especially in the S, fail to pronounce linking r before an initial vowel of the following word (*more ice* mɔə aɪs, *when the war ends* hwɛn ðə wɔə ɛndz). Omission of r before a vowel within a word (ˈvɛ·ɪ for ˈvɛrɪ) is regarded as substandard.

§83. In vocabulary entries, when pronunciation fragments are added, the use of (r must be observed. The rule is simple: If the added fragment begins with a vowel sound, the r is sounded in the E and S; if it begins with a consonant sound, the r is not heard in the E and S:—

labor ˈlebɚ; ES ˈlebə(r; |-ed -d |-ing -brɪŋ, -bərɪŋ

Here ES ˈlebə(r means ˈlebər or ˈlebə according as a vowel sound immediately follows or not. When -*ed* -d is added, being a consonant sound (*e* silent), we are to understand ES ˈlebəd beside N ˈlebɚd; but when -*ing* -ɪŋ is added, with its vowel sound, then the r is sounded and the ES and the N pronunciations are alike ˈlebrɪŋ or ˈlebərɪŋ.

§84. For the pronunciation of the N in words like *labor* ˈlebɚ, when a vowel sound is added (*laboring* ˈlebərɪŋ), then -ər replaces -ɚ, since there is no significant difference between ˈlebɚ·ɪŋ and ˈlebɚ·rɪŋ. When, as often, *laboring* is contracted, then vowel ɚ becomes consonant r (ˈlebrɪŋ). Likewise in the entry *farrier* ˈfærɪɚ; ES ˈfærɪ·ə(r; |-*y* -ɪ, the pronunciation of the derivative *farriery* becomes ˈfærɪərɪ, which is also right for the E and S, because a vowel follows -ə(r and therefore r is retained.

INTRUSIVE r

§85. Though not recorded in the vocabulary, intrusive r is appropriately described here. Following the regular habits of his speech a cultivated Easterner or Southerner might normally pronounce *straighter and straighter* ˈstretər ən ˈstretə, sounding final r before the vowel and dropping it at the end. Following the same habits, he might pronounce *strata on strata* ˈstretər ɒn ˈstretə, likewise sounding r before the vowel and not at the end. Both procedures are unconscious and phonetically natural.

When the final r is spelt (*straighter*) and pronounced before a vowel it is called Linking **r**; when it is not spelt but is pronounced before a vowel, it is called Intrusive **r**. The frequency of intrusive r among cultivated Easterners, Southerners, and British is no longer a matter of doubt except to the uninformed. It is perhaps less frequent in the S than in the E. Words ending in the sound -ə (*Victoria, sofa, idea*) are more apt to show it than are those ending in other vowels. Its use is perhaps less consistent than that of linking **r**. The same educated Southerner said ðɪs ˈmætə ɪz ˈdɪfrənt who said ə ˈgretə ðən ˈdʒonər ɪz hɪə.

WORD ELEMENTS OMITTED FROM THE VOCABULARY

§86. To save space and relieve the reader from the distraction of needless information, words having certain suffixes with regular pronunciation are often omitted from the vocabulary; as those with -*dom* (*heathendom*), -*hood* (*motherhood*), -*ish* (*darkish*), -*ment* (*announcement*). See §89.

§87. The -(*e*)*s* plural of regular nouns, the third person singular present indicative of verbs, and the possessive case ending of nouns are regularly omitted from the vocabulary, except for words ending in a sibilant sound (s, z, ʃ, ʒ, tʃ, dʒ), where they are regularly given. If the plural and the possessive sound alike, only one is given. If they differ, both are given (see *house*). The possessive plural of regular nouns, formed by adding the apostrophe (') but no sound, is omitted.

Certain nouns ending in a s or z sound closely preceded by a s or z sound vary in current usage in forming the possessive. Unfortunately some printing shops follow their own rules in this, and do not always agree with others or with general usage. Current literary usage in this is set forth in *Webster's New International Dictionary, Second Edition*, at the word *possessive*, and the present work follows this, with a very few exceptions where usage is divided.

The following rules, fully illustrated, will enable the reader to form the regular plural of nouns, the possessive case, and the third singular of verbs, in all cases where these are not recorded in the vocabulary.

§88. Pronunciation of the Plural and Possessive Singular of Nouns and the Third Singular Present of Verbs

Rule I. Add the sound **s** when the stem of the noun or verb ends in any of the voiceless consonant sounds **p, t, k, f, θ**. Examples follow:

1. Plural of nouns.
   cap-s kæp-s, *gate-s* get-s, *oak-s* ok-s, *cliff-s* klɪf-s, *growth-s* groθ-s. Words like *leaf* lif—*leaves* livz, *oath* oθ—*oaths* oðz will be found in the vocabulary.
2. Possessives in -'s follow the same rule.
   Philip's ˈfɪləp-s, *Kate's* ket-s, *Isaac's* ˈaɪzək-s, *Joseph's* ˈdʒozəf-s, *Edith's* ˈidɪθ-s.
3. Third singular present indicatives follow the same rule.
   keep-s kip-s, *get-s* gɛt-s, *look-s* lʊk-s, *chafe-s* tʃef-s, *froth-s* frɔθ-s.

Rule II. Add the sound **z** when the stem of the noun or verb ends in any of the voiced consonant sounds **b, d, g, v, ð, m, n, ŋ, l**, or in any vowel sound (all vowel sounds are voiced):

1. Plural of nouns.

    robe-s rob-z, *bed-s* bɛd-z, *rogue-s* rog-z, *stove-s* stov-z, *lathe-s* leð-z, *rim-s* rɪm-z, *bone-s* bon-z, *thing-s* θɪŋ-z, *ball-s* bɔl-z; (vowels) *sea-s* si-z, *citi-es* ˈsɪtɪ-z, *day-s* de-z, *ma-s* mɑ-z, *law-s* lɔ-z, *hoe-s* ho-z, *value-s* ˈvælju-z, *shoe-s* ʃu-z, *fur-s* fɝ-z, fɝ-z, *bar-s* bɑr-z (§26), bɑː-z, *paper-s* ˈpepɚ-z, *sofa-s* ˈsofə-z, *tie-s* taɪ-z, *cow-s* kau-z, *toy-s* tɔɪ-z, *cue-s* kju-z, kɪu-z.

2. Possessives in -'s follow the same rule.

    Rob's rɑb-z, *Adelaide's* ˈædlˌed-z, *Meg's* mɛg-z, *Olive's* ˈɑlɪv-z, *Blythe's* blaɪð-z, *Tom's* tɑm-z, *John's* dʒɑn-z, *Harding's* ˈhɑrdɪŋ-z, *Will's* wɪl-z; (vowels) *Lee's* li-z, *Betty's* ˈbɛtɪ-z, *Ray's* re-z, *ma's* mɑ-z, *Esau's* ˈisɔ-z, *Joe's* dʒo-z, *Andrew's* ˈændru-z, *Burr's* bɝ-z, bɝ-z, *Wilbur's* ˈwɪlbɚ-z, *Sarah's* ˈsɛrə-z, *Nye's* naɪ-z, *Howe's* hau-z, *Roy's* rɔɪ-z, *Hugh's* hju-z, hɪu-z.

3. Third singular present indicatives follow the same rule.

    rub-s rʌb-z, *hide-s* haɪd-z, *lag-s* læg-z, *save-s* sev-z, *breathe-s* brið-z, *come-s* kʌm-z, *run-s* rʌn-z, *sing-s* sɪŋ-z, *feel-s* fil-z; (vowels) *see-s* si-z, *piti-es* ˈpɪtɪ-z, *stay-s* ste-z, *thaw-s* θɔ-z, *go-es* go-z, *woo-es* wu-z, *stir-s* stɝ-z, stɝ-z, *scatter-s* ˈskætɚ-z, *subpoena-s* səˈpinə-z, *tri-es* traɪ-z, *allow-s* əˈlau-z, *employ-s* ɪmˈplɔɪ-z, *hew-s* hju-z, hɪu-z.

    (Rules I & II also apply to the pronunciation of -'s, the unstressed form of *is, has*.)

Rule III. Plurals, possessives in -'s, and third singulars of words ending in the remaining sounds, —the sibilants s, ʃ, tʃ, z, ʒ, dʒ,—are regularly given in the vocabulary. These add the syllable -ɪz or -əz (for variation in the vowel, see -*ed* in the vocabulary): *face-s* ˈfes-ɪz, *Nash's* ˈnæʃ-ɪz, *catch-es* ˈkætʃ-ɪz, *nose-s* ˈnoz-ɪz, *rouge-s* ˈruʒ-ɪz, *George's* ˈdʒɔrdʒ-ɪz.

PREFIXES AND SUFFIXES TREATED IN THE VOCABULARY

§89. Following is a list of word elements, chiefly initial or final, many of which have variant pronunciations. These elements are treated in the vocabulary in alphabetical order.

Where they are not found attached to head words in the vocabulary (as *prideful*, cf *pride*), the reader can add them with their pronunciations. If they are found in the vocabulary with their head words, variant pronunciations not listed at the full word can be found by consulting the separate element in the vocabulary, as, e.g., at *goodness* (see -*ness*) or at *mate* (see -*ed*).

-able	-edly	-hood
-age	-edness	i-, -i-
-ally *see* -ically	em- *see* en-	-ia
-ana	en-	-ial *see* -ia
-ate	-er	-ian *see* -ia
-ative	-es	-ible *see* -able
be-	-ese	-ically
-bly	-ess	-ie *see* -y
-d *see* -ed	-est	-iel *see* -ia
de-	-et	-ien *see* -ia
-dom	ex-	il- *see* in-
e-	-ey *see* -y	im- *see* in-
-ed	-ful	in-

-ing	-ment	-ship
-io, -ion, -ious *see* -ia	-ness	-sia
-ish	-or	-sion
-ism	-ous	-some
-ity	-ow	sub-
-ius *see* -ia	pre-	-tia
-ive	pro-	-tion
-less	re-	un-
-like	-ry	up-
-ly	-s *see* -es	wh-
-man	se-	-y

VARIANTS

§90. Certain classes of variant pronunciations found in cultivated American speech are described here in order to avoid excessive complication of the vocabulary entries. These variants are only those in wide use by cultivated speakers, and do not include those confined to local dialect or substandard speech.

MEDIAL UNACCENTED -*i*-

§91. Medial unaccented short *i* ɪ not followed by a vowel may become -ə- in nearly all words (*editor* ˈɛdɪtɚ, ˈɛdətɚ). When final ɪ becomes medial by the addition of a suffix, this change from ɪ to ə must often be assumed, as in *fragmentary* ˈfrægmənˌtɛrɪ |-*ly* -lɪ = ˈfrægmənˌtɛrɪlɪ or -ˌtɛrəlɪ. See also *i*-, -*i*- in the vocabulary.

UNACCENTED ɪ BEFORE ANOTHER VOWEL

§92. When the vowel sound ɪ (variously spelt) is immediately followed by another vowel sound (*radiate, oceanic, Ephraim, periodic, radio, medium, immediate*), the ɪ sound tends toward i, and thus might properly be shown as in ˈrediˌet, ˌoʃiˈænɪk, ˈifriəm, ˌpɪriˈɑdɪk, ˈrediˌo, ˈmidiəm, ɪˈmidiɪt. But this would greatly complicate the vocabulary, especially when derivatives vary from the head word, as in *study* ˈstʌdɪ |-*ing* ˈstʌdɪŋ, and even so would not fully show the extent of the variation of the ɪ. This variation is therefore not shown in the vocabulary. In reading a transcription like ɪˈmidɪt the variation will be made automatically.

THE ɔ SOUND (*WAR, HORSE, ALL*)

§93. In most of America ɔ appears to be rather unstable. In most positions except before ɪ final or r plus a consonant (*war, horse*), ɔ varies with many speakers to ɒ or ɑ. A similar variation is reported from Canada. In words in which the sound occurs before l plus a consonant (*walnut, Waldo, salt*), which in Brit have either ɔ or ɒ, the variants ɑ and ɒ are very common in America.

In New England ɒ is an extremely common substitute for ɔ, many speakers having only one phoneme (usually of ɒ quality) in such words as *cot* and *caught* or *collar* and *caller*. In spite of these widespread variants, our collections appear to justify the somewhat regular recording of the standard historical ɔ sound in the appropriate words.

ε FOR æ IN *CARRY, CHARITY*

§94. In words like *carry* ˈkærɪ, *marry* ˈmærɪ, *charity* ˈtʃærətɪ, *comparison* kəmˈpærəsṇ, having historical "short *a*" (æ) before r plus a vowel, a widespread pronunciation with ε (ˈkɛrɪ, ˈmɛrɪ. ˈtʃɛrətɪ, kəmˈpɛrəsṇ) is heard in the North and Canada, especially from the younger generations. Many of these speakers pronounce *marry, merry*, and *Mary* all alike —ˈmɛrɪ. This variant appears to be rare in the South, and for New England the *L.A.* shows only a very small percentage with ε.

DREARY, WEARY, POOR

§95. In words like *dreary, weary*, formerly having the vowel sound i before the **r**, while the general tendency is to lower the i to ɪ, some speakers use the higher i, and many use an intermediate vowel somewhat nearer to i than is the ɪ of *bit*. When the r is final or followed by a consonant (*year, beard*), the i sound is less apt to occur. Likewise ʊr (*poor*) varies to ur.

EASTERN AND SOUTHERN ɔə(r

§96. In words like *form* fɔrm; ES fɔəm, both pronunciations fɔəm and fɔːm are used in the East and the South. In the vocabulary only ɔə is given. This is done, however, with the implication that in such words the vowel varies between ɔə and ɔː, so that for speakers who do not usually pronounce ɔə in such words the symbol ɔə must be taken also to suggest ɔː. In longer words ɔə is more likely to be reduced to ɔ, especially if unaccented. This reduction is shown in such a word as *formality* fɔrˈmælətɪ; ES fɔˈmælətɪ. No sharp line can be drawn. The same speaker may say fɔəm in one breath and fɔːm or fɔm in the next, according to style of speech.

EASTERN AND SOUTHERN ɑə(r

§97. In words like *farm* fɑrm; ES fɑːm, or *far* fɑr; ES fɑː(r, an ə glide is less commonly heard after the ɑ (fɑəm, fɑə(r) than after ɔ in words like *form* (fɔəm). With some speakers in the East and South, however, this is consciously present, so that there is a definite distinction between *father* ˈfɑðə(r and *farther* ˈfɑəðə(r, even when the words are of equal length. As with ɔə(r, the pronunciation ɑə(r is commoner in the shorter words than in longer ones. Thus a speaker may say lɑədʒ for *large*, but ˈlɑːdʒə(r for *larger*. This glide ə after ɑ being much less frequent than after ɔ, it is not shown in the vocabulary.

WORDS LIKE *BOARD*

§98. Besides the two types **bord** and **bɔrd**, regularly shown in the vocabulary, a pronunciation of *board* is heard from some speakers, especially in the North, with a vowel sound about midway between o and ɔ (phonetic symbol ǫ, a lowered o or a raised ɔ). Such speakers also pronounce the same vowel ǫ in words like *horse, form* (pronounced by others hɔrs, fɔrm), so that in their speech *hoarse* is like *horse, boarder* is like *border*, etc. Thus these speakers pronounce all such words uniformly with ǫ, while other speakers that do not distinguish *hoarse* from *horse*, etc., pronounce them uniformly with ɔ.[4]

⁴ See Kenyon, *American Pronunciation*, 10th ed. §§366–372.

EASTERN AND SOUTHERN VOWEL IN *BIRD*

§99. In words like *bird, further* the first pronunciation for Eastern and Southern is **bɜd, ˈfɜˈðə(r**. In both the E and the S, however, a very large number of speakers pronounce ɝ instead of ɜ, saying **bɝd, ˈfɝˈðə(r** (not **ˈfɜˈðə** nor **ˈfɝˈðɚ**), with *r*-coloring in the accented vowel. It is to be noted that this pronunciation is heard from those who otherwise "drop their *r*'s," and it is confined to the stressed vowel. In this type of pronunciation the ə in *further* remains ə as with those who say **ˈfɜˈðə**. Thus such speakers would pronounce *The further part is better* **ðə ˈfɝˈðə pɑːt ɪz ˈbɛtə**.

This fact has long been known for Southern speech, but it has also recently been demonstrated for New England by the workers on the *L.A.*, and the same combination of ɝ with otherwise "*r*-less" pronunciation is heard in New York City. These facts have been fully verified by the present editors. Hence, in the vocabulary such words as *furthermore* are regularly represented for ES as **ˈfɜˈðəˌmoə(r, ˈfɝˈðəˌmoə(r**.

ɜɪ FOR THE VOWEL IN *BIRD*

§100. With many speakers in various parts of the South, and in New York City, a former r sound after ɜ, except when final (*fur*) or followed only by an inflectional ending (*furs*), is changed into something like ɪ, so that a word like *bird* is pronounced **bɜɪd**.[5]

Whether the NYC ɜɪ in *bird* (popularly but wrongly represented as *boid*) is historically connected with the Southern sound is unknown. But the NYC sound, commonly regarded as local dialect, is used by many educated speakers there, who recognize the sound in their own speech; and in the South it is also used by people of unquestioned cultivation.

EASTERN VARIATION BETWEEN ɑ AND a

§101. In the East, especially New England, the sound ɑ when spelt with *a* (*father, bar, calm*) varies with many speakers toward the sound **a**. A similar sound, but less prevalent, has been reported from near Williamsburg, Va. Since this variant is highly characteristic of New England, it is usually recorded, either in the vocabulary or in a page heading over the appropriate words. But it is not invariably recorded with less common words, and is then to be assumed as a possible variant.

EASTERN VARIATION BETWEEN æ, a, AND ɑ
IN WORDS LIKE *ASK*

§102. In the class of words spelt with *a* that is followed by a voiceless fricative s, f, or θ (*ask, chaff, bath*) or by a nasal plus a consonant (*example, demand*), in which British usually has ɑ, Eastern pronunciation (less commonly Eastern Virginian, see next section) varies between æ, a, and ɑ. The findings of the *L.A.* and the present editors' collections clearly indicate that, with a few exceptions (cf *half, calf, laugh, aunt*), the sound æ in these words in New England and New York City is at least as frequent as a, and usually more frequent than ɑ. In the vocabulary this variation is regularly shown by use of the plus sign, meaning "also," as at the word *fast* **fæst**; E + **fast, fɑst**. For other uses of the plus sign see §80.

---

[5] See Kemp Malone, *Studies for William A. Read*, University, La., 1940, p. 137. The same fact has also been observed by others.

WORDS LIKE *ASK* IN EASTERN VIRGINIA

§103. The words referred to in the preceding section (*ask, last, craft, path, chance,* etc.), in the vicinity of Richmond and Williamsburg, Va., are often pronounced with ɑ, less frequently with a. This pronunciation appears to be somewhat less common now than formerly. The historical and cultural importance of this region precludes regarding this merely as a localism. Yet to list this pronunciation of those words as a regular variant for Southern pronunciation as a whole would give a disproportionate impression, as well as complicate the vocabulary entries. It is therefore to be understood at those entries of such words containing the item "E + -a-, -ɑ-" that in eastern Virginia such words are also sometimes pronounced with ɑ, less often with a.

ɒ FOR ɑ IN *FATHER*

§104. In parts of the South the ɑ sound as in *father* ˈfɑðə(r is retracted or raised in the direction of ɔ (*all*) without wholly reaching ɔ, but resembling the intermediate ɒ (§12). The same variant is becoming common in New York City. As a result, we sometimes find the roles of *a* and *o* apparently reversed, *a* being pronounced ɒ and *o* being pronounced ɑ. Thus a native of NYC pronounced *margin* ˈmɒːdʒɪn and *Arthur* ˈɒːθə, while in the same breath he pronounced *Conning Tower* ˈkɑnɪŋˌtaʊə.

VARIANTS OF THE DIPHTHONG aʊ

§105. For the vowel sound in *out, ground*, one symbol aʊ is used in the vocabulary. This is an inclusive symbol, here serving for all varieties of this diphthong in cultivated American speech. Outside of the South the principal varieties are aʊ and ɑʊ. In aʊ the first element often varies slightly toward ɜ. aʊ and ɑʊ are so nearly alike that most hearers do not notice the difference. These two show no important geographical distribution, and often vary from speaker to speaker. A common variant, very general, is ɑ for aʊ before r (*our* aʊr, ɑr).

§106. In the South are several varieties. These never distinguish words otherwise alike, but there are geographical and sometimes social distinctions. The most striking of these are found in Virginia and bordering North Carolina. In Virginia, mainly east of the Blue Ridge, a diphthong approximately ɜʊ (often written əʊ but with stressed first element) is used before voiceless consonants (*out* ɜʊt, *house* hɜʊs), while æʊ is used before voiced sounds and finally (*ground* græʊnd, *houses* ˈhæʊzɪz, *cow* kæʊ). ɜʊ varies somewhat, especially to ʌʊ or oʊ. æʊ varies to aʊ or ɑʊ. Besides, the influence of analogy often breaks down the distinction before voiceless and voiced sounds, giving, e.g., *house* hɜʊs—*houses* ˈhɜʊzɪz, or hæʊs—ˈhæʊzɪz. In the western and southwestern parts of Virginia the tendency is to use æʊ in all positions, with variation to aʊ or ɑʊ.[6]

Perhaps owing in part to the influence of eastern Virginia, similar varieties are occasionally found in other parts of the South, but appear not to prevail there. The commonest varieties for the South as a whole are æʊ and aʊ, with intermediate shades. The form æʊ often becomes æə (*down* dæʊn, dæən).

---

[6] E. F. Shewmake, "Laws of Pronunciation in Eastern Virginia," *Mod. Lang. Notes*, XI, 8 (Dec. 1925), pp. 489–492. See also *American Speech*, XVIII, 1 (Feb. 1943), pp. 33–38.

Guy S. Lowman, "The Treatment of aʊ in Virginia," *Proc. of the Second International Congress of Phonetic Sciences*, Cambridge, 1936, pp. 122–125.

Argus Tresidder, "Notes on Virginia Speech," *American Speech*, XVI, 2 (April 1941), pp. 112–116.

Unpublished material in the *L.A.* was also consulted.

In parts of Canada (Ontario, Nova Scotia, and probably elsewhere) a distinction is found similar to that of eastern Virginia, the singular of *house* being hȝʊs or hoʊs and the plural 'haʊzɪz or 'hɑʊzɪz.

VARIANTS OF THE DIPHTHONG aɪ

§107. As with aʊ, so only one symbol aɪ is used in the vocabulary for the "long *i*" sound (*white* hwaɪt, *rise* raɪz). Outside of the South the principal varieties are aɪ (with a often varying slightly toward ȝ) and ɑɪ. The comments on the relation of aʊ to ɑʊ apply to that of aɪ to ɑɪ.

§108. In the South the varieties partly behave like those of aʊ. In Virginia east of the Blue Ridge many speakers use a sound approximately ʌɪ (varying toward ȝɪ) before voiceless consonants (*white* hwʌɪt, *wife* wʌɪf) but aɪ before voiced consonants and finally (*rise* raɪz, *wives* waɪvz, *high* haɪ). In some other parts of the South (as in the Carolinas) a similar distinction is found.

Another distinction, found, e.g., in Virginia and the Carolinas and probably elsewhere, is the use of aɪ or ʌɪ before voiceless consonants (*wife* waɪf, wʌɪf), but simple a or a: before voiced and finally (*wives* wavz, wa:vz, *why* hwa, hwa:, *mighty tired* 'mʌɪtɪ ta:d). The simple a, less frequently ɑ, for aɪ is fairly common in many parts of the South (Virginia, North Carolina, South Carolina, Texas, etc.). As with aʊ, analogy (as *wife—wives*) tends to break down the distinction wʌɪf—waɪvz or waɪf—wavz, yielding such pairs as waɪf—waɪvz or waf—wavz.[7] For the South as a whole aɪ may safely be taken as the prevailing sound.

As with aʊ, so with aɪ a distinction similar to that in Virginia between *wife* wʌɪf and *wives* waɪvz is also found in Ontario and eastern Canada, probably reflecting a situation found in several Scottish dialects.

VARIATION BETWEEN ju, ɪu, AND u

§109. In words containing "long *u*" there is variation between the sounds ju, ɪu, and u too complicated to be fully described here.[8] Some misunderstanding has existed as to the prevalence of the diphthong ɪu in cultivated American English. Apparently many suppose that words like *duty*, *new* have but two pronunciations—either djutɪ or dutɪ, nju or nu; or that words like *accuse* have but one—ə'kjuz. Grandgent, however, long ago demonstrated the frequency of ɪu in America[9] in collections that showed ɪu in 35 to 60 per cent of the speakers tested, according to the class of words used. Other American observers have confirmed his findings. Grandgent also accurately described the diphthong as ɪ with tongue drawn back somewhat (symbol ɪ) followed by u with tongue pushed forward (symbol ʉ), and either having more stress on ɪ than on ʉ or having about equal stress on both elements, and with the ʉ usually longer than the ɪ.

The same speaker often varies between ɪu and ju, for ɪu easily shades into ju as the ɪ receives less stress and thus becomes more like consonantal j. It was thus that modern ju developed from Early Modern ɪu in all words that now have ju, and many Americans have retained the older ɪu (except initially) along with other features of Early Modern English.

[7] See Shewmake and Tresidder, as cited above, footnote 6.
[8] See Kenyon, *American Pronunciation*, 8th ed., §§341–350.
[9] *Mod. Lang. Notes*, VI, 8 (1891), pp. 466–467

In one variant of this diphthong the first element has the tongue drawn back as far as to the position for an advanced u (ʉ), so that the diphthong merges into a monophthongal ʉ. Both ɪu and this ʉ are used by many Americans to distinguish words from similar words that have u; as *brewed* brɪud, brʉd, distinct from *brood* brud, or *lute* lɪut, lʉt, distinct from *loot* lut.

Present knowledge of the distribution and prevalence of ju, ɪu, and u in the words concerned does not always permit of an accurate order of frequency in the vocabulary. Such order as has been verified is there shown. For example, it appears certain that words like *assume* are prevailingly pronounced with u. But in the main all that is attempted is to give the three (or two) current sounds (*duty* ˈdjutɪ, ˈdɪutɪ, ˈdutɪ; *blue* blu, blɪu; *accuse* əˈkjuz, əˈkɪuz) without insistence on order of frequency, all the pronunciations being in cultivated American use.

In the vocabulary the symbol ɪu is always to be taken to mean ʉ. See §§40, 41.

UNACCENTED *U* IN WORDS LIKE *CALCULATE*, *CONGRATULATE*, *EDUCATE*, *NATURE*, *VERDURE*

§110. In familiar speech unaccented *u* as in *calculate* is most commonly -jə- (ˈkælkjəˌlet) unless another vowel follows (*evacuate* ɪˈvækjuˌet). It often varies between -jə- and -ju- according to style of speech.

In colloquial pronunciation of words like *congratulate, educate*, unaccented -*tu*- and -*du*- most commonly are -tʃə- (kənˈgrætʃəˌlet, -ˈgrætʃu-) and -dʒə- (ˈɛdʒəˌket, ˈɛdʒu-), unless a vowel follows (*eventuate* ɪˈvɛntʃuˌet, *graduate* ˈgrædʒuˌet). In dissyllables the unaccented ending -*ture* is usually -tʃɚ, ES -tʃə(r, in common words (*nature* ˈnetʃɚ; ES ˈnetʃə(r), and -*dure* is usually -dʒɚ, ES -dʒə(r (*verdure* ˈvɝdʒɚ, -dʒur; ES -dʒə(r, -dʒuə(r). See *Webster's New International Dictionary, Second Edition*, Guide to Pronunciation, §249, seventh paragraph. In words of three or more syllables not accented on the penult the unaccented ending -*ture* is commonly -tʃɚ or -tʃur according to style or to familiarity of the word (*miniature* ˈmɪnɪtʃɚ, ˈmɪnɪətʃɚ, ˈmɪnɪəˌtʃur). If -*ture* has a light accent then it is -ˌtʃur (*literature* ˈlɪtərəˌtʃur). Initial unaccented "long *u*" is ju- or ju- according to style (*unite* juˈnaɪt, juˈnaɪt).

SOUTHERN ɪ FOR ɛ BEFORE NASAL SOUNDS

§111. In parts of the South the sound of ɛ before m, n, or ŋ (*stem, men, length*) is replaced by, or tends in the direction of, ɪ (stɪm, mɪn, lɪŋkθ). This pronunciation is not equally distributed over the South and apparently is not equally acceptable in all types of Southern speech. Its omission from the vocabulary is not intended to imply disapproval of it.

VARIATION BETWEEN n AND ŋ BEFORE k OR g

§112. When the letter *n* ends the syllable before a k or a g sound, it usually represents the sound ŋ if the next syllable is final and wholly unaccented, as in *congress* ˈkaŋgrəs, *Concord* ˈkaŋkəd (compare the pronunciation ˈkankɔrd, where the final syllable has an unmarked subordinate accent). In other situations there is much wavering between n and ŋ that has no bearing on acceptability and is therefore often not shown in the vocabulary.

For the substitution of n for ŋ in -*ing* words, see -*ing* in the vocabulary.

THE SOUNDS OF *WH*

§113. In words spelt with *wh* (*whale* **hwel,** *when* **hwɛn,** *wheel* **hwil,** etc.) many speakers omit the **h** element and pronounce plain **w,** thus making homophones of *whale, wail* **wel;** *when, wen* **wɛn;** *wheel, weal* **wil;** etc. This is clearly not the prevailing pronunciation for America as a whole, but it appears to be somewhat on the increase, perhaps owing to the influence of Southern British speech. In the vocabulary only **hw** is given for such words. See also *wh-* in the vocabulary.

SYLLABIC ļ, n̩, m̩, VARYING WITH əl, ən, əm

§114. In a great many words there is frequent variation between a syllabic consonant and ə plus a nonsyllabic consonant. In the vocabulary, as a rule, only the one deemed to be colloquially most usual is given. Examples of such variation are: *apple* **ˈæpļ, ˈæpəl;** *happen* **ˈhæpən, ˈhæpn̩, ˈhæpm̩** (when -pm̩ results from assimilation of -pn̩, -pəm never occurs); *trouble* **ˈtrʌbļ, ˈtrʌbəl;** *buckle* **ˈbʌkļ, ˈbʌkəl;** *struggle* **ˈstrʌgļ, ˈstrʌgəl;** *castle* **ˈkæsļ, ˈkæsəl;** *drizzle* **ˈdrɪzļ, ˈdrɪzəl;** *prism* **ˈprɪzəm, ˈprɪzm̩** (see *-ism* in the vocabulary); *mason* **ˈmesn̩, ˈmesən;** *prison* **ˈprɪzn̩, ˈprɪzən;** *bacon* **ˈbekən, ˈbekn̩, ˈbekŋ** (see §24, 3d par.); *wagon* **ˈwægən, ˈwægn̩, ˈwægŋ;** *monopoly* **məˈnapļɪ, məˈnapəlɪ;** *obelisk* **ˈabļˌɪsk, ˈabəˌlɪsk** (for the accent see §52); *assassinate* **əˈsæsn̩ˌet, əˈsæsəˌnet.**

But in many words, while it is phonetically possible to pronounce either form, one of the forms is decidedly prevalent and the other either rare or un-English. Thus *cotton* **ˈkatn̩,** *hidden* **ˈhɪdn̩,** *little* **ˈlɪtļ,** *cradle* **ˈkredļ,** and such words as *didn't* **ˈdɪdn̩t,** *oughtn't* **ˈɔtn̩t,** *couldn't* **ˈkudn̩t,** *wouldn't* **ˈwudn̩t** in standard speech are not pronounced **ˈkatən, ˈhɪdən, ˈlɪtəl, ˈkredəl, ˈdɪdənt, ˈɔtənt, ˈkudənt, ˈwudənt.** An alternative pronunciation with -əl, -ən, -əm is much less usual when the syllabic consonant is final and follows a consonant made with the same position of the tongue point or of the lips (-tn̩, -dn̩, -tļ, -dļ, -nļ). Syllabic m̩ is less frequent and is heard chiefly after the homorganic **p** (*open* **ˈopm̩,** *keep 'em* **ˈkipm̩**) or **b** (*album* **ˈælbm̩,** *rob 'em* **ˈrabm̩**).

m is not syllabic after **t** (*bottom* **ˈbatəm**) or **d** (*Adam* **ˈædəm**), though the ə may be very quick. Nasals are not syllabic after nasals (*common* **ˈkamən,** *venom* **ˈvɛnəm,** *cannon* **ˈkænən,** *minimum* **ˈmɪnəməm**) or after **l** (*stolen* **ˈstolən** or **stoln** with nonsyllabic **n,** *column* **ˈkaləm**). **n** is not usually syllabic after **nd** (*London* **ˈlʌndən**), but is often so after **nt** (*mountain* **ˈmauntn̩**). Consonants are not syllabic after vowels.

In medial position alternation is frequent even after homorganic consonants (*fatally* **ˈfetļɪ, ˈfetəlɪ;** *Adelaide* **ˈædļˌed, ˈædəˌled;** *scrutiny* **ˈskrutn̩ɪ, ˈskrutənɪ;** *ordinal* **ˈɔrdn̩əl, ˈɔrdənəl**).

In some cases the difference distinguishes words otherwise alike. Thus in Eastern and Southern, **ˈsætn̩** means "satin," while **ˈsætən** means "Saturn"; **ˈbɪtn̩** means "bitten," while **ˈbɪtən** means "bittern"; **ˈpætn̩** means "paten" or "patten," while **ˈpætən** means "pattern"; **ˈfɔəmļɪ** means "formally," while **ˈfɔəməlɪ** means "formerly."

ADDITION OR OMISSION OF CONSONANTS

§115. Certain consonant sounds are inserted or omitted very generally in American English which are not regularly shown as variants in the vocabulary. Thus a **t** sound is often inserted between **n** and the **s** sound (*sense* **sɛns, sɛnts,** like *cents* **sɛnts**), between **n** and ʃ (*mansion* **ˈmænʃən, ˈmænt·ʃən,** *intention* **ɪnˈtɛnʃən, ɪnˈtɛnt·ʃən,** cf *luncheon* **ˈlʌntʃən**), between **n** and θ (*ninth* **naɪnθ, naɪntθ,** *tenth* **tɛnθ, tɛntθ**), between l and θ (*health* **hɛlθ, hɛltθ**), between l and s (*false* **fɔls, fɔlts,** like *faults*), between l and ʃ (*Welsh* **wɛlʃ, wɛltʃ,** cf *Welch*); and a **p** sound between **m** and **f** (*comfort* **'kʌmfət, 'kʌmpfət,** *camphor* **'kæmfə, 'kæmpfə,** cf *campfire*).

Omissions: **d** is often omitted between **n** and **z** (*lends* **lɛndz, lɛnz,** like *lens*) or between l and **z** (*fields* **fildz, filz,** like *feels*). The first element of **tʃ** is often omitted after **n** (*bench* **bɛntʃ, bɛnʃ,** *luncheon* **'lʌntʃən, 'lʌnʃən**) or after l (*filch* **fɪltʃ, fɪlʃ,** cf *Walsh, Welsh*), and the first element of **dʒ** is often omitted after **n** (*revenge* **rɪ'vɛndʒ, rɪ'vɛnʒ**), less frequently after l (*bulge* **bʌldʒ, bʌlʒ**).

LENGTHENED s REPLACING sts

§116. When the ending **s** is added to words in **-st** (*nests, beasts, rests*) the **t** sound is very often omitted, and the two **s** sounds combine into one long **s** (symbol **s:**). Thus *nests, beasts, rests* are often pronounced **nɛs:, bis:, rɛs:.**

PROPER NAMES

§117. For personal and place names the variant pronunciations given in the vocabulary often refer to different persons or places. Whenever the information was available, the variants have been referred to particular persons or places, but to do so in all cases is beyond the scope of this work.

CANADIAN VARIANTS

§118. In its most noticeable feature—the treatment of the *r* sound—most Canadian speech resembles the speech of the North in the US. The Midwesterner who visits Ontario or southern Quebec feels at home in the matter of speech. Direct British influence is, however, noticeable in details of both pronunciation and vocabulary. The pronunciations **'aɪðə** and **'naɪðə** are rather more frequent than in the East in the US. For *rather* and *can't* **'raðə** and **kɑnt** are often heard. For *dictionary* (and similar words) **'dɪkʃənrɪ** is heard beside **'dɪkʃən‚ɛrɪ.** For *laboratory* **lə'bɔrətrɪ** is heard beside **'læbrə‚torɪ.** For *terrible* **'tɛrɪbl** is heard beside **'tɛrəbḷ.** **sə'dʒɛst** for *suggest*, and **'frædʒaɪl** for *fragile*, are frequent. Scottish influence is apparent in Canada, especially in the use of the intermediate **a** for **æ** in "flat *a*" words (*hat, man,* etc.), in Nova Scotia and Alberta, and probably elsewhere. For the **aʊ** diphthong, **oʊ** (§106) and **u** are heard, probably also reflecting Scottish influence.

JUNCTIONAL, OR SANDHI, FORMS

§119. Pronunciations resulting from the effect of an initial sound of a following word (*did you* **'dɪdʒu,** *goes shopping* **goʒ 'ʃɑpɪŋ,** *sand pile* **'sæn‚paɪl**), or of a final sound of a preceding word (*bag and baggage* **'bæɡṇ'bæɡɪdʒ,** *good enough* **‚gʊdṇ'ʌf**), are only occasionally recorded in the vocabulary.

SPELLING PRONUNCIATION

§120. The term Spelling Pronunciation is used to designate a pronunciation which replaces that handed on by word of mouth in the spoken language and conforms in some respect more closely to the spelling, which is in some degree unphonetic—fails to correspond with the established pronunciation. Such pronunciations originate, as the *Oxford Dictionary* puts it, by taking a "shot" at the word from the spelling. Every such pronunciation is at first an error (departs from established usage); but innumerable pronunciations of this origin have come to be so general that they are now in unquestioned good standing. For examples see *Bentham, Waltham, Horsham;* and for fuller treatment see Kenyon, *American Pronunciation,* 8th ed., §§142–150.

DISSIMILATION

§121. A phonetic tendency known as Dissimilation is seen in English words in which an *r* sound in one syllable is lost if there is another *r* sound in the word. Thus in those regions where *r* is usually sounded in all positions the commonest colloquial pronunciation of *surprise* is sə'praɪz. Here the presence of the second **r** has led to the loss of the first (that is, in this case, the change of ɚ to ə by loss of its *r*-coloring). This tendency was pointed out for American English by Hempl (*Dialect Notes,* I, vi, 1893). Sometimes instead of being lost the **r** is changed to **l**, as it was in *Salisbury* (formerly *Sarisberie,* cf *Sarum*), or in *Salop* 'Shropshire,' from *Sloppesberie,* earlier *Shrobbesberie* 'Shrewsbury.'

Another example of *r* loss is 'gʌvənɚ, the prevailing pronunciation of *governor* in the North. That this is due to the other *r* sound and not to slovenly pronunciation is shown by the fact that the same speakers who say 'gʌvənɚ do not omit the *r* sound in *governess, govern, governing, governance, government,* which have no second **r**.

R-dissimilation does not often occur in regions where **r** is pronounced only before a vowel, though it might occur there in such a word as *preparatory* if pronounced pə'pærə,torɪ, and it may have operated in some words before a second **r** was dropped by the regular loss of **r** in the '*r*-less' regions. The loss of the first *r* in ES *governor* 'gʌvənə(r is not due to *r*-dissimilation, for similar loss is regular in ES *governess* 'gʌvənɪs, *govern* 'gʌvən, which have no other *r;* and *surprise* in ES is sə'praɪz for the same reason that *survive* in ES is sə'vaɪv.

Other examples of dissimilation are: *Bourchier* (cf *Boucher*), *Canterbury, catercornered, caterpillar, elderberry, February, Marylebone, northerner, southerner, Northrup, Otterburn, paraphernalia, particular* (the schoolmastered pronunciation pɑr'tɪkjələ is perhaps a reaction against this), *Pendergast, reservoir, reverbatory, St. Bernard, thermometer, Waterbury.*

The pronunciations sə'praɪz and 'gʌvənɚ are "correct" forms, not because they are phonetically normal, but solely because they are in wide use by cultivated speakers. The same dissimilation is also seen in some pronunciations not so prevalent as to be generally acceptable; as *Arthur, corner, interpret, perform, performance, proportion, secretary, Shrewsbury, Swarthmore.*

ANGLICIZING

§122. A pronouncing dictionary of English must deal with the pronunciation of foreign words that have become more or less a part of the English language. With wholly foreign words it has, strictly speaking, nothing to do. However, a few foreign words or phrases and some foreign names have been entered which are somewhat in use in America but which have as yet no settled English pronunciation. These are given with their foreign pronunciation only, and are so labeled.

For the much larger body of foreign words that have become more or less Anglicized in use, meaning, and pronunciation, the editors follow the same guide as for fully English words—

they try to ascertain and report cultivated usage. But it is just this area of the language in which usage is most unsettled and uncertain, and where dictionary editors must bring to bear certain linguistic principles to supplement the uncertain evidence of usage. Some of these principles and considerations are:—

(1) The English language has shown great vigor and stability in assimilation of foreign material—in making it native. Until comparatively recent times foreign words fully adopted into English use have been adjusted to English laws of sound and accent. In Great Britain especially this is still usual. By radio one often hears foreign words pronounced in the English way by the best-educated leaders of that country; as, for example, the pronunciation ˈnæzɪ for *Nazi*. Whether or not this ever becomes a settled pronunciation, it shows the tendency; and many similar cases could be cited, which are in keeping with English tradition, and are by no means blunders.[10]

(2) The question often arises, Why not pronounce foreign words, especially names, with their foreign sounds? The answer, too little understood, is simple: except for the fractional percentage who speak the foreign language like a native, it is impossible, as the history of sound changes in past borrowings clearly shows. Very few English sounds are exactly like the foreign ones or those spelt with corresponding letters. This is deceptive to those not expert in foreign language. Examples abound. Many apparently suppose, for example, that they are pronouncing *Monticello* as Italian when they call it ˌmɑntɪˈtʃɛlo. In fact, they are giving approximately the Italian sound to three out of the ten sounds (m, tʃ, ɛ), and omitting one. An attempt, sometimes heard, to pronounce *envelope* in the French way by saying ˈɑnvəˌlop results in giving approximately the French sound to the v and the p. The l and all the vowels are quite different, and the n is not in the French word. The pronunciation of the fully Americanized name *Valparaiso* as ˌvalpəˈraɪzo is not a very successful attempt at the Spanish ˌbalparaˈiso. The American gəˈrɑʒ has two consonants of the French gɑˈraːʒ (g, ʒ, the r's being different) and one of its vowels—in the wrong syllable. The underlying fact is, that the speaker not fully conversant with a foreign language in attempting to imitate the foreign pronunciation substitutes his own nearest sounds for the foreign sounds, with a result unacceptable to the native speaker of the foreign language.

Often, too, the attempt to use foreign pronunciations misses the mark. Thus the word *valet* is not from Modern French but from Old French, and has been English (with a t sound) for some 400 years. Neither of the hybrid pronunciations væˈle or ˈvæle comes very near to the French vaˈlɛ. The case of *Calais* is similar. For several centuries an English name (for 200 years an English town), it was, and is, pronounced ˈkælɪs in the English way (like *palace* ˈpælɪs from OF *palais*), as in Shakespeare (spelt *Callis, Callice*) and later English poets (riming with *malice, Alice*). The present frequently heard kæˈle, ˈkælɪ are as far from Modern French kɑˈlɛ or kaˈlɛ as væˈle or ˈvælɪ is from French vaˈlɛ.

The attempt to show knowledge of a foreign language by similar rough or even ludicrous attempts at the foreign pronunciation often shows ignorance instead. Such inaccurate hybrid pronunciations are, however, often taken up by many otherwise well-informed speakers, and so get established in good use, in the same way that hundreds of other linguistic errors and blunders have attained to good standing (witness Dr. Johnson's recommendation of *ache* for

---

[10] See Brander Matthews's defense of this tradition in *Society for Pure English Tract No. V.*

ake); and a dictionary based on usage must recognize them. Consequently many hybrid pronunciations of foreign derivatives are here given, for, however inaccurate, usage has established them.

(3) Wherever there is room for doubt as to actual usage, however, our policy has been to lean toward the long-established English tradition of full Anglicizing. Certain foreign sounds will, if the words become general, inevitably shift to native English sounds—as French **a** is sure to become either English **æ** or **α**. In most cases the actual foreign pronunciation is added in parentheses, so that the user of the dictionary can adopt the foreign pronunciation if he chooses. And for those who prefer to follow the English tradition the appended foreign pronunciation may serve to show the inaccuracy of some of the attempted imitations.

PRONUNCIATION OF LATIN WORDS

§123. Latin words not usually being American colloquial English, as a rule only the orthodox English Latin pronunciation is given. The so-called Roman pronunciation is very inconsistent in actual practice. Some form of it is sometimes added if it has become widely current in actual use (cf *cum laude*).

MISCELLANEOUS SUGGESTIONS

§124.   1. The Key to pronunciation found at the bottom of every pair of open pages in the vocabulary contains the common English sounds. Each illustrative word in boldface type shows the sound of both vowel and consonant symbols. For fuller information about the phonetic alphabet and its use in this book, see Introduction, §§3–47.

2. The basis of pronunciation in this dictionary is Cultivated Colloquial English—conversational style, not formal public address or public reading. For discussion of colloquial English, see Introduction, §§1–2.

3. A Colloquialism is not a Localism or Slang. See Introduction, §§1–2, with the definition of *Colloquial* there quoted from *Webster's New International Dictionary, Second Edition*.

4. For acceptable pronunciations not regularly listed in the vocabulary, see Introduction, *Variants*, §§90–119.

5. Certain classes of words have Shifting or Variable Accent. For information on this and on accent and stress in general, see Introduction, §§48–54.

6. For treatment of Regional Variations, see Introduction, §§76–85.

7. For the pronunciation of Foreign Words, see §122 on Anglicizing.

8. Too much importance should not be attached to the Order in which the variant pronunciations are given in the vocabulary. Several factors govern this order. See Introduction, §§57–58.

9. It is idle to insist on the "correct" pronunciation of words not yet established in general oral use. The correct pronunciation will be whatever usage finally settles on, regardless of whether it agrees with etymology, spelling, or analogy.

10. "The pronunciation is the actual living form or forms of a word, that is, *the word*

itself, of which the current spelling is only a symbolization—generally, indeed, only the traditionally-preserved symbolization of an earlier form."—*Oxford English Dictionary*.

11. "While we are entitled to display a certain fastidious precision in our saying of words that only the educated use, we deserve not praise but censure if we decline to accept the popular pronunciation of popular words."—H. W. Fowler, *Dictionary of Modern English Usage*.

12. "I do not believe in the feasibility of imposing one particular form of pronunciation on the English-speaking world."—Daniel Jones, *An English Pronouncing Dictionary*, 4th ed.

ABBREVIATIONS

Abbreviated names of English counties are listed in the vocabulary

+	also	*Can*	Canada, -dian
abbr.	abbreviation, -ated	*cf*	compare
acct	accent, -uation	*ch.*	church
acc. to	according to	*Chauc.*	Chaucer
adj	adjective	*chem.*	chemistry
adv	adverb	*Chin*	China, -nese
Afr	Africa, -can	*co.*	county
Ala	Alabama	*Col*	Colorado
Alas	Alaska	*colloq.*	colloquial, -ly
Am	American	*conj*	conjunction
Amer	America	*Conn*	Connecticut
Am Sp	American Spanish (with PI)	*cons., conss.*	consonant, -nants
anat.	anatomy	*Cornw*	Cornwall
Anglic.	Anglicize, -d	*Cumb*	Cumberland
apos.	apostle	*Czech*	Czechish
Arab	Arabic, Arabian	*Dan*	Danish
arch.	archaic	*dat*	dative
Arg	Argentine, -na	*Del*	Delaware
Ark	Arkansas	*Dev*	Devonshire
art.	article	*dial.*	dialect, -al, -ally
attrib.	attributive	*Du*	Dutch
Austral	Australia	E	Eastern, East
aux	auxiliary	*Egyp*	Egypt, -ptian
BBC	British Broadcasting Corporation	*emph.*	emphatic, -phasis
		EN	Eastern and Northern
bef.	before	*Eng*	English
Belg	Belgium, Belgian	*Engd*	England
Bib.	Bible	*erron.*	erroneous, -ly
Bol	Bolivia	ES	Eastern and Southern
bor.	borough	*esp.*	especially
bot.	botany, botanist	*etym.*	etymology
Braz	Brazil	*fem.*	feminine, female
Brit	British	*Finl*	Finland
C	Canada, -dian	*Fla*	Florida
c (before		*Flem*	Flemish
numerals)	*circa*, about	*Fr*	French
c, cc (after		*freq.*	frequent, -ly
numerals)	century, -ries	*Ga*	Georgia
CA	Central America, -can	*gen*	genitive
Cal	California	*geog.*	geography, -phic, -ically
Camb	Cambridge	*geol.*	geology

(1)

geom.	geometry, -trical	*Mod E*	Modern English
Ger	German	*M. of Ven.*	*Merchant of Venice*
Gk	Greek	*mt., mts.*	mountain, -s
gram.	grammar, -matical	*mus.*	music
Heb	Hebrew	*myth.*	mythology, -logical
Hind	Hindi	N	Northern, North
hist.	historical, -ly	*n*	noun
Hung	Hungarian	*naut.*	nautical
Ia	Iowa	*NB*	New Brunswick, Can.
Ice	Iceland, -ic	*NC*	North Carolina
Id	Idaho	*NEngd*	New England
Ill	Illinois	*Neth*	Netherlands
Ind	Indiana	*NH*	New Hampshire
inf	infinitive	*Nicar*	Nicaragua
infreq.	infrequent, -ly	*NJ*	New Jersey
intj	interjection	*NMex*	New Mexico
Ir	Irish	*Norw*	Norwegian
Irel	Ireland	*NY*	New York
isl.	island	*NYC*	New York City
It	Italian	*NZ*	New Zealand
IW	Isle of Wight	*O*	Ohio
Jap	Japanese	*occas.*	occasional, -ly
Kan	Kansas	*OE*	Old English
Ky	Kentucky	*OED*	*Oxford English Dictionary*
L	Latin		*=Oxford Dictionary*
L.A.	*Linguistic Atlas of the US*	*OF*	Old French
	and Canada	*o. f.*	old-fashioned
La	Louisiana	*Okla*	Oklahoma
LI	Long Island	*Oreg*	Oregon
loc.	local, -ly	*Oxf*	Oxford, -shire
Lond	London	*Pa*	Pennsylvania
Mass	Massachusetts	*Pal*	Palestine
math.	mathematics	*perh.*	perhaps
Md	Maryland	*Pers*	Persia, -n
ME	Middle English	*pers*	person (grammar)
Me	Maine	*pers.*	personal
meas.	measure	*Pg*	Portuguese
Mich	Michigan	*Phil*	Philippine
mil.	military	*phil.*	philosopher
Minn	Minnesota	*PI*	Philippine Islands
Miss	Mississippi	*pl*	plural
Mo	Missouri	*poet.*	poetic, -al, poetry
mod.	modern	*Pol*	Polish

Port	Portugal	*surg.*	surgery
poss	possessive	*Sus*	Sussex
pptc	past participle	*Sw*	Swedish
prep	preposition	*Swtz*	Switzerland
pres	present	*syl.*	syllable
pro	pronoun	*Tasm*	Tasmania
prob.	probably	*Tenn*	Tennessee
pron.	pronunciation, pronounce, pronounced	*Tex*	Texas
		trans	transitive
ptc	participle, -cipial	*unstr.*	unstressed
rel	relative pronoun	*Uru*	Uruguay
relig.	religion, -ious	*US*	United States
RI	Rhode Island	*v*	verb
riv.	river	*Va*	Virginia
Rom	Roman	*var.*	variant
Rus	Russian	*vil.*	village
S	Southern, South	*vocab.*	vocabulary
S Amer, SA	South America, -can	*volc.*	volcano
SC	South Carolina	*vow.*	vowel, -s
Sc	Scottish, Scotch	*Vt*	Vermont
Scand	Scandinavian	W	Western, West
schol.	scholar	*w.*	with
Scotl	Scotland	*W²*	*Webster's New International Dictionary, Second Edition*
sculp.	sculptor		
SD	South Dakota		
sg	singular	*Wash*	Washington (state)
Shak.	Shakespeare	*WI*	West Indies
Som	Somersetshire	*Wis*	Wisconsin
Sp	Spanish	*WPacif*	West Pacific
sp.	spelling, spelt	*WVa*	West Virginia
sp. pr., sp. pron.	spelling pronunciation	*Yks*	Yorkshire

In the vocabulary, entries and other spelling forms (except catchwords) are in light roman type, pronunciations and all sounds are in **boldface,** and explanatory matter is in *italic* (except the regional labels E, S, N, W).

Occasionally, earlier spellings of an entry word, with dates of their occurrence in records, are shown as evidence of pronunciation or of other significant facts in the history of the word. Cf. the entries Bicester, kiln.

ADDENDA

A PRONOUNCING DICTIONARY OF AMERICAN ENGLISH

An asterisk (*) marks words already recorded in the main vocabulary.
The plus sign (+) is to be read "also."

adieux *2d pl of* adieu* ə'djuz, ə'dɪuz, ə'duz
  (*Fr* a'djø)
Aguilar *Col* 'ægwɪ͵lɑr; ES -͵lɑːɪr, E+-͵lɑːɪr
Ahsahka *Id* ə'sɑkə
Alamosa *Col* ͵ælə'mosə, *loc.*+-'musə, -sɪ
Algonquian*, -quin*+-nk-
Amish 'amɪʃ, 'æmɪʃ
Athol* *NY* 'eθəl |A- Springs 'eθəl, 'æθəl
Attu *Alas isl.* 'ætu
bateaux *pl of* bateau* bæ'toz (*Fr* ba'to)
Baugh bɔ—*from* Bach, *cf* Reidenbach, Utah*
Benld *Ill loc.* bə'nɛl, *older* bɛn'ɛldi *from* Ben
  L. Dorsey—*cf* Gnadenhutten*, Ypres*,
  Yreka*, Yvonne*, *in which also the name of*
  a letter replaces its usual sound.
Biloxi *Miss* bə'lɑksɪ, -'lʌk-; ES+-'lɒk-
Blackstone* *cf variant spelling* Blaxton
Blanchester *O* 'blæn͵tʃɛstə, -tʃɪs-; ES -tə(r
Bogalusa *La* ͵bogə'lusə
Bogoslof Isl. *Alas* 'bogəs͵lɑf, -͵lɒf, -͵lɔf
Bois Blanc Isl. *Mich* 'bab͵lo'aɪlənd; ES+
  'bɒb-; (*Fr* bwa'blɑ̃)
Boise* *Id*+'bɔɪzɪ
Bollinger *Mo* 'balɪndʒɚ; ES -dʒə(r, 'bɒl-
Bonar*, *Horatius* 'banɚ; ES 'banə(r, 'bɒn-
Bon Homme *SD* ban'ham; ES+bɒn'hɒm
Borger *Tex* 'bɔrgɚ; ES 'bɔəgə(r
Boscawen* *NH loc.* 'baskwaɪn, 'bɒs-
Boston*+'bɔstən, 'bɒstən (§114)
Botolph* *loc.*+bə'tɒl ͵strit
Bouckville *NY* 'baukvɪl
Bouquet *NY* bo'kɛt, bə'kɛt
Broadalbin *NY* brɔd'ɔlbɪn, -'ælbɪn
Broome* *NY co. now more often* brum
Bruneau *Id* 'bruno
Buchman 'bukmən, 'bʌk- (*Ger* 'buːxman)
Buchmanism*, -ite*+'bukmən-
Burleigh *ND* 'bɝlɪ; ES 'bɜlɪ, 'bɜˑlɪ

Busti *NY* 'bʌstaɪ
Cache *Utah* kæʃ |-'s -ɪz
Cadiz* *spell Sp city* Cádiz; *pron.*+kə'dɪz
Cahaba *Ala riv.* kə'habə, kə'hɒbə
Cahoon *surname* kə'hun—*see* Calhoon *below*
Calhoon = Calhoun*—*cf* Colquhoun*
Canaseraga *NY* ͵kænəsə'rɑgə
Canastota *NY* ͵kænə'stotə
Caneadea *NY* ͵kænə'diə ('Canea͵dea 'Road)
Canisteo *NY* ͵kænə'stio
Canyon de Chelly *Ariz* 'kænjəndə'ʃe
Cape Girardeau *Mo* 'kɛpdʒə'rɑrdo, -də; ES
  -'rɑːdo, E+-'raːdo
Capulin *NMex mt.* kə'pjuln, kə'pɪuln
Celoron* *NY*+'sɛlə͵ron, 'sɛlərən
Cerf *surname* sɝf; ES sɜf, sɜˑf
charm *var. sp. of* chirm* '*din of birds*'
Chateaugay *NY* 'ʃætə͵ge, 'ʃætəgɪ
Chehalis *Wash* tʃɪ'helɪs |-'s -ɪz
Cheney *Am vils., surname* 'tʃinɪ
Cheningo *NY* ʃə'nɪŋgo
Chesuncook *Me* tʃɪ'sʌnkuk
Chichester* *NY* 'tʃaɪ͵tʃɛstə; ES -tə(r
chile con carne, -li 'tʃɪlɪkən'kɑrnɪ, -kɑn'k-;
  ES -'kɑːnɪ, -kɒn'k-, E+-'kaːnɪ
Chittenango *NY* ͵tʃɪtn̩'æŋgo, tʃɪt'næŋgo
Churchill*+-͵hɪl—*cf* Northampton*
Cleburne *Ala, Ark, Tex* 'klibɚn; ES 'klibən
climatic klaɪ'mætɪk |-al -l̩ |-ally -l̩ɪ, -ɪklɪ
Cochise *Ariz* ko'tʃis |-'s -ɪz
Coconino *Ariz* ͵kokə'nino
Coeur D'Alene *Id* ͵kɔrd'len; ES ͵kɔəd-
cognizable*+kag'naɪzəbl̩, kɒg-
Columbiana *O* kə͵lʌmbɪ'ænə
Combahee *SC* ͵kambə'hi, kʌm'bi; ES+
  ͵kɒmbə'hi
Conewango *NY* ͵kanə'waŋgo, -'wɒŋ-; ES+
  ͵kɒn-

Key: *See in full §§3–47.* bee bi |pity 'pɪtɪ (§6) |rate ret |yet jɛt |sang sæŋ |angry 'æŋ·grɪ
|bath bæθ; E baθ (§10) |ah ɑ |far fɑr |watch watʃ, wɒtʃ (§12) |jaw dʒɔ |gorge gɔrdʒ |go go
|full ful |tooth tuθ |further 'fɝðɚ; ES 'fɜˑðə |custom 'kʌstəm |while hwaɪl |how hau |toy tɔɪ
|using 'juzɪŋ |fuse fjuz, fɪuz |dish dɪʃ |vision 'vɪʒən |Eden 'idn̩ |cradle 'kredl̩ |keep 'em 'kipm̩

(liii)

Corinth* *NY, Vt, loc.*+kə'rɪnθ, krɪnθ
Costilla *Col* kas'tiə, kɒs-, -'tijə (*Am Sp* kɔs'tija)
coxcombic* *at ES read:*+kɒks'kɒmɪk
Coxsackie *NY* kuk'sakɪ, kak-, -'sækɪ; ES+ kɒk-
cross bun 'krɔs'bʌn, 'krɒs- ('hot ˌcross 'bun)
Crummel, -mmles 'krʌm|(z)—*from* Cromwell
Cunard* *accent*+*as in* 'Cuˌnard 'Line
Cuprum *Id* 'kjuprəm, 'kɪu-, 'ku-
Dahlia* *NY vil.* 'delɪə, 'deljə; *see p. vi*
Darien* *Ga* 'derɪən
Depauville *NY* dɪ'povɪl, dɪ'pɔvɪl
De Ruyter *NY* dɪ'raɪtə; ES dɪ'raɪtə(r
Desha *Ark* də'ʃe
dilettantes *pl* ˌdɪlə'tæntɪz |-ti -'tænti
diphosgene*+-'fazdʒin; ES+-'fɒz-
Domremy-la-Pucelle*+Domrémy- dŏre'mi-
Dorcheat *La riv.* 'dɔrtʃit; ES 'dɔətʃit
Dravosburg *Pa* drə'vosbɜ·g: ES -bɜg, -bɝg
Dumas* *Ark* 'dumæs, 'dju-, 'dɪu-
Dunsany* *Brit*+dʌn'sænɪ
Duplin *NC* 'djuplɪn, 'dɪu-, 'du-
Duryea *Pa* dur'je, 'durje; ES duə'je, 'duəje
Ecorse *Mich* 'ikɔrs; ES 'ikɔəs |-'s -ɪz
Edgecombe *NC*, -comb *Me, Wash* 'ɛdʒkəm
Edina *Minn* ɪ'daɪnə, i'daɪnə
Elberta ɛl'bɜtə; ES ɛl'bɜtə, ɛl'bɝtə
elegiast ɪ'lidʒɪˌæst, ə'lidʒɪˌæst
Eoanthropus* *put* ˌio'ænθrəpəs *first*
Ephrata *Pa* 'ɛfrətə, *Wash* ɪ'fretə
Ephratah *Bible* 'ɛfrətə, *NY* ɪ'fretə
Esarey, Logan 'ɛzərɪ
Etowah *Ala, Tenn* 'ɛtəˌwa, -ˌwɒ, -wə
Eulalie *Poe's poem* julə'li (*Fr* øla'li)
existentialism ˌɛgzɪs'tɛnʃəlˌɪzəm, ˌɛksɪs-
Falconer* *NY*+'fælkənə; ES 'fælkənə(r
Faust* *NY village* fɔst
Fayette fe'ɛt, fe'jɛt ('Fayˌette 'City)
Fernandina *Fla* ˌfɜnən'dinə; ES ˌfɜn-, ˌfɝn-
Finisterre* *add:* (*Sp* ˌfinis'tɛrrɛ)
Folsom *Cal, NMex* 'folsəm, *surname* -o-, -ɑ-
Forsyth* *NY loc.* 'fɔrsaɪθ; ES 'fɔəsaɪθ
Franconia *NH* fræŋ'konɪə
Fremont* *NY loc.* 'fremɒnt, -mɒnt
frow '*froe*' fro |frow '*woman*' frau
Galway* *NY loc.* 'gælwe
Gansevoort* *NY* 'gænzvɜt, -vurt; ES -vət, -vuət

Ghent* *NY, Minn* g-, *Ky* dʒ-, *WVa* dʒ-, g-
Godeffroy *NY* 'gadfrɪ, 'gɒd-, *cf* Godfrey*
Gogebic *Mich* go'gibɪk
Gouverneur* *NY*+ˌgʌvə'nur, ˌguvə-, §121, *loc.*+-'nɜ; ES -'nuə(r, -'nɜ(r, -'nɜ
Gouverneur Morris ˌgʌvə'nɪr, ˌgʌvə-, §121; ES ˌgʌvə'nɪə(r; ('Gouverˌneur 'Morris)
Gravenstein *apple* 'grævənˌstaɪn, -ˌstin
greengage 'grin'gedʒ ('greenˌgage 'plum)
Grosvenor 'grovnə, *NY bay loc.* 'gravnə; ES -nə(r, 'grɒvnə(r
haberdasher* *sometimes* 'hæbəˌdæʃə (§121)
Hahn *surname* han, hɒn—*cf* Baugh, Utah*
Hallowell 'hæləˌwɛl, -wəl, *Me loc.* 'hɒl-
Hampstead*+'hæmstɛd, 'hæmstɪd
Hapsburg* *see also* Habsburg*
Haralson *Ga* 'hærəlsn̩
Healdsburg *Cal* 'hildzbɜg, -lz-; ES -ɜ-, -ɝ-
Healdton *Okla* 'hildtən, 'hiltən
Hempstead *NY* 'hɛmpstɛd, 'hɛmst-, -stɪd
Henlopen *Del cape* hɛn'lopən
Henrico *Va* hɛn'raɪko
Hermosa *Cal* hə'mosə, hɜ-; ES hə-, hɜ-, hɝ-
Hialeah *Fla* ˌhaɪə'liə
Hindman *Ky* 'haɪnmən, 'haɪndmən
Holbrook *Ariz, Mass* 'holbruk
Honeoye *NY* 'hʌnɪˌɔɪ
Hoosic*+'huzɪk
Houma *La* 'humə, 'homə
Huerfano *Col* 'wɛrfəˌno, 'wɜ-; ES 'wɛə-, 'wɜ-, 'wɝ-; *loc.*+ɔrfəˌno
Hyndman *Id mt.* 'haɪnmən, 'haɪndmən
Indianola *Ia, Miss* ˌɪndɪə'nolə
Ingraham*+'ɪŋgrəm, 'ɪngrəm
Ischua *NY* 'ɪʃuə, *loc.*+'ɪʃəˌwe—*cf* Nashua*
Ishpeming *Mich* 'ɪʃpɪˌmɪŋ
Itawamba *Miss* ˌɪtə'wambə, -'wɒmbə
Iuka *Miss* aɪ'jukə
Jacquard* *acct*+*as in* 'Jacˌquard 'loom
Java* *NY* 'dʒevə
Juliana*+dʒul'jænə, dʒɪul-
Kalevala*+'kalɪˌvala
Kalispell *Mont* ˌkælə'spɛl, 'kæləˌspɛl
Kegonsa *Wis lake* kɪ'gansə; ES+-'gɒnsə
Kinderhook *NY* 'kɪndəˌhuk; ES 'kɪndəˌhuk
Kineo *Me mt.* 'kɪnɪˌo
Kissimmee *Fla* kɪ'sɪmɪ
Koshkonong *Wis* 'kaʃkəˌnaŋ; ES+'kɒʃkə-ˌnɒŋ
Kossuth* *Ia* kə'suθ, ka-, kɒ-

Key: *See in full* §§3–47. bee bi |pity 'pɪtɪ (§6) |rate ret |yet jet |sang sæŋ |angry 'æŋ·grɪ |bath bæθ; E baθ (§10) |ah ɑ |far fɑr |watch watʃ, wɒtʃ (§12) |jaw dʒɔ |gorge gɔrdʒ |go go

Kotzebue *Alas* ˈkɑtsəˌbju, -ˌbɪu; ES+ˈkɒt-
La Crosse *Wis* ləˈkrɔs, -ˈkrɒs |-ˈs -ɪz
La Garita *Cal* ˌlɑgəˈritə
La Habra *Cal* ləˈhɑbrə
Lampasas *Tex* læmˈpæsəs |-sas' -səs
Lassellsville *NY* ˈlæs|zˌvɪl—*cf* Lascelles*
Latah *Id* ˈletɔ, leˈtɔ—*cf* Utah*
Lavaca *Tex* ləˈvækə
Ledyard*+ˈlɛdʒɚd; ES ˈlɛdʒəd
Leelanau *Mich* ˈliləˌnɔ
Lenox *var. sp. of* Lennox* ˈlɛnəks |-ˈs -ɪz
leukemia, -kae- luˈkimɪə, lɪu- |-mic -mɪk
Ligonier* *acct*+, *esp. attrib.*, ˈLigoˌnier
literatus *sg of* literati* ˌlɪtəˈretəs
Livengood *Alas vil.*, *surname* ˈlaɪvənˌgʊd
Lonaconing *Md* ˌlonəˈkonɪŋ
Loogootee *Ind* ləˈgotɪ
Loup *Nebr* lup
Lycoming* *Pa co. loc.*+-ˈkom-, -ˈkʌm-; *NY
vil.* laɪˈkomɪŋ
McDermott məkˈdɝmət; ES -ˈdɝmət, -ˈdɝ-
McDiarmid məkˈdɝmɪd; ES -ˈdɝmɪd, -ˈdɝ-
Mahopac *NY* ˈmeoˌpæk, ˈmeəˌpæk
Mannering *surname* ˈmænərɪŋ=Manwaring*,
    Mainwaring*, Maynwaring*
Matteawan* *NY*+, *esp. attrib.*, ˈMatteaˌwan
Mazomanie *Wis* ˌmezəˈmenɪ, ˌmezo-
Mebane *NC* ˈmæbɪn
Montgomery*+məntˈgʌmrɪ, -ˈgʌmərɪ
Montour* *accent*+*as in* ˈMonˌtour ˈFalls
Morenci *Mich* məˈrɛnsɪ
Morris, Gouverneur, *see* Gouverneur Morris
Munising *Mich* ˈmjunəsɪŋ, ˈmɪunəsɪŋ
Muscatatuck *Ind riv.* mʌsˈkætəˌtʌk
Mycenae* *NY loc.* məˈsinə—*cf* məˈzurə
Nauvoo* *accent*+*as in* ˈNauˌvoo ˈstreets
Navarino *NY* ˌnævəˈraɪno
Neligh *Nebr* ˈnilɪ
Neodesha *Kan* ˌniədəˈʃe
Nescopeck *Pa* ˈnɛskəˌpɛk
Neshoba *Miss* nɪˈʃobə
Nevada* *O loc.* nəˈvedə, nɪ-
Newbern* *Tenn*+-bɝn; ES -bɝn, -bɝn
Newfane *NY*, *Vt* ˈnjuˌfen, ˈnɪu-, ˈnu-; *Vt loc.*
    +ˌNewˈfane, *also spelt* New Fane
Nisei ˈnise, niˈse
Nootka*+ˈnʊtkə, ˈnutka, ˈnutkɔ—*cf* Utah*
Nueces *Tex* njuˈesɪs, nɪu-, nu-
Nunda *Ill, NY, loc.* nʌnˈde

Obion *Tenn* oˈbaɪən
Oceana* *WVa* ˌosɪˈænə
Ocheltree *Kan* ˈok|ˌtri, ˈok|trɪ
Ochiltree *Tex* ˈak|ˌtri, ˈak|trɪ; ES+ˈɒk-; *Scotl*
    ˈok|ˌtri, -trɪ (*Sc* ˈoxɪl-, ˈox|-)
Okanagan *Can* ˌokəˈnagən
Okanogan *Wash* ˌokəˈnagən, -ˈnɒgən
Okemah *Okla* oˈkimə, oˈkima
Oktibbeha *Miss* akˈtɪbɪˌhɔ; ES+ɒk-
Olathe *Kan* oˈleθɪ, əˈleθɪ, -θə
Olean *NY* ˈolɪˌæn, ˌolɪˈæn
Olneyville *RI* ˈonɪˌvɪl—*cf* Olney*
Olustee *Ala, Fla, Okla* oˈlʌstɪ, əˈlʌstɪ
Onawa *Ia* ˈɑnəwə; ES+ˈɒnəwə
Onaway *Mich* ˈɑnəˌwe; ES+ˈɒnəˌwe
Onondaga* *NY loc.*+ˌɑnəˈdɔgə
Onoville *NY* ˈɑnəˌvɪl; ES+ˈɒnəˌvɪl
Opelika *Ala* ˌopəˈlaɪkə, ˌopɪˈlaɪkə
Oregonian ˌɔrəˈgonɪən, ˌɑr-, ˌɒr-
Oriskany *NY* əˈrɪskənɪ, oˈrɪskənɪ
Orleans* *US, accent*+*as in* ˈOrˌleans ˈCo.
Osakis *Minn* oˈsekɪs |-ˈs -ɪz
Oskaloosa *Ia* ˌaskəˈlusə; ES+ˌɒskəˈlusə
Ossining* *NY*+ˈasnɪŋ; ES+ˈɒsnɪŋ
Otsego *NY* atˈsigo; ES+ɒtˈsigo
Ottumwa *Ia* əˈtʌmwə, aˈtʌmwə; ES+
    ɒˈtʌmwə
Outagamie *Wis* ˌautəˈgæmɪ
Ovid* *Mich, NY, occas. pers. name* ˈovɪd
Owyhee *Id* əˈwaɪhi, oˈwaɪhi
Palestine* *Tex loc.* ˈpæləsˌtin
Palomar *Cal* ˌpæləˈmar; ES -ˈma:(r, E+
    -ˈma:(r; *accent*+*as in* ˈPaloˌmar ˈMountain
Passaconaway *NH* ˌpæsəˈkanəˌwe; ES+
    -ˈkɒn-
Pehlevi 'Pahlavi' ˈpeləˌvi |Pehlvi ˈpelvi
Pend Oreille *Id, Wash* ˌpandəˈre, ˌpɛn-
phosgene*+ˈfazdʒin; ES+ˈfɒzdʒin
Picabo *Id loc.* ˈpɪkəˌbu, *elsewhere*+ˈpikəˌbu
pileated ˈpaɪlɪˌetɪd, ˈpɪlɪˌetɪd
Piqua* *O*+ˈpɪkwe—*cf* Pickaway*
Pithecanthropus* *put second pron. first*
Poestenkill *NY* ˈpusnˌkɪl, ˈpostnˌkɪl
princess* *Brit*+prɪnˈsɛs, *but* ˈprɪnsɪs *when at-
    trib.*, *as in* ˈPrincess ˈMary
Pulaski* *US*+pəˈlæskɪ, pju-, pɪu-
Pushmataha *Okla* ˌpuʃməˈtɔhɔ, -ˈtaha
Puyallup *Wash* pjuˈæləp, pɪuˈæləp
Rahway *NJ* ˈrɔwe
Ramapo *NY vil.*, *NY, NJ riv.* ˈræməˌpo

|full fʊl |tooth tuθ |further ˈfɝðɚ; ES ˈfɝðə |custom ˈkʌstəm |while hwaɪl |how haʊ |toy tɔɪ
|using ˈjuzɪŋ |fuse fjuz, fɪuz |dish dɪʃ |vision ˈvɪʒən |Eden ˈidn̩ |cradle ˈkredl̩ |keep 'em ˈkipm̩

Rangeley *Me* ˈrendʒlɪ

Rantoul *Ill* rænˈtul (ˈRanˌtoul ˈschools)

Raton* *Col* rəˈtun, ræ-; *NMex* rəˈton, rɑ-

Reidenbach *surname* ˈraɪdn̩ˌbɑ—*cf* Baugh

Rensselaer* *NY*+ˌrɛnslˈɪr; ES -ˈɪə(r; *accent* +*as in* ˈRensseˌlaer ˈboy

Robson* *surname*+ˈrɑbsn̩

Sabinal *Tex* ˌsæbəˈnæl (ˈSabiˌnal ˈbank)

Sacandaga *NY* ˌsækənˈdɔgə

Sagadahoc* *Me*, *put acct* ˌSagadaˈhoc *first*

Salida *Col* səˈlaɪdə (*Sp* saˈliðɑ)

Salina *Kan* səˈlaɪnə

Salinas *Cal* səˈlinəs |-ˈs -ɪz

Saluda *NC, SC, Va, Ind* səˈludə

San Bernardino* *Cal*+-ˌbɚnəˈdino, *§121*

Santanoni *NY* ˌsæntəˈnonɪ (ˈSantaˌnoni ˈMt.)

Sapulpa *Okla* səˈpʌlpə

sarsaparilla*+ˌsæspəˈrɪlə, ˌsæsəpə-

Saugerties *NY* ˈsɔgɚtɪz, -ˌtiz; ES ˈsɔgə-

Sauquoit *NY* səˈkwɔɪt

Schaefer, -ffer ˈʃefɚ; ES ˈʃefə(r

Schaghticoke *NY* ˈskætɪˌkʊk, ˈʃætɪ-, -ˌkok

Schenevus *NY* skəˈnivəs |-ˈs -ɪz

Schrader ˈʃredɚ; ES ˈʃredə(r

Schroeder ˈʃredɚ, ˈʃrodɚ; ES -də(r; (*Ger* ˈʃrøːdər)

Schuylkill* *SE Pa loc.*+-ˈskukl̩

sermonic sɝˈmɑnɪk; ES sɝ-, sɝ-, -ˈmɒnɪk

Shafer ˈʃefɚ; ES ˈʃefə(r

Shaffer ˈʃefɚ, ˈʃæfɚ; ES -fə(r

shafts *'thills'* ʃævz, ʃæfts; E+ʃɑ-, ʃɑ-; *see* §124.11

Shelbina *Mo* ʃɛlˈbaɪnə

shindig* *accent*+ˈʃɪnˌdɪg

slaver *'slave dealer'* ˈslevɚ; ES ˈslevə(r

slaver *'drool'* ˈslævɚ; ES ˈslævə(r; |-ed -d |-ing ˈslævərɪŋ, ˈslævrɪŋ

soot* *cf* boot **but**, foot fʊt, flood flʌd

submersible səbˈmɝsəbl̩; ES -ˈmɝs-, -ˈmɝs-

Suckow *surname* ˈsuko

Suffolk*+ˈsʌfək

Sylacauga *Ala* ˌsɪləˈkɔgə

Tahoe *Cal* ˈtɑho, ˈteho

Talcott, Tallcott ˈtɔlkət, ˈtælkət

Talladega *Ala* ˌtæləˈdigə

Tallulah *La* təˈlulə

Taughannock Falls *NY* təˈgænək, tɔˈgænək

Tazewell *Ill, Va* ˈtæzwɛl, ˈtezwɛl, -wəl

Tehuacana *Tex* tɪˈwakənə, -ˈwɒk-

Tidioute *Pa* ˈtɪdɪˌut, ˌtɪdɪˈut

Tionesta *Pa* ˌtaɪəˈnɛstə

Totowa *NJ* ˈtotəwə

Tucumcari *NMex* ˈtukəmˌkɛrɪ, -ˌkærɪ; S -æ-

Tuolumne *Cal* ˈtwɑləmnɪ, ˈtwɒləmnɪ

Tuscola *Mich, Ill* tʌsˈkolə

Tyrone* *Pa*, *acct*+*as in* ˈtaɪˌron ˈstrɪts

Uhrichsville *O* ˈjʊrɪksˌvɪl

Umatilla *Oreg* ˌjuməˈtɪlə

Unadilla *NY* ˌjunəˈdɪlə, *loc.*+ˌʌnəˈdɪlə; *acct*+ *as in* ˈUnaˌdilla ˈForks

Upshire *Engd* ˈʌpʃɪr, -ʃɚ; ES -ʃɪə(r, -ʃə(r

Upshur *surname, WVa co.* ˈʌpʃɚ; ES ˈʌpʃə(r

Uvalde *Tex* juˈvældɪ

Valois ˈvælwɑ, -wɒ (*Fr* vaˈlwa), *NY* vəˈlɔɪs

Vandalia *Am places* vænˈdeljə

Venango *Pa, Nebr* vəˈnæŋgo

Venezuela*+ˌvɛnzuˈilə, ˌvɛnəzuˈilə

Vergennes *Vt, Ill* vɚˈdʒɛnz; ES və-; |-ˈs -ɪz

vernacular*+vɚˈnækjələ (*§121*)

Vevay *Swtz Co. Ind* ˈvivɪ, *older* viˈve (*§6*)

Vevey *Switzerland* vəˈve (*Fr* vəˈvɛ)

Vienna* *some Am places*+vaɪˈɛnə

Vigo *Ind* ˈvaɪgo, ˈvigo

Vinita *Okla* vəˈnitə

Waban *Mass* ˈwɑbən

Wabasha *Minn* ˈwɑbəˌʃɔ, ˈwɒbə-, ˈwɔbə-

Wadena *Minn* wɑˈdinə, wɒˈdinə|

Waha *Id* ˈwɑhɔ—*cf* Omaha*, Utah*, Baugh

Walthall *Miss* ˈwɔlθɔl—*cf* Waltham*

Wamego *Kan* wɑˈmigo, wɒ-, wa-

Wappingers *NY* ˈwapɪndʒɚz, ˈwɒp-; ES -dʒəz

Wasatch ˈwɔsætʃ, wɔˈsætʃ (ˈWaˌsatch ˈMts.)

Washingtonian ˌwaʃɪŋˈtonɪən, ˌwɔʃ-, ˌwɒʃ-

Washtenaw *Mich* ˈwaʃtəˌnɔ, ˈwɒʃ-, ˈwɔʃ-

Watauga *NC, Tenn* wɑˈtɔgə, wɒˈtɔgə, wə-

Watervliet *NY* ˈwɔtɚˌvlit, ˈwɑ-, ˈwɒ-, -vlˌit; ES -tə-; *acct*+ˌWaterˈvliet

Watseka *Ill* wɑtˈsikə, wɒtˈsikə

Waubesa *Wis lake* wɔˈbisə

Waunakee *Wis* ˌwɔnəˈki (ˈWaunaˌkee ˈmail)

Waupaca *Wis* wɔˈpækə

Waupun *Wis* wɔˈpʌn (ˈWauˌpun ˈschools)

Wauseon *O* ˈwɔsɪˌɑn, -ˌɒn, ˌwɔsɪˈɑn, -ˈɒn

Weehawken *NJ* wiˈhɔkən

Weiser *Id* ˈwizɚ; ES ˈwizə(r

Wetumka *Okla* wɪˈtʌmkə |-mpka *Ala* wɪ-ˈtʌmpkə

Wigtownshire* *put* ˈwɪgtənˌʃɪr *first*

Winder *Ga* ˈwaɪndɚ; ES ˈwaɪndə(r

Winnetka *Ill* wɪˈnɛtkə

Wolcott* *NY loc.* ˈwɔlkət

woollen *variant spelling of* woolen*

Zeigler *Ill* ˈzɪglɚ; ES ˈzɪglə(r

Ziebach *SD* ˈziˈbɑk, -ˈbɑ, -ˈbɔ—*cf* Baugh

A
PRONOUNCING DICTIONARY
OF
AMERICAN ENGLISH

A, a *letter* e |*pl* A's, As, *poss* A's ez

a *indef. art.* ə, *emph. or hesitating* e—*The use of* e, *the stressed form of* a, *in places where the unstressed* ə *belongs, often gives an artificial effect to public address.*

a, a- *unstressed form of* on ə (a begging, a-foot, afire)

Aachen 'ɑkən, 'ɑxən (*Ger* 'ɑːxən)

Aaron 'ɛrən, 'ærən, 'erən; S 'ærən, 'erən

abacá ˌɑbə'kɑ

aback ə'bæk

abacus 'æbəkəs |-es -ɪz |-ci -ˌsaɪ

abaft ə'bæft; E+ə'bɑft, ə'bɑft

abalone, A- ˌæbə'lonɪ

Abana 'æbənə

abandon *n* ə'bændən (*Fr* abɑ̃'dõ)

abandon *v* ə'bændən |-ed -d

abase ə'bes |-s -ɪz |-d -t |-dly -ɪdlɪ

abash ə'bæʃ |-es -ɪz |-ed -t |-edly -ɪdlɪ

abatable ə'betəbḷ

abate ə'bet |abated ə'betɪd

abatis 'æbətɪs, ə'bætɪs |-es -ɪz |-ed -t

abattoir ˌæbə'twɑr, -'twɔr; ES -'twɑː(r, -'twɔə(r; (*Fr* aba'twaːr)

abbacy 'æbəsɪ

Abbana 'æbənə

abbé 'æbe, æ'be (*Fr* a'be)

abbess 'æbɪs, 'æbes |abbesses 'æbɪsɪz

Abbeville *US* 'æbɪˌvɪl; S+-vḷ; *France* ab'vil

abbey 'æbɪ |Abbeyville, Abby- 'æbɪˌvɪl

abbot 'æbət

Abbotsford 'æbətsfəd; ES 'æbətsfəd

abbreviate ə'brivɪˌet |-ated -ˌetɪd

abbreviation əˌbrivɪ'eʃən

ABC 'e'bi'si |ABC's, ABCs 'e'bi'siz ('AˌB'C ˌbook)

abdicate 'æbdəˌket |-cated -ˌketɪd

abdication ˌæbdə'keʃən

Abdiel 'æbdɪəl, -dɪɛl, -dj-

abdomen 'æbdəmən, æb'domən, əb-

abdominal æb'dɑmənḷ, əb-; ES+-'dɒm-; |-ly -ɪ

abduce æb'djus, -'dɪus, -'dus |-s -ɪz |-d -t

abduct æb'dʌkt, əb- |-ed -ɪd |-ction -kʃən

abeam ə'bim

abecedarian ˌebɪsɪ'dɛrɪən, -'der-

Á Becket, -ett ə'bɛkɪt

abed ə'bɛd

Abednego ə'bɛdnɪˌgo

Abel 'ebḷ

Abelard 'æbḷˌɑrd; ES 'æbḷˌɑːd; (*Fr* abe'laːr)

Aberdeen ˌæbə'din; ES ˌæbə'din; ('Aberˌdeen 'Angus) |-shire -ʃɪr, -ʃə; ES -ʃɪə(r, -ʃə(r

Abergavenny *Eng town* ˌæbəgə'vɛnɪ, *family* ˌæbə'gɛnɪ, *Shak.* Aburgany ˌæbə'gɛnɪ; ES ˌæbə-

aberrance æb'ɛrəns |-ancy -ənsɪ |-ant -ənt

aberration ˌæbə'reʃən

Aberystwyth ˌæbə'ɪstwɪθ

abet ə'bɛt |-ted -ɪd |-ter, -tor -ə; ES -ə(r

abeyance ə'beəns |-ant -ənt

abhor əb'hɔr, æb-; ES -'hɔə(r; |-red -d

abhorrence əb'hɔrəns, æb-, -'hɑr-, -'hɒr- |-ent -ənt

Abhorson əb'hɔrsṇ; ES -'hɔəsṇ

abidance ə'baɪdṇs

Key: See in full §§3–47. bee bi |pity 'pɪtɪ (§6) |rate ret |yet jɛt |sang sæŋ |angry 'æŋ·grɪ |bath bæθ; E baθ (§10) |ah ɑ |far fɑr |watch wɑtʃ, wɒtʃ (§12) |jaw dʒɔ |gorge gɔrdʒ |go go |full fʊl |tooth tuθ |further 'fɝðə; ES 'fɝðə |custom 'kʌstəm |while hwaɪl |how haʊ |toy tɔɪ |using 'juzɪŋ |fuse fjuz, fɪuz |dish dɪʃ |vision 'vɪʒən |Eden 'idṇ |cradle 'kredḷ |keep 'em 'kipm̩

abide ə'baɪd |past abode ə'bod or abided
ə'baɪdɪd |pptc abode ə'bod or abided
ə'baɪdɪd, rarely abidden ə'bɪdn̩
Abigail 'æbə,gel, 'æbəg|
Abijah ə'baɪdʒə
Abilene US 'æbə,lin, Syria ,æbə'linɪ
ability ə'bɪlətɪ
Abimelech ə'bɪmə,lɛk
Abinadab ə'bɪnə,dæb
Abingdon 'æbɪŋdən |-gton -tən
ab initio 'æbɪ'nɪʃɪ,o
abject æb'dʒɛkt, 'æbdʒɛkt ('ab,ject 'look)
abjection æb'dʒɛkʃən
abjuration ,æbdʒu'reʃən
abjure əb'dʒur, æb-, -'dʒɪur; ES -'dʒuə(r,
-'dʒɪuə(r; |-d -d
ablation æb'leʃən
ablative 'æblətɪv, 'æblɪtɪv
ablaut 'ablaut, 'æblaut (Ger 'aplaut)
ablaze ə'blez
able 'ebl |-ler 'eblɚ; ES -lə(r; |-lest 'eblɪst
-able unstressed ending -əb|—often omitted
from the vocab. when the pron. can be found
by adding -əb| to the head pron. The corre-
sponding adverb ending is -ably -əblɪ. For
the addition of -bly -blɪ when the head word
does not end in -able, see the suffix -bly.
able-bodied 'ebl̩'badɪd; ES+-'bɒd-; ('able-
,bodied 'man)
ablution æb'luʃən, əb-, -'lɪuʃən
ably 'eblɪ
abnegate 'æbnɪ,get |-gated -,getɪd
abnegation ,æbnɪ'geʃən
Abner 'æbnɚ; ES 'æbnə(r
abnormal æb'nɔrml̩, əb-; ES -'nɔəml̩; |-ly -ɪ
abnormality ,æbnɔr'mælətɪ; ES -nɔ'mælətɪ
abnormity æb'nɔrmətɪ; ES -'nɔəmətɪ
aboard ə'bord, ə'bɔrd; ES ə'boəd, E+ə'bɔəd
abode ə'bod
abolish ə'balɪʃ; ES+ə'bɒl-; |-es -ɪz |-ed -t
abolition ,æbə'lɪʃən |-ism -,ɪzəm |-ist -ɪst
abominable ə'bamnəb|, -mən-; ES+ə'bɒm-;
|-bly -blɪ
abominate ə'bamə,net; ES+ə'bɒm-; |-d -ɪd
aboriginal ,æbə'rɪdʒən| |-ly -ɪ |-ne -,ni
abort ə'bɔrt; ES ə'bɔət; |-ed -ɪd
aborticide ə'bɔrtə,saɪd; ES ə'bɔətə-
abortifacient ə,bɔrtə'feʃənt; ES ə,bɔətə-
abortion ə'bɔrʃən; ES ə'bɔəʃən

Abou ben Adhem 'æbubɛn'ædəm, 'abubɛn-
'adɛm
abound ə'baund |-ed -ɪd
about ə'baut
about-face n ə'baut,fes |-s -ɪz
about-face v ə,baut'fes |-s -ɪz |-d -t
about-ship v ə,baut'ʃɪp |-ped -t
above ə'bʌv
aboveboard ə'bʌv,bord, -,bɔrd; ES -,boəd,
E+-,bɔəd
aboveground ə'bʌv,graund
abrade ə'bred, æb'red |-d -ɪd
Abraham 'ebrə,hæm, 'ebrɪ-, -həm
Abram 'ebrəm
abrasion ə'breʒən, æb'r- |-sive -sɪv, -zɪv
abreaction ,æbrɪ'ækʃən
abreast ə'brɛst
abridge ə'brɪdʒ |-s -ɪz |-d -d |-dly -ɪdlɪ
abroad ə'brɔd
abrogable 'æbrəgəb|
abrogate 'æbrə,get, -ro- |-gated -,getɪd
abrogation ,æbrə'geʃən, -ro-
abrupt ə'brʌpt, æb'rʌpt
Absalom 'æbsələm
abscess 'æb,sɛs, -sɪs |-es -ɪz |-ed -t
abscissa æb'sɪsə |-s -z |-sae -si
abscission æb'sɪʒən, æb'sɪʃən
abscond æb'skand, əb-; ES+-'skɒnd; |-ed
-ɪd
absence 'æbsn̩s |absences 'æbsn̩sɪz |-sent
-sn̩t
absent v æb'sɛnt, əb- |-ed -ɪd
absentee ,æbsn̩'ti ('absen,tee 'land,lord)
absent-minded 'æbsn̩t'maɪndɪd
absinthe, -th 'æbsɪnθ, æb'sɪnθ
absolute 'æbsə,lut, -,lɪut, -s|,jut |-ly -lɪ,
emph.+,abso'lutely, 'abso'lutely
absolution ,æbsə'luʃən, -'lɪuʃən, -s|'juʃən
absolutism 'æbsəlut,ɪzəm, -lɪut-, -s|jut-
absolutist 'æbsə,lutɪst, -,lɪut-, -s|,jutɪst
absolve æb'salv, əb-, -'sɒlv, -'z- |-d -d
absorb əb'sɔrb, æb-, -'z-; ES -ɔəb; |-ed -d
|-edly -ɪdlɪ
absorbefacient əb,sɔrbə'feʃənt, æb-, -,z-; ES
-ɔəb-
absorbent əb'sɔrbənt, æb-, -'z-; ES -ɔəb-
absorption əb'sɔrpʃən, æb-; ES -'sɔəp-;
|-tive -tɪv
abstain əb'sten, æb- |-ed -d

abstemious æb'stɪmɪəs, əb-, -mjəs
abstention æb'stɛnʃən, əb-
absterge æb'stɝdʒ, əb-; ES -'stɝdʒ, -'stɝ·dʒ;
 |-s -ɪz |-d -d |-gent -ənt
abstersion æb'stɝʃən; ES -'stɝʃ-, -'stɝʃ-
abstinence 'æbstənəns |-s -ɪz
abstract adj æb'strækt ('ab‚stract 'thought)
abstract n 'æbstrækt
abstract v æb'strækt, əb-; 'abridge,' 'trace
 title' 'æbstrækt |-ed -ɪd
abstractedly æb'stræktɪdlɪ
abstraction æb'strækʃən, əb- |-tive -tɪv
abstriction æb'strɪkʃən
abstruse æb'strus, əb-, -'strɪus
absurd əb'sɝd, æb-, -'z-; ES -ɝd, -ɝd; |-ity
 -ətɪ
Abukir ‚æbu'kɪr, ‚ɑ-, ə'bukɚ; ES -'kɪə(r,
 -kə(r
abulia ə'bjulɪə, ə'bɪul-, ‚æbju'lɪə
abundance ə'bʌndəns |abundant ə'bʌndənt
Abury 'ɛbərɪ = Avebury
abuse n ə'bjus, ə'bɪus |-s -ɪz
abuse v ə'bjuz, ə'bɪuz |-s -ɪz |-d -d
abusive ə'bjusɪv, ə'bɪusɪv
abut ə'bʌt |-ted -ɪd |-ment -mənt |-tal -l̩
Abydos ə'baɪdɑs, -dəs; ES+-dɒs; |-'s -ɪz
abysm ə'bɪzəm |abysmal ə'bɪzml̩ |-ally
 -zml̩ɪ
abyss ə'bɪs |-es -ɪz |-al -l̩
Abyssinia ‚æbə'sɪnɪə, -'sɪnjə |-n -n
acacia ə'keʃə
academe ‚ækə'dim
academic ‚ækə'dɛmɪk |-al -l̩ |-ally -l̩ɪ, -ɪklɪ
academician ə‚kædə'mɪʃən, ‚ækədə-
academicism ‚ækə'dɛmə‚sɪzəm
academy ə'kædəmɪ
Acadia ə'kedɪə, -djə |-n -n—see also Cajun
acanthus ə'kænθəs |-es -ɪz |-thi -θaɪ
a cappella 'ɑ kə'pɛlə (It ‚ɑkkɑp'pɛllɑ)
acariasis ‚ækə'raɪəsɪs
acarid 'ækərɪd
acatalectic e‚kæt|'ɛktɪk, ə-, æ-, ‚ekæt|-,
 ‚ækæt|-
acaudal e'kɔdl̩, ə-, æ-
Accad 'ækæd = Akkad
Accadia ə'kedɪə, ə'kɑ-, -djə |-dian -dɪən,
 -djən
accede æk'sid, ək- |-ceded -'sidɪd
accelerable æk'sɛlərəbl̩, ək-

accelerando æk‚sɛlə'rændo, ək- (It ɑt‚tʃele-
 'rɑndo)
accelerant æk'sɛlərənt, ək-
accelerate æk'sɛlə‚ret, ək- |-rated -‚retɪd
acceleration æk‚sɛlə'reʃən, ək-, ‚æksɛlə-
accelerative æk'sɛlə‚retɪv, ək- |-tor -tɚ; ES
 -tə(r
accent n 'æksɛnt, less freq. 'æksn̩t
accent v 'æksɛnt, æk'sɛnt, ək- |-ed -ɪd
accentual æk'sɛntʃuəl, ək- |-ly -ɪ
accentuate æk'sɛntʃu‚et, ək- |-ated -‚etɪd
accentuation æk‚sɛntʃu'eʃən, ək-, ‚æksɛntʃu-
accept ək'sɛpt, ɪk-, æk- |-ed -ɪd |-able -əbl̩
 |-bly -blɪ
acceptability ək‚sɛptə'bɪlətɪ, ɪk-, æk-,
 ‚æksɛptə-
acceptance ək'sɛptəns, ɪk-, æk- |-s -ɪz
acceptation ‚æksɛp'teʃən
access 'æksɛs |-es -ɪz
accessary æk'sɛsərɪ, ək- |-ries -rɪz
accessibility æk‚sɛsə'bɪlətɪ, ək-, ‚æksɛsə-
accessible æk'sɛsəbl̩, ək- |-bly -blɪ
accession æk'sɛʃən, ək- |-ed -d
accessorial ‚æksə'sorɪəl, -'sɔr-; S -'sor-
accessory æk'sɛsərɪ, ək-
accidence 'æksədəns |-dent -dənt
accidental ‚æksə'dɛntl̩ |-ly -ɪ
acclaim ə'klem |acclaimed ə'klemd
acclamation ‚æklə'meʃən
acclimate ə'klaɪmɪt, 'æklə‚met |-d -ɪd
acclimation ‚æklə'meʃən
acclimatization ə‚klaɪmətə'zeʃən, -aɪ'z-
acclimatize ə'klaɪmə‚taɪz |-s -ɪz |-d -d
acclivity ə'klɪvətɪ
accolade ‚ækə'led, -'lɑd |-d -ɪd
Accomac 'ækə‚mæk
accommodate ə'kɑmə‚det; ES+-'kɒm-; |-d
 -ɪd
accommodation ə‚kɑmə'deʃən; ES+-‚kɒm-
accompaniment ə'kʌmpənɪmənt, ə'kʌmpnɪ-
accompanist ə'kʌmpənɪst, ə'kʌmpnɪst
accompany ə'kʌmpənɪ |-nyist -nɪɪst
accomplice ə'kɑmplɪs; ES+-'kɒm-; |-s -ɪz
accomplish ə'kɑmplɪʃ; ES+-'kɒm-; |-es -ɪz
 |-ed -t
accord ə'kɔrd; ES ə'kɔəd; |-ed -ɪd
accordance ə'kɔrdn̩s; ES ə'kɔəd-; |-dant
 -dn̩t
accordion ə'kɔrdɪən; ES ə'kɔədɪən

|full fʊl |tooth tuθ |further 'fɝðɚ; ES 'fɝðə |custom 'kʌstəm |while hwaɪl |how haʊ |toy tɔɪ
|using 'juzɪŋ |fuse fjuz, fɪuz |dish dɪʃ |vision 'vɪʒən |Eden 'idn̩ |cradle 'kredl̩ |keep 'em 'kipm̩

accost ə'kɔst, ə'kɒst |-ed -ɪd
accouchement ə'kuʃmã, -mənt (Fr akuʃ'mã)
accoucheur ˌæku'ʃɝ; ES ˌæku'ʃɜ(r, -'ʃɝ; (Fr
aku'ʃœːr)
accoucheuse ˌæku'ʃɝz |-s -ɪz (Fr aku'ʃøːz)
account ə'kaʊnt |accounted ə'kaʊntɪd
accountability əˌkaʊntə'bɪlətɪ
accountable ə'kaʊntəbḷ |-bly -blɪ
accountancy ə'kaʊntənsɪ |-tant -tənt
accouter, -tre ə'kutɚ; ES ə'kutə(r; |-(e)d -d
accredit ə'krɛdɪt |-ed -ɪd
accrete ə'krit, æ'krit |-d -ɪd
accretion ə'kriʃən, æ'kriʃən
accrual ə'kruəl, ə'krɪuəl, æ-
accrue ə'kru, ə'krɪu, æ- |-d -d
accumbency ə'kʌmbənsɪ |-bent -bənt
accumulate ə'kjumjəˌlet, ə'kɪum- |-d -ɪd
|-tive -ɪv |-tor -ɚ; ES -ə(r
accumulation əˌkjumjə'leʃən, əˌkɪum-
accuracy 'ækjərəsɪ
accurate 'ækjərɪt
accursed ə'kɝ·sɪd, -st; ES ə'kɜs-, ə'kɝ·s-;
|-sedly -sɪdlɪ
accurst ə'kɝst; ES ə'kɜst, ə'kɝst
accusal ə'kjuzḷ, ə'kɪuzḷ
accusation ˌækjə'zeʃən, ˌækjʊ-
accusative ə'kjuzətɪv, ə'kɪuz-
accusatorial əˌkjuzə'torɪəl, əˌkɪuz-, -'tɔr-;
S -'tor-
accusatory ə'kjuzəˌtorɪ, ə'kɪuz-, -ˌtɔrɪ; S
-ˌtorɪ
accuse ə'kjuz, ə'kɪuz |-s -ɪz |-d -d
accustom ə'kʌstəm |-ed -d
ace es |aces 'esɪz
acentric e'sɛntrɪk, ə-, æ-
acephalous e'sɛfələs, ə-, æ-
acerbate v 'æsɚˌbet; ES 'æsə-; |-d -ɪd
acerbate adj ə'sɝbɪt; ES ə'sɜb-, ə'sɝb-
acerbity ə'sɝbətɪ; ES ə'sɜb-, ə'sɝb-
acetamide ˌæsə'tæmaɪd, ə'sɛtəˌmaɪd, -mɪd
|-mid -mɪd
acetanilide ˌæsə'tænḷˌaɪd, -ḷɪd |-lid -ḷɪd
acetate 'æsəˌtet |-tated -ˌtetɪd
acetic ə'sitɪk, ə'sɛtɪk
acetify ə'sɛtəˌfaɪ |-fied -ˌfaɪd
acetone 'æsəˌton
acetyl 'æsəˌtɪl |-ene -ˌin ə'sɛtḷˌin
Achaea ə'kiə |Achaia ə'keə, ə'kaɪə |-n -n
Achates ə'ketiz |-tes' -tiz

ache ek |ached ekt—Before 1700 the verb was
spelt ake, and the noun was pronounced etʃ,
pl 'etʃɪz.
Achean ə'kiən
Acheron 'ækəˌran, -rən; ES+-ˌrɒn
achieve ə'tʃiv |-d -d |-ment -mənt
Achilles ə'kɪliz |-es' -iz
Achitophel ə'kɪtəˌfɛl
achromatic ˌækrə'mætɪk, -ro- ('achroˌmatic
'lens)
achromic e'kromɪk, ə-, æ-
acid 'æsɪd |acidic ə'sɪdɪk, æ'sɪdɪk
acidify ə'sɪdəˌfaɪ, æ- |-fied -ˌfaɪd
acidimeter ˌæsɪ'dɪmətɚ; ES -tə(r
acidity ə'sɪdətɪ, æ-
acidosis ˌæsɪ'dosɪs
acidulate ə'sɪdʒəˌlet, æ- |-d -ɪd |-lous -ləs
aciform 'æsɪˌfɔrm; ES -ˌfɔəm
acknowledge ək'nalɪdʒ, æk-, ɪk-, -ədʒ; ES+
-'nɒl-; |-d -d
aclinic e'klɪnɪk, ə-, æ-
acme 'ækmɪ, 'ækmi
acne 'æknɪ, 'ækni
acolyte 'ækəˌlaɪt
Acoma 'akəˌma, -mə
acorn 'ekɚn, 'ekɔrn; ES 'ekən, 'ekɔən;—The
second pron. arises from false etymology.
acotyledon ˌekatḷ'idṇ, əˌkat-, æˌkat-; ES+
-ɒt-; |-ous -'idṇəs, -'ɛdṇəs
acoustic ə'kustɪk, ə'kaʊstɪk |-al -ḷ |-ally -ḷɪ,
-ɪklɪ
acoustician ˌækus'tɪʃən, -kaʊs-, əˌkus-,
əˌkaʊs-
acquaint ə'kwent |-ed -ɪd
acquaintance ə'kwentəns |-s -ɪz
acquiesce ˌækwɪ'ɛs |-s -ɪz |-d -t |-nce -ṇs |-nt
-ṇt
acquire ə'kwaɪr; ES ə'kwaɪə(r; |-d -d |-rable
-əbḷ
acquisition ˌækwə'zɪʃən
acquit ə'kwɪt |-ted -ɪd |-tal -ḷ |-tance -ṇs
acre 'ekɚ; ES 'ekə(r
acreage 'ekərɪdʒ, 'ekrɪdʒ |-s -ɪz
acre-foot 'ekɚ'fʊt; ES 'ekə-; |-feet -'fit
acre-inch 'ekɚ'ɪntʃ |-es -ɪz
acrid 'ækrɪd |-ine -ˌin, -ɪn |-in -ɪn
acridity æ'krɪdətɪ, ə-
acrimonious ˌækrə'monɪəs, -njəs
acrimony 'ækrəˌmonɪ

Key: See in full §§3–47. bee bi |pity 'pɪtɪ (§6) |rate ret |yet jɛt |sang sæŋ |angry 'æŋ·grɪ
|bath bæθ; E baθ (§10) |ah ɑ |far fɑr |watch wɑtʃ, wɒtʃ (§12) |jaw dʒɔ |gorge gɔrdʒ |go go

acrobat ˈækrəˌbæt
acrobatic ˌækrəˈbætɪk |-al -ḷ |-ally -ḷɪ, -ɪklɪ
acrogen ˈækrədʒən, -dʒɪn
acromegalic ˌækromɪˈgælɪk |-megaly -ˈmɛgəlɪ
acrophobia ˌækrəˈfobɪə
acropolis əˈkrɑpəlɪs; ES+-ˈkrɒp-; |-lises
  -lɪsɪz |Gk pl -leis -ˌles
across əˈkrɔs, əˈkrɒs
acrostic əˈkrɔstɪk, əˈkrɒs-
act ækt |acted ˈæktɪd
Actaeon ækˈtiən
actinic ækˈtɪnɪk |-ally -ḷɪ, -ɪklɪ
actinism ˈæktɪnˌɪzəm
actinium ækˈtɪnɪəm
action ˈækʃən |-able -əbḷ, -ʃnəbḷ |-bly -blɪ
Actium ˈæktɪəm, ˈækʃɪəm
activate ˈæktəˌvet |-vated -ˌvetɪd
activation ˌæktəˈveʃən
active ˈæktɪv |-vism -ˌɪzəm |-vist -ɪst
activity ækˈtɪvətɪ
actor ˈæktɚ; ES ˈæktə(r
actress ˈæktrɪs |-es -ɪz
actual ˈæktʃʊəl, -tʃʊl
actuality ˌæktʃʊˈælətɪ
actually ˈæktʃʊəlɪ, -tʃʊlɪ, -tʃəlɪ
actuarial ˌæktʃʊˈɛrɪəl, -ˈer-
actuary ˈæktʃʊˌɛrɪ
actuate ˈæktʃʊˌet |-ated -ˌetɪd
acuity əˈkjuətɪ, əˈkɪuətɪ
acumen əˈkjumɪn, əˈkɪu-, -mən
acute əˈkjut, əˈkɪut
acyclic eˈsaɪklɪk, eˈsɪk-
A.D. ˈeˈdi, ˈænoˈdɑməˌnaɪ; ES+-ˈdɒm-
ad æd
Ada(h) ˈedə
adage ˈædɪdʒ |-s -ɪz
adagio əˈdɑdʒo, əˈdɑdʒɪˌo (It aˈda:dʒo)
Adair əˈdɛr, əˈdær; E əˈdɛə(r, ES əˈdæə(r
Adaline ˈædḷˌaɪn, -ˌin
Adam ˈædəm |Adams ˈædəmz |Adams's
  ˈædəmzɪz
adamant ˈædəˌmænt
adamantine ˌædəˈmæntɪn, -tin, -taɪn
Adamic, Louis ˈluɪˈædəmɪk, ˈluɪs-, ˈlɪuɪ(s)-
adapt əˈdæpt |-ed -ɪd
adaptability əˌdæptəˈbɪlətɪ
adaptable əˈdæptəbḷ
adaptation ˌædəpˈteʃən, ˌædæp-
adaptive əˈdæptɪv

add æd |added ˈædɪd
Addams ˈædəmz |Addams's ˈædəmzɪz
addend ˈædɛnd, əˈdɛnd
addendum əˈdɛndəm, æ- |-da -də
adder ˈædɚ; ES ˈædə(r
addible ˈædəbḷ
addict n ˈædɪkt
addict v əˈdɪkt |-ed -ɪd |-ction -kʃən
Addis Ababa ˈædɪsˈabəbə, ˈadɪs-
Addison ˈædəsṇ
additament əˈdɪtəmənt
addition əˈdɪʃən, æ- |-al -ḷ |-ally -ḷɪ
additive ˈædətɪv
addle ˈædḷ |-d -d |-ling ˈædḷɪŋ, ˈædlɪŋ
addlebrain ˈædḷˌbren
addlebrained ˈædḷˈbrend (ˈaddleˌbrained ˈboy)
addleheaded ˈædḷˈhɛdɪd
addlepated ˈædḷˈpetɪd
address n əˈdrɛs, ˈædrɛs |-es -ɪz
address v əˈdrɛs |-es -ɪz |-ed -t
addressee ədrɛsˈi, ˌædrɛsˈi
adduce əˈdjus, əˈdɪus, əˈdus |-s -ɪz |-d -t
adducible, -ceable əˈdjusəbḷ, əˈdɪus-, əˈdus-
adduct əˈdʌkt |-ed -ɪd
adduction əˈdʌkʃən |-tive -tɪv |-tor -tɚ; ES
  -tə(r
Adel eˈdɛl
Adela ˈædḷə
Adelaide ˈædḷˌed
Adelbert ˈædḷbɚt, əˈdɛlbɚt, college əˈdɛlbɚt;
  ES -bət
Adelina ˌædḷˈaɪnə, -ˈinə
Adeline ˈædḷˌaɪn, -ˌin
Adelphi əˈdɛlfɪ, -faɪ
Aden ˈedṇ, ˈadṇ
adenoid ˈædṇˌɔɪd |-ism -ˌɪzəm
adenoidal ˌædṇˈɔɪdḷ
adept n ˈædɛpt, əˈdɛpt
adept adj əˈdɛpt
adequacy ˈædəkwəsɪ |-quate -kwɪt
adhere ədˈhɪr, æd-; ES -ˈhɪə(r, S+-ˈhɛə(r;
  |-nce -əns |-nt -ənt
adhesion ədˈhiʒən, æd- |-sive -sɪv
adhibit ædˈhɪbɪt |-ed -ɪd
ad hoc ˈædˈhɑk; ES+-ˈhɒk
ad hominem ˈædˈhɑməˌnɛm; ES+-ˈhɒm-
adieu əˈdju, əˈdɪu, əˈdu
ad infinitum ˈædˌɪnfəˈnaɪtəm
ad interim ˈædˈɪntərɪm

---

adipose 'ædə‚pos
adiposity ‚ædə'pasətɪ; ES+-'pɒs-
Adirondack ‚ædə'rɑndæk; ES+-'rɒn-
adit 'ædɪt
adjacency ə'dʒesn̩sɪ |-cent -sn̩t
adjectival ‚ædʒɪk'taɪv|, 'ædʒɪktɪv| |-ly -ɪ
adjective 'ædʒɪktɪv |-ly -lɪ
adjoin ə'dʒɔɪn |-ed -d |-edly -ɪdlɪ, ə'dʒɔɪndlɪ
adjourn ə'dʒɜ˞n; ES ə'dʒɜn, ə'dʒɜ˞n; |-ed -d
adjudge ə'dʒʌdʒ |-s -ɪz |-d -d
adjudicate ə'dʒudɪ‚ket, ə'dʒɪu- |-d -ɪd
adjudication ə‚dʒudɪ'keʃən, ə‚dʒɪu-
adjunct 'ædʒʌŋkt
adjuration ‚ædʒu'reʃən
adjure ə'dʒur, ə'dʒɪur; ES -ə(r; |-d -d
adjust ə'dʒʌst |-ed -ɪd |-able -əb| |-bly
-blɪ
adjutancy 'ædʒətənsɪ |-tant -tənt
Adler 'ɑdlɚ, 'æd-; ES -lə(r
ad-lib v æd'lɪb |-bed -d
ad libitum 'æd'lɪbɪtəm
administer əd'mɪnəstɚ, æd-; ES -tə(r; |-ed
-d |-ing -tərɪŋ, -trɪŋ
administrable əd'mɪnəstrəb|, æd-
administrate əd'mɪnə‚stret, æd- |-d -ɪd |-tive
-ɪv
administration əd‚mɪnə'streʃən, æd-, ‚æd-
mɪnə-
administrator əd'mɪnə‚stretɚ, æd-; ES -tə(r
administratress əd‚mɪnə'stretrɪs, ‚ædmɪnə-
|-es -ɪz
administratrix əd‚mɪnə'stretrɪks, ‚ædmɪnə-
|-es -ɪz |-trices -trɪ‚siz
admirable 'ædmərəb| |-bly -blɪ
admiral 'ædmərəl |-ty -tɪ
admiration ‚ædmə'reʃən
admire əd'maɪr; ES -'maɪə(r; |-d -d |-dly
-ɪdlɪ, -dlɪ
admissibility əd‚mɪsə'bɪlətɪ, æd-
admissible əd'mɪsəb|, æd- |-bly -blɪ
admission əd'mɪʃən, æd-
admit əd'mɪt, æd- |-ted -ɪd |-tance -n̩s
admix æd'mɪks, əd- |-es -ɪz |-ed -t
admixture æd'mɪkstʃɚ, əd-; ES -tʃə(r
admonish əd'manɪʃ, æd-; ES+-'mɒn-; |-es
-ɪz |-ed -t
admonition ‚ædmə'nɪʃən
admonitory əd'manə‚torɪ, æd-, -‚tɔrɪ; S
-‚torɪ, ES+-'mɒn-

ad nauseam 'æd'nɔʃɪ‚æm, often -'nɔz-,
-'nɑs-
ado ə'du
adobe ə'dobɪ
adolescence ‚æd|'ɛsn̩s |-cy -ɪ |-cent -sn̩t
Adolf, -lph 'ædɑlf, 'ædɒlf, 'ed-
Adolphus ə'dɑlfəs, ə'dɒl- |-'s -ɪz
Adonais ‚ædə'ne·ɪs |-'s -ɪz
Adonijah ‚ædə'naɪdʒə
Adonis ə'donɪs |-'s -ɪz
adopt ə'dapt; ES+ə'dɒpt; |-ed -ɪd
adoptability ə‚daptə'bɪlətɪ; ES+ə‚dɒp-
adoptable ə'daptəb|; ES+ə'dɒp-
adoption ə'dapʃən; ES+ə'dɒp-; |-tive -tɪv
adorable ə'dorəb|, ə'dɔr-; S ə'dor-; |-bly
-blɪ
adoration ‚ædə'reʃən
adore ə'dor, ə'dɔr; ES ə'doə(r, E+ə'dɔə(r;
|-d -d
adorn ə'dɔrn; ES ə'dɔən; |-ed -d
adown ə'daun
adrenal æd'rin| |-in æd'rɛn|ɪn
Adrian 'edrɪən |Adriana ‚edrɪ'ænə, -'enə
Adrianople ‚edrɪən'op|
Adriatic ‚edrɪ'ætɪk
adrift ə'drɪft
adroit ə'drɔɪt
adsorb æd'sɔrb; ES -'sɔəb; |-ed -d
adsorption æd'sɔrpʃən; ES -'sɔəpʃən
adulate 'ædʒə‚let |-d -ɪd |-tion ‚ædʒə'leʃən
adulatory 'ædʒələ‚torɪ, -‚tɔrɪ; S -‚torɪ
Adullam ə'dʌləm |-ite -‚aɪt
adult ə'dʌlt, 'ædʌlt ('a‚dult 'school)
adulterant ə'dʌltərənt, -trənt
adulterate adj ə'dʌltərɪt, -‚ret
adulterate v ə'dʌltə‚ret |-d -ɪd
adulteration ə‚dʌltə'reʃən
adulterer ə'dʌltərɚ; ES -tərə(r; |-tery -tərɪ,
-trɪ
adulteress ə'dʌltərɪs, -trɪs |-es -ɪz
adulterine ə'dʌltərɪn, -‚raɪn
adulterous ə'dʌltərəs, -trəs
adumbrate æd'ʌmbret, 'ædəm‚bret |-d -ɪd
adumbration ‚ædəm'breʃən, ‚ædʌm-
adust ə'dʌst
ad valorem ‚ædvə'lorəm, -'lɔrəm, -əm; S
-'lor-
advance əd'væns; E+-'vɑns, -'vɑns; |-s -ɪz
|-d -t

Key: See in full §§3–47. bee bi |pity 'pɪtɪ (§6) |rate ret |yet jɛt |sang sæŋ |angry 'æŋ·grɪ |bath bæθ; E baθ (§10) |ah ɑ |far fɑr |watch watʃ, wɒtʃ (§12) |jaw dʒɔ |gorge gɔrdʒ |go go

advantage əd'væntɪdʒ; E+-'van-, -'vɑn-;
|-s -ɪz |-d -d
advantageous ˌædvən'tedʒəs, -væn-
advent, A- 'ædvɛnt |-ism -ˌɪzəm |-ist -ɪst
adventitious ˌædvɛn'tɪʃəs, ˌædvən-
adventive æd'vɛntɪv
adventure əd'vɛntʃɚ; ES -tʃə(r; |-d -d |-ring
-'vɛntʃərɪŋ, -'vɛntʃrɪŋ |-rous -tʃərəs, -tʃrəs
adventurer əd'vɛntʃərɚ; ES -tʃərə(r
adventuresome əd'vɛntʃɚsəm; ES -'vɛn-
tʃəsəm
adventuress əd'vɛntʃərɪs, -tʃrɪs |-es -ɪz
adverb 'ædvɝb; ES 'ædvɝb, -vɝb
adverbial əd'vɝbɪəl, æd-, -bjəl; ES -'vɝb-,
-'vɝb-; |-ly -ɪ
adversary 'ædvɚˌsɛrɪ; ES 'ædvə-
adversative əd'vɝsətɪv, æd-; ES -'vɝs-,
-'vɝs-
adverse əd'vɝs, æd-, 'ædvɝs; ES -ɝs, -ɝs;
('winds ad'verse, 'adˌverse 'winds)
adversity əd'vɝsətɪ; ES -'vɝs-, -'vɝs-
advert əd'vɝt, æd-; ES -'vɝt, -'vɝt; |-ed -ɪd
advertence əd'vɝtn̩s, æd-; ES -'vɝt-, -'vɝt-;
|-cy -ɪ |-tent -tn̩t
advertise, -ize 'ædvɚˌtaɪz, ˌædvɚ'taɪz; ES
-və-; |-s -ɪz |-d -d
advertisement, -tize- ˌædvɚ'taɪzmənt, əd-
'vɝtɪz-, -tɪs-; ES ˌædvə-, -'vɝt-, -'vɝt-
advertising, -tiz- n 'ædvɚˌtaɪzɪŋ; ES 'ædvə-
advice əd'vaɪs |-s -ɪz
advisability ədˌvaɪzə'bɪlətɪ
advisable əd'vaɪzəbl̩ |-bly -blɪ
advise əd'vaɪz |-s -ɪz |-d -d |-dly -ɪdlɪ
advisement əd'vaɪzmənt
adviser, -sor əd'vaɪzɚ; ES -'vaɪzə(r; |-sory
-zərɪ
advocacy 'ædvəkəsɪ
advocate n 'ædvəkɪt -ˌket
advocate v 'ædvəˌket |-d -ɪd
advowson əd'vauzn̩
adz, adze ædz |-(e)s -ɪz |-(e)d -d
adzuki æd'zukɪ
Aeacus 'iəkəs |-'s -ɪz
Aëdes e'idiz |-des' -diz
aedile 'idaɪl
Aegean i'dʒiən |-geon -'dʒiən
Aegeus myth. 'idʒjus, -dʒus |-'s -ɪz
Aegina i'dʒaɪnə
aegis 'idʒɪs |-es -ɪz

Aegisthus i'dʒɪsθəs |-'s -ɪz
Aegospotami, -mos ˌigəs'pɑtəˌmaɪ, -məs; ES
+-'pɒt-
Ælfred 'ælfrɪd, 'ælfrəd, 'ælfɚd; ES -frɪd,
-frəd, -fəd
Ælfric 'ælfrɪk
Aemilia i'mɪlɪə |-lius -lɪəs |-lius's -lɪəsɪz
Aeneas ɪ'niəs, i- |-'s -ɪz
Aeneid ɪ'niɪd, i-, -əd
Aeolia i'olɪə |-n -n
Aeolis 'iəlɪs |-'s -ɪz |-t -t |-m -ˌlɪzəm
Aeolus 'iələs, Vt mt. loc. i'oləs |-'s -ɪz
aeon 'iən, 'iɑn; ES+'iɒn
aerate 'eəˌret |-d -ɪd |-tion ˌeə'reʃən
aerial 'airy' e'ɪrɪəl, 'ɛrɪəl, 'ærɪəl; S e'ɪr-,
'ær-; radio 'ɛrɪəl, 'ɛrɪəl |-ly -ɪ
aerie 'ɛrɪ, 'ærɪ, 'ɪrɪ; S 'ærɪ, 'ɪrɪ
aeriform e'ɪrəˌfɔrm, 'ɛrə-, 'ærə-; ES e'ɪrə-
ˌfɔəm, 'ærə-, E+'ɛrə-
aerify e'ɪrəˌfaɪ, 'ɛrə-, 'ærə-; S e'ɪrə-, 'ærə-;
|-fied -ˌfaɪd
aerobic ˌeə'robɪk, ɛ'robɪk |-ally -l̩ɪ
aerodrome 'ɛrəˌdrom, 'ærə-; S 'ærə-
aerodynamics ˌɛrodaɪ'næmɪks, ˌæro-, ˌeəro-;
S ˌæro-, ˌeəro-
aerology ˌeə'rɑlədʒɪ; ES+-'rɒl-
aeromechanic ˌɛromɪ'kænɪk, ˌæro-, ˌeəro-; S
ˌæro-, ˌeəro-
aerometer ˌeə'rɑmətɚ; ES -'rɑmətə(r, -'rɒm-
aeronaut 'ɛrəˌnɔt, 'ærə-; S 'ærə-
aeronautic ˌɛrə'nɔtɪk, ˌærə-; S ˌærə-
aeroplane 'ɛrəˌplen, 'ærə-; S 'ærə-
aerostat 'ɛrəˌstæt, 'ærə-; S 'ærə-
aerostatic ˌɛrə'stætɪk, ˌærə-; S ˌærə-
aerostation ˌɛro'steʃən, ˌæro-; S ˌæro-
aery 'airy' 'ɛrɪ, 'ærɪ; S 'ærɪ
aery 'nest' 'ɛrɪ, 'ærɪ, 'ɪrɪ; S 'ærɪ, 'ɪrɪ
Aeschines 'ɛskəˌniz |-'s -ɪz
Aeschylus 'ɛskələs |-'s -ɪz
Aesculapius ˌɛskjə'lepɪəs |-'s -ɪz |-pian
-pɪən
Aesop 'isɑp, 'isɒp; ES+'isɒp
aesthesia ɛs'θiʒə, -ʒɪə |-thesis -'θisɪs
aesthete 'ɛsθit
aesthetic ɛs'θɛtɪk |-al -l̩ |-ally -l̩ɪ, -ɪklɪ
aestheticism ɛs'θɛtəˌsɪzəm |-thetics -'θɛtɪks
aestival 'ɛstəvl̩, ɛs'taɪvl̩
aestivate 'ɛstəˌvet |-d -ɪd |-tion ˌɛstə'veʃən
aes triplex, A- T- 'iz'traɪplɛks

|full fʊl |tooth tuθ |further 'fɝðɚ; ES 'fɝðə |custom 'kʌstəm |while hwaɪl |how hau |toy tɔɪ
|using 'juzɪŋ |fuse fjuz, fɪuz |dish dɪʃ |vision 'vɪʒən |Eden 'idn̩ |cradle 'kredl̩ |keep 'em 'kipm̩

aestuary ˈɛstʃʊˌɛrɪ
aetheling ˈæθəlɪŋ, ˈæðəlɪŋ (OE ˈæð-)
Æthelstan ˈæθəlˌstæn, ˈæðəl-, -stən (OE ˈæð-)
Aethiop ˈiθɪˌɑp; ES+-ˌɒp
Aethiopia ˌiθɪˈopɪə |-n -n
Aethiopic ˌiθɪˈɑpɪk, -ˈopɪk; ES+-ˈɒpɪk
aetiology ˌitɪˈɑlədʒɪ; ES+-ˈɒl-
Aetna ˈɛtnə
afar əˈfɑr; ES əˈfɑːr, E+əˈfɑːr
affability ˌæfəˈbɪlətɪ
affable ˈæfəbl̩ |-bly -blɪ
affair əˈfɛr, əˈfær; E əˈfɛər, ES əˈfæər
affect əˈfɛkt |-ed -ɪd
affectation ˌæfɪkˈteʃən, ˌæfɛk-
affection əˈfɛkʃən |-ed -d |-ate -ɪt
affective əˈfɛktɪv, æˈf-
afferent ˈæfərənt
affiance əˈfaɪəns |-s -ɪz |-d -t |-ant -ənt
affidavit ˌæfəˈdevɪt
affiliate n, adj əˈfɪlɪɪt, -ˌet
affiliate v əˈfɪlɪˌet |-d -ɪd
affiliation əˌfɪlɪˈeʃən
affinity əˈfɪnətɪ
affirm əˈfɝm; ES əˈfɝm, əˈfɜm; |-ed -d
affirmable əˈfɝməbl̩; ES əˈfɝm-, əˈfɜm-; |-bly -blɪ
affirmation ˌæfɚˈmeʃən; ES ˌæfə-
affirmative əˈfɝmətɪv; ES əˈfɝm-, əˈfɜm-
affirmatory əˈfɝməˌtorɪ, -ˌtɔrɪ; ES əˈfɝməˌtorɪ, əˈfɝm-, E+-ˌtɔrɪ
affix n ˈæfɪks |-es -ɪz
affix v əˈfɪks |-es -ɪz |-ed -t
afflatus əˈfletəs
afflict əˈflɪkt |-ed -ɪd
affliction əˈflɪkʃən |-tive -tɪv
affluence ˈæfluəns, -flɪu- |-ent -ənt
afflux ˈæflʌks |-es -ɪz
afford əˈford, əˈfɔrd; ES əˈfoəd, E+əˈfɔəd; |-ed -ɪd
afforest əˈfɔrɪst, əˈfɑr-, əˈfɒr- |-ed -ɪd
affranchise əˈfræntʃaɪz |-s -ɪz |-d -d
affranchisement əˈfræntʃɪzmənt
affray əˈfre |-ed -d
affricate n ˈæfrɪkɪt
affricate v ˈæfrɪˌket |-d -ɪd
affricative əˈfrɪkətɪv
affright əˈfraɪt |-ed -ɪd
affront əˈfrʌnt |-ed -ɪd

affy əˈfaɪ |affied əˈfaɪd
afghan, A- ˈæfgən, -gæn
Afghanistan æfˈgænəˌstæn, ˌæfgænəˈstæn
afield əˈfild
afire əˈfaɪr; ES əˈfaɪə(r
aflame əˈflem
afloat əˈflot
aflutter əˈflʌtɚ; ES əˈflʌtə(r
afoot əˈfʊt
afore əˈfor, əˈfɔr; ES əˈfoə(r, E+əˈfɔə(r
afore-mentioned əˈforˈmɛnʃənd, əˈfɔr-; ES see afore; (aˈfore-ˌmentioned ˈact)
aforesaid əˈforˌsɛd, əˈfɔr-; ES see afore
aforethought əˈforˌθɔt, əˈfɔr-; ES see afore
aforetime əˈforˌtaɪm, əˈfɔr-; ES see afore
a fortiori ˈeˌforʃɪˈoraɪ, -ˌfɔrʃɪˈɔr-; ES -ˌfoəʃɪˈoraɪ, E+-ˌfɔəʃɪˈɔraɪ
afoul əˈfaʊl
afraid əˈfred; S+əˈfrɛd
afreet ˈæfrit
afresh əˈfrɛʃ
Afric ˈæfrɪk |-a -ə |-an -ən
Afrikaans ˌæfrɪˈkɑnz, -ˈkɑns
Afrikander ˌæfrɪˈkændɚ; ES -də(r
Afro-American ˈæfroəˈmɛrəkən
aft æft; E+aft, ɑft
after ˈæftɚ; ES ˈæftə(r, E+ˈaf-, ˈɑf-
afterbirth ˈæftɚˌbɝθ; ES ˈæftəˌbɝθ, ˈæftəˌbɜθ, E+ˈaf-, ˈɑf-
afterbrain ˈæftɚˌbren; ES see after
afterdamp ˈæftɚˌdæmp; ES see after
afterdeck ˈæftɚˌdɛk; ES see after
after-dinner adj ˈæftɚˈdɪnɚ; ES ˈæftəˈdɪnə(r, E+ˈaf-, ˈɑf-; (ˈafter-ˌdinner ˈmints)
aftereffect ˈæftərəˌfɛkt; E+ˈaf-, ˈɑf-
afterglow ˈæftɚˌglo; ES see after
afterimage ˈæftɚˌɪmɪdʒ; E+ˈaf-, ˈɑf-; |-s -ɪz
afterlife ˈæftɚˌlaɪf; ES see after
aftermath ˈæftɚˌmæθ; ES see after; |-ths -θs
aftermost ˈæftɚˌmost, -məst; ES see after
afternoon ˌæftɚˈnun; ES see after; (ˈafterˌnoon ˈtea)
aftertaste ˈæftɚˌtest; ES see after
afterthought ˈæftɚˌθɔt; ES see after
afterward ˈæftɚwɚd; ES ˈæftəwəd, E+ˈaf-, ˈɑf-; |-s -z— A dissimilated pron. ˈæftɚwɚd is often heard (§121).
Agag ˈegæg

---

again ə'gɛn, *less freq. or poet.* ə'gen
against ə'gɛnst, *less freq. or poet.* ə'genst
Agamemnon ˌægə'mɛmnən, -nɑn; ES+-nɒn
agape ə'gep, ə'gæp
agar 'egɑr, 'egɚ, 'ɑgɑr; ES -gɑ:(r, -gə(r
agar-agar 'egɑr'egɑr; ES 'egɑr'egɑ:(r
agaric 'ægərɪk, ə'gærɪk
Agassiz 'ægəsɪ |Agassiz's 'ægəsɪz
agate *n* 'ægɪt, 'ægət
agate *adv* ə'get
Agatha 'ægəθə
agave, A- ə'gevɪ
Agawam 'ægəˌwɔm, -ˌwɑm, -ˌwɒm
agaze ə'gez
age edʒ |ages 'edʒɪz |*past & pptc* aged edʒd
-age *unstressed ending* -ɪdʒ, -ədʒ. *In the
vocab. when only* -ɪdʒ *is given, it is to be
understood that many speakers pronounce*
-ədʒ.
aged *'old'* 'edʒɪd, *'of the age of'* edʒd
agelong 'edʒ'lɔŋ, -'lɒŋ; S+-'lɑŋ; ('ageˌlong
'drift)
agency 'edʒənsɪ |agent 'edʒənt
agenda *pl* ə'dʒɛndə |*sg* agendum ə'dʒɛndəm
ageratum ˌædʒə'retəm
Ageratum ə'dʒɛrətəm, ˌædʒə'retəm
agglomerate *adj, n* ə'glɑmərɪt, -ˌret; ES+
-'glɒm-
agglomerate *v* ə'glɑməˌret; ES+-'glɒm-; |-d
-ɪd
agglomeration əˌglɑmə'reʃən; ES+-ˌglɒm-
agglutinate *adj* ə'glutn̩ɪt, -'glɪu-, -ˌet
agglutinate *v* ə'glutn̩ˌet, -'glɪu- |-d -ɪd |-tive
-tɪv
agglutination əˌglutn̩'eʃən, -ˌglɪu-
aggrandize 'ægrənˌdaɪz, ə'græn- |-s -ɪz |-d -d
aggrandizement ə'grændɪzmənt
aggravate 'ægrəˌvet |-d -ɪd |-tion ˌægrə'veʃən
aggregate *n, adj* 'ægrɪgɪt, -ˌget
aggregate *v* 'ægrɪˌget |-d -ɪd |-tive -ɪv
aggregation ˌægrɪ'geʃən
aggregatory 'ægrɪgəˌtorɪ, -ˌtɔrɪ; S -ˌtorɪ
aggress ə'grɛs |-es -ɪz |-ed -t
aggression ə'grɛʃən |-sive -sɪv
aggressor ə'grɛsɚ; ES ə'grɛsə(r
aggrieve ə'griv |-d -d |-dly -ɪdlɪ
aghast ə'gæst; E+ə'gɑst, ə'gɑst
agile 'ædʒəl, 'ædʒɪl |-ly -dʒɪllɪ, -dʒɪlɪ
agility ə'dʒɪlətɪ

Agincourt 'ædʒɪnˌkort, -ˌkɔrt; ES -ˌkoət, E+
-ˌkɔət
agio 'ædʒo, 'ædʒɪˌo (*It* 'ɑ:dʒo)
agiotage 'ædʒətɪdʒ, 'ædʒɪə-
agitate 'ædʒəˌtet |-d -ɪd |-tor -ɚ; ES -ə(r
agitation ˌædʒə'teʃən
Aglaia ə'gleə
aglet 'æglɪt
agley ə'glaɪ=agly *'asquint'*
aglow ə'glo
agly ə'glaɪ=agley—*in Burns rimed with
joy, then pronounced* dʒaɪ
agnat 'ægnæt |agnate 'ægnet
Agnes 'ægnɪs, -nəs |-'s -ɪz
Agnew 'ægnju, -nɪu, -nu
agnostic æg'nɑstɪk; ES+-'nɒs-; |-ism
-təˌsɪzəm
Agnus Dei 'ægnəs'diaɪ
ago ə'go
agog ə'gɑg, ə'gɒg
agonize 'ægəˌnaɪz |-s -ɪz |-d -d
agony 'ægənɪ |-ied -d
agora 'ægərə |-s -z |-rae -ˌri
agoraphobia ˌægərə'fobɪə
agouti ə'gutɪ
agrarian ə'grɛrɪən, ə'grer- |-ism -ˌɪzəm
agree ə'gri |-d -d |-able -əbɭ |-bly -blɪ
agreeability əˌgriə'bɪlətɪ
Agricola ə'grɪkələ
agricultural ˌægrɪ'kʌltʃərəl |-ly -ɪ |-ist -ɪst
agriculture 'ægrɪˌkʌltʃɚ; ES -tʃə(r
agriculturist ˌægrɪ'kʌltʃərɪst
agrimony 'ægrəˌmonɪ
Agrippa ə'grɪpə
agrology ə'grɑlədʒɪ; ES+-'grɒl-
agronomic ˌægrə'nɑmɪk; ES+-'nɒm-; |-al -ɭ
agronomy ə'grɑnəmɪ; ES+-'grɒn-; |-mist
-mɪst
aground ə'graʊnd
ague 'egju |-d -d |aguing 'egjuɪŋ
Aguecheek 'egjuˌtʃik
aguinaldo, A- ˌagi'naldo (*Sp* ˌagi'naldo)
ah ɑ
aha ə'hɑ, ɑ'hɑ, 'ɑ'hɑ
Ahab 'ehæb
Ahasuerus əˌhæzju'ɪrəs, əˌhæzu- |-'s -ɪz
Ahaz 'ehæz |-'s -ɪz
ahead ə'hɛd
ahem ə'hɛm, ʔm̩ʔm̩ʔm̩ʔm̩ *&c.*

Aherne əˈhɜ·n; ES əˈhɜn, əˈhɜ·n
Ahithophel, Ahito- əˈhɪtəˌfɛl
Ahmed ˈɑmɪd, ˈɑmɛd
ahorse əˈhɔrs; ES əˈhɔəs
ahorseback əˈhɔrsˌbæk; ES əˈhɔəs-
Ahoskie əˈhɑskɪ; ES+əˈhɒs-
ahoy əˈhɔɪ
ahungered əˈhʌŋgəd; ES -gəd
Ai ˈeaɪ
aid ed |aided ˈedɪd
Aïda ɑˈidə
aide ed
aide-de-camp ˈeddəˈkæmp, ˈeddəˈkã̃ (Fr
    ɛddəˈkã̃)
aides-de-camp ˈedzdəˈkæmp, ˈedzdəˈkã̃ (Fr
    ɛddəˈkã̃)
aiglet ˈeglɪt
aigrette ˈegrɛt, eˈgrɛt
Aiken ˈekɪn, -ən
ail el |ailed eld |-ment -mənt
ailanthus, A- eˈlænθəs |-es -ɪz
Aileen ˈelin, ˈaɪ-, eˈlin, aɪ-
aileron ˈeləˌrɑn; ES+-ˌrɒn
Ailsa ˈelsə, Sc ˈɛlsə
aim em |aimed emd
ain't ent
Ainu ˈaɪnu
air ɛr, ær; E ɛə(r, ES æə(r
air-cool ˈɛrˌkul, ˈær-; ES see air; |-ed -d
air-cooled adj ˈɛrˈkuld, ˈær-; ES see air;
    (ˈairˌcooled ˈmotor)
aircraft ˈɛrˌkræft, ˈær-; E ˈɛə-, ˈæə-, -ˌkraft,
    -ˌkraft; S ˈæəˌkræft
airdrome ˈɛrˌdrom, ˈær-; ES see air
air-dry ˈɛrˌdraɪ, ˈær-; ES see air; |-ied -d
Airedale ˈɛrˌdel, ˈær-; ES see air
airfield ˈɛrˌfild, ˈær-; ES see air
airfoil ˈɛrˌfɔɪl, ˈær-; ES see air
airily ˈɛrəlɪ, ˈær-, -ɪlɪ; S ˈær-
airplane ˈɛrˌplen, ˈær-; ES see air
airport ˈɛrˌport, ˈær-, -ˌpɔrt; E ˈɛəˌpoət,
    ˈæə-, -ˌpɔət; S ˈæəˌpoət
airproof ˈɛrˈpruf, ˈær-; ES see air
airship ˈɛrˌʃɪp, ˈær-; ES see air
airsick ˈɛrˌsɪk, ˈær-; ES see air
airt ɛrt, ært, ert; E ɛət, ES æət, eət
airtight ˈɛrˈtaɪt, ˈær-; ES see air
airway ˈɛrˌwe, ˈær-; ES see air
airy ˈɛrɪ, ˈærɪ; S ˈærɪ

aisle aɪl |aisled aɪld |-less ˈaɪllɪs
Aisne en (Fr ɛːn)
aitch etʃ |aitches ˈetʃɪz |-bone -ˌbon
Aix eks |-'s -ɪz (Fr ɛks)
Aix-la-Chapelle ˈekslɑʃæˈpɛl (Fr ɛkslaʃaˈpɛl)
ajar əˈdʒɑr; ES əˈdʒɑː(r, E+əˈdʒɑː(r
Ajax ˈedʒæks |-'s -ɪz
Akbar ˈækbɑr; ES -bɑː(r, E+-baː(r
ake 'to ache' ek |-d -t
À Kempis əˈkɛmpɪs |-'s -ɪz
Akenside ˈekɪnˌsaɪd, ˈekən-
akimbo əˈkɪmbo
akin əˈkɪn
Akkad ˈækæd
Akkadian əˈkedɪən, əˈkɑd-
Akron ˈækrən |-ite -ˌaɪt
à la ˈɑlə, ˈɑlɑ (Fr ala)
Alabama ˌæləˈbæmə |-n -n |-mian -mɪən
alabamine ˌæləˈbæmin, -ɪn
alabaster ˈæləˌbæstə; ES -tə(r, E+-ˌbas-,
    -ˌbɑs-
à la carte ˌɑləˈkɑrt; ES -ˈkɑːt, E+-ˈkaːt;
    (Fr alaˈkart)
alack əˈlæk
alacrity əˈlækrətɪ
Aladdin əˈlædɪn, əˈlædn̩
Alamannic ˌæləˈmænɪk
alameda ˌæləˈmedə
Alameda ˌæləˈmidə, -ˈmedə (Sp ˌalaˈmeða)
alamo ˈæləˌmo, ˈal- (Sp ˈalaˌmo)
Alamo ˈæləˌmo
alamode ˌɑləˈmod, ˌælə- (Fr alaˈmɔ̈d)
Åland ˈɑlənd, ˈɔ-
Alarbus əˈlɑrbəs; ES əˈlɑːb-; |-'s -ɪz
Alaric ˈælərɪk
alarm əˈlɑrm; ES əˈlɑːm, E+əˈlaːm
alarum əˈlærəm, əˈlɛrəm; S əˈlærəm
alary ˈelərɪ, ˈæl-
alas əˈlæs; E+əˈlas, əˈlɑs
Alaska əˈlæskə |-n -n
Alastor əˈlæstə, -tɔr; ES -tə(r, -tɔə(r
alate ˈelet |alated ˈeletɪd
alb ælb
Alban ˈɔlbən
alban chem. ˈælbən
Albania ælˈbenɪə, -njə |-n -n
Albans ˈɔlbənz |-'s -ɪz
Albany ˈɔlbənɪ
albatross ˈælbəˌtrɔs, -ˌtrɒs |-es -ɪz

albeit ɔl'biːt
Albemarle 'ælbə,marl; ES -,muːl, E+ -,maːl
Albert 'ælbət; ES 'ælbət
Alberta æl'bɝtə; ES -'bɝtə, -'bɝtə
Albigenses ,ælbɪ'dʒɛnsiz
albinism 'ælbə,nɪzəm
albino æl'baɪno |-binoism -,ɪzəm
Albion 'ælbɪən, -bjən
Albright 'ɔlbraɪt
Albro 'ɔlbro, cf Aldborough
album 'ælbəm, -bm̩
albumen æl'bjumən, -'bɪum-
albumin æl'bjumɪn, -'bɪum- |-ate -ɪt, -,et
albuminoid æl'bjumɪ,nɔɪd, -'bɪum- |-nose -,nos |-nous -nəs
Albuquerque 'ælbə,kɝkɪ, ,ælbə'kɝkɪ, -bjʊ-; ES -ɝ-, -ɝ-
alburnum æl'bɝnəm; ES -'bɝn-, -'bɝn-
Alcaeus æl'siəs |-'s -ɪz
Alcaic æl'ke·ɪk
alcaide æl'ked (Sp al'kaiðe)
alcalde æl'kældɪ (Sp al'kalde)
Alcatraz 'ælkə,træz, ,ælkə'træz (Am Sp ,alka'tras)
alcazar, A- æl'kæzɚ; ES -zə(r; (Sp al'kaθar)
Alcestis æl'sɛstɪs |-'s -ɪz
alchemist 'ælkəmɪst |-my -mɪ
Alcibiades ,ælsə'baɪə,diz |-'s -ɪz
Alcides æl'saɪdiz |-des' -diz
Alcinoüs æl'sɪnʊəs |-'s -ɪz
Alcmene ælk'minɪ
Alcoa æl'koə
alcohol 'ælkə,hɔl, -,hɒl, -,hɑl |-ism -,ɪzəm
alcoholic ,ælkə'hɔlɪk, -'hɒl-, -'hɑl- |-ally -|ɪ, -ɪklɪ
alcoholicity ,ælkəhɔl'ɪsətɪ, -hɒl-, -hɑl-
Alcoran ,ælko'rɑn, -'ræn
Alcott 'ɔlkət
alcove 'ælkov
Alcuin 'ælkwɪn
Alcyone æl'saɪə,ni
Alda 'ɔldə
Aldan Pa 'ɔldən, Russia al'dɑn
Aldborough 'ɔld,bɝo, 'ɔl,b-, -ə; ES -,bɝr-, -,bʌr-, -,bɝ-; Brit 'ɔldbərə, 'ɔlb-, -brə
Aldebaran æl'dɛbərən
aldehyde 'ældə,haɪd
Alden 'ɔldɪn, -dən

alder 'ɔldɚ; ES 'ɔldə(r
alderman 'ɔldɚmən; ES 'ɔldə-; |-men -mən
aldermanic ,ɔldɚ'mænɪk; ES ,ɔldə-
Alderney 'ɔldɚnɪ; ES 'ɔldənɪ
Aldershot 'ɔldɚ,ʃɑt; ES 'ɔldə,ʃɑt, -,ʃɒt
Aldine 'ɔldaɪn, 'ɔldin
Aldington 'ɔldɪŋtən
Aldrich 'ɔldrɪtʃ |-'s -ɪz
ale el
aleatory 'elɪə,torɪ, -,tɔrɪ; S -,torɪ
alee ə'li
alehouse 'el,haʊs |-ses -zɪz
Alemannic ,ælə'mænɪk
alembic ə'lɛmbɪk
Alençon ə'lɛnsən, -sɑn, -sɒn (Fr alɑ̃'sõ)
Aleppo ə'lɛpo
alert ə'lɝt; ES ə'lɝt, ə'lɝt; |-ed -ɪd
Alethea ,ælə'θiə, ə'liθɪə
Aleut 'ælɪ,ut
Aleutian ə'luʃən, ə'lɪu-
alewife 'el,waɪf |-wives -,waɪvz
Aleyn 'ælɪn, -ən
Alexander ,ælɪg'zændɚ, ,ɛlɪg-; ES -'zændə(r; |-dra -drə |-dria -drɪə |-drian -drɪən |-drine -drɪn
Alexas ə'lɛksəs |-xas' -ksəs
alexin ə'lɛksɪn
Alexis ə'lɛksɪs |-xis' -ksɪs
alfalfa, A- æl'fælfə
Alfonso æl'fɑnzo, -so; ES+-'fɒn-
Alford 'ɔlfɚd; ES 'ɔlfəd
Alfred 'ælfrɪd, -frəd, -fɚd; ES -frɪd, -frəd, -fəd
Alfreda æl'fridə ('Al,freda 'Burroughs)
Alfredian æl'fridɪən
alfresco æl'fresko
Alfric 'ælfrɪk
alga 'ælgə |algae 'ældʒi
algebra 'ældʒəbrə
algebraic ,ældʒə'bre·ɪk |-al -| |-ally -|ɪ, -ɪklɪ
algebraist 'ældʒə,bre·ɪst
Algeciras ,ældʒɪ'sɪrəs |-'s -ɪz (Sp ,alxe'θiras)
Alger 'ældʒɚ; ES 'ældʒə(r
Algeria æl'dʒɪrɪə |-n -n
Algerine ,ældʒə'rin
Algernon 'ældʒɚnən; ES 'ældʒə-
algid 'ældʒɪd
Algiers æl'dʒɪrz; ES -'dʒɪəz, S+-'dʒɛəz; |-'s -ɪz

Algol ˈælgɑl, -gɒl
Algoma ælˈgomə
Algona ælˈgonə
Algonkian ælˈgaŋkɪən, -ˈgɒŋ-
Algonquian ælˈgaŋkɪən, -kwɪən, -ˈgɒŋ-
Algonquin ælˈgaŋkɪn, -kwɪn, -ˈgɒŋ-
algorism ˈælgəˌrɪzəm |algorithm ˈælgəˌrɪðəm
Alhambra ælˈhæmbrə
alias ˈelɪəs |-es -ɪz
Ali Baba ˈælɪˈbæbə, ˈɑlɪˈbɑbə
alibi ˈæləˌbaɪ |-ed -d
Alice ˈælɪs |-ˈs -ɪz
Alicia əˈlɪʃɪə
alien ˈeljən, ˈelɪən
Aliena Shak. ˌelɪˈinə
alienability ˌeljənəˈbɪlətɪ, ˌelɪən-
alienable ˈeljənəbl̩, ˈelɪən-
alienate ˈeljənˌet, ˈelɪən- |-d -ɪd
alienation ˌeljənˈeʃən, ˌelɪən-
alienism ˈeljənˌɪzəm, ˈelɪən- |-ist -ɪst
alight adv əˈlaɪt
alight v əˈlaɪt |-ed -ɪd or alit əˈlɪt
align əˈlaɪn |-ed -d
alike əˈlaɪk
aliment n ˈæləmənt
aliment v ˈæləˌment |-ed -ɪd
alimental ˌæləˈmentl̩ |-ly -ɪ
alimentary ˌæləˈmentərɪ, -ˈmentrɪ
alimentation ˌæləmenˈteʃən
alimony ˈæləˌmonɪ
aline əˈlaɪn |-d -d
Aline əˈlin
aliquant ˈæləkwənt |-quot -kwət
Aliquippa ˌæləˈkwɪpə
Alison ˈæləsn̩
alit past & pptc of alight əˈlɪt
alive əˈlaɪv
alizarin əˈlɪzərɪn |-rine -rɪn -ˌrin
alkahest ˈælkəˌhest
alkalescence ˌælkəˈlesn̩s |-cy -ɪ |-nt -n̩t
alkali ˈælkəˌlaɪ
alkalify ˈælkələˌfaɪ, ælˈkælə- |-fied -ˌfaɪd
alkaline ˈælkəˌlaɪn, -lɪn
alkalinity ˌælkəˈlɪnətɪ
alkalize ˈælkəˌlaɪz |-s -ɪz |-d -d
alkaloid ˈælkəˌlɔɪd |-al ˌælkəˈlɔɪdl̩
Alkoran ˌælkoˈran, -ˈræn
all ɔl
Allah ˈælə, ˈɑlə

all-American ˈɔləˈmɛrəkən
Allan ˈælən
Allardice ˈælɚˌdaɪs; ES ˈælə-; |-ˈs -ɪz
all-around ˈɔləˈraʊnd (ˈall-aˌround ˈskill)
allay əˈle |-ed -d
Allegan ˈæləgən
Allegany Md, NY ˈæləˌgenɪ
allegation ˌæləˈgeʃən
allege əˈlɛdʒ |-s -ɪz |-d -d |-dly -ɪdlɪ
Alleghany NC, Va ˈæləˌgenɪ
Allegheny Pa city, riv., college ˈæləˌgenɪ
allegiance əˈlidʒəns |-s -ɪz
allegoric ˌæləˈgɔrɪk, -ˈgɑr-, -ˈgɒr- |-al -l̩
    |-ally -l̩ɪ, -ɪklɪ
allegorist ˈæləˌgorɪst, -ˌgɔr-, ˈæləgərɪst; S
    -ˌgor-, -ˌgər-
allegoristic ˌæləgəˈrɪstɪk
allegorize ˈæləgəˌraɪz |-s -ɪz |-d -d
allegory ˈæləˌgorɪ, -ˌgɔrɪ; S -ˌgorɪ
allegretto ˌæləˈgrɛto (It ˌalleˈgretto)
allegro əˈlegro, əˈlɛgro (It alˈle:gro)
Alleine ˈælɪn, -ən
allelomorph əˈliləˌmɔrf, -ˈlɛl-; ES -ˌmɔəf
alleluia ˌæləˈlujə, -ˈlɪujə
allemande ˌæləˈmænd (Fr alˈmã:d)
Allen ˈælɪn, -ən
Allenby ˈælɪnbɪ, -ən-
Allentown ˈælɪnˌtaʊn, -ən-
allergic əˈlɝdʒɪk; ES -ˈlɜdʒ-, -ˈlɝdʒ-
allergy ˈælədʒɪ; ES ˈælədʒɪ
Allerton ˈælətən; ES ˈælətən
alleviate əˈlivɪˌet |-d -ɪd |-tion əˌlivɪˈeʃən
alley ˈælɪ |-ed -d
Alleyn ˈælɪn, -ən
Allhallows ˌɔlˈhæloz, -ləz
alliance, A- əˈlaɪəns |-s -ɪz |-d -t
allied əˈlaɪd (ˈalˌlied ˈarmies)
Allies ˈælaɪz, əˈlaɪz
alligator ˈæləˌgetɚ; ES -ˌgetə(r
Allingham ˈælɪŋəm
Allison ˈæləsn̩
alliterate əˈlɪtəˌret |-d -ɪd |-tive -ɪv
alliteration əˌlɪtəˈreʃən, ˌælɪtə-
allocable ˈæləkəbl̩
allocate ˈæləˌket, ˈælo- |-d -ɪd
allocation ˌæləˈkeʃən, ˌælo-
allocution ˌæləˈkjuʃən, ˌælo-, -ˈkɪu-
allomorph ˈæləˌmɔrf; ES -ˌmɔəf
allomorphic ˌæləˈmɔrfɪk; ES -ˈmɔəf-

Key: See in full §§3-47. bee **bi** |pity ˈpɪtɪ (§6) |rate ret |yet jet |sang sæŋ |angry ˈæŋ·grɪ
|bath bæθ; E baθ (§10) |ah ɑ |far fɑr |watch wɑtʃ, wɒtʃ (§12) |jaw dʒɔ |gorge gɔrdʒ |go go

allopath ˈæləˌpæθ |-ths -θs
allopathic ˌæləˈpæθɪk
allopathist əˈlɑpəθɪst; ES+-ˈlɒp-; |-thy -θɪ
allot əˈlɑt; ES+əˈlɒt; |-ted -ɪd
allotrope ˈæləˌtrop
allotropic ˌæləˈtrɑpɪk; ES+-ˈtrɒp-; |-al -|
  |-ally -ɪ, -ɪklɪ
allotropy əˈlɑtrəpɪ; ES+əˈlɒt-
allover n ˈɔlˌovɚ; ES -ˌovə(r
allover adj ˈɔlˈovɚ; ES -ˈovə(r; (ən ˈɔlˈovɚ
  wən)
allow əˈlaʊ |-ed -d |-edly -ɪdlɪ
allowable əˈlaʊəb| |-bly -blɪ
allowance əˈlaʊəns |-s -ɪz
Alloway ˈæləˌwe
alloy n ˈælɔɪ, əˈlɔɪ
alloy v əˈlɔɪ |-ed -d
all-round ˈɔlˈraʊnd (ˈall-ˌround ˈhelp)
allspice ˈɔlˌspaɪs |-s -ɪz
Allston ˈɔlstən
allude əˈlud, əˈlɪud |-d -ɪd
allure əˈlʊr, əˈlɪur; ES əˈlʊə(r, əˈlɪuə(r
allusion əˈluʒən, əˈlɪuʒən, æ-
allusive əˈlusɪv, əˈlɪusɪv
alluvial əˈluvɪəl, əˈlɪuv-, -vjəl
alluvion əˈluvɪən, əˈlɪuv- |-vium -vɪəm -via
  -vɪə
ally n ˈælaɪ, əˈlaɪ
ally v əˈlaɪ |allied əˈlaɪd
Allyn ˈælaɪn, -lɪn, -lən
almagest ˈælməˌdʒɛst
Alma US ˈælmə, Russia ˈɑlmə
Alma Mater ˈælməˈmetɚ, ˈɑlməˈmɑtɚ; ES
  -tə(r;—The hybrid ˈælməˈmɑtɚ is frequently heard.
almanac ˈɔlməˌnæk, ˈɒlmənɪk
Alma-Tadema ˈælməˈtædɪmə
almighty, A- ɔlˈmaɪtɪ (ˈalˌmighty ˈtruth)
Almon ˈælmən
almond ˈɑmənd, ˈæmənd—ˈæmənd, now less
  freq., is preserved by some old families. In
  NEngd ˈælmənd is freq.
almoner ˈælmənɚ, ˈɑmənɚ; ES -nə(r
almonry ˈælmənrɪ, ˈɑmənrɪ
almost ɔlˈmost, ˈɔlˌmost (ˈdone, alˈmost;
  ˈalˌmost ˈdone)
alms ɑmz |-giving -ˌgɪvɪŋ |-house -ˌhaʊs
almuce ˈælmjus, -mɪus |-s -ɪz
Aln æln, loc.+el, ˈalən, jɛl

Alne ɔn
Alnmouth ˈælnˌmaʊθ, -məθ, loc.+ˈelməθ,
  ˈjɛlməθ
Alnwick ˈænɪk, loc. ˈanɪk
aloe ˈælo |-s -z
aloft əˈlɔft, əˈlɒft
aloha əˈloə, ɑˈlohɑ
alone əˈlon
along əˈlɔŋ, əˈlɒŋ; S+əˈlɑŋ
alongshore əˈlɔŋˌʃor, əˈlɒŋ-, -ˌʃɔr; E -ˌʃoə(r,
  -ˌʃɔə(r; S -ˌʃoə(r, əˈlɑŋ-
alongside əˈlɔŋˈsaɪd, əˈlɒŋ-; S+əˈlɑŋ-:
  (aˈlongˈside it, aˈlongˌside a ˈbarge)
Alonso, -zo əˈlɑnzo; ES+əˈlɒn-
aloof əˈluf
aloud əˈlaʊd
alow əˈlo
Aloysius ˌæloˈɪsɪəs, -ˈɪʃəs |-'s -ɪz
alp ælp
alpaca ælˈpækə
Alpena ælˈpinə
alpenhorn ˈælpɪnˌhɔrn, -pən-; ES -ˌhɔən
alpenstock ˈælpɪnˌstɑk, -pən-; ES+-ˌstɒk
alpha, A- ˈælfə
alphabet ˈælfəˌbɛt
alphabetic ˌælfəˈbɛtɪk |-al -| |-ally -ɪ, -ɪklɪ
alphabetize ˈælfəbəˌtaɪz |-s -ɪz |-d -d
Alphaeus, -phe- Bib. ælˈfiəs, ˈælf- |-'s -ɪz
Alpheus mod. name ˈælfɪəs, myth. ælˈfiəs
Alphonse ælˈfanz, -ˈfɒnz, -ˈfɔnz |-'s -ɪz (Fr
  alˈfõːs)
Alphonso ælˈfanzo, -so; ES+-ˈfɒn-
Alpine ˈælpaɪn, -pɪn
Alps ælps
already ɔlˈrɛdɪ
alright ɔlˈraɪt
Alsace ælˈses, ˈælsæs |-'s -ɪz (Fr alˈzas)
Alsace-Lorraine ˈælˌsesloˈren, -lɒ-, ˈælˌsæs-
Alsatia ælˈseʃɪə, -ʃə |-tian -ʃən
alsike ˈælsaɪk, ˈɔl-
also ˈɔlso
Altai ælˈtaɪ, ælˈteˈaɪ |Altaic ælˈteˈɪk
Altair ælˈtaˈɪr; ES -ɪə(r
Altamaha ˌɔltəməˈhɔ
altar ˈɔltɚ; ES ˈɔltə(r; |-ed -d
altarpiece ˈɔltɚˌpis; ES ˈɔltə-; |-s -ɪz
altazimuth ælˈtæzəməθ
alter ˈɔltɚ; ES ˈɔltə(r; |-ed -d |-ing ˈɔltərɪŋ,
  ˈɔltrɪŋ

|full fʊl |tooth tuθ |further ˈfɝðɚ; ES ˈfɜðə |custom ˈkʌstəm |while hwaɪl |how haʊ |toy tɔɪ
|using ˈjuzɪŋ |fuse fjuz, fɪuz |dish dɪʃ |vision ˈvɪʒən |Eden ˈidn̩ |cradle ˈkredl̩ |keep 'em ˈkipm̩

alterant ˈɔltərənt
alteration ˌɔltəˈreʃən |-rative ˈɔltəˌretɪv
altercate ˈɔltəˌket, ˈæl-; ES -tə-
altercation ˌɔltəˈkeʃən, ˌæl-; ES -tə-
alter ego ˈæltəˈigo, -ˈɛgo
alternant ɔlˈtɜ·nənt, æl-; ES -ˈtɜn-, -ˈtɝn-
alternate n, adj ˈɔltənɪt, ˈæl-; ES -tə-; |-ly -lɪ,
    acct+alˈternate(ly)
alternate v ˈɔltəˌnet, ˈæl-; ES -tə-; |-d -ɪd
alternation ˌɔltəˈneʃən, ˌæl-; ES -tə-
alternative ɔlˈtɜ·nətɪv, æl-; ES -ˈtɜn-, -ˈtɝn-
alternator ˈɔltəˌnetə, ˈæl-; ES -təˌnetə(r
Altgeld ˈɔltgɛld (Ger ˈaltgɛlt)
Althaea ælˈθiə
althea, A- ælˈθiə
althorn ˈæltˌhɔrn; ES -ˌhɔən
although, altho ɔlˈðo
altimeter ælˈtɪmətə, ˈæltəˌmitə; ES -tə(r
altissimo ælˈtɪsəˌmo (It alˈtissiˌmo)
altitude ˈæltəˌtjud, -ˌtɪud, -ˌtud
altitudinal ˌæltəˈtjudn̩l, -ˈtɪud-, -ˈtud-
Altman ˈɔltmən
alto ˈælto
alto-cumulus ˌæltoˈkjumjələs, -ˈkɪum- |-es
    -ɪz |-li -ˌlaɪ
altogether ˌɔltəˈgɛðə; ES -ˈgɛðə(r
Alton ˈɔltn̩
Altoona ælˈtunə
alto-relievo ˈæltoˈrɪˈlivo (It -rilievo ˈalto-ri-
    ˈlje:vo)
alto-stratus ˈæltoˈstretəs |-es -ɪz |-ti -taɪ
altruism ˈæltrʊˌɪzəm |-ist -ɪst
altruistic ˌæltrʊˈɪstɪk |-ally -l̩ɪ, -ɪklɪ
Altus ˈæltəs |-'s -ɪz
aludel ˈæljʊˌdɛl
alum ˈæləm |-ed -d
alumina əˈlumɪnə, əˈlɪu-
aluminium ˌæljəˈmɪnɪəm
aluminum əˈlumɪnəm, əˈlɪu- |-nous -nəs
alumna əˈlʌmnə |alumnae əˈlʌmni
alumnus əˈlʌmnəs |-'s -ɪz |-ni -naɪ
Alva ˈælvə
alveolar ælˈviələ; ES -ˈviələ(r
alveolus ælˈviələs |-li -ˌlaɪ
alway ˈɔlwe
always ˈɔlwɪz, ˈɔlwez, ˈɔlwəz; S ˈɔlwez, -wɪz
alyssum, A- əˈlɪsəm
am stressed ˈæm, ˌæm; unstr. əm, m
A.M., a.m. ˈeˈɛm

Amabel ˈæməˌbɛl
Amadis ˈæmədɪs |-'s -ɪz
Amador ˈæməˌdor, -ˌdɔr; ES -ˌdoə(r, E+
    -ˌdɔə(r; (Sp ˌamaˈðɔr)
amain əˈmen
Amalek ˈæməˌlɛk |-ite ˈæmələˌkaɪt
amalgam əˈmælgəm
amalgamate adj əˈmælgəmɪt, -ˌmet
amalgamate v əˈmælgəˌmet |-d -ɪd
amalgamation əˌmælgəˈmeʃən
Amanda əˈmændə
amanita, A- ˌæməˈnaɪtə, -ˈnitə
amanuensis əˌmænjʊˈɛnsɪs |-sis' -sɪs |pl -nses
    -ˈɛnsiz
amaranth ˈæməˌrænθ |-ths -θs
amaranthine ˌæməˈrænθɪn
Amarillo ˌæməˈrɪlo
amaryllis, A- ˌæməˈrɪlɪs |-lises -lɪsɪz
Amasa ˈæməsə
amass əˈmæs |-es -ɪz |-ed -t
amateur n ˈæməˌtʃʊr, -ˌtɪur, -ˌtur, -tʃə,
    -tə, ˌæməˈtɝ; ES ˈæməˌtʃʊə(r, -ˌtɪuə(r,
    -ˌtuə(r, -tʃə(r, -tə(r, ˌæməˈtɝ(r, -ˈtɝ; (Fr
    amaˈtœːr)—see note below
amateur adj ˈæməˌtʃʊr, -ˌtɪur, -ˌtur, -tʃə,
    -tə; ES ˈæməˌtʃʊə(r, -ˌtɪuə(r, -ˌtuə(r,
    -tʃə(r, -tə(r; (Fr amaˈtœːr)—Other prons.
    were reported. The 1st, most freq., accords
    best with the habits of English. The 2d, 3d,
    4th, & 5th are normal variations of the 1st.
amateurish ˌæməˈtɝɪʃ, -ˈtjurɪʃ, -ˈtɪur-, -ˈtur-;
    ES+-ˈtɝɪʃ
amative ˈæmətɪv
amatory ˈæməˌtorɪ, -ˌtɔrɪ; S -ˌtorɪ
amaze əˈmez |-s -ɪz |-d -d |-dly -ɪdlɪ
Amaziah ˌæməˈzaɪə
Amazon, a- ˈæməˌzɑn, -zn̩; ES+-ˌzɒn
Amazonian, a- ˌæməˈzonɪən
ambage ˈæmbɪdʒ |-s -ɪz or as L ambages
    æmˈbedʒiz
ambassador æmˈbæsədə, əm-; ES -də(r
ambassadorial æmˌbæsəˈdorɪəl, əm-, -ˈdɔr-;
    S -ˈdor-
ambassadress æmˈbæsədrɪs, əm- |-es -ɪz
amber ˈæmbə; ES ˈæmbə(r; |-ed -d
ambergris ˈæmbəˌgris, -grɪs; ES ˈæmbə-
ambidexter ˌæmbəˈdɛkstə; ES -ˈdɛkstə(r;
    |-trous -trəs
ambidexterity ˌæmbədɛksˈtɛrətɪ

Key: See in full §§3–47. bee bi |pity ˈpɪtɪ (§6) |rate ret |yet jɛt |sang sæŋ |angry ˈæŋ·grɪ
|bath bæθ; E baθ (§10) |ah ɑ |far fɑr |watch wɑtʃ, wɒtʃ (§12) |jaw dʒɔ |gorge gɔrdʒ |go go

ambient **'æmbɪənt**

ambiguity **‚æmbɪ'gjuətɪ, -'gɪuətɪ**

ambiguous **æm'bɪgjuəs**

ambition **æm'bɪʃən** |-tious **-ʃəs**

ambivalence **æm'bɪvələns** |-cy **-ɪ** |-ent **-ənt**

amble **'æmbḷ** |-d **-d** |-ling **'æmblɪŋ, 'æmbḷɪŋ**

ambler, A- **'æmblɚ**; ES **'æmblə(r**

Ambleside **'æmbḷ‚saɪd**

Ambridge **'æmbrɪdʒ** |-'s **-ɪz**

Ambrose **'æmbroz** |-'s **-ɪz**

ambrosia **æm'broʒɪə, -ʒə** |-l **-l** |-lly **-lɪ** |-n **-n**

Ambrosian **æm'broʒɪən, -ʒən**

ambrotype **'æmbrə‚taɪp, -bro-**

ambry **'æmbrɪ**

ambsace **'emz‚es, 'æmz-** |-s **-ɪz**

ambulance **'æmbjələns** |-s **-ɪz** |-d **-t** |-nt **-nt**

ambulate **'æmbjə‚let** |-d **-ɪd**

ambulation **‚æmbjə'leʃən**

ambulatory **'æmbjələ‚torɪ, -‚tɔrɪ**; S **-‚torɪ**

ambuscade **‚æmbəs'ked** |-d **-ɪd**

ambush **'æmbʊʃ** |-es **-ɪz** |-ed **-t**

ameba **ə'mibə** |-s **-z** |-bae **-bi** |-n **-n**

amebean **‚æmɪ'biən**

amebic **ə'mibɪk** |ameboid **ə'mibɔɪd**

ameer **ə'mɪr**; ES **ə'mɪə(r**

Amelia **ə'miljə**

ameliorate **ə'miljə‚ret** |-d **-ɪd**

amelioration **ə‚miljə'reʃən**

amen **'e'mɛn**; *worship* **'e'mɛn, 'ɑ-**; *singing* **'ɑ'mɛn**

Amen *Egyp god* **'ɑmən**

amenable **ə'minəbḷ, ə'mɛn-** |-bly **-blɪ**

Amen Corner **'e‚mɛn'kɔrnɚ**; ES **-'kɔənə(r**

amend **ə'mɛnd** |-ed **-ɪd** |-s **ə'mɛndz, ə'mɛnz**

amenity **ə'mɛnətɪ**

ament *'catkin'* **'æmənt, 'emənt**

ament *'moron'* **'emənt**

amentia **e'mɛnʃɪə, ə'mɛnʃɪə**

amerce **ə'mɝs**; ES **ə'mɜs, ə'mɝs**; |-s **-ɪz** |-d **-t**

America **ə'mɛrəkə, ə'mɛrɪkə** |-n **-n** |-nism **-n‚ɪzəm**

Americana **ə‚mɛrə'kenə, -'kænə, -'kɑnə**

Americanize **ə'mɛrəkən‚aɪz** |-s **-ɪz** |-d **-d**

Americus **ə'mɛrɪkəs** |-'s **-ɪz**

Americus Vespucius **ə'mɛrɪkəs vɛs'pjuʃəs, -'pɪu-**

Amerigo Vespucci **ə'mɛrɪ‚go vɛs'putʃɪ** (*It* **‚ame'ri:go ves'puttʃi**)

Amerind **'æmə‚rɪnd** |-ian **‚æmə'rɪndɪən**

Amesbury **'emz‚bɛrɪ, -bərɪ**

amethyst **'æməθɪst**

Amfortas *Ger* **ɑm'fɔrtɑs**

Amherst **'æmɚst**; ES **'æməst**

amiability **‚emɪə'bɪlətɪ**

amiable **'emɪəbḷ** |-bly **-blɪ**

amic **'æmɪk**

amicability **‚æmɪkə'bɪlətɪ**

amicable **'æmɪkəbḷ** |-bly **-blɪ**

amice **'æmɪs** |-s **-ɪz**

amid *prep* **ə'mɪd**

amide *chem.* **'æmaɪd, 'æmɪd** |-mid **-mɪd**

amidine **'æmɪ‚din, -dɪn** |-din **-dɪn**

amido **ə'mido, 'æmɪ‚do**

amidships **ə'mɪdʃɪps**

amidst **ə'mɪdst**

Amiens *Shak.* **'æmɪənz**, *Dublin street* **'emjənz**, *Fr city* **'æmɪənz** |-'s **-ɪz** (*Fr* **a'mjæ**)

amine **ə'min** |amin **'æmɪn**

amino **ə'mino**

amir **ə'mɪr**; ES **ə'mɪə(r**

amiss **ə'mɪs**

Amite **ə'mit**

amitosis **‚æmə'tosɪs**

amity **'æmətɪ** |Amityville **'æmətɪ‚vɪl**

ammeter **'æm‚mitɚ, 'æ‚mitɚ**; ES **-‚mitə(r**

ammine **'æmin**

ammino **'æmɪ‚no**

Ammon **'æmən**

ammonia **ə'monjə, -nɪə** |-niac **ə'monɪ‚æk**

ammoniacal **‚æmə'naɪəkḷ**

ammoniate **ə'monɪ‚et** |-d **-ɪd**

ammonite **'æmə‚naɪt**

Ammonite **'æmən‚aɪt**

ammonium **ə'monɪəm**

ammunition **‚æmjə'nɪʃən**

amnesia **æm'niʒɪə, -ʒə**

amnesty **'æm‚nɛstɪ, 'æmnəstɪ**

amoeba **ə'mibə** |-s **-z** |-bae **-bi** |-n **-n**

amoebaean **‚æmɪ'biən**

amoebic **ə'mibɪk** |amoeboid **ə'mibɔɪd**

amok **ə'mʌk, ə'mɑk, ə'mɒk**

among **ə'mʌŋ** |-st **-st, -kst**

amoral **e'mɔrəl, e'mɑrəl, e'mɒrəl**

Amorite **'æmə‚raɪt**

amorous **'æmərəs**

amorphism **ə'mɔrfɪzəm**; ES **ə'mɔəf-**

amorphous **ə'mɔrfəs**; ES **ə'mɔəfəs**

amort **ə'mɔrt**; ES **ə'mɔət**

amortization ˌæmɚtəˈzeʃən, əˌmɔrt-, -aɪˈz-;
ES ˌæmə-, əˌmɔɔt-
amortize ˈæmɚˌtaɪz, əˈmɔrtaɪz; ES ˈæmə-,
əˈmɔɔ-; |-s -ɪz |-d -d
Amory ˈemɚɪ
Amos ˈeməs |-'s -ɪz
Amoskeag ˌæməsˈkɛg
amount əˈmaʊnt |-ed -ɪd
amour əˈmʊr, æ-; ES -ˈmʊə(r
amour-propre *Fr* amurˈprɔ̈pɽ
Amoy əˈmɔɪ
amperage æmˈpɪrɪdʒ, ˈæmˌpɪrɪdʒ |-s -ɪz
Ampère æmˈpɪr, ˈæmpɛr; ES -ˈpɪə(r, -pɛə(r;
(*Fr* ɑ̃ˈpɛːr)
ampere ˈæmpɪr, æmˈpɪr; ES -pɪə(r, -ˈpɪə(r
ampersand ˈæmpɚsˌænd, ˌæmpɚsˈænd; ES
-pəs-
amphetamine æmˈfɛtəˌmin, -mɪn
amphibian æmˈfɪbɪən |-bious -bɪəs
amphibrach ˈæmfɪˌbræk
amphictyon æmˈfɪktɪən |-y -ɪ
amphictyonic æmˌfɪktɪˈɑnɪk; ES+-ˈɒn-
Amphion æmˈfaɪən
amphitheater, -tre ˈæmfəˌθiətɚ, -ˌθɪə-; ES
-tə(r
amphora ˈæmfərə |-s -z |-rae -ˌri
ample ˈæmpḷ |-r -plɚ; ES -plə(r; |-st -plɪst
amplification ˌæmpləfəˈkeʃən
amplifier ˈæmpləˌfaɪɚ; ES -ˌfaɪ-ə(r
amplify ˈæmpləˌfaɪ |-fied -ˌfaɪd
amplitude ˈæmpləˌtjud, -ˌtɪud, -ˌtud
amply ˈæmplɪ
ampulla æmˈpʌlə, -ˈpʊlə |-s -z |-lae -li
amputate ˈæmpjəˌtet, ˈæmpjʊ- |-d -ɪd
amputation ˌæmpjəˈteʃən, -pjʊ-
Amritsar ʌmˈrɪtsɚ; ES -ˈrɪtsə(r
Amsterdam *US* ˈæmstɚˌdæm, *Neth*+ˌæmstɚ-
ˈdæm; ES -stɚ-; (*Du* ˌɑmstərˈdɑm)
Amstutz ˈæmstʌts |-es -ɪz (*Ger* ˈɑmʃtʊts)
amuck əˈmʌk
amulet ˈæmjəlɪt
Amundsen ˈɑmənsṇ, ˈɑmʊndsṇ
Amur ɑˈmʊr; ES ɑˈmʊə(r
amuse əˈmjuz, əˈmɪuz |-s -ɪz |-d -d |-dly
-ɪdlɪ
amusive əˈmjuzɪv, əˈmɪuzɪv
Amy ˈemɪ
amygdalin əˈmɪgdəlɪn |-line -lɪn, -ˌlaɪn
amyl ˈæmɪl |-ase -ɪˌles |-ene -ɪˌlin

amylolysis ˌæmɪˈlɑləsɪs; ES+-ˈlɒl-
amylose ˈæmɪˌlos |amylum ˈæmɪləm
Amyot ˈemɪət (*Fr* aˈmjo)
Amzi ˈæmzaɪ
an *unstressed* ən, ṇ; *rarely stressed* ˈæn, ˌæn
ana ˈenə, ˈɑnə
-ana -ˈenə, -ˈænə, -ˈɑnə
Anabaptist ˌænəˈbæptɪst
anabasis, A- əˈnæbəsɪs |-bases -bəˌsiz
anabolism əˈnæbḷˌɪzəm
anachronism əˈnækrəˌnɪzəm
anachronistic əˌnækrəˈnɪstɪk |-al -ḷ |-ally
-ḷɪ, -ɪklɪ
anachronous əˈnækrənəs
anaclinal ˌænəˈklaɪnḷ
anaclitic ˌænəˈklɪtɪk
anacoluthia ˌænəkəˈluθɪə, -ˈlɪuθ-
anacoluthic ˌænəkəˈluθɪk, -ˈlɪuθ- |-ally -ḷɪ,
-ɪklɪ
anacoluthon ˌænəkəˈluθɑn, -ˈlɪuθ-, -ɒn, -ən
anaconda, A- ˌænəˈkɑndə; ES+-ˈkɒn-
Anacortes ˌænəˈkɔrtɪz, -tɛz, -təs; ES -ˈkɔə-;
|-'s -ɪz
Anacostia ˌænəˈkɑstɪə, -ˈkɒs-, -ˈkɔs-
Anacreon əˈnækrɪən, -ˌɑn; ES+-ˌɒn
Anacreontic əˌnækrɪˈɑntɪk; ES+-ˈɒntɪk
anacrusis ˌænəˈkrusɪs, -ˈkrɪu- |-cruses -siz
Anadarko ˌænəˈdɑrko; ES -ˈdɑːko, E+
-ˈdɑːko
anadem ˈænəˌdɛm
anadromous əˈnædrəməs
anaemia əˈnimɪə |-mic -mɪk
anaerobe ænˈeəˌrob
anaerobic ænˌeəˈrobɪk, ˌænɛˈrobɪk
anaesthesia ˌænəsˈθiʒə, -ʒɪə
anaesthetic ˌænəsˈθɛtɪk |-ally -ḷɪ, -ɪklɪ
anaesthetist əˈnɛsθətɪst
anaesthetize əˈnɛsθəˌtaɪz |-s -ɪz |-d -d
anaglyph ˈænəˌglɪf
anagoge ˌænəˈgodʒɪ |-gogy ˈænəˌgodʒɪ
anagogic ˌænəˈgadʒɪk; ES+-ˈgɒdʒ-; |-al -ḷ
|-ally -ḷɪ, -ɪklɪ
anagram ˈænəˌgræm
anagrammatic ˌænəgrəˈmætɪk |-al -ḷ |-ally
-ḷɪ, -ɪklɪ
Anaheim ˈænəˌhaɪm
Anak ˈenæk |-s -s |-im ˈænəˌkɪm |-ims
ˈænəˌkɪmz
anal ˈenḷ |-ly -ɪ

Key: See in full §§3–47. bee bi |pity ˈpɪtɪ (§6) |rate ret |yet jɛt |sang sæŋ |angry ˈæŋ·grɪ
|bath bæθ; E baθ (§10) |ah ɑ |far fɑr |watch wɑtʃ, wɒtʃ (§12) |jaw dʒɔ |gorge gɔrdʒ |go go

analects 'ænəˌlɛkts |analecta ˌænəˈlɛktə
analgesia ˌænælˈdʒiziə, -sɪə |-sic -zɪk, -sɪk
analogic ˌæn|ˈɑdʒɪk; ES+-ˈɒdʒ-; |-al -|
  |-ally -|ɪ, -ɪklɪ
analogist əˈnælədʒɪst
analogize əˈnæləˌdʒaɪz |-s -ɪz |-d -d
analogous əˈnæləgəs
analogue 'æn|ˌɔg, -ˌɑg, -ˌɒg
analogy əˈnælədʒɪ
analphabetic ˌænælfəˈbɛtɪk |-al -| |-ally -|ɪ,
  -ɪklɪ
analysable 'æn|ˌaɪzəb|
analyse 'æn|ˌaɪz |-s -ɪz |-d -d
analysis əˈnæləsɪs |-yses -əˌsiz
analyst 'æn|ɪst
analytic ˌæn|ˈɪtɪk |-al -| |-ally -|ɪ, -ɪklɪ
analytics ˌæn|ˈɪtɪks
analyzable 'æn|ˌaɪzəb|
analyze 'æn|ˌaɪz |-s -ɪz |-d -d
Anam əˈnæm
Ananias ˌænəˈnaɪəs |-'s -ɪz
anapaest, -pest 'ænəˌpɛst
anapaestic, -pes- ˌænəˈpɛstɪk |-al -| |-ally -|ɪ,
  -ɪklɪ
anaphora əˈnæfərə |-l -l
anaphoric ˌænəˈfɔrɪk, -ˈfɑr-, -ˈfɒr- |-al -|
anaphylaxis ˌænəfəˈlæksɪs
anaplasty 'ænəˌplæstɪ |-tic ˌænəˈplæstɪk
anarch 'ænɑrk; ES 'ænɑːk, E+-ɑːk
anarchic ænˈɑrkɪk; ES -ˈɑːk-, E+-ˈɑːk-; |-al
  -| |-ally -|ɪ, -ɪklɪ
anarchism 'ænɚˌkɪzəm; ES 'ænə-
anarchist 'ænɚkɪst; ES 'ænəkɪst; |-chy -kɪ
anarchistic ˌænɚˈkɪstɪk; ES ˌænə-
anastigmatic ˌænəstɪgˈmætɪk, ˌænæstɪg-,
  ænˌæs-
anastomosis ˌænəstəˈmosɪs, əˌnæstə- |-moses
  -ˈmosiz
anastrophe əˈnæstrəfɪ
anathema əˈnæθəmə
anathematize əˈnæθəməˌtaɪz |-s -ɪz |-d -d
Anatolia ˌænəˈtolɪə |-n -n
anatomic ˌænəˈtɑmɪk; ES+-ˈtɒm-; |-al -|
  |-ally -|ɪ, -ɪklɪ
anatomist əˈnætəmɪst |-my -mɪ
anatomize əˈnætəˌmaɪz |-s -ɪz |-d -d
Anaxagoras ˌænæksˈægərəs |-'s -ɪz
ancestor 'ænsɛstɚ; ES -sɛstə(r
ancestral ænˈsɛstrəl |-ly -ɪ |-try 'ænsɛstrɪ

ancestress 'ænsɛstrɪs |-es -ɪz
Anchises ænˈkaɪsiz, æŋ- |-ses' -siz
anchor 'æŋkɚ; ES 'æŋkə(r; |-ed -d |-ing
  'æŋkərɪŋ, 'æŋkrɪŋ
anchorage 'æŋkərɪdʒ, -krɪdʒ |-s -ɪz
anchoress 'æŋkərɪs, -krɪs |-es -ɪz
anchoret 'æŋkərɪt, -ɛt
anchorite 'æŋkəˌraɪt
anchovy 'ænˌtʃovɪ, 'æntʃəvɪ, ænˈtʃovɪ
anchusa ænˈtʃuzə, -ˈtʃɪuzə (L æŋˈkjuzə,
  -ˈkɪu-)
ancien régime Fr ɑ̃sjæ̃·reˈʒim
ancient 'enʃənt
ancillary 'ænsəˌlɛrɪ, Brit ænˈsɪlərɪ
ancress 'æŋkrɪs |-es -ɪz=anchoress
and usually unstressed: before vowels ənd, ɛnd,
  n̩d ('sno ənd 'aɪs, 'hɛd n̩d 'ɑrm); before
  consonants and often before vowels ən ('mæn
  ən 'bɪst), ɛn, n̩ ('rɑd n̩ 'gʌn, 'fɛs n̩ 'aɪz),
  n ('bʌtɚ n 'ɛgz); after p or b often m̩ ('kʌp m̩
  'sosɚ, 'rʌb m̩ 'palɪʃ); after k or g often ŋ
  ('dʒæk ŋ 'dʒɪl, 'bæg ŋ 'bægɪdʒ); stressed
  or in pause: before vowels 'ænd, ˌænd, or
  before consonants 'æn, ˌæn. The forms with
  -d occur in ordinary speech before vowels
  ('fri ənd 'izɪ) or l, r, w, hw, j ('ɝl ənd 'lɛt),
  but those without -d are also common there
  ('stɑp ən 'ɪt), and are regular before other
  consonants ('go ən 'si, 'traɪ ən 'dʊ ɪt).
Andalusia ˌændəˈluʒə, -ˈlɪu-, -ʃə |-n -n
Andaman 'ændəmən
andante ænˈdæntɪ, ɑnˈdɑntɪ (It ɑnˈdɑnte)
Andean ænˈdiən, 'ændɪən
Andersen 'ændɚsn̩; ES 'ændəsn̩; |-son -sn̩
Andes 'ændiz |-des' -diz
andiron 'ændˌaɪɚn, -ˌaɪrn; ES -ˌaɪ·ən, -ˌaɪən
Andorra ænˈdɔrə, -ˈdɑrə, -ˈdɒrə
Andover 'ændovɚ; ES -dovə(r; Mass loc.+
  'ændəvə(r
Andrade ænˈdrɑdɪ
André 'ændrɪ, 'ɑndre
Andrea del Sarto 'ɑndrɪədɛlˈsɑrto; ES
  -ˈsɑːto; (It ɑnˈdrɛːadelˈsɑrto)
Andreas 'ændrɪəs |-'s -ɪz
Andrew 'ændru, 'ændrɪu |-s -z |-s's -zɪz
Androcles 'ændrəˌkliz |-'s -ɪz
Androclus 'ændrəkləs |-'s -ɪz
androgen 'ændrədʒən, -dʒɪn |-ic ˌændrə-
  'dʒɛnɪk

|full fʊl |tooth tuθ |further 'fɝðɚ; ES 'fɝðə |custom 'kʌstəm |while hwaɪl |how haʊ |toy tɔɪ
|using 'juzɪŋ |fuse fjuz, fɪuz |dish dɪʃ |vision 'vɪʒən |Eden 'idn̩ |cradle 'kredl̩ |keep 'em 'kipm̩

androgynous æn'drædʒənəs; ES+-'drɒdʒ-
Andromache æn'dramǝki; ES+-'drɒm-
Andromeda æn'dramɪdǝ; ES+-'drɒm-
Andronicus ˌændrǝ'naɪkǝs, *Shak.* æn'dranɪ-
  kǝs; ES+-'drɒn-; |-'s -ɪz
Andros 'ændrɑs, -drǝs; ES+-drɒs; |-'s -ɪz
Androscoggin ˌændrǝ'skɑgɪn, -'skɒg-
anear ǝ'nɪr; ES ǝ'nɪǝ(r, S+ǝ'njɛǝ(r, ǝ'njɪǝ(r,
  ǝ'nɛǝ(r
anecdotal ˌænɪk'dotḷ ('anecˌdotal 'speech)
anecdote 'ænɪkˌdot |-d -ɪd |-tage -ɪdʒ
anecdotic ˌænɪk'datɪk; ES+-'dɒt-; |-al -ḷ
  |-ally -ḷɪ, -ɪklɪ
anele ǝ'nil |-d -d
anelectric ˌænɪ'lɛktrɪk
anemia ǝ'nimɪǝ |-mic -mɪk
anemometer ˌænǝ'mamǝtǝ; ES -'mamǝtǝ(r,
  -'mɒm-
anemometric ˌænǝmǝ'mɛtrɪk |-al -ḷ |-ally -ḷɪ,
  -ɪklɪ
anemone, A- ǝ'nɛmǝˌni
anent ǝ'nɛnt
aneroid 'ænǝˌrɔɪd
anesthesia ˌænǝs'θiʒǝ, -ʒɪǝ
anesthetic ˌænǝs'θɛtɪk |-ally -ḷɪ, -ɪklɪ
anesthetist ǝ'nɛsθǝtɪst
anesthetize ǝ'nɛsθǝˌtaɪz |-s -ɪz |-d -d
aneurysm, -rism 'ænjǝˌrɪzǝm
anew ǝ'nju, ǝ'nɪu, ǝ'nu
anfractuous æn'fræktʃʊǝs
angary 'æŋgǝrɪ
angel, A- 'endʒǝl
Angela 'ændʒǝlǝ
angelic æn'dʒɛlɪk |-al -ḷ |-ally -ḷɪ, -ɪklɪ
Angelica æn'dʒɛlɪkǝ
Angelina ˌændʒǝ'linɛ, -'laɪnǝ
Angell 'endʒǝl
Angelo 'ændʒǝˌlo
Angelus 'ændʒǝlǝs |-es -ɪz
anger 'æŋgǝ; ES 'æŋgǝ(r; |-ed -d |-ing
  'æŋgǝrɪŋ, 'æŋgrɪŋ
angerly 'æŋgǝlɪ; ES 'æŋgǝlɪ
Angers 'ændʒǝz, 'æŋgǝz; ES -ǝz; |-'s -ɪz
  (*Fr* ã'ʒe)
Angevin 'ændʒǝvɪn
Angiers *Shak.* 'ændʒɪrz; ES 'ændʒɪǝz; |-'s
  -ɪz
angina æn'dʒaɪnǝ, *in medicine often* 'ændʒɪnǝ
angina pectoris æn'dʒaɪnǝ'pɛktǝrɪs

angiosperm 'ændʒɪoˌspɝm; ES -ˌspɝm,
  -ˌspɝm
angle 'æŋgḷ |-d -d |-ling 'æŋglɪŋ, 'æŋgḷɪŋ
angler 'æŋglǝ; ES 'æŋglǝ(r
Angles 'æŋgḷz
Anglesey, -sea 'æŋgḷsɪ
angleworm 'æŋgḷˌwɝm; ES -ˌwɝm, -ˌwɝm
Anglia 'æŋglɪǝ
Anglican 'æŋglɪkǝn
Anglicism 'æŋglǝˌsɪzǝm |-cist -sɪst
Anglicize 'æŋglǝˌsaɪz |-s -ɪz |-d -d
Anglify 'æŋglǝˌfaɪ |-fied -ˌfaɪd
Anglin 'æŋglɪn
Anglist 'æŋglɪst |-ics æŋ'glɪstɪks
Anglo-American 'æŋgloǝ'mɛrǝkǝn
Anglo-Catholic 'æŋglo'kæθǝlɪk, -'kæθlɪk
Anglo-Catholicism 'æŋglokǝ'θalǝˌsɪzǝm; ES
  + -'θɒl-
Anglo-Egyptian 'æŋglo·ɪ'dʒɪpʃǝn
Anglo-French 'æŋglo'frɛntʃ
Anglo-Indian 'æŋglo'ɪndɪǝn, -djǝn
Anglo-Irish 'æŋglo'aɪrɪʃ
Anglo-Japanese 'æŋgloˌdʒæpǝ'niz
Anglomania ˌæŋglǝ'menɪǝ, -glo- |-niac -nɪˌæk
Anglo-Norman 'æŋglo'nɔrmǝn; ES -'nɔǝmǝn
Anglophile 'æŋglǝˌfaɪl, -glo-
Anglophobe 'æŋglǝˌfob, -glo-
Anglophobia ˌæŋglǝ'fobɪǝ, -glo-
Anglo-Saxon 'æŋglo'sæksṇ |-dom -dǝm |-ism
  -ˌɪzǝm
Angola æŋ'golǝ, æn-
Angora æŋ'gorǝ, æn-, -'gɔrǝ, 'æŋgǝrǝ; S
  -'gorǝ, -gǝrǝ
angostura ˌæŋgǝs'tjurǝ, -'tɪurǝ, -'turǝ
angry 'æŋgrɪ |-grily -grǝlɪ, -grɪlɪ
angstrom 'æŋstrǝm
anguish 'æŋgwɪʃ |-es -ɪz |-ed -t
angular 'æŋgjǝlǝ; ES 'æŋgjǝlǝ(r
angularity ˌæŋgjǝ'lærǝtɪ
angulate *adj* 'æŋgjǝlɪt, -ˌlet
angulate *v* 'æŋgjǝˌlet |-d -ɪd
Angus 'æŋgǝs |-'s -ɪz
angustura ˌæŋgǝs'tjurǝ, -'tɪurǝ, -'turǝ
anhungered ǝn'hʌŋgǝd; ES -'hʌŋgǝd
anhydride æn'haɪdraɪd, -drɪd |-drid -drɪd
anhydrous æn'haɪdrǝs
anil 'ænɪl
anile 'ænaɪl, 'enaɪl
aniline 'ænḷˌin, -ɪn |-in -ɪn

Key: See in full §§3–47. bee bi |pity 'pɪtɪ (§6) |rate ret |yet jɛt |sang sæŋ |angry 'æŋ·grɪ
|bath bæθ; E baθ (§10) |ah ɑ |far fɑr |watch watʃ, wɒtʃ (§12) |jaw dʒɔ |gorge gɔrdʒ |go go

anility ə'nɪlətɪ

animadversion ˌænəmæd'vɝʒən, -'vɝʃ-; ES -'vɝ-, -'vɝ-

animadvert ˌænəmæd'vɝt; ES -'vɝt, -'vɝt; |-ed -ɪd

animal 'ænəmḷ |-ly -ɪ

animalcula pl ˌænə'mælkjələ

animalculae pl ˌænə'mælkjəˌli

animalcule ˌænə'mælkjʊl, -kɪʊl

animalculism ˌænə'mælkjəˌlɪzəm

animalculum ˌænə'mælkjələm |-la -lə |-lae -ˌli

animalism 'ænəmḷˌɪzəm

animality ˌænə'mælətɪ

animate adj 'ænəmɪt

animate v 'ænəˌmet |-d -ɪd |-tion ˌænə'meʃən

animism 'ænəˌmɪzəm |animistic ˌænə'mɪstɪk

animosity ˌænə'masətɪ; ES+-'mɒs-

animus 'ænəməs

anion 'ænˌaɪən

anise 'ænɪs

aniseed, anisseed 'ænɪˌsid, 'ænɪsˌsid

anisometric ˌænaɪsə'mɛtrɪk, ænˌaɪsə-

anisotropic ˌænaɪsə'trɑpɪk, ænˌaɪsə-; ES+ -'trɒp-; |-al -ḷ |-ally -ḷɪ, -ɪklɪ

Anita ə'nitə

Anjou 'ændʒu (Fr ã'ʒu)

Ankara 'æŋkərə, 'ɑŋkərə

ankh æŋk

ankle 'æŋkḷ |ankled 'æŋkḷd

anklebone 'æŋkḷˌbon, -'bon

anklet 'æŋklɪt

ankus 'æŋkəs, 'ʌŋkəʃ |-es -ɪz

ankylose 'æŋkəˌlos |-s -ɪz |-d -t

ankylosis ˌæŋkə'losɪs

anlace 'ænlɪs, -ləs |-s -ɪz

Ann æn

anna, A- 'ænə

Annabel, -lle 'ænəˌbɛl

Annabella ˌænə'bɛlə

annals 'ænḷz |annalist 'ænḷɪst

Annam ə'næm

Annamese ˌænə'miz

Annapolis ə'næpḷɪs, -plɪs, -əs |-'s -ɪz

Ann Arbor æn'ɑrbɚ; ES -'ɑ:bə(r, E+ -'ɑ:bə(r

annates 'ænɪts, 'ænets |annat 'ænæt

Anne æn

anneal ə'nil |-ed -d

Anne Arundel 'æn·ə'rʌndḷ

annelid 'ænḷɪd

annex n 'ænɛks |-es -ɪz |-ation ˌænɛks'eʃən

annex v ə'nɛks |-es -ɪz |-ed -t

Annie 'ænɪ

annihilate ə'naɪəˌlet |-d -ɪd |-lable -ləbḷ

annihilation əˌnaɪə'leʃən

anniversary ˌænə'vɝsərɪ, -srɪ; ES -'vɝs-, -'vɝs-

anno Domini 'æno'dɑməˌnaɪ; ES+-'dɒm-

annotate 'ænoˌtet |-d -ɪd |-tion ˌæno'teʃən

annotator 'ænoˌtetɚ; ES -ˌtetə(r

announce ə'naʊns |-s -ɪz |-d -t

annoy ə'nɔɪ |-ed -d |-ance -əns |-ances -ənsɪz

annual 'ænjʊəl, 'ænjʊl |-ly -ɪ

annuitant ə'nuətənt, ə'nɪu-, ə'nju- |-ity -ətɪ

annul ə'nʌl |-led -d

annular 'ænjələ; ES -lə(r

annulet 'ænjəlɪt

annulus 'ænjələs |-es -ɪz |-li -ˌlaɪ

annum 'ænəm

annunciate ə'nʌnʃɪˌet, -sɪ- |-d -ɪd

annunciation, A- əˌnʌnsɪ'eʃən, -ʃɪ-

annunciator ə'nʌnʃɪˌetɚ, -sɪ-; ES -ˌetə(r

Annunzio, d' də'nunzɪˌo (It dɑn'nuntsjo)

anociassociation əˌnosɪəˌsosɪ'eʃən, -ˌsoʃɪ-

anociation əˌnosɪ'eʃən, əˌnoʃɪ-

anode 'ænod |-dic æn'ɑdɪk; ES+-'rdɪk

anodize 'ænoˌdaɪz |-s -ɪz |-d -d

anodyne 'ænəˌdaɪn, 'æno-

anoint ə'nɔɪnt |-ed -ɪd

Anoka ə'nokə

anolyte 'ænəˌlaɪt

anomalism ə'naɪ mḷˌɪzəm; ES+-'nɒm-

anomalistic əˌnaməl'ɪstɪk; ES+-ˌnɒm-; |-al -ḷ |-ally -ḷɪ, -ɪklɪ

anomaly ə'naməlɪ; ES+-'nɒm-; |-lous -ləs

anon ə'nan, ə'nɒn

anonym, -e 'ænəˌnɪm |-nymity ˌænə'nɪmətɪ

anonymous ə'nanəməs; ES+ə'nɒn-

anopheles, A- ə'nafəˌliz; ES+-'nɒf-

another ə'nʌðɚ; ES ə'nʌðə(r

Anschluss Ger 'anʃlus

Anselm 'ænsɛlm

anserine 'gooselike' 'ænsəˌraɪn, -rɪn

anserine chem. 'ænsəˌrin, -rɪn

Anson 'ænsṇ

Ansonia æn'sonɪə

|full fʊl |tooth tuθ |further 'fɝðɚ; ES 'fɝðə |custom 'kʌstəm |while hwaɪl |how haʊ |toy tɔɪ |using 'juzɪŋ |fuse fjuz, fɪuz |dish dɪʃ |vision 'vɪʒən |Eden 'idṇ |cradle 'kredḷ |keep 'em 'kipm̩

Anstruther 'ænstrʌðɚ; ES -ðə(r
answer 'ænsɚ; ES 'ænsə(r, E+'an-, 'ɑn-;
|-ed -d |-ing -sərɪŋ, -srɪŋ
answerable 'ænsərəb|, -srə- |-bly -blɪ; E see
answer
ant ænt
antacid ænt'æsɪd
Antaeus æn'tiəs |-'s -ɪz
antagonism æn'tægə,nɪzəm |-nist -nɪst
antagonistic æn,tægə'nɪstɪk, ,æntægə- |-al -|
|-ally -|ɪ, -ɪklɪ
antagonize æn'tægə,naɪz |-s -ɪz |-d -d
antalkali ænt'ælkə,laɪ
antarctic ænt'ɑrktɪk, now rare -'ɑrtɪk; ES
-'ɑ:-, E+-'ɑ:-; ('ant,arctic 'circle)
Antarctica ænt'ɑrktɪkə; ES -'ɑ:k-, E+-'ɑ:k-
Antares æn'tɛriz, -'tær-; S -'tær-; |-es' -iz
ante 'æntɪ
anteater 'ænt,itɚ; ES -,itə(r
ante bellum 'æntɪ'bɛləm
antecede ,æntə'sid |-d -ɪd
antecedence ,æntə'sidn̩s |-cy -ɪ |-dent -dn̩t
antecessor ,æntə'sɛsɚ; ES -'sɛsə(r
antechamber 'æntɪ,tʃembɚ; ES -,tʃembə(r
antedate 'æntɪ,det, ,æntɪ'det |-d -ɪd
antediluvian ,æntɪdɪ'luvɪən, -'lɪuv-
antelope 'ænt|,op
ante meridiem 'æntɪmə'rɪdɪ,ɛm, -'rɪdɪəm
antenna æn'tɛnə |-s -z |-nae -ni
Antenor æn'tinɚ, -nɔr; ES -nə(r, -nɔə(r
antepenult ,æntɪ'pinʌlt, -pɪ'nʌlt
antepenultimate ,æntɪpɪ'nʌltəmɪt
anterior æn'tɪrɪɚ; ES -'tɪrɪ·ə(r
anteriority ,æntɪrɪ'ɔrətɪ, -'ɑr-, -'ɒr-
anteroom 'æntɪ,rum, -,rʊm
anthelion ænt'hilɪən, æn'θilɪən |-s -z |-lia
-lɪə—The 2d is not a spelling pron. Gk
has θ.
anthelmintic ,ænθɛl'mɪntɪk
anthem 'ænθəm—a sp. pron. (OE antefn, ME
antem, 16c anthem with Latinized sp.
of t)
anther 'ænθɚ; ES 'ænθə(r
anthill 'ænt,hɪl
anthologize æn'θɑlə,dʒaɪz; ES+-'θɒl-; |-s
-ɪz |-d -d
anthology æn'θɑlədʒɪ; ES+-'θɒl-
Anthony 'æntənɪ, 'æntn̩ɪ, 'æntn̩ɪ
anthozoan ,ænθə'zoən

anthracene 'ænθrə,sin
anthracite 'ænθrə,saɪt
anthracnose æn'θræknos
anthrax 'ænθræks |-es -ɪz
anthropocentric ,ænθrəpo'sɛntrɪk
anthropogenesis ,ænθrəpo'dʒɛnəsɪs
anthropogenetic ,ænθrə,podʒə'nɛtɪk
anthropography ,ænθrə'pɑgrəfɪ, -'pɒg-
anthropoid 'ænθrə,pɔɪd
anthropological ,ænθrəpə'lɑdʒɪk|; ES+
-'lɒdʒ-; |-ly -ɪ, -ɪklɪ
anthropology ,ænθrə'pɑlədʒɪ; ES+-'pɒl-;
|-gist -dʒɪst
anthropometric ,ænθrəpo'mɛtrɪk |-al -| |-ally
-|ɪ, -ɪklɪ
anthropometry ,ænθrə'pamətrɪ; ES+-'pɒm-
anthropomorphic ,ænθrəpo'mɔrfɪk; ES
-'mɔəf-; |-al -| |-ally -|ɪ, -ɪklɪ |-phism
-fɪzəm
anthropomorphosis ,ænθrəpo'mɔrfəsɪs; ES
-'mɔəf-
anthropomorphous ,ænθrəpo'mɔrfəs; ES
-'mɔəfəs
anthroponomy ,ænθrə'panəmɪ; ES+-'pɒn-
anthropophagi ,ænθrə'pafə,dʒaɪ; ES+-'pɒf-;
|-gite -,dʒaɪt |-gous -gəs
anti n 'æntaɪ, 'æntɪ |-s -z
antiadministration ,æntɪəd,mɪnə'streʃən
antiaircraft ,æntɪ'ɛr,kræft, -'ær-; E -'ɛə-,
-'æə-, -,kraft, -,krɑft; S -'æə,kræft
antibiosis ,æntɪbaɪ'osɪs |-otic -'atɪk; ES+
-'ɒtɪk
antibody 'æntɪ,badɪ; ES+-,bɒdɪ
antic 'æntɪk |-ked -t
anticatalyst ,æntɪ'kæt|ɪst
anticathode ,æntɪ'kæθod
antichlor 'æntɪ,klor, -,klɔr; ES -,kloə(r, E+
-,klɔə(r
antichrist 'æntɪ,kraɪst
anticipant æn'tɪsəpənt
anticipate æn'tɪsə,pet |-d -ɪd |-tive -ɪv
anticipation æn,tɪsə'peʃən, ,æntɪsə-
anticipatory æn'tɪsəpə,torɪ, -,tɔrɪ; S -,torɪ
anticlastic ,æntɪ'klæstɪk
anticlerical ,æntɪ'klɛrɪk|
anticlimax ,æntɪ'klaɪmæks |-es -ɪz |-ed -t
anticline 'æntɪ,klaɪn |-clinal ,æntɪ'klaɪn|
Anticosti ,æntə'kɑstɪ, -'kas-, -'kɒs-
anticyclone ,æntɪ'saɪklon

Key: See in full §§3–47. bee bi |pity 'pɪtɪ (§6) |rate ret |yet jɛt |sang sæŋ |angry 'æŋ·grɪ
|bath bæθ; E baθ (§10) |ah ɑ |far fɑr |watch wɑtʃ, wɒtʃ (§12) |jaw dʒɔ |gorge gɔrdʒ |go go

anticyclonic ˌæntɪsaɪˈklɑnɪk; ES+-ˈklɒn-;
|-ally -ḷɪ, -ɪklɪ
antidotal ˈæntɪˌdotḷ, ˌæntɪˈdotḷ |-ly -ˈdotḷɪ
antidote ˈæntɪˌdot |-d -ɪd
Antietam ænˈtitəm
antifat ˌæntɪˈfæt (ˈantiˌfat ˈtreatment)
Antifederalist ˌæntɪˈfedərəlɪst, -ˈfɛdrəl-
antifreeze ˌæntɪˈfriz |-s -ɪz
antigen ˈæntədʒən -dʒɪn
Antigone ænˈtɪgəˌni
Antigonus ænˈtɪgənəs |-ˈs -ɪz
Antigua ænˈtigə, ænˈtigwə
anti-imperialism ˌæntɪˌɪmˈpɪrɪəlˌɪzəm |-ist- ɪst
anti-imperialistic ˌæntɪˌɪmˌpɪrɪəlˈɪstɪk
antiknock ˌæntɪˈnak; ES+-ˈnɒk
antilabor ˌæntɪˈlebɚ; ES -ˈlebə(r
Antilles ænˈtɪliz
antilogarithm ˌæntɪˈlɔgəˌrɪðəm, -ˈlɑg-, -ˈlɒg-
antilynching ˌæntɪˈlɪntʃɪŋ
antimacassar ˌæntɪməˈkæsɚ; ES -ˈkæsə(r
antimask, -sque ˈæntɪˌmæsk; E+-ˌmask,
-ˌmɑsk
antimonsoon ˌæntɪmɑnˈsun; ES+-mɒn-
antimony ˈæntəˌmonɪ
antimonyl ˈæntɪməˌnɪl
antinomian, A- ˌæntɪˈnomɪən
antinomy ænˈtɪnəmɪ
Antioch ˈæntɪˌak; ES+-ˌɒk
Antiochus ænˈtaɪəkəs |-ˈs -ɪz
antipathetic ænˌtɪpəˈθɛtɪk ˌæntɪpə- |-al -ḷ
|-ally -ḷɪ, -ɪklɪ
antipathy ænˈtɪpəθɪ
antiperiodic ˌæntɪˌpɪrɪˈɑdɪk; ES+-ˈɒd-
antiphlogistic ˌæntɪfloˈdʒɪstɪk
Antipholus ænˈtɪfələs |-ˈs -ɪz
antiphon ˈæntəˌfan, -fən; ES+-ˌfɒn
antiphonal ænˈtɪfənḷ |-ly -ɪ |-phony -fənɪ
antiphonary ænˈtɪfəˌnɛrɪ
antipodal ænˈtɪpədḷ
antipode ˈæntɪˌpod |pl antipodes ænˈtɪpəˌdiz
antipodean ænˌtɪpəˈdiən, ˌæntɪpə-
antipope ˈæntɪˌpop
antiputrid ˌæntɪˈpjutrɪd, -ˈpɪu-
antiquarian ˌæntɪˈkwɛrɪən, -ˈkwer-
antiquary ˈæntɪˌkwɛrɪ
antiquate ˈæntəˌkwet |-d -ɪd
antique ænˈtik (ˈanˌtique ˈtable)
antiquity ænˈtɪkwətɪ
antirrhinum, A- ˌæntɪˈraɪnəm

antirust ˌæntɪˈrʌst
antisaloon ˌæntɪsəˈlun
antiscorbutic ˌæntɪskɔrˈbjutɪk, -ˈbɪu-; ES
-skɔə-
anti-Semitic ˌæntɪsəˈmɪtɪk |-ally -ḷɪ, -ɪklɪ
anti-Semitism ˌæntɪˈsɛməˌtɪzəm
antisepsis ˌæntəˈsɛpsɪs
antiseptic ˌæntəˈsɛptɪk |-ally -ḷɪ, -ɪklɪ
antisepticize ˌæntəˈsɛptəˌsaɪz |-s -ɪz |-d -d
antiserum ˌæntɪˈsɪrəm
antislavery ˌæntəˈslevrɪ, -ˈslevərɪ
antisocial ˌæntɪˈsoʃəl
antistrophe ænˈtɪstrəfɪ, -ˌfi
antistrophic ˌæntɪˈstrafɪk, -ˈstrof-; ES+
-ˈstrɒf-; |-ally -ḷɪ, -ɪklɪ
antitank ˌæntɪˈtæŋk (ˈantiˌtank ˈgun)
antithesis ænˈtɪθəsɪs |-theses -θəˌsiz
antithetic ˌæntɪˈθɛtɪk |-al -ḷ |-ally -ḷɪ, -ɪklɪ
antitoxic ˌæntɪˈtaksɪk; ES+-ˈtɒk-; |-xin
-ksɪn
antitrades ˈæntɪˌtredz
antitrust ˌæntɪˈtrʌst
antitype ˈæntəˌtaɪp
antitypic ˌæntɪˈtɪpɪk |-al -ḷ |-ally -ḷɪ, -ɪklɪ
Antium ˈæntɪəm, -ʃɪəm
antivivisection ˌæntɪˌvɪvəˈsɛkʃən |-ist -ɪst
antiwar ˌæntɪˈwɔr; ES -ˈwɔə(r
antler ˈæntlɚ; ES ˈæntlə(r; |-ed -d
Antoinette ˌæntwaˈnet (Fr ɑ̃twaˈnɛt)
Antonia ænˈtonɪə
Antoninus ˌæntəˈnaɪnəs |-ˈs -ɪz
Antonio ænˈtonɪˌo, -njo
Antonius ænˈtonɪəs |-ˈs -ɪz
antonomasia ˌæntənoˈmeʒə, -ʒɪə
Antony ˈæntənɪ, ˈæntnɪ
antonym ˈæntəˌnɪm
antonymous ænˈtanəməs; ES+-ˈtɒn-
antre ˈæntɚ; ES ˈæntə(r
Antrim ˈæntrɪm
antrum ˈæntrəm
Antwerp ˈæntwɝp; ES -wɜp, -wɝp
anus ˈenəs |-es -ɪz |-ni -naɪ
anvil ˈænvɪl |-ed -d
anxiety æŋˈzaɪətɪ, æŋˈz-
anxious ˈæŋkʃəs, ˈæŋʃəs
any ˈɛnɪ, unstressed occas. ənɪ, nɪ (ˈgatnɪ
ˈbet?)
anybody ˈɛnɪˌbadɪ, -ˌbʌdɪ, -bədɪ; ES+
-ˌbɒdɪ

|full fʊl |tooth tuθ |further ˈfɝðɚ; ES ˈfɝðə |custom ˈkʌstəm |while hwaɪl |how haʊ |toy tɔɪ
|using ˈjuzɪŋ |fuse fjuz, fɪuz |dish dɪʃ |vision ˈvɪʒən |Eden ˈidn̩ |cradle ˈkredḷ |keep 'em ˈkipm̩

Those words below in which the ɑ sound is spelt o are often pronounced with ɒ in E and S

anyhow 'ɛnɪˌhaʊ

anyone 'ɛnɪˌwʌn, -wən (ˌɛnɪwən'ɛls)

anything 'ɛnɪˌθɪŋ

anyway 'ɛnɪˌwe |-s -z

anywhere 'ɛnɪˌhwɛr, -ˌhwæːr; E -ˌhwɛə(r, ES -ˌhwæːə(r

anywhere else 'ɛnɪˌhwɛr'ɛls, -ˌhwæːr-, -hwəˈ'ɛls

anywise 'ɛnɪˌwaɪz

Anzac 'ænzæk

A one, A 1 'e'wʌn

Aonian e'onɪən

aorist 'eərɪst

aoristic ˌeə'rɪstɪk |-ally -ḷɪ, -ɪklɪ

aorta e'ɔrtə; ES e'ɔətə

apace ə'pes

apache *'gangster'* ə'paʃ, ə'pæʃ |-s -ɪz (*Fr* a'paʃ)

Apache *Indian* ə'pætʃɪ

Apalachee, -chi ˌæpə'lætʃɪ, -tʃɪ

Apalachicola ˌæpəˌlætʃɪ'kolə

apanage 'æpənɪdʒ |-s -ɪz |-d -d

apart ə'pɑrt; ES ə'pɑ:t, E+ə'pɑ:t

apartment ə'pɑrtmənt; ES ə'pɑ:t-, E+ə'pɑ:t-

apartmental əpɑrt'mɛntḷ; ES əpɑ:t-, E+ əpɑ:t-

apathetic ˌæpə'θɛtɪk |-al -ḷ |-ally -ḷɪ, -ɪklɪ

apathy 'æpəθɪ

ape ep |aped ept

apeak ə'pik

Apemantus ˌæpɪ'mæntəs |-'s -ɪz

Apennines 'æpəˌnaɪnz

aperient ə'pɪrɪənt

aperiodic ˌepɪrɪ'ɑdɪk; ES+-'ɒd-; |-ally -ḷɪ, -ɪklɪ

aperitif *Fr* aperi'tif

aperitive ə'pɛrətɪv

aperture 'æpətʃɚ; ES 'æpətʃə(r; |-d -d

apery 'epərɪ

apetalous e'pɛtḷəs

apex 'epɛks |-es -ɪz |apices 'æpɪˌsiz, 'e- |-ed -t

aphaeresis ə'fɛrəsɪs, æ-

aphasia ə'feʒə, -ʒɪə

aphelion æ'filɪən, ə- |-s -z |-lia -lɪə

apheresis ə'fɛrəsɪs, æ-

aphesis 'æfəsɪs

aphid 'efɪd, 'æfɪd

aphis, A- 'efɪs, 'æfɪs |-es -ɪz |aphides 'æfɪˌdiz

aphorism 'æfəˌrɪzəm |-ist -rɪst

aphoristic ˌæfə'rɪstɪk |-al -ḷ |-ally -ḷɪ, -ɪklɪ

aphorize 'æfəˌraɪz |-s -ɪz |-d -d

aphrodisiac ˌæfrə'dɪzɪˌæk

Aphrodite ˌæfrə'daɪtɪ

A P I 'e͵pi'aɪ, asɔsjaˈsjŏ fŏne'tik æːtɛrnasjŏ-'nal, *cf* I P A

apian 'epɪən

apiarian ˌepɪ'ɛrɪən, -'er-

apiarist 'epɪərɪst

apiary 'epɪˌɛrɪ

apical 'æpɪkḷ, 'e- |-ly -ɪ

apices 'æpɪˌsiz, 'e-

apicultural ˌepɪ'kʌltʃərəl

apiculture 'epɪˌkʌltʃɚ; ES -tʃə(r

apiece ə'pis

Apis 'epɪs

apish 'epɪʃ

aplenty ə'plɛntɪ

aplomb ə'plam, ə'plɒm (*Fr* a'plŏ)

apocalypse, A- ə'pɑkəˌlɪps |-s -ɪz

apocalyptic əˌpɑkə'lɪptɪk |-al -ḷ |-ally -ḷɪ, -ɪklɪ

apocopate *adj* ə'pɑkəpɪt, -ˌpet

apocopate *v* ə'pɑkəˌpet |-d -ɪd

apocopation əˌpɑkə'peʃən

apocope ə'pɑkəpɪ, -ˌpi

apocrypha, A- ə'pɑkrəfə |-l -l |-lly -lɪ

apodeictic, -deik- ˌæpə'daɪktɪk |-al -ḷ |-ally -ḷɪ, -ɪklɪ

apodictic ˌæpə'dɪktɪk |-al -ḷ |-ally -ḷɪ, -ɪklɪ

apodosis ə'pɑdəsɪs |-doses -dəˌsiz

apogee 'æpəˌdʒi

Apollinaris əˌpɑlə'nɛrɪs, -'nærɪs, -'nerɪs

Apollo ə'pɑlo

Apollodorus əˌpɑlə'dorəs, -'dɔr-; S -'dor-; |-'s -ɪz

Apollonius ˌæpə'lonɪəs |-'s -ɪz

Apollos ə'pɑləs |-'s -ɪz

Apollyon ə'pɑljən

apologetic əˌpɑlə'dʒɛtɪk |-al -ḷ |-ally -ḷɪ, -ɪklɪ

apologia ˌæpə'lodʒɪə

apologist ə'pɑlədʒɪst |-gy -dʒɪ

apologize ə'pɑləˌdʒaɪz |-s -ɪz |-d -d

apologue 'æpəˌlɔg, -ˌlɑg, -ˌlɒg

apophthegm 'æpəˌθɛm

Key: See in full §§3–47. bee bi |pity 'pɪtɪ (§6) |rate ret |yet jɛt |sang sæŋ |angry 'æŋ·grɪ |bath bæθ; E bɑθ (§10) |ah ɑ |far fɑr |watch wɑtʃ, wɒtʃ (§12) |jaw dʒɔ |gorge gɔrdʒ |go go

Those words below in which the ɑ *sound is spelt* o *are often pronounced with* ɒ *in E and S*

apophthegmatic ˌæpəθɛgˈmætɪk |-al -l̩ |-ally -l̩ɪ, -ɪklɪ

apoplectic ˌæpəˈplɛktɪk |-al -l̩ |-ally -l̩ɪ, -ɪklɪ

apoplexed ˈæpəˌplɛkst |apoplexy ˈæpəˌplɛksɪ

aport əˈport, əˈpɔrt; ES əˈpoət, E+əˈpɔət

aposiopesis ˌæpəˌsaɪəˈpisɪs

apostasy əˈpɑstəsɪ

apostate əˈpɑstet, -tɪt

apostatize əˈpɑstəˌtaɪz |-s -ɪz |-d -d

a posteriori ˈepɑsˌtɪrɪˈoraɪ, -ˈɔr-; S -ˈor-

apostle əˈpɑsl̩

apostolate əˈpɑstl̩ɪt, -ˌet

apostolic ˌæpəsˈtɑlɪk |-al -l̩ |-ally -l̩ɪ, -ɪklɪ

apostrophe əˈpɑstrəfɪ

apostrophize əˈpɑstrəˌfaɪz |-s -ɪz |-d -d

apothecary əˈpɑθəˌkɛrɪ

apothegm ˈæpəˌθɛm

apothegmatic ˌæpəθɛgˈmætɪk |-al -l̩ |-ally -l̩ɪ, -ɪklɪ

apotheosis əˌpɑθɪˈosɪs, ˌæpəˈθiəsɪs

Appalachia ˌæpəˈlætʃɪə

Appalachian ˌæpəˈlætʃɪən, -ˈletʃ-, -tʃən

Appalachians ˌæpəˈlætʃənz, -ˈletʃ-, -ɪənz

appall, -al əˈpɔl |-ed, -led -d

appanage ˈæpənɪdʒ |-s -ɪz |-d -d

Appanoose ˌæpəˈnus |-'s -ɪz

apparatus ˌæpəˈretəs, -ˈrætəs |pl -tuses -ˌəsɪz |L pl -ratus -ˈretəs

apparel əˈpærəl |-ed -d

apparent əˈpærənt, əˈpɛr-; S əˈpær-

apparition ˌæpəˈrɪʃən

apparitor əˈpærətɚ; ES -tə(r

appeal əˈpil |-ed -d |-able -əbl̩

appealability əˌpiləˈbɪlətɪ

appear əˈpɪr; ES əˈpɪə(r, S+əˈpɛə(r, əˈpjɛə(r; |-ed -d

appearance əˈpɪrəns; S+əˈpɛr-, əˈpjɛr-; |-s -ɪz

appeasable əˈpizəbl̩ |-bly -blɪ

appease əˈpiz |-s -ɪz |-d -d

appellant əˈpɛlənt

appellate əˈpɛlɪt |-tive -ɪv, -lətɪv

appellation ˌæpəˈleʃən

appellee ˌæpəˈli

appellor əˈpɛlɔr, ˌæpəˈlɔr; ES -ɔə(r

append əˈpɛnd |-ed -ɪd |-age -ɪdʒ |-ages -ɪdʒɪz

appendant əˈpɛndənt

appendectomy ˌæpənˈdɛktəmɪ

appendices əˈpɛndəˌsiz

appendicitis əˌpɛndəˈsaɪtɪs

appendix əˈpɛndɪks |-es -ɪz |-dices -dəˌsiz

apperceive ˌæpɚˈsiv; ES ˌæpə-; |-d -d

apperception ˌæpɚˈsɛpʃən; ES ˌæpə-; |-tive -tɪv

appertain ˌæpɚˈten; ES ˌæpə-; |-ed -d

appetence ˈæpətəns |-cy -ɪ |-tent -tənt

appetite ˈæpəˌtaɪt |-titive -ˌtaɪtɪv

appetize ˈæpəˌtaɪz |-s -ɪz |-d -d

appetizer ˈæpəˌtaɪzɚ; ES -ˌtaɪzə(r

Appian ˈæpɪən

applaud əˈplɔd |-ed -ɪd |-able -əbl̩ |-bly -blɪ

applause əˈplɔz |-s -ɪz

apple ˈæpl̩ |-d -d |-ling ˈæpl̩ɪŋ, ˈæplɪŋ

applejack ˈæpl̩ˌdʒæk

apple pie ˈæpl̩ˈpaɪ (ˈapple-ˌpie ˈorder)

applesauce ˈæpl̩ˌsɔs

Appleton ˈæpl̩tən

appliable əˈplaɪəbl̩ |-bly -blɪ

appliance əˈplaɪəns |-s -ɪz |-ant -ənt

applicability ˌæplɪkəˈbɪlətɪ

applicable ˈæplɪkəbl̩, əˈplɪk- |-bly -blɪ

applicant ˈæpləkənt

application ˌæpləˈkeʃən

applicative ˈæpləˌketɪv |-tor -tɚ; ES -tə(r

applicatory ˈæpləkəˌtorɪ, -ˌtɔrɪ; S -ˌtorɪ

applied əˈplaɪd |appliedly əˈplaɪ-ɪdlɪ

appliqué ˌæplɪˈke (Fr apliˈke)

apply əˈplaɪ |applied əˈplaɪd

appoint əˈpɔɪnt |-ed -ɪd |-ive -ɪv

appointee əpɔɪnˈti, ˌæpɔɪnˈti, əˈpɔɪnti

appointor əˈpɔɪntɚ, əpɔɪnˈtɔr; ES -tə(r, -ˈtɔə(r

Appomattox ˌæpəˈmætəks |-'s -ɪz |-toc -tək

apportion əˈporʃən, əˈpɔr-; ES əˈpoəʃən, E+əˈpɔə-; |-ed -d |-ing -ʃənɪŋ, -ʃnɪŋ

appose əˈpoz, æ- |-s -ɪz |-d -d |-sable -əbl̩

apposite ˈæpəzɪt

apposition ˌæpəˈzɪʃən

appositive əˈpɑzətɪv

appraise əˈprez |-s -ɪz |-d -d |-sal -l̩

appreciable əˈpriʃɪəbl̩, -ʃəbl̩ |-bly -blɪ

appreciate əˈpriʃɪˌet |-d -ɪd

appreciation əˌpriʃɪˈeʃən |-tive əˈpriʃɪˌetɪv

appreciatory əˈpriʃɪəˌtorɪ, -ˌtɔrɪ; S -ˌtorɪ

apprehend ˌæprɪˈhɛnd |-ed -ɪd

|full fʊl |tooth tuθ |further ˈfɝðɚ; ES ˈfɝðə |custom ˈkʌstəm |while hwaɪl |how haʊ |toy tɔɪ |using ˈjuzɪŋ |fuse fjuz, fɪuz |dish dɪʃ |vision ˈvɪʒən |Eden ˈidn̩ |cradle ˈkredl̩ |keep 'em ˈkipm̩

Words below in which a *before* r (farm) *is sounded* ɑ *are often pronounced in E with* a (fɑ:m)

apprehensible ˌæprɪˈhɛnsəbļ |-bly -blɪ

apprehension ˌæprɪˈhɛnʃən |-sive -sɪv

apprentice əˈprɛntɪs |-s -ɪz |-d -t |-ship -ˌʃɪp

appressed əˈprɛst, æ-

apprise, -ze ʻadviseʼ əˈpraɪz |-s -ɪz |-d -d

apprize, -se ʻappraiseʼ əˈpraɪz |-s -ɪz |-d -d

approach əˈprotʃ |-es -ɪz |-ed -t

approachability əˌprotʃəˈbɪlətɪ

approachable əˈprotʃəbļ

approbate ˈæprəˌbet |-d -ɪd |-tion ˌæprəˈbeʃən

approbatory əˈprobəˌtorɪ, -ˌtɔrɪ; S -ˌtorɪ

appropriable əˈproprɪəbļ

appropriate adj əˈproprɪɪt

appropriate v əˈproprɪˌet |-d -ɪd |-tive -ɪv

appropriation əˌproprɪˈeʃən

approve əˈpruv |-d -d |-dly -ɪdlɪ |-val -ļ

approximate adj əˈpraksəmɪt; ES+əˈprɒks-

approximate v əˈpraksəˌmet; ES+əˈprɒks-; |-d -ɪd

approximation əˌpraksəˈmeʃən; ES+ əˌprɒks-

appurtenance əˈpɝtņəns; ES əˈpɜt-, əˈpɝt-; |-s -ɪz |-ant -ənt

apricot ˈeprɪˌkɑt, ˈæp-; ES+-ˌkɒt

April ˈeprəl, ˈeprɪl

a priori ˈepraɪˈoraɪ, -ˈɔr-; S -ˈoraɪ

apriority ˌepraɪˈɔrətɪ, -ˈɑr-, -ˈɒr-

apron ˈeprən, ˈepɚn; ES ˈeprən, ˈepən; |-ed -d—The older pron. ˈepɚn, ˈepən is by no means rare, and appears from the L.A. to be very common in NEngd.

apropos ˌæprəˈpo

apse æps |apses ˈæpsɪz

apsis ˈæpsɪs |apsides ˈæpsɪˌdiz

apt æpt

apterous ˈæptərəs

apteryx ˈæptəˌrɪks |-es -ɪz

aptitude ˈæptəˌtjud, -ˌtɪud, -ˌtud

Apuleius ˌæpjuˈliəs |-ʼs -ɪz

Apulia əˈpjulɪə, əˈpɪulɪə

aqua ˈækwə, ˈe- |-s -z |aquae -wi

aqua fortis ˈækwəˈfɔrtɪs, ˈe-; ES -ˈfɔətɪs

aqualon ˈækwəˌlɑn; ES+-ˌlɒn

aquamarine ˌækwəməˈrin

aquaplane ˈækwəˌplen

aqua regia ˈækwəˈridʒɪə, ˈe-

aquarium əˈkwɛrɪəm, əˈkwer- | s -z |-ria -rɪə

Aquarius əˈkwɛrɪəs, əˈkwer- |-ʼs -ɪz

aquatic əˈkwætɪk, əˈkwɑt-, əˈkwɒt-

aquatint ˈækwəˌtɪnt

aqua vitae ˈækwəˈvaɪtɪ

aqueduct ˈækwɪˌdʌkt

aqueous ˈekwɪəs, ˈæk-

Aquidneck əˈkwɪdnɛk

Aquila ˈækwɪlə |-lae -ˌli— Bible+əˈkwɪlə, perh. by association with Priscilla (Rom. 16:3).

aquiline ˈækwəˌlaɪn, -lɪn

Aquinas əˈkwaɪnəs |-ʼs -ɪz

Aquitaine ˌækwɪˈten |-tania -ɪə

ar ɑr; ES ɑ:(r

Arab ˈærəb, now less freq. ˈeræb

Arabella ˌærəˈbɛlə

arabesque ˌærəˈbɛsk

Arabia əˈrebɪə, -bjə |-n -n

Arabic, a- ˈærəbɪk

arabis, A- ˈærəbɪs |-es -ɪz

arable ˈærəbļ

Araby ˈærəbɪ

Arachne əˈræknɪ

arachnid əˈræknɪd |-noid -nɔɪd

Aragon ˈærəˌgan, -gən; ES+-ˌgɒn; (Sp ˌarɑˈgɒn)

Aral ˈɛrəl, ˈærəl, ˈerəl; S ˈærəl, ˈerəl

Aram ˈerəm, ˈɛrəm, ˈærəm; S ˈerəm, ˈærəm

Aramaean, -mean ˌærəˈmiən |-maic -ˈme·ɪk

Aransas əˈrænsəs |-sasʼ -səs

Arapaho, -hoe əˈræpəˌho

Ararat ˈærəˌræt

arbalest, -list ˈɑrbəlɪst; ES ˈɑ:b-

arbiter ˈɑrbɪtɚ; ES ˈɑ:bɪtə(r

arbitrable ˈɑrbətrəbļ; ES ˈɑ:b-

arbitrage ʻarbitrationʼ ˈɑrbətrɪdʒ; ES ˈɑ:b-; |-s -ɪz

arbitrage commerce ˈɑrbətrɪdʒ, ˌɑrbəˈtraʒ; ES ˈɑ:b-, ˌɑ:b-; |-s -ɪz |-d -d

arbitral ˈɑrbətrəl; ES ˈɑ:b-

arbitrament ɑrˈbɪtrəmənt; ES ɑˈbɪt-

arbitrarily ˈɑrbəˌtrerəlɪ; ES ˈɑ:b-; esp. if emph. ˌɑrbɪˈtrarily

arbitrary ˈɑrbəˌtrɛrɪ; ES ˈɑ:b-

arbitrate ˈɑrbəˌtret; ES ˈɑ:b-; |-d -ɪd

arbitration ˌɑrbəˈtreʃən; ES ˌɑ:b-

arbitrator ˈɑrbəˌtretɚ; ES ˈɑ:bəˌtretə(r

arbitress ˈɑrbətrɪs; ES ˈɑ:b-; |-es -ɪz

Arblay, dʼ ˈdɑrble; ES ˈdɑ:ble

Words below in which a *before* r (farm) *is sounded* ɑ *are often pronounced in* E *with* a (fa:m)

arbor, A- 'ɑrbɚ; ES 'ɑ:bə(r; |-ed -d
arboraceous ˌɑrbə'reʃəs; ES ˌɑ:bə-
arboreal ɑr'borɪəl, -'bɔr-; ES ɑ'borɪəl, E+
-'bɔrɪəl
arborescent ˌɑrbə'rɛsn̩t; ES ˌɑ:bə-; |-nce
-sn̩s
arboretum ˌɑrbə'ritəm; ES ˌɑ:bə-
arboriculture 'ɑrbərɪˌkʌltʃɚ; ES 'ɑ:bərɪ-
ˌkʌltʃə(r
arborvitae, arbor vitae 'ɑrbɚ'vaɪtɪ; ES
'ɑ:bə-
Arbuckle 'ɑrbʌk|; ES 'ɑ:b-
Arbuthnot ɑr'bʌθnət, 'ɑrbəθˌnɑt; ES ɑ:-,
'ɑ:-, -ˌnɒt
arbutus ɑr'bjutəs, -'bru-; ES ɑ:-; |-es -ɪz
arc ɑrk; ES ɑ:k; |arced, arcked ɑrkt; ES ɑ:kt
Arc, Jeanne d' *Fr* ʒɑ:n'dark
arcade ɑr'ked; ES ɑ:'ked; |-d -ɪd
Arcadia ɑr'kedɪə; ES ɑ'ked-; |-n -n
Arcady 'ɑrkədɪ; ES 'ɑ:k-
arcanum ɑr'kenəm; ES ɑ:'ken-; |-na -nə
arced ɑrkt; ES ɑ:kt
arch ɑrtʃ; ES ɑ:tʃ; |-es -ɪz |-ed -t
Archaean ɑr'kiən; ES ɑ:'kiən
archaeological ˌɑrkɪə'lɑdʒɪk|; ES ˌɑ:kɪə'lɑdʒ-,
-'lɒdʒ-; |-ly -ɪ, -ɪklɪ
archaeology ˌɑrkɪ'ɑlədʒɪ; ES ˌɑ:kɪ'ɑl-, -'ɒl-;
|-gist -dʒɪst
archaeopteryx, A- ˌɑrkɪ'ɑptərɪks; ES
ˌɑ:kɪ'ɑp-, -'ɒp-; |-es -ɪz
Archaeornis ˌɑrkɪ'ɔrnɪs; ES ˌɑ:kɪ'ɔənɪs
archaic ɑr'ke·ɪk; ES ɑ:-; |-al -| |-ally -|ɪ,
-ɪklɪ
archaism 'ɑrkɪˌɪzəm, 'ɑrke-; ES 'ɑ:k-
archaistic ˌɑrkɪ'ɪstɪk, ˌɑrke-; ES ˌɑ:k-
archaize 'ɑrkɪˌaɪz, 'ɑrke-; ES 'ɑ:k-; |-s -ɪz
|-d -d
archangel, A- 'ɑrk'endʒəl, -ˌendʒəl; ES 'ɑ:k-
archangelic ˌɑrkæn'dʒɛlɪk; ES ˌɑ:k-; |-al -|
archbishop ˌɑrtʃ'bɪʃəp; ES 'ɑ:tʃ-; ('Arch-
ˌbishop 'Laud)
archbishopric ˌɑrtʃ'bɪʃəprɪk; ES ˌɑ:tʃ-
Archbald 'ɑrtʃbɔld; ES 'ɑ:tʃ-; |-bold -bold
archdeacon 'ɑrtʃ'dikən, -ˌdikən; ES 'ɑ:tʃ-
archdiocese 'ɑrtʃ'daɪəˌsis, -sɪs; ES 'ɑ:tʃ-;
|-s -ɪz
archducal ˌɑrtʃ'djuk|, -'dru-, -'du-; ES
ˌɑ:tʃ-

archduchess 'ɑrtʃ'dʌtʃɪs, -ˌdʌtʃɪs; ES 'ɑ:tʃ-;
|-es -ɪz
archduchy 'ɑrtʃ'dʌtʃɪ; ES 'ɑ:tʃ-
archduke 'ɑrtʃ'djuk, -'druk, -'duk, -ˌd-; ES
'ɑ:tʃ-
Archean ɑr'kiən; ES ɑ:'kiən
arched ɑrtʃt; ES ɑ:tʃt
archenemy 'ɑrtʃ'ɛnəmɪ, -ˌɛnəmɪ; ES 'ɑ:tʃ-
archeological ˌɑrkɪə'lɑdʒɪk|; ES ˌɑ:kɪə'lɑdʒ-,
-'lɒdʒ-; |-ly -ɪ, -ɪklɪ
archeology ˌɑrkɪ'ɑlədʒɪ; ES ˌɑ:kɪ'ɑl-, -'ɒl-;
|-gist -dʒɪst
Archeozoic ˌɑrkɪə'zo·ɪk; ES ˌɑ:kɪə-
archer, A- 'ɑrtʃɚ; ES 'ɑ:tʃə(r; |-y -ɪ
archetype 'ɑrkəˌtaɪp; ES 'ɑ:kə-
archfiend 'ɑrtʃ'find, -ˌfind; ES 'ɑ:tʃ-
Archibald 'ɑrtʃəˌbɔld; ES 'ɑ:tʃ-
Archidamus ˌɑrkɪ'deməs; ES ˌɑ:kɪ-; |-'s -ɪz
archidiaconal ˌɑrkɪdaɪ'ækən|; ES ˌɑ:kɪ-
archiepiscopacy ˌɑrkɪə'pɪskəpəsɪ; ES ˌɑ:kɪ-;
|-pal -p|
Archimedean ˌɑrkɪ'midɪən, -mɪ'diən; ES
ˌɑ:kɪ-
Archimedes ˌɑrkə'midiz; ES ˌɑ:k-; |-des'
-diz
archipelagic ˌɑrkɪpə'lædʒɪk; ES ˌɑ:kɪ-
archipelago ˌɑrkə'pɛləˌgo; ES ˌɑ:kə-
architect 'ɑrkəˌtɛkt; ES 'ɑ:kə-
architectonic ˌɑrkɪtɛk'tɑnɪk; ES ˌɑ:kɪtɛk'tɑn-,
-'tɒn-; |-al -| |-ally -|ɪ, -ɪklɪ
architectural ˌɑrkə'tɛktʃərəl; ES ˌɑ:kə-;
|-ly -ɪ
architecture 'ɑrkəˌtɛktʃɚ; ES 'ɑ:kəˌtɛktʃə(r
architrave 'ɑrkəˌtrev; ES 'ɑ:kə-; |-d -d
archival ɑr'kaɪv|; ES ɑ:'kaɪv|
archive 'ɑrkaɪv; ES 'ɑ:k-; |-s -z |-d -d
archivist 'ɑrkəvɪst; ES 'ɑ:k-
archivolt 'ɑrkəˌvolt; ES 'ɑ:kə-
archon 'ɑrkɑn, -kən; ES 'ɑ:kɑn, -kɒn, -kən
archpriest 'ɑrtʃ'prist; ES 'ɑ:tʃ-; |-hood -hʊd
|-ship -ʃɪp
archway 'ɑrtʃˌwe; ES 'ɑ:tʃ-
arcing 'ɑrkɪŋ; ES 'ɑ:kɪŋ
Arcite 'ɑrsaɪt, ɑr'saɪt; ES 'ɑ:s-, ɑ:'s-
arcked ɑrkt; ES ɑ:kt; |-cking -kɪŋ
Arcola ɑr'kolə; ES ɑ:'k-
arctic 'ɑrktɪk, *now rare* 'ɑrtɪk; ES 'ɑ:-;
|-s -s

|full fʊl |tooth tuθ |further 'fɝðɚ; ES 'fɜðə |custom 'kʌstəm |while hwaɪl |how haʊ |toy tɔɪ
|using 'juzɪŋ |fuse fjuz. fɪuz |dish dɪʃ |vision 'vɪʒən |Eden 'idn̩ |cradle 'kredl̩ |keep 'em 'kipm̩

Words below in which a *before* r (farm) *is sounded* ɑ *are often pronounced in* E *with* a (fa:m)

Arcturus ɑrk'tjʊrəs, -'tɪʊr-, -'tʊr-; ES ɑ:k-; |-'s -ɪz

arcuate 'ɑrkjuɪt, -ˌet; ES 'ɑ:k-; |-d -ˌetɪd

Arden 'ɑrdn̩; ES 'ɑ:dn̩

ardent 'ɑrdn̩t; ES 'ɑ:d-; |-ncy -n̩sɪ

Ardmore 'ɑrdmor, -mɔr; ES 'ɑ:dmoə(r, E+-mɔə(r

ardor 'ɑrdɚ; ES 'ɑ:də(r

arduous 'ɑrdʒuəs; ES 'ɑ:dʒ-

are *measure* ɛr, ær, ɑr; E ɛə(r, ES æə(r, ɑ:(r

are *v stressed* 'ɑr, ˌɑr; ES 'ɑ:(r, ˌɑ:(r; *unstr.* ɚ; ES ə(r; |'re -r; ES -ə(r; *see* we're, you're, they're

area 'ɛrɪə, 'ɛrɪə |-way -ˌwe

arena ə'rinə

aren't ɑrnt; ES ɑ:nt

Areopagite ˌærɪ'ɑpəˌdʒaɪt, -ˌgaɪt; ES+-'ɒp-

Areopagitic ˌærɪˌɑpə'dʒɪtɪk; ES+-ˌɒp-; |-a -ə

Areopagus ˌærɪ'ɑpəgəs; ES+-'ɒp-; |-'s -ɪz

Ares 'ɛriz, 'ɛriz, 'æriz; S 'ɛriz, 'æriz; |-res' -riz

Arethusa ˌærɪ'θjuzə, -'θɪu-, -'θu-

argal *'argol'* 'ɑrgl̩; ES 'ɑ:gl̩

argal *'ergo'* 'ɑrgl̩; ES 'ɑ:gl̩—*In Shak.'s day* argal *was pron.* 'ærgl̩ *and* ergo 'ærgɔ.

argali 'ɑrgəlɪ; ES 'ɑ:gəlɪ

argent 'ɑrdʒənt; ES 'ɑ:dʒənt

argental ɑr'dʒɛntl̩; ES ɑ:'dʒɛntl̩; |-teous -tɪəs |-tic -tɪk

argentiferous ˌɑrdʒən'tɪfərəs; ES ˌɑ:dʒən-

Argentina ˌɑrdʒən'tinə; ES ˌɑ:dʒən-

Argentine 'ɑrdʒənˌtin, -ˌtaɪn; ES 'ɑ:dʒ-

argentine 'ɑrdʒəntɪn, -ˌtaɪn; ES 'ɑ:dʒ-

Argentinian ˌɑrdʒən'tɪnɪən; ES ˌɑ:dʒ-

argentite 'ɑrdʒənˌtaɪt; ES 'ɑ:dʒ-

argentous ɑr'dʒɛntəs; ES ɑ:'dʒɛn-

argil 'ɑrdʒɪl; ES 'ɑ:dʒɪl

Argive 'ɑrdʒaɪv; ES 'ɑ:dʒaɪv

Argo 'ɑrgo; ES 'ɑ:go

argol 'ɑrgl̩; ES 'ɑ:gl̩

argon 'ɑrgɑn; ES 'ɑ:gɑn, -gɒn

Argonaut 'ɑrgəˌnɔt; ES 'ɑ:gə-

Argonautic ˌɑrgə'nɔtɪk; ES ˌɑ:gə-

Argonne 'ɑrgɑn; ES 'ɑ:gɑn, -gɒn (*Fr* ɑr'gǒn)

Argos 'ɑrgɑs, -gəs; ES 'ɑ:gɑs, -gɒs, -gəs; |-'s -ɪz

argosy 'ɑrgəsɪ; ES 'ɑ:gəsɪ

argot 'ɑrgo, 'ɑrgət; ES 'ɑ:g-

argue 'ɑrgju; ES 'ɑ:g-; |-d -d

argument 'ɑrgjəmənt; ES 'ɑ:g-

argumental ˌɑrgjə'mɛntl̩; ES ˌɑ:g-

argumentation ˌɑrgjəmɛn'teʃən; ES ˌɑ:g-

argumentative ˌɑrgjə'mɛntətɪv; ES ˌɑ:g-

Argus 'ɑrgəs; ES 'ɑ:g-; |-'s -ɪz

Argus-eyed 'ɑrgəsˌaɪd; ES 'ɑ:g-

Argyll, -gyle ɑr'gaɪl; ES ɑ:'g-; |-shire -ʃɪr, -ʃɚ; ES -ʃɪə(r, -ʃə(r

Argyrol 'ɑrdʒəˌrɔl, -ˌrɑl; ES 'ɑ:dʒ-, -ˌrɒl

aria 'ɑrɪə, 'ɛrɪə, 'ærɪə; S 'ɑrɪə, 'ærɪə

Ariadne ˌærɪ'ædnɪ

Arian 'ɛrɪən, 'ærɪən, 'ɛrɪən; S 'ærɪən, 'er-

arid 'ærɪd |-ity ə'rɪdətɪ, æ-

Ariel 'ɛrɪəl, 'ɛrɪəl, 'ærɪəl; S 'ɛrɪəl, 'ær-

Aries 'ɛriz, 'ɛriz, 'æriz, -rɪˌiz; S 'ɛr-, 'ær-; |-es' -iz |*gen* Arietis ə'raɪətɪs

aright ə'raɪt

Ariosto ˌærɪ'ɑsto, -'ɒs-, -'os- (*It* ˌɑri'ɔsto)

arise ə'raɪz |-s -ɪz |arose ə'roz |arisen ə'rɪzn̩

Aristides ˌærə'staɪdiz |-des' -diz

aristocracy ˌærə'stɑkrəsɪ; ES+-'stɒk-

aristocrat ə'rɪstəˌkræt, 'ærɪstə-

aristocratic əˌrɪstə'krætɪk, ˌærɪstə- |-al -l̩ |-ally -l̩ɪ, -ɪklɪ

Aristophanes ˌærə'stɑfəˌniz; ES+-'stɒf-

Aristotelian ˌærɪstə'tilɪən, əˌrɪstə-, -ljən

Aristotle 'ærəˌstɑtl̩; ES+-ˌstɒtl̩

arithmetic *n* ə'rɪθməˌtɪk

arithmetic *adj* ˌærɪθ'mɛtɪk |-al -l̩ |-ally -lɪ, -ɪklɪ

arithmetician əˌrɪθmə'tɪʃən, ˌærɪθmə-

Arius 'ɛrɪəs, 'ær-, 'er-, ə'raɪəs; S 'ær-, 'er-, ə'raɪəs; |-'s -ɪz

Arizona ˌærə'zonə |-nan -nən |-nian -nɪən

ark ɑrk; ES ɑ:k; |-ed -t

Arkansan ɑr'kænzən; ES ɑ:'kæn-

Arkansas *state* 'ɑrkənˌsɔ, *o. f.* ɑr'kænzəs; *riv.* 'ɑrkənˌsɔ, *loc.*+ɑr'kænzəs, -z; *city in Ark* 'ɑrkənˌsɔ, *loc.*+ɑr'kænzəs, -z; *city in Kan* 'ɑrkənˌsɔ, *loc.* ɑr'kænzəs, -z; ES 'ɑ:kənˌsɔ, ɑ:'kænzəs, S+'ɑ:kɪnˌsɔ; |*poss* 'Arkanˌsas's -ˌsɔz |Ar'kansas' -zəs

Arkansawyer 'ɑrkənˌsɔjɚ; ES 'ɑ:kənˌsɔjə(r

Arkwright 'ɑrkˌraɪt; ES 'ɑ:k-

Arlen 'ɑrlɪn, -ən; ES 'ɑ:l-

Arlington 'ɑrlɪŋtən; ES 'ɑ:l-

Key: *See in full* §§3–47. bee bi |pity 'pɪtɪ (§6) |rate ret |yet jɛt |sang sæŋ |angry 'æŋ·grɪ |bath bæθ; E bɑθ (§10) |ah ɑ |far fɑr |watch wɑtʃ, wɒtʃ (§12) |jaw dʒɔ |gorge gɔrdʒ |go go

Words below in which a *before* r (farm) *is sounded* ɑ *are often pronounced in* E *with* a (fɑːm)

Arliss 'ɑrlıs; ES 'ɑːl-; |-'s -ız

arm ɑrm; ES ɑːm; |-ed -d

armada, A- ɑr'mɑdə, -'meɪdə; ES ɑː'm-

armadillo ˌɑrmə'dɪlo; ES ˌɑːmə-

Armageddon ˌɑrmə'gɛdn̩; ES ˌɑːmə-

armament 'ɑrməmənt; ES 'ɑːmə-

armature 'ɑrmətʃɚ, -ˌtʃʊr; ES 'ɑːmətʃə(r, -ˌtʃʊə(r

armchair 'ɑrmˌtʃɛr, -ˌtʃær; E 'ɑːmˌtʃɛə(r, ES -ˌtʃæə(r; *acct+*'ɑrm'chair

Armenia ɑr'minɪə; ES ɑ'min-; |-n -n

armful 'ɑrmˌfʊl; ES 'ɑːm-; |-s -z

armhole 'ɑrmˌhol; ES 'ɑːm-

Arminian ɑr'mɪnɪən; ES ɑ'mɪn-

Arminius ɑr'mɪnɪəs; ES ɑ'mɪn-; |-'s -ız

armipotent ɑr'mɪpətənt; ES ɑ'mɪp-; |-ence -əns

armistice 'ɑrməstɪs; ES 'ɑːm-; |-s -ız

Armitage 'ɑrmətɪdʒ; ES 'ɑːm-; |-'s -ız

armlet 'ɑrmlɪt; ES 'ɑːm-

armor 'ɑrmɚ; ES 'ɑːmə(r; |-ed -d

armor-bearer 'ɑrmɚˌbɛrɚ, -ˌbærɚ; E 'ɑːməˌbɛrə(r, ES -ˌbærə(r

armor-clad 'ɑrmɚˌklæd; ES 'ɑːmə-

armorer 'ɑrmərɚ; ES 'ɑːmərə(r

armorial ɑr'morɪəl, -'mɔr-; ES ɑ'morɪəl, E+-'mɔr-

Armoric ɑr'mɔrɪk, -'mɑr-, -'mɒr-; ES ɑː'm-; |-a -ə |-an -ən

armory 'ɑrmərɪ; ES 'ɑːmərɪ

armpit 'ɑrmˌpɪt; ES 'ɑːm-

arms ɑrmz; ES ɑːmz

Armstrong 'ɑrmstrɔŋ, -strɒŋ; ES 'ɑːm-

army 'ɑrmɪ; ES 'ɑːmɪ; |-mied -mɪd

arnica 'ɑrnɪkə; ES 'ɑːn-

Arno 'ɑrno; ES 'ɑːno

Arnold 'ɑrn̩d; ES 'ɑːn̩d

aroint ə'rɔɪnt

aroma ə'romə

Aroostook ə'rustʊk, *loc.*+-tɪk

arose ə'roz

around ə'raʊnd

arouse ə'raʊz |-s -ız |-d -d |-sal -|

ARP, A.R.P. 'eˌɑr'pi; ES 'eˌɑ'pi

arpeggio ɑr'pɛdʒɪˌo, -dʒo; ES ɑ'p-

arquebus 'ɑrkwɪbəs; ES 'ɑːk-; |-es -ız

arquebusier ˌɑrkwɪbəs'ɪr; ES ˌɑːkwɪbəs'ɪə(r

arrack 'ærək

Arragon 'ærəˌgɑn, -gən; ES+-ˌgɒn; (*Sp* ˌɑrɑ'gɒn)

arraign ə'ren |-ed -d

arrange ə'rendʒ |-s -ız |-d -d

arrant 'ærənt

arras, A- 'ærəs |-es -ız (*Fr* a'rɑːs)

array ə're |-ed -d

arrear ə'rɪr; ES ə'rɪə(r, S+ə'rɛə(r; |-s -z

arrearage ə'rɪrɪdʒ |-s -ız

arrest ə'rɛst |-ed -ıd

Arrighi ə'rigi, ɑ- (*It* ɑr'riːgi)

arris 'ærɪs |-es -ız

arrive ə'raɪv |-d -d |-val -|

arrogance 'ærəgəns |-cy -ı |-gant -gənt

arrogate 'ærəˌget, 'æro- |-d -ıd

arrow 'æro, 'ærɑ |-ed -d |-ing 'ærəwɪŋ

arrowhead 'æroˌhɛd, 'ærə-

arrowroot 'æroˌrut, 'ærə-, -ˌrʊt

arrowy 'ærəwɪ

arroyo ə'rɔɪo

arsenal 'ɑrsn̩əl, 'ɑrsnəl; ES 'ɑːsn̩əl, 'ɑːsnəl

arsenate *n* 'ɑrsn̩ˌet, -ıt; ES 'ɑːsn̩-

arsenate *v* 'ɑrsn̩ˌet; ES 'ɑːsn̩-; |-d -ıd

arsenic *n, v* 'ɑrsn̩ɪk, 'ɑrsnɪk; ES 'ɑːs-; |-ked -t

arsenic *adj* ɑr'sɛnɪk; ES ɑ'sɛnɪk; |-al -|

arsenide 'ɑrsn̩ˌaɪd, -ıd; ES 'ɑːsn̩-

arsenious ɑr'sinɪəs; ES ɑ'sin-

arsenite 'ɑrsn̩ˌaɪt; ES 'ɑːsn̩-

arsine ɑr'sin; ES ɑ'sin

arsis 'ɑrsɪs; ES 'ɑːsɪs; |arses -siz

arson 'ɑrsn̩; ES 'ɑːsn̩

arsphenamine ˌɑrsfɛnə'min, -'æmɪn; ES ˌɑːs-

art *n* ɑrt; ES ɑːt; |-y -ı

art *v* 2 *pers: stressed* 'ɑrt, ˌɑrt; ES 'ɑːt, ˌɑːt; *unstr.* ɑrt, ɚt; ES ɑt, ət

Artaxerxes ˌɑrtə'zɝksiz; ES ˌɑːtə'zɝk-, ˌɑːtə-'zɝk-; |xes' -ksiz

artefact 'ɑrtıˌfækt; ES 'ɑːtı-

Artemidorus ˌɑrtəmı'dorəs, -'dɔr-; ES ˌɑːtəmı'dor-, E+-'dɔr-; |-'s -ız

Artemis 'ɑrtəmɪs; ES 'ɑːt-; |-'s -ız

Artemus 'ɑrtəməs; ES 'ɑːt-; |-'s -ız

arterial ɑr'tɪrɪəl; ES ɑ'tɪr-

arteriosclerosis ɑr'tɪrɪˌosklɪ'rosɪs; ES ɑ'tɪr-

artery 'ɑrtərɪ; ES 'ɑːtərɪ

artesian ɑr'tiʒən; ES ɑː't-; ('ɑrtıˌtesian 'well)

Artesius ɑr'tiʒəs; ES ɑː't-; |-'s -ız

|full fʊl |tooth tuθ |further 'fɝðɚ; ES 'fɝðə |custom 'kʌstəm |while hwaɪl |how haʊ |toy tɔɪ |using 'juzɪŋ |fuse fjuz, fɪuz |dish dɪʃ |vision 'vɪʒən |Eden 'idn̩ |cradle 'kred| |keep 'em 'kipm̩

Words below in which a *before* r (farm) *is sounded* ɑ *are often pronounced in E with* a (fa:m)

Arteveld ˈɑrtəˌvɛlt; ES ˈɑ:tə-

artful ˈɑrtfəl; ES ˈɑ:t-; |-ly -ɪ

Arthabaska ˌɑrθəˈbæskə; ES ˌɑ:θə-

arthritic ɑrˈθrɪtɪk; ES ɑ:ˈθrɪtɪk; |-al -l̩

arthritis ɑrˈθraɪtɪs; ES ɑ:ˈθr-; |-tes -tiz

arthropod ˈɑrθrəˌpɑd; ES ˈɑ:θrəˌpɑd, -ˌpɒd

Arthur ˈɑrθɚ; ES ˈɑ:θə(r;—*In the occas. pron.* ˈɑθɚ *the first* r *is lost by dissimilation* (§121).

Arthurian ɑrˈθjʊrɪən, -ˈθɪʊr-, -ˈθʊr-; ES ɑˈθ-

artichoke ˈɑrtɪˌtʃok; ES ˈɑ:tɪ-

article ˈɑrtɪkl̩; ES ˈɑ:tɪ-; |-d -d |-ling -klɪŋ, -kl̩ɪŋ

articular ɑrˈtɪkjəlɚ; ES ɑˈtɪkjələ(r

articulate *adj* ɑrˈtɪkjəlɪt; ES ɑˈtɪk-

articulate *v* ɑrˈtɪkjəˌlet; ES ɑˈtɪk-; |-d -ɪd

articulation ɑrˌtɪkjəˈleʃən, ˌɑrtɪkjə-; ES ɑˌtɪk-, ˌɑ:tɪk-

Artie ˈɑrtɪ; ES ˈɑ:tɪ

artifact ˈɑrtɪˌfækt; ES ˈɑ:tɪ-

artifice ˈɑrtəfɪs; ES ˈɑ:tə-; |-s -ɪz

artificer ɑrˈtɪfəsɚ; ES ɑˈtɪfəsə(r

artificial ˌɑrtəˈfɪʃəl; ES ˌɑ:tə-; |-ly -ɪ

artificiality ˌɑrtəˌfɪʃɪˈælɪtɪ, -fɪˈʃælɪtɪ; ES ˌɑ:tə-

artillery ɑrˈtɪlərɪ; ES ɑˈtɪl-; |-rist -rɪst

artisan ˈɑrtəzn̩; ES ˈɑ:təzn̩; |-ship -ˌʃɪp

artist ˈɑrtɪst; ES ˈɑ:tɪst; |-ry -rɪ

artiste ɑrˈtist; ES ɑ:ˈtist; (*Fr* arˈtist)

artistic ɑrˈtɪstɪk; ES ɑ:ˈtɪs-; |-al -l̩ |-ally -l̩ɪ, -ɪklɪ

artless ˈɑrtlɪs; ES ˈɑ:tlɪs

Artois ɑrˈtwa, -ˈtwɒ; ES ɑ:ˈt-; (*Fr* arˈtwa)

arty ˈɑrtɪ; ES ˈɑ:tɪ

Arundel *Engd, Can* ˈærəndl̩, *Sus loc.* ˈɑrndl̩ (Arndle *1788*); *Md* əˈrʌndl̩ (*see* Anne Arundel)

Arveragus ɑrˈvɛrəgəs; ES ɑˈvɛr-; |-'s -ɪz

Arviragus ɑrˈvɪrəgəs; ES ɑˈvɪr-; |-'s -ɪz

Aryan ˈɛrɪən, ˈær-, ˈɑr-, -rjən; S ˈær-, ˈer-, ˈɑr-

arytenoid ˌærɪˈtɪnɔɪd, əˈrɪtn̩ˌɔɪd

as *Rom weight* æs |asses ˈæsɪz

as *adv, etc: unstressed* əz, z, s; *rarely stressed* ˈæz, ˌæz

Asa ˈesə

asafetida, -foet- ˌæsəˈfɛtɪdə, æsˈfɛtɪdə

Asaph ˈæsəf, ˈesəf, ˈesæf

asbestos, -us æsˈbɛstəs, æz-

Asbury ˈæzˌbɛrɪ, -bərɪ

Ascalon *sword & Pal vil.* ˈæskəˌlan, -ˌlɒn, -lən

Ascanius əˈskenɪəs, æ- |-'s -ɪz

ascend əˈsɛnd |-ed -ɪd

ascendance, -ence əˈsɛndəns |-cy -ɪ |-nt -nt

ascension, A- əˈsɛnʃən

ascent əˈsɛnt

ascertain ˌæsɚˈten; ES ˌæsə-; |-ed -d

ascetic əˈsɛtɪk |-al -l̩ |-ally -l̩ɪ, -ɪklɪ

asceticism əˈsɛtəˌsɪzəm

Asch, Sholem ˈʃoləmˈæʃ (*Yiddish* ˈʃolɛmˈaʃ)

Ascham, a- ˈæskəm

Asclepias æsˈklipɪəs |-pius -pɪəs |-'s -ɪz

ascot, A- ˈæskət

ascribe əˈskraɪb |-d -d

Ascue ˈæskju, -kɪu

Ascutney əˈskʌtnɪ, *loc. often* ˈskʌtnɪ

asepsis əˈsɛpsɪs, e-, æ-

aseptic əˈsɛptɪk, e-, æ- |-ally -l̩ɪ, -ɪklɪ

asexual eˈsɛkʃʊəl, ə-, æ- |-ly -ɪ

Asgard ˈæsgɑrd, ˈæz-; ES -gɑ:d

ash, A- æʃ |-es -ɪz |-ed -t

ashamed əˈʃemd |-medly -mɪdlɪ

Ashanti əˈʃæntɪ

Ashburn ˈæʃbɚn; ES ˈæʃbən

Ashburnham *Mass* ˈæʃbɚnˌhæm; ES -bən-; *Engd* ˈæʃˌbɚnəm; ES -ˌbɜn-, -ˌbʒn-

Ashburton ˈæʃbɚtn̩; ES ˈæʃbətn̩

Ashby-de-la-Zouch ˈæʃbɪˌdɛləˈzuʃ, -dələ- |-'s -ɪz

Ashdod ˈæʃdɑd; ES+-dɒd

Ashdown ˈæʃˌdaʊn

ashes ˈæʃɪz |ashen ˈæʃən

Asheville ˈæʃvɪl; S+-vl̩

Ashkelon ˈæʃkəˌlan, -ˌlɒn, -lən

ashlar, -ler ˈæʃlɚ; ES ˈæʃlə(r

Ashmole ˈæʃmol |-an æʃˈmolɪən

Ashokan əˈʃokən

ashore əˈʃor, əˈʃɔr; ES əˈʃoə(r, E+əˈʃɔə(r

Ashtabula ˌæʃtəˈbjulə, -ˈbɪʊlə

Ashtoreth ˈæʃtərɪθ, -ˌreθ |*pl* -taroth -ˌroθ, -ˌrɒθ

Ashuelot ˈæʃwɪˌlat; ES+-ˌlɒt; *loc.*+ˌæʃuˈɪlət, ˌæʃəˈwɪlət, æʃˈwɪlət

Asia ˈeʒə, ˈeʃə |-n -n —ˈeʒə *prevails in US*, ˈeʃə *in Engd.*

Asiatic ˌeʒɪˈætɪk, ˌeʃ- |-al -l̩ |-ally -l̩ɪ, -ɪklɪ
aside əˈsaɪd
asinine ˈæsn̩ˌaɪn |-ninity ˌæsəˈnɪnətɪ
ask 'newt' æsk
ask v æsk; E ask, æsk, ɑsk; |-ed -skt, -st
askance əˈskæns |askant əˈskænt
Askelon sword ˈæskəˌlɑn, -ˌlɒn, -lən
askew əˈskju, əˈskɪu
Askew ˈæskju, -kɪu
aslant əˈslænt; E+əˈslɑnt, əˈslɑnt
asleep əˈslip
aslope əˈslop
Asmodeus ˌæzmoˈdiəs, ˌæs- |-'s -ɪz
asp æsp
asparagus əˈspærəgəs
Aspasia æsˈpeʒɪə, -ʃɪə
aspect ˈæspɛkt—in Shak. æˈspɛkt
aspen ˈæspɪn, -pən
asperges, A- əˈspɝˈdʒiz; ES əˈspɝ-, əˈspɝˈ-
aspergillum, A- ˌæspɚˈdʒɪləm; ES ˌæspə-; |-s -z |-la -lə
asperity æsˈpɛrətɪ, əˈspɛr-
asperse əˈspɝs; ES əˈspɜs, əˈspɝˈs; |-s -ɪz |-d -t
aspersion əˈspɝˈʒən, -ʃən; ES əˈspɝ-, əˈspɝˈ-
aspersorium ˌæspɚˈsorɪəm, -ˈsɔr-; ES ˌæspə-ˈsor-, E+-ˈsɔr-; |-s -z |-ria -rɪə
asphalt ˈæsfɔlt, -fælt |-ed -ɪd
asphaltic æsˈfɔltɪk, -ˈfæltɪk
asphaltum æsˈfæltəm
asphodel ˈæsfəˌdɛl
asphyxia æsˈfɪksɪə |-iate -ɪˌet |-iated -ɪˌetɪd
asphyxiation æsˌfɪksɪˈeʃən ˌæsfɪksɪ-
aspic ˈæspɪk
aspidistra, A- ˌæspɪˈdɪstrə
Aspinwall ˈæspɪnˌwɔl
aspirant əˈspaɪrənt, ˈæspərənt
aspirate n, adj ˈæspərɪt, ˈæsprɪt
aspirate v ˈæspəˌret |-d -ɪd |-tion ˌæspəˈreʃən
aspirator ˈæspəˌretɚ; ES -ˌretə(r
aspiratory əˈspaɪrəˌtorɪ, -ˌtɔrɪ; S -ˌtorɪ
aspire əˈspaɪr; ES əˈspaɪə(r; |-d -d
aspirin ˈæspərɪn, -prɪn
asquint əˈskwɪnt
Asquith ˈæskwɪθ
ass 'donkey' æs, 'blockhead' æs, ɑs |-es -ɪz
assafetida, -foet- ˌæsəˈfɛtɪdə, æsˈfɛt-
assagai ˈæsəˌgaɪ
assai əˈsɑ·i

assail əˈsel |-ed -d |-ant -ənt
Assam æˈsæm, ˈæsæm
assassin əˈsæsɪn |-ate -sn̩ˌet |-ated -sn̩ˌetɪd
assassination əˌsæsn̩ˈeʃən
assault əˈsɔlt |-ed -ɪd
assay n əˈse, ˈæse
assay v əˈse |-ed -d
assegai ˈæsəˌgaɪ
assemblage əˈsɛmblɪdʒ |-s -ɪz
assemble əˈsɛmbl̩ |-d -d |-ling əˈsɛmblɪŋ, -bl̩ɪŋ
assembly əˈsɛmblɪ |-man -mən, -ˌmæn |-men -mən, -ˌmɛn
assent əˈsɛnt |-ed -ɪd
assentation ˌæsɛnˈteʃən
assenter, -or əˈsɛntɚ; ES əˈsɛntə(r
Asser ˈæsɚ; ES ˈæsə(r
assert əˈsɝt; ES əˈsɜt, əˈsɝt; |-ed -ɪd
assertion əˈsɝˈʃən; ES əˈsɜʃ-, əˈsɝˈʃ-; |-tive -tɪv |-tory -tərɪ
assess əˈsɛs |-es -ɪz |-ed -t |-or -ɚ; ES -ə(r
assessorial ˌæsəˈsorɪəl, -ˈsɔr-; S -ˈsor-
asset ˈæsɛt |-s -s
asseverate əˈsɛvəˌret |-d -ɪd
asseveration əˌsɛvəˈreʃən
assibilate əˈsɪbl̩ˌet |-d -ɪd
assibilation əˌsɪbl̩ˈeʃən
assiduity ˌæsəˈdjuətɪ, -ˈdɪu-, -ˈdu-
assiduous əˈsɪdʒuəs
assign əˈsaɪn |-ed -d
assignability əˌsaɪnəˈbɪlətɪ
assignable əˈsaɪnəbl̩ |-bly -blɪ
assignat ˈæsɪgˌnæt (Fr asiˈɲa)
assignation ˌæsɪgˈneʃən
assignee əsaɪˈni, ˌæsəˈni, ˌæsaɪ-
assigner əˈsaɪnɚ; ES -nə(r
assignor əsaɪˈnɔr, ˌæsəˈnɔr; ES -ˈnɔə(r
assimilability əˌsɪml̩əˈbɪlətɪ
assimilable əˈsɪml̩əbl̩
assimilate n əˈsɪml̩ɪt, -ˌet
assimilate v əˈsɪml̩ˌet |-d -ɪd |-tive -ɪv
assimilation əˌsɪml̩ˈeʃən
assimilatory əˈsɪml̩əˌtorɪ, -ˌtɔrɪ; S -ˌtorɪ
Assiniboia əˌsɪnəˈbɔɪə
Assiniboine əˈsɪnəˌbɔɪn
Assisi əˈsizɪ (It ɑsˈsiːzi)
assist əˈsɪst |-ed -ɪd |-ance -əns |-ant -ənt
assize əˈsaɪz |-s -ɪz |-d -d
associable əˈsoʃɪəbl̩, -ʃəbl̩

|full fʊl |tooth tuθ |further ˈfɝˈðɚ; ES ˈfɝˈðə |custom ˈkʌstəm |while hwaɪl |how haʊ |toy tɔɪ
|using ˈjuzɪŋ |fuse fjuz, fɪuz |dish dɪʃ |vision ˈvɪʒən |Eden ˈidn̩ |cradle ˈkredl̩ |keep 'em ˈkipm̩

associate *n, adj* ə'soʃɪt, -ˌet
associate *v* ə'soʃɪˌet |-d -ɪd |-tive -ɪv
association əˌsosɪ'eʃən, əˌsoʃɪ——*It is doubt-ful which of these prons. prevails.*
assoil ə'sɔɪl |-ed -d
assonance 'æsənəns |-s -ɪz |-d -t |-nant -nənt
assort ə'sɔrt; ES ə'sɔət; |-ed -ɪd
assuage ə'swedʒ |-s -ɪz |-d -d
assuasive ə'swesɪv
assume ə'sum, ə'sɪum, ə'sjum |-d -d
assumpsit ə'sʌmpsɪt
assumption, A- ə'sʌmpʃən |-tive -tɪv
assurance ə'ʃurəns |-s -ɪz
assure ə'ʃur; ES ə'ʃuə(r; |-d -d |-dly -ɪdlɪ
assurgency ə's3ˈdʒənsɪ; ES ə's3dʒ-, ə's3ˈdʒ-; |-ent -ənt
Assyria ə'sɪrɪə |-n -n
Assyriology əˌsɪrɪ'alədʒɪ; ES+-'ɒl-; |-gist -dʒɪst
Astarte æs'tartɪ; ES -'ta:tɪ, E+-'ta:tɪ
astatic e'stætɪk, ə-, æ- |-ally -ḷɪ, -ɪklɪ
Astell 'æstḷ
aster, A- 'æstɚ; ES 'æstə(r
asterisk 'æstəˌrɪsk
asterism 'æstəˌrɪzəm
astern ə'st3ˈn; ES ə'st3n, ə'st3ˈn
asteroid 'æstəˌrɔɪd |-al ˌæstə'rɔɪdḷ
asthenia æs'θinɪə, ˌæsθə'naɪə
asthma 'æzmə, 'æsmə
asthmatic æz'mætɪk, æs- |-al -ḷ |-ally -ḷɪ, -ɪklɪ
astigmatic ˌæstɪg'mætɪk |-al -ḷ |-ally -ḷɪ, -ɪklɪ
astigmatism ə'stɪgməˌtɪzəm
astir ə'st3ˈ; ES ə'st3(r, ə'st3ˈ
astonish ə'stanɪʃ; ES+-'stɒn-; |-es -ɪz |-ed -t
astony ə'stanɪ; ES+-'stɒn-; |-nied -nɪd
Astor 'æstɚ; ES 'æstə(r
Astoria æs'torɪə, -'tɔrɪə; S -'torɪə
astound ə'staund |-ed -ɪd
astrachan, A- 'æstrəkən
astraddle ə'strædḷ
astragal 'æstrəgḷ
astrakhan 'æstrəkən
Astrakhan ˌæstrə'kæn
astral 'æstrəl |-ly -ɪ
astray ə'stre

astride ə'straɪd
astringe ə'strɪndʒ |-s -ɪz |-d -d
astringency ə'strɪndʒənsɪ |-gent -dʒənt
astrolabe 'æstrəˌleb
astrologer ə'stralədʒɚ; ES ə'stralədʒə(r, -'strɒl-; |-gy -dʒɪ -gist -dʒɪst
astrologic ˌæstrə'ladʒɪk; ES+-'lɒdʒ-; |-al -ḷ |-ally -ḷɪ, -ɪklɪ
astronomer ə'stranəmɚ; ES ə'stranəmə(r, -'strɒn-; |-my -mɪ
astronomic ˌæstrə'namɪk; ES+-'nɒm-; |-al -ḷ |-ally -ḷɪ, -ɪklɪ
Astrophel 'æstrəˌfɛl
astrophotographic 'æstrəˌfotə'græfɪk
astrophotography ˌæstrəfo'tagrəfɪ, -'tɒg-
astrophysical ˌæstro'fɪzɪkḷ |-icist -ɪsɪst
astrophysics ˌæstro'fɪzɪks
astrosphere 'æstrəˌsfɪr; ES-ˌsfɪə(r, S+-ˌsfɛə(r
astrut ə'strʌt
astute ə'stjut, -'strut, -'stut
Astyanax ə'staɪəˌnæks |-'s -ɪz
Asuncion *Am Sp* asun'sjon
asunder ə'sʌndɚ; ES ə'sʌndə(r
asylum ə'saɪləm |-s -z |-la -lə
asymmetric ˌesɪ'mɛtrɪk, ˌæ- |-al -ḷ |-ally -ḷɪ, -ɪklɪ
asymmetry e'sɪmɪtrɪ, æ-
asymptote 'æsɪmˌtot, 'æsɪmp-
asymptotic ˌæsɪm'tatɪk, -sɪmp-; ES+-'tɒt-; |-al -ḷ |-ally -ḷɪ, -ɪklɪ
asynchronous e'sɪŋkrənəs, æ-, -'sɪn-
asyndeton ə'sɪndətən, -ˌtan; ES+-ˌtɒn
at *stressed* 'æt, ˌæt; *unstr.* ət, ɪt
Atalanta ˌætḷ'æntə
at all *'to any degree'* ə'tɔl, ət'ɔl—*In* ət'ɔl *the* t *is not aspirated and is usually voiced. This is also the pron. when* at all *is an ordinary prepositional phrase, as in* It stops at some stations, but not at all. *Cf* It stops at no small stations at all (ə'tɔl).
atamasco ˌætə'mæsko
atar 'ætɚ; ES 'ætə(r
Atascosa ˌætə'skosə
atavic ə'tævɪk |atavism 'ætəˌvɪzəm
atavistic ˌætə'vɪstɪk |-ally -ḷɪ, -ɪklɪ
ataxia ə'tæksɪə |ataxy ə'tæksɪ
Atchafalaya əˌtʃæfə'laɪə, ˌtʃæfə-, æˌtʃæfə-
Atchison 'ætʃɪsn̩
Ate, ate *myth.* 'etɪ, 'eti

Key: *See in full §§3–47.* bee **bi** |pity 'pɪtɪ (§6) |rate ret |yet jɛt |sang sæŋ |angry 'æŋ·grɪ |bath bæθ; E baθ (§10) |ah ɑ |far fɑr |watch watʃ, wɒtʃ (§12) |jaw dʒɔ |gorge gɔrdʒ |go go

ate *past of* eat et—*The past tense* ɛt, *occas.
in cultivated S, is spelt* ate *in Engd, but
properly belongs to the old past spelling
form* eat (*cf* threat, sweat), *as does also the
old past pron.* it (*cf* meat, seat). *See* eat.

-ate *unstressed ending* -ɪt, -ət—*In the vocab.
when only the pron.* -ɪt *is given, it is to be
understood that many speakers pronounce
-ət, as in* gamut ˈgæmət. *When more or less
stressed* (*with or without accent mark*), -ate
is pronounced -et, *as in* permeate ˈpɝmɪˌet,
mandate ˈmændet, oblate ˈablet.

atelier ˈætlˌje (*Fr* atəˈlje)

Athabasca, -ka ˌæθəˈbæskə |-n -n

athanasia ˌæθəˈneʒɪə

Athanasian ˌæθəˈneʒən

Athanasius ˌæθəˈneʃɪəs, -ʃəs |-ʼs -ɪz

athanasy əˈθænəsɪ

Athapascan ˌæθəˈpæskən

atheism ˈeθɪˌɪzəm |atheist ˈeθɪɪst

atheistic ˌeθɪˈɪstɪk |-al -ḷ |-ally -ḷɪ, -ɪklɪ

atheling ˈæθəlɪŋ, ˈæðəlɪŋ (*OE* ˈæð-)

Athelstan ˈæθəlˌstæn, ˈæðəl-, -stən (*OE* ˈæð-)

Athena əˈθinə |Athene əˈθini

athenaeum, A-, -neum ˌæθəˈniəm

Athenian əˈθinɪən

Athens ˈæθɪnz, -ənz |-ʼs -ɪz |*N Y* +ˈeθ-

Atherton ˈæθɚtən; ES ˈæθətən

athirst əˈθɝst; ES əˈθɜst, əˈθɝst

athlete ˈæθlit

athletic æθˈlɛtɪk |-s -s |-ally -ḷɪ, -ɪklɪ

Athlone æθˈlon

Athol *Mass* ˈæθal, -θɒl, -θəl

Atholl, -ole *Scotl* ˈæθəl

at home, at-home ətˈhom—*The pron.* əˈtom,
freq. in Engd, is rare in US.

Athos ˈæθas, ˈe-, -θɒs

athwart əˈθwɔrt; ES əˈθwɔət; |-ship -ʃɪp

atilt əˈtɪlt

atingle əˈtɪŋgḷ

-ative *ending* -ˌetɪv, -ətɪv, *as in* cumulative,
operative, *etc. When the main accent is on
the second syllable before* -ative, *there is
usually a secondary accent on the* -a- *of*
-ative (in ˈiˈtiˌative ɪˈnɪʃˈ·ɪˌe·tɪv); *but in
familiar words some speakers often pronounce* -ative *without accent* (-ətɪv), *as*
ɪˈnɪʃɪətɪv. *When only* -ˌetɪv *is given,* -ətɪv
is to be understood as a possible variant.

Atkins ˈætkɪnz |-ʼs -ɪz |-kinson ˈætkɪnsṇ

Atlanta ətˈlæntə, æt-

atlantean, A- ˌætlænˈtiən

atlantes *pl of* atlas ətˈlæntiz, æt-

Atlantic ətˈlæntɪk

Atlantis ətˈlæntɪs |-ʼs -ɪz

atlas, A- ˈætləs |-es -ɪz |atlantes ətˈlæntiz,
æt-

atman, A- ˈatmən

Atmore ˈætmor, -mɔr; ES -moə(r, E+
-mɔə(r

atmosphere ˈætməsˌfɪr; ES -ˌfɪə(r, S+
-ˌfɛə(r

atmospheric ˌætməsˈfɛrɪk |-al -ḷ |-ally -ḷɪ,
-ɪklɪ

atoll ˈætal, -tɒl, əˈtal, -ˈtɒl

atom ˈætəm |-ism -ˌɪzəm |-y -ɪ

atomic əˈtamɪk, æ-; ES+-ˈtɒm-; |-al -ḷ |-ally
-ḷɪ, -ɪklɪ

atomicity ˌætəˈmɪsətɪ

atomization ˌætəməˈzeʃən, -aɪˈz-

atomize ˈætəmˌaɪz |-s -ɪz |-d -d

atonal eˈtonḷ, æ- |-ly -ɪ |-ity ˌetoˈnælətɪ

atone əˈton |-d -d

atonic əˈtanɪk, e-, æ-; ES+-ˈtɒn-

atonicity ˌætəˈnɪsətɪ, ˌe-, -toˈn-

atony ˈætənɪ

atop əˈtap; ES+əˈtɒp

atrabilious ˌætrəˈbɪljəs

Atreus ˈetrus, -trɪus, ˈetrɪ·əs |-ʼs -ɪz

atrip əˈtrɪp

atrium ˈetrɪəm |-s -z |-ria -rɪə

atrocious əˈtroʃəs

atrocity əˈtrasətɪ; ES+-ˈtrɒs-

atrophy ˈætrəfɪ |-phied -fɪd

atropine ˈætrəˌpin, -pɪn |-pin -pɪn

Atropos ˈætrəˌpas; ES+-ˌpɒs; |-ʼs -ɪz

attach əˈtætʃ |-es -ɪz |-ed -t

attaché ˌætəˈʃe, əˈtæʃe (*Fr* ataˈʃe)

attack əˈtæk |-ed -t

attain əˈten |-ed -d

attainable əˈtenəbḷ |-bility əˌtenəˈbɪlətɪ

attainder əˈtendɚ; ES əˈtendə(r

attaint əˈtent |-ed -ɪd

attainture əˈtentʃɚ; ES əˈtentʃə(r

Attala *Miss* ˈætlə |Attalla *Ala* əˈtælə

attar ˈætɚ; ES ˈætə(r

attemper əˈtɛmpɚ; ES -pə(r; |-ed -d |-ing
əˈtɛmpərɪŋ, əˈtɛmprɪŋ

|full fʊl |tooth tuθ |further ˈfɝðɚ; ES ˈfɜðə |custom ˈkʌstəm |while hwaɪl |how haʊ |toy tɔɪ
|using ˈjuzɪŋ |fuse fjuz, fɪuz |dish dɪʃ |vision ˈvɪʒən |Eden ˈidṇ |cradle ˈkredḷ |keep ʼem ˈkipṃ

attempt əˈtɛmpt |-ed -ɪd
attend əˈtɛnd |-ed -ɪd |-ance -əns |-ant -ənt
attent əˈtɛnt
attention əˈtɛnʃən |-tive -tɪv
attenuate *adj* əˈtɛnjuɪt
attenuate *v* əˈtɛnjuˌet |-d -ɪd
attenuation əˌtɛnjuˈeʃən
Atterbury ˈætɚˌbɛrɪ, -bərɪ; ES ˈætə-
attest əˈtɛst |-ed -ɪd |-ation ˌætɛsˈteʃən
attic ˈætɪk
Attic ˈætɪk |-a -ə |-ism ˈætɪˌsɪzəm
Attila ˈætl̩ə
attire əˈtaɪr; ES əˈtaɪə(r; |-d -d
attitude ˈætəˌtjud, -ˌtɪud, -ˌtud
attitudinize ˌætəˈtjudn̩ˌaɪz, -ˈtɪud-, -ˈtud- |-s -ɪz |-d -d
Attleboro ˈætl̩ˌbɝo, -ə; ES -ˌbɜr-, -ˌbʌr-, -ˌbɝ-
Attlee, Atlee ˈætlɪ, ˈætli
attorn əˈtɝn; ES əˈtɜn, əˈtɝn; |-ed -d
attorney əˈtɝnɪ; ES əˈtɜnɪ, əˈtɝnɪ
attract əˈtrækt |-ed -ɪd
attractability əˌtræktəˈbɪlətɪ
attraction əˈtrækʃən |-tive -tɪv
attribute *n* ˈætrəˌbjut, -ˌbrɪut
attribute *v* əˈtrɪbjut |-d -bjətɪd |-tive -bjətɪv
attribution ˌætrəˈbjuʃən, -ˈbrɪu-
attrite *adj* əˈtraɪt |-d -ɪd
attrition əˈtrɪʃən, æ-
attune əˈtjun, əˈtɪun, əˈtun |-d -d
atwain əˈtwen
Atwater ˈætˌwɔtɚ, -ˌwɑtɚ, -ˌwɒtɚ; ES -tə(r
atypic eˈtɪpɪk, æ- |-al -l̩ |-ally -l̩ɪ, -ɪklɪ
au *Fr* o
Aubrey, -bry ˈɔbrɪ
auburn, A- ˈɔbɚn; ES ˈɔbən
Auckland ˈɔklənd
auction ˈɔkʃən |-ed -d
auctioneer ˌɔkʃənˈɪr; ES -ˈɪə(r, S+-ˈɛə(r
audacious ɔˈdeʃəs |-dacity ɔˈdæsətɪ
audibility ˌɔdəˈbɪlətɪ
audible ˈɔdəbl̩ |-bly -blɪ
audience ˈɔdɪəns, -djəns |-s -ɪz |-ent -dɪənt
audile ˈɔdɪl
audio ˈɔdɪˌo |audiogram ˈɔdɪəˌgræm
audiometer ˌɔdɪˈɑmətɚ; ES -ˈɑmətə(r, -ˈɒm-
audiphone, A- ˈɔdəˌfon
audit ˈɔdɪt |-ed -ɪd |-or -ɚ; ES -ə(r
audition ɔˈdɪʃən |-ed -d |-ing -ʃənɪŋ, -ʃnɪŋ
auditorium ˌɔdəˈtorɪəm, -ˈtɔr-; S -ˈtor-
auditory ˈɔdəˌtorɪ, -ˌtɔrɪ; S -ˌtorɪ
Audley ˈɔdlɪ
Audrey ˈɔdrɪ
Audubon ˈɔdəˌbɑn; ES+-ˌbɒn
Auer ˈaʊɚ; ES ˈaʊ·ə(r
au fait oˈfe (*Fr* oˈfɛ)
Aufidius ɔˈfɪdɪəs |-'s -ɪz
auf Wiedersehen *Ger* aʊfˈvi:dərˌze:ən
Augeas ɔˈdʒiəs |-'s -ɪz |-gean -ˈdʒiən
augend ˈɔdʒɛnd
auger ˈɔgɚ; ES ˈɔgə(r
aught ɔt
Auglaize ɔˈglez |-'s -ɪz
augment *n* ˈɔgmɛnt
augment *v* ɔgˈmɛnt |-ed -ɪd |-ative -ətɪv
augmenter ɔgˈmɛntɚ; ES -ˈmɛntə(r
au gratin oˈgrɑtn̩, oˈgrætn̩, -tɪn (*Fr* ograˈtæ̃)
Augsburg ˈɔgzbɝg; ES -bɜg, -bɝg; (*Ger* ˈaʊksbʊrk)
augur ˈɔgɚ; ES ˈɔgə(r; |-ed -d |-ing -gərɪŋ, -grɪŋ
augury ˈɔgjərɪ
august ɔˈgʌst (ˈauˌgust ˈoffice)
August ˈɔgəst
Augusta ɔˈgʌstə, əˈgʌs- |-tan -tən
Augustine *saint* ˈɔgəsˌtin, əˈgʌstɪn, ɔ-; *isl. Alas* ˈɔgəstɪn
Augustinian ˌɔgəsˈtɪnɪən
Augustus ɔˈgʌstəs, əˈgʌs- |-'s -ɪz
au jus *Fr* oˈʒy
auk ɔk |-let -lɪt
auld ɔld
Aulis ˈɔlɪs |-'s -ɪz
Ault ɔlt
Aumerle ɔˈmɝl; ES ɔˈmɜl, ɔˈmɝl
au naturel *Fr* onatyˈrɛl
aunt ænt; E ant, ɑnt, ænt—*Sporadic instances of* ant, ɑnt *occur in the N and S.*
aura ˈɔrə |-s -z |-rae -ri
aural ˈɔrəl |-ly -ɪ
Aurangzeb ˈɔrʌŋˈzɛb
aureate *adj* ˈɔrɪɪt, -ˌet
aureate *v* ˈɔrɪˌet |-d -ɪd
Aurelia ɔˈrilɪə, -ljə |-n -n
Aurelius ɔˈrilɪəs |-'s -ɪz
aureole ˈɔrɪˌol |-d -d
au revoir ˌorəˈvɔr; ES -ˈvɔə(r; (*Fr* orəˈvwa:r)

Key: *See in full §§3–47.* bee bi |pity ˈpɪtɪ (§6) |rate ret |yet jɛt |sang sæŋ |angry ˈæŋ·grɪ |bath bæθ; E baθ (§10) |ah ɑ |far fɑr |watch wɑtʃ, wɒtʃ (§12) |jaw dʒɔ |gorge gɔrdʒ |go go

auric 'ɔrɪk
auricle 'ɔrɪkl̩
auricular ɔ'rɪkjələ; ES -lə(r
auriculate adj ɔ'rɪkjəlɪt |-lated -ˌletɪd
auriferous ɔ'rɪfərəs
Auriga ɔ'raɪgə |gen Aurigae ɔ'raɪdʒi
Aurignacian ˌɔrɪg'neʃən
aurist 'ɔrɪst
aurochs 'brɑks; ES+-ɒks
aurora, A- ɔ'rorə, ə-, -'rɔrə; S -'rorə; |-s -z
|-rae -ri
aurora australis ɔ'rorə ɔs'trelɪs, ə-, -'rɔrə; S
-'rorə
aurora borealis ɔ'rorə ˌborɪ'ælɪs, ə-, -'rɔrə
ˌbɔrɪ-, -'elɪs; S -'rorə ˌborɪ-
auroral ɔ'rorəl, ə-, -'rɔrəl; S -'rorəl; |-ly -ɪ
aurorean ɔ'rorɪən, ə-, -'rɔr-; S -'ror-
Aurorian ɔ'rorɪən, -'rɔr-; S -'ror-
aurum 'ɔrəm |aurous 'ɔrəs
Aurungzeb, -ebe 'ɔrʌŋ'zɛb, -'zib
Ausable, Au Sable ɔ'sebl̩ ('Au,sable 'Chasm)
auscultate 'ɔskəlˌtet |-d -ɪd
auscultation ˌɔskəl'teʃən
Auslander 'ɔsˌlændɚ, 'aʊs-; ES -ˌlændə(r
Ausonia ɔ'sonɪə |-n -n
auspex 'ɔspɛks |pl auspices 'ɔspɪˌsiz
auspice 'ɔspɪs |-s -ɪz
auspicial ɔ'spɪʃəl |-cious -ʃəs
Austen 'ɔstɪn, -tən
Auster 'ɔstɚ; ES 'ɔstə(r
austere ɔ'stɪr; ES ɔ'stɪə(r, S+ɔ'stɛə(r
austerity ɔ'stɛrətɪ
Austerlitz 'ɔstɚˌlɪts; ES 'ɔstə-; |-'s -ɪz (Ger
'aʊstər-)
Austin 'ɔstɪn, -tən
austral 'ɔstrəl
Australasia ˌɔstrəl'eʒə, -ʃə |-n -n
Australia ɔ'streljə |-n -n
Austrasia ɔ'streʒə, -ʃə |-n -n
Austria 'ɔstrɪə |-n -n
Austria-Hungary 'ɔstrɪə'hʌŋgərɪ
Austro-Hungarian 'ɔstrohʌŋ'gɛrɪən, -'ger-
Austronesian ˌɔstro'niʒən, -ʃən
autarch 'ɔtɑrk; ES -tɑ:k, E+-tɑ:k; |-y -ɪ
autarchic ɔ'tɑrkɪk; ES ɔ'tɑ:k-, E+ɔ'tɑ:k-;
|-al -l̩
autarky 'ɔtɑrkɪ; ES -tɑ:kɪ, E+-tɑ:kɪ; |-kist
-kɪst
authentic ɔ'θɛntɪk |-al -l̩ |-ally -l̩ɪ |-icly -ɪklɪ

authenticate ɔ'θɛntɪˌket |-d -ɪd
authentication ɔˌθɛntɪ'keʃən, ˌɔθɛntɪ-
authenticity ˌɔθən'tɪsətɪ, -θɛn-
author 'ɔθɚ; ES 'ɔθə(r; |-ess -ɪs |-esses -ɪsɪz
authoritarian əˌθɔrə'tɛrɪən, əˌθɑr-, əˌθɒr-,
-'ter- |-ism -ˌɪzəm
authoritative ə'θɔrəˌtetɪv, ə'θɑr-, ə'θɒr-
authority ə'θɔrətɪ, ə'θɑr-, ə'θɒr-
authorization ˌɔθərə'zeʃən, -aɪ'z-
authorize 'ɔθəˌraɪz |-s -ɪz |-d -d
autism 'ɔtɪzəm |-ist -ɪst |-tistic ɔ'tɪstɪk
auto 'ɔto
autobiographic ˌɔtəˌbaɪə'græfɪk |-al -l̩ |-ally
-l̩ɪ, -ɪklɪ
autobiography ˌɔtəbaɪ'ɑgrəfɪ, -bɪ-, -'ɒg-
autochthon ɔ'tɑkθən; ES+-'tɒk-; |-s -z
|-es -ˌiz
autochthonous ɔ'tɑkθənəs; ES+-'tɒk-
autoclave 'ɔtəˌklev |-d -d
autocracy ɔ'tɑkrəsɪ; ES+-'tɒk-
autocrat 'ɔtəˌkræt
autocratic ˌɔtə'krætɪk |-al -l̩ |-ally -l̩ɪ, -ɪklɪ
auto-da-fé ˌɔtodə'fe |pl autos- ˌɔtoz-
autogenous ɔ'tadʒənəs; ES+-'tɒdʒ-
autogiro, A- ˌɔto'dʒaɪro
autograph 'ɔtəˌgræf; E+-ˌgraf, -ˌgrɑf
autographic ˌɔtə'græfɪk |-al -l̩ |-ally -l̩ɪ,
-ɪklɪ
autography ɔ'tagrəfɪ, -'tɒg-
autogyro, A- ˌɔto'dʒaɪro
autohypnosis ˌɔtohɪp'nosɪs
autoinfection ˌɔto·ɪn'fɛkʃən
autointoxication ˌɔto·ɪnˌtaksə'keʃən; ES+
-ˌtɒk-
Autolycus ɔ'taləkəs; ES+-'tɒl-; |-'s -ɪz
automat 'ɔtəˌmæt
automata ɔ'tamətə; ES+-'tɒm-
automatic ˌɔtə'mætɪk |-al -l̩ |-ally -l̩ɪ, -ɪklɪ
automatism ɔ'taməˌtɪzəm; ES+-'tɒm-
automaton ɔ'taməˌtan, -tən; ES+ɔ'tɒmə-
ˌtɒn, -tən; |-s -z |-ta -tə
automobile adj ˌɔtə'mobɪl
automobile n 'ɔtəməˌbil, ˌɔtə'mobil, ˌɔtəmə-
'bil
automotive ˌɔtə'motɪv
autonomic ˌɔtə'namɪk; ES+-'nɒm-; |-al -l̩
|-ally -l̩ɪ, -ɪklɪ
autonomist ɔ'tanəmɪst; ES+-'tɒn-; |-mous
-məs |-my -mɪ

|full fʊl |tooth tuθ |further 'fɝðɚ; ES 'fɝðə |custom 'kʌstəm |while hwaɪl |how haʊ |toy tɔɪ
|using 'juzɪŋ |fuse fjuz, fɪuz |dish dɪʃ |vision 'vɪʒən |Eden 'idn̩ |cradle 'kredl̩ |keep 'em 'kipm̩

autopsy 'ɔtɑpsɪ, 'ɔtəpsɪ; ES+-tɒp-
autos-da-fé pl ˌɔtozdə'fe
autosuggestion ˌɔtəsəg'dʒɛstʃən, -sə'dʒɛs-
autumn 'ɔtəm |-al ɔ'tʌmn̩| |-ally ɔ'tʌmn̩ɪ
Auvergne o'vɜˑn; ES o'vɜn, o'vɜˑn; (Fr o'vɛrˌɲ, ɔ̃-)
aux Fr o
auxiliary ɔg'zɪljərɪ, -'zɪlərɪ, -'zɪlɪˌɛrɪ
avail ə'vel |-ed -d
availability əˌvelə'bɪlətɪ
available ə'veləb̩l |-bly -blɪ
avalanche 'ævl̩ˌæntʃ; E+-ˌantʃ, -ˌɑntʃ; |-s -ɪz |-d -t
Avalon, -llon 'ævl̩ˌan, -ˌɒn (Fr ava'lõ)
avarice 'ævərɪs, 'ævrɪs |-cious ˌævə'rɪʃəs
avast ə'væst; E+ə'vast, ə'vɑst
avatar ˌævə'tɑr; ES -'tɑː(r, E+-'tɑː(r
avaunt ə'vɔnt, ə'vɒnt, ə'vɑnt
ave, A- 'evɪ, 'ave
Avebury, Abury 'ebərɪ, 'evˌbɛrɪ, -bərɪ
Ave Maria 'avɪmə'riə
Ave Maria Lane Lond 'evɪmə ˌraɪə'len
Ave Mary 'evɪ'mɛrɪ, -'mɛːrɪ, -'merɪ, -'mærɪ
avenge ə'vɛndʒ |-s -ɪz |-d -d
avens 'ævɪnz, -ənz |-es -ɪz
Aventine 'ævənˌtaɪn, -tɪn
aventurine, -in ə'vɛntʃərɪn
avenue 'ævəˌnu, -ˌnɪu, -ˌnju
aver 'assert' ə'vɜˑ; ES ə'vɜ(r, ə'vɜˑ; |-red -d
aver 'horse' 'evɚ; ES 'evə(r
average 'ævrɪdʒ, 'ævərɪdʒ |-s -ɪz |-d -d
Avernus ə'vɜˑnəs; ES ə'vɜ-, ə'vɜˑ-; |-'s -ɪz
averse ə'vɜˑs; ES ə'vɜs, ə'vɜˑs
aversion ə'vɜˑʒən, -ʃən; ES ə'vɜ-, ə'vɜˑ-
avert ə'vɜˑt; ES ə'vɜt, ə'vɜˑt; |-ed -ɪd
Avery 'evərɪ, 'evrɪ
Aves pl of Avis 'eviz
Avesta ə'vɛstə
avian 'evɪən
aviary 'evɪˌɛrɪ
aviate 'evɪˌet, 'æv- |-d -ɪd |-tor -ɚ; ES -ə(r
aviation ˌevɪ'eʃən, ˌævɪ-
aviculture 'evɪˌkʌltʃɚ; ES -ˌkʌltʃə(r
avid 'ævɪd |avidity ə'vɪdətɪ
Avignon ə'vinjõ, ə'vɪnjən (Fr avi'ɲõ)
Avoca ə'vokə
avocado ˌɑvə'kɑdo, ˌævə-
avocation ˌævə'keʃən, ˌævo-
avocet 'ævəˌsɛt

avoid ə'vɔɪd |-ed -ɪd |-ance -ɳs
avoirdupois ˌævɚdə'pɔɪz; ES ˌævə-
Avon 'evən, 'ævən, Warwickshire 'evən, Scotl 'evən, an
Avon Lake, Avon Park 'evan, -ɒn
avoset 'ævəˌsɛt
avouch ə'vautʃ |-es -ɪz |-ed -t
avow ə'vau |-ed -d |-al -əl |-edly -ɪdlɪ
avuncular ə'vʌŋkjəlɚ; ES -jələ(r; |-late -lɪt
await ə'wet |-ed -ɪd
awake ə'wek |past awoke ə'wok or awaked ə'wekt |pptc awaked ə'wekt or awoke ə'wok
awaken ə'wekən |-ed -d |-ing -kənɪŋ, -knɪŋ
award ə'wɔrd; ES ə'wɔəd; |-ed -ɪd
aware ə'wɛr, ə'wær; E ə'wɛə(r, ES ə'wæə(r
awash ə'waʃ, ə'wɔʃ, ə'wɒʃ
away ə'we
awe ɔ |-d -d
aweary ə'wɪrɪ, ə'wɪrɪ; S+ə'wɛrɪ
awedness 'ɔdnɪs
aweful 'ɔful |-ly -ɪ
aweigh ə'we
aweless 'ɔlɪs |awelessness 'ɔlɪsnɪs
awesome 'ɔsəm
awful 'impressive' 'ɔful |-ly -ɪ
awful 'great,' 'ugly' 'ɔfl̩ |-ly 'ɔfl̩ɪ, 'ɔflɪ
awheel ə'hwil
awhile ə'hwaɪl
awkward 'ɔkwɚd; ES 'ɔkwəd
awl ɔl
awless 'ɔlɪs |awlessness 'ɔlɪsnɪs
awlless 'ɔllɪs
awn ɔn |-ed -d
awning 'ɔnɪŋ
awoke ə'wok |awoken arch. ə'wokən
awork ə'wɜˑk; ES ə'wɜk, ə'wɜˑk
awry ə'raɪ
ax, axe æks |axes 'æksɪz |axed ækst
axes pl of axis 'æksiz
axial 'æksɪəl |-ly -ɪ
axil 'æksɪl |axile 'æksɪl, -aɪl
axilla æk'sɪlə |-s -z |-lae -li
axillary 'æksəˌlɛrɪ
axiom 'æksɪəm
axiomatic ˌæksɪə'mætɪk |-al -l̩ |-ally -l̩ɪ, -ɪklɪ
axis 'æksɪs |axes 'æksiz
axle 'æks̩l |-d -d

axletree ˈæksḷˌtri, -trɪ
Axminster ˈæksˌmɪnstɚ; ES -ˌmɪnstə(r
axolotl ˈæksəˌlɑtḷ; ES+-ˌlɒtḷ
ay *intj 'alas!'* e
ay, aye *'always'* e—ay *is the better spelling*
ayah ˈɑjə
Aydelotte ˈedḷˌɑt; ES+-ˌɒt
Ayden ˈedṇ
aye, ay *'yes'* aɪ—aye *is the better spelling*
Ayer ɛr, ær; E ɛə(r, ES æə(r
Aylesbury ˈelzˌbɛrɪ, -bərɪ
Aylmer ˈelmɚ; ES ˈelmə(r
Ayr ɛr, ær; E ɛə(r, ES æə(r
Ayres ɛrz, ærz; E ɛəz, ES æəz; |-'s -ɪz
Ayrshire ˈɛrʃɪr, ˈær-, -ʃɚ; E ˈɛəʃɪə(r, -ʃə(r, ES ˈæə-
Ayscough, -cue ˈæskju, ˈes-, -kɪu
Ayton, Aytoun ˈetṇ
Azalea əˈzelɪə |azalea əˈzeljə

Azazel əˈzezəl, ˈæzəˌzɛl
Azerbaijan ˌɑzɚbaɪˈdʒɑn, ˌæzɚ-; ES -zə-
azimuth ˈæzəməθ |-al ˌæzəˈmʌθəl
azine ˈæzin, -ɪn |-in -ɪn
Azof ˈɑzɑf, -zɒf
azoic əˈzo·ɪk
azole ˈæzol, əˈzol
Azores əˈzorz, ˈezorz, -ɔrz; ES -oəz, E+ -ɔəz
azorite ˈæzəˌraɪt
azote ˈæzot, əˈzot
azoth ˈæzɑθ, -ɒθ
Azov ˈɑzɑf, -zɒf, ˈezɑv, ˈezɒv
Azrael ˈæzrɪəl
Aztec ˈæztɛk |-an -ən
azure ˈæʒɚ, ˈeʒɚ; ES -ʒə(r; |-d -d
azurine ˈæʒərɪn, -ˌaɪn
azurite ˈæʒəˌraɪt
Azusa əˈzusə

B

B, b *letter* bi |*pl* B's, Bs, *poss* B's biz
baa bæ:, ba:, bɑ: |3 *sg* baaes, *pl n* baas -z |-ed -d |-ing -ɪŋ
Baal ˈbeəl, bel
babbitt, B- ˈbæbɪt |-ed -ɪd
babble ˈbæbḷ |-d -d |-ling ˈbæbḷɪŋ, -blɪŋ
babe beb
Babel ˈbebḷ, ˈbæbḷ
Bab el Mandeb ˈbæbˌɛlˈmændɛb, ˈbɑbˌɛlˈmɑn-
baboo, babu ˈbɑbu
baboon bæˈbun, bəˈbun
baby ˈbebɪ |-bied -bɪd
Babylon ˈbæbḷən
Babylonia ˌbæbḷˈonɪə, -njə |-n -n
baccalaureate ˌbækəˈlɔrɪt
baccarat, -ra ˌbækəˈrɑ, ˈbækəˌrɑ (*Fr* bakaˈra)
Bacchae ˈbæki
bacchanal ˈbækənḷ, -ˌnæl
Bacchanalia, b- ˌbækəˈnelɪə, -ljə |-n -n
bacchant ˈbækənt |-s -s |-es bəˈkæntiz, bæ-
bacchante bəˈkæntɪ, -ˈkænt, bæ-, ˈbækənt
Bacchic, b- ˈbækɪk |-al -ḷ
Bacchus ˈbækəs |-'s -ɪz
Bach bɑk, bɑx (*Ger* bɑx)

Bacheller ˈbætʃɑlɚ, ˈbætʃlɚ; ES -lə(r
bachelor ˈbætʃɑlɚ, ˈbætʃlɚ; ES -lə(r
Bachman ˈbækmən, ˈbɑk- (*Ger* ˈbɑxmɑn)
bacillary ˈbæsḷˌɛrɪ, ˈbæsɪˌl-
bacillus bəˈsɪləs |-li -laɪ
back bæk |-ed -t |-ache -ˌek
backbite ˈbækˌbaɪt |-bit -ˌbɪt |-bitten -ˌbɪtṇ
backbone ˈbækˈbon, -ˌbon |-d -d
backfire *n* ˈbækˌfaɪr; ES -ˌfaɪə(r
backfire *v* ˈbækˌfaɪr, -ˈfaɪr; ES -aɪə(r; |-d -d
backgammon ˈbækˌgæmən, ˌbækˈgæmən
background ˈbækˌgraʊnd
backhand ˈbækˈhænd, -ˌhænd |-ed -ɪd (ˈbackˌhand(ed) ˈstroke)
backlash ˈbækˌlæʃ |-es -ɪz |-ed -t
backlog ˈbækˌlɔg, -ˌlɑg, -ˌlɒg
backset ˈbækˌsɛt
backslide ˈbækˌslaɪd, ˈbækˈslaɪd |-slid -ˌslɪd, -ˈslɪd |-slidden -ˌslɪdṇ, -ˈslɪdṇ
backspace ˈbækˌspes |-s -ɪz |-d -t
backspin ˈbækˌspɪn
backstage *adv* ˈbækˈstedʒ, *adj* ˈbækˌstedʒ
backstay ˈbækˌste |-ed -d
backstroke ˈbækˌstrok
backswept ˈbækˌswɛpt

|full fʊl |tooth tuθ |further ˈfɝðɚ; ES ˈfɝðə |custom ˈkʌstəm |while hwaɪl |how haʊ |toy tɔɪ |using ˈjuzɪŋ |fuse fjuz, fɪuz |dish dɪʃ |vision ˈvɪʒən |Eden ˈidṇ |cradle ˈkredḷ |keep 'em ˈkipm̩

backward 'bækwəd; ES -wəd; |-s -z
backwash 'bæk₁wɑʃ, -₁wɔʃ, -₁wɒʃ |-es -ɪz |-ed -t
backwater 'bæk₁wɔtɚ, -₁wɑtɚ, -₁wɒtɚ; ES -tə(r
backwoods 'bæk'wʊdz, 'bæk₁wʊdz |-man, -men -mən
bacon, B- 'bekən, 'bekŋ
Baconian be'konɪən, bə-, -njən
bacteria bæk'tɪrɪə |-l -l |sg -ium -m
bactericide bæk'tɪrə₁saɪd
bacterin 'bæktərɪn
bacteriological 'bæk₁tɪrɪə'lɑdʒɪk|, bæk₁tɪrɪə-; ES+-'lɒdʒ-
bacteriologist 'bæk₁tɪrɪ'ɑlədʒɪst, bæk₁tɪrɪ-; ES+-'ɒl-; |-gy -dʒɪ
bacteriolysis 'bæk₁tɪrɪ'ɑləsɪs, bæk₁tɪrɪ-; ES+-'ɒl-
bacteriophage bæk'tɪrɪə₁fedʒ |-s -ɪz
Bactria 'bæktrɪə |-n -n
bad bæd
bade past of bid bæd
Baden US 'bedṇ, Germany 'bɑdṇ (Ger 'ba:dən)
Baden-Powell 'bedṇ'poəl
badge bædʒ |-s -ɪz |-d -d
badger, B- 'bædʒɚ; ES 'bædʒə(r; |-ed -d |-ing 'bædʒərɪŋ, 'bædʒrɪŋ
Badgworthy 'bædʒərɪ = Bagworthy
badinage 'bædnɪdʒ, ₁bædɪ'nɑʒ (Fr badi'na:ʒ)
badminton, B- 'bædmɪntən
Badon 'bedṇ
Baeda 'bidə, cf Bede
Baedeker 'bedɪkɚ, -də-; ES -kə(r; (Ger 'be:dəkər)
baff bæf |-ed -t (Sc baf)
Baffin 'bæfɪn
baffle 'bæf| |-d -d |-ling -'bæf|ɪŋ, -flɪŋ
baffy 'bæfɪ (Sc 'bafɪ)
bag bæg |-ged -d |-man, -men -mən
bagasse bə'gæs (Fr ba'gas)
bagatelle ₁bægə'tɛl
Bagdad 'bægdæd, bag'dad ('Bag₁dad 'rail-₁way)
Bagehot 'bædʒət
bagful 'bæg₁fʊl |-s -z
baggage 'bægɪdʒ |-s -ɪz
Bagot 'bægət
bagpipe 'bæg₁paɪp

Bagworthy Lorna Doone 'bædʒərɪ
bah bɑ, ba, bæ |-ed -d
Bahai bə'hɑ·i |-haism -'hɑ·ɪzəm
Bahama bə'hemə, loc. and Brit bə'hɑmə |-s -z
Bahia bə'hiə (Pg ba'ia)
Baikal baɪ'kɑl
bail bel |-ed -d |-ee 'bel'i
bailey, B- 'belɪ |-liff -lɪf
bailiwick 'belə₁wɪk
Baillie 'belɪ
bailsman 'belzmən |-men -mən
Bainbridge 'benbrɪdʒ |-'s -ɪz
Baird berd, bærd; E bɛəd, ES bæəd
bairn bɛrn, bærn, bern; E bɛən, ES bæən, beən
bait bet |baited 'betɪd
baize bez |baizes 'bezɪz |-d -d
bake bek |baked bekt
bakehouse 'bek₁haʊs |-houses -₁haʊzɪz
Bakelite, b- 'bekə₁laɪt, 'beklaɪt
baker, B- 'bekɚ; ES 'bekə(r; |-kery -kərɪ, -krɪ
baking-powder 'bekɪŋ₁paʊdɚ, 'bekŋ-; ES -də(r
baksheesh, -shish 'bækʃɪʃ
Baku bɑ'ku
Balaam 'beləm
Balaclava, -klava ₁bælə'klɑvə
balalaika ₁bælə'laɪkə
balance 'bæləns |-s -ɪz |-d -t
Balanga bə'lɑŋgə (Sp ba'laŋga)
balata 'bælətə
Balboa bæl'boə
balboa coin bɑl'boə
balbriggan, B- bæl'brɪgən
balcony 'bælkənɪ |balconied 'bælkənɪd
bald bɔld
baldachin 'bældəkɪn, 'bɔl-
Balder, -dr 'bɔldɚ; ES 'bɔldə(r
balderdash 'bɔldɚ₁dæʃ; ES 'bɔldə-
baldhead 'bɔld₁hɛd
bald-headed 'bɔld'hɛdɪd ('bald-₁headed 'man)
baldpate 'bɔld₁pet |-pated -'petɪd
baldric 'bɔldrɪk, 'bɔdrɪk |-ked -t
Baldwin 'bɔldwɪn, -dɪn
bale, B- bel |baled beld
Bâle bɑl
Balearic ₁bælɪ'ærɪk, bə'lɪrɪk

---

baleen bə'lin
balefire 'bel,faɪr; ES 'bel,faɪə(r
baleful 'belfəl |-ly -ɪ
baler 'belɚ; ES 'belə(r
Balfour 'bælfʊr; ES 'bælfuə(r
Baliol 'beljəl, 'belɪəl
balk bɔk |balked bɔkt |balky 'bɔkɪ
Balkan 'bɔlkən
Balkanize 'bɔlkən,aɪz |-s -ɪz |-d -d
ball bɔl |balled bɔld
ballad 'bæləd |balladry 'bælədrɪ
ballade bə'lɑd, bæ'lɑd (Fr ba'lad)
ball-and-socket 'bɔlən'sɑkɪt; ES+-'sɒk-
Ballantrae ,bælən'tre, 'bæləntrɪ
Ballard 'bælɚd; ES 'bæləd
ballast 'bæləst |ballasted 'bæləstɪd
ballerina ,bælə'rinə |-s -z (It ,balle'ri:na)
ballet 'bæle, 'bælɪ, bæ'le (Fr ba'lɛ)
Ballinger 'bælɪndʒɚ; ES -dʒə(r
Balliol 'beljəl, 'belɪəl
ballistic bæ'lɪstɪk, bə- |-s -s
ballonet ,bælə'nɛt
balloon bə'lun, b̩'un |-ed -d
ballot 'bælət |balloted 'bælətɪd
Ballou bə'lu, bæ'lu
ballproof 'bɔl'pruf ('ball,proof 'armor)
ballroom 'bɔl,rum, -,rʊm
ballyhoo 'bælɪ,hu, ,bælɪ'hu |-ed -d
Ballymena ,bælɪ'minə
balm bɑm |balmed bɑmd |balmy 'bɑmɪ; |E+
-a-
Balmoral bæl'mɔrəl, -'mɑrəl, -'mɒrəl
balneal 'bælnɪəl
balneology ,bælnɪ'alədʒɪ; ES+-'ɒl-
baloney bə'lonɪ, b̩'onɪ
balsa 'bɔlsə, 'bɑlsə
balsam 'bɔlsəm |-ed -d
balsamic bɔl'sæmɪk, bæl'sæmɪk |-al -l̩ |-ally
-l̩ɪ, -ɪklɪ
baltered 'bɔltɚd; ES -təd; cf blood-boltered
Balthazar bæl'θæzɚ; ES -'θæzə(r; Shak.
,bælθə'zɑr, -tə'zɑr; ES -'zɑ:(r
Baltic 'bɔltɪk
Baltimore 'bɔltə,mor, -,mɔr; ES -,moə(r,
E+-,mɔə(r; loc. 'bɔltəmɚ, -mə(r
Baluchistan bə,lutʃɪ'stæn, -'stan, bə'lutʃɪ-
,stæn, -,stan, -ukɪ-
baluster 'bæləstɚ; ES -tə(r; |-ed -d
balustrade ,bælə'stred |-straded -'stredɪd

Balzac 'bælzæk (Fr. bal'zak)
bambino bæm'bino, bam- |-ni -ni (It
bam'bi:no)
bamboo bæm'bu ('bam,boo 'pole)
bamboozle bæm'buz̩ |-ed -d |-ling -zlɪŋ,
-z̩ɪŋ
ban bæn |banned bænd
banal 'ben̩, bə'næl, -'nal, 'bæn̩ (Fr ba'nal)
banality bə'nælətɪ, be-, bæ-
banana bə'nænə
Banbury 'bæn,bɛrɪ, 'bæm-, -bərɪ, -brɪ
Bancroft 'bænkrɔft, 'bæŋ-, -krɒft
band bænd |banded 'bændɪd
bandage 'bændɪdʒ |-s -ɪz |-d -d
bandanna bæn'dænə
bandbox 'bænd,baks, 'bæn-; ES+-,bɒks;
|-es -ɪz
bandeau bæn'do, 'bændo
Bandelier ,bænd̩'ɪr; ES -'ɪə(r, S+-'ɛə(r
Bandello bæn'dɛlo (It ban'dɛllo)
banderole 'bændə,rol
bandicoot 'bændɪ,kut
bandit 'bændɪt |-ry -rɪ |-ditti bæn'dɪtɪ
bandmaster 'bænd,mæstɚ, 'bæn-; ES
-,mæstə(r, E+-,mas-, -,mɑs-
bandog 'bæn,dɔg, -,dɒg
bandoleer ,bændə'lɪr; ES -'lɪə(r, S+-'lɛə(r
bandore bæn'dor, 'bændor, -ɔr; ES -oə(r,
E+-ɔə(r
bandsman 'bændzmən, 'bænz- |-men -mən
bandstand 'bænd,stænd, 'bæn-
bandy 'bændɪ |bandied 'bændɪd
bandy-legged 'bændɪ'lɛgɪd, -'lɛgd, 'bændɪ-
,lɛgɪd, -,lɛgd
bane ben |-d -d |-ful -fəl |-fully -fəlɪ
Banff bæmf |-shire -ʃɪr, -ʃɚ; ES -ʃɪə(r,
-ʃə(r
bang bæŋ |banged bæŋd
bang 'bhang' bæŋ
Bangkok 'bæŋkak, bæŋ'kak; ES+-ɒk
bangle 'bæŋg̩ |-d -d |bangling 'bæŋglɪŋ,
-glɪŋ
Bangor Me 'bæŋgɔr, -gɚ, Wales, Irel 'bæŋgɚ;
ES -gɔə(r, -gə(r
banish 'bænɪʃ |-es -ɪz |-ed -t
banister 'bænɪstɚ; ES -tə(r; |-ed -d
banjo 'bændʒo |-ed -d
banjorine ,bændʒə'rin
bank bæŋk |banked bæŋkt

|full fʊl |tooth tuθ |further 'fɝðɚ; ES 'fɜðə |custom 'kʌstəm |while hwaɪl |how haʊ |toy tɔɪ
|using 'juzɪŋ |fuse fjuz, fɪuz |dish dɪʃ |vision 'vɪʒən |Eden 'idn̩ |cradle 'kred̩ |keep 'em 'kipm̩

Words below in which a *before* r (farm) *is sounded* ɑ *are often pronounced in* E *with* a (fɑːm)

bankrupt 'bæŋkrʌpt, -rəpt |-ed -ɪd |-ptcy
-ptsɪ, -psɪ
Bankside 'bæŋk,saɪd
banner 'bænɚ; ES 'bænə(r
banneret *knight* 'bænərɪt, -ˌrɛt
banneret, -ette *banner* ˌbænə'rɛt
bannock 'bænək
Bannockburn 'bænəkˌbɝn, ˌbænək'bɝn; ES
-ɜn, -ɜn
banns, bans bænz
banquet 'bæŋkwɪt, 'bæn- |-ed -ɪd
banquette bæŋ'kɛt
Banquo 'bæŋkwo, 'bæn-, -ko
banshee, -shie 'bænʃi, bæn'ʃi
Banta 'bæntə, *publisher* 'bɑntə
Bantam, b- 'bæntəm
banter 'bæntɚ; ES 'bæntə(r; |-ed -d |-ing
-tərɪŋ, -trɪŋ
Banting 'bæntɪŋ
bantingize 'bæntɪŋˌaɪz |-s -ɪz |-d -d
Bantu 'bæn'tu, 'bɑn- ('Banˌtu 'language)
banyan 'bænjən, 'bænjæn
banzai 'bɑn'zɑ·i, 'bɑn'zɑɪ
baobab 'beoˌbæb, 'bɑoˌbæb
baptism 'bæptɪzəm
baptismal bæp'tɪzml̩ |-ly -ɪ
Baptist 'bæptɪst
Baptista Minola bæp'tɪstə'mɪnələ
baptistery 'bæptɪstrɪ, -tərɪ |baptistry -trɪ
baptize bæp'taɪz |-s -ɪz |-d -d
bar bɑr; ES bɑː(r; |-red -d
Barabas *Marlowe* 'bærəbəs |-'s -ɪz
Barabbas *Bible* bə'ræbəs, *in Shak.* 'bærəbəs
|-'s -ɪz
Baraboo 'bɛrəˌbu, 'bær-; S 'bær-
Baraca bə'rækə
Barak 'bɛrək, 'bærək, 'beræk
barb bɑrb; ES bɑːb; |-ed -d, -ɪd
Barbados, -oes bɑr'bedoz, 'bɑrbəˌdoz; ES
bɑː-, 'bɑː-b-
Barbara 'bɑrbərə, -brə; ES 'bɑː-b-
barbarian bɑr'bɛrɪən, -'bær-, -'ber-, -jən;
ES bɑ-
barbaric bɑr'bærɪk; ES bɑː-; |-ally -ḷɪ, -ɪklɪ
barbarism 'bɑrbəˌrɪzəm; ES 'bɑːbəˌrɪzəm
barbarity bɑr'bærətɪ; ES bɑ-
barbarous 'bɑrbərəs, -brəs; ES 'bɑː-b-
Barbary 'bɑrbərɪ; ES 'bɑːbərɪ

barbecue 'bɑrbɪˌkju, -ˌkɪu; ES 'bɑː-; |-d -d
barbel 'bɑrbl̩; ES 'bɑːbl̩
barber, B- 'bɑrbɚ; ES 'bɑːbə(r; |-ed -d |-ing
-bərɪŋ, -brɪŋ
barberry 'bɑrˌbɛrɪ, -bərɪ; ES 'bɑː-
Barberton 'bɑrbɚtən; ES 'bɑːbətən
barbette bɑr'bɛt; ES bɑ-'bɛt
barbican, B- 'bɑrbɪkən; ES 'bɑː-
Barbour 'bɑrbɚ; ES 'bɑːbə(r
Barca 'bɑrkə; ES 'bɑː-; |*pl Eng* -cas -kəz, *Sp*
-cas -kɑs, *It* -che -ke
barcarole, -rolle 'bɑrkəˌrol; ES 'bɑːkəˌrol
Barcelona ˌbɑrsl̩'onə; ES ˌbɑ-'; (*Sp* ˌbɑrθe-
'lona)
Barclay 'bɑrklɪ, -le; ES 'bɑːk-
bard bɑrd; ES bɑːd; |-ic -ɪk
Bardolph 'bɑrdɑlf, -dɒlf; ES 'bɑːˑ
bare bɛr, bær; E bɛə(r, ES bæə(r; |-d -d
bareback 'bɛrˌbæk, 'bær-; E 'bɛə-, ES
'bæə-
barefaced 'bɛr'fest, 'bær-; E 'bɛə-, ES 'bæə-;
|-cedly -sɪdlɪ, -stlɪ ('bareˌfaced 'lie)
barefoot 'bɛrˌfut, 'bær-; E 'bɛə-, ES 'bæə-;
|-ed -ɪd
barehead 'bɛrˌhɛd, 'bær-; E 'bɛə-, ES 'bæə-
bareheaded 'bɛr'hɛdɪd, 'bær-; E 'bɛə-, ES
'bæə-
baresark 'bɛrˌsɑrk, 'bær-; E 'bɛəˌsɑːk, ES
'bæə-
bargain 'bɑrgɪn; ES 'bɑːgɪn; |-ed -d
barge bɑrdʒ; ES bɑːdʒ; |-s -ɪz |-d -d
bargeman 'bɑrdʒmən; ES 'bɑːdʒ-; |-men
-mən
Barham, *Richard* 'bærəm
baric 'bærɪk
Baring-Gould 'bɛrɪŋ'guld, 'bærɪŋ-; S 'bær-
barite 'bɛraɪt, 'bæraɪt, 'beraɪt; S 'bær-, 'ber-
baritone 'bærəˌton
barium 'bɛrɪəm, 'bær-, 'ber-; S 'bær-, 'ber-
bark bɑrk; ES bɑːk; |-ed -t
barkeeper 'bɑrˌkipɚ; ES 'bɑːˌkipə(r
barkentine 'bɑrkənˌtin; ES 'bɑːk-
Barker, b- 'bɑrkɚ; ES 'bɑːkə(r
barley 'bɑrlɪ; ES 'bɑːlɪ; |-corn -ˌkɔrn; ES
-ˌkɔən
barm bɑrm; ES bɑːm
barmaid 'bɑrˌmed; ES 'bɑːˌmed
Barmecide 'bɑrməˌsaɪd; ES 'bɑːm-

Key: *See in full §§3–47.* bee bi |pity 'pɪtɪ (§6) |rate ret |yet jɛt |sang sæŋ |angry 'æŋ·grɪ
|bath bæθ; E bɑθ (§10) |ah ɑ |far fɑr |watch wɑtʃ, wɒtʃ (§12) |jaw dʒɔ |gorge gɔrdʒ |go go

Words below in which a *before* r (farm) *is sounded* ɑ *are often pronounced in E with* a (fɑːm)
Words below that have æ *before* r (carry ˈkærɪ) *are often pronounced in N with* ɛ (ˈkɛrɪ, §94)

bar mizvah, mitz- ˈbɑrˈmɪtsvə; ES ˈbɑː-
barn bɑrn; ES bɑːn; |-ed -d
Barnabas ˈbɑrnəbəs; ES ˈbɑːnə-; |-ʼs -ɪz
Barnaby ˈbɑrnəbɪ; ES ˈbɑːnəbɪ
barnacle ˈbɑrnəkḷ, ˈbɑrnɪ-; ES ˈbɑːn-; |-d -d
Barnard ˈbɑrnəd; ES ˈbɑːnəd
Barnardine ˈbɑrnəˌdin; ES ˈbɑːnə-
barn door ˈbɑrnˈdor, -ˈdɔr; ES ˈbɑːnˈdoə(r,
E+-ˈdɔə(r; (ˈbarn-ˌdoor ˈfowl)
Barnegat ˌbɑrnɪˈgæt; ES ˌbɑːnɪ-; (ˈBarneˌgat
ˈBay)
Barnet(t) ˈbɑrnɪt; ES ˈbɑːnɪt; *acct*+Barˈnett
Barnstable *Mass* ˈbɑrnstəbḷ; ES ˈbɑːn-
Barnstaple *Dev* ˈbɑrnstəpḷ; ES ˈbɑːn-; *loc.*
-stəbḷ (*spelt* -ple 1086, -ble 1421)
barnstorm ˈbɑrnˌstɔrm; ES ˈbɑːnˌstɔəm;
|-ed -d
Barnum ˈbɑrnəm; ES ˈbɑːnəm
barnyard ˈbɑrnˌjard; ES ˈbɑːnˌjɑːd
barogram ˈbærəˌgræm
barograph ˈbærəˌgræf; E+-ˌgraf, -ˌgrɑf
barographic ˌbærəˈgræfɪk
barometer bəˈrɑmətə; ES bəˈrɑmətə(r, -ˈrɒm-
barometric ˌbærəˈmɛtrɪk |-al -ḷ |-ally -ḷɪ, -ɪklɪ
baron, B- ˈbærən |-age -ɪdʒ |-ages -ɪdʒɪz
baroness ˈbærənɪs |-es -ɪz
baronet ˈbærənɪt, -ˌnɛt |-ed -ɪd |-age -ɪdʒ
|-ages -ɪdʒɪz |-cy -sɪ
barong b ˈrɔŋ, bɑˈrɔŋ, -ˈrɒŋ
barony ˈbærənɪ |-nial bəˈronɪəl
baroque bəˈrok (*Fr* baˈrɔ̆k)
baroscope ˈbærəˌskop
barouche bəˈruʃ, bæ- |-s -ɪz
barque bɑrk; ES bɑːk
barrack ˈbærək |-ed -t
barracuda ˌbærəˈkudə
barrage '*act of barring*,' '*bar*' ˈbɑrɪdʒ |-s -ɪz
barrage *mil.* bəˈrɑʒ |-s -ɪz |-d -d
barrator ˈbærətə; ES ˈbærətə(r; |-try -trɪ
Barré, *Isaac* ˈbærɪ, *hence next*
Barre *Mass, Vt* ˈbærɪ
barrel ˈbærəl, ˈbærl, ˈbærɪl |-ed -d
barren ˈbærən |-ness ˈbærənnɪs
barret, Barrett ˈbærɪt
barette bəˈrɛt
barricade *n* ˌbærəˈked, ˈbærəˌked
barricade *v* ˌbærəˈked |-d -ɪd

Barrie ˈbærɪ
barrier ˈbærɪə; ES ˈbærɪ·ə(r
Barrington ˈbærɪŋtən
barrister ˈbærɪstə; ES ˈbærɪstə(r
barroom ˈbɑrˌrum, -ˌrʊm; ES ˈbɑːˌr-
barrow, B- ˈbæro, -rə
Barry ˈbærɪ
Barrymore ˈbærəˌmor, -ˌmɔr; ES -ˌmoə(r, E+
-ˌmɔə(r
Bartas, du djubɑrˈtas, dru-, du-; ES -bɑːˈtas;
(*Fr* dybarˈtɑːs) |-ʼs -ɪz
bartender ˈbɑrˌtɛndə; ES ˈbɑːˌtɛndə(r
barter ˈbɑrtə; ES ˈbɑːtə(r; |-ed -d |-ing
-tərɪŋ, -trɪŋ
Bartholomew bɑrˈθɑləˌmju, -ˌmɪu; ES
bɑˈθɑl-, -ˈθɒl-
Bartimeus ˌbɑrtɪˈmiəs; ES ˌbɑːtə-; |-ʼs -ɪz
bartizan ˈbɑrtəzn̩, ˌbɑrtəˈzæn; ES ˈbɑːtə-,
ˌbɑːtə-
Bartlett ˈbɑrtlɪt, -lət; ES ˈbɑːt-
Baruch *Bible* ˈbɛrək, ˈbærək, ˈberək, -rʊk;
S ˈbær-, ˈber-
Baruch *Bernard* bəˈruk
barytone ˈbærəˌton
basal ˈbesḷ |-ly -ɪ
basalt bəˈsɔlt, ˈbæsɔlt
basaltic bəˈsɔltɪk, bæ-
bascule ˈbæskjul, ˈbæskɪul
base bes |bases ˈbesɪz |based best
baseball ˈbesˌbɔl, ˈbesˌbɒl
baseboard ˈbesˌbord, -ˌbɔrd; ES -ˌboəd, E+
-ˌbɔəd
baseborn ˈbesˈbɔrn; ES -ˈbɔən; (ˈbaseˌborn
ˈserf)
Basel ˈbɑzḷ—*see* Basle
basement ˈbesmənt
bases *pl of* base ˈbesɪz
bases *pl of* basis ˈbesɪz
bash bæʃ |bashes ˈbæʃɪz |bashed bæʃt
Bashan ˈbeʃæn, ˈbeʃən
bashaw bəˈʃɔ
bashful ˈbæʃfəl |bashfully ˈbæʃfəlɪ
bashi-bazouk ˈbæʃɪbəˈzuk
basic ˈbesɪk |-ally -ḷɪ, -ɪklɪ
basicity beˈsɪsətɪ
basil, B- ˈbæzḷ, -zɪl
basilica bəˈsɪlɪkə, bəˈzɪlɪkə

basilisk ˈbæsəˌlɪsk ˈbæzəˌlɪsk
basin ˈbesn̩ |basined ˈbesn̩d
basinet ˈbæsənɪt
Basingstoke ˈbezɪŋˌstok
basis ˈbesɪs |bases ˈbesiz
bask bæsk; E+bask, bɑsk; |-ed -t
basket ˈbæskɪt; E+ˈbaskɪt, ˈbɑskɪt
basketball ˈbæskɪtˌbɔl; E+ˈbas-, ˈbɑs-
basketful ˈbæskɪtˌful; E+ˈbas-, ˈbɑs-; |-s -z
basketry ˈbæskɪtrɪ; E+ˈbas-, ˈbɑs-
Basle bɑl
Basque bæsk
Basra ˈbʌsrə
bas-relief ˌbɑ·rɪˈlif, ˌbæs-, ˈbɑ·rɪˌlif, ˈbæs-
bass *fish* bæs |basses ˈbæsɪz
bass *music* bes |basses ˈbesɪz
Bassanio bəˈsanɪˌo, bəˈsanjo—*trisyllabic in Shak.*
basset, B- ˈbæsɪt
Bassianus ˌbæsɪˈenəs |-'s -ɪz
bassinet ˌbæsəˈnɛt, ˈbæsəˌnɛt
basso ˈbæso
bassoon bæˈsun, bəˈsun, -ˈzun
basso-relievo ˈbæso·rɪˈlivo (*It* -rilievo ˈbasso-rɪˈljɛːvo)
basswood ˈbæsˌwud
bast bæst
bastard ˈbæstəd; ES ˈbæstəd
baste best |basted ˈbestɪd |basting ˈbestɪŋ
bastille bæsˈtil (*Fr* basˈtiːj)
bastinado ˌbæstəˈnedo
bastion ˈbæstʃən, ˈbæstɪən
Basutoland bəˈsutoˌlænd
bat bæt |batted ˈbætɪd
Bataan bəˈtan, ba-, bæ-
Batavia bəˈtevɪə, -ˈtevjə
batch bætʃ |batches ˈbætʃɪz |batched bætʃt
bate bet |bated ˈbetɪd
bateau bæˈto
bath, B- bæθ; E+baθ, bɑθ; |-ths -ðz |-th's -θs
bathe beð |bathed beðd |bathing ˈbeðɪŋ
bathetic bəˈθɛtɪk
bathhouse ˈbæθˌhaus; E+ˈbaθ-, ˈbɑθ-
bathos ˈbeθɑs; ES+-ɒs
bathroom ˈbæθˌrum, -ˌrum; E+ˈbaθ-, ˈbɑθ-
Bathsheba bæθˈʃibə, ˈbæθʃɪbə
Bathurst ˈbæθəst; ES ˈbæθəst
batik ˈbatik, bæˈtik, bə-, ˈbætɪk
batiste bæˈtist, bə- (*Fr* baˈtist)

baton bæˈtan, ˈbætn̩, bæˈtɔ̃; ES+-ˈtɒn; (*Fr* baˈtɔ̃)
Baton Rouge ˈbætn̩ˈruʒ |-'s -ɪz
batrachian bəˈtrekɪən
batsman ˈbætsmən |-men ˈbætsmən
batswing ˈbætsˌwɪŋ
battalion bəˈtæljən, bæˈtæljən
batten ˈbætn̩ |-ed -d |-ing ˈbætn̩ɪŋ, ˈbætnɪŋ
batter ˈbætə; ES ˈbætə(r; |-ed -d
battery ˈbætərɪ, ˈbætrɪ
battle ˈbætl̩ |-d -d |-ling ˈbætl̩ɪŋ, ˈbætlɪŋ
Battle Creek ˈbætl̩ˈkrɪk, -ˈkrik
battledore ˈbætl̩ˌdor, -ˌdɔr; ES -ˌdoə(r, E+-ˌdɔə(r
battlement *n* ˈbætl̩mənt
battlement *v* ˈbætl̩ˌmɛnt |-mented -ˌmɛntɪd
battleplane ˈbætl̩ˌplen
battleship ˈbætl̩ˌʃɪp
battue bæˈtu, bæˈtɪu, bæˈtju (*Fr* baˈty)
batty ˈbætɪ
bauble ˈbɔbl̩
Baucis ˈbɔsɪs |Baucis' ˈbɔsɪs
baudekin ˈbɔdəkɪn
Bausch and Lomb ˈbɔʃənˈlam, -ˈlɒm-, -ˈlɔm
bauxite ˈbɔksaɪt, ˈbozaɪt
Bavaria bəˈvɛrɪə, bəˈverɪə |-n -n
bawcock ˈbɔˌkak; ES+ˈbɔˌkɒk
bawd bɔd |bawdry ˈbɔdrɪ |bawdy ˈbɔdɪ
bawl bɔl |bawled bɔld
bay be |bayed bed
bayard, B- ˈbeəd, *Am statesmen* ˈbaɪəd; ES -əd
Bayeux beˈju (*Fr* baˈjø)
bayonet ˈbeənɪt |bayoneted ˈbeənɪtɪd, -ˌnɛtɪd
Bayonne *US* beˈon, beˈjon; *France, Fr* baˈjɔ̃n
bayou ˈbaɪu, ˈbaɪju
Bayreuth baɪˈrɔɪt, ˈbaɪrɔɪt (*Ger* baɪˈrɔyt)
bazaar bəˈzar; ES bəˈzaː(r, E+-ˈzaː(r
B.C. ˈbiˈsi
bdellium ˈdɛlɪəm
be *v stressed* ˈbi, ˌbi; *unstr.* bɪ
be- *unstressed prefix* bɪ-, bə- — *Usually only one pron. is given in the vocab. Where bə- is given, usually bɪ- would represent a somewhat more careful style; where bɪ- is given, bə- may often be substituted bef. conss., esp. in a more familiar style. When followed by l, bl̩- is a common variant* (believe bl̩ˈiv).

Key: *See in full §§3–47.* bee bi |pity ˈpɪtɪ (§6) |rate ret |yet jɛt |sang sæŋ |angry ˈæŋ·grɪ |bath bæθ; E baθ (§10) |ah ɑ |far far |watch watʃ, wɒtʃ (§12) |jaw dʒɔ |gorge gɔrdʒ |go go

The **bɪ-** *type with many speakers has the usual tendency toward* **bi-.**

beach **bitʃ** |-es **-ɪz** |-ed **-t**
beachcomber **'bitʃ,komɚ**; ES **-,komə(r**
beacon **'bikən** |-ed **-d** |-ing **'bikənɪŋ, -knɪŋ**
Beaconsfield *in Bucks* **'bɛkənz,fild**
Beaconsfield *Lord* **'bikənz,fild**
bead **bid** |beaded **'bidɪd**
beadle **'bidl̩** |-dom **-dəm** |-ry **-rɪ**
beadroll **'bid,rol**
beadsman **'bidzmən** |-men **-mən**
beadwork **'bid,wɝk**; ES **-,wɝk, -,wɝk**
beagle, B- **'bigl̩**
beak **bik** |-ed **-t**
beaked *adj* **bikt, 'bikɪd**
beaker **'bikɚ**; ES **'bikə(r**
beam **bim** |-ed **-d**
beam-ends **'bim'ɛndz, -,ɛndz, -nz**
bean **bin** |-ed **-d**
beano **'bino**
beanstalk **'bin,stɔk**
bear *n* **bɛr, bær**; E **bɛə(r,** ES **bæə(r**
bear *v* **bɛr, bær**; E **bɛə(r,** ES **bæə(r**; |bore **bor, bɔr**; ES **boə(r,** E+**bɔə(r**; |borne **born, bɔrn**; ES **boən,** E+**bɔən**
beard **bɪrd**; ES **bɪəd,** S+**bɛəd**; |-ed **-ɪd**
Beard **bɪrd, bɛrd, bærd**; ES **bɪəd, bɛəd, bæəd**
bearer **'bɛrɚ, 'bærɚ**; E **'bɛrə(r,** ES **'bærə(r**
bearskin **'bɛr,skɪn, 'bær-**; E **'bɛə-,** ES **'bæə-**
beast **bist** |beasted **'bistɪd** |-ly **-lɪ**
beat **bit** |*past* beat **bit** |*pptc* beaten **'bitn̩** *or* beat **bit**
beatific **,biə'tɪfɪk** |-al **-l̩** |-ally **-l̩ɪ, -ɪklɪ**
beatification **bɪ,ætəfə'keʃən**
beatify **bɪ'ætə,faɪ** |-fied **-,faɪd**
beatitude **bɪ'ætə,tjud, -,tɪud, -,tud**
Beatrice *fem. name* **'biətrɪs,** *in Dante* **'biətrɪs** (*It* **,bea'tri:tʃe**) |-'s **-ɪz**
Beatrix **'biətrɪks** |-'s **-ɪz**
Beattie, -tty **'bitɪ, 'betɪ**
beau **bo** |-s, -x **-z** |-ed **-d**
Beaucaire **bo'kɛr, -'kær**; E **-'kɛə(r,** ES **-'kæə(r;** (*Fr* **bo'kɛːr**)
Beauchamp *Eng name* **'bitʃəm** (*Fr* **bo'ʃɑ̃**)
Beauclerc, -rk **'bo,klɛr, -,klær, -,klɑrk**; E **-,klɛə(r,** ES **-,klæə(r, -,klɑːk**
Beaufort **'bofɚt,** *SC* **'bjufɚt, 'bɪu-,** *NC* **'bo-**; ES **-fɚt**

beau geste *Fr* **bo'ʒɛst**
beau ideal **'boaɪ'diəl, -'dil, -'dɪəl**
Beaulieu *Engd* **'bjulɪ, 'bɪulɪ**
Beaumarchais **,bomar'ʃe**; ES **-mɑ:'ʃe;** (*Fr* **bomar'ʃɛ**)
beau monde **bo'mɑnd, -'mɒnd** (*Fr* **bo'mõːd**)
Beaumont **'bomɑnt, -mɒnt**
Beauregard **'borə,gɑrd**; ES **-,gɑ:d,** E+**-,gɑ:d**
beauteous **'bjutɪəs, 'bɪu-**
beautiful **'bjutəfəl, 'bɪu-** |-ly **-fəlɪ, -flɪ**
beautify **'bjutə,faɪ, 'bɪu-** |-fied **-,faɪd**
beauty **'bjutɪ, 'bɪutɪ**
Beauvais **bo've** (*Fr* **bo'vɛ**)
beaux **boz**
beaux-arts *Fr* **bo'zɑːr**
Beaven **'bɛvən**
beaver, B- **'bivɚ**; ES **'bivə(r**
becalm **bɪ'kɑm**; E+**-'kɑm**; |-ed **-d**
became **bɪ'kem**
because **bɪ'kɔz, bə-, -'kɒz, -'kʌz**
bechance **bɪ'tʃæns**; E+**-'tʃɑns, -'tʃɒns**; |-s **-ɪz** |-d **-t**
becharm **bɪ'tʃɑrm**; ES **-'tʃɑːm,** E+**-'tʃɑːm;** |-ed **-d**
Bechuana **,betʃu'ɑnə, ,bɛkju-** |-land **-,lænd**
beck **bɛk** |-ed **-t**
becket, B- **'bɛkɪt**
beckon **'bɛkən** |-ed **-d** |-ing **'bɛkənɪŋ, -knɪŋ**
becloud **bɪ'klaud** |-ed **-ɪd**
become **bɪ'kʌm** |became **bɪ'kem** |become **bɪ'kʌm**
Becquerel **bɛk'rɛl** (**'Becque,rel 'rays**)
bed **bɛd** |bedded **'bɛdɪd**
bedabble **bɪ'dæbl̩** |-d **-d** |-ling **-'dæblɪŋ, -bl̩ɪŋ**
bedaub **bɪ'dɔb** |-ed **-d**
bedazzle **bɪ'dæzl̩** |-d **-d** |-ling **-'dæzlɪŋ, -zl̩ɪŋ**
bedbug **'bɛd,bʌg**
bedchamber **'bɛd,tʃembɚ**; ES **-,tʃembə(r**
bedclothes **'bɛd,kloz, -,kloðz**
bedcover **'bɛd,kʌvɚ**; ES **-,kʌvə(r**
bedding **'bɛdɪŋ**
Beddoes **'bɛdoz** |-'s **-ɪz**
Bede **bid,** *Latinized* Baeda **'bidə**
bedeck **bɪ'dɛk** |-ed **-t**
Bedel, -ll **'bidl̩, bə'dɛl**
bedesman **'bidzmən** |-men **-mən**
bedevil **bɪ'dɛvl̩** |-ed **-d** |-ing **-'dɛvlɪŋ, -vl̩ɪŋ**
bedew **bɪ'dju, -'dɪu, -'du** |-ed **-d**

|full **ful** |tooth **tuθ** |further **'fɝðɚ**; ES **'fɝðə** |custom **'kʌstəm** |while **hwaɪl** |how **hau** |toy **tɔɪ**
|using **'juzɪŋ** |fuse **fjuz, fɪuz** |dish **dɪʃ** |vision **'vɪʒən** |Eden **'idn̩** |cradle **'kredl̩** |keep 'em **'kipm̩**

bedfellow ˈbɛdˌfɛlo, -ə
Bedford ˈbɛdfəd; ES ˈbɛdfəd; |-shire -ˌʃɪr,
-ʃɚ; ES -ˌʃɪə(r, -ʃə(r
bedight bɪˈdaɪt
bedim bɪˈdɪm |-med -d
Bedivere ˈbɛdəˌvɪr; ES -ˌvɪə(r
bedizen bɪˈdɪzn̩, -ˈdaɪzn̩ |-ed -d |-ing -zn̩ɪŋ,
-znɪŋ—bɪˈdaɪzn̩ is chiefly Brit.
bedlam, B- ˈbɛdləm |-ite -ˌaɪt
Bedloe ˈbɛdlo
bedmate ˈbɛdˌmet
Bedouin ˈbɛduɪn
bedpan ˈbɛdˌpæn
bedplate ˈbɛdˌplet
bedraggle bɪˈdrægl̩ |-d -d |-ling -ˈdræglɪŋ,
-gl̩ɪŋ
bedrid ˈbɛdˌrɪd |bedridden ˈbɛdˌrɪdn̩
bedrock ˈbɛdˈrɑk, -ˌrɑk; ES+-ɒk
bedroll ˈbɛdˌrol
bedroom ˈbɛdˌrum, -ˌrʊm, -rəm
bedroom door ˈbɛdˌrʊmˈdor, ˈbɛdrəm-, -ˈdɔr;
ES -ˈdoə(r, E+-ˈdɔə(r
Beds short for Bedfordshire bɛdz
bedside ˈbɛdˌsaɪd
bedsore ˈbɛdˌsor, -ˌsɔr; ES -ˌsoə(r, E+
-ˌsɔə(r
bedspread ˈbɛdˌsprɛd
bedspring ˈbɛdˌsprɪŋ
bedstaff ˈbɛdˌstæf; E+-ˌstaf, -ˌstɑf; |-staves
-ˌstevz
bedstead ˈbɛdˌstɛd, -stɪd
bedstraw ˈbɛdˌstrɔ
bedtime ˈbɛdˌtaɪm
bedward ˈbɛdwəd; ES ˈbɛdwəd
bee bi
beech ˈbitʃ |-es -ɪz |-en -ən
beechnut ˈbitʃnət, -ˌnʌt
beef n bif |-'s -s |beeves bivz or beefs bifs
beef v bif |beefs bifs |beefed bift
beefeater ˈbifˌitɚ; ES -ˌitə(r
beefsteak ˈbifˌstek
beehive ˈbiˌhaɪv
beeline ˈbiˈlaɪn (ˈbeeˌline ˈflight)
Beelzebub bɪˈɛlzɪˌbʌb
been bɪn, bɛn—bin occurs chiefly as a Briticism, esp. in Canada. bɛn is most apt to
occur when unstressed.
beer, B- bɪr; ES bɪə(r, S+bɛə(r
Beersheba bɪrˈʃibə, ˈbɪrʃɪbə; ES bɪə-, ˈbɪə-

beeswax ˈbizˌwæks |-es -ɪz |-ed -t
beeswing ˈbizˌwɪŋ |-ed -d
beet bit
Beethoven ˈbetovən, ˈbet·hovən; Lond square
ˈbit·hovən (Ger ˈbe:t·ho:vən)
beetle ˈbitl̩ |-d -d |-ling ˈbitlɪŋ, ˈbitl̩ɪŋ
beetle-browed ˈbitl̩ˈbraud (ˈbeetle-ˌbrowed
ˈface)
beetlehead ˈbitl̩ˌhɛd |-ed ˈbitl̩ˈhɛdɪd
beetroot ˈbitˌrut, -ˌrʊt
beeves bivz
befall bɪˈfɔl |-fell -ˈfɛl |-fallen -ˈfɔlən, -ln
befit bɪˈfɪt |-ted -ɪd
befog bɪˈfɑg, -ˈfɔg, -ˈfɒg |-ged -d
befool bɪˈful |-ed -d
before bɪˈfor, bə-, -ˈfɔr; ES -ˈfoə(r, E+
-ˈfɔə(r; |-hand -ˌhænd |-time -ˌtaɪm
befoul bɪˈfaul |-ed -d
befriend bɪˈfrɛnd |-ed -ɪd
befuddle bɪˈfʌdl̩ |-d -d |-ling -ˈfʌdlɪŋ, -dl̩ɪŋ
beg bɛg |begged bɛgd
begad bɪˈgæd
began bɪˈgæn
begat bɪˈgæt
beget bɪˈgɛt |-got -ˈgɑt, arch. -gat -ˈgæt
|-gotten -ˈgɑtn̩ or -got -ˈgɑt; |ES +-ˈgɒt(n̩
beggar ˈbɛgɚ; ES ˈbɛgə(r; |-ed -d |-ing
-gərɪŋ, -grɪŋ |-ly -lɪ |-y -ɪ
begin bɪˈgɪn |-gan -ˈgæn |-gun -ˈgʌn |-ning
-ɪŋ
begird bɪˈgɝd |past -girt -ˈgɝt or -girded
-ˈgɝdɪd |pptc -girt -ˈgɝt; | ES -ɝ-, -ɜ-
begohm ˈbɛgˌom
begone bɪˈgɔn, -ˈgɒn, much less freq. -ˈgɑn
begonia, B- bɪˈgonjə, -nɪə
begot bɪˈgɑt; ES+-ˈgɒt; |-ten -n̩
begrime bɪˈgraɪm |-d -d
begrudge bɪˈgrʌdʒ |-s -ɪz |-d -d
beguile bɪˈgaɪl |-d -d
begum n ˈbigəm
begum v bɪˈgʌm |-med -d
begun bɪˈgʌn
behalf bɪˈhæf; E -ˈhaf, -ˈhæf, -ˈhɑf
behave bɪˈhev |-d -d
behavior bɪˈhevjɚ; ES -ˈhevjə(r; |-ism -ˌɪzəm
behavioristic bɪˌhevjəˈrɪstɪk |-ally -ļɪ, -ɪklɪ
behead bɪˈhɛd |-ed -ɪd
beheld bɪˈhɛld
behemoth bɪˈhiməθ, ˈbiəməθ

Key: See in full §§3–47. bee bi |pity ˈpɪtɪ (§6) |rate ret |yet jɛt |sang sæŋ |angry ˈæŋ·grɪ
|bath bæθ; E baθ (§10) |ah ɑ |far fɑr |watch watʃ, wɒtʃ (§12) |jaw dʒɔ |gorge gɔrdʒ |go go

behest bɪˈhɛst
behind bɪˈhaɪnd |-hand bɪˈhaɪndˌhænd
behold bɪˈhold |-held -ˈhɛld |arch. pptc
  -holden -ˈholdən
behoof bɪˈhuf |-s -s
behoove bɪˈhuv |-d -d
behove bɪˈhov |-d -d
Behring ˈbɪrɪŋ, ˈbɛrɪŋ, ˈberɪŋ
beige beʒ |-s -ɪz (Fr bɛ:ʒ)
being ˈbiɪŋ
Beirut ˈberut, beˈrut
bejewel bɪˈdʒuəl, -ˈdʒɪuəl |-ed -d
bel bɛl
Bel god bɛl, abbr. name bɛl
Bela, Belah ˈbilə
belabor bɪˈlebɚ; ES -ˈlebə(r; |-ed -d |-ing
  -ˈlebərɪŋ, -ˈlebrɪŋ
Belarius bəˈlɛrɪəs, -ˈlær-, -ˈler- |-ˈs -ɪz
belate bɪˈlet |-d -ɪd
belaud bɪˈlɔd |-ed -ɪd
belay bɪˈle |-ed -d
belch, B- bɛltʃ |-es -ɪz |-ed -t
beldam ˈbɛldəm |-dame -dəm, -dem
beleaguer bɪˈligɚ; ES -ˈligə(r; |-ed -d |-ing
  -ˈligərɪŋ, -ˈligrɪŋ
Belfast US ˈbɛlfæst, Irel ˈbɛlfæst, bɛlˈfæst;
  E+-ast, -ɑst
belfry ˈbɛlfrɪ |-fried -frɪd
Belgian ˈbɛldʒɪən, -dʒən |-gium -dʒɪəm,
  -dʒəm
Belgic ˈbɛldʒɪk
Belgrade bɛlˈgred, ˈbɛlgred
Belgravia bɛlˈgrevɪə
Belial ˈbilɪəl, -ljəl
belie bɪˈlaɪ |-d -d
belief bəˈlif, bļˈif, bɪˈlif
believe bəˈliv, bļˈiv, bɪˈliv |-d -d
belike bɪˈlaɪk
Belinda bəˈlɪndə
Belisarius ˌbɛləˈsɛrɪəs, -ˈser- |-ˈs -ɪz
Belisha beacon bəˈliʃəˈbikən
belittle bɪˈlɪtļ |-d -d |-ling -ˈlɪtlɪŋ, -tlɪŋ
belive bɪˈlaɪv
Belize bɛˈliz
Belknap ˈbɛlnæp, bɛlˈnæp
bell, B- bɛl |belled bɛld
belladonna ˌbɛləˈdɑnə; ES+-ˈdɒnə
Bellaire bəˈlɛr, bɛ-, -ˈlær; E -ˈlɛə(r, ES
  -ˈlæə(r

Bellamy ˈbɛləmɪ
bellboy ˈbɛlˌbɔɪ
belle, B- bɛl
Bellefontaine O bɛlˈfauntṇ, -ɑn-, -ɒn-, -tɪn
Bellerophon bəˈlɛrəfən, -ˌfɑn, -ˌfɒn
Bellerus bəˈlɪrəs, -ˈlirəs |-ˈs -ɪz
belles-lettres bɛlˈlɛtrə, -tɚ; ES -trə, -tə(r;
  (Fr bɛlˈlɛtṛ)
belletrist bɛlˈlɛtrɪst |-ic ˌbɛllɛˈtrɪstɪk
bellicose ˈbɛləˌkos
bellicosity ˌbɛləˈkasətɪ; ES+-ˈkɒs-
belligerence bəˈlɪdʒərəns |-cy -ɪ |-ent -ənt
Bellingham US ˈbɛlɪŋˌhæm, Engd ˈbɛlɪndʒəm
Bellini beˈlini (It belˈli:ni)
bellmouthed ˈbɛlˌmauðd, -θt
Belloc bɛˈlak; ES+-ˈlɒk
Bellona bəˈlonə, bɛ-
bellow ˈbɛlo, ˈbɛlə |-ed -d |-ing ˈbɛləwɪŋ
bellows ˈbɛloz, -əz, -əs |double pl bellowses
  ˈbɛləsɪz
Bellows Falls ˈbɛlozˈfɔlz, ˈbɛləz- |-ˈs -ɪz
bellwether ˈbɛlˌwɛðɚ; ES -ˌwɛðə(r
belly ˈbɛlɪ |bellied ˈbɛlɪd
Belmont ˈbɛlmant, -mɒnt
Beloit bəˈlɔɪt
belong bəˈlɔŋ, -ˈlɒŋ; S+-ˈlaŋ; |-ed -d
belove bɪˈlʌv |-d -d
beloved adj bɪˈlʌvɪd, -ˈlʌvd
below bəˈlo
Belshazzar bɛlˈʃæzɚ; ES -ˈʃæzə(r
belt bɛlt |belted ˈbɛltɪd
Beluchistan bəˌlutʃɪˈstæn, -ˈstɑn, bəˈlutʃɪ-
  ˌstæn, -ˌstɑn, -ukɪ-
belvedere, B- ˌbɛlvəˈdɪr; ES -ˈdɪə(r
belying ptc of belie bɪˈlaɪɪŋ
bemaul bɪˈmɔl |-ed -d
bemazed bɪˈmezd
bemean bɪˈmin |-ed -d
bemire bɪˈmaɪr; ES -ˈmaɪə(r; |-d -d
Bemis ˈbimɪs |-ˈs -ɪz
bemoan bɪˈmon |-ed -d
bemock bɪˈmak, -ˈmɒk, -ˈmɔk |-ed -t
bemuddle bɪˈmʌdļ |-d -d |-ling -ˈmʌdlɪŋ,
  -dlɪŋ
bemuse bɪˈmjuz, -ˈmɪuz |-s -ɪz |-d -d |-dly
  -ɪdlɪ
Ben bɛn
bename bɪˈnem |-d -d |pptc -d -d or -nempt
  -ˈnɛmpt or -nempted -ˈnɛmptɪd

|full fʊl |tooth tuθ |further ˈfɝðɚ; ES ˈfɝðə |custom ˈkʌstəm |while hwaɪl |how haʊ |toy tɔɪ
|using ˈjuzɪŋ |fuse fjuz, fɪuz |dish dɪʃ |vision ˈvɪʒən |Eden ˈidṇ |cradle ˈkredļ |keep 'em ˈkipṃ

Benares bə'nɑrɪz |-'s -ɪz
Ben Avon *Pa* bɛn'ævən, *Scotl* -'evən, bɛn'ɑn
bench bɛntʃ |-es -ɪz |-ed -t
bend bɛnd |bent bɛnt, *arch.* bended 'bɛndɪd
beneath bɪ'niθ, -'niθ̬
benedicite, B- ˌbɛnə'dɪsətɪ, *Chauc.* ˌbɛndɪs'te
Benedick 'bɛnəˌdɪk
benedict, B- 'bɛnəˌdɪkt
benedictine *liquor* ˌbɛnə'dɪktɪn
Benedictine *monk* ˌbɛnə'dɪktɪn, -tin
benediction ˌbɛnə'dɪkʃən
Benedictus ˌbɛnɪ'dɪktəs |-es -ɪz
benefaction ˌbɛnə'fækʃən
benefactor 'bɛnəˌfæktɚ, ˌbɛnə'fæktɚ; ES
-tə(r
benefactress 'bɛnəˌfæktrɪs, ˌbɛnə'fæktrɪs |-es
-ɪz
benefic bə'nɛfɪk
benefice 'bɛnəfɪs |-s -ɪz, -ˌfɪsɪz |-d -t
beneficence bə'nɛfəsn̩s |-cent -sn̩t
beneficial ˌbɛnə'fɪʃəl |-ly -ɪ
beneficiary ˌbɛnə'fɪʃərɪ, -'fɪʃɪˌɛrɪ
benefit 'bɛnəfɪt |-ted -ɪd, -ˌfɪtɪd
Beneš 'bɛnɛʃ |-'s -ɪz
Benet 'bɛnɪt
Benét be'ne
benevolence bə'nɛvələns, -vləns |-s -ɪz |-lent
-lənt
Benewah 'bɛnəˌwa, -ˌwɒ
Bengal bɛn'gɔl, bɛŋ- ('Benˌgal 'tiger)
Bengalese ˌbɛngə'liz, ˌbɛŋ-
Bengali bɛn'gɔlɪ, bɛŋ-
Bengasi, -ghazi bɛn'gazɪ, bɛŋ-
Benicia bə'niʃə
benighted bɪ'naɪtɪd
benign bɪ'naɪn
benignancy bɪ'nɪgnənsɪ |-nant -nənt |-gnity
-nətɪ
benison 'bɛnəzn̩, -sn̩
Benjamin 'bɛndʒəmən
Ben Lomond bɛn'lomənd
Ben More bɛn'mor, -'mɔr; ES -'moə(r, E+
-'mɔə(r
Bennett 'bɛnɪt
Ben Nevis bɛn'nɛvɪs, -'nivɪs |-'s -ɪz
Bennington 'bɛnɪŋtən
Benoni bə'nonaɪ, bɛ-
Benson 'bɛnsn̩
bent bɛnt

Bentham 'bɛnθəm, 'bɛntəm—'bɛnθəm *is a
sp. pron.*
benthos 'bɛnθɒs; ES+-θɒs
Benton 'bɛntən
benumb bɪ'nʌm |-ed -d |-edness -'nʌmdnɪs,
-ɪdnɪs
Ben Venue ˌbɛnvə'nu, -'nɪu, -'nju
Benvolio bɛn'volɪˌo, -ljo
Ben Vorlich, Voir- bɛn'vɔrlɪk; ES -'vɔə-; (*Sc*
-'vɔrlɪx)
benzaldehyde bɛn'zældəˌhaɪd
benzene, -zine 'bɛnzin, bɛn'zin
benzoate bɛn'zo·ɪt, -et
benzoic bɛn'zo·ɪk
benzoin 'bɛnzo·ɪn, bɛn'zo-
benzol 'bɛnzol, -zal, -zɒl |-zole -zol
Beowulf 'beəˌwʊlf
bepaint bɪ'pent |-ed -ɪd
bequeath bɪ'kwiθ̬ |-ed -d |-al -əl
bequest bɪ'kwɛst
berate bɪ'ret |-rated -'retɪd
Berber 'bɝbɚ; ES 'bɜbə(r, 'bɝbə(r
Berbera 'bɝbərə; ES 'bɜ-, 'bɝ-
berceuse *Fr* bɛr'sø:z
Berea bə'riə |-n -n
bereave bə'riv |-d -d *or* -reft -'rɛft
Berengaria ˌbɛrɪŋ'gɛrɪə, -'gɛr-
Berenice ˌbɛrə'naɪsɪ
Beresford 'bɛrɪzfɚd, -rɪs-; ES -fəd
beret bə're, 'bɛrɪt (*Fr* be'rɛ)
bergamot 'bɝgəˌmat; ES 'bɜ-, 'bɝ-, -ˌmɒt
Bergen *NJ* 'bɝgən, *NY* 'bɝdʒɪn, *Norw,
Neth* 'bɝgən, 'bɛrgən; ES 'bɜ-, 'bɝ-, 'bɛə-
Bergerac 'bɝdʒəˌræk; ES 'bɜ-, 'bɝ-; (*Fr*
bɛrʒə'rak)
Bergson 'bɝgsn̩, 'bɛrg-; ES 'bɜg-, 'bɝg-,
'bɛəg-; (*Fr* bɛrg'sɔ̃n, bɛrk-) |-ism -ˌɪzəm
berhyme, -rime bɪ'raɪm |-d -d
beribboned bɪ'rɪbənd
beriberi 'bɛrɪ'bɛrɪ
Bering 'bɪrɪŋ, 'bɛr- 'ber-
beringed bɪ'rɪŋd
Berkeley *US* 'bɝklɪ, *Engd* 'barklɪ; ES 'bɝk-,
'bɝk-, 'ba:k-, E+'ba:k-
Berkhamsted, -mpstead 'bɝkəmˌstɛd, *loc.*+
'bark-; ES 'bɜk-, 'bɝk-, 'ba:k-;—*The
Brit pron. is* 'bɝkəmstɪd, *loc.*+'ba:k-; *the
corresponding Am is as given above.*
Berkley 'bɝklɪ; ES 'bɝklɪ, 'bɝk-

Key: *See in full* §§3–47. bee bi |pity 'pɪtɪ (§6) |rate ret |yet jɛt |sang sæŋ |angry 'æŋ·grɪ
|bath bæθ; E baθ (§10) |ah ɑ |far fɑr |watch watʃ, wɒtʃ (§12) |jaw dʒɔ |gorge gɔrdʒ |go go

Berks *in Engd short for* Berkshire **'bɑrks**;
ES **'bɑːks**; *Pa* **bɝks**; ES **bɑks, bɝks**
Berkshire *US* **'bɝkʃɪr, -ʃɚ,** *Engd* **'bɑrkʃɪr,
-ʃɚ**; ES **'bɑkʃɪə(r, 'bɝkʃɪə(r, 'bɑːk-, -ʃə(r**
berlin **bɝ'lɪn, bɚ'lɪn, 'bɝlɪn**; ES **bɝ'lɪn, bɝ-,
bə-, 'bɜlɪn, 'bɝ-**
Berlin *US* **'bɝlɪn**; ES **'bɜlɪn, 'bɝ-;** *Germany*
bɝ'lɪn, bɚ'lɪn; ES **bɝ'lɪn, bɝ-, bə-;** *(Ger*
bɛr'liːn) ('Ber₍lin 'wool)
Berlioz **'bɛrlɪ₍oz**; ES **'bɛəlɪ₍oz;** *(Fr* **bɛr'ljöːz,
-'ljoːz)**
berm, -e **bɝm**; ES **bɜm, bɝm**
Bermuda **bɚ'mjudə, -'mɪudə**; ES **bə-;** |-dian
-dɪən
Bern, -e *US* **bɝn,** *Swtz* **bɝn, bɛrn**; ES **bɜn,
bɝn, bɛən;** *(Fr, Ger* **bɛrn)**
Bernard **'bɝnəd, 'bɝnɑrd, bɚ'nɑrd;** ES
'bɜnəd, 'bɝnəd, -nɑːd, bə'nɑːd, E+-ɑːd;
(Fr **bɛr'naːr)**
Bernardo **bɚ'nɑrdo**; ES **bə'nɑːdo,** E+-'naː-
Berners **'bɝnɚz**; ES **'bɜnəz, 'bɝnəz**
Bernhardt **'bɝnhɑrt**; ES **'bɜnhɑːt, 'bɝnhɑːt;**
(Fr **bɛr'naːr)**
Bernice **'bɝnɪs, bɚ'nis**; ES **'bɜnɪs, 'bɝ-,
bə'nis;** |-'s -ɪz
Bernicia **bɚ'nɪʃɪə**; ES **bə'nɪʃ-**
bernicle **'bɑrnɪk|**; ES **'bɑːn-;** =barnacle
Berowne **bɪ'run**
berretta **bə'rɛtə**
berrigan **'bɛrɪgən**
berry **'bɛrɪ** |berried **'bɛrɪd**
berserk **'bɝsɝk**; ES **'bɜsɜk, 'bɝsɝk;** |-er -ɚ;
ES **-ə(r**
berth **bɝθ**; ES **bɜθ, bɝθ;** |-ths **-θs**
Bertha, b- **'bɝθə**; ES **'bɜθə, 'bɝθə**
Bertillon *system* **'bɝt|₍ɑn, -₍ɒn**; ES **'bɝt-,
'bɝt-;** *(Fr* **bɛrti'jõ)**
Bertram **'bɝtrəm**; ES **'bɜtrəm, 'bɝt-**
Bertrand **'bɝtrənd**; ES **'bɜt-, 'bɝt-;** *(Fr*
bɛr'trɑ̃)
bertrandite **'bɝtrənd₍aɪt**; ES **'bɜt-, 'bɝt-**
beruffled **bɪ'rʌf|d**
Berwick *US* **'bɝwɪk**; ES **'bɜwɪk, 'bɝ-;** *Scott*
'bɛrɪk
Berwickshire **'bɛrɪk₍ʃɪr, -ʃɚ**; ES **-₍ʃɪə(r, -ʃə(r**
Berwyn **'bɝwɪn**; ES **'bɜwɪn, 'bɝ-**
beryl **'bɛrəl, -ɪl**
beryllium **bə'rɪlɪəm**
Besant, *Annie* **'bɛzn̩t,** *Sir Walter* **bə'zænt**

besant **'bɛzn̩t, bə'zænt**
beseech **bɪ'sitʃ** |-es -ɪz |-sought -'sɔt
beseem **bɪ'sim** |-ed -d
beseen **bɪ'sin**
beset **bɪ'sɛt**
beshrew **bɪ'ʃru, -'ʃrɪu,** *arch.* **bɪ'ʃro** |-ed-d
beside **bɪ'saɪd** |-s -z
besiege **bɪ'sidʒ** |-s -ɪz |-d -d
besmear **bɪ'smɪr**; ES **-'smɪə(r,** S+-'smɛə(r;
|-ed -d
besmirch **bɪ'smɝtʃ**; ES **-'smɜtʃ, -'smɝtʃ;** |-es
-ɪz |-ed -t
besom **'bizəm** |-ed -d
besot **bɪ'sɑt;** ES+-'sɒt; |-ted -ɪd
besought **bɪ'sɔt**
bespake **bɪ'spek**
bespangle **bɪ'spæŋg|** |-ed -d |-ling -glɪŋ,
-glɪŋ
bespatter **bɪ'spætɚ**; ES **-'spætə(r;** |-ed -d
bespeak **bɪ'spik** |-spoke -'spok |-spoken
-'spokən
bespouse **bɪ'spaʊz** |-s -ɪz |-d -d
bespread **bɪ'sprɛd**
besprent **bɪ'sprɛnt**
besprinkle **bɪ'sprɪŋk|** |-d -d |-ling -klɪŋ,
-k|ɪŋ
Bess **bɛs** |Bess's **'bɛsɪz** |-ie -ɪ
Bessarabia **₍bɛsə'rebɪə** |-n -n
Bessemer **'bɛsəmɚ**; ES **'bɛsəmə(r**
best **bɛst** |bested **'bɛstɪd**
best-dressed **'bɛst'drɛst** ('best-₍dressed 'man)
bestead, -sted *adj* **bɪ'stɛd**
bestead *v* **bɪ'stɛd** |*past* -steaded -'stɛdɪd
|*pptc* -stead -'stɛd
bestial **'bɛstʃəl, -tɪəl** |-ly -ɪ
bestiality **₍bɛstʃɪ'ælətɪ, ₍bɛstɪ-**
bestiary **'bɛstɪ₍ɛrɪ**
bestir **bɪ'stɝ**; ES **-'stɜ(r, -'stɝ;** |-red -d
best-known **'bɛst'non**
best-liked **'bɛst'laɪkt** ('best-₍liked 'play)
bestow **bɪ'sto** |-ed -d |-al -əl
bestraddle **bɪ'stræd|** |-d -d |-ling -dlɪŋ, -d|ɪŋ
bestrew **bɪ'stru, -'strɪu** |-ed -d |-ed -d *or*
-n -n
bestride **bɪ'straɪd** |-strode -'strod |-stridden
-'strɪdn̩
bestrow **bɪ'stro** |-ed -d |-ed -d *or* -n -n
bet **bɛt** |*past & pptc* bet **bɛt** *or* betted **'bɛtɪd**
beta *Gk letter* **'betə, 'bitə**

|full **fʊl** |tooth **tuθ** |further **'fɝðɚ**; ES **'fɝðə;** |custom **'kʌstəm** |while **hwaɪl** |how **haʊ** |toy **tɔɪ**
|using **'juzɪŋ** |fuse **fjuz, fɪuz** |dish **dɪʃ** |vision **'vɪʒən** |Eden **'idn̩** |cradle **'kred|** |keep 'em **'kipm̩**

Beta, b- *'beet'* 'bitə
betaine 'bitɪ‚in
betake bɪ'tek |-took -'tʊk |-taken -'tekən
betel 'bitḷ
Betelgeuse, -geux 'bitḷ‚dʒuz, 'bɛtḷ‚dʒʒz |-'s -ɪz
bête noire 'bet'nwɑr; ES -'nwɑ:(r; *(Fr* bɛ:t'nwɑ:r)
Bethany 'bɛθənɪ
bethel, B- 'bɛθəl
Bethesda bə'θɛzdə
bethink bɪ'θɪŋk |-thought -'θɔt
Bethlehem 'bɛθlɪəm, 'bɛθlɪ‚hɛm
Bethnal 'bɛθnəl
bethought bɪ'θɔt
Bethphage 'bɛθfədʒɪ, -‚dʒi
Bethsaida bɛθ'seədə
Bethune *surnames, US places* bə'θjun, -'θɪun, -'θun, 'bitṇ
Béthune bə'θjun, -'θɪun, -'θun *(Fr* be'tyn)
betide bɪ'taɪd |-d -ɪd *or arch.* -tid -'tɪd
betimes bɪ'taɪmz
betoken bɪ'tokən |-ed -d |-ing -'tokənɪŋ, -knɪŋ
betook bɪ'tʊk
betray bɪ'tre |-ed -d |-al -əl
betroth bɪ'trɔθ, -'trɒθ, -'troð |-ed -θt, -ðd |-al -əl
Betsy 'bɛtsɪ
better 'bɛtɚ; ES 'bɛtə(r; |-ed -d
bettor 'bɛtɚ; ES 'bɛtə(r
Bettws-y-Coed 'bɛtəzɪ'ko·ɪd, -sɪ-
Betty 'bɛtɪ
between bə'twin
betwixt bə'twɪkst
Beulah 'bjulə, 'bɪulə
Bevan 'bɛvən
bevel 'bɛvḷ |-ed -d |-ing 'bɛvlɪŋ, 'bɛvḷɪŋ
Beven 'bɛvən
beverage 'bɛvrɪdʒ, 'bɛvərɪdʒ |-s -ɪz
Beveridge 'bɛvrɪdʒ, 'bɛvərɪdʒ |-'s -ɪz
Beverley, -ly 'bɛvɚlɪ; ES 'bɛvəlɪ
Bevier bɪ'vɪr; ES -'vɪə(r
Bevis 'bivɪs, 'bɛvɪs |-'s- ɪz
bevy 'bɛvɪ
bewail bɪ'wel |-ed -d
beware bɪ'wɛr, -'wær; E -'wɛə(r, ES -'wæə(r; |-d -d
beweep bɪ'wip |-wept -'wɛpt
Bewick 'bjuɪk, 'bɪuɪk

bewilder bɪ'wɪldɚ; ES -'wɪldə(r; |-ed -d |-ing -'wɪldrɪŋ, -'wɪldərɪŋ
bewitch bɪ'wɪtʃ |-es -ɪz |-ed -t
bewray bɪ're |-ed -d
Bexar *Tex, loc.* bær, bæə(r *(Sp* 'bɛxar)
bey be
beyond bɪ'jɑnd, bɪ'ɑnd, -'jɒnd, -'ɒnd
Beyrouth 'berut, be'rut
Beza 'bizə
bezant, bezz- 'bɛzṇt, bə'zænt
bezel, -il 'bɛzḷ |-ed -d
bezique bə'zik
bezonian bə'zonɪən
bhang bæŋ
Bianca bɪ'æŋkə *(It* 'bjaŋkɑ)
biannual baɪ'ænjʊəl |-ly -ɪ
Biarritz 'bɪə‚rɪts *(Fr* bja'rits)
bias 'baɪəs |-es -ɪz |-ed -t
bib bɪb |bibbed bɪbd
bibber 'bɪbɚ; ES 'bɪbə(r
bibcock 'bɪb‚kɑk; ES+-‚kɒk
bibelot 'bɪblo *(Fr* bi'blo)
Bible 'baɪbḷ
Biblical 'bɪblɪkḷ |-ly -ɪ, -ɪklɪ
Biblicism 'bɪblɪ‚sɪzəm |-cist -sɪst
bibliographer ‚bɪblɪ'ɑgrəfɚ, -'ɒg-; ES -fə(r; |-phy -fɪ
bibliographic ‚bɪblɪə'græfɪk |-al -ḷ |-ally -ḷɪ, -ɪklɪ
bibliolater ‚bɪblɪ'ɑlətɚ; ES -'ɑlətə(r, -'ɒl-; |-try -trɪ
bibliomania ‚bɪblɪə'menɪə, -njə |-iac -ɪ‚æk
bibliophile 'bɪblɪə‚fɪl |-phile -‚faɪl
bibulosity ‚bɪbjə'lɑsətɪ; ES+-'lɒs-
bibulous 'bɪbjələs
bicameral baɪ'kæmərəl
bicarbonate baɪ'kɑrbənɪt, -‚net; ES -'kɑ:b-, E+-'kɑ:b-
bicaudal baɪ'kɔdḷ |-date -det
bice baɪs
bicentenary baɪ'sɛntə‚nɛrɪ, ‚baɪsɛn'tɛnərɪ; *Brit* -'tin-, -'tɛn-
bicentennial ‚baɪsɛn'tɛnɪəl |-ly -ɪ
biceps 'baɪsɛps |-es -ɪz
Bicester 'bɪstɚ; ES 'bɪstə(r; (Bister *1634*)
bichlorid baɪ'klorɪd, -'klɔr-; S -'klor-; |-ide -aɪd, -ɪd
bichromate *n* baɪ'kromɪt, -met
bichromate *v* baɪ'kromet |-d -ɪd

Key: See in full §§3–47. bee bi |pity 'pɪtɪ (§6) |rate ret |yet jɛt |sang sæŋ |angry 'æŋ·grɪ |bath bæθ; E baθ (§10) |ah ɑ |far fɑr |watch wɑtʃ, wɒtʃ (§12) |jaw dʒɔ |gorge gɔrdʒ |go go

bicker 'bɪkɚ; ES 'bɪkə(r; |-ed -d |-ing 'bɪkərɪŋ,
  'bɪkrɪŋ
Bickerstaff 'bɪkɚˌstæf; ES 'bɪkə-, E+-ˌstaf,
  -ˌstaf
Bicknell 'bɪknəl
bicolor 'baɪˌkʌlɚ; ES -ˌkʌlə(r; |-ed -d
biconcave baɪ'kankev, -'kaŋ-, ˌbaɪkan'kev;
  ES+-ɒ-
biconvex baɪ'kanvɛks, ˌbaɪkan'vɛks; ES+
  -ɒn-
bicron 'baɪkran, 'bɪk-; ES+-krɒn
bicuspid baɪ'kʌspɪd |-ate -ˌet
bicycle 'baɪˌsɪkl̩, 'baɪsɪkl̩ |-d -d |-ling -klɪŋ,
  -kl̩ɪŋ
bicyclic 'of bicycles' baɪ'sɪklɪk, 'baɪsɪk-
bicyclic 'two-cycled' baɪ'saɪklɪk, -'sɪk-
bicyclist 'b. rider' 'baɪˌsɪklɪst, -sɪklɪst
bid 'ask' bɪd |past bade, bad bæd or bid bɪd
  |pptc bidden 'bɪdn̩ or bid bɪd
bid 'offer' bɪd |past & pptc bid bɪd
biddable 'bɪdəbl̩ |-bly -blɪ
Biddeford Me 'bɪdəfɚd; ES 'bɪdəfəd
biddy 'bɪdɪ
bide baɪd |past bode bod or bided 'baɪdɪd
  |pptc bided 'baɪdɪd
Bideford Engd 'bɪdəfɚd; ES 'bɪdəfəd
bidentate baɪ'dɛntet
Biela 'bilə
biennial baɪ'ɛnɪəl |-ly -ɪ
bier bɪr; ES bɪə(r, S+bɛə(r
biff bɪf |biffed bɪft
bifid 'baɪfɪd
biflex 'baɪflɛks
bifocal adj baɪ'fokl̩ ('biˌfocal 'lenses)
bifocal n 'baɪfokl̩, baɪ'fokl̩ |-s -z
bifurcate adj 'baɪfɚˌket, baɪ'fɝkɪt; ES 'baɪfə-,
  -'fɜkɪt, -'fɝkɪt
bifurcate v 'baɪfɚˌket, baɪ'fɝket; ES 'baɪfə-,
  -'fɜket, -'fɝket; |-d -ɪd
bifurcation ˌbaɪfɚ'keʃən; ES ˌbaɪfə-
big bɪg
bigamist 'bɪgəmɪst |-mous -məs |-my -mɪ
Bigelow 'bɪgəˌlo, 'bɪglo
bighead 'bɪgˌhɛd |-ed 'bɪg'hɛdɪd
bighorn 'bɪgˌhɔrn; ES -ˌhɔən
Big Horn riv. 'bɪg'hɔrn; ES -'hɔən; (The
  'Big 'Horn, 'Big ˌHorn 'River)
bight baɪt |bighted 'baɪtɪd
Biglow 'bɪglo

bigot, B- 'bɪgət |-ed -ɪd |-ry -rɪ
bigwig 'bɪgˌwɪg |-ged -d |-gery -ərɪ, -rɪ
bijou 'biʒu, bɪ'ʒu
bike baɪk
bilabial baɪ'lebɪəl
bilabiate baɪ'lebɪˌet, -bɪt
Bilaspur bɪ'læspur, -'las-; ES -puə(r
bilateral baɪ'lætərəl |-ly -ɪ
Bilbao bɪl'bao
bilberry 'bɪlˌbɛrɪ, -bərɪ
bilbo 'bɪlbo
Bildad 'bɪldæd
bile baɪl
bilge bɪldʒ |-s -ɪz |-d -d
biliary 'bɪlɪˌɛrɪ
bilinear baɪ'lɪnɪɚ; ES -'lɪnɪ·ə(r
bilingual baɪ'lɪŋgwəl |-ism -ˌɪzəm |-ly -ɪ
bilious 'bɪljəs
biliteral baɪ'lɪtərəl |-ism -ˌɪzəm
bilk bɪlk |bilked bɪlkt
bill bɪl |billed bɪld |-able -əbl
billboard 'bɪlˌbord, -ˌbɔrd; ES -ˌboəd, E+
  -ˌbɔəd
Billerica Mass 'bɪlrɪkə
Billericay Engd ˌbɪlə'rɪkɪ
billet 'bɪlɪt |-ed -ɪd
billet-doux 'bɪlɪ'du |pl -doux -'duz (Fr
  bijɛ'du)
billfold 'bɪlˌfold
billhead 'bɪlˌhɛd
billiard 'bɪljɚd; ES 'bɪljəd; |-s -z
billingsgate, B- 'bɪlɪŋzˌget, -gɪt
billion 'bɪljən |-aire ˌbɪljən'ɛr, -'ær; E -'ɛə(r,
  ES -'æə(r; |-th -θ |-ths -θs
billow 'bɪlo, 'bɪlə |-ed -d |-ing 'bɪləwɪŋ |-y
  'bɪləwɪ
billposter 'bɪlˌpostɚ; ES -ˌpostə(r
billsticker 'bɪlˌstɪkɚ; ES -ˌstɪkə(r
billy, B- 'bɪlɪ
bilobate baɪ'lobet |-d -ɪd
bimanual baɪ'mænjuəl |-ly -ɪ
bimensal baɪ'mɛnsl̩
bimester baɪ'mɛstɚ; ES -'mɛstə(r
bimetallic ˌbaɪmə'tælɪk
bimetallism baɪ'mɛtl̩ˌɪzəm |-ist -ɪst
bimonthly baɪ'mʌnθlɪ
bin bɪn |binned bɪnd
binary 'baɪnərɪ |-nate -net
binaural bɪn'ɔrəl

|full fʊl |tooth tuθ |further 'fɝðɚ; ES 'fɝðə |custom 'kʌstəm |while hwaɪl |how haʊ |toy tɔɪ
|using 'juzɪŋ |fuse fjuz, fɪuz |dish dɪʃ |vision 'vɪʒən |Eden 'idn̩ |cradle 'kredl̩ |keep 'em 'kipm̩

bind baɪnd |bound baʊnd |*arch pptc* bounden 'baʊndən

binder 'baɪndɚ; ES 'baɪndə(r; |-y -dərɪ, -drɪ

bine baɪn

Binet bɪ'ne, bi- (*Fr* bi'nɛ)

Bingen 'bɪŋən

Bingham 'bɪŋəm |-ton -tən

Bingley 'bɪŋlɪ

bingo 'bɪŋgo

binnacle, binocle 'bɪnəkl̩

binocular baɪ'nakjələɚ, bɪ-; ES -'nakjələ(r, -'nɒk-

binomial baɪ'nomɪəl |-ly -ɪ

Binyon 'bɪnjən

biochemic ˌbaɪo'kɛmɪk |-al -l̩ |-ally -l̩ɪ, -ɪklɪ

biochemistry ˌbaɪo'kɛmɪstrɪ

biogenesis ˌbaɪo'dʒɛnəsɪs

biogenetic ˌbaɪodʒə'nɛtɪk |-al -l̩ |-ally -l̩ɪ, -ɪklɪ

biogeography ˌbaɪodʒi'agrəfɪ, -'ɒg-

biographer baɪ'agrəfɚ, bɪ-, -'ɒg-; ES -fə(r

biographic ˌbaɪə'græfɪk |-al -l̩ |-ally -l̩ɪ, -ɪklɪ

biography baɪ'agrəfɪ, bɪ-, -'ɒg-

biologic ˌbaɪə'ladʒɪk; ES+-'lɒdʒ-; |-al -l̩ |-ally -l̩ɪ, -ɪklɪ

biology baɪ'alədʒɪ; ES+-'ɒl-; |-gist -dʒɪst

biometric ˌbaɪə'mɛtrɪk |-al -l̩ |-ally -l̩ɪ, -ɪklɪ

biometry baɪ'amətrɪ; ES+-'ɒm-

Bion 'baɪən

Biondello ˌbiən'dɛlo

biophysics ˌbaɪo'fɪzɪks |-cal -kl̩

biotic baɪ'atɪk; ES+-'ɒt-; |-al -l̩

biotite 'baɪəˌtaɪt

biparous 'bɪpərəs

bipartisan baɪ'partəzn̩; ES -'pɑ:t-, E+-'pɑ:t-; |-ship -ˌʃɪp

bipartite baɪ'partaɪt; ES -'pɑ:t-, E+-'pɑ:t-

biped 'baɪpɛd |-al -l̩, 'bɪpədl̩

bipetalous baɪ'pɛtl̩əs

bipinnate baɪ'pɪnet

biplane 'baɪˌplen

bipolar baɪ'polɚ; ES -'polə(r

bipolarity ˌbaɪpo'lærətɪ

biquadratic ˌbaɪkwad'rætɪk, -kwɒd-

birch bɝtʃ; ES bɜtʃ, bɝtʃ; |-es -ɪz |ed -t |-en -ən

bird bɝd; ES bɜd, bɝd; |-ed -ɪd |-ie -ɪ

birdbath 'bɝdˌbæθ; ES 'bɜd-, 'bɝd-, E+ -ˌbaθ, -ˌbaθ; |-ths -ðz

birdhouse 'bɝdˌhaʊs; ES 'bɜd-, 'bɝd-; |-ses -zɪz

birdlime 'bɝdˌlaɪm; ES 'bɜd-, 'bɝd-

birdseed 'bɝdˌsid; ES 'bɜd-, 'bɝd-

bird's-eye 'bɝdzˌaɪ; ES 'bɜdz-, 'bɝdz-

biretta bə'rɛtə

Birkenhead 'bɝkənˌhɛd; ES 'bɜk-, 'bɝk-; *loc.* ˌBirken'head

birl bɝl; ES bɜl, bɝl; |-ed -d

Birmingham *US* 'bɝmɪŋˌhæm, -ŋəm, *Engd* 'bɝmɪŋəm; ES 'bɜm-, 'bɝm-

Biron 'baɪrən, *in Shak.* bɪ'run *spelt* Berowne

birr bɝ; ES bɜ(r, bɝ; |-ed -d

Birrell 'bɪrəl

birth bɝθ; ES bɜθ, bɝθ; |-ths -θs |-day -ˌde

birthmark 'bɝθˌmark; ES 'bɜθˌmɑːk, 'bɝθ-ˌmɑːk, E+-ˌmɑːk

birthplace 'bɝθˌples; ES 'bɜθ-, 'bɝθ-; |-s -ɪz

birthright 'bɝθˌraɪt; ES 'bɜθ-, 'bɝθ-

bis bɪs

Biscay 'bɪskɪ, -ke

biscuit 'bɪskɪt

bisect *n* 'baɪsɛkt

bisect *v* baɪ'sɛkt |-ed -ɪd |-ction -kʃən

bishop, B- 'bɪʃəp |-ric -rɪk

Bismarck 'bɪzmark; ES -mɑːk, E+-mɑːk; (*Ger* 'bɪs-)

bismuth 'bɪzməθ |-al -əl

bismuthic bɪz'mjuθɪk, -'mɪu-, -'mʌθɪk

bison 'baɪsn̩, -zn̩

Bispham 'bɪspəm

bisque bɪsk

bister, -tre 'bɪstɚ; ES 'bɪstə(r

bisulphate baɪ'sʌlfet

bisulphid baɪ'sʌlfɪd |-ide -aɪd, -ɪd

bisulphite baɪ'sʌlfaɪt

bisymmetric ˌbaɪsɪ'mɛtrɪk |-al -l̩ |-ally -l̩ɪ, -ɪklɪ

bisymmetry baɪ'sɪmɪtrɪ

bit bɪt |bitted 'bɪtɪd

bitch bɪtʃ |bitches 'bɪtʃɪz |-ed -t

bite baɪt |bit bɪt |bitten 'bɪtn̩

bitstock 'bɪtˌstak, -ˌstɒk

bitt bɪt |bitted 'bɪtɪd

bitten 'bɪtn̩

bitter 'bɪtɚ; ES 'bɪtə(r; |-s -z

bittern 'bɪtɚn; ES 'bɪtən

Key: See in full §§3–47. bee bi |pity 'pɪtɪ (§6) |rate ret |yet jɛt |sang sæŋ |angry 'æŋ·grɪ |bath bæθ; E baθ (§10) |ah ɑ |far fɑr |watch watʃ, wɒtʃ (§12) |jaw dʒɔ |gorge gɔrdʒ |go go

bitternut 'bɪtənət, -ˌnʌt; ES 'bɪtə-
bitterroot 'bɪtəˌrut, -ˌrʊt; ES 'bɪtə-
bittersweet 'bɪtəˌswit, -'swit; ES 'bɪtə-
bitumen bɪ'tjumən, -'tɪu-, -'tu-, 'bɪtʃumən
bituminous bɪ'tjumənəs, baɪ-, -'tɪu-, -'tu-
bivalence baɪ'veləns, 'bɪvələns |-cy -ɪ |-nt
-nt
bivalve 'baɪˌvælv |-d -d
bivouac 'bɪvʊˌæk, 'bɪvwæk |-ked -t
biweekly baɪ'wiklɪ
biyearly baɪ'jɪrlɪ; ES -'jɪəlɪ, S+-'jɛəlɪ
bizarre bɪ'zɑr; ES -'zɑ:(r, E+-'za:(r
Bizet bɪ'ze (Fr bi'zɛ)
Björnson 'bjɜ˞nsn̩; ES 'bjɜn-, 'bjɜ˞n-; (Norw
'bjø:rnsɔn)
blab blæb |blabbed blæbd
black blæk |blacked blækt
blackamoor 'blækəˌmʊr; ES -ˌmʊə(r
black-and-blue 'blækən'blu, 'blækn̩'blu,
-'blɪu
blackball 'blækˌbɔl |-ed -d
black-berried 'blæk'bɛrɪd ('black-ˌberried
'elder)
blackberry 'blækˌbɛrɪ, -bərɪ |-ried -d
blackbird 'blækˌbɜ˞d; ES -ˌbɜd, -ˌbɜ˞d
blackboard 'blækˌbord, -ˌbɔrd; ES -ˌboəd,
E+-ˌbɔəd
Blackburn 'blækbən; ES 'blækbən
blackcap 'blækˌkæp
blackcock 'blækˌkɑk; ES+-ˌkɒk
blackdamp 'blækˌdæmp
blacken 'blækən |-ed -d |-ing 'blækənɪŋ,
-knɪŋ
black-eyed 'blæk'aɪd ('black-ˌeyed 'Susan)
Blackfeet 'blækˌfit
blackfellow 'blækˌfɛlo, -ˌfɛlə
blackfish 'blækˌfɪʃ
Blackfoot 'blækˌfʊt |-feet -ˌfit
Blackfriars 'blækˌfraɪəz, -'fraɪəz; ES -ˌfraɪ·əz,
-'fraɪ·əz
blackguard 'blægəd, 'blægard; ES 'blægəd,
-gɑ:d, E+-ga:d; |-ed -ɪd |-ry -rɪ
blackhead 'blækˌhɛd
Blackheath 'blækˌhiθ, -'hiθ
blackjack 'blækˌdʒæk |-ed -t
Black Jack 'blæk'dʒæk
blackleg 'blækˌlɛg
blacklist 'blækˌlɪst |-ed -ɪd
blackmail 'blækˌmel |-ed -d

Blackmore 'blækmor, -mɔr; ES -moə(r, E+
-mɔə(r
blacksmith 'blæksmɪθ |-ths -θs |-ing -ˌsmɪθɪŋ
Blackstone 'blækˌston, -stən
black-throated 'blæk'θrotɪd ('black-ˌthroated
'warbler)
Blackwells 'blækˌwɛlz, -wəlz
bladder 'blædə; ES 'blædə(r; |-ed -d |-ing
'blædərɪŋ, -drɪŋ
blade bled |bladed 'bledɪd
blah blɑ
blain blen |blained blend
Blaine blen
Blake blek
blamable 'bleməbl̩ |-bly -blɪ
blame blem |-ed -d |able -əbl̩ |-bly -blɪ
blameful 'blemfəl |-ly -ɪ
blameless 'blemlɪs
blameworthy 'blemˌwɜ˞ðɪ; ES -ˌwɜðɪ, -ˌwɜ˞ðɪ
Blanc, Mont mɑnt'blæŋk, mɒnt- (Fr mõ'blɑ̃)
blanch blæntʃ; E+blɑntʃ, blantʃ; |-es -ɪz
|-ed -t
Blanch(e) blæntʃ; E+blɑntʃ, blantʃ; |-'s
-ɪz
blancmange blə'mɑnʒ, -mɑndʒ
Blanco 'blæŋko
bland blænd
blandish 'blændɪʃ |-es -ɪz |-ed -t
blank blæŋk |blanked blæŋkt
blankbook 'blæŋkˌbʊk, -'bʊk
blanket 'blæŋkɪt |-ed -ɪd
blare blɛr, blær; E blɛə(r, ES blæə(r; |-d -d
blarney, B- 'blɑrnɪ; ES 'blɑ:nɪ, E+'blɑ:nɪ
blasé blɑ'ze, 'blaze (Fr blɑ'ze)
blaspheme blæs'fim |-d -d
blasphemous 'blæsfɪməs |-my -mɪ, older
blæs'fim-
blast blæst; E+blɑst, blɑst; |-ed -ɪd
blastoderm 'blæstəˌdɜ˞m; ES -ˌdɜm, -ˌdɜ˞m
blastula 'blæstʃʊlə
blat blæt |blatted 'blætɪd
blatancy 'bletn̩sɪ |blatant 'bletn̩t
blather 'blæðə; ES 'blæðə(r; |-ed -d |-ing
'blæðrɪŋ, 'blæðərɪŋ
blatherskite 'blæðəˌskaɪt; ES 'blæðə-
blaze blez |blazes 'blezɪz |blazed blezd
blazon 'blezn̩ |-ed -d |-ing 'blezn̩ɪŋ, -znɪŋ
blazonry 'blezn̩rɪ
bleach blitʃ |bleaches 'blitʃɪz |-ed -t

bleachers 'blitʃɚz; ES 'blitʃəz
bleachery 'blitʃərɪ
bleak blik
blear blɪr; ES blɪə(r, S+blɛə(r; |-ed -d
blearedness 'blɪrɪdnɪs; S+'blɛr-
bleat blit |bleated 'blitɪd
bleb blɛb |-bed -d
bleed blid |bled blɛd
blemish 'blɛmɪʃ |-es -ɪz |-ed -t
blench blɛntʃ |blenches 'blɛntʃɪz |-ed -t
blend blɛnd |blended 'blɛndɪd or blent blɛnt
blende blɛnd
Blenheim 'blɛnəm (Ger Blindheim 'blɪnt-
haɪm)
Blennerhassett ˌblɛnɚ'hæsɪt; ES ˌblɛnə-
blenny 'blɛnɪ
blent blɛnt
bless blɛs |blesses 'blɛsɪz |blessed, blest
blɛst
blessed adj 'blɛsɪd |-ly -lɪ |-ness -nɪs
blessing 'blɛsɪŋ
blest blɛst
blether 'blɛðɚ; ES 'blɛðə(r
blew blu, blɪu
blight blaɪt |blighted 'blaɪtɪd
blighty, B- 'blaɪtɪ
blimp blɪmp
blind blaɪnd |blinded 'blaɪndɪd
blindfold 'blaɪndˌfold, 'blaɪn- |-ed -ɪd
blindman's buff 'blaɪndˌmænz'bʌf, 'blaɪn-
blindness 'blaɪndnɪs, 'blaɪnnɪs
blindworm 'blaɪndˌwɝm; ES -ˌwɝm, -ˌwɝm
blink blɪŋk |blinked blɪŋkt
bliss blɪs |blisses 'blɪsɪz |-ful -fəl |-fully
-fəlɪ
blister 'blɪstɚ; ES 'blɪstə(r; |-ed -d |-ing
'blɪstərɪŋ, 'blɪstrɪŋ
blithe blaɪð |-some -səm
Blithedale 'blaɪðˌdel
blitz blɪts |-es -ɪz |-ed -t
Blitzkrieg 'blɪtsˌkrig (Ger -ˌkri:k)
blizzard 'blɪzɚd; ES 'blɪzəd
bloat blot |bloated 'blotɪd
blob blab; ES+blɒb; |-bed -d
bloc blak; ES+blɒk
Bloch blak; ES+blɒk
block blak; ES+blɒk; |-ed -t
blockade bla'ked; ES+blɒ-; |-d -ɪd
blockhead 'blakˌhɛd; ES+'blɒk-

blockhouse 'blakˌhaʊs; ES+'blɒk-; |-ses
-zɪz
Bloemfontein 'blumfənˌten, -fan-, -fɒn-
blond, -e bland, blɒnd
Blondel trouvère blan'dɛl, blɒn-; Brit name
'blʌndl
blood blʌd |blooded 'blʌdɪd |-ily -ɪ, -ɪlɪ
blood-boltered 'blʌdˌboltɚd, -ˌbɒltəd; ES
-təd; cf baltered
bloodcurdling 'blʌdˌkɝdlɪŋ; ES -ˌkɝd-, -ˌkɝd-
bloodguilty 'blʌdˌgɪltɪ
bloodhound 'blʌdˌhaʊnd |-ed -ɪd
bloodletting 'blʌdˌlɛtɪŋ
blood-red 'blʌd'rɛd ('blood-ˌred 'wine)
bloodroot 'blʌdˌrut, -ˌrʊt
bloodshed 'blʌdˌʃɛd
bloodshot 'blʌdˌʃat; ES+-ˌʃɒt
bloodstain 'blʌdˌsten |-ed -d
bloodsucker 'blʌdˌsʌkɚ; ES -ˌsʌkə(r
bloodthirsty 'blʌdˌθɝstɪ; ES -ˌθɝstɪ, -ˌθɝstɪ
bloom blum |bloomed blumd |-age -ɪdʒ
bloomers 'blumɚz; ES 'bluməz
bloomery 'blumərɪ
Bloomfield 'blumˌfild
Bloomington 'blumɪŋtən
Bloomsbury 'blumzˌbɛrɪ, -bərɪ
blossom, B- 'blasəm; ES+'blɒsəm; |-ed -d
blot blat; ES+blɒt; |-ted -ɪd
blotch blatʃ; ES+blɒtʃ; |-es -ɪz |-ed -t
blotter 'blatɚ; ES 'blatə(r, 'blɒt-
blotto 'blato; ES+'blɒto
Blount blaʊnt, blʌnt
blouse blaʊs, blaʊz |-s -ɪz |-d -t, -d
blow of wind blo |blew blu, blɪu |blown blon
or slang blowed blod
blow 'blossom' blo |blew blu, blɪu |blown
blon
blowfly 'bloˌflaɪ
blowgun 'bloˌgʌn
blowhole 'bloˌhol
blown blon
blowoff 'bloˌɔf, -ˌɒf
blowout 'bloˌaʊt
blowpipe 'bloˌpaɪp
blowtorch 'bloˌtɔrtʃ; ES -ˌtɔətʃ; |-es -ɪz
blowup 'bloˌʌp
blowzed blaʊzd |blowzy 'blaʊzɪ
blubber 'blʌbɚ; ES 'blʌbə(r; |-ed -d |-ing
'blʌbrɪŋ, 'blʌbərɪŋ |-y -brɪ, -bərɪ

blucher ˈblutʃɚ, ˈblukɚ; ES -ə(r
Blücher ˈblutʃɚ, ˈblukɚ; ES -ə(r; (*Ger* ˈblyxər)
bludgeon ˈblʌdʒən |-ed -d
blue blu, blɪu |-d -d
Bluebeard ˈblu͜ɪbɪrd, ˈblɪu-; ES -ˌbɪəd, S+ -ˌbɛəd
bluebell ˈblu͜ɪbɛl, ˈblɪu-
blueberry ˈblu͜ɪbɛrɪ, ˈblɪu-, -bərɪ
bluebird ˈblu͜ɪbɝd, ˈblɪu-; ES -ˌbɜd, -ˌbɝd
blue-black ˈbluˈblæk, ˈblɪu- (ˈblue-ˌblack ˈdye)
blue-blooded ˈbluˈblʌdɪd, ˈblɪu-
bluebonnet ˈblu͜ɪbɑnɪt, ˈblɪu-; ES+-ˌbɒnɪt
bluebottle ˈblu͜ɪbɑtl̩, ˈblɪu-; ES+-ˌbɒtl̩
bluecoat ˈblu͜ɪkot, ˈblɪu-
blue-eyed ˈbluˈaɪd, ˈblɪu- (ˈblue-ˌeyed ˈboy)
bluefish ˈblu͜ɪfɪʃ, ˈblɪu- |-ˈs -ɪz
bluegill ˈblu͜ɪgɪl, ˈblɪu-
bluegrass ˈblu͜ɪgræs, ˈblɪu-; E+-ˌgras, -ˌgrɑs
blueing ˈbluɪŋ, ˈblɪuɪŋ |-ish -ɪʃ
bluejacket ˈblu͜ɪdʒækɪt, ˈblɪu-
blue-jay ˈblu͜ɪdʒe, ˈblɪu-
blue-pencil ˈbluˈpɛnsl̩, ˈblɪu- |-ed -d
blueprint ˈblu͜ɪprɪnt, ˈblɪu- |-ed -ɪd
Blue Ridge ˈbluˈrɪdʒ, ˈblɪu- (ˈBlue ˌRidge ˈMts.)
blues bluz, blɪuz
blue-sky law ˈbluˈskaɪˌlɔ, ˈblɪu-
bluestocking ˈblu͜ɪstɑkɪŋ, ˈblɪu-; ES+-ˌstɒk-
bluet ˈbluɪt, ˈblɪuɪt
bluff blʌf |bluffed blʌft
bluing ˈbluɪŋ, ˈblɪuɪŋ |-ish -ɪʃ
blunder ˈblʌndɚ; ES -də(r; |-ed -d |-ing ˈblʌndrɪŋ, ˈblʌndərɪŋ
blunderbuss ˈblʌndɚˌbʌs; ES ˈblʌndə-; |-es -ɪz
blunge blʌndʒ |blunges ˈblʌndʒɪz |-d -d
blunt, B- blʌnt |blunted ˈblʌntɪd
blur blɝ; ES blɜ(r, blɝ; |-red -d
blurb blɝb; ES blɜb, blɝb; |-ed -d
blurry ˈblɝɪ; ES ˈblɜrɪ, ˈblɝɪ
blurt blɝt; ES blɜt, blɝt; |-ed -ɪd
blush blʌʃ |blushes ˈblʌʃɪz |blushed blʌʃt
bluster ˈblʌstɚ; ES ˈblʌstə(r; |-ed -d |-ing ˈblʌstərɪŋ, ˈblustrɪŋ |-y -tərɪ, -trɪ
-bly -blɪ, *ending of advs corresponding to adjs in* -able -əbl̩. *In the vocab. this is regularly added to such adjs in* -able *as have corre-*

sponding advs, to show the change from syllabic | *in* -əbl̩ *to nonsyllabic* l *in* -əblɪ (dependable dɪˈpɛndəbl̩ |-bly (dɪˈpɛndə)-blɪ).

When |-bly -blɪ *immediately follows* |-able -əbl̩, *if the head word does not end in* -able (pardon ˈpɑrdn̩ |-ed -d |-able -əbl̩ |bly -blɪ), *in this case exceptionally the ending* -blɪ *is to be referred, not as usual to the head word, but to the immediately preceding form, and pronounced* -əblɪ, *thus* (*cf* pardon *in the vocab.*): pardon ˈpɑrdn̩ |-ed -d |-able (ˈpɑr)dnəbl̩, (ˈpɑr)dn̩əbl̩ |-bly (ˈpɑrdnə)blɪ, (ˈpɑrdn̩ə)blɪ. *In such cases, also, the form in* -bly -(ə)blɪ *includes any variant prons. of the form in* -able, *as in this example. The same statements apply to words in* -ible -əbl̩ *with added* |-bly -blɪ.

Blyth blaɪð, blaɪ |Blythe blaɪð
Bʼnai Bʼrith bəˈne·bəˈriθ, -ˈbrɪθ
boa ˈboə
Boadicea ˌboədɪˈsiə
Boanerges ˌboəˈnɝdʒiz; ES -ˈnɜ-, -ˈnɝ-; |-gesʼ -dʒiz
boar bor, bɔr; ES boə(r, E+bɔə(r
board bord, bɔrd; ES boəd, E+bɔəd; |-ed -ɪd
boarder ˈbordɚ, ˈbɔr-; ES ˈboədə(r, E+ˈbɔə-
boardinghouse ˈbordɪŋˌhaʊs, ˈbɔrd-; ES ˈboəd-, E+ˈbɔəd-; |-ses -zɪz
boardwalk ˈbordˌwɔk, ˈbɔrd-; ES ˈboəd-, E+ˈbɔəd-
boarhound ˈborˌhaʊnd, ˈbɔr-; ES ˈboə-, E+ˈbɔə-
Boas, *Franz* ˈboas, *Frederick S.* ˈboæz |-ʼs -ɪz
boast bost |boasted ˈbostɪd
boat bot |boated ˈbotɪd; |*NEngd*+bɒt (§46)
boatful ˈbotˌful |-s -z
boatman, -men ˈbotmən
boatswain, bosun ˈbosn̩, *occas.* ˈbotˌswen
Boaz *Bible* ˈboæz |-ʼs -ɪz
bob bab; ES+bɒb; |-bed -d
bobbin ˈbabɪn; ES+ˈbɒbɪn; |-ed -d
bobbinet ˌbabəˈnɛt; ES+ˌbɒb-
bobby ˈbabɪ; ES+ˈbɒbɪ
bobcat ˈbabˌkæt; ES+ˈbɒb-
bobolink ˈbabl̩ˌɪŋk; ES+ˈbɒb-
bobsled ˈbabˌslɛd; ES+ˈbɒb-; |-ed -ɪd

|full fʊl |tooth tuθ |further ˈfɝðɚ; ES ˈfɝðə |custom ˈkʌstəm |while hwaɪl |how haʊ |toy tɔɪ |using ˈjuzɪŋ |fuse fjuz, fɪuz |dish dɪʃ |vision ˈvɪʒən |Eden ˈidn̩ |cradle ˈkredl̩ |keep ʼem ˈkipm̩

Those words below in which the ɑ sound is spelt o are often pronounced with ɒ in E and S

bobsleigh ˈbabˌsle |-ed -d
bobstay ˈbabˌste
bobtail ˈbabˌtel
bobtailed ˈbabˈteld (ˈbobˌtailed ˈox)
bobwhite ˈbabˈhwaɪt
Boccaccio boˈkatʃɪˌo (*It* bokˈkattʃo)
Boche, b- baʃ, bɔʃ, boʃ |-s -ɪz
bock bak
bode *past of bide* bod
bode *v* bod |boded ˈbodɪd
bodice ˈbadɪs |-s -ɪz
bodied ˈbadɪd
bodiless ˈbadɪlɪs, ˈbad｜ ɪs
bodily ˈbad｜ ɪ, -dɪlɪ
bodkin ˈbadkɪn
Bodleian badˈliən, ˈbadliən
Bodley ˈbadlɪ
Bodmin ˈbadmɪn
body ˈbadɪ |-died -d |-guard ˌ-gard; ES
 -ˌgɑːd, E+-ˌgɑːd
Boeotia biˈoʃɪə, -ʃə |-tian -ʃən, -ʃiən
Boer bor, bɔr, bʊr; ES boə(r, bʊə(r, E+
 bɔə(r
Boethius boˈiθɪəs *or* |Boetius boˈiʃɪəs |-'s -ɪz
Boeuf Bayou ˈbɛfˈbaɪu, -ˈbaɪju
bog bag, bɔg, bɒg |-ged -d
bogey ˈbogɪ
boggle ˈbagｌ, ˈbɒgｌ |-d -d |-ling -glɪŋ, -gｌ ɪŋ
bogie ˈbogɪ
Bogota *US* bəˈgotə, *SAmer* ˌbogəˈta, -ˈtɔ
 (*Sp* ˌbogoˈta)
bogtrotter ˈbagˌtratɚ; ˈbɔg-, ˈbɒg-; ES
 -ˌtratə(r
bogus ˈbogəs |-es -ɪz
bogy ˈbogɪ
bohea boˈhi
Bohemia boˈhimɪə, -mjə |-n -n |-nism -nˌɪzəm
Bohn bon
Bohr bor, bɔr; ES boə(r, E+bɔə(r
boil bɔɪl |boiled bɔɪld
Boise ˈbɔɪsɪ
boisterous ˈbɔɪstərəs, -trəs
Bok bak
Bokhara boˈkarə
bola ˈbolə |bolas ˈboləs |-ses -sɪz
bold bold
boldface ˈboldˌfes
bold-faced ˈboldˈfest (ˈbold-ˌfaced ˈlie)

bold-facedly ˈboldˈfesɪdlɪ, -ˈfestlɪ
bole bol |boled bold
bolero boˈlero, -ˈlero
Boleyn ˈbʊlɪn=Bullen (*in Shak.* Anne
 Bullen)
bolide ˈbolaɪd, -lɪd
Bolingbroke ˈbalɪŋˌbrʊk, ˈbʊl-, ˈbol- —*All
 except* ˈbʊlɪŋˌbrʊk *are spelling pronunciations. The original was* Bul- *and the last
 part is the word* brook.
bolivar ˈbaləvɚ; ES ˈbaləvə(r
Bolivar *US* ˈbaləvɚ; ES ˈbaləvə(r
Bolivar *SAmer* boˈlivar; ES -vɑː(r; (*Sp*
 boˈliβar)
Bolivia, b- bəˈlɪvɪə |-n -n (*Sp* boˈliβja)
boll bol |bolled bold
bollard ˈbalɚd; ES ˈbaləd
bollworm ˈbolˌwɝm; ES -ˌwɜm, -ˌwɝm
bolly ˈbolɪ
bolo ˈbolo |-ed -d
Bologna *city* bəˈlonjə (*It* boˈloɲɲa)
Bologna *sausage* bəˈlonə, -ˈlonjə, -ˈlonɪ
bolometer boˈlamətɚ; ES -ˈlamətə(r
boloney bəˈlonɪ, bｌ ˈonɪ
Bolshevik, b- ˈbalʃəˌvɪk, ˈbol- |-vism -ˌvɪzəm
 |-vist -vɪst
bolster ˈbolstɚ; ES ˈbolstə(r; |-ed -d
bolt bolt |bolted ˈboltɪd; |*NEngd*+bȫlt
 (*§46*)
bolthead ˈboltˌhed
Bolton ˈboltｎ
boltrope ˈboltˌrop
bolus ˈboləs |-es -ɪz
bomb bam; *less freq.* bʌm |-ed -d
bombard *n* ˈbambard; ES ˈbambɑːd, E+
 -bɑːd
bombard *v* bamˈbard; ES bamˈbɑːd, E+
 -ˈbɑːd; |-ed -ɪd
bombardier ˌbambɚˈdɪr; ES ˌbambəˈdɪə(r,
 S+-ˈdɛə(r
bombasine ˌbambəˈzin, ˈbambəˌzin
bombast ˈbambæst
bombastic bamˈbæstɪk |-al -ｌ |-ally -ｌ ɪ, -ɪklɪ
Bombay bamˈbe (ˈBomˌbay ˈduck)
bombazine ˌbambəˈzin, ˈbambəˌzin
bomber ˈbamɚ; ES ˈbamə(r
bombproof ˈbamˈpruf (ˈbombˌpɪoof ˈshelter)
bombshell ˈbamˌʃɛl, ˈbʌmˌʃɛl

Key, *See in full §§3–47.* bee bi |pity ˈpɪtɪ (§6) |rate ret |yet jɛt |sang sæŋ |angry ˈæŋˌgrɪ
|bath bæθ; E bɑθ (§10) |ah ɑ |far fɑr |watch watʃ, wɒtʃ (§12) |jaw dʒɔ |gorge gɔrdʒ |go go

Those words below in which the ɑ sound is spelt o are often pronounced with ɒ in E and S

Bon bon
Bona 'bonə
bona fide 'bonə'faɪdɪ
bonanza bo'nænzə
Bonaparte 'bonəˌpɑrt; ES -ˌpɑːt, E+-ˌpɑːt;
|-tist -ɪst
Bonar 'banɚ, 'bon-; ES -nɚ(r
bonbon 'banˌban (*Fr* bõ'bõ)
bond band |bonded 'bandɪd |-age -ɪdʒ
bondholder 'bandˌholdɚ; ES -ˌholdə(r
bondmaid 'bandˌmed |-man -mən |-men
-mən
bondsman, -men 'bandzmən, 'banz-
bondwoman 'bandˌwʊmən, -ˌwum- |-men
-ˌwɪmɪn, -ən
bone bon |-d -d |-r -ɚ; ES -ə(r; |*NEngd*+
bõn (*§46*)
bone-dry 'bon'draɪ ('bone-ˌdry 'wood)
boneset 'bonˌsɛt |-ter -ɚ; ES -ə(r
bonfire 'banˌfaɪr; ES -ˌfaɪə(r; |-d -d
Bonheur bə'nɝ, bɔ-; ES -'nɝ(r, -'nɝ; (*Fr*
bõ'nœːr)
bonhomie, -mmie ˌbanə'mi, 'banəˌmi (*Fr*
bõnõ'mi)
Boniface 'banəˌfes |-'s -ɪz
bonito bə'nito
bon mot *Fr* bõ'mo |*Eng pl* bons mots bõ'moz,
Fr -'mo
Bonn ban
bonne *Fr* bõn
bonnet 'banɪt |-ed -ɪd
bonny 'banɪ
bonspiel 'banspil, -spəl
bon ton *Fr* bõ'tõ
bonus 'bonəs |-es-ɪz |-ed -t
bon vivant *Fr* bõvi'vã
bon voyage *Fr* bõvwa'jaːʒ
bony 'bonɪ; *NEngd*+ 'bõnɪ (*§46*)
boo bu |booed bud
boob bub |boobery 'bubərɪ |booby 'bubɪ
boodle 'budl̩ |-d -d |-ling 'budlɪŋ, 'budl̩ɪŋ
boohoo *n* 'buˌhu
boohoo *intj, v* ˌbu'hu |-ed -d
book bʊk |booked bʊkt |-ish -ɪʃ
bookbinder 'bʊkˌbaɪndɚ; ES -ˌbaɪndə(r; |-y
-dərɪ, -drɪ
bookcase 'bʊkˌkes |-s -ɪz
bookkeeper 'bʊkˌkipɚ; ES -ˌkipə(r

booklore 'bʊkˌlor, -ˌlɔr; ES -ˌloə(r, E+
-ˌlɔə(r
bookmaker 'bʊkˌmekɚ; ES -ˌmekə(r
Bookman 'bʊkmən
bookman 'bʊkmən, -ˌmæn |-men -mən,
-ˌmɛn
bookmark 'bʊkˌmark; ES -ˌmaːk, E+
-ˌmaːk
bookplate 'bʊkˌplet
bookrack 'bʊkˌræk
bookseller 'bʊkˌsɛlɚ; ES -ˌsɛlə(r
bookstall 'bʊkˌstɔl
bookworm 'bʊkˌwɝm; ES -ˌwɝm, -ˌwɝm
boom bum |boomed bumd
boomerang 'buməˌræŋ, 'bumˌræŋ
boon bun |booned bund
boondoggle 'bunˌdagl̩, -ˌdɒgl̩ |-d -d |-ling
-glɪŋ, -gl̩ɪŋ
Boone bun
Boonesboro 'bunzˌbɝo, -ə; ES -ˌbɝr-, -ˌbʌr-,
-ˌbɝ-
boor bʊr; ES bʊə(r; |-ish -ɪʃ
boost bust |boosted 'bustɪd
boot but |booted 'butɪd |-black -ˌblæk
bootee bu'ti
Boötes bo'otiz |*gen* -tis -tɪs
booth buθ, buð |-ths -ðz |-'s -θs, -ðz
Booth buθ, buð |-th's -θs, -ðz
Boothbay 'buθˌbe
bootjack 'butˌdʒæk
bootleg 'butˌlɛg |-ged -d |-ger -ɚ; ES -ə(r
bootstrap 'butˌstræp
booty 'butɪ
booze buz |boozes 'buzɪz |boozed buzd |-zy -ɪ
bopeep, B- bo'pip
Borachio bo'ratʃɪˌo, -kɪˌo
boracic bo'ræsɪk
borage 'bɝɪdʒ, 'bɒrɪdʒ, 'barɪdʒ, 'bɒrɪdʒ;
ES+, 'bɝr-, 'bʌr-
Borah 'borə, 'bɔrə; S 'borə
borate *n* 'boret, 'bɔr-, -rɪt; S 'bor-
borate *v* 'boret, 'bɔr-; S 'boret; |-d -ɪd
borax 'boræks, 'bɔr-; S 'boræks
Bordeaux bɔr'do; ES bɔə'do
Borden 'bɔrdn̩; ES 'bɔədn̩; |-town -ˌtaʊn
border 'bɔrdɚ; ES 'bɔədə(r; |-ed -d |-ing
-dərɪŋ, -drɪŋ, |-land -ˌlænd
bore bor, bɔr; ES boə(r, E+bɔə(r; |-d -d

|full fʊl |tooth tuθ |further 'fɝðɚ; ES 'fɝðə |custom 'kʌstəm |while hwaɪl |how haʊ |toy tɔɪ
|using 'juzɪŋ |fuse fjuz, fɪuz |dish dɪʃ |vision 'vɪʒən |Eden 'idn̩ |cradle 'kredl̩ |keep 'em 'kipm̩

Those words below in which the ɑ sound is spelt o are often pronounced with ɒ in E and S

boreal 'bɔrɪəl, 'bɔr-; S 'bɔrɪəl
borealis ˌbɔrɪ'ælɪs, ˌbɔrɪ-, -'elɪs; S ˌbɔrɪ-
Boreas 'bɔrɪəs, 'bɔr-; S 'bor-; |-'s -ɪz
boredom 'bɔrdəm, 'bɔr-; ES 'boə-, E+'bɔə-
borer 'bɔrɚ, 'bɔrɚ; ES 'bɔrə(r, E+'bɔrə(r
boresome 'bɔrsəm, 'bɔr-; ES 'boəsəm, E+
 'bɔə-
Borghese bɔr'gezɪ; ES bɔə-; (*It* bor'ge:se)
Borgia 'bɔrdʒə, -dʒɪə; ES 'bɔə-
Borglum, Gutzon 'gʌtsn̩'bɔrgləm; ES -'bɔəg-
boric 'bɔrɪk, 'bɔr-; S 'bɔrɪk
Boris 'bɔrɪs, 'bɔr-; S 'bɔrɪs; |-'s -ɪz
born bɔrn; ES bɔən
borne born, bɔrn; ES boən, E+bɔən
Borneo 'bɔrnɪˌo, 'bɔr-; ES 'boən-, 'bɔən-
Borodino ˌbɔrə'dino, ˌbar-, ˌbɒr-
boron 'bɔrɑn, 'bɔr-; S 'bɔrɑn
borough 'bɝo, 'bɝə; ES 'bɜr-, 'bʌr-, 'bɝ-
borrow, B- 'bɔro, -ə, 'bar-, 'bɒr-; |-ed -d |-ing
 -rəwɪŋ
bort bɔrt; ES bɔət
borzoi 'bɔrzɔɪ; ES 'bɔə-
boscage 'baskɪdʒ |-s -ɪz
Boscawen *NH* 'baskəwən, 'baskwɪn, *Brit
 name* bɑs'kɔ·ən, -'kɔ·ən
Boscobel 'baskəˌbɛl
bosh bɑʃ |boshes 'bɑʃɪz |boshed bɑʃt
bosk bɑsk |-age -ɪdʒ |-ages -ɪdʒɪz |-y -ɪ
bo's'n 'bosn̩ = boatswain
Bosnia 'bɑznɪə |-n -n
bosom 'buzəm, 'buzəm |-ed -d
Bosphorus 'bɑsfərəs |-porus -pərəs |-'s -ɪz
boss *n 'knob', 'chief'* bɔs, bɒs |-es -ɪz |-ed -t
boss *v 'emboss', 'order'* bɔs, bɒs |-es -ɪz |-ed -t
boss *'cow'* bɑs, bɒs
bossy *'officious'* 'bɔsɪ, 'bɒsɪ
bossy *'cow'* 'basɪ, 'bɒsɪ
Boston, b- 'bɔstn̩, 'bɒstn̩—ɔ *prevails in
 N Engd*
Bostonian bɔs'tonɪən, bɒs-
bosun 'bosn̩ = boatswain
Boswell 'bazwɛl, 'bɒz-, -wəl |-ian baz'wɛlɪən
Bosworth 'bazwɚθ, 'bɒz-, 'bɔz-; ES -wɚθ
bot *'bott'* bat
bot *'bote'* bot
botanic bo'tænɪk |-al -] |-ally -]ɪ, -ɪklɪ
botanist 'batn̩ɪst |botany 'batn̩ɪ
botanize 'batn̩ˌaɪz |-s -ɪz |-d -d

botch batʃ |-es -ɪz |-ed -t |-edly -ɪdlɪ
bote bot
Botetourt 'batəˌtɝt; ES -ˌtɜt, -ˌtɝt
botfly 'batˌflaɪ
both boθ; *N Engd*+bɔθ (*§46*)
bother 'baðɚ; ES 'baðə(r; |-ed -d |-ing
 'baðərɪŋ, 'baðrɪŋ |-some -səm |-ation
 ˌbaðə'reʃən
Bothnia 'baθnɪə
Bothwell 'baθwɛl, 'baθ-, -wəl
Botolph 'batəlf, *Boston street loc.* bə'tɒlf
bott bat
Botticelli ˌbatɪ'tʃɛlɪ (*It* ˌbotti'tʃɛlli)
bottle 'batl̩ |-d -d |-ling 'batlɪŋ, 'batlɪŋ
bottom, B- 'batəm |-ed -d |-less -lɪs
Bottome bə'tom = Bottom, bottom
bottomry 'batəmrɪ |-ried -d
botulism 'batʃəˌlɪzəm
Botulph 'batəlf
Botzaris bo'tsarɪs |-'s -ɪz
Boucher 'bautʃɚ; ES 'bautʃə(r
Boucicault 'busɪˌkɔlt (*Fr* busi'ko)
bouclé bu'kle
boudoir bu'dwar, -'dwɔr; ES -'dwa:(r,
 -'dwɔə(r
bough bau |boughed baud
bought bɔt |boughten 'bɔtn̩
Boughton *various persons* 'botn̩, 'bɔtn̩, 'bautn̩
bouillabaisse ˌbuljə'bes (*Fr* buja'bɛs)
bouillon 'buljan, -jɒn, bul'jan, -'jɒn (*Fr
 bu'jõ*)
boulder, B- 'boldɚ; ES 'boldə(r; |-ed -d
boulevard 'buləˌvard, 'bul-; ES -ˌva:d, E+
 -ˌva:d; (*Fr* bul'va:r)
Boulle, Boule bul
Boulogne bu'lon, bə-, -'lɔɪn (*Fr* bu'lɔɲ)
Boult bolt
boun *arch.* baun, *Sc* bun |-(e)d -d
bounce bauns |bounces 'baunsɪz |bounced
 baunst
bound *past & pptc of* bind baund
bound *n, adj, v* baund |-ed -ɪd |-ary -ərɪ, -rɪ
bounden 'baundən
bounteous 'bauntɪəs
bountiful 'bauntəfəl |-ly -ɪ, -flɪ
bounty 'bauntɪ |bountied 'bauntɪd
bouquet *flowers* bo'ke, bu'ke (*Fr* bu'kɛ)
bouquet *'aroma'* bu'ke (*Fr* bu'kɛ)

Key: See in full *§§3–47.* bee **bi** |pity 'pɪtɪ (§6) |rate ret |yet jɛt |sang sæŋ |angry 'æŋ·grɪ
|bath bæθ; E baθ (§10) |ah ɑ |far fɑr |watch wɑtʃ, wɒtʃ (§12) |jaw dʒɔ |gorge gɔrdʒ |go go

Bourbon ˈbʊrbən; ES ˈbʊəb-; |-ism -ˌɪzəm
|*Ky co. loc.* ˈbɜˑbən; ES ˈbɜb-, ˈbɜˑb-
bourbon *whiskey* ˈbʊrbən, ˈbɜˑb-; ES ˈbʊəb-,
ˈbɜb-, ˈbɜˑb-
Bourchier *Eng name* ˈbaʊtʃɚ (*cf §121*); ES
ˈbaʊtʃə(r; *Lord Berners* ˈbʊrtʃɪɚ; ES
ˈbʊətʃɪˑə(r
bourdon ˈbʊrdn̩, ˈbordn̩, ˈbɔrdn̩; ES ˈbʊədn̩,
ˈbɔədn̩, E+ˈbɔədn̩
bourg bʊrg; ES bʊəg; (*Fr* buːr)
bourgeois '*middle-class*' bʊrˈʒwa, ˈbʊrʒwa;
ES bʊə-, ˈbʊə-; (*Fr* burˈʒwa)
bourgeois *type* bɚˈdʒɔɪs, bɜ-; ES bə-, bɜ-, bɜˑ-
bourgeoise, *pl* -ses bʊrˈʒwaz; ES bʊə-; (*Fr*
burˈʒwaːz)
bourgeoisie, ˌbʊrʒwaˈzi; ES ˌbʊə-; (*Fr*
burʒwaˈzi)
bourgeon ˈbɜˑdʒən; ES ˈbɜdʒ-, ˈbɜˑdʒ-; |-ed -d
bourn, -e '*limit*,' '*brook*' born, bɔrn, bʊrn;
ES bɔən, bʊən, E+bɔən
Bournemouth ˈbornməθ, ˈbɔrn-, ˈbʊrn-; ES
ˈbɔən-, ˈbʊən-, E+ˈbɔən-
bourse bʊrs; ES bʊəs; |-s -ɪz
bouse *naut.* baʊs, baʊz |-s -ɪz |-d -t, -d
bouse, -ze '*drink*' buz, baʊz |-s -ɪz |-d -d |-sy,
-zy -ɪ
boustrophedon ˌbʊstrəˈfidn̩ |-ic buˌstrafə-
ˈdɑnɪk; ES+-ˌstrɔfəˈdɒnɪk
bout baʊt
boutonniere ˌbutn̩ˈjɛr; ES -ˈjɛə(r; (*Fr*
butɔ̃ˈnjɛːr)
Bovary ˌbovəˈri (*Fr* bovaˈri) |-rism, -rysm
ˈbovəˌrɪzəm
bovine ˈbovaɪn
bow *n*, *v* '*prow*,' '*nod*' baʊ |bowed baʊd
bow *n*, *v* '*weapon*,' '*curve*,' '*violin bow*' bo
|bowed bod
Bowdich, Bowditch ˈbaʊdɪtʃ |-'s -ɪz
Bowdler ˈbaʊdlɚ; ES ˈbaʊdlə(r
Bowdlerize ˈbaʊdləˌraɪz |-s -ɪz |-d -d
Bowdoin ˈbodn̩
bowel ˈbaʊəl, baʊl |-s -z |-ed -d
bower '*arbor*,' *cards* ˈbaʊɚ, baʊr; ES ˈbaʊ·ə(r,
baʊə(r; |-ed -d |-ing ˈbaʊərɪŋ, ˈbaʊrɪŋ |-y -ɪ
bower '*fiddler*' ˈboɚ; ES ˈbo·ə(r
bowie ˈbo·ɪ, ˈbu·ɪ
bowknot ˈboˌnat, ˈboˈnat; ES+-ˌnɒt, -ˈnɒt
bowl bol |-s -z |bowled bold
bowlder ˈboldɚ; ES ˈboldə(r

bowleg ˈboˌlɛg
bow-legged ˈboˈlɛgɪd, -ˈlɛgd (ˈbow-ˌlegged
ˈdog)
Bowles bolz |-'s -ɪz
bowline *naut.* ˈbolɪn, -ˌlaɪn
bowling green, B- G- ˈbolɪŋˈgrin
bowman, B- '*archer*' ˈbomən |-men -mən
bowman '*front oarsman*' baʊmən |-men -mən
Bowmanville ˈbomənˌvɪl
bown(e) baʊn, *Sc* bun |-(e)d -d
Bowness boˈnɛs |-'s -ɪz
bowse '*drink*' buz, baʊz |-s -ɪz |-d -d |-sy -zɪ
bowshot ˈboˌʃat; ES+-ˌʃɒt
bowsprit ˈbaʊˌsprɪt, ˈbo-
bowstring ˈboˌstrɪŋ |-ed -d *or* -strung -ˌstrʌŋ
bowyer ˈbojɚ; ES ˈbojə(r
bowze '*drink*' buz, baʊz |-s -ɪz |-d -d |-zy -zɪ
box baks; ES+bɒks; |-es -ɪz |-ed -t
boxer, B- ˈbaksɚ; ES ˈbaksə(r, ˈbɒks-
boxful ˈbaksˌfʊl; ES+ˈbɒks-; |-s -z
boxwood ˈbaksˌwʊd; ES+ˈbɒks-
boy bɔɪ |-hood -hʊd
boycott ˈbɔɪˌkat, -ˌkɒt; |-ed -ɪd
Boyesen ˈbɔɪəsn̩
Boyet bɔɪˈɛt (*Fr* bwaˈjɛ)
Boyle bɔɪl
Boyne bɔɪn
boys-and-girls ˈbɔɪzn̩ˈgɜˑlz; ES -ˈgɜlz, -ˈgɜˑlz
Boz baz, bɒz—*pron.* boz *by Dickens for* 'Mose'
Bozzaris boˈzærɪs |-'s -ɪz
Brabant brəˈbænt, ˈbrabənt (*Fr* braˈbã),
Shak. ˈBrabant
Brabantio brəˈbænʃo, -ˈbanʃo, -ʃɪˌo
brabble ˈbræbl̩ |-d -d |-ling ˈbræbl̩ɪŋ, -blɪŋ
brace bres |braces ˈbresɪz |braced brest
bracelet ˈbreslɪt |-ed -ɪd
brach brætʃ |-es -ɪz
brachial ˈbrekɪəl, ˈbræk-
brachiopod ˈbrækɪəˌpad, ˈbrek-; ES+-ˌpɒd
brachycephalic ˌbrækɪsəˈfælɪk |-lism -ˈsɛfə-
ˌlɪzəm
bracing ˈbresɪŋ
bracken ˈbrækən |-ed -d
Brackenbury ˈbrækənˌbɛrɪ, -bərɪ
Brackenridge ˈbrækənˌrɪdʒ |-'s -ɪz
bracket ˈbrækɪt |-ed -ɪd
brackish ˈbrækɪʃ
bract brækt |-ed -ɪd |-eal -ɪəl
brad bræd |bradded ˈbrædɪd |-awl -ˌɔl

Braddock 'brædək
Bradford 'brædfəd; ES 'brædfəd
Bradshaw 'brædʃɔ
Bradwardine 'brædwə˞dɪn, -ˌaɪn; ES -wəd-
brae bre
brag bræg |bragged brægd
Bragg bræg
braggadocio ˌbrægə'doʃɪˌo
braggart 'brægə˞t; ES 'brægət
Brahe bra (*Dan* 'bra·ɛ)
Brahma *Hindu god* 'bramə, *fowl* 'bramə, 'bremə
Brahman 'bramən |-s -z |-ism -ˌɪzəm
Brahmanic bra'mænɪk |-al -ḷ
Brahmaputra ˌbramə'putrə
Brahmin 'bramɪn |-ism -ˌɪzəm
Brahminic bra'mɪnɪk |-al -ḷ
Brahms bramz (*Ger* bra:ms) |-'s -ɪz
braid bred |braided 'bredɪd
brail brel |brailed breld
Braille brel |brailled breld (*Fr* bra:j)
brain bren |brained brend
brainpan 'brenˌpæn
brainsick 'brenˌsɪk
Braintree 'brentrɪ, -ˌtri, *in Engd loc.*+ 'bran-
braise brez |braises 'brezɪz |braised brezd
Braithwaite 'breθwet, *in Engd loc.*+ 'breθɪt—
cf. Breathitt
brake *arch. past of* break brek
brake *n, v* brek |braked brekt |-age -ɪdʒ
brakeman, -men 'brekmən
brakesman, -men 'breksmən
bramble 'bræmbḷ |-d -d |-ling -blɪŋ |bly -blɪ
bran, B- bræn
brancard 'bræŋkə˞d; ES 'bræŋkəd
branch bræntʃ; E+brantʃ, brantʃ; |-es -ɪz |-ed -t
brand brænd |branded 'brændɪd
Brandeis 'brændaɪs |-'s -ɪz
Brandenburg 'brændənˌbɝg; ES -ˌbɝg, -ˌbɝg; (*Ger* 'brandənˌburk)
brandied 'brændɪd
brandish 'brændɪʃ |-es -ɪz |-ed -t
brand-new 'bræn'nju, 'brænd-, -'nɪu, -'nu
Brandon 'brændən
brandtail 'brænˌtel
brandy 'brændɪ |brandied 'brændɪd
Brandywine 'brændɪˌwaɪn
Brangwaine 'bræŋwen

bran-new 'bræn'nju, -'nɪu, -'nu
brant brænt
brantail 'brænˌtel
brash bræʃ
brasier 'breʒə˞; ES 'breʒə(r
brass bræs; E+bras, bras; |-es -ɪz |-ed -t
brassard 'bræsard; ES 'bræsa:d, E+-a:d
brassart 'bræsə˞t; ES 'bræsət
brassie, -y, -ey 'bræsɪ; E+'brasɪ, 'brasɪ
brassière brə'zɪr, ˌbræsɪ'ɛr; ES -'zɪə(r, -'ɛə(r
brass-smith 'bræsˌsmɪθ; E+'bras-, 'bras-; |-ths -θs
brassware 'bræsˌwɛr, -ˌwær; E -ˌwɛə(r, -ˌwæə(r, 'bras-, 'bras-; S 'bræsˌwæə(r
brasswork 'bræsˌwɝk; ES -ˌwɝk, -ˌwɝk, E+ 'bras-, 'bras-
brassy 'bræsɪ; E+'brasɪ, 'brasɪ
brat bræt |-ling -lɪŋ |-tish -ɪʃ
Brathwaite 'breθwet
Bratislava ˌbratɪˌslavə, ˌbratɪ'slavə
brattice 'brætɪs |-s -ɪz |-d -t
Brattleboro 'brætḷˌbɝo, -ˌbɝə; ES -ˌbɝr-, -ˌbʌr-, -ˌbɝ-
Brauwer 'brauə˞; ES 'brau·ə(r
bravado brə'vado, -'vedo |-ed -d
brave brev |braved brevd |-ry -ərɪ, -rɪ
bravo '*well done!*' 'bravo
bravo '*villain*' 'bravo, 'brevo
bravura brə'vjurə, -'vɪurə (*It* bra'vu:ra)
braw *Sc* brɔ, bra
brawl brɔl |brawled brɔld
brawn brɔn |brawned brɔnd |-edness -ɪdnɪs
bray bre |brayed bred
braze brez |brazes 'brezɪz |brazed brezd
brazen 'brezn̩ |-ed -d |-ing 'breznɪŋ, -znɪŋ
brazenfaced 'breznˌfest |-ly -'fesɪdlɪ ('brazen-ˌfaced 'lie)
brazenness 'breznnɪs
brazier '*brassworker*' 'breʒə˞, 'brezɪə˞; ES 'breʒə(r, -zɪ·ə(r
brazier *for hot coals* 'breʒə˞; ES 'breʒə(r
Brazil, b- brə'zɪl, bə'zɪl |-ian -jən
brazilin 'bræzḷɪn
Brazos 'bræzəs
Brea 'briə
breach britʃ |breaches 'britʃɪz |-ed -t
bread brɛd |breaded 'brɛdɪd
Breadalbane brɛd'ɔlbən
bread-and-butter 'brɛdn̩'bʌtə˞; ES -'bʌtə(r

Key: *See in full* §§3–47. bee bi |pity 'pɪtɪ (§6) |rate ret |yet jɛt |sang sæŋ |angry 'æŋ·grɪ |bath bæθ; E baθ (§10) |ah ɑ |far far |watch watʃ, wɒtʃ (§12) |jaw dʒɔ |gorge gɔrdʒ |go go

breadfruit ˈbrɛdˌfrut, -ˌfrɪut
breadstuff ˈbrɛdˌstʌf
breadth brɛdθ, brɛtθ |-ths -θs
breadwinner ˈbrɛdˌwɪnɚ; ES -ˌwɪnə(r
break brek |*past* broke brok *or arch.* brake
 brek |*pptc* broken ˈbrokən *or arch. or slang*
 broke brok; |*N Engd*+brŏk(ən)
breakable ˈbrekəbļ |-bly -blɪ
breakage ˈbrekɪdʒ |-s -ɪz
breakbone ˈbrekˌbon
breakdown ˈbrekˌdaʊn
breakfast ˈbrɛkfəst |-ed -ɪd
breakneck ˈbrekˌnɛk
Breakspeare ˈbrekˌspɪr; ES -ˌspɪə(r, S+
 -ˌspɛə(r
breakup ˈbrekˌʌp
breakwater ˈbrekˌwɔtɚ, -ˌwɑtɚ, -ˌwɒtɚ; ES
 -tə(r
bream brim |breamed brimd
breast brɛst |breasted ˈbrɛstɪd |-band -ˌbænd
breastbone ˈbrɛstˈbon, -ˌbon
Breasted ˈbrɛstɪd
breastpin ˈbrɛstˌpɪn, ˈbrɛs-
breastplate ˈbrɛstˌplet, ˈbrɛs-
breastsummer ˈbrɛstˌsʌmɚ, ˈbrɛsəmɚ; ES
 -ˌsʌmə(r, -səmə(r
breastwork ˈbrɛstˌwɝk; ES -ˌwɜk, -ˌwɝk
breath brɛθ |-ths -θs |-less -lɪs |-y -ɪ
breathe bri ̆ð |breathed bri ̆ðd
breathed *adj ‘having (such) b.,’ ‘voiceless’*
 brɛθt
Breathitt ˈbrɛθɪt, *cf* Braithwaite
breccia ˈbrɛtʃɪə, ˈbrɛʃɪə (*It* ˈbrettʃa)
Breckenridge, Breckinridge ˈbrɛkənrɪdʒ |-’s
 -ɪz
Brecknock ˈbrɛknək, -nak, -nɒk |-shire -ˌʃɪr,
 -ʃɚ; ES -ˌʃɪə(r, -ʃə(r
Brecon ˈbrɛkən
bred *past & pptc of* breed brɛd
brede *n arch.* brid
breech britʃ, brɪtʃ |-es -ɪz |-ed -t
breechblock ˈbritʃˌblak, ˈbrɪtʃ-; ES+-ˌblɒk
breechcloth ˈbritʃˌklɔθ, ˈbrɪtʃ-, -ˌklɒθ |-ths
 -ðz, -θs
breeches *garment* ˈbrɪtʃɪz
breeching ˈbrɪtʃɪŋ, ˈbritʃɪŋ—*Those familiar
 with harness call it* ˈbrɪtʃɪŋ.
breechloader ˈbritʃˈlodɚ, ˈbrɪtʃ-; ES -ˈlodə(r
breech-pin ˈbritʃˌpɪn, ˈbrɪtʃ-

breed brid |bred brɛd
breeks briks
Breese ˈbriz |-’s -ɪz
breeze briz |breezes ˈbrizɪz |breezed brizd
Bremen *US* ˈbrimən, *Germany* ˈbremən,
 ˈbrɛmən (*Ger* ˈbre:mən)
Bremerton ˈbrɛmɚtən; ES ˈbrɛmətən
Brenner ˈbrɛnɚ; ES ˈbrɛnə(r
Brereton ˈbrɪrtņ; ES ˈbrɪətņ, S+ˈbrɛə-
Br’er Rabbit brɚˈræbɪt; ES brəˈræbɪt
Breslau ˈbrɛslɔ (*Ger* ˈbreslaʊ)
Brest brɛst
Brest Litovsk ˈbrɛstlɪˈtɔfsk, -ˈtɒfsk
brethren, B- ˈbrɛðrɪn, -rən
Breton ˈbrɛtņ (*Fr* brəˈtõ)
breve briv
brevet brəˈvɛt, ˈbrɛvɪt |-ed -ɪd |-cy -ˈvɛtsɪ
breviary ˈbrivɪˌɛrɪ, ˈbrɛvɪ-
brevier brəˈvɪr; ES -ˈvɪə(r, S+-ˈvɛə(r
brevity ˈbrɛvətɪ
brew bru, brɪu |-ed -d |-ery -ərɪ, -rɪ
brewer, B- ˈbruɚ, ˈbrɪuɚ; ES -ə(r
Brewster ˈbrustɚ, ˈbrɪu-; ES -stə(r
Brian ˈbraɪən
Briand ˈbriand (*Fr* briˈã)
briar ˈbraɪɚ; ES ˈbraɪ·ə(r
Briarean braɪˈɛrɪən, -ˈer- |-reus -rɪəs |-reus’s
 -rɪəsɪz
briarroot ˈbraɪɚˌrut, -ˌrʊt; ES ˈbraɪ·ə-
bribe braɪb |bribed braɪbd |-ry -ərɪ, -rɪ
bric-a-brac ˈbrɪkəˌbræk]-kery -ərɪ, -rɪ
brick brɪk |bricked brɪkt
brickbat ˈbrɪkˌbæt |-ted -ɪd
brickkiln ˈbrɪkˌkɪl, -ˌkɪln—*cf* kiln
bricklayer ˈbrɪkˌleɚ; ES -ˌle·ə(r
brickle ˈbrɪkļ
brick-red ˈbrɪkˈrɛd (ˈbrick-ˌred ˈpaint)
brickwork ˈbrɪkˌwɝk; ES -ˌwɜk, -ˌwɝk
brickyard ˈbrɪkˌjard; ES -ˌjɑːd, E+-ˌjɑːd
bridal ˈbraɪdļ |-ly -ɪ
bride braɪd |brided ˈbraɪdɪd
bride-ale, brideale ˈbraɪdˌel
bridechamber ˈbraɪdˌtʃembɚ; ES -ˌtʃembə(r
bridegroom ˈbraɪdˌgrum, -ˌgrʊm
bridesmaid ˈbraɪdzˌmed
bridesman ˈbraɪdzmən, -ˌmæn |-men -mən
bridewell, B- ˈbraɪdwɛl, -wəl
bridge brɪdʒ |bridges ˈbrɪdʒɪz |-d -d
bridgehead ˈbrɪdʒˌhɛd

|full fʊl |tooth tuθ |further ˈfɝðɚ; ES ˈfɝðə |custom ˈkʌstəm |while hwaɪl |how haʊ |toy tɔɪ
|using ˈjuzɪŋ |fuse fjuz, fɪuz |dish dɪʃ |vision ˈvɪʒən |Eden ˈidņ |cradle ˈkredļ |keep ’em ˈkipm̩

Those words below in which the ɑ sound is spelt o are often pronounced with ɒ in E and S

Bridgeport 'brɪdʒ͵port, -͵pɔrt; ES -͵poət, E+ -'pɔət

Bridges 'brɪdʒɪz |Bridges' 'brɪdʒɪz

bridget, B- 'brɪdʒɪt

Bridgewater, -dgw- 'brɪdʒ͵wɔtɚ, -͵watɚ, -͵wɒtɚ; ES -tə(r;—*formerly* -Walter

bridgework 'brɪdʒ͵wɝk; ES -͵wɜk, -͵wɝk

Bridgman 'brɪdʒmən

bridle 'braɪdḷ |-d -d |-ling 'braɪdlɪŋ, -dḷɪŋ

bridleless 'braɪdḷlɪs

Brie bri

brief brif |briefed brift

brier 'braɪɚ; ES 'braɪ·ə(r; |-ed -d

brierroot 'braɪɚ͵rut, -͵rʊt; ES 'braɪ·ə-

brieve briv

brig brɪg

brigade brɪ'ged |-gaded -'gedɪd

brigadier ͵brɪgə'dɪr; ES -'dɪə(r, S+-'dɛə(r

brigand 'brɪgənd |-ed -ɪd |-age -ɪdʒ

brigandine 'brɪgən͵din, -͵daɪn

brigantine 'brɪgən͵tin, -͵taɪn

Brigham 'brɪgəm

bright, B- braɪt

brighten 'braɪtṇ |-ed -d |-ing 'braɪtṇɪŋ, -tnɪŋ

brighteyes, B- 'braɪt͵aɪz

Brighton 'braɪtṇ

Bright's disease 'braɪtsdɪ͵ziz

brill brɪl

brilliance 'brɪljəns |-cy -ɪ |-iant -jənt

brilliantine *n* 'brɪljən͵tin, *v* ͵brɪljən'tin |-d -d

brim brɪm |brimmed brɪmd

brimful, -ll 'brɪm'fʊl ('hearts 'brɪm'fʊl, 'brim͵ful 'eye)

brimmer 'brɪmɚ; ES 'brɪmə(r; |-ed -d

brimstone 'brɪm͵ston

brinded 'brɪndɪd

Brindisi 'brɪndəzɪ (*It* 'brindizi)

brindle 'brɪndḷ |brindled 'brɪndḷd

brine braɪn |brined braɪnd

bring brɪŋ |brought brɔt

bringing-up 'brɪŋɪŋ ʌp

brink brɪŋk

briny 'braɪnɪ

brio 'brio

brioche 'brioʃ, 'briaʃ, -ɒʃ (*Fr* bri'ɔʃ)

briquette, -quet brɪ'kɛt |-(e)d -ɪd

Brisbane 'brɪzben, -bən

Briseis braɪ'siɪs |-'s -ɪz

brisk brɪsk |brisked brɪskt |-en -ən |-ened -ənd

brisket 'brɪskɪt

bristle 'brɪsḷ |-d -d |-ling 'brɪslɪŋ, -sḷɪŋ

bristly 'brɪsḷɪ, 'brɪslɪ

Bristol 'brɪstḷ (Bristow *in 1142*)

Bristow *US* 'brɪsto

Britain 'brɪtṇ, 'brɪtən |-tish -tɪʃ

Britannia brɪ'tænɪə, -njə |-ic -ɪk |-ica -ɪkə

Briticism 'brɪtə͵sɪzəm

Briton 'brɪtṇ, 'brɪtən

Brittain 'brɪtṇ, 'brɪtən

Brittany 'brɪtṇɪ

brittle 'brɪtḷ |brittlely 'brɪtḷɪ, 'brɪtḷɪ |-r -tḷɚ, -tḷɚ; ES -ə(r; |-st -tḷɪst, -tḷɪst

Britton 'brɪtṇ, 'brɪtən

Brno 'bɝno; ES 'bɜno, 'bɝno

broach brotʃ |broaches 'brotʃɪz |-ed -t

broad brɔd |-ax, -axe -͵æks |-axes -͵æksɪz

broadbill 'brɔd͵bɪl

broadbrim, B- 'brɔd͵brɪm

broad-brimmed 'brɔd'brɪmd ('broad-͵brimmed 'hat)

broadcast 'brɔd͵kæst; E+-͵kast, -͵kɑst; |*past & pptc* -cast, *radio*+-casted -ɪd

broadcloth 'brɔd͵klɔθ, -͵klɒθ |-ths -θs

broaden 'brɔdṇ |-ed -d |-ing 'brɔdṇɪŋ, -dnɪŋ

broad-gauge 'brɔd͵gedʒ |-s -ɪz

broad-gauged 'brɔd'gedʒd ('broad-͵gauged 'mind)

broadleaf, B- 'brɔd͵lif

broad-minded 'brɔd'maɪndɪd

Broad Ripple 'brɔd͵rɪpḷ

broadside *n, v* 'brɔd͵saɪd |-d -ɪd

broadside *adv* 'brɔd'saɪd, -͵saɪd

broadsword 'brɔd͵sord, -͵sɔrd; ES -͵soəd, E+ -͵sɔəd

Broadview 'brɔd͵vju, -͵vɪu, -'v-

Broadway 'brɔd͵we

Brobdignag *erron. for next*

Brobdingnag 'brabdɪŋ͵næg |-ian ͵brabdɪŋ-'nægɪən

brocade bro'ked |-caded -'kedɪd

brocatel, -lle ͵brakə'tɛl

broccoli 'brakəlɪ, 'braklɪ (*It* 'brɔkkoli)

brochure bro'ʃjʊr, -'ʃɪur, -'ʃʊr; ES -ʊə(r; (*Fr* brɔ'ʃy:r)

brock brak

Key: *See in full §§3–47.* bee bi |pity 'pɪtɪ (§6) |rate ret |yet jɛt |sang sæŋ |angry 'æŋ·grɪ |bath bæθ; E baθ (§10) |ah ɑ |far fɑr |watch watʃ, wɒtʃ (§12) |jaw dʒɔ |gorge gɔrdʒ |go go

Those words below in which the ɑ *sound is spelt* o *are often pronounced with* ɒ *in E and S*

Brockport ˈbrɑkˌport, -ˌpɔrt; ES -ˌpoət, E+
  -ˌpɔət
Brockton ˈbrɑktən
brocoli ˈbrɑkəlɪ, ˈbrɑklɪ
Brodhead ˈbrɑdˌhɛd, ˈbrɑd-
brogan ˈbrogən
brogue brog |brogued brogd
broider ˈbrɔɪdɚ; ES -də(r; |-ed -d |-ing
  ˈbrɔɪdərɪŋ, ˈbrɔɪdrɪŋ
broil brɔɪl |broiled brɔɪld
brokage ˈbrokɪdʒ
broke brok; *N Engd*+brōk (*§46*)
broken ˈbrokən; *N Engd*+ˈbrōkən (*§46*);
  |-ness -kənnɪs
broken-down ˈbrokənˈdaʊn
brokenhearted ˈbrokənˈhɑrtɪd; ES -ˈhɑːtɪd,
  E+-ˈhɑːtɪd
broken-winded ˈbrokənˈwɪndɪd
broker ˈbrokɚ; ES ˈbrokə(r
brokerage ˈbrokərɪdʒ, ˈbrokrɪdʒ
bromal ˈbromæl
bromate ˈbromet |-mated -metɪd
Brom Bones ˈbrɑmˈbonz |-ʼs -ɪz
Bromfield ˈbrɑmˌfild
bromic ˈbromɪk
bromide ˈbromaɪd, -mɪd |bromid ˈbromɪd
bromine ˈbromin, -mɪn |bromin ˈbromɪn
Bromley ˈbrʌmlɪ, ˈbrɑm-
Bromwich ˈbrʌmɪdʒ, ˈbrɑm-, -wɪtʃ |-ʼs -ɪz
bronchi *pl* ˈbrɑŋkaɪ
bronchia *pl* ˈbrɑŋkɪə
bronchial ˈbrɑŋkɪəl |-ly -ɪ
bronchitis brɑnˈkaɪtɪs, brɑŋ- |-chitic -ˈkɪtɪk
broncho *see* bronco
bronchoscope ˈbrɑŋkəˌskop
bronchus ˈbrɑŋkəs |bronchi ˈbrɑŋkaɪ
bronco ˈbrɑŋko |-buster -ˌbʌstɚ; ES -tə(r
Bronson ˈbrɑnsn̩, ˈbrɑnsn̩
Brontë ˈbrɑntɪ
Brontosaurus, b- ˌbrɑntəˈsɔrəs |-ʼs -ɪz
Bronx brɑŋks |-ʼs -ɪz |-ville -vɪl
bronze brɑnz |bronzes ˈbrɑnzɪz |-d -d
brooch brotʃ, brutʃ |-es -ɪz |-ed -t
brood brud |brooded ˈbrudɪd
brook brʊk |brooked brʊkt |-let -lɪt
Brooke brʊk
Brookline ˈbrʊklaɪn |-lyn -lɪn
broom brum, brʊm |-ed -d

broomcorn ˈbrumˌkɔrn, ˈbrʊm-; ES -ˌkɔən
Broome *NY county* brum
broomrape ˈbrumˌrep, ˈbrʊm-
broomstick ˈbrumˌstɪk, ˈbrʊm-
broth brɔθ, brɒθ |-ths -θs
brothel ˈbrɔθəl, ˈbrɒθəl, -ðəl
brother ˈbrʌðɚ; ES -ðə(r; |-ed -d |-ing
  ˈbrʌðərɪŋ, ˈbrʌðrɪŋ
brotherhood ˈbrʌðɚˌhʊd; ES ˈbrʌðə-
brother-in-law ˈbrʌðərɪnˌlɔ, ˈbrʌðɚnˌlɔ; ES
  ˈbrʌðərɪnˌlɔ, ˈbrʌðənˌlɔ
brotherly ˈbrʌðɚlɪ; ES ˈbrʌðəlɪ
brothers-in-law ˈbrʌðɚzɪnˌlɔ, ˈbrʌðɚzn̩ˌlɔ; ES
  ˈbrʌðəzɪnˌlɔ, ˈbrʌðəzn̩ˌlɔ
brougham ˈbruəm, brum, ˈbroəm
Brougham brum, ˈbruəm
brought brɔt
Broun, *Heywood* ˈbrun
brow braʊ |browed braʊd
Broward ˈbraʊɚd; ES ˈbraʊ·əd
browbeat ˈbraʊˌbit |*past* -beat -ˌbit |*pptc*
  -beaten -ˌbitn̩
Brower braʊɚ; ES ˈbraʊ·ə(r
brown braʊn |-ed -d |-ness ˈbraʊnnɪs
Brown(e) braʊn
Brownell ˈbraʊnɛl, braʊˈnɛl
brown-eyed ˈbraʊnˈaɪd (ˈbrown-ˌeyed ˈSusan)
Brownian ˈbraʊnɪən
brownie ˈbraʊnɪ
Browning ˈbraʊnɪŋ
brownstone ˈbraʊnˌston
Brownsville ˈbraʊnzvɪl; S+-vl̩
browntail ˈbraʊnˌtel
brown-tailed ˈbraʊnˈteld (ˈbrown-ˌtailed
  ˈmoth)
browse braʊz |browses ˈbraʊzɪz |-d -d
Bruce brus, brɪus |-ʼs -ɪz
bruckle ˈbrʌkl̩
Bruges ˈbrudʒɪz, bruʒ (*Fr* bry:ʒ) |Brugesʼ
  ˈbrudʒɪz |Brugesʼs ˈbruʒɪz
Brugmann ˈbrugmən (*Ger* ˈbrugman)
bruin ˈbruɪn, ˈbrɪuɪn
bruise bruz, brɪuz |-s -ɪz |-d -d
bruit brut, brɪut |-ed -ɪd
brumal ˈbruml̩, ˈbrɪuml̩
brume brum, brɪum
brummagem, B- ˈbrʌmədʒəm
Brummell ˈbrʌml̩

Brunanburh 'brunən‚bɝg; ES -‚bɜg, -‚bɝg; (OE 'brunan‚burx)

Brundisium brʌn'dɪzɪəm

Brunelleschi ‚brun∫'ɛskɪ (It ‚brunel'lɛski)

brunet, -tte bru'nɛt, brɪu-

Brunhild 'brunhɪld (Ger 'bru:nhɪlt)

Brunhilde brun'hɪldə (Ger bru:n'hɪldə)

Bruno 'bruno, 'brɪuno

Brunswick 'brʌnzwɪk, -zɪk

brunt brʌnt |brunted 'brʌntɪd

brush, B- brʌʃ |brushes 'brʌʃɪz |-ed -t

brushbush 'brʌʃ‚buʃ |-es -ɪz

brushland 'brʌʃ‚lænd

brushwood 'brʌʃ‚wʊd

brusque brʌsk, brʊsk (Fr brysk)

Brussells 'brʌs∫z |-ls' -∫z

Brussells sprouts 'brʌs∫'sprauts, 'brʌs∫z's-

Brut brut, brɪut

brutal 'brut∫, 'brɪut∫ |-ly -ɪ

brutality bru'tælətɪ, brɪu-

brutalization ‚brut∫ə'zeʃən, ‚brɪut∫-, -aɪ'z-

brutalize 'brut∫‚aɪz, 'brɪut∫- |-s -ɪz |-d -d

brute brut, brɪut |-tify -ə‚faɪ |-tified -ə‚faɪd

brutish 'brutɪʃ, 'brɪutɪʃ

Brutus 'brutəs, 'brɪutəs |-'s -ɪz

Bruyere bru'jɛr; ES -'jɛə(r; (Fr bry'jɛ:r)

Bryan 'braɪən |-ism -‚ɪzəm

Bryant 'braɪənt

Bryce braɪs |-'s -ɪz

Brynhild 'brɪnhɪld (Scand 'bryn-)

Brynmawr, -maur Wales brɪn'mɔr; ES -'mɔə(r; (S. Welsh brin'maur)

Bryn Mawr Pa brɪn'mɔr, loc. -'mar; ES -'mɔə(r, -'ma:(r

bryology braɪ'alədʒɪ; ES+-'ɒl-

bryony 'braɪənɪ

bryophyte 'braɪə‚faɪt

Brython 'brɪθən |Brythonic brɪ'θanɪk; ES+ -'θɒn-

bubble 'bʌb∫ |-d -d |-ling 'bʌblɪŋ, 'bʌb∫ɪŋ

bubble and squeak 'bʌb∫ən'skwik

bubbler 'bʌblɚ, 'bʌb∫ɚ; ES -ə(r; |-bly -blɪ, -b∫ɪ

bubo 'bjubo, 'brɪubo

bubonalgia ‚bjubən'ældʒɪə, ‚brɪu-

bubonic bju'banɪk, brɪu-; ES+-'bɒnɪk

buccal 'bʌk∫ |-ly -ɪ

buccaneer ‚bʌkə'nɪr; ES -'nɪə(r, S+-'nɛə(r; |-ed -d

Bucephalus bju'sɛfələs, brɪu- |-'s -ɪz

Buchan 'bʌkən (Sc 'bʌxən)

Buchanan bju'kænən, brɪu-, bə-

Bucharest ‚bjukə'rɛst, ‚brɪu-, ‚bu- —acct + 'Bucha‚rest

Buchmanism 'bʌkmən‚ɪzəm |-ite -‚aɪt

Buchtel 'buktl (Ger 'buxtəl)

buck, B- bʌk |bucked bʌkt

buckaroo 'bʌkə‚ru, ‚bʌkə'ru

buckayro bʌk'ero

buckboard 'bʌk‚bord, -‚bɔrd; ES -‚boəd, E+ -‚bɔəd

bucket 'bʌkɪt |-ed -ɪd |-ful -‚fʊl |-fuls -‚fʊlz

buckeye 'bʌk‚aɪ |-d -d

Buckhannon bʌk'hænən

Buckingham US 'bʌkɪŋ‚hæm, Engd 'bʌkɪŋəm

Buckinghamshire 'bʌkɪŋəm‚ʃɪr, -ʃɚ; ES -‚ʃɪə(r, -ʃə(r

buckle, B- 'bʌk∫ |-d -d |-ling 'bʌklɪŋ, -k∫ɪŋ

buckler from buckle 'bʌklɚ, 'bʌk∫ɚ; ES -ə(r

buckler 'shield' 'bʌklɚ; ES 'bʌklə(r

Bucknell Pa coll. 'bʌknɛl, bʌk'nɛl; Eng places 'bʌknəl

bucko 'bʌko

buckra 'bʌkrə

buckram 'bʌkrəm |-ed -d

Bucks Pa & short for Buckinghamshire bʌks

bucksaw 'bʌk‚sɔ

buckshot 'bʌk‚ʃat; ES+-‚ʃɒt

buckskin 'bʌk‚skɪn |-ned -d

buckthorn 'bʌk‚θɔrn; ES -‚θɔən

bucktooth 'bʌk‚tuθ |-teeth -‚tiθ

buckwheat 'bʌk‚hwit

bucolic, B- bju'kalɪk, brɪu-; ES+-'kɒl-

Bucovina ‚bukə'vinə

Bucyrus bju'saɪrəs, brɪu- |-'s -ɪz

bud bʌd |budded 'bʌdɪd

Budapest ‚bjudə'pɛst, ‚brɪudə-, ‚budə-

Buddha 'budə |-ddhism -dɪzəm |-ddhist -dɪst

Buddhistic bud'ɪstɪk |-al -∫

buddy 'bʌdɪ

budge bʌdʒ |budges 'bʌdʒɪz |budged bʌdʒd

budget 'bʌdʒɪt |-ed -ɪd |-ary 'bʌdʒɪ‚tɛrɪ

Budle 'bjud∫, 'brɪud∫

Buell 'bjuəl, 'brɪuəl

Buena Vista US 'bjunə'vɪstə, 'brɪu-; CA 'bwena'vista (Sp 'bwena'βista)

Buenos Aires 'bonəs'ɛrɪz, -'ærɪz, -'erɪz, 'bwenəs'aɪrɪz (Sp 'bwenɔs'aires)—In the

---

19th c. a common Anglicized form in both Engd & America was 'bonəs'ɛrz, -'ærz; E -'ɛəz, ES -'æəz—*see §122.*

buff bʌf |buffed bʌft

buffalo, B- 'bʌf|ˌo |-ed -d

buffer 'bʌfɚ; ES 'bʌfə(r; |-ed -d

buffet *'stroke,' 'strike'* 'bʌfɪt |-ed -ɪd

buffet *'sideboard'* bʌ'fe, bə-, bu-, *Brit* 'bʌfɪt

buffet *'restaurant'* bu'fe, 'bufe (*Fr* by'fɛ)

bufflehead 'bʌf|ˌhɛd

buffo 'bufo (*It* 'buffo)

Buffon 'bʌfən (*Fr* by'fõ)

buffoon bʌ'fun |-ed -d |-ery -ərɪ, -rɪ

Bufo 'bjufo, 'bɪu-

Buford 'bjufɚd, 'bɪu-; ES -fəd

Bug *riv.* bug, bʌg

bug bʌg |bugged bʌgd

bugaboo 'bʌgəˌbu

bugbane 'bʌgˌben

bugbear 'bʌgˌbɛr, -ˌbær; E -ˌbɛə(r, ES -ˌbæə(r

buggy 'bʌgɪ |-gies -z

bugle 'bjug|, 'bɪu- |-d -d |-ling -glɪŋ, -g|ɪŋ

bugloss 'bjuglɑs, 'bɪu-, -glɒs, -glɔs |-es -ɪz

Buhl *US* bjul, bɪul, bul

Buhl *Fr cabinetmaker* bul

buhl bul |-work -ˌwɝk; ES -ˌwɜk, -ˌwɝk

buhrstone 'bɝˌston; ES 'bɜ-, 'bɝ-

Buick 'bjuɪk, 'bɪuɪk

build bɪld |built bɪlt *or arch.* builded -ɪd

built-in 'bɪlt'ɪn ('built-ˌin 'cupboard)

Bukarest, Bukha- ˌbjukə'rɛst, ˌbɪu-, ˌbu- — *acct+* 'Bukaˌrest

Bukhara bu'karə

Bukovina ˌbukə'vinə

bulb bʌlb |bulbed bʌlbd

bulbose 'bʌlbos |bulbous 'bʌlbəs

bulbul 'bulbul

Bulfinch 'bulˌfɪntʃ |-'s -ɪz

Bulgar 'bʌlgɚ, 'bul-, -gar; ES -gə(r, -ga:(r

Bulgaria bʌl'gɛrɪə, bul-, -'ger- |-n -n

bulge bʌldʒ; S+buldʒ; |-s -ɪz |-d -d

bulk bʌlk, *esp. S* bulk |-ed -t |-y -ɪ

bulkhead 'bʌlkˌhɛd, *esp. S* 'bulk-

bull, B- bul |bulled buld

bulla 'bulə, 'bʌlə |-lae -i

bullace 'bulɪs, -əs |-s -ɪz

Bullcalf 'bulˌkæf; E -ˌkaf, -ˌkɑf, -ˌkæf

bulldog 'bulˌdɔg, -ˌdɒg

bulldoze 'bulˌdoz |-s -ɪz |-d -d

Bullen 'bulɪn=Boleyn

bullet 'bulɪt |-ed -ɪd

bullethead 'bulɪtˌhɛd

bulletheaded 'bulɪt'hɛdɪd ('bulletˌheaded 'boy)

bulletin 'bulətṇ, -tɪn

bulletproof *v* 'bulɪtˌpruf |-ed -t

bulletproof *adj* 'bulɪt'pruf ('bulletˌproof 'hat)

bullfight 'bulˌfaɪt

bullfinch, B- 'bulˌfɪntʃ |-es -ɪz

bullfrog 'bulˌfrɑg, -ˌfrɔg, -ˌfrɒg; S -ˌfrɔg, -ˌfrɑg, -ˌfrɒg

bullhead 'bulˌhɛd

bullheaded 'bul'hɛdɪd ('bullˌheaded 'obstinacy)

bullion 'buljən

Bullitt 'bulɪt

Bulloch 'bulək

bullock, B- 'bulək

Bullokar 'buləˌkar; ES -ˌka:(r

Bull Run 'bul'rʌn

bull's-eye 'bulzˌaɪ

bully 'bulɪ |bullied 'bulɪd

bulrush 'bulˌrʌʃ |-es -ɪz

bulwark 'bulwɚk; ES -wək; |-ed -t

Bulwer 'bulwɚ; ES 'bulwə(r

Bulwer-Lytton 'bulwɚ'lɪtṇ; ES 'bulwə-

bum bʌm |bummed bʌmd

bumblebee 'bʌmb|ˌbi

bumblepuppy 'bʌmb|ˌpʌpɪ

bumboat 'bʌmˌbot

bump bʌmp |bumped bʌmpt |-er -ɚ; ES -ə(r

bumpkin 'bʌmpkɪn

bumptious 'bʌmpʃəs

bun bʌn

bunch bʌntʃ |bunches 'bʌntʃɪz |-ed -t

bunco 'bʌŋko |-ed -d

buncombe, B- 'bʌŋkəm

bund bʌnd |bunded 'bʌndɪd

Bund bund (*Ger* bunt)

bundle 'bʌnd| |-d -d |-ling 'bʌndlɪŋ, -d|ɪŋ

bung bʌŋ |bunged bʌŋd

bungalow 'bʌŋgəˌlo

Bungay 'bʌŋgɪ

bunghole 'bʌŋˌhol

bungle 'bʌŋg| |-d -d |-ling 'bʌŋglɪŋ, -g|ɪŋ

bunion 'bʌnjən, -jɪn

bunk bʌŋk |bunked bʌŋkt

|full ful |tooth tuθ |further 'fɝðɚ; ES 'fɝðə |custom 'kʌstəm |while hwaɪl |how haʊ |toy tɔɪ |using 'juzɪŋ |fuse fjuz, fɪuz |dish dɪʃ |vision 'vɪʒən |Eden 'idṇ |cradle 'kredḷ |keep 'em 'kipṃ

bunko 'bʌŋko |-ed -d
bunkum 'bʌŋkəm
bunny 'bʌnɪ
Bunsen 'bʌnsn̩ (Ger 'bunzən)
bunt bʌnt |bunted 'bʌntɪd |bunting 'bʌntɪŋ
buntline 'bʌntlɪn, -laɪn
Bunyan 'bʌnjən, -jɪn
Buonaparte 'bonəˌpɑrt; ES -ˌpɑ:t, E+-ˌpɑ:t;
  (Fr bu̯ɔna'part, bwŏn-)
buoy bɔɪ, 'bu·ɪ |-ed -d
buoyancy 'bɔɪənsɪ, 'bujən- |-ant -ənt
buprestid bju'prɛstɪd, bɪu-
bur bɝ; ES bɜ(r, bɝ; |-red -d
Burbage 'bɝbɪdʒ; ES 'bɜ-, 'bɝ-; |-'s -ɪz
Burbank, b- 'bɝbæŋk; ES 'bɜ-, 'bɝ-; |-ed -t
burberry 'bɝˌbɛrɪ, -bərɪ; ES 'bɜ-, 'bɝ-
burble 'bɝbl̩; ES 'bɜbl̩, 'bɝbl̩; |-d -d |-ling
  -blɪŋ, -bl̩ɪŋ
burbot 'bɝbət; ES 'bɜbət, 'bɝbət
burden 'bɝdn̩; ES 'bɜdn̩, 'bɝdn̩; |-ed -d
  |-ing -dn̩ɪŋ, -dnɪŋ |-some -səm
Burdett(e) bɝ'dɛt; ES bɜ-
Burdett-Couts 'bɝdɛt'kuts, bɝ'dɛt-; ES 'bɜ-,
  'bɝ-, bə- |-'s -ɪz
burdock 'bɝˌdɑk; ES 'bɜ-, 'bɝ-, -ˌdɒk
bureau 'bjʊro, -rə, 'bɪʊ-
bureaucracy bju'rɑkrəsɪ, bɪu-; ES+-'rɒk-
bureaucrat 'bjʊrəˌkræt, 'bɪʊ-
burette, -ret bju'rɛt, bɪu-
burg bɝg; ES bɜg, bɝg; |-age -ɪdʒ
burgeon 'bɝdʒən; ES 'bɜdʒ-, 'bɝdʒ-; |-ed -d
Bürger Ger 'byrgər
burgess, B- 'bɝdʒɪs; ES 'bɜdʒ-, 'bɝdʒ-;
  |-es -ɪz
Burgettstown 'bɝdʒɪtsˌtaʊn; ES 'bɜdʒ-,
  'bɝdʒ-
burgh bɝg; ES bɜg, bɝg; (Sc 'bʌro, -ə)
Burgh, de dɪ'bɝg; ES dɪ'bɜg, dɪ'bɝg
burgher, B- 'bɝgɚ; ES 'bɜgə(r, 'bɝgə(r
Burghley, -leigh 'bɝlɪ; ES 'bɜlɪ, 'bɝlɪ
burglar 'bɝglɚ; ES 'bɜglə(r, 'bɝglə(r; |-y -ɪ
burglarize 'bɝgləˌraɪz; ES 'bɜg-, 'bɝg-; |-s
  -ɪz |-d -d
burgle 'bɝgl̩; ES 'bɜgl̩, 'bɝgl̩; |-d -d |-ling
  -glɪŋ, -gl̩ɪŋ
burgomaster 'bɝgəˌmæstɚ; ES 'bɜgəˌmæstə(r,
  'bɝgə-, E+-ˌmas-, -ˌmɑs-
burgonet 'bɝgəˌnɛt; ES 'bɜg-, 'bɝg-
burgoo, -gout 'bɝgu, bɝ'gu; ES -ɜ-, -ɝ-

Burgoyne bɝ'gɔɪn; ES bə'gɔɪn
burgrave 'bɝgrev; ES 'bɜ-, 'bɝ-
Burgundian bɝ'gʌndɪən; ES bə'gʌn-
Burgundy 'bɝgəndɪ; ES 'bɜgən-, 'bɝgən-
burial 'bɛrɪəl
burin 'bjʊrɪn, 'bɪʊ-
burke, B- bɝk; ES bɜk, bɝk; |-d -t
burl bɝl; ES bɜl, bɝl; |-ed -d
burlap 'bɝlæp; ES 'bɜ-, 'bɝ-; |-ped -t
Burleson 'bɝlɪsn̩; ES 'bɜl-, 'bɝl-
burlesque bɝ'lɛsk, bɜ'lɛsk; ES bə'lɛsk, bɜ-
  bɝ-; |-d -t ('burˌlesque 'play)
Burley, b- 'bɝlɪ; ES 'bɜlɪ, 'bɝlɪ
Burlingame 'bɝlɪŋˌgem, -ɪŋəm; ES 'bɜl-,
  'bɝl-; The 1st is a sp. pron. Same word as
  Burlingham.
Burlingham 'bɝlɪŋˌhæm, -ɪŋəm; ES 'bɜ-,
  'bɝ-
Burlington 'bɝlɪŋtən; ES 'bɜlɪŋ-, 'bɝlɪŋ-
burly 'bɝlɪ; ES 'bɜlɪ, 'bɝlɪ
Burma 'bɝmə; ES 'bɜmə, 'bɝmə; |-n -n
Burmese bɝ'miz; ES bɜ'miz, bɝ'miz
burn bɝn; ES bɜn, bɝn; |-ed -d or -t -t
Burne-Jones 'bɝn'dʒonz; ES 'bɜn-, 'bɝn-;
  |-'s -ɪz
Burnell 'bɝnl̩; ES 'bɜnl̩, 'bɝnl̩
burner 'bɝnɚ; ES 'bɜnə(r, 'bɝnə(r
burnet B- 'bɝnɪt; ES 'bɜnɪt, 'bɝnɪt
Burnett bɝ'nɛt, 'bɝnɪt; ES bɜ-, bɝ-, 'bɜ-,
  'bɝ-
Burney 'bɝnɪ; ES 'bɜnɪ, 'bɝnɪ
Burnham 'bɝnəm; ES 'bɜnəm, 'bɝnəm
burnish 'bɝnɪʃ; ES 'bɜ-, 'bɝ-; |-es -ɪz |-ed -t
burnoose, -nous bɝ'nus, 'bɝnus; ES bə-,
  'bɜ-, 'bɝ-; |-(e)s -ɪz |-(e)d -t
Burns bɝnz; ES bɜnz, bɝnz; |-'s- ɪz |-ian -ɪən
burnside, B- 'bɝnˌsaɪd; ES 'bɜn-, 'bɝn-;
  |-s -z
burnt bɝnt; ES bɜnt, bɝnt
Burntisland 'bɝnt'aɪlənd; ES 'bɜnt-, 'bɝnt-;
  Sc+'brʌnt-
burr, B- bɝ; ES bɜ(r, bɝ; |-ed -d
Burrillville 'bɝəlˌvɪl, 'bɝl-; ES 'bɜr-, 'bʌr-,
  'bɝ-, 'bɜl-, 'bɝl-
Burritt 'bɝɪt; ES 'bɜrɪt, 'bʌrɪt, 'bɝɪt
burro 'bɝo, 'bʊro, -ə; ES 'bɜr-, 'bʌr-, 'bɝ-,
  'bʊr-
Burroughs 'bɝoz, -əz; ES 'bɜr-, 'bʌr-, 'bɝ-;
  |-'s -ɪz

Key: See in full §§3-47. bee bi |pity 'pɪtɪ (§6) |rate ret |yet jɛt |sang sæŋ |angry 'æŋ·grɪ
|bath bæθ; E baθ (§10) |ah ɑ |far fɑr |watch wɑtʃ, wɒtʃ (§12) |jaw dʒɔ |gorge gɔrdʒ |go go

burrow 'bɜˑo, -ə; ES 'bɜr-, 'bʌr-, 'bɜ-; |-ed -d
burrowing 'bɜˑəwɪŋ; ES 'bɜrəwɪŋ, 'bʌr-, 'bɜˑ-
Burrows 'bɜˑoz, -əz; ES 'bɜr-, 'bʌr-, 'bɜ-;
|-'s -ɪz
burrstone 'bɜˑ‚ston; ES 'bɜ-, 'bɜˑ-
bursa 'bɜˑsə; ES 'bɜsə, 'bɜˑsə; |-s -z |-sae -si
bursar 'bɜˑsɚ; ES 'bɜsə(r, 'bɜˑsə(r; |-y -ɪ
burse bɜˑs; ES bɜs, bɜˑs; |-s -ɪz
burst bɜˑst; ES bɜst, bɜˑst
burstone 'bɜˑ‚ston; ES 'bɜ-, 'bɜˑ-
burthen 'bɜˑðən; ES 'bɜðən, 'bɜˑðən; |-ed -d
Burton 'bɜˑtn̩; ES 'bɜtn̩, 'bɜˑtn̩
bury 'bɛrɪ |buried 'bɛrɪd
Bury places 'bɛrɪ, surname 'bɛrɪ, 'bjʊrɪ, 'bɪu-
burying ground 'bɛrɪɪŋ‚graʊnd
bus bʌs |busses, buses 'bʌsɪz
busby, B- 'bʌzbɪ
Busch bʊʃ |-'s -ɪz
bush bʊʃ |bushes 'bʊʃɪz |bushed bʊʃt
bushel 'bʊʃəl |-ed -d |-ing 'bʊʃəlɪŋ, 'bʊʃlɪŋ
bushing 'bʊʃɪŋ
bushman, B-, -men 'bʊʃmən
Bushnell 'bʊʃnəl
bushranger 'bʊʃ‚rendʒɚ; ES -‚rendʒə(r
bushwhack 'bʊʃ‚hwæk |-ed -t |-er -ɚ; ES -ə(r
bushy, B- 'bʊʃɪ
busily 'bɪzl̩ɪ, -zɪlɪ
business 'occupation' 'bɪznɪs |-es -ɪz
business, busy- 'activity' 'bɪzɪnɪs
businesslike 'bɪznɪs‚laɪk
businessman 'bɪznɪs‚mæn |-men -‚mɛn
Busiris bju'saɪrɪs, bɪu- |-'s -ɪz
busk bʌsk |busked bʌskt
buskin 'bʌskɪn |-ed -d
busman, -men 'bʌsmən
Busra, -rah 'bʌsrə = Basra
buss bʌs |busses 'bʌsɪz |bussed bʌst
bust n, v bʌst |busted 'bʌstɪd
bustard 'bʌstɚd; ES 'bʌstəd
busticate 'bʌstə‚ket |-d -ɪd
bustle 'bʌsl̩ |-d -d |-ling 'bʌslɪŋ, 'bʌslɪŋ
busy 'bɪzɪ |busied 'bɪzɪd
busybody 'bɪzɪ‚badɪ; ES+ -‚bɒdɪ
busyness 'bɪzɪnɪs
but unstressed bət, stressed or hesit. 'bʌt, ‚bʌt
but-and-ben 'bʌtn̩'bɛn
butane 'bjuten, 'bɪu-, bju'ten, bɪu-
butcher 'bʊtʃɚ; ES 'bʊtʃə(r; |-ed -d |-ing
'bʊtʃərɪŋ, 'bʊtʃrɪŋ |-y -ɪ, -tʃrɪ

butcherbird 'bʊtʃɚ‚bɜˑd; ES 'bʊtʃə‚bɜd,
'bʊtʃə‚bɜˑd
butcher-knife 'bʊtʃɚ‚naɪf; ES 'bʊtʃə-; |-ives
-aɪvz
Bute bjut, bɪut
butler, B- 'bʌtlɚ; ES 'bʌtlə(r; |-y -ɪ
butt, B- bʌt |butted 'bʌtɪd
butte, B- bjut, bɪut
butter 'bʌtɚ; ES 'bʌtə(r; |-ed -d
butter-and-eggs 'bʌtən'ɛgz, 'bʌtərənd'ɛgz;
ES 'bʌtən-, 'bʌtərənd-
buttercup 'bʌtɚ‚kʌp; ES 'bʌtə-
butterfat 'bʌtɚ‚fæt; ES 'bʌtə-
butterfingers 'bʌtɚ‚fɪŋgɚz; ES 'bʌtə‚fɪŋgəz
butterfly 'bʌtɚ‚flaɪ; ES 'bʌtə-; |-flies -‚flaɪz
|-flied -‚flaɪd
Butterick 'bʌtərɪk, 'bʌtrɪk
butterine 'bʌtə‚rin, -rɪn
butterman 'bʌtɚ‚mæn, -mən; ES 'bʌtə-;
|-men -‚mɛn, -mən
Buttermere 'bʌtɚ‚mɪr; ES 'bʌtə‚mɪə(r, S+
-‚mɛə(r
buttermilk 'bʌtɚ‚mɪlk; ES 'bʌtə-
butternut 'bʌtɚnət, -‚nʌt; ES 'bʌtə-
butterscotch 'bʌtɚ'skatʃ; ES 'bʌtə'skatʃ,
-'skɒtʃ; |-es -ɪz ('butter‚scotch 'flavor)
Butterwick 'bʌtɚrɪk, 'bʌtɚwɪk; ES 'bʌtərɪk,
'bʌtəwɪk
Butterworth 'bʌtɚwɚθ, -‚wɜˑθ; ES 'bʌtəwəθ,
-‚wɜθ, 'bʌtə‚wɜˑθ
buttery 'like butter' 'bʌtərɪ
buttery 'pantry' 'bʌtrɪ, 'bʌtərɪ
buttle 'bʌtl̩ |-d -d |-ling 'bʌtl̩ɪŋ, 'bʌtlɪŋ
buttock 'bʌtək |buttocked 'bʌtəkt
button, B- 'bʌtn̩ |-ed -d |-ing 'bʌtn̩ɪŋ, -tnɪŋ
buttonhole 'bʌtn̩‚hol |-d -d
buttonhook 'bʌtn̩‚hʊk
buttonwood 'bʌtn̩‚wʊd
buttress 'bʌtrɪs |-es -ɪz |-ed -t
Butts bʌts |-'s -ɪz
butts and bounds 'bʌtsn̩'baʊndz, -nz
buttstock 'bʌt‚stak, -‚stɒk
butyl 'bjutl̩, 'bɪu-
butylene 'bjutl̩‚in, 'bɪu-
butyric bju'tɪrɪk, bɪu- |-ally -l̩ɪ, -ɪklɪ
butyrin 'bjutərɪn, 'bɪu-
buxom 'bʌksəm
Buxton 'bʌkstən
buy baɪ |bought bɔt

buzz bʌz |buzzes 'bʌzɪz |buzzed bʌzd
buzzard 'bʌzəd; ES 'bʌzəd
Buzzard's Bay 'bʌzədz'be; ES 'bʌzədz-
by stressed 'baɪ, ˌbaɪ; unstr. baɪ, bə
by-and-by 'baɪən'baɪ, 'baɪm'baɪ
bye baɪ
bye-bye n 'baɪˌbaɪ
bye-bye intj 'baɪ'baɪ, 'baɪˌbaɪ
byelaw 'baɪˌlɔ
by-form 'baɪˌfɔrm; ES -ˌfɔəm
bygone 'baɪˌgɔn, -ˌgɒn, much less freq. -ˌgɑn
bylaw 'baɪˌlɔ
byname 'baɪˌnem |-d -d
Bynner 'bɪnɚ; ES 'bɪnə(r
by-pass 'baɪˌpæs; E+-ˌpas, -ˌpɑs; |-es -ɪz
  |-ed -t
bypast 'baɪˌpæst; E+-ˌpast, -ˌpɑst
bypath 'baɪˌpæθ; E+-ˌpaθ, -ˌpɑθ; |-ths -ðz
byplay 'baɪˌple
by-product 'baɪˌprɑdəkt, -dʌkt; ES+-ˌprɒd-
Byrd bɝd; ES bɜd, bɝd

byre baɪr; ES baɪə(r
Byrne bɝn; ES bɜn, bɝn
byrnie 'bɝnɪ; ES 'bɜnɪ, 'bɝnɪ
byroad 'baɪˌrod
Byrom 'baɪrəm
Byron 'baɪrən |-esque ˌbaɪrən'ɛsk
Byronian baɪ'ronɪən
Byronic baɪ'rɑnɪk; ES+-'rɒn-; |-ally -ˌlɪ,
  -ɪklɪ
Byronism 'baɪrənˌɪzəm
byssal 'bɪsl̩
Bysshe bɪʃ |-'s -ɪz
byssus 'bɪsəs |byssuses 'bɪsəsɪz |-ssi -saɪ
bystander 'baɪˌstændɚ; ES -ˌstændə(r
bystreet 'baɪˌstrit
byway 'baɪˌwe
byword 'baɪˌwɝd; ES -ˌwɜd, -ˌwɝd
Byzantian bɪ'zænʃən, -'zæntɪən
Byzantine bɪ'zæntɪn, 'bɪznˌtaɪn, -ˌtin
Byzantinism bɪ'zæntɪnˌɪzəm
Byzantium bɪ'zænʃɪəm, -'zæntɪəm

C

C, c letter si |pl C's, Cs, poss C's siz
cab kæb
cabal kə'bæl |caballed kə'bæld
cabala, cabbala 'kæbələ
cabalistic ˌkæbə'lɪstɪk
cabaret 'kæbəˌrɛt, 'café' ˌkæbə're (Fr kaba're)
cabbage 'kæbɪdʒ |-s -ɪz |-d -d (Shak. cabidge)
Cabell 'kæbl̩
cabin 'kæbɪn |cabined 'kæbɪnd
cabinet 'kæbənɪt |-maker -ˌmekɚ; ES -ə(r
cabinetwork 'kæbənɪtˌwɝk; ES -ˌwɜk, -ˌwɝk
cable 'kebl̩ |-d -d |-ling 'keblɪŋ, 'keblɪŋ
cablegram 'keblˌgræm
cabman 'kæbmən |cabmen 'kæbmən, -ˌmɛn
cabob kə'bɑb; ES+kə'bɒb
caboose kə'bus |cabooses kə'busɪz
Cabot 'kæbət
cabriolet ˌkæbrɪə'le, ˌkæbrɪə'lɛt (Fr kabriŏ'le)
cacao kə'keo, kə'kao
cache kæʃ |caches 'kæʃɪz |cached kæʃt
cachet kæ'ʃe, 'kæʃe (Fr ka'ʃɛ)
cachexia kə'kɛksɪə |cachexy kə'kɛksɪ
cachinate 'kækəˌnet |-nated -ˌnetɪd

cachination ˌkækə'neʃən
cachou kə'ʃu, kæ'ʃu (Fr ka'ʃu)
cacique kə'sik
cackle 'kækl̩ |-d -d |-ling 'kæklɪŋ, -klɪŋ
cacodemon ˌkækə'dimən
cacoethes ˌkæko'iθɪz, -is
cacogenics ˌkækə'dʒɛnɪks
cacophonic ˌkækə'fɑnɪk; ES+-'fɒnɪk
cacophonous kæ'kɑfənəs, kə-; ES+-'kɒf-
cacophony kæ'kɑfənɪ, kə-; ES+-'kɒf-
cactus 'kæktəs |-es -ɪz |cacti 'kæktaɪ
cad kæd
cadaver kə'dævɚ, kə'devɚ; ES -və(r
cadaverous kə'dævərəs, kə'dævrəs
caddie 'kædɪ
caddis, -ice 'kædɪs |-(e)s -ɪz |-(e)d -ι
caddy 'kædɪ
Cade ked
cadence 'kedns |-s -ɪz |-cy -ɪ |-dent -dn̩t
cadenza kə'dɛnzə (It ka'dɛntsa)
cadet kə'dɛt
cadge kædʒ |cadges 'kædʒɪz |cadged kædʒd
Cadillac 'kædlˌæk

Cadiz *Spain* ˈkedɪz, *PI* ˈkadis, *O* ˈkædɪz,
ˈkedɪz |-'s -ɪzɪz, -isɪz (*Sp* ˈkaðiθ)
Cadman ˈkædmən
cadmium ˈkædmɪəm
Cadmus ˈkædməs |Cadmus's ˈkædməsɪz
Cadnam ˈkædnəm—*cf* Puttenham
Cadogan kəˈdʌgən
cadre ˈkadɚ; ES ˈkadə(r; *mil.*+ˈkædrɪ
caduceus kəˈdjusɪəs, -ˈdɪu-, -ˈdu- |-cei -sɪˌaɪ
Cadwal ˈkædwɑl, -wɒl, -wɔl
Cadwallader kædˈwɑlədɚ, -ˈwɒl-, -ˈwɔl-; ES
-də(r
caecum ˈsikəm |caeca ˈsikə
Caedmon ˈkædmən |-ian kædˈmonɪən |-ic
kædˈmɑnɪk; ES+-ˈmɒnɪk
Caen ˈkeən, ˈkan (*Fr* kã)
Caesar ˈsizɚ; ES ˈsizə(r
Caesarea ˌsɛsəˈriə, ˌsɛz- |-rean -ˈriən
Caesarean, -ian *surg.* sɪˈzɛrɪən, -ˈzær-, -ˈzer-
caesium ˈsizɪəm
caesura sɪˈʒurə, sɪˈzjurə, -ˈzɪurə |-l -l
café kəˈfe, kæˈfe
café-au-lait kəˈfe·oˈle, ˌkæfɪoˈle (*Fr* kafeoˈlɛ)
cafeteria ˌkæfəˈtɪrɪə, -təˈriə
caffeine, -in ˈkæfiin, -ˌin, ˈkæfin
cage kedʒ |cages ˈkedʒɪz |caged kedʒd
cahoot kəˈhut |-s -s
Caiaphas ˈkeəfəs, ˈkaɪ- |Caiaphas's -fəsɪz
Cain ken
cairn kɛrn, kærn; E kɛən, ES kæən
Cairo *Egypt* ˈkaɪro, *US* ˈkero, ˈkɛro
caisson ˈkesn̩
Caithness ˈkeθnɛs, keθˈnɛs |-'s -ɪz
caitiff ˈketɪf |caitiffs ˈketɪfs
Caius ˈkeəs, *Cambridge college* kiz
cajole kəˈdʒol |cajoled kəˈdʒold |-ry -ərɪ
Cajun, -jan, -jen ˈkedʒən—*see* Acadian
cake kek |caked kekt |caky ˈkekɪ
calabash ˈkæləˌbæʃ |calabashes ˈkæləˌbæʃɪz
calaboose ˈkæləˌbus, ˌkæləˈbus |-s -ɪz
Calabria kəˈlebrɪə |-brian -brɪən
Calais *US* ˈkælɪs; *France* ˈkælɪs, ˈkæle (*mod.
Fr* kaˈlɛ)—*in* Shaks. ˈCallis, ˈCallice. "*A
town which once sent members to the English
Parliament has a right to an English name.*"
—*John Sargeaunt. See* §122.
calamitous kəˈlæmətəs |calamity kəˈlæmətɪ
calash kəˈlæʃ |calashes kəˈlæʃɪz |-ed -t
Calaveras ˌkæləˈvɛrəs, -ˈverəs |-'s -ɪz

calcareous kælˈkɛrɪəs, -ˈkær-, -ˈker-
Calchas ˈkælkəs |Calchas's ˈkælkəsɪz
calcify ˈkælsəˌfaɪ |calcified ˈkælsəˌfaɪd
calcimine ˈkælsəˌmaɪn, -mɪn |-d -d
calcine ˈkælsaɪn, -sɪn |-d -d
calcite ˈkælsaɪt |calcitic kælˈsɪtɪk
calcium ˈkælsɪəm
calculable ˈkælkjələbl̩ |-bly -blɪ
calculate ˈkælkjəˌlet |-lated -ˌletɪd
calculation ˌkælkjəˈleʃən
calculator ˈkælkjəˌletɚ; ES -ˌletə(r
calculus ˈkælkjələs |-es -ɪz |-li -ˌlaɪ
Calcutta kælˈkʌtə
Calderon ˈkɔldərən (*Sp* ˌkaldeˈrɔn)
caldron ˈkɔldrən |-ed -d
Caldwell ˈkɔldwɛl, ˈkɔldwəl, *Yks loc.* ˈkɔdwɛl
Caleb ˈkeləb, ˈkelɪb
Caledonia ˌkæləˈdonɪə, -ˈdonjə |-n -n
calendar ˈkæləndɚ, ˈkælɪn-; ES -də(r; |-ed -d
calender ˈkæləndɚ, ˈkælɪn-; ES -də(r; |-ed -d
calends ˈkæləndz, ˈkælɪndz, -nz
calendula kəˈlɛndʒələ, -dʒulə
calenture ˈkælənˌtʃuɚ, -tʃɚ; ES -ˌtʃuə(r,
-tʃə(r
Calexico kəˈlɛksɪˌko
calf kæf; E kaf, kɑf, kæf; |-'s -s, -vz |-lves -vz
calf's-foot ˈkævzˌfut; E ˈkavz-, ˈkɑvz-, ˈkævz-;
—ˈkævz- *is not the plural, but the older
possessive singular.*
calfskin ˈkæfˌskɪn; E ˈkaf-, ˈkɑf-, ˈkæf-
Calgary ˈkælgərɪ
Calhoun kəˈhun, kælˈhun
Caliban ˈkæləˌbæn
caliber, -bre ˈkæləbɚ; ES ˈkæləbə(r; |-(e)d -d
calibrate ˈkæləˌbret |-brated -ˌbretɪd
calibration ˌkæləˈbreʃən
calico ˈkæləˌko
Calicut ˈkæləˌkʌt, ˈkæləkət
California ˌkæləˈfɔrnjə, *esp. NEngd* -nɪə; ES
-ˈfɔən-
Caligula kəˈlɪgjulə
caliper ˈkæləpɚ; ES ˈkæləpə(r; |-ed -d
caliph ˈkelɪf, ˈkælɪf |-ate ˈkæləˌfet, -fɪt
calisthenics ˌkæləsˈθɛnɪks
calix ˈkelɪks |calices ˈkæləˌsiz
calk kɔk |calked kɔkt
call kɔl |called kɔld |-er -ɚ; ES -ə(r
calla ˈkælə
Callahan ˈkæləˌhæn

Callao *Peru* ka'jɑo, *US* 'kælɪˌo (*Am Sp*
 ka'jao)
Callaway 'kæləˌwe
Calles 'kajɛs (*Am Sp* 'kajes)
calligrapher kə'lɪgrəfɚ; ES -fə(r; |-phy -fɪ
calligraphic ˌkælə'græfɪk
calling 'kɔlɪŋ
Calliope kə'laɪəˌpi, -pɪ |Kallyope 'kælɪˌop
calliper 'kæləpɚ; ES 'kæləpə(r; |-ed -d
callisthenics ˌkæləs'θɛnɪks
Callisto kə'lɪsto
callosity kə'lɑsətɪ, kæ-; ES+-'lɒs-
callous 'kæləs |-es -ɪz |-ed -t
callow 'kælo, 'kælə |-er 'kæləwɚ; ES -wə(r;
 |-est 'kæləwɪst
callus 'kæləs |-es -ɪz |-li -laɪ |-ed -t
calm kɑm; E kɑm, kam; |-ed -d
calomel 'kæləmḷ, 'kæləˌmɛl
caloric kə'lɔrɪk, kə'lɑrɪk, -'lɒr-
calorie, -y 'kælərɪ |-rific ˌkælə'rɪfɪk
calorimeter ˌkælə'rɪmətɚ; ES -tə(r
Calphurnia kæl'fɝnɪə, -njə; ES -'fɝn-, -'fɝn-
Calpurnia kæl'pɝnɪə, -njə; ES -'pɝn-, -'pɝn-
calumet, C- 'kæljʊˌmɛt, -mɪt, -mət, ˌkæljʊ-
 'mɛt
calumniate kə'lʌmnɪˌet |-d -ɪd
calumniation kəˌlʌmnɪ'eʃən
calumniatory kə'lʌmnɪəˌtorɪ, -ˌtɔrɪ; S -ˌtorɪ
calumny 'kæləmnɪ
Calvary 'kælvərɪ
calve kæv; E kav, kɑv, kæv; |-d -d
calves-foot 'kævzˌfʊt; E 'kavz-, 'kɑvz-,
 'kævz-
Calvin 'kælvɪn |-ism -ˌɪzəm |-ist -ɪst
Calvinistic ˌkælvə'nɪstɪk |-al -ḷ |-ally -ḷɪ, -ɪklɪ
calx kælks |calxes 'kælksɪz |calces 'kælsiz
Calydon 'kæləˌdɑn; ES+-ˌdɒn
Calydonian ˌkælə'donɪən, -'donjən
Calypso kə'lɪpso
calyx 'kelɪks, 'kæl- |-es -ɪz |calyces 'kæləˌsiz
cam kæm |cammed kæmd
camaraderie ˌkɑmə'rɑdərɪ, -ˌri (*Fr* kamara-
 'dri)
camarilla ˌkæmə'rɪlə (*Sp* kama'riʎa)
camber 'kæmbɚ; ES 'kæmbə(r; |-ed -d
cambium 'kæmbɪəm, 'kæmbjəm
Cambodia kæm'bodɪə, kæm'bodjə
Cambria 'kæmbrɪə |Cambrian 'kæmbrɪən
cambric 'kembrɪk

Cambridge 'kembrɪdʒ |-'s -ɪz |-shire -ˌʃɪr, -ʃɚ;
 ES -ˌʃɪə(r, -ʃə(r
Cambs *short for* Cambridgeshire kæmz,
 kæmbz
Cambyses kæm'baɪsiz |-ses' -siz
Camden 'kæmdən
came *past of* come kem
camel 'kæmḷ
camellia kə'mɛlɪə, -'milɪə, -ljə
camelopard kə'mɛləˌpɑrd; ES -ˌpɑ:d, E+
 -ˌpa:d
Camelot 'kæməˌlɑt; ES+-ˌlɒt
Camembert 'kæməmˌbɛr, -ˌbær; E -ˌbɛə(r,
 ES -ˌbæə(r; (*Fr* kamɑ̃'bɛ:r)
cameo 'kæmɪˌo, 'kæmjo |-ed -d
camera 'kæmərə |-s -z |-rae -ˌri
Cameron 'kæmərən, 'kæmrən
Cameroon ˌkæmə'run |-roons -'runz
Camilla kə'mɪlə
Camille kə'mil (*Fr* ka'mi:j)
Camillo kə'mɪlo
camisole 'kæməˌsol
Camoëns 'kæmoˌɛnz |Camoëns's 'kæmoˌɛnzɪz
camomile 'kæməˌmaɪl
camouflage 'kæməˌflɑʒ, 'kæmʊ- |-s -ɪz |-d -d
 (*Fr* kamu'fla:ʒ)
camp kæmp |camped kæmpt
Campagna kɑm'pɑnjə, kæm- (*It* kɑm'pɑɲˌɲa)
campaign kæm'pen |campaigned kæm'pend
Campania kæm'penɪə
campanile ˌkæmpə'nilɪ |-s -z |-li -li
Campaspe kæm'pæspɪ
Campbell 'kæmḷ, 'kæmbḷ |-ite -ˌaɪt
Campeius kæm'piəs |-'s -ɪz
campfire 'kæmpˌfaɪr; ES -ˌfaɪə(r
camphene 'kæmfin, kæm'fin
camphor 'kæmfɚ, 'kæmpfɚ; ES -fə(r
campstool 'kæmpˌstul
Campton 'kæmptən
campus 'kæmpəs |campuses 'kæmpəsɪz
can *n, v* kæn |canned kænd
can *aux. v stressed* 'kæn, ˌkæn; *unstr.* kən, kn̩,
 kŋ (ˌaɪkŋ'go)
Cana 'kenə
Canaan 'kenən |Canaanite 'kenənˌaɪt
Canada 'kænədə |-dian kə'nedɪən
canaille kə'nel (*Fr* ka'nɑ:j)
Canajoharie ˌkænədʒo'hærɪ
canal kə'næl |-nalled, -naled -'næld

canalization kə͵nælə'zeʃən, ͵kænǀə-, -aɪ'z-
canalize kə'nælaɪz, 'kænǀ͵aɪz ǀ-s -ɪz ǀ-d -d
Canal Zone kə'nælͺzon
Canandaigua ͵kænən'degwə
canape 'kænəpɪ (Fr kana'pe)
canard kə'nard; ES kə'na:d; (Fr ka'na:r)
canary, C- kə'nɛrɪ, kə'nɛrɪ
Canberra 'kænbərə
cancel 'kænsǀ ǀ-ed -d ǀ-ing -sǀɪŋ, -slɪŋ
cancellation ͵kænsǀ'eʃən
cancellous 'kænsələs
cancer, C- 'kænsɚ; ES 'kænsə(r; ǀCancri
  'kæŋkraɪ
cancerous 'kænsərəs, 'kænsrəs
candelabrum ͵kændǀ'ebrəm ǀ-s -z ǀ-bra -brə
candent 'kændənt
candescent kæn'dɛsn̩t ǀ-scence -sn̩s
candid 'kændɪd, 'kændəd
Candida 'kændɪdə
candidate 'kændə͵det, -dɪt ǀ-dacy -dəsɪ
Candide kan'did, kæn- (Fr kã'did)
Candish 'kændɪʃ ǀ-'s -ɪz = Cavendish
candle kændǀ ǀ-d -d ǀ-ling 'kændlɪŋ, -dǀɪŋ
candlelight 'kændǀ͵laɪt, 'kændǀ͵aɪt
Candlemas 'kændǀməs ǀ-es -ɪz
candlestick 'kændǀ͵stɪk
candor 'kændɚ; ES 'kændə(r
candy 'kændɪ ǀcandied 'kændɪd
candytuft 'kændɪ͵tʌft
cane ken ǀcaned kend
canescent kə'nɛsn̩t ǀcanescence kə'nɛsn̩s
Canidius kə'nɪdɪəs ǀ-'s -ɪz
canine 'kenaɪn, kə'naɪn
canister 'kænɪstɚ; ES 'kænɪstə(r
canker 'kæŋkɚ; ES 'kæŋkə(r; ǀ-ed -d ǀ-ing
  'kæŋkərɪŋ, -krɪŋ
cankerous 'kæŋkərəs, 'kæŋkrəs
cankerworm 'kæŋkɚ͵wɝm; ES 'kæŋkə͵wɜm,
  -kə͵wɝm
canna 'kænə
Cannae 'kæni (mod. It Canne 'kanne)
cannel 'kænǀ
canner 'kænɚ; ES 'kænə(r; ǀ-y 'kænərɪ
Cannes kæn, kænz (Fr kan) ǀ-'s kænz, 'kænzɪz
cannibal 'kænəbǀ ǀcannibalism 'kænəbǀ͵ɪzəm
cannikin 'kænəkɪn
canning, C- 'kænɪŋ
cannon, C- 'kænən ǀ-ed -d ǀ-ry -rɪ
cannonade ͵kænən'ed ǀ-d -ɪd

cannoneer ͵kænən'ɪr; ES ͵kænən'ɪə(r, S+
  -'ɛə(r
cannot formal colloq. 'kænat, kæ'nat, kə'nat
  'kænət. The usual familiar form is can't.
  Emph. kə'nat, kæ'nat, 'kæn'nat; ES+-ɒt
canny 'kænɪ
canoe kə'nu
canon 'kænən ǀ-ed -d
cañon 'kænjən ǀ-ed -d
Canon City 'kænjən'sɪtɪ
canoness 'kænənɪs ǀ-es -ɪz
canonic kə'nanɪk; ES+-'nɒn-; ǀ-al -ǀ ǀ-ally -ǀɪ,
  -ɪklɪ
canonicity ͵kænən'ɪsətɪ
canonization ͵kænənə'zeʃən, -aɪ'z-
canonize 'kænən͵aɪz ǀ-s -ɪz ǀ-d -d
Canonsburg 'kænənz͵bɝg; ES -͵bɜg, -͵bɝg
Canopic kə'nopɪk
Canopus kə'nopəs ǀ-'s -ɪz ǀCanopi kə'nopaɪ
canopy 'kænəpɪ ǀcanopied 'kænəpɪd
Canossa kə'nasə, kə'nɒsə, kə'nɔsə (It
  ka'nɔssa)
canst stressed 'kænst, ͵kænst; unstr. kənst
cant kænt ǀcanted 'kæntɪd
can't kænt; E kant, kant, kænt
Cantabrigian ͵kæntə'brɪdʒɪən
cantaloupe, -lope 'kæntǀ͵op, mainly Brit -͵up
cantankerous kæn'tæŋkərəs, -krəs
cantata kæn'tatə, kən-, -'tætə
canteen kæn'tin
canter 'kæntɚ; ES 'kæntə(r; ǀ-ed -d ǀ-ing
  'kæntərɪŋ, 'kæntrɪŋ
Canterbury 'kæntɚ͵bɛrɪ, 'kæntɚ-; ES
  'kæntə-;—In the second pron. ɚ is lost by
  dissimilation (§121).
canticle 'kæntɪkǀ
cantilever 'kæntǀ͵ɛvɚ, 'kæntǀ͵ivɚ; ES -və(r
cantle 'kæntǀ ǀ-d -d
canto 'kænto
canton n 'kæntən, -tan, kæn'tan; ES+-ɒn
canton v 'divide' 'kæntən, kæn'tan; ES+-ɒn;
  'quarter troops' kæn'tan, -'ton, -'tun; ES+
  -'tɒn; ǀ-ed -d
Canton China kæn'tan; ES+-'tɒn; US 'kæntən, 'kæntn̩
Cantonese ͵kæntən'iz
cantonment kæn'tanmənt, -'tun-, -'ton-;
  ES+-'tɒn-
cantor 'kæntɔr, -tɚ; ES 'kæntɔə(r, -tə(r

Words below in which a *before* r (farm) *is sounded* ɑ *are often pronounced in E with* a (fɑ:m)
Words below that have æ *before* r (carry 'kærɪ) *are often pronounced in N with* ɛ ('kɛrɪ, §94)

Canuck kə'nʌk

Canute kə'nut, kə'nɪut, kə'njut

canvas 'kænvəs |canvases 'kænvəsɪz |-ed -t

canvasback 'kænvəs,bæk

canvass 'kænvəs |-es -ɪz |-ed -t

canyon, C- 'kænjən |canyoned 'kænjənd

caoutchouc 'kutʃuk, kau'tʃuk

cap kæp |capped kæpt

capability ,kepə'bɪlətɪ

capable 'kepəbḷ |capably 'kepəblɪ

capacious kə'peʃəs

capacitance kə'pæsətəns

capacitate kə'pæsə,tet |-tated -,tetɪd |-ity -ətɪ

cap and gown 'kæpən'gaun, 'kæpm̩'gaun

cap-a-pie ,kæpə'pi

caparison kə'pærəsn̩ |-ed -d

cape kep

cape *writ* 'kepi

Cape Breton 'kep'brɪtn̩, -'brɛtn̩, *loc.* kə'brɪtn̩

Capel, -ll 'kæpḷ, 'kepḷ

Capella kə'pɛlə

Capen 'kepən

Cape of Good Hope 'kepəv'gud,hop, -'hop

caper 'kepɚ; ES 'kepə(r; |-ed -d

capercaillie ,kæpɚ'keljɪ; ES ,kæpə-; |-cailzie -'keljɪ, -'kelzɪ

Capernaum kə'pɝnɪəm; ES -'pɝn-, -'pɝn-

Capet 'kepɪt, 'kæpɪt (*Fr* ka'pɛ)

Capetian kə'piʃən

Cape Town, Capetown 'kep'taun, -,taun

Caphis 'kefɪs |-'s -ɪz

capias 'kepɪəs |-es -ɪz

capillary 'kæpḷ,ɛrɪ; *Brit* kə'pɪlərɪ; |-arity ,kæpḷ'ærətɪ

capital 'kæpətḷ |-ly -ɪ |-ism -,ɪzəm |-ist -ɪst

capitalization ,kæpətḷə'zeʃən, -aɪ'z-

capitalize 'kæpətḷ,aɪz |-s -ɪz |-d -d

capitate 'kæpə,tet |-d -ɪd |-tion ,kæpə'teʃən

Capitol, c- 'kæpətḷ |-ine -,aɪn

capitular kə'pɪtʃəlɚ; ES -lə(r; |-lary -,lɛrɪ

capitulate kə'pɪtʃə,let |-lated -,letɪd

capitulation kə,pɪtʃə'leʃən

capon 'kepan, 'kepən; ES+-pɒn

capote kə'pot

Cappadocia ,kæpə'doʃɪə, -ʃə |-n -n

capper, C- 'kæpɚ; ES 'kæpə(r

Capri 'kapri

capriccio kə'pritʃɪ,o (*It* ka'prittʃo)

capriccioso kə,pritʃɪ'oso (*It* kaprit'tʃo:so)

caprice kə'pris |caprices kə'prisɪz

capricious kə'prɪʃəs, *often* -'priʃ-, *cf* caprice

Capricorn 'kæprɪ,kɔrn; ES 'kæprɪ,kɔən

Capron 'kepɚn; ES 'kepən; *cf* apron

capsize kæp'saɪz |-s -ɪz |-d -d

capstan 'kæpstən

capsular 'kæpsələ, -sjulə; ES -lə(r

capsule 'kæpsḷ, 'kæpsjul |-d -d

captain 'kæptɪn, 'kæptən, 'kæptn̩ |-cy -sɪ

caption 'kæpʃən |-ed -d |-tious -ʃəs

captivate 'kæptə,vet |captivated 'kæptə,vetɪd

captive 'kæptɪv |-d -d |-vity kæp'tɪvətɪ

captor 'kæptɚ; ES 'kæptə(r

capture 'kæptʃɚ; ES 'kæptʃə(r; |-d -d

Capua 'kæpjuə (*It* 'kapwa)

Capuchin 'kæpju,tʃɪn, -,ʃɪn

Capucius kə'pjuʃəs, -'pɪu- |-'s -ɪz

Capulet 'kæpjə,lɛt, 'kæpjəlɪt

capybara ,kæpɪ'barə

car kar; ES ka:(r; |-red -d

carabao ,karə'bao

carabineer, -nier ,kærəbə'nɪr; ES -'nɪə(r, S+ -'nɛə(r

Caracas kə'rakəs |-'s -ɪz (*Sp* ka'rakas)

carack 'kærək

caracole 'kærə,kol |-col -,kal, -,kɒl

Caractacus kə'ræktəkəs |-'s -ɪz

Caradoc 'kærə,dak, kə'rædək; ES+-,dɒk;= Cradock; *geol.* kə'rædək

carafe kə'ræf; E+-'raf, -'raf

caramel 'kærəml |-ed -d—*In many places* 'karml *is often heard.*

caramelize 'kærəml,aɪz |-s -ɪz |-d -d

carapace 'kærə,pes |-s -ɪz |-d -t

carat 'kærət

caravan 'kærə,væn |-ed -d

caravanserai ,kærə'vænsə,raɪ, -,re |-sary -rɪ

caravel, -elle 'kærə,vɛl

caraway 'kærə,we

carbazole 'karbə,zol; ES 'ka:-; |-zol -,zal, -,zɒl

carbide 'karbaɪd, -bɪd; ES 'ka:b-

carbine 'karbaɪn; ES 'ka:baɪn

carbineer ,karbə'nɪr; ES ,ka:bə'nɪə(r, S+ -'nɛə(r

Words below in which a *before* r (farm) *is sounded* ɑ *are often pronounced in E with* a (fa:m)
Words below that have æ *before* r (carry ˈkærɪ) *are often pronounced in N with* ɛ (ˈkɛrɪ, §94)

carbinol ˈkɑrbəˌnol; ES ˈkɑ:bə-

carbohydrate ˌkɑrboˈhaɪdret; ES ˌkɑ:bo-

carbolated ˈkɑrbəˌletɪd; ES ˈkɑ:bə-

carbolic kɑrˈbɑlɪk; ES kɑ:ˈbɑlɪk, -ˈbɒlɪk

carbolize ˈkɑrbəˌlaɪz; ES ˈkɑ:bə-; |-s -ɪz |-d -d

carbon, C- ˈkɑrbən, -bən; ES ˈkɑ:bɑn, -bɒn, -bən

carbonaceous ˌkɑrbəˈneʃəs; ES ˌkɑ:bə-

carbonate n ˈkɑrbənɪt, -ˌnet; ES ˈkɑ:bə-

carbonate v ˈkɑrbəˌnet; ES ˈkɑ:bə-; |-d -ɪd

Carbondale ˈkɑrbənˌdel; ES ˈkɑ:bən-

carbonic kɑrˈbɑnɪk; ES kɑ:ˈbɑnɪk, -ˈbɒnɪk

carboniferous ˌkɑrbəˈnɪfərəs; ES ˌkɑ:bə-

carbonize ˈkɑrbənˌaɪz; ES ˈkɑ:bən-; |-s -ɪz |-d -d

carbonyl ˈkɑrbəˌnɪl; ES ˈkɑ:bə-

carborundum, C- ˌkɑrbəˈrʌndəm; ES ˌkɑ:bə-

carboxyl kɑrˈbɑksɪl; ES kɑ:ˈbɑksɪl, -ˈbɒksɪl

carboy ˈkɑrbɔɪ; ES ˈkɑ:bɔɪ; |-ed -d

carbuncle ˈkɑrbʌŋkļ; ES ˈkɑ:bʌŋkļ; |-d -d

carburate ˈkɑrbəˌret, -bjə-; ES ˈkɑ:b-; |-d -ɪd

carburation ˌkɑrbəˈreʃən, -bjə-; ES ˌkɑ:b-

carburator ˈkɑrbəˌretɚ, -bjə-; ES ˈkɑ:b-, -tə(r

carburet ˈkɑrbəˌret, -bjə-; ES ˈkɑ:b-; |-ed -ɪd

carburetion ˌkɑrbəˈreʃən, -bjə-; ES ˌkɑ:b-

carburetor, -ttor ˈkɑrbəˌretɚ, -bjəˌretɚ; ES ˈkɑ:b-, -tə(r

carburize ˈkɑrbəˌraɪz, -bjə-; ES ˈkɑ:b-; |-s -ɪz |-d -d

carcajou ˈkɑrkəˌdʒu, -ˌʒu; ES ˈkɑ:kə-

carcass, -case ˈkɑrkəs; ES ˈkɑ:kəs; |-es -ɪz |-ed -t

Carchemish ˈkɑrkəˌmɪʃ; ES ˈkɑ:k-

carcinogen kɑrˈsɪnədʒən, -dʒɪn, ˈkɑrsənə-; ES kɑ-, ˈkɑ:s-

carcinoma ˌkɑrsəˈnomə; ES ˌkɑ:sə-; |-s -z |-ta -tə

card kɑrd; ES kɑ:d; |-ed -ɪd

cardamom, -mum ˈkɑrdəməm; ES ˈkɑ:də-; |-mon -mən

cardboard ˈkɑrdˌbord, -ˌbɔrd; ES ˈkɑ:dˌboəd, E+-ˌbɔəd

cardcase ˈkɑrdˌkes; ES ˈkɑ:d-; |-s -ɪz

Cárdenas ˈkɑrdɪˌnɑs; ES ˈkɑ:d-; (Sp ˈkɑrðeˌnɑs)

cardiac ˈkɑrdɪˌæk; ES ˈkɑ:dɪ-

cardiacal kɑrˈdaɪəkļ; ES kɑˈdaɪəkļ

Cardiff ˈkɑrdɪf; ES ˈkɑ:dɪf

Cardigan, c- ˈkɑrdɪgən; ES ˈkɑ:dɪ-; |-shire -ˌʃɪr, -ʃɚ; ES -ˌʃɪə(r, -ʃə(r

cardinal, C- ˈkɑrdņəl, -dnəl; ES ˈkɑ:d-; |-ly -ɪ

cardiograph ˈkɑrdɪəˌgræf; ES ˈkɑ:dɪə-, E+-ˌgrɑf, -ˌgrɑf

carditis kɑrˈdaɪtɪs; ES kɑ:ˈdaɪtɪs

Cardozo kɑrˈdozo; ES kɑ:ˈdozo

care kɛr, kær; E kɛə(r, ES kæə(r; |-d -d

careen kəˈrin |careened kəˈrind

career kəˈrɪr; ES kəˈrɪə(r, S+-ˈrɛə(r; |-ed -d

carefree ˈkɛrˌfri, ˈkær-; E ˈkɛə-, ES ˈkæə-

careful ˈkɛrfəl, ˈkær-; E ˈkɛə-, ES ˈkæə-; |-ly -ɪ

careless ˈkɛrlɪs, ˈkær-; E ˈkɛə-, ES ˈkæə-

caress kəˈrɛs |caresses kəˈrɛsɪz |-ed -t

caret ˈkærət, ˈkerət

caretaker ˈkɛrˌtekɚ, ˈkær-; E ˈkɛəˌtekə(r, ES ˈkæə-

Carew kəˈru, -ˈrɪu, ˈkɛru, ˈke-, -rɪu, -rɪ

careworn ˈkɛrˌworn, ˈkær-, -ˌwɔrn; E ˈkɛəˌwoən, ˈkæə-, -ˌwɔən; S ˈkæəˌwoən

Carey ˈkɛrɪ, ˈkɛ:rɪ, ˈkerɪ, ˈkærɪ; S ˈkerɪ, ˈkærɪ;—Some speakers distinguish Carey from Kerry by a longer ɛ.

carf kɑrf; ES kɑ:f

carfare ˈkɑrˌfɛr, -ˌfær; E ˈkɑ:ˌfɛə(r, ES -ˌfæə(r

cargo ˈkɑrgo; ES ˈkɑ:go

Carhart ˈkɑrˌhɑrt; ES ˈkɑ:ˌhɑ:t

Carib ˈkærɪb |-al -] |-an -ən

Caribbean ˌkærəˈbiən, kəˈrɪbɪən

Caribbee, -ibee ˈkærəˌbi |-s -z

Caribian 'Cariban' kəˈrɪbɪən—see Carib

caribou, C- ˈkærəˌbu

caricature ˈkærɪkətʃɚ, -ˌtʃʊr; ES -tʃə(r, -ˌtʃʊə(r; |-d -d |-rist -ɪst

caries ˈkɛrɪz, ˈke-, -rɪˌiz

carillon ˈkærəˌlɑn, -ˌlɒn, -lən, kəˈrɪljən |-ed -d (Fr kariˈjɔ̃)

Carinthia kəˈrɪnθɪə |-n -n

cariole ˈkærɪˌol, -ˌol

cark kɑrk; ES kɑ:k; |-ed -t

carl, -e, C- kɑrl; ES kɑ:l

Carleton ˈkɑrltən; ES ˈkɑ:l-

Carlile kɑrˈlaɪl, kə-; ES kɑ:ˈlaɪl, kə-

carlin, -e ˈkɑrlɪn; ES ˈkɑ:lɪn

|full fʊl |tooth tuθ |further ˈfɝðɚ; ES ˈfɝðə |custom ˈkʌstəm |while hwaɪl |how haʊ |toy tɔɪ |using ˈjuzɪŋ |fuse fjuz, fɪuz |dish dɪʃ |vision ˈvɪʒən |Eden ˈidņ |cradle ˈkredļ |keep 'em ˈkipm̩

Words below in which a *before* r (farm) *is sounded* ɑ *are often pronounced in E with* a (fɑːm)
Words below that have æ *before* r (carry ˈkærɪ) *are often pronounced in N with* ɛ (ˈkɛrɪ, §94)

car-line ˈkɑrˌlaɪn; ES ˈkɑː-
carling *naut.* ˈkɑrlɪŋ; ES ˈkɑːlɪŋ
Carlisle kɑrˈlaɪl, kɚ-; ES kɑːˈlaɪl, kə-
Carlotta kɑrˈlɑtə; ES kɑːˈlɑtə, -ˈlɒtə
Carlovingian ˌkɑrləˈvɪndʒɪən; ES ˌkɑːlə-
Carlsbad ˈkɑrlzbæd; ES ˈkɑːlzbæd
Carlsruhe ˈkɑrlzruə; ES ˈkɑːlzruə
Carlton ˈkɑrltən; ES ˈkɑːltən
Carlyle kɑrˈlaɪl, kɚ-; ES kɑːˈlaɪl, kə-
carmagnole ˌkɑrmənˈjol; ES ˌkɑː-; (*Fr* karma-ˈɲɔl)
Carman ˈkɑrmən; ES ˈkɑːmən
Carmarthen kɚˈmɑrðən; ES kəˈmɑːˈðən; |-shire -ˌʃɪr, -ʃɚ; ES -ˌʃɪə(r, -ʃə(r
Carmel ˈkɑrml; ES ˈkɑːml; *Cal* Carˈmel
Carmen ˈkɑrmən; ES ˈkɑːmən
Carmi ˈkɑrmaɪ; ES ˈkɑːmaɪ
Carmichael ˈkɑrmaɪkl; ES ˈkɑːmaɪkl
carminative kɑrˈmɪnətɪv; ES kɑˈmɪnətɪv
carmine ˈkɑrmɪn, -maɪn; ES ˈkɑːm-; |-d -d
carnage ˈkɑrnɪdʒ; ES ˈkɑːn-; |-s -ɪz |-d -d
carnal ˈkɑrnl; ES ˈkɑːnl; |-ly -ɪ
Carnarvon kɚˈnɑrvən; ES kəˈnɑːvən; |-shire -ˌʃɪr, -ʃɚ; ES -ˌʃɪə(r, -ʃə(r
Carnatic kɑrˈnætɪk; ES kɑːˈnætɪk
carnation kɑrˈneʃən; ES kɑːˈneʃən; |-ed -d
Carnegie kɑrˈnegɪ, kɚ-; ES kɑːˈnegɪ, kə-; (ˈCarˌnegie ˈHall)
carnelian kɑrˈniljən; ES kɑːˈniljən
Carniola ˌkɑrnɪˈolə; ES ˌkɑːnɪ-; |-n -n (*It* kɑrˈnjɔːla)
carnival ˈkɑrnəvl; ES ˈkɑːnəvl
Carnivora kɑrˈnɪvərə; ES kɑˈnɪvərə
carnivore ˈkɑrnəˌvor, -ˌvɔr; ES ˈkɑːnəˌvoə(r, E+-ˌvɔə(r
carnivorous kɑrˈnɪvərəs; ES kɑˈnɪvərəs
Carnot *Am name* ˈkɑrnət, -nɑt; ES ˈkɑːnət, -nɑt, -nɒt, *Fr name* kɑrˈno; ES kɑːˈno
carob ˈkærəb
caroche kəˈrotʃ, -ˈroʃ |-s -ɪz |-d -t
carol, C- ˈkærəl, kærl |-ed -d
Carolina ˌkærəˈlaɪnə—*see* N. & S. Carolina
Caroline ˈkærəˌlaɪn, -lɪn
Carolingian ˌkærəˈlɪndʒɪən
Carolinian ˌkærəˈlɪnɪən
carom ˈkærəm |caromed ˈkærəmd
carotid kəˈrɑtɪd; ES+-ˈrɒtɪd

carouse kəˈrauz |-s -ɪz |-d -d |-sal -l
carousel ˌkærəˈzɛl, ˌkæru-
carp kɑrp; ES kɑːp; |-ed -t
carpal ˈkɑrpl; ES ˈkɑːpl
Carpathian kɑrˈpeθɪən, -θjən; ES kɑˈpeθ-
carpe diem ˈkɑrpɪˈdaɪɛm; ES ˈkɑːpɪ-
carpel ˈkɑrpl; ES ˈkɑːpl; |-lary -ˌɛrɪ
Carpentaria ˌkɑrpənˈtɛrɪə, -ˈter-; ES ˌkɑː-p-
carpenter, C- ˈkɑrpəntɚ, ˈkɑrpm̩tɚ; ES ˈkɑːp-, -tə(r; |-ed -d |-ing -tərɪŋ, -trɪŋ |-try -trɪ
carpet ˈkɑrpɪt; ES ˈkɑːpɪt; |-ed -ɪd
carpetbag ˈkɑrpɪtˌbæg; ES ˈkɑːpɪt-; |-ged -d |-ger -ɚ; ES -ə(r
carpus ˈkɑrpəs; ES ˈkɑːpəs; |-es -ɪz |-pi -paɪ
Carr kɑr; ES kɑː(r
carrack ˈkærək
Carrara kəˈrɑrə (*It* kɑrˈrɑːrɑ)
carraway ˈkærəˌwe
Carrel kəˈrɛl
carrettina ˌkɑrəˈtinə (*It* ˌkɑrretˈtiːnɑ)
carriage ʹvehicleʹ ˈkærɪdʒ |-s -ɪz; ʹfreight chargeʹ ˈkærɪɪdʒ
carrier ˈkærɪɚ; ES ˈkærɪ·ə(r
Carrington ˈkærɪŋtən
carriole ˈkærɪˌol, -ˌəl
carrion ˈkærɪən
Carrizo kəˈrizo (*Am Sp* kaˈrriso)
Carroll ˈkærəl |-ton -tən
carronade ˌkærəˈned
carrot ˈkærət |-ed -ɪd
carrousel ˌkærəˈzɛl, ˌkæru-
Carruthers kəˈrʌðɚz; ES -ˈrʌðəz; |-ʹs -ɪz
carry ˈkærɪ |carried ˈkærɪd
carryall ˈkærɪˌɔl = cariole, carriole
Carshalton kɚˈʃɔltn̩; ES kə-
Carson ˈkɑrsn̩; ES ˈkɑːsn̩
Carstairs, -stares ˈkɑrstɛrz, -stærz; E ˈkɑːstɛəz, ES -stæəz
cart kɑrt; ES kɑːt; |-ed -ɪd |-age -ɪdʒ |-ful -ˌful
Cartagena ˌkɑrtəˈdʒinə; ES ˌkɑːtə-
carte kɑrt; ES kɑːt
carte blanche ˈkɑrtˈblɑnʃ; ES ˈkɑːt-; |*pl.* cartes ˈkɑrts-; ES ˈkɑːts-; (*Fr* kɑrtˈblɑ̃ːʃ)
cartel ˈkɑrtl, kɑrˈtɛl; ES ˈkɑː-, kɑː-
carter, C- ˈkɑrtɚ; ES ˈkɑːtə(r
Carteret ˈkɑrtərɪt; ES ˈkɑːtə-

Key: *See in full §§3–47.* bee bi |pity ˈpɪtɪ (§6) |rate ret |yet jɛt |sang sæŋ |angry ˈæŋ·grɪ |bath bæθ; E bɑθ (§10) |ah ɑ |far fɑr |watch wɑtʃ, wɒtʃ (§12) |jaw dʒɔ |gorge gɔrdʒ |go go

Words below in which a *before* r *(farm) is sounded* ɑ *are often pronounced in* E *with* a *(fa:m)*

Cartesian kɑr'tiʒən; ES kɑ:'tiʒən
Carthage 'kɑrθɪdʒ; ES 'kɑ:θɪdʒ; |-'s -ɪz
Carthaginian ˌkɑrθə'dʒɪnɪən; ES ˌkɑ:θə-
Carthusian kɑr'θjuʒən, -'θɪu-; ES kɑ:-
Cartier ˌkɑrtɪ'e, kɑr'tje; ES ˌkɑ:-, kɑ:-;
  (Fr kar'tje)
cartilage 'kɑrtḷɪdʒ; ES 'kɑ:t-; |-s -ɪz
cartilaginous ˌkɑrtḷ'ædʒənəs; ES ˌkɑ:t-
cartle 'kɑrtḷ; ES 'kɑ:tḷ
cartogram 'kɑrtəˌgræm; ES 'kɑ:tə-
cartograph 'kɑrtəˌgræf; ES 'kɑ:tə-, E+
  -ˌgraf, -ˌgrɑf
cartographer kɑr'tɑgrəfɚ, -'tɒg-; ES kɑ-,
  -fə(r; |-phy -fɪ
cartographic ˌkɑrtə'græfɪk; ES ˌkɑ:tə-; |-al
  -ḷ |-ally -ḷɪ, -ɪklɪ
carton, C- 'kɑrtṇ, -tan; ES 'kɑ:t-, -tɒn
cartoon kɑr'tun; ES kɑ:'tun; |-ed -d |-ist -ɪst
cartouche, -ch kɑr'tuʃ; ES kɑ:'tuʃ; |-s -ɪz
cartridge 'kɑrtrɪdʒ; ES 'kɑ:trɪdʒ; |-s -ɪz
cart-track 'kɑrtˌtræk; ES 'kɑ:t-
cartulary 'kɑrtʃʊˌlerɪ; ES 'kɑ:tʃʊˌlerɪ
cartwright, C- 'kɑrtˌraɪt; ES 'kɑ:t-
Caruso kə'ruso (It kɑ'ru:zo)
Caruthers kə'rʌðɚz; ES kə'rʌðəz; |-'s -ɪz
carve kɑrv; ES kɑ:v; |-d -d |arch. pptc -n -ən
carvel 'kɑrvḷ
carven 'kɑrvən; ES 'kɑ:vən
Cary 'kɛrɪ, 'kɛ:rɪ, 'kerɪ, 'kærɪ; S 'kerɪ, 'kærɪ;
  see note at Carey
caryatid ˌkærɪ'ætɪd |-s -z |-es -ˌiz
casaba kə'sɑbə
Casabianca ˌkæsəbɪ'æŋkə (It ˌkasa'bjaŋka)
Casablanca ˌkɑsə'blɑŋkə, ˌkæsə'blæŋkə
Casanova ˌkæzə'novə (It ˌkasa'nɔ:va)
Casaubon kə'sɔbən (Fr kazo'bõ)
Casca 'kæskə
cascade, C- kæs'ked |-caded -'kedɪd
cascara kæs'kɛrə, -'kerə (Sp 'kaskara)
cascarilla ˌkæskə'rɪlə
cascaron ˌkæskə'ron (Am Sp ˌkaska'ron)
Casco 'kæsko
case, C- kes |cases 'kesɪz |cased kest
casease 'kesɪˌes
caseate 'kesɪˌet |-d -ɪd
casefy 'kesəˌfaɪ |-fied -ˌfaɪd
caseharden 'kesˌhɑrdṇ, -'hɑrdṇ; ES -ˌhɑ:dṇ,
  -'hɑ:dṇ; |-ed -d |-ing -dṇɪŋ, -dnɪŋ

casein 'kesɪɪn
case-knife 'kesˌnaɪf, -'naɪf |-ives -aɪvz
casemate 'kesˌmet |-mated -ˌmetɪd
casement, C- 'kesmənt |-ed -ɪd
caseose 'kesɪˌos |caseous 'kesɪəs
casern, -e kə'zɝn; ES -'zɜn, -'zɝn
Casey 'kesɪ, Ill 'kezɪ
caseworm 'kesˌwɝm; ES -ˌwɜm, -ˌwɝm
cash kæʃ |cashes 'kæʃɪz |cashed kæʃt
casha 'kæʃə
cash-and-carry 'kæʃən'kærɪ
cashaw kə'ʃɔ
cashbook 'kæʃˌbʊk
cashboy 'kæʃˌbɔɪ
cashew kə'ʃu, -'ʃɪu, 'kæʃ-
cashier n, v kæ'ʃɪr; ES -'ʃɪə(r, S+-'ʃɛə(r;
  |-ed -d ('cash,ier 'Jones)
cashmere cloth 'kæʃmɪr; ES -mɪə(r
Cashmere India kæʃ'mɪr; ES -'mɪə(r
cashoo kə'ʃu = catechu
casimere, -mire 'kæsəˌmɪr, 'kæzə-; ES -ˌmɪə(r
Casimir 'kæsəˌmɪr; ES -ˌmɪə(r
casing 'kesɪŋ
casino, C- kə'sino |-s -z |-ni -ni
cask kæsk; E+kask, kɑsk; |-ed -t
casket 'kæskɪt; E 'kæs-, much less freq.
  'kas-, 'kɑs-; |-ed -ɪd
Caslon 'kæzlən
Caspar, -per 'kæspɚ; ES 'kæspə(r
Caspian 'kæspɪən
casque 'kæsk |casqued 'kæskt |-quet 'kæskɪt
Cass kæs |Cass's 'kæsɪz
cassaba kə'sɑbə
Cassandra kə'sændrə
cassation kæ'seʃən
cassava kə'savə
Cassel, -ll 'kæsḷ
casserole 'kæsəˌrol |-d -d
Cassia 'kæʃɪə |cassia 'kæʃə
Cassiepeia ˌkæsɪə'piə
Cassil 'kæsḷ
cassimere 'kæsəˌmɪr; ES -ˌmɪə(r
cassino kə'sino
Cassio 'kæʃɪˌo, 'kæʃjo
Cassiopeia, -pea ˌkæsɪə'piə |-n -n
Cassius 'kæʃəs, 'kæʃɪəs |-'s -ɪz
cassock 'kæsək |-ed -t
cassowary 'kæsəˌwɛrɪ

cast kæst; ES+kast, kɑst
Castalia kæs'telɪə |-n -n
castanet ˌkæstə'nɛt
castaway 'kæstəˌwe; E+'kast-, 'kɑst-
caste kæst; E+kast, kɑst
castellan 'kæstələn
castellate 'kæstəˌlet |-d -ɪd
caster 'kæstɚ; ES 'kæstə(r, E+'kas-, 'kɑs-
Casterbridge 'kæstɚˌbrɪdʒ; ES 'kæstɚ-; |-'s -ɪz
castigate 'kæstəˌget |-d -ɪd
castigation ˌkæstə'geʃən
Castile kæs'til ('Casˌtile 'soap), NY kæs'taɪl
Castilian kæs'tɪljən, -lɪən
cast-iron adj 'kæst'aɪɚn; ES 'kæst'aɪ·ən, E+'kast-, 'kɑst-; ('cast-ˌiron 'pipe)
castle, C- 'kæsl̩; E+'kasl̩, 'kɑsl̩; |-d -d |-ling 'kæslɪŋ, 'kæsl̩ɪŋ
Castlereagh 'kæsl̩ˌre; E+'kasl̩-, 'kɑsl̩-; acct+ˌCastle'reagh
castoff n 'kæstˌɔf, -ˌɒf; E+'kast-, 'kɑst-
castor, C- 'kæstɚ; ES 'kæstə(r, E+'kas-, 'kɑs-
castrate 'kæstret |-d -ɪd
casual 'kæʒʊəl, 'kæʒʊl |-ly -ɪ |-ty -tɪ
casuist 'kæʒʊɪst |-ry -rɪ
casuistic ˌkæʒʊ'ɪstɪk |-al -l̩ |-ally -l̩ɪ, -ɪklɪ
casus belli 'kesəs'bɛlaɪ
Caswell 'kæzwəl, -wɛl
cat kæt |catted 'kætɪd
catabolism kə'tæbl̩ˌɪzəm
catachresis ˌkætə'krisɪs |-chreses -'krisiz
catachrestic ˌkætə'krɛstɪk |-al -l̩ |-ally -l̩ɪ, -ɪklɪ
cataclinal ˌkætə'klaɪnl̩
cataclysm 'kætəˌklɪzəm |-al ˌkætə'klɪzml̩
cataclysmic ˌkætə'klɪzmɪk |-ally -l̩ɪ, -ɪklɪ
catacomb 'kætəˌkom
catacumbal ˌkætə'kʌmbl̩
catafalque 'kætəˌfælk
Catahoula ˌkætə'hulə
Catalan 'kætlən, 'kætl̩ˌæn
catalase 'kætl̩ˌes
catalectic ˌkætl̩'ɛktɪk
catalepsis ˌkætl̩'ɛpsɪs |-leptic -'ɛptɪk
catalepsy 'kætl̩ˌɛpsɪ
Catalina, c- ˌkætl̩'inə
catalogue, -log 'kætl̩ˌɔg, -ˌɑg, -ˌɒg |-d, -ged -d
Catalonia ˌkætl̩'onɪə |-n -n
catalpa, C- kə'tælpə, occas. kə'tɒlpə

catalysis kə'tæləsɪs |-yses -əˌsiz
catalyst 'kætlɪst |-lytic ˌkætl̩'ɪtɪk
catalyze 'kætl̩ˌaɪz |-s -ɪz |-d -d
catamaran ˌkætəmə'ræn
catamount 'kætəˌmaʊnt
Catania kə'tenɪə, -njə (It ka'ta:njɑ)
catapult 'kætəˌpʌlt |-ed -ɪd
cataract 'kætəˌrækt |-ed -ɪd
catarrh kə'tɑr; ES kə'tɑ:(r, E+-'ta:(r; |-ed -d |-al -əl |-ally -əlɪ
Catasauqua ˌkætə'sɔkwə
catastasis kə'tæstəsɪs |-tases -təˌsiz
catastrophe kə'tæstrəfɪ
catastrophic ˌkætə'strɑfɪk; ES+-'strɒf-; |-al -l̩ |-ally -l̩ɪ, -ɪklɪ
Catawba, c- kə'tɔbə
Catawissa ˌkætə'wɪsə
catbird 'kætˌbɝd; ES -ˌbɜd, -ˌbɝd
catboat 'kætˌbot
catcall 'kætˌkɔl |-ed -d
catch kætʃ, not infreq. kɛtʃ |-es -ɪz |caught kɔt
catchall 'kætʃˌɔl
catcher 'kætʃɚ, 'kɛtʃɚ; ES -tʃə(r
catchpenny 'kætʃˌpɛnɪ
catchpole, -poll 'kætʃˌpol |-d, -ed -d
catchup 'kætʃəp, 'kɛtʃəp
catchword 'kætʃˌwɝd; ES -ˌwɜd, -ˌwɝd
cate ket |cates kets
catechesis ˌkætə'kisɪs |-cheses -'kisiz
catechetical ˌkætə'kɛtɪkl̩ |-ly -ɪ
catechism 'kætəˌkɪzəm |-chist -kɪst
catechistic ˌkætə'kɪstɪk |-al -l̩ |-ally -l̩ɪ, -ɪklɪ
catechize 'kætəˌkaɪz |-s -ɪz |-d -d
catechu 'kætəˌtʃu
catechumen ˌkætə'kjumən, -'kɪu- |-al -l̩ |-ate -ˌet |-ism -ˌɪzəm
categorical ˌkætə'gɔrɪkl̩, -'gar-, -'gɒr- |-ly -ɪ
category 'kætəˌgorɪ, -ˌgɔrɪ; S -ˌgorɪ
catena kə'tinə |-s -z |-nae -ni |-ry -rɪ
catenate 'kætṇˌet |-d -ɪd
cater 'ketɚ; ES 'ketə(r; |-ed -d |-ing 'ketərɪŋ, 'ketrɪŋ
catercornered 'kætəˌkɔrnɚd, 'kætɚ-; ES 'kætəˌkɔənəd—In 'kætəˌkɔrnɚd the first ɚ was lost by dissimilation (§121).
cater-cousin 'ketɚˌkʌzṇ; ES 'ketə-
caterer 'ketərɚ; ES 'ketərə(r
Caterina ˌkætə'rinə (It kate'ri:na)
caterpillar 'kætəˌpɪlɚ, 'kætɚ-; ES 'kætə-

Key: See in full §§3–47. bee bi |pity 'pɪtɪ (§6) |rate ret |yet jɛt |sang sæŋ |angry 'æŋ·grɪ |bath bæθ; E baθ (§10) |ah ɑ |far far |watch watʃ, wɒtʃ (§12) |jaw dʒɔ |gorge gɔrdʒ |go go

ˌpɪlə(r; |-ed -d—*In* ˈkætəˌpɪlɚ *the first ɚ was lost by dissimilation (§121).*

caterwaul ˈkætɚˌwɔl; ES ˈkætə-; |-ed -d

Catesby ˈketsbɪ

catfall ˈkætˌfɔl

catfish ˈkætˌfɪʃ |-ˈs -ɪz

catgut ˈkætˌgʌt (ˈkætgət ˈstrɪŋ)

Catharine ˈkæθrɪn, ˈkæθərɪn

catharsis kəˈθɑrsɪs; ES -ˈθɑːs-, E+-ˈθɑːs-

cathartic kəˈθɑrtɪk; ES -ˈθɑːt-, E+-ˈθɑːt-; |-al -ļ |-ally -ļɪ, -ɪklɪ

Cathay kəˈθe, kæˈθe

Cathcart ˈkæθkɚt, -kɑrt; ES -kət, -kɑːt, E+ -kɑːt

cathead ˈkætˌhɛd |-ed -ɪd

cathedra kəˈθidrə, ˈkæθɪdrə

cathedral kəˈθidrəl

Cather ˈkæðɚ; ES ˈkæðə(r

Catherine ˈkæθrɪn, ˈkæθərɪn

Catherwood ˈkæθɚˌwʊd; ES ˈkæθə-

catheter ˈkæθətɚ; ES ˈkæθətə(r

Cathleen ˈkæθlin

cathode ˈkæθod

cathodic kəˈθɑdɪk; ES+-ˈθɒd-; |-al -ļ |-ally -ļɪ, -ɪklɪ

cat-hole ˈkætˌhol

catholic, C- ˈkæθəlɪk, ˈkæθlɪk

catholicism, C- kəˈθɑləˌsɪzəm; ES+-ˈθɒl-

catholicity ˌkæθəˈlɪsətɪ

catholicize kəˈθɑləˌsaɪz; ES+-ˈθɒl-; |-s -ɪz |-d -d

catholicon kəˈθɑləkən; ES+-ˈθɒl-

Catiline ˈkætļˌaɪn

cation ˈkætˌaɪən

catkin ˈkætkɪn

Catlettsburg ˈkætlɪtsˌbɝg; ES -ˌbɝg, -ˌbɝg

catmint ˈkætˌmɪnt

catnip ˈkætnɪp, -nəp

Cato ˈketo

cat-o'-nine-tails ˌkætəˈnaɪnˌtelz, ˌkætņˈaɪn-

Catoosa kəˈtusə

catoptric kəˈtɑptrɪk; ES+-ˈtɒp-; |-s -s |-al -ļ |-ally -ļɪ, -ɪklɪ

cat-rigged ˈkætˌrɪgd

Catron kəˈtrɑn; ES+-ˈtrɒn

cat's-cradle ˈkætsˌkredļ

cat's-ear ˈkætsˌɪr; ES -ˌɪə(r, S+-ˌɛə(r

cat's-eye ˈkætsˌaɪ

Catskill ˈkætsˌkɪl

cat's-paw ˈkætsˌpɔ

catsup ˈkætsəp, ˈketʃəp

cattail ˈkætˌtel

Cattaraugus ˌkætəˈrɔgəs |-ˈs -ɪz

Cattegat ˈkætɪˌgæt, ˌkætɪˈgæt

Cattell kəˈtɛl, kæ-

cattish ˈkætɪʃ |catty ˈkætɪ

cattle ˈkætļ |-less ˈkætļɪs

Catullus kəˈtʌlɪs |-ˈs -ɪz

Catulus ˈkætʃələs |-ˈs -ɪz

catwalk ˈkætˌwɔk

Caucasia kɔˈkeʒə, -ˈkeʃə

Caucasian kɔˈkeʒən, -ˈkeʃən, -ˈkæʒən, -ˈkæʃən

Caucasus ˈkɔkəsəs |-sus' -səs

caucus ˈkɔkəs |-es -ɪz |-ed -t

caudal ˈkɔdļ |-ly -ɪ

caudate ˈkɔdet |-d -ɪd

caudicle ˈkɔdɪkļ

Caudine ˈkɔdaɪn

caudle ˈkɔdļ |-d -d |-ling ˈkɔdlɪŋ, -dļɪŋ

Caudle ˈkɔdļ, *cf* Caldwell

caught kɔt

caul kɔl

cauldron ˈkɔldrən |-ed -d

cauliflower ˈkɔləˌflauɚ; ES -ˌflau·ə(r

caulk kɔk |caulked kɔkt

causal ˈkɔzļ |-ly -ɪ |-ity kɔˈzælətɪ

causation kɔˈzeʃən |causative ˈkɔzətɪv

cause kɔz |causes ˈkɔzɪz |caused kɔzd

causerie ˌkozəˈri (*Fr* koz'ri)

causeway ˈkɔzˌwe |-wayed -ˌwed

causey ˈkɔzɪ |-ed -d

caustic ˈkɔstɪk |-ly -lɪ |-al -ļ |-ally -ļɪ

cautel ˈkɔtļ

cauterization ˌkɔtərəˈzeʃən, -aɪˈz-

cauterize ˈkɔtəˌraɪz |-s -ɪz |-d -d |-tery -rɪ

caution ˈkɔʃən |-ed -d |-ing ˈkɔʃənɪŋ, -ʃnɪŋ

cautionary ˈkɔʃənˌɛrɪ

cautious ˈkɔʃəs

cavalcade ˌkævļˈked |-caded -ˈkedɪd

cavalier, C- ˌkævəˈlɪr; ES -ˈlɪə(r, S+-ˈlɛə(r

cavalry ˈkævļrɪ |-man, -men -mən

cavatina ˌkævəˈtinə (*It* ˌkavaˈtiːna)

cave, C- kev |caved kevd

caveat ˈkevɪˌæt

caveat emptor ˈkevɪˌætˈɛmptɔr; ES -tɔə(r

cave-in ˈkevˌɪn

Cavell, *Edith* ˈkævļ

Cavendish, c-, Candish ˈkævəndɪʃ, *loc.*+
 ˈkændɪʃ |-ˈs -ɪz
cavern ˈkævən; ES ˈkævən; |-ed -d |-ous -əs
caviar, -are ˌkævɪˈɑr, ˈkævɪˌɑr; ES -ˈɑ:(r,
 -ˌɑ:(r;—*in Hamlet* caviary, *probably pron.*
 ˌkævɪˈærɪ
cavie ˈkevɪ
cavil ˈkævl̩, -vɪl |-ed -d |-ing ˈkævl̩ɪŋ, -vlɪŋ
Cavite kəˈvite, kɑ-
cavity ˈkævətɪ |cavitied ˈkævətɪd
cavort kəˈvɔrt; ES -ˈvɔət; |-ed -ɪd
Cavour kəˈvur; ES -ˈvuə(r; (*It* kɑˈvu:r)
cavy ˈkevɪ
caw kɔ |cawed kɔd
Cawdor ˈkɔdɚ; ES ˈkɔdə(r
Cawnpore, -pur kɔnˈpor, -ˈpɔr, -ˈpur; ES
 -ˈpoə(r, -ˈpuə(r, E+-ˈpɔə(r
Caxton ˈkækstən
cay ke, ki, *in West Indies usually* ki
cayenne, C- kaɪˈɛn, keˈɛn (ˈcayˌenne ˈpepper)
cayman ˈkemən |caymans ˈkemənz
Cayman *isls.* kaɪˈmɑn
Cayuga keˈugə, -ˈjugə, kɪˈugə, ˈkjugə
Cayuse, c- kaɪˈjus, -ˈjɪus
Cazenovia ˌkæzəˈnovɪə
cease sis |ceases ˈsisɪz |ceased sist
Cebu seˈbu
Cecil *Md co.* ˈsisl̩, -sɪl, *pers. name* ˈsisl̩,ˈsɛsl̩,
 -sɪl
Cecilia sɪˈsɪljə, -ˈsɪlɪə, -ˈsiljə
Cecily ˈsɛsl̩ɪ, ˈsɪsl̩ɪ
Cecropia sɪˈkropɪə
cedar ˈsidɚ; ES ˈsidə(r; |-ed -d
cede sid |ceded ˈsidɪd
cedilla sɪˈdɪlə
Cedric ˈsɛdrɪk, ˈsidrɪk
cee si
ceil sil |ceiled sild |ceiling ˈsilɪŋ
celandine ˈsɛlənˌdaɪn
Celebes ˈsɛləˌbiz, səˈlibiz
celebrant ˈsɛləbrənt
celebrate ˈsɛləˌbret |-brated -ˌbretɪd
celebration ˌsɛləˈbreʃən
celebrity səˈlɛbrətɪ
celerity səˈlɛrətɪ
celery ˈsɛlərɪ
celesta səˈlɛstə
celeste, C- səˈlɛst
celestial, C- səˈlɛstʃəl |-ly -ɪ

Celia ˈsiljə, *in Shak.* ˈsilɪə
celiac ˈsilɪˌæk
celibate ˈsɛləbɪt, -ˌbet |-bacy -bəsɪ
Celina səˈlaɪnə
cell sɛl |celled sɛld
cellar ˈsɛlɚ; ES ˈsɛlə(r; |-ed -d
cellarage ˈsɛlərɪdʒ |-s -ɪz
cellarer ˈsɛlərɚ; ES ˈsɛlərə(r
Cellini tʃɛˈlini (*It* tʃɛlˈli:ni)
cellist, ˈcellist ˈtʃɛlɪst
cello, ˈcello ˈtʃɛlo |-s -z |-li -i
cellophane, C- ˈsɛləˌfen |-d -d
cellular ˈsɛljələ; ES ˈsɛljələ(r
cellulate ˈsɛljəˌlet |-d -ɪd
cellule ˈsɛljul
celluloid, C- ˈsɛljəˌlɔɪd, ˈsɛlə-
cellulose ˈsɛljəˌlos |-s -ɪz |-d -t |-lous -ləs
Celoron ˈsɛləˌrɑn, -ˌrɒn
Celotex, c- ˈsɛləˌtɛks
Celsius ˈsɛlsɪəs |-ˈs -ɪz
celt sɛlt
Celt sɛlt |-ist -ɪst
Celtic ˈsɛltɪk |-ally -l̩ɪ, -ɪklɪ
Celticism ˈsɛltəˌsɪzəm |-cist -sɪst
cement səˈmɛnt |-ed -ɪd
cementation ˌsimənˈteʃən, ˌsɛmən-
cemetery ˈsɛməˌtɛrɪ, ˈsɛmɪtrɪ
Cenci ˈtʃɛntʃɪ (*It* ˈtʃɛntʃi)
Cenis səˈni
cenobite ˈsɛnəˌbaɪt, ˈsin-
cenotaph ˈsɛnəˌtæf
Cenozoic ˌsinəˈzo·ɪk, ˌsɛnə-
cense sɛns |censes ˈsɛnsɪz |censed sɛnst
censer ˈsɛnsɚ; ES ˈsɛnsə(r
censor ˈsɛnsɚ; ES ˈsɛnsə(r; |-ed -d
censorial sɛnˈsorɪəl, -ˈsɔr-; S -ˈsor-
censorious sɛnˈsorɪəs, -ˈsɔr-; S -ˈsor-
censorship ˈsɛnsɚˌʃɪp; ES ˈsɛnsə-
censurability ˌsɛnʃərəˈbɪlətɪ
censurable ˈsɛnʃərəbl̩ |-bly -blɪ
censure ˈsɛnʃɚ; ES ˈsɛnʃə(r; |-d -d |-ring
 ˈsɛnʃərɪŋ, ˈsɛnʃrɪŋ
census ˈsɛnsəs |-es -ɪz |-ed -t |-sus' -səs
cent sɛnt |cental ˈsɛntl̩
centaur ˈsɛntɔr; ES ˈsɛntɔə(r
Centaurus, c- sɛnˈtɔrəs |*gen* & *pl* -ri -raɪ
 |-ˈs -ɪz
centavo sɛnˈtavo
centenarian ˌsɛntəˈnɛrɪən, -ˈner-; -ism -ˌɪzəm

Key: See in full §§3–47.   bee bi |pity ˈpɪtɪ (§6) |rate ret |yet jɛt |sang sæŋ |angry ˈæŋ·grɪ
|bath bæθ; E baθ (§10) |ah ɑ |far fɑr |watch wɑtʃ, wɒtʃ (§12) |jaw dʒɔ |gorge gɔrdʒ |go go

centenary ˈsɛntəˌnɛrɪ, sɛnˈtɛnərɪ, *mainly Brit*
  sɛnˈtinərɪ

centennial sɛnˈtɛnɪəl, -njəl |-ly -ɪ

center, -tre ˈsɛntɚ; ES ˈsɛntə(r; |-(e)d -d
  |-(r)ing ˈsɛntərɪŋ, ˈsɛntrɪŋ

centerboard, -tre- ˈsɛntɚˌbord, -ˌbɔrd; ES
  ˈsɛntəˌboəd, E+-ˌbɔəd

center-fire, -tre- ˈsɛntɚˈfaɪr; ES ˈsɛntəˈfaɪə(r;
  (ˈcenter-ˌfire ˈshell)

centerpiece, -tre- ˈsɛntɚˌpis; ES ˈsɛntə-;
  |-s -ɪz

centesimal sɛnˈtɛsəml̩ |-ly -ɪ

centesimo sɛnˈtɛsəˌmo

centiar ˈsɛntɪˌɑr; ES -ˌɑː(r

centiare ˈsɛntɪˌɛr, -ˌær; E -ˌɛə(r, ES -ˌæə(r

centigrade ˈsɛntəˌgred

centigram, -mme ˈsɛntəˌgræm

centiliter, -tre ˈsɛntl̩ˌitɚ; ES -tə(r

centillion sɛnˈtɪljən

centime ˈsantim, sɑnˈtim (*Fr* sãˈtim)

centimeter, -tre ˈsɛntəˌmitɚ; ES -ˌmitə(r;
  (*Fr* sãti'mɛtr̯)

centimeter-gram-second, -tre- ˈsɛntəˌmitɚ-
  ˈgræmˈsɛkənd; ES -ˌmitə-

centimo ˈsɛntəˌmo

centipede ˈsɛntəˌpid

centistere ˈsɛntəˌstɪr; ES -ˌstɪə(r

Centlivre sɛntˈlɪvɚ, -ˈlivɚ; ES
  -ˈlɪvə(r, -ˈliv-

centner ˈsɛntnɚ; ES ˈsɛntnə(r; (*Ger* ˈtsɛntnər)

cento ˈsɛnto

central ˈsɛntrəl |-ly -ɪ |-ism -ˌɪzəm |-ist -ɪst

Centralia sɛnˈtrelɪə, -ljə

centrality sɛnˈtrælətɪ

centralization ˌsɛntrələˈzeʃən, -aɪˈz-

centralize ˈsɛntrəlˌaɪz |-s -ɪz |-d -d

centric ˈsɛntrɪk |-al -l̩ |ally -l̩ɪ, -ɪklɪ

centrifugal sɛnˈtrɪfjʊgl̩ |-ly -ɪ

centrifuge ˈsɛntrəˌfjudʒ, -ˌfɪudʒ |-s -ɪz

centripetal sɛnˈtrɪpətl̩ |-ly -ɪ

centrist, C- ˈsɛntrɪst

centrosphere ˈsɛntrəˌsfɪr; ES -ˌsfɪə(r, S+
  -ˌsfɛə(r

centuple ˈsɛntʊpl̩, -tjʊ-, sɛnˈtʊpl̩, -ˈtɪu-,
  -ˈtju- |-d -d |-ling -plɪŋ, -pl̩ɪŋ

centurial sɛnˈtjʊrɪəl, -ˈtɪurɪəl, -ˈtʊr-

centurion sɛnˈtjʊrɪən, -ˈtɪurɪən, -ˈtʊr-

century ˈsɛntʃərɪ |-ried -d

cephalic səˈfælɪk, sɛ-

Cephalonia ˌsɛfəˈlonɪə, -njə |-n -n

cephalopod ˈsɛfələˌpad; ES+-ˌpɒd

Cephalopoda ˌsɛfəˈlapədə; ES+-ˈlɒp-

cephalothorax ˌsɛfələˈθoræks, -ˈθɔr-; S -ˈθor-;
  |-es -ɪz

cephalous ˈsɛfələs

Cephalus ˈsɛfələs |-'s -ɪz

Cephas ˈsifəs |-'s -ɪz

Cepheus ˈsifjus, ˈsifɪəs |-'s -ɪz

ceramic səˈræmɪk |-s -s

cerate ˈsɪret

Cerberus ˈsɝbərəs; ES ˈsɜb-, ˈsɝb-; |-'s -ɪz

cere sɪr; ES sɪə(r, S+sɛə(r; |-d -d

cereal ˈsɪrɪəl

cerebellar ˌsɛrəˈbɛlɚ; ES -ˈbɛlə(r

cerebellum ˌsɛrəˈbɛləm |-s -z |-la -lə

cerebral ˈsɛrəbrəl |-ly -ɪ

cerebrate ˈsɛrəˌbret |-brated -ˌbretɪd

cerebration ˌsɛrəˈbreʃən

cerebrospinal ˌsɛrəbroˈspaɪnl̩

cerebrum ˈsɛrəbrəm |-s -z |-bra -brə

cerecloth ˈsɪrˌklɔθ, -ˌklɒθ; ES ˈsɪə-; |-ths -ðz,
  -θs

cerement ˈsɪrmənt; ES ˈsɪəmənt

ceremonial ˌsɛrəˈmonɪəl, -njəl |-ly -ɪ

ceremonious ˌsɛrəˈmonɪəs, -njəs

ceremony ˈsɛrəˌmonɪ

Ceres ˈsɪriz, ˈsiriz |-res' -riz

Cereus, c- ˈsɪrɪəs, ˈsi- |-es -ɪz

cerif, -iph ˈsɛrɪf=serif

Cerigo ˈtʃɛrɪˌgo (*It* ˈtʃɛːrɪˌgo)

Cerimon ˈsɛrɪˌman, -ˌmɒn

cerise səˈriz, -ˈris |-s -ɪz

cerium ˈsɪrɪəm

Cerro Gordo ˈsɛroˈgɔrdo; ES -ˈgɔədo

certain ˈsɝtn̩, -ɪn, -ən; ES ˈsɜt-, ˈsɝt-; |-ty -tɪ

certes ˈsɝtiz; ES ˈsɜt-, ˈsɝt-

certifiable ˈsɝtəˌfaɪəbl̩; ES ˈsɜtə-, ˈsɝtə-;
  |-bly -blɪ

certificate *n* sɚˈtɪfəkɪt; ES səˈtɪf-

certificate *v* sɚˈtɪfəˌket; ES sə-; |-d -ɪd

certification '*certifying*' ˌsɝtəfəˈkeʃən; ES
  ˌsɜtə-, ˌsɝtə-

certification '*certificating*' sɚˌtɪfəˈkeʃən; ES
  sə-

certify ˈsɝtəˌfaɪ; ES ˈsɜtə-, ˈsɝtə-; |-fied -ˌfaɪd

certiorari ˌsɝʃɪəˈrɛrɪ, -ˈrɛrɪ; ES ˌsɜʃɪ-, ˌsɝʃɪ-

certitude ˈsɝtəˌtjud, -ˌtɪud; -ˌtud; ES ˈsɜt-,
  ˈsɝt-

|full fʊl |tooth tuθ |further ˈfɝðɚ; ES ˈfɝðə |custom ˈkʌstəm |while hwaɪl |how haʊ |toy tɔɪ
|using ˈjuzɪŋ |fuse fjuz, fɪuz |dish dɪʃ |vision ˈvɪʒən |Eden ˈidn̩ |cradle ˈkredl̩ |keep 'em ˈkipm̩

cerulean səˈruliən, -ˈriuliən, -ljən
cerumen səˈrumən, -ˈriumən
ceruse ˈsɪrus, səˈrus
Cervantes sɚˈvæntiz; ES sə-; |-tesʔ -tiz (Sp θerˈβantes)
cervical ˈsɚvɪk‖; ES ˈsɚv-, ˈsɚˈv-
cervix ˈsɚvɪks; ES ˈsɚv-, ˈsɚˈv-; |-es -ɪz |cervices sɚˈvaɪsiz; ES sə-
César ˈsezɑr; ES ˈsezɑː(r, E+-zaː(r; (Fr seˈzaːr)
Cesarea ˌsɛsəˈriə, ˌsɛz- |-rean -ˈriən
Cesarean, c-, -ian surg. sɪˈzɛrɪən, -ˈzær-, -ˈzer-
cesium ˈsiziəm
cessation sɛˈseʃən
cession ˈsɛʃən
cesspit ˈsɛsˌpɪt
cesspool ˈsɛsˌpul
cestode ˈsɛstod
cestus, C- ˈsɛstəs |-es -ɪz
cesura sɪˈʒurə, sɪˈzjurə, -ˈzɪurə |-l -l
Cetacea sɪˈteʃə |cetacean sɪˈteʃən
Cetus ˈsitəs |gen Ceti ˈsitaɪ
cevitamic ˌsivaɪˈtæmɪk
Ceylon sɪˈlɑn; ES+-ˈlɒn; |-ese ˌsiləˈniz
Ceyx ˈsiɪks |-ʼs -ɪz
Cézanne sɪˈzæn (Fr seˈzan)
cf. ʽcompareʼ ˈsiˈɛf, kənˈfɚ; ES -ˈfɚ(r, -ˈfɚ
chabouk, -buk ˈtʃabʊk
Chaco ˈtʃako
Chad tʃæd, tʃad
Chadds Ford ˈtʃædzˈford, -ˈfɔrd; ES -ˈfoəd, E+-ˈfɔəd
Chadron ˈʃædrən
Chaeronea ˌkɛrəˈniə
chafe tʃef |chafed tʃeft
Chafee ˈtʃefɪ, ˈtʃæfɪ
chafer ˈtʃefɚ; ES ˈtʃefə(r, |-y -ɪ
chaff tʃæf; E+tʃaf, tʃɑf; |-ed -t
Chaffee ˈtʃæfɪ, ˈtʃefɪ
chaffer ˈtʃæfɚ; ES ˈtʃæfə(r; |-ed -d |-ing ˈtʃæfərɪŋ, ˈtʃæfrɪŋ
Chaffey ˈtʃæfɪ, ˈtʃefɪ
chaffinch ˈtʃæˌfɪntʃ, ˈtʃæfˌfɪntʃ |-es -ɪz
Chagres ˈtʃagrɛs
chagrin ʃəˈgrɪn |-ed -d
Chagrin Falls ʃəˈgrɪnˈfɔlz, loc.+ˈʃugrɪn-, ˈʃægrɪn-
chain tʃen |chained tʃend
chain-stitch ˈtʃenˌstɪtʃ |-es -ɪz |-ed -t

chainwork ˈtʃenˌwɚk; ES -ˌwɜk, -ˌwɝk
chair tʃɛr, tʃær; E tʃɛə(r, ES tʃæə(r; |-ed -d
chairman ˈtʃɛrmən, ˈtʃær-; E ˈtʃɛə-, ES ˈtʃæə-; |-men -mən |-ship -ˌʃɪp
chaise ʃez |chaises ˈʃezɪz |chaised ʃezd
chaise longue ˈʃezˈlɔŋg, -ˈlɒŋg (Fr ʃɛːzˈlŏg)
Chalcedon ˈkælsɪdən, -ˌdɑn, -ˌdɒn
chalcedony kælˈsɛdṇɪ, ˈkælsəˌdonɪ
chalcid ˈkælsɪd
chalcography kælˈkɑgrəfɪ, -ˈkɒg-
chalcographic ˌkælkəˈgræfɪk |-al -l̩
chalcopyrite ˌkælkəˈpaɪraɪt, -ˈpɪr-
Chaldaic kælˈde·ɪk |-al -l̩
Chaldea kælˈdiə |-n -n |-dee kælˈdi, ˈkældi
chaldron ˈtʃɔldrən
chalet ʃæˈle, ˈʃælɪ (Fr ʃaˈlɛ)
Chalfont Bucks ˈtʃælfənt, loc. ˈtʃafənt
chalice ˈtʃælɪs |-s -ɪz |-d -t
chalk tʃɔk |chalked tʃɔkt
challenge ˈtʃælɪndʒ, -əndʒ |-s -ɪz·|-d -d
challis, -llie ˈʃælɪ
Chalmers ˈtʃælmɚz, ˈtʃɑm-, ˈtʃɒm-; ES -əz; |-ʼs -ɪz
cham dial. ʻI amʼ tʃæm
cham ʻkhanʼ kæm
chamade ʃəˈmad
chamber ˈtʃembɚ; ES -bə(r; |-ed -d |-ing ˈtʃembərɪŋ, ˈtʃembrɪŋ
chamberer ˈtʃembərɚ; ES ˈtʃembərə(r
chamberlain ˈtʃembɚlɪn; ES ˈtʃembə-
Chamberlain, -lin ˈtʃembɚlɪn; ES ˈtʃembə-
chambermaid ˈtʃembɚˌmed; ES ˈtʃembə-
chambray ˈʃæmbre
chameleon kəˈmiliən, -ljən
chamfer ˈtʃæmfɚ; ES ˈtʃæmfə(r; |-ed -d |-ing ˈtʃæmfərɪŋ, ˈtʃæmfrɪŋ
chamois, -mmy ˈʃæmɪ
chamomile ˈkæməˌmaɪl
Chamonix, -mouny ˈʃæmənɪ (Fr ʃamuˈni)
champ tʃæmp |champed tʃæmpt
champac, -pak ˈtʃæmpæk, ˈtʃʌmpʌk
champagne ʃæmˈpen |-d -d
Champagne ʃæmˈpen (Fr ʃãˈpaɲ)
champaign ʃæmˈpen, ˈtʃæmpen
Champaign Ill ʃæmˈpen
champerty ˈtʃæmpɚtɪ; ES ˈtʃæmpətɪ
champion, C- ˈtʃæmpɪən |-ed -d |-ship -ˌʃɪp
Champlain ʃæmˈplen
Champlin ˈtʃæmplɪn

Words below in which a *before* r (farm) *is sounded* ɑ *are often pronounced in* E *with* a (fɑːm)

Champs Élysées *Fr* ʃãzeli'ze
chance tʃæns; E+tʃɑns, tʃɑns; |-s -ɪz |-d -t
chancel 'tʃæns|; E+'tʃɑn-, 'tʃɑn-
chancellery 'tʃænsələrɪ, -slərɪ; E+'tʃɑn-,
'tʃɑn-
chancellor, C- 'tʃænsələ, -slə; ES -lə(r, E+
'tʃɑn-, 'tʃɑn-; |-ship -,ʃɪp
Chancellorsville 'tʃænsələz,vɪl, -slɚz-; ES
-ləz-, E+'tʃɑn-, 'tʃɑn-
chancery 'tʃænsərɪ; E+'tʃɑn-, 'tʃɑn-
chancre 'ʃæŋkɚ; ES 'ʃæŋkə(r
chancy, -cey 'tʃænsɪ; E+'tʃɑn-, 'tʃɑn-
chandelier ,ʃændl|'ɪr; ES -'ɪə(r, S+-'ɛə(r
chandler, C- 'tʃændlɚ; ES -dlə(r, E+'tʃɑn-,
'tʃɑn-
Chandos 'tʃændɑs, 'ʃæn-; ES+-dɒs; |-'s -ɪz
Chandragupta ,tʃʌndrə'guptə
Changchun 'tʃɑŋ'tʃʊn
change tʃendʒ |changes 'tʃendʒɪz |-d -d
changeability ,tʃendʒə'bɪlətɪ
changeable 'tʃendʒəb| |-bly -blɪ
changeling 'tʃendʒlɪŋ
Chang Kai-shek 'tʃɑŋ'kaɪ'ʃɛk, 'tʃæŋ-
channel 'tʃæn| |channeled 'tʃæn|d
Channing 'tʃænɪŋ
chanson 'ʃænsən, -sɑn, -sɒn (*Fr* ʃã'sõ)
chant tʃænt; E+tʃɑnt, tʃɑnt; |-ed -ɪd
chantey, -ty 'ʃæntɪ, 'tʃæn-; E+-an-, -ɑn-
chanticleer 'tʃæntɪ,klɪr; ES -,klɪə(r, S+
-,klɛə(r
Chantilly *Va, France* ʃæn'tɪlɪ (*Fr* ʃãti'ji)
chantress 'tʃæntrɪs; E+'tʃɑnt-, 'tʃɑnt-; |-es
-ɪz
chantry, C- 'tʃæntrɪ; E+'tʃɑnt-, 'tʃɑnt-
Chanute tʃə'nut, ʃə'nut
chaos 'keɑs; ES+'kens; |-es -ɪz
chaotic ke'ɑtɪk; ES+-'ɒtɪk; |-al -| |-ally -|ɪ,
-ɪklɪ
chap *'fellow'*, *'crack'* tʃæp |chapped tʃæpt
chap *'jaw'* tʃæp—*cf* chop *'jaw'*
chaparajos ,tʃɑpə'rɑhos |-rejos -'rehos
chaparral ,tʃæpə'ræl
chaparreras, -pareras ,tʃɑpə'rerɑs
chapbook 'tʃæp,bʊk
chape tʃep
chapeau ʃæ'po |-x, -s -z (*Fr* ʃa'po)
chapel, C- 'tʃæp| |-ed -d |-ing 'tʃæplɪŋ, -plɪŋ
chaperajos ,tʃɑpə'rahos

chaperon, -one 'ʃæpə,ron |-ed -d |-age -ɪdʒ
chapfallen 'tʃæp,fɔlən, -,fɔln—*cf* chopfallen
chaplain 'tʃæplɪn |-cy -sɪ |-ship -,ʃɪp
chaplet 'tʃæplɪt |-ed -ɪd
Chaplin 'tʃæplɪn
Chapman, c- 'tʃæpmən |-men -mən
Chappell, -pple 'tʃæp|
chappie, -ppy 'tʃæpɪ
chaptalize 'ʃæpt|,aɪz |-s -ɪz |-d -d
chapter 'tʃæptɚ; ES -tə(r; |-ed -d |-ing
'tʃæptərɪŋ, -trɪŋ
Chapultepec tʃə'pʌltə,pek (*Sp* tʃa,pulte'pek)
char tʃɑr; ES tʃɑ:(r; |-red -d
charabanc 'ʃærə,bæŋk, -,bæŋ (*Fr* ʃara'bã)
character 'kærɪktɚ, -ək-; ES -tə(r; |-ed -d
|-ing -tərɪŋ, -trɪŋ
characteristic ,kærɪktə'rɪstɪk, ,kærək- |-al -|
|-ally -|ɪ, -ɪklɪ
characterization ,kærɪktrə'zeʃən, -ək-, -tərə-,
-aɪ'z-
characterize 'kærɪktə,raɪz, 'kærək- |-s -ɪz
|-d -d
charactery 'kærɪktərɪ, -ək-, -trɪ
charade ʃə'red
charcoal 'tʃɑr,kol; ES 'tʃɑ:,kol; |-ed -d
chard tʃɑrd; ES tʃɑːd
Chardon 'ʃɑrdn̩; ES 'ʃɑːdn̩
chare tʃɛr, tʃær; E tʃɛə(r, ES tʃæə(r; |-d -d
charge tʃɑrdʒ; ES tʃɑːdʒ; |-s -ɪz |-d -d |-able
-əb| |-bly -blɪ
chargé d'affaires ʃɑr'ʒedæ'fɛr, -'fær; E
ʃɑ:'ʒedæ'fɛə(r, ES -'fæə(r; |*pl* chargés
-'ʒez- (*Fr* ʃarʒeda'fɛːr)
charily 'tʃɛrəlɪ, 'tʃær-, 'tʃer-, -ɪlɪ; S 'tʃær-,
'tʃer-
chariness 'tʃɛrɪnɪs, 'tʃær-, 'tʃer-; S 'tʃær-,
'tʃer-
Charing Cross 'tʃærɪŋ'krɔs, 'tʃer-, -'krɒs; S
'tʃærɪŋ-; ('Charing ,Cross 'Road)
chariot 'tʃærɪət |-ed -ɪd
charioteer ,tʃærɪət'ɪr; ES -'ɪə(r, S+-'ɛə(r
charitable 'tʃærətəb| |-bly -blɪ
Chariton 'ʃerətn̩, 'ʃær-; S 'ʃær-
charity 'tʃærətɪ
charivari ʃə,rɪvə'ri, ,ʃɪvə'ri, ,ʃɑrɪ'vɑrɪ—*In*
,ʃɪvə'ri *the first* r *is lost by dissimilation*
(§121). *Cf* shivaree
charkha, -ka 'tʃʌrkə; ES 'tʃʌ:kə

Words below in which a *before* r (farm) *is sounded* ɑ *are often pronounced in* E *with* a (fa:m)

charlatan 'ʃɑrlətņ; ES 'ʃɑ:lə-; |-ism -ˌɪzəm
|-ry -rɪ

charlatanic ˌʃɑrlə'tænɪk; ES ˌʃɑ:lə-; |-al -|
|-ally -|ɪ, -ɪklɪ

Charlecote 'tʃɑrlkət, -kot; ES 'tʃɑ:l-

Charlemagne 'ʃɑrləˌmen; ES 'ʃɑ:lə-; (Fr
ʃɑrlə'maɲ)

Charleroi Pa ˌʃɑrlə'rɔɪ, 'ʃɑrləˌrɔɪ; ES ˌʃɑ:l-,
'ʃɑ:l-; |Belg -roi, -roy Fr ʃɑrlə'rwɑ

Charles tʃɑrlz; ES tʃɑ:lz; |-'s -ɪz |-ton -tən
|-town -ˌtaʊn

Charley, -ie 'tʃɑrlɪ; ES 'tʃɑ:lɪ

charlock 'tʃɑrlək; ES 'tʃɑ:lək

Charlotte *fem. name* 'ʃɑrlət, *US places* 'ʃɑrlət,
ʃɚ'lɑt; ES 'ʃɑ:l-, ʃə-, -'lɒt

Charlottenburg ʃɑr'lɑtņˌbɝg; ES ʃɑ'lɑtņˌbɜg,
-'lɒt-, -ˌbɜg (Ger ʃɑr'lɒtənˌbʊrk)

charlotte russe 'ʃɑrlət'rus, -'ruʃ; ES 'ʃɑ:lət-

Charlottesville 'ʃɑrlətsˌvɪl; ES 'ʃɑ:l-, S+-v|

Charlton 'tʃɑrltən; ES 'tʃɑ:l-

charm tʃɑrm; ES tʃɑ:m; |-ed -d |-edly -ɪdlɪ

charmeuse ʃɑr'mɜz; ES ʃɑ:-; (Fr ʃɑr'mø:z)

Charmian 'tʃɑrmɪən, 'kɑrm-; ES 'tʃɑ:m-,
'kɑ:m-

charnel 'tʃɑrn|; ES 'tʃɑ:n|

Charon 'kɛrən, 'kærən, 'kerən; S 'kærən,
'kerən

charpoy, -pai 'tʃɑr'pɔɪ, -'paɪ; ES 'tʃɑ:-

chart tʃɑrt; ES tʃɑ:t; |-ed -ɪd

charter 'tʃɑrtɚ; ES 'tʃɑ:tə(r; |-ed -d |-ing
-tərɪŋ, -trɪŋ

Charterhouse, c- 'tʃɑrtɚˌhaʊs; ES 'tʃɑ:tə-

chartograph 'kɑrtəˌgræf; ES 'kɑ:tə-, E+
-ˌgraf, -ˌgrɑf

chartographer kɑr'tɑgrəfɚ, -'tɒg-; ES kɑ-,
-fə(r; |-phy -fɪ

chartographic ˌkɑrtə'græfɪk; ES ˌkɑ:tə-

Chartres 'ʃɑrtrə, ʃɑrt; ES 'ʃɑ:t-, ʃɑ:t; (Fr
ʃɑrtȓ)

chartreuse, C- ʃɑr'trɜz; ES ʃɑ:-; (Fr ʃɑr'trø:z)

chartulary 'kɑrtʃʊˌlɛrɪ; ES 'kɑ:tʃʊˌlɛrɪ

charwoman 'tʃɑrˌwʊmən, -ˌwu-; ES 'tʃɑ:-;
|-men -ˌwɪmɪn, -ən

chary 'tʃɛrɪ, 'tʃɛ:rɪ, 'tʃærɪ, 'tʃɛrɪ; S 'tʃærɪ,
'tʃɛrɪ—*Some speakers distinguish* chary
from cherry *by a longer* ɛ.

Charybdis kə'rɪbdɪs |-'s -ɪz |-dian -dɪən

chase, C- tʃes |chases 'tʃesɪz |chased tʃest

chasm 'kæzəm, *much less freq.* 'kæzm̩ |-ed -d

chasmal 'kæzm| |chasmic 'kæzmɪk

chassé ʃæ'se |-d -d—*cf* sashay

chasseur ʃæ'sɝ; ES -'sɜ(r, -'sɝ; (Fr ʃɑ'sœ:r)

chassis 'ʃæsɪ, 'ʃæsɪs |pl chassis 'ʃæsɪz

chaste tʃest

chasten 'tʃesņ |-ed -d |-ing 'tʃesņɪŋ, -snɪŋ

chastise tʃæs'taɪz |-s -ɪz |-d -d

chastisement 'tʃæstɪzmənt, tʃæs'taɪzmənt

chastity 'tʃæstətɪ

chasuble 'tʃæzjʊb|, 'tʃæs-

chat tʃæt |chatted 'tʃætɪd

château ʃæ'to |pl -teaux -'toz (Fr ʃɑ'to)

Chateaubriand ʃæ'tobrɪənd, -ˌɑnd (Fr
ʃɑtobri'ɑ̃)

Château-Thierry ʃæ'totɪə'ri (Fr ʃɑtotjɛ'ri)

chatelain 'ʃæt|ˌen (Fr ʃɑ'tlæ)

chatelaine 'ʃæt|ˌen (Fr ʃɑ'tlɛn)

Chatham 'tʃætəm, *US places*+'tʃæt·hæm,
-æm

Chatillon *Shak.* ʃæ'tɪljən (Fr ʃɑti'jõ)

Chattahoochee ˌtʃætə'hutʃɪ

Chattanooga ˌtʃætņ'ugə, ˌtʃætə'nugə

chattel 'tʃæt| |-ed -d

chatterbox 'tʃætɚˌbɑks; ES 'tʃætəˌbaks,
-ˌbɒks; |-es -ɪz

Chatterton 'tʃætɚtən; ES 'tʃætətən

Chattooga tʃə'tugə

Chaucer 'tʃɔsɚ; ES 'tʃɔsə(r; |-ism -ˌɪzəm

Chaucerian tʃɔ'sɪrɪən

chauffer '*stove*' 'tʃɔfɚ; ES 'tʃɔfə(r

chauffeur 'ʃofɚ, ʃo'fɝ; ES 'ʃofə(r, ʃo'fɜ(r, -'fɝ;
|-ed -d

chaulmoogra, -mugra tʃɔl'mugrə

Chauncey 'tʃɔnsɪ, 'tʃɒnsɪ, 'tʃɑnsɪ, 'tʃænsɪ

chaunt tʃɔnt, tʃɒnt, tʃɑnt |-ed -ɪd

Chautauqua, c- ʃə'tɔkwə |-n -n

chauvinism 'ʃovɪnˌɪzəm |-ist -ɪst

chauvinistic ˌʃovɪ'nɪstɪk |-al -| |-ally -|ɪ, -ɪklɪ

chaw tʃɔ |chawed tʃɔd

Chazy 'ʃezɪ, ʃe'zi ('Chazy's 'Landing)

cheap tʃip |-ed -t

cheapen 'tʃipən |-ed -d |-ing 'tʃipənɪŋ, -pnɪŋ

Cheapside 'tʃipˌsaɪd, -'saɪd

cheat, C- tʃit |cheated 'tʃitɪd

Cheatham 'tʃitəm—*cf* Cheetham, Chetham

Cheboygan ʃɪ'bɔɪgən

check tʃɛk |checked tʃɛkt |-book -ˌbʊk

checker 'tʃɛkɚ; ES 'tʃɛkə(r; |-ed -d |-ing 'tʃɛkərɪŋ, 'tʃɛkrɪŋ

checkerboard 'tʃɛkɚˌbord, -ˌbɔrd; ES 'tʃɛkə-ˌboəd, E+-ˌbɔəd; |-ed -ɪd

checkmate 'tʃɛkˌmet |-mated -ˌmetɪd

checkoff 'tʃɛkˌɔf, -ˌɒf

checkrein 'tʃɛkˌren

checkroom 'tʃɛkˌrum, -ˌrʊm

checkrow 'tʃɛkˌro |-ed -d

checkstrap 'tʃɛkˌstræp

Cheddar 'tʃɛdɚ; ES 'tʃɛdə(r

cheek tʃik |cheeked tʃikt

cheekbone 'tʃikˌbon, -'bon

Cheeke tʃik

cheekily 'tʃikḷɪ, -ɪlɪ

cheep tʃip |cheeped tʃipt

cheer tʃɪr; ES tʃɪə(r, S+tʃɛə(r; |-ed -d

cheerful 'tʃɪrfəl; ES 'tʃɪə-, S+'tʃɛə-; |-ly -ɪ

cheerily 'tʃɪrəlɪ, -ɪlɪ

cheerio 'tʃɪrɪˌo

cheerly 'tʃɪrlɪ; ES 'tʃɪəlɪ, S+'tʃɛəlɪ

cheese tʃiz |cheeses 'tʃizɪz |cheesed tʃizd

cheesecake 'tʃizˌkek

cheesecloth 'tʃizˌklɔθ, -ˌklɒθ |-ths -ðz, -θs

cheesemonger 'tʃizˌmʌŋgɚ; ES -ˌmʌŋgə(r

cheeseparing 'tʃizˌpɛrɪŋ, -ˌpærɪŋ; S -ˌpærɪŋ

cheetah 'tʃitə

Cheetham 'tʃitəm—cf Cheatham

chef ʃɛf

chef-d'oeuvre ʃe'dœvrə (Fr ʃɛ'dœ:vr)

Chefoo 'tʃʃi'fu

Cheke tʃik

Chekov 'tʃɛkɔf, -ɒf

chela 'claw' 'kilə |chelae 'kili

chela 'disciple' 'tʃelə

chela measure 'kelə

Chelan ʃə'læn

Chelmsford Mass 'tʃɛmzfɚd, 'tʃɛlmz-, Engd 'tʃɛlms-, 'tʃɛms-; ES -fəd

Chelonia kə'lonɪə |chelonian kə'lonɪən

Chelsea 'tʃɛlsɪ

Cheltenham 'tʃɛltnəm, 'tʃɛltṇəm

chemic 'kɛmɪk |-al -ḷ |-ally -ḷɪ, -ɪklɪ

chemise ʃə'miz |-s -ɪz |-sette ˌʃɛmɪ'zɛt

chemist 'kɛmɪst |-ry -rɪ

Chemnitz 'kɛmnɪts |-'s -ɪz

Chemosh 'kimɑʃ, -mɒʃ |-'s -ɪz

chemotherapy ˌkɛmo'θɛrəpɪ

Chemung ʃɪ'mʌŋ

chemurgic kɛm'ɝdʒɪk; ES -'ɜdʒ-, -'ɝdʒ-; |-al -ḷ

chemurgy 'kɛmɝdʒɪ; ES -ɜdʒɪ, -ɝdʒɪ

Chenango ʃɪ'næŋgo

chenille ʃə'nil

Cheops 'kiɑps; ES+'kiɒps |-'s -ɪz

Chepstow 'tʃɛpsto

cheque tʃɛk |-r -ɚ; ES -ə(r; |-red -ɚd; ES -əd; |-ring 'tʃɛkərɪŋ, 'tʃɛkrɪŋ

chequerboard 'tʃɛkɚˌbord, -ˌbɔrd; ES 'tʃɛkə-ˌboəd, E+-ˌbɔəd; |-ed -ɪd

Cheraw 'tʃɪrɔ, tʃɪ'rɔ

Cherbourg 'ʃɛrburg; ES 'ʃɛəbuəg; (Fr ʃɛr'bu:r)

cherish 'tʃɛrɪʃ |-es -ɪz |-ed -t

Cherith 'kɪrɪθ, 'tʃɪrɪθ

Cherokee 'tʃɛrəˌki, ˌtʃɛrə'ki

cheroot ʃə'rut

cherry 'tʃɛrɪ |cherried 'tʃɛrɪd

Chersonese, c- 'kɝsəˌniz; ES 'kɜsə-, 'kɝsə-

chert tʃɝt; ES tʃɜt, tʃɝt

cherub 'tʃɛrəb |-s -z |-im -ɪm, 'tʃɛrjubɪm |-in -ɪn, -jubɪn

cherubic tʃə'rubɪk, -'rɪubɪk |-al -ḷ |-ally -ḷɪ, -ɪklɪ

chervonets tʃɛr'vɒnɪts |pl chervontsi tʃɛr-'vɒntsi

Cherwell 'tʃɑrwəl, -wɛl; ES 'tʃɑ:-

Chesaning 'tʃɛsnɪŋ

Chesapeake tʃɛs'pik, ˌtʃɛsə'pik ('Chesaˌpeake 'Bay)

Chesham 'tʃɛʃəm, less freq. 'tʃɛsəm—'tʃɛʃəm is a sp. pron. Cf Bentham

Cheshire 'tʃɛʃɪr, 'tʃɛʃɚ; ES 'tʃɛʃɪə(r, -ʃə(r

chess tʃɛs |chesses 'tʃɛsɪz

chessboard 'tʃɛsˌbord, -ˌbɔrd; ES -ˌboəd, E+-ˌbɔəd

chessman 'tʃɛsˌmæn, -mən |-men -ˌmɛn, -mən

chest tʃɛst |chested 'tʃɛstɪd

Chester, c- 'tʃɛstɚ; ES 'tʃɛstə(r

Chesterfield 'tʃɛstɚˌfild; ES 'tʃɛstə-

Chesterton 'tʃɛstɚtən; ES 'tʃɛstətən, -tṇ

Chester White 'tʃɛstɚ'hwaɪt; ES 'tʃɛstə-

chestnut 'tʃɛsnət, -ˌnʌt

chestnut-roan 'tʃɛsnət'ron ('chestnutˌroan 'mare)

chetah 'tʃitə

Chetham 'tʃɛtəm—cf Cheatham

cheval-de-frise ʃə'vældə'friz |pl -vaux- -'vo-

|full fʊl |tooth tuθ |further 'fɝðɚ; ES 'fɜðə |custom 'kʌstəm |while hwaɪl |how haʊ |toy tɔɪ |using 'juzɪŋ |fuse fjuz, fɪuz |dish dɪʃ |vision 'vɪʒən |Eden 'idṇ |cradle 'kredḷ |keep 'em 'kipm̩

cheval-glass ʃəˈvælˌglæs; E+-ˌglas, -ˌglas; |-es -ɪz

chevalier ˌʃevəˈlɪr; ES -ˈlɪə(r, S+-ˈlɛə(r

Cheviot *Hills, sheep* ˈtʃevɪət, ˈtʃiv-; *O vil.* ˈʃivɪət, ˈʃev-; |Ch-, ch- *cloth* ˈʃevɪət, ˈtʃevɪət

Chevrolet ˌʃevrəˈle

chevron ˈʃevrən |-ed -d

chevy, C- ˈtʃevɪ |chevied ˈtʃevɪd

chew, C- tʃu, tʃɪu |-ed -d

chewink tʃɪˈwɪŋk

Cheyenne ʃaɪˈɛn

Cheyne ˈtʃenɪ, ˈtʃen

chi *Gk letter* kaɪ

Chian ˈkaɪən

Chiang Kai-shek tʃɪˈaŋˈkaɪˈʃɛk, ˈtʃʃjaŋ-

Chianti, c- kɪˈæntɪ (*It* ˈkjanti)

chiaroscuro kɪˌarəˈskjuro, -ˈskɪuro (*It* ˌkjɑːroˈskuːro)

chibouk, -que tʃɪˈbuk, -ˈbuk

chic ʃik, ʃɪk

Chicago ʃəˈkago, -ˈkɒgo, -ˈkɔgo, ʃɪ-, -ə |-ed -d |-goan -gəwən

chicane ʃɪˈken |-caned -ˈkend |-canery -ˈkenərɪ

Chichen Itzá tʃiˈtʃɛnitˈsa

Chichester ˈtʃɪtʃɪstɚ; ES ˈtʃɪtʃɪstə(r

chick tʃɪk

chickadee ˈtʃɪkəˌdi, ˌtʃɪkəˈdi

Chickahominy ˌtʃɪkəˈhamənɪ; ES+-ˈhɒm-

Chickamauga ˌtʃɪkəˈmɔgə (ˈChickaˌmauga ˈCreek)

chickaree ˈtʃɪkəˌri

Chickasaw ˈtʃɪkəˌsɔ

Chickasawhay ˌtʃɪkəˈsɔwe |-wha -wə

Chickasha ˈtʃɪkəˌʃe

chicken ˈtʃɪkɪn, -ən

chickenhearted ˈtʃɪkɪnˈhartɪd, -ən-; ES -ˈhɑːtɪd, E+-ˈhaːtɪd; (ˈchickenˌhearted ˈhero)

chicken-pox ˈtʃɪkɪnˌpaks, -ən-; ES+-ˌpɒks

Chickering ˈtʃɪkərɪŋ, ˈtʃɪkrɪŋ

chickweed ˈtʃɪkˌwid

chicle ˈtʃɪkl̩, ˈtʃikl̩ (*Sp* ˈtʃikle)

Chico ˈtʃiko

Chicopee ˈtʃɪkəˌpi, -pɪ

chicory ˈtʃɪkərɪ, ˈtʃɪkrɪ

chicot ˈtʃiko (*Fr* ʃiˈko)

Chicot ˈʃiko

chide tʃaɪd |*past* chid tʃɪd *or* chided ˈtʃaɪdɪd |*pptc* chid tʃɪd *or* chidden ˈtʃɪdn̩ *or* chided ˈtʃaɪdɪd

Chidley ˈtʃɪdlɪ

chief tʃif |-tain -tɪn |-taincy -tɪnsɪ

chield tʃild |chiel tʃil

chiffon ʃɪˈfan, -ˈfɒn, ˈʃɪfən

chiffonier ˌʃɪfəˈnɪr; ES -ˈnɪə(r, S+-ˈnɛə(r, -ˈnjɛə(r

chigger ˈtʃɪgɚ; ES ˈtʃɪgə(r

chignon ˈʃinjan, -jɒn (*Fr* ʃiˈjõ)

chigoe ˈtʃɪgo

Chihuahua tʃɪˈwawa, -ˈwɒwɒ

chilblain ˈtʃɪlˌblen |-ed -d |-s -z

child, C-(e) tʃaɪld |-ed -ɪd |*pl see* children

childbearing ˈtʃaɪldˌberɪŋ, -ˌbærɪŋ; S -ˌbær-

childbirth ˈtʃaɪldˌbɝθ; ES -ˌbɝθ, -ˌbɝθ |-ths -θs

Childermas ˈtʃɪldɚməs; ES ˈtʃɪldə-

childhood ˈtʃaɪldˌhud

childlike ˈtʃaɪldˌlaɪk

children ˈtʃɪldrən, -drɪn, -dɚn; ES -drən, -drɪn, -dən

Childress ˈtʃaɪldrɪs |-'s -ɪz

Chile ˈtʃɪlɪ |-an -ən |-lian -lɪən (*Sp* ˈtʃile)

Chili *US* ˈtʃɪlɪ, *NY* ˈtʃaɪlaɪ

chili, -le ˈtʃɪlɪ

Chilkat ˈtʃɪlkæt

Chilkoot ˈtʃɪlkut

chill tʃɪl |chilled tʃɪld

chilli ˈtʃɪlɪ

Chillicothe ˌtʃɪləˈkɑθɪ; ES+-ˈkɒθɪ; (ˈChilliˌcothe ˈRoad)

Chillingworth ˈtʃɪlɪŋwɚθ, -ˌwɝθ; ES -wəθ, -ˌwɝθ, -ˌwɝθ

Chillon ʃəˈlan, -ˈlɒn, ˈʃilən (*Fr* ʃiˈjõ)

chilly ˈtʃɪlɪ

Chiltern ˈtʃɪltɚn; ES ˈtʃɪltən

chimaera kəˈmɪrə, kaɪ-

chimb tʃaɪm

Chimborazo ˌtʃɪmbəˈrezo, -ˈrazo (*Am Sp* ˌtʃimboˈraso) |+ ˌʃ-

chime tʃaɪm |chimed tʃaɪmd

chimera kəˈmɪrə, kaɪˈmɪrə

chimerical kəˈmɪrɪkl̩, kaɪ- |-ly -ɪ, -ɪklɪ

chimney ˈtʃɪmnɪ |chimneyed ˈtʃɪmnɪd

chimpanzee ˌtʃɪmpænˈzi, tʃɪmˈpænzɪ, ˌʃ-, ʃ-

chin tʃɪn |chinned tʃɪnd

China, c- ˈtʃaɪnə |-man, -men -mən

Those words below in which the ɑ sound is spelt o are often pronounced with ɒ in E and S

chinaware ˈtʃaɪnəˌwɛr, -ˌwær; E -ˌwɛə(r, ES -ˌwæə(r

chincapin ˈtʃɪŋkəpɪn

chinch ˈtʃɪntʃ |-es -ɪz

chinchilla, C- tʃɪnˈtʃɪlə

chincough ˈtʃɪnˌkɔf, -ˌkɒf

chine tʃaɪn |chined tʃaɪnd

Chinee tʃaɪˈni

Chinese tʃaɪˈniz |-'s -ɪz (ˈChiˌnese ˈcabbage)

chink tʃɪŋk |chinked tʃɪŋkt

chinkapin ˈtʃɪŋkəpɪn

Chino-Japanese ˈtʃaɪnoˌdʒæpəˈniz

Chinook, c- tʃɪˈnuk, -ˈnʊk

chinquapin ˈtʃɪŋkəpɪn

chinse, chintze *naut.* tʃɪnts |-d -t

chintz tʃɪnts |chintzes ˈtʃɪntsɪz

Chios ˈkaɪɑs, -ɒs

chip tʃɪp |chipped tʃɪpt

Chipewayan ˌtʃɪpəˈweən

Chipewyan ˌtʃɪpəˈwaɪən

chipmunk ˈtʃɪpmʌŋk

Chippawa ˈtʃɪpəˌwa, -ˌwɒ, -ˌwe, -wə

Chippendale ˈtʃɪpənˌdel

Chippenham ˈtʃɪpənəm

chipper ˈtʃɪpɚ; ES ˈtʃɪpə(r; |-ed -d |-ing ˈtʃɪpərɪŋ, ˈtʃɪprɪŋ

Chippewa ˈtʃɪpəˌwa, -ˌwɒ, -ˌwe, -wə |-way -ˌwe

chippy ˈtʃɪpɪ

chirk tʃɝk; ES tʃɜk, tʃɝk; |-ed -t

chirm, charm tʃɝm, tʃɑrm; ES tʃɜm, tʃɝm, tʃɑ:m

chirograph ˈkaɪrəˌgræf; E+-ˌgraf, -ˌgraf

chirographer kaɪˈragrəfɚ, -ˈrɒg-; ES -fə(r; |-phy -fɪ

chirographic ˌkaɪrəˈgræfɪk |-al -ḷ

Chiron ˈkaɪran, -rɒn, -rən

chiropody kaɪˈrapədɪ |-dist -dɪst

chiropracter ˈkaɪrəˌpræktɚ; ES -ˌpræktə(r

chiropractic ˌkaɪrəˈpræktɪk

chirp tʃɝp; ES tʃɜp, tʃɝp; |-ed -t

chirr tʃɝ; ES tʃɜ(r, tʃɝ; |-ed -d

chirrup ˈtʃɪrəp, ˈtʃɝəp; ES+ˈtʃɜr-, ˈtʃʌr-

chirurgeon kaɪˈrɝdʒən; ES -ˈrɜdʒ-, -ˈrɝdʒ-

chirurgery kaɪˈrɝdʒərɪ; ES -ˈrɜdʒ-, -ˈrɝdʒ-

chirurgic kaɪˈrɝdʒɪk; ES -ˈrɜdʒ-, -ˈrɝdʒ-

Chisago ˌtʃɪsəˈgo

chisel ˈtʃɪzḷ |-ed -d |-ing ˈtʃɪzlɪŋ, -zḷɪŋ

Chisholm ˈtʃɪzəm |Chisolm ˈtʃɪzəm

Chiswick ˈtʃɪzɪk

chit tʃɪt |chitted ˈtʃɪtɪd

chitchat ˈtʃɪtˌtʃæt |-ty -ɪ

chiton ˈkaɪtn̩, -tan, -tɒn

Chittenden ˈtʃɪtn̩dən

chitter ˈtʃɪtɚ; ES ˈtʃɪtə(r; |-ed -d

chitterling ˈtʃɪtɚlɪŋ; ES ˈtʃɪtə-

chivalric ˈʃɪvḷrɪk, ʃɪˈvælrɪk |-rous ˈʃɪvḷrəs

chivalry ˈʃɪvḷrɪ—*The historical pron.* ˈtʃɪvḷrɪ *is now rare.*

chive tʃaɪv

Chivers ˈtʃɪvɚz; ES ˈtʃɪvəz

chlamys ˈklemɪs, ˈklæm- |-es -ɪz |-mydes ˈklæmɪˌdiz

Chloë ˈklo·ɪ

chloral ˈklorəl, ˈklɔr-; S ˈklorəl

chlorate ˈklorɪt, ˈklɔr-, -ret; S ˈklor-

chloric ˈklorɪk, ˈklɔr-; S ˈklorɪk

chlorid ˈklorɪd, ˈklɔr-; S ˈklorɪd; |-ride -raɪd, -rɪd

chlorin ˈklorɪn, ˈklɔr-; S ˈklorɪn; |-rine -rin, -rɪn

chlorinate ˈklorɪˌnet, ˈklɔr-; S ˈklor-; |-d -ɪd

chlorite ˈkloraɪt, ˈklɔr-; S ˈkloraɪt

chloroform ˈklorəˌfɔrm, ˈklɔrə-; ES ˈklorəˌfɔəm, E+ˈklɔrə-

chlorophyll, -yl ˈklorəˌfɪl, ˈklɔrə-; S ˈklorə-

chloroplast ˈklorəˌplæst, ˈklɔrə-; S ˈklorə-

chlorous ˈklorəs, ˈklɔr-; S ˈklorəs

Choate tʃot

choate *adj* ˈkoet

chock tʃak |chocked tʃakt

chockablock ˈtʃakəˈblak

chock-full ˈtʃakˈfʊl

chocolate ˈtʃɔklɪt, -kəlɪt, ˈtʃak-, ˈtʃɒk-; S ˈtʃak-, ˈtʃɒk-, ˈtʃɔk-

Chocorua tʃəˈkɔrəwə, ʃə-, -ˈkar, -ˈkɒr-

Choctaw ˈtʃaktɔ

choice tʃɔɪs |choices ˈtʃɔɪsɪz

choir kwaɪr; ES kwaɪə(r; |-ed -d

choirboy ˈkwaɪrˌbɔɪ; ES ˈkwaɪə-

choke tʃok |choked tʃokt; |*N Engd*+tʃɔk (§46)

chokebore ˈtʃokˌbor, -ˌbɔr; ES -ˌboə(r, E+ -ˌbɔə(r; |-d -d

chokecherry ˈtʃokˌtʃɛrɪ

chokedamp ˈtʃokˌdæmp

choke-full ˈtʃokˈfʊl

|full fʊl |tooth tuθ |further ˈfɝðɚ; ES ˈfɝðə |custom ˈkʌstəm |while hwaɪl |how haʊ |toy tɔɪ
|using ˈjuzɪŋ |fuse fjuz, fɪuz |dish dɪʃ |vision ˈvɪʒən |Eden ˈidn̩ |cradle ˈkredḷ |keep 'em ˈkipm̩

Those words below in which the ɑ *sound is spelt* o *are often pronounced with* ɒ *in E and S*

chold *dial.* '*I would*' tʃʊd
choler 'kalɚ; ES 'kalə(r
cholera 'kalərə
choleric 'kalərık
cholesterol kə'lɛstə‚rol
Cholmley, -meley, -mondeley, Chomley 'tʃʌmlı
choose tʃuz |-s -ız |chose tʃoz |chosen 'tʃozn̩
chop '*jaw*' tʃap |-s -s = chap
chop *v* tʃap |chopped tʃapt
chopfallen 'tʃap‚fɔlən, -‚fɔln
Chopin 'ʃopæn, ʃo'pæn (*Fr* ʃo'pæ̃)
chopin, -e *measure* 'tʃapın
chopine, -in '*patten*' 'tʃapın, tʃo'pin
choppy 'tʃapı
chopstick 'tʃap‚stık
chop suey, sooy 'tʃap'suı, -'sıuı
choral *adj* 'korəl, 'kɔrəl; S 'korəl |-ly -ı
choral, -e *n* ko'ral, kɔ-, 'korəl, 'kɔr-; S ko'ral, 'korəl
Chorazin ko'rezın
chord kɔrd; ES kɔəd; |-ed -ıd
chore tʃor, tʃɔr; ES tʃoə(r, E+tʃɔə(r; |-d -d
chorea ko'riə, kɔ-; S ko'riə; |-l -l |-reic -'riık
choreography ‚korı'agrəfı, ‚kɔ-, -'ɒg-; S ‚ko-
choric 'korık, 'kɔr-, 'kar-, 'kɒr-
chorister 'kɔrıstɚ, 'kar-, 'kɒr-; ES -tə(r
chorography ko'ragrəfı, kɔ-, -'rɒg-; S ko-
choroid 'korɔıd, 'kɔr-; S 'kor-
chortle 'tʃɔrtl̩; ES 'tʃɔətl̩; |-d -d |-ling -t|ıŋ, -tl̩ıŋ
chorus 'korəs, 'kɔrəs; S 'korəs; |-es -ız |-ed -t
chose *past of* choose tʃoz
chose '*property*' ʃoz |choses 'ʃozız
chosen *pptc of* choose 'tʃozn̩
Chosen '*Korea*' 'tʃo'sɛn
chough tʃʌf
chouse tʃaʊs |-s -ız
chow tʃaʊ
chowchow 'tʃaʊ‚tʃaʊ
chowder 'tʃaʊdɚ; ES 'tʃaʊdə(r; |-ed -d |-ing 'tʃaʊdərıŋ, -drıŋ
chow mein 'tʃaʊ'men
Chrestien, -ét-, de Troyes *Fr* kretjæ̃də'trwa
chrestomathy krɛs'taməθı
chrism 'krızəm |-ed -d
chrismal 'krızml̩ |chrismale krız'meli
chrisom 'krızəm

crisscross 'krıs‚krɔs, -‚krɒs |-es -ız
Christ *Jesus* kraıst, *given name* krıst, krıs
Christabel 'krıstə‚bɛl
Christchurch 'kraıst‚tʃɝtʃ; ES -‚tʃɜtʃ, -‚tʃ3tʃ
christcross 'krıs‚krɔs, -‚krɒs |-es -ız
christen 'krısn̩ |-ed -d |-ing 'krısn̩ıŋ, -snıŋ
Christendom 'krısn̩dəm
Christian 'krıstʃən
Christiana ‚krıstı'ænə
Christiania ‚krıstı'anıə, krıs'tjanıə
Christianity ‚krıstʃı'ænıtı, krıs'tʃænətı
Christianize 'krıstʃən‚aız |-s -ız |-d -d
Christie 'krıstı
Christina krıs'tinə |-tine -'tin ('Chris‚tina 'Day)
Christlike 'kraıst‚laık |Christly 'kraıstlı
Christmas 'krısməs |-es -ız |-ed -t
Christmastide 'krısməs‚taıd
Christopher 'krıstəfɚ; ES 'krıstəfə(r
Christy 'krıstı
chroma 'kromə
chromate 'kromet |-d -ıd
chromatic kro'mætık |-al -l̩ |-ally -lı, -ıklı
chromatin 'kromətın
chrome krom |chromed kromd |chromic 'kromık
chromium 'kromıəm
chromo 'kromo
chromolithograph ‚kromo'lıθə‚græf; E+-‚graf, -‚graf
chromosome 'kromə‚som
chromosphere 'kromə‚sfır; ES -‚sfıə(r, S+-‚sfɛə(r
chronic 'kranık |-al -l̩ |-ally -lı, -ıklı
chronicle 'kranık|l̩ |-d -d |-ling -k|ıŋ, -klıŋ
chronicler 'kranıklɚ; ES -klə(r
Chronicles 'kranık|z
chronograph 'kranə‚græf; E+-‚graf, -‚graf
chronographic ‚kranə'græfık |-al -l̩ |-ally -lı, -ıklı
chronologer krə'nalədʒɚ; ES -dʒə(r; |-gy -dʒı |-gist -dʒıst
chronologic ‚kranə'ladʒık |-al -l̩ |-ally -lı, -ıklı
chronometer krə'namətɚ; ES -'namətə(r; |-try -trı
chronometric ‚kranə'mɛtrık |-al -l̩ |-ally -lı, -ıklı

chronoscope 'krɑnə͵skop; ES+'krɒn-
chronoscopic ͵krɑnə'skɑpɪk |-ally -ļɪ, -ɪklɪ
chronoscopy kro'nɑskəpɪ; ES+-'nɒs-
chrysalid 'krɪsḷɪd
chrysalis 'krɪsḷɪs |-es -ɪz |-lides krɪ'sælə͵diz
chrysanthemum krɪs'ænθəməm
Chryseis kraɪ'siɪs |-'s -ɪz
Chrysler 'kraɪslɚ; ES 'kraɪslə(r
chrysoberyl 'krɪsə͵bɛrəl, -ɪl
chrysolite 'krɪsḷ͵aɪt
chrysoprase 'krɪsə͵prez
Chrysostom 'krɪsəstəm, krɪs'ɑstəm, -'ɒs-
chthonian 'θonɪən |-onic 'θɑnɪk; ES+'θɒn-
chub tʃʌb |chubbed 'tʃʌbɪd
chubby 'tʃʌbɪ |chubbily 'tʃʌbḷɪ, -ɪlɪ
chuck tʃʌk |chucked tʃʌkt
chuck-full 'tʃʌk'fʊl
chuckle 'tʃʌkḷ |-d -d |-ling 'tʃʌklɪŋ, -kļɪŋ
chucklehead 'tʃʌkḷ͵hɛd
chud dial. 'I would' tʃʊd
chuff tʃʌf |chuffed tʃʌft
chug tʃʌg |chugged tʃʌgd
chukker, -kar 'tʃʌkɚ; ES 'tʃʌkə(r
Chulmleigh 'tʃʌmlɪ
chum tʃʌm |chummed tʃʌmd |-my -ɪ
chump tʃʌmp |chumped tʃʌmpt
Chungking 'tʃʊŋ'kɪŋ
chunk tʃʌŋk |chunked tʃʌŋkt
church, C- tʃɝtʃ; ES tʃɜtʃ, tʃɝtʃ; |-es -ɪz |-ed-t
Churchill 'tʃɝtʃɪl, -əl; ES 'tʃɜtʃ-, 'tʃɝtʃ-
churchman, C-, -men 'tʃɝtʃmən; ES see
  church
churchwarden 'tʃɝtʃ'wɔrdn̩, -͵wɔrdn̩; ES
  'tʃɝtʃ'wɔədn̩, 'tʃɝtʃ'wɔədn̩, -͵wɔədn̩
churchyard 'tʃɝtʃ͵jɑrd; ES 'tʃɝtʃ͵jɑːd, 'tʃɝtʃ-
  jɑːd, E+-͵jɑːd
churl tʃɝl; ES tʃɜl, tʃɝl; |-ed -d |-ish -ɪʃ
churn tʃɝn; ES tʃɜn, tʃɝn; |-ed -d
churr tʃɝ; ES tʃɜ(r, tʃɝ; |-ed -d
chute ʃut |chuted 'ʃutɪd
chutney, -nee 'tʃʌtnɪ
Chuzzlewit 'tʃʌzḷ͵wɪt
chyle kaɪl |chylous 'kaɪləs
chyme kaɪm |chymous 'kaɪməs
Cibber 'sɪbɚ; ES 'sɪbə(r
ciborium sɪ'borɪəm, -'bɔr-; S -'bor-; |-s -z
  |-ia -ɪə
cicada sɪ'kedə, -'kɑdə
cicatrix 'sɪkətrɪks |-es -ɪz |-trices ͵sɪkə'traɪsiz

cicatrize 'sɪkə͵traɪz |-s -ɪz |-d -d
cicely 'sɪsḷɪ |-lies -ḷɪz
Cicely 'sɪsḷɪ
Cicero 'sɪsə͵ro |-nian ͵sɪsə'ronɪən
cicerone ͵sɪsə'ronɪ, ͵tʃɪtʃə'ronɪ (It ͵tʃitʃe-
  'roːne)
Cid sɪd (Sp θið)
cider 'saɪdɚ; ES 'saɪdə(r
cider-mill 'saɪdɚ͵mɪl; ES 'saɪdə-
cider-press 'saɪdɚ͵prɛs; ES 'saɪdə-; |-es -ɪz
cigar sɪ'gɑr; ES sɪ'gɑː(r, E+-'gɑː(r
cigarette, -ret ͵sɪgə'rɛt, 'sɪgə͵rɛt
cilia pl 'sɪlɪə |sg cilium 'sɪlɪəm
ciliary 'sɪlɪ͵ɛrɪ
ciliate 'sɪlɪɪt, 'sɪlɪ͵et |-ated -͵etɪd
Cilicia sə'lɪʃə, -ʃɪə |-n -n
cilium 'sɪlɪəm
Cimabue ͵tʃɪmə'buɪ (It ͵tʃima'buːe)
Cimarron 'sɪmə͵rɑn, ͵sɪmə'rɑn (Am Sp
  ͵sima'rrɔn)
Cimber 'sɪmbɚ; ES 'sɪmbə(r
cimex 'saɪmɛks |cimices 'sɪmə͵siz
Cimmerian sə'mɪrɪən
cinch sɪntʃ |cinches 'sɪntʃɪz |cinched sɪntʃt
cinchona, C- sɪn'konə
Cincinnati ͵sɪnsə'nætɪ, -'nætə; E+-'nɑt-;—
  -tɪ & -tə seem about equally frequent loc.
  and generally.
Cincinnatus ͵sɪnsə'netəs |-'s -ɪz
cincture 'sɪŋktʃɚ; ES 'sɪŋktʃə(r; |-d -d
cinder 'sɪndɚ; ES 'sɪndə(r; |-ed -d |-ing
  'sɪndrɪŋ, 'sɪndərɪŋ
Cinderella ͵sɪndə'rɛlə
cinema 'sɪnəmə
cinematograph ͵sɪnə'mætə͵græf; E+-͵graf,
  -͵grɑf
cinematography ͵sɪnəmə'tɑgrəfɪ, -'tɒg-
cineraria, C- ͵sɪnə'rɛrɪə, -'rer-
cinerarium ͵sɪnə'rɛrɪəm, -'rer- |pl -ria -rɪə
cinerary 'sɪnə͵rɛrɪ
Cingalese ͵sɪŋgə'liz
Cinna 'sɪnə
cinnabar 'sɪnə͵bɑr; ES -͵bɑː(r, E+-͵bɑː(r
cinnamon 'sɪnəmən |-ed -d
cinque sɪŋk
cinquefoil 'sɪŋk͵fɔɪl
Cinque Ports 'sɪŋk'ports, -'pɔrts; ES -'poəts,
  E+-'pɔəts
C I O 'si͵aɪ'o

|full fʊl |tooth tuθ |further 'fɝðɚ; ES 'fɝðə |custom 'kʌstəm |while hwaɪl |how haʊ |toy tɔɪ
|using 'juzɪŋ |fuse fjuz, fɪuz |dish dɪʃ |vision 'vɪʒən |Eden 'idn̩ |cradle 'kredḷ |keep 'em 'kipm̩

cion *'scion'* 'saɪən

Cipango sɪ'pæŋgo

cipher 'saɪfɚ; ES 'saɪfə(r; |-ed -d |-ing 'saɪfrɪŋ, 'saɪfərɪŋ

cipolin 'sɪpəlɪn

circa 's3˞kə; ES 's3kə, 's3˞kə

Circassia sɚ'kæʃɪə, -ʃə; ES sə-; |-n -n

Circe 's3˞sɪ, -si; ES 's3s-, 's3˞s-

circinate 's3˞sn̩ˌet; ES 's3s-, 's3˞s-

circle 's3˞k!; ES 's3k!, 's3˞k!; |-d -d |-ling -klɪŋ, -k!ɪŋ

circlet 's3˞klɪt; ES 's3k-, 's3˞k-

circuit 's3˞kɪt; ES 's3kɪt, 's3˞kɪt; |-ed -ɪd

circuitous sɚ'kjuɪtəs, -'kɪu-; ES sə-; |-ty -tɪ

circular 's3˞kjələ˞; ES 's3kjələ(r, 's3˞kjələ(r

circularity ˌs3˞kjə'lærətɪ; ES ˌs3k-, ˌs3˞k-

circularize 's3˞kjələˌraɪz; ES 's3k-, 's3˞k-; |-s -ɪz |-d -d

circulate 's3˞kjəˌlet; ES 's3k-, 's3˞k-; |-d -ɪd

circulation ˌs3˞kjə'leʃən; ES ˌs3k-, ˌs3˞k-

circulatory 's3˞kjələˌtorɪ, -ˌtɔrɪ; ES 's3kjələ-ˌtorɪ, 's3˞k-, E+-ˌtɔrɪ

circumambient ˌs3˞kəm'æmbɪənt; ES ˌs3k-, ˌs3˞k-

circumambulate ˌs3˞kəm'æmbjəˌlet; ES ˌs3k-, ˌs3˞k-; |-d -ɪd

circumaviate ˌs3˞kəm'evɪˌet; ES ˌs3k-, ˌs3˞k-; |-d -ɪd

circumcise 's3˞kəmˌsaɪz; ES 's3k-, 's3˞k-; |-s -ɪz |-d -d

circumcision ˌs3˞kəm'sɪʒən; ES ˌs3k-, ˌs3˞k-

circumference sɚ'kʌmfərəns, sə'kʌm-; ES sə-; |-s -ɪz—*In the 2d pron. ɚ has become ə by r-dissimilation (§121).*

circumferential sɚˌkʌmfə'renʃəl; ES sə-; |-ly -ɪ

circumflex 's3˞kəmˌfleks; ES 's3k-, 's3˞k-; |-es -ɪz |-ed -t

circumfluent sɚ'kʌmflʊənt; ES sə-

circumfuse ˌs3˞kəm'fjuz, -'fɪuz; ES ˌs3k-, ˌs3˞k-; |-s -ɪz |-d -d

circumjacence ˌs3˞kəm'dʒesn̩s; ES ˌs3k-, ˌs3˞k-; |-cy -ɪ |-cent -sn̩t

circumlocution ˌs3˞kəmlo'kjuʃən, -'kɪu-; ES ˌs3k-, ˌs3˞k-

circumlocutory ˌs3˞kəm'lɑkjəˌtorɪ, -ˌtɔrɪ; ES ˌs3k-, ˌs3˞k-, -'lɒk-, E+-ˌtɔrɪ

circumnavigable ˌs3˞kəm'nævəgəb!; ES ˌs3k-, ˌs3˞k-

circumnavigate ˌs3˞kəm'nævəˌget; ES ˌs3k-, ˌs3˞k-; |-d -ɪd |-tor -ɚ; ES -ə(r

circumnavigation ˌs3˞kəmˌnævə'geʃən; ES ˌs3k-, ˌs3˞k-

circumpolar ˌs3˞kəm'polɚ; ES ˌs3kəm'polə(r, ˌs3˞kəm'polə(r

circumscribe ˌs3˞kəm'skraɪb; ES ˌs3k-, ˌs3˞k-; |-d -d ('circumˌscribed 'halo)

circumscription ˌs3˞kəm'skrɪpʃən; ES ˌs3k-, ˌs3˞k-

circumspect 's3˞kəmˌspekt; ES 's3k-, 's3˞k-

circumspection ˌs3˞kəm'spekʃən; ES ˌs3k-, ˌs3˞k-; |-tive -tɪv

circumstance 's3˞kəmˌstæns; ES 's3k-, 's3˞k-; |-s -ɪz |-d -t

circumstantial ˌs3˞kəm'stænʃəl; ES ˌs3k-, ˌs3˞k-; |-ly -ɪ

circumstantiality ˌs3˞kəmˌstænʃɪ'ælətɪ; ES ˌs3k-, ˌs3˞k-

circumstantiate ˌs3˞kəm'stænʃɪˌet; ES ˌs3k-, ˌs3˞k-; |-d -ɪd

circumvallation ˌs3˞kəmvæ'leʃən; ES ˌs3k-, ˌs3˞k-

circumvent ˌs3˞kəm'vent; ES ˌs3k-, ˌs3˞k-; |-ed -ɪd |-vention -'venʃən

circus, C- 's3˞kəs; ES 's3k-, 's3˞k-; |-es -ɪz

Cirencester 'saɪrənˌsestɚ, 'sɪsɪtɚ, 'sɪzɪtɚ; ES -tə(r—*All these prons. (including the -ɚ) are used in Cirencester and vicinity. The BBC (in 1936) recommended* 'sɪsɪtər, 'saɪərənˌsestər.

cirque s3˞k; ES s3k, s3˞k

cirrhosis sɪ'rosɪs

cirro-cumulus ˌsɪro'kjumjələs, -'kɪum- |-li -ˌlaɪ

cirrose 'sɪros

cirro-stratus ˌsɪro'stretəs |-ti -taɪ

cirrus 'sɪrəs |cirri 'sɪraɪ |cirrous 'sɪrəs

cisalpine, C- sɪs'ælpaɪn, -pɪn

cisco, C- 'sɪsko

cismontane, C- sɪs'mɑnten; ES+-'mɒn-

cispadane 'sɪspəˌden, sɪs'peden

cist sɪst, kɪst=kist

Cistercian sɪs't3˞ʃən; ES -'t3ʃ-, -'t3˞ʃ-

cistern 'sɪstɚn; ES 'sɪstən

citable 'saɪtəb!

citadel, C- 'sɪtəd!, -ˌdɛl

citation saɪ'teʃən

cite saɪt |cited 'saɪtɪd |citeable 'saɪtəb!

cithara 'sɪθərə

---

cither 'sɪðɚ; ES 'sɪðə(r; |-n -n
citied 'sɪtɪd
citify 'sɪtɪ,faɪ |-fied -,faɪd
citizen 'sɪtəzn̩, -sn̩ |-ry -rɪ |-ship -,ʃɪp
citrate 'sɪtret, -rɪt |-d -ɪd |-ric -rɪk
citriculture 'sɪtrɪ,kʌltʃɚ; ES -,kʌltʃə(r
citrine 'sɪtrɪn
Citroën 'sɪtro,ɛn
citron 'sɪtrən |-ade ,sɪtrən'ed
citronella ,sɪtrən'ɛlə
citrus, C- 'sɪtrəs |citrous 'sɪtrəs
Città del Vaticano It tʃit'ta·del,vati'ka:no
cittern 'sɪtɚn; ES 'sɪtən
city 'sɪtɪ |citied 'sɪtɪd
city-state 'sɪtɪ'stet
Ciudad Trujillo Am Sp sju'ðaðtru'hijo
civet 'sɪvɪt |-ed -ɪd
civic 'sɪvɪk |-s -s |-ally -,lɪ, -ɪklɪ
civil 'sɪvl̩, less freq. 'sɪvɪl |-ly -ɪ
civilian sə'vɪljən |civility sə'vɪlətɪ
civilizable 'sɪvl̩,aɪzəbl̩
civilization ,sɪvl̩ə'zeʃən, -aɪ'z-
civilize 'sɪvl̩,aɪz |-s -ɪz |-d -d
clabber 'klæbɚ; ES -bə(r; |-ed -d |-ing
   'klæbərɪŋ, 'klæbrɪŋ
clack klæk |clacked klækt
Clackamas 'klækəməs |-'s -ɪz
Clackmannan klæk'mænən |-shire -,ʃɪr, -ʃɚ;
   ES -,ʃɪə(r, -ʃə(r
clad klæd
Claiborne 'klebɚn; ES 'klebən
Claibornian kle'bornɪən, -'bɔrn-; ES -'boən-,
   E+-'bɔən-
claim klem |claimed klemd |-ant -ənt
Clair(e) kler, klær; E klɛə(r, ES klæə(r
clairvoyance kler'vɔɪəns, klær-; E klɛə-, ES
   klæə-; |-ant -ənt
Clallam 'klæləm
clam klæm |clammed klæmd
clamant 'klemənt
clambake 'klæm,bek
clamber 'klæmbɚ; ES -bə(r; |-ed -d |-ing
   'klæmbərɪŋ, 'klæmbrɪŋ
clammy 'klæmɪ |-mily -m,lɪ, -mɪlɪ
clamor 'klæmɚ; ES 'klæmə(r; |-ed -d |-ing
   'klæmrɪŋ, 'klæmərɪŋ
clamorous 'klæmərəs, 'klæmrəs
clamp klæmp |clamped klæmpt
clamshell 'klæm,ʃɛl

clan klæn |clanned klænd |-nish -ɪʃ
clandestine klæn'dɛstɪn
clang klæŋ |clanged klæŋd
clangor 'klæŋgɚ, 'klæŋɚ; ES -ə(r; |-ed -d
   |-ous -əs
clank klæŋk |clanked klæŋkt
clansman 'klænzmən |-men -mən
clap klæp |clapped klæpt
clapboard 'klæbɚd, 'klæbord, 'klæp,bord,
   -ɔrd; ES 'klæbəd, 'klæboəd, 'klæp,boəd,
   E+-ɔəd; |-ed -ɪd
clapper 'klæpɚ; ES 'klæpə(r; |-ed -d |-ing
   'klæpərɪŋ, 'klæprɪŋ
clapperclaw 'klæpɚ,klɔ; ES 'klæpə-; |-ed -d
claptrap 'klæp,træp
claque klæk
Clara 'klɛrə, 'klærə; S 'klærə
clarabella, C- ,klærə'bɛlə
Clare klɛr, klær; E klɛə(r, ES klæə(r
Claremont 'klɛrmɑnt, 'klær-; E 'klɛə-, ES
   'klæə-, -mɑnt
Claremore 'klɛrmor, 'klær-, -mɔr; E
   'klɛəmoə(r, 'klæə-, -mɔə(r; S 'klæəmoə(r
Clarence 'klærəns |-'s -ɪz
Clarendon, c- 'klærəndən
claret 'klærət, -ɪt
Claribel 'klærə,bɛl
Clarice 'klærɪs |-'s -ɪz
clarification ,klærəfə'keʃən
clarify 'klærə,faɪ |-fied -,faɪd
Clarinda klə'rɪndə
clarinet ,klærə'nɛt ('clari,net 'solo)
clarion, C- 'klærɪən
clarionet ,klærɪə'nɛt
Clarissa klə'rɪsə
clarity 'klærətɪ
Clark, -e klɑrk; ES klɑ:k, E+klɑ:k
Clarksburg 'klɑrksbɚg; ES 'klɑ:ksbɚg,
   'klɑ:ksbɚg, E+'klɑ:ks-
clary 'klɛrɪ, 'klærɪ; S 'klærɪ
clash klæʃ |clashes 'klæʃɪz |clashed klæʃt
clasp klæsp; E+klɑsp, klɑsp; |-ed -t
class klæs; E+klɑs, klɑs; |-es -ɪz |-ed -t
classic 'klæsɪk |-al -l̩ |-ally -l̩ɪ, -ɪklɪ
classicalism 'klæsɪkl̩,ɪzəm |-ist -ɪst
classicality ,klæsə'kælətɪ
classicism 'klæsə,sɪzəm |-cist -sɪst
classifiable 'klæsə,faɪəbl̩
classification ,klæsəfə'keʃən

|full fʊl |tooth tuθ |further 'fɝðɚ; ES 'fɝðə |custom 'kʌstəm |while hwaɪl |how haʊ |toy tɔɪ
|using 'juzɪŋ |fuse fjuz, fɪuz |dish dɪʃ |vision 'vɪʒən |Eden 'idn̩ |cradle 'kredl̩ |keep 'em 'kipm̩

classify ˈklæsəˌfaɪ |-fied -ˌfaɪd
classman ˈklæsmən; E+ˈklas-, ˈklɑs-; |-men -mən
classmate ˈklæsˌmet; E+ˈklas-, ˈklɑs-
classroom ˈklæsˌrum, -ˌrʊm; E+ˈklas-, ˈklɑs-
clatter ˈklætɚ; ES ˈklætə(r; |-ed -d
Claude Lorrain ˈklɔdloˈren, -lɔ-, -lɒ- (Fr klodlɔˈræ̃)
Claudia ˈklɔdɪə |-n -n |-ius -s |-ius's -sɪz
Claudio ˈklɔdɪˌo, ˈklɔdjo
clause klɔz |clauses ˈklɔzɪz |-d -d |-sal -ļ
claustral ˈklɔstrəl
claustrophobia ˌklɔstrəˈfobɪə
clavate ˈklevet |-d -ɪd
clave arch. past of cleave klev
Claverhouse ˈklævərəs, ˈklævɚz, ˈklævəˌhaʊs; ES ˈklævərəs, ˈklævəz, ˈklævəˌhaʊs; |-'s -ɪz, Brit+ˈklev-
clavichord ˈklævəˌkɔrd; ES -ˌkɔəd
clavicle ˈklævəkļ
clavier 'keyboard' ˈklævɪɚ, kləˈvɪr, 'instrument' kləˈvɪr; ES ˈklævɪ·ə(r, kləˈvɪə(r
claw klɔ |clawed klɔd
clay, C- kle |clayed kled
Clayhanger ˈkleˌhæŋɚ; ES -ˌhæŋə(r
claymore ˈklemor, -mɔr; ES -moə(r, E+ -mɔə(r
Clayton ˈkletn̩
clean klin |cleaned klind |-ness ˈklinnɪs
clean-cut ˈklinˈkʌt (ˈcleanˌcut ˈedges)
cleanly adj ˈklɛnlɪ
cleanly adv ˈklinlɪ
cleanse klɛnz |cleanses ˈklɛnzɪz |-d -d
cleanup n ˈklinˌʌp
clear klɪr; ES klɪə(r, S+klɛə(r; |-ed -d
clearance ˈklɪrəns; S+ˈklɛr-; |-s -ɪz
clear-cut ˈklɪrˈkʌt; ES ˈklɪəˈkʌt, S+ˈklɛə-
clear-eyed ˈklɪrˈaɪd; S+ˈklɛr-; (ˈclear-ˌeyed ˈox)
Clearfield ˈklɪrˌfild; ES ˈklɪə-, S+ˈklɛə-
clearheaded ˈklɪrˈhɛdɪd; ES ˈklɪə-, S+ˈklɛə-
clearing ˈklɪrɪŋ; S+ˈklɛrɪŋ; |-house -ˌhaʊs
clear-sighted ˈklɪrˈsaɪtɪd; ES ˈklɪə-, S+ˈklɛə-
clearstarch ˈklɪrˌstɑrtʃ; E ˈklɪəˌstɑːtʃ, -ˌstɑːtʃ; S ˈklɪəˌstɑːtʃ, ˈklɛə-; |-es -ɪz |-ed -t
clearstory ˈklɪrˌstorɪ, -ˌstɔrɪ; E ˈklɪə-; S ˈklɪəˌstorɪ, ˈklɛə-
Clearwater ˈklɪrˌwɔtɚ, -ˌwɑtɚ, -ˌwɒtɚ; ES ˈklɪəˌwɔtə(r, -ˌwɑt-, -ˌwɒt-, S+ˈklɛə-

cleat klit |cleated ˈklitɪd
cleavable ˈklivəbļ
cleavage ˈklivɪdʒ |-s -ɪz
cleave 'cling' kliv |past & pptc cleaved klivd |arch. past clave klev or clove klov
cleave 'split' kliv |past cleft klɛft or cleaved klivd or clove klov; arch. clave klev |pptc cleft klɛft or cleaved klivd or cloven ˈklovən; arch. clove klov
Cleaveland, Moses ˈklivlənd
cleek klik |-ed -t
clef klɛf
cleft klɛft
cleistogamus klaɪsˈtɑgəməs, -ˈtɒg-
clematis, C- ˈklɛmətɪs |-es -ɪz
Clemenceau ˌklɛmənˈso (Fr klemɑ̃ˈso)
Clemens ˈklɛmənz |-'s -ɪz
clement, C- ˈklɛmənt |clemency ˈklɛmənsɪ
Clementina ˌklɛmənˈtinə
Clementine fem. name ˈklɛmənˌtin, -ˌtaɪn
Clementine 'of Clement' ˈklɛməntɪn, -ˌtaɪn
clench klɛntʃ |clenches ˈklɛntʃɪz |-ed -t
Cleomenes kliˈɑməˌniz; ES+-ˈɒm-; |-'s -ɪz
Cleon ˈklian, -ɒn
Cleopatra ˌkliəˈpetrə, -ˈpɑtrə, -ˈpætrə
clepsydra ˈklɛpsɪdrə |-s -z |-drae -ˌdri
cleptomania ˌklɛptəˈmenɪə |-iac -ɪˌæk
clerestory ˈklɪrˌstorɪ, -ˌstɔrɪ; E ˈklɪə-; S ˈklɪəˌstorɪ, ˈklɛə-
clergy ˈklɝdʒɪ; ES ˈklɜdʒɪ, ˈklɝdʒɪ; |-man -mən |-men -mən
cleric ˈklɛrɪk |-al -ļ |-ally -ļɪ, -ɪklɪ
clerk klɝk; ES klɜk, klɝk; Brit. klɑːk, klɑrk; |-ed -t |-ly -lɪ
Clerkenwell ˈklɝkənˌwɛl; ES ˈklɜk-, ˈklɝk-; loc. ˈklɑːkənwəl
Clermont ˈklɝmant; ES ˈklɛəmant, -mɒnt
Clevedon ˈklivdən
Cleveland ˈklivlənd
clever ˈklɛvɚ; ES ˈklɛvə(r; |-er ˈklɛvərɚ, ˈklɛvrɚ; ES -rə(r; |-est -ɪst, -vrɪst
Cleves klivz |-'s -ɪz
clevis ˈklɛvɪs |-es -ɪz
clew klu, klɪu |-ed -d
cliché kliˈʃe
click klɪk |clicked klɪkt
clickety-clack ˈklɪkətɪˈklæk |-click -ˈklɪk
client ˈklaɪənt |-ed -ɪd |-age -ɪdʒ
clientele ˌklaɪənˈtɛl

---

cliff klɪf |cliffed klɪft
Clifford 'klɪfɚd; ES 'klɪfəd
Clifton 'klɪftən |-ia klɪf'tonɪə
climacteric klaɪ'mæktərɪk, ˌklaɪmæk'tɛrɪk
climacterical ˌklaɪmæk'tɛrɪk| |-ly -ɪ
climactic klaɪ'mæktɪk |-al -| |-ally -|ɪ, -ɪklɪ
climate 'klaɪmɪt |-d -ɪd |-tal -ɪt|, -ət|
climatology ˌklaɪmə'talədʒɪ; ES+-'tɒl-
climature 'klaɪməˌtʃʊr; ES -ˌtʃʊə(r
climax 'klaɪmæks |-es -ɪz |-ed -t
climb klaɪm |climbed klaɪmd |-er -ɚ; ES -ə(r
clime klaɪm
clinch, C- klɪntʃ |-es -ɪz |-ed -t
Clinedinst 'klaɪndɪnst
cling klɪŋ |clung klʌŋ |-stone -ˌston
clinic 'klɪnɪk |-al -| |-ally -|ɪ, -ɪklɪ
clinician klɪ'nɪʃən
clink klɪŋk |clinked klɪŋkt |-er -ɚ; ES -ə(r
clinker-built 'klɪŋkɚˌbɪlt; ES 'klɪŋkə-
clinkety-clink 'klɪŋkətɪ'klɪŋk
clinometer klaɪ'namətɚ, klɪ-; ES -'namətə(r, -'nɒm-
clinometric ˌklaɪnə'mɛtrɪk |-al -|
Clinton 'klɪntən
Clio 'klaɪo
clip klɪp |clipped klɪpt |-per -ɚ; ES -ə(r
clique klik, klɪk
Clitheroe 'klɪðəˌro
clitoris 'klaɪtərɪs, 'klɪtərɪs |-es -ɪz
Clitus 'klaɪtəs |-'s -ɪz
Clive klaɪv
Cliveden 'klɪvdən
cloaca klo'ekə |-s -z |-acae -'esi
cloak klok |cloaked klokt; |N Engd+klɔ̃k
cloakroom 'klokˌrum, -ˌrʊm
cloche kloʃ |cloches 'kloʃɪz (Fr klɔ̃ʃ)
clock klak; ES+klɒk; |-ed -t
clockwise 'klakˌwaɪz; ES+'klɒk-
clockwork 'klakˌwɝk; ES 'klakˌwɜk, -ˌwɝ̃k, 'klɒk-
clod klad; ES+klɒd; |-ded -ɪd
clodhopper 'kladˌhapɚ; ES 'kladˌhapə(r, 'klɒdˌhɒpə(r
clodpate 'kladˌpet; ES+'klɒd-; |-d -ɪd
clodpoll, -pole 'kladˌpol; ES+'klɒd-
clog klag, klɒg, klɔg |-ged -d
cloisonné ˌklɔɪzə'ne (Fr klwazɔ̃'ne)
cloister 'klɔɪstɚ; ES -stə(r; |-ed -d |-ing 'klɔɪstərɪŋ, 'klɔɪstrɪŋ |-tral -trəl

clootie 'klutɪ, Sc 'klytɪ
Cloquet klo'ke
close adj klos; N Engd+klɔ̃s (§46)
close n 'end' kloz |-s -ɪz
close n 'enclosed place' klos |-s -ɪz
close v kloz |closes 'klozɪz |closed klozd
closefisted 'klos'fɪstɪd ('closeˌfisted 'miser)
close-fitting 'klos'fɪtɪŋ
close-grained 'klos'grend
close-hauled 'klos'hɔld
close-lipped 'klos'lɪpt ('close-ˌlipped 'smile)
close-mouthed 'klos'mauðd, -'mauθt
closet 'klazɪt, 'klɒzɪt |-ed -ɪd
close-up 'klosˌʌp
closure 'kloʒɚ; ES 'kloʒə(r; |-d -d
clot klat; ES+klɒt; |-ted -ɪd
Cloten 'klotn̩
cloth klɔθ, klɒθ |-ths 'pieces of cloth' -ðz, 'kinds of cloth' -θs |-'s -θs
clothe v kloð |clothes kloðz |clothed kloðd—
  Note that the 3 sg pres is not kloz, the usual pron. of the noun clothes, which occurs far oftener.
clothes n kloz, kloðz—kloz has been the cultivated colloq. pron. for 200 yrs. Dr. Johnson says "always clo's," Sheridan (1780) & Walker (1791) give only kloz. Oxf. Dict. calls it "vulgar or careless." Fowler (Mod. Eng. Usage) denies this and says kloz is the usual pron. [in Engd]. Webster has correctly labeled kloz 'Colloq.' for some 70 yrs. The L. A. shows an overwhelming majority for kloz. The verb clothes kloðz keeps its ð from clothe kloð & clothed kloðd. The noun has no sg kloð.
clothesbasket 'klozˌbæskɪt, 'kloðz-; E+-ˌbas-, -ˌbɑs-
clothesbrush 'klozˌbrʌʃ, 'kloðz- |-es -ɪz
clotheshorse 'klozˌhɔrs, 'kloðz-; ES -ˌhɔəs; |-s -ɪz
clothesline 'klozˌlaɪn, 'kloðz-
clothespin 'klozˌpɪn, 'kloðz-
clothespress 'klozˌprɛs, 'kloðz- |-es -ɪz
clothes-wringer 'klozˌrɪŋɚ, 'kloðz-; ES -ˌrɪŋə(r
clothier 'kloðjɚ, -ðɪɚ; ES 'kloðjə(r, -ɪ·ə(r
clothing 'kloðɪŋ
Clotho 'kloθo
cloths 'pieces of cloth' klɔðz, klɒðz; 'kinds of cloth' klɔθs, klɒθs

---

|full fʊl |tooth tuθ |further 'fɝðɚ; ES 'fɝðə |custom 'kʌstəm |while hwaɪl |how hau |toy tɔɪ
|using 'juzɪŋ |fuse fjuz, fɪuz |dish dɪʃ |vision 'vɪʒən |Eden 'idn̩ |cradle 'kredl̩ |keep 'em 'kipm̩

Those words below in which the ɑ sound is spelt o are often pronounced with ɒ in E and S

cloture 'klotʃɚ, -tʃur; ES 'klotʃə(r, -tʃuə(r;
  |-d -d
cloud klaud |clouded 'klaudɪd
cloudburst 'klaud,bɝst; ES -,bɜst, -,bɝst
cloud-capped 'klaud,kæpt
cloudland 'klaud,lænd
cloudlet 'klaudlɪt
clough klʌf, klau
Clough klʌf, *Irel* klɒx
clout klaut |clouted 'klautɪd
clove *'spice'* klov |cloved klovd
clove *past of* cleave klov
Clovelly klo'vɛlɪ
cloven 'klovən
cloven-footed 'klovən'futɪd ('cloven-,footed
  'ox)
cloven-hoofed 'klovən'huft, -'huft
clover 'klovɚ; ES 'klovə(r; |-ed -d
clover-leaf *adj* 'klovɚ,lif; ES 'klovə-
Clovis 'klovɪs |-'s -ɪz
clown klaun |-ed -d |-age -ɪdʒ |-ery -ərɪ
cloy klɔɪ |-ed -d |-edness -ɪdnɪs
club klʌb |clubbed klʌbd
clubbable, clubable 'klʌbəbl̩
clubfoot 'klʌb'fut, -,fut
clubfooted 'klʌb'futɪd ('club,footed 'sophisms)
clubland 'klʌb,lænd
clubman 'klʌbmən, -,mæn |-men -mən,
  -,mɛn
clubwoman 'klʌb,wumən, -,wum- |-men
  -,wɪmɪn, -ən
cluck klʌk |clucked klʌkt
clue klu, klɪu |-d -d
clumber 'klʌmbɚ; ES 'klʌmbə(r
clump klʌmp |clumped klʌmpt
clumsy 'klʌmzɪ |-sily -zəlɪ, -zɪlɪ
clung klʌŋ
Cluniac 'klunɪ,æk, 'klɪunɪ-
Cluny 'klunɪ, 'klɪunɪ (*Fr* kly'ni)
cluster 'klʌstɚ; ES -tə(r; |-ed -d |-ing
  'klʌstrɪŋ, 'klʌstərɪŋ
clutch klʌtʃ |clutches 'klʌtʃɪz |-ed -t
clutter 'klʌtɚ; ES 'klʌtə(r; |-ed -d
Clutton-Brock 'klʌtn̩'brɑk
Clyde klaɪd |-bank -,bæŋk |-sdale -z,del
Clymer 'klaɪmɚ; ES 'klaɪmə(r
Clytemnestra, -taem- 'klaɪtəm'nɛstrə
Cnidus 'naɪdəs |-'s -ɪz

Cnossus 'nɑsəs |-sus' -səs
Cnut kə'nut, -'nɪut, -'njut=Canute
coach kotʃ |coaches 'kotʃɪz |coached kotʃt
coach-and-four 'kotʃən'for, -'fɔr; ES -'foə(r,
  E+-'fɔə(r
Coachella ,koə'tʃɛlə
coachman 'kotʃmən |-men -mən
coact ko'ækt |-ed -ɪd |-ction -kʃən |-ive -ɪv
coadjutor ko'ædʒətɚ, ,koə'dʒutɚ; ES -tə(r
coagulate ko'ægjə,let |-d -ɪd |-lant -lənt
coagulation ko,ægjə'leʃən, ,koægjə-
Coahoma ,koə'homə
Coahuila ,koə'wilə
coal kol |coaled kold
coalesce ,koə'lɛs |-s -ɪz |-d -t
coalescence ,koə'lɛsn̩s |-cy -ɪ |-cent -sn̩t
Coalinga ,koə'lɪŋgə
coalition ,koə'lɪʃən ('coa,lition 'party)
coalless 'kollɪs
coaming 'komɪŋ
coarse kors, kɔrs; ES koəs, E+kɔəs
coarse-grained 'kors'grend, 'kɔrs-; ES 'koəs-,
  E+'kɔəs-
coarsen 'korsn̩, 'kɔrsn̩; ES 'koəsn̩, E+'kɔəsn̩;
  |-ed -d |-ing -sn̩ɪŋ, -snɪŋ
coast kost |coasted 'kostɪd |-al -l̩ |-ally -lɪ
coastward 'kostwɚd; ES 'kostwəd
coastways 'kost,wez |-wise -,waɪz
coat kot |coated 'kotɪd; |*NEngd*+kɔt (§46)
coati ko'ɑtɪ
coattail 'kot,tel |-ed -d
coauthor ko'ɔθɚ; ES -'ɔθə(r; |-ship -,ʃɪp
coax koks |coaxes 'koksɪz |coaxed kokst;
  |*NEngd*+kɔks (§46)
coaxal ko'æksl̩ |-xial -ksɪəl |-xially -ksɪəlɪ
cob kab |-bed -d
cobalt, C- 'kobɔlt
Cobbett 'kabɪt
cobble 'kabl̩ |-d -d |-ling 'kablɪŋ, -bl̩ɪŋ
cobbler 'kablɚ; ES 'kablə(r; |-y -ɪ
cobblestone 'kabl̩,ston
Cobden 'kabdən
Cóbh kov
Cobham 'kabəm, 'kabm̩
Coblenz 'koblɛnts |-'s -ɪz
Cobleskill 'kobl̩z,kɪl, 'kobl̩,skɪl
Cobourg *Can* 'kobɝg; ES 'kobɜg, -bɝg
cobra 'kobrə

Key: See in full §§3–47. bee bi |pity 'pɪtɪ (§6) |rate ret |yet jɛt |sang sæŋ |angry 'æŋ·grɪ
|bath bæθ; E baθ (§10) |ah ɑ |far fɑr |watch watʃ, wɒtʃ (§12) |jaw dʒɔ |gorge gɔrdʒ |go go

Those words below in which the ɑ sound is spelt o are often pronounced with ɒ in E and S

Coburg *Germany* ˈkobɝg; ES -bɜg, -bɝg; *(Ger* K- ˈkoːburk)

Coburn ˈkobɝn; ES ˈkobən; *cf* Cockburn

cobweb ˈkabˌwɛb |-webbery -ˌwɛbərɪ, -brɪ

coca ˈkokə

cocaine, -ain koˈken, ˈkoken |-ism -ˈkenɪzəm

coccus ˈkakəs |cocci ˈkaksaɪ

coccygeal kakˈsɪdʒɪəl

coccyx ˈkaksɪks |-es -ɪz |coccyges kakˈsaɪdʒiz

Cochin, c- ˈkotʃɪn, ˈkatʃɪn

Cochin China ˈkotʃɪnˈtʃaɪnə, ˈkatʃ-

cochineal ˌkatʃəˈnil (ˈcochiˌneal ˈdye)

cochlea ˈkaklɪə |cochleae ˈkaklɪˌi

cochlear ˈkaklɪɚ; ES ˈkaklɪ·ə(r

Cochran, -e ˈkakrən

cock kak |cocked kakt

cockade kakˈed |-aded -ˈedɪd

cock-a-doodle ˌkakəˈdudl̩ |-d -d

cock-a-doodle-doo ˈkakəˌdudl̩ˈdu

cock-a-hoop ˌkakəˈhup, -ˈhup

Cockaigne kaˈken

cockalorum ˌkakəˈlorəm, -ˈlɔrəm; S -ˈlorəm

cock-and-bull story ˈkakənˈbulˌstorɪ, ˈkakŋ-, -ˌstɔrɪ; S -ˌstorɪ

cockatoo ˌkakəˈtu (ˈcockaˌtoo ˈorchis)

cockatrice ˈkakətrɪs |-s -ɪz

cockboat ˈkakˌbot

Cockburn ˈkobɝn; ES ˈkobən; *cf* Coburn

cockchafer ˈkakˌtʃefɚ; ES -ˌtʃefə(r

cockcrow ˈkakˌkro

cocker ˈkakɚ; ES ˈkakə(r; |-ed -d |-ing ˈkakərɪŋ, ˈkakrɪŋ

cockerel ˈkakərəl, ˈkakrəl

Cockermouth ˈkakɚməθ, -ˌmauθ; ES ˈkakə-

cockeye ˈkakˌaɪ |-d -d

cockfight ˈkakˌfaɪt

cockhorse ˈkakˈhɔrs; ES -ˈhɔəs; |-s -ɪz (a ˈcockˌhorse ˈair)

cockle ˈkakl̩ |-d -d |-ling ˈkaklɪŋ, ˈkakl̩ɪŋ

cocklebur ˈkakl̩ˌbɝ; ES -ˌbɜ(r, -ˌbɝ

cockleshell ˈkakl̩ˌʃɛl

cockloft ˈkakˌlɔft, -ˌlɒft

cockney, C- ˈkaknɪ |-ism -ˌɪzəm

cockpit ˈkakˌpɪt

cockroach ˈkakˌrotʃ |-es -ɪz

cockscomb ˈkaksˌkom |-ed -d |-ry -rɪ

cockshot ˈkakˌʃat

cockshut ˈkakˌʃʌt

cocksure ˈkakˈʃur; ES -ˈʃuə(r; (ˈcockˌsure ˈplan)

cockswain ˈkaksn̩, ˈkakˌswen

cocktail ˈkakˌtel |-ed -d

coco ˈkoko

cocoa ˈkoko, ˈkokə

coconut, cocoa- ˈkokənət, ˈkokəˌnʌt

cocoon kəˈkun, kuˈkun

Cocos ˈkokas

cocotte koˈkat, kə- *(Fr* kɔˈkɔt)

cocytus, C- koˈsaɪtəs |-'s -ɪz

cod, C- kad |codded ˈkadɪd

C.O.D. ˈsiˌoˈdi

coda ˈkodə

Coddington ˈkadɪŋtən

coddle ˈkadl̩ |-d -d |-ling ˈkadlɪŋ, ˈkadl̩ɪŋ

code kod |coded ˈkodɪd

codefendant ˌkodɪˈfɛndənt

codeine ˈkodɪˌin, ˈkodin |-dein -dɪɪn

codex ˈkodɛks |-es -ɪz |codices ˈkodəˌsiz, ˈkad- —*The* o *in* codices *is by analogy with the singular. The long* o *of Latin becomes short in English, as in* orator, prominent, solitude, nominal, *etc.*

codfish ˈkadˌfɪʃ |-'s -ɪz

codger ˈkadʒɚ; ES ˈkadʒə(r

codices ˈkodəˌsiz, ˈkad- —*see* codex

codicil ˈkadəsl̩, -ˌsɪl

codify ˈkadəˌfaɪ, ˈkod- |-fied -ˌfaɪd

codling ˈkadlɪŋ

codpiece ˈkadˌpis |-pieces -ˌpisɪz

Cody ˈkodɪ

coed, co-ed ˈkoˈɛd, ˈkoˌɛd (ˈcoˌed ˈcollege)

coeducation ˌkoɛdʒəˈkeʃən |-al -l̩ |-ally -l̩ɪ

coefficient ˌkoəˈfɪʃənt, ˌkoˌɪ-

coeliac ˈsilɪˌæk

coempt koˈɛmpt |-ed -ɪd |-ption -pʃən

coenobite ˈsɛnəˌbaɪt, ˈsin-

coequal koˈikwəl |-ed -d |-ly -ɪ

coequality ˌkoˌiˈkwalətɪ, ˈkwɒl-

coerce koˈɝs; ES -ˈɜs, -ˈɝs; |-s -ɪz |-d -t

coercion koˈɝʃən; ES -ˈɜʃən, -ˈɝʃən |-cive -sɪv

coeternal ˌkoˌiˈtɝnl̩; ES -ˈtɜnl̩, -ˈtɝnl̩; |-ly -ɪ

Coeur de Lion ˌkɝdəˈliən, -ˈlian; ES ˌkɜ-, ˌkɝ-; *(Fr* kœrdəˈljɔ̃)

coeval koˈivl̩ |-ly -ɪ |-ity ˌkoˈɪˈvælətɪ

coexecutor ˌkoɪgˈzɛkjətɚ; ES -ˈzɛkjətə(r

|full fʊl |tooth tuθ |further ˈfɝðɚ; ES ˈfɝðə |custom ˈkʌstəm |while hwaɪl |how hau |toy tɔɪ |using ˈjuzɪŋ |fuse fjuz, fɪuz |dish dɪʃ |vision ˈvɪʒən |Eden ˈidn̩ |cradle ˈkredl̩ |keep 'em ˈkipm̩

Those words below in which the ɑ sound is spelt o are often pronounced with ɒ in E and S

coexist ˌko·ɪgˈzɪst |-ed -ɪd |-ence -əns |-ent -ənt

coextend ˌko·ɪkˈstɛnd |-ed -ɪd |-tensive -nsɪv

coffee, C- ˈkɔfɪ, ˈkɒfɪ, *much less freq.* ˈkɑfɪ |-house -ˌhaʊs |-pot -ˌpɑt—*In* coffee ɔ *clearly prevails in all regions of US.*

coffer ˈkɔfɚ, ˈkɒfɚ; ES -fə(r; |-dam -ˌdæm

Coffeyville ˈkɔfɪˌvɪl, ˈkɒfɪ-; S+-vl̩

coffin, C- ˈkɔfɪn, ˈkɒfɪn |-ed -d

Coffman ˈkɔfmən, ˈkɒf-, ˈkɑf-

cog kɑg, kɒg, *less freq.* kɔg |-ged -d

cogence ˈkodʒəns |-cy -ɪ |-gent -dʒənt

cogitable ˈkadʒɪtəbl̩

cogitate ˈkadʒəˌtet |-d -ɪd |-tive -ɪv

cogitation ˌkadʒəˈteʃən

cognac ˈkonjæk, ˈkan- (*Fr* kɔˈɲak)

cognate ˈkagnet

cognition kagˈnɪʃən |cognitive ˈkagnətɪv

cognizable ˈkagnəzəbl̩ |-bly -blɪ

cognizance ˈkagnəzəns, ˈkan- |-s -ɪz |-nt -nt

cognomen kagˈnomən |-s -z |-nomina -ˈnamənə

cogwheel ˈkagˌhwil, ˈkɒg-, *less freq.* ˈkɔg-

cohabit koˈhæbɪt |-ed -ɪd

cohabitation ˌkohæbəˈteʃən

Cohasset koˈhæsɪt

coheir koˈɛr, -ˈær; E -ˈɛə(r, ES -ˈæə(r; |-ess -ɪs |-esses -ɪsɪz

cohere koˈhɪr; ES koˈhɪə(r, S+-ˈhɛə(r

coherence koˈhɪrəns; S+-ˈhɛr-; |-ent -ənt

coherer koˈhɪrɚ; ES -ˈhɪrə(r, S+-ˈhɛrə(r

cohesion koˈhiʒən |-hesive -ˈhisɪv

Cohoes koˈhoz |-ʼs -ɪz

cohort ˈkohɔrt; ES ˈkohɔət

cohortative koˈhɔrtətɪv; ES -ˈhɔət-

coif kɔɪf |coifed kɔɪft

coiffeur kwɑˈfɚ ; ES -ˈfɜ(r, -ˈfɚ; (*Fr* kwa-ˈfœːr)

coiffure kwɑˈfjʊr, -ˈfɪʊr; ES -ˈfjʊə(r, -ˈfɪʊə(r; (*Fr* kwaˈfyːr)

coign, -e kɔɪn

coil kɔɪl |coiled kɔɪld

coin kɔɪn |-ed -d |-age -ɪdʒ |-ages -ɪdʒɪz

coincide ˌko·ɪnˈsaɪd |-cided -ˈsaɪdɪd

coincidence koˈɪnsədəns |-s -ɪz |-cy -ɪ |-nt -nt

coincidental koˌɪnsəˈdɛntl̩, ˌko·ɪn- |-ly -ɪ

coincidently koˈɪnsədəntlɪ

coinsurance ˌko·ɪnˈʃʊrəns |-s -ɪz

coinsure ˌko·ɪnˈʃʊr; ES -ˈʃʊə(r; |-d -d

coir kɔɪr; ES kɔɪə(r

coistrel, -il ˈkɔɪstrəl

coition koˈɪʃən

coitus ˈko·ɪtəs

coke kok |coked kokt

Coke kʊk, kok

colander ˈkʌləndɚ, ˈkɑl-; ES -də(r

Colbert *Am name* ˈkɑlbɚt, ˈkɔl-, ˈkol-; ES -bət; *Fr name* kɔlˈbɛːr

Colby ˈkolbɪ

Colchester ˈkɑlˌtʃɛstɚ; ˈkoltʃɪstɚ; ES -tə(r

colchicum, C- ˈkaltʃɪkəm

Colchis ˈkalkɪs |-ʼs -ɪz

cold kold |colded ˈkoldɪd

cold-blooded ˈkoldˈblʌdɪd, -ˌblʌdɪd (ˈcold-ˌblooded ˈmalice)

cold-hearted ˈkoldˈhɑrtɪd; ES -ˈhɑːtɪd, E+-ˈhɑːtɪd

cold-shoulder *v* ˈkoldˈʃoldɚ; ES -ˈʃoldə(r; |-ed -d |-ing -ˈʃoldərɪŋ, -ˈʃoldrɪŋ

coldslaw ˈkolˌslɔ, ˈkold-

Coldstream ˈkoldˌstrim

cole kol

Coleman ˈkolmən

coleopterous ˌkolɪˈaptərəs, ˌkalɪ-

Coleridge ˈkolrɪdʒ, *not infreq.* ˈkolərɪdʒ |-ʼs -ɪz

coleslaw ˈkolˌslɔ

Colet ˈkalɪt

coleus, C- ˈkolɪəs |-es -ɪz

Coleville ˈkolvɪl

colewort ˈkolˌwɚt; ES -ˌwɜt, -ˌwɚt

Colfax ˈkolfæks |-ʼs -ɪz

colic ˈkalɪk |colicky ˈkalɪkɪ

Colin ˈkalɪn

Coliseum ˌkaləˈsiəm

colitis koˈlaɪtɪs

collaborate kəˈlæbəˌret |-d -ɪd |-tor -ɚ; ES -ə(r; |-tive -ɪv

collaboration kəˌlæbəˈreʃən

collage kəˈlaʒ, ko- |-gist -ɪst (*Fr* kɔˈlaːʒ)

collapse kəˈlæps |-s -ɪz |-d -t |-sible -əbl̩

collapsibility kəˌlæpsəˈbɪlətɪ

collar ˈkalɚ; ES ˈkalə(r; |-ed -d

collarbone ˈkalɚˌbon, -ˌbon; ES ˈkalə-

collaret, -tte ˌkaləˈrɛt

collate kaˈlet, kə-, ˈkalet |-d -ɪd

collateral kəˈlætərəl |-ly -ɪ

Those words below in which the ɑ *sound is spelt* o *are often pronounced with* ɒ *in E and S*

collation kɑˈleʃən, kə-
colleague *n* ˈkɑlig
colleague *v* kəˈlig, kɑ- |-leagued -ˈligd
collect *n* ˈkɑlɛkt
collect *v* kəˈlɛkt |-ed -ɪd
collectanea ˌkɑlɛkˈtenɪə
collectibility, -ability kəˌlɛktəˈbɪlətɪ
collectible, -able kəˈlɛktəbḷ
collection kəˈlɛkʃən
collective kəˈlɛktɪv |-ism -ˌɪzəm |-ist -ɪst
collectivistic kəˌlɛktəˈvɪstɪk |-ally -ḷɪ, -ɪklɪ
collector kəˈlɛktɚ; ES -ˈlɛktə(r; |-ship -ˌʃɪp
colleen ˈkɑlin, kəˈlin
college ˈkɑlɪdʒ |-s -ɪz
college-bred ˈkɑlɪdʒˈbrɛd (ˈcollege-ˌbred ˈman)
collegian kəˈlidʒən, -dʒɪən |-giate -dʒɪɪt, -dʒɪt
collet ˈkɑlɪt |-ed -ɪd
Colleton ˈkɑlətṇ
collide kəˈlaɪd |-lided -ˈlaɪdɪd
collie ˈkɑlɪ
collied ˈkɑlɪd
collier ˈkɑljɚ; ES ˈkɑljə(r; |-y -ɪ
collimate ˈkɑləˌmet |-d -ɪd |-tion ˌkɑləˈmeʃən
Collingwood ˈkɑlɪŋˌwʊd
Collins ˈkɑlɪnz |-ˈs -ɪz
Collinwood ˈkɑlɪnˌwʊd
collision kəˈlɪʒən |-al -ḷ
collocate ˈkɑloˌket |-d -ɪd |-tion ˌkɑloˈkeʃən
collodion kəˈlodɪən
colloid ˈkɑlɔɪd |-al kəˈlɔɪdḷ
collop ˈkɑləp |colloped ˈkɑləpt
colloquial kəˈlokwɪəl |-ly -ɪ |-ism -ˌɪzəm
colloquiality kəˌlokwɪˈælətɪ
colloquy ˈkɑləkwɪ
collude kəˈlud, -ˈlɪud |-d -ɪd
collusion kəˈluʒən, -ˈlɪuʒən |-sive -sɪv
Colman ˈkolmən
Cologne, c- kəˈlon (*Ger* Köln, C- kœln)
Colombia kəˈlʌmbɪə (*Sp* koˈlɔmbja) |-n -n
Colombo kəˈlʌmbo, kəˈlɑmbo
Colón koˈlɑn, -ˈlon (*Am Sp* koˈlon)
colon ˈkolən
colon *coin* koˈlon |-s -z |-es -es
colonel ˈkɝnḷ; ES ˈkɜnḷ, ˈkɝnḷ; |-ed -d |-cy -sɪ
colonial kəˈlonɪəl |-ism -ˌɪzəm
colonist ˈkɑlənɪst
colonization ˌkɑlənəˈzeʃən, -aɪˈz- |-ist -ɪst
colonize ˈkɑləˌnaɪz |-s -ɪz |-d -d

colonnade ˌkɑləˈned |-naded -ˈnedɪd
colony ˈkɑlənɪ
colophon ˈkɑləˌfɑn, -fən
color ˈkʌlɚ; ES ˈkʌlə(r; |-ed -d
colorable ˈkʌlərəbḷ |-bly -blɪ
Colorado ˌkɑləˈrædo, -ˈrɑdo |-dan -dən—*Observers disagree as to whether* ˌkɑləˈrædo *or* -ˈrɑdo *prevails in the state.* *There is little doubt that in the US as a whole* ˌkɑləˈrædo *prevails.*
coloration ˌkʌləˈreʃən
coloratura ˌkʌlərəˈtjʊrə, ˌkɑl-, -ˈtɪʊrə, -ˈtʊrə
colorature ˈkʌlərəˌtʃʊr, ˈkɑl-; ES -ˌtʃʊə(r
color-bearer ˈkʌlɚˌbɛrɚ, -ˌbærɚ; E ˈkʌlə-ˌbɛrə(r, ES -ˌbærə(r
color-blind ˈkʌlɚˌblaɪnd; ES ˈkʌlə-
colorful ˈkʌlɚfəl; ES ˈkʌlə-; |-ly -ɪ
colorimeter ˌkʌləˈrɪmətɚ; ES -ˈrɪmətə(r
colossal kəˈlɑsḷ |-ly -ɪ
Colosseum ˌkɑləˈsiəm
Colossian kəˈlɑʃən |-s -z
colossus kəˈlɑsəs |-es -ɪz |-ssi -saɪ |-sus' -səs
colporteur, -ter ˈkɑlˌportɚ, -ˌpɔrtɚ; ES -ˌpoətə(r, E+-ˌpɔətə(r; (*Fr* kɔlpɔrˈtœːr)
Colquhoun kəˈhun
colt, C- kolt |colted ˈkoltɪd; |*NEngd*+költ (§46)
colter ˈkoltɚ; ES ˈkoltə(r; |-ed -d
Colton ˈkoltṇ
Colum ˈkɑləm
Columb ˈkɑləm
Columba kəˈlʌmbə
Columbia kəˈlʌmbɪə, -bjə |-n -n
columbine, C- ˈkɑləmˌbaɪn
columbium kəˈlʌmbɪəm
Columbus kəˈlʌmbəs |-ˈs -ɪz
column ˈkɑləm, *humorous* ˈkɑljəṁ |-ed -d
columnar kəˈlʌmnɚ; ES -ˈlʌmnə(r
columniation '*columning*' kəˌlʌmnɪˈeʃən
columnist ˈkɑləmnɪst, ˈkɑləmnɪst
Colusa kəˈlusə, kəˈlɪusə
Colvin ˈkolvɪn, ˈkɑl-
coma '*stupor*' ˈkomə |-s -z
coma '*comet's head*' ˈkomə |-ae -i
Comanche koˈmæntʃɪ |-chean -tʃɪən
comatose ˈkɑməˌtos, ˈkomə-
comb kom |combed komd; |*NEngd*+köm (§46)

|full fʊl |tooth tuθ |further ˈfɝðɚ; ES ˈfɜðə |custom ˈkʌstəm |while hwaɪl |how haʊ |toy tɔɪ
|using ˈjuzɪŋ |fuse fjuz, fɪuz |dish dɪʃ |vision ˈvɪʒən |Eden ˈidṇ |cradle ˈkredḷ |keep 'em ˈkipṃ

Those words below in which the ɑ *sound is spelt* o *are often pronounced with* ɒ *in E and S*

comb '*valley*' kum

combat *n* 'kɑmbæt, 'kʌm-

combat *v* 'kɑmbæt, 'kʌm-, kəm'bæt |-ted -ɪd

combatant 'kɑmbətənt, 'kʌm-

combative kəm'bætɪv, 'kɑmbətɪv, 'kʌm-

combe kum

comber 'komɚ; ES 'komə(r

combination ˌkɑmbə'neʃən

combinative 'kɑmbəˌnetɪv, kəm'baɪnətɪv

combine *n* 'kɑmbaɪn, kəm'baɪn

combine *v* kəm'baɪn |-bined -'baɪnd |-dly -ɪdlɪ

combings 'komɪŋz

combust kəm'bʌst |-ed -ɪd

combustibility kəmˌbʌstə'bɪlətɪ

combustible kəm'bʌstəbḷ |-bly -blɪ

combustion kəm'bʌstʃən

come *n malting* kom, kum

come *v* kʌm |came kem |come kʌm—*in un-stressed position often* kəm (kəm'ɪn!)

come-and-go 'kʌmən'go

comedian kə'midɪən

comédienne kəˌmidɪ'ɛn (*Fr* kȫme'djɛn)

comedy 'kɑmədɪ

comely 'kʌmlɪ

comestible kə'mɛstəbḷ

comet 'kɑmɪt

comfit 'kʌmfɪt, 'kɑm-

comfort 'kʌmfɚt; ES -fət; |-ed -ɪd

comfortable 'kʌmfɚtəbḷ; ES 'kʌmfətəbḷ

comforter 'kʌmfɚtɚ, 'kʌmfətɚ; ES -fətə(r;— 'kʌmfətɚ *shows r-dissimilation* (*§121*).

comfry 'kʌmfrɪ

comic 'kɑmɪk |-al -ḷ |-ally -ḷɪ, -ɪklɪ

Cominius kə'mɪnɪəs, -njəs |-'s -ɪz

Comintern ˌkɑmɪn'tɝn, 'kɑmɪnˌtɝn; ES -ɜn, -ɝn

comitatus ˌkɑmɪ'tetəs

comity 'kɑmətɪ

comma 'kɑmə |-ed -d

command kə'mænd; ES+-'mɑnd, -'mɒnd; |-ed -ɪd

commandant ˌkɑmən'dænt, -'dɑnt

commandeer ˌkɑmən'dɪr; ES -'dɪə(r, S+ -'dɛə(r; |-ed -d

commander ˌkə'mændɚ; ES -də(r, E+ -'mɑnd-, -'mɒnd-

commander in chief kə'mændərɪn'tʃif; E+ -'mɑnd-, -'mɒnd-

commandment kə'mændmənt, -'mænmənt; E+-an-, -ɑn-

commemorate kə'mɛməˌret |-rated -ˌretɪd

commemoration kəˌmɛmə'reʃən

commence kə'mɛns |-s -ɪz |-d -t |-ment -mənt

commend kə'mɛnd |-ed -ɪd

commendable kə'mɛndəbḷ |-bly -blɪ

commendation ˌkɑmən'deʃən, ˌkɑmɛn-

commendatory kə'mɛndəˌtorɪ, -ˌtɔrɪ; S -ˌtorɪ

commensurability kəˌmɛnʃərə'bɪlətɪ, -ˌmɛnsərə-

commensurable kə'mɛnʃərəbḷ, -'mɛnsərə- |-bly -blɪ

commensurate *adj* kə'mɛnʃərɪt, -'mɛnsə-

commensurate *v* kə'mɛnʃəˌret, -'mɛnsə- |-d -ɪd

commensuration kəˌmɛnʃə'reʃən, -ˌmɛnsə-

comment *n* 'kɑmɛnt

comment *v* 'kɑmɛnt, *less freq.* kə'mɛnt |-ed -ɪd

commentary 'kɑmənˌtɛrɪ

commentator 'kɑmənˌtetɚ; ES -ˌtetə(r

commerce *n* 'kɑmɚs, -mɝs; ES 'kɑməs, -mɜs, -mɝs

commerce *v* kə'mɝs; ES -'mɜs, -'mɝs; |-s -ɪz |-d -t

commercial kə'mɝʃəl; ES -'mɜʃ-, -'mɝʃ-; |-ly -ɪ |-ism -ˌɪzəm

commercialization kəˌmɝʃələ'zeʃən, -aɪ'z-; ES -ˌmɜʃ-, -ˌmɝʃ-

commercialize kə'mɝʃəlˌaɪz; ES -'mɜʃ-, -'mɝʃ-; |-s -ɪz |-d -d

comminate 'kɑməˌnet |-nated -ˌnetɪd

commination ˌkɑmə'neʃən

commingle kə'mɪŋgḷ |-d -d

comminute 'kɑməˌnjut, -ˌnɪut, -ˌnut |-d -ɪd

comminution ˌkɑmə'njuʃən, -'nɪu-, -'nu-

commiserable kə'mɪzərəbḷ

commiserate kə'mɪzəˌret |-rated -ˌretɪd

commiseration kəˌmɪzə'reʃən

commiserative kə'mɪzəˌretɪv

commissar ˌkɑmə'sɑr; ES -'sɑ:(r, E+-'sɑ:(r

commissariat ˌkɑmə'sɛrɪət, -'sær-, -'ser-

commissary 'kɑməˌsɛrɪ

commission kə'mɪʃən |-ed -d

commissionaire kəˌmɪʃən'ɛr, -'ær; E -'ɛə(r, ES -'æə(r

commissioner kə'mɪʃənɚ, -'mɪʃnɚ; ES -nə(r

commit kə'mɪt |-ted -ɪd |-tal -ḷ

Those words below in which the a sound is spelt o are often pronounced with ɒ in E and S

committee kə'mɪtɪ |-d -d |-man -mən, -ˌmæn |-men -mən, -ˌmɛn

commix kə'mɪks, ka- |-es -ɪz |-ed -t

commixture kə'mɪkstʃɚ, ka-; ES -'mɪkstʃə(r

commode kə'mod

commodious kə'modɪəs

commodity kə'madətɪ

commodore 'kaməˌdor, -ˌdɔr; ES -ˌdoə(r, E+ -ˌdɔə(r

common 'kamən |-ed -d |-ness 'kamənnɪs

commonage 'kamənɪdʒ |-s -ɪz

commonality ˌkamən'ælətɪ

commonalty 'kamənəltɪ

commonplace 'kamənˌples |-s -ɪz

common-sense *adj* 'kamən'sɛns ('common-'sense ˌway)

commonweal 'kamənˌwil

commonwealth 'kamənˌwɛlθ, 'kamən'wɛlθ

commotion kə'moʃən

communal 'kamjʊn|, kə'mjun|, -'mɪu- |-ism -ˌɪzəm |-ist -ɪst |-ly -ɪ

commune *n* 'kamjun, -mɪun

commune *v* kə'mjun, -'mɪun |-d -d

communicability kəˌmjunɪkə'bɪlətɪ, -ˌmɪun-

communicable kə'mjunɪkəb|, -'mɪun- |-bly -blɪ

communicant kə'mjunɪkənt, -'mɪun-

communicate kə'mjunəˌket, -'mɪun- |-d -ɪd

communication kəˌmjunə'keʃən, -ˌmɪun-

communicative kə'mjunəˌketɪv, -'mɪun-

communion kə'mjunjən, -'mɪun-

communiqué kəˌmjunə'ke, -ˌmɪun-

communism 'kamjʊˌnɪzəm |-ist -nɪst

communistic ˌkamjʊ'nɪstɪk |-al -| |-ally -|ɪ, -ɪklɪ

community kə'mjunətɪ, -'mɪun-

communize 'kamjʊˌnaɪz |-s -ɪz |-d -d

commutable kə'mjutəb|, -'mɪut-

commutate 'kamjʊˌtet |-d -ɪd |-ter -ɚ; ES -ə(r

commutation ˌkamjʊ'teʃən

commute kə'mjut, -'mɪut |-d -ɪd |-r -ɚ; ES -ə(r

Como 'komo

compact *adj* kəm'pækt ('comˌpact 'mass)

compact *n* 'kampækt

compact *v* kəm'pækt |-ed -ɪd

companion kəm'pænjən |-ed -d |-ship -ˌʃɪp

companionable kəm'pænjənəb| |bly -blɪ

companionate *adj* kəm'pænjənɪt

companionway kəm'pænjənˌwe

company 'kʌmpənɪ, 'kʌmpnɪ |-nied -nɪd

comparability ˌkampərə'bɪlətɪ

comparable 'kampərəb|, -prəb| |-bly -blɪ

comparative kəm'pærətɪv

compare kəm'pɛr, -'pær; E -'pɛə(r, ES -'pæə(r

Comparetti ˌkampə'rɛtɪ (*It* ˌkompa'retti)

comparison kəm'pærəsn̩

compartment kəm'partmənt; ES -'pɑːt-, E+ -'pɑːt-

compass 'kʌmpəs |-es -ɪz |-ed -t

compassion kəm'pæʃən |-ed -d |-ate -ɪt

compatibility kəmˌpætə'bɪlətɪ

compatible kəm'pætəb| |-bly -blɪ

compatriot kəm'petrɪət, *less freq.* -'pæt-

compeer kəm'pɪr, 'kampɪr; ES -ɪə(r, S+-ɛə(r

compel kəm'pɛl |-led -d

compellable kəm'pɛləb| |-bly -blɪ

compend 'kampend |-ious kəm'pendɪəs

compendium kəm'pendɪəm |-s -z |-dia -dɪə

compensable kəm'pensəb|

compensate 'kampənˌset, -pɛn-, kəm'pɛnset |-d -ɪd

compensation ˌkampən'seʃən, -pɛn-

compensative 'kampənˌsetɪv, kəm'pɛnsətɪv

compensatory kəm'pensəˌtorɪ, -ˌtɔrɪ; S -ˌtorɪ

compete kəm'pit |-peted -'pitɪd

competence 'kampətəns |-s -ɪz |-cy -ɪ |-nt -nt

competition ˌkampə'tɪʃən

competitive kəm'petətɪv |-tor -tɚ; ES -tə(r

compilation ˌkampl̩'eʃən, -pɪ'leʃən

compile kəm'paɪl |-piled -'paɪld

complacence kəm'plesn̩s |-cy -ɪ |-cent -sn̩t

complain kəm'plen |-ed -d |-ant -ənt |-t -t

complaisance kəm'plezn̩s, 'kamplɪˌzæns |-sant -zn̩t, -ˌzænt

complement *n* 'kampləmənt

complement *v* 'kampləˌmɛnt |-ed -ɪd

complemental ˌkamplə'mɛnt| |-ly -ɪ

complementary ˌkamplə'mɛntərɪ, -'mɛntrɪ

complete kəm'plit |-d -ɪd |-tion -'pliʃən

complex *n* 'kamplɛks |-es -ɪz

complex *adj* kəm'plɛks, 'kamplɛks ('comˌplex 'act)

complex *v* kəm'plɛks |-es -ɪz |-ed -t

complexion, -plection kəm'plɛkʃən |-ed -d

Those words below in which the ɑ *sound is spelt* o *are often pronounced with* ɒ *in E and S*

complexity kəm'plɛksətɪ
compliance kəm'plaɪəns |-cy -ɪ |-ant -ənt
complicate *adj* 'kɑmpləkɪt
complicate *v* 'kɑmplə‚ket |-cated -‚ketɪd
complication ‚kɑmplə'keʃən
complice 'kɑmplɪs |-s -ɪz
complicity kəm'plɪsətɪ
compliment *n* 'kɑmpləmənt
compliment 'kɑmplə‚mɛnt |-ed -ɪd
complimentary ‚kɑmplə'mɛntərɪ, -'mɛntrɪ
complin 'kɑmplɪn |-pline -plɪn, -plaɪn
comply kəm'plaɪ |-plied -'plaɪd
component kəm'ponənt |-ed -ɪd
comport kəm'port, -'pɔrt; ES -'poət, E+
  -'pɔət; |-ed -ɪd
compose kəm'poz |-s -ɪz |-d -d |-dly -ɪdlɪ
composite kəm'pazɪt |-d -ɪd |-tor -ɚ; ES -ə(r
compos mentis 'kɑmpəs'mɛntɪs
compost 'kɑmpost |-ed -ɪd, -pəstɪd
composure kəm'poʒɚ; ES -'poʒə(r
compote 'kɑmpot |-poted -potɪd
compound *n* 'kɑmpaʊnd
compound *adj* kɑm'paʊnd ('com‚pound
  'word)
compound *v* kɑm'paʊnd, kəm- |-ed -ɪd
comprehend ‚kɑmprɪ'hɛnd |-ed -ɪd |-ible -əbl̩
comprehensibility ‚kɑmprɪ‚hɛnsə'bɪlətɪ
comprehensible ‚kɑmprɪ'hɛnsəbl̩ |-bly -blɪ
comprehension ‚kɑmprɪ'hɛnʃən |-sive -sɪv
compress *n* 'kɑmprɛs |-es -ɪz
compress *v* kəm'prɛs |-es -ɪz |-ed -t |-edly
  -ɪdlɪ, -'prɛstlɪ
compressibility kəm‚prɛsə'bɪlətɪ
compressible kəm'prɛsəbl̩ |-bly -blɪ
compression kəm'prɛʃən |-sive -'prɛsɪv |-sor
  -'prɛsɚ; ES -ə(r
comprise, -ze kəm'praɪz |-s -ɪz |-d -d
compromise 'kɑmprə‚maɪz |-s -ɪz |-d -d
comptometer, C- kɑmp'tɑmətɚ; ES -'tɑmətə(r
Compton 'kɑmptən, 'kʌmptən
comptroller kən'trolɚ; ES -lə(r; |-ship -‚ʃɪp
compulsion kəm'pʌlʃən |-sive -sɪv |-sory -sərɪ
compunction kəm'pʌŋkʃən |-tious -ʃəs
compurgation ‚kɑmpɚ'geʃən, -pə-; ES -pɜ-,
  -pɝ-, -pə-
computability kəm‚pjutə'bɪlətɪ, -‚pɪut-
computable kəm'pjutəbl̩, -'pɪut-, 'kɑmpjutə-
  |-bly -blɪ

computation ‚kɑmpjə'teʃən, -pjʊ-
compute kəm'pjut, -'pɪut |-d -ɪd
comrade 'kɑmræd, 'kʌm-, -rɪd
Comstock 'kʌmstɑk, -stɒk, -stɔk
Comte kɔnt (*Fr* kõt)
Comus 'koməs |-'s -ɪz
con '*against*' kɑn
con '*study*' kɑn |conned kɑnd
con amore ‚kɑnə'morɪ, -'mɔrɪ; S -'morɪ; (*It*
  ‚konɑ'mo:re)
Conan 'kɑnən, 'konən
Conant 'konənt
conation ko'neʃən |-al -l̩ |-tive 'kɑnətɪv
concatenate kɑn'kætn̩‚et, kən- |-d -ɪd
concatenation ‚kɑnkætn̩'eʃən, kən‚kætn̩-
concave *n* 'kɑnkev, 'kɑŋ-
concave *adj* kɑn'kev, kən- ('con‚cave 'surface)
concave *v* kɑn'kev, kən- |-d -d |-cavity
  -'kævətɪ
concavo-concave kɑn'kevokɑn'kev
concavo-convex kɑn'kevokɑn'vɛks
conceal kən'sil |-ed -d |-edly -ɪdlɪ
concede kən'sid |-ceded -'sidɪd
conceit kən'sit |-ed -ɪd
conceivability kən‚sivə'bɪlətɪ
conceivable kən'sivəbl̩ |-bly -blɪ
conceive kən'siv |-ceived -'sivd
concentrate 'kɑnsn̩‚tret, -sɛn- |-d -ɪd
concentration ‚kɑnsn̩'treʃən, -sɛn-
concentric kən'sɛntrɪk |-al -l̩ |-ally -l̩ɪ, -ɪklɪ
Concepción kən‚sɛpsɪ'on (*Am Sp* kɔn-
  sɛp'sjon)
concept 'kɑnsɛpt |-ption, C- kən'sɛpʃən
conceptual kən'sɛptʃʊəl, -tʃʊl |-ly -ɪ
concern kən'sɜn; ES -'sɜn, -'sɜn; |-ed -d
  |-edly -ɪdlɪ
concert *n* 'kɑnsɜt, -sɚt; ES -sɜt, -sɝt, -sət
concert *v* kən'sɜt; ES -'sɜt, -'sɝt; |-ed -ɪd
concertina ‚kɑnsɚ'tinə; ES ‚kɑnsə-
concertmaster 'kɑnsɚt‚mæstɚ; ES 'kɑnsət-
  ‚mæstə(r, E+-‚mas-, -‚mas-
concertmeister 'kɑnsɚt‚maɪstɚ; ES 'kɑnsət-
  ‚maɪstə(r; (*Ger* Konzert- kɔn'tsɛrt‚maɪstər)
concerto kən'tʃɛrto; ES -'tʃɛəto; (*It* kon-
  'tʃɛrto)
concession kən'sɛʃən
concessionaire kən‚sɛʃən'ɛr, -'ær; E -'ɛə(r,
  ES -'æə(r

Those words below in which the ɑ *sound is spelt* o *are often pronounced with* ɒ *in E and S*

concessionary kənˈsɛʃənˌɛrɪ
concessive kənˈsɛsɪv
conch kɑŋk, kɒŋk |-ed -t
Concho ˈkɑntʃo |Conchos ˈkɑntʃos |-s's -sɪz
conchology kɑŋˈkɑlədʒɪ, kɒŋ- |-gist -dʒɪst
concierge ˌkɑnsɪˈɛrʒ; ES -ˈɛɜʒ; (Fr kõˈsjɛrʒ)
conciliable kənˈsɪlɪəbḷ
conciliate kənˈsɪlɪˌet |-ated -ˌetɪd
conciliation kənˌsɪlɪˈeʃən
conciliatory kənˈsɪlɪəˌtorɪ, -ˌtɔrɪ; S -ˌtorɪ
concise kənˈsaɪs |-cision kənˈsɪʒən
conclave ˈkɑnklev, ˈkɑŋ-
conclude kənˈklud, -ˈklɪud |-d -ɪd
conclusion kənˈkluʒən, -ˈklɪuʒən |-sive -sɪv
concoct kɑnˈkɑkt, kən- |-ed -ɪd |-ction -kʃən
concomitance kɑnˈkɑmətəns, kən- |-cy -ɪ
|-ant -ənt
concord ˈkɑnkɔrd, -ˈkɑŋ-; ES -kɔəd
Concord Mass, NH ˈkɑŋkɚd; ES ˈkɑŋkəd;
elsewhere in US, towns & grape ˈkɑnkɔrd;
ES ˈkɑnkɔəd
concordance kɑnˈkɔrdṇs, kən-; ES -ˈkɔəd-;
|-s -ɪz |-d -t |-dant -dṇt
concordat kɑnˈkɔrdæt; ES -ˈkɔədæt
Concordia kɑnˈkɔrdɪə; ES -ˈkɔədɪə
concourse ˈkɑnkors, ˈkɑŋ-, -kɔrs; ES -koəs,
E+-kɔəs; |-s -ɪz
concrete adj kɑnˈkrit, ˈkɑnkrit, much less freq.
kɑŋ-, ˈkɑŋ- (ˈconˌcrete ˈact)
concrete n ˈkɑnkrit, kɑnˈkrit, much less freq.
ˈkɑŋ-, kɑŋ-
concrete v 'congeal' kɑnˈkrit; 'cement' ˈkɑnkrit,
kɑnˈkrit |-d -ɪd—see n
concretion kɑnˈkriʃən—see n
concubinage kɑnˈkjubənɪdʒ, -ˈkɪub-
concubine ˈkɑŋkjuˌbaɪn, ˈkɑn-
concupiscence kɑnˈkjupəsṇs, -ˈkɪu- |-cent
-sṇt
concur kənˈkɝ; ES -ˈkɝ(r, -ˈkɝ; |-red -d
concurrence kənˈkɝəns; ES -ˈkɝr-, -ˈkʌr-,
-ˈkɝ-; |-cy -ɪ |-ent -ənt
concussion kənˈkʌʃən |-sive -sɪv
condemn kənˈdɛm |-ed -d |-ing -ɪŋ
condemnable 'subject to condemnation' kən-
ˈdɛməbḷ, 'fit to be condemned' kənˈdɛmnəbḷ
|-bly -blɪ
condemnation ˌkɑndɛmˈneʃən, -dəm-
condemnatory kənˈdɛmnəˌtorɪ, -ˌtɔrɪ; S -ˌtorɪ

condensability kənˌdɛnsəˈbɪlətɪ
condensable kənˈdɛnsəbḷ
condensate kənˈdɛnset
condensation ˌkɑndɛnˈseʃən
condense kənˈdɛns |-s -ɪz |-d -t |-dly -ɪdlɪ
condescend ˌkɑndɪˈsɛnd |-ed -ɪd
condescendence ˌkɑndɪˈsɛndəns |-dent -dənt
condescension ˌkɑndɪˈsɛnʃən
condign kənˈdaɪn (ˈconˌdign ˈcensure)
condiment ˈkɑndəmənt
condition kənˈdɪʃən |-ed -d |-ing -ʃənɪŋ, -ʃnɪŋ
conditional kənˈdɪʃənḷ, -ʃnəl |-ly -ɪ
condole kənˈdol |-d -d
condolence kənˈdoləns, ˈkɑndələns |-s -ɪz
condominium ˌkɑndəˈmɪnɪəm
condone kənˈdon |-d -d |-nation ˌkɑndoˈneʃən
condor ˈkɑndɚ; ES ˈkɑndə(r
condottiere It ˌkɑndotˈtjɛːre
conduce kənˈdjus, -ˈdɪus |-s -ɪz |-d -t |-cive -ɪv
conduct n ˈkɑndʌkt
conduct v kənˈdʌkt |-ed -ɪd
conductance kənˈdʌktəns |-s -ɪz
conductibility kənˌdʌktəˈbɪlətɪ
conductible kənˈdʌktəbḷ
conduction kənˈdʌkʃən |-tive -tɪv
conductivity ˌkɑndʌkˈtɪvətɪ
conductor kənˈdʌktɚ; ES -ˈdʌktə(r
conduit ˈkɑndɪt, ˈkɑndʊɪt
cone kon |coned kond
Conejos kəˈneɑs, -ˈnehəs, -ˈnehos |-ˈs -ɪz
(Am Sp koˈnehos)
Conemaugh ˈkɑnəˌmɔ
conenose ˈkɑnˌnoz |-s -ɪz
Conestoga ˌkɑnəˈstogə
coney ˈkonɪ, ˈkʌnɪ—see cony
Coney ˈkonɪ
confab ˈkɑnfæb
confabulate kənˈfæbjəˌlet |-lated -ˌletɪd
confabulation kənˌfæbjəˈleʃən
confect n ˈkɑnfɛkt
confect v kənˈfɛkt |-ed -ɪd |-ction -kʃən
confectionary kənˈfɛkʃənˌɛrɪ
confectioner kənˈfɛkʃənɚ, -kʃnɚ; ES -nə(r
confectionery kənˈfɛkʃənˌɛrɪ
confederacy, C- kənˈfɛdərəsɪ, -ˈfɛdrəsɪ
confederate, C- n, adj kənˈfɛdərɪt, -ˈfɛdrɪt
confederate v kənˈfɛdəˌret |-d -ɪd |-tive -ɪv
confederation kənˌfɛdəˈreʃən

Those words below in which the a *sound is spelt* o *are often pronounced with* ɒ *in E and S*

confer kən'fɜ˞; ES -'fɜ(r, -'fɜ˞; |-red -d
conferee ˌkɑnfə'ri
conference 'kɑnfərəns |-s -ɪz
confess kən'fɛs |-es -ɪz |-ed -t |-edly -ɪdlɪ
Confessio Amantis kən'fɛʃɪˌo ə'mæntɪs
confession kən'fɛʃən |-al -|̩ |-ary -ˌɛrɪ
confessor kən'fɛsɚ; ES -'fɛsə(r
confetti kən'fɛtɪ (*It* kon'fɛtti)
confidant, -nte ˌkɑnfə'dænt, 'kɑnfəˌdænt
confide kən'faɪd |-fided -'faɪdɪd
confidence 'kɑnfədəns |-s -ɪz |-dent -dənt
confidential ˌkɑnfə'dɛnʃəl |-ly -ɪ
configuration kənˌfɪgjə'reʃən |-al -|̩ |-ally -|ɪ
confine *n* 'kɑnfaɪn
confine *v* kən'faɪn |-d -d |-dly -ɪdlɪ
confirm kən'fɜ˞m; ES -'fɜm, -'fɜ˞m; |-ed -d
    |-edly -ɪdlɪ |-atory -əˌtorɪ, -əˌtɔrɪ; S -əˌtorɪ
confirmation ˌkɑnfɚ'meʃən; ES ˌkɑnfə-
confirmative kən'fɜ˞mətɪv; ES -'fɜm-, -'fɜ˞m-
confiscate 'kɑnfɪsˌket, kən'fɪsket |-d -ɪd
confiscation ˌkɑnfɪs'keʃən
confiscatory kən'fɪskəˌtorɪ, -ˌtɔrɪ; S -ˌtorɪ
confiture 'kɑnfɪˌtʃur; ES -ˌtʃuə(r
conflagrate 'kɑnfləˌgret |-grated -ˌgretɪd
conflagration ˌkɑnflə'greʃən
conflate kən'flet |-d -ɪd |-tion -'fleʃən
conflict *n* 'kɑnflɪkt
conflict *v* kən'flɪkt |-ed -ɪd |-ction -kʃən
confluence 'kɑnfluəns, -flɪu- |-s -ɪz |-ent -ənt
conflux 'kɑnflʌks |-es -ɪz
conform kən'fɔrm; ES -'fɔəm; |-ed -d
conformable kən'fɔrməb|̩; ES -'fɔəm-; |-bly
    -blɪ
conformance kən'fɔrməns; ES -'fɔəm-; |-s -ɪz
conformation ˌkɑnfɔr'meʃən; ES -fɔə-
conformist kən'fɔrmɪst; ES -'fɔəm-
conformity kən'fɔrmətɪ; ES -'fɔəm-
confound kɑn'faund, kən-; '*damn*' 'kɑn'faund
    |-ed -ɪd
confrere 'kɑnfrɛr; ES -frɛə(r
confront kən'frʌnt |-ed -ɪd
Confucian kən'fjuʃən, -'fru- |-ism -ˌɪzəm
Confucius kən'fjuʃəs, -'fru- |-'s -ɪz
confuse kən'fjuz, -'fruz |-s -ɪz |-d -d |-dly
    -ɪdlɪ, -dlɪ
confusion kən'fjuʒən, -'fruʒən
confutation ˌkɑnfju'teʃən, -fru-
confutative kən'fjutətɪv, -'fru-

confute kən'fjut, -'frut |-d -ɪd
Congaree ˌkɑŋgə'ri
congé 'kɑnʒe (*Fr* kõ'ʒe)
congeal kən'dʒil |-ed -d
congee 'kɑndʒi
congener 'kɑndʒɪnɚ; ES -nə(r
congenial kən'dʒinjəl |-ly -ɪ
congeniality kənˌdʒinɪ'ælətɪ, -ˌdʒinjɪ'ælətɪ,
    -ˌdʒin'jælətɪ
congenital kən'dʒɛnət|̩ |-ly -ɪ
conger, C- 'kɑŋgɚ; ES 'kɑŋgə(r
congeries kɑn'dʒɪriz, -'dʒɪrɪˌiz
congest kən'dʒɛst |-ed -ɪd |-ive -ɪv |-stion
    -stʃən
conglobate kɑn'globet, 'kɑŋgloˌbet
conglomerate *n, adj* kən'glɑmərɪt; -'glɑmrɪt
conglomerate *v* kən'glɑməˌret |-rated -ˌretɪd
conglomeration kənˌglɑmə'reʃən
Congo 'kɑŋgo
congratulate kən'grætʃəˌlet |-lated -ˌletɪd
congratulation kənˌgrætʃə'leʃən
congratulatory kən'grætʃələˌtorɪ, -ˌtɔrɪ; S
    -ˌtorɪ
congregate 'kɑŋgrɪˌget |-gated -ˌgetɪd
congregation ˌkɑŋgrɪ'geʃən |-al -|̩, -ʃnəl |-ally
    -|ɪ, -ʃnəlɪ
Congregational ˌkɑŋgrɪ'geʃən|̩, -ʃnəl |-ism
    -ˌɪzəm |-ist -ɪst
congress 'kɑŋgrəs, -ɪs |-es ɪz |-ed -t
congressional kən'grɛʃən|̩, -ʃnəl |-ly -ɪ
congressman 'kɑŋgrəsmən |-men -mən
congresswoman 'kɑŋgrəsˌwumən, -ˌwu- |-men
    -ˌwɪmɪn, -ən
Congreve 'kɑngriv, 'kɑŋ-
congruence 'kɑŋgruəns, 'kɑnˌgruəns, -ˌgrɪu-
    |-s -ɪz |-cy -ɪ |-ent -ənt
congruity kən'gruətɪ, -'grɪu-
congruous 'kɑŋgruəs
conic 'kɑnɪk |-al -|̩ |-ally -|ɪ, -ɪklɪ
conifer 'konəfɚ, 'kɑn-; ES -fə(r
coniferous ko'nɪfərəs
Coningsby 'kʌnɪŋzbɪ
Coniston 'kɑnɪstən
conjectural kən'dʒɛktʃərəl |-ly -ɪ
conjecture kən'dʒɛktʃɚ; ES -tʃə(r; |-d -d
    |-ring -'dʒɛktʃərɪŋ, -'dʒɛktʃrɪŋ
conjoin kən'dʒɔɪn |-ed -d |-edly -ɪdlɪ |-t -t
conjugal 'kɑndʒug|̩ |-ly -ɪ

Key: *See in full* §§3–47. bee bi |pity 'pɪtɪ (§6) |rate ret |yet jɛt |sang sæŋ |angry 'æŋ·grɪ
|bath bæθ; E baθ (§10) |ah ɑ |far fɑr |watch wɑtʃ, wɒtʃ (§12) |jaw dʒɔ |gorge gɔrdʒ |go go

Those words below in which the ɑ sound is spelt o are often pronounced with ɒ in E and S

conjugality ˌkʌndʒuˈgæləti
conjugate *n, adj* ˈkʌndʒugɪt, -ˌget
conjugate *v* ˈkʌndʒəˌget |-gated -ˌgetɪd
conjugation ˌkʌndʒəˈgeʃən
conjunct kənˈdʒʌŋkt (ˈconˌjunct ˈverb)
conjunction kənˈdʒʌŋkʃən |-tive -tɪv
conjunctiva ˌkʌndʒʌŋkˈtaɪvə
conjunctivitis kənˌdʒʌŋktəˈvaɪtɪs
conjuncture kənˈdʒʌŋktʃɚ; ES -tʃə(r; |-ral -əl
conjuration ˌkʌndʒuˈreʃən
conjure *'juggle'* ˈkʌndʒɚ, ˈkʌn-; ES -dʒə(r; |-d -d
conjure *'implore'* kənˈdʒur, -ˈdʒɪur; ES -ə(r; |-d -d
conjurer, -or *'juggler'* ˈkʌndʒərɚ, ˈkʌn-; ES -rə(r
conjurer, -or *'petitioner'* kənˈdʒurɚ, -ˈdʒɪu-; ES -rə(r
conjuror *'coswearer'* kɑnˈdʒurɚ, -ˈdʒɪu-; ES -rə(r
Conkling ˈkʌŋklɪŋ
Connacht ˈkʌnəxt, -nət
Connaught ˈkʌnɔt
Conneaut ˈkʌnɪˌɔt
connect kəˈnɛkt |-ed -ɪd |-ible, -able -əbļ
Connecticut kəˈnɛtɪkət—*The Brit pron.* kəˈnɛktɪkət, *based on the current erroneous spelling, has no Am currency.*
connection, -nexion kəˈnɛkʃən |-ctive -ktɪv
Connelly ˈkʌnļɪ
conning ˈkʌnɪŋ
conniption kəˈnɪpʃən
connivance kəˈnaɪvəns |-s -ɪz |-cy -ɪ |-ant -ənt
connive kəˈnaɪv |-nived -ˈnaɪvd |-vent -ənt
connoisseur ˌkʌnəˈsɝ; ES -ˈsɜ(r, -ˈsɝ; (*Fr* connaisseur könɛˈsœːr)
connotation ˌkʌnəˈteʃən
connotative ˈkʌnəˌtetɪv, kəˈnotətɪv
connote kəˈnot |-noted -ˈnotɪd
connubial kəˈnubɪəl, -ˈnɪub-, -ˈnjub- |-ly -ɪ
conoid ˈkonɔɪd
conquer ˈkʌŋkɚ, ˈkɒŋkɚ, ˈkɔŋkɚ; ES -kɚ; |-ed -d |-ing -kərɪŋ, -krɪŋ |-or -ɚ; ES -ə(r
conquest ˈkʌŋkwɛst, ˈkɒŋ-
conquistador kɑnˈkwɪstəˌdɔr; ES -ˌdɔə(r
Conrad, -e ˈkʌnræd
Conroe ˈkʌnro
consanguine kʌnˈsæŋgwɪn

consanguineous ˌkʌnsæŋˈgwɪnɪəs |-nity -nətɪ
conscience ˈkʌnʃəns |-s -ɪz
conscientious ˌkʌnʃɪˈɛnʃəs, ˌkʌnsɪ-
conscionable ˈkʌnʃənəbļ |-bly -blɪ
conscious ˈkʌnʃəs
conscribe kənˈskraɪb |-scribed -ˈskraɪbd
conscript *n, adj* ˈkʌnskrɪpt
conscript *v* kənˈskrɪpt |-ed -ɪd |-ption -pʃən
consecrate ˈkʌnsɪˌkret |-crated -ˌkretɪd
consecration ˌkʌnsɪˈkreʃən
consecutive kənˈsɛkjətɪv
consensus kənˈsɛnsəs |-suses -səsɪz
consent kənˈsɛnt |-ed -ɪd |-ient -ˈsɛnʃənt
consequence ˈkʌnsəˌkwɛns |-s -ɪz |-quent -ˌkwɛnt
consequential ˌkʌnsəˈkwɛnʃəl |-ly -ɪ
consequentiality ˌkʌnsəˌkwɛnʃɪˈælətɪ
conservable kənˈsɝvəbļ; ES -ˈsɜv-, -ˈsɝv-
conservancy kənˈsɝvənsɪ; ES -ˈsɜv-, -ˈsɝv-
conservation ˌkʌnsɚˈveʃən; ES ˌkʌnsə-
conservatism kənˈsɝvəˌtɪzəm; ES -ˈsɜv-, -ˈsɝv-
conservative kənˈsɝvətɪv; ES -ˈsɜv-, -ˈsɝv-
conservatoire kənˌsɝvəˈtwar; ES -ˌsɜvə-ˈtwaː(r, -ˌsɝvəˈtwaː(r; (*Fr* kõservaˈtwaːr)
conservator *'preserver'* ˈkʌnsɚˌvetɚ, kənˈsɝvətɚ, *bank officer* kənˈsɝvətɚ; ES ˈkʌnsəˌvetə(r, kənˈsɜvətə(r, kənˈsɝvətə(r
conservatory kənˈsɝvəˌtorɪ, -ˌtɔrɪ; ES kənˈsɝvəˌtorɪ, -ˈsɜv-, E+-ˌtɔrɪ
conserve *n* ˈkʌnsɝv, kənˈsɝv; ES -ɜv, -ɝv
conserve *v* kənˈsɝv; ES -ˈsɜv, -ˈsɝv; |-d -d
Conshohocken ˌkʌnʃəˈhɑkən
consider kənˈsɪdɚ; ES -ˈsɪdə(r; |-ed -d |-ing -ˈsɪdərɪŋ, -ˈsɪdrɪŋ
considerable kənˈsɪdərəbļ, -ˈsɪdrəbļ |-bly -blɪ
considerate kənˈsɪdərɪt, -ˈsɪdrɪt
consideration kənˌsɪdəˈreʃən
consign kənˈsaɪn |-ed -d
consignee ˌkʌnsaɪˈni, -sɪˈni
consigner kənˈsaɪnɚ; ES -ˈsaɪnə(r
consignment kənˈsaɪnmənt
consignor kənˈsaɪnɚ; ES -ˈsaɪnə(r; (ˌconsignˈee & ˌconsignˈor)
consist kənˈsɪst |-ed -ɪd
consistence kənˈsɪstəns |-cy -ɪ |-ent -ənt
consistory kənˈsɪstərɪ, -ˈsɪstrɪ
consociate *n, adj* kənˈsoʃɪt, -ʃɪˌet

|full fʊl |tooth tuθ |further ˈfɝðɚ; ES ˈfɜðə |custom ˈkʌstəm |while hwaɪl |how haʊ |toy tɔɪ
|using ˈjuzɪŋ |fuse fjuz, fɪuz |dish dɪʃ |vision ˈvɪʒən |Eden ˈidṇ |cradle ˈkredļ |keep 'em ˈkipṃ

Those words below in which the ɑ sound is spelt o are often pronounced with ɒ in E and S

consociate *v* kənˈsoʃɪˌet |-ated -ˌetɪd

consociation kənˌsosɪˈeʃən, -ˌsoʃɪ-

consol ˈkɑnsɑl, kənˈsɑl |-s -z

consolable kənˈsoləbļ |-bly -blɪ

consolation ˌkɑnsəˈleʃən

consolatory kənˈsɑləˌtorɪ, -ˌtɔrɪ; S -ˌtorɪ

console *n* ˈkɑnsol

console *v* kənˈsol |-soled -ˈsold

consolidate kənˈsɑləˌdet |-dated -ˌdetɪd

consolidation kənˌsɑləˈdeʃən

consommé ˌkɑnsəˈme

consonance ˈkɑnsənəns |-cy -ɪ |-ant -ənt

consonantal ˌkɑnsəˈnæntļ |-ly -ɪ

consonantly ˈkɑnsənəntlɪ

consort *n* ˈkɑnsɔrt; ES -sɔət

consort *v* kənˈsɔrt; ES -ˈsɔət; |-ed -ɪd

consortium kənˈsɔrʃɪəm; ES -ˈsɔəʃ-; |-ia -ɪə

conspectus kənˈspɛktəs |-es -ɪz

conspicuous kənˈspɪkjʊəs

conspirator kənˈspɪrətɚ; ES -tə(r; |-acy -əsɪ

conspiratorial kənˌspɪrəˈtorɪəl, -ˈtɔr-; S -ˈtor-; |-ly -ɪ

conspire kənˈspaɪr; ES -ˈspaɪə(r; |-d -d

conspirer kənˈspaɪrɚ; ES -ˈspaɪrə(r

constable ˈkɑnstəbļ, ˈkʌn- —*The sp. pron. is now more freq. than the traditional one; see next.*

Constable ˈkʌnstəbļ

constabulary kənˈstæbjəˌlɛrɪ

Constance ˈkɑnstəns |-'s -ɪz

constancy ˈkɑnstənsɪ |-tant -tənt

Constantine ˈkɑnstənˌtaɪn, -ˌtin

Constantinople ˌkɑnstæntəˈnopļ, -stæntṇˈopļ

constellation ˌkɑnstəˈleʃən

consternate ˈkɑnstɚˌnet; ES ˈkɑnstə-; |-d -ɪd

consternation ˌkɑnstɚˈneʃən; ES ˌkɑnstə-

constipate ˈkɑnstəˌpet |-pated -ˌpetɪd

constipation ˌkɑnstəˈpeʃən

constituency kənˈstɪtʃʊənsɪ |-ent -ənt

constitute ˈkɑnstəˌtjut, -ˌtrut, -ˌtut |-d -ɪd

constitution ˌkɑnstəˈtjuʃən, -ˈtru-, -ˈtu- |-al -ļ |-ally -ļɪ

constitutionality ˌkɑnstəˌtjuʃənˈælətɪ -ˌtrɪu-, -ˌtu-

constitutive ˈkɑnstəˌtjutɪv, -ˌtrɪu-, -ˌtu

constrain kənˈstren |-ed -d |-edly -ɪdlɪ |-t -t

constrict kənˈstrɪkt |-ed -ɪd |-or -ɚ; ES -ə(r

constriction kənˈstrɪkʃən |-tive -tɪv

construable kənˈstruəbļ, -ˈstrɪu-

construct *adj* kənˈstrʌkt (ˈconˌstruct ˈstate)

construct *n* ˈkɑnstrʌkt

construct *v* kənˈstrʌkt |-ed -ɪd

construction kənˈstrʌkʃən |-al -ļ |-ally -ļɪ |-tive -tɪv

construe kənˈstru, -ˈstrɪu |-d -d—*in Shak.* conster ˈkɑnstɚ

consubstantial ˌkɑnsəbˈstænʃəl |-ly -ɪ

consubstantiality ˌkɑnsəbˌstænʃɪˈælətɪ

consubstantiate ˌkɑnsəbˈstænʃɪˌet |-ed -ɪd

consubstantiation ˌkɑnsəbˌstænʃɪˈeʃən

consuetude ˈkɑnswɪˌtjud, -ˌtrud, -ˌtud

consuetudinary ˌkɑnswɪˈtjudṇˌɛrɪ, -ˈtrud-, -ˈtud-

consul ˈkɑnsļ |-ship -ˌʃɪp

consular ˈkɑnsļɚ, ˈkɑnsjələ; ES -ə(r

consulate ˈkɑnsļɪt, ˈkɑnsjəlɪt

consult *n* ˈkɑnsʌlt, kənˈsʌlt

consult *v* kənˈsʌlt |-ed -ɪd |-ant -ṇt

consultation ˌkɑnsļˈteʃən

consultative kənˈsʌltətɪv

consultatory kənˈsʌltəˌtorɪ, -ˌtɔrɪ; S -ˌtorɪ

consultory kənˈsʌltərɪ

consumable kənˈsuməbļ, -ˈsɪum-, -ˈsjum-

consume kənˈsum, -ˈsɪum, -ˈsjum |-d -d |-dly -ɪdlɪ

consumer kənˈsumɚ, -ˈsɪumɚ, -ˈsjumɚ; ES -ə(r

consummate *adj* kənˈsʌmɪt

consummate *v* ˈkɑnsəˌmet |-mated -ˌmetɪd

consummation ˌkɑnsəˈmeʃən

consumption kənˈsʌmpʃən |-tive -tɪv

contact ˈkɑntækt |-ed -ɪd

contagion kənˈtedʒən |-gious -dʒəs

contain kənˈten |-ed -d

contaminate kənˈtæməˌnet |-nated -ˌnetɪd

contamination kənˌtæməˈneʃən

contemn kənˈtɛm |-ed -d |-edly -nɪdlɪ

contemnible kənˈtɛmnəbļ |-bly -blɪ

contemner kənˈtɛmɚ; ES -ˈtɛmə(r

contemnor kənˈtɛmnɚ; ES -ˈtɛmnə(r

contemplable kənˈtɛmpləbļ

contemplate ˈkɑntəmˌplet, kənˈtɛmplet |-d -ɪd

contemplation ˌkɑntəmˈpleʃən

contemplative ˈkɑntəmˌpletɪv, kənˈtɛmplətɪv

contemporaneity kənˌtɛmpərəˈniətɪ

contemporaneous kənˌtɛmpəˈreniəs

Key: See in full §§3–47. bee bi |pity ˈpɪt (§6) |rate ret |yet jɛt |sang sæŋ |angry ˈæŋ·grɪ |bath bæθ; E baθ (§10) |ah ɑ |far fɑr |watch wɑtʃ. wɒtʃ (§12) |jaw dʒɔ |gorge gɔrdʒ |go go

Those words below in which the ɑ *sound is spelt* o *are often pronounced with* ɒ *in E and S*

contemporary kən'tɛmpə‚rɛrɪ

contempt kən'tɛmpt

contemptible kən'tɛmptəbl̩ |-bly -blɪ

contemptuous kən'tɛmptʃʊəs

contend kən'tɛnd |-ed -ɪd

content *n 'satisfaction'* kən'tɛnt, *'what is contained'* 'kantɛnt, kən'tɛnt

content *adj, v* kən'tɛnt |-ed -ɪd

contention kən'tɛnʃən |-al -l̩ |-tious -ʃəs

conterminous kən'tɝmənəs; ES -'tɜm-, -'tɝm-

contest *n* 'kantɛst

contest *v* kən'tɛst |-ed -ɪd |-ant -ənt

context 'kantɛkst

contextual kən'tɛkstʃʊəl, kan- |-ly -ɪ

contexture kən'tɛkstʃɝ, kan-; ES -'tɛkstʃə(r

contiguity ‚kantɪ'gjuətɪ, -'gɪu-

contiguous kən'tɪgjʊəs

continence 'kantənəns |-cy -ɪ |-nent -nənt

continental ‚kantə'nɛntl̩ |-ly -ɪ

contingence kən'tɪndʒəns |-cy -ɪ |-gent -dʒənt

continual kən'tɪnjʊəl |-ly -ɪ

continuance kən'tɪnjʊəns |-s -ɪz |-ant -ənt

continuation kən‚tɪnjʊ'eʃən

continue kən'tɪnjʊ |-d -d |-dly -jʊdlɪ

continuity ‚kantə'nuətɪ, -'nɪu-, -'nju-

continuous kən'tɪnjʊəs |-nuum -njʊəm |-nua -njʊə

contort kən'tɔrt; ES -'tɔət; |-ed -ɪd

contortion kən'tɔrʃən; ES -'tɔəʃən

contour 'kantʊr; ES -tʊə(r; |-ed -d

contra 'kantrə

contraband 'kantrə‚bænd |-age -ɪdʒ |-ist -ɪst

contrabandism 'kantrəbænd‚ɪzəm

contrabass 'kantrə‚bes |-es -ɪz

contraception ‚kantrə'sɛpʃən |-tive -tɪv

contraclockwise ‚kantrə'klak‚waɪz

contract *n* 'kantrækt

contract *v 'shrink'* kən'trækt, *'make a contract'*+'kantrækt |-ed -ɪd

contractible kən'træktəbl̩ |-bly -blɪ

contractile kən'træktl̩, -tɪl

contractility ‚kantræk'tɪlətɪ

contraction kən'trækʃən |-tive -tɪv

contractor 'kantræktɝ, kən'træktɝ; ES -tə(r

contractual kən'træktʃʊəl |-ly -ɪ

contradict ‚kantrə'dɪkt |-ed -ɪd

contradiction ‚kantrə'dɪkʃən |-tory -tərɪ, -trɪ

contradistinction ‚kantrədɪ'stɪŋkʃən |-tive -tɪv

contraindication ‚kantrə‚ɪndə'keʃən

contralto kən'trælto

contraposition ‚kantrəpə'zɪʃən

contraption kən'træpʃən

contrapuntal ‚kantrə'pʌntl̩ |-ly -ɪ

contrariety ‚kantrə'raɪətɪ

contrarily 'kantrərəlɪ, *esp. if emph.* kən-'trɛrəlɪ, -'trer-

contrarious kən'trɛrɪəs, -'trer-

contrariwise 'kantrɛrɪ‚waɪz

contrary *'opposite'* 'kantrɛrɪ; *'perverse'* 'kantrɛrɪ, kən'trɛrɪ, -'trerɪ

contrast *n* 'kantræst

contrast *v* kən'træst |-ed -ɪd

contravene ‚kantrə'vin |-vened -'vind

contravention ‚kantrə'vɛnʃən

contredanse *Fr* kõtrə'dãːs

contretemps *Fr* kõtrə'tã

contribute kən'trɪbjut |-d -bjətɪd

contribution ‚kantrə'bjuʃən, -'brɪuʃən

contributor kən'trɪbjətɝ; ES -tə(r

contributory kən'trɪbjə‚torɪ, -‚tɔrɪ; S -‚torɪ

contrite 'kantraɪt, kən'traɪt ('con‚trite 'heart, 'hearts con'trite)

contrition kən'trɪʃən

contrivance kən'traɪvəns |-s -ɪz |-cy -ɪ

contrive kən'traɪv |-d -d

control kən'trol |-trolled -'trold

controllable kən'troləbl̩ |-bly -blɪ

controller kən'trolɝ; ES -'trolə(r; |-ship -‚ʃɪp

controversial ‚kantrə'vɝʃəl, -sɪəl; ES -'vɝ-, -'vɝ-; |-ly -ɪ

controversy 'kantrə‚vɝsɪ; ES -‚vɝsɪ, -‚vɝsɪ

controvert 'kantrə‚vɝt, ‚kantrə'vɝt; ES -ɝt; |-ed -ɪd

controvertible ‚kantrə'vɝtəbl̩; ES -'vɝt-, -'vɝt-; *acct+*'contro‚vertible |-bly -blɪ

contumacious ‚kantjʊ'meʃəs, ‚kantʊ-

contumacy 'kantjuməsɪ, 'kantʊ-

contumelious ‚kantjʊ'milɪəs, ‚kantʊ-

contumely 'kantjʊməlɪ, 'kantʊ-, -‚milɪ, kən'tjuməlɪ, -'trɪu-, -'tu- —*Only a bookword. Formerly* 'kantjʊ‚milɪ, *as in Chapman and probably Shak. Hood has* kən-'tjumɪlɪ (*rime gloomily*).

contuse kən'tjuz, -'trɪuz, -'tuz |-s -ɪz |-d -d

|full fʊl |tooth tuθ |further 'fɝðɝ; ES 'fɝðə |custom 'kʌstəm |while hwaɪl |how haʊ |toy tɔɪ
|using 'juzɪŋ |fuse fjuz, frɪuz |dish dɪʃ |vision 'vɪʒən |Eden 'idn̩ |cradle 'kredl̩ |keep 'em 'kipm̩

Those words below in which the ɑ sound is spelt o are often pronounced with ɒ in E and S

contusion kən'tjuʒən, -'truʒ-, -'tuʒ-
conundrum kə'nʌndrəm
convalesce ˌkanvə'lɛs |-s -ɪz |-d -t
convalescence ˌkanvə'lɛsn̩s |-cy -ɪ |-scent -sn̩t
convection kən'vɛkʃən |-al -l̩
convenance 'kanvəˌnans |-s -ɪz (*Fr* kõv'nã:s)
convene kən'vin |-vened -'vind
convenience kən'vinjəns |-s -ɪz |-ient -jənt
convent 'kanvent
conventical kən'vɛntɪkl̩ |-ly -ɪ
conventicle kən'vɛntɪkl̩ |-d -d
convention kən'vɛnʃən |-al -l̩, -ʃnəl |-ally -l̩ɪ, -ʃnəlɪ
conventionalism kən'vɛnʃənl̩ˌɪzəm, -ʃnəl- |-ist -ɪst
conventionality kənˌvɛnʃən'ælətɪ
conventionalize kən'vɛnʃənl̩ˌaɪz, -ʃnəl- |-s -ɪz |-d -d
conventual kən'vɛntʃʊəl |-ly -ɪ
converge kən'vɝˑdʒ; ES -'vɝˑdʒ, -'vɝˑdʒ; |-s -ɪz |-d -d
convergence kən'vɝˑdʒəns; ES -'vɝˑdʒ-, -'vɝˑdʒ-; |-cy -ɪ |-gent -dʒənt
conversance 'kanvɝsn̩s, kən'vɝˑsn̩s; ES -vəs-, -'vɝˑs-, -'vɝˑs-; |-cy -ɪ |-sant -sn̩t
conversation ˌkanvɝ'seʃən; ES ˌkanvə-; |-al -l̩ |-ally -l̩ɪ
conversationalist ˌkanvɝ'seʃənl̩ɪst, -ʃnəl-; ES ˌkanvə-
converse *n* 'kanvɝs; ES -vɝs, -vɝs; |-s -ɪz
converse *adj* kən'vɝs; ES -'vɝs, -'vɝs; ('conˌverse 'wind)
converse *v* kən'vɝs; ES -'vɝs, -'vɝs; |-s -ɪz |-d -t
conversion kən'vɝʃən, -ʒən; ES -'vɝ-, -'vɝ-
convert *n* 'kanvɝt; ES -vɝt, -vɝt
convert *v* kən'vɝt; ES -'vɝt, -'vɝt; |-ed -ɪd
convertibility kənˌvɝtə'bɪlətɪ; ES -ˌvɝt-, -ˌvɝt-
convertible kən'vɝtəbl̩; ES -'vɝt-, -'vɝt-; |-bly -blɪ
convex *adj* kan'vɛks, kən- ('conˌvex 'surface)
convex *n, v* 'kanvɛks |-es -ɪz |-ed -t, *v*+ kən'vɛks
convexity kən'vɛksətɪ
convey kən've |-ed -d |-ance -əns |-ances -ənsɪz

convict *n* 'kanvɪkt
convict *v* kən'vɪkt |-ed -ɪd |-ction -kʃən
convince kən'vɪns |-s -ɪz |-d -t |-dly -ɪdlɪ
convivial kən'vɪvɪəl |-ly -ɪ
conviviality kənˌvɪvɪ'ælətɪ
convocation ˌkanvə'keʃən |-al -l̩ |-ally -l̩ɪ
convoke kən'vok |-voked -'vokt
convolute 'kanvəˌlut, -ˌlɪut |-d -ɪd
convolution ˌkanvə'luʃən, -'lɪuʃən, -vl̩'juʃən
convolvulus, C- kən'valvjələs |-es -ɪz |-li -ˌlaɪ
convoy *n* 'kanvɔɪ
convoy *v* kən'vɔɪ |-ed -d
convulse kən'vʌls |-s -ɪz |-d -t |-dly -ɪdlɪ
convulsion kən'vʌlʃən |-sive -sɪv
Conway 'kanwe
Conwell 'kanwɛl
cony 'konɪ, 'kʌnɪ—*When the word was popular, it was pron.* 'kʌnɪ; *since it became a book-word, sp. pron. has prevailed.*
conycatcher 'konɪˌkætʃɚ, 'kʌnɪ-; ES -ˌkætʃə(r
coo ku |cooed kud
cook kʊk |cooked kʊkt |-ery -ərɪ, -rɪ |-y, -ie -ɪ
cool kul |cooled kuld
Cooley 'kulɪ
cool-headed 'kul'hɛdɪd ('cool-ˌheaded 'move)
Coolidge 'kulɪdʒ |-'s -ɪz
coolie, -ly 'kulɪ
coolly 'kulɪ, 'kullɪ
coomb, coombe, coom '*valley*' kum
coon kun |cooned kund
co-op ko'ap, 'koˌap
coop kup, kʊp; S kʊp, kup; |-ed -t
cooper, C- 'kupɚ, 'kʊpɚ; E -pə(r; S 'kupə(r, 'kup-; |-ed -d |-ing -pərɪŋ, -prɪŋ
co-operate *adj* ko'apərɪt, -'aprɪt
co-operate *v* ko'apəˌret |-rated -ˌretɪd
co-operation koˌapə'reʃən, ˌkoapə-
co-operative ko'apəˌretɪv, -'aprətɪv
Cooperstown 'kupɚzˌtaʊn, 'kʊp-; E -pəz-; S 'kupəz-, 'kup-
co-opt ko'apt |-opted -'aptɪd
co-ordinate, *n, adj* ko'ɔrdn̩ɪt, -ˌet; ES -'ɔəd-
co-ordinate *v* ko'ɔrdn̩ˌet; ES -'ɔəd-; |-d -ɪd
co-ordination koˌɔrdn̩'eʃən; ES -ˌɔədn̩'eʃən
co-ordinative ko'ɔrdn̩ˌetɪv; ES -'ɔədn̩ˌetɪv
Coos *NH* ko'as, 'koas; *Oreg* kus
coot kut |cooted 'kutɪd
cop kap |copped kapt
copal 'kopl̩, 'kopæl

Key: *See in full §§3–47.* bee bi |pity 'pɪtɪ (§6) |rate ret |yet jɛt |sang sæŋ |angry 'æŋ·grɪ |bath bæθ; E baθ (§10) |ah ɑ |far fɑr |watch watʃ, wɒtʃ (§12) |jaw dʒɔ |gorge gɔrdʒ |go go

Those words below in which the ɑ *sound is spelt* o *are often pronounced with* ɒ *in E and S*

coparcenary ko'pɑrsn̩ˌɛrɪ; ES -'pɑːs-, E+ -'pɑːs-

coparcener ko'pɑrsn̩ɚ; ES -'pɑːsn̩ə(r, E+ -'pɑːs-

copartner ko'pɑrtnɚ; ES -'pɑːtnə(r, E+ -'pɑːt-

cope kop |coped kopt

copeck, -pec 'kopɛk

Copeland 'koplənd

Copenhagen ˌkopən'hegən (*Dan* ˌkøpn̩'haʊn)

Copernicus ko'pɝnɪkəs; ES -'pɜn-, -'pɝn-; |-'s -ɪz |-can -kən

copestone 'kopˌston

Cophetua ko'fɛtʃʊə

Copiah kə'paɪə, ko-

copier 'kapɪɚ; ES 'kapɪ·ə(r

coping 'kopɪŋ

copious 'kopɪəs

Coplay 'kaplɪ |Copley 'kaplɪ

copper 'kapɚ; ES 'kapə(r; |-ed -d |-ing 'kapərɪŋ, 'kaprɪŋ

copperas 'kapərəs, 'kaprəs

Copperfield 'kapɚˌfild; ES 'kapə-

copperhead, C- 'kapɚˌhɛd; ES 'kapə-

copperplate '*engraving*' 'kapɚˌplet; ES 'kapə-

copperplate '*engrave*' 'kapɚˌplet; ES 'kapə-; |-d -ɪd

copper-plate '*plate with copper*' 'kapɚ'plet; ES 'kapə-; |-d -ɪd ('copper-ˌplated 'medal)

coppersmith 'kapɚˌsmɪθ; ES 'kapə-; |-ths -θs

coppice 'kapɪs |-s -ɪz |-d -t

copra 'kaprə

copse kaps |copses 'kapsɪz |copsed kapst

Copt kapt |Coptic 'kaptɪk

copula 'kapjələ

copulate *adj* 'kapjəlɪt

copulate *v* 'kapjəˌlet |-lated -ˌletɪd

copulation ˌkapjə'leʃən |-tive 'kapjəˌletɪv

copy 'kapɪ |copied 'kapɪd |-pyist -ɪst

copybook 'kapɪˌbʊk

copyhold 'kapɪˌhold

copyright 'kapɪˌraɪt |-ed -ɪd

coquet ko'kɛt |-quetted -'kɛtɪd

coquetry 'kokɪtrɪ, ko'kɛtrɪ

coquette ko'kɛt |-quetted -'kɛtɪd

Coquille ko'kil

Cora 'korə, 'kɔrə; S 'korə

coracle 'kɔrəkl̩, 'kar-, 'kɒr-

coral 'kɔrəl, 'kar-, 'kɒr-, 'kor- |-ed -d

Coran ko'ran, -'ræn

Coraopolis ˌkorɪ'apl̩ɪs, -plɪs, ˌkorə'ˀap-, ˌkɔr-; S ˌkor-

corbel 'kɔrbl̩; ES 'kɔəbl̩; |-ed -d

corbie 'kɔrbɪ; ES 'kɔəbɪ

Corcoran 'kɔrkərən; ES 'kɔəkərən

cord kɔrd; ES kɔəd; |-ed -ɪd |-age -ɪdʒ

Cordelia kɔr'dɪljə; ES kɔə'dɪljə

Cordell kɔr'dɛl; ES kɔə'dɛl ('Cor̩dell 'Hull)

cordial 'kɔrdʒəl; ES 'kɔədʒ-; *Brit* -dɪəl |-ly -ɪ

cordiality kɔr'dʒælətɪ; ES kɔ-; *Brit* -dɪ'æl-

cordillera, C- kɔr'dɪlərə, ˌkɔrdɪl'jɛrə; ES kɔ-, ˌkɔə-; (*Am Sp* ˌkɔrði'jera)

cordite 'kɔrdaɪt

Córdoba 'kɔrdovə; ES 'kɔə-; (*Sp* 'kɔrðoβa)

cordoba 'kɔrdəbə; ES 'kɔə-

cordon 'kɔrdn̩; ES 'kɔədn̩; |-ed -d

Cordova 'kɔrdəvə; ES 'kɔə-; |-n -n— *some US places* Cor'dova

corduroy ˌkɔrdə'rɔɪ; ES ˌkɔədə-; ('cordu̩roy 'road)

cordwain 'kɔrdwen; ES 'kɔəd-; |-er -ɚ; ES -ə(r

cordwood 'kɔrdˌwʊd; ES 'kɔəd-

core kor, kɔr; ES koə(r, E+kɔə(r; |-d -d

Corea ko'riə |-n -n

corelation ˌko·rɪ'leʃən

coreligionist ˌko·rɪ'lɪdʒənɪst

corella kə'rɛlə

Corelli kə'rɛlɪ

coreopsis ˌkorɪ'apsɪs, ˌkɔrɪ-; S ˌkorɪ-

corespondent ˌko·rɪ'spandənt

Corfu 'kɔrfju, -fɪu, kɔr'fu; ES 'kɔə-, kɔə-

Corgi 'kɔrgɪ; ES 'kɔəgɪ

coriander ˌkorɪ'ændɚ, ˌkɔrɪ-; ES ˌkorɪ'ændə(r, E+ˌkɔrɪ-

Corin 'kɔrɪn, 'kar-, 'kɒr-

Corinna kə'rɪnə

Corinth 'kɔrɪnθ, 'kar-, 'kɒr- |-ian kə'rɪnθɪən

Coriolanus ˌkorɪə'lenəs, ˌkar-, ˌkɒr- |-'s -ɪz

Corioles kə'raɪəˌliz, -lɪz |-'s -ɪz |-li -ˌlaɪ

cork, C- kɔrk; ES kɔək; |-ed -t

corival ko'raɪvl̩, kə-

corkscrew 'kɔrkˌskru, -ˌskrɪu; ES 'kɔək-

Corliss 'kɔrlɪs; ES 'kɔəlɪs; |-'s -ɪz

corm kɔrm; ES kɔəm

cormorant 'kɔrmərənt; ES 'kɔəm-

|full fʊl |tooth tuθ |further 'fɝðɚ; ES 'fɜðə |custom 'kʌstəm |while hwaɪl |how haʊ |toy tɔɪ
|using 'juzɪŋ |fuse fjuz, fɪuz |dish dɪʃ |vision 'vɪʒən |Eden 'idn̩ |cradle 'kredl̩ |keep 'em 'kipm̩

corn kɔrn; ES kɔən; |-ed -d |-cake -ˌkek |-cob -ˌkɑb; ES+-ˌkɒb

cornea ˈkɔrnɪə; ES ˈkɔənɪə

Corneille kɔrˈne; ES kɔəˈne (Fr kɔrˈnɛ:j)

cornel ˈkɔrnḷ, -nɛl; ES ˈkɔən-

Cornelia kɔrˈnɪljə, kɚ-; ES kɔəˈnɪljə, kə-

cornelian 'carnelian' kɔrˈnɪljən, kɚ-; ES kɔə-, kə-

Cornelius kɔrˈnɪljəs, kɚ-; ES kɔə-, kə-; |-'s -ɪz

Cornell kɔrˈnɛl; ES kɔəˈnɛl; (ˈCorˌnell ˈcap)

corneous ˈkɔrnɪəs; ES ˈkɔənɪəs

corner ˈkɔrnɚ; ES ˈkɔənə(r; |-ed -d—A dissimilated pron. ˈkɒnɚ is sometimes heard (§121).

cornerstone ˈkɔrnɚˌston; ES ˈkɔənə-

cornerways ˈkɔrnɚˌwez; ES ˈkɔənə-; |-wise -ˌwaɪz

cornet ˈkɔrnɪt, kɔrˈnɛt, musical instr. kɔrˈnɛt; ES ˈkɔə-, kɔə-

cornettist, -netist kɔrˈnɛtɪst; ES kɔə-

corn-flour ˈkɔrnˌflaʊr; ES ˈkɔənˌflaʊə(r

cornflower ˈkɔrnˌflaʊɚ; ES ˈkɔənˌflaʊ·ə(r

cornice ˈkɔrnɪs; ES ˈkɔənɪs; |-s -ɪz |-d -t

Cornish ˈkɔrnɪʃ; ES ˈkɔənɪʃ; |-man, -men -mən

cornstarch ˈkɔrnˌstɑrtʃ, -ˈstɑrtʃ; ES ˈkɔənˌstɑːtʃ, -ˈstɑːtʃ, E+-aːtʃ

cornucopia ˌkɔrnəˈkopɪə; ES ˌkɔənə-; |-n -n

Cornwall ˈkɔrnwɔl, -wəl; ES ˈkɔən-

Cornwallis kɔrnˈwɒlɪs, -ˈwɒl-, -ˈwɑl-; ES kɔən-; |-'s -ɪz

corody ˈkɔrədɪ, ˈkɑr-, ˈkɒr-

corolla kəˈrɑlə; ES+-ˈrɒlə

corollary ˈkɔrəˌlɛrɪ, ˈkɑr-, ˈkɒr-, Brit kə-ˈrɒlərɪ

corona, C- kəˈronə |-s -z |-nae -ni

coronach ˈkɔrənəx, ˈkɑr-, ˈkɒr-

coronal n ˈkɔrənḷ, ˈkɑr-, ˈkɒr-

coronal adj kəˈronḷ, ˈkɔrənḷ, ˈkɑr-, ˈkɒr-; |-ly -ɪ

coronary ˈkɔrəˌnɛrɪ, ˈkɑr-, ˈkɒr-

coronation ˌkɔrəˈneʃən, ˌkɑr-, ˌkɒr-

coroner ˈkɔrənɚ, ˈkɑr-, ˈkɒr-; ES -nə(r

coronet ˈkɔrənɪt, ˈkɑr-, ˈkɒr- |-ed -ɪd, -ˌnɛtɪd

Corot kəˈro

corporal ˈkɔrpərəl, ˈkɔrprəl; ES ˈkɔəp-; |-ly-ɪ

corporality ˌkɔrpəˈrælətɪ; ES ˌkɔəp-

corporate adj ˈkɔrpərɪt, ˈkɔrprɪt; ES ˈkɔəp-

corporate v ˈkɔrpəˌret; ES ˈkɔəp-; |-d -ɪd

corporation ˌkɔrpəˈreʃən; ES ˌkɔəp-

corporeal kɔrˈporɪəl, -ˈpɔr-; ES kəˈporɪəl, E+-ˈpɔrɪəl; |-ly -ɪ

corporeity ˌkɔrpəˈriətɪ; ES ˌkɔəp-

corposant ˈkɔrpəˌzænt; ES ˈkɔəp-

corps kor, kɔr; ES koə(r, E+kɔə(r; |pl -ps -z

corpse kɔrps; ES kɔəps; |-s -ɪz

corpulence ˈkɔrpjələns; ES ˈkɔəp-; |-cy -ɪ |-nt -nt

corpus ˈkɔrpəs; ES ˈkɔəp-; |-es -ɪz |-pora -pərə

Corpus Christi ˈkɔrpəsˈkrɪstɪ; ES ˈkɔəp-; Church +-taɪ

corpuscular kɔrˈpʌskjələ; ES kəˈpʌskjələ(r

corpuscle ˈkɔrpəsḷ, ˈkɔrpʌsḷ; ES ˈkɔəp-

corpus delicti ˈkɔrpəsdɪˈlɪktaɪ; ES ˈkɔəp-

corral kəˈræl |-led -d

correct kəˈrɛkt |-ed -ɪd

correction kəˈrɛkʃən |-tive -tɪv

correctitude kəˈrɛktəˌtjud, -ˌtɪud, -ˌtud

corrector kəˈrɛktɚ; ES -ˈrɛktə(r

Corregidor kəˈrɛgəˌdɔr; ES -ˌdɔə(r; (Am Sp kɔˌrrɛhiˈðɔr)

correlate ˈkɔrəˌlet, ˈkɑr-, ˈkɒr- |-d -ɪd

correlation ˌkɔrəˈleʃən, ˌkɑr-, ˌkɒr-

correlative kəˈrɛlətɪv |-vity kəˌrɛləˈtɪvətɪ

correspond ˌkɔrəˈspɑnd, ˌkɑr-, ˌkɒr-; ES+-ˈspɒnd; |-ed -ɪd |-ence -əns |-ent -ənt

corridor ˈkɔrədɚ, ˈkɑr-, ˈkɒr-, geog.+-ˌdɔr; ES -də(r, -ˌdɔə(r; |-ed -d

corrie ˈkɔrɪ, ˈkɑrɪ, ˈkɒrɪ

Corrigan ˈkɔrəgən, ˈkɑr-, ˈkɒr-

corrigendum ˌkɔrɪˈdʒɛndəm, ˌkɑr-, ˌkɒr- |-da -də

corrigibility ˌkɔrədʒəˈbɪlətɪ, ˌkɑr-, ˌkɒr-

corrigible ˈkɔrədʒəbḷ, ˈkɑr-, ˈkɒr- |-bly -blɪ

corrival kəˈraɪvḷ

corrobboree, -ri n kəˈrɑbərɪ; ES+-ˈrɒb-

corroborant kəˈrɑbərənt; ES+-ˈrɒb-

corroborate adj kəˈrɑbərɪt; ES+-ˈrɒb-

corroborate v kəˈrɑbəˌret; ES+-ˈrɒb-; |-d -ɪd |-tive -tɪv

corroboration kəˌrɑbəˈreʃən; ES+-ˌrɒb-

corroboratory kəˈrɑbərəˌtorɪ, -ˌtɔrɪ; S -ˌtɔrɪ

corroboree, -ri n kəˈrɑbərɪ; ES+-ˈrɒb-

corroboree v kəˈrɑbəˌri |-d -d

corrode kəˈrod |-roded -ˈrodɪd

corrosion kəˈroʒən |-sive -sɪv

corrugate adj ˈkɔrəgɪt, ˈkɔrjə-, ˈkɑr-, ˈkɒr-, -ˌget

Those words below in which the ɑ *sound is spelt* o *are often pronounced with* ɒ *in E and S*

corrugate *v* ˈkɔrəˌget, ˈkɔrjə-, ˈkar-, ˈkɒr-
|-d -ɪd
corrugation ˌkɔrəˈgeʃən, ˌkɔrjə-, ˌkar-, ˌkɒr-
corrupt kəˈrʌpt |-ed -ɪd |-ption -pʃən
corruptibility kəˌrʌptəˈbɪlətɪ
corruptible kəˈrʌptəbļ |-bly -blɪ
Corry ˈkɔrɪ, ˈkarɪ, ˈkɒrɪ
corsage kɔrˈsɑʒ; ES kɔəˈsɑʒ; |-s -ɪz
corsair ˈkɔrsɛr, -sær; E ˈkɔəsɛə(r, ES -sæə(r
corse kɔrs; ES kɔəs; |-s -ɪz
corselet *'armor'* ˈkɔrslɪt; ES ˈkɔəs-; *'under-
garment'* ˌkɔrsļˈɛt; ES ˌkɔəs-
corset ˈkɔrsɪt; ES ˈkɔəsɪt; |-ed -ɪd
Corsica ˈkɔrsɪkə; ES ˈkɔəsɪkə; |-n -n
Corsicana ˌkɔrsɪˈkænə; ES ˌkɔəs-
corslet ˈkɔrslɪt; ES ˈkɔəslɪt
Corson ˈkɔrsņ; ES ˈkɔəsņ
cortege kɔrˈteʒ, -ˈtɛʒ; ES kɔə-; (*Fr* körˈtɛːʒ)
Cortes *Sp & Pg legisl.* ˈkɔrtɪz; ES ˈkɔət-;
(*Sp* ˈkɔrtes, *Pg* ˈkɔrtɛʃ)
Cortes, -ez *Sp soldier* ˈkɔrtɛz; ES ˈkɔətɛz;
(*Sp* kɔrˈtes) |-ʼs -ɪz
cortex ˈkɔrtɛks; ES ˈkɔə-; |-es -ɪz |-tices
-tɪˌsiz
cortez kɔrˈtes; ES kɔə; |-es -ɪz
cortical ˈkɔrtɪkļ; ES ˈkɔə-; |-ly -ɪ
corticate *adj* ˈkɔrtɪkɪt, -ˌket; ES ˈkɔə-;
|-cated -ˌketɪd
Cortland ˈkɔrtlənd, ˈkɔrt-; ES ˈkɔət-, E+
ˈkɔət-
corundum kəˈrʌndəm
coruscant kəˈrʌskənt
coruscate ˈkɔrəsˌket, ˈkar-, ˈkɒr- |-d -ɪd
coruscation ˌkɔrəsˈkeʃən, ˌkar-, ˌkɒr-
Corvallis kɔrˈvælɪs; ES kɔə-; |-ʼs -ɪz
corvée kɔrˈve; ES kɔəˈve; (*Fr* körˈve)
corvette, -vet kɔrˈvɛt; ES kɔəˈvɛt
Corybant ˈkɔrəˌbænt, ˈkar-, ˈkɒr- |-s -s |-es
ˌkɔrəˈbæntiz |-ic ˌkɔrəˈbæntɪk
Corydon ˈkɔrədņ, ˈkar-, ˈkɒr-, -ˌdɑn, -ˌdɒn
Coryell ˌkɔrɪˈɛl, ˌkɔr-; S ˌkɔr-
corymb ˈkɔrɪmb, ˈkar-, ˈkɒr-, -ɪm
coryphaeus ˌkɔrəˈfiəs, ˌkar-, ˌkɒr- |-es -ɪz
|-phaei -ˈfiaɪ
coryphee ˌkɔrəˈfe, ˌkarəˈfe, ˌkɒrəˈfe |-s -z
(*Fr* köriˈfe)
coryza kəˈraɪzə
cose *'kos'* kos

cose *'coze'* koz |coses ˈkozɪz |cosed kozd
cosecant koˈsikənt, -kænt
cosey *'cozy'* ˈkozɪ
Cosgrave ˈkazgrev, ˈkɒz-
Coshocton kəˈʃaktən
cosie *'cozy'* ˈkozɪ
cosignatory koˈsɪgnəˌtorɪ, -ˌtɔrɪ; S -ˌtorɪ
cosine ˈkosaɪn
Cos lettuce ˈkasˌlɛtɪs, ˈkɒs-, -əs
cosmetic kazˈmɛtɪk |-al -ļ |-ally -ļɪ, -ɪklɪ
cosmic ˈkazmɪk |-al -ļ |-ally -ļɪ, -ɪklɪ
cosmogony kazˈmagənɪ, -ˈmɒg-
cosmographic ˌkazməˈgræfɪk |-al -ļ |-ally -lɪ,
-ɪklɪ
cosmography kazˈmagrəfɪ, -ˈmɒg-
cosmology kazˈmalədʒɪ
cosmopolitan ˌkazməˈpalətņ |-ism -ˌɪzəm
cosmopolitanize ˌkazməˈpalətņˌaɪz |-s -ɪz |-d -d
cosmopolite kazˈmapəˌlaɪt
cosmos ˈkazməs, -mas |-es -ɪz
Cossack ˈkasæk, ˈkɒs-, -ək
cosset ˈkasɪt, ˈkɒsɪt |-ed -ɪd
cost kɔst, kɒst
costa ˈkastə |-tae -ti |-tal -tļ |-tally -tļɪ
costard, C- ˈkastəd; ES ˈkastəd
Costa Rica ˈkastəˈrikə, ˈkɒs-, ˈkɔs-, ˈkos-
|-n -n
costermonger ˈkastəˌmʌŋgə, ˈkɒs-; ES
-təˌmʌŋgə(r
costive ˈkastɪv, ˈkɒs-
costly ˈkɔstlɪ, ˈkɒst-
costmary ˈkastˌmɛrɪ, ˈkɒst-, -ˌmærɪ; S
-ˌmærɪ, -ˌmɛrɪ
costrel ˈkastrəl, ˈkɒs-
costume *n* ˈkastjum, ˈkɒs-, -tɪum, -tum
costume *v* kasˈtjum, kɒs-, -ˈtɪum, -ˈtum |-d -d
|-r -ə; ES -ə(r
costumier kasˈtjumɪə; -ˈtɪum-, -ˈtum-; ES
-ɪ·ə(r; (*Fr* köstyˈmje)
cosy *'cozy'* ˈkozɪ
cot kat |cotted ˈkatɪd—*see* cote
cotangent koˈtændʒənt
cotangential ˌkotænˈdʒɛnʃəl
cote kot—cot *& cote are distinct, but related,
words in the oldest English, but have become
confused in spelling.*
cotemporaneous koˌtɛmpəˈrenɪəs, ˈkotɛmpə-
cotemporary koˈtɛmpəˌrɛrɪ

|full fʊl |tooth tuθ |further ˈfɝðə; ES ˈfɝðə |custom ˈkʌstəm |while hwaɪl |how haʊ |toy tɔɪ
|using ˈjuzɪŋ |fuse fjuz, fɪuz |dish dɪʃ |vision ˈvɪʒən |Eden ˈidņ |cradle ˈkredļ |keep ʼem ˈkipm̩

Those words below in which the a sound is spelt o are often pronounced with ɒ in E and S

cotenant ko'tɛnənt |-ancy -ənsɪ

coterie 'kotərɪ

coterminous ko'tɝmənəs; ES -'tɜm-, -'tɝm-

cothurnus ko'θɝnəs; ES -'θɜn-, -'θɝn-; |-ni -naɪ

cotidal ko'taɪdl̩

cotillion, -llon ko'tɪljən

Cotopaxi ˌkotə'pæksɪ (*Am Sp* ˌkoto'pa·hi)

Cotswold 'kɑtswold, -wəld |-s -z

cottage 'kɑtɪdʒ |-s -ɪz |-d -d

cotter, -ar 'kɑtɚ; ES 'kɑtə(r

Cotterell 'kɑtərəl, 'kɑtrəl

cottier 'kɑtɪɚ; ES 'kɑtɪ·ə(r

cotton, C- 'kɑtn̩ |-ed -d

Cottonian kɑ'tonɪən

cottonmouth 'kɑtn̩ˌmaʊθ |-ths -ðz

cottonseed 'kɑtn̩ˌsid

cottontail 'kɑtn̩ˌtel

cottonwood 'kɑtn̩ˌwʊd

Cottrell 'kɑtrəl

cotyledon ˌkɑtl̩'idn̩ |-ous -'idnəs, -'ɛdnəs

couch kaʊtʃ |couches 'kaʊtʃɪz |couched kaʊtʃt

Couch kaʊtʃ, kutʃ |-'s -ɪz

couchant 'kaʊtʃənt

Coudersport 'kaʊdɚzˌport; ES 'kaʊdəzˌpoət, E+-ˌpɔət

Coué ku'e

Coues kaʊz |-'s -ɪz

cougar 'kugɚ; ES 'kugə(r

cough kɔf, kɒf |-ed -t

Coughlin 'kɔglən, 'kɒg-

could *stressed* 'kʊd, ˌkʊd; *unstr.* kəd

couldest 'kʊdɪst

couldn't 'kʊdn̩t, *before some conss.*+'kʊdn̩ ('kʊdn̩'se)—*The pron.* 'kʊdənt *is substandard.*

couldst *stressed* 'kʊdst, ˌkʊdst; *unstr.* kədst

coulee 'kulɪ (*Fr* coulée ku'le)

coulomb, C- ku'lɑm, -'lɒm

coulter, C- 'koltɚ; ES 'koltə(r; |-ed -d

Coulton 'koltn̩

council 'kaʊnsl̩

Council Bluffs 'kaʊnsl̩'blʌfs

councilman 'kaʊnsl̩mən |-men -mən

councilor, -llor 'kaʊnsl̩ɚ, -slɚ; ES -ə(r

counsel 'kaʊnsl̩ |-ed -d |-ing 'kaʊnsl̩ɪŋ, -slɪŋ

counselor, -llor 'kaʊnsl̩ɚ, -slɚ; ES -ə(r

count kaʊnt |counted 'kaʊntɪd

countenance 'kaʊntənəns |-s -ɪz |-d -t

counter 'kaʊntɚ; ES 'kaʊntə(r; |-ed -d

counteraccusation ˌkaʊntɚˌækju'zeʃən

counteract ˌkaʊntɚ'ækt |-ed -ɪd

counteraction ˌkaʊntɚ'ækʃən ('action & 'counterˌaction)

counterattack *n* 'kaʊntərəˌtæk

counterattack *v* ˌkaʊntərə'tæk |-ed -t

counterattraction ˌkaʊntərə'trækʃən

counterbalance *n* 'kaʊntɚˌbæləns; ES -tə-; |-s -ɪz

counterbalance *v* ˌkaʊntɚ'bæləns; ES -tə-; |-s -ɪz |-d -t

counterblast 'kaʊntɚˌblæst; ES -tə-, E+-ˌblast, -ˌblɑst

counterchange *v* ˌkaʊntɚ'tʃendʒ; ES -tə-; |-s -ɪz |-d -d

countercharge *n* 'kaʊntɚˌtʃɑrdʒ; ES 'kaʊntɚˌtʃɑ:dʒ, E+-ˌtʃɑ:dʒ; |-s -ɪz

countercharge *v* ˌkaʊntɚ'tʃɑrdʒ; ES ˌkaʊntɚ'tʃɑ:dʒ, E+-'tʃɑ:dʒ; |-s -ɪz |-d -d

countercheck *n* 'kaʊntɚˌtʃɛk; ES 'kaʊntɚ-

counterclaim *n* 'kaʊntɚˌklem; ES 'kaʊntɚ-

counterclaim *v* ˌkaʊntɚ'klem; ES ˌkaʊntɚ-; |-ed -d

counterclockwise ˌkaʊntɚ'klɑkˌwaɪz; ES ˌkaʊntɚ'klɑk-

counterdemonstration ˌkaʊntɚˌdɛmən'streʃən; ES ˌkaʊntɚ-

counterespionage ˌkaʊntɚ'ɛspɪənɪdʒ, -ə'spaɪənɪdʒ

counterfeit 'kaʊntɚfɪt; ES 'kaʊntɚ-; |-ed -ˌfɪtɪd

counterfoil 'kaʊntɚˌfɔɪl; ES 'kaʊntɚ-

counterirritant ˌkaʊntɚ'ɪrətənt

counterjumper 'kaʊntɚˌdʒʌmpɚ; ES 'kaʊntɚˌdʒʌmpə(r

countermand *n* 'kaʊntɚˌmænd; ES 'kaʊntɚ-, E+-ˌmand, -ˌmɑnd

countermand *v* ˌkaʊntɚ'mænd; ES ˌkaʊntɚ-, E+-'mand, -'mɑnd; |-ed -ɪd ('counterˌmand 'orders)

countermarch *n* 'kaʊntɚˌmɑrtʃ; ES 'kaʊntɚˌmɑ:tʃ, E+-ˌmɑ:tʃ; |-es -ɪz

countermarch *v* ˌkaʊntɚ'mɑrtʃ; ES ˌkaʊntɚ-'mɑ:tʃ, E+-'mɑ:tʃ; |-es -ɪz |-ed -t

countermine *n* 'kaʊntɚˌmaɪn; ES 'kaʊntɚ-

Key: *See in full §§3–47.* bee bi |pity 'pɪtɪ (§6) |rate ret |yet jɛt |sang sæŋ |angry 'æŋ·grɪ |bath bæθ; E bɑθ (§10) |ah ɑ |far fɑr |watch wɑtʃ, wɒtʃ (§12) |jaw dʒɔ |gorge gɔrdʒ |go go

countermine v ˌkaʊntɚˈmaɪn; ES ˌkaʊntə-; |-d -d

countermove ˈkaʊntɚˌmuv; ES ˈkaʊntə-

counteroffensive ˌkaʊntərəˈfɛnsɪv (ofˈfensive & ˈcounterofˌfensive)

counterpane ˈkaʊntɚˌpen; ES ˈkaʊntə-; |-d -d

counterpart ˈkaʊntɚˌpɑrt; ES ˈkaʊntəˌpɑːt, E+-ˌpɑːt

counterplot n, v ˈkaʊntɚˌplɑt; ES ˈkaʊntə-ˌplɑt, -ˌplɒt; |-ted -ɪd

counterpoint ˈkaʊntɚˌpɔɪnt; ES ˈkaʊntə-

counterpoise n, v ˈkaʊntɚˌpɔɪz; ES ˈkaʊntə-; |-s -ɪz |-d -d

counterproposal ˈkaʊntɚprəˌpozḷ; ES ˈkaʊntə-

counterreformation ˌkaʊntɚˌrɛfɚˈmeʃən; ES ˌkaʊntəˌrɛfəˈmeʃən

counterrevolution ˌkaʊntɚˌrɛvəˈluʃən, -ˈlɪuʃən, -ˌrɛvḷˈjuʃən; ES ˌkaʊntə-; |-ary -ˌɛrɪ

counterscarp ˈkaʊntɚˌskɑrp; ES ˈkaʊntə-ˌskɑːp, E+-ˌskɑːp

countershaft ˈkaʊntɚˌʃæft; ES ˈkaʊntə-, E+ -ˌʃɑft, -ˌʃɑft

countersign n ˈkaʊntɚˌsaɪn; ES ˈkaʊntə-

countersign v ˈkaʊntɚˌsaɪn, ˌkaʊntɚˈsaɪn; ES -tə-; |-ed -d

countersignature ˌkaʊntɚˈsɪgnətʃɚ; ES ˌkaʊntəˈsɪgnətʃə(r; (ˈsignature & ˈcounter-ˌsignature)

countersink n ˈkaʊntɚˌsɪŋk; ES ˈkaʊntə-

countersink v ˈkaʊntɚˌsɪŋk, ˌkaʊntɚˈsɪŋk; ES -tə-; |-sunk -ˌsʌŋk, -ˈsʌŋk

counterstatement ˈkaʊntɚˌstetmənt; ES ˈkaʊntə-

counterstroke ˈkaʊntɚˌstrok; ES ˈkaʊntə-

countersuggestion ˈkaʊntɚsəgˌdʒɛstʃən, -sə-ˌdʒɛstʃən; ES ˈkaʊntə-

counterthrust ˈkaʊntɚˌθrʌst; ES ˈkaʊntə-

countervail ˌkaʊntɚˈvel; ES ˌkaʊntə-; |-ed -d

counterweigh ˌkaʊntɚˈwe; ES ˌkaʊntə-; |-ed -d

counterweight ˈkaʊntɚˌwet; ES ˈkaʊntə-

counterwork n ˈkaʊntɚˌwɝk; ES ˈkaʊntə-ˌwɝk, -ˌwɝk

counterwork v ˌkaʊntɚˈwɝk; ES ˌkaʊntə-ˈwɝk, -ˈwɝk

countess ˈkaʊntɪs |-es -ɪz

countinghouse ˈkaʊntɪŋˌhaʊs |-ses -zɪz

country ˈkʌntrɪ |-trified, -tryf- ˈkʌntrɪˌfaɪd

country-bred ˈkʌntrɪˈbrɛd (ˈcountry-ˌbred ˈman)

country-dance ˈkʌntrɪˈdæns, -ˌdæns; E+ -ans, -ans; |-s -ɪz

countryfolk ˈkʌntrɪˌfok

countryman ˈkʌntrɪmən |-men -mən

countryseat ˈkʌntrɪˌsit, -ˈsit

countryside ˈkʌntrɪˌsaɪd (ˈwhole ˈcountry-ˈside)

country-style ˈkʌntrɪˌstaɪl, -ˈstaɪl

country-wide ˈkʌntrɪˈwaɪd

countrywoman ˈkʌntrɪˌwʊmən, ˌwu- |-women -ˌwɪmɪn, -ən

county ˈkaʊntɪ

coup 'upset', 'drink' kop, kup |-ed -t

coup 'stroke' ku

coup de grâce Fr kudəˈgrɑːs

coup de main Fr kudəˈmæ̃

coup d'état ˈkudeˈta (Fr kudeˈta)

coupé 'carriage' kuˈpe; 'auto' kup, less freq. kuˈpe

couple ˈkʌpḷ |-d -d |-ling ˈkʌplɪŋ, ˈkʌplɪŋ

coupler ˈkʌplɚ; ES ˈkʌplə(r

couplet ˈkʌplɪt

coupling n ˈkʌplɪŋ

coupon ˈkupɑn, ˈkju-, ˈkɪu-, -pɒn

courage ˈkɝɪdʒ; ES ˈkɝɪdʒ, ˈkʌr-, ˈkɝ-; |-d -d

courageous kəˈredʒəs

courante kuˈrant (Fr kuˈrɑ̃)

courier ˈkʊrɪɚ, ˈkɝɪɚ; ES ˈkʊrɪ·ə(r, ˈkɝ-, ˈkʌr-, ˈkɝ-

course kors, kɔrs, esp. in 'of course' kurs; ES koəs, kuəs, E+kɔəs |-s -ɪz |-d -t

courser ˈkorsɚ, ˈkɔr-; ES ˈkoəsə(r, E+ ˈkɔə-

court kort, kɔrt; ES koət, E+kɔət; |-ed -ɪd

courteous ˈkɝtɪəs; ES ˈkɝtɪəs, ˈkɝt-

courtesan, -zan ˈkortəzṇ, ˈkɔrt-, ˈkɝt-; ES ˈkoət-, ˈkɝt-, ˈkɝt-, E+ˈkɔət-

courtesy 'politeness' ˈkɝtəsɪ; ES ˈkɝtəsɪ, ˈkɝt-

courtesy 'curtsy' kɝtsɪ; ES ˈkɝtsɪ, ˈkɝt-; |-ied -d

Courthope ˈkortəp, ˈkɔrt-, -ˌhop; ES ˈkoət-, E+ˈkɔət-

courthouse ˈkortˌhaʊs, ˈkɔrt-; ES ˈkoət-, E+ ˈkɔət-; |-ses -zɪz

courtier ˈkortɪɚ, ˈkɔrt-, -tjɚ; ES ˈkoətɪ·ə(r, -tjə(r, E+ˈkɔət-

courtly ˈkortlɪ, ˈkɔrt-; ES ˈkoət-, E+ˈkɔət-

court-martial ˈkortˈmɑrʃəl, ˈkɔrt-; ES ˈkoət-

|full fʊl |tooth tuθ |further ˈfɝðɚ; ES ˈfɝðə |custom ˈkʌstəm |while hwaɪl |how haʊ |toy tɔɪ ʃusing ˈjuzɪŋ |fuse fjuz, fɪuz |dish dɪʃ |vision ˈvɪʒən |Eden ˈidṇ |cradle ˈkredḷ |keep 'em ˈkipm̩

'maːʃəl, E+'kɔət-, -'maːʃəl; |-ed -d |-ing
-ʃəlɪŋ, -ʃlɪŋ
court-plaster 'kort‚plæstɚ, 'kɔrt-; ES 'kɔət-
‚plæstə(r, E+'kɔət-, -‚plas-, -‚plas-
courtroom 'kort‚rum, 'kɔrt-, -‚rʊm; ES
'kɔət-, E+'kɔət-
courtship 'kortʃɪp, 'kɔrt-; ES 'kɔət-, E+
'kɔət-
courtyard 'kort‚jɑrd, 'kɔrt-; ES 'kɔət‚jɑːd,
E+'kɔət-, -‚jɑːd
cousin 'kʌzn̩ |-ed -d |-ing 'kʌznɪŋ, 'kʌznɪŋ
cousin-german 'kʌzn̩'dʒɝmən; ES -'dʒɜm-,
-'dʒɝm-; |pl cousins- 'kʌznz-
Cousins 'kʌznz |-'s -ɪz
couth kuθ
couturier Fr kuty'rje |fem -rière -'rjɛːr
Couzens 'kʌznz |-'s -ɪz
cove kov |coved kovd
covenant, C- 'kʌvənənt, 'kʌvnənt |-ed -ɪd
covenanter, -or 'kʌvənəntɚ, 'kʌvn-; ES -tə(r
Covenanter 'kʌvə‚næntɚ, ‚kʌvə'næntɚ; ES
-tə(r
Covent 'kʌvənt, 'kɑv-; ES+'kɒv-
Coventry 'kʌvəntrɪ, 'kɑv-; ES+'kɒv-; |-ied
-d—Both ɑ(ɒ) and ʌ appear to be historical.
cover 'kʌvɚ; ES 'kʌvə(r; |-ed -d |-ing
'kʌvərɪŋ, 'kʌvrɪŋ
coverage 'kʌvərɪdʒ, 'kʌvrɪdʒ |-s -ɪz
Coverdale 'kʌvɚ‚del; ES 'kʌvə-
covering n 'kʌvrɪŋ
coverlet 'kʌvɚlɪt; ES 'kʌvə-
Coverley 'kʌvɚlɪ; ES 'kʌvə-
coverlid 'kʌvɚ‚lɪd; ES 'kʌvə-
covert 'kʌvɚt; ES 'kʌvət
coverture 'kʌvɚtʃɚ; ES 'kʌvətʃə(r
covet 'kʌvɪt |-ed -ɪd |-ous -əs
covey 'kʌvɪ |-ed -d
covin 'kʌvɪn
Covina ko'vinə
Covington 'kʌvɪŋtən
cow kau |cowed kaud
·coward, C- 'kauɚd; ES 'kau-əd; |-ice -ɪs
cowbell 'kau‚bɛl
cowbird 'kau‚bɝd; ES -‚bɜd, -‚bɝd
cowboy 'kau‚bɔɪ
cowcatcher 'kau‚kætʃɚ, -‚kɛtʃɚ; ES -tʃə(r
cower 'kauɚ; ES 'kau·ə(r; |-ed -d |-ing
'kauərɪŋ, 'kaurɪŋ
Cowes kauz |-'s -ɪz

cowherd 'kau‚hɝd; ES -‚hɜd, -‚hɝd
cowhide 'kau‚haɪd |-d -ɪd
cowl, C- kaul |-ed -d
Cowley 'kaulɪ
cowlick 'kau‚lɪk
cowling, C- 'kaulɪŋ
co-worker ko'wɝkɚ; ES -'wɜkə(r, -'wɝkə(r
cowpea 'kau‚pi
Cowpens SC 'kau‚pɛnz, loc.+'kʌpɪnz
Cowper 'kupɚ, 'kaupɚ; ES -pə(r;—the same
word as Cooper, 'kaupɚ being a spelling
pronunciation.
cowpox 'kau‚pɑks; ES+-‚pɒks
cowpuncher 'kau‚pʌntʃɚ; ES -‚pʌntʃə(r
cowrie, -ry 'kaurɪ
cowskin 'kau‚skɪn
cowslip 'kau‚slɪp—cf oxlip
cox kaks; ES+kɒks; |-es -ɪz
coxcomb 'kaks‚kom; ES+'kɒks-; |-ry -rɪ
coxcombic kaks'kɑmɪk, -'kom-; ES+-'kɒm-;
|-al -] |-ally -ļɪ, -ɪklɪ
coxswain 'kaksn̩, 'kak‚swen; ES+'kɒk-
coy kɔɪ |coyed kɔɪd
coyote kaɪ'ot, kaɪ'otɪ, 'kaɪot
coz kʌz
coze koz |cozes 'kozɪz |cozed kozd
cozen 'kʌzn̩ |-ed -d |-ing 'kʌznɪŋ, 'kʌznɪŋ
cozenage 'kʌzn̩ɪdʒ, 'kʌznɪdʒ
cozy 'kozɪ
Cozzens 'kʌznz |-'s -ɪz
crab kræb |crabbed kræbd
Crabbe kræb
crabbed adj 'kræbɪd |-ly -lɪ
crabby 'kræbɪ
crack kræk |cracked krækt
crackajack 'krækə‚dʒæk
crackbrain 'kræk‚bren
crackbrained 'kræk'brend ('crack‚brained
'wits)
cracker 'krækɚ; ES 'krækə(r
crackerjack 'krækɚ‚dʒæk; ES 'krækə-
crackle 'krækļ |-d -d |-ling 'kræklɪŋ, -kļɪŋ-
crackling n 'kræklɪŋ
cracknel 'kræknļ
cracksman 'kræksmən |-men -mən
crack-up 'kræk‚ʌp
Cracow 'kreko, 'krækau (see Kraków)
Craddock 'krædək
cradle 'kredļ |-d -d |-ling 'kredļɪŋ, 'kredlɪŋ

Cradock ˈkrædək=Caradoc *knight*
craft kræft; ES+kraft, krɑft; |-y -ɪ
craftsman ˈkræftsmən; E+ˈkrafts-, ˈkrɑfts-;
  |-men -mən |-manship -mənˌʃɪp
crag kræg |cragged ˈkrægɪd |-gy -ɪ
Craigenputtock ˌkregənˈpʌtək
Craigie ˈkregɪ
crake krek |craked krekt
crakow ˈkrækaʊ
cram kræm |crammed kræmd
crambo ˈkræmbo
cramp kræmp |cramped kræmpt
crampon ˈkræmpən
cranage ˈkrenɪdʒ
Cranage ˈkrænɪdʒ |-'s -ɪz
cranberry ˈkrænˌbɛrɪ, -bərɪ
Crandall ˈkrændḷ
crane, C- kren |craned krend
Cranford ˈkrænfɚd; ES ˈkrænfəd
cranial ˈkrenɪəl |-ly -ɪ
craniological ˌkrenɪəˈlɑdʒɪkḷ; ES+-ˈlɒdʒ-;
  |-ly -ɪ
craniology ˌkrenɪˈɑlədʒɪ; ES+-ˈɒl-
craniometer ˌkrenɪˈɑmətɚ; ES -ˈɑmətə(r,
  -ˈɒm-
craniometric ˌkrenɪəˈmɛtrɪk |-al -ḷ |-ally -ḷɪ,
  -ɪkḷɪ
craniometry ˌkrenɪˈɑmətrɪ; ES+-ˈɒm-
cranium ˈkrenɪəm |-s -z |-nia -nɪə
crank kræŋk |cranked kræŋkt
crankcase ˈkræŋkˌkes |-cases -ˌkesɪz
crankle ˈkræŋkḷ |-d -d |-ling ˈkræŋkḷɪŋ, -klɪŋ
crankpin ˈkræŋkˌpɪn
crankshaft ˈkræŋkˌʃæft; E+-ˌʃaft,-ˌʃɑft
Cranmer ˈkrænmɚ; ES ˈkrænmə(r
crannog ˈkrænəg
cranny ˈkrænɪ |crannied ˈkrænɪd
Cranston ˈkrænstən
crape krep |craped krept
crappie ˈkræpɪ, ˈkrɑpɪ
craps kræps
crapulous ˈkræpjʊləs
crash kræʃ |-es -ɪz |-ed -t
Crashaw ˈkræʃɔ
crasis ˈkresɪs |crases ˈkresiz
crass kræs
Crassus ˈkræsəs |-sus' -səs
cratch, C- krætʃ |cratches ˈkrætʃɪz
Cratchit ˈkrætʃɪt

crate kret |crated ˈkretɪd
crater ˈkretɚ; ES ˈkretə(r; |-ed -d
cravat krəˈvæt |-vatted -ˈvætɪd
crave krev |craved krevd
craven ˈkrevən |-ed -d |-ing ˈkrevənɪŋ, -vnɪŋ
cravenette, C- ˌkrævəˈnɛt, ˌkrev- |-d -ɪd
craving ˈkrevɪŋ
craw krɔ
crawfish ˈkrɔˌfɪʃ |-es -ɪz |-ed -t
Crawford ˈkrɔfəd; ES ˈkrɔfəd; |-sville -zˌvɪl
crawl krɔl |crawled krɔld |-y -ɪ
Crawley ˈkrɔlɪ
crayfish ˈkreˌfɪʃ |-'s -ɪz
crayon ˈkreən |crayoned ˈkreənd
craze krez |crazes ˈkrezɪz |crazed krezd
crazy ˈkrezɪ |crazily ˈkrezḷɪ, -zɪlɪ
creak krik |creaked krikt
cream krim |creamed krimd |-ery -ərɪ,
  ˈkrimrɪ
cream-faced ˈkrimˈfest (ˈcream-ˌfaced ˈloon)
crease kris |creases ˈkrisɪz |creased krist
creasy ˈkrisɪ
create krɪˈet |created krɪˈetɪd |-tion -ˈeʃən
creative krɪˈetɪv |-tor -tɚ; ES -tə(r
creature ˈkritʃɚ; ES ˈkritʃə(r; |-ral -əl
crèche krɛʃ, krɛʃ |-s -ɪz (*Fr* krɛːʃ)
Crécy ˈkresɪ (*Fr* kreˈsi)
credence ˈkridn̩s |-dent -dn̩t
credential krɪˈdɛnʃəl |-ed -d
credibility ˌkrɛdəˈbɪlətɪ
credible ˈkrɛdəbḷ |-bly -blɪ
credit ˈkrɛdɪt |credited ˈkrɛdɪtɪd
creditability ˌkrɛdɪtəˈbɪlətɪ
creditable ˈkrɛdɪtəbḷ |-bly -blɪ
creditor ˈkrɛdɪtɚ; ES ˈkrɛdɪtə(r
credo, C- ˈkrido, ˈkredo
credulity krəˈdulətɪ, -ˈdɪu-, -ˈdju-
credulous ˈkrɛdʒələs
Cree kri
creed krid |creeded ˈkridɪd
creek krik, krɪk—krɪk *is much less freq. in the*
  S, but appears to be the native form in the
  N & E. krik, *originally a North British dia-*
  lect form, is still native in the Appalachians.
  According to Horn's, Jordan's, and Luick's
  Historical English Grammars, krɪk *repre-*
  sents the original word (ME crike), *later*
  altered to krik *and then spelt* creek. *Crike is*
  much the earlier recorded form. At first krɪk

|full fʊl |tooth tuθ |further ˈfɝðɚ; ES ˈfɝðə |custom ˈkʌstəm |while hwaɪl |how haʊ |toy tɔɪ
|using ˈjuzɪŋ |fuse fjuz, fɪuz |dish dɪʃ |vision ˈvɪʒən |Eden ˈidn̩ |cradle ˈkredḷ |keep 'em ˈkipm̩

was not a spelling pronunciation, but the spelling creek *doubtless encouraged its spread. Luick thinks that American* krɪk *represents the normal standard English development.*

Creek krik

creel kril |creeled krild

creep krip |crept krɛpt |-er 'kripɚ; ES -pə(r

creepmouse 'krip͵maʊs |-'s -ɪz |-mice -͵maɪs

creese kris |creeses 'krisɪz

Creighton 'kretn̩, 'kraitn̩

cremate 'krimet |-d -ɪd |-tor -ɚ; ES -ə(r

crematory 'krimə͵torɪ, 'krɛm-, -͵tɔrɪ; S -͵tɔrɪ

crème de menthe *Fr* krɛmdə'mãt

Cremona krɪ'monə

crenate 'krinet |-d -ɪd |-tion krɪ'neʃən

crenel 'krɛn̩l |creneled 'krɛn̩ld

crenelate, -ll- 'krɛn̩͵et |-d -ɪd

crenelation, -ll- ͵krɛn̩l'eʃən

Creole, c- 'kriol

Creon 'krian, -ɒn

creosote 'kriə͵sot |creosoted 'kriə͵sotɪd

crepe, crêpe krep |-d -t

crepe de Chine ͵krepdə'ʃin

crepitant 'krɛpətənt |-itate -͵tet |-tated -͵tetɪd

crept krɛpt

crepuscle krɪ'pʌs̩l |-cular -kjələɚ; ES -lə(r

crescendo krə'ʃɛndo, -'sɛn- (*It* kre'ʃɛndo)

crescent 'krɛsn̩t |-ed -ɪd

cresol 'krisol

cress krɛs |cresses 'krɛsɪz |cressed krɛst

cresset 'krɛsɪt

Cressida *in Shak.* 'krɛsɪdə—*see* Criseyde

Cressy 'krɛsɪ (*Fr* Crécy kre'si)

crest krɛst |crested 'krɛstɪd

crestfallen 'krɛst͵fɔlən, -͵fɔln

Crestline 'krɛstlaɪn, 'krɛslaɪn

cretaceous krɪ'teʃəs

Crete krit |Cretan 'kritn̩

cretin 'kritɪn |-ism -͵ɪzəm, -tn̩-

cretonne krɪ'tan, -'tɒn, 'kritan, -tɒn

crevasse krə'væs |-s -ɪz |-d -t

crevice 'krɛvɪs |-s -ɪz |-d -t

crew kru, krɪu

Crewe kru, krɪu

crewel 'kruəl, 'krɪuəl

crib krɪb |cribbed krɪbd

cribbage 'krɪbɪdʒ |-s -ɪz |-d -d

cribwork 'krɪb͵wɝk; ES -͵wɜk, -͵wɝk

Crichton 'kraitn̩

crick krɪk |cricked krɪkt

cricket 'krɪkɪt |-ed -ɪd |-er -ɚ; ES -ə(r

cricoid 'kraikɔid

cried kraid

crier 'kraiɚ; ES 'krai·ə(r

cries kraiz

Crile krail

crime kraim |crimed kraimd

Crimea krai'miə, krɪ- |-n -n

criminal 'krɪmən̩l, 'krɪmn̩l |-ly -ɪ

criminality ͵krɪmə'nælətɪ

criminate 'krɪmə͵net |-nated -͵netɪd

crimination ͵krɪmə'neʃən

criminologic ͵krɪmənə'ladʒɪk, ͵krɪmnə-; ES+ -'lɒdʒ-; |-al -l̩|

criminologist ͵krɪmə'nalədʒɪst, krɪm'nal-; ES+-'nɒl-; |-gy -dʒɪ

crimp krɪmp |crimped krɪmpt

crimple 'krɪmpl̩ |-d -d |-ling -'krɪmplɪŋ, -plɪŋ

crimson 'krɪmzn̩ |crimsoned 'krɪmzn̩d

cringe krɪndʒ |cringes 'krɪndʒɪz |-d -d

cringle 'krɪŋgl̩

crinkle 'krɪŋkl̩ |-d -d |-ling 'krɪŋklɪŋ, -kl̩ɪŋ

crinkly 'krɪŋklɪ

crinoid 'krainɔid, 'krɪn-

crinoline 'krɪn̩ɪn, -͵in

cripple 'krɪpl̩ |-d -d |-ling 'krɪplɪŋ, -pl̩ɪŋ

Cripple Creek 'krɪpl̩'krɪk, -'krɪk

Cripplegate 'krɪpl̩͵get, -gɪt

Criseyde *in Chaucer* krɪ'sedə

crisis 'kraisɪs |crises 'kraisiz

crisp krɪsp |crisped krɪspt

crisscross 'krɪs͵krɔs, -͵krɒs |-es -ɪz |-ed -t

Cristobal krɪs'tobl̩ (*Sp* kris'toβal)

criterion krai'tɪrɪən |-teria -'tɪrɪə

critic 'krɪtɪk |-al -l̩ |-ally -lɪ, -ɪklɪ

criticaster 'krɪtɪk͵æstɚ; ES -͵æstə(r

criticism 'krɪtə͵sɪzəm

criticize 'krɪtə͵saɪz |-s -ɪz |-d -d

critique krɪ'tik

Crito 'kraito

Crittendon 'krɪtn̩dən

croak krok |croaked krokt

croaker, C- 'krokɚ; ES 'krokə(r

Croat 'kroæt, -ət

Croatia kro'eʃə, -ʃɪə |-n -n

Croce 'krotʃɪ (*It* 'kro:tʃe)

crochet *n* 'kratʃit; ES+'krɒtʃit

crochet *v* kro'ʃe |-cheted -'ʃed |-cheting -'ʃe·ɪŋ

---

crock krɑk; ES+krɒk; |-ed -t |-ery -ərɪ, -rɪ	crossbreed *n* 'krɔs,brid, 'krɒs-
Crockett 'krɑkɪt; ES+'krɒkɪt	crossbreed *v* 'krɔs'brid, 'krɒs-, -,brid |-bred
crocodile 'krɑkə,daɪl; ES+'krɒk-	-'brɛd, -,brɛd
crocodilian ,krɑkə'dɪlɪən; ES+,krɒk-	crosscut 'krɔs,kʌt, 'krɒs-
crocus, C- 'krokəs |-es -ɪz |-ci -saɪ	crosse krɔs, krɒs |-s -ɪz
Croesus 'krisəs |-sus' -səs	cross-examination 'krɔsɪg,zæmə'neʃən, 'krɒs-
croft krɔft, krɒft	cross-examine 'krɔsɪg'zæmɪn, 'krɒs- |-d -d
Croix krɔɪ (*Fr* krwa)	cross-eye 'krɔs,aɪ, 'krɒs-
Croix de guerre *Fr* krwad 'gɛːr	cross-eyed 'krɔs'aɪd, 'krɒs- ('cross-,eyed
Croker 'krokɚ; ES 'krokə(r	'bear)
crokinole, C- 'krokə,nol	cross-fertilization 'krɔs,fɝtlə'zeʃən, 'krɒs-,
Cro-Magnon kro'mægnan, -nɒn (*Fr*	-aɪ'z-; ES -,fɜtl-, -,fɝtl-
kroma'nõ)	cross-fertilize 'krɔs'fɝtl,aɪz, 'krɒs-; ES -'fɜtl-,
Cromarty 'krɑmɚtɪ; ES 'krɑmətɪ, 'krɒm-	-'fɝtl-; |-s -ɪz |-d -d
cromlech 'krɑmlɛk; ES+'krɒm-	cross-gartered 'krɔs'gɑrtɚd, 'krɒs-; ES
Crompton 'krɑmptən; ES+'krɒmp-	-'gɑ:təd, E+-'gɑ:təd
Cromwell 'krɑmwəl, -wɛl, 'krʌm-; ES+	cross-grained 'krɔs'grend, 'krɒs-
'krɒm-	crosshatch 'krɔs,hætʃ, 'krɒs- |-es -ɪz |-ed -t
Cromwellian krɑm'wɛlɪən, -ljən; ES+krɒm-	cross-legged 'krɔs'lɛgɪd, -'lɛgd, 'krɒs- ('sit
crone kron	,cross-'legged, 'cross-,legged 'knight)
Cronus 'kronəs |-'s -ɪz	crossover *n* 'krɔs,ovɚ, 'krɒs-; ES -,ovə(r
crony 'kronɪ |cronied 'kronɪd	crosspatch 'krɔs,pætʃ, 'krɒs- |-es -ɪz
crook kruk |crooked krukt	crosspiece 'krɔs,pis, 'krɒs- |-s -ɪz
crookback 'kruk,bæk |-ed -t	cross-pollinate 'krɔs'pɑlə,net, 'krɒs-; ES+
crooked *adj* 'krukɪd	-'pɒl-; |-d -ɪd
Crookes kruks |-'s -ɪz	cross-pollination 'krɔs,pɑlə'neʃən, 'krɒs-;
crookneck 'kruk,nɛk |-ed -t	ES+-,pɒl-
croon krun |crooned krund	cross-purpose 'krɔs'pɝpəs, 'krɒs-; ES -'pɜp-,
crop krɑp; ES+krɒp; |-ped -t	-'pɝp-; |-s -ɪz
crop-eared 'krɑp'ɪrd; ES 'krɑp'ɪəd, 'krɒp-,	cross-question 'krɔs'kwɛstʃən, 'krɒs- |-ed -d
S+-'ɛəd; ('crop-,eared 'cur)	crossruff 'krɔs,rʌf, 'krɒs- |-ed -t
cropper 'krɑpɚ; ES 'krɑpə(r, 'krɒp-	cross-section *v* 'krɔs'sɛkʃən, 'krɒs- |-ed -d
croppie 'krɑpɪ; ES+'krɒpɪ	cross-stitch 'krɔs,stɪtʃ, 'krɒs- |-es -ɪz |-ed -t
croquet kro'ke |croqueted kro'ked |-ing	crosstrees 'krɔs,triz, 'krɒs-
-'ke·ɪŋ	crossways 'krɔs,wez, 'krɒs- |-wise -,waɪz
croquette kro'kɛt	crossword 'krɔs,wɝd, 'krɒs-; ES -,wɜd, -,wɝd
croquignole 'krokə,nol, -kɪn,jol (*Fr* krõki'nöl)	crotch krɑtʃ; ES+krɒtʃ; |-es -ɪz |-ed -t
crore kror, krɔr; ES kroə(r, E+krɔə(r	crotched *adj* 'krɑtʃt, 'krɑtʃɪd; ES+'krɒtʃ-
Crosby 'krɔzbɪ, 'krɒz-, 'krɑz-	crotchet 'krɑtʃɪt; ES+'krɒtʃɪt; |-ed -ɪd
crosier, C- 'kroʒɚ; ES 'kroʒə(r; |-ed -d	Crothers 'krʌðɚz; ES 'krʌðəz; |-'s -ɪz
cross krɔs, krɒs |-es -ɪz |-ed -t	croton, C- krotn̩
crossbar 'krɔs,bɑr, 'krɒs-; ES -,bɑ:(r, E+	crouch krautʃ |crouches 'krautʃɪz |-ed -t
-,bɑ:(r; |-red -d	croup krup |-ed -t
crossbeam 'krɔs,bim, 'krɒs-	crouper *'crupper'* 'krupɚ, 'krupɚ; ES -pə(r
crossbill 'krɔs,bɪl, 'krɒs-	croupier 'krupɪɚ; ES 'krupɪ·ə(r
crossbones 'krɔs,bonz, 'krɒs-	crouton kru'tɑn, -'tɒn (*Fr* kru'tõ)
crossbow 'krɔs,bo, 'krɒs- |-man -mən |-men	crow kro |*past* crew kru, krɪu *or* crowed krod
-mən	|*pptc* crowed krod
crossbred 'krɔs'brɛd, 'krɒs- ('cross,bred 'dog)	crowbar 'kro,bɑr; ES -,bɑ:(r, E+-,bɑ:(r

\|full fʊl \|tooth tuθ \|further 'fɝðɚ; ES 'fɝðə \|custom 'kʌstəm \|while hwaɪl \|how haʊ \|toy tɔɪ
\|using 'juzɪŋ \|fuse fjuz, fɪuz \|dish dɪʃ \|vision 'vɪʒən \|Eden 'idn̩ \|cradle 'kredl̩ \|keep 'em 'kipm̩

crowd kraud |crowded 'kraudıd

Crowell 'kroəl

crowfoot 'kro͟ıfʊt |pl -feet -ıfit, plant -foots -ıfʊts

Crowley 'krolı, 'kraʊlı

crown kraun |crowned 'kraʊnd

crownpiece 'kraʊnıpis |-pieces -ıpisız

crow's-foot 'krozıfʊt |-feet -ıfit

crow's-nest 'krozınɛst

Croydon 'krɔıdn̩

crozier, C- 'kroʒɚ; ES 'kroʒə(r; |-ed -d

cruces pl of crux 'krusiz, 'krıusiz

crucial 'kruʃəl, 'krıuʃəl |-ly -ı

cruciate adj 'kruʃıt, 'krıu-, -ıͺet

cruciate v 'kruʃıͺet, 'krıu- |-ated -ͺetıd

crucible 'krusəbl̩, 'krıu- |-d -d

crucifix 'krusəıfıks, 'krıu- |-es -ız

crucifixion ͺkrusə'fıkʃən, ͺkrıu-

cruciform 'krusəıfɔrm, 'krıu-; ES -ıfɔəm

crucify 'krusəıfaı, 'krıu- |-fied -ıfaıd

crude krud, krıud |-dity -ətı

cruel 'kruəl, 'krıuəl |-ly -ı |-ty -tı

cruet 'kruɪt, 'krıuɪt

Cruikshank 'krʊkͺʃæŋk

cruise kruz, krıuz |-s -ız |-d -d

cruiser 'kruzɚ, 'krıuzɚ; ES -zə(r

cruller 'krʌlɚ; ES 'krʌlə(r

crumb, C- krʌm |crumbed krʌmd

crumble 'krʌmbl̩ |crumbled 'krʌmbl̩d |-bly -blı

crump krʌmp |crumped krʌmpt

crumpet 'krʌmpıt

crumple 'krʌmpl̩ |-d -d |-ling 'krʌmplıŋ, -pl̩ıŋ

crumply 'krʌmplı

crunch krʌntʃ |crunches 'krʌntʃız |-ed -t

crupper 'krʌpɚ, 'krʊpɚ; ES -pə(r

crural 'krurəl, 'krıurəl

crusade, C- kru'sed, krıu- |-d -ıd

cruse kruz, krıuz, -s |-s -ız

crush krʌʃ |crushes 'krʌʃız |crushed krʌʃt

Crusoe 'kruso, 'krıuso

crust krʌst |crusted 'krʌstıd

crustacean krʌs'teʃən |-ceous -ʃəs

crutch krʌtʃ |crutches 'krʌtʃız |-ed -t

crux krʌks |-es -ız |cruces 'krusiz, 'krıu-

cry kraı |cried kraıd |-baby -ıbebı

cryolite 'kraıəͺlaıt

crypt krıpt |crypted 'krıptıd

cryptic 'krıptık |-al -l̩ |-ally -lı, -ıklı

cryptogam 'krıptəͺgæm |-ic ͺkrıptə'gæmık

cryptogamous krıp'tagəməs, -'tɒg- |-my -mı

cryptogram 'krıptəͺgræm

cryptograph 'krıptəͺgræf; E+-ͺgraf, -ͺgraf

cryptographer krıp'tagrəfɚ, -'tɒg-; ES -fə(r; |-phy -fı

cryptographic ͺkrıptə'græfık |-al -l̩ |-ally -lı, -ıklı

crystal, C- 'krıstl̩ |-ed -d

crystalline 'krıstl̩ın, -ͺaın, poet.+krıs'tæl-

crystallization ͺkrıstl̩ə'zeʃən, -aı'z-

crystallize 'krıstl̩ͺaız |-s -ız |-d -d

crystallography ͺkrıstl̩'agrəfı, -'ɒg-

crystalloid 'krıstl̩ͺɔıd |-al ͺkrıstl̩'ɔıdl̩

Ctesiphon 'tɛsəͺfan, -ͺfɒn

cub kʌb |cubbed kʌbd

Cuba 'kjubə, 'kıubə |-n -n (Sp 'kuβa)

cubbyhole 'kʌbıͺhol

cube kjub, kıub |-d -d

cubeb 'kjubɛb, 'kıubɛb

cubic 'kjubık, 'kıu- |-al -l̩ |-ally -lı |-icly -ıklı

cubicle 'kjubıkl̩, 'kıu-

cubism 'kjubızəm, 'kıub- |-ist -ıst

cubistic kju'bıstık, kıu-

cubit 'kjubıt, 'kıubıt |-ed -ıd

cuboid 'kjubɔıd, 'kıubɔıd

Cuchulainn, -llin ku'kʌlın, 'kuxʊlın

cucking-stool 'kʌkıŋͺstul

cuckold 'kʌkl̩d |-ed -ıd |-ry -rı

cuckoo 'kʊku, ku'ku |-ed -d

cuckooflower 'kʊkuͺflaʊɚ; ES -ͺflau·ə(r

cucumber 'kjukʌmbɚ, 'kıu-; ES -kʌmbə(r

cud kʌd

Cudahy 'kʌdəhı

cuddle 'kʌdl̩ |-d -d |-ling 'kʌdlıŋ, 'kʌdl̩ıŋ

cuddly 'kʌdlı

cuddy, C- 'kʌdı

cudgel 'kʌdʒəl |cudgeled 'kʌdʒəld

cue kju, kıu |cued kjud, kıud

cuff kʌf |cuffed kʌft

Cufic 'kjufık, 'kıu-

cuirass kwı'ræs |-es -ız |-ed -t

cuirassier ͺkwırə'sır; ES -'sıə(r

cuisine kwı'zin

cuisse kwıs |cuisses 'kwısız

cul-de-sac 'kʌldə'sæk, 'kʊl- (Fr kyd'sak, kyt-)

Culebra ku'lebrə

culex, C- 'kjulɛks, 'kıu- |-lices -lıͺsiz

culinary 'kjuləͺnɛrı, 'kıulə-

cull kʌl |culled kʌld
Cullen ˈkʌlɪn, -ən
cullender ˈkʌləndɚ, ˈkʌlɪn-; ES -də(r
cullion ˈkʌljən |-ry -rɪ
Culloden kəˈlɑdn̩, -ˈlɒdn̩, -ˈlɒdn̩
culm kʌlm |culmed kʌlmd
culminate ˈkʌlməˌnet |-nated -ˌnetɪd
culmination ˌkʌlməˈneʃən
culpability ˌkʌlpəˈbɪlətɪ
culpable ˈkʌlpəbl̩ |-bly -blɪ
Culpeper ˈkʌlpepɚ; ES ˈkʌlpepə(r
culprit ˈkʌlprɪt
cult kʌlt
cultivability ˌkʌltəvəˈbɪlətɪ
cultivable ˈkʌltəvəbl̩ |-bly -blɪ
cultivate ˈkʌltəˌvet |-vated -ˌvetɪd
cultivation ˌkʌltəˈveʃən
cultivator ˈkʌltəˌvetɚ; ES -ˌvetə(r
cultural ˈkʌltʃərəl |-ly -ɪ
culture ˈkʌltʃɚ; ES ˈkʌltʃə(r; |-d -d
culver, C- ˈkʌlvɚ; ES ˈkʌlvə(r
culverin ˈkʌlvərɪn
culvert ˈkʌlvɚt; ES ˈkʌlvət; |-ed -ɪd
cumber ˈkʌmbɚ; ES ˈkʌmbə(r; |-ed -d |-ing
ˈkʌmbrɪŋ, ˈkʌmbərɪŋ
Cumberland ˈkʌmbɚlənd; ES ˈkʌmbə-
cumbersome ˈkʌmbɚsəm; ES ˈkʌmbə-
cumbrance ˈkʌmbrəns |-s -ɪz |-brous -brəs
Cumbria ˈkʌmbrɪə |-n -n
cumin, cumm- ˈkʌmɪn
cum laude ˈkʌmˈlɔdɪ, ˈkʊmˈlaʊdɪ
Cummings ˈkʌmɪŋz |-ʼs -ɪz
Cummins ˈkʌmɪnz |-ʼs -ɪz
cumquat ˈkʌmkwɑt, -kwɒt
cumshaw ˈkʌmʃɔ
cumulate adj ˈkjumjəlɪt, ˈkɪʊm-, -ˌlet
cumulate v ˈkjumjəˌlet, ˈkɪʊm- |-lated -ˌletɪd
cumulation ˌkjumjəˈleʃən, ˌkɪʊmjə-
cumulative ˈkjumjəˌletɪv, ˈkɪʊmjə-
cumulo-cirrus ˌkjumjəloˈsɪrəs, ˌkɪʊm- |-ri -raɪ
cumulo-nimbus ˌkjumjəloˈnɪmbəs, ˌkɪʊm-
|-bi -baɪ
cumulo-stratus ˌkjumjəloˈstretəs, ˌkɪʊm- |-ti
-taɪ
cumulous ˈkjumjələs, ˈkɪʊm-
cumulus ˈkjumjələs, ˈkɪʊm- |-es -ɪz |-li -ˌlaɪ
Cunard kjʊˈnɑrd, kɪʊ-; ES -ˈnɑːd, E+-ˈnɑːd
cunctator kʌŋkˈtetɚ; ES -ˈtetə(r; |-ship -ʃɪp
cuneate ˈkjunɪt, ˈkɪʊn-, -rˌet

cuneiform ˈkjunɪəˌfɔrm, ˈkɪʊn-, -nɪˌfɔrm,
kjuˈnɪə-, kɪʊ-; ES -ˌfɔəm
cuniform ˈkjunɪfɔrm, ˈkɪʊnɪ-; ES -ˌfɔəm
cunner ˈkʌnɚ; ES ˈkʌnə(r
cunning ˈkʌnɪŋ
Cunningham ˈkʌnɪŋˌhæm, ˈkʌnɪŋəm
cup kʌp |cupped kʌpt
cupalo, -olo ˈkjupəˌlo, ˈkɪʊ- |-ed -d—ˈkjupəˌlo
represents a 17c variant of cupola still widely
heard in US.
cupbearer ˈkʌpˌberɚ, -ˌbærɚ; E -ˌberə(r, ES
-ˌbærə(r
cupboard ˈkʌbɚd; ES ˈkʌbəd; |-ed -ɪd
cupful ˈkʌpˌfʊl |-s -z
Cupid, c- ˈkjupɪd, ˈkɪʊpɪd
cupidity kjuˈpɪdətɪ, kɪʊ-
cupola ˈkjupələ, ˈkɪʊ- |-ed -d—see cupalo
cupreous ˈkjuprɪəs, ˈkɪʊp- |-rous -rəs |-ric -rɪk
cur kɝ; ES kɜ(r, kɝ
curability ˌkjʊrəˈbɪlətɪ, ˌkɪʊrə-
curable ˈkjʊrəbl̩, ˈkɪʊr- |-bly -blɪ
Curaçao, c-, -çoa ˌkjʊrəˈso, ˌkɪʊrə-
curacy ˈkjʊrəsɪ, ˈkɪʊrəsɪ
Curan ˈkɝən; ES ˈkɜrən, ˈkʌrən, ˈkɝən
curassow ˈkjʊrəˌso, ˈkɪʊrə-
curate ˈkjʊrɪt, ˈkɪʊrɪt
curative ˈkjʊrətɪv, ˈkɪʊ-
curator kjuˈretɚ, kɪʊˈretɚ, law+ˈkjʊrətɚ,
ˈkɪʊr-; ES -tə(r
curatorial ˌkjʊrəˈtorɪəl, ˌkɪʊrə-, -ˈtɔr-; S
-ˈtor-
curb kɝb; ES kɜb, kɝb; |-ed -d |-stone -ˌston
curculio kɝˈkjulɪˌo, -ˈkɪʊlɪ-; ES kɜ-, kɝ-
curd kɝd; ES kɜd, kɝd; |-ed -ɪd
curdle ˈkɝdl̩; ES ˈkɜdl̩, ˈkɝdl̩; |-d -d |-ling
-dl̩ɪŋ, -dlɪŋ
cure kjʊr, kɪʊr; ES -ə(r; |-d -d
curé kjuˈre, kɪʊˈre (Fr kyˈre)
cure-all ˈkjʊrˌɔl, ˈkɪʊrˌɔl
curette kjuˈrɛt, kɪʊ- |-d -ɪd
curfew ˈkɝfju, -fɪu; ES ˈkɜ-, ˈkɝ-
curia ˈkjʊrɪə, ˈkɪʊrɪə |-iae -ɪˌi
Curie, c- ˈkjuri, ˈkɪʊ-, kjuˈri, kɪʊ- (Fr kyˈri)
curio, C- ˈkjʊrɪˌo, ˈkɪʊrɪ-
curiosity ˌkjʊrɪˈɑsətɪ, ˌkɪʊrɪ-; ES+-ˈɒs-
curious ˈkjʊrɪəs, ˈkɪʊrɪ-
curl kɝl; ES kɜl, kɝl; |-ed -d
curlew ˈkɝlu, -lɪu, ˈkɝlju; ES ˈkɜ-, ˈkɝ-
curlicue ˈkɝlɪˌkju, -ˌkɪu; ES ˈkɜlɪ-, ˈkɝlɪ-

|full fʊl |tooth tuθ |further ˈfɝðɚ; ES ˈfɝðə |custom ˈkʌstəm |while hwaɪl |how haʊ |toy tɔɪ
|using ˈjuzɪŋ |fuse fjuz, fɪuz |dish dɪʃ |vision ˈvɪʒən |Eden ˈidn̩ |cradle ˈkredl̩ |keep ʼem ˈkipm̩

curmudgeon kə'mʌdʒən; ES kə-
currant 'kɝənt; ES 'kɜrənt, 'kʌr-, 'kɝ-
currency 'kɝənsɪ; ES 'kɜrənsɪ, 'kʌr-, 'kɝ-
current 'kɝənt; ES 'kɜrənt, 'kʌr-, 'kɝ-
curricle 'kɝɪk]; ES 'kɜrɪk], 'kʌr-, 'kɝ-;
|-d -d |-ling -klɪŋ, -k|ɪŋ
curricular kə'rɪkjələ; ES -lə(r
curriculum kə'rɪkjələm |-s -z |-la -lə
currier, C- 'kɝɪə; ES 'kɜrɪ·ə(r, 'kʌrɪ-, 'kɝɪ-
Currier and Ives 'kɝɪən'aɪvz, 'kɝɪərənd'aɪvz;
  ES 'kɜrɪən'aɪvz, 'kʌrɪən'aɪvz, 'kɝɪən'aɪvz,
  'kɜrɪərənd'aɪvz 'kʌrɪərənd'aɪvz, 'kɝɪərənd-
  'aɪvz
currish 'kɝɪʃ; ES 'kɜrɪʃ, 'kɝ-
curry 'kɝɪ; ES 'kɜrɪ, 'kʌrɪ, 'kɝɪ; |-ied -d
  |-comb -ˌkom
curse kɝs; ES kɜs, kɝs; |-s -ɪz |-d -t
cursed adj 'kɝsɪd, kɝst; ES 'kɜs-, 'kɝs-,
  kɜst, kɝst; |-ly -ɪdlɪ
cursive 'kɝsɪv; ES 'kɜs-, 'kɝs-; |-sory -sərɪ
cursorial kɝ'sorɪəl, -'sɔr-; ES kɜ'sorɪəl, kɝ-,
  E+-'sɔr-
Cursor Mundi 'kɝsɔr'mʌndaɪ, 'kɝsɔ-, -dɪ;
  ES 'kɜsɔə-, -sə-, 'kɝsɔə-, 'kɝsə-
curst kɝst; ES kɜst, kɝst
curt kɝt; ES kɜt, kɝt
curtail kɝ'tel, kə-; ES kɜ-, kɝ-, kə-; |-ed -d
  ('curˌtail 'spending)
curtain 'kɝtn̩, -tɪn, -tən; ES 'kɜt-, 'kɝt-;
  |-ed -d |-ing -ɪŋ, -tnɪŋ
curtal 'kɝt]; ES 'kɜt], 'kɝt]
curtesy 'kɝtəsɪ; ES 'kɜt-, 'kɝt-
curtilage 'kɝt|ɪdʒ; ES 'kɜt-, 'kɝt-; |-s -ɪz
Curtis, -ss 'kɝtɪs; ES 'kɜt-, 'kɝt-; |-'s -ɪz
curtsy -sey 'kɝtsɪ; ES 'kɜt-, 'kɝt-; |-ied -d
curule 'kjurʊl, 'kɪur-, -rul
curvature 'kɝvətʃə; -ˌtʃur; ES 'kɝvətʃə(r,
  'kɝvətʃə(r, -ˌtʃuə(r
curve kɝv; ES kɜv, kɝv; |-d -d |-dly -ɪdlɪ
curvet n 'kɝvɪt; ES 'kɜv-, 'kɝv-
curvet v 'kɝvɪt, kə'vɛt; ES 'kɜvɪt, 'kɝv-,
  kə'vɛt; |-(t)ed -ɪd
curvilineal ˌkɝvə'lɪnɪəl; ES ˌkɜvə-, ˌkɝvə-;
  |-ear -ɪə; ES -ɪ·ə(r
Curwood 'kɝˌwʊd; ES 'kɜˌwʊd, 'kɝ-
Curzon 'kɝzn̩; ES 'kɜzn̩, 'kɝzn̩
Cusco 'kusko
cusec 'kjusɛk, 'kɪusɛk
Cush kʌʃ |-'s -ɪz |-ite -aɪt |-itic kʌʃ'ɪtɪk

cushaw kə'ʃɔ
Cushing 'kuʃɪŋ
Cushman 'kuʃmən
cushion 'kuʃən, -ɪn |-ed -d
cusp kʌsp |cusped kʌspt |-id -ɪd |-idal -ɪd]
cuspate 'kʌspɪt, -pet |-d -petɪd
cuspidate 'kʌspɪˌdet |-dated -ˌdetɪd
cuspidor 'kʌspəˌdɔr; ES -ˌdɔə(r
cuss kʌs |cusses 'kʌsɪz |cussed kʌst
cussed adj 'kʌsɪd |-ly -lɪ
cuss-word 'kʌsˌwɝd; ES -ˌwɝd, -ˌwɝd
custard 'kʌstəd; ES 'kʌstəd
Custer 'kʌstə; ES 'kʌstə(r
Custis 'kʌstɪs |-'s -ɪz
custodial kʌs'todɪəl |-an -ən |-anship -ənˌʃɪp
custody 'kʌstədɪ
custom 'kʌstəm |-ed -d
customarily 'kʌstəmˌɛrəlɪ, esp. if emph.
  ˌkʌstə'mɛrəlɪ
customary 'kʌstəmˌɛrɪ
customer 'kʌstəmə; ES 'kʌstəmə(r
customhouse 'kʌstəmˌhaus |-ses -zɪz
custom-made 'kʌstəm'med ('customˌmade
  'hat)
cut kʌt
cut-and-fill 'kʌtn̩'fɪl
cutaneous kju'tenɪəs, kɪu-
cutaway 'kʌtəˌwe
cutback 'kʌtˌbæk
cute kjut, kɪut
Cuthbert 'kʌθbət; ES 'kʌθbət
cuticle 'kjutɪk], 'kɪut-
cutlass, -las 'kʌtləs |-es -ɪz
cut-leaf 'kʌtˌlif |-leaved -ˌlivd
cutler 'kʌtlə; ES 'kʌtlə(r; |-ess -ɪs |-y -ɪ
cutlet 'kʌtlɪt
cutoff 'kʌtˌɔf, -ˌɒf
cutout 'kʌtˌaut
cutover 'kʌtˌovə; ES -ˌovə(r
cutpurse 'kʌtˌpɝs; ES -ˌpɝs, -ˌpɝs; |-s -ɪz
cut-rate 'kʌt'ret ('cut-ˌrate 'store)
cutter 'kʌtə; ES 'kʌtə(r
cutthroat 'kʌtˌθrot
cutting 'kʌtɪŋ
cuttle, C- 'kʌt] |-bone -ˌbon |-fish -ˌfɪʃ
cutty 'kʌtɪ
Cuttyhunk 'kʌtɪˌhʌŋk
cutworm 'kʌtˌwɝm; ES -ˌwɝm, -ˌwɝm
Cuvier 'kjuvɪˌe, 'kɪu- (Fr ky'vje)

Cuyahoga kaɪˈhagə, ˌkaɪə-, kə-, -ˈhɒgə, -ˈhɔgə, old-fash. -ˈhogə
Cuyahoga Falls kəˈhagəˈfɔlz, kaɪ-, -ˈhɒgə-, -ˈhɔgə-, old-fash. -ˈhogə-
Cuzco ˈkusko
cyanamide ˌsaɪəˈnæmaɪd, saɪˈænəˌmaɪd, -mɪd |-mid -mɪd
cyanate ˈsaɪəˌnet
cyanic saɪˈænɪk
cyanide ˈsaɪəˌnaɪd, -nɪd |-nid -nɪd |-d -ɪd
cyanogen saɪˈænədʒən, -dʒɪn
cyanosis ˌsaɪəˈnosɪs
Cybele, c- ˈsɪbḷˌi
Cyclades ˈsɪkləˌdiz
cyclamen ˈsɪkləmən, -ˌmɛn
cycle ˈsaɪkḷ |-d -d |-ling ˈsaɪklɪŋ, ˈsaɪkḷɪŋ
cyclic ˈsaɪklɪk, ˈsɪk- |-al -ḷ |-ally -ḷɪ, -ɪklɪ
cyclist ˈsaɪklɪst, ˈsaɪkḷɪst
cycloid ˈsaɪklɔɪd |-al saɪˈklɔɪdḷ |-ally saɪˈklɔɪdḷɪ
cyclometer saɪˈklɑmətɚ; ES -ˈklɑmətə(r, -ˈklɒm-
cyclone ˈsaɪklon |-d -d
cyclonic saɪˈklɑnɪk; ES+-ˈklɒn-; |-al -ḷ |-ally -ḷɪ, -ɪklɪ
Cyclopean, c- ˌsaɪkləˈpiən
cyclopedia, -paed- ˌsaɪkləˈpidɪə
cyclopedic, -paed- ˌsaɪkləˈpidɪk |-al -ḷ |-ally -ḷɪ, -ɪklɪ
Cyclops ˈsaɪklɑps; ES+-klɒps; |-es -ɪz |-clopes saɪˈklopiz
cyclorama ˌsaɪkləˈræmə, -ˈrɑmə
cygnet ˈsɪgnɪt
Cygnus ˈsɪgnəs |-'s -ɪz |gen Cygni ˈsɪgnaɪ
cylinder ˈsɪlɪndɚ; ES -də(r; |-ed -d |-ing ˈsɪlɪndrɪŋ, -dərɪŋ
cylindric sɪˈlɪndrɪk |-al -ḷ |-ally -ḷɪ, -ɪklɪ
cymbal ˈsɪmbḷ |-ed -d |-ing ˈsɪmbḷɪŋ, -blɪŋ
cymbalist ˈsɪmbḷɪst, ˈsɪmblɪst

Cymbeline ˈsɪmbḷˌin
cyme saɪm |cymose ˈsaɪmos, saɪˈmos
cymous ˈsaɪməs
Cymric ˈsɪmrɪk, ˈkɪmrɪk |-ry -rɪ
Cynewulf ˈkɪnɪˌwʊlf
cynic ˈsɪnɪk |-al -ḷ |-ally -ḷɪ, -ɪklɪ
cynicism ˈsɪnəˌsɪzəm |-cist -sɪst
cynocephalic ˌsɪnoseˈfælɪk, ˌsaɪno-
cynocephalus ˌsɪnoˈsɛfələs, ˌsaɪ- |-lous -ləs
cynosure ˈsaɪnəˌʃʊr, ˈsɪnə-; ES -ˌʃʊə(r
Cynthia ˈsɪnθɪə |Cynthiana ˌsɪnθɪˈænə
cypher ˈsaɪfɚ; ES ˈsaɪfə(r; |-ed -d |-ing ˈsaɪfrɪŋ, ˈsaɪfərɪŋ
cypress ˈsaɪprəs |-es -ɪz |-ed -t
Cyprian ˈsɪprɪən
cyprinoid ˈsɪprəˌnɔɪd
Cypriot ˈsɪprɪət |-ote -ˌot
cypripedium, C- ˌsɪprəˈpidɪəm |-dia -dɪə
Cyprus, c- ˈsaɪprəs |-'s -ɪz
Cyrano de Bergerac ˈsɪrəˌnodəˈbɝdʒəˌræk; ES -ˈbɜdʒ-, -ˈbɝdʒ-; (Fr siranodbɛrʒəˈrak)
Cyrenaic ˌsɪrəˈneˈɪk, ˌsaɪrə- |-naica -ˈneəkə
Cyrene pers. name saɪˈrin, Gk city saɪˈrini
Cyril ˈsɪrəl, -ɪl
Cyrus ˈsaɪrəs |-'s -ɪz
cyst sɪst |-ed -ɪd |-itis sɪsˈtaɪtɪs
Cythera sɪˈθɪrə
Cytherea ˌsɪθəˈriə |-n -n
cytology saɪˈtɑlədʒɪ; ES+-ˈtɒl-; |-gist -st
cytoplasm ˈsaɪtəˌplæzəm |-ic ˌsaɪtəˈplæzmɪk
czar zɑr; ES zɑ:(r, E+za:(r
czarevitch ˈzɑrəˌvɪtʃ; E+ˈzɑrə-; |-'s -ɪz
czarevna zɑˈrɛvnə; E+zɑ-
czarina zɑˈrinə; E+zɑ-
Czech tʃɛk |-ic -ɪk |-ish -ɪʃ
Czechoslovak, Czecho-Sl- ˌtʃɛkəˈslovæk, -vɑk
Czechoslovakia, Czecho-Sl- ˌtʃɛkəsloˈvækɪə, -ˈvɑk-, -kjɑ |-n -n
Czernowitz ˈtʃɛrnəˌvɪts |-'s -ɪz

D

D, d *letter* di |*pl* D's, Ds, *poss* D's diz
-d *ending see* -ed
'd *abbr. spelling of unstressed* had, would, *as in*
I'd aɪd, he'd hid, she'd ʃid, it'd ɪtəd, we'd
wid, you'd jud, they'd ðed, there'd ðɛrd,
ðɛəd, *etc.*
dab dæb |dabbed dæbd
dabble 'dæbļ |-d -d |-ling 'dæbļɪŋ, 'dæblɪŋ
dabster 'dæbstɚ; ES 'dæbstə(r
da capo *It* dɑ'kɑːpo
dace des |daces 'desɪz
dachshund 'dɑksˌhʊnd, 'dæksˌhʌnd (*Ger*
'dɑksˌhʊnt
Dacia 'deʃɪə, 'deʃə |-n -n
dacoit də'kɔɪt |dacoitage də'kɔɪtɪdʒ |-y -ɪ
dactyl, D- 'dæktɪl, -tļ |Dactyli 'dæktɪˌlaɪ
dactylic dæk'tɪlɪk
dad dæd |daddy 'dædɪ
dado 'dedo |dadoed 'dedod
Daedalus 'dɛdļəs |Daedalus's 'dɛdļəsɪz
daemon 'dimən |-s -z |daemones 'dimənˌiz
daffodil 'dæfəˌdɪl |-dilly -ˌdɪlɪ
daffy 'dæfɪ
daffydowndilly 'dæfɪˌdaʊn'dɪlɪ
Dafoe 'defo
daft dæft; E+daft, dɑft
dag dæg |dagged dægd
dagger 'dægɚ; ES 'dægə(r
daggle 'dægļ |-d -d |daggling 'dæglɪŋ, -glɪŋ
Dago '*Italian*' 'dego; *Darfur Negro* 'dɑgo
Dagobert 'dægəbɚt, 'dægoˌbɝt; ES 'dægə-
bət, 'dægoˌbɝt, -ˌbɝt
Dagon 'degɑn, -gən; ES+'degɒn
Daguerre *Fr* dɑ'gɛːr
daguerreotype də'gɛrəˌtaɪp, də'gɛrɪə-
Dahl dɑl
Dahlgren 'dælgrɪn, -ən
dahlia 'dæljə, 'dɑljə, 'deljə—*The regular
Anglicized form is* 'deljə, *prevalent in Engd
and formerly in Amer.* 'dɑljə *is formed on
Sw* Dahl, *and* 'dæljə *is an Am modification
of* 'dɑljə.
Dahomey də'homɪ, dɑ'home
Dail Eireann 'dɔɪl'ɛrən, 'dɑɪl-, -'ɛrən
daily, D- 'delɪ
daimio 'daɪmjo
Daimler 'demlɚ, 'daɪmlɚ; ES -lə(r

daimon 'daɪmɑn; ES+'daɪmɒn
Daingerfield 'dendʒɚˌfild; ES 'dendʒə-
Dai Nippon 'daɪ nɪ'pɑn, -'pɒn, 'nɪp'pɑn, -'pɒn
(*Jap* 'njɪppon)
dainty 'dentɪ |-tily 'dentļɪ, -tɪlɪ
dairy 'dɛrɪ, 'dɛːrɪ, 'derɪ |-man -mən, -ˌmæn
|-men -mən, -ˌmɛn—*Some speakers distin-
guish* dairy *from* Derry *by a longer* ɛ.
dais 'de·ɪs, des |daises 'de·ɪsɪz, 'desɪz—"*The
dissyllabic pronunciation of* dais *is a 'shot' at
the word from the spelling.*"—*OED.*
daisy 'dezɪ |daisied 'dezɪd
dak, dawk dɔk, dɑk
Dakar dɑ'kɑr, də-; ES -'kɑː(r, E+-'kɑː(r
Dakin 'dekɪn
Dakota də'kotə, dɪ'kotə
Dalai Lama də'laɪ'lɑmə, 'dɑlaɪ-
dale del |-man, -men -mən |-sman, -smen
-zmən
Dalhousie *college* dæl'haʊzɪ, *Quebec* dæl'huzɪ
Dallas 'dæləs, *Texas loc.*+'dælɪs |-'s -ɪz
dalles, D- dælz
dalliance 'dælɪəns, 'dæljəns |-s -ɪz
dally 'dælɪ |dallied 'dælɪd
Dalmatia dæl'meʃɪə, -'meʃə |-n -n
dalmatic, D- dæl'mætɪk
Dalrymple 'dælrɪmpļ, dæl'rɪmpļ
Dalton 'dɔltn̩
Daly 'delɪ
Dalzel, -ll, -ziel *Am name* dæl'zɛl; *Scotl*
dɑl'jɛl, -'zɛl, dɪ'ɛl, di'ɛl, də'ɛl
dam dæm |dammed dæmd
damage 'dæmɪdʒ |-s -ɪz |-d -d
Damariscotta ˌdæmərɪ'skɑtə; ES+-'skɒtə;
loc. ˌdæmə'skɒtɪ
Damascene 'dæməˌsin, ˌdæmə'sin
Damascus də'mæskəs |-'s -ɪz
damask 'dæməsk
dame dem
Damien 'demɪən, -mjən (*Fr* dɑ'mjæ̃)
damn dæm |-ed -d |damning 'dæmɪŋ,
'dæmnɪŋ
damnable 'dæmnəbļ |-bly -blɪ |-ation dæm-
'neʃən
damnatory 'dæmnəˌtorɪ, -ˌtɔrɪ; S 'dæmnə-
ˌtorɪ
damnify 'dæmnəˌfaɪ |damnified 'dæmnəˌfaɪd

Words below in which a *before* r (farm) *is sounded* ɑ *are often pronounced in* E *with* a (fa:m)

Damocles ˈdæməˌkliz |Damocles's ˈdæmə-
ˌklizɪz

Damon ˈdemən

damosel, -zel ˈdæməˌzɛl |-zell ˌdæməˈzɛl

damosella ˌdæməˈzɛlə

damp dæmp |damped dæmpt

dampen ˈdæmpən |-ed -d |-ing -pənɪŋ, -pnɪŋ

damper ˈdæmpɚ; ES ˈdæmpə(r

Dampier ˈdæmpɪr, ˈdæmpɪ·ɚ, -pjɚ; ES -pɪə(r,
-pɪ·ə(r, -pjə(r

Damrosch ˈdæmrɑʃ; ES+-rɒʃ; |-'s -ɪz

damsel ˈdæmzl̩

damson ˈdæmzn̩

Dan dæn

Dana ˈdenə

Danaë ˈdænɪˌi

Danai ˈdænɪˌaɪ

Danbury ˈdænˌbɛrɪ, ˈdænbərɪ

dance dæns; E+dɑns, dɑns; |-s -ɪz |-d -t

dandelion ˈdændl̩ˌaɪən, ˈdændɪˌlaɪən

dander ˈdændɚ; ES ˈdændə(r

Dandie ˈdændɪ

dandify ˈdændɪˌfaɪ |-fied -ˌfaɪd

dandle ˈdændl̩ |-d -d |-ling ˈdændlɪŋ, ˈdændl̩ɪŋ

dandler ˈdændlɚ; ES ˈdændlə(r

dandruff ˈdændrəf

dandy ˈdændɪ

Dane den |-geld -ˌgɛld |-lagh, -law -ˌlɔ

Danenhower ˈdænənˌhaʊɚ; ES -ˌhaʊ·ə(r

danger ˈdendʒɚ; ES ˈdendʒə(r; |-ous -əs,
-dʒrəs

Dangerfield ˈdendʒɚˌfild; ES ˈdendʒə-

dangle ˈdæŋgl̩ |-d -d |-ling ˈdæŋglɪŋ, -gl̩ɪŋ

Daniel ˈdænjəl, old-fash. ˈdænl̩ |-s -z

Danielson Conn ˈdænl̩sn̩, ˈdænjəlsn̩

Danish ˈdenɪʃ

Danite ˈdænaɪt

dank dæŋk

d'Annunzio dəˈnunzɪˌo (It danˈnuntsjo)

danseuse dɑnˈsɜz, dæn- |-s -ɪz (Fr dãsøːz)

Dante ˈdæntɪ, ˈdɑntɪ (It ˈdante)

Dantean ˈdæntɪən, dænˈtiən, ˈdɑn-, dɑn-

Dantesque dænˈtɛsk, dɑn-

Danton ˈdæntən, Fr leader ʒɔ̃rʒ ʒɑːk dɑ̃ˈtõ

Danube ˈdænjub, ˈdænjub |-bian dænˈjubɪən

Danvers ˈdænvɚz; ES ˈdænvəz; |-'s -ɪz

Danzig ˈdæntsɪg (Ger ˈdɑntsɪx)

dap dæp |dapped dæpt

Daphne ˈdæfnɪ

Daphnis ˈdæfnɪs |Daphnis's ˈdæfnɪsɪz

dapper ˈdæpɚ; ES ˈdæpə(r

dapple ˈdæpl̩ |-d -d |-ling ˈdæplɪŋ, -pl̩ɪŋ

dapple-gray ˈdæpl̩ˈgre (ˈdapple-ˌgray ˈmare)

Darbishire ˈdɑrbɪˌʃɪr, -ʃɚ; ES ˈdɑːbɪˌʃɪə(r,
-ʃə(r

Darby ˈdɑrbɪ; ES ˈdɑːbɪ

Dardanelles ˌdɑrdn̩ˈɛlz; ES ˌdɑːd-

Dardanius dɑrˈdenɪəs; ES dɑ-; |-'s -ɪz

dare dɛr, dær; E dɛə(r, ES dæə(r; |-d -d
or durst dɜst; ES dɜst, dɝst; pptc -d -d

daredevil ˈdɛrˌdɛvl̩, ˈdær-; E ˈdɛə-, ES ˈdæə-;
|-try -trɪ

daren't dɛrnt, dærnt; E dɛənt, ES dæənt

Dares ˈdɛrɪz, ˈdærɪz, ˈderɪz; S ˈdærɪz, ˈderɪz;
|-es' -ɪz

Darfur dɑrˈfur, ˈdɑrfɚ; ES dɑːˈfuə(r, ˈdɑːfə(r

daric ˈdærɪk

Darien Panama ˌdɛrɪˈɛn, ˌdær-, ˈdɛrɪˌɛn,
ˈdær-, -ən; S ˌdær-, ˈdær-; Conn -ˈɛn

daring ˈdɛrɪŋ, ˈdærɪŋ; S ˈdærɪŋ

Darius dəˈraɪəs |Darius's dəˈraɪəsɪz

Darjeeling, -jil- dɑrˈdʒilɪŋ; ES dɑːˈdʒ-

dark dɑrk; ES dɑːk; |darked dɑrkt; ES dɑːkt

darken ˈdɑrkən; ES ˈdɑːk-; |-ed -d |-ing
-kənɪŋ, -knɪŋ

darkey ˈdɑrkɪ; ES ˈdɑːkɪ

darkling ˈdɑrklɪŋ; ES ˈdɑːklɪŋ

darkroom ˈdɑrkˌrum, -ˌrʊm; ES ˈdɑːk-

darksome ˈdɑrksəm; ES ˈdɑːksəm

darky ˈdɑrkɪ; ES ˈdɑːkɪ

Darlan ˈdɑrlən; ES ˈdɑːl-; (Fr darˈlɑ̃)

darling ˈdɑrlɪŋ; ES ˈdɑːlɪŋ

Darmstadt ˈdɑrmˌstat; ES ˈdɑːm-; (Ger
ˈdɑrmˌʃtat)

darn dɑrn; ES dɑːn; |-ed -d |-edest -dɪst

Darnal, -ll ˈdɑrnl̩; ES ˈdɑːnl̩

Darnay dɑrˈne; ES dɑːˈne

darnel ˈdɑrnl̩; ES ˈdɑːnl̩

Darnel, -ll ˈdɑrnl̩, dɑrˈnɛl; ES ˈdɑːnl̩, dɑːˈnɛl

Darnley ˈdɑrnlɪ; ES ˈdɑːnlɪ

Darrow ˈdæro, -ə

Darsie ˈdɑrsɪ; ES ˈdɑːsɪ

dart dɑrt; ES dɑːt; |-ed -ɪd

Dartford ˈdɑrtfɚd; ES ˈdɑːtfəd

dartle ˈdɑrtl̩; ES ˈdɑːtl̩; |-d -d |-ling -tl̩ɪŋ,
-tlɪŋ

|full fʊl |tooth tuθ |further ˈfɝðɚ; ES ˈfɜðə |custom ˈkʌstəm |while hwaɪl |how haʊ |toy tɔɪ
|using ˈjuzɪŋ |fuse fjuz, fɪuz |dish dɪʃ |vision ˈvɪʒən |Eden ˈidn̩ |cradle ˈkredl̩ |keep 'em ˈkipm̩

Words below in which a before r (farm) is sounded ɑ are often pronounced in E with a (fɑːm)

Dartmoor 'dɑrtˌmur, -ˌmor, -ˌmɔr; ES 'dɑːt-ˌmuə(r, -ˌmoə(r, E+-ˌmɔə(r
Dartmouth 'dɑrtməθ; ES 'dɑːtməθ
Darwin 'dɑrwɪn; ES 'dɑːwɪn; |-ism -ˌɪzəm
Darwinian dɑr'wɪnɪən; ES dɑ'wɪnɪən
Dasent 'desn̩t
dash dæʃ |dashes 'dæʃɪz |-ed -t |-edly -ɪdlɪ
dashboard 'dæʃˌbord, -ˌbɔrd; ES 'dæʃˌboəd, E+-ˌbɔəd
dastard 'dæstəd; ES 'dæstəd
data 'detə, 'dætə, 'dɑtə
datary 'detərɪ |dataria də'tɛrɪə, de-, -'ter-
date det |dated 'detɪd
dative 'detɪv
datum 'detəm |data 'detə, 'dætə, 'dɑtə
daub dɔb |daubed dɔbd
Daubeney 'dɔbənɪ, 'dɔbnɪ
Daubigny do'binjɪ (Fr dobi'ŋi)
Daudet do'de, 'dode (Fr do'dɛ)
daughter 'dɔtə; ES 'dɔtə(r
daughter-in-law 'dɔtərɪnˌlɔ, 'dɔtənˌlɔ; ES 'dɔtərɪnˌlɔ, 'dɔtənˌlɔ
daughters-in-law 'dɔtəzɪnˌlɔ, 'dɔtəzn̩ˌlɔ; ES 'dɔtəzɪnˌlɔ, 'dɔtəzn̩ˌlɔ
daunt dɔnt, dɒnt, dɑnt |-ed -ɪd |-less -lɪs
dauphin 'dɔfɪn |-ess -ɪs, -ˌɛs (Fr do'fæ̃)
davenport, D- 'dævənˌport, 'dævm̩ˌport, -ˌpɔrt; ES -ˌpoət, E+-ˌpɔət
Daventry 'dævəntrɪ, loc. 'dentrɪ
David 'devɪd |-son -sn̩
Davies 'devɪz, 'devɪs, 'devɪz |-'s -ɪz
Daviess 'devɪs |-'s -ɪz
da Vinci, Leonardo ˌliə'nɑrdo də'vɪntʃɪ; ES -'nɑːdo; (It ˌleo'nɑrdo dɑ'vintʃi)
Davis 'devɪs |Davis's 'devɪsɪz |-on -n̩
davit 'dævɪt
Davy 'devɪ
daw dɔ
dawdle 'dɔdl̩ |-d -d |-ling 'dɔdlɪŋ, 'dɔdl̩ɪŋ
Dawes dɔz |Dawes's 'dɔzɪz
dawk dɔk, dɑk
dawn dɔn |dawned dɔnd
Dawson 'dɔsn̩
day, D- de |-book -ˌbuk |-break -ˌbrek
Dayak 'daɪæk
daydream 'deˌdrim |-ed -d
dayflower 'deˌflauə, -ˌflaur; ES -ˌflau·ə(r, -ˌflauə(r

daylight 'deˌlaɪt
daylight-saving 'deˌlaɪt'sevɪŋ ('daylight-ˌsaving 'time)
dayspring 'deˌsprɪŋ
daystar 'deˌstɑr; ES 'deˌstɑː(r
daytime 'deˌtaɪm
Dayton 'detn̩ |-ian de'tonɪən
Daytona de'tonə
daze dez |dazes 'dezɪz |dazed dezd |-dly -ɪdlɪ
dazzle 'dæzl̩ |-d -d |-ling 'dæzlɪŋ, dæzl̩ɪŋ
de- prefix. When wholly unaccented, de- varies between dɪ- and də-. When only one of these is given in the vocab., it is to be understood that the other is used by many speakers, or often by the same speaker in different styles. The dɪ- type with many speakers has the usual tendency toward di-.
deacon 'dikən |-ed -d |-ate -ɪt |-ess -ɪs |-esses -ɪsɪz
dead dɛd |deaded 'dɛdɪd |-ly -lɪ
deaden 'dɛdn̩ |-ed -d |-ing 'dɛdn̩ɪŋ, 'dɛdnɪŋ
deadeye, D- 'dɛdˌaɪ
deadfall 'dɛdˌfɔl
deadhead 'dɛdˌhɛd |-headed -ˌhɛdɪd
deadliness 'dɛdlɪnɪs
deadlock 'dɛdˌlɑk; ES+-ˌlɒk; |-ed -t
deadwood, D- 'dɛdˌwud
deaf dɛf, now much less freq. dif
deaf-and-dumb 'dɛfənˈdʌm ('deaf-and-'dumb ˌschool, 'deaf-and-ˌdumb 'boy)
deafen 'dɛfən |-ed -d |-ing 'dɛfənɪŋ, 'dɛfnɪŋ
deaf-mute 'dɛfˈmjut, -'mɪut, -ˌmjut, -ˌmɪut
deal dil |dealt dɛlt
dean din |deaned dind |-ery -ərɪ, -rɪ |-ship -ʃɪp
Dean(e) din
dear dɪr; ES dɪə(r, S+dɛə(r, djɛə(r
Dearborn 'dɪrbən, -ˌbɔrn; ES 'dɪəbən, -ˌbɔən, S+'dɛə-, 'djɛə-
dearth dɝθ; ES dɜθ, dɝθ; |-ths -θs
deary, -ie 'dɪrɪ; S+'dɛrɪ, 'djɛrɪ
death dɛθ |-ths -θs |-ly -lɪ |-like -ˌlaɪk
deathbed 'dɛθˌbɛd
deathblow 'dɛθˌblo
death's-head 'dɛθsˌhɛd
deathwatch 'dɛθˌwatʃ, -ˌwɒtʃ, -ˌwɔtʃ |-es -ɪz
Deauville 'dovɪl (Fr do'vil)
debacle de'bɑkl̩, dɪ-, -'bækl̩ (Fr de'bɑːkl̩)
debar dɪ'bɑr; ES -'bɑː(r; |-red -d

debark dɪˈbɑrk; ES -ˈbɑːk, E+-ˈbɑːk; |-ed -t
debarkation ˌdibɑrˈkeʃən; ES -bɑː-, E+-bɑː-
debase dɪˈbes |-s -ɪz |-d -t |-dness -ɪdnɪs
debatable, -bateable dɪˈbetəbḷ
debate dɪˈbet |-bated -ˈbetɪd
debauch dɪˈbɔtʃ |-es -ɪz |-ed -t |-edly -ɪdlɪ
debauchee ˌdɛbəˈtʃi, -ˈʃi
debauchery dɪˈbɔtʃərɪ, -tʃrɪ
debenture dɪˈbɛntʃɚ; ES -ˈbɛntʃə(r; |-d -d
debilitate dɪˈbɪləˌtet |-tated -ˌtetɪd
debilitation dɪˌbɪləˈteʃən
debility dɪˈbɪlətɪ
debit ˈdɛbɪt |debited ˈdɛbɪtɪd
debonair, -aire ˌdɛbəˈnɛr, -ˈnær; E -ˈnɛə(r,
  ES -ˈnæə(r
Deborah ˈdɛbərə
debouch dɪˈbuʃ |-es -ɪz |-ed -t
debris, dé- dəˈbri, ˈdebri, Brit ˈdɛbri
Debs dɛbz |-ˈs -ɪz
debt dɛt |debtor ˈdɛtɚ; ES ˈdɛtə(r
debunk diˈbʌŋk |-ed -t
De Burgh dɪˈbɝg; ES -ˈbɝg, -ˈbɝg
Debussy dəˈbjusɪ, -ˈbɪu- (Fr dəbyˈsi)
debut dɪˈbju, de-, -ˈbɪu, ˈdebju, -bɪu |-ed -d
  (Fr deˈby)
debutante ˌdɛbjuˈtɑnt ˈdɛbjəˌtænt
decade ˈdɛked, dɛkˈed
decadence dɪˈkedn̩s, ˈdɛkədəns |-cy -ɪ |-dent
  dɪˈkednt, ˈdɛkədənt
decagon ˈdɛkəˌgɑn; ES+-ˌgɒn
decagram, -mme ˈdɛkəˌgræm
decahedral ˌdɛkəˈhidrəl
decahedron ˌdɛkəˈhidrən |-s -z |-dra -drə
decalcify diˈkælsəˌfaɪ |-fied -ˌfaɪd
decalescence ˌdikəˈlɛsn̩s |-scent -sn̩t
decaliter, -tre ˈdɛkəˌlitɚ; ES -ˌlitə(r
Decalogue, -log ˈdɛkəˌlɔg, -ˌlɑg, -ˌlɒg
Decameron dɪˈkæmərən, dɛ-
decameter verse dɪˈkæmətɚ; ES -ˈkæmətə(r
decameter, -tre meas. ˈdɛkəˌmitɚ; ES -tə(r
decamp dɪˈkæmp |-camped -ˈkæmpt
de Camp dɪˈkæmp
decanal ˈdɛkənḷ, dɪˈkenḷ |-ly -ɪ
decane ˈdɛken
decant dɪˈkænt |-ed -ɪd |-er -ɚ; ES -ə(r
decantation ˌdikænˈteʃən
decapitate dɪˈkæpəˌtet |-tated -ˌtetɪd
decapitation dɪˌkæpəˈteʃən, ˌdikæpə-
decapod ˈdɛkəˌpɑd; ES+-ˌpɒd

Decapolis dɪˈkæpəlɪs |-ˈs -ɪz
decarbonate diˈkɑrbənˌet; ES -ˈkɑːb-, E+
  -ˈkɑːb-; |-ated -ˌetɪd
decarbonize diˈkɑrbənˌaɪz; ES -ˈkɑːb-, E+
  -ˈkɑːb-; |-s -ɪz |-d -d
decarburize diˈkɑrbjəˌraɪz, -ˈkɑrbə-; ES
  -ˈkɑːb-, E+-ˈkɑːb-
decasyllable ˈdɛkəˌsɪləbḷ |-bic ˌdɛkəsɪˈlæbɪk
decathlon dɪˈkæθlɑn; ES+-lɒn
Decatur dɪˈketɚ; ES -ˈketə(r
decay dɪˈke |-cayed -ˈked
Deccan ˈdɛkən
decease dɪˈsis |-s -ɪz |-d -t
decedent dɪˈsidn̩t
deceit dɪˈsit |-ful -fəl |-fully -fəlɪ
deceive dɪˈsiv |-ceived -ˈsivd
decelerate diˈsɛləˌret |-rated -ˌretɪd
deceleration diˌsɛləˈreʃən, ˌdisɛlə-
December dɪˈsɛmbɚ; ES -ˈsɛmbə(r
decemvir dɪˈsɛmvɚ; ES -ˈsɛmvə(r; |-s -z |-i
  -ˌaɪ
decemvirate dɪˈsɛmvərɪt, -ˌret, -vrɪt
decency ˈdisn̩sɪ |decent ˈdisn̩t
decennial dɪˈsɛnɪəl |-ly -ɪ
decenter, -tre diˈsɛntɚ; ES -ˈsɛntə(r; |-(e)d -d
  |-(r)ing -ˈsɛntərɪŋ, -ˈsɛntrɪŋ
decentralization ˌdisɛntrələˈzeʃən, diˌsɛn-,
  -aɪˈz-
decentralize diˈsɛntrəlˌaɪz |-s -ɪz |-d -d
deception dɪˈsɛpʃən |-tive -tɪv
decibel ˈdɛsəˌbɛl
decide dɪˈsaɪd |-cided -ˈsaɪdɪd
deciduous dɪˈsɪdʒʊəs
decigram, -mme ˈdɛsəˌgræm
decile, -il ˈdɛsɪl
deciliter, -tre ˈdɛsəˌlitɚ; ES -ˌlitə(r
decillion diˈsɪljən |-th -θ |-ths -θs
decimal ˈdɛsəmḷ |-ly -ɪ
decimate ˈdɛsəˌmet |-d -ɪd |-tion ˌdɛsəˈmeʃən
decimeter, -tre ˈdɛsəˌmitɚ; ES -ˌmitə(r
decipher dɪˈsaɪfɚ; ES -ˈsaɪfə(r; |-ed -d |-ing
  -ˈsaɪfərɪŋ, -ˈsaɪfrɪŋ
decision dɪˈsɪʒən |-al -ḷ
decisive dɪˈsaɪsɪv
decistere ˈdɛsəˌstɪr; ES -ˌstɪə(r
Decius ˈdiʃɪəs, -ʃəs |-ˈs -ɪz
deck dɛk |decked dɛkt |-house -ˌhaʊs
deckle, -ckel ˈdɛkḷ
deckle-edged ˈdɛkḷˈɛdʒd (ˈdeckle-ˌedgedˈbond)

declaim dɪ'klem |-claimed -'klemd
declamation ˌdɛklə'meʃən
declamatory dɪ'klæməˌtorɪ, -ˌtɔrɪ; S -ˌtorɪ
declaration ˌdɛklə'reʃən
declarative dɪ'klærətɪv
declaratory dɪ'klærəˌtorɪ, -ˌtɔrɪ; S -ˌtorɪ
declare dɪ'klɛr, -'klær; E -'klɛə(r, ES
-'klæə(r; |-d -d |-dly -ɪdlɪ |-r -ɚ; ES -ə(r
declension dɪ'klɛnʃən |-al -l |-ally -lɪ
declinable dɪ'klaɪnəbl
declination ˌdɛklə'neʃən |-al -l
decline dɪ'klaɪn |-clined -'klaɪnd
declivitous dɪ'klɪvətəs |-ty -tɪ
decoct dɪ'kakt; ES+-'kɒkt; |-ed -ɪd
decoction dɪ'kakʃən; ES+-'kɒk-; |-tive -tɪv
decode di'kod |-coded -'kodɪd
decollate dɪ'kalet; ES+-'kɒl-; |-d -ɪd
décolleté ˌdekal'te, -kalə'te, -kɒl- (Fr de-
kɔl'te)
decolorant di'kʌlərənt
decolorate di'kʌləˌret |-rated -ˌretɪd
decoloration ˌdikʌlə'reʃən
decolorize di'kʌləˌraɪz |-s -ɪz |-d -d
decompose ˌdikəm'poz |-s -ɪz |-d -d
decomposition ˌdikampə'zɪʃən; ES+-kɒm-
decompound ˌdikəm'paund |-ed -ɪd
decompress ˌdikəm'prɛs |-es -ɪz |-ed -t
décor de'kɔr; ES -'kɔə(r; (Fr de'kɔ:r)
Decorah dɪ'korə, -'kɔrə; S -'korə
decorate 'dɛkəˌret |-d -ɪd -tion ˌdɛkə'reʃən
decorative 'dɛkəˌretɪv |-tor -tɚ; ES -tə(r
decorous 'dɛkərəs, dɪ'korəs; EN+-'kɔr-
decorum dɪ'korəm, -'kɔr-; S -'korəm
decoy n dɪ'kɔɪ, 'dikɔɪ
decoy v dɪ'kɔɪ |-ed -d
decrease n 'dikris, di'kris, dɪ- |-s -ɪz
decrease v dɪ'kris, ˌdi- |-s -ɪz |-d -t ('de-
ˌcreased 'buying)
decree dɪ'kri |-creed -'krid
decrement 'dɛkrəmənt
decrepit dɪ'krɛpɪt
decrepitude dɪ'krɛpəˌtjud, -ˌtɪud, -ˌtud
decrescendo ˌdikrə'ʃɛndo, ˌde- (It ˌdekre-
'ʃendo)
decretal dɪ'kritl
decry dɪ'kraɪ |-cried -'kraɪd |-crial -'kraɪəl
decumbent dɪ'kʌmbənt
decuple 'dɛkjupl, dɛk'jupl |-d -d |-ling -plɪŋ,
-plɪŋ

decurrent dɪ'kɝənt; ES -'kɜr-, -'kʌr-, -'kɝ-
Dedham 'dɛdəm
dedicate 'dɛdəˌket |-d -ɪd |-tor -ɚ; ES -ə(r
dedication ˌdɛdə'keʃən
dedicatory 'dɛdəkəˌtorɪ, -ˌtɔrɪ; S -ˌtorɪ
deduce dɪ'djus, -'dɪus, -'dus |-s -ɪz |-d -t
deducibility dɪˌdjusə'bɪlətɪ, -ˌdɪus-, -ˌdus-
deducible dɪ'djusəbl, -'dɪus-, -'dus- |-bly
-blɪ
deduct dɪ'dʌkt |-ed -ɪd |-ible -əbl
deduction dɪ'dʌkʃən |-tive -tɪv
Dee di
dee 'die² di
dee 'damn³ di |-d -d
dee letter di
deed did |deeded 'didɪd
deem dim |deemed dimd
Deems dimz |-'s -ɪz
deemster 'dimstɚ; ES 'dimstə(r
deep dip
deepen 'dipən |-ed -d |-ing 'dipənɪŋ, 'dipnɪŋ
deep-mouthed 'dip'mauðd, -θt ('deep-
ˌmouthed 'bay)
deep-rooted 'dip'rutɪd, -'rʊtɪd
deep-sea 'dip'si ('deep-'sea ˌlife)
deep-seated 'dip'sitɪd ('deep-ˌseated 'faith)
deer dɪr; ES dɪə(r, S+dɛə(r, djɛə(r; |-hound
-ˌhaund |-skin -ˌskɪn |-stalking -ˌstɔkɪŋ
Deerfield 'dɪr,fild; ES 'dɪə,fild, S+'dɛə-,
'djɛə-
deface dɪ'fes |-s -ɪz |-d -t |-able -əbl
de facto dɪ'fækto
defalcate dɪ'fælket, -'fɔl- |-d -ɪd |-tor -ɚ; ES
-ə(r
defalcation ˌdifæl'keʃən, -fɔl-
defamation ˌdɛfə'meʃən, ˌdi-
defamatory dɪ'fæməˌtorɪ, -ˌtɔrɪ; S -ˌtorɪ
defame dɪ'fem |-famed -'femd
default dɪ'fɔlt |-ed -ɪd
defeasibility dɪˌfizə'bɪlətɪ
defeasible dɪ'fizəbl
defeat dɪ'fit |-ed -ɪd |-ism -ɪzəm |-ist -ɪst
defecate 'dɛfəˌket |-d -ɪd |-tion ˌdɛfə'keʃən
defect dɪ'fɛkt, 'difɛkt
defection dɪ'fɛkʃən |-tive -tɪv
defend dɪ'fɛnd |-ed -ɪd |-ant -ənt
defense, Brit -ce dɪ'fɛns |-s -ɪz |-sive -ɪv
defensibility dɪˌfɛnsə'bɪlətɪ
defensible dɪ'fɛnsəbl |-bly -blɪ

defer dɪˈfɝ; ES -ˈfɜ(r, -ˈfɝ; |-red -d
deference ˈdɛfərəns
deferential ˌdɛfəˈrɛnʃəl |-ly -ɪ
deferrer dɪˈfɝɚ; ES -ˈfɜrə(r, -ˈfɝə(r
defiance, D- dɪˈfaɪəns |-s -ɪz |-ant -ənt
deficiency dɪˈfɪʃənsɪ |-cient -ʃənt
deficit ˈdɛfəsɪt, *Brit* + dɪˈfɪsɪt
defier dɪˈfaɪɚ; ES -ˈfaɪ·ə(r
defile *'befoul'* dɪˈfaɪl |-filed -ˈfaɪld
defile *'march off'* dɪˈfaɪl, ˈdifaɪl |-d -d
defile *n* dɪˈfaɪl, ˈdifaɪl
definable dɪˈfaɪnəbl̩ |-bly -blɪ
define dɪˈfaɪn |-fined -ˈfaɪnd
definite ˈdɛfənɪt |-tion ˌdɛfəˈnɪʃən
definitive dɪˈfɪnətɪv
deflate dɪˈflet |-d -ɪd |-flation -ˈfleʃən
deflationary dɪˈfleʃənˌɛrɪ
deflect dɪˈflɛkt |-ed -ɪd
deflection, -flexion dɪˈflɛkʃən
deflower dɪˈflaʊɚ; ES -ˈflaʊ·ə(r; |-ed -d
Defoe, De Foe dɪˈfo
deforce dɪˈfors, -ˈfɔrs; ES -ˈfoəs, E+-ˈfɔəs;
  |-s -ɪz |-d -t
deforest dɪˈfɔrɪst, -ˈfɑr-, -ˈfɒr- |-ed -ɪd
deforestation dɪˌfɔrɪsˈteʃən, -ˌfɑr-, -ˌfɒr-, ˌdif-
deform dɪˈfɔrm; ES -ˈfɔəm; |-ed -d |-edly
  -ɪdlɪ
deformation ˌdifɔrˈmeʃən, ˌdɛfɚ-; ES ˌdifɔə-,
  ˌdɛfə-
deformity dɪˈfɔrmətɪ; ES -ˈfɔəmətɪ
defraud dɪˈfrɔd |-ed -ɪd
defray dɪˈfre |-ed -d |-able -əbl̩ |-al -əl
defrock diˈfrɑk; ES+-ˈfrɒk; |-ed -t
defrost diˈfrɔst, -ˈfrɒst |-ed -ɪd
deft dɛft
defunct dɪˈfʌŋkt
defy *n* dɪˈfaɪ, ˈdifaɪ
defy *v* dɪˈfaɪ |-fied -ˈfaɪd
degenerate *adj* dɪˈdʒɛnərɪt, -ˈdʒɛnrɪt |-racy
  -rəsɪ, -nrəsɪ
degenerate *v* dɪˈdʒɛnəˌret |-d -ɪd |-tive -ɪv
degeneration dɪˌdʒɛnəˈreʃən, ˌdidʒənə-
deglutinate dɪˈglutn̩ˌet, -ˈglʊt- |-d -ɪd
deglutition ˌdiglʊˈtɪʃən, -glɪʊ-
degrade dɪˈgred |-d -ɪd |-dation ˌdɛgrəˈdeʃən
degree dɪˈgri |-d -d
De Groot dəˈgrot = Grotius
degum diˈgʌm |-gummed -ˈgʌmd
dehisce dɪˈhɪs |-s -ɪz |-d -t |-nce -n̩s |-nt -n̩t

dehorn diˈhɔrn; ES -ˈhɔən; |-ed -d
dehydrate diˈhaɪdret |-drated -dretɪd
deictic ˈdaɪktɪk |-al -l̩ |-ally -l̩ɪ, -ɪklɪ
deification ˌdiəfəˈkeʃən
deiform ˈdiəˌfɔrm; ES -ˌfɔəm
deify ˈdiəˌfaɪ |-fied -ˌfaɪd
deign den |deigned dend
Dei gratia ˈdiaɪˈgreʃɪə
deil dil
Deiphobus diˈɪfəbəs |-'s -ɪz
Deira ˈdeərə
Deirdre ˈdɪrdrɪ, ˈdɛrdrɪ; ES ˈdɪə-, ˈdɛə-; *Ir*
  ˈderdre
deism ˈdiɪzəm |-ist -ɪst
deistic diˈɪstɪk |-al -l̩ |-ally -l̩ɪ, -ɪklɪ
deity ˈdiətɪ
deject dɪˈdʒɛkt |-ed -ɪd |-ction -kʃən
déjeuné, -ner *n* ˈdeʒəˌne (*Fr* deʒœˈne)
de jure diˈdʒʊrɪ, -ˈdʒɪʊrɪ
De Kalb dɪˈkælb
Dekker ˈdɛkɚ; ES ˈdɛkə
dekle ˈdɛkl̩
De Koven dɪˈkovən
Delafield ˈdɛləˌfild
Delagoa ˌdɛləˈgoə (ˈDelaˌgoa ˈBay)
delaine, D- dəˈlen
de la Mare, D- ˈdɛləˌmɛr, -ˌmær; E -ˌmɛə(r,
  ES -ˌmæə(r; *acct* + ˌde la ˈMare
Delamere ˈdɛləˌmɪr; ES -ˌmɪə(r, S+-ˌmɛə(r
De Land dɪˈlænd
Deland dɪˈlænd, *Brit name* ˈdilənd
Delano ˈdɛləˌno
De la Pole ˌdɛləˈpol
delate dɪˈlet |-lated -ˈletɪd
Delavan ˈdɛləvən
Delaware ˈdɛləˌwɛr, -ˌwær; E -ˌwɛə(r, ES
  -ˌwæə(r
Delawarean ˌdɛləˈwɛrɪən, -ˈwær-; S -ˈwærɪən
De La Warr ˈdɛləˌwɛr -ˌwær; E -ˌwɛə(r, ES
  -ˌwæə(r
delay dɪˈle |-layed -ˈled
dele ˈdilɪ |deled ˈdilɪd
delectable dɪˈlɛktəbl̩ |-bly -blɪ
delectation ˌdilɛkˈteʃən, dɪˌlɛkˈteʃən
delegate *n* ˈdɛləˌget, ˈdɛləgɪt |-gacy -gəsɪ
delegate *v* ˈdɛləˌget |-d -ɪd |-tion ˌdɛləˈgeʃən
de Lesseps dəˈlɛsəps (*Fr* dəlɛˈsɛps) |-'s -ɪz
delete dɪˈlit |-leted -ˈlitɪd |-letion -ˈliʃən
deleterious ˌdɛləˈtɪrɪəs

|full fʊl |tooth tuθ |further ˈfɝðɚ; ES ˈfɜðə |custom ˈkʌstəm |while hwaɪl |how haʊ |toy tɔɪ
|using ˈjuzɪŋ |fuse fjuz, fɪuz |dish dɪʃ |vision ˈvɪʒən |Eden ˈidn̩ |cradle ˈkredl̩ |keep 'em ˈkipm̩

delft, D- dɛlft |-ware -ˌwɛr, -ˌwær; E
 -ˌwɛə(r, ES -ˌwæə(r
Delhi US 'dɛlhaɪ, India 'dɛlɪ
Delia 'dɪljə, -lɪə |-n -n
deliberate adj dɪ'lɪbərɪt, -brɪt
deliberate v dɪ'lɪbəˌret |-d -ɪd |-tion dɪˌlɪbə-
 'reʃən
deliberative dɪ'lɪbəˌretɪv |-tor -tɚ; ES -tə(r
delicate 'dɛləkət, -kɪt |-cacy -kəsɪ
delicatessen ˌdɛləkə'tɛsn̩
delicious dɪ'lɪʃəs
delight dɪ'laɪt |-ed -ɪd |-ful -fəl |-fully -fəlɪ
Delilah dɪ'laɪlə
delimit dɪ'lɪmɪt |-ed -ɪd
delimitation dɪˌlɪmə'teʃən, ˌdɪlɪmə-
delineate dɪ'lɪnɪˌet |-d -ɪd |-tion dɪˌlɪnɪ'eʃən
delineative dɪ'lɪnɪˌetɪv |-tor -tɚ; ES -tə(r
delinquency dɪ'lɪŋkwənsɪ |-quent -kwənt
deliquesce ˌdɛlə'kwɛs |-s -ɪz |-d -t
deliquescence ˌdɛlə'kwɛsn̩s |-cent -sn̩t
delirium dɪ'lɪrɪəm |-s -z |-ria -rɪə |-rious -rɪəs
Delisle, De l'Isle US dɪ'laɪl, Fr name də'lil
Delitzsch 'dɛlɪtʃ |-'s -ɪz
Delius 'dɪlɪəs |-'s -ɪz
deliver dɪ'lɪvɚ; ES -'lɪvə(r; |-ed -d |-ing
 -'lɪvərɪŋ, -'lɪvrɪŋ |-ance -vərəns, -vrəns
deliverer dɪ'lɪvərɚ, -'lɪvrɚ; ES -rə(r; |-very
 -vərɪ, -vrɪ
dell, D- dɛl |Della 'dɛlə
Della Robbia ˌdɛlə'rabɪə, -'rɒb- (It ˌdella-
 'robbja)
Delmarva dɛl'marvə; ES -'ma:və, E+
 -'ma:və
Delmonico dɛl'manɪˌko, -'mɒn-
Delos 'dilas, -lɒs |-'s -ɪz
delouse di'laus, -'lauz |-s -ɪz |-d -t, -d
Delphi 'dɛlfaɪ |-phian -fɪən |-phic -fɪk
delphinium, D- dɛl'fɪnɪəm |-s -z
Delphos 'dɛlfəs, -fas, -fɒs |-'s -ɪz
Del Rio dɛl'rio
Delsarte dɛl'sart; ES -'sa:t, E+-'sa:t
del Sarto, Andrea 'andrɪədɛl'sarto; ES
 -'sa:to, E+-'sa:to; (It an'drɛ:adel'sarto)
delta, D- 'dɛltə |-ic dɛl'te·ɪk |-toid 'dɛltɔɪd
delude dɪ'lud, -'lɪud |-d -ɪd
deluge 'dɛljudʒ |-s -ɪz |-d -d
delusion dɪ'luʒən, -'lɪuʒən
delusive dɪ'lusɪv, -'lɪus- |-sory -sərɪ
de luxe dɪ'lʊks, -'lʌks (Fr də'lyks)

delve dɛlv |delved dɛlvd
demagnetization ˌdimægnətə'zeʃən, diˌmæg-,
 -aɪ'z-
demagnetize di'mægnəˌtaɪz |-s -ɪz |-d -d
demagogic ˌdɛmə'gadʒɪk, -'gɒdʒ-, -'gag-,
 -'gɒg- |-al -| |-ally -ɪ, -ɪklɪ
demagogism 'dɛməˌgɔgɪzəm, -ˌgag-, -ˌgɒg-
demagogue, -gog 'dɛməˌgɔg, -ˌgag, -ˌgɒg
 |-guery -ərɪ, -rɪ
demagogy 'dɛməˌgodʒɪ, -ˌgɔgɪ, -ˌgagɪ, -ˌgɒgɪ
demand dɪ'mænd; E+-'mand, -'mand; |-ed
 -ɪd
demarcate dɪ'market, 'dimarˌket; ES -a:k-,
 E+-a:k-; |-d -ɪd
demarcation ˌdimar'keʃən; ES -ma:'k-, E+
 -ma:'k-
Demas 'dimas |-'s -ɪz
dematerialize ˌdimə'tɪrɪəlˌaɪz |-s -ɪz |-d -d
demean dɪ'min |-ed -d |-or -ɚ; ES -ə(r
dement dɪ'mɛnt |-ed -ɪd |-ia -'mɛnʃɪə, -ʃə
demerit di'mɛrɪt |-ed -ɪd
demesne dɪ'men, -'min |-nial -ɪəl
Demeter dɪ'mitɚ; ES -'mitə(r
Demetrius dɪ'mitrɪəs |-'s -ɪz
demigod 'dɛməˌgad, -ˌgɒd
demijohn 'dɛməˌdʒan, -ˌdʒɒn
demilitarize di'mɪlətəˌraɪz |-s -ɪz |-d -d
demimondaine ˌdɛmɪman'den, -mɒn- (Fr
 dəmimõ'dɛn)
demimonde 'dɛmɪˌmand, -ˌmɒnd, ˌdɛmɪ'm-
 (Fr dəmi'mõ:d)
Deming 'dɛmɪŋ
demirep 'dɛmɪˌrɛp
demise dɪ'maɪz |-s -ɪz |-d -d
demisemiquaver ˌdɛmɪ'sɛməˌkwevɚ; ES
 -ˌkwevə(r
demission dɪ'mɪʃən |-ary -ˌɛrɪ
demit n dɪ'mɪt, 'dimɪt
demit v dɪ'mɪt |-ted -ɪd
demitasse 'dɛməˌtæs, -ˌtas (Fr dəmi'ta:s)
demitint 'dɛmɪˌtɪnt
demiurge 'dɛmɪˌɝdʒ; ES -ˌɜdʒ, -ˌɝdʒ; |-s -ɪz
demobilization ˌdimoblə'zeʃən, dɪˌmoblə-,
 -aɪ'z-
demobilize di'moblˌaɪz |-s -ɪz |-d -d
democracy də'makrəsɪ; ES+-'mɒk-
democrat, D- 'dɛməˌkræt
democratic ˌdɛmə'krætɪk |-al -| |-ally -ɪ,
 -ɪklɪ

democratize də'makrə₋taɪz; ES+-'mɒk-; |-s
-ɪz |-d -d
Democritus dɪ'makrɪtəs; ES+-'mɒk-; |-'s -ɪz
Demogorgon ₋dimə'gɔrgən, ₋dɛmə-; ES
-'gɔɔgən
demography dɪ'magrəfɪ, di-, -'mɒg-
demoiselle ₋dɛmwa'zɛl (Fr dəmwa'zɛl)
demolish dɪ'malɪʃ; ES+-'mɒl-; |-es -ɪz |-ed -t
demolition ₋dɛmə'lɪʃən, ₋dimə-
demon 'dimən
demonetization di₋manətə'zeʃən, -₋mʌn-,
-aɪ'z-; ES+-₋mɒn-
demonetize di'manə₋taɪz, -'mʌn-; ES+
-'mɒn-; |-s -ɪz |-d -d
demoniac dɪ'monɪ₋æk
demoniacal ₋dimə'naɪək| |-ly -ɪ, -əklɪ
demonic di'manɪk; ES+-'mɒn-; |-al -|
demonism 'dimən₋ɪzəm |-ist -ɪst
demonolater ₋dimən'alətɚ; ES -'alətə(r,
-'ɒl-; |-try -trɪ |-logy -lədʒɪ
demonstrability ₋dɛmənstrə'bɪlətɪ, dɪ₋man-
strə-; ES+-₋mɒn-
demonstrable 'dɛmənstrəb|, dɪ'manstrə-;
ES+-'mɒn-; |-bly -blɪ
demonstrant dɪ'manstrənt; ES+-'mɒn-
demonstrate 'dɛmən₋stret |-strated -₋stretɪd
demonstration ₋dɛmən'streʃən
demonstrative dɪ'manstrətɪv; ES+-'mɒn-; in
sense 'showy'+'dɛmən₋stretɪv
demonstrator 'dɛmən₋stretɚ; ES -₋stretə(r
demoralization dɪ₋mɔrələ'zeʃən, -₋mar-,
-₋mɒr-, -aɪ'z-
demoralize dɪ'mɔrəl₋aɪz, -'mar-, -'mɒr- |-s -ɪz
|-d -d
De Morgan dɪ'mɔrgən; ES -'mɔəgən
demos 'dimas, -mɒs |-mi -maɪ
Demosthenes dɪ'masθə₋niz, -'mɒs- |-'s -ɪz
demote dɪ'mot |-moted -'motɪd |-tion -'moʃən
demotics di'matɪks; ES+-'mɒt-
demount di'maʊnt |-able -əb|
dempster 'dɛmpstɚ; ES -stə(r
demulcent dɪ'mʌlsnt
demur dɪ'mɝ; ES -'mɝ(r, -'mɝ; |-red -d
demure dɪ'mjʊr, -'mɪʊr; ES -'mjʊə(r,
-'mɪʊə(r
demurrage dɪ'mɝɪdʒ; ES -'mɝr-, -'mʌr-,
-'mɝ-
demurrer 'objector' dɪ'mɝɚ; ES -'mɝə(r,
-'mɝə(r

demurrer 'objection' dɪ'mɝɚ; ES -'mɝə(r,
-'mʌr-, -'mɝə(r
demy dɪ'maɪ
den dɛn |denned dɛnd
denarius dɪ'nɛrɪəs, -'ner- |-s -ɪz |-rii -rɪ₋aɪ
denary 'dɛnərɪ, 'dinərɪ
denationalize di'næʃən|₋aɪz, -ʃnəl- |-s -ɪz
|-d -d
denaturalization di₋nætʃrələ'zeʃən, -aɪ'z-
denaturalize di'nætʃrəl₋aɪz, -tʃərəl- |-s -ɪz
|-d -d
denaturant di'netʃərənt
denature di'netʃɚ; ES -tʃə(r; |-d -d |-ring
-'netʃərɪŋ, -'netʃrɪŋ
Denbigh 'dɛnbɪ |-shire -₋ʃɪr, -ʃɚ; ES -₋ʃɪə(r,
-ʃə(r
dendrite 'dɛndraɪt
dendroid 'dɛndrɔɪd |-al dɛn'drɔɪd|
dendrology dɛn'dralədʒɪ; ES+-'drɒl-
Deneb 'dɛnɛb
dengue 'dɛŋgɪ, 'dɛŋge
Denham 'dɛnəm
denial dɪ'naɪəl, -'naɪl |-able -'naɪəb|
denier 'contradicter' dɪ'naɪɚ; ES -'naɪ₋ə(r
denier coin də'nɪr; ES -'nɪə(r; (Fr də'nje)
denigrate 'dɛnə₋gret |-grated -₋gretɪd
denim 'dɛnəm, 'dɛnɪm
Denis 'dɛnɪs |-'s -ɪz (Fr də'ni)
Denise də'niz |-'s -ɪz
Denison 'dɛnəsn
denitrate di'naɪtret |-trated -tretɪd
denizen 'dɛnəzn |-ed -d
Denmark 'dɛnmark; ES -ma:k, E+-ma:k
Dennis 'dɛnɪs |-'s -ɪz
Dennison 'dɛnəsn
Denny 'dɛnɪ |-s -s |-s's -sɪz
denominate adj dɪ'namənɪt, -₋net; ES+
-'nɒm-
denomination dɪ₋namə'neʃən; ES+-₋nɒm-;
|-al -|, -ʃnəl |-ally -|ɪ, -ʃnəlɪ |-alism -|₋ɪzəm,
-ʃnəl-
denominative dɪ'namə₋netɪv, -nətɪv; ES+
-'nɒm-
denominator dɪ'namə₋netɚ; ES-'namə₋netə(r,
-'nɒm-
denotation ₋dino'teʃən
denotative dɪ'notətɪv, esp. in contrast with
connotative 'dino₋tetɪv
denote dɪ'not |-noted -'notɪd

denouement de'numã (Fr denu'mã)
denounce dɪ'nauns |-s -ɪz |-d -t
de novo di'novo
dense dɛns |density 'dɛnsətɪ
dent dɛnt |dented 'dɛntɪd
dental 'dɛntḷ |-ly -ɪ
dentate 'dɛntet |-tated -tetɪd |-tion dɛn'teʃən
denticulate adj dɛn'tɪkjəlɪt, -ˌlet |-d -ɪd
dentifrice 'dɛntəˌfrɪs |-s -ɪz
dentilabial ˌdɛntɪ'lebɪəl
dentin 'dɛntɪn |dentine 'dɛntin, -tɪn
dentist 'dɛntɪst |-ry -rɪ
dentition dɛn'tɪʃən
Denton 'dɛntən
denture 'dɛntʃɚ; ES 'dɛntʃə(r; |-ral -əl
denudation ˌdinju'deʃən, ˌdɛn-, -nɪu-, -nu-
denude dɪ'njud, -'nɪud, -'nud |-d -ɪd
denunciate dɪ'nʌnsɪˌet, -ʃɪ- |-d -ɪd |-tive -ɪv
denunciation dɪˌnʌnsɪ'eʃən, -ʃɪ'eʃən
denunciatory dɪ'nʌnsɪəˌtorɪ, -ʃɪ-, -ˌtɔrɪ; S
   -ˌtorɪ
Denver 'dɛnvɚ; ES 'dɛnvə(r
deny dɪ'naɪ |denied dɪ'naɪd
Denys 'dɛnɪs |-'s -ɪz (Fr də'ni)
deodand 'diəˌdænd
deodar 'diəˌdɑr; ES -ˌdɑ:(r, E+-ˌdɑ:(r
deodorant di'odərənt
deodorize di'odəˌraɪz |-s -ɪz |-d -d
Deo gratias 'dio'greʃɪˌæs
Deo volente 'diovo'lɛntɪ
deoxidize di'ɑksəˌdaɪz; ES+-'ɒks-; |-s -ɪz
   |-d -d
depart dɪ'pɑrt; ES -'pɑ:t, E+-'pɑ:t; |-ed -ɪd
   |-ment -mənt
departmental dɪˌpɑrt'mɛntḷ, ˌdipɑrt-; ES
   -ɑ:t-, E+-ɑ:t-; |-ly -ɪ
departure dɪ'pɑrtʃɚ; ES -'pɑ:tʃə(r, E+-'pɑ:t-
depend dɪ'pɛnd |-ed -ɪd
dependability dɪˌpɛndə'bɪlətɪ
dependable dɪ'pɛndəbḷ |-bly -blɪ
dependence dɪ'pɛndəns |-cy -ɪ
dependent, -ant dɪ'pɛndənt
Depere dɪ'pɪr; ES -'pɪə(r
Depew dɪ'pju, -'pɪu
depict dɪ'pɪkt |-ed -ɪd
depiction dɪ'pɪkʃən |-ture -tʃɚ; ES -tʃə(r
depilate 'dɛpəˌlet |-lated -ˌletɪd
depilatory dɪ'pɪləˌtorɪ, -ˌtɔrɪ; S -ˌtorɪ
deplete dɪ'plit |-d -ɪd |-tion -'pliʃən

deplorable dɪ'plorəbḷ, -'plɔr-; S -'plor-; |-bly
   -blɪ
deplore dɪ'plor, -'plɔr; ES -'ploə(r, E+
   -'plɔə(r; |-d -d
deploy dɪ'plɔɪ |-ed -d
deplume dɪ'plum, -'plɪum |-d -d
depolarization ˌdipolərə'zeʃən, diˌpol-, -aɪ'z-
depolarize dɪ'poləˌraɪz |-s -ɪz |-d -d
depone dɪ'pon |-d -d |-nt -ənt
depopulate di'pɑpjəˌlet; ES+-'pɒp-; |-d -ɪd
depopulation ˌdipɑpjə'leʃən, diˌpɑp-; ES+
   -ɒp-
deport dɪ'port, -'pɔrt; ES -'poət, E+-'pɔət;
   |-ed -ɪd
deportation ˌdipor'teʃən, -pɔr-; ES -poə-,
   E+-pɔə-
deportee ˌdipor'ti, -pɔr-; ES -poə-, E+-pɔə-
deportment dɪ'portmənt, -'pɔrt-; ES -'poət-,
   E+-'pɔət-
depose dɪ'poz |-s -ɪz |-d -d |-sal -ḷ
deposit, D- dɪ'pazɪt; ES+-'pɒz-; |-ed -ɪd
depositary dɪ'pazəˌtɛrɪ; ES+-'pɒz-
deposition ˌdɛpə'zɪʃən, ˌdi-
depositor dɪ'pazɪtɚ; ES -'pazɪtə(r, -'pɒz-
depository dɪ'pazəˌtorɪ, -ˌtɔrɪ; S -ˌtorɪ,
   ES+-'pɒz-
depot 'dipo, Brit usually 'dɛpo
depravation ˌdɛprə'veʃən
deprave dɪ'prev |-d -d |-pravity -'prævətɪ
deprecate 'dɛprəˌket |-d -ɪd |-tive -ɪv
deprecation ˌdɛprə'keʃən
deprecatory 'dɛprəkəˌtorɪ, -ˌtɔrɪ; S -ˌtorɪ
depreciable dɪ'priʃɪəbḷ
depreciate dɪ'priʃɪˌet |-ated -ˌetɪd
depreciation dɪˌpriʃɪ'eʃən
depreciative dɪ'priʃɪˌetɪv |-tor -tɚ; ES -tə(r
depreciatory dɪ'priʃɪəˌtorɪ, -ˌtɔrɪ; S -ˌtorɪ
depredate 'dɛprɪˌdet |-d -ɪd |-tor -ɚ; ES -ə(r
depredation ˌdɛprɪ'deʃən
depress dɪ'prɛs |-es -ɪz |-ed -t |-ant -ṇt
depression dɪ'prɛʃən |-sive -'prɛsɪv
deprival dɪ'praɪvḷ
deprivation ˌdɛprə'veʃən
deprive dɪ'praɪv |-prived -'praɪvd
de profundis ˌdiprə'fʌndɪs
Deptford 'dɛtfɚd; ES 'dɛtfəd
depth dɛpθ |-ths -θs
Depue dɪ'pju, -'pɪu
deputation ˌdɛpjə'teʃən

depute dɪ'pjut, -'pɪut |-d -ɪd
deputize 'dɛpjə,taɪz |-s -ɪz |-d -d |-ty -tɪ
De Quincey, -cy dɪ'kwɪnsɪ
derail di'rel |-railed -'reld
derange dɪ'rendʒ |-s -ɪz |-d -d
Derby Engd 'darbɪ, 'dɝbɪ; Am races 'dɝbɪ,
    less freq. 'darbɪ; Eng races 'darbɪ; US
    places 'dɝbɪ; ES 'da:bɪ, 'dɜbɪ, 'dɝbɪ,
    E+'da:bɪ; |-shire -,ʃɪr, -ʃɚ; ES -,ʃɪə(r, -ʃə(r
    —The Brit pron. of all these is 'da:bɪ, 'darbɪ,
    less freq. 'dɜbɪ, 'dɝbɪ.
derby 'dɝbɪ; ES 'dɜbɪ, 'dɝbɪ; Brit 'da:bɪ,
    'darbɪ
derelict 'dɛrə,lɪkt |-ction ,dɛrə'lɪkʃən
deride dɪ'raɪd |-rided -'raɪdɪd
de rigueur Fr dəri'gœːr
derision dɪ'rɪʒən |-risible dɪ'rɪzəbḷ
derisive dɪ'raɪsɪv |-sory -sərɪ
derivable dɪ'raɪvəbḷ |-bly -blɪ
derivation ,dɛrə'veʃən
derivative də'rɪvətɪv
derive də'raɪv |-rived -'raɪvd
derma 'dɝmə; ES 'dɜmə, 'dɝmə
dermatitis ,dɝmə'taɪtɪs; ES ,dɜmə-, ,dɝmə-
dermatological ,dɝmətə'ladʒɪkḷ; ES ,dɜmə-,
    ,dɝmə-, -'lɒdʒ-
dermatology ,dɝmə'talədʒɪ; ES ,dɜmə-,
    ,dɝmə-, -'tɒl-; |-gist -dʒɪst
dermis 'dɝmɪs; ES 'dɜmɪs, 'dɝmɪs
Dermott 'dɝmət; ES 'dɜmət, 'dɝmət
Derna 'dɛrnə; ES 'dɛənə
dernier 'dɝnɪɚ; ES 'dɜnɪ·ə(r, 'dɝn-; (Fr
    dɛr'nje)
dernier cri Fr dɛrnje'kri
dernier ressort Fr dɛrnjərə'sɔːr
derogate 'dɛrə,get |-gated -,getɪd
derogation ,dɛrə'geʃən
derogative dɪ'ragətɪv, -'rɒg-
derogatory dɪ'ragə,torɪ, -'rɒg-, -,tɔrɪ; S
    -,tɔrɪ; |-rily -rəlɪ
Deronda də'randə; ES+-'rɒn-
derrick, D- 'dɛrɪk |-ed -t
derring-do 'dɛrɪŋ'du
derringer, D- 'dɛrɪndʒɚ; ES -dʒə(r
Derry 'dɛrɪ
dervish 'dɝvɪʃ; ES 'dɜv-, 'dɝv-; |-es -ɪz
Derwent 'dɝwənt, -wɛnt; ES 'dɜ-, 'dɝ-
descant n 'dɛskænt
descant v dɛs'kænt, dɪ'skænt |-ed -ɪd

Descartes de'kart; ES -'ka:t, E+-'ka:t; (Fr
    de'kart, dɛ-)
descend dɪ'sɛnd |-ed -ɪd |-ible, -able -əbḷ
descendant n, adj dɪ'sɛndənt
descendent adj dɪ'sɛndənt
descent dɪ'sɛnt
Deschamps Fr de'ʃɑ̃, dɛ-
Deschutes de'ʃut
describable dɪ'skraɪbəbḷ |-bly -blɪ
describe dɪ'skraɪb |-scribed -'skraɪbd
description dɪ'skrɪpʃən |-tive -tɪv
descry dɪ'skraɪ |-scried -'skraɪd
Desdemona ,dɛzdə'monə
desecrate 'dɛsɪ,kret |-crated -,kretɪd
desecration ,dɛsɪ'kreʃən
desensitization ,disɛnsətə'zeʃən, di,sɛn-,
    -aɪ'z-
desensitize di'sɛnsə,taɪz |-s -ɪz |-d -d
desert 'merit' dɪ'zɝt; ES -'zɜt, -'zɝt
desert 'a waste' 'dɛzɚt; ES 'dɛzət
desert 'abandon' dɪ'zɝt; ES -'zɜt, -'zɝt; |-ed
    -ɪd
desertion dɪ'zɝʃən; ES -'zɜʃ-, -'zɝʃ-
deserve dɪ'zɝv; ES -'zɜv, -'zɝv; |-d -d |-dly
    -ɪdlɪ
deshabille ,dɛzə'bil, cf Fr déshabillé dezabi'je
    & Eng dishabille
desiccant 'dɛsəkənt
desiccate 'dɛsə,ket |-d -d |-tive -ɪv
desiderate dɪ'sɪdə,ret |-rated -,retɪd
desideratum dɪ,sɪdə'retəm |-rata -'retə
design dɪ'zaɪn |-signed -'zaɪnd |-edly -ɪdlɪ
designate adj 'dɛzɪgnɪt, 'dɛs-, -,net
designate v 'dɛzɪg,net, 'dɛs- |-d -ɪd
designation ,dɛzɪg'neʃən, ,dɛs-
designative 'dɛzɪg,netɪv, 'dɛs-
designee ,dɛzɪg'ni, ,dɛs-
desirability dɪ,zaɪrə'bɪlətɪ
desirable dɪ'zaɪrəbḷ |-bly -blɪ
desire dɪ'zaɪr; ES dɪ'zaɪə(r; |-d -d |-dly -ɪdlɪ
    |-rous -əs
desist dɪ'zɪst |-ed -ɪd |-ance -əns |-ive -ɪv
desk dɛsk |desked dɛskt
Des Moines dɪ'mɔɪn, -'mɔɪnz |-'s -z, -nzɪz
desolate adj 'dɛsḷɪt
desolate v 'dɛsḷ,et |-d -ɪd |-tor -ɚ; ES -ə(r
De Soto dɪ'soto, -'sotə
despair dɪ'spɛr, -'spær; E -'spɛə(r, ES
    -'spæə(r; |-ed -d

despatch dɪˈspætʃ |-es -ɪz |-ed -t=dispatch
desperado ˌdɛspəˈredo
desperate ˈdɛsprɪt, -pərɪt |-tion ˌdɛspəˈreʃən
despicable ˈdɛspɪkɪb|, less freq. dɪˈspɪkəb|
|-bly -blɪ
despise dɪˈspaɪz |-s -ɪz |-d -d |-dness -ɪdnɪs
despite dɪˈspaɪt |-d -ɪd |-ful -fəl |-fully -fəlɪ
Des Plaines dɛsˈplenz (Fr deˈplɛn)
despoil dɪˈspɔɪl |-ed -d
despoliation dɪˌspolɪˈeʃən
despond dɪˈspɑnd, -ˈspɒnd |-ed -ɪd |-ence
-əns |-ency -ənsɪ |-ent -ənt
despot ˈdɛspət, -pɑt; ES+-pɒt
despotic dɪˈspɑtɪk; ES+-ˈspɒt-; |-al -|̩ |-ally
-|ɪ |-ly -lɪ
despotism ˈdɛspətˌɪzəm
despumate dɪˈspjumet, -ˈspɪu-, ˈdɛspjuˌmet
|-d -ɪd
desquamate ˈdɛskwəˌmet |-mated -ˌmetɪd
dessert dɪˈzɝt; ES -ˈzɜt, -ˈzɝt; |-spoon -ˌspun,
-ˌspʊn
de Stijl dəˈstil
destination ˌdɛstəˈneʃən
destine ˈdɛstɪn |-d -d |-tiny -tənɪ
destitute ˈdɛstəˌtjut, -ˌtɪut, -ˌtut |-d -ɪd
destitution ˌdɛstəˈtjuʃən, -ˈtɪu-, -ˈtu-
destroy dɪˈstrɔɪ |-ed -d |-er -ɚ; ES -ə(r
destructibility dɪˌstrʌktəˈbɪlətɪ
destructible dɪˈstrʌktəb|
destruction dɪˈstrʌkʃən |-tive -tɪv
destructivity ˌdistrʌkˈtɪvətɪ, dɪˌstrʌkˈtɪv-
desuetude ˈdɛswɪˌtjud, -ˌtɪud, -ˌtud
desulphurize diˈsʌlfəˌraɪz, -fjə- |-s -ɪz |-d -d
desultory ˈdɛs|ˌtorɪ, -ˌtɔrɪ; S -ˌtorɪ; |-rily
-rəlɪ, -rɪlɪ
detach dɪˈtætʃ |-es -ɪz |-ed -t |-edly -ɪdlɪ
detachability dɪˌtætʃəˈbɪlətɪ
detachable dɪˈtætʃəb| |-bly -blɪ
detail n ˈditel, dɪˈtel
detail v dɪˈtel |-ed -d |-edly -ɪdlɪ
detain dɪˈten |-ed -d
detect dɪˈtɛkt |-ed -ɪd |-able -əb| |-bly -blɪ
detection dɪˈtɛkʃən |-tive -tɪv |-tor -tɚ; ES
-tə(r
detent dɪˈtɛnt
detention dɪˈtɛnʃən
deter dɪˈtɝ; ES -ˈtɜ(r, -ˈtɝ; |-red -d
deterge dɪˈtɝdʒ; ES -ˈtɜdʒ, -ˈtɝdʒ; |-s -ɪz
|-d -d |-nce -əns |-ncy -ənsɪ |-nt -ənt

deteriorate dɪˈtɪrɪəˌret |-rated -ˌretɪd
deterioration dɪˌtɪrɪəˈreʃən
determinable dɪˈtɝmɪnəb|; ES -ˈtɜm-, -ˈtɝm-;
|-bly -blɪ
determinant dɪˈtɝmənənt; ES -ˈtɜm-, -ˈtɝm-
determinate adj dɪˈtɝmənɪt; ES -ˈtɜm-,
-ˈtɝm-; n -nɪt, -ˌnet
determination dɪˌtɝməˈneʃən; ES -ˌtɜm-,
-ˌtɝm-
determine dɪˈtɝmɪn; ES -ˈtɜm-, -ˈtɝm-; |-d -d
|-dly -dlɪ, -ɪdlɪ |-nism -ˌɪzəm |-nist -ɪst
deterrent dɪˈtɝrənt, -ˈtɛr-; ES -ˈtɜr-, -ˈtʌr-,
-ˈtɝ-, -ˈtɛr-
detest dɪˈtɛst |-ed -ɪd |-able -əb| |-bly -blɪ
detestation ˌditɛsˈteʃən
dethrone dɪˈθron, di- |-d -d
de Tocqueville dɪˈtɑkvɪl, -ˈtɒk- (Fr dətɔkˈvil)
detonate ˈdɛtəˌnet, -to- |-d -ɪd |-tor -ɚ; ES
-ə(r
detonation ˌdɛtəˈneʃən, -to-
detour ˈditur, dɪˈtur |-ed -d
detract dɪˈtrækt |-ed -ɪd |-or -ɚ; ES -ə(r
detraction dɪˈtrækʃən |-tory -tərɪ
detrain diˈtren |-trained -ˈtrend
detriment ˈdɛtrəmənt
detrimental ˌdɛtrəˈmɛnt| |-ly -ɪ
detrition dɪˈtrɪʃən
detritus dɪˈtraɪtəs
Detroit dɪˈtrɔɪt |-er -ɚ; ES -ə(r
de trop Fr dəˈtro
Deucalion djuˈkelɪən, dɪu-, du-, -ljən
deuce djus, dɪus, dus |-s -ɪz |-d -ɪd, -t |-d|y -dly
-ɪdlɪ
Deuel ˈdjuəl, ˈdɪuəl, ˈduəl
deus ex machina ˈdiəsˌɛksˈmækɪnə
deuterium djuˈtɪrɪəm, dɪu-, du-
Deuteronomy ˌdjutəˈranəmɪ, ˌdɪu-, ˌdu-;
ES+-ˈrɒn-
Deutsches Reich Ger ˈdɔytʃəsˌraɪx
Deutschland Ger ˈdɔytʃˌlɑnt
De Valera dəvəˈlɛrə, -ˈlerə, -ˈlɪrə
devaluate diˈvæljuˌet |-ated -ˌetɪd
devaluation ˌdivæljuˈeʃən
devastate ˈdɛvəsˌtet |-tated -ˌtetɪd
devastation ˌdɛvəsˈteʃən
develop dɪˈvɛləp |-ed -t
De Vere dɪˈvɪr; ES -ˈvɪə(r
Devereux ˈdɛvəˌru, -ˌrɪu
deviate ˈdivɪˌet |-d -ɪd |-tion ˌdivɪˈeʃən

device dɪ'vaɪs |-vices -'vaɪsɪz	dey de
devil 'dɛvl̩ |-ed -d |-ing 'dɛvlɪŋ, 'dɛvl̩ɪŋ	Dhaulagiri ˌdaʊlə'gɪrɪ
devilfish 'dɛvl̩ˌfɪʃ |-'s -ɪz	dhole dol
devilish 'dɛvl̩ɪʃ, 'dɛvl̩ɪʃ	dhoti, dhooti 'dotɪ
devil-may-care ˌdɛvl̩mɪ'kɛr, -'kær; E -'kɛə(r,	dhow daʊ
ES -'kæə(r; ('devil-may-ˌcare 'wit)	diabase 'daɪəˌbes |-sic ˌdaɪə'besɪk
devilment 'dɛvl̩mənt	diabetes ˌdaɪə'bitɪs, -tiz
devilry 'dɛvl̩rɪ |deviltry 'dɛvl̩trɪ	diabetic ˌdaɪə'bɛtɪk, -'bitɪk |-al -l̩
devious 'divɪəs, -vjəs	diablerie dɪ'ɑblərɪ (Fr djablə'ri)
devisable dɪ'vaɪzəbl̩	diabolic ˌdaɪə'bɑlɪk; ES+-'bɒl-; |-al -l̩ |-ally
devise dɪ'vaɪz |-s -ɪz |-d -d |-sal -l̩	-lɪ, -ɪklɪ
devisee dɪˌvaɪz'i, ˌdɛvɪ'zi (deˌvis'ee & de-	diabolism daɪ'æbəˌlɪzəm
ˌvis'or)	diachronic ˌdaɪə'krɑnɪk; ES+-'krɒn-
devisor dɪ'vaɪzɚ, dɪˌvaɪz'ɔr; ES -ə(r, -'ɔə(r	diacid daɪ'æsɪd
devitalization diˌvaɪtl̩ə'zeʃən, ˌdivaɪt-, -aɪ'z-	diaconate daɪ'ækənɪt, -ˌnet |-nal -nl̩
devitalize di'vaɪtl̩ˌaɪz |-s -ɪz |-d -d	diacritic ˌdaɪə'krɪtɪk |-al -l̩ |-ally -lɪ, -ɪklɪ
Devizes dɪ'vaɪzɪz |-zes' -zɪz	diadem 'daɪəˌdɛm |-demed -ˌdɛmd
devoice di'vɔɪs |-s -ɪz |-d -t	diaeresis daɪ'ɛrəsɪs |-eses -əˌsiz
devoid dɪ'vɔɪd	diagnose 'daɪəg'nos, -'noz |-s -ɪz |-d -t, -d
devoir də'vwɑr, 'dɛvwɑr; ES -wɑ:(r; (Fr	diagnosis ˌdaɪəg'nosɪs |-noses -'nosiz
də'vwa:r)	diagnostic ˌdaɪəg'nɑstɪk; ES+-'nɒs-; |-ally
devolution ˌdɛvə'luʃən, -'lɪuʃən, -vl̩'juʃən	-lɪ, -ɪklɪ
devolve dɪ'vɑlv, -'vɒlv |-d -d	diagnostician ˌdaɪəgnɑs'tɪʃən; ES+-nɒs-
Devon 'dɛvən |Devonian də'vonɪən	diagonal daɪ'ægənl̩ |-ly -ɪ, -'ægnəlɪ
Devonport 'dɛvənˌport, 'dɛvm̩-, -ˌpɔrt; ES	diagram 'daɪəˌgræm |-(m)ed -d
-ˌpoət, E+-ˌpɔət	diagrammatic ˌdaɪəgrə'mætɪk |-al -l̩ |-ally
Devonshire 'dɛvənˌʃɪr, -ʃɚ; ES -ˌʃɪə(r, -ʃə(r	-lɪ, -ɪklɪ
devote dɪ'vot |-d -ɪd	dial 'daɪəl, daɪl |-ed -d
devotee ˌdɛvə'ti	dialect 'daɪəˌlɛkt
devotion dɪ'voʃən |-al -l̩ |-ally -lɪ	dialectal ˌdaɪə'lɛktl̩ |-ly -ɪ
devour dɪ'vaʊr; ES -'vaʊə(r; |-ed -d |-ing	dialectic ˌdaɪə'lɛktɪk |-al -l̩ |-ally -lɪ, -ɪklɪ
-'vaʊrɪŋ	dialectician ˌdaɪəlɛk'tɪʃən
devout dɪ'vaʊt	dialectology ˌdaɪəlɛk'tɑlədʒɪ; ES+-'tɒl-
De Vries də'vris |-'s -ɪz	dialogist daɪ'ælədʒɪst
dew dju, dɪu, du |-ed -d	dialogue, -log 'daɪəˌlɔg, -ˌlɑg, -ˌlɒg |-d, -ged -d
Dewar 'djuɚ, 'dɪuɚ, 'duɚ; ES -ə(r	dialysis daɪ'æləsɪs |-yses -əˌsiz
dewberry 'djuˌbɛrɪ, 'dɪu-, 'du-, -bərɪ	dialytic ˌdaɪə'lɪtɪk |-ally -lɪ, -ɪklɪ
dewdrop 'djuˌdrɑp, 'dɪu-, 'du-; ES+-ˌdrɒp	diamagnetic ˌdaɪəmæg'nɛtɪk |-ally -lɪ, -ɪklɪ
Dewey 'djuɪ, 'dɪuɪ, 'duɪ	diamagnetism ˌdaɪə'mægnəˌtɪzəm
Dewitt, De-Witt v dɪ'wɪt |-ed -ɪd	diameter daɪ'æmətɚ; ES -'æmətə(r
dewlap 'djuˌlæp, 'dɪu-, 'du- |-ped -t	diametric ˌdaɪə'mɛtrɪk |-al -l̩ |-ally -lɪ, -ɪklɪ
dewy 'djuɪ, 'dɪuɪ, 'duɪ	diamond 'daɪmənd, 'daɪə- |-ed -ɪd—'daɪmənd
dexter, D- 'dɛkstɚ; ES 'dɛkstə(r	is common from the 16c (often spelt dimond),
dexterity dɛks'tɛrətɪ	being found in Shak., Milton, Pope, Cowper,
dexterous 'dɛkstrəs, -tərəs	Keats, Tennyson.
dextral 'dɛkstrəl |-ly -ɪ	Dian 'daɪən |Diana daɪ'ænə
dextrin 'dɛkstrɪn |-trine -trɪn, -trin	dianthus, D- daɪ'ænθəs |-es -ɪz
dextrose 'dɛkstros	diapason ˌdaɪə'pezn̩, -'pesn̩
dextrous 'dɛkstrəs	diaper 'daɪəpɚ; ES 'daɪəpə(r; |-ed -d

|full fʊl |tooth tuθ |further 'fɝðɚ; ES 'fɝðə |custom 'kʌstəm |while hwaɪl |how haʊ |toy tɔɪ |using 'juzɪŋ |fuse fjuz, fɪuz |dish dɪʃ |vision 'vɪʒən |Eden 'idn̩ |cradle 'kredl̩ |keep 'em 'kipm̩

diaphanous daɪˈæfənəs
diaphone ˈdaɪəˌfon
diaphonic ˌdaɪəˈfɑnɪk; ES+-ˈfɒn-; |-al -ḷ
diaphoresis ˌdaɪəfəˈrɪsɪs
diaphoretic ˌdaɪəfəˈrɛtɪk |-al -ḷ
diaphragm ˈdaɪəˌfræm |-ed -d
diaphragmatic ˌdaɪəfrægˈmætɪk |-ally -ḷɪ, -ɪklɪ
diarchy ˈdaɪɑrkɪ; ES -ɑːkɪ, E+-ɑːkɪ
diarist ˈdaɪərɪst
diarrhea, -rrhoea ˌdaɪəˈrɪə
diary ˈdaɪərɪ
Diaspora daɪˈæspərə
diastase ˈdaɪəˌstes
diastole daɪˈæstəˌli
diastolic ˌdaɪəˈstɑlɪk; ES+-ˈstɒl-
diastrophism daɪˈæstrəˌfɪzəm
diathermic ˌdaɪəˈθɝˑmɪk; ES -ˈθɜːm-, -ˈθɝˑm-
diathermy ˈdaɪəˌθɝˑmɪ; ES -ˌθɜːmɪ, -ˌθɝˑmɪ
diatom ˈdaɪətəm, -ˌtɑm; ES+-ˌtɒm
diatomaceous ˌdaɪətəˈmeʃəs
diatonic ˌdaɪəˈtɑnɪk; ES+-ˈtɒn-; |-al -ḷ |-ally -ḷɪ, -ɪklɪ
diatribe ˈdaɪəˌtraɪb |-tribed -ˌtraɪbd
Díaz ˈdiəs |-'s -ɪz
dib dɪb |dibbed dɪbd
dibase ˈdaɪˌbes |-sic daɪˈbesɪk
dibble ˈdɪbḷ |-d -d |-ling ˈdɪblɪŋ, ˈdɪbḷɪŋ
dice daɪs |diced daɪst |-'s -ɪz
dichlorid daɪˈklorɪd, -ˈklɔr-; S -ˈklor-; |-ride -raɪd, -rɪd
dichotomous daɪˈkɑtəməs; ES+-ˈkɒt-; |-my -mɪ
dichromatic ˌdaɪkroˈmætɪk |-tism daɪˈkroməˌtɪzəm
Dick dɪk
dickcissel dɪkˈsɪsḷ, ˈdɪkˌs-
Dickens, d- ˈdɪkɪnz |-'s -ɪz |-ian dɪˈkɛnzɪən
dicker ˈdɪkɚ; ES ˈdɪkə(r; |-ed -d |-ing ˈdɪkərɪŋ, ˈdɪkrɪŋ
Dickinson, Dicken- ˈdɪkɪnsṇ
dicotyledon ˌdaɪkɑtḷˈidṇ, daɪˌkɑt-; ES+-ɒt-; |-ous -ˈidṇəs, -ˈɛdṇəs
dictaphone, D- ˈdɪktəˌfon
dictate n ˈdɪktet
dictate v ˈdɪktet, dɪkˈtet |-d -ɪd
dictation dɪkˈteʃən
dictator ˈdɪktetɚ, dɪkˈtetɚ; ES -tər; |-ship -ˌʃɪp

dictatorial ˌdɪktəˈtorɪəl, -ˈtɔr-; S -ˈtor-; |-ly -ɪ
dictic ˈdɪktɪk |-al -ḷ |-ally -ḷɪ, -ɪklɪ
diction ˈdɪkʃən
dictionary ˈdɪkʃənˌɛrɪ, as a Briticism+ˈdɪkʃənərɪ, -ʃənrɪ, -ʃnərɪ
dictograph, D- ˈdɪktəˌgræf; E+-ˌgraf, -ˌgrɑf
dictum ˈdɪktəm |-s -z |-ta -tə
did dɪd—for forms see do
didactic daɪˈdæktɪk |-al -ḷ |-ally -ḷɪ, -ɪklɪ
diddest ˈdɪdɪst—see do
diddle ˈdɪdḷ |-d -d |-ling ˈdɪdlɪŋ, ˈdɪdḷɪŋ
Diderot ˈdidəˌro (Fr diˈdro)
didest ˈdɪdɪst—see do
didn't ˈdɪdṇt, before some conss.+ˈdɪdṇ (ˌdɪdṇˈgo)—The pron. ˈdɪdənt is substandard.
Dido, d- ˈdaɪdo
didst dɪdst—see do
Didymus ˈdɪdəməs |-'s -ɪz
die 'cube' daɪ |pl dice daɪs
die 'tool' daɪ |pl dies daɪz
die 'expire' daɪ |died daɪd
die-hard ˈdaɪˌhɑrd; ES -ˌhɑːd, E+-ˌhɑːd
dielectric ˌdaɪəˈlɛktrɪk |-al -ḷ |-ally -ḷɪ, -ɪklɪ
Dieman, van væn ˈdimən
Dieppe dɪˈɛp (Fr djɛp)
dieresis daɪˈɛrəsɪs |-eses -əˌsiz
dies 'expires,' 'colors,' 'tools' daɪz
dies 'day' ˈdaɪɪz
Dies, Martin daɪz |-'s -ɪz
Diesel ˈdizḷ, ˈdisḷ
Dies Irae ˈdaɪizˈaɪri
diet ˈdaɪət |-ed -ɪd |-ary ˈdaɪəˌtɛrɪ
dietetic ˌdaɪəˈtɛtɪk |-al -ḷ |-ally -ḷɪ, -ɪklɪ
dietician ˌdaɪəˈtɪʃən |-titian -ˈtɪʃən
differ ˈdɪfɚ; ES -fə(r; |-ed -d |-ing ˈdɪfrɪŋ, ˈdɪfərɪŋ
difference ˈdɪfrəns, ˈdɪfəns, ˈdɪfərəns; ES -frəns, -fər-, -fəns; |-s -ɪz |-nt -nt
differentia ˌdɪfəˈrɛnʃɪə |-tiae -ʃɪˌi
differential ˌdɪfəˈrɛnʃəl |-ly -ɪ
differentiate ˌdɪfəˈrɛnʃɪˌet |-ated -ˌetɪd
differentiation ˌdɪfəˌrɛnʃɪˈeʃən
difficile ˌdɪfəˈsil, formerly dɪˈfɪsḷ
difficult ˈdɪfəˌkʌlt, ˈdɪfəkəlt, -kḷt
difficulty ˈdɪfəˌkʌltɪ, -kəltɪ, -kḷtɪ
diffidence ˈdɪfədəns |-dent -dənt
diffract dɪˈfrækt |-ed -ɪd |-ction -kʃən

diffuse, *adj* dɪˈfjus, -ˈfɪus
diffuse *v* dɪˈfjuz, -ˈfɪuz |-s -ɪz |-d -d |-dly -ɪdlɪ
diffusibility dɪˌfjuzəˈbɪlətɪ, -ˌfɪuz-
diffusible dɪˈfjuzəbļ, -ˈfɪuz- |-bly -blɪ
diffusion dɪˈfjuʒən, -ˈfɪu- |-sive -sɪv
dig dɪg |*past & pptc* dug dʌg, *or arch.* digged
　digd
digamma daɪˈgæmə
digest *n* ˈdaɪdʒɛst
digest *v* dəˈdʒɛst, daɪˈdʒɛst |-ed -ɪd
digestibility dəˌdʒɛstəˈbɪlətɪ, daɪ-
digestible dəˈdʒɛstəbļ, daɪ- |-bly -blɪ
digestion dəˈdʒɛstʃən, daɪ- |-gestive -ˈdʒɛstɪv
digger ˈdɪgɚ; ES ˈdɪgə(r; |digging ˈdɪgɪŋ
Diggory ˈdɪgərɪ
dight daɪt |*past & pptc* dight daɪt, *or* dighted
　ˈdaɪtɪd
Dighton ˈdaɪtn̩
digit ˈdɪdʒɪt |-al -ļ |-ally -ļɪ
digitalin ˌdɪdʒəˈtelɪn
digitalis ˌdɪdʒəˈtelɪs, -ˈtælɪs
digitate *adj* ˈdɪdʒəˌtet |-d -ɪd
digitigrade ˈdɪdʒɪtɪəˌgred |-ism -gredˌɪzəm
dignify ˈdɪgnəˌfaɪ |-fied -ˌfaɪd
dignitary ˈdɪgnəˌtɛrɪ
dignity ˈdɪgnətɪ
digraph ˈdaɪgræf; E+-graf, -grɑf
digress dəˈgrɛs, daɪ- |-es -ɪz |-ed -t
digression dəˈgrɛʃən, daɪ- |-sive -ˈgrɛsɪv
dihedral daɪˈhidrəl |-dron -drən
Dijk, van væn ˈdaɪk
Dijon ˈdiʒɑn, -ʒɒn, diˈʒ- (*Fr* diˈʒõ)
dike daɪk |-d -t
dilantin daɪˈlæntɪn
dilapidate dəˈlæpəˌdet |-dated -ˌdetɪd
dilapidation dəˌlæpəˈdeʃən
dilatation ˌdɪləˈteʃən, ˌdaɪlə-
dilate daɪˈlet, dɪ- |-d -ɪd |-lation -ˈleʃən
dilatory ˈdɪləˌtorɪ, -ˌtɔrɪ; S -ˌtɔrɪ; |-rily -rəlɪ,
　-rɪlɪ
dilemma dəˈlɛmə, daɪ-
dilettante ˌdɪləˈtæntɪ |-ism -tɪˌɪzəm |-tism
　-ˈtæntɪzəm
diligence ˈdɪlədʒəns |-s -ɪz |-gent -dʒənt
dill dɪl
Dillon ˈdɪlən
dillydally ˈdɪlɪˌdælɪ |-ied -d
diluent ˈdɪljʊənt
dilute dɪˈlut, daɪ-, -ˈlɪut |-d -ɪd |-tion -ʃən

diluvial dɪˈluvɪəl, -ˈlɪu- |-an -ən
dim dɪm |dimmed dɪmd
dime daɪm
dimension dəˈmɛnʃən |-ed -d |-al -ļ |-ally -ļɪ
dimeter ˈdɪmətɚ; ES ˈdɪmətə(r
diminish dəˈmɪnɪʃ |-es -ɪz |-ed -t
diminuendo dəˌmɪnjʊˈɛndo
diminution ˌdɪməˈnjuʃən, -ˈnɪu-, -ˈnu-
diminutive dəˈmɪnjətɪv
dimissory ˈdɪməˌsorɪ, dəˈmɪsərɪ; EN+-ˌsɔrɪ
dimity ˈdɪmətɪ
Dimmesdale ˈdɪmzdel
Dimond ˈdaɪmənd
dimorphism daɪˈmɔrfɪzəm; ES -ˈmɔəf-
dimple ˈdɪmpļ |-d -d |-ling ˈdɪmplɪŋ, -pļɪŋ
din dɪn |dinned dɪnd
Dinah ˈdaɪnə
dinar dɪˈnɑr; ES -ˈnɑː(r
dine daɪn |dined daɪnd
ding dɪŋ |dinged dɪŋd
dingdong ˈdɪŋˌdɔŋ, -ˌdɒŋ; S+-ˌdɑŋ; |-ed -d
dinghy, -gey, -gy ˈdɪŋgɪ
dinghy ˈdɪŋgļ |-d -d |-ling ˈdɪŋglɪŋ, -gļɪŋ
dingo ˈdɪŋgo
dingy *'dinghy'* ˈdɪŋgɪ
dingy *'dusky'* ˈdɪndʒɪ
dinkey, -ky ˈdɪŋkɪ
Dinmont, d- ˈdɪnmənt, -mɑnt; ES+-mɒnt
dinner ˈdɪnɚ; ES ˈdɪnə(r
dinnerware ˈdɪnɚˌwɛr, -ˌwær; E ˈdɪnəˌwɛə(r,
　ES -ˌwæə(r
dinosaur ˈdaɪnəˌsɔr; ES -ˌsɔə(r
Dinosauria ˌdaɪnəˈsɔrɪə |d-n ˌdaɪnəˈsɔrɪən
dinosaurus ˌdaɪnəˈsɔrəs, -rai -raɪ
dinothere ˈdaɪnəˌθɪr; ES -ˌθɪə(r
Dinotherium ˌdaɪnəˈθɪrɪəm
dint dɪnt |dinted ˈdɪntɪd
Dinwiddie dɪnˈwɪdɪ, ˈdɪnwɪdɪ
diocesan daɪˈɑsəsn̩, ˈdaɪəˌsɪsn̩; ES+-ˈɒs-
diocese ˈdaɪəˌsɪs |-s -ɪz
Diocles ˈdaɪəˌkliz |-'s -ɪz
Diocletian ˌdaɪəˈkliʃən
Diodorus ˌdaɪəˈdorəs, -ˈdɔr-; S -ˈdor-; |-'s -ɪz
Diogenes daɪˈɑdʒəˌniz; ES+-ˈɒdʒ-; |-'s -ɪz
Diomed ˈdaɪəˌmɛd |-mede -ˌmid
Diomedes ˌdaɪəˈmidɪz |-des' -diz
Dion ˈdaɪən
Dionysia ˌdaɪəˈnɪʃɪə, -sɪə |-iac -ˈnɪsɪˌæk
Dionysian ˌdaɪəˈnɪʃən, -ˈnɪsɪən

Dionysius ˌdaɪəˈnɪʃɪəs, -ˈnɪsɪəs |-ˈs -ɪz
Dionysus ˌdaɪəˈnaɪsəs |-sus' -səs
Dionyza ˌdaɪəˈnaɪzə
diopter daɪˈaptɚ; ES -ˈaptə(r, -ˈɒp-
dioptric daɪˈaptrɪk; ES+-ˈɒp-; |-s -s
diorama ˌdaɪəˈræmə, -ˈramə
diorite ˈdaɪəˌraɪt
Dioscuri ˌdaɪəˈskjʊraɪ, -ˈskɪʊ- |-rian -rɪən
dioxide daɪˈaksaɪd, -ɪd; ES+-ˈɒks-; |-id -ɪd
dip dɪp |dipped dɪpt
diphase ˈdaɪˌfez |-phasic daɪˈfezɪk
diphosgene daɪˈfasdʒin; ES+-ˈfɒs-
diphtheria dɪfˈθɪrɪə, dɪp-; S+-ˈθɛr-; |-l -l
diphtheretic ˌdɪfθəˈrɛtɪk, ˌdɪp- |-ally -|ɪ, -ɪklɪ
diphthong ˈdɪfθɔŋ, ˈdɪp-, -θɒŋ |-ed -d
diphthongal dɪfˈθɔŋg|, dɪp-, -ˈθɔŋ|, -ˈθɒŋ-
|-ly -ɪ
diphthongization ˌdɪfθɔŋəˈzeʃən, ˌdɪp-,
-θɔŋgə-, -θɒŋ-, -aɪˈz-
diphthongize ˈdɪfθɔŋˌaɪz, ˈdɪp-, -θɔŋˌgaɪz,
-θɒŋ- |-s -ɪz |-d -d
diplococcus ˌdɪpləˈkakəs; ES+-ˈkɒk-; |-ci
-ksaɪ
diploma dɪˈplomə |-s -z |-ed -d |-cy -sɪ
diplomat ˈdɪpləˌmæt |-ist dɪˈplomətɪst
diplomatic ˌdɪpləˈmætɪk |-al -| |-ally -|ɪ, -ɪklɪ
dipody ˈdɪpədɪ
dipolar daɪˈpolɚ; ES -ˈpolə(r; |-pole ˈdaɪˌpol
dipper ˈdɪpɚ; ES ˈdɪpə(r
dipsomania ˌdɪpsəˈmenɪə |-maniac -ˈmenɪˌæk
dipterous ˈdɪptərəs
dire daɪr; ES daɪə(r
direct dəˈrɛkt, daɪ- |-ed -ɪd |-ive -ɪv
direction dəˈrɛkʃən, daɪ- |-al -| |-ally -|ɪ
director dəˈrɛktɚ, daɪ-; ES -tə(r; |-ate -ɪt
|-ship -ˌʃɪp
directorial dəˌrɛkˈtorɪəl, ˌdaɪrɛk-, -ˈtɔr-; S
-ˈtor-; |-ly -ɪ
directory dəˈrɛktərɪ, -ˈrɛktrɪ
directress dəˈrɛktrɪs, daɪ- |-es -ɪz
directrix dəˈrɛktrɪks, daɪ- |-es -ɪz |for any that
desire it -trices ˌdaɪrɛkˈtraɪsiz
direful ˈdaɪrfəl; ES ˈdaɪəfəl; |-ly -ɪ
dirge dɝdʒ; ES dɜdʒ, dɝdʒ; |-s -ɪz |-d -d
dirigibility ˌdɪrədʒəˈbɪlətɪ
dirigible ˈdɪrədʒəb|, Brit + dɪˈrɪdʒəb|
dirk, D- dɝk; ES dɜk, dɝk; |-ed -t
dirt dɝt; ES dɜt, dɝt; |-ed -ɪd |-y -ɪ |-ied -ɪd
|-ily -|ɪ, -ɪlɪ

Dis dɪs |-ˈs -ɪz
disability ˌdɪsəˈbɪlətɪ
disable dɪsˈeb|, dɪz- |-d -d
disabuse ˌdɪsəˈbjuz, -ˈbɪuz |-s -ɪz |-d -d
disaccord ˌdɪsəˈkɔrd; ES -ˈkɔəd; |-ed -ɪd
disaccustom ˌdɪsəˈkʌstəm |-ed -d
disadvantage ˌdɪsədˈvæntɪdʒ; E+-ˈvan-,
-ˈvɑn-; |-s -ɪz |-d -d
disadvantageous dɪsˌædvənˈtedʒəs, ˌdɪsæd-
vən-
disaffect ˌdɪsəˈfɛkt |-ed -ɪd |-ction -kʃən
disagree ˌdɪsəˈgri |-d -d |-able -əb| |-bly -blɪ
disallow ˌdɪsəˈlaʊ |-ed -d |-ance -əns
disannul ˌdɪsəˈnʌl |-led -d
disappear ˌdɪsəˈpɪr; ES -ˈpɪə(r, S+-ˈpɛə(r,
-ˈpjɛə(r; |-ed -d |-ance -əns |-ances -ənsɪz
disappoint ˌdɪsəˈpɔɪnt |-ed -ɪd |-ment -mənt
disapprobation ˌdɪsæprəˈbeʃən, dɪsˌæprə-
disapprove ˌdɪsəˈpruv |-d -d |-val -v|
disarm dɪsˈarm, dɪz-; ES -ˈa:m, E+-ˈa:m; |-ed
-d |-ament -əmənt
disarrange ˌdɪsəˈrendʒ |-s -ɪz |-d -d
disarray ˌdɪsəˈre |-ed -d
disaster dɪzˈæstɚ; ES -ˈæstə(r, E+-ˈas-,
-ˈɑs-; |-trous -trəs
disavow ˌdɪsəˈvaʊ |-ed -d |-edly -ɪdlɪ |-al -əl
disband dɪsˈbænd |-ed -ɪd
disbar dɪsˈbar; ES -ˈba:(r, E+-ˈba:(r; |-red -d
disbark dɪsˈbark; ES -ˈba:k, E+-ˈba:k; |-ed -t
disbelieve ˌdɪsbəˈliv |-d -d |-lief -ˈlif
disburden dɪsˈbɝdn̩; ES -ˈbɝdn̩, -ˈbɝdn̩;
|-ed -d
disburse dɪsˈbɝs; ES -ˈbɝs, -ˈbɝs; |-s -ɪz
|-d -t
disc dɪsk
discard n ˈdɪskard; ES -ka:d, E+-ka:d
discard v dɪsˈkard; ES -ˈka:d, E+-ˈka:d; |-ed
-ɪd
discern dɪˈzɝn, -ˈsɝn; ES -ɝn, -ɝn; |-ed -d
|-ible -əb| |-bly -blɪ
discharge dɪsˈtʃardʒ; ES -ˈtʃa:dʒ, E+
-ˈtʃa:dʒ; |-s -ɪz |-d -d
disciple, D- dɪˈsaɪp| |-d -d |-ship -ˌʃɪp
disciplinable ˈdɪsəˌplɪnəb|
disciplinarian ˌdɪsəplɪnˈɛrɪən, -ˈer-
disciplinary ˈdɪsəplɪnˌɛrɪ
discipline n ˈdɪsəplɪn
discipline v ˈdɪsəˌplɪn |-d -d
disclaim dɪsˈklem |-ed -d

Key: *See in full §§3–47.* bee bi |pity ˈpɪtɪ (§6) |rate ret |yet jɛt |sang sæŋ |angry ˈæŋ·grɪ
|bath bæθ; E baθ (§10) |ah ɑ |far fɑr |watch watʃ, wɒtʃ (§12) |jaw dʒɔ |gorge gɔrdʒ |go go

disclose dıs'kloz |-s -ız |-d -d |-sure -ʒɚ; ES -ʒə(r

discolor dıs'kʌlɚ; ES -'kʌlə(r; |-ed -d

discoloration ˌdıskʌlə'reʃən, dıs͵kʌlə-

discombobulate ˌdıskəm'bab|͵et; ES+-'bɒb-; |-d -ıd

discomfit dıs'kʌmfıt |-ed -ıd |-ure -fıtʃɚ; ES -fıtʃə(r

discomfort dıs'kʌmfɚt; ES -'kʌmfət; |-ed -ıd

discommode ˌdıskə'mod |-d -ıd

discompose ˌdıskəm'poz |-s -ız |-d -d |-dly -ıdlı |-sure -'poʒɚ; ES -'poʒə(r

disconcert ˌdıskən'sɚt; ES -'sɚt, -'sɝt; |-ed -ıd

disconnect ˌdıskə'nɛkt |-ed -ıd

disconnection, -nexion ˌdıskə'nɛkʃən

disconsolate dıs'kans|ıt; ES+-'kɒn-

disconsolation ˌdıskansə'leʃən, dıs͵kansə-; ES+-ɒn-

discontent ˌdıskən'tɛnt |-ed -ıd

discontinuance ˌdıskən'tınjuəns |-s -ız

discontinuation ˌdıskən͵tınju'eʃən

discontinue ˌdıskən'tınju |-d -d |-uous -juəs

discontinuity ˌdıskantə'nuətı, -'nıu-, -'nju-; ES+-kɒn-

discord n 'dıskɔrd; ES -kɔəd

discord v dıs'kɔrd; ES -'kɔəd; |-ed -ıd

discordance dıs'kɔrdn̩s; ES -'kɔəd-; |-s -ız |-dant -dn̩t

discount n 'dıskaunt

discount v 'dıskaunt, dıs'kaunt |-ed -ıd

discountenance dıs'kauntənəns |-s -ız |-d -t

discourage dıs'kɝıdʒ; ES -'kɝr-, -'kʌr-, -'kɝ-; |-s -ız |-d -d

discourse n 'dıskors, dı'skors, -ɔrs; ES -oəs, E+-ɔəs; |-s -ız

discourse v dı'skors, -'skɔrs; ES -'skoəs, E+-'skɔəs; |-s -ız |-d -t

discourteous dıs'kɝtıəs; ES -'kɝt-, -'kɝt-; |-esy -əsı

discover dı'skʌvɚ; ES -'skʌvə(r; |-ed -d |-ing -'skʌvərıŋ, -'skʌvrıŋ |-y -'skʌvrı, -vərı

discredit dıs'krɛdıt |-ed -ıd

discreditable dıs'krɛdıtəb|l̩ |-bly -blı

discreet dı'skrit

discrepance dı'skrɛpəns |-cy -ı |-ant -ənt

discrete dı'skrit

discretion dı'skrɛʃən |-al -l̩ |-ally -l̩ı

discretionary dı'skrɛʃən͵ɛrı

discriminate adj dı'skrımənıt

discriminate v dı'skrımə͵net |-d -ıd |-tive -ıv

discrimination dı͵skrımə'neʃən

discriminatory dı'skrımənə͵torı, -͵tɔrı; S -͵torı

discrown dıs'kraun |-ed -d

discursive dı'skɝsıv; ES -'skɝs-, -'skɝs-; |-sory -sərı

discus 'dıskəs |-es -ız |disci 'dısaı

discuss dı'skʌs |-es -ız |-ed -t |-ion -'skʌʃən

disdain dıs'den, dız- |-ed -d

disdainful dıs'denfəl, dız- |-ly -ı

disease dı'ziz |-s -ız |-d -d |-dly -ıdlı

disembark ˌdısım'bark; ES -'bɑːk, E+-'bɑːk; |-ed -t

disembarkation ˌdısembar'keʃən, dıs͵ɛm-; ES -bɑː-, E+-bɑː-

disembarrass ˌdısım'bærəs, -ıs |-es -ız |-ed -t

disembody ˌdısım'badı; ES+-'bɒdı; |-ied -d

disembowel ˌdısım'bauəl, -'baul |-ed -d

disenchant ˌdısın'tʃænt; E+-'tʃant, -'tʃant; |-ed -ıd

disencumber ˌdısın'kʌmbɚ; ES -'kʌmbə(r; |-ed -d |-ing -'kʌmbərıŋ, -'kʌmbrıŋ

disenfranchise ˌdısın'fræntʃaız |-s -ız |-d -d

disenfranchisement ˌdısın'fræntʃızmənt

disengage ˌdısın'gedʒ |-s -ız |-d -d |-dness -ıdnıs, -dnıs

disentangle ˌdısın'tæŋg|l̩ |-d -d |-ling -'tæŋglıŋ, -'tæŋg| lıŋ

disestablish ˌdısə'stæblıʃ |-es -ız |-ed -t

disesteem ˌdısə'stim |-ed -d

disfavor dıs'fevɚ; ES -'fevə(r; |-ed -d |-ing -'fevərıŋ, -'fevrıŋ

disfiguration ˌdısfıgjɚ'reʃən, dıs͵fıgjə-

disfigure dıs'fıgjɚ; ES -'fıgjə(r; |-d -d

disfranchise dıs'fræntʃaız |-s -ız |-d -d

disfranchisement dıs'fræntʃızmənt

disgorge dıs'gɔrdʒ; ES -'gɔədʒ; |-s -ız |-d -d -t

disgrace dıs'gres |-s -ız |-d -t

disgraceful dıs'gresfəl |-ly -ı

disgruntle dıs'grʌnt|l̩ |-d -d

disguise dıs'gaız |-s -ız |-d -d |-dly -ıdlı

disgust dıs'gʌst, dız- |-ed -ıd

dish dıʃ |dishes 'dıʃız |dished dıʃt

dishabille ˌdısə'bil, cf deshabille

disharmonious ˌdıs·har'monıəs; ES -ha-, E -hadisharmony dɪs'harmənɪ; ES -'hɑːm-, E+ -'haːm-

dishcloth 'dɪʃˌklɔθ, -ˌklɒθ |-ths -ðz, -θs

dishearten dɪs'hartn̩; ES -'hɑːtn̩, E+-'haːtn̩; |-ed -d |-ing -tnɪŋ, -tn̩ɪŋ

disherison dɪs'hɛrəzn̩ |-ed -d

dishevel dɪ'ʃɛvl̩ |-ed -d |-ing -'ʃɛvl̩ɪŋ, -vlɪŋ

dishful 'dɪʃˌfʊl |-s -z

dishonest dɪs'anɪst, dɪz-; ES+-'ɒn-; |-y -ɪ

dishonor dɪs'anɚ, dɪz-; ES -'anə(r, -'ɒn-; |-able -əbl̩ |-bly -blɪ

disillusion ˌdɪsɪ'luʒən, -'lɪu- |-ed -d

disinclination ˌdɪsɪnklə'neʃən, dɪsˌɪnklə-

disincline ˌdɪsɪn'klaɪn |-clined -'klaɪnd

disinfect ˌdɪsɪn'fɛkt, ˌdɪsn̩- |-ed -ɪd |-ant -ənt |-ction -kʃən

disingenuous ˌdɪsɪn'dʒɛnjʊəs, ˌdɪsn̩-

disinherit ˌdɪsɪn'hɛrɪt, ˌdɪsn̩- |-ed -ɪd

disintegrable dɪs'ɪntəgrəbl̩

disintegrate dɪs'ɪntəˌgret |-grated -ˌgretɪd

disintegration ˌdɪsɪntə'greʃən, dɪsˌɪntə-

disinter ˌdɪsɪn'tɝ; ES -'tɝ(r, -'tɜ; |-red -d

disinterested dɪs'ɪntərəstɪd, -'ɪntrɪstɪd, -'ɪntə-ˌrɛstɪd—*see* interesting

disjoin dɪs'dʒɔɪn |-ed -d |-t -t |-ted -tɪd

disjunct dɪs'dʒʌŋkt |-ction -kʃən |-ive -ɪv

disk dɪsk |-ed -t

dislike dɪs'laɪk |-liked -'laɪkt

dislocate 'dɪsloˌket, dɪs'loket |-d -ɪd

dislocation ˌdɪslo'keʃən

dislodge dɪs'ladʒ; ES+-'lɒdʒ; |-s -ɪz |-d -d

disloyal dɪs'lɔɪəl, -'lɔjəl |-ly -ɪ |-ty -tɪ

dismal 'dɪzml̩ |-ly -ɪ

dismantle dɪs'mæntl̩ |-d -d |-ling -tl̩ɪŋ, -tlɪŋ

dismast dɪs'mæst; E+-'mast, -'mast; |-ed -ɪd

dismay dɪs'me, dɪz- |-ed -d |-edness -dnɪs, -ɪdnɪs

dismember dɪs'mɛmbɚ; ES -'mɛmbə(r; |-ed -d |-ing -'mɛmbrɪŋ, -'mɛmbərɪŋ

dismiss dɪs'mɪs |-ed -d |-al -l̩

dismount dɪs'maʊnt |-ed -ɪd

disobedience ˌdɪsə'bidɪəns |-ent -ənt

disobey ˌdɪsə'be |-ed -d

disoblige ˌdɪsə'blaɪdʒ |-s -ɪz |-d -d

disorder dɪs'ɔrdɚ, dɪz-; ES -'ɔədə(r; |-ed -d |-ing -dərɪŋ, -drɪŋ

disorganic ˌdɪsɔr'gænɪk; ES -ɔə'gæn-

disorganization dɪsˌɔrgənə'zeʃən, ˌdɪsɔr-; ES -ˌɔəgənə-, -ˌɔəg-, -aɪ'z-

disorganize dɪs'ɔrgəˌnaɪz; ES -'ɔəgə-; |-s -ɪz |-d -d

disown dɪs'on, dɪz- |-ed -d

disparage dɪ'spærɪdʒ |-es -ɪz |-d -d

disparate 'dɪspərɪt |disparity dɪs'pærətɪ

dispart dɪs'part; ES -'paːt, E+-'paːt; |-ed -ɪd

dispassion dɪs'pæʃən |-ed -d |-ate -ɪt

dispatch dɪ'spætʃ |-es -ɪz |-ed -t

dispel dɪ'spɛl |-led -d

dispensable dɪ'spɛnsəbl̩

dispensary dɪ'spɛnsərɪ

dispensation ˌdɪspən'seʃən, -pɛn-

dispensatory dɪ'spɛnsəˌtorɪ, -ˌtɔrɪ; S -ˌtorɪ

dispense dɪ'spɛns |-s -ɪz |-d -d

disperse dɪ'spɝs; ES -'spɝs, -'spɜs; |-s -ɪz |-d -t |-sal -l̩

dispersion dɪ'spɝʃən, -'spɝʒ-; ES -'spɝ-, -'spɜ-; |-sive -sɪv

dispirit dɪ'spɪrɪt |-ed -ɪd

displace dɪs'ples |-s -ɪz |-d -t

display dɪ'sple |-ed -d

displease dɪs'pliz |-s -ɪz |-d -d

displeasure dɪs'plɛʒɚ; ES -'plɛʒə(r; |-d -d

disport dɪ'sport, -'spɔrt; ES -'spoət, E+ -'spɔət; |-ed -ɪd

disposable dɪ'spozəbl̩ |-sal -zl̩

dispose dɪ'spoz |-s -ɪz |-d -d

disposition ˌdɪspə'zɪʃən

dispossess ˌdɪspə'zɛs |-es -ɪz |-ed -t

disposure dɪ'spoʒɚ; ES -'spoʒə(r

dispraise dɪs'prez |-s -ɪz |- d -d

disprize dɪs'praɪz |-s -ɪz |- d -d

disproof dɪs'pruf ('proof and 'disˌproof)

disproportion ˌdɪsprə'porʃən, -'pɔr-; ES -'poə-, E+-'pɔə-; |-al -l̩ |-ally -l̩ɪ |-ate -ɪt

disprove dɪs'pruv |-proved -'pruvd |-val -l̩

disputable dɪ'spjutəbl̩, -'sprut-, 'dɪspjutəbl̩ |-bly -blɪ—*The accentuation of* dis'putable *like* dis'pute *has inevitably won its way into good use.*

disputant 'dɪspjutənt, dɪ'spjutn̩t, -'sprut-

disputation ˌdɪspju'teʃən |-tious -ʃəs

disputative dɪ'spjutətɪv, -'sprut-

dispute dɪ'spjut, -'sprut |-d -ɪd

disqualification ˌdɪskwaləfə'keʃən, dɪsˌkw-, -wɒl-

disqualify dɪs'kwaləˌfaɪ, -'kwɒl- |-fied -ˌfaɪd

disquiet dɪs'kwaɪət |-ed -ɪd

disquietude dɪs'kwaɪəˌtjud, -ˌtrud, -ˌtud

Key: *See in full §§3–47.* bee **bi** |pity **'pɪtɪ** (§6) |rate **ret** |yet **jɛt** |sang **sæŋ** |angry **'æŋ·grɪ** |bath **bæθ**; E **baθ** (§10) |ah **ɑ** |far **fɑr** |watch **watʃ, wɒtʃ** (§12) |jaw **dʒɔ** |gorge **gɔrdʒ** |go **go**

disquisition ˌdɪskwə'zɪʃən
Disraeli dɪz'relɪ
disrate dɪs'ret |-rated -'retɪd
disregard ˌdɪsrɪ'gɑrd; ES -'gɑːd, E+-'gɑːd;
|-ed -ɪd
disrelish dɪs'rɛlɪʃ |-es -ɪz |-ed -t
disrepair ˌdɪsrɪ'pɛr, -'pær; E -'pɛə(r, ES
-'pæə(r
disreputability dɪsˌrɛpjətə'bɪlətɪ, ˌdɪsrɛp-
disreputable dɪs'rɛpjətəbl̩ |-bly -blɪ
disrepute ˌdɪsrɪ'pjut, -'pɪut
disrespect ˌdɪsrɪ'spɛkt |-ed -ɪd
disrespectful ˌdɪsrɪ'spɛktfəl |-ly -ɪ
disrobe dɪs'rob |-robed -'robd
disrupt dɪs'rʌpt |-ed -ɪd |-ption -pʃən |-ive -ɪv
dissatisfaction ˌdɪssætɪs'fækʃən, ˌdɪsæt- |-tory
-tərɪ
dissatisfy dɪs'sætɪsˌfaɪ, dɪ'sæt- |-fied -ˌfaɪd
dissect dɪ'sɛkt |-ed -ɪd |-ction -kʃən
disseize dɪs'siz |-s -ɪz |-d -d
dissemblance dɪ'sɛmbləns
dissemble dɪ'sɛmbl̩ |-d -d |-ling -blɪŋ, -bl̩ɪŋ
disseminate dɪ'sɛməˌnet |-nated -ˌnetɪd
dissemination dɪˌsɛmə'neʃən
dissension dɪ'sɛnʃən
dissent dɪ'sɛnt |-ed -ɪd |-er -ɚ; ES -ə(r
dissentience dɪ'sɛnʃəns |-cy -ɪ |-ent -ənt
dissert dɪ'sɝt; ES -'sɝt, -'sɜt; |-ed -ɪd
dissertation ˌdɪsɚ'teʃən; ES ˌdɪsə-
disservice dɪs'sɝvɪs; ES -'sɝv-, -'sɜv-; |-s -ɪz
|-d -t
dissever dɪ'sɛvɚ; ES -'sɛvə(r; |-ed -d |-ing
-'sɛvərɪŋ, -'sɛvrɪŋ
dissidence 'dɪsədəns |-dent -dənt
dissimilar dɪ'sɪmələ, dɪs's-; ES -'sɪmələ(r
dissimilarity dɪˌsɪmə'lærətɪ, dɪsˌs-, ˌdɪssɪm-
dissimilate dɪ'sɪməˌlet, dɪs's- |-d -ɪd
dissimilation dɪˌsɪmə'leʃən, dɪsˌs-, ˌdɪssɪm-
dissimilitude ˌdɪssɪ'mɪləˌtjud, -ˌtɪud, -ˌtud
dissimulate dɪ'sɪmjəˌlet |-lated -ˌletɪd
dissimulation dɪˌsɪmjə'leʃən
dissipate 'dɪsəˌpet |-d -ɪd |-tion ˌdɪsə'peʃən
dissociate dɪ'soʃɪˌet |-ated -ˌetɪd
dissociation dɪˌsosɪ'eʃən, -ˌsoʃɪ-
dissociative dɪ'soʃɪˌetɪv
dissolubility dɪˌsaljə'bɪlətɪ; ES+-ˌsɒl-
dissoluble dɪ'saljəbl̩; ES+-'sɒl-;—*The accentuation* dis'soluble *has displaced* 'dissoluble
by analogy of 'soluble *and* dis'solve.

dissolute 'dɪsəˌlut, -ˌlɪut, 'dɪsl̩ˌjut
dissolution ˌdɪsə'luʃən, -'lɪu-, -sl̩'juʃən
dissolve dɪ'zalv, -'zɒlv |-d -d |-nt -ənt
dissonance 'dɪsənəns |-s -ɪz |-cy -ɪ |-ant -ənt
dissuade dɪ'swed |-d -ɪd
dissuasion dɪ'sweʒən |-sive -'swesɪv
dissyllabic ˌdɪssɪ'læbɪk, ˌdɪsɪ-
dissyllable dɪ'sɪləbl̩, 'dɪsˌsɪləbl̩
distaff 'dɪstæf; E+'dɪstaf, 'dɪstɑf
distain dɪ'sten |-ed -d
distal 'dɪstl̩ |-ly -ɪ
distance 'dɪstəns |-s -ɪz |-d -t |-tant -tənt
distaste dɪs'test |-tasted -'testɪd
distasteful dɪs'testfəl |-ly -ɪ
distemper dɪs'tɛmpɚ; ES -pə(r; |-ed -d
|-pərɪŋ, -prɪŋ
distend dɪ'stɛnd |-ed -ɪd
distensible dɪ'stɛnsəbl̩
distention, -sion dɪ'stɛnʃən
distich 'dɪstɪk
distill, -til dɪ'stɪl |-(l)ed -d
distillate 'dɪstl̩ɪt, -ˌet
distillation ˌdɪstl̩'eʃən, -stɪl-
distiller dɪ'stɪlɚ; ES -'stɪlə(r; |-y -ɪ
distinct dɪ'stɪŋkt |-ction -kʃən |-ctive -ktɪv
distingué ˌdɪstæŋ'ge, dɪ'stæŋge (*Fr* distæ̃'ge)
distinguish dɪ'stɪŋgwɪʃ |-es -ɪz |-ed -t
distinguishable dɪ'stɪŋgwɪʃəbl̩ |-bly -blɪ
distort dɪs'tɔrt; ES -'tɔət; |-ed -ɪd
distortion dɪs'tɔrʃən; ES -'tɔəʃən
distract dɪ'strækt |-ed -ɪd
distraction dɪ'strækʃən |-tive -tɪv
distrain dɪ'stren |-ed -d |-t -t
distrait dɪ'stre |-e -t (*Fr* dis'trɛ(t))
distraught dɪ'strɔt
distress dɪ'strɛs |-es -ɪz |-ed -t |-edly -ɪdlɪ
distressful dɪ'strɛsfəl |-ly -ɪ
distributable dɪ'strɪbjətəbl̩
distribute dɪ'strɪbjut |-d -bjətɪd |-tive -bjətɪv
distribution ˌdɪstrə'bjuʃən, -'bɪuʃən
distributor dɪ'strɪbjətɚ; ES -tə(r
district 'dɪstrɪkt |-ed -ɪd
distrust dɪs'trʌst |-ed -ɪd
distrustful dɪs'trʌstfəl |-ly -ɪ
disturb dɪ'stɝb; ES -'stɝb, -'stɜb; |-ed -d
|-ance -əns |-ances -ənsɪz
disulphate, -fate daɪ'sʌlfet
disulphide, -fide daɪ'sʌlfaɪd, -fɪd |-phid, -fid
-fɪd

Those words below in which the ɑ sound is spelt o are often pronounced with ɒ in E and S

disunion dɪsˈjunjən
disunite ˌdɪsjuˈnaɪt |-nited -ˈnaɪtɪd
disuse *n* dɪsˈjus |-s -ɪz
disuse *v* dɪsˈjuz |-s -ɪz |-d -d
disyllable dɪˈsɪləbl̩ |disyllabic ˌdɪsɪˈlæbɪk
ditch dɪtʃ |ditches ˈdɪtʃɪz |ditched dɪtʃt
dither ˈdɪðɚ; ES -ə(r; |-ed -d |-ing -ˈðərɪŋ,
  -ˈðrɪŋ
dithyramb ˈdɪθəˌræm, -ˌræmb
dithyrambic ˌdɪθəˈræmbɪk |-ally -l̩ɪ, -ɪklɪ
ditto ˈdɪto |-ed -d
ditty ˈdɪtɪ |-ied -d
diuretic ˌdaɪjuˈrɛtɪk |-al -l̩ |-ally -l̩ɪ, -ɪklɪ
diurnal daɪˈɝnl̩; ES -ˈɜnl̩, -ˈɝnl̩; |-ly -ɪ
diva ˈdivə
divagate ˈdaɪvəˌget |-d -ɪd |-tion ˌdaɪvəˈgeʃən
divalent daɪˈvelənt, ˈdɪvələnt
divan ˈdaɪvæn, dɪˈvæn
divaricate dəˈværəˌket, daɪ- |-d -ɪd
divarication dəˌværəˈkeʃən, daɪ-
dive daɪv |*past* dove dov *or* dived daɪvd |*pptc*
  dived daɪvd
diver ˈdaɪvɚ; ES ˈdaɪvə(r
diverge dəˈvɝdʒ, daɪ-; ES -ˈvɝdʒ, -ˈvɝdʒ;
  |-s -ɪz |-d -d |-nce -əns |-ncy -ənsɪ |-nt -ənt
divers 'swimmers,' 'various' ˈdaɪvɚz; ES
  ˈdaɪvəz
diverse dəˈvɝs, daɪ-; ES -ˈvɝs, -ˈvɝs;
  (ˈdiˌverse ˈforces)
diversification dəˌvɝsəfəˈkeʃən, daɪ-; ES
  -ˌvɝs-, -ˌvɝs-
diversify dəˈvɝsəˌfaɪ, daɪ-; ES -ˈvɝs-, -ˈvɝs-;
  |-fied -ˌfaɪd
diversion dəˈvɝʒən, daɪ-, -ʃən; ES -ˈvɝ-,
  -ˈvɝ-
diversity dəˈvɝsətɪ, daɪ-; ES -ˈvɝs-, -ˈvɝs-
divert dəˈvɝt, daɪ-; ES -ˈvɝt, -ˈvɝt; |-ed -ɪd
divertisement dəˈvɝtɪzmənt; ES -ˈvɝt-, -ˈvɝt-
divertissement *Fr* divɛrtisˈmã
Dives ˈdaɪviz |-ves' -viz
divest dəˈvɛst, daɪ- |-ed -ɪd
divide dəˈvaɪd |-vided -ˈvaɪdɪd
dividend ˈdɪvəˌdɛnd
divination ˌdɪvəˈneʃən
divine dəˈvaɪn |-vineness -ˈvaɪnnɪs
divinity dəˈvɪnətɪ
divisibility dəˌvɪzəˈbɪlətɪ
divisible dəˈvɪzəbl̩ |-bly -blɪ

division dəˈvɪʒən |-al -l̩ |-ally -l̩ɪ
divisive dəˈvaɪsɪv
divisor dəˈvaɪzɚ; ES -ˈvaɪzə(r; |-ry -ɪ
divorce dəˈvors, -ˈvɔrs; ES -ˈvoəs, E+-ˈvɔəs;
  |-s -ɪz |-d -t
divorcé, -cée dəˌvorˈse, -ˌvɔr-; ES -ˌvoə-,
  E+-ˌvɔə-; |-cee -ˈsi (*Fr* divörˈse)
divot ˈdɪvət
divulge dəˈvʌldʒ |-s -ɪz |-d -d |-nce -əns
Dixie ˈdɪksɪ
Dixon ˈdɪksn̩
dizen ˈdɪzn̩, ˈdaɪzn̩ |-ed -d |-ing -zn̩ɪŋ, -znɪŋ
dizzy ˈdɪzɪ |dizzied ˈdɪzɪd
Dnepropetrovsk ˌdnjɛpropjɛˈtrɔfsk
Dnieper ˈnipɚ; ES ˈnipə(r
Dniester ˈnistɚ; ES ˈnistə(r
do *music, Jap geography* do
do *v stressed forms:*—|do ˈdu, ˌdu |*2 sg arch.*
  dost ˈdʌst, ˌdʌst *or* doest ˈduɪst, ˌduɪst
  |*3 sg* does ˈdʌz, ˌdʌz *or arch.* doth ˈdʌθ,
  ˌdʌθ *or* doeth ˈduɪθ, ˌduɪθ |*past 2 sg arch.*
  didst ˈdɪdst, ˌdɪdst *or* diddest, didest
  ˈdɪdɪst, ˌdɪdɪst |*past 1 & 3 sg, 1–3 pl* did
  ˈdɪd, ˌdɪd |*pptc* done ˈdʌn, ˌdʌn; *unstressed*
  forms (*auxiliaries*):—|do *bef. vowels* du
  (ˌso du ˈaɪ); *bef. conss.* də (ˌso də ˈðe)
  |dost dəst (ˈhwaɪ dəst ðau ˌpaɪn wɪðˈɪn?)
  |doth dəθ (dəθ ˈæsk ə ˈdrɪŋk dɪˈvaɪn) |does
  dəz (ˌhau dəz ɪt ˈlʊk?), dz (ˌhaudzɪt ˈsim?),
  ts (ˌhwʌtsɪt ˈmætɚ?) |did dɪd (ˌhwɛn dɪd
  ɪt ˈkʌm?), dəd (ˌhau dəd ˈhi ˌno?), d
  (ˌhaudɪt ˈgo? ˌhaud ðe ˈlaɪk ɪt?)
doable ˈduəbl̩
dob dab, dɒb |-bed -d
Dobbin, d- ˈdabɪn
Dobell doˈbɛl
Dobruja, -dja ˈdobrudʒə
Dobson, d- ˈdabsn̩
docent ˈdosn̩t (*Ger* dozent doˈtsɛnt)
docibility ˌdasəˈbɪlətɪ
docile ˈdasl̩, ˈdasɪl |-ly -ɪ
docility doˈsɪlətɪ, daˈsɪl-
dock dak |docked dakt |-age -ɪdʒ
docket ˈdakɪt |-ed -ɪd
dockyard ˈdakˌjard; ES -ˌjɑːd, E+-ˌjɑːd
doctor ˈdaktɚ; ES -tə(r; |-ed -d |-ing ˈdak-
  tərɪŋ, ˈdaktrɪŋ
doctoral ˈdaktərəl |-ly -ɪ |-rate -tərɪt, -trɪt

Those words below in which the ɑ sound is spelt o are often pronounced with ɒ in E and S

doctrinaire ˌdɑktrɪˈnɛr, -ˈnær; ES -ˈnɛə(r, ES -ˈnæə(r

doctrine ˈdɑktrɪn |-al -] |-ally -ļɪ

document *n* ˈdɑkjəmənt |-al ˌdɑkjəˈmɛnt]

document *v* ˈdɑkjəˌmɛnt |-ed -ɪd

documentary ˌdɑkjəˈmɛntərɪ, -trɪ |-rily -rəlɪ

documentation ˌdɑkjəmɛnˈteʃən

dodder ˈdɑdɚ; ES ˈdɑdə(r; |-ed -d |-ing ˈdɑdərɪŋ, ˈdɑdrɪŋ

dodecagon doˈdɛkəˌgɑn, -gən

dodecahedron ˌdodɛkəˈhidrən |-s -z |-dra -drə

Dodecanese ˌdodɛkəˈnis, doˌdɛk- |-nesus -ˈnisəs

dodge, D- dɑdʒ |-s -ɪz |-d -d|-r -ɚ; ES -ə(r

Dodgson ˈdɑdʒsən

dodo ˈdodo

Dodona doˈdonə

doe, D- do

does dʌz—*for forms see* do

doesn't ˈdʌzn̩t, *before some conss.*+ˈdʌzn̩ (ˌdʌznˈkɛr)—ˈdʌzənt *is substandard*

doest ˈduɪst—*for forms see* do

doeth ˈduɪθ—*for forms see* do

doff dɑf, dɒf, dɔf |-ed -t

dog dɔg, dɒg, *much less freq.* dɑg |-ged -d

Dogberry, d- ˈdɔgˌbɛrɪ, ˈdɒg-, -bərɪ

dogcart ˈdɔgˌkɑrt, ˈdɒg-; ES -ˌkɑ:t, E+-ˌkɑ:t

doge dodʒ |-'s -ɪz

dog-ear ˈdɔgˌɪr ˈdɒg-; ES -ˌɪə(r, S+-ˌɛə(r; |ed -d

dogged *adj* ˈdɔgɪd, ˈdɒg-

dogger ˈdɔgɚ, ˈdɒgɚ; ES -ə(r

doggerel ˈdɔgərəl, ˈdɒg-, ˈdɑg-, -grəl

dogie ˈdogɪ

dogma ˈdɔgmə, ˈdɒg-, ˈdɑg- |-tism -ˌtɪzəm |-tist -tɪst

dogmatic dɔgˈmætɪk, dɒg-, dɑg- |-al -] |-ally -ļɪ, -ɪklɪ

dogmatize ˈdɔgməˌtaɪz, ˈdɒg-, ˈdɑg- |-s -ɪz |-d -d

dog-tired ˈdɔgˈtaɪrd, ˈdɒg-; ES -ˈtaɪəd

dogtooth ˈdɔgˌtuθ, ˈdɒg- |-teeth -ˌtiθ |-ed -θt, -ðd

dogtrot ˈdɔgˌtrɑt, ˈdɒg-

dogwatch ˈdɔgˌwɑtʃ, ˈdɒg-, -ˌwɒtʃ, -ˌwɔtʃ |-es -ɪz

dogwood ˈdɔgˌwʊd, ˈdɒg-

dogy ˈdogɪ

doily ˈdɔɪlɪ

doings ˈduɪŋz, *humorous* ˈduɪnz

doit dɔɪt

Dolabella ˌdɑləˈbɛlə

dolce far niente ˈdoltʃɪˌfɑr·nɪˈɛntɪ; ES -fɑ:- (*It* ˈdoltʃeˌfɑrˈnjɛnte)

doldrum ˈdɑldrəm |-s -z

dole dol |doled dold |-ful -fəl |-fully -fəlɪ

dolerite ˈdɑləˌraɪt

Dolgelly dɑlˈgɛθlɪ, -ˈgɛlɪ (*Welsh* dolˈgeɬi)

Dolgeville ˈdɑldʒvɪl

dolichocephalic ˈdɑlɪˌkosəˈfælɪk

doll dɑl, dɒl, dɔl |-ed -d

dollar ˈdɑlɚ; ES ˈdɑlə(r

Dollard ˈdɑlɚd; ES ˈdɑləd

dolly, D- ˈdɑlɪ, ˈdɒlɪ, ˈdɔlɪ

dolman ˈdɑlmən |-s -z

dolmen ˈdɑlmɛn |-s -z

dolomite ˈdɑləˌmaɪt

Dolomites ˈdɑləˌmaɪts

dolor ˈdolɚ; ES ˈdolə(r; |-ous ˈdalərəs, ˈdol-

Dolores dəˈlorɪs, -ɪz, -ˈlɔr-; S -ˈlor-; |-'s -ɪz

dolphin ˈdɑlfɪn

dolt dolt; *N Engd*+dȫlt (*§46*)

-dom *unstressed ending* -dəm—*Many words in* -dom *are omitted from the vocab.*

domain doˈmen |-ial -ɪəl

Dombey ˈdɑmbɪ

dome dom |domed domd |domal ˈdomļ

domesday, D- ˈdumzˌde=doomsday

domestic dəˈmɛstɪk |-al -] |-ally -ļɪ, -ɪklɪ

domesticate dəˈmɛstəˌket |-cated -ˌketɪd

domestication dəˌmɛstəˈkeʃən

domesticity ˌdomɛsˈtɪsətɪ, dəˌmɛsˈtɪsətɪ

domicile ˈdɑməsļ, -sɪl |-d -d

domiciliary ˌdɑməˈsɪlɪˌɛrɪ

dominance ˈdɑmənəns |-cy -ɪ |-nant -nənt

dominate ˈdɑməˌnet |-d -ɪd |-tion ˌdɑməˈneʃən

domineer ˌdɑməˈnɪr; ES -ˈnɪə(r, S+-ˈnɛə(r, -ˈnjɛə(r; |-ed -d

Domingo dəˈmɪŋgo

Dominic ˈdɑmənɪk

Dominica dəˈmɪnɪkə, ˌdɑməˈnikə |-n -n

dominical dəˈmɪnɪk]

dominie ˈdɑmənɪ, '*pastor*'+ˈdomənɪ

dominion dəˈmɪnjən

domino ˈdɑməˌno

|full fʊl |tooth tuθ |further ˈfɝðɚ; ES ˈfɝðə |custom ˈkʌstəm |while hwaɪl |how haʊ |toy tɔɪ |using ˈjuzɪŋ |fuse fjuz, fɪuz |dish dɪʃ |vision ˈvɪʒən |Eden ˈidn̩ |cradle ˈkredļ |keep 'em ˈkipm̩

Those words below in which the ɑ sound is spelt o are often pronounced with ɒ in E and S

Domitian dəˈmɪʃən, -ʃɪən |-tius -ʃəs, -ʃɪəs
  |-tius's -əsɪz
Domremy-la-Pucelle *Fr* dŏrəmilapyˈsɛl
don, D- dan |donned dand
Don Adriano de Armado ˌdan·adrɪˈanoˌdear-
  ˈmado; ES -ɑːˈmado
Donalbain ˈdanl̩ˌben
Donald ˈdanld |-son ˈdanl̩sn̩, ˈdanl̩dsən
donate ˈdonet |-nated -netɪd |-tion doˈneʃən
Donatello ˌdanəˈtɛlo (*It* ˌdonaˈtɛllo)
Donati doˈnatɪ
donative ˈdanətɪv, ˈdon-
Donatus doˈnetəs |-'s -ɪz
Doncaster ˈdaŋkæstɚ, ˈdan-; ES -kæstə(r
done dʌn
done for ˈdʌnˌfɔr; ES -ˌfɔə(r
done up ˈdʌnˈʌp
done with ˈdʌnˌwɪð, -ˌwɪθ
donee doˈni
Donegal ˈdanɪˌgɔl, ˌdanɪˈgɔl
Donelson ˈdanl̩sn̩
Don Giovanni ˌdan·dʒɪəˈvanɪ, -dʒo- (*It*
  ˌdondʒoˈvanni)
Dongola ˈdaŋgələ
Donizetti ˌdanəˈzetɪ, (*It* ˌdoniˈdzetti)
donjon ˈdʌndʒən, ˈdan-
Don Juan danˈdʒuən, -ˈdʒɪuən (*Sp* dɔn-
  ˈxwan)
donkey ˈdaŋkɪ, ˈdɒŋkɪ, ˈdɔŋkɪ, ˈdʌŋkɪ
Donley ˈdanlɪ
donna, D- ˈdanə (*It* ˈdɒnnɑ)
Donne dʌn
Donnelly ˈdanl̩ɪ, ˈdanlɪ
Donnithorne ˈdanəˌθɔrn; ES -ˌθɔən
Donnybrook ˈdanɪˌbrʊk
Donohue ˈdanəˌhju, -ˌhɪu, -ˌhu, ˈdʌn-
donor ˈdonɚ; ES ˈdonə(r; (doˈni ən doˈnɔr)
Donora doˈnorə, -ˈnɔrə; S -ˈnorə
do-nothing ˈduˌnʌθɪŋ
Don Pedro danˈpidro
Don Quixote ˌdankɪˈhotɪ, danˈkwɪksət (*Sp*
  -kiˈxote)
don't dont, *bef. some conss. often* don (donˈtek
  ɪt), *bef.* n *often* don, do (donˈno, doˈno),
  bef. p, b, m *often* domp (dompprɪˈtend ˌtu,
  dompbəˈliv ɪt, dompˈmaɪnd ɪt), *bef.* k, g
  often doŋ, doŋk (doŋˈkær, doŋkˈkær,
  doŋˈgo, doŋkˈgo); |*N Engd*+dɔ̃nt (*§46*)

doodlebug ˈdudl̩ˌbʌg
doom dum |doomed dumd
doomsday, D- ˈdumzˌde
Doon(e) dun
door, D- dor, dɔr; ES doə(r, E+dɔə(r; |-ed -d
doorjamb ˈdorˌdʒæm, ˈdɔr-; ES ˈdoə-,
  E+ˈdɔə-
doorman ˈdorˌmæn, -mən |-men -ˌmɛn, -mən
doornail ˈdorˌnel, ˈdɔr-, -ˈnel; ES ˈdoə-,
  E+ˈdɔə-
dooryard ˈdorˌjard, ˈdɔr-; ES ˈdoəˌjaːd,
  E+ˈdɔə-, -ˌjaːd
dope dop |doped dopt
dor, -rr dɔr; ES dɔə(r
Dora ˈdorə, ˈdɔrə; S ˈdorə
Dorcas ˈdɔrkəs; ES ˈdɔəkəs; |-'s -ɪz
Dorchester ˈdɔrˌtʃɛstɚ, ˈdɔrtʃɪstɚ; ES ˈdɔə-,
  -tə(r
Dordogne dɔrˈdɔnjə (*Fr* dŏrˈdɔ̃ɲ)
Dordrecht ˈdɔrdrɛkt, -drɛxt
Doré doˈre, dɔ-; S doˈre; (*Fr* dŏˈre)
Dorian ˈdorɪən, ˈdɔr-; S ˈdorɪən
Doric ˈdɔrɪk, ˈdar-, ˈdɒr-
Doricles ˈdɔrəˌkliz, ˈdar-, ˈdɒr- |-'s -ɪz
Dorigen ˈdɔrəgɪn, -gən, ˈdar-, ˈdɒr-
Doris ˈdɔrɪs, ˈdar-, ˈdɒr- |-'s -ɪz
Dorking ˈdɔrkɪŋ; ES ˈdɔəkɪŋ
dormancy ˈdɔrmənsɪ; ES ˈdɔəm-; |-mant
  -mənt
dormer ˈdɔrmɚ; ES ˈdɔəmə(r; |-ed -d
dormitory ˈdɔrməˌtorɪ, -ˌtɔrɪ; ES ˈdɔəməˌtorɪ,
  E+-ˌtɔrɪ
dormouse ˈdɔrˌmaʊs; ES ˈdɔə-; |-'s -ɪz |-mice
  -ˌmaɪs |-mice's -ˌmaɪsɪz
dormy, -mie ˈdɔrmɪ; ES ˈdɔəmɪ
Dorothea ˌdɔrəˈθiə, ˌdar-, ˌdɒr-
Dorothy ˈdɔrəθɪ, ˈdar-, ˈdɒr-
Dorrit ˈdɔrɪt, ˈdar-, ˈdɒr-
dorsal ˈdɔrsl̩; ES ˈdɔəsl̩; |-ly -ɪ
Dorset ˈdɔrsɪt; ES ˈdɔəsɪt; |-shire -ˌʃɪr, -ʃɚ;
  ES -ˌʃɪə(r, -ʃə(r
Dortmund ˈdɔrtmənd; ES ˈdɔət-; (*Ger*
  ˈdɔrtmʊnt)
dory- D- ˈdorɪ, ˈdɔrɪ; S ˈdorɪ
dos-à-dos *Fr* dozaˈdo
dosage ˈdosɪdʒ |-s -ɪz
dose dos |doses ˈdosɪz |dosed dost; |*N Engd*+
  dɔ̈s (*§46*)

Key: See in full §§3–47. bee bi |pity ˈpɪtɪ (§6) |rate ret |yet jɛt |sang sæŋ |angry ˈæŋ·grɪ
|bath bæθ; E baθ (§10) |ah ɑ |far fɑr |watch watʃ, wɒtʃ (§12) |jaw dʒɔ |gorge gɔrdʒ |go go

Dos Passos dɑs'pæsos; ES+dɒs-; |-sos' -sos
dossier 'dɑsɪ‚e, 'dɑsɪɚ; ES 'dɑsɪ‚e, 'dɑsɪ‚ə(r, 'dɒs-; (Fr do'sje)
dost dʌst—see do
Dostoevski ‚dɑstɔ'jɛfskɪ, ‚dɒs-
dot 'dowry' dɑt; ES+dɒt; (Fr döt)
dot 'point' dɑt; ES+dɒt; |-ted -ɪd
dotard 'dotɚd; ES 'dotəd
dote dot |doted 'dotɪd |dotage 'dotɪdʒ
doth dʌθ—see do
Dothan 'doθən, 'doθæn
Dotheboys Hall 'duðə‚bɔɪz'hɔl
dotterel 'dɑtərəl; ES+'dɒt-
Douai, -ay du'e ('Dou‚ai 'Bible)
double 'dʌbḷ |-d -d |-ling 'dʌblɪŋ, 'dʌbḷɪŋ
double-barreled 'dʌbḷ'bærəld
double-breasted 'dʌbḷ'brɛstɪd
double-cross 'dʌbḷ'krɔs, -'krɒs |-es -ɪz |-ed -t
double-edged 'dʌbḷ'ɛdʒd, -'ɛdʒɪd
double-entendre 'dublạn'tɑndrə (Fr dublã-'tã:dr)
double-faced 'dʌbḷ'fest |-facedly -'fesɪdlɪ
double-leaded 'dʌbḷ'lɛdɪd
double-lived 'dʌbḷ'laɪvd ('double-‚lived 'bards)
double-quick 'dʌbḷ'kwɪk ('double-‚quick 'time)
doublet 'dʌblɪt |-ed -ɪd
doubletree 'dʌbḷ‚tri, -trɪ
double-U letter 'dʌb·lju, 'dʌbḷju, 'dʌbju
doubloon dʌ'blun
doubly 'dʌblɪ
doubt daʊt |-ed -ɪd |-ful -fəl |-fully -fəlɪ
Douce daʊs, dus |-'s -ɪz
douceur du'sɝ; ES -'sɝ(r, -'sɝ; (Fr du'sœ:r)
douche duʃ |douches 'duʃɪz |douched duʃt
Dougal, -ll 'dugḷ
dough do |doughed dod |-y -ɪ |-boy -‚bɔɪ
Dougherty 'doɚtɪ, 'dɔɚtɪ, 'dɑhɚtɪ; ES 'doɚ-, 'dɔɚ-, 'dɑhə-
doughfaced 'do‚fest
doughnut 'donət, -‚nʌt
doughty 'daʊtɪ
Douglas, -ss 'dʌgləs |-'s -ɪz
dour dur, dʊr, daʊr; ES dʊə(r, dʊə(r, daʊə(r
Dousabel 'dusə‚bɛl
douse daʊs |douses 'daʊsɪz |doused daʊst
dove 'pigeon' dʌv
dove 'dived' dov
Dove Eng name dʌv, Ger name 'dovə

dovecot 'dʌv‚kɑt; ES+-‚kɒt;—see cot
dovecote 'dʌv‚kot—see cot, cote
Dovedale 'dʌv‚del
Dover 'dovɚ; ES 'dovə(r
dovetail 'dʌv‚tel |-tailed -‚teld
Dow daʊ
dowager 'daʊədʒɚ; ES 'daʊədʒə(r
Dowagiac də'wɒdʒæk
Dowden 'daʊdn̩
dowdy 'daʊdɪ
dowel 'daʊəl |-ed -d
dower 'daʊɚ; ES 'daʊ·ə(r; |-ed -d |-ing 'daʊərɪŋ, 'daʊrɪŋ
down daʊn |downed daʊnd
down-and-out 'daʊnən'aʊt, 'daʊnənd'aʊt
downcast 'daʊn‚kæst; E+-‚kast, -‚kɑst
downfall 'daʊn‚fɔl |-en -ən, -‚fɔln
downgrade adj, adv 'daʊn'gred, cf upgrade
downhearted 'daʊn'hɑrtɪd; ES -'hɑ:t-, E+-'hɑ:t-
downhill n 'daʊn‚hɪl, daʊn'hɪl
Downing 'daʊnɪŋ
downpour 'daʊn‚por, -‚pɔr, -‚pur; ES -‚poə(r, -‚pʊə(r, E+-‚pɔə(r
downright adj 'daʊn‚raɪt
downright adv 'daʊn‚raɪt, daʊn'raɪt
downside 'daʊn'saɪd, 'daʊn‚saɪd
downstage adj, adv, v 'daʊn'stedʒ |-s -ɪz |-d -d
downstairs n daʊn'stɛrz, -'stærz; E -'stɛəz, ES -'stæəz; acct+'down‚stairs, adj, adv 'down'stairs
downstream adj, adv 'daʊn'strim; v daʊn-'strim |-ed -d
downtown n daʊn'taʊn, 'daʊn‚taʊn
downtown adj, adv 'daʊn'taʊn ('up‚town & 'down‚town)
downtrodden 'daʊn'trɑdn̩; ES+-'trɒdn̩
downward 'daʊnwɚd; ES 'daʊnwəd |-s -z
dowry 'daʊrɪ
dowsabel 'daʊsə‚bɛl
doxology dɑks'ɑlədʒɪ; ES+dɒks'ɒl-
doyen 'dɔɪən (Fr dwa'jæ̃)
Doyle dɔɪl
Doylestown 'dɔɪlz‚taʊn
doze doz |dozes 'dozɪz |dozed dozd
dozen 'stun' 'dozn̩ |-ed -d
dozen 'twelve' 'dʌzn̩ |-ed -d
dozy 'dozɪ
drab dræb |drabbed dræbd

|full fʊl |tooth tuθ |further 'fɝðɚ; ES 'fɝðə |custom 'kʌstəm |while hwaɪl |how haʊ |toy tɔɪ
|using 'juzɪŋ |fuse fjuz, fɪuz |dish dɪʃ |vision 'vɪʒən |Eden 'idn̩ |cradle 'kredḷ |keep 'em 'kipm̩

drabble 'dræb| |-d -d |-ling 'dræblıŋ, -b|ıŋ
drachm dræm
drachma 'drækmə |-s -z |-mae -mi
Draco 'dreko |*gen* Draconis dre'konıs
Draconian dre'konıən
Dracula 'drækjulə
Dracut 'drekət
draff dræf
draft dræft; E+draft, draft; |-ed -ıd
draftsman 'dræftsmən; E+'draft-, 'draft-;
|-men -mən
drag dræg |dragged drægd
draggle 'dræg| |-d -d |-ling 'dræglıŋ, -g|ıŋ
draggly 'dræglı
dragnet 'dræg,nɛt
dragoman 'drægəmən |-mans -mənz |-men
-mən
dragon 'drægən |-et -ıt |-fly -,flaı
dragonnade ,drægə'ned
dragoon drə'gun |-ed -d |-age -ıdʒ
dragrope 'dræg,rop
drain dren |drained drend |-age -ıdʒ
drake, D- drek
dram dræm
drama 'dramə, 'dræmə, 'dramə, *rarely*
'dremə
dramatic drə'mætık |-al -| |-ally -|ı, -ıklı
dramatis personae 'dræmətıspə'soni; ES
-pə-
dramatization ,dræmətə'zeʃən, -aı'z-
dramatize 'dræmə,taız |-s -ız |-d -d
dramaturgic ,dræmə'tɜˑdʒık; ES -'tɜdʒ-,
-'tɜˑdʒ-
dramaturgy 'dræmə,tɜˑdʒı; ES -,tɜdʒı, -,tɜˑdʒı
dramshop 'dræm,ʃap; ES+-,ʃɒp
drank dræŋk
drape drep |-d -t |-r -ɚ; ES -ə(r; |-ry -ərı, -rı
drastic 'dræstık |-ally -|ı, -ıklı
drat dræt |dratted 'drætıd
draught dræft; E+draft, draft; |-ed -ıd
draughtsman 'dræftsmən; E+'draft-, 'draft-;
|-men -mən
Drava 'dravə
Dravida 'dravıdə |-vidian drə'vıdıən
draw drɔ |drew dru, drıu |drawn drɔn
drawbar 'drɔ,bar; ES -,ba:(r, E+-,ba:(r
drawboard 'drɔ,bord, -,bɔrd; ES -,boəd,
E+-,bɔəd
drawbridge 'drɔ,brıdʒ |-s -ız

drawee drɔ'i
drawer '*one who draws*' 'drɔɚ; ES 'drɔ·ə(r
drawer *of a dresser* drɔr; ES drɔə(r; |-s -z
drawing-room 'drɔ·ıŋ,rum, -,rum
drawknife 'drɔ,naıf |-knives -,naıvz
drawl drɔl |drawled drɔld
drawn drɔn
drawshave 'drɔ,ʃev
dray dre |-ed -d |-age -ıdʒ |-man, -men -mən
Drayton 'dretn̩
dread drɛd |-ed -ıd |-ful -fəl |-fully -fəlı
dreadnought, -naught, D- 'drɛd,nɔt
dream drim |dreamed drimd *or* dreamt
drɛmpt
dreamland 'drim,lænd, -lənd
drear drır; ES drıə(r, S+drɛə(r
dreary 'drırı, 'drırı; S+'drɛrı
dredge drɛdʒ |-s -ız |-d -d
dregs drɛgz
Dreiser 'draısɚ, -zɚ; ES 'draısə(r, -zə(r
drench drɛntʃ |-es -ız |-ed -t
Dresden 'drɛzdən
dress drɛs |-es -ız |-ed *or* drest 'drɛst
dressmaker 'drɛs,mekɚ; ES -,mekə(r
dress suit 'drɛs'sut, -'sıut, -'sjut ('drɛss-'suit
,case, 'dress-,suit ,case)
drew, D- dru, drıu
Dreyfus 'drefəs, 'draı- |-'s -ız (*Fr* drɛ'fys)
dribble 'drıb| |-d -d |-ling 'drıblıŋ, -b|ıŋ
dribbler 'drıblɚ; ES 'drıblə(r
driblet, dribb- 'drıblıt
dried draıd
drier 'draıɚ; ES 'draı·ə(r
dries draız
drift drıft |drifted 'drıftıd |-wood -,wud
drill drıl |drilled drıld
drily 'draılı
drink drıŋk |drank dræŋk |drunk drʌŋk
drinkable 'drıŋkəb| |-bly -blı
Drinkwater 'drıŋk,wɔtɚ, -,watɚ, -,wɒtɚ; ES
-tə(r
drip drıp |dripped drıpt
drippings 'drıpıŋz
drivable, driveable 'draıvəb|
drive draıv |drove drov |driven 'drıvən
drivel 'drıv| |-ed -d |-ing 'drıv|ıŋ, -vlıŋ
driveling *adj* 'drıvlıŋ
driveway 'draıv,we
drizzle 'drız| |-d -d |-ling 'drızlıŋ, -z|ıŋ

Key: See in full §§3–47. bee bi |pity 'pıtı (§6) |rate ret |yet jɛt |sang sæŋ |angry 'æŋ·grı
|bath bæθ; E baθ (§10) |ah a |far far |watch watʃ, wɒtʃ (§12) |jaw dʒɔ |gorge gɔrdʒ |go go

drizzly 'drɪzlɪ
Drogheda 'drɔədə, 'drɔ·ɪdə
drogher, droger 'drogɚ; ES 'drogə(r
droll drol |-ed -d |ery -ərɪ |-y 'drolɪ, -olɪ
dromedary 'drɑmə͵dɛrɪ, 'drʌm-; ES+-'drɒm-
Dromio 'dromjo, 'dromɪ͵o
drone dron |droned drond |-age -ɪdʒ
Drood drud
drool drul |drooled druld
droop drup |drooped drupt
drop drɑp; ES+drɒp; |-ped, -t -t
drop-forge 'drɑp'fɔrdʒ, -'fordʒ; ES -'foədʒ, -'fɔədʒ; |-s -ɪz |-d -d—see forge
droplet 'drɑplɪt; ES+'drɒp-
droplight 'drɑp͵laɪt; ES+'drɒp-
dropper 'drɑpɚ; ES 'drɑpə(r, 'drɒp-
dropsical 'drɑpsɪk|; ES+'drɒp-; |-ly -ɪ
dropsy 'drɑpsɪ; ES+'drɒp-; |-ied -d
dropt drɑpt; ES+drɒpt
droshky 'drɑʃkɪ; ES+'drɒʃ-
Drosophila, d- dro'sɑfələ; ES+-'sɒf-; |-lae -͵li
dross drɔs, drɒs |-es -ɪz |-ed -t
drought draʊt
drouth draʊθ |-ths -θs—Drouth is not an error for drought, but a normal historical variant in wide American use.
drove drov |droved drovd
drover 'drovɚ; ES 'drovə(r
drown draʊn |drowned draʊnd
drowse draʊz |-s -ɪz |-d -d
drowsy 'draʊzɪ |-sily 'draʊz|ɪ, -zɪlɪ
drub drʌb |drubbed drʌbd |-bing -ɪŋ
drudge drʌdʒ |-s -ɪz |-d -d |-ry -ərɪ, -rɪ
drug drʌg |drugged drʌgd |-gist -ɪst
drugget 'drʌgɪt
drugstore 'drʌg͵stor, -͵stɔr; ES -͵stoə(r, E+-͵stɔə(r
druid, D- 'druɪd, 'drɪuɪd
druidic dru'ɪdɪk, drɪu- |-al -|
drum drʌm |drummed drʌmd |-mer -ɚ; ES -ə(r
drumfire 'drʌm͵faɪr; ES -͵faɪə(r
drumhead 'drʌm͵hɛd
drumlin 'drʌmlɪn
Drummond 'drʌmənd
drumstick 'drʌm͵stɪk
drunk drʌŋk |-en -ən |-ard -ɚd; ES -əd
drunkenness 'drʌŋkənnɪs

drupaceous dru'peʃəs, drɪu-
drupe drup, drɪup |-let -lɪt
Drury Lane 'drʊrɪ'len, 'drɪʊrɪ-
Drusilla dru'sɪlə, drɪu-
dry draɪ |dried draɪd
dryad 'draɪəd, -æd
Dryasdust 'draɪəz͵dʌst
Dryburgh 'draɪ͵bɜ·o, -ə; ES -͵bɜr-, -͵bʌr-, -͵bɜr-; Brit 'draɪbərə
dry-clean 'draɪ'klin, -͵klin |-ed -d
Dryden 'draɪdn̩
dryer 'draɪɚ; ES 'draɪ·ə(r
dryly 'draɪlɪ
dry-nurse 'draɪ͵nɜ·s; ES -͵nɜs, -͵nɜ·s; |-s -ɪz |-d -t
drysalter 'draɪ͵sɔltɚ; ES -͵sɔltə(r; |-y -ɪ
dry-shod 'draɪ'ʃɑd; ES -'ʃɒd
'dst 'wouldst' dst
dual 'djuəl, 'drɪuəl, 'duəl |-ism -͵ɪzəm
dualistic ͵djuəl'ɪstɪk, ͵drɪu-, ͵du- |-ally -|ɪ, -ɪklɪ
duality dju'ælətɪ, drɪu-, du-
dub dʌb |dubbed dʌbd
Du Barry dju'bærɪ, drɪu- du- (Fr dyba'ri)
Du Bartas djubar'tas, drɪu-, du-; ES -ba:'tas; (Fr dybar'ta:s) |-'s -ɪz
dubiety dju'baɪətɪ, drɪu-, du-
dubious 'djubɪəs, 'drɪu-, 'du-
dubitable 'djubɪtəb|, 'drɪu-, 'du- |-bly -blɪ
dubitate 'djubə͵tet, 'drɪu-, 'du- |-d -ɪd |-tive -ɪv
dubitation ͵djubə'teʃən, ͵drɪu- ͵du-
Dublin 'dʌblɪn
Dubois, Du Bois də'bɔɪs, du-, 'dubɔɪs |-'s -ɪz
Dubuque də'bjuk, du-, -'brɪuk
ducal 'djuk|, 'drɪu-, 'du- |-ly -ɪ
Du Cange dju'kændʒ, drɪu-, du- |-'s -ɪz (Fr dy'kɑ̃:ʒ)
ducat 'dʌkət
duce It 'du:tʃe
Duchesne in Utah du'ʃen, drɪu-; Fr name dy'ʃɛ:n
duchess 'dʌtʃɪs |-'s -ɪz
duchy 'dʌtʃɪ
duck dʌk |ducked dʌkt |-ling 'dʌklɪŋ
duct dʌkt |-ed -ɪd
ductile 'dʌkt|, -tɪl |-ly -ɪ
ductility dʌk'tɪlətɪ
dud dʌd

|full fʊl |tooth tuθ |further 'fɝðɚ; ES 'fɜðə |custom 'kʌstəm |while hwaɪl |how haʊ |toy tɔɪ |using 'juzɪŋ |fuse fjuz, frɪuz |dish dɪʃ |vision 'vɪʒən |Eden 'idn̩ |cradle 'kredl̩ |keep 'em 'kipm̩

Duddon 'dʌdn̩
dude djud, dɪud, dud
dudgeon 'dʌdʒən
Dudley 'dʌdlɪ
due dju, dɪu, du
duel 'djuəl, 'dɪu-, 'du- |-ed -d |-ist -ɪst
duello dju'ɛlo, dɪu-, du- (*It* du'ɛllo)
duenna dju'ɛnə, dɪu-, du-
duet dju'ɛt, dɪu-, du- |-ted -ɪd
duff dʌf |duffed dʌft |-el -l̩ |-er -ɚ; ES -ə(r
dug dʌg
Dugdale 'dʌgdel
dugong 'dugɑŋ, -gɒŋ, -gɔŋ
dugout 'dʌgˌaut
dugway 'dʌgˌwe
duke djuk, dɪuk, duk |-dom -dəm |-ry -ərɪ
dulcet 'dʌlsɪt
dulcimer 'dʌlsəmɚ; ES 'dʌlsəmə(r
Dulcinea dʌl'sɪnɪə, ˌdʌlsə'nɪə (*Sp* ˌdulθi'nea)
dulia dju'laɪə, dɪu-, du-
dull dʌl |dulled dʌld |-ard -ɚd; ES -əd
dully 'dʌllɪ, 'dʌlɪ
Duluth də'luθ, du-, -'lɪuθ
Dulwich 'dʌlɪdʒ, -ɪtʃ |-'s -ɪz
duly 'djulɪ, 'dɪulɪ, 'dulɪ
Dumain dju'men, dɪu-, du-
Dumas dju'ma, dɪu-, du-, *acct+*'Dumas (*Fr* dy'ma)
Du Maurier dju'mɔrɪˌe, dɪu-, du- (*Fr* dymɔ̃'rje)
dumb dʌm |-ed -d |-bell -ˌbɛl
Dumbarton dʌm'bartn̩; ES -'baːtn̩, E+ -'baːtn̩; |-shire -ˌʃɪr, -ˌʃɚ; ES -ˌʃɪə(r, -ˌʃə(r
dumdum 'dʌmdʌm
dumfound, dumbf- dʌm'faund |-ed -ɪd
Dumfries dʌm'fris |-shire -ʃɪr, -ʃɚ; ES -ʃɪə(r, -ʃə(r
dummy 'dʌmɪ |-ied -d
dump dʌmp |dumped dʌmpt |-ling -lɪŋ
dun dʌn |dunned dʌnd
Dunbar *US* 'dʌnbɑr; ES -baː(r, E+-baː(r; *Scotl* Dun'bar
Duncan 'dʌŋkən
Duncannon dʌn'kænən
dunce dʌns |dunces 'dʌnsɪz
Dunciad 'dʌnsɪˌæd
Dundas dʌn'dæs |-'s -ɪz
Dundee dʌn'di ('Dunˌdee 'road)
dunderhead 'dʌndɚˌhɛd; ES 'dʌndə-

dunderpate 'dʌndɚˌpet; ES 'dʌndə-
Dundreary, d- dʌn'drɪrɪ
dune djun, dɪun, dun
Dun Edin, Dunedin dʌn'idn̩, -dɪn
Dunellen dʌn'ɛlɪn
Dunfermline dʌn'fɝmlɪn, dʌm-; ES -'fɝm-, -'fɝm-; *loc.+*-'fɛrm-, -'farm-
dung dʌŋ |-ed -d
dungaree, -ri ˌdʌŋgə'ri
dungeon 'dʌndʒən |-ed -d
dung-fork 'dʌŋˌfɔrk; ES -ˌfɔək
dunghill 'dʌŋˌhɪl
Dunkard 'dʌŋkɚd; ES 'dʌŋkəd
Dunker 'dʌŋkɚ; ES 'dʌŋkə(r
Dunkirk *US* 'dʌnkɝk; ES -kɝk, -kɝk, *France* 'Dunkirk, Dun'kirk
Dunmore dʌn'mor, -'mɔr; ES -'moə(r, E+-'mɔə(r
Dunmow 'dʌnmo
dunnage 'dʌnɪdʒ |-s -ɪz |-d -d
Duns dʌnz, dʌns |-'s -ɪz
Dunsany dʌn'senɪ
Dunsinane 'dʌnsəˌnen, ˌdʌnsə'nen
Dunsmuir 'dʌnzmjur, -mɪur
Duns Scotus 'dʌnz'skotəs, *earlier* 'dʌns- |-'s -ɪz
Dunstan 'dʌnstən
Dunster 'dʌnstɚ; ES 'dʌnstə(r
duo *It* 'duːo
duo- 'djuo, 'dɪuo, 'duo, -ə
duodecimal ˌdjuə'dɛsəml̩, ˌdɪuə-, ˌduə- |-ly -ɪ |-mo -ˌmo
duodenal ˌdjuə'dinl̩, ˌdɪuə-, ˌduə- |-num -nəm |-na -nə
duologue 'djuəˌlɔg, 'dɪuə-, 'duə-, -ˌlɑg, -ˌlɒg
dupe djup, dɪup, dup |-d -t |-ry -ərɪ, -rɪ
duple 'djupl̩, 'dɪupl̩, 'dupl̩
duplex 'djuplɛks, 'dɪu-, 'du- |-es -ɪz |-ed -t
duplicate, *n, adj* 'djupləkɪt, 'dɪu-, 'du-, -ˌket
duplicate *v* 'djupləˌket, 'dɪu-, 'du- |-d -ɪd |-tor -ɚ; ES -ə(r
duplication ˌdjuplə'keʃən, ˌdɪu-, ˌdu-
duplicity dju'plɪsətɪ, dɪu-, du-
Dupont 'djupant, 'dɪu-, 'du-; ES+-pɒnt; *acct+*Du'pont ('Duˌpont 'product)
Duquesne dju'ken, dɪu-, du-
Du Quoin dju'kɔɪn, dɪu-, du-
durability ˌdjurə'bɪlətɪ, ˌdɪur-, ˌdur-
durable 'djurəbl̩, 'dɪur-, 'dur- |-bly -blɪ

---

duralumin, D- djʊˈræljəˌmɪn, dɪʊ-, dʊ-

durance ˈdjʊrəns, ˈdɪʊr-, ˈdʊr-

Durand djʊˈrænd, dɪʊ-, dʊ-

Durango djʊˈræŋgo, dɪʊ-, dʊ-

Durant djʊˈrænt, dɪʊ-, dʊ-

duration djʊˈreʃən, dɪʊ-, dʊ-

durative ˈdjʊrətɪv, ˈdɪʊr-, ˈdʊr-

Durazzo dʊˈratso

Durban ˈdɝbən, dɝˈbæn; ES ˈdɜb-, ˈdɝb-, də-

durbar ˈdɝbar; ES ˈdɜbɑː(r, ˈdɝbɑː(r, E+-baː(r

D'Urberville ˈdɝbɚˌvɪl; ES ˈdɜbə-, ˈdɝbə-

Durbeyfield ˈdɝbɪˌfild; ES ˈdɜbɪ-, ˈdɝbɪ-

dure djʊr, dɪʊr, dʊr; ES -ə(r; |-d -d

duress ˈdjʊrɪs, ˈdɪʊr-, ˈdʊr-, acct+duˈress

D'Urfey, Durfey ˈdɝfɪ; ES ˈdɜfɪ, ˈdɝfɪ

Durham ˈdɝəm; ES ˈdɜrəm, ˈdʌr-, ˈdɝ-

during ˈdʊrɪŋ, ˈdɪʊrɪŋ, ˈdjʊrɪŋ

durn dɝn; ES dɜn, dɝn; |-ed -d |-edest -dɪst

Duroc ˈdjʊrak, ˈdɪʊr-, ˈdʊr-; ES+-ɒk

durst dɝst; ES dɜst, dɝst |-stn't -sn̩t—before some conss.+-sn̩ (ˌdɝsn̩ˈgo)

durum ˈdjʊrəm, ˈdɪʊr-, ˈdʊr-

Duse ˈduzɪ (It ˈduːze)

dusk dʌsk |dusked dʌskt

Düsseldorf ˈdɪsl̩ˌdɔrf, ˈdʌs|-; ES -ˌdɔəf; (Ger ˈdysəlˌdɔrf)

dust dʌst |dusted ˈdʌstɪd

dustman ˈdʌstmən |-men -mən

dustpan ˈdʌstˌpæn, ˈdʌsˌpæn

dustproof ˈdʌstˈpruf (ˈdustˌproof ˈbearings)

Dutch dʌtʃ |dutches ˈdʌtʃɪz |dutched dʌtʃt

Dutchman ˈdʌtʃmən |-men -mən

Dutchman's-breeches ˈdʌtʃmənzˈbrɪtʃɪz

duteous ˈdjutɪəs, ˈdɪu-, ˈdu-

dutiable ˈdjutɪəbl̩, ˈdɪu-, ˈdu-

dutiful ˈdjutɪfəl, ˈdɪu-, ˈdu- |-ly -ɪ

duty ˈdjutɪ, ˈdɪu-, ˈdu-

duty-free ˈdjutɪˈfri, ˈdɪu-, ˈdu-

duumvir djuˈʌmvɚ, dɪu-, du-; ES -ˈʌmvə(r; |-ate -ɪt

Duxbury ˈdʌksˌbɛrɪ, -bərɪ

Duyckinck ˈdaɪkɪŋk

Dvina dviˈna

Dvořák ˈdvɔrʒak, dəˈvɔrʒak, ˈvɔrʒæk, ˈvɔrʃæk; ES -ɔə-

dwarf dwɔrf; ES dwɔəf; |-ed -t |-ish -ɪʃ

dwarvish ˈdwɔrvɪʃ; ES ˈdwɔəvɪʃ

dwell dwɛl |dwelt dwɛlt, arch. dwelled dwɛld

dwelling ˈdwɛlɪŋ

dwindle ˈdwɪndl̩ |-d -d |-ling ˈdwɪndl̩ɪŋ, -dlɪŋ

Dwight dwaɪt

Dyak ˈdaɪæk

dyarchy ˈdaɪarkɪ; ES -aːkɪ, E+-aːkɪ

Dyce daɪs |-'s -ɪz

Dyck, van vænˈdaɪk

dye daɪ |dyed daɪd |-ing -ɪŋ |-r -ɚ; ES -ə(r

dyed-in-the-wool ˈdaɪdn̩ðəˈwʊl, ˈdaɪdɪnðə-

dyeing from dye ˈdaɪɪŋ

dyestuff ˈdaɪˌstʌf

dying from die ˈdaɪɪŋ

Dyke, van vænˈdaɪk

dyke daɪk |dyked daɪkt

Dykema ˈdaɪkəmə

Dykstra ˈdaɪkstrə

Dymond ˈdaɪmənd

dynameter daɪˈnæmətɚ; ES -ˈnæmətə(r

dynamic daɪˈnæmɪk |-al -l̩ |-ally -l̩ɪ, -ɪklɪ

dynamism ˈdaɪnəˌmɪzəm |-mist -mɪst

dynamite ˈdaɪnəˌmaɪt |-mited -ˌmaɪtɪd

dynamo ˈdaɪnəˌmo

dynamometer ˌdaɪnəˈmamətɚ; ES -ˈmamətə(r, -ˈmɒm-

dynast ˈdaɪnæst, ˈdaɪnəst

dynastic daɪˈnæstɪk |-al -l̩ |-ally -l̩ɪ, -ɪklɪ

dynasty ˈdaɪnəstɪ, ˈdaɪnæstɪ—ˈdɪnəstɪ is mainly Brit.

dyne daɪn

Dysart ˈdaɪzɚt, -zart; ES ˈdaɪzət, -zaːt

dysentery ˈdɪsn̩ˌtɛrɪ

dysgenic dɪsˈdʒɛnɪk

Dyson ˈdaɪsn̩

dyspepsia dɪˈspɛpʃə, -ʃɪə

dyspeptic dɪˈspɛptɪk |-al -l̩ |-ally -l̩ɪ, -ɪklɪ

dysphasia dɪsˈfeʒə, -ʒɪə

dyspnea, -noea dɪspˈnɪə

dysprosium dɪsˈprosɪəm, -ˈproʃɪəm

|full fʊl |tooth tuθ |further ˈfɝðɚ; ES ˈfɝðə |custom ˈkʌstəm |while hwaɪl |how haʊ |toy tɔɪ |using ˈjuzɪŋ |fuse fjuz, fɪuz |dish dɪʃ |vision ˈvɪʒən |Eden ˈidn̩ |cradle ˈkredl̩ |keep 'em ˈkipm̩

E

E, e *letter* i |*pl* E's, Es, *poss* E's ɪz
e- *word initial. When unstressed, this varies as*
i-, ɪ-, ɛ-, *or* ə- *according to style of speech or*
commonness of the word. ə- *is esp. freq. be-*
fore l (elect ɪ'lɛkt, ə'lɛkt). *When only one*
or two prons. are given in the vocab., it is to
be understood that one or more of the others
are used by many speakers.

each itʃ |each's 'itʃɪz
Eads idz |Eads's 'idzɪz
eager 'igɚ; ES 'igə(r
eagle 'ig‖ |eaglet 'iglɪt
eagre 'igɚ, 'egɚ; ES 'igə(r, 'egə(r
Eakins 'ekɪnz |-'s -ɪz
Eames emz, imz |Eames's 'emzɪz, 'imzɪz
Eamon de Valera 'ɪəmən dəvə'lɛrə, -'lɛrə,
-'lɪrə
ean in |eaned ind |eanling 'inlɪŋ
ear ɪr; ES ɪə(r, S+ɛə(r; |-ed -d
earache 'ɪr‚ek; S+'ɛr‚ek
eardrop 'ɪr‚drɑp; ES 'ɪə‚drɑp, 'ɪə‚drɒp,
S+'ɛə-
eardrum 'ɪr‚drʌm; ES 'ɪə‚drʌm, S+'ɛə-
earl ɝl; ES ɜl, ɝl; |-dom -dəm
early 'ɝlɪ; ES 'ɜlɪ, 'ɝlɪ
earmark 'ɪr‚mɑrk; E 'ɪə‚mɑːk, -‚mɑːk; S
'ɪə‚mɑːk, 'ɛə-
earn ɝn; ES ɜn, ɝn; |-ed -d
earnest 'ɝnɪst, -əst; ES 'ɜn-, 'ɝn-
earnings 'ɝnɪŋz; ES 'ɜnɪŋz, 'ɝn-
earphone 'ɪr‚fon; ES 'ɪə‚fon, S+'ɛə-
earring 'ɪr‚rɪŋ; ES 'ɪə‚rɪŋ, S+'ɛə‚rɪŋ
Earsdon 'ɪrzdən; ES 'ɪəz-; *loc.*+'jɔzn̩
earshot 'ɪr‚ʃɑt; ES 'ɪə‚ʃɑt, 'ɪə‚ʃɒt, S+'ɛə-
earth ɝθ; ES ɜθ, ɝθ; |-th's -θs
earthborn 'ɝθ‚bɔrn; ES 'ɝθ‚bɔən, 'ɝθ‚bɔən
earthbound 'ɝθ‚baʊnd; ES 'ɝθ-, 'ɝθ-
earthen 'ɝθən; ES 'ɝθən, 'ɝθən
earthenware 'ɝθən‚wɛr, -‚wær; E 'ɝθən-
‚wɛə(r, 'ɝθ-, ES -‚wæə(r
earthling 'ɝθlɪŋ; ES 'ɝθlɪŋ, 'ɝθlɪŋ
earthly 'ɝθlɪ; ES 'ɝθlɪ, 'ɝθlɪ
earthquake 'ɝθ‚kwek; ES 'ɝθ-, 'ɝθ-
earthshine 'ɝθ‚ʃaɪn; ES 'ɝθ-, 'ɝθ-
earthward 'ɝθwɚd; ES 'ɝθwəd, 'ɝθwəd
earthwork 'ɝθ‚wɝk; ES 'ɝθ‚wɜk, 'ɝθ‚wɝk
earthworm 'ɝθ‚wɝm; ES 'ɝθ‚wɜm, 'ɝθ‚wɝm

earwig 'ɪr‚wɪg; ES 'ɪə‚wɪg, S+'ɛə-; |-wigged
-‚wɪgd
Easdale 'iz‚del
ease iz |-s -ɪz |-d -d |-ful -fəl |-fully -fəlɪ
easel 'iz‖
easement 'izmənt
easily 'izlɪ, 'izɪlɪ
Easley 'izlɪ
east, E- ist
Eastbourne 'ist‚bɔrn, -‚bɔrn, -bɚn; ES 'ist-
‚boən, -bən, E+-‚bɔən
Eastcheap 'ist‚tʃip, 'is‚tʃip
Easter 'istɚ; ES 'istə(r
easterly 'istɚlɪ; ES 'istəlɪ
eastern 'istɚn; ES 'istən; |-er -ɚ; ES -ə(r;
|-most -‚most, -məst—'istənɚ *is sometimes*
heard by r-dissimilation (§121).
Eastertide 'istɚ‚taɪd; ES 'istə‚taɪd
East Greenwich *RI* 'ist'grɪnwɪtʃ, *loc.*+
-'grɪnɪdʒ, -ɪtʃ
Eastham 'istəm, *Mass loc.*+'istæm
East Ham 'ist'hæm
Eastman 'istmən
Easton 'istən
eastward 'istwɚd; ES 'istwəd
easy 'izɪ |-going -'goɪŋ ('easy‚going 'man)
eat it |ate et |eaten 'itn̩ |eat *dial. past* ɛt, it—
ɛt *is occas. in cultivated S, see* ate.
eatable 'itəb‖
Eaton 'itn̩ |Eatonton 'itn̩tən |-town 'itn̩‚taʊn
Eau Claire ‚o'klɛr, ‚o'klær; E ‚o'klɛə(r, ES
‚o'klæə(r
Eau de Cologne ‚odəkə'lon
eaves ivz
eavesdrop 'ivz‚drɑp; ES+-‚drɒp; |-ped -t
ebb ɛb |ebbed ɛbd |ebb-tide 'ɛb'taɪd, -‚taɪd
Ebenezer ‚ɛbə'nizɚ; ES ‚ɛbə'nizə(r
Ebensburg 'ɛbənz‚bɝg; ES -‚bɜg, -‚bɝg
ebon 'ɛbən |ebony 'ɛbənɪ
ebriate *adj* 'ibrɪɪt |ebriated 'ibrɪ‚etɪd
ebriety i'braɪətɪ
Ebro 'ibro, 'ebro
ebullience ɪ'bʌljəns, ɪ'bʌlɪəns |-cy -ɪ |-nt -nt
ebullition ‚ɛbə'lɪʃən
écarté ‚ekɑr'te; ES ‚ekɑː'te; (*Fr* ekar'te)
ecce homo 'ɛksɪ'homo, 'ɛkɛ-
eccentric ɪk'sɛntrɪk, ɛk- |-al -‖ |-ally -‖ɪ, -ɪklɪ

eccentricity ˌɛksən'trɪsətɪ, ˌɛksɛn-

Ecclefechan ˌɛkḷ'fɛkən, -'fɛxən

Eccles 'ɛkḷz |-'s -ɪz

Ecclesiastes ɪˌklizɪ'æstiz |-tes' -tiz

ecclesiastic ɪˌklizɪ'æstɪk |-al -ḷ |-ally -ḷɪ, -ɪklɪ

ecclesiasticism ɪˌklizɪ'æstəˌsɪzəm

Ecclesiasticus ɪˌklizɪ'æstɪkəs |-'s -ɪz

echelon 'ɛʃəˌlɑn, -ˌlɒn (Fr ɛʃ'lõ)

echinoderm ɛ'kaɪnəˌdɝm, 'ɛkɪnə-; ES -ˌdɝm, -ˌdɝm

echinus ɛ'kaɪnəs |echini ɛ'kaɪnaɪ

echo 'ɛko |echoed 'ɛkod |-ing 'ɛkəwɪŋ

echoic ɛ'ko·ɪk

éclair e'klɛr, e'klær, ɪ-; E -'klɛə(r, ES -'klæə(r

éclat ɪ'klɑ, e'klɑ (Fr e'kla)

eclectic ɪk'lɛktɪk, ɛk- |-ticism -ˌsɪzəm

eclipse ɪ'klɪps |eclipses ɪ'klɪpsɪz |-d -t

ecliptic ɪ'klɪptɪk, i-

eclogue 'ɛklɒg, -lɑg, -lɒg

ecology i'kɑlədʒɪ; ES+-'kɒl-

economic ˌikə'nɑmɪk, ˌɛk-; ES+-'nɒm-; |-s -s |-al -ḷ |-ally -ḷɪ, -ɪklɪ

economist ɪ'kɑnəmɪst, i-; ES+-'kɒn-

economize ɪ'kɑnəˌmaɪz, i-; ES+-'kɒn-; |-s -ɪz |-d -d |-my -mɪ

ecru 'ɛkru, 'ekru, e'kru (Fr e'kry)

ecstasy 'ɛkstəsɪ

ecstatic ɪk'stætɪk, ɛk- |-ally -ḷɪ, -ɪklɪ

ectoderm 'ɛktəˌdɝm; ES -ˌdɝm, -ˌdɝm

ectoplasm 'ɛktəˌplæzəm

Ecuador 'ɛkwəˌdɔr; ES 'ɛkwəˌdɔə(r

Ecuadorian ˌɛkwə'dɔrɪən, -'dɔr-; S -'dɔrɪən

ecumenic ˌɛkju'mɛnɪk |-al -ḷ |-ally -ḷɪ, -ɪklɪ

eczema 'ɛksəmə, 'ɛgzəmə, -ɪmə, ɪg'zimə

-ed, -d ending of the past and pptc, and of certain adjectives. Pronounced -t after voiceless consonant sounds except t (walk-ed wɔk-t, price-d praɪs-t, reach-ed ritʃ-t); pronounced -d after vowel and voiced consonants sounds except d (paw-ed pɔ-d, free-d fri-d, dragg-ed dræg-d, prize-d praɪz-d, horn-ed hɔrn-d, age-d edʒ-d); pronounced -ɪd or -əd after t & d (state-d 'stet-ɪd, -əd, fatt-ed 'fæt-ɪd, -əd, wood-ed 'wʊd-ɪd, -əd, raid-ed 'red-ɪd, -əd, padd-ed 'pæd-ɪd, -əd); in a few adjectives pronounced -ɪd, -əd also after other consonants than t & d (age-d 'edʒ-ɪd, -əd, crabb-ed 'kræb-ɪd, -əd, bless-ed 'blɛs-ɪd,

-əd, two-legg-ed 'tu'lɛg-ɪd, -əd). With different speakers the unstressed vowel of -ed (when sounded at all) varies from a sound like that in bit bɪt to one like the last vowel in method 'mɛθəd. Very often it is a sound made with the tongue higher than the central position (that for ə), and back of that for ɪ (phonetic symbol ɪ). In the vocabulary, as a rule, only the pronunciation -ɪd is given, it being understood that many speakers instead pronounce -ɪd, or (fewer in the E & S) -əd as in method 'mɛθəd. The difference between -əd & -ɪd or -əz & -ɪz is sometimes phonemic—used to distinguish words otherwise alike, as quotaed (Jefferson) 'kwotəd, quoted 'kwotɪd, or Louisa's lu'izəz, Louise's lu'izɪz, and often in ES: Caesars 'sizəz, seizes 'sizɪz or mattered 'mætəd, matted 'mætɪd.

Edam 'idəm, 'idæm (Du e'dɑm)

Edda 'ɛdə

eddy, E- 'ɛdɪ |eddied 'ɛdɪd

Eddystone light 'ɛdɪstən, Pa bor. 'ɛdɪˌston

edelweiss 'edḷˌvaɪs |-es -ɪz

edema i'dimə |-mata -mətə |-tous -təs

Eden 'idṇ |-ton 'idṇtən

Edgar 'ɛdgɚ; ES 'ɛdgə(r

edge ɛdʒ |edges 'ɛdʒɪz |edged ɛdʒd

Edgerton 'ɛdʒɚtən; ES 'ɛdʒətən

edgeways 'ɛdʒˌwez |edgewise 'ɛdʒˌwaɪz

Edgeworth 'ɛdʒwɚθ; ES 'ɛdʒwəθ

edible 'ɛdəbḷ |edibility ˌɛdə'bɪlətɪ

edict 'idɪkt

edification ˌɛdəfə'keʃən

edifice 'ɛdəfɪs |edifices 'ɛdəfɪsɪz |-d -t

edify 'ɛdəˌfaɪ |edified 'ɛdəˌfaɪd

edile 'idaɪl

Edinburg US 'ɛdṇˌbɝg, 'ɛdɪn-; ES -ˌbɝg, -ˌbɝg

Edinburgh Scotl 'ɛdṇˌbɝo, 'ɛdɪn-, -ə; ES -ˌbɝr-, -ˌbʌr-, -ˌbɝ-; (Brit. pron. 'ɛdɪnbrə, 'ɛdṇ-, -bərə, -ˌbʌrə)

Edison 'ɛdəsṇ

edit 'ɛdɪt |edited 'ɛdɪtɪd

Edith 'idɪθ

edition ɪ'dɪʃən, i'dɪʃən

editor 'ɛdɪtɚ; ES 'ɛdɪtə(r; -ship -ˌʃɪp

editorial ˌɛdə'tɔrɪəl, -'tɔr-; S -'tor-; |-ly -ɪ

-edly ending of advs formed on -ed words, as

designedly dɪ'zaınıdlı—*Advs in* -edly *are
only given in the vocabulary when the pron.
cannot be inferred from the form in* -ed, *as*
disguised dɪs'gaɪzd *but* disguisedly dɪs-
'gaɪzıdlı. *But* disgustedly dɪs'gʌstıdlı *is
not entered, since the pron. can be found by
adding* -lı *directly to* dɪs'gʌstıd. *For the
vowels in* -edly *see* -ed *&* -ly *in the vocab.
The pron. of* -edness *as* -ıdnıs *or* -dnıs
usually follows that of -edly.

Edmondson, -nson 'ɛdmənsn̩
Edmonton 'ɛdməntən
Edmund 'ɛdmənd, *before some conss.*+'ɛdmən
  ('ɛdmənd'smıθ, 'ɛdmən'smıθ)
Edmundston 'ɛdmənstən
Edna 'ɛdnə
-edness *ending, see* -edly
Edom 'idəm |Edomite 'idəm‚aıt
educability ‚ɛdʒəkə'bılətı, ‚ɛdʒʊ-
educable 'ɛdʒəkəbl̩, 'ɛdʒʊ-
educate 'ɛdʒə‚ket, 'ɛdʒʊ- |-d -ıd
educator 'ɛdʒə‚ketɚ, 'ɛdʒʊ-; ES -‚ketə(r
education ‚ɛdʒə'keʃən, ‚ɛdʒʊ-
educational ‚ɛdʒə'keʃənl̩, ‚ɛdʒʊ-, -ʃnəl |-ist
  -ıst |-ly -ı
educative 'ɛdʒə‚ketıv, 'ɛdʒʊ-
educe ı'djus, ı'dıus, ı'dus, i- |-s -ız |-d -t
eductive ı'dʌktıv, i- |-tion -kʃən
Edward 'ɛdwɚd; ES 'ɛdwəd; |-s -z |-s's -zız
Edwardian, -dean ɛd'wɔrdıən; ES ɛd'wɔədıən
Edwin 'ɛdwın |Edwina ɛd'winə, -'wınə
eel il
eelgrass 'il‚græs; E+-‚gras, -‚gras
eelpout 'il‚paʊt
e'en in
e'er ɛɚ; ES ɛə(r
eerie, -ry 'ırı, 'ırı
ef ɛf
efface ı'fes, ɛ- |-faces -'fesız |-faced -'fest
effect ə'fɛkt, ı'fɛkt, ɛ- |-fected -'fɛktıd
effective ə'fɛktıv, ı-
effector ə'fɛktɚ, ı-; ES -'fɛktə(r
effectual ə'fɛktʃʊəl, -tʃʊl, ı- |-ly -ı
effectuality ə‚fɛktʃʊ'ælətı, ı-
effectuate ə'fɛktʃʊ‚et, ı- |-ated -‚etıd
effeminacy ə'fɛmənəsı, ı- |-nate -nıt
efferent 'ɛfərənt
effervesce ‚ɛfɚ'vɛs; ES ‚ɛfə'vɛs; |-s -ız |-d -t
  |-cence -ns̩ |-cent -n̩t

effete ɛ'fit, ı-
efficacious ‚ɛfə'keʃəs
efficacy 'ɛfəkəsı
efficiency ə'fıʃənsı, ı-, |-ent -ənt
Effie 'ɛfı
effigy 'ɛfədʒı
Effingham *US* 'ɛfıŋ‚hæm; *Engd* -ıŋəm
effloresce ‚ɛflo'rɛs, -flɔ-; S -flo-; |-s -ız |-d -t
  |-cence -ns̩ |-cency -ns̩ı
effluence 'ɛfluəns, 'ɛflıuəns |-s -ız
effluvium ɛ'fluvıəm, ı-, -'flıu- |-via -vıə
efflux 'ɛflʌks |effluxes 'ɛflʌksız
effort 'ɛfɚt; ES 'ɛfət
effrontery ə'frʌntərı, ı-
effulge ɛ'fʌldʒ, ı- |-s -ız |-d -d |-nce -əns
  |-ncy -ənsı |-nt -ənt
effuse *adj* ɛ'fjus, ı-, -'fıus |-sive -ıv
effuse *v* ɛ'fjuz, ı-, -'fıuz |-s -ız |-d -d
effusion ə'fjuʒən, ı-, ɛ-, -'fıuʒən
eft ɛft |eftsoon ɛft'sun |-soons -'sunz
e.g. 'i'dʒi, ıg'zɛmplaı'greʃıə, fərıg'zæmpl̩
egad ı'gæd, i'gæd
egalitarian ı‚gælə'tɛrıən, i-, -'ter-
Egbert 'ɛgbɚt; ES 'ɛgbət
Egerton 'ɛdʒɚtən; ES 'ɛdʒətən
egest i'dʒɛst |-ed -ıd
Egeus *myth.* 'idʒjus, -dʒus, *Shak.* i'dʒiəs
  |-'s -ız
egg ɛg |egged ɛgd
Eggleston 'ɛgl̩z‚tən, 'ɛgl̩‚stən
eggnog 'ɛg‚nag, 'ɛg‚nag, -'nɒg, -‚nɒg
eggplant 'ɛg‚plænt; E+-‚plant, -‚plant
eggshell 'ɛg‚ʃɛl
egis 'idʒıs |egises 'idʒısız
Eglamore 'ɛglə‚mor, -‚mɔr; ES -‚moə(r,
  E+-‚mɔə(r; |-mour -‚mur; ES -‚muə(r
eglantine 'ɛglən‚taın, -‚tin
ego 'igo, 'ɛgo |-ism -‚ızəm |-ist -ıst
egocentric ‚igo'sɛntrık, ‚ɛgo-
egotism 'igə‚tızəm, 'ɛg- |-tist -tıst
egotistic ‚igə'tıstık, ‚ɛg- |-al -l̩ |-ally -l̩ı, -ıklı
egregious ı'gridʒəs, ı'gridʒıəs
egress *n* 'igrɛs |egresses 'igrɛsız
egress *v* ı'grɛs, i- |-es -ız |-ed -t
egret 'igrıt, -grɛt, 'ɛ-
Egypt 'idʒəpt, 'idʒıpt |-ptian ı'dʒıpʃən, i-
Egyptology ‚idʒıp'talədʒı; ES+-'tɒl-
eh e, ɛ *and various other inquiring sounds*
eider 'aıdɚ; ES 'aıdə(r

Key: See in full §§3–47. bee bi |pity 'pıtı (§6) |rate ret |yet jɛt |sang sæŋ |angry 'æŋ‚grı
|bath bæθ; E baθ (§10) |ah ɑ |far fɑr |watch wɑtʃ, wɒtʃ (§12) |jaw dʒɔ |gorge gɔrdʒ |go go

Eiffel 'aɪfḷ

eight et |eighth etθ |eighty 'etɪ |-ieth -ɪɪθ |-ieths -ɪɪθs

eighteen e'tin, 'e'tin ('eigh‚teen 'years)

eightfold adj, adv 'et'fold ('eight‚fold 'loss)

eightpenny 'et‚penɪ, -pənɪ

eikon, E- 'aɪkɑn; ES+'aɪkɒn

Eileen aɪ'lin ('Ei‚leen 'Johnson)

Einstein 'aɪnstaɪn |-ian aɪn'staɪnɪən

Eire 'erə, 'ɛrə |Eireann 'erən, 'ɛrən

eisteddfod e'stɛðvad, ɛ-, -vɒd

either 'iðɚ, much less freq. 'aɪðɚ; ES -ðə(r

ejaculate ɪ'dʒækjə‚let, i'dʒækjʊ- |-d -ɪd

ejaculation ɪ‚dʒækjə'leʃən, i‚dʒækjʊ-

ejaculatory ɪ'dʒækjələ‚torɪ, i'dʒækjʊ-, -‚tɔrɪ; S -‚torɪ

eject n 'idʒɛkt

eject v ɪ'dʒɛkt, i- |-jected -'dʒɛktɪd

ejecta i'dʒɛktə

ejection ɪ'dʒɛkʃən, i- |-tment -'dʒɛktmənt

eke adv ik

eke v ik |eked ikt

el ɛl

elaborate adj ɪ'læbərɪt, ə-, -'læbrɪt

elaborate v ɪ'læbə‚ret, ə- |-rated -‚retɪd

elaboration ɪ‚læbə'reʃən, ə-

Elaine ɪ'len, ə'len

Elam 'iləm |-ite -‚aɪt |-itic ‚ilə'mɪtɪk

élan Fr e'lɑ̃

eland 'ilənd

elapse ɪ'læps, ə- |-s -ɪz |-d -t

elastic ɪ'læstɪk, ə- |-ally -|ɪ, -ɪklɪ

elasticity ɪ‚læs'tɪsətɪ, ə-, ‚ilæs'tɪsətɪ

elate ɪ'let, i- |-lated -'letɪd

elation ɪ'leʃən, i-

Elba 'ɛlbə

Elbe ɛlb (Ger 'ɛlbə)

Elbert 'ɛlbɚt; ES 'ɛlbət

elbow 'ɛl‚bo |elbowed 'ɛl‚bod

elbowroom 'ɛlbo‚rum, -‚rʊm

eld ɛld

elder 'ɛldɚ; ES 'ɛldə(r

elderberry 'ɛldɚ‚bɛrɪ, 'ɛldə-, -bərɪ, -brɪ; ES 'ɛldə-; The second pron. results from r-dissimilation (§121).

elderly 'ɛldɚlɪ; ES 'ɛldəlɪ

eldest 'ɛldɪst

Eldora ɛl'dorə, -'dɔrə; S -'dorə

El Dorado myth. ‚ɛldə'rado, Ark city -'redo

Eldorado Calif ‚ɛldə'rado; Ill, Kas, Mo ‚ɛldə'redo

eldritch, E- 'ɛldrɪtʃ |Eldritch's 'ɛldrɪtʃɪz

Eleanor 'ɛlənɚ, 'ɛlɪnɚ; ES -nə(r

Eleanora ‚ɛlə'norə, ‚ɛlɪə-, -'nɔrə; S -'norə

Eleazar, -er ‚ɛlɪ'ezɚ; ES ‚ɛlɪ'ezə(r

elecampane ‚ɛləkəm'pen, ‚ɛlɪ-

elect ɪ'lɛkt, ə'lɛkt |-lected -'lɛktɪd

election ɪ'lɛkʃən, ə'lɛkʃən

electioneer ɪ‚lɛkʃən'ɪr, ə-; ES -'ɪə(r, S+-'ɛə(r; |-ed -d

elective ɪ'lɛktɪv, ə'lɛktɪv

elector ɪ'lɛktɚ, ə-; ES -'lɛktə(r

electoral ɪ'lɛktərəl, ə- |-ly -ɪ |-rate -rɪt, -trɪt

Electra ɪ'lɛktrə

electress ɪ'lɛktrɪs, ə- |-es -ɪz

electric ɪ'lɛktrɪk, ə- |-al -|̣ |-ally -|ɪ, -ɪklɪ

electrician ɪ‚lɛk'trɪʃən, ə-, ‚ilɛk'trɪʃən

electricity ɪ‚lɛk'trɪsətɪ, ə-, ‚ilɛk'trɪsətɪ

electrification ɪ‚lɛktrəfə'keʃən, ə-

electrify ɪ'lɛktrə‚faɪ, ə- |-fied -‚faɪd

electro ɪ'lɛktro, ə-

electroanalysis ɪ‚lɛktroə'næləsɪs, ə-

electrochemical ɪ‚lɛktro'kɛmɪkḷ, ə- |-ly -ɪ

electrochemist ɪ‚lɛktro'kɛmɪst, ə- |-ry -rɪ

electrocute ɪ'lɛktrə‚kjut, ə-, -‚krut |-d -ɪd

electrocution ɪ‚lɛktrə'kjuʃən, ə-, -'kruʃən

electrode ɪ'lɛktrod, ə-

electrodeposit ɪ‚lɛktrodɪ'pazɪt, ə-; ES+ -'pɒzɪt

electrodynamics ɪ‚lɛktrodaɪ'næmɪks, ə-

electroencephalograph ɪ‚lɛktro·ɛn'sɛfələ‚græf, ə-; E+-‚graf, -‚grɑf

electrograph ɪ'lɛktro‚græf, ə-; E+-af, -ɑf

electrokinetics ɪ‚lɛktrokɪ'nɛtɪks, ə-, -kaɪ-

electrolysis ɪ‚lɛk'trɑləsɪs, ə-; ES+-'trɒl-

electrolyte ɪ'lɛktrə‚laɪt, ə-

electrolytic ɪ‚lɛktrə'lɪtɪk, ə-

electrolyze ɪ'lɛktrə‚laɪz, ə- |-s -ɪz |-d -d

electromagnet ɪ‚lɛktro'mægnɪt, ə-

electromagnetic ɪ‚lɛktromæg'nɛtɪk, ə- |-s -s

electromagnetism ɪ‚lɛktro'mægnə‚tɪzəm, ə-

electrometallurgy ɪ‚lɛktro'mɛtḷ‚ɝdʒɪ, ə-, -mɛ-'tælə‚dʒɪ; ES -‚ɜdʒɪ, -‚ɝdʒɪ, -'tælədʒɪ

electrometer ɪ‚lɛk'trɑmətɚ, ə-, ‚ilɛk-; ES -'trɑmətə(r, -'trɒmətə(r

electromotive ɪ‚lɛktrə'motɪv, ə-

electromotor ɪ‚lɛktrə'motɚ, ə-; ES -'motə(r

electron ɪ'lɛktrɑn, ə-; ES+-trɒn

|full fʊl |tooth tuθ |further 'fɝðɚ; ES 'fɜðə |custom 'kʌstəm |while hwaɪl |how haʊ |toy tɔɪ |using 'juzɪŋ |fuse fjuz, fɪuz |dish dɪʃ |vision 'vɪʒən |Eden 'idṇ |cradle 'kredḷ |keep 'em 'kipm̩

electroplate ɪˈlɛktrəˌplet, ə- |-d -ɪd
electroscope ɪˈlɛktrəˌskop, ə-
electroscopic ɪˌlɛktrəˈskɑpɪk, ə-; ES+-ˈskɒp-
electrostatic ɪˌlɛktrəˈstætɪk, ə- |-al -l̩ |-ally
-lɪ, -ɪklɪ
electrotherapeutic ɪˌlɛktroˌθɛrəˈpjutɪk, ə-,
-ˈpɪu- |-al -l̩
electrotherapy ɪˌlɛktroˈθɛrəpɪ, ə-
electrotype ɪˈlɛktrəˌtaɪp, ə- |-d -t
electrum ɪˈlɛktrəm, ə-
electuary ɪˈlɛktʃʊˌɛrɪ, ə-
eleemosynary ˌɛləˈmɑsn̩ˌɛrɪ, ˌɛlɪə-; ES+
-ˈmɒs-
elegance ˈɛləgəns |-cy -ɪ |-gant -gənt
elegiac ɪˈlɪdʒɪˌæk, ə-, ˌɛləˈdʒaɪæk, -ək
elegiacal ˌɛləˈdʒaɪəkl̩
elegize ˈɛləˌdʒaɪz |-s -ɪz |-d -d
elegy ˈɛlədʒɪ |-gist -dʒɪst
element ˈɛləmənt
elemental ˌɛləˈmɛntl̩ |-ly -ɪ |-tary -tərɪ, -trɪ
Elena ˈɛlənə
Eleonora ˌɛləˈnorə, ˌɛlɪə-, -ˈnɔrə; S -ˈnorə
elephant ˈɛləfənt |-a ˌɛləˈfæntə
elephantiasis ˌɛləfənˈtaɪəsɪs, -fæn-
elephantine ˌɛləˈfæntin, -taɪn, -tɪn
Eleusinian ˌɛljuˈsɪnɪən
Eleusis ɛˈlusɪs, ə-, -ˈlɪusɪs |-sis' -sɪs
elevate ˈɛləˌvet |-d -ɪd |-tor -ɚ; ES -ə(r
elevation ˌɛləˈveʃən
eleven ɪˈlɛvən, ɪˈlɛvm̩, ə- |-th -ənθ |-ths -ənθs
elf ɛlf |-'s -s |elves ɛlvz |-in -ɪn
elfish ˈɛlfɪʃ, ˈɛlvɪʃ
elflock ˈɛlfˌlɑk; ES+-ˌlɒk
Elfrida ɛlˈfridə
Elgar ˈɛlgɚ; ES ˈɛlgə(r
Elgin US ˈɛldʒɪn; C, Scotl, Lord, marble
ˈɛlgɪn
Elginshire ˈɛlgɪnˌʃɪr, -ʃɚ; ES -ˌʃɪə(r, -ʃə(r
El Greco ɛlˈgrɛko, -ˈgreko
Eli ˈilaɪ
Elia ˈilɪə
Elias ɪˈlaɪəs |-'s -ɪz
elicit ɪˈlɪsɪt |-ed -ɪd
elide ɪˈlaɪd |-lided -ˈlaɪdɪd
eligibility ˌɛlɪdʒəˈbɪlətɪ
eligible ˈɛlɪdʒəbl̩ |-bly -blɪ
Elihu Bible ɪˈlaɪhju, -hɪu; Am name ˈɛləˌhju,
-ˌhɪu
Elijah ɪˈlaɪdʒə, ə-

Elimelech ɪˈlɪməˌlɛk, ə-
eliminate ɪˈlɪməˌnet, ə- |-nated -ˌnetɪd
elimination ɪˌlɪməˈneʃən, ə-
Elinor ˈɛlɪnɚ; ES ˈɛlɪnə(r
Eliot ˈɛlɪət, ˈɛljət
Eliphalet ɪˈlɪfəlɪt, ə-
Eliphaz ˈɛləˌfæz |-'s -ɪz
Elis ˈilɪs |-'s -ɪz
Elisabeth ɪˈlɪzəbəθ, ə-—see Elizabeth
Elisha ɪˈlaɪʃə, ə-
elision ɪˈlɪʒən
elite ɪˈlit, eˈlit
elixir ɪˈlɪksɚ; ES ɪˈlɪksə(r
Eliza ɪˈlaɪzə
Elizabeth ɪˈlɪzəbəθ, ə- |-ton -tən |-town
-ˌtaʊn—spelt with z in the 1611 Bible
Elizabethan ɪˌlɪzəˈbiθən, ə-, -ˈbɛθən, ɪˈlɪzə-
ˌbeθən
elk ɛlk
Elkanah ˈɛlkənə, ɛlˈkenə
Elkhart ˈɛlkˌhɑrt; ES -ˌhɑːt, E+-ˌhɑːt
ell ɛl—The n sound was lost from ell (OE eln
measure) in the same way as from kiln, mill,
Milne.
Ella ˈɛlə
Ellen ˈɛlɪn, -ən
Ellesmere ˈɛlzmɪr; ES -mɪə(r
Ellice Islands ˈɛlɪsˈaɪləndz, -lənz
Elliott ˈɛlɪət, ˈɛljət
ellipse ɪˈlɪps, ə- |-s -ɪz
ellipsis ɪˈlɪpsɪs, ə- |-pses -psiz
ellipsoid ɪˈlɪpsɔɪd, ə-
ellipsoidal ɪˌlɪpˈsɔɪdl̩, ə-, ˌɛlɪpˈsɔɪdl̩
elliptic ɪˈlɪptɪk, ə- |-al -l̩ |-ally -lɪ, -ɪklɪ
ellipticity ɪˌlɪpˈtɪsətɪ, ə-, ˌɛlɪpˈtɪsətɪ
Ellis ˈɛlɪs |-'s -ɪz
Ellsworth ˈɛlzwɚθ; ES ˈɛlzwəθ
elm ɛlm
Elmer ˈɛlmɚ; ES ˈɛlmə(r
Elmira ɛlˈmaɪrə
Elmo ˈɛlmo
El Modena ˌɛlmoˈdinə
Elmore ˈɛlmor, -mɔr; ES -moə(r, E+-mɔə(r
elocution ˌɛləˈkjuʃən, -ˈkɪu-, -ary -ˌɛrɪ
Elohim ɛˈlohɪm, -him |-hist -hɪst |-hism
-hɪzəm
Elohistic ˌɛloˈhɪstɪk
eloign, eloin ɪˈlɔɪn |-ed -d
Eloise 'Heloise' ˌeloˈiz, Eng name ˌɛləˈwiz

elongate ɪ'lɔŋget, ɪ'lɒŋ-; S+ɪ'laŋ-; |-gated -getɪd

elongation ɪˌlɔŋ'geʃən, ɪˌlɒŋ-, ˌilɔŋ-, ˌilɒŋ-; S+-aŋ-

elope ɪ'lop, ə- |-d -t

eloquence 'ɛləkwəns |-quent -kwənt

El Paso ɛl'pæso

Elphinstone 'ɛlfɪnstən

Elsa 'ɛlsə (Ger 'ɛlzɑ:)

El Salvador ɛl'sælvəˌdɔr; ES -ˌdɔə(r; (Sp -ˌsalβa'ðɔr)

Elsass Ger 'ɛlzɑs

else ɛls |else's 'ɛlsɪz

El Segundo ˌɛlsə'gʌndo, -'gʊn-

elsewhere 'ɛlsˌhwɛr, -ˌhwær; E -ˌhwɛə(r, ES -ˌhwæə(r

Elsie 'ɛlsɪ

Elsinore 'ɛlsəˌnor, -ˌnɔr; ES -ˌnoə(r, E+ -ˌnɔə(r; acct+ˌElsi'nore

Elsmere 'ɛlzmɪr; ES -mɪə(r

Elspeth 'ɛlspəθ

Elsworthy 'ɛlzwɝˈðɪ; ES -wɝˈðɪ, -wɝˈðɪ

Eltham Kent 'ɛltəm, 'ɛlθəm—'ɛlθəm is a sp. pron.

elucidate ɪ'lusəˌdet, ɪ'lɪus- |-d -ɪd

elucidation ɪˌlusə'deʃən, ɪˌlɪus-

elude ɪ'lud, ɪ'lɪud |-d -ɪd

elusive ɪ'lusɪv, ɪ'lɪusɪv |-sory -sərɪ

elves ɛlvz

Elvira ɛl'vaɪrə

elvish 'ɛlvɪʃ

Ely 'ilɪ, pers. name+'ilaɪ, cf Eli

Elyot 'ɛlɪət, 'ɛljət

Elyria ɪ'lɪrɪə, ə-

Elysia ɪ'lɪʒɪə, ɪ'lɪzɪə

Elysian ɪ'lɪʒən, ɪ'lɪʒɪən

Elysium ɪ'lɪʒɪəm, ɪ'lɪzɪəm

elzevir, E- 'ɛlzəvɚ, -ˌvɪr; ES -və(r, -ˌvɪə(r

em ɛm

'em unstressed only əm, after p or b+m̩ (keep 'em 'kɪpm̩, mob 'em 'mabm̩)—When unstressed, hem, the native Eng word for 'them,' lost its h sound just as do he, her, his, him when unstressed. Hem and hit lost the letter h also. The mistaken belief that 'em is an abbreviation of them has led some to avoid it, but it is in excellent colloquial use.

em- unstressed prefix ɪm-, ɛm——see en-

emaciate ɪ'meʃɪˌet |-ated -ˌetɪd

emaciation ɪˌmeʃɪ'eʃən, ɪˌmesɪ-

emanate 'ɛməˌnet |-d -ɪd |-tion ˌɛmə'neʃən

emancipate ɪ'mænsəˌpet |-pated -ˌpetɪd

emancipation ɪˌmænsə'peʃən

Emanuel ɪ'mænjuəl, -ˌɛl

emasculate ɪ'mæskjəˌlet |-lated -ˌletɪd

emasculation ɪˌmæskjə'leʃən

embalm ɪm'bɑm |-ed -d

embank ɪm'bæŋk |-ed -t

embar ɛm'bar; ES -'bɑ:(r, E+-'ba:(r; |-red -d

embarcation ˌɛmbar'keʃən; ES -bɑ:-, E+ -ba:-

embargo ɪm'bargo; ES -'bɑ:-, E+-'ba:-; |-ed -d

embark ɪm'bark; ES -'bɑ:k, E+-'ba:k; |-ed -t

embarkation ˌɛmbar'keʃən; ES -bɑ:-, E+ -ba:-

embarrass ɪm'bærəs, -ɪs |-es -ɪz |-ed -t

embassador ɪm'bæsədɚ; ES -'bæsədə(r

embassage 'ɛmbəsɪdʒ |-s -ɪz |-bassy -bəsɪ

embattle ɛm'bætl̩ |-d -d |-ling -'bætl̩ɪŋ, -tl̩ɪŋ

embay ɛm'be |-ed -d

embed ɪm'bɛd |-ded -ɪd

embellish ɪm'bɛlɪʃ |-es -ɪz |-ed -t

ember 'ɛmbɚ; ES 'ɛmbə(r

embezzle ɪm'bɛzl̩ |-ed -d |-ling -'bɛzlɪŋ, -zl̩ɪŋ

embitter ɪm'bɪtɚ; ES -'bɪtə(r; |-ed -d

emblaze ɛm'blez |-s -ɪz |-d -d

emblazon ɛm'blezn̩ |-ed -d |-ing -zn̩ɪŋ, -znɪŋ

emblem 'ɛmbləm |-ed -d

emblematic ˌɛmblə'mætɪk |-al -l̩ |-ally -lɪ, -ɪklɪ

embodiment ɪm'badɪmənt; ES+-'bɒdɪ-

embody ɪm'badɪ; ES+-'bɒdɪ; |-ied -d

embolden ɪm'boldn̩ |-ed -d |-ing -dn̩ɪŋ, -dnɪŋ

embolic ɛm'balɪk; ES+-'bɒl-

embolism 'ɛmbəˌlɪzəm |-lus -ləs |-li -ˌlaɪ

embonpoint Fr ãbõ'pwæ̃

embosom ɛm'buzəm, -'buzəm |-ed -d

emboss ɪm'bɔs, -'bɒs |-es -ɪz |-ed -t

embouchure ˌambu'ʃur; ES -'ʃuə(r; (Fr ãbu'ʃy:r)

embow ɛm'bo |-ed -d

embowel ɛm'bauəl, -'baul |-ed -d

embower ɛm'bauɚ; ES -'bau·ə(r; |-ed -d |-ing -'bauərɪŋ, -'baurɪŋ

embrace ɪm'bres |-s -ɪz |-d -t

embraceor ɛm'bresɚ; ES -'bresə(r; |-cery -ɪ

embracer ɪm'bresɚ; ES -'bresə(r

|full fʊl |tooth tuθ |further 'fɝˈðɚ; ES 'fɝˈðə |custom 'kʌstəm |while hwaɪl |how hau |toy tɔɪ |using 'juzɪŋ |fuse fjuz, fɪuz |dish dɪʃ |vision 'vɪʒən |Eden 'idn̩ |cradle 'kredl̩ |keep 'em 'kɪpm̩

embranchment ɛm'bræntʃmənt; E+-'brantʃ-,
-'brantʃ-
embrasure ɛm'breʒɚ; ES -'breʒə(r; |-d -d
embrocate 'ɛmbro̩ket |-cated -̩ketɪd
embrocation ̩ɛmbro'keʃən
embroider ɪm'brɔɪdɚ; ES -'brɔɪdə(r; |-ed -d
|-ing -dərɪŋ, -drɪŋ |-y -dərɪ, -drɪ
embroil ɛm'brɔɪl |-ed -d
embrown ɛm'braʊn |-ed -d
embrue ɛm'bru, -'brɪu |-d -d
embryo 'ɛmbrɪ̩o
embryologic ̩ɛmbrɪə'lɑdʒɪk; ES+-'lɒdʒ-; |-al
-l̩ |-ally -l̩ɪ, -ɪklɪ
embryologist ̩ɛmbrɪ'ɑlədʒɪst; ES+-'ɒl-; |-gy
-dʒɪ
embryonic ̩ɛmbrɪ'ɑnɪk; ES+-'ɒn-; |-ally -l̩ɪ,
-ɪklɪ
Emden 'ɛmdən
emeer ə'mɪr; ES ə'mɪə(r; |-ate -ɪt
Emeline 'ɛmə̩laɪn, -̩lin
emend ɪ'mɛnd |-ed -ɪd
emendate 'imən̩det |-dated -̩detɪd
emendation ̩imɛn'deʃən, -mən-, ̩ɛmən-
'deʃən
emendator 'imən̩detɚ, 'ɛmən-; ES -̩detə(r
emendatory ɪ'mɛndə̩torɪ, -̩tɔrɪ; S -̩torɪ
emerald 'ɛmərəld, 'ɛmrəld
emerge ɪ'mɝdʒ; ES ɪ'mɜdʒ, ɪ'mɝdʒ; |-s -ɪz
|-d -d
emergence ɪ'mɝdʒəns; ES ɪ'mɜdʒ-, ɪ'mɝdʒ-;
|-cy -ɪ |-gent -dʒənt
emeritus ɪ'mɛrətəs |-ti -̩taɪ
emersed i'mɝst; ES i'mɜst, i'mɝst
emersion i'mɝʃən, -ʒən; ES -'mɜ-, -'mɝ-
Emerson 'ɛmɚsn̩; ES 'ɛməsn̩
emery 'ɛmərɪ, 'ɛmrɪ |-ied -d
emetic ɪ'mɛtɪk |-al -l̩ |-ally -l̩ɪ, -ɪklɪ
emigrant 'ɛməgrənt, -̩grænt
emigrate 'ɛmə̩gret |-d -ɪd |-tion ̩ɛmə'greʃən
émigré 'ɛmə̩gre (Fr emi'gre)
Emil 'iml̩
Emilia ɪ'mɪlɪə, ɪ'mɪljə
Emily 'ɛml̩ɪ
eminence 'ɛmənəns |-cy -ɪ |-nent -nənt
emir ə'mɪr; ES ə'mɪə(r; |-ate -ɪt
emissary 'ɛmə̩sɛrɪ
emission ɪ'mɪʃən
emit ɪ'mɪt |emitted ɪ'mɪtɪd
Emma 'ɛmə

Emmanuel ɪ'mænjʊəl
Emmaus ɛ'meəs, 'ɛmɪəs |-'s -ɪz
Emmeline 'ɛmə̩laɪn, -̩lin
emmet, E- 'ɛmɪt
Emmetsburg, Emmits- 'ɛmɪts̩bɝg; ES -̩bɝg,
-̩bɝg
emollient ɪ'mɑljənt, -lɪənt; ES+-'mɒl-
emolument ɪ'mɑljəmənt; ES+-'mɒl-
Emory 'ɛmərɪ
emotion ɪ'moʃən |-al -l̩, -ʃnəl |-ally -l̩ɪ, -ʃnəlɪ
emotionalism ɪ'moʃənl̩̩ɪzəm, -'moʃnəl̩ɪzəm
emotionality ɪ̩moʃən'ælətɪ
emotionalization ɪ̩moʃənlə'zeʃən, -ʃnələ-,
-aɪ'z-
emotionalize ɪ'moʃənl̩̩aɪz, -ʃnəl- |-s -ɪz |-d -d
emotive ɪ'motɪv
empale ɪm'pel |-d -d
empanel ɪm'pænl̩ |-ed -d
empathic ɛm'pæθɪk |-ally -l̩ɪ, -ɪklɪ
empathy 'ɛmpəθɪ
Empedocles ɛm'pɛdə̩kliz |-'s -ɪz
emperor 'ɛmpərɚ; ES 'ɛmpərə(r
empery 'ɛmpərɪ
emphasis 'ɛmfəsɪs |-phases -fə̩siz
emphasize 'ɛmfə̩saɪz |-s -ɪz |-d -d
emphatic ɪm'fætɪk |-al -l̩ |-ally -l̩ɪ, -ɪklɪ
empire 'ɛmpaɪr; ES 'ɛmpaɪə(r
empiric ɛm'pɪrɪk |-al -l̩ |-ally -l̩ɪ, -ɪklɪ
empiricism ɛm'pɪrə̩sɪzəm |-cist -sɪst
emplacement ɪm'plesmənt
employ ɪm'plɔɪ |-ed -d |-ment -mənt
employee, -ye, -yé ɪm'plɔɪ·i, ̩ɛmplɔɪ'i
employer ɪm'plɔɪɚ, -'plɔjɚ; ES -'plɔɪ·ə(r,
-'plɔjə(r
empoison ɛm'pɔɪzn̩ |-ed -d |-ing -zn̩ɪŋ, -znɪŋ
Emporia ɛm'porɪə, -'pɔr-; S -'porɪə
emporium ɛm'porɪəm, -'pɔr-; S -'porɪəm; |-s
-z |-ia -ɪə
empower ɪm'paʊɚ; ES -'paʊ·ə(r; |-ed -d |-ing
-'paʊrɪŋ, -'paʊərɪŋ
empress 'ɛmprɪs |-es -ɪz
emprise, -ze ɛm'praɪz |-s -ɪz
emption 'ɛmpʃən |-al -l̩
empty 'ɛmptɪ |-ied -d
empurple ɛm'pɝpl̩; ES -'pɝpl̩, -'pɝpl̩; |-d -d
|-ling -plɪŋ, -pl̩ɪŋ
empyema ̩ɛmpɪ'imə, -paɪ- |-mata -'imətə,
-'ɛmətə
empyreal ɛm'pɪrɪəl, ̩ɛmpə'riəl, -paɪ-

empyrean ˌɛmpəˈriən, -paɪ-
emu ˈimju, ˈimɪu
emulate adj ˈɛmjəlɪt
emulate v ˈɛmjəˌlet |-lated -ˌletɪd |-tive -ɪv
emulation ˌɛmjəˈleʃən
emulator ˈɛmjəˌletɚ; ES -ˌletə(r
emulous ˈɛmjələs
emulsification ɪˌmʌlsəfəˈkeʃən
emulsify ɪˈmʌlsəˌfaɪ |-fied -ˌfaɪd
emulsion ɪˈmʌlʃən
en ɛn
en- *prefix* ɪn-, ɛn-—*When wholly unstressed in
familiar words, pronounced* ɪn-, *sometimes*
ən-. *Since words vary in familiarity, and
since styles and personal habits vary, many
such words are pronounced with either* ɪn- *or*
ɛn-. *Observe that many such words are spelt
with either en- or in-, as endorse, indorse.
These facts will explain seeming inconsistencies in the pron. of such words in the vocabulary. The same statements apply to the
variant em-. In these prefixes, ɪm-, ɪn- are
heard in more familiar words; cf* ɪmˈbɛzl̩
with ɛmˈblezn̩, *or* ɪˈnæml̩ *with* ɛnˈklæsp.
enable ɪnˈebl̩ |-d -d |-ling -ˈeblɪŋ, -ˈebl̩ɪŋ
enact ɪnˈækt |-ed -ɪd |-ive -ɪv |-ory -ərɪ
enamel ɪˈnæml̩ |-ed -d |-ing -ml̩ɪŋ, -mlɪŋ
enamor ɪnˈæmɚ; ES -ˈæmə(r; |-ed -d
en bloc ɛnˈblɑk; ES+-ˈblɒk; (*Fr* ɑ̃ˈblɔ̃k)
encage ɛnˈkedʒ |-s -ɪz |-d -d
encamp ɪnˈkæmp |-ed -t |-ment -mənt
encase ɪnˈkes |-s -ɪz |-d -t
encaustic ɛnˈkɔstɪk |-ally -l̩ɪ, -ɪklɪ
enceinte ɛnˈsent (*Fr* ɑ̃ˈsæ̃t)
Enceladus ɛnˈsɛlədəs |-ʼs -ɪz
encephalic ˌɛnsəˈfælɪk
encephalitis ˌɛnsɛfəˈlaɪtɪs, ɛnˌsɛfə-
encephalon ɛnˈsɛfəˌlɑn, -ˌlɒn |-la -lə
enchain ɛnˈtʃen |-chained -ˈtʃend
enchant ɪnˈtʃænt; E+-ˈtʃɑnt, -ˈtʃɑnt |-ed -ɪd
|-ress -rɪs |-resses -rɪsɪz
enchase ɛnˈtʃes |-s -ɪz |-d -t
encircle ɪnˈsɝkl̩; ES -ˈsɜkl̩, -ˈsɝkl̩; |-d -d
|-ling -klɪŋ, -kl̩ɪŋ
Encke ˈɛŋkə
enclasp ɛnˈklæsp; E+-ˈklasp, -ˈklɑsp; |-ed -t
enclave n ˈɛnklev (*Fr* ɑ̃ˈklɑːv)
enclave v ɛnˈklev |-claved -ˈklevd
enclitic ɛnˈklɪtɪk |-al -l̩ |-ally -l̩ɪ, -ɪklɪ

enclose ɪnˈkloz |-s -ɪz |-d -d
enclosure ɪnˈkloʒɚ; ES -ˈkloʒə(r
encomiast ɛnˈkomɪˌæst
encomiastic ɛnˌkomɪˈæstɪk |-al -l̩ |-ally -l̩ɪ,
-ɪklɪ
encomium ɛnˈkomɪəm |-s -z |-comia -mɪə
encompass ɪnˈkʌmpəs |-es -ɪz |-ed -t
encore n, v ˈɑŋkor, ˈɑn-, -kɔr; ES -koə(r,
E+-kɔə(r; |-d -d—v+enˈcore
encounter ɪnˈkaʊntɚ; ES -ˈkaʊntə(r; |-ed -d
|-ing -tərɪŋ, -trɪŋ
encourage ɪnˈkɝɪdʒ; ES -ˈkɜr-, -ˈkʌr-, -ˈkɝ-;
|-s -ɪz |-d -d
encrimson ɛnˈkrɪmzn̩ |-ed -d
encroach ɪnˈkrotʃ |-es -ɪz |-ed -t
encrust ɪnˈkrʌst |-ed -ɪd
encumber ɪnˈkʌmbɚ; ES -ˈkʌmbə(r; |-ed -d
|-ing -bərɪŋ, -brɪŋ
encumbrance ɪnˈkʌmbrəns |-s -ɪz
encyclical ɛnˈsɪklɪkl̩, -ˈsaɪk-
encyclopedia, -paed- ɪnˌsaɪkləˈpidɪə
encyclopedic, -paed- ɪnˌsaɪkləˈpidɪk |-al -l̩
|-ally -l̩ɪ, -ɪklɪ
encyclopedism, -paed- ɪnˌsaɪkləˈpidɪzəm |-ist
-ɪst
encyst ɛnˈsɪst |-ed -ɪd
end ɛnd |ended ˈɛndɪd
endanger ɪnˈdendʒɚ; ES -ˈdendʒə(r; |-ed -d
|-ing -dʒərɪŋ, -dʒrɪŋ
endear ɪnˈdɪr; ES -ˈdɪə(r, S+-ˈdɛə(r, -ˈdjɛə(r;
|-ed -d
endeavor ɪnˈdɛvɚ; ES -ˈdɛvə(r; |-ed -d |-ing
-ˈdɛvərɪŋ, -ˈdɛvrɪŋ
endemic ɛnˈdɛmɪk |-al -l̩ |-ally -l̩ɪ, -ɪklɪ
Enderby ˈɛndɚbɪ; ES ˈɛndəbɪ
endermic ɛnˈdɝmɪk; ES -ˈdɜm-, -ˈdɝm-; |-al
-l̩ |-ally -l̩ɪ, -ɪklɪ
Endicott ˈɛndɪˌkɑt, -kət; ES+-ˌkɒt
endive ˈɛndaɪv, ˈɑndiv (*Fr* ɑ̃ˈdiːv)
endlong ˈɛndˌlɔŋ, -ˌlɒŋ; S+-ˌlɑŋ
endmost ˈɛndˌmost, ˈɛnˌmost
endocarditis ˌɛndokɑrˈdaɪtɪs; ES -kɑː-, E+
-kɑː-
endocardium ˌɛndoˈkɑrdɪəm; ES -ˈkɑːd-,
E+-ˈkɑːd-
endocarp ˈɛndoˌkɑrp; ES -ˌkɑːp, E+-ˌkɑːp
endocrin ˈɛndoˌkrɪn
endocrine ˈɛndoˌkraɪn |-nal ˌɛndoˈkraɪnl̩
endocrinology ˌɛndokraɪˈnɑlədʒɪ; ES+-ˈnɒl-

endoderm ˈɛndoˌdɝm; ES -ˌdɜm, -ˌdɝm
endogamy ɛnˈdagəmɪ, -ˈdɒg-
endogenous ɛnˈdadʒənəs; ES+-ˈdɒdʒ-
endolymph ˈɛndoˌlɪmf, -ˌlɪmpf
endoparasite ˌɛndoˈpærəˌsaɪt
endoplasm ˈɛndoˌplæzəm
Endor ˈɛndɚ, -dɔr; ES ˈɛndə(r, -dɔə(r
endorse ɪnˈdɔrs; ES -ˈdɔəs; |-s -ɪz |-d -t
endorsee ɪnˌdɔrˈsi, ˌɛndɔrˈsi; ES -ˌdɔə-, -dɔə-
endoscope ˈɛndəˌskop
endothelium ˌɛndoˈθilɪəm |-lia -lɪə
endothermic ˌɛndoˈθɝmɪk; ES -ˈθɜm-, -ˈθɝm-
endow ɪnˈdau |endowed ɪnˈdaud
endue ɪnˈdju, -ˈdɪu, -ˈdu |-d -d
endurance ɪnˈdjʊrəns, -ˈdɪʊr-, -ˈdʊr-
endure ɪnˈdjʊr, -ˈdɪʊr, -ˈdʊr; ES -ə(r
endways ˈɛndˌwez |-wise -ˌwaɪz
Endymion ɛnˈdɪmɪən
Eneas ɪˈniəs |-'s -ɪz
Eneid ɪˈniɪd, -əd
enema ˈɛnəmə
enemy ˈɛnəmɪ
energetic ˌɛnɚˈdʒɛtɪk; ES ˌɛnə-; |-al -ļ |-ally -ļɪ, -ɪklɪ
energize ˈɛnɚˌdʒaɪz; ES ˈɛnə-; |-s -ɪz |-d -d
energy ˈɛnɚdʒɪ; ES ˈɛnədʒɪ
enervate adj ɪˈnɝvɪt; ES ɪˈnɜv-, ɪˈnɝv-
enervate v ˈɛnɚˌvet; ES ˈɛnə-; |-d -ɪd
enervation ˌɛnɚˈveʃən; ES ˌɛnə-
enfeeble ɪnˈfibļ |-d -d |-ling -blɪŋ, -bļɪŋ
enfeoff ɛnˈfɛf |-ed -t
Enfield ˈɛnfild
enfilade ˌɛnfəˈled |-laded -ˈledɪd
enfold ɪnˈfold |-ed -ɪd
enforce ɪnˈfors, -ˈfɔrs; ES -ˈfoəs, E+-ˈfɔəs; |-s -ɪz |-d -t |-dly -ɪdlɪ
enfranchise ɛnˈfræntʃaɪz |-s -ɪz |-d -d
enfranchisement ɛnˈfræntʃɪzmənt
engage ɪnˈgedʒ |-s -ɪz |-d -d |-dly -ɪdlɪ
engarland ɛnˈgarlənd; ES -ˈga:l-, E+-ˈga:l-; |-ed -ɪd
Engedi ɛnˈgidaɪ
Engels Ger ˈɛŋəls
engender ɪnˈdʒɛndɚ; ES -ˈdʒɛndə(r; |-ed -d |-ing -ˈdʒɛndrɪŋ, -ˈdʒɛndərɪŋ
engine ˈɛndʒən |-d -d |-ry -rɪ
engineer ˌɛndʒəˈnɪr; ES -ˈnɪə(r, S+-ˈnɛə(r, -ˈnjɛə(r; |-ed -d
engird ɛnˈgɝd; ES -ˈgɜd, -ˈgɝd; |-ed -ɪd

England ˈɪŋglənd |-er -ɚ; ES -ə(r; freq. ˈɪŋlənd, which many regard as careless
Englefield ˈɛŋgļˌfild
Englewood ˈɛŋgļˌwud
English ˈɪŋglɪʃ |-ed -t |-man -mən |-men -mən |-ry -rɪ |-woman -ˌwumən, -ˌwu- |-women -ˌwɪmɪn, -ən—freq. ˈɪŋlɪʃ; see England
engorge ɛnˈgɔrdʒ; ES -ˈgɔədʒ; |-s -ɪz |-d -d
engraft ɛnˈgræft; E+-ˈgraft, -ˈgrɑft; |-ed -ɪd
engrain ɪnˈgren |-ed -d |-edly -ɪdlɪ
engrave ɪnˈgrev |-graved -ˈgrevd
engross ɪnˈgros |-es -ɪz |-ed -t |-edly -ɪdlɪ
engulf ɪnˈgʌlf |-ed -t
enhance ɪnˈhæns; E+-ˈhans, -ˈhɑns; |-s -ɪz |-d -t
enharmonic ˌɛnharˈmanɪk; ES -ha:ˈmanɪk, -ˈmɒn-, E+-ha:-; |-al -ļ |-ally -ļɪ, -ɪklɪ
Enid ˈinɪd
enigma ɪˈnɪgmə
enigmatic ˌɛnɪgˈmætɪk, ˌi- |-al -ļ |-ally -ļɪ, -ɪklɪ
enjambment, -bement ɪnˈdʒæmmənt (Fr ãʒãbˈmã)
enjoin ɪnˈdʒɔɪn |-ed -d
enjoy ɪnˈdʒɔɪ |-ed -d
enkindle ɪnˈkɪndļ |-d -d |-ling -dlɪŋ, -dļɪŋ
enlace ɪnˈles |-s -ɪz |-d -t
enlarge ɪnˈlardʒ; ES -ˈla:dʒ, E+-ˈla:dʒ; |-s -ɪz |-d -d |-dly -ɪdlɪ, -dlɪ
enlighten ɪnˈlaɪtn̩ |-ed -d |-ing -tn̩ɪŋ, -tnɪŋ
enlist ɪnˈlɪst |-ed -ɪd
enliven ɪnˈlaɪvən |-ed -d |-ing -vənɪŋ, -vnɪŋ
en masse ɛnˈmæs (Fr ãˈmas)
enmesh ɛnˈmɛʃ |-es -ɪz |-ed -t
enmity ˈɛnmətɪ
ennoble ɪˈnobļ, ɛnˈnobļ |-d -d |-ling -ˈnoblɪŋ, -ˈnobļɪŋ
ennui ˈanwi (Fr ãˈnɥi)
Enobarb ˈinəˌbarb, ˈɛnə-; ES -ˌba:b, E+-ˌba:b
Enobarbus ˌinəˈbarbəs, ˌɛnə-; ES -ˈba:b-, E+-ˈba:b-; |-'s -ɪz
Enoch ˈinək
enorm ɪˈnɔrm; ES ɪˈnɔəm
enormous ɪˈnɔrməs; ES ɪˈnɔəməs; |-mity -mətɪ
Enos ˈinəs |-'s -ɪz
enough əˈnʌf, ɪˈnʌf—after t, d, s, z, often n̩ˈʌf (gudn̩ˈʌf, ðætsn̩ˈʌf)

enounce i'naʊns |-s -ız |-d -t
enow ı'naʊ
enplane ɛn'plen |-planed -'plend
enquire ın'kwaır; ES -'kwaıə(r; |-d -d |-ry -ı
enrage ın'redʒ |-s -ız |-d -d |-dly -ıdlı, -dlı
enrapture ın'ræptʃɚ; ES -'ræptʃə(r; |-d -d
enravish ɛn'rævıʃ |-es -ız |-ed -t
enregister ɛn'redʒıstɚ; ES -tə(r; |-ed -d |-ing
  -trıŋ, -tərıŋ
enrich ın'rıtʃ |-es -ız |-ed -t
enrobe ɛn'rob |-robed -'robd
enroll, -ol ın'rol |-(l)ed -d
enroot ɛn'rut, -'rʊt |-ed -ıd
Enroughty ɛn'raʊtı—'dɑːbı is not a pronunciation of Enroughty, but a substitution for
  it.
en route ɑn'rut (Fr ã'rut)
ensample ɛn'sæmpļ; E+-'sampļ, -'sɑmpļ
ensanguine ɛn'sæŋgwın |-d -d
ensconce ɛn'skɑns; ES+-'skɒns; |-s -ız |-d -t
ensemble ɑn'sɑmbļ (Fr ã'sãːbl)
enshade ɛn'ʃed |-shaded -'ʃedıd
enshrine ın'ʃraın |-d -d
enshroud ɛn'ʃraʊd |-ed -ıd
ensign n 'ɛnsaın, mil.+'ɛnsņ
ensign v ɛn'saın |-ed -d
ensilage 'ɛnsịıdʒ
ensile ɛn'saıl, 'ɛnsaıl |-d -d
enslave ın'slev |-slaved -'slevd
ensnare ɛn'snɛr, -'snær; E -'snɛə(r, ES
  -'snæə(r; |-d -d
ensphere ɛn'sfır; ES -'sfıə(r, S+-'sfɛə(r
ensue ɛn'su, -'sıu, -'sju |-d -d
en suite ɑn'swit (Fr ã'sɥit)
ensure ın'ʃʊr; ES -'ʃʊə(r; |-d -d
enswathe ɛn'sweð |-swathed -'sweðd
entablature ɛn'tæblətʃɚ; ES -tʃə(r
entablement ɛn'tebļmənt
entail ın'tel |-ed -d
entangle ın'tæŋgļ |-d -d |-ling -glıŋ, -gļıŋ
entelechy ɛn'tɛləkı
entente ɑn'tant (Fr ã'tãːt)
enter 'ɛntɚ; ES -tə(r; |-ed -d |-ing -tərıŋ,
  -trıŋ
enteric ɛn'tɛrık |-ritis ¸ɛntə'raıtıs
enteron 'ɛntə¸rɑn; ES+-¸rɒn
enterprise 'ɛntɚ¸praız, 'ɛntə-; ES 'ɛntə-; |-s
  -ız |-d -d—In the second pron. ɚ becomes ə
  by dissimilation (§121).

entertain ¸ɛntɚ'ten; ES ¸ɛntə-; |-ed -d
enthrall, -al ın'θrɔl |-(l)ed -d
enthrone ın'θron |-d -d
enthronize ɛn'θronaız |-s -ız |-d -d
enthuse ın'θjuz, -'θıuz, -'θuz |-s -ız |-d -d
enthusiasm ın'θjuzı¸æzəm, -'θıuz-, -'θuz-
  |-ast -¸æst
enthusiastic ın¸θjuzı'æstık, -¸θıuz-, -¸θuz- |-al
  -ļ |-ally -ļı, -ıklı
enthymeme 'ɛnθə¸mim
entice ın'taıs |-s -ız |-d -t
entire ın'taır; ES -'taıə(r; |-ty -tı ('en¸tire
  'length)
entitle ın'taıtļ |-d -d |-ling -tļıŋ, -tļıŋ
entity 'ɛntətı
entoil ɛn'tɔıl |-ed -d
entomb ın'tum |-ed -d |-ment -'tummənt
entomologic ¸ɛntəmə'lɑdʒık; ES+-'lɒdʒ-;
  |-al -ļ |-ally -ļı, -ıklı
entomologist ¸ɛntə'malədʒıst; ES+-'mɒl-;
  |-gy -dʒı
entourage ¸ɑntu'rɑʒ (Fr ãtu'raːʒ)
entr'acte ɑn'trækt (Fr ã'trakt)
entrails 'ɛntrəlz
entrain ın'tren |-ed -d
entrance n 'ɛntrəns |-s -ız |-trant -trənt
entrance v ın'træns; E+-'trans, -'trɑns; |-s
  -ız |-d -t |-dly -ıdlı
entrap ın'træp |-trapped -'træpt
entreasure ɛn'trɛʒɚ; ES -'trɛʒə(r; |-d -d
entreat ın'trit |-ed -ıd |-y -ı
entree 'antre (Fr ã'tre)
entremets 'antrə¸me |pl -mets -¸mez (Fr
  ãtrə'mɛ)
entrench ın'trɛntʃ |-es -ız |-ed -t
entre nous Fr ãtrə'nu
entrepôt 'antrə¸po (Fr ãtrə'po)
entrepreneur ¸antrəprə'nɝ; ES -'nɜ(r, -'nɝ;
  (Fr ãtrəprə'nœːr)
entropy 'ɛntrəpı
entrust ın'trʌst |-ed -ıd
entry 'ɛntrı
entwine ın'twaın |-d -d
entwist ɛn'twıst |-ed -ıd
enucleate adj ı'njuklııt, ı'nıu-, ı'nu-, -¸et
enucleate v ı'njuklı¸et, ı'nıu-, ı'nu- |-d -ıd
enucleation ı¸njuklı'eʃən, ı¸nıu-, ı¸nu-
enumerate ı'njumə¸ret, ı'nıu-, ı'nu- |-d -ıd
enumeration ı¸njumə'reʃən, ı¸nıu-, ı¸nu-

enunciate ı'nʌnsı,et, -ʃı- |-d -ıd
enunciation ı,nʌnsı'eʃən, ı,nʌnʃı-
enure ın'jur; ES ın'juə(r; |-d -d
envelop n, v ın'vɛləp |-ed -t
envelope n 'ɛnvə,lop, 'an-, ın'vɛləp (Fr
ã'vlɔp)—'anvə,lop is pseudo-French.
envelopment ın'vɛləpmənt
envenom ɛn'vɛnəm |-ed -d
enviable 'ɛnvıəbl̩ |-bly -blı |-vious -vıəs
environ v ın'vaırən |-ed -d
environs n ın'vaırənz, 'ɛnvərənz
envisage ɛn'vızıdʒ |-s -ız |-d -d
envision ɛn'vıʒən |-ed -d
envoy 'postscript' 'ɛnvɔı (Fr ã'vwa)
envoy 'messenger' 'ɛnvɔı
envy 'ɛnvı |-ied -ıd
enwrap ɛn'ræp |-wrapped -'ræpt
enwreathe ɛn'rið |-d -d
enzym 'ɛnzım |-zyme - zaım, -zım
Eoanthropus ,ıoæn'θropəs |-'s -ız
Eocene 'ıə,sin
Eohippus ,ıo'hıpəs |-'s -ız
Eolia i'olıə |-n -n
Eolis 'ıəlıs |-'s -ız |-t -t |-m -,lızəm
eolith 'ıə,lıθ |-ths -θs -ıc ,ıə'lıθık
Eolus 'ıələs, Vt mt. loc. i'oləs |-'s -ız
eon 'ıən, 'ıan; ES+'ıɒn
Eos 'ıas; ES+-ɒs; |-'s -ız
eosin 'ıə,sın
Eothen i'oθɛn
Epaminondas ɛ,pæmə'nandəs; ES+-'nɒn-
eparch 'ɛpark; ES 'ɛpɑ:k, E+-a:k
epaulet, -tte 'ɛpə,lɛt, 'ɛpəlıt
epencephalon ,ɛpɛn'sɛfə,lan, -,lɒn
ephah 'ifə
ephedrine, -in ɛ'fɛdrın, chem.+'ɛfə,drin
ephemera, E- ə'fɛmərə |-s -z |-rae -,ri
ephemeral ə'fɛmərəl |-ly -ı |-rid -rıd
Ephesian ı'fiʒən
Ephesus 'ɛfəsəs, -zəs |-us' -əs
ephod 'ɛfəd, 'i-, -fad; ES+-fɒd
Ephraim 'ifrıəm |-ite -,aıt
epic 'ɛpık |-al -l̩ |-ally -lı |-ly -lı
epicene 'ɛpə,sin
epicenter, -tre 'ɛpı,sɛntə; ES -,sɛntə(r
Epictetus ,ɛpık'titəs |-'s -ız
epicure 'ɛpı,kjur, -,kıur; ES -ə(r
Epicurean ,ɛpıkju'rıən, -kıu'rıən |-ism -,ızəm
epicurism 'ɛpıkju,rızəm, -kıu-

Epicurus ,ɛpı'kjurəs, -'kıurəs |-'s -ız
epicycle 'ɛpə,saıkl̩
epicyclic ,ɛpə'saıklık, -'sık- |-al -l̩
epidemic ,ɛpə'dɛmık |-al -l̩ |-ally -lı, -ıklı
epidermic ,ɛpə'dɜmık; ES -'dɜm̩-, -'dɜm-;
|-al -l̩ |-ally -lı, -ıklı
epidermis ,ɛpə'dɜmıs; ES -'dɜm-, -'dɜm-;
|-mal -ml̩
epigene 'ɛpə,dʒin |-genesis ,ɛpə'dʒɛnəsıs
epiglottal ,ɛpə'glatl̩; ES+-'glɒtl̩
epiglottis ,ɛpə'glatıs; ES+-'glɒt-; |-es -ız
epigram 'ɛpə,græm
epigrammatic ,ɛpəgrə'mætık |-al -l̩ |-ally -lı,
-ıklı
epigraph 'ɛpə,græf; E+-,graf, -,grɑf
epigraphy ɛ'pıgrəfı
epilepsy 'ɛpə,lɛpsı
epileptic ,ɛpə'lɛptık |-al -l̩ |-ally -lı, -ıklı
epilogue, -log 'ɛpə,lɔg, -,lag, -,lɒg |-d, -ged -d
Epimenides ,ɛpə'mɛnə,diz |-'s -ız
Épinal 'ɛpınl̩ (Fr epi'nal)
Epiphany ı'pıfənı
epiphyte 'ɛpı,faıt |-tic ,ɛpı'fıtık
Epipsychidion ,ɛpısaı'kıdıən, -sı'kıdıən
Epirus ɛ'paırəs |-'s -ız
episcopacy ı'pıskəpəsı
episcopal, E- ı'pıskəpl̩ |-ly -ı
episcopalian, E- ı,pıskə'peljən, -lıən
episcopate ı'pıskəpıt, -,pet
episode 'ɛpə,sod, -,zod
episodic ,ɛpə'sadık, -'zad-; ES+-ɒd-; |-al -l̩
|-ally -lı, -ıklı
epistemology ı,pıstə'malədʒı; ES+-'mɒl-
epistle ı'pısl̩
epistolary ı'pıstə,lɛrı
epistyle 'ɛpı,staıl
epitaph 'ɛpə,tæf; ES+-,taf, -,tɑf; |-ed -t
epithalamium ,ɛpıθə'lemıəm |-s -z |-lamia
-mıə
epithelium ,ɛpə'θilıəm |-s -z |-lia -lıə
epithet 'ɛpə,θɛt |-theted -,θɛtıd
epithetic ,ɛpə'θɛtık |-al -l̩ |-ally -lı, -ıklı
epitome ı'pıtəmı
epitomize ı'pıtə,maız |-s -ız |-d -d
epoch 'ɛpək |-al -l̩ |-ally -lı—'ıpɒk is mainly
Brit.
epode 'ɛpod
eponym 'ɛpə,nım |-ous ɛ'panəməs; ES+
-'pɒn-

---

epos 'εpɑs; ES+-ɒs; |-es -ɪz
Epping 'εpɪŋ
epsilon 'εpsələn, -ˌlɑn, -ˌlɒn, Brit εp'saɪlən
Epsom 'εpsəm
Epworth 'εpwɚθ; ES 'εpwəθ
equable 'εkwəbl̩, 'ik- |-bly -blɪ
equal 'ikwəl |-ed -d |-ly -ɪ
equalitarian ɪˌkwɑlə'tεrɪən, -ˌkwɒl-, -'ter-
equality ɪ'kwɑlətɪ, ɪ'kwɒl-
equalization ˌikwələ'zeʃən, -aɪ'z-
equalize 'ikwəlˌaɪz |-s -ɪz |-d -d
equanimity ˌikwə'nɪmətɪ
equate ɪ'kwet |equated ɪ'kwetɪd
equation ɪ'kweʒən, -ʃən |-al -l̩ |-ally -lɪ
equator ɪ'kwetɚ; ES ɪ'kwetə(r
equatorial ˌikwə'torɪəl, ˌεk-, -'tɔr-; S -'tor-;
|-ly -ɪ
equerry 'εkwərɪ
equestrian ɪ'kwεstrɪən |-ienne ɪˌkwεstrɪ'εn
equiangular ˌikwɪ'æŋgjələ; ES -'æŋgjələ(r
equidistance ˌikwə'dɪstəns |-tant -tənt
equilateral ˌikwə'lætərəl |-ly -ɪ
equilibrant i'kwɪləbrənt
equilibrate ˌikwə'laɪbret, ɪ'kwɪləˌbret |-d -ɪd
equilibrist ɪ'kwɪləbrɪst
equilibrium ˌikwə'lɪbrɪəm |-s -z |-ria -rɪə
equine 'ikwaɪn
equinoctial ˌikwə'nɑkʃəl; ES+-'nɒk-; |-ly -ɪ
equinox 'ikwəˌnɑks; ES+-ˌnɒks; |-es -ɪz
equip ɪ'kwɪp |equipped ɪ'kwɪpt
equipage 'εkwəpɪdʒ |-s -ɪz
equipoise 'εkwəˌpɔɪz, 'i- |-s -ɪz |-d -d
equiponderance ˌikwɪ'pɑndərəns; ES+-'pɒn-
equiponderate ˌikwɪ'pɑndəˌret; ES+-'pɒn-;
|-d -ɪd
equipotential ˌikwɪpo'tεnʃəl
equisetum ˌεkwə'sitəm |-s -z |-ta -tə
equitable 'εkwɪtəbl̩ |-bly -blɪ
equitation ˌεkwɪ'teʃən
equity 'εkwətɪ
equivalence ɪ'kwɪvələns |-cy -ɪ |-lent -lənt
equivocal ɪ'kwɪvəkl̩ |-ly -ɪ, -əklɪ
equivocate ɪ'kwɪvəˌket |-cated -ˌketɪd
equivocation ɪˌkwɪvə'keʃən
equivoque, -oke 'εkwɪˌvok
er intj of hesitation ə, əː, ʌ, ʌː of various
lengths. This spelling originated with writers
who did not sound the r. It is a blunder in
reading to pronounce it ɚ or ɝ.

-er ending of agent nouns (maker) and the
comparative degree (slower) -ɚ; ES -ə(r. In
the vocab. usually omitted when its sound can
be added directly to that of the head word, as
make mek, maker 'mek-ɚ; ES 'mek-ə(r;
slow slo, slower 'slo-ɚ; ES 'slo-ə(r. When
-ɚ follows -r-, as in blusterer 'blʌs·tə·rɚ,
'blʌs·trɚ, or syllabic l̩ or n̩, as in handler
'hænd·l̩·ɚ, 'hænd·lɚ, or fastener 'fæs·n̩·ɚ,
'fæs·nɚ, there are usually the same alterna-
tives as in the addition of -ing in similar
cases. See also -est.

era 'ɪrə, 'irə
eradiate i'redɪˌet |-ated -ˌetɪd
eradicable ɪ'rædɪkəbl̩
eradicate ɪ'rædɪˌket |-d -ɪd |-tor -ɚ; ES -ə(r
eradication ɪˌrædɪ'keʃən
erase ɪ'res |-s -ɪz |-d -t |-r -ɚ; ES -ə(r
Erasmus ɪ'ræzməs |-'s -ɪz
Erastus ɪ'ræstəs |-'s -ɪz
erasure ɪ'reʒɚ, ɪ'reʃɚ; ES -ə(r
Erath i'ræθ
erbium 'ɝbɪəm; ES 'ɝb-, 'ɝb-
ere εr, ær; ES εə(r, æə(r
Erebus 'εrəbəs |-'s -ɪz
Erechtheum ˌεrɪk'θiəm
Erechtheus ɪ'rεkθjus, -θɪus |-'s -ɪz
erect ɪ'rεkt |-ed -ɪd |-ile -l̩, -ɪl
erectility ɪˌrεk'tɪlətɪ, ˌirεk'tɪlətɪ
erection ɪ'rεkʃən
erelong εr'lɒŋ, ær-, -'lɔŋ; ES εə-, æə-,
S+-'lɑŋ
eremite 'εrəˌmaɪt
erenow εr'naʊ, ær-; ES εə-, æə-
Eretria ɪ'ritrɪə, ɪ'rεt- |-n -n
erewhile εr'hwaɪl, ær-; ES εə-, æə-
Erewhon 'εrəhwən
erg ɝg; ES ɝg, ɝg
ergo 'ɝgo; ES 'ɝgo, 'ɝgo; see argal
ergon 'ɝgɑn; ES 'ɝgɑn, 'ɝ-, -gɒn
ergosterol ɚ'gɑstəˌrol; ES ə'gɑs-, ə'gɒs-
ergot 'ɝgət; ES 'ɝgət, 'ɝgət
Eric 'εrɪk |-son, -riccson 'εrɪksn̩
Erie 'ɪrɪ; S+'iri
Erin 'εrɪn, 'ɪrɪn
Erinys ɪ'rɪnɪs, ɪ'raɪnɪs |-'s -ɪz |pl Erinyes
ɪ'rɪnɪˌiz
Eris 'ɪrɪs, 'irɪs, 'εrɪs |-'s -ɪz
Eritrea ˌεrɪ'triə |-n -n (It eri'trɛːɑ)

|full fʊl |tooth tuθ |further 'fɝðɚ; ES 'fɝðə |custom 'kʌstəm |while hwaɪl |how haʊ |toy tɔɪ
|using 'juzɪŋ |fuse fjuz, fɪuz |dish dɪʃ |vision 'vɪʒən |Eden 'idn̩ |cradle 'kredl̩ |keep 'em 'kipm̩

erlking ˈɝlˌkɪŋ; ES ˈɜl-, ˈɝl-—*The pronuncia-*
tion ˈɛrlˌkɪŋ *is a mixture of Ger and Eng.*
The Ger is Erlkönig ˈɛrlˌkønɪx.
Erma ˈɝmə; ES ˈɜmə, ˈɝmə
Ermengarde ˈɝmənˌgard; ES ˈɜmənˌgɑːd,
ˈɝm-
ermine ˈɝmɪn; ES ˈɜmɪn, ˈɝm-; |-d **-d**
Erminia ɝˈmɪnɪə; ES ɜˈmɪnɪə, ɝ-
erne, ern ɝn; ES ɜn, ɝn
Ernest ˈɝnɪst; ES ˈɜnɪst, ˈɝ-
Ernestine *fem. name* ˈɝnɪsˌtin; ES ˈɜ-, ˈɝ-
Ernestine *adj* ˈɝnɪstɪn; ES ˈɜ-, ˈɝ-
erode ɪˈrod |-d **-ɪd**
Eroica ɪˈroˑɪkə
Eros ˈɪrɑs, ˈi-, ˈɛ-, -rɒs |-ˈs **-ɪz**
erosion ɪˈroʒən
erotic ɪˈratɪk; ES+-ˈrɒt-; |-al **-ḷ** |-ally **-ḷɪ,**
-ɪklɪ
eroticism ɪˈratəˌsɪzəm; ES+-ˈrɒt-
Erpingham ˈɝpɪŋˌhæm, ˈɝpɪŋəm; ES ˈɜp-,
ˈɝp-; *in Shak.* ˈErpingˌham
err ɝ; ES ɜ(r, ɝ; |-ed **-d**
errand ˈɛrənd
errant ˈɛrənt |-ry **-rɪ**
errata ɪˈretə, ɛ-, -ˈratə
erratic əˈrætɪk |-al **-ḷ** |-ally **-ḷɪ, -ɪklɪ**
erratum ɪˈretəm, ɛ-, -ˈrat- |-ta **-tə**
erring ˈɝɪŋ; ES ˈɜrɪŋ, ˈɝɪŋ; *less freq.* ˈɛrɪŋ
erroneous əˈronɪəs, ɛ-
error ˈɛrɚ; ES ˈɛrə(r
ersatz *Ger* ɛrˈzats
Erse ɝs; ES ɜs, ɝs
Erskine ˈɝskɪn; ES ˈɜs-, ˈɝs-
erst ɝst; ES ɜst, ɝst; |-while -ˌhwaɪl
eruct ɪˈrʌkt |-ed **-ɪd** |-ate **-et** |-ated **-etɪd**
eructation ɪˌrʌkˈteʃən, ˌɪrʌk-
erudite ˈɛruˌdaɪt, ˈɛrju-
erudition ˌɛruˈdɪʃən, ˌɛrju-
erupt ɪˈrʌpt |-ed **-ɪd** |-ption **-pʃən**
Ervine ˈɝvɪn; ES ˈɜvɪn, ˈɝ-
Erwin ˈɝwɪn; ES ˈɜwɪn, ˈɝ-
erysipelas ˌɛrəˈsɪpḷəs, ˌɪrə-
erythrocyte ɪˈrɪθroˌsaɪt, ɛ-
-es, -s *ending for pl & poss of nouns, & for 3*
sg pres of verbs. *Pron.* -s *after voiceless*
consonant sounds except s, ʃ, tʃ (cap-s
kæp-s, Kate's ket-s, chafe-s tʃef-s); *pron.*
z *after vowel & voiced consonant sounds ex-*
cept z, ʒ, dʒ (ball-s bɔl-z, Joe's dʒo-z,

save-s sev-z); *pron.* -ɪz *or* -əz *after the*
voiceless and voiced sibilants s, ʃ, tʃ, z, ʒ, dʒ
(face-s ˈfes-ɪz, Nash's ˈnæʃ-ɪz, catch-es
ˈkætʃ-ɪz, nose-s ˈnoz-ɪz, rouge-s ˈruʒ-ɪz,
George's ˈdʒɔrdʒ-ɪz). *For the variation in*
unstressed vowel between -ɪz & -əz, *see fuller*
statement of the same variation at -ed *in the*
vocab., and for full illustration of the ending
-es, -s *see* §88.
Esau ˈisɔ
escadrille ˌɛskəˈdrɪl (*Fr* ɛskaˈdriːj)
escalade ˌɛskəˈled |-laded -ˈledɪd
escalator, E- ˈɛskəˌletɚ; ES -ˌletə(r
escalop, -ll- ɛˈskaləp, ɛˈskæləp; ES+-ˈskɒl-;
|-ed **-t**
Escalus ˈɛskələs |-ˈs **-ɪz**
Escanes ˈɛskəˌniz |-ˈs **-ɪz**
escapade ˈɛskəˌped, ˌɛskəˈped
escape əˈskep, ɪ-, ɛ- |-d **-t** |-pism -ɪzəm |-pist
-ɪst
escarp ɛˈskarp; ES ɛˈskaːp, E+ɛˈskaːp;
|-ed **-t**
eschatological ˌɛskætəˈladʒɪkḷ; ES+-ˈlɒdʒ-
eschatologist ˌɛskəˈtalədʒɪst; ES+-ˈtɒl-; |-gy
-dʒɪ
escheat ɛsˈtʃit |-ed **-ɪd** |-age **-ɪdʒ**
eschew ɛsˈtʃu, -ˈtʃɪu |-ed **-d** |-al **-əl**
Escorial ɛsˈkorɪəl, -ˈkɔr-; S -ˈkor-; (*Sp*
eskoriˈal)
escort *n* ˈɛskɔrt; ES ˈɛskɔət
escort *v* ɪˈskɔrt; ES ɪˈskɔət; |-ed **-ɪd**
escritoire ˌɛskrɪˈtwar, -ˈtwɔr; ES -ˈtwaː(r,
-ˈtwɔə(r; (*Fr* écritoire ekriˈtwaːr)
escrow ˈɛskro, ɛˈskro
esculent ˈɛskjələnt
escutcheon ɪˈskʌtʃən |-ed **-d**
Esdraelon ˌɛzdrəˈilən, ˌɛs-
Esdras ˈɛzdrəs |-ˈs **-ɪz**
-ese *word ending* (Chinese, Burmese) -ˈiz, -ˌiz,
-iz; *in America much less often* -s
esker, -kar ˈɛskɚ; ES ˈɛskə(r
Eskimo ˈɛskəˌmo |-mauan, -moan ˌɛskəˈmoən
Esmeralda ˌɛzməˈrældə
Esmond ˈɛzmənd
esophagus iˈsafəgəs; ES+-ˈsɒf-; |-es **-ɪz** |-gi
-ˌdʒaɪ
Esopus iˈsopəs |-ˈs **-ɪz**
esoteric ˌɛsəˈtɛrɪk |-al **-ḷ** |-ally **-ḷɪ, -ɪklɪ**
espalier ɛˈspæljɚ; ES -jə(r; |-ed **-d**

Key: *See in full* §§3–47. bee bi |pity ˈpɪtɪ (§6) |rate ret |yet jɛt |sang sæŋ |angry ˈæŋ·grɪ
|bath bæθ; E baθ (§10) |ah ɑ |far fɑr |watch watʃ, wɒtʃ (§12) |jaw dʒɔ |gorge gɔrdʒ |go go

especial ə'spɛʃəl |-ly -ɪ, -ʃlɪ
esperance 'ɛspərəns |-s -ɪz
Esperanto ˌɛspə'rɑnto, -'rænto
espial ɪ'spaɪəl
espionage 'ɛspɪənɪdʒ, ə'spaɪənɪdʒ (Fr espion-
  nage ɛspjɔ̃'na:ʒ)
esplanade ˌɛsplə'ned, -'nɑd
espouse ɪ'spaʊz |-s -ɪz |-d -d |-sal -ļ
esprit ɛ'spri
esprit de corps ɛ'spridə'kor, -'kɔr; ES -'koə(r,
  E+-'kɔə(r; (Fr ɛsprid'kö:r)
espy ə'spaɪ |-ied -d
Espy 'ɛspɪ
Esquimau 'ɛskəˌmo |-maux -ˌmo, -ˌmoz
  |-mauan ˌɛskə'moən
esquire ə'skwaɪr; ES ə'skwaɪə(r; |-d -d
ess ɛs |esses 'ɛsɪz
-ess fem. ending -ɪs, -əs; if lightly accented,
  esp. in verse, sometimes -ɛs. In the vocab.
  if only -ɪs is given, it is to be understood that
  -əs and -ɛs are also possible. Often omitted
  when the pron. can be found by adding -ɪs,
  -əs, -ɛs to the head pronunciation.
essay 'composition' 'ɛsɪ, 'ɛse; 'trial' ɛ'se,
  'ɛse
essay 'try' ə'se, ɛ'se |-ed -d
esse 'ɛsɪ
Essen 'ɛsņ
essence 'ɛsņs |-s -ɪz
Essene 'ɛsin, ɛ'sin
essential ə'sɛnʃəl |-ly -ɪ |-ity ə,sɛnʃɪ'ælətɪ
Essex 'ɛsɪks |-'s -ɪz
-est unstressed superlative & archaic 2 sg pres
  ending -ɪst or -əst; if lightly stressed, esp.
  in verse, sometimes -ɛst. In the vocab. if
  only -ɪst is given, it is to be understood that
  many speakers (fewer in the E & S) also
  pronounce -əst as in August 'ɔgəst. For the
  vowel see also -ed.
establish ə'stæblɪʃ |-es -ɪz |-ed -t
estaminet Fr ɛstami'nɛ
estate ə'stet |-d -ɪd
esteem ə'stim |-ed -d
Estella ɛ'stɛlə |Estelle ɛ'stɛl
ester 'ɛstɚ; ES 'ɛstə(r
Estes 'ɛstɪz |-tes' -tɪz
Esther 'ɛstɚ; ES 'ɛstə(r
esthesia ɛs'θiʒə, -ʒɪə |-thesis -'θisɪs
esthete 'ɛsθit

esthetic ɛs'θɛtɪk |-al -ļ |-ally -ļɪ, -ɪklɪ
estheticism ɛs'θɛtəˌsɪzəm |-thetics -'θɛtɪks
Esthonia ɛs'tonɪə, -'θon- |-n -n=Estonia
estimable 'ɛstəməbļ |-bly -blɪ
estimate n 'ɛstəmɪt, -ˌmet
estimate v 'ɛstəˌmet |-d -ɪd |-tion ˌɛstə'meʃən
estival 'ɛstəvļ, ɛs'taɪvļ
estivate 'ɛstəˌvet |-d -ɪd |-tion ˌɛstə'veʃən
Estmere 'ɛstmɪr; ES -mɪə(r, S+-mɛə(r
Estonia ɛs'tonɪə |-n -n
estop ɛ'stɑp; ES+ɛ'stɒp; |-ped -t |-pel -ļ
estovers ɛ'stovɚz; ES -vəz
estrange ə'strendʒ |-s -ɪz |-d -d |-dness -ɪdnɪs,
  -dnɪs
estray ɪ'stre
estreat ɪ'strit |-ed -ɪd
estrous 'ɛstrəs, 'ɪs-
estrum 'ɛstrəm, 'ɪs- |-trus -trəs |-truses
  -trəsɪz
estuary 'ɛstʃʊˌɛrɪ |-arial ˌɛstʃʊ'ɛrɪəl
esurient ɪ'sjʊrɪənt, ɪ'sɪʊr-, ɪ'sʊr-
et 'and' ɛt
-et unstressed word terminal, as in pocket,
  tablet, comet, carpet, rivet, etc. -ɪt, -ət.
  In the vocab. when only -ɪt is given, it is to
  be understood that many speakers (fewer in
  the E & S) also pron. -ət as in pilot 'paɪlət.
eta Gk letter 'etə, 'itə
etaoin 'ɛtɪˌɔɪn—cf shrdlu
et cetera ɛt'sɛtərə, -'sɛtrə |-s -z
etch ɛtʃ |etches 'ɛtʃɪz |etched ɛtʃt
eternal ɪ'tɝnļ; ES ɪ'tɜnļ, ɪ'tɝnļ; |-ly -ɪ
eternalize ɪ'tɝnļˌaɪz; ES ɪ'tɜn-, ɪ'tɝn-; |-s -ɪz
  |-d -d
eterne ɪ'tɝn; ES ɪ'tɜn, ɪ'tɝn |-nity -ətɪ
eternization ɪ,tɝnə'zeʃən, -aɪ'z-; ES ɪ,tɜn-,
  ɪ,tɝn-
eternize ɪ'tɝnaɪz; ES ɪ'tɜn-, ɪ'tɝn-; |-s -ɪz
  |-d -d
Ethan 'iθən
ethane 'ɛθen
Ethel 'ɛθəl
Ethelbald 'ɛθəlˌbɔld
Ethelbert 'ɛθəlbɚt; ES -bət
Ethelberta ˌɛθəl'bɝtə; ES -'bɜtə, -'bɝtə
Ethelred 'ɛθəlˌred |Ethelwulf 'ɛθəlˌwʊlf
ether 'iθɚ; ES 'iθə(r
ethereal ɪ'θɪrɪəl |-ly -ɪ
ethereality ɪ,θɪrɪ'ælətɪ

|full fʊl |tooth tuθ |further 'fɝðɚ; ES 'fɝðə |custom 'kʌstəm |while hwaɪl |how haʊ |toy tɔɪ
|using 'juzɪŋ |fuse fjuz, fɪuz |dish dɪʃ |vision 'vɪʒən |Eden 'idņ |cradle 'kredļ |keep 'em 'kipm̩

Etherege 'εθərɪdʒ |-'s -ɪz
etherization ˌiθərə'zeʃən, -aɪ'z-
etherize 'iθəˌraɪz |-s -ɪz |-d -d
ethic 'εθɪk |-al -ļ |-ally -ļɪ, -ɪklɪ
Ethiop 'iθɪˌɑp; ES+-ˌɒp
Ethiopia ˌiθɪ'opɪə |-n -n
Ethiopic ˌiθɪ'ɑpɪk, -'opɪk; ES+-'ɒp-
ethmoid 'εθmɔɪd
ethnic 'εθnɪk |-al -ļ |-ally -ļɪ, -ɪklɪ
ethnographic ˌεθnə'græfɪk |-al -ļ |-ally -ļɪ,
-ɪklɪ
ethnography εθ'nɑgrəfɪ, -'nɒg-
ethnologic ˌεθnə'lɑdʒɪk; ES+-'lɒdʒ-; |-al -ļ
|-ally -ļɪ, -ɪklɪ
ethnology εθ'nɑlədʒɪ; ES+-'nɒl-
ethos 'iθɑs; ES+-θɒs
ethyl, E- 'εθəl, -ɪl
ethylate 'εθəˌlet |-lated -ˌletɪd
ethylene 'εθəˌlin
ethylic ɪ'θɪlɪk
etiology ˌitɪ'ɑlədʒɪ; ES+-'ɒl-
etiquette 'εtɪˌkεt
Etna, e- 'εtnə
Eton 'itṇ |-tonian i'tonɪən
Etruria ɪ'trʊrɪə |-n -n
Etruscan ɪ'trʌskən
Ettrick 'εtrɪk
étude e'tjud, e'tɪud, e'tud (Fr e'tyd)
etymologic ˌεtəmə'lɑdʒɪk; ES+-'lɒdʒ-; |-al
-ļ |-ally -ļɪ, -ɪklɪ
etymologist ˌεtə'mɑlədʒɪst; ES+-'mɒl-; |-gy
-dʒɪ
etymologize ˌεtə'mɑləˌdʒaɪz; ES+-'mɒl-; |-s
-ɪz |-d -d
etymon 'εtəˌmɑn, -ˌmɒn |-s -z |-ma -mə
Euboea ju'bɪə |-n -n |-boic -'bo·ɪk
eucalypt 'jukəˌlɪpt |-ic ˌjukə'lɪptɪk
eucalyptus, E- ˌjukə'lɪptəs |-es -ɪz |-ti -taɪ
Eucharist 'jukərɪst
Eucharistic ˌjukə'rɪstɪk |-al -ļ |-ally -ļɪ, -ɪklɪ
euchre 'jukɚ; ES 'jukə(r; |-d -d |-ring -kərɪŋ,
-krɪŋ
Euclid 'juklɪd |-ean ju'klɪdɪən
eudaemon, -dem- ju'dimən |-monia ˌjudɪ-
'monɪə
eudiometer ˌjudɪ'ɑmətɚ; ES -'amətə(r, -'ɒm-
eudiometric ˌjudɪə'mεtrɪk |-al -ļ |-ally -ļɪ,
-ɪklɪ
Eudora ju'dorə, -'dɔrə; S -'dorə

Euganean ˌjugə'niən, ju'genɪən
Eugene ju'dʒin |-nia -ɪə |-nius -ɪəs |-nius's
-ɪəsɪz
eugenic ju'dʒεnɪk |-al -ļ |-ally -ļɪ, -ɪklɪ
Eugénie Fr øʒe'ni
eugenism 'judʒəˌnɪzəm |-nist -nɪst
Eulalia ju'lelɪə, -ljə
eulogia ju'lodʒɪə |-giae -dʒɪˌi
eulogist 'julədʒɪst |-gy -dʒɪ
eulogistic ˌjulə'dʒɪstɪk |-al -ļ |-ally -ļɪ, -ɪklɪ
eulogize 'juləˌdʒaɪz |-s -ɪz |-d -d
Eumenides ju'mεnəˌdiz
Eunice 'junɪs |-'s -ɪz
eunuch 'junək
eupepsia ju'pεpʃə, -ʃɪə |-ptic -tɪk
Euphemia ju'fimɪə
euphemism 'jufəˌmɪzəm |-mist -mɪst
euphemistic ˌjufə'mɪstɪk |-al -ļ |-ally -ļɪ,
-ɪklɪ
euphonic ju'fɑnɪk; ES+-'fɒn-; |-al -ļ |-ally
-ļɪ, -ɪklɪ
euphony 'jufənɪ |-phonious ju'fonɪəs
Euphorbia, e- ju'fɔrbɪə; ES -'fɔəb-
Euphrates ju'fretiz, in Shak. 'jufrəˌtiz |-tes'
-tiz
Euphronius ju'fronɪəs |-'s -ɪz
Euphrosyne ju'frɑsəˌni, -'frɒs-
Euphues 'jufjuˌiz |-'s -ɪz
euphuism 'jufjuˌɪzəm |-ist -ɪst
euphuistic ˌjufju'ɪstɪk |-al -ļ |-ally -ļɪ, -ɪklɪ
Eurasia ju'reʒə, -'reʃə |-n -n
Eureka, e- ju'rikə
eurhythmic ju'rɪðmɪk |-al -ļ |-my -mɪ
Euripedes ju'rɪpəˌdiz |-'s -ɪz
Euroclydon ju'rɑklɪˌdɑn; ES+-'rɒklɪˌdɒn
Europa ju'ropə
Europe 'jʊrəp |-an ˌjʊrə'piən
europium ju'ropɪəm
Eurus 'jʊrəs |-'s -ɪz
Eurydice ju'rɪdəˌsi
eurythmic ju'rɪðmɪk |-al -ļ |-my -mɪ
Eusebius ju'sibɪəs |-'s -ɪz
Eustace 'justɪs, -təs |-'s -ɪz
Eustachian ju'stekɪən, -ʃɪən, -ʃən
Eustis 'justɪs |-'s -ɪz
Euston 'justən
Eutaw 'jutɔ
eutectic ju'tεktɪk
Euterpe ju'tɝpɪ; ES -'tɜpɪ, -'tɝpɪ

euthanasia ˌjuθəˈneʒə, -ʒɪə
euthenics juˈθɛnɪks |-ist ˈjuθənɪst
euxenite ˈjuksəˌnaɪt
Euxine ˈjuksɪn, -aɪn
Eva ˈivə, ˈɛvə
evacuant ɪˈvækjuənt
evacuate ɪˈvækjuˌet |-d -ɪd |-tion ɪˌvækjuˈeʃən
evacuee ɪˈvækjuˌi, ɪˌvækjuˈi, -ˈe (Fr evaˈkɥe)
evadable, -ible ɪˈvedəbļ
evade ɪˈved |evaded ɪˈvedɪd
evaluate ɪˈvæljuˌet |-d -ɪd |-tion ɪˌvæljuˈeʃən
Evan ˈɛvən
Evander ɪˈvændɚ; ES ɪˈvændə(r
evanesce ˌɛvəˈnɛs |-s -ɪz |-d -t
evanescence ˌɛvəˈnɛsņs |-cy -ɪ |-ent -ņt
evangel ɪˈvændʒəl
evangelic ˌivænˈdʒɛlɪk, ˌɛvən- |-al -ļ |-ally -ļɪ, -ɪklɪ
Evangeline ɪˈvændʒəˌlin, -lɪn, -ˌlaɪn
evangelism ɪˈvændʒəˌlɪzəm |-list -lɪst
evangelistic ɪˌvændʒəˈlɪstɪk |-ally -ļɪ, -ɪklɪ
evangelize ɪˈvændʒəˌlaɪz |-s -ɪz |-d -d
evanish ɪˈvænɪʃ |-es -ɪz |-ed -t
Evans ˈɛvənz |-'s -ɪz |-ville -ˌvɪl
Evanston ˈɛvənˌstən, ˈɛvənzˌtən
evaporability ɪˌvæpərəˈbɪlətɪ
evaporable ɪˈvæpərəbļ, -prəbļ
evaporate ɪˈvæpəˌret |-rated -ˌretɪd
evaporation ɪˌvæpəˈreʃən
Evarts ˈɛvɚts; ES ˈɛvəts; |-'s -ɪz
evasion ɪˈveʒən |-sive -sɪv
eve iv
Eve iv
Eveleth ˈɛvəlɪθ
Evelina ˌɛvəˈlaɪnə, -ˈlinə
Eveline ˈɛvəˌlaɪn, -lɪn, ˈɛvlɪn
Evelyn ˈɛvəlɪn, ˈɛvlɪn, ˈivlɪn
even ˈivən |-fall -ˌfɔl
evener ˈivnɚ, ˈivənɚ; ES -nə(r
evenhanded ˈivənˈhændɪd (ˈevenˌhanded ˈjustice)
evening ˈivnɪŋ
evenness ˈivənnɪs
evensong ˈivənˌsɔŋ, -ˌsɒŋ; S+-ˌsɑŋ
event ɪˈvɛnt
eventide ˈivənˌtaɪd
eventual ɪˈvɛntʃuəl |-ly -ɪ, ɪˈvɛntʃulɪ
eventuality ɪˌvɛntʃuˈælətɪ

eventuate ɪˈvɛntʃuˌet |-ated -ˌetɪd
ever ˈɛvɚ; ES ˈɛvə(r
Everest ˈɛvrɪst, ˈɛvərɪst
Everett, -itt ˈɛvrɪt, ˈɛvərɪt
everglade, E- ˈɛvɚˌgled; ES ˈɛvəˌgled
evergreen ˈɛvɚˌgrin; ES ˈɛvəˌgrin
everlasting ˌɛvɚˈlæstɪŋ; ES ˌɛvə-, E+-ˈlast-, -ˈlɑst-; (ˈeverˌlasting ˈwhipˌcord)
evermore ˌɛvɚˈmor, -ˈmɔr; ES -ˈmoə(r, E+-ˈmɔə(r
eversion iˈvɝʃən, -ʒən; ES iˈvɝ-, iˈvɝ-
evert iˈvɝt; ES iˈvɝt, iˈvɝt; |-ed -ɪd
every ˈɛvrɪ, ˈɛvərɪ
everybody ˈɛvrɪˌbadɪ, -ˌbʌdɪ, -bədɪ; ES+-ˌbɒdɪ
everyday ˈɛvrɪˈde (ˈeveryˌday ˈclothes)
Everyman ˈɛvrɪˌmæn
everyone ˈɛvrɪˌwʌn, -wən
everything ˈɛvrɪˌθɪŋ
everywhere ˈɛvrɪˌhwɛr, -ˌhwær; E -ˌhwɛə(r, ES -ˌhwæə(r
Evesham ˈivʃəm, ˈivzəm, loc.+ˈiʃəm, ˈisəm
evict ɪˈvɪkt |-ed -ɪd |-ction ɪˈvɪkʃən
evidence ˈɛvədəns |-s -ɪz |-d -t |-dent -dənt
evidential ˌɛvəˈdɛnʃəl |-ly -ɪ
evidently ˈɛvədəntlɪ, -dɛntlɪ, sometimes if emphatic ˌɛvəˈdɛntlɪ
evil ˈivļ, formal, esp. in church,+ˈivɪl |-ly -ɪ, ˈivlɪ
evince ɪˈvɪns |-s -ɪz |-d -t
eviscerate ɪˈvɪsəˌret |-rated -ˌretɪd
evisceration ɪˌvɪsəˈreʃən
evocable ˈɛvəkəbļ |-cation ˌɛvoˈkeʃən
evocative ɪˈvakətɪv, ɪˈvok-; ES+-ˈvɒk-
evoke ɪˈvok |evoked ɪˈvokt
evolute n, adj, v ˈɛvəˌlut, -ˌlɪut |-d -ɪd
evolution ˌɛvəˈluʃən, -ˈlɪu-, ɛvļˈjuʃən |-ary -ˌɛrɪ
evolve ɪˈvalv, ɪˈvɒlv |-d -d
Ewart ˈjuɚt; ES ˈjuˑət
ewe ju, jo—The historical variant jo is still common among sheep breeders both in England and America.
Ewen ˈjuɪn, -ən
ewer ˈjuɚ; ES ˈjuˑə(r
Ewers ˈjuɚz, jurz; ES ˈjuˑəz, juəz; |-'s -ɪz
Ewing ˈjuɪŋ
ex ɛks |exes ˈɛksɪz
ex- prefix. When quite unaccented, the vowel

|full fʊl |tooth tuθ |further ˈfɝðɚ; ES ˈfɝðə |custom ˈkʌstəm |while hwaɪl |how haʊ |toy tɔɪ |using ˈjuzɪŋ |fuse fjuz, fɪuz |dish dɪʃ |vision ˈvɪʒən |Eden ˈidņ |cradle ˈkredļ |keep 'em ˈkipm̩

is usually ɪ *in current speech, less freq.* ə *or*
ɛ, *of the two* ə *being more likely in rapid*
speech & ɛ *in careful. In the vocab. when*
only ɪ *is given, it is to be understood that* ə
or ɛ *may also occur.*

exacerbate ɪgˈzæsəˌbet, ɪkˈsæs-; ES -æsə-;
|-d -ɪd
exacerbation ɪgˌzæsəˈbeʃən, ɪkˌsæs-; ES
-æsə-
exact ɪgˈzækt |-ed -ɪd |-ction -kʃən
exactitude ɪgˈzæktəˌtjud, -ˌtɪud, -ˌtud
exactly ɪgˈzæktlɪ, ɪgˈzæklɪ
exaggerate ɪgˈzædʒəˌret |-d -ɪd |-tive -ɪv
exaggeration ɪgˌzædʒəˈreʃən
exalt ɪgˈzɔlt |-ed -ɪd |-ation ˌɛgzɔlˈteʃən
exam ɪgˈzæm |-ination ɪgˌzæməˈneʃən
examine ɪgˈzæmɪn |-d -d |-nee ɪgˌzæməˈni
example ɪgˈzæmp|; E+-ˈzam-, -ˈzam-; |-d -d
|-ling -plɪŋ, -plɪŋ
exanimate *adj* ɪgˈzænəmɪt, -ˌmet
exanimate *v* ɪgˈzænəˌmet |-mated -ˌmetɪd
exarch ˈɛksark; ES ˈɛksa:k, E+-a:k
exasperate ɪgˈzæspəˌret |-reted -ˌretɪd
exasperation ɪgˌzæspəˈreʃən
Excalibur ɛksˈkæləbə; ES -bə(r
ex cathedra ˌɛkskəˈθidrə, ɛksˈkæθɪdrə
excavate ˈɛkskəˌvet |-d -ɪd |-tor -ə; ES -ə(r
excavation ˌɛkskəˈveʃən
exceed ɪkˈsid |-ed -ɪd
excel ɪkˈsɛl |-celled -ˈsɛld
excellence ˈɛksləns |-cy -ɪ |-ent -ənt
excelsior ɪkˈsɛlsɪə; ES -ˈsɛlsɪ·ə(r
except ɪkˈsɛpt |-ed -ɪd |-ption -ˈsɛpʃən
exceptionable ɪkˈsɛpʃənəb|, -ʃnəb| |-bly -blɪ
exceptional ɪkˈsɛpʃən|, -ʃnəl |-ly -ɪ
excerpt *n* ˈɛksɝpt; ES -sɝpt, -sɝpt
excerpt *v* ɪkˈsɝpt; ES -ˈsɝpt, -ˈsɝpt; |-ed -ɪd
|-ption -pʃən
excess ɪkˈsɛs |-es -ɪz |-ed -t (ˈɛkˌsɛs ˈret)
exchange ɪksˈtʃendʒ |-s -ɪz |-d -d
exchangeability ɪksˌtʃendʒəˈbɪlətɪ
exchangeable ɪksˈtʃendʒəb| |-bly -blɪ
exchequer ɪksˈtʃɛkə, ˈɛkstʃɛkə; ES -kə(r
excise *n* ɪkˈsaɪz (ˈexˌcise ˈduty)
excise *v* ɪkˈsaɪz |-s -ɪz |-d -d
excision ɪkˈsɪʒən
excitability ɪkˌsaɪtəˈbɪlətɪ
excitable ɪkˈsaɪtəb|
excitation ˌɛksaɪˈteʃən

excitatory ɪkˈsaɪtəˌtɔrɪ, -ˌtorɪ; S -ˌtorɪ
excite ɪkˈsaɪt |-cited -ˈsaɪtɪd
exclaim ɪkˈsklem |-ed -d
exclamation ˌɛkskləˈmeʃən
exclamatory ɪkˈsklæməˌtorɪ, -ˌtɔrɪ; S -ˌtorɪ
exclave ˈɛksklev
exclude ɪkˈsklud, -ˈsklɪud |-d -ɪd
exclusion ɪkˈskluʒən, -ˈsklɪu- |-sive -sɪv
excogitate ɛksˈkadʒəˌtet; ES+-ˈkɒdʒ-; |-d
-ɪd
excogitation ɛksˌkadʒəˈteʃən; ES+-ˌkɒdʒ-
excommunicable ˌɛkskəˈmjunɪkəb|, -ˈmɪun-
excommunicate ˌɛkskəˈmjunəˌket, -ˈmɪun-
|-d -ɪd
excommunication ˌɛkskəˌmjunəˈkeʃən, -ˌmɪun-
excoriate ɪkˈskorɪˌet, -ˈskɔr-; S -ˈskor-; |-d -ɪd
excoriation ɪkˌskorɪˈeʃən, ˌɛkskorɪ-, -kɔr; S
-kor-
excrement ˈɛkskrɪmənt
excremental ˌɛkskrɪˈmɛnt| |-tary -tərɪ
excrescence ɪkˈskrɛsn̩s |-cy -ɪ |-scent -sn̩t
excreta ɛkˈskritə |-tal -t|
excrete ɪkˈskrit |-d -ɪd |-tion -ˈskriʃən
excretory ˈɛkskrɪˌtorɪ, -ˌtɔrɪ; S -ˌtorɪ
excruciate ɪkˈskruʃɪˌet, -ˈskrɪu- |-d -ɪd
excruciation ɪkˌskruʃɪˈeʃən, -ˌskrɪu-, -sɪ-
exculpate ˈɛkskʌlˌpet, ɪkˈskʌlpet |-d -ɪd
exculpation ˌɛkskʌlˈpeʃən
exculpatory ɪkˈskʌlpəˌtorɪ, -ˌtɔrɪ; S -ˌtorɪ
excursion ɪkˈskɝʒən, -ʃən; ES -ˈskɝʒ-, -ˈskɝʒ-;
|-sive -sɪv
excursus ɛkˈskɝsəs; ES -ˈskɝsəs-, -ˈskɝs-; |-es
-ɪz
excusability ɪkˌskjuzəˈbɪlətɪ, -ˌskɪuz-
excusable ɪkˈskjuzəb|, -ˈskɪuz- |-bly -blɪ
excusatory ɪkˈskjuzəˌtorɪ, -ˈskɪuz-, -ˌtɔrɪ; S
-ˌtorɪ
excuse *n* ɪkˈskjus, -ˈskɪus |-s -ɪz
excuse *v* ɪkˈskjuz, -ˈskɪuz |-s -ɪz |-d -d
Exe ɛks |-ˈs -ɪz
execrable ˈɛksɪkrəb|, |-bly -blɪ
execrate ˈɛksɪˌkret |-crated -ˌkretɪd
execration ˌɛksɪˈkreʃən
execratory ˈɛksɪkrəˌtorɪ, -ˌtɔrɪ, -ˌkretɔrɪ; S
-ˌtorɪ, -ˌkretərɪ
executable ˈɛksɪˌkjutəb|, -ˌkɪut-, ɪgˈzɛkjutəb|
executant ɪgˈzɛkjutənt
execute ˈɛksɪˌkjut, -ˌkɪut |-d -ɪd
execution ˌɛksɪˈkjuʃən, -ˈkɪu-

executive ɪgˈzɛkjʊtɪv

executor *ˈperformer* ˈɛksɪˌkjutɚ, -ˌkɪu-, *law* ɪgˈzɛkjətɚ; ES -tə(r

executory ɪgˈzɛkjəˌtorɪ, -ˌtɔrɪ; S -ˌtorɪ

executrix ɪgˈzɛkjətrɪks |-es -ɪz |*L pl* -trices ɪgˌzɛkjəˈtraɪsɪz

exegesis ˌɛksəˈdʒɪsɪs |-geses -ˈdʒisiz

exegetic ˌɛksəˈdʒɛtɪk |-al -l̩ |-ally -l̩ɪ, -ɪklɪ

exemplar ɪgˈzɛmplɚ; ES -ˈzɛmplə(r; |-y -ɪ

exemplification ɪgˌzɛmpləfəˈkeʃən

exemplify ɪgˈzɛmpləˌfaɪ |-fied -ˌfaɪd

exempli gratia ɪgˈzɛmplaɪˈgreʃɪə

exempt ɪgˈzɛmpt |-ed -ɪd |-ption -pʃən

exequatur ˌɛksɪˈkwetɚ; ES -ˈkweta(r

exequy ˈɛksɪkwɪ |-quies -kwɪz

exercise ˈɛksɚˌsaɪz; ES ˈɛksə-; |-s -ɪz |-d -d

exercitation ɪgˌzɝsɪˈteʃən; ES -ˌzɝ-, -ˌzɝ-

exert ɪgˈzɝt; ES -ˈzɜt, -ˈzɜt; |-ed -ɪd

exertion ɪgˈzɝʃən; ES -ˈzɜʃ-, -ˈzɜʃ-

Exeter ˈɛksɪtɚ; ES ˈɛksɪtə(r

exeunt ˈɛksɪənt, ˈɛksɪˌʌnt

exhalant ɛksˈhelənt, ɪgˈzelənt

exhalation ˌɛksəˈleʃən, ˌɛgzə-

exhale ɛksˈhel, ɪgˈzel |-d -d

exhaust ɪgˈzɔst |-ed -ɪd |-ion -stʃən |-ive -ɪv

exhibit ɪgˈzɪbɪt |-ed -ɪd

exhibition ˌɛksəˈbɪʃən |-ism -ˌɪzəm |-ist -ɪst

exhibitive ɪgˈzɪbɪtɪv

exhibitory ɪgˈzɪbəˌtorɪ, -ˌtɔrɪ; S -ˌtorɪ

exhilarate ɪgˈzɪləˌret |-d -ɪd |-rant -rənt

exhilaration ɪgˌzɪləˈreʃən

exhort ɪgˈzɔrt; ES -ˈzɔət; |-ed -ɪd

exhortation ˌɛgzɔˈteʃən, ˌɛksɔ-, -ɔrˈteʃən; ES ˌɛgzɔ-, ˌɛksɔ-, -ɔəˈteʃən

exhume ɪgˈzjum, ɪkˈsjum, -ɪum, -um |-d -d

exigence ˈɛksədʒəns |-cy -ɪ |-gent -dʒənt

exiguity ˌɛksəˈgjuətɪ, -ˈgɪu-

exiguous ɪgˈzɪgjʊəs, ɪkˈsɪg-

exile *n* ˈɛgzaɪl, ˈɛksaɪl

exile *v* ˈɛgzaɪl, ˈɛksaɪl, ɪgˈzaɪl |-d -d

exist ɪgˈzɪst |-ed -ɪd |-ence -əns |-ent -ənt

exit ˈɛgzɪt, ˈɛksɪt |-ed -ɪd

ex libris ɛksˈlaɪbrɪs

Exmoor ˈɛksˌmʊr; ES -ˌmʊə(r

Exmouth ˈɛksˌmaʊθ, ˈɛksməθ

exodontia ˌɛksəˈdɑnʃə, -ʃɪə; ES+-ˈdɒn-

exodus, E- ˈɛksədəs |-es -ɪz

ex officio ˌɛksəˈfɪʃɪˌo

exogamy ɛksˈɑgəmɪ, -ˈɒg-

exonerate ɪgˈzɑnəˌret; ES+-ˈzɒn-; |-d -ɪd

exorable ˈɛksərəbl̩

exorbitance ɪgˈzɔrbətəns; ES -ˈzɔəb-; |-nt -nt

exorcise, -ze ˈɛksɔrˌsaɪz; ES ˈɛksɔə-; |-s -ɪz |-d -d |-cism -ˌsɪzəm

exordium ɪgˈzɔrdɪəm, ɪkˈs-; ES -ˈzɔəd-; |-s -z |-ia -ɪə

exoskeleton ˌɛksoˈskɛlətn̩ |-tal -tl̩

exoteric ˌɛksəˈtɛrɪk |-al -l̩ |-ally -l̩ɪ, -ɪklɪ

exotic ɪgˈzɑtɪk; ES+-ˈzɒt-; |-ally -l̩ɪ, -ɪklɪ

expand ɪkˈspænd |-ed -ɪd

expanse ɪkˈspæns |-s -ɪz |-sion -ʃən |-sive -ɪv

expansibility ɪkˌspænsəˈbɪlətɪ

expansible ɪkˈspænsəbl̩ |-bly -blɪ

expansile ɪkˈspænsl̩, -sɪl

ex parte ɛksˈpɑrtɪ; ES -ˈpɑːtɪ, E+-ˈpaːtɪ

expatiate ɪkˈspeʃɪˌet |-d -ɪd

expatiation ɪkˌspeʃɪˈeʃən

expatriate *adj* ɛksˈpetrɪɪt, -ˌet

expatriate *v* ɛksˈpetrɪˌet |-d -ɪd

expatriation ɛksˌpetrɪˈeʃən, ˌɛkspetrɪ-

expect ɪkˈspɛkt |-ed -ɪd

expectance ɪkˈspɛktəns |-cy -ɪ |-ant -ənt

expectation ˌɛkspɛkˈteʃən

expectorant ɪkˈspɛktərənt

expectorate ɪkˈspɛktəˌret |-rated -ˌretɪd

expectoration ɪkˌspɛktəˈreʃən

expedience ɪkˈspidɪəns |-cy -ɪ |-ent -ənt

expedite ˈɛkspɪˌdaɪt |-dited -ˌdaɪtɪd

expedition ˌɛkspɪˈdɪʃən |-ary -ˌɛrɪ |-tious -ʃəs

expel ɪkˈspɛl |-led -d |-lant, -lent -ənt

expend ɪkˈspɛnd |-ed -ɪd

expenditure ɪkˈspɛndɪtʃɚ, -ˌtʃʊr; ES -tʃə(r, -ˌtʃʊə(r

expense ɪkˈspɛns |-s -ɪz |-sive -ɪv

experience ɪkˈspɪrɪəns; S+-ˈspɛr-; |-s -ɪz |-d -t

experiential ɪkˌspɪrɪˈɛnʃəl; S+-ˌspɛr-; |-ly -ɪ

experiment ɪkˈspɛrəmənt

experimental ɪkˌspɛrəˈmɛntl̩, ˌɛkspɛrə- |-ly -ɪ |-ism -ˌɪzəm |-ist -ɪst

experimentation ɪkˌspɛrəmɛnˈteʃən, -mən-

expert *n* ˈɛkspɝt; ES -spɜt, -spɝt

expert *adj* ɪkˈspɝt, ˈɛkspɝt; ES -pɜt, -pɝt (ˈexˌpert ˈworkman)

expert *v* ɪkˈspɝt; ES -ˈspɜt, -ˈspɝt; |-ed -ɪd

expiable ˈɛkspɪəbl̩

expiate ˈɛkspɪˌet |-d -ɪd |-tion ˌɛkspɪˈeʃən

expiatory ˈɛkspɪəˌtorɪ, -ˌtɔrɪ; S -ˌtorɪ

|full fʊl |tooth tuθ |further ˈfɝðɚ; ES ˈfɝðə |custom ˈkʌstəm |while hwaɪl |how haʊ |toy tɔɪ
|using ˈjuzɪŋ |fuse fjuz, fɪuz |dish dɪʃ |vision ˈvɪʒən |Eden ˈidn̩ |cradle ˈkredl̩ |keep 'em ˈkipm̩

expiration ˌɛkspəˈreʃən
expiratory ɪkˈspaɪrəˌtorɪ, -ˌtɔrɪ; S -ˌtorɪ
expire ɪkˈspaɪr; ES -ˈspaɪə(r; |-d -d
expiry ɪkˈspaɪrɪ, ˈɛkspərɪ
explain ɪkˈsplen |-ed -d
explanation ˌɛkspləˈneʃən
explanatory ɪkˈsplænəˌtorɪ, -ˌtɔrɪ; S -ˌtorɪ
expletive ˈɛksplɪtɪv
explicable ˈɛksplɪkəbḷ, less freq. ɪkˈsplɪkəbḷ—
cf inexplicable
explicate ˈɛksplɪˌket |-d -ɪd |-tive -ɪv
explication ˌɛksplɪˈkeʃən
explicatory ˈɛksplɪkəˌtorɪ, -ˌtɔrɪ; S -ˌtorɪ;
Brit ˈɛksplɪˌketərɪ, ɪksˈplɪkətərɪ, -trɪ
explicit 'here ends' ˈɛksplɪsɪt
explicit 'precise' ɪkˈsplɪsɪt
explode ɪkˈsplod |-d -ɪd
exploit n ˈɛksplɔɪt, ɪkˈsplɔɪt
exploit v ɪkˈsplɔɪt |-ed -ɪd
exploitation ˌɛksplɔɪˈteʃən
exploration ˌɛkspləˈreʃən, -splo-
exploratory ɪkˈsplorəˌtorɪ, -ˈsplɔrəˌtɔrɪ; S
ɪkˈsplorəˌtorɪ
explore ɪkˈsplor, -ˈsplɔr; ES ɪkˈsploə(r, E+
-ˈsplɔə(r; |-d -d
explosion ɪkˈsploʒən |-sive -sɪv
exponent ɪkˈsponənt
exponential ˌɛkspoˈnɛnʃəl |-ly -ɪ
export n ˈɛksport, -pɔrt; ES -poət, E+-pɔət
export v ɪksˈport, -ˈpɔrt; ES ɪksˈpoət, E+
-ˈpɔət; |-ed -ɪd—acct+ˈexport, esp. in con-
trast to import v.
exportation ˌɛksporˈteʃən, -pɔr-; ES -poə-,
E+-pɔə-
expose ɪkˈspoz |-s -ɪz |-d -d |-dness -ɪdnɪs,
-dnɪs
exposé ˌɛkspoˈze
exposition ˌɛkspəˈzɪʃən
expositor ɪkˈspazɪtə; ES ɪkˈspazɪtə(r, -ˈspɒz-;
|-tory -ˌtorɪ, -ˌtɔrɪ; S -ˌtorɪ
ex post facto ˈɛksˌpostˈfækto
expostulate ɪkˈspɑstʃəˌlet; ES+-ˈspɒs-; |-d
-ɪd
expostulation ɪkˌspɑstʃəˈleʃən; ES+-ˌspɒs-
expostulatory ɪkˈspɑstʃələˌtorɪ, -ˌtɔrɪ; S
-ˌtorɪ, ES+-ˈspɒs-
exposure ɪkˈspoʒə; ES -ˈspoʒə(r
expound ɪkˈspaund |-ed -ɪd
ex-president ˈɛksˈprɛzədənt, -ˈprɛzdənt

express ɪkˈsprɛs |-es -ɪz |-ed -t |-ive -ɪv
expressible ɪkˈsprɛsəbḷ |-bly -blɪ
expression ɪkˈsprɛʃən |-ism -ˌɪzəm |-ist -ɪst
expressionistic ɪkˌsprɛʃənˈɪstɪk
expressman ɪkˈsprɛsmən |-men -mən
expropriate ɛksˈproprɪˌet |-d -ɪd
expropriation ɛksˌproprɪˈeʃən, ˌɛkspropri-
expulsion ɪkˈspʌlʃən |-sive -sɪv
expunction ɪkˈspʌŋkʃən
expunge ɪkˈspʌndʒ |-s -ɪz |-d -d
expurgate adj ˈɛkspɝˌgɪt, -ˌget; ES -pə-
expurgate v ˈɛkspɝˌget, ɪkˈspɝget; ES
ˈɛkspə-, -ˈspɝ-, -ˈspɝ-; |-d -ɪd
expurgation ˌɛkspɝˈgeʃən; ES ˌɛkspə-
expurgatory ɪkˈspɝgəˌtorɪ, -ˌtɔrɪ; ES ɪk-
ˈspɝgəˌtorɪ, -ˈspɝ-, E+-ˌtɔrɪ
exquisite ˈɛkskwɪzɪt, less freq. ɪkˈskwɪzɪt
exscind ɛkˈsɪnd |-ed -ɪd
exsect ɛkˈsɛkt |-ed -ɪd
exsert ɛkˈsɝt; ES -ˈsɝt, -ˈsɝt; |-ed -ɪd
ex-service ˈɛksˈsɝvɪs; ES -ˈsɝv-, -ˈsɝv-
exsiccate ˈɛksɪˌket |-d -ɪd
exsufflicate adj ɛksˈsʌflɪˌket, -kɪt
extant ɪkˈstænt, ˈɛkstənt
extemporal ɪkˈstɛmpərəl |-ly -ɪ
extemporaneity ɪkˌstɛmpərəˈniətɪ
extemporaneous ɪkˌstɛmpəˈreniəs
extemporary ɪkˈstɛmpəˌrɛrɪ |-rarily -rəlɪ, esp.
if emph. ɪkˌstɛmpəˈrerəlɪ
extempore ɪkˈstɛmpərɪ, -ˌri
extemporize ɪkˈstɛmpəˌraɪz |-s -ɪz |-d -d
extend ɪkˈstɛnd |-ed -ɪd
extensibility ɪkˌstɛnsəˈbɪlətɪ
extensible ɪkˈstɛnsəbḷ
extensile ɪkˈstɛnsḷ, -sɪl
extensimeter ˌɛkstɛnˈsɪmətə; ES -ˈsɪmətə(r
extension ɪkˈstɛnʃən |-sive -sɪv
extensometer ˌɛkstɛnˈsamətə; ES -ˈsamətə(r,
-ˈsɒm-
extensor ɪkˈstɛnsə, as L -sɔr; ES -sə(r,
-sɔə(r
extent ɪkˈstɛnt
extenuate ɪkˈstɛnjuˌet |-d -ɪd |-tive -ɪv
extenuation ɪkˌstɛnjuˈeʃən
extenuatory ɪkˈstɛnjuəˌtorɪ, -ˌtɔrɪ-; S -ˌtorɪ
exterior ɪkˈstɪrɪə; ES -ˈstɪrɪ·ə(r
exteriorize ɪkˈstɪrɪəˌraɪz |-s -ɪz |-d -d
exterminable ɪkˈstɝmɪnəbḷ; ES -ˈstɝm-,
-ˈstɝm-

---

exterminate ɪkˈstɝməˌnet; ES -ˈstɜm-, -ˈstɝm-; |-d -ɪd |-tor -ɚ; ES -ə(r
extermination ɪkˌstɝməˈneʃən; ES -ˌstɜm-, -ˌstɝm-
external ɪkˈstɝnḷ; ES -ˈstɜnḷ, -ˈstɝnḷ; |-ly -ɪ
externality ˌɛkstɚˈnælətɪ; ES ˌɛkstə-
exterritorial ˌɛkstɛrəˈtorɪəl, -ˈtɔr-; S -ˈtor-; |-ly -ɪ
exterritoriality ɛksˌtɛrəˌtorɪˈælətɪ, ˌɛkstɛrə-, -ˌtɔr-; S -ˌtor-
extinct ɪkˈstɪŋkt |-ction -ˈstɪŋkʃən
extinguish ɪkˈstɪŋgwɪʃ |-es -ɪz |-ed -t
extirpate ˈɛkstɚˌpet, ɪkˈstɝpet; ES -stə-, -ˈstɜ-, -ˈstɝ-; |-d -ɪd
extirpation ˌɛkstɚˈpeʃən; ES ˌɛkstə-
extol, -ll ɪkˈstɑl, -ˈstɒl, -ˈstol |-(l)ed -d
Exton ˈɛkstən
extort ɪkˈstɔrt; ES -ˈstɔət; |-ed -ɪd
extortion ɪkˈstɔrʃən; ES -ˈstɔəʃən; |-ary -ˌɛrɪ |-ate -ɪt
extra ˈɛkstrə—ˈɛkstrɪ *is often heard from educated speakers, esp. before a vowel* (extra allowance).
extract *n* ˈɛkstrækt
extract *v* ɪkˈstrækt |-ed -ɪd |-ction -kʃən
extractable, -ible ɪkˈstræktəbḷ
extracurricular ˌɛkstrəkəˈrɪkjəlɚ; ES -lə(r
extraditable ˈɛkstrəˌdaɪtəbḷ
extradite ˈɛkstrəˌdaɪt |-dited -ˌdaɪtɪd
extradition ˌɛkstrəˈdɪʃən
extrados ɛkˈstredɑs; ES+-dɒs; |-es -ɪz
extrajudicial ˌɛkstrədʒuˈdɪʃəl, -dʒɪu- |-ly -ɪ
extralegal ˌɛkstrəˈligḷ |-ly -ɪ
extramarital ˌɛkstrəˈmærətḷ |-ly -ɪ
extramundane ˌɛkstrəˈmʌnden
extramural ˌɛkstrəˈmjurəl, -ˈmɪu- |-ly -ɪ
extraneous ɪkˈstrenɪəs
extraofficial ˌɛkstrɪəˈfɪʃəl, ˌɛkstrə·əˈfɪʃəl
extraordinarily ɪkˈstrɔrdṇˌɛrəlɪ, *esp. if emph.* ɪkˌstrɔrdṇˈɛrəlɪ; ES -əədṇ-
extraordinary ɪkˈstrɔrdṇˌɛrɪ, *envoy* ˌɛkstrəˈɔrdṇˌɛrɪ, -trɪ-; ES -əədṇ-
extraterritorial ˌɛkstrəˌtɛrəˈtorɪəl, -ˈtɔr-; S -ˈtor-; |-ly -ɪ
extraterritoriality ˌɛkstrəˌtɛrəˌtorɪˈælətɪ, -ˌtɔr-; S -ˌtor-
extravagance ɪkˈstrævəgəns |-cy -ɪ |-ant -ənt
extravaganza ɪkˌstrævəˈgænzə
extravert *n* ˈɛkstrəˌvɝt; ES -ˌvɜt, -ˌvɝt

extravert *v* ˌɛkstrəˈvɝt; ES -ˈvɜt, -ˈvɝt; |-ed -ɪd
extreme ɪkˈstrim (the ˈexˌtreme ˈverge)
extremism ɪkˈstrimɪzəm |-ist -ɪst
extremity ɪkˈstrɛmətɪ
extricable ˈɛkstrɪkəbḷ |-bly -blɪ
extricate ˈɛkstrɪˌket |-cated -ˌketɪd
extrication ˌɛkstrɪˈkeʃən
extrinsic ɛkˈstrɪnsɪk |-al -ḷ |-ally -ḷɪ, -ɪklɪ
extrorse ɛkˈstrɔrs; ES -ˈstrɔəs
extroversion ˌɛkstroˈvɝʃən, -ˈvɝʒ-; ES -ˈvɝ-, -ˈvɝ-
extrovert *n* ˈɛkstroˌvɝt; ES -ˌvɜt, -ˌvɝt
extrovert *v* ˌɛkstroˈvɝt; ES -ˈvɜt, -ˈvɝt; |-ed -ɪd
extrude ɪkˈstrud, -ˈstrɪud |-d -ɪd
extrusion ɪkˈstruʒən, -ˈstrɪu- |-sive -sɪv
exuberance ɪgˈzjubərəns, -ˈzɪu-, -ˈzu- |-cy -ɪ |-ant -ənt
exude ɪgˈzjud, -ˈzɪud, -ˈzud, ɪkˈsjud, -ˈsɪud, -ˈsud |-d -ɪd |exudation ˌɛksjuˈdeʃən
exult ɪgˈzʌlt |-ed -ɪd |-ant -ṇt
exultation ˌɛgzʌlˈteʃən, ˌɛksʌl-
-ey *ending see* -y
eyas ˈaɪəs |-es -ɪz
Eyck, van vænˈaɪk
eye aɪ |eyed aɪd |-ful -ˌfʊl |-fuls -ˌfʊlz
eyeglass ˈaɪˌglæs; E+-ˌglas, -ˌglɑs; |-es -ɪz
eyehole ˈaɪˌhol
eyelash ˈaɪˌlæʃ |-es -ɪz
eyeless ˈaɪlɪs
eyelet ˈaɪlɪt |-ed -ɪd |-lid ˈaɪˌlɪd
eye-minded ˈaɪˈmaɪndɪd (ˈeye-ˌminded ˈman)
eye-opener ˈaɪˌopənɚ, -ˌopnɚ; ES -nə(r
eyeservant ˈaɪˌsɝvənt; ES -ˌsɜv-, -ˌsɝv-
eyeservice ˈaɪˌsɝvɪs; ES -ˌsɜv-, -ˌsɝv-
eyeshot ˈaɪˌʃɑt; ES+-ˌʃɒt
eyesight ˈaɪˌsaɪt
eyesore ˈaɪˌsor, -ˌsɔr; ES -ˌsoə(r, E+-ˌsɔə(r
eyestrain ˈaɪˌstren
eyetooth ˈaɪˈtuθ, -ˌtuθ |-teeth -ˈtiθ, -ˌtiθ
eyewash ˈaɪˌwɑʃ, -ˌwɔʃ, -ˌwɒʃ |-es -ɪz
eyewater ˈaɪˌwɔtɚ, -ˌwɑtɚ, -ˌwɒtɚ; ES -tə(r
eyewitness ˈaɪˈwɪtnɪs, -ˌwɪt- |-es -ɪz |-ed -t
eyne *'eyes'* aɪn
eyre, E- ɛr, ær; E ɛə(r, ES æə(r
eyrie, -ry ˈɛrɪ, ˈærɪ, ˈɪrɪ; S ˈærɪ, ˈɪrɪ
Ezekiel ɪˈzikɪəl, -kjəl
Ezra ˈɛzrə

F

F, f *letter* ɛf |*pl* F's, Fs, *poss* F's ɛfs
fa *music* fɑ
Faber *Eng name* ˈfebɚ, *Ger name* ˈfabɚ; ES -bə(r
Fabian ˈfebɪən |-ism -ˌɪzəm |-ist -ɪst
Fabius ˈfebɪəs |-'s -ɪz
fable ˈfebḷ |-d -d |-ling ˈfeblɪŋ, -bḷɪŋ
Fabre ˈfabɚ, ˈfabrə; ES -bə(r, -brə; (*Fr* fabr)
fabric ˈfæbrɪk |-ation ˌfæbrɪˈkeʃən
fabricate ˈfæbrɪˌket |-d -ɪd |-tor -ɚ; ES -ə(r
Fabrikoid ˈfæbrɪˌkɔɪd
fabulous ˈfæbjələs
Fabyan ˈfebɪən
façade fəˈsad, fæˈsad |-d -ɪd (*Fr* faˈsad)
face fes |faces ˈfesɪz |faced fest
facet ˈfæsɪt |-ed -ɪd
facetiae fəˈsiʃɪˌi
facetious fəˈsiʃəs
facial ˈfeʃəl |-ly -ɪ
facile ˈfæsḷ, -sɪl
facilely ˈfæsḷɪ, -sḷɪ, -sɪlɪ, -sɪllɪ
facilitate fəˈsɪləˌtet |-tated -ˌtetɪd
facilitation fəˌsɪləˈteʃən
facility fəˈsɪlətɪ
facing ˈfesɪŋ
facsimile fækˈsɪməlɪ, -ˈsɪməˌli |-s -z
fact fækt |facts fækts, fæks
faction ˈfækʃən |-tious -ʃəs
factitious fækˈtɪʃəs
factitive ˈfæktətɪv
factor ˈfæktɚ; ES ˈfæktə(r; |-ed -d |-ing ˈfæktərɪŋ, ˈfæktrɪŋ
factorial fækˈtorɪəl, -ˈtɔrɪəl; S -ˈtorɪəl
factory ˈfæktrɪ, ˈfæktərɪ
factotum fækˈtotəm
factual ˈfæktʃuəl |-ly -ɪ
facultative ˈfækḷˌtetɪv
faculty ˈfækḷtɪ
fad fæd |faddish ˈfædɪʃ |faddist ˈfædɪst
fade fed |faded ˈfedɪd
faeces ˈfisɪz
faerie, -ry, F- ˈfeərɪ, ˈfɛrɪ, ˈfeːrɪ, ˈfærɪ; S ˈfeərɪ, ˈfærɪ, ˈfɛrɪ—*Some speakers distinguish* faerie & fairy *from* ferry *by a longer* ɛ.
Faeroes ˈfɛroz, ˈfæroz, ˈferoz; S ˈfæroz, ˈferoz

fag fæg |fagged fægd
Fagin ˈfegɪn
fagot, fagg- ˈfægət |-ed -ɪd
Fahrenheit ˈfærənˌhaɪt, ˈfarən-
faience faɪˈɑns, feˈɑns (*Fr* faˈjãːs)
fail fel |failed feld |-ure -jɚ; ES -ʒ(r
fain fen
faineant ˈfenɪənt, -njənt (*Fr* feneˈã)
faint fent |fainted ˈfentɪd
fainthearted ˈfentˈhɑrtɪd; ES -ˈhɑːtɪd, E+ -ˈhaːt-; (ˈfaintˌhearted ˈhero)
fair fɛr, fær; E fɛə(r, ES fæə(r; |-ed -d |-er -ɚ; ES -ə(r
Fairfax ˈfɛrˌfæks, ˈfær-; E ˈfɛə-, ES ˈfæə-; |-fax's -ˌfæksɪz
Fair Haven, Fairhaven ˈfɛrˈhevən, ˈfær-; E ˈfɛə-, ES ˈfæə-
fair-lead ˈfɛrˌlid, ˈfær-; E ˈfɛə-, ES ˈfæə-
fair-minded ˈfɛrˈmaɪndɪd, ˈfær-; E ˈfɛə-, ES ˈfæə-
Fairport ˈfɛrˌport, ˈfær-, -ˌpɔrt; E ˈfɛəˌpoət, ˈfæə-, -ˌpɔət; S ˈfæəˌpoət
fair-spoken ˈfɛrˈspokən, ˈfær-; E ˈfɛə-, ES ˈfæə-; (ˈfair-ˌspoken ˈman)
Fairview ˈfɛrˌvju, ˈfær-, -ˌvɪu; E ˈfɛə-, ES ˈfæə-
fairway ˈfɛrˌwe, ˈfær-; E ˈfɛə-, ES ˈfæə-
Fairweather ˈfɛrˌwɛðɚ, ˈfær-; E ˈfɛəˌwɛðə(r, ES ˈfæə-
fairy ˈfɛrɪ, ˈfeːrɪ, ˈfærɪ; S ˈfærɪ, ˈfɛrɪ; |-land -ˌlænd—*see note at* faerie
fait accompli *Fr* fɛtakõˈpli
faith feθ |-ths -θs |-ful -fəl |-fully -fəlɪ
Faiyum faɪˈjum
fake fek |faked fekt |faker ˈfekɚ; ES ˈfekə(r
fakir fəˈkɪr, ˈfekɚ; ES fəˈkɪə(r, ˈfekə(r
Falangist fəˈlændʒɪst
falchion ˈfɔltʃən, ˈfɔlʃən
falcon ˈfɔlkən, *esp. among falconers* ˈfɔkən
Falconbridge ˈfɔkənˌbrɪdʒ, ˈfɔlkən- |-'s -ɪz
Falconer ˈfɔknɚ, ˈfɔlkənɚ; ES -nə(r
falderal ˈfældəˌræl—*see* folderol
Falernian fəˈlɝnɪən, fæ-; ES -ˈlɜn-, -ˈlɜn-
Falkirk ˈfɔlkɝk, ˈfɔk-; ES -kɜk, -kɝk
Falkland ˈfɔklənd, ˈfɔlklənd
Falkner ˈfɔknɚ; ES ˈfɔknə(r
fall fɔl |fell fɛl |fallen ˈfɔlən, fɔln

Key: *See in full* §§3–47. bee bi |pity ˈpɪtɪ (§6) |rate ret |yet jɛt |sang sæŋ |angry ˈæŋ·grɪ |bath bæθ; E baθ (§10) |ah ɑ |far fɑr |watch watʃ, wɒtʃ (§12) |jaw dʒɔ |gorge gɔrdʒ |go go

Words below that have æ before r (carry **'kærı**) *are often pronounced in N with* ε (**'kεrı**, *§94*)
Words below in which a *before* r (farm) *is sounded* ɑ *are often pronounced in E with* a (fɑːm)

fallacy **'fæləsı** |-lacious fə'leʃəs
fallibility ˌfælə'bılətı
fallible **'fæləbḷ** |fallibly **'fæləblı**
Falloden **'fælədn̩**
Fallon **'fælən**
Fallopian fə'lopıən, fæ-
fallow **'fælo**, **'fælə** |-ed -d |-ing **'fæləwıŋ**
Falmouth **'fælməθ**
false fɔls |falsed fɔlst
falsehearted **'fɔls'hɑrtıd**; ES **'fɔls'hɑːtıd**;
    ('false,hearted 'knave)
falsehood **'fɔls·hud**
falsetto fɔl'seto, -'setə
falsification ˌfɔlsəfə'keʃən
falsify **'fɔlsəˌfaı** |falsified **'fɔlsəˌfaıd**
falsity **'fɔlsətı**
Falstaff **'fɔlstæf**; E+-staf, -stɑf
Falstaffian fɔl'stæfıən; E+-'stɑf-, -'stɑf-
falter **'fɔltɚ**; ES **'fɔltə(r**; |-ed -d |-ing **'fɔltərıŋ**
    'fɔltrıŋ
fame fem |famed femd |famous **'feməs**
familiar fə'mıljɚ; ES fə'mıljə(r
familiarity fəˌmılı'ærətı, fəˌmıljı'ærətı, fə-
    ˌmıl'jærətı
familiarize fə'mıljəˌraız |-s -ız |-d -d
family **'fæmlı**, **'fæməlı**
famine **'fæmın**
famish **'fæmıʃ** |famishes **'fæmıʃız** |-ed -t
fan fæn |fanned fænd
fanatic fə'nætık |-al -ḷ |-ally -ḷı, -ıklı
fanaticism fə'nætəˌsızəm
fanciful **'fænsıfəl** |-ly -ı
fancy **'fænsı** |fancied **'fænsıd**
fancy-free **'fænsı'fri** ('fancy-ˌfree 'maiden)
fandango fæn'dæŋgo
fane fen
Faneuil **'fænḷ**, **'fænjəl**, -juəl, *older* **'fʌnḷ**
fanfare **'fænˌfer**, -ˌfær; E -ˌfeə(r, ES -ˌfæə(r
fanfaron **'fænfəˌran**; ES+-ˌrɒn
fanfaronade ˌfænfərə'ned, -færə-
fang fæŋ |fanged fæŋd
fangle **'fæŋgḷ** |fangled **'fæŋgḷd**
fanlight **'fænˌlaıt** |-ed -ıd
fanner **'fænɚ**; ES **'fænə(r**
fantail **'fænˌtel** |fantailed **'fænˌteld**
fan-tan **'fænˌtæn**
fantasia fæn'teʒıə, -ʒə, -zıə (*It* ˌfanta'ziːɑ)

fantasm **'fæntæzəm**
fantastic fæn'tæstık |-al -ḷ |-ally -ḷı, -ıklı
fantasy **'fæntəsı**, **'fæntəzı** |-ied -d
far fɑr; ES fɑː(r
farad **'færəd**, **'færæd**
Faraday, f- **'færədı**, **'færəˌde**
faradic fə'rædık, fæ'rædık
faraway *adj, n* **'fɑrə'we** ('fɑrəˌway 'look)
farce fɑrs; ES fɑːs; |-s -ız |-d -t
farcical **'fɑrsıkḷ**; ES **'fɑːsıkḷ**; |-ly -ı, -ıklı
fardle **'fɑrdḷ**; ES **'fɑːdḷ**
fare fer, fær; E feə(r, ES fæə(r; |-ed -d
farewell *intj* **'fer'wεl**, **'fær-**; ES *see* fare
farewell *n* ˌfer'wεl, ˌfær-; ES *see* fare; ('fare-
    ˌwell 'speech)
farfetched **'fɑr'fεtʃt**; ES **'fɑː-**; ('fɑrˌfetched
    'pun)
far-flung **'fɑr'flʌŋ**; ES **'fɑː'flʌŋ**
far-forth **'fɑrˌforθ**, -ˌfɔrθ; ES **'fɑːˌfoəθ**, E+
    -ˌfɔəθ; *acct varies*
Fargo **'fɑrgo**; ES **'fɑːgo**
Faribault **'fεrəˌbo**, **'færəˌbo**; S **'færəˌbo**
farina fə'rinə, -'raınə |-naceous ˌfærə'neʃəs
farinose **'færəˌnos**
farm fɑrm; ES fɑːm; |-ed -d |-er -ɚ; ES -ə(r
farmer-general **'fɑrmɚ'dʒεnərəl**, -'dʒεnrəl;
    ES **'fɑːmə-**
farmhouse **'fɑrmˌhaus**; ES **'fɑːmˌhaus**; |-ses
    -zız
farmstead **'fɑrmˌsted**; ES **'fɑːmˌsted**
farmyard **'fɑrmˌjɑrd**; ES **'fɑːmˌjɑːd**
Farne Islands **'fɑrnˌaıləndz**, -ənz; ES **'fɑːn-**
Farnham **'fɑrnəm**; ES **'fɑːn-**
faro **'fεro**, **'færo**; S **'færo**
Faroe **'fεro**, **'færo**, **'fero**
Faroese ˌfεro'iz, ˌfær-, ˌfer-
far-off *n, adj* **'fɑr'ɔf**, -'ɒf ('fɑrˌoff 'look)
Farquhar **'fɑrkwɚ**, -kwɑr, -kɚ; ES **'fɑːkwə(r**,
    -kwɑː(r, -kə(r
farrago fə'rego, fə'rago
Farragut **'færəgət**, **'færəˌgʌt**
Farrand **'færənd**
Farrar **'færɚ**; ES **'færə(r**; *Geraldine* fə'rɑr;
    ES fə'rɑː(r
far-reaching **'fɑr'ritʃıŋ**; ES **'fɑː'ritʃıŋ**
Farrell **'færəl**
Farrer **'færɚ**; ES **'færə(r**

|full fʊl |tooth tuθ |further **'fɝðɚ**; ES **'fɝðə**; |custom **'kʌstəm** |while hwaıl |how haʊ |toy tɔı
|using **'juzıŋ** |fuse fjuz, fruz |dish dıʃ |vision **'vıʒən** |Eden **'idn̩** |cradle **'kredḷ** |keep 'em **'kipm̩**

Words below that have æ before r (carry 'kærɪ) *are often pronounced in N with* ɛ ('kɛrɪ, §94)
Words below in which a *before* r (farm) *is sounded* ɑ *are often pronounced in E with* a (fɑːm)

farrier 'færɪɚ; ES 'færɪ·ə(r; |-y -ɪ
farrow 'færo, -ə |-ed -d |-ing 'færəwɪŋ
farse fɑrs; ES fɑːs; |-s -ɪz |-d -t
farseeing 'fɑr'siɪŋ; ES 'fɑː'siɪŋ
farsighted 'fɑr'saɪtɪd; ES 'fɑː'saɪtɪd
farther 'fɑrðɚ; ES 'fɑːðə(r; |-most -ˌmost, -məst
farthest 'fɑrðɪst; ES 'fɑːðɪst
farthing 'fɑrðɪŋ; ES 'fɑːðɪŋ
farthingale 'fɑrðɪŋˌgel; ES 'fɑːðɪŋˌgel
fasces 'fæsiz *L pl of* fascis 'fæsɪs
fasciate 'fæʃɪˌet |fasciated 'fæʃɪˌetɪd
fascicle 'fæsɪk] |fasicled 'fæsɪk]d
fascinate 'fæsn̩ˌet |-d -ɪd |-tor -ɚ; ES -ə(r
fascination ˌfæsn̩'eʃən
fascine fæ'sin, fə'sin |-d -d
fascis 'fæsɪs |*pl* fasces 'fæsiz
Fascism 'fæʃˌɪzəm |-ist -ɪst
Fascisti fə'ʃɪsti, fæ'ʃɪsti (*It* fɑ'ʃisti)
Fascistic fə'ʃɪstɪk |-ally -ḷɪ, -ɪklɪ
fashion 'fæʃən |-ed -d |-ing 'fæʃənɪŋ, 'fæʃnɪŋ
fashionable 'fæʃnəb], 'fæʃənəb] |-bly -blɪ
Fashoda fə'ʃodə
fast fæst; E+fast, fɑst; |-ed -ɪd
fasten 'fæsn̩; E+'fɑsn̩, 'fɑsn̩; |-ed -d |-ing -snɪŋ, -sn̩ɪŋ
fastidious fæs'tɪdɪəs, -djəs
fastness 'fæstnɪs |-es -ɪz; E *see* fast
Fastolf, -e 'fæstɑlf, -tɒlf
fat fæt |fatted 'fætɪd
fatal 'fetḷ |-ly -ɪ |-ism -ˌɪzəm |-ist -ɪst
fatalistic ˌfetḷ'ɪstɪk |-ally -ḷɪ, -ɪklɪ
fatality fe'tælətɪ, fə'tælətɪ, fɪ'tælətɪ
Fata Morgana 'fɑtəmɔr'gɑnə; ES -mɔə'gɑnə
father 'fɑðɚ; ES -ðə(r, E+'fɑð-; |-hood -ˌhʊd
father-in-law 'fɑðɚɪnˌlɔ, 'fɑðɚnˌlɔ; ES 'fɑ-ðərɪnˌlɔ, 'fɑðənˌlɔ, E+'fɑð-
fatherland 'fɑðɚˌlænd; ES 'fɑðɚ-, E+'fɑðə-
fathers-in-law 'fɑðɚzɪnˌlɔ, 'fɑðɚzn̩ˌlɔ; ES 'fɑðəzɪnˌlɔ, 'fɑðəzn̩ˌlɔ, E+'fɑð-
fathom 'fæðəm |fathomed 'fæðəmd
fatigable 'fætɪgəb]
fatigate 'fætɪˌget |fatigated 'fætɪˌgetɪd
fatigue fə'tig |fatigued fə'tigd
Fatima 'fætɪmə, 'fɑtɪmə
fatling 'fætlɪŋ
fatten 'fætn̩ |-ed -d |-ing 'fætn̩ɪŋ, 'fætnɪŋ

fattish 'fætɪʃ |fatty 'fætɪ
fatuitous fə'tjuətəs, -'trʊ-, -'tu- |-ity -ətɪ
fatuous 'fætʃʊəs
fat-witted 'fæt'wɪtɪd ('fat-ˌwitted 'Falstaff)
fauces 'fɔsiz
faucet 'fɔsɪt, *occas.* 'fæsɪt, 'fɑsɪt
Faucit 'fɔsɪt
faugh fɔ, pf, *and various puffs of breath*
Faulconbridge 'fɔkənˌbrɪdʒ, 'fɔlkən- |-'s -ɪz
Faulkner 'fɔknɚ; ES 'fɔknə(r
fault fɔlt |faulted 'fɔltɪd |faulty 'fɔltɪ
faultfinding 'fɔltˌfaɪndɪŋ
faun fɔn |fauna 'fɔnə
Fauntleroy 'fɔntləˌrɔɪ, 'fɒnt-, 'fɑnt-
Fauquier fɔ'kɪr; ES -'kɪə(r, S+-'kɛə(r
Faust faʊst |Faustian 'faʊstɪən, 'fɒs-
Faustus 'fɔstəs |Faustus's 'fɔstəsɪz
faux pas 'fo'pɑ |*pl* -'pɑz (*Fr pl* -'pɑ)
Faversham 'fævɚʃəm; ES 'fævə-
favor 'fevɚ; ES 'fevə(r; |-ed -d |-ing 'fevrɪŋ, 'fevərɪŋ |-able 'fevrəb], 'fevərəb] |-bly -blɪ
favorite 'fevrɪt, 'fevərɪt |-tism -ˌɪzəm
Fawcett 'fɔsɪt
Fawkes fɔks |Fawkes's |'fɔksɪz
fawn fɔn |fawned fɔnd
fay fe
Fayal faɪ'ɑl
Fayum faɪ'jum
faze fez |fazes 'fezɪz |fazed fezd—*less properly spelt* feaze
feal '*turf*' fil
fealty 'fiəltɪ, 'filtɪ
fear fɪr; ES fɪə(r, S+fɛə(r, fjɪə(r, fjɛə(r; |-ful -fəl |-fully -fəlɪ, -flɪ
fearnought 'fɪrˌnɔt; ES 'fɪə-, S+'fɛə-, 'fjɪə-, 'fjɛə-
fearsome 'fɪrsəm; ES 'fɪəsəm, S+'fɛə-, 'fjɪə-, 'fjɛə-
feasance 'fizn̩s
feasibility ˌfizə'bɪlətɪ
feasible 'fizəb] |-bly -blɪ
feast fist |feasted 'fistɪd
feat fit
feather 'fɛðɚ; ES 'fɛðə(r; |-ed -d |-ing 'fɛðərɪŋ, 'fɛðrɪŋ
featherbrain 'fɛðɚˌbren; ES 'fɛðə-; |-ed -d
featherhead 'fɛðɚˌhɛd; ES 'fɛðə-; |-ed -ɪd

featherstitch 'fɛðɚˌstɪtʃ; ES 'fɛðə-; |-es -ɪz
|-ed -t
featherweight 'fɛðɚˌwet; ES 'fɛðə-
feathery 'fɛðərɪ, 'fɛðrɪ
feature 'fitʃɚ; ES 'fitʃə(r; |-d -d
feaze 'feeze' fiz |-s -ɪz |-d -d, cf faze
febrifuge 'fɛbrɪˌfjudʒ, -ˌfrudʒ |-s -ɪz
febrile 'fibrəl, 'fɛb-
February 'fɛbruˌɛrɪ, 'fɛbjuˌɛrɪ, -ərɪ—Loss of
r in 'fɛbjuˌɛrɪ is due to dissimilation and the
influence of 'dʒænjuˌɛrɪ (§121).
feces 'fisiz
feckless 'fɛklɪs
feculence 'fɛkjuləns |-lent -lənt
fecund 'fikənd, 'fɛk-, -ʌnd
fecundate 'fikənˌdet, 'fɛk- |-d -ɪd
fecundity fɪ'kʌndətɪ
fed fɛd
federacy 'fɛdərəsɪ
federal, F- 'fɛdərəl, 'fɛdrəl |-ly -ɪ |-ist -ɪst
federalize 'fɛdərəlˌaɪz, 'fɛdrəl- |-s -ɪz |-d -d
federate n, adj 'fɛdərɪt, 'fɛdrɪt
federate, v 'fɛdəˌret |-d -ɪd
federation ˌfɛdə'reʃən
fedora, F- fɪ'dorə, -'dɔrə; S -'dorə
fee fi |past & pptc feed fid
feeble 'fibl̩ |-bly -blɪ |-bler -blɚ; ES -blə(r;
|-blest -blɪst
feeble-minded 'fibl̩'maɪndɪd ('feeble-ˌminded
'man)
feed past & pptc of fee fid
feed v fid |fed fɛd
feedback 'fidˌbæk
feel fil |felt fɛlt
feere 'mate' arch. fɪr; ES fɪə(r, S+fɛə(r
fee-simple 'fi'sɪmpl̩
feet fit
feeze fiz |feezes 'fiziz |-d -d
feign fen |feigned fend |-edly -ɪdlɪ
feint fent |feinted 'fentɪd
feldspar 'fɛldˌspɑr, 'fɛl-; ES -ˌspɑ:(r, E+
-ˌspɑ:(r
Felicia fə'lɪʃɪə, -ʃə
felicitate fə'lɪsəˌtet |-tated -ˌtetɪd
felicitation fəˌlɪsə'teʃən
felicity fə'lɪsətɪ |-tous -təs
feline 'filaɪn
Felix 'filɪks |-'s -ɪz
fell past of fall fɛl

fell n, v, adj fɛl |felled fɛld
fellah 'fɛlə |Arab pl -ahin, -aheen ˌfɛlə'hin
fellmonger 'fɛlˌmʌŋgɚ; ES -gə(r
felloe 'wheel rim' 'fɛlo, -ə—Felloe, mainly
Brit, comes from the OE pl felga; cf felly.
fellow 'fɛlo, 'fɛlə |-ed -d |-ship -ˌʃɪp
felly 'wheel rim' 'fɛlɪ—Felly, Am and Brit,
comes from the OE dative sg felge; cf felloe.
felly adv 'cruelly' 'fɛllɪ, 'fɛlɪ
felon 'fɛlən |-y -ɪ |-lonious fə'lonɪəs, fɛ-
felsite 'fɛlsaɪt
felspar 'fɛlˌspɑr; ES -ˌspɑ:(r, E+-ˌspɑ:(r
felt past & pptc of feel fɛlt
felt n, v fɛlt |felted 'fɛltɪd
felucca fə'lʌkə, fɛ-
female 'fimel
feme fɛm
feme covert 'fɛm'kʌvɚt; ES -'kʌvət
feme sole 'fɛm'sol
feminacy 'fɛmənəsɪ |-neity ˌfɛmə'niətɪ
feminie 'fɛmənɪ
feminine 'fɛmənɪn |feminineness 'fɛmənɪnnɪs
femininity ˌfɛmə'nɪnətɪ
feminism 'fɛməˌnɪzəm |-nist -nɪst
femme de chambre Fr famdə'ʃɑ̃:br
femoral 'fɛmərəl
femur 'fimɚ; ES -mə(r; |-s -z |-mora 'fɛmərə
fen fɛn
fence fɛns |-s -ɪz |-d -t
fencible 'fɛnsəbl̩
fend fɛnd |fended 'fɛndɪd |-er -ɚ; ES -ə(r
Fénelon 'fɛnl̩ˌɑn, -ˌɒn (Fr fen'lõ)
Fenian 'finɪən, -njən |-ism -ˌɪzəm
fennel 'fɛnl̩
Fennimore Wis, Feni- Cooper 'fɛnəˌmor,
-ˌmɔr; ES -ˌmoə(r, E+-ˌmɔə(r
fenny 'fɛnɪ
Fenton 'fɛntən
fenugreek 'fɛnjuˌgrik
feod fjud, frud |-al -l̩ |-ary -ərɪ
feodality fju'dælətɪ, fru-
feoff fɛf, fif |-ed -t
feoffee fɛf'i, fif'i
feoffor 'fɛfɚ, 'fifɚ; ES -ə(r; (fɛf'i ən fɛf'ɔr)
feracious fə'reʃəs, fɛ-
feral 'fɪrəl
Ferber 'fɝbɚ; ES 'fɝbə(r, 'fɝbə(r
fer-de-lance Fr fɛrdə'lɑ̃:s
Ferdinand 'fɝdn̩ˌænd; ES 'fɝd-, 'fɝd-

|full ful |tooth tuθ |further 'fɝðɚ; ES 'fɝðə |custom 'kʌstəm |while hwaɪl |how haʊ |toy tɔɪ
|using 'juzɪŋ |fuse fjuz, fruz |dish dɪʃ |vision 'vɪʒən |Eden 'idn̩ |cradle 'kredl̩ |keep 'em 'kipm̩

fere *'mate' arch.* fɪr; ES fɪə(r, S+fɛə(r
feretory 'fɛrəˌtorɪ, -ˌtɔrɪ; S -ˌtorɪ
Ferguson, -sson 'fɝ·gəsn̩; ES 'fɝg-, 'fɝ·g-
Feringi fə'rɪŋgɪ
ferly 'fɝ·lɪ, 'fɛrlɪ; ES 'fɝlɪ, 'fɛəlɪ, 'fɝ·lɪ
ferment *n* 'fɝ·ment; ES 'fɝ-, 'fɝ·-
ferment *v* fə·'ment; ES fə-; |-ed -ɪd |-able -əb|
fermentation ˌfɝ·mən'teʃən, -mɛn-; ES ˌfɝ-, ˌfɝ·-
fern fɝn; ES fɝn, fɝ·n; |-ery -ərɪ, -rɪ
ferocious fə'roʃəs, fɪ-, *emph.*+'fi'roʃəs
ferocity fə'rasətɪ, fɪ-; ES+-'rɒs-
Ferrara fə'rɑrə, fɛ- (*It* fer'rɑːrɑ)
ferrate 'fɛret |-d -ɪd
ferret 'fɛrɪt |-ed -ɪd
ferriage 'fɛrɪɪdʒ |-s -ɪz
ferric 'fɛrɪk
ferrite 'fɛraɪt
ferroconcrete ˌfɛro'kɑnkrit, -kən'krit; ES+-ɒn-
ferromagnetic ˌfɛromæg'nɛtɪk
ferrous 'fɛrəs
ferruginous fɛ'rudʒənəs, fə-
ferrule *'ring'* 'fɛrəl |-d -d
ferry 'fɛrɪ |-ied -d |-boat -ˌbot
fertile 'fɝ·t|; ES 'fɝt|, 'fɝ·t|; |-tilely -t|ɪ, -t|ɪ
fertility fɝ·'tɪlətɪ; ES fɝ-, fɝ·-
fertilization ˌfɝ·t|ə'zeʃən, -aɪ'z-; ES ˌfɝt-, ˌfɝ·t-
fertilize 'fɝ·t|ˌaɪz; ES 'fɝt-, 'fɝ·t-; |-s -ɪz |-d -d
ferule *'ruler'* 'fɛrəl, 'fɛrul |-d -d
fervency 'fɝ·vənsɪ; ES 'fɝv-, 'fɝ·v-; |-ent -ənt
fervid 'fɝ·vɪd; ES 'fɝvɪd, 'fɝ·v-
fervor 'fɝ·vɚ; ES 'fɝvə(r, 'fɝ·və(r
fescue 'fɛskju, 'fɛskɪu
Fessenden 'fɛsn̩dən
festal 'fɛst| |-ly -ɪ
Feste 'fɛstɪ
fester 'fɛstɚ; ES -tə(r; |-ed -d |-ing 'fɛstərɪŋ, 'fɛstrɪŋ
festival 'fɛstəv|
festive 'fɛstɪv |-vity fɛs'tɪvətɪ
festoon fɛs'tun |-ed -d |-ery -ərɪ
fetal 'fit| |-ism -ˌɪzəm
fetation fi'teʃən
fetch fɛtʃ |fetches 'fɛtʃɪz |fetched fɛtʃt
fete, fête fet |-d -ɪd (*Fr* fɛːt)
feterita ˌfɛtə'ritə
feticide 'fitəˌsaɪd |-dal ˌfitə'saɪd|

fetid 'fɛtɪd, 'fitɪd
fetish, -ich 'fitɪʃ, 'fɛtɪʃ |-ed -t
fetlock 'fɛtˌlɑk; ES+-ˌlɒk; |-ed -t
fetter 'fɛtɚ; ES 'fɛtə(r; |-ed -d
fettle 'fɛt| |-d -d |-ling 'fɛt|ɪŋ, 'fɛtlɪŋ
fetus 'fitəs |-es -ɪz
Fetzer 'fɛtsɚ; ES 'fɛtsə(r
feu fju, fɪu |-ed -d
feud fjud, frud |-ist -ɪst
feudal 'fjud|, 'frud| |-ism -ˌɪzəm |-ist -ɪst |-ly -ɪ
feudalize 'fjud|ˌaɪz, 'frud- |-s -ɪz |-d -d
feudatory 'fjudəˌtorɪ, 'frud-, -ˌtɔrɪ; S -ˌtorɪ
fever 'fivɚ; ES 'fivə(r; |-ed -d |-ing 'fivərɪŋ, 'fivrɪŋ |-ous -vərəs, -vrəs
feverfew 'fivɚˌfju, -ˌfɪu; ES 'fivə-
Feversham 'fɛvɚʃəm; ES 'fɛvə-
few, F- fju, fru
Fewkes fjuks, fruks |-'s -ɪz
fey fe
fez, F- fɛz |fezzes 'fɛzɪz |fezzed fɛzd
fiacre fɪ'akɚ; ES -'akə(r; (*Fr* fjakr̩)
fiancé ˌfiɑn'se, fiˌɑn'se, fi'ɑnse (*Fr* fjɑ̃'se)
fiancée *pron. like* fiancé
Fianna Fail 'fiənə'fɔɪl, -'faɪl
fiasco fɪ'æsko
fiat 'faɪət, 'faɪæt |-ed -ɪd
fib fɪb |fibbed fɪbd
fiber, -bre 'faɪbɚ; ES 'faɪbə(r; |-ed, -d -d
fibril 'faɪbrəl, -brɪl |-led -d
fibrin 'faɪbrɪn |-ation ˌfaɪbrɪ'neʃən
fibrinogen faɪ'brɪnədʒən, -ˌdʒɛn
fibroid 'faɪbrɔɪd |fibrous 'faɪbrəs
fibster 'fɪbstɚ; ES 'fɪbstə(r
fibula 'fɪbjələ |-s -z |-lae -ˌli
Fichte 'fɪxtə |-tean -tɪən |-teanism -tɪənˌɪzəm
fichu 'fɪʃu, -ʃɪu, -ʃju (*Fr* fi'ʃy)
fickle 'fɪk|
fico 'fiko
fictile 'fɪkt|, -tɪl
fiction 'fɪkʃən |-al -| |-ally -|ɪ
fictitious fɪk'tɪʃəs |fictive 'fɪktɪv
fid fɪd |fidded 'fɪdɪd
fiddle 'fɪd| |-d -d |-ling 'fɪdlɪŋ, 'fɪd|ɪŋ
fiddle-dee-dee ˌfɪd|'di'di, ˌfɪd|dɪ'di
fiddle-faddle 'fɪd|ˌfæd| |-d -d |-ling -d|ɪŋ, -dlɪŋ
fiddlehead 'fɪd|ˌhɛd
fiddler 'fɪdlɚ, 'fɪd|ɚ; ES -ə(r

Key: *See in full* §§3–47.　bee bi |pity 'pɪtɪ (§6) |rate ret |yet jɛt |sang sæŋ |angry 'æŋ·grɪ |bath bæθ; E baθ (§10) |ah ɑ |far fɑr |watch watʃ, wɒtʃ (§12) |jaw dʒɔ |gorge gɔrdʒ |go go

fiddlestick 'fɪdḷ,stɪk
Fidele fɪ'dili
Fidelia fɪ'diljə, -lɪə
Fidelio fɪ'delɪo, -ljo
fidelity faɪ'dɛlətɪ, fə-
fidget 'fɪdʒɪt |-ed -ɪd
fiducial fɪ'duʃəl, -'dɪu-, -'dju- |-ly -ɪ
fiduciary fɪ'duʃɪ,ɛrɪ, -'dɪu-, -'dju-, -ʃərɪ
fie faɪ |fie-fie adj, v 'faɪ,faɪ |-d -d
fief fif
field, F- fild |-ed -ɪd
fieldfare 'fild,fɛr, -,fær; E -,fɛə(r, ES -,fæə(r
Fielding 'fildɪŋ
fieldpiece 'fild,pis |-s -ɪz
fiend find |fiends findz, finz
fierce fɪrs; ES fɪəs, S+fɛəs, fjɛəs
fiery 'faɪrɪ, 'faɪərɪ
Fiesole fi'ezəlɪ (It 'fjɛːzole)
fiesta fɪ'ɛstə (Sp 'fjesta)
fife, F- faɪf |-d -t |-shire -ʃɪr, -ʃɚ; ES -ʃɪə(r, -ʃə(r
fifteen fɪf'tin, 'fɪf'tin ('fɪf,teen 'men)
fifteenth fɪf'tinθ, 'fɪf- |-ths -θs
fifth fɪfθ |-ths -θs
fifty 'fɪftɪ |-tieth -tɪɪθ |-fold -'fold ('fifty,fold 'loss)
fig fɪg
Figaro 'fɪgə,ro (Fr figa'ro)
fight faɪt |fought fɔt
figment 'fɪgmənt |figmental fɪg'mɛntḷ
figurate adj 'fɪgjərɪt
figurate v 'fɪgjə,ret |-d -ɪd
figuration ,fɪgjə'reʃən
figurative 'fɪgjərətɪv, 'fɪgərətɪv, 'fɪgrətɪv
figure 'fɪgjɚ, 'fɪgɚ; ES -ə(r; |-d -d |-ring -gjərɪŋ, -gərɪŋ, -grɪŋ—In America 'fɪgɚ, -ə(r is less freq.
figurehead 'fɪgjɚ,hɛd, 'fɪgɚ-; ES 'fɪgjə-, -gə-
figurine ,fɪgjə'rin
Fiji 'fidʒi |Figian fi'dʒɪən, 'fidʒɪən
filament n 'fɪləmənt |filimented 'fɪləməntɪd
filament v 'fɪlə,mɛnt |-ed -ɪd
filar 'faɪlɚ; ES -lə(r
filbert 'fɪlbɚt; ES 'fɪlbət
filch fɪltʃ |-es -ɪz |-ed -t
file faɪl |filed faɪld
filet 'fillet' 'fɪlɪt |fileted 'fɪlɪtɪd
filet de sole Eng 'fɪlɪəv'sol, Fr filɛ d'sɔl
filet mignon fi'le min'jɔ̃ (Fr filɛ mi'ɲ̃ɔ)

filial 'fɪlɪəl, -ljəl |-ly -ɪ
filiate 'fɪlɪ,et |-d -d |-tion ,fɪlɪ'eʃən
filibuster 'fɪlə,bʌstɚ; ES -,bʌstə(r; |-ed -d |-ing -,bʌstərɪŋ, -trɪŋ
filibusterer ,fɪlə'bʌstərɚ; ES -rə(r; |-terism -tə,rɪzəm |-terous -tərəs, -trəs
filiform 'fɪlə,fɔrm, 'faɪlə-; ES -,fɔəm
filigree 'fɪlə,gri |-d -d
filing 'faɪlɪŋ
Filipino ,fɪlə'pino |fem -pina -'pinə, -ɑ
fill fɪl |filled fɪld
fillet 'fɪlɪt |filleted 'fɪlɪtɪd
fillip 'fɪləp |filliped 'fɪləpt
Fillmore 'fɪlmor, -mɔr; ES -moə(r, E+-mɔə(r
filly 'fɪlɪ
film fɪlm |filmed fɪlmd
filose 'faɪlos
filter 'fɪltɚ; ES -tə(r; |-ed -d |-ing 'fɪltərɪŋ, 'fɪltrɪŋ
filterable 'fɪltərəbḷ, 'fɪltrəbḷ
filth fɪlθ |-ths -θs |-y -ɪ |filthily 'fɪlθəlɪ
filtrable 'fɪltrəbḷ
filtrate n 'fɪltret, 'fɪltrɪt
filtrate v 'fɪltret |-d -ɪd |-tion fɪl'treʃən
fin fɪn |finned fɪnd
finable 'faɪnəbḷ
finagle fə'negḷ |-nagler -'neglɚ; ES -lə(r
final 'faɪnḷ |-ism -,ɪzəm |-ist -ɪst |-ly -ɪ
finale fɪ'nalɪ (It fi'nɑːle)
finality faɪ'nælətɪ
finance fə'næns, 'faɪnæns |-s -ɪz |-d -t
financial fə'nænʃəl, faɪ'nænʃəl |-ly -ɪ
financier ,fɪnən'sɪr, ,faɪnən-; ES -'sɪə(r; |-ed -d
finback 'fɪn,bæk
finch fɪntʃ |finches 'fɪntʃɪz |finched fɪntʃt
Finchley 'fɪntʃlɪ
find faɪnd |found faʊnd
fin de siècle Fr fæɛdə'sjɛkḷ
Findlay 'fɪnlɪ, less freq. 'fɪndlɪ
fine faɪn |fined faɪnd |fineness 'faɪnnɪs
fineable 'faɪnəbḷ
finery 'faɪnərɪ
finespun 'faɪn'spʌn ('fine,spun 'theory)
finesse fə'nɛs |-s -ɪz |-d -t
Fingal 'fɪŋgḷ
finger 'fɪŋgɚ; ES 'fɪŋgə(r; |-ed -d |-ing 'fɪŋgərɪŋ, 'fɪŋgrɪŋ

|full fʊl |tooth tuθ |further 'fɝðɚ; ES 'fɝðə |custom 'kʌstəm |while hwaɪl |how haʊ |toy tɔɪ
|using 'juzɪŋ |fuse fjuz, fɪuz |dish dɪʃ |vision 'vɪʒən |Eden 'idn̩ |cradle 'kredḷ |keep 'em 'kipm̩

fingerer 'fɪŋgərɚ; ES -rə(r
fingerling 'fɪŋgəlɪŋ; ES 'fɪŋgə-
fingernail 'fɪŋgɚˌnel, ˌfɪŋgɚ'nel; ES -gə-
fingerprint 'fɪŋgɚˌprɪnt; ES 'fɪŋgə-; |-ed -ɪd
finial 'fɪnɪəl, 'faɪnɪəl
finical 'fɪnɪk| |-ly -ɪ, -ɪklɪ
finicking 'fɪnɪkɪŋ |-cky -kɪ
finikin 'fɪnɪkɪn
finis 'faɪnɪs |finises 'faɪnɪsɪz |+ 'fɪnɪs
finish 'fɪnɪʃ |-es -ɪz |-ed -t
Finistère Fr finis'tɛːr
Finisterre ˌfɪnɪs'tɛr; ES -'tɛə(r
finite 'faɪnaɪt
finitude 'fɪnəˌtjud, 'faɪnə-, -ˌtɪud, -ˌtud
Finland 'fɪnlənd
finland 'home of fish' 'fɪnˌlænd
Finlay 'fɪnlɪ |Finley 'fɪnlɪ
Finn fɪn |-ish -ɪʃ
finnan haddie 'fɪnən'hædɪ
finny 'fɪnɪ
fiord fjord, fjɔrd; ES fjoəd, E+fjɔəd
fipple 'fɪp|
fir fɝ; ES fɜ(r, fɝ; |-ry -ɪ
fire faɪr; ES faɪə(r; |-d -d |-ring 'faɪrɪŋ
firearm 'faɪrˌɑrm; ES -ˌɑːm, E+-ˌɑːm
fireball 'faɪrˌbɔl; ES 'faɪə-
firebird 'faɪrˌbɝd; ES 'faɪəˌbɜd, 'faɪəˌbɝd
firebox 'faɪrˌbɑks; ES 'faɪəˌbɑks, -ˌbɒks; |-es -ɪz
firebrand 'faɪrˌbrænd; ES 'faɪə-; |-ed -ɪd
firebreak 'faɪrˌbrek; ES 'faɪə-
firebrick 'faɪrˌbrɪk; ES 'faɪə-
firebug 'faɪrˌbʌg; ES 'faɪə-
firecracker 'faɪrˌkrækɚ; ES 'faɪəˌkrækə(r
firedamp 'faɪrˌdæmp; ES 'faɪə-
firedog 'faɪrˌdɔg, -ˌdɒg; ES 'faɪə-
firedrake 'faɪrˌdrek; ES 'faɪə-
fire-eater 'faɪrˌitɚ; ES 'faɪrˌitə(r
firefang 'faɪrˌfæŋ; ES 'faɪə-; |-ed -d
firefly 'faɪrˌflaɪ; ES 'faɪə-
fireguard 'faɪrˌgɑrd; ES 'faɪəˌgɑːd, E+-ˌgɑːd
firelock 'faɪrˌlɑk; ES 'faɪəˌlɑk, -ˌlɒk
fireman 'faɪrmən; ES 'faɪəmən; |-men -mən
fireplace 'faɪrˌples; ES 'faɪə-; |-s -ɪz
fireproof adj 'faɪr'pruf; ES 'faɪə-; ('fireˌproof 'vault)
fireproof v 'faɪrˌpruf; ES 'faɪə-; |-ed -t
fireside 'faɪrˌsaɪd; ES 'faɪə-
firetrap 'faɪrˌtræp; ES 'faɪə-

firewarden 'faɪrˌwɔrdn̩; ES 'faɪəˌwɔədn̩
firewater 'faɪrˌwɔtɚ, -ˌwɑtɚ, -ˌwɒtɚ; ES 'faɪə-, -tə(r
firewood 'faɪrˌwʊd; ES 'faɪə-
firework 'faɪrˌwɝk; ES 'faɪəˌwɜk, -ˌwɝk; |-s -s
firkin 'fɝkɪn; ES 'fɜkɪn, 'fɝ-; |-ed -d
firm fɝm; ES fɜm, fɝm; |-ed -d
firmament 'fɝməmənt; ES 'fɜm-, 'fɝm-
firman 'fɝmən, fɚ'man; ES 'fɜm-, 'fɝm-, fə-
Firman pers. name 'fɝmən; ES 'fɜm-, 'fɝm-
first fɝst; ES fɜst, fɝst
first-born 'fɝst'bɔrn; ES 'fɜst'bɔən, 'fɝst'bɔən
first-class 'fɝst'klæs; ES 'fɜst-, 'fɝst-, E+-'klas, -'klɑs; ('first-ˌclass 'fare)
firsthand 'fɝst'hænd; ES 'fɜst-, 'fɝst-
firstling 'fɝstlɪŋ; ES 'fɜst-, 'fɝst-
firstly 'fɝstlɪ; ES 'fɜstlɪ, 'fɝstlɪ
first-rate 'fɝs'tret, 'fɝst'ret; ES 'fɜ-, 'fɝ-
firth fɝθ; ES fɜθ, fɝθ; |-ths -θs
fisc fɪsk
fiscal 'fɪsk| |-ly -ɪ
fish fɪʃ |fishes 'fɪʃɪz |fished fɪʃt
fisher, F- 'fɪʃɚ; ES 'fɪʃə(r; |-man, -men -mən
fishery 'fɪʃərɪ
fishhook 'fɪʃˌhʊk, 'fɪʃʊk
fishmonger 'fɪʃˌmʌŋgɚ; ES -ˌmʌŋgə(r
fishwife 'fɪʃˌwaɪf |-'s -s, -vz |-wives -ˌwaɪvz
fishy 'fɪʃɪ
fisk, F- fɪsk
fissile 'fɪs|, 'fɪsɪl
fission 'fɪʃən |-ed -d
fissure 'fɪʃɚ; ES 'fɪʃə(r; |-d -d
fist fɪst |fisted 'fɪstɪd |-ic -ɪk |-ical -ɪk|
fisticuff 'fɪstɪˌkʌf |-ed -t
fistula 'fɪstʃʊlə |-s -z |-lae -ˌli
fit fɪt |fitted 'fɪtɪd
Fitch fɪtʃ |Fitch's 'fɪtʃɪz
fitchew 'fɪtʃu, 'fɪtʃɪu
fitful 'fɪtfəl |-ly -ɪ
fitting 'fɪtɪŋ
Fitzgerald fɪts'dʒɛrəld
FitzGerald Eng poet fɪts'dʒɛrəld
Fitzhugh fɪts'hju, -'hɪu ('Fitzˌhugh 'Lee)
Fitzsimmons fɪt'sɪmənz, fɪts's- |-'s -ɪz
Fitzwalter 'fɪts'wɔltɚ; ES -ˌwɔltə(r
Fitzwater 'fɪtsˌwɔtɚ, -ˌwɑtɚ, -ˌwɒtɚ; ES -tə(r; formerly Fitzwalter

Fiume *It* 'fju:me
five faɪv |-r 'faɪvɚ; ES -vǝ(r
fivefold *adj, adv* 'faɪv'fold ('five,fold 'loss)
fivepence 'faɪvpǝns, *now less freq.* 'fɪpǝns
fivepenny 'faɪv,pɛnɪ, -pǝnɪ
fix fɪks |fixes 'fɪksɪz |fixed, fixt fɪkst |-edly -ɪdlɪ
fixate 'fɪkset |-d -ɪd |-tion fɪks'eʃǝn
fixative 'fɪksǝtɪv
fixity 'fɪksǝtɪ
fixt fɪkst
fixture 'fɪkstʃɚ; ES 'fɪkstʃǝ(r
fizgig 'fɪz,gɪg
fizz fɪz |-es -ɪz |-ed -d |-y -ɪ
fizzle 'fɪzl̩ |-d -d |-ling 'fɪzlɪŋ, 'fɪzl̩ŋ
fjord fjord, fjɔrd; ES fjoǝd, E+fjɔǝd
flabbergast 'flæbɚ,gæst; ES 'flæbǝ-; |-ed -ɪd
flabby 'flæbɪ
flabellum flǝ'bɛlǝm |-bella -'bɛlǝ
flaccid 'flæksɪd |-ity flæk'sɪdǝtɪ
flag flæg |flagged flægd
flagellant 'flædʒǝlǝnt, flǝ'dʒɛlǝnt
flagellate 'flædʒǝ,let |-d -ɪd
flageolet ,flædʒǝ'lɛt
flaggy 'flægɪ
flagitious flǝ'dʒɪʃǝs
flagman 'flægmǝn |-men -mǝn
flagon 'flægǝn
flagrancy 'flegrǝnsɪ |flagrant 'flegrǝnt
flagship 'flæg,ʃɪp
Flagstad 'flægstæd
flagstaff, F- 'flæg,stæf; E+-,staf, -,staf; |-s -s—*The pl* flagstaves -,stevz *is rare in America.*
flagstone 'flæg,ston
Flaherty 'flæɚtɪ; ES 'flæ·ǝtɪ
flail flel |flailed fleld
flair flɛr, flær; E flɛǝ(r, ES flæǝ(r; |-ed -d
flake flek |flaked flekt |flaky 'flekɪ
flam flæm |flammed flæmd
flambeau 'flæmbo |-beaux *or* -beaus -boz
flamboyance flæm'bɔɪǝns |-cy -ɪ |-ant -ǝnt
flame flem |flamed flemd
flame-color 'flem,kʌlɚ; ES -,kʌlǝ(r; |-ed -d
flamingo flǝ'mɪŋgo, flæ-
Flaminius flǝ'mɪnɪǝs, -njǝs |-'s -ɪz
flan *pastry* flæn (*Fr* flɑ̃)
Flanders 'flændɚz; ES 'flændǝz; |-'s -ɪz
flange flændʒ |-s -ɪz |-d -d

flank flæŋk |flanked flæŋkt
flannel 'flænl̩ |-ed -d
flannelette, -let ,flænl̩'ɛt
flap flæp |flapped flæpt
flapdoodle 'flæp,dudl̩
flapjack 'flæp,dʒæk
flapper 'flæpɚ; ES 'flæpǝ(r; |-ed -d
flare flɛr, flær; E flɛǝ(r, ES flæǝ(r; |-d -d
flare-up 'flɛr,ʌp, 'flær,ʌp; S 'flær,ʌp
flash flæʃ |flashes 'flæʃɪz |flashed flæʃt
flashboard 'flæʃ,bord, -,bɔrd; ES -,boǝd, E+-,bɔǝd
flashlight 'flæʃ,laɪt |-ed -ɪd
flask flæsk; E+flask, flɑsk
flat flæt |flatted 'flætɪd
flatboat 'flæt,bot
flatcar 'flæt,kɑr; ES -,kɑ:(r, E+-,kɑ:(r
flatfish 'flæt,fɪʃ |-es -ɪz
flat-footed 'flæt'futɪd ('flat-,footed 'way)
flathead, F- 'flæt,hɛd
flatiron 'flæt,aɪɚn, -,aɪrn; ES -,aɪ·ǝn, -,aɪǝn
flatten 'flætn̩ |-ed -d |-ing 'flætn̩ɪŋ, -tnɪŋ
flatter 'flætɚ; ES -tǝ(r; |-ed -d |-ing 'flætǝrɪŋ, 'flætrɪŋ
flattery 'flætǝrɪ, 'flætrɪ
flatulence 'flætʃǝlǝns |-cy -ɪ |-lent -lǝnt
flatus 'fletǝs |-es -ɪz
flatways 'flæt,wez |flatwise 'flæt,waɪz
flaunt flɔnt, flɒnt, flɑnt |-ed -ɪd
flauntily 'flɔntl̩ɪ, 'flɒnt-, 'flɑnt-
flautist 'flɔtɪst
Flavius 'flevɪǝs, -vjǝs |-'s -ɪz
flavor 'flevɚ; ES -vǝ(r; |-ing 'flevrɪŋ, -vǝrɪŋ
flaw flɔ |flawed flɔd |-less -lɪs |-y 'flɔ·ɪ
flax flæks |flaxes 'flæksɪz |-ed -t |-en -n̩
flaxseed 'flæks,sid, 'flæk,sid
flay fle |flayed fled
flea fli |-bane -,ben |-bite -,baɪt
flea-bitten 'fli,bɪtn̩
Fleance 'flɪǝns |-'s -ɪz
Fleay fle
fleck flɛk |flecked flɛkt
Flecknoe 'flɛkno
flection 'flɛkʃǝn |-al -l̩
fled *past & pptc of* flee flɛd
fledge flɛdʒ |-s -ɪz |-d -d |-dgling, -dgeling -lɪŋ
flee fli |fled flɛd
fleece flis |fleeces 'flisɪz |fleeced flist

fleer *'gibe'* flɪr; ES flɪə(r, S+flɛə(r; |-ed -d
fleer *'one whe flees'* 'fliɚ; ES 'fli·ə(r
fleet flit |fleeted 'flitɪd
Fleming 'flɛmɪŋ |Flemish 'flɛmɪʃ
flense, flence flɛns |-s -ɪz |-d -t
flesh flɛʃ |fleshes 'flɛʃɪz |fleshed flɛʃt
fleshly 'flɛʃlɪ |fleshy 'flɛʃɪ
fleshpot 'flɛʃˌpat; ES+-ˌpɒt
fletch flɛtʃ |-es -ɪz |-ed -t
fletcher 'flɛtʃɚ; ES 'flɛtʃə(r
Fletcherism 'flɛtʃəˌrɪzəm |-rite -ˌraɪt
Fletcherize 'flɛtʃəˌraɪz |-s -ɪz |-d -d
fleur-de-lis ˌflɜdə'li, -'lis; ES ˌflɜ-, ˌflɝ-; |pl
  -lis -'liz or -lises -'lisɪz
flew *'dog's lip'* flu, flɪu |-s -z |-ed -d
flew *past of* fly flu, flɪu
flex flɛks |flexes 'flɛksɪz |flexed flɛkst
flexibility ˌflɛksə'bɪlətɪ
flexible 'flɛksəbl̩ |-bly -blɪ
flexion 'flɛkʃən |-al -l̩
Flexner 'flɛksnɚ; ES 'flɛksnə(r
flexor 'flɛksɚ; ES 'flɛksə(r
flexure 'flɛkʃɚ; ES 'flɛkʃə(r; |-xuous -kʃuəs
flibbertigibbet, F- 'flɪbɚtɪˌdʒɪbɪt; ES 'flɪbə-
flick flɪk |flicked flɪkt
flicker 'flɪkɚ; ES 'flɪkə(r; |-ed -d |-ing
  'flɪkərɪŋ, 'flɪkrɪŋ
flier 'flaɪɚ; ES 'flaɪ·ə(r
flies flaɪz
flight flaɪt |-y -ɪ
flimflam 'flɪmˌflæm |-med -d
flimsy 'flɪmzɪ
flinch flɪntʃ |flinches 'flɪntʃɪz |-ed -t
flinder 'flɪndɚ; ES 'flɪndə(r
fling flɪŋ |flung flʌŋ
flint, F- flɪnt |flinted 'flɪntɪd
flintlock 'flɪntˌlak; ES+-ˌlɒk
Flintshire 'flɪntʃɪr, -ʃɚ; ES -ʃɪə(r, -ʃə(r
flip flɪp |flipped flɪpt
flippancy 'flɪpənsɪ |-ant -ənt
flirt flɝt; ES flɜt, flɝt; |-ed -ɪd
flirtatious flɚ'teʃəs; ES flɜ-, flɝ-
flit flɪt |flitted 'flɪtɪd
flitch flɪtʃ |flitches 'flɪtʃɪz |-ed -t
flite flaɪt |-d -ɪd |-ting 'flaɪtɪŋ
flitter 'flɪtɚ; ES 'flɪtə(r; |-ed -d
flivver 'flɪvɚ; ES 'flɪvə(r; |-ed -d |-ing
  'flɪvərɪŋ, 'flɪvrɪŋ
float flot |floated 'flotɪd |-age -ɪdʒ

floatation flo'teʃən
floc flak; ES+flɒk
floccose 'flakos, fla'kos; ES+-ɒk-
flocculence 'flakjələns; ES+'flɒk-; |-nt -nt
flock flak; ES+flɒk; |-ed -t
Flodden 'fladn̩; ES+'flɒdn̩
floe flo
flog flag, flɒg, flɔg |-ged -d
flood flʌd |flooded 'flʌdɪd |-gate -ˌget
floodlight 'flʌdˌlaɪt |-ed -ɪd
floor flor, flɔr; ES floə(r, E+flɔə(r
floorcloth 'florˌklɔθ, 'flɔr-, -ˌklɒθ; ES 'floə-,
  E+'flɔə-; |-ths -ðz, -θs
flooring 'florɪŋ, 'flɔrɪŋ; S 'florɪŋ
floorwalker 'florˌwɔkɚ, 'flɔr-; ES 'floəˌwɔkə(r,
  E+'flɔə-
flop flap; ES+flɒp; |-ped -t |-py -ɪ
Flora 'florə, 'flɔrə; S 'florə
floral 'florəl, 'flɔrəl; S 'florəl
Florala flo'rælə, fla-, flɒ-
Florence 'florəns, 'flar-, 'flɔr- |-'s -ɪz |-entine
  -ənˌtin
flores 'floriz, 'flɔriz; S 'floriz
florescence flo'rɛsn̩s, flɔ-; S flo-; |-nt -n̩t
Floresville 'florisˌvɪl, 'flɔr-; S 'flo-, S+-vl̩
floriculture 'florɪˌkʌltʃɚ, 'flɔ-; ES 'florɪ-
  ˌkʌltʃə(r, E+'flɔ-
florid 'florɪd, 'flarɪd, 'flɒrɪd
Florida 'florədə, 'flar-, 'flɔr- |-n -n
Floridian flo'rɪdɪən, flɔ-, fla-, flɒ-
Florimel 'florəˌmɛl, 'flar-, 'flɔr-
florin 'florɪn, 'flar-, 'flɔr-, 'flɒrɪn
florist 'florɪst, 'flɔr-, 'flar-, 'flɒr-
Florizel 'florəˌzɛl, 'flar-, 'flɔr-
floss flɔs, flɒs |-es -ɪz |-ed -t
flota 'flotə
flotage 'flotɪdʒ |-s -ɪz
flotation flo'teʃən
flotilla flo'tɪlə
flotsam 'flatsəm; ES+'flɒtsəm; *less freq.*
  'flotsəm (*19c* floatsome)
flounce flauns |flounces 'flaunsɪz |-d -t
flounder 'flaundɚ; ES -də(r; |-ed -d |-ing
  'flaundərɪŋ, 'flaundrɪŋ
flour flaur; ES flauə(r; |-ed -d
flourish 'flɝɪʃ; ES 'flɜrɪʃ, 'flʌrɪʃ, 'flɝɪʃ; |-es
  -ɪz |-ed -t
flout flaut |flouted 'flautɪd
flow flo |flowed flod

---

flower ˈflauɚ, flaur; ES ˈflau·ə(r, flauə(r;
 |-ed -d
flower-de-luce ˈflaurdɪˈlus, -ˈlrus; ES ˈflauə-;
 |-s -ɪz
floweret ˈflaurɪt
flowerpot ˈflaurˌpat; ES ˈflauəˌpat, -ˌpɒt
flowery ˈflaurɪ, ˈflauərɪ
flown flon
flu flu, flɪu
fluctuate ˈflʌktʃuˌet |-ated -ˌetɪd |-ant -ənt
fluctuation ˌflʌktʃuˈeʃən
flue flu, flɪu
Fluellen fluˈɛlɪn, -ən
fluent ˈfluənt, ˈflɪuənt |-ency -ənsɪ
fluff flʌf |-fluffed flʌft
Flügel ˈfligl (Ger ˈfly:gəl)
fluid ˈfluɪd, ˈflɪuɪd
fluidity fluˈɪdətɪ, flɪu-
fluke fluk, flɪuk |-d -t |-ky -ɪ
flume, F- flum, flɪum
flummery ˈflʌmərɪ
flummox ˈflʌməks |-es -ɪz |-ed -t
flung flʌŋ
flunk flʌŋk |flunked flʌŋkt
fluor ˈfluɚ, ˈflɪuɚ; ES -ə(r
fluoresce ˌfluəˈrɛs, ˌflɪu- |-s -ɪz |-d -t |-nce -ns
 |-nt -nt
fluoric fluˈɔrɪk, flɪu-, -ˈarɪk, -ˈɒrɪk
fluorine ˈfluəˌrin, ˈflɪu-, -rɪn |-rin -rɪn
fluorite ˈfluəˌraɪt ˈflɪu-
fluoroscope ˈfluərəˌskop, ˈflɪu-
flurry ˈflɝɪ; ES ˈflɜrɪ, ˈflʌrɪ, ˈflɝɪ
flush flʌʃ |flushes ˈflʌʃɪz |flushed flʌʃt
fluster ˈflʌstɚ; ES ˈflʌstə(r; |-ed -d |-ing
 ˈflʌstərɪŋ, ˈflʌstrɪŋ
flustrate ˈflʌstret |-terate -təˌret, -tret |-d -ɪd
flute flut, flɪut |-d -ɪd
flutter ˈflʌtɚ; ES ˈflʌtə(r; |-ed -d
fluty ˈflutɪ, ˈflɪutɪ
Fluvanna fluˈvænə, flɪu-
fluvial ˈfluvɪəl, ˈflɪu-
flux flʌks |fluxes ˈflʌksɪz |fluxed flʌkst
fluxion ˈflʌkʃən
fly flaɪ |flew flu, flɪu |flown flon
flyaway ˈflaɪəˌwe
flycatcher ˈflaɪˌkætʃɚ; ES -ˌkætʃə(r
flyer ˈflaɪɚ; ES ˈflaɪ·ə(r
flyleaf ˈflaɪˌlif |-leaves -ˌlivz
flyproof ˈflaɪˈpruf (ˈflyˌproof ˈointment)

flyspeck ˈflaɪˌspɛk |-ed -t
flyte flaɪt |-d -ɪd |-ting -ɪŋ
flytrap ˈflaɪˌtræp
flyweight ˈflaɪˌwet
flywheel ˈflaɪˌhwil
foal fol |foaled fold
foam fom |foamed fomd
f.o.b. ˈɛfˌoˈbi
fob fab; ES+fɒb; |-bed -d
focal ˈfokl |-ly -ɪ
focalize ˈfoklˌaɪz |-s -ɪz |-d -d
Foch fɔʃ, fak (Fr fɔ̃ʃ, Ger fɔk)
focus ˈfokəs |-es -ɪz |-ed -t |foci ˈfosaɪ
fodder ˈfadɚ; ES ˈfadə(r, ˈfɒd-; |-ed -d |-ing
 -dərɪŋ, -drɪŋ
foe fo
foehn fen (Ger fø:n)
foeman ˈfomən |-men -mən
foetal ˈfitl |-ism -ˌɪzəm
foetation fiˈteʃən
foeticide ˈfitəˌsaɪd |-dal ˌfitəˈsaɪdl
foetus ˈfitəs |-es -ɪz
fog fag, fɔg, fɒg |-ged -d |-gy -ɪ
foghorn ˈfagˌhɔrn, ˈfɔg-, ˈfɒg-; ES -ˌhɔən
fogy ˈfogɪ
foible ˈfɔɪbl
foie gras Fr fwaˈgra
foil fɔɪl |foiled fɔɪld
foison ˈfɔɪzn
foist fɔɪst |foisted ˈfɔɪstɪd
fold fold |folded ˈfoldɪd
folderol ˈfaldəˌral; ES+ˈfɒldəˌrɒl
Folger ˈfoldʒɚ; ES ˈfoldʒə(r
foliage ˈfolɪɪdʒ |-s -ɪz |-d -d
foliate adj ˈfolɪt, -ˌet
foliate v ˈfolɪˌet |-ated -ˌetɪd
folio ˈfolɪˌo, -ljo |-ed -d
folium ˈfolɪəm |-s -z |-lia -ə
folk fok |-s -s; N Engd+fɔ̃ks (§46)
Folkestone ˈfokˌston, Brit ˈfokstən
folklore ˈfokˌlor, -ˌlɔr; ES -ˌloə(r, E+-ˌlɔə(r
folkmoot ˈfokˌmut |folkmote, -mot ˈfokˌmot
folkway ˈfokˌwe
Follansbee ˈfalənzbɪ; ES+ˈfɒl-
follicle ˈfalɪkl; ES+ˈfɒl-
follow ˈfalo, -ə; ES+ˈfɒl-; |-ed -d |-ing -ləwɪŋ
follow-up ˈfaloˌʌp, ˈfaləˌwʌp; ES+ˈfɒl-
folly ˈfalɪ; ES+ˈfɒlɪ
foment n ˈfomɛnt

|full ful |tooth tuθ |further ˈfɝðɚ; ES ˈfɝðə |custom ˈkʌstəm |while hwaɪl |how hau |toy tɔɪ
|using ˈjuzɪŋ |fuse fjuz, fruz |dish dɪʃ |vision ˈvɪʒən |Eden ˈidn̩ |cradle ˈkredl̩ |keep 'em ˈkipm̩

foment *v* fo'mɛnt |-ed -ɪd ('foment 'trouble)
fomentation ˌfomən'teʃən, -mɛn-
fond fɑnd, fɒnd
fondant 'fɑndənt, 'fɒn-
Fond du Lac 'fɑndӡə͵læk, -dӡʊ-, 'fɑndə-,
  'fɒn-
fondle 'fɑndḷ, 'fɒn- |-d -d |-ling -dlɪŋ, -dḷɪŋ
fondler 'fɑndlɚ, 'fɒn-; ES -lə(r
fondue 'fɑndu, fɑn'du, -ɒn- (*Fr* fõ'dy)
font fɑnt; ES+fɒnt
Fontaine, La læfɑn'ten, -fɒn- (*Fr* lafõ'tɛn)
Fontainebleau 'fɑntɪn͵blo, ˌfɑntɪn'blo, -ɒn-
  (*Fr* fõtɛn'blo)
fontanel, -lle ˌfɑntə'nɛl; ES+ˌfɒn-
Foochow 'fu'tʃaʊ (*Chin* -'dӡo)
food fud |foodstuff 'fud͵stʌf
fool ful |fooled fuld |-ery -ərɪ
foolhardy 'ful͵hɑrdɪ; ES -͵hɑ:dɪ, E+-͵hɑ:dɪ
foolish 'fulɪʃ
foolproof 'ful'pruf ('fool͵proof 'gadget)
foolscap 'fulz͵kæp, *paper often* 'ful͵skæp
foot fʊt |footed 'fʊtɪd |-age -ɪdӡ |-ing -ɪŋ
football 'fʊt͵bɔl
footboard 'fʊt͵bord, -͵bɔrd; ES -͵boəd, E+
  -͵bɔəd
footboy 'fʊt͵bɔɪ
footbridge 'fʊt͵brɪdӡ |-s -ɪz
foot-candle 'fʊt'kændḷ
footfall 'fʊt͵fɔl
footgear 'fʊt͵gɪr; ES -͵gɪə(r, S+-͵gɛə(r
foothill 'fʊt͵hɪl
foothold 'fʊt͵hold
footle 'fʊtḷ |-d -d |-ling 'fʊtlɪŋ, 'fʊtḷɪŋ
footlights 'fʊt͵laɪts
footling *adv, adj* 'fʊtlɪŋ
foot-loose 'fʊt͵lus
footman 'fʊtmən |-men -mən
footmark 'fʊt͵mɑrk; ES -͵mɑ:k, E+-͵mɑ:k
footnote 'fʊt͵not |-d -ɪd
footpad 'fʊt͵pæd
footpath 'fʊt͵pæθ; E+-͵pɑθ, -͵pɒθ |-ths -ðz
foot-pound 'fʊt'paʊnd
footprint 'fʊt͵prɪnt |-ed -ɪd
footrest 'fʊt͵rɛst
footrope 'fʊt͵rop
footsore 'fʊt͵sor, -͵sɔr; ES -͵soə(r, E+-͵sɔə(r
footstep 'fʊt͵stɛp
footstock 'fʊt͵stɑk; ES+-͵stɒk
footstool 'fʊt͵stul

foot-ton 'fʊt'tʌn
footway 'fʊt͵we
footwear 'fʊt͵wɛr, -͵wær; E -͵wɛə(r, ES
  -͵wæə(r
footwork 'fʊt͵wӡk; ES -͵wӡk, -͵wɝk
footworn 'fʊt͵worn, -͵wɔrn; ES -͵woən,
  E+-͵wɔən
foozle 'fuzḷ |-d -d |-ling 'fuzḷɪŋ, 'fuzlɪŋ
fop fɑp; ES+fɒp; |-pery -ərɪ, -rɪ
for *stressed* 'fɔr, ˌfɔr; ES 'fɔə(r, ˌfɔə(r; *unstr.*
  fɚ; ES fə(r
forage 'fɔrɪdӡ, 'fɑr-, 'fɒr- |-s -ɪz |-d -d
Foraker 'fɔrəkɚ, 'fɑr-, 'fɒr-; ES -kə(r
foramen fo'remən |-s -z |foramina fo-
  'ræmənə
forasmuch ˌfɔrəz'mʌtʃ
foray 'fɔre, 'fɑre, 'fɒre |-ed -d
forbade fɚ'bæd; ES fə'bæd
forbear *'ancestor'* 'fɔr͵bɛr, -͵bær; E 'fɔə͵bɛə(r,
  ES -͵bæə(r
forbear *v* fɔr'bɛr, fɚ-, -'bær; E fɔə'bɛə(r, fə-,
  ES -'bæə(r; |-bore -'bor, -'bɔr; ES -'boə(r,
  E+-'bɔə(r; |-borne -'born, -'bɔrn; ES
  -'boən, E+-'bɔən; ('bear and 'for͵bear)
forbearance fɔr'bɛrəns, fɚ-, -'bærəns; E fɔə-,
  fə-; S fɔə'bærəns, fə-
Forbes-Robertson 'fɔrbz'rɑbɚtsṇ; ES 'fɔəbz-
  'rɑbətsṇ, -'rɒb-
forbid fɚ'bɪd; ES fə'bɪd; |-bad, -bade -'bæd
  |-bidden -'bɪdṇ |-dance -ṇs
forbore fɔr'bor, fɚ-, -'bɔr; ES fɔə'boə(r, fə-,
  E+-'bɔə(r; |-rne -n
forby, -bye fɔr'baɪ; ES fɔə'baɪ
force fors, fɔrs; ES foəs, E+fɔəs; |-s -ɪz |-d -t
  |-dly -ɪdlɪ
forceable *'coerceable'* 'forsəbḷ, 'fɔrs-; ES
  'foəs-, E+'fɔəs-
forceful 'forsfəl, 'fɔrs-; ES 'foəs-, E+'fɔəs-;
  |-ly -ɪ
forcemeat 'fors͵mit, 'fɔrs-; ES 'foəs-, E+
  'fɔəs-
forceps 'forsəps; ES 'fɔəsəps
forcible *'violent'* 'forsəbḷ, 'fɔrs-; ES 'foəs-,
  E+'fɔəs-; |-bly -blɪ
ford, F- ford, fɔrd; ES foəd, E+fɔəd; |-ed -ɪd
Fordham 'fordəm, 'fɔr-; ES 'foədəm, E+
  'fɔə-
fordo fɔr'du; ES fɔə-; |-does -'dʌz |-did -'dɪd
  |-done -'dʌn

Fordyce 'fɔrdaɪs; ES 'fɔə-; |-'s -ɪz, *Scotl*
For'dyce
fore for, fɔr; ES fɔə(r, E+fɔə(r
fore-and-aft 'fɔrən'æft, 'fɔr-, -ənd-; E+-'aft,
-'ɑft; S 'fɔrən(d)'æft
forearm *n* 'fɔr̩ɑrm, 'fɔr-; ES 'fɔr̩ɑːm,
E+'fɔr-, -̩ɑːm
forearm *v* for'ɑrm, fɔr-; ES for'ɑːm, E+fɔr-,
-'ɑːm; |-ed -d
forebear '*ancestor*' 'fɔr̩bɛr, 'fɔr-, -̩bær; E
'fɔə̩bɛə(r, 'fɔə-, -̩bæə(r; S 'fɔə̩bæə(r
forebode for'bod, fɔr-; ES fɔə-, E+fɔə-; |-d
-ɪd |-ding -ɪŋ
forebrain 'fɔr̩bren, 'fɔr-; ES 'fɔə-, E+'fɔə-
forecast *n* 'fɔr̩kæst, 'fɔr-; ES 'fɔə-, E+'fɔə-,
-̩kast, -̩kɑst
forecast *v* for'kæst, fɔr-; ES fɔə-, E+fɔə-,
-'kast, -'kɑst; |*past* -cast, -casted -ɪd
|*acct*+'fɔr̩cast(ed)
forecastle *naut.* 'foksl̩, *as sp. pron.* 'fɔr̩kæsl̩,
'fɔr-; ES 'fɔə-, E+'fɔə-, -̩kasl̩, -̩kɑsl̩
foreclose for'kloz, fɔr-; ES fɔə-, E+fɔə-; |-s
-ɪz |-d -d |-sure -ʒɚ; ES -ʒə(r
foredo for'du, fɔr-; ES fɔə-, E+fɔə-; |-does
-'dʌz |-did -'dɪd |-done -'dʌn
foredoom *n* 'fɔr̩dum, 'fɔr-; ES 'fɔə-, E+'fɔə-
foredoom *v* for'dum, fɔr-; ES fɔə-, E+fɔə-;
|-ed -d
forefather 'fɔr̩fɑðɚ, 'fɔr-; ES 'fɔə̩fɑðə(r,
E+'fɔə-, -̩fɑðə(r
forefend for'fɛnd, fɔr-; ES fɔə-, E+fɔə-;
|-ed -ɪd
forefinger 'fɔr̩fɪŋgɚ, 'fɔr-; ES 'fɔə̩fɪŋgə(r,
E+'fɔə-
forefoot 'fɔr̩fʊt, 'fɔr-; ES 'fɔə-, E+'fɔə-;
|-feet -̩fit—*acct*+'fɔre'f-
foregather for'gæðɚ, fɔr-; ES fɔə'gæðə(r,
E+fɔə-; |-ed -d |-ing -'gæðərɪŋ, -'gæðrɪŋ
forego for'go, fɔr-; ES fɔə-, E+fɔə-; |-went
-'wɛnt |-gone -'gɔn, -'gɒn, *less freq.* -'gɑn
foregoing for'go·ɪŋ, fɔr-; ES fɔə-, E+fɔə-;
('fɔre̩going 'day)
foregone for'gɔn, fɔr-, -'gɒn; ES fɔə-, E+fɔə-;
('fɔre̩gone con'clusion)
foreground 'fɔr̩graʊnd, 'fɔr-; ES 'fɔə-, E+
'fɔə-
forehand 'fɔr̩hænd, 'fɔr-; ES 'fɔə-, E+'fɔə-
forehanded 'fɔr'hændɪd, 'fɔr-; ES 'fɔə-,
E+'fɔə-

forehead 'fɔrɪd, 'far-, 'fɒr-, -əd, 'fɔr̩hɛd
foreign 'fɔrɪn, 'far-, 'fɒr-, -ən |-ness -nɪs
forejudge for'dʒʌdʒ, fɔr-; ES fɔə-, E+fɔə-;
|-s -ɪz |-d -d
foreknow for'no, fɔr-; ES fɔə-, E+fɔə-;
|-knew -'nju, -'nɪu, -'nu |-known -'non
foreknowledge 'fɔr̩nalɪdʒ, 'fɔr-; ES 'fɔə̩nal-,
-̩nɒl-, E+'fɔə-; *acct*+fore'knowledge
forelady 'fɔr̩ledɪ, 'fɔr-; ES 'fɔə-, E+'fɔə-
foreland 'fɔrlənd, 'fɔr-; ES 'fɔə-, E+'fɔə-
foreleg 'fɔr̩lɛg, 'fɔr-; ES 'fɔə-, E+'fɔə-;
acct+'fore'leg
forelimb 'fɔr̩lɪm, 'fɔr-; ES 'fɔə-, E+'fɔə-;
acct+'fore'limb
forelock 'fɔr̩lak, 'fɔr-; ES 'fɔə̩lak, -̩lɒk,
E+'fɔə-
foreman 'fɔrmən, 'fɔr-; ES 'fɔə-, E+'fɔə-
|-men -mən
foremast 'fɔr̩mæst, 'fɔr-; ES 'fɔə̩mæst,
E+'fɔə-, -̩mast, -̩mɑst
foremost 'fɔr̩most, 'fɔr-, -məst; ES 'fɔə-,
E+'fɔə-
forename 'fɔr̩nem, 'fɔr-; ES 'fɔə-, E+'fɔə-;
|-d -d
forenoon for'nun, fɔr-; ES fɔə-, E+fɔə-;
('fɔre̩noon 'task)
forensic fə'rɛnsɪk, fo- |-al -l̩ |-ally -l̩ɪ, -ɪklɪ
foreordain ̩fɔrɔr'den, ̩fɔr-; ES ̩fɔrɔə'den,
E+̩fɔr-; |-ed -d
foreordinate *v* for'ɔrdn̩̩et, fɔr-; ES for'ɔədn̩-,
E+fɔr-; |-d -ɪd
foreordination ̩fɔrɔrdn̩'eʃən, ̩fɔr-; ES ̩fɔr-
ɔdn̩-, E+̩fɔr-
Forepaugh 'fɔr̩pɔ, 'fɔr-; ES 'fɔə-, E+'fɔə-
forepaw, F- 'fɔr̩pɔ, 'fɔr-; ES 'fɔə-, E+'fɔə-
forequarter 'fɔr̩kwɔrtɚ, 'fɔr-; ES 'fɔə-
̩kwɔətə(r, E+'fɔə-
forerun for'rʌn, fɔr-; ES fɔə'rʌn, E+fɔə-;
|-ran -'ræn |*pptc* -run -'rʌn |-ner -ɚ; ES
-ə(r; *acct*+'fore̩runner
foresaid 'fɔr̩sɛd, 'fɔr-; ES 'fɔə-, E+'fɔə-
foresail 'fɔr̩sel, 'fɔr-; ES 'fɔə-, E+'fɔə-
foresee for'si, fɔr-; ES fɔə-, E+fɔə-; |-saw
-'sɔ |-seen -'sin
foreshadow *n* 'fɔr̩ʃædo, 'fɔr-, -ə; ES 'fɔə-,
E+'fɔə-
foreshadow *v* for'ʃædo, fɔr-, -ə; ES fɔə-,
E+fɔə-; |-ed -d |-ing -'ʃædəwɪŋ
foreshank 'fɔr̩ʃæŋk, 'fɔr-; ES 'fɔə-, E+'fɔə-

|full fʊl |tooth tuθ |further 'fɝðɚ; ES 'fɝðə |custom 'kʌstəm |while hwaɪl |how haʊ |toy tɔɪ
|using 'juzɪŋ |fuse fjuz, fɪuz |dish dɪʃ |vision 'vɪʒən |Eden 'idn̩ |cradle 'kredl̩ |keep 'em 'kipm̩

foresheet 'fɔrˌʃit, 'fɔr-; ES 'foə-, E+'fɔə-

foreshore 'fɔrˌʃor, 'fɔrˌʃɔr; ES 'foəˌʃoə(r, E+'fɔəˌʃɔə(r

foreshorten for'ʃɔrtn̩, fɔr-; ES foə'ʃɔətn̩, E+ fɔə-; |-ed -d |-ing -tn̩ɪŋ, -tnɪŋ

foreside 'fɔrˌsaɪd, 'fɔr-; ES 'foə-, E+'fɔə-; acct+'fore'side

foresight 'fɔrˌsaɪt, 'fɔr-; ES 'foə-, E+'fɔə-

foresighted 'for'saɪtɪd, 'fɔr-; ES 'foə-, E+ 'fɔə-; ('foreˌsighted 'act)

foreskin 'fɔrˌskɪn, 'fɔr-; ES 'foə-, E+'fɔə-

forespeak for'spik, fɔr-; ES foə-, E+fɔə-; |-spoke -'spok |-spoken -'spokən

forest 'fɔrɪst, 'far-, 'fɒr-, -əst |-ed -ɪd |-ry -rɪ

forestall for'stɔl, fɔr-; ES foə-, E+fɔə-; |-ed -d

forestation ˌfɔrɪs'teʃən, ˌfar-, ˌfɒr-

foretaste n 'fɔrˌtest, 'fɔr-; ES 'foə-, E+'fɔə-

foretaste v for'test, fɔr-; ES foə-, E+fɔə-; |-d -ɪd

foretell for'tɛl, fɔr-; ES foə-, E+fɔə-; |-told -'told

forethink for'θɪŋk, fɔr-; ES foə-, E+fɔə-; |-thought -'θɔt

forethought n 'fɔrˌθɔt, 'fɔr-; ES 'foə-, E+'fɔə-

foretime 'fɔrˌtaɪm, 'fɔr-; ES 'foə-, E+'fɔə-

foretimed 'timed before' for'taɪmd, fɔr-; ES foə-, E+fɔə-

foretoken n 'fɔrˌtokən, 'fɔr-; ES 'foə-, E+'fɔə-

foretoken v for'tokən, fɔr-; ES foə-, E+fɔə-; |-ed -d |-ing -'tokənɪŋ, -'toknɪŋ

foretop 'fɔrˌtap, 'fɔr-; ES 'foəˌtap, -ˌtɒp, E+'fɔə-

fore-topmast for'tapˌmæst, fɔr-; ES foə'tap-, ˌmæst, -'tɒp-, E+fɔə-, -ˌmast, -ˌmɑst

fore-topsail for'tapˌsel, naut. -s|, fɔr-; ES foə'tap-, -'tɒp-, E+fɔə-

forever fɔr'ɛvɚ; ES -'ɛvə(r

forevermore fɚˌɛvɚ'mor, -'mɔr; ES fɚˌɛvə-'moə(r, E+-'mɔə(r

forewarn for'wɔrn, fɔr-; ES foə'wɔən, E+ fɔə-; |-ed -d

forewent past of forego for'wɛnt, fɔr-; ES foə-, E+fɔə-

forewoman 'fɔrˌwumən, 'fɔr-, -ˌwum-; ES 'foə-, E+'fɔə-; |-women -ˌwɪmɪn, -mən— see woman

foreword 'fɔrˌwɝd, 'fɔr-; ES 'foəˌwɝd, 'foə-ˌwɝd, E+'fɔə-

foreyard 'fɔrˌjard, 'fɔr-; ES 'foəˌja:d, E+ 'fɔə-, -ˌja:d

Forfar 'fɔrfɚ; loc. 'fɒrfər; ES 'fɔəfə(r; |-shire -ˌʃɪr, -ʃɚ; ES -ˌʃɪə(r, -ʃə(r

forfeit 'fɔrfɪt; ES 'fɔəfɪt; |-ed -ɪd

forfeiture 'fɔrfɪtʃɚ; ES 'fɔəfɪtʃə(r

forfend fɔr'fɛnd; ES fɔə'fɛnd; |-ed -ɪd

forgather fɔr'gæðɚ; ES fɔə'gæðə(r; |-ed -d |-ing -'gæðərɪŋ, -'gæðrɪŋ

forgave fɚ'gev; ES fə'gev

forge fɔrdʒ, fordʒ; ES foədʒ, fɔədʒ; |-s -ɪz |-d -d—The pron. with ɔ by many who say ford, forθ, etc., results from ME double forms 'fɔrdʒə & 'fɔːrdʒə.

forger 'fɔrdʒɚ, 'fordʒɚ; ES 'foədʒə(r, 'fɔə-; |-y -ɪ—see forge

forget fɚ'gɛt; ES fə-; |past -got -'gat |pptc -gotten, -got -'gatn̩, -'gat; |ES+-'gɒt(n̩)

forgetful fɚ'gɛtfəl; ES fə-; |-ly -ɪ

forgetive 'fɔrdʒətɪv, 'for-; ES 'foədʒ-, 'fɔədʒ-—see forge

forget-me-not fɚ'gɛtmɪˌnat; ES fə'gɛtmɪˌnat, -ˌnɒt

forgettable fɚ'gɛtəb|; ES fə-

forgive fɚ'gɪv; ES fə-; |-gave -'gev |-given -'gɪvən |-ness -nɪs

forgo fɔr'go; ES fɔə'go; |-went -'wɛnt |-gone -'gɔn, -'gɒn, less freq. -'gan

forgot fɚ'gat; ES fə'gat, -'gɒt; |-ten -n̩

forjudge fɔr'dʒʌdʒ; ES fɔə-; |-s -ɪz |-d -d

fork fɔrk; ES fɔək; |-ed -t

forked adj fɔrkt, 'fɔrkɪd; ES fɔək-

forlorn fɚ'lɔrn; ES fə'lɔən; |-ness -nɪs

form fɔrm; ES fɔəm; |-ed -d |-al -] |-ally -ɪ—The pron. form for the sense 'rank,' 'bench,' once current in Engd, comes from a ME variant furme, fourme 'fuːrmə. Cf course.

formaldehyde fɔr'mældəˌhaɪd; ES fɔ'mæl-

formalin, F- 'fɔrməlɪn; ES 'fɔəm-

formalism 'fɔrmlˌɪzəm; ES 'fɔəm-; |-ist -ɪst

formality fɔr'mælətɪ; ES fɔ-

formalize 'fɔrmlˌaɪz; ES 'fɔəm-; |-s -ɪz |-d -d

formant 'fɔrmənt; ES 'fɔəm-

format 'fɔrmæt (Fr fɔr'ma)

formation fɔr'meʃən; ES fɔə-

formative 'fɔrmətɪv; ES 'fɔəm-

forme fɔrm; ES fɔəm

former 'fɔrmɚ; ES 'fɔəmə(r; |-ly -lɪ— 'fɔrməlɪ, by r-dissimilation, is often heard,

leading to easier confusion with formally
(*§121*).

formic ˈfɔrmɪk; ES ˈfɔəm-; |-ary -ˌɛrɪ

formicate *adj* ˈfɔrmɪkɪt; ES ˈfɔəm-

formicate *v* ˈfɔrmɪˌket; ES ˈfɔəm-; |-d -ɪd

formidable ˈfɔrmɪdəbļ; ES ˈfɔəm-; |-bly -blɪ
—*Brit*+fɔˈmɪd-

Formosa fɔrˈmosə; ES fɔə-

formula ˈfɔrmjələ; ES ˈfɔəm-; |-s -z |-lae -ˌli
|-lary -ˌlɛrɪ

formulate ˈfɔrmjəˌlet; ES ˈfɔəm-; |-d -ɪd

formulation ˌfɔrmjəˈleʃən; ES ˌfɔəm-

fornicate ˈfɔrnɪˌket; ES ˈfɔən-; |-d -ɪd

fornication ˌfɔrnɪˈkeʃən; ES ˌfɔən-

Forres ˈfɔrɪs, ˈfɑrɪs, ˈfɒrɪs, -ɪz |-'s -ɪsɪz, -ɪzɪz

Forrest ˈfɔrɪst, ˈfɑrɪst, ˈfɒrɪst

forsake fɚˈsek; ES fə-; |-sook -ˈsʊk |-saken
-ˈsekən

forsooth fɚˈsuθ; ES fə-ˈsuθ

forspend fɔrˈspɛnd; ES fɔə-; |-spent -ˈspɛnt

forswear fɔrˈswɛr, -ˈswær; E fɔəˈswɛə(r, ES
fɔəˈswæə(r; |-swore -ˈswor, -ˈswɔr; ES
-ˈswoə(r, E+-ˈswɔə(r; |-sworn -ˈsworn,
-ˈswɔrn; ES -ˈswoən, E+-ˈswɔən

Forsyte ˈfɔrsaɪt; ES ˈfɔəsaɪt

Forsyth fɚˈsaɪθ; ES fəˈsaɪθ

forsythia, F- fɚˈsɪθɪə, fɔr-, -ˈsaɪθ-, -θjə; ES
fə-, fɔ-; *The 1st pron. follows English Latin
tradition, as in* Lydia (*L* Lȳdia); *the 2d,
the analogy of* Forsyth.

fort fort, fɔrt; ES foət, E+fɔət

forte '*strong point*' fort, fɔrt; ES foət, E+fɔət

forte *music* ˈfɔrtɪ, -te; ES ˈfɔət-

Fortescue ˈfɔrtɪsˌkju, -ˌkɪu; ES ˈfɔət-

forth, F- forθ, fɔrθ; ES foəθ, E+fɔəθ

forthcoming ˈforθˈkʌmɪŋ, ˈfɔrθ-; ES ˈfoəθ-,
E+ˈfɔəθ-

forthright *adj, adv* forθˈraɪt, fɔrθ-; ES foəθ-,
E+fɔəθ-; (ˈforthˌright ˈmind)

forthwith forθˈwɪθ, fɔrθ-, -ˈwɪð; ES foəθ-,
E+fɔəθ-

fortification ˌfɔrtəfəˈkeʃən; ES ˌfɔətə-

fortify ˈfɔrtəˌfaɪ; ES ˈfɔətə-; |-fied -ˌfaɪd

Fortinbras ˈfɔrtņˌbræs, ˈfɔrtɪn-; ES ˈfɔət-

fortissimo fɔrˈtɪsəˌmo; ES fɔˈtɪs-; (*It* for-
ˈtissiˌmo)

fortitude ˈfɔrtəˌtjud, -ˌtɪud, -ˌtud; ES ˈfɔət-

fortnight ˈfɔrtnaɪt, ˈfort-, -nɪt, -nət; ES
ˈfɔət-, ˈfoət-; |-ly -lɪ—*All the pronuncia-*

tions of fortnight *here given are regular
phonetic or analogical developments.*

fortress ˈfɔrtrɪs, -trəs; ES ˈfɔət-; |-es -ɪz
|-ed -t

fortuitous fɔrˈtjuətəs, -ˈtɪu-, -ˈtu-; ES fɔ-;
|-tism -ˌtɪzəm |-ty -tɪ

Fortuna fɔrˈtjunə, -ˈtɪu-, -ˈtu-; ES fɔə-

fortune ˈfɔrtʃən; ES ˈfɔə-; |-nate -ɪt

fortuneteller ˈfɔrtʃənˌtɛlɚ; ES ˈfɔətʃənˌtɛlə(r

forty ˈfɔrtɪ; ES ˈfɔətɪ; |-tieth -tɪθ |-fold -ˈfold

forty-niner ˌfɔrtɪˈnaɪnɚ; ES ˌfɔətɪˈnaɪnə(r

forum ˈforəm, ˈfɔrəm; S ˈforəm; |-s -z |-ra -rə

forward ˈfɔrwɚd; ES ˈfɔəwəd; |-s -z—*Some
good speakers still use the historical pron.*
ˈfɔrɚd; ES ˈfɔrəd.

forwent *past of* forgo fɔrˈwɛnt; ES fɔə-

forwhy fɔrˈhwaɪ; ES fɔəˈhwaɪ

fosse fɔs, fɒs |-s -ɪz |-d -t

fossil ˈfɑsļ, ˈfɒsļ; |-ize -ˌaɪz |-izes -ˌaɪzɪz |-ized
-ˌaɪzd

foster, F- ˈfɔstɚ, ˈfɑs-, ˈfɒs-; ES -tə(r; |-ed -d
|-ing -tərɪŋ, -trɪŋ

Fostoria fɔsˈtorɪə, fɒs-, -ˈtɔr-; S -ˈtor-

Fotheringay ˈfɑðərɪŋˌge, -ðrɪŋ-; ES+ˈfɒð-

fought fɔt

foul faʊl |-ed -d |-ly ˈfaʊllɪ, ˈfaʊlɪ

foulard fuˈlɑrd, fəˈlɑrd; ES -ˈlɑːd, E+-ˈlɑːd

foul-breathed ˈfaʊlˈbrɛθt

foulmouthed ˈfaʊlˈmaʊðd, -θt |-thedly -ðɪdlɪ

foulness ˈfaʊlnɪs |-es -ɪz

Foulness ˌfaʊlˈnɛs |-'s -ɪz

found *past & pptc of* find faʊnd

found *v* faʊnd |founded ˈfaʊndɪd

foundation faʊnˈdeʃən |-al -ļ |-ally -ļɪ

founder *n* ˈfaʊndɚ; ES -də(r; |-dress -drɪs

founder *v* ˈfaʊndɚ; ES -də(r; |-ed -d |-ing
ˈfaʊndərɪŋ, -drɪŋ

foundery ˈfaʊndərɪ, ˈfaʊndrɪ |-dry -drɪ

fount faʊnt

fountain ˈfaʊntņ, -tɪn, -tən

four for, fɔr; ES foə(r, E+fɔə(r

Fourdrinier furˈdrɪnɪɚ; ES fuəˈdrɪnɪ·ə(r

four-flush ˈforˈflʌʃ, ˈfɔr-; ES ˈfoə-, E+ˈfɔə-;
|-es -ɪz |-ed -t |-er -ɚ; ES -ə(r

fourfold *adj, adv* ˈforˈfold, ˈfɔr-; ES ˈfoə-,
E+ˈfɔə-

four-footed ˈforˈfʊtɪd, ˈfɔr-; ES ˈfoə-, E+ˈfɔə-

Fourier ˌfurɪˈe, ˈfurɪɚ; ES ˌfurɪˈe, ˈfurɪ·ə(r;
(*Fr* fuˈrje)

Fourierism ˈfʊrɪɚˌɪzəm |-ist -ɪst

four-in-hand ˈfɔrɪnˌhænd, ˈfɔr-; S ˈfor-

four-legged ˈforˈlɛgɪd, ˈfɔr-, -ˈlɛgd; ES ˈfoə-, E+ˈfɔə-

four-masted ˈforˈmæstɪd, ˈfɔr-; ES ˈfoə-, E+ˈfɔə-, -ˈmast-, -ˈmast-

four-o'clock ˈforəˌklak, ˈfɔrə-; ES ˈforəˌklak, -ˌklɒk, E+ˈfɔrə-

fourpence ˈforpəns, ˈfɔr-; ES ˈfoə-, E+ˈfɔə-; |-penny -ˌpɛnɪ, -pənɪ

four-poster ˈforˈpostɚ, ˈfɔr-; ES ˈfoəˈpostə(r, E+ˈfɔə-

fourscore ˈforˈskor, ˈfɔrˈskɔr; ES ˈfoəˈskoə(r, E+ˈfɔəˈskɔə(r; (ˈfourˌscore and ˈten)

foursome ˈforsəm, ˈfɔr-; ES ˈfoə-, E+ˈfɔə-

foursquare ˈforˈskwɛr, ˈfɔr-, -ˈskwær; E ˈfoəˈskwɛə(r, ˈfɔə-, -ˈskwæə(r; S ˈfoə-ˈskwæə(r; (ˈfourˌsquare ˈroom)

fourteen forˈtin, fɔr-; ES foə-, E+fɔə-; (ˌhe's ˈfourˈteen, ˈfourˌteen ˈmen)

fourteenth forˈtinθ, fɔr-; ES foə-, E+fɔə-; |-ths -θs—acct+ˈfourˈteenth

fourth forθ, fɔrθ; ES foəθ, E+fɔəθ; |-ths -θs

four-wheel adj, n ˈforˌhwil, ˈfɔr-; ES ˈfoə-, E+ˈfɔə-

four-wheeled ˈforˈhwild, ˈfɔr-; ES ˈfoə-, E+ˈfɔə-; (ˈfour-ˌwheeled ˈtruck)

fouter, -tre ˈfutɚ; ES ˈfutə(r

fowl faʊl |fowled faʊld |fowling ˈfaʊlɪŋ

fox faks; ES+fɒks; |-es -ɪz |-ed -t |-glove -ˌglʌv |-hound -ˌhaʊnd |-tail -ˌtel

foy v fɔɪ |-ed -d

foyer 'pilot' ˈfɔɪɚ; ES ˈfɔɪ·ə(r

foyer 'lobby' ˈfɔɪɚ, ˈfɔɪ·e; ES ˈfɔɪ·ə(r, ˈfɔɪ·e; (Fr fwaˈje)

fra, F- fra

fracas ˈfrekəs |-es -ɪz; Brit ˈfræka, pl -kaz

fraction ˈfrækʃən |-ed -d |-al -ļ |-ally -ļɪ

fractionate ˈfrækʃənˌet |-d -ɪd

fractious ˈfrækʃəs

fracture ˈfræktʃɚ; ES -tʃə(r; |-d -d

frae stressed ˈfre, ˌfre; unstr. fre, frɪ

fragile ˈfrædʒəl, -dʒɪl |-gilely -dʒəlɪ, -dʒɪlɪ, -əlɪ, -ɪlɪ

fragility fræˈdʒɪlətɪ, frə-

fragment ˈfrægmənt

fragmental frægˈmɛntļ |-ly -ɪ

fragmentary ˈfrægmənˌtɛrɪ |-ly -lɪ, esp. if emph. ˌfrægmənˈtɛrəlɪ

fragrance ˈfregrəns |-cy -ɪ |-ant -ənt

frail frel |-ly ˈfrelɪ, ˈfrelɪ |-ty -tɪ

fraise frez |-s -ɪz |-d -d

frame frem |-d -d

frame-up ˈfremˌʌp

framework ˈfremˌwɜ˞k; ES -ˌwɜk, -ˌwɜ˞k

Framingham Mass ˈfremɪŋˌhæm, Engd -mɪŋəm

franc fræŋk

France fræns; E+frans, frɑns; |-'s -ɪz

Frances ˈfrænsɪs E+ˈfran-, ˈfrɑn-; |-ces' -sɪs

Francesca franˈtʃɛska (It franˈtʃeska)

franchise ˈfræntʃaɪz |-s -ɪz |-d -d

franchisement ˈfræntʃɪzmənt

Francis ˈfrænsɪs; E+ˈfran-, ˈfrɑn-; |-cis' -sɪs

Francisca frænˈsɪskə |-can -kən |-co -ko

Franck fraŋk (Fr frɑ̃:k, Ger fraŋk)

Francke, Kuno ˈkunoˈfraŋkə

Franco-American ˈfræŋkoəˈmɛrəkən

Franco-British ˈfræŋkoˈbrɪtɪʃ

Franco-German ˈfræŋkoˈdʒɜ˞mən; ES -ˈdʒɜm-, -ˈdʒɜ˞m-

Francophile ˈfræŋkəˌfaɪl

Francophobe ˈfræŋkəˌfob |-bia ˌfræŋkəˈfobɪə

Franco-Prussian ˈfræŋkoˈprʌʃən

frangible ˈfrændʒəbļ |-bility ˌfrændʒəˈbɪlətɪ

frangipane ˈfrændʒəˌpen

frangipani ˌfrændʒɪˈpænɪ, -ˈpɑnɪ

frank, F- fræŋk |-ed -t

Frankenstein ˈfræŋkənˌstaɪn, -kɪn-

Frankfort ˈfræŋkfɚt; ES ˈfræŋkfət

Frankfurt ˈfræŋkfɚt; ES ˈfræŋkfət; (Ger ˈfraŋkfurt)

frankfurter, F- ˈfræŋkfɚtɚ; ES ˈfræŋkfətə(r

frankincense ˈfræŋkɪnˌsɛns

franklin, F- ˈfræŋklɪn |-ite -ˌaɪt

frankpledge ˈfræŋkˌplɛdʒ |-s -ɪz

frantic ˈfræntɪk |-ly -lɪ |-ally -ļɪ

frappé fræˈpe |-ed -d (Fr fraˈpe)

Fraser ˈfrezɚ, ˈfreʒɚ; ES -ə(r; (Sc ˈfreːʒər)

frater ˈfretɚ; ES ˈfretə(r

fraternal frəˈtɜ˞nļ, fre-; ES -ˈtɜnļ, -ˈtɜ˞nļ; |-ly -ɪ

fraternity frəˈtɜ˞nətɪ; ES -ˈtɜn-, -ˈtɜ˞n-

fraternize ˈfrætɚˌnaɪz, ˈfret-; ES -tə-; |-s -ɪz |-d -d

fratricide ˈfrætrəˌsaɪd, ˈfretrə-

fratricidal ˌfrætrəˈsaɪdļ, ˌfretrə-

fraud frɔd |-ful -fəl |-fully -fəlɪ

Key: See in full §§3–47. bee bi |pity ˈpɪtɪ (§6) |rate ret |yet jɛt |sang sæŋ |angry ˈæŋ·grɪ |bath bæθ; E baθ (§10) |ah ɑ |far fɑr |watch watʃ, wɒtʃ (§12) |jaw dʒɔ |gorge gɔrdʒ |go go

fraudulence ˈfrɔdʒələns |-cy -ɪ |-lent -lənt
fraught frɔt
Fraunhofer ˈfraʊnˌhofəˌ; ES -ˌhofə(r
fray fre |-ed -d
Frazer ˈfrezəˌ, ˈfreʒəˌ; ES -ə(r; (Sc ˈfreːʒər)
Frazier ˈfreʒəˌ; ES ˈfreʒə(r; cf Fraser, Frazer
frazzle ˈfræzl̩ |-d -d |-ling ˈfræzlɪŋ, -zl̩ɪŋ
freak frik
freckle ˈfrɛkl̩ |-d -d |-ling ˈfrɛklɪŋ, -kl̩ɪŋ
Frederic, -ick ˈfrɛdərɪk, ˈfrɛdrɪk
Frederica ˌfrɛdəˈrikə
Fredericksburg ˈfrɛdrɪksˌbɝg; ES -ˌbɝg,
-ˌbɝg
Fredonia NY, Kan friˈdonɪə; Colombia fre-
ˈdonjə (Am Sp freˈðonja)
free fri |freer ˈfriəˌ; ES ˈfri·ə(r
freeboard ˈfriˌbord, -ˌbɔrd; ES -ˌbɔəd, E+
-ˌbɑəd
freebooter ˈfriˌbutəˌ; ES -ˌbutə(r
freeborn ˈfriˌbɔrn; ES -ˌbɔən
Freeborn ˈfribəˌn; ES ˈfribən
freedman, F- ˈfridmən |-men -mən
freedom, F- ˈfridəm
freedwoman ˈfridˌwʊmən, -ˌwu- |-men
-ˈwɪmɪn, -ən—see woman
free-for-all ˈfrifəˈɔl (ˈfree-for-ˌall ˈfight)
freehand ˈfriˌhænd
freehanded ˈfriˈhændɪd
freehold ˈfriˌhold
freeman, F- ˈfrimən |-men -mən
Freemason ˈfriˌmesn̩, ˌfriˈmesn̩ |-ry -rɪ
freer, F- ˈfriəˌ; ES ˈfri·ə(r
free-soil, F- ˈfriˈsɔɪl (ˈFree-ˌsoil ˈparty)
free-spoken ˈfriˈspokən
freestone, F- ˈfriˌston
freethinker ˈfriˈθɪŋkəˌ; ES -ˈθɪŋkə(r
freeze, F- friz |-s -ɪz |froze froz |frozen ˈfrozn̩
Freiburg ˈfraɪbɝg; ES -bɝg, -bɝg; (Ger
ˈfraɪbʊrk)
freight fret |freighted ˈfretɪd
Frémont John C. ˈfrimɑnt, -mɒnt, frɪˈm-
Fremont O ˈfrimɑnt, -mɒnt
French frɛntʃ |-'s -ɪz |-man, -men -mən
|-woman -ˌwʊmən |-women -ˌwɪmɪn, -ən—
see woman
Frenchify ˈfrɛntʃəˌfaɪ |-fied -ˌfaɪd
Freneau frɪˈno, fre-
frenetic frəˈnɛtɪk, frɪ- |-al -l̩ |-ally -l̩ɪ
frenzy ˈfrɛnzɪ |-ied -d

frequence ˈfrikwəns |-s -ɪz |-cy -ɪ |-nt -nt
frequent v frɪˈkwɛnt |-ed -ɪd
Frere frɪr; ES frɪə(r, S+frɛə(r
fresco ˈfrɛsko |-ed -d
fresh frɛʃ |-es -ɪz |-ed -t
freshen ˈfrɛʃən |-ed -d |-ing ˈfrɛʃənɪŋ, -ʃnɪŋ
freshet ˈfrɛʃɪt
freshman ˈfrɛʃmən |-men -mən
Fresno ˈfrɛzno
fret frɛt |-ted -ɪd |-ful -fəl |-fully -fəlɪ
fretsome ˈfrɛtsəm
fretwork ˈfrɛtˌwɝk; ES -ˌwɝk, -ˌwɝk
Freud frɔɪd (Ger frɔyt) |Freudian ˈfrɔɪdɪən
Frey fre, Swiss statesm. fraɪ
Freya ˈfreə |Freyja ˈfrejə
friable ˈfraɪəbl̩
friar, F- ˈfraɪəˌ, fraɪr; ES ˈfraɪ·ə(r, fraɪə(r
friary ˈfraɪərɪ
fribble ˈfrɪbl̩ |-d -d |-ling ˈfrɪblɪŋ, -bl̩ɪŋ
fricassee ˌfrɪkəˈsi |-d -d
fricative ˈfrɪkətɪv
friction ˈfrɪkʃən |-ed -d
Friday ˈfraɪdɪ—spelt Fridy in 1642
fried past & pptc of fry fraɪd
friedcake ˈfraɪdˌkek
friend frɛnd |-ly -lɪ |-ship -ʃɪp, ˈfrɛnʃɪp
frier 'fryer' ˈfraɪəˌ; ES ˈfraɪ·ə(r
Fries Sw bot., Ger philos. fris; Am schol. friz
|-'s -ɪz
fries from fry fraɪz
Friesian ˈfriʒən |-sic -zɪk |-sish -zɪʃ
Friesland ˈfrizlənd, -ˌlænd
frieze friz |-s -ɪz |-d -d
frigate ˈfrɪgɪt
Frigg frɪg |Frigga ˈfrɪgɑ
fright fraɪt |-ed -ɪd
frighten ˈfraɪtn̩ |-ed -d |-ing ˈfraɪtn̩ɪŋ, -tnɪŋ
frightful ˈfraɪtfəl |-ly -ɪ
frigid ˈfrɪdʒɪd |-ity frɪˈdʒɪdətɪ
frijol, -e ˈfrihol, -ˈhol
frill frɪl |-ed -d
fringe frɪndʒ |-s -ɪz |-d -d
frippery ˈfrɪpərɪ
Frisian ˈfrɪʒən, ˈfrɪʒɪən
frisk frɪsk |-ed -t
frit frɪt
frith frɪθ |-ths -θs
fritillary ˈfrɪtl̩ˌɛrɪ
fritter ˈfrɪtəˌ; ES ˈfrɪtə(r; |-ed -d

---

frivol ˈfrɪvl̩ |-ed -d |-ing ˈfrɪvl̩ɪŋ, -vlɪŋ
frivolity frɪˈvɑlətɪ; ES+-ˈvɒl-
frivolous ˈfrɪvələs, ˈfrɪvləs
friz, -zz frɪz |frizzes ˈfrɪzɪz |frizzed frɪzd
frizzle ˈfrɪzl̩ |-d -d |-ling ˈfrɪzl̩ɪŋ, -zlɪŋ
fro fro
Fröbel ˈfrebl̩ (Ger ˈfrø:bəl)
Frobisher ˈfrobɪʃɚ; ES ˈfrobɪʃə(r
frock frɑk; ES+frɒk; |-ed -t
froe fro
Froebel ˈfrebl̩ (Ger ˈfrø:bəl)
frog frɑg, frɔg, frɒg; S frɔg, frɑg, frɒg; |-eye
 -ˌaɪ
Frohman ˈfromən
Froissart ˈfrɔɪsɑrt; ES -sɑ:t, E+-sa:t; (Fr
 frwɑˈsa:r)
frolic ˈfrɑlɪk; ES+ˈfrɒlɪk; |-some -səm
from stressed ˈfrɑm, ˌfrɑm, ˈfrɒm, ˌfrɒm,
 ˈfrʌm, ˌfrʌm; unstr. frəm
Frome Eng rivs. & places frum—A sp. pron.
 from is also heard in Engd.
frond frɑnd, frɒnd
Fronde Fr frõ:d
front frʌnt |fronted ˈfrʌntɪd |-age -ɪdʒ |-ages
 -ɪdʒɪz |-al -l̩ |-ally -l̩ɪ
Frontenac ˈfrɑntəˌnæk, ˈfrɒn-, in C+Fr
 frõtəˈnak
frontier frʌnˈtɪr, frɑn-, frɒn-, ˈfrʌntɪr, ˈfrɑn-,
 ˈfrɒn-; ES -ˈtɪə(r, -tɪə(r, S+-ˈtɛə(r, -tɛə(r;
 |-sman -zmən |-smen -zmən
frontispiece ˈfrʌntɪsˌpis, ˈfrɑn-; ES+ˈfrɒn-;
 |-s -ɪz
frontlet ˈfrʌntlɪt
frore arch. fror, frɔr; ES froə(r, E+frɔə(r
frost frɔst, frɒst |-ed -ɪd |-ing -ɪŋ
frostbite ˈfrɔstˌbaɪt, ˈfrɒst- |-bit -ˌbɪt |-bitten
 -ˌbɪtn̩
frostflower ˈfrɔstˌflauɚ, ˈfrɒst-, -ˌflaur; ES
 -ˌflau·ə(r, -ˌflauə(r
frostwork ˈfrɔstˌwɝk, ˈfrɒst-; ES -ˌwɜk,
 -ˌwɝk
froth frɔθ, frɒθ |-ths -θs |-ed -t
Froude frud
frou-frou ˈfrufru
frounce frauns |-s -ɪz |-d -t
frouzy ˈfrauzɪ
froward ˈfroɚd, ˈfrowɚd; ES -əd, -wəd
frown fraun |-ed -d
frowsty ˈfraustɪ

frowzy ˈfrauzɪ
froze froz |frozen ˈfrozn̩
fructification ˌfrʌktəfəˈkeʃən
fructify ˈfrʌktəˌfaɪ |-fied -ˌfaɪd |-tose -tos
fructuous ˈfrʌktʃuəs
frugal ˈfrugl̩, ˈfrɪugl̩ |-ity fruˈgælətɪ, frɪu-
fruit frut, frɪut |-ed -ɪd |-ful -fəl |-fully -fəlɪ
fruitcake ˈfrutˌkek, ˈfrɪut-
fruiterer ˈfrutərɚ, ˈfrɪut-; ES -tərə(r
fruition fruˈɪʃən, frɪu-
frumenty ˈfruməntɪ, ˈfrɪu-
frump frʌmp |-ed -t
frustrate ˈfrʌstret |-d -ɪd |-tion frʌsˈtreʃən
frustrum erron. for frustum ˈfrʌstrəm |-s -z
 |-tra -trə
frustum ˈfrʌstəm |-s -z |-ta -tə
fry fraɪ |fried fraɪd |fryer ˈfraɪɚ; ES -ə(r
Fryeburg ˈfraɪbɝg; ES -bɜg, -bɝg
fuchsia, F- ˈfjuʃə, ˈfɪu-, -ʃɪə, generic ˈfuksɪə
fuchsin ˈfuksɪn |-sine -sɪn, -sɪn
fuddle ˈfʌdl̩ |-d -d |-ling ˈfʌdl̩ɪŋ, ˈfʌdlɪŋ
fudge fʌdʒ |fudges ˈfʌdʒɪz |fudged fʌdʒd
Fuegian fjuˈidʒɪən, frʊ-, ˈfwedʒ-
Fuehrer ˈfɪrɚ, ˈfjʊ-; ES -rə(r; (Ger ˈfy:rər)
fuel ˈfjuəl, ˈfrʊəl |-ed -d
fugacious fjuˈgeʃəs, frʊ-
fugitive ˈfjudʒətɪv, ˈfɪu-
fugleman ˈfjuglˌmən, ˈfɪu- |-men -mən
fugue fjug, frʊg |-d -d
Führer ˈfɪrɚ, ˈfjʊ-; ES -rə(r; (Ger ˈfy:rər)
Fuji ˈfudʒi |Fujiyama ˌfudʒɪˈjamə
-ful unstressed ending forming adjectives (play-
 ful), pron. -fəl, -fl̩, less freq. -ful. Only the
 pron. -fəl is given in the vocabulary, it being
 understood that -fl̩ is a common variant, and
 -ful a less freq. one, being heard chiefly in
 formal style or consciously careful speech.
 Many adjectives in -ful are omitted from the
 vocabulary.
-ful half-stressed ending of compound nouns
 (cupful ˈkʌpˌful).
-ful, -full stressed second element of compound
 adjectives (brimful, -ll ˈbrɪmˈful, -ˌful, half-
 full ˈhæfˈful, -ˌful).
fulcrum ˈfʌlkrəm |-s -z |-ra -rə
fulfill, -fil fulˈfɪl |-(l)ed -d
fulgent ˈfʌldʒənt |-gid -dʒɪd
fulgor ˈfʌlgɚ; ES -gə(r; |-ous -əs
full ful |fulled fuld |fully ˈfulɪ

fullback ˈfʊlˌbæk

fuller ˈfʊlɚ; ES ˈfʊlə(r; |-ed -d

fulmar ˈfʊlmɚ; ES ˈfʊlmə(r

fulminate ˈfʌlməˌnet |-d -ɪd |-nant -nənt

fulmination ˌfʌlməˈneʃən |-nous ˈfʌlmənəs

fulsome ˈfʊlsəm, ˈfʌl-

Fulton ˈfʊltn̩

Fulvia ˈfʌlvɪə, -vjə

fulvous ˈfʌlvəs

fumarole ˈfjuməˌrol, ˈfɪu-

fumatory ˈfjuməˌtorɪ, ˈfɪu-, -ˌtɔrɪ; S -ˌtorɪ

fumble ˈfʌmbl̩ |-d -d |-ling ˈfʌmblɪŋ, -bl̩ɪŋ

fume fjum, fɪum |-d -d

fumet ˈfjumɪt, ˈfɪu- |fumette fjuˈmɛt, fɪu-

fumigate ˈfjuməˌget, ˈfɪu- |-d -ɪd

fumiter ˈfjumətɚ, ˈfɪu-; ES -tə(r

fumitory ˈfjuməˌtorɪ, ˈfɪu-, -ˌtɔrɪ; S -ˌtorɪ

fumy ˈfjumɪ, ˈfɪumɪ

fun fʌn |funned fʌnd

function ˈfʌŋkʃən |-ed -d |-al -l̩ |-ally -l̩ɪ

functionary ˈfʌŋkʃənˌɛrɪ

fund fʌnd |funded ˈfʌndɪd

fundament ˈfʌndəmənt

fundamental ˌfʌndəˈmɛntl̩ |-ly -ɪ |-ism -ˌɪzəm
    |-ist -ɪst

fundus ˈfʌndəs |-es -ɪz

Fundy ˈfʌndɪ

funeral ˈfjunərəl, ˈfɪu-

funereal fjuˈnɪrɪəl, fɪu- |-ly -ɪ

funest fjuˈnɛst, fɪu-

fungi ˈfʌndʒaɪ

fungicide ˈfʌndʒəˌsaɪd

fungoid ˈfʌŋgɔɪd |-al fʌŋˈgɔɪdl̩

fungous adj ˈfʌŋgəs

fungus n ˈfʌŋgəs |-es -ɪz |fungi ˈfʌndʒaɪ

funicle ˈfjunɪkl̩, ˈfɪu-

funicular fjuˈnɪkjələ, fɪu-; ES -lə(r

funk fʌŋk |funked fʌŋkt

funnel ˈfʌnl̩ |-ed -d

funny ˈfʌnɪ

fur fɝ; ES fɝ(r, fɝ; |-red -d

furbelow ˈfɝbl̩ˌo; ES ˈfɝ-, ˈfɝ-; |-ed -d

furbish ˈfɝbɪʃ; ES ˈfɝ-, ˈfɝ-; |-es -ɪz |-ed -t

furcate adj ˈfɝket, -kɪt; ES ˈfɝ-, ˈfɝ-

furcate v ˈfɝket; ES ˈfɝ-, ˈfɝ-; |-d -ɪd

furfur ˈfɝfɚ; ES ˈfɝfə(r, ˈfɝfə(r; |-es -ˌɪz |-al
    -ˌæl

furibund ˈfjurɪˌbʌnd, ˈfɪu-

furious ˈfjurɪəs, ˈfɪu-

furl fɝl; ES fɝl, fɝl; |-ed -d

furlong ˈfɝlɔŋ, -lɒŋ; ES ˈfɝ-, ˈfɝ-, S+-lɑŋ

furlough ˈfɝlo; ES ˈfɝlo, ˈfɝlo

furmenty ˈfɝməntɪ; ES ˈfɝ-, ˈfɝ-

furmity ˈfɝmətɪ; ES ˈfɝ-, ˈfɝ-

furnace ˈfɝnɪs, -əs; ES ˈfɝ-, ˈfɝ-; |-s -ɪz

Furnas ˈfɝnɪs, -əs; ES ˈfɝ-, ˈfɝ-; |-'s -ɪz

Furness, -niss ˈfɝnɪs, -əs; ES ˈfɝ-, ˈfɝ-; |-'s
    -ɪz

furnish ˈfɝnɪʃ; ES ˈfɝ-, ˈfɝ-; |-es -ɪz |-ed -t

furniture ˈfɝnɪtʃɚ; ES ˈfɝnɪtʃə(r, ˈfɝnɪtʃə(r

Furnival, -all ˈfɝnəvl̩; ES ˈfɝn-, ˈfɝn-

furor ˈfjurɔr, ˈfɪu-; ES -rɔə(r

furrier ˈfɝɪɚ; ES ˈfɝɪ·ə(r, ˈfʌr-, ˈfɝɪ·ə(r

furring ˈfɝɪŋ; ES ˈfɝɪŋ, ˈfɝɪŋ

furrow ˈfɝo, -ə; ES ˈfɝr-, ˈfʌr-, ˈfɝ-; |-ed -d

furrowing ˈfɝəwɪŋ; ES ˈfɝəwɪŋ, ˈfʌr-, ˈfɝ-

furry ˈfɝɪ; ES ˈfɝɪ, ˈfɝɪ

further ˈfɝðɚ; ES ˈfɝðə(r, ˈfɝðə(r; |-ed -d
    |-ing -ðərɪŋ, -ðrɪŋ |-ance -əns, -ðrəns

furthermore ˈfɝðɚˌmor, ˈfɝðə-, -ˌmɔr; ES
    ˈfɝðəˌmoə(r, ˈfɝðəˌmoə(r, E+-ˌmɔə(r;—In
    the 2d pron. ɚ has become ə by dissimilation
    (§121).

furthermost ˈfɝðɚˌmost; ES ˈfɝðə-, ˈfɝðə-

furthest ˈfɝðɪst; ES ˈfɝ-, ˈfɝ-

furtive ˈfɝtɪv; ES ˈfɝ-, ˈfɝ-

fury ˈfjurɪ, ˈfɪurɪ

furze fɝz; ES fɝz, fɝz; |-s -ɪz |-d -d

fusain ˈfjuzen, ˈfɪu-, fjuˈzen, fɪu- (Fr fyˈzæ̃)

fuscous ˈfʌskəs

fuse fjuz, fɪuz |-s -ɪz |-d -d

fusee gun fjuˈzi, fɪu-

fusée mus. Fr fyˈze

fusel ˈfjuzl̩, ˈfɪu-, -s|

fuselage ˈfjuzl̩ɪdʒ, ˈfɪu-, -ˌɑʒ; |-s -ɪz (Fr
    fyzˈlaːʒ)

fusibility ˌfjuzəˈbɪlətɪ, ˈfɪu-

fusible ˈfjuzəbl̩, ˈfɪu- |-bly -blɪ

fusiform ˈfjuzəˌfɔrm, ˈfɪu-; ES -ˌfɔəm

fusil ˈfjuzl̩, ˈfɪu-, -zɪl

fusilier, -eer ˌfjuzl̩ˈɪr, ˌfɪu-; ES -ˈɪə(r, S+
    -ˈɛə(r

fusillade ˌfjuzl̩ˈed, ˌfɪu- |-d -ɪd

fusion ˈfjuʒən, ˈfɪu-

fuss fʌs |fusses ˈfʌsɪz |fussed fʌst

fustian ˈfʌstʃən

fustic ˈfʌstɪk

fustigate ˈfʌstəˌget |-d -ɪd |-tor -ɚ; ES -ə(r

|full fʊl |tooth tuθ |further ˈfɝðɚ; ES ˈfɝðə |custom ˈkʌstəm |while hwaɪl |how haʊ |toy tɔɪ
|using ˈjuzɪŋ |fuse fjuz, fɪuz |dish dɪʃ |vision ˈvɪʒən |Eden ˈidn̩ |cradle ˈkredl̩ |keep 'em ˈkipm̩

fusty 'fʌstɪ |-tily -t|ɪ, -tɪlɪ
futhorc, -rk 'fuθɔrk; ES 'fuθɔək
futile 'fjut|, 'fɪu-, -tɪl |-ly -ɪ
futilitarian ˌfjutɪlə'tɛrɪən, ˌfɪu-, -'ter-, -rjən,
    acct+fuˌtili'tarian
futility fju'tɪlətɪ, fɪu-
Futrall 'fjutrəl, 'fɪu-
Futrell 'fjutrəl, 'fɪu-
Futrelle fju'trɛl, fɪu-

futtock 'fʌtək
future 'fjutʃɚ, 'fɪu-; ES -tʃə(r; |-rism -ˌɪzəm
    |-ist -ɪst
futuristic ˌfjutʃə'rɪstɪk, ˌfɪu-
futurity fju'tʊrətɪ, fɪu-, -'tɪʊr-, -'tjʊr- |-ric
    -rɪk
fuze fjuz, fɪuz |-s -ɪz |-d -d
fuzee fju'zi, fɪu-
fuzz fʌz |fuzzes 'fʌzɪz |fuzzed fʌzd |-y -ɪ

G

G, g letter dʒi |pl G's, Gs, poss G's dʒiz
gab gæb |gabbed gæbd
gabardine, -ber- 'gæbɚˌdin, ˌgæbɚ'din; ES
    -bə-
gabble 'gæb| |-d -d |-ling 'gæb|ɪŋ, 'gæblɪŋ
gabby 'gæbɪ
gable 'geb| |-d -d |-ling 'geb|ɪŋ, 'geblɪŋ
Gabriel 'gebrɪəl
gad, G- gæd |gadded 'gædɪd
gadabout 'gædəˌbaʊt
Gadarine ˌgædə'rin, 'gædəˌrin
Gades 'gediz |-es' -ɪz
gadfly 'gædˌflaɪ
gadget 'gædʒɪt
gadolinium ˌgædə'lɪnɪəm, -'lɪnjəm
Gadsden 'gædzdən
Gadshill 'gædzˌhɪl
gadzooks 'gæd'zuks, 'gæd'zʊks
Gaea 'dʒiə
Gaekwar 'dʒikwɑr; ES 'dʒikwɑ:(r
Gael gel |Gaelic 'gelɪk |Gaelicist 'geləsɪst
gaff gæf |gaffed gæft
gaffer 'gæfɚ; ES 'gæfə(r
gaff-topsail 'gæf'tɑps|, -ˌsel; ES+-'tɒp-
gag gæg |gagged gægd
gage gedʒ |gages 'gedʒɪz |gaged gedʒd
Gaia 'geə, 'gaɪə
gaiety 'geətɪ |gaily 'gelɪ
gaillardia ge'lɑrdɪə, gɪ-; ES -'lɑ:dɪə, E+
    -'lɑ:d-
gain gen |-ed -d |-ful -fəl |-fully -fəlɪ
Gainesville 'genzvɪl; S+-v|
gainly 'genlɪ
gainsay gen'se |-says -'sez, -'sɛz |-said -'sed,
    -'sɛd, acct+'gainˌsay, -ˌsaid

Gainsborough 'genzˌbɝo, -ə; ES -ˌbɝ-,
    -ˌbʌr-, -ˌbɝ-; Brit -bərə, -brə
Gairdner 'gɑrdnɚ, 'gerd-, 'gærd-; ES
    'gɑ:dnə(r, 'gæəd-, E+'gɑ:d-, 'gɛəd-
gait get |gaited 'getɪd
gaiter 'getɚ; ES 'getə(r
Gaius 'geəs, 'gaɪəs |-'s -ɪz
gala 'gelə
galactic gə'læktɪk
galactose gə'læktos
Galahad 'gæləˌhæd
Galapagos gə'lɑpəˌgos (Sp ga'lapagɔs)
Galashiels ˌgælə'ʃilz
Galatea ˌgælə'tiə
Galatia gə'leʃə, gə'leʃɪə |-tians -ʃənz, -ʃɪənz
Galax, g- 'gelæks |-'s -ɪz |-ias gə'læksɪəs
galaxy 'gæləksɪ |-xian gə'læksɪən
Galba 'gælbə
gale gel |galed geld
Galen 'gelən, 'gelɪn
galena, G- gə'linə
Galesburg 'gelzbɝg; ES -bɝg, -bɝg
Galicia gə'lɪʃɪə, -'lɪʃə |-cian -ʃɪən, -ʃən
Galilee 'gæləˌli |Galilean ˌgælə'liən
Galileo ˌgælə'lio (It ˌgali'lɛ:o)
galingale 'gælɪnˌgel, 'gælɪŋˌgel
Galion 'gælɪən
gall gɔl |galled gɔld
Gall gɔl, gal, gæl
gallant adj 'brave' 'gælənt
gallant adj 'amorous' gə'lænt, 'gælənt
gallant n 'gælənt, gə'lænt |-ry 'gæləntrɪ
gallant v gə'lænt |gallanted gə'læntɪd
Gallatin 'gælətɪn
galleass 'gælɪˌæs, 'gælɪəs |-es -ɪz

Key: See in full §§3–47. bee bi |pity 'pɪtɪ (§6) |rate ret |yet jɛt |sang sæŋ |angry 'æŋ·grɪ
|bath bæθ; E bɑθ (§10) |ah ɑ |far fɑr |watch wɑtʃ, wɒtʃ (§12) |jaw dʒɔ |gorge gɔrdʒ |go go

galleon ˈgælɪən, ˈgæljən	Gambia ˈgæmbɪ·ə
gallery ˈgælərɪ, -lrɪ |-ied -d	Gambier O ˈgæmˌbɪr; ES -ˌbɪə(r; loc.+gæm-
galley ˈgælɪ	ˈbɪr
gallfly ˈgɔlˌflaɪ	gambier ˈgæmˌbɪr; ES -ˌbɪə(r
Gallia ˈgælɪə	gambit ˈgæmbɪt
galliard ˈgæljɚd; ES ˈgæljəd	gamble ˈgæmbl̩ |-d -d |-ling ˈgæmblɪŋ,
galliardise ˈgæljɚdˌiz; ES ˈgæljədˌiz	ˈgæmbl̩ɪŋ
gallic, G- ˈgælɪk	gambrel ˈgæmbrəl |gambreled ˈgæmbrəld
Gallicism ˈgæləˌsɪzəm	Gambrinus gæmˈbraɪnəs |-ˈs -ɪz
Galli-Curci ˈgɑlɪˈkurtʃɪ, ˈgælɪˈkɝtʃɪ; ES	game gem |-d -d |-some -səm
-ˈkuə-, -ˈkɝ-, -ˈkɝ·-; (It ˈgɑlliˈkurtʃi)	gamecock ˈgemˌkɑk; ES+-ˌkɒk
gallimaufry ˌgæləˈmɔfrɪ	gamester ˈgemstɚ; ES ˈgemstə(r
gallinaceous ˌgæləˈneʃəs	gamete ˈgæmit, gəˈmit, gæˈmit
gallinule ˈgæləˌnjul, -ˌnɪul, -ˌnul	gamin ˈgæmɪn (Fr gaˈmæ̃)
Gallipoli gəˈlɪpəlɪ, gəˈlɪpəˌli	gamma ˈgæmə
Gallipolis O ˌgæləpəˈlis |-lis's -ˈlisɪz	gammer ˈgæmɚ; ES ˈgæmə(r
gallipot ˈgæləˌpɑt; ES+-ˌpɒt	gammon ˈgæmən
Gallitzin Pa gəˈlɪtsɪn	Gamp gæmp
gallium ˈgælɪəm	gamut ˈgæmət
gallivant ˈgæləˌvænt, ˌgæləˈvænt |-ed -ɪd	gamy ˈgemɪ
gall-less ˈgɔllɪs	gan gæn
gallnut ˈgɔlˌnʌt	Gananoque ˌgænəˈnok, loc.+-ˈnɑkwɪ (Fr ga-
galloglass ˈgæloˌglæs |-glasses -ˌglæsɪz	naˈnɔk)
gallon ˈgælən	gander ˈgændɚ; ES ˈgændə(r
gallop ˈgæləp |galloped ˈgæləpt	Gandhi ˈgɑndɪ, ˈgɑndi, ˈgændi, ˈgændɪ
Galloway ˈgæləˌwe	ganef ˈgɑnəf
gallowglass ˈgæloˌglæs |-glasses -ˌglæsɪz	gang gæŋ |ganged gæŋd |ganging ˈgæŋɪŋ
gallows ˈgæloz, -əz |gallowses rare ˈgæloziz,	gange gændʒ |-s -ɪz |-d -d
-ləzɪz |dial. gallus ˈgæləs |galluses ˈgæləsɪz	Ganges ˈgændʒiz |Ganges' ˈgændʒiz
gallstone ˈgɔlˌston	gangling ˈgæŋglɪŋ |-gly -glɪ
Gallup ˈgæləp	ganglion ˈgæŋglɪən |ganglia ˈgæŋglɪə
Gallus ˈgæləs |-li -laɪ |-'s -ɪz	gangplank ˈgæŋˌplæŋk
galop ˈgæləp |galoped ˈgæləpt	gangrene ˈgæŋgrin, ˈgæn-, gæŋˈgrin, gæn-
galore gəˈlor, -ˈlɔr; ES -ˈloə(r, E+-ˈlɔə(r	|-d -d
galosh gəˈlɑʃ; ES+-ˈlɒʃ; |-es -ɪz	gangster ˈgæŋstɚ; ES ˈgæŋstə(r
Galsworthy ˈgɔlzˌwɝˈðɪ, ˈgælz-; ES -ˌwɝði,	gangue gæŋ
-ˌwɝˈðɪ; Dev ˈgælzərɪ	gangway ˈgæŋˌwe
galumph gəˈlʌmf |galumphed gəˈlʌmft	gannet, G- ˈgænɪt
Galvani gælˈvɑnɪ (It gɑlˈvɑːni)	ganof ˈgɑnəf
galvanic gælˈvænɪk |galvanism ˈgælvəˌnɪzəm	ganoid ˈgænɔɪd |ganoidal gəˈnɔɪdl̩
galvanize ˈgælvəˌnaɪz |-s -ɪz |-d -d	Gans gænz |-'s -ɪz (Ger gɑns)
galvanometer ˌgælvəˈnɑmətɚ; ES -ˈnɑmət(r,	Gansevoort ˈgænsvurt; ES -vuət
-ˈnɒm-; |-metry -mətrɪ	gantlet ˈgæntlɪt—see gauntlet
galvanoscope gælˈvænəˌskop, ˈgælvənəˌskop	gantline ˈgæntˌlaɪn
Galveston ˈgælvɪstn̩, ˈgælvəstn̩	gantry ˈgæntrɪ
Galway ˈgɔlwe	Ganymede ˈgænəˌmid
gam gæm |gammed gæmd	gaol dʒel |gaoled dʒeld, formerly gel, geld—
Gamaliel gəˈmelɪəl, gəˈmeljəl	"Some..again are boring their very Noses
Gambetta gæmˈbɛtə	with hot Irons, in rage that they cannot come

\|full fʊl \|tooth tuθ \|further ˈfɝˈðɚ; ES ˈfɝðə \|custom ˈkʌstəm \|while hwaɪl \|how haʊ \|toy tɔɪ
\|using ˈjuzɪŋ \|fuse fjuz, fɪuz \|dish dɪʃ \|vision ˈvɪʒən \|Eden ˈidn̩ \|cradle ˈkredl̩ \|keep 'em ˈkipm̩

Words below in which a *before* r *(farm) is sounded* ɑ *are often pronounced in* E *with* a *(*fɑːm*)*
Words below that have æ *before* r *(carry* ˈkærɪ*) are often pronounced in* N *with* ɛ *(*ˈkɛrɪ, *§94)*

to a Resolution, whether they shall say..
Jayl or Gaol."—R. L'Estrange (OED).
gaolbird ˈdʒelˌbɜd; ES -ˌbɜd, -ˌbɝd
gap gæp |gapped gæpt
gape gep, gæp |gaped gept, gæpt—see gaup
gapingstock ˈgepɪŋˌstak, ˈgæp-; ES+-ˌstɒk
gar gɑr; ES gɑː(r
garage gəˈrɑʒ, gəˈrɑdʒ, ˈgærɑʒ |-s -ɪz |-d -d
(Fr gaˈraːʒ)—The fully Anglicized ˈgærɪdʒ
(cf carriage ˈkærɪdʒ) is not general in
American cultivated use.
Garand ˈgærənd
garb gɑrb; ES gɑːb; |-ed -d
garbage ˈgɑrbɪdʒ; ES ˈgɑːbɪdʒ
garble ˈgɑrbļ; ES ˈgɑːbļ; |-d -d |-ling -bļɪŋ,
-blɪŋ
garboard ˈgɑrˌbord, -ˌbɔrd; ES ˈgɑːˌboəd,
E+-ˌbɔəd
Garcia ˈgɑrʃɪə, -ʃə, -sɪə, Col gɑrˈsiə; ES -ɑː-;
(Am Sp gɑrˈsiə)
garden ˈgɑrdṇ, ˈgɑrdɪn; ES ˈgɑːdṇ, -dɪn
gardener, G- ˈgɑrdnɚ, ˈgɑrdṇɚ; ES ˈgɑːd-
gardenia gɑrˈdinɪə, -njə; ES gɑˈdin-
Gardiner ˈgɑrdnɚ, ˈgɑrdnɚ, ˈgɑrdɪnɚ; ES
ˈgɑːdnə(r, -dnə(r, -dɪnə(r
Gardner ˈgɑrdnɚ; ES ˈgɑːdnə(r
Gareth ˈgærɪθ, ˈgærəθ
Garfield ˈgɑrfild; ES ˈgɑːfild
Gargantua gɑrˈgæntʃʊə; ES gɑˈgæntʃʊə;
|-n -n
gargle ˈgɑrgļ; ES ˈgɑːgļ; |-d -d |-ling -glɪŋ,
-glɪŋ
gargoyle ˈgɑrgɔɪl; ES ˈgɑːgɔɪl; |-d -d
Gargrave ˈgɑrgrev; ES ˈgɑːgrev
Garibaldi ˌgærəˈbɔldɪ (It ˌgariˈbaldi)
garish ˈgɛrɪʃ, ˈgærɪʃ; S ˈgærɪʃ
garland, G- ˈgɑrlənd; ES ˈgɑːlənd; |-ed -ɪd
garlic ˈgɑrlɪk; ES ˈgɑːlɪk
garment ˈgɑrmənt; ES ˈgɑːmənt; |-ed -ɪd
garner ˈgɑrnɚ; ES ˈgɑːnə(r; |-ed -d
garnet ˈgɑrnɪt; ES ˈgɑːnɪt; |-ed -ɪd
garnish ˈgɑrnɪʃ; ES ˈgɑːnɪʃ; |-es -ɪz |-ed -t
garnishee ˌgɑrnɪˈʃi; ES ˌgɑː-; |-d -d
garniture ˈgɑrnɪtʃɚ; ES ˈgɑːnɪtʃə(r
Garrard ˈgærɚd; ES ˈgærəd
garret ˈgærɪt
Garrett ˈgærɪt |-sville -sˌvɪl

Garrick ˈgærɪk
garrison ˈgærəsṇ |-ed -d
garrote, -tte gəˈrot, gəˈrɑt; ES+-ˈrɒt; |-d -ɪd
garrulity gəˈrulətɪ, gəˈrɪulətɪ
garrulous ˈgærələs, ˈgærjələs
Garry ˈgærɪ
garter ˈgɑrtɚ; ES ˈgɑːtə(r; |-ed -d
garth gɑrθ; ES gɑːθ; |-ths -θs
Gary ˈgɛrɪ, ˈgɛːrɪ, ˈgærɪ, ˈgerɪ; S ˈgerɪ, ˈgærɪ—
Some speakers distinguish Gary from Gerry
by a longer ɛ.
gas n gæs |gases ˈgæsɪz |gassy ˈgæsɪ
gas v gæs |gasses ˈgæsɪz |gassed gæst
Gascoigne gæsˈkɔɪn, ˈgæskɔɪn, ˈgæskɪn
Gascon ˈgæskən |Gascony ˈgæskənɪ
gasconade ˌgæskənˈed |-aded -ˈedɪd
gaseous ˈgæsɪəs, ˈgæsjəs, ˈgæz-
gash gæʃ |gashes ˈgæʃɪz |gashed gæʃt
gasiform ˈgæsəˌfɔrm; ES -ˌfɔəm
gasify ˈgæsəˌfaɪ |-fied -ˌfaɪd
Gaskell ˈgæskļ
gasket ˈgæskɪt |gasketed ˈgæskɪtɪd
gaslight ˈgæsˌlaɪt |-lighted -ˌlaɪtɪd
gasoline, -lene ˈgæsļˌin, ˌgæsļˈin, ˈgæz-,
ˌgæz-
gasometer gæsˈɑmətɚ; ES -ˈɑmətə(r, -ˈɒmə-
tə(r
gasp gæsp; E+gɑsp, gɑsp; |-ed -t
Gaspé gæsˈpe (Fr gasˈpe) (ˈGasˌpé ˈtourist)
gaspergou ˌgæspɚˈgu, ˈgæspɚˌgu; ES -pə-
gastight ˈgæsˈtaɪt (ˈgasˌtight ˈjoint)
Gaston US ˈgæstən; Fr name gæsˈtɔn, -ˈtɑn,
-ˈtɒn (Fr gasˈtõ)
gastric ˈgæstrɪk |gastritis gæsˈtraɪtɪs
gastroenteritis ˈgæstroˌɛntəˈraɪtɪs
gastronomic ˌgæstrəˈnɑmɪk; ES+-ˈnɒmɪk;
|-al -ļ |-ally -ļɪ, -ɪklɪ
gastronomy gæsˈtrɑnəmɪ; ES+-ˈtrɒnəmɪ
gastropod ˈgæstrəˌpɑd; ES+-ˌpɒd
gastroscope ˈgæstrəˌskop
gat gæt
gate get |gated ˈgetɪd |-way -ˌwe
gate-leg ˈgetˌlɛg |gate-legged ˈgetˌlɛgd
Gath gæθ
gather ˈgæðɚ; ES ˈgæðə(r; |-ed -d |-ing
ˈgæðrɪŋ, ˈgæðərɪŋ
Gatling ˈgætlɪŋ

Gatun gɑ'tun
gauche goʃ
gaucherie ˌgoʃə'ri, 'goʃəˌri (Fr goʃ'ri)
Gaucho 'gautʃo
gaud gɔd |gaudy 'gɔdɪ |-ed -ɪd
gauffer 'gɔfɚ, 'gɒfɚ, 'gɑfɚ; ES -fə(r; |-ed -d
 |-ing -fərɪŋ, -frɪŋ
gauge gedʒ |gauges 'gedʒɪz |gauged gedʒd
Gaul gɔl
gaunt, G- gɔnt, gɒnt, gant
gauntlet 'gɔntlɪt, 'gɒnt-, 'gant—cf gantlet
gaup gɔp |gauped gɔpt—see gape
gauss gaus |gausses 'gausɪz
Gauss Christian, Karl gaus; Clarence gɔs
 |-'s -ɪz
Gautama 'gɔtəmə
gauze gɔz |gauzes 'gɔzɪz |gauzy 'gɔzɪ
gave gev
gavel 'gæv| |-ed -d |-ing 'gævlɪŋ, 'gævlɪŋ
gavelkind 'gæv|ˌkaɪnd
Gawain 'gɑwɪn, 'gɔwɪn
gawk gɔk |gawky 'gɔkɪ
gay ge |gayety 'geətɪ
Gaza Palestine 'gezə, Mozambique 'gɑzə
gaze gez |gazes 'gezɪz |gazed gezd
gazelle gə'zɛl
gazette gə'zɛt |gazetted gə'zɛtɪd
gazetteer ˌgæzə'tɪr; ES -'tɪə(r, S+-'tɛə(r
Gdynia gə'dɪnjə, -nɪə (Pol 'gdiɲa)
gear gɪr; ES gɪə(r, S+gɛə(r; |-ed -d |-shift
 -ˌʃɪft
Geauga dʒɪ'ɔgə
gecko 'gɛko
Geddes 'gɛdɪz, -ɪs |-'s -ɪz
gee dʒi |geed dʒid
geese gis |geese's 'gisɪz
geest gist
geezer 'gizɚ; ES 'gizə(r
Geffrey 'dʒɛfrɪ
Gehenna gɪ'hɛnə
Gehrkens 'gɝkɪnz, 'gɛr-; ES 'gɝ-, 'gɝ-,
 'gɛə-; |-'s -ɪz
Geierstein 'gaɪɚˌstaɪn; ES 'gaɪə-
Geikie 'gikɪ
geisha 'geʃə
gel chem. dʒɛl |gelled dʒɛld
gelatin, -e 'dʒɛlətn̩ |-(e)d -d
gelatinate dʒə'lætn̩ˌet |-d -ɪd |-nous -əs
gelation dʒɛl'eʃən, dʒə'l-

geld n gɛld
geld v gɛld |gelded 'gɛldɪd or gelt gɛlt
Gelderland 'gɛldɚlənd; ES 'gɛldə-
gelding 'gɛldɪŋ
gelid 'dʒɛlɪd |-ity dʒə'lɪdətɪ, dʒɛ-
gelt past & pptc of geld gɛlt
gem dʒɛm |gemmed dʒɛmd
geminate n, adj 'dʒɛmənɪt
geminate v 'dʒɛməˌnet |-d -ɪd
gemination ˌdʒɛmə'neʃən
Gemini 'dʒɛməˌnaɪ, as intj 'dʒɪmənɪ
gemot, -e gə'mot
gemsbok 'gɛmzbɑk; ES+-bɒk
gendarme 'ʒandɑrm; ES -dɑːm, E+-dɑːm;
 |-ry -ərɪ, -rɪ (Fr ʒɑ̃'darm)
gender 'dʒɛndɚ; ES -də(r; |-ed -d |-ing -dərɪŋ,
 -drɪŋ
gene dʒin
genealogical ˌdʒɛnɪə'lɑdʒɪk|, ˌdʒinɪ-; ES+
 -'lɒdʒ-; |-ly -ɪ
genealogy ˌdʒinɪ'ælədʒɪ, ˌdʒɛnɪ-, -'ɑlədʒɪ;
 ES+-'ɒl-; |-gist -st; The ɑ or ɒ sound is
 found in all parts of the US and in Canada.
 The -ology words have influenced it.
genera pl of genus 'dʒɛnərə
general 'dʒɛnərəl, 'dʒɛnrəl |-cy -sɪ
generalissimo ˌdʒɛnərəl'ɪsəˌmo, ˌdʒɛnrəl-
generality ˌdʒɛnə'rælətɪ
generalization ˌdʒɛnərələ'zeʃən, 'dʒɛnrəl-,
 -aɪ'z-
generalize 'dʒɛnərəlˌaɪz, 'dʒɛnrəl- |-s -ɪz
 |-d -d
generally 'dʒɛnərəlɪ, 'dʒɛnrəlɪ
generalty 'dʒɛnərəltɪ, 'dʒɛnrəltɪ
generate 'dʒɛnəˌret |-d -ɪd |-tor -ɚ; ES -ə(r
generation ˌdʒɛnə'reʃən
generic dʒə'nɛrɪk |-al -| |-ally -ʃɪ, -ɪklɪ
generosity ˌdʒɛnə'rɑsətɪ; ES+-'rɒs-
generous 'dʒɛnərəs, 'dʒɛnrəs
Genesee ˌdʒɛnə'si ('Geneˌsee 'River)
Geneseo ˌdʒɛnə'sio
genesis, G- 'dʒɛnəsɪs |pl geneses 'dʒɛnəˌsiz
Genest, Genêt dʒə'nɛt, ʒə'ne (Fr ʒə'nɛ)
genet, -tte 'dʒɛnɪt, dʒə'nɛt
genetic dʒə'nɛtɪk |-al -| |-ally -ʃɪ, -ɪklɪ |-s -s
geneticism dʒə'nɛtəˌsɪzəm |-cist -sɪst
Geneva dʒə'nivə |-van -vən
Genevese ˌdʒɛnə'viz
Genevieve 'dʒɛnəˌviv, ˌdʒɛnə'viv

Genevieve, -viève *saint* **'dʒɛnə,viv** (*Fr*
ʒən'vjɛ:v)
Genghis Khan **'dʒɛn·gɪz'kɑn, 'dʒɛŋgɪz-**
genial *'cheerful'* **'dʒinjəl** |-ly -ɪ
genial *'generative'* **'dʒiniəl**
genial *'of the chin'* dʒɪ'naɪəl
geniality ,dʒini'ælətɪ, -n'jæl-, -njɪ'ælətɪ
genic **'dʒɛnɪk**
geniculate *adj* dʒə'nɪkjəlɪt
genie **'dʒini**
genii **'dʒiniaɪ**
genital **'dʒɛnətl**
genitival ,dʒɛnə'taɪvl| |-ly -ɪ
genitive **'dʒɛnətɪv**
genito-urinary ,dʒɛnəto'jʊrə,nɛrɪ
geniture **'dʒɛnɪtʃɚ**; ES -tʃə(r
genius **'dʒinjəs,** *'spirit'* +-nɪəs |-'s -ɪz |*pl*
geniuses **'dʒinjəsɪz,** *'spirits'* genii **'dʒini,aɪ**
Gennesaret gə'nɛsərɪt, dʒə-
Genoa *Italy* **'dʒɛnəwə, dʒə'noə** (*It* Genova
'dʒɛ:nova); *US* dʒə'noə
Genoese ,dʒɛnə'wiz
genotype **'dʒɛno,taɪp**
genotypic ,dʒɛno'tɪpɪk |-al -l| |-ally -lɪ, -ɪklɪ
genre **'ʒɑnrə** (*Fr* ʒɑ̃:r)
genro **'gɛn'ro**
gens dʒɛnz |*pl* gentes **'dʒɛntiz**
Genseric **'dʒɛnsərɪk, 'gɛn-**
gent dʒɛnt
genteel dʒɛn'til |-ly -'tillɪ, -'tilɪ
gentes *pl of* gens **'dʒɛntiz**
gentian **'dʒɛnʃən, -ʃiən**
gentile, G- **'dʒɛntaɪl**
gentilesse **'dʒɛntl,ɛs,** *ME* **'dʒɛntɪ,lɛssə**
gentility dʒɛn'tɪlətɪ
gentle **'dʒɛntl| |-d -d |-ling -tlɪŋ, -tlɪŋ |-r -tlɚ;**
ES -tlə(r; |-st -tlɪst, -tlɪst
gentlefolk **'dʒɛntl,fok** |-s -s
gentleman **'dʒɛntl|mən** |-men -mən |-ly -lɪ
gentlewoman **'dʒɛntl,wʊmən, -,wʊ-** |-men
-,wɪmɪn, -ən—*see* woman
gently **'dʒɛntlɪ**
gentrice **'dʒɛntrɪs**
gentry **'dʒɛntrɪ**
genuflect **'dʒɛnju,flɛkt** |-ed -ɪd
genuflection, -flexion ,dʒɛnju,flɛkʃən
genuflexuous ,dʒɛnju'flɛkʃʊəs
genuine **'dʒɛnjʊɪn** |-ineness **'dʒɛnjʊɪnnɪs**
Genung dʒɪ'nʌŋ

genus **'dʒinəs** |*pl* genera **'dʒɛnərə** |*less freq.*
-es -ɪz
geocentric ,dʒio'sɛntrɪk |-al -l| |-ally -lɪ, -ɪklɪ
geochemistry ,dʒio'kɛmɪstrɪ
geode **'dʒiod**
geodesic ,dʒiə'dɛsɪk, -'dis- |-al -l|
geodesist dʒi'ɑdəsɪst; ES+-'ɒd-
geodesy dʒi'ɑdəsɪ; ES+-'ɒd-
geodetic ,dʒiə'dɛtɪk |-al -l| |-ally -lɪ, -ɪklɪ
Geoffrey **'dʒɛfrɪ**
geographer dʒi'ɑgrəfɚ, -'ɒg-; ES -fə(r
geographic ,dʒiə'græfɪk |-al -l| |-ally -lɪ, -ɪklɪ
geography dʒi'ɑgrəfɪ, -'ɒg-
geoid **'dʒiɔɪd** |-al dʒi'ɔɪdl|
geologic ,dʒiə'lɑdʒɪk; ES+-'lɒdʒ-; |-al -l|
|-ally -lɪ, -ɪklɪ
geologist dʒi'ɑlədʒɪst; ES+-'ɒl-
geologize dʒi'ɑlə,dʒaɪz; ES+-'ɒl-; |-s -ɪz
|-d -d
geology dʒi'ɑlədʒɪ; ES+-'ɒl-
geomancer **'dʒiə,mænsɚ;** ES -sə(r; |-cy -sɪ
geometer dʒi'ɑmətɚ; ES -'ɑmətə(r, -'ɒm-
geometric ,dʒiə'mɛtrɪk |-al -l| |-ally -lɪ, -ɪklɪ
geometrician ,dʒiəmə'trɪʃən, dʒi,əmə-; ES+
-,ɒm-
geometrize dʒi'ɑmə,traɪz; ES+-'ɒm-; |-s -ɪz
|-d -d
geometry dʒi'ɑmətrɪ; ES+-'ɒm-
geomorphic ,dʒiə'mɔrfɪk; ES -'mɔə-
geophysics ,dʒio'fɪzɪks
geopolitics ,dʒio'pɑlətɪks; ES+-'pɒl-
geoponic ,dʒiə'pɑnɪk; ES+-'pɒnɪk; |-al -l|
George dʒɔrdʒ; ES dʒɔədʒ; |-'s -ɪz
Georgette dʒɔr'dʒɛt; ES dʒɔə-
Georgia **'dʒɔrdʒə, -dʒɪə;** ES **'dʒɔədʒ-;** |-n -n
Georgiana dʒɔr'dʒænə, -dʒɪ'ænə; ES dʒɔə-
georgic, G- **'dʒɔrdʒɪk;** ES **'dʒɔə-;** |-al -l|
geostatic ,dʒiə'stætɪk |-s -s
geosyncline ,dʒio'sɪnklaɪn |-nal -sɪn'klaɪnl|
geotectonic ,dʒiotɛk'tɑnɪk; ES+-'tɒn-
geotropic ,dʒiə'trɑpɪk; ES+-'trɒpɪk
geotropism dʒi'ɑtrə,pɪzəm; ES+-'ɒt-
gerah **'gɪrə, 'gɪrə**
Geraint dʒə'rent
Gerald **'dʒɛrəld** |-ine -,in, -ɪn
geranium dʒə'renɪəm, -njəm
Gerard dʒə'rard; ES -'ra:d, E+-'ra:d; *Brit*+
'dʒɛrɑ:d, -rəd
gerent **'dʒɪrənt**

Key: *See in full §§3-47.* bee bi |pity **'pɪtɪ** (§6) |rate ret |yet jɛt |sang sæŋ |angry **'æŋ·grɪ**
|bath bæθ; E baθ (§10) |ah ɑ |far fɑr |watch wɑtʃ, wɒtʃ (§12) |jaw dʒɔ |gorge gɔrdʒ |go go

gerfalcon 'dʒɜˌfɔlkən, -ˌfɔkən; ES 'dʒɜ-, 'dʒɜ-

Gergesenes 'gɜˈgəˌsinz; ES 'gɜ-, 'gɜ-

Gerhard 'gɜˈhɑrd; ES 'gɜhɑːd, 'gɜ-, E+-hɑːd

Gerizim gə'raızım, 'gɛrəzım

germ dʒɜˈm; ES dʒɜm, dʒɜˈm

german 'dʒɜˈmən; ES 'dʒɜm-, 'dʒɜˈm-

German 'dʒɜˈmən; ES 'dʒɜˈm-, 'dʒɜˈm-; |-ism -ˌızəm |-y -ı

germander dʒɜˈ'mændə; ES dʒə'mændə(r

germane dʒɜˈ'men, dʒə-; ES dʒɜ-, dʒɜˈ-, dʒə-; |-maneness -'mennıs

Germanic dʒɜˈ'mænık, dʒə-; ES dʒɜ-, dʒɜˈ-, dʒə-

germanium dʒɜˈ'menıəm, -njəm; ES dʒɜ-, dʒɜˈ-

Germantown 'dʒɜˈmənˌtaʊn; ES 'dʒɜm-, 'dʒɜˈm-

germen 'dʒɜˈmın, -ən; ES 'dʒɜm-, 'dʒɜˈm-; |-s -z |-mina -mınə

germicide 'dʒɜˈməˌsaıd; ES 'dʒɜm-, 'dʒɜˈm-

germinal 'dʒɜˈmən]; ES 'dʒɜm-, 'dʒɜˈm-; |-ly -ı

germinant 'dʒɜˈmənənt; ES 'dʒɜm-, 'dʒɜˈm-

germinate 'dʒɜˈməˌnet; ES 'dʒɜm-, 'dʒɜˈm-; |-d -ıd |-tive -ıv

germination ˌdʒɜˈmə'neʃən; ES ˌdʒɜm-, ˌdʒɜˈm-

Gerontius dʒə'rantıəs; ES+-'rɒn-; |-'s -ız

Gerrard 'dʒɛrəd; ES 'dʒɛrəd

Gerrold 'dʒɛrəld

Gerry 'gɛrı

gerrymander 'gɛrıˌmændə, 'dʒɛrı-; ES -də(r

Gertrude 'gɜˈtrud; ES 'gɜt-, 'gɜt-

gerund 'dʒɛrənd, -ʌnd |-ive dʒə'rʌndıv

Geryon 'dʒırıən, 'gɛrıən |-es dʒı'raıəˌniz, gə-gest, -e dʒɛst

Gestapo gə'stapo (Ger gə'ʃtapo)

gestate 'dʒɛstet |-d -ıd |-tion dʒɛs'teʃən

gesticulate dʒɛs'tıkjəˌlet |-d -ıd

gesticulation ˌdʒɛstıkjə'leʃən, dʒɛsˌtık-

gesticulatory dʒɛs'tıkjələˌtorı, -ˌtɔrı; S -ˌtɔrı

gestion 'dʒɛstʃən

gesture 'dʒɛstʃə; ES -tʃə(r; |-d -d

get gɛt |past got gat, arch. gat gæt |pptc got gat or gotten 'gatn; ES+gɒt(n) — in unstressed position often gıt (wı ˌkænt gıt'ın)

get-at-able gɛt'ætəb], gıt'ætəb]

getaway 'gɛtəˌwe

Gethsemane gɛθ'sɛmənı

Gettysburg 'gɛtızˌbɜˈg; ES -ˌbɜg, -ˌbɜˈg

getup 'gɛtˌʌp

gewgaw 'gjugɔ, 'gıu- |-ed -d |-ry -rı

geyser 'spring' 'gaızə, 'gaısə, water-heater Brit 'gizə; ES -ə(r

ghast arch. gæst |-ful -fəl |-fully -fəlı

ghastly 'gæstlı; E+'gast-, 'gɑst-

ghat, ghaut gɔt

ghazi, G- 'gazi

ghee gi

Ghent Belg gɛnt, O dʒɛnt

gherkin 'gɜˈkın; ES 'gɜk-, 'gɜˈk-

ghetto 'gɛto

Ghibelline 'gıb]ın, -ˌin

Ghoorka 'gʊrkə; ES 'gʊəkə

ghost gost |-ed -ıd |-ly -lı

ghoul gul |-ish -ıʃ

Ghurka 'gʊrkə; ES 'gʊəkə

ghyl 'ravine' gıl

giant 'dʒaıənt |-ess -ıs |-esses -ısız

giaour dʒaʊr; ES dʒaʊə(r

gib, G- gıb

gibber v 'jabber' 'dʒıbə, 'gıbə; ES -bə(r; |-ed -d |-ing -bərıŋ, -brıŋ |-ish -bərıʃ, -brıʃ

gibber n 'hump' 'gıbə; ES 'gıbə(r

gibbet 'dʒıbıt |-ed -ıd

gibbon, G- 'gıbən

gibbosity gı'basətı; ES+-'bɒs-; |-bous 'gıbəs

gib-cat 'Gilbert cat' 'gıbˌkæt

gibe dʒaıb |gibed dʒaıbd

Gibeon 'gıbıən |-ites -ˌaıts

giblet 'dʒıblıt

Gibralter dʒıb'rɔltə; ES -tə(r

Gibson 'gıbsn̩

giddy 'gıdı

Gideon 'gıdıən |-s -z |-ite -ˌaıt

Gielgud 'gilgud

gier-eagle 'dʒırˌig]

gift gıft |gifted 'gıftıd

gig gıg |gigged gıgd

gigantean ˌdʒaıgæn'tıən |-tesque -'tɛsk

gigantic dʒaı'gæntık |-ally -]ı, -ıklı ('giˌgantic 'hound)

gigantism 'dʒaıgænˌtızəm, dʒaı'gæntızəm

gigantomachy ˌdʒaıgæn'taməkı; ES+-'tɒm-

giggle 'gıg] |-d -d |-ling 'gıglıŋ, 'gıg]ıŋ

giglet 'gıglıt

gigolo 'dʒıgəˌlo (Fr ʒiḡɔ'lo)

|full fʊl |tooth tuθ |further 'fɜˈðə; ES 'fɜˈðə |custom 'kʌstəm |while hwaıl |how haʊ |toy tɔı |using 'juzıŋ |fuse fjuz, fıuz |dish dıʃ |vision 'vıʒən |Eden 'idn̩ |cradle 'kred] |keep 'em 'kipm̩

gigue ʒig
Gila ˈhilə
gilbert, G- ˈgɪlbɚt; ES -bət
Gilbert and Ellice Islands ˈgɪlbɚtn̩ˈɛlɪs-
ˌaɪləndz, -lənz; ES -bət-
Gilbertian gɪlˈbɝtɪən; ES -ˈbɜt-, -ˈbɝt-
Gilboa gɪlˈboə
Gilchrist ˈgɪlkrɪst
gild gɪld |gilded ˈgɪldɪd or gilt gɪlt
Gilead ˈgɪlɪəd |-ites -ˌaɪts
Giles dʒaɪlz |-'s -ɪz
Gilfillan gɪlˈfɪlən
gill 'quarter pint' dʒɪl
Gill Jack & Gill dʒɪl
gill 'ravine' gɪl
gill of a fish gɪl |gilled gɪld
Gillespie gɪˈlɛspɪ
Gillett, -e dʒəˈlɛt, ˈdʒɪlɪt
Gillian ˈdʒɪlɪən, -ljən
gillie, -y 'servant,' 'serve' ˈgɪlɪ |-d -d
Gilliss ˈgɪlɪs |-'s -ɪz
gill-less ˈgɪllɪs
gillyflower ˈdʒɪlɪˌflauɚ, -ˌflaur; ES -ˌflau·ə(r,
-ˌflauə(r
gilt past & pptc of gild gɪlt
gilt-edged ˈgɪltˈɛdʒd (ˈgilt-ˌedged ˈbook)
gimbals ˈdʒɪmbl̩z, ˈgɪm-
gimcrack ˈdʒɪmˌkræk
gimlet ˈgɪmlɪt |-ed -ɪd
gimmal ˈgɪml̩, ˈdʒɪml̩ |-ed -d
gimmick ˈgɪmɪk
gimp 'trimming' gɪmp |-ed -t
gin 'begin' gɪn |past gan gæn |pptc gun gʌn
gin liquor dʒɪn
gin machine dʒɪn |ginned dʒɪnd
Ginevra dʒɪˈnɛvrə
ginger ˈdʒɪndʒɚ; ES -dʒə(r; |-ly -lɪ |-bread
-ˌbrɛd |-snap -ˌsnæp
gingham ˈgɪŋəm |-ed -d
gingival dʒɪnˈdʒaɪvl̩, ˈdʒɪndʒəvl̩
gingko, ginko ˈgɪŋko, ˈdʒɪŋko
gink gɪŋk
Ginn gɪn
ginseng, -sing ˈdʒɪnsɛŋ, -sɪŋ
Giotto ˈdʒɑto, ˈdʒɒto (It ˈdʒɔtto)
gip dʒɪp |-ped -t
gip 'cut fish' gɪp |-ped -t
gipon dʒɪˈpɑn, ˈdʒɪpɑn; ES+-ɒn
gipsy ˈdʒɪpsɪ

giraffe dʒəˈræf; E+-ˈrɑf, -ˈrɑf
girandole ˈdʒɪrənˌdol
Girard dʒəˈrɑrd; ES -ˈrɑ:d, E+-ˈrɑ:d
gird 'encircle' gɝd |past & pptc girt gɝt or
girded ˈgɝdɪd; |ES -3-, -ɝ-
gird 'sill,' 'sneer' gɝd; ES gɜd, gɝd; |-ed -ɪd
girdle ˈgɝdl̩; ES ˈgɜdl̩, ˈgɝdl̩; |-d -d |-ling
-dl̩ɪŋ, -dlɪŋ |-ler -dlɚ, -dl̩ɚ; ES -dlə(r,
-dl̩ə(r
girl gɝl, much less freq. gɛrl; ES gɜl, gɝl, gɛəl;
|-hood -hud
Girondist dʒəˈrɑndɪst; ES+-ˈrɒn-
girt gɝt; ES gɜt, gɝt; |-ed -ɪd
girth gɝθ; ES gɜθ, gɝθ; |-ths -θs |-ed -t
gisarme gɪˈzɑrm; ES -ˈzɑ:m, E+-ˈzɑ:m
Gissing ˈgɪsɪŋ
gist dʒɪst
gittern ˈgɪtɚn; ES ˈgɪtən
give gɪv |gave gev |given ˈgɪvən
give-and-take ˈgɪvənˈtek
giveaway ˈgɪvəˌwe
given ˈgɪvən
Giza ˈgizə |Gizeh ˈgizɛ
gizzard ˈgɪzɚd; ES ˈgɪzəd
glabrous ˈglebrəs
glacé glæˈse (Fr glaˈse)
glacial ˈgleʃəl, -ʃɪəl |-ly -ɪ
glaciate ˈgleʃɪˌet |-d -ɪd
glacier ˈgleʃɚ; ES ˈgleʃə(r; Brit usually
ˈglæsɪə, ˈglæsjə
glacis ˈglesɪs, ˈglæsɪs (Fr glaˈsi) |-es -ɪz
glad glæd |gladded ˈglædɪd
gladden, G- ˈglædn̩ |-ed -d |-ing ˈglædn̩ɪŋ,
-dnɪŋ
glade gled
gladiator ˈglædɪˌetɚ; ES -ˌetə(r
gladiatorial ˌglædɪəˈtorɪəl, -ˈtɔr-; S -ˈtor-
gladiola ˌglædɪˈolə, gləˈdaɪələ |pl -s -z
gladiolus plant ˌglædɪˈoləs |pl -es -ɪz |-li -laɪ
Gladiolus the genus gləˈdaɪələs |pl -li -ˌlaɪ
gladsome ˈglædsəm
Gladstone ˈglædˌston, -stən—W. E. Gladstone pronounced his name ˈgladˌston
(Wyld).
Gladys ˈglædɪs |-'s -ɪz
glair gler, glær; E glɛə(r, ES glæə(r; |-ed -d
|-eous -ɪəs |-y -ɪ
glaive glev |glaived glevd
Glamis Scotl glɑmz, in Shak. ˈglɑmɪs |-'s -ɪz

Glamorganshire glə'mɔrgən‚ʃɪr, -ʃɚ; ES
-'mɔəgən‚ʃɪə(r, -ʃə(r
glamorous 'glæmərəs, 'glæmrəs
glamour, -mor 'glæmɚ; ES 'glæmə(r
glance glæns; E+glans, glɑns; |-s -ɪz |-d -t
gland glænd
glanders 'glændɚz; ES 'glændəz
glandular 'glændʒələ; ES 'glændʒələ(r; |-lous
-ləs
glandule 'glændʒul
glans glænz |pl glandes 'glændiz
Glansdale 'glænz‚del, -d|
glare glɛr, glær; E glɛə(r, ES glæə(r; |-d -d
Glarus Swtz 'glɑrəs (Fr Glaris gla'ris), Wis
'glærəs |-'s -ɪz
Glasgow 'glæsgo, 'glæz-, 'glæsko, Brit+'gla-
glass glæs; E+glas, glɑs; |-es -ɪz |-ed -t
glassful 'glæs‚ful; E+'glas-, 'glɑs-; |-s -z
glasshouse 'glæs‚haʊs; E+'glas-, 'glɑs-;
|-houses -‚haʊzɪz
glassmaker 'glæs‚mekɚ; ES -‚mekə(r, E+
'glas-, 'glɑs-
glassman 'glæsmən; E+'glas-, 'glɑs-; |-men
-mən
glassware 'glæs‚wɛr, -‚wær; E -‚wɛə(r,
-‚wæə(r, 'glas-, 'glɑs-; S 'glæs‚wæə(r
glasswork 'glæs‚wɝk; ES -‚wɜk, -‚wɝk,
E+'glas-, 'glɑs-
Glastonbury 'glæstən‚bɛrɪ, 'glæsn̩-, -bərɪ
Glaswegian glæs'widʒən, -dʒɪən
Glauber 'glaʊbɚ; ES 'glaʊbə(r
glaucoma glɔ'komə
glaucous, G- 'glɔkəs
glaze glez |glazes 'glezɪz |glazed glezd
glazier 'gleʒɚ; ES 'gleʒə(r
gleam glim |-ed -d
glean glin |-ed -d
glebe glib
glee gli |-ful -fəl |-fully -fəlɪ |-man -mən
|-men -mən
glee v 'squint' gli |gleed glid—see agley
gleet glit |gleeted 'glitɪd
glen glɛn
Glencairn glɛn'kɛrn, -'kærn; E -'kɛən, ES
-'kæən
Glencoe US 'glɛnko, Scotl glɛn'ko
Glendower 'glɛndaʊɚ, glɛn'daʊɚ; ES -ə(r
Glengarry glɛn'gærɪ
gley v 'squint' glaɪ |gleyed glaɪd—see agley

glib glɪb |glibbed glɪbd
glide glaɪd |glided 'glaɪdɪd |-r -ɚ; ES -ə(r
glim glɪm
glimmer 'glɪmɚ; ES -ə(r; |-ed -d |-ing 'glɪm-
ərɪŋ, 'glɪmrɪŋ
glimpse glɪmps |-s -ɪz |-d -t
glint glɪnt |glinted 'glɪntɪd
glissade glɪ'sɑd, -'sed |-d -ɪd
glissando glɪ'sɑndo |pl -di -di (pseudo-It)
glisten 'glɪsn̩ |-ed -d |-ing 'glɪsn̩ɪŋ, -snɪŋ
glister 'glɪstɚ; ES -tə(r; |-ed -d |-ing 'glɪstərɪŋ,
'glɪstrɪŋ
glitter 'glɪtɚ; ES -tə(r; |-ed -d
gloam glom |-ed -d |-ing -ɪŋ
gloat glot |gloated 'glotɪd
global 'glob| |-ly -ɪ
globate 'globet |-d -ɪd
globe glob |globed globd
globeflower 'glob‚flaʊɚ, -‚flaʊr; ES -‚flaʊ·ə(r,
-‚flaʊə(r
globoid 'globɔɪd
globose 'globos, glo'bos |-bous 'globəs
globular 'glɑbjələ; ES 'glɑbjələ(r, 'glɒb-
globule 'glɑbjul; ES+'glɒb-
globulin 'glɑbjəlɪn; ES+'glɒb-
Glocester 'glɑstɚ, 'glɒs-; ES -tə(r
glockenspiel 'glɑkən‚spil; ES+'glɒk-; (Ger
'glɔkən‚ʃpi:l)
glomerate adj 'glɑmərɪt, -mrɪt; ES+'glɒm-
glomerate v 'glɑmə‚ret; ES+'glɒm-; |-d -ɪd
glomeration ‚glɑmə'reʃən; ES+‚glɒm-
gloom glum |gloomed glumd |-y -ɪ
Gloria 'glorɪə, 'glɔr-; S 'glorɪə; |G- Patri
-'pɑtrɪ, -'petraɪ
Gloriana ‚glorɪ'ænə, ‚glɔr-, -'enə; S ‚glor-
glorification ‚glorəfə'keʃən, ‚glɔr-; S ‚glor-
glorify 'glorə‚faɪ, 'glɔr-; S 'glor-; |-fied -‚faɪd
|-fier -‚faɪɚ; ES -‚faɪ·ə(r
glorious 'glorɪəs, 'glɔr-; S 'glor-
glory 'glorɪ, 'glɔrɪ; S 'glorɪ; |-ried -rɪd
Glos. abbr. for Gloucestershire glɑs, glɒs, glɔs
gloss glɔs, glɒs |-es -ɪz |-ed -t
glossary 'glɑsərɪ, 'glɒs-, 'glɔs-
Gloster Ga, La, Minn, Miss 'glɑstɚ, 'glɒs-;
ES -tə(r
glottal 'glɑt|; ES+'glɒt|
glottalize 'glɑt|‚aɪz; ES+'glɒt-; |-s -ɪz |-d -d
glottis 'glɑtɪs; ES+'glɒt-; |-es -ɪz
Gloucester 'glɑstɚ, 'glɒs-, 'glɔs-; ES -tə(r; in

Engd loc. ˈglɔs- |-shire -ˌʃɪr, -ʃɚ; ES -ˌʃɪə(r, -ʃəˈr	*freq.* gən — *in unstressed position often* gʊ (ˌlɛts gʊˈɪn), *or* gə (ˌlɛts gəˈdaʊn)
Glouster *O* ˈglaʊstɚ; ES ˈglaʊstə(r	goad god |goaded ˈgodɪd
glove glʌv |gloved glʌvd	go-ahead *adj* ˈgoəˈhɛd (ˈgo-aˈhead ˌchap,
Gloversville ˈglʌvɚzˌvɪl; ES -vəz-	ˈgo-aˌhead ˈspirit)
glow glo |glowed glod	go-ahead *n* ˈgoəˌhɛd
glower ˈglaʊɚ; ES ˈglaʊ·ə(r; |-ed -d |-ing ˈglaʊrɪŋ, ˈglaʊərɪŋ	goal gol |-ed -d, *children's game*+gul
glowfly ˈgloˌflaɪ	goalkeeper ˈgolˌkipɚ; ES -ˌkipə(r
glowworm ˈgloˌwɝm; ES -ˌwɜm, -ˌwɝm	goalless ˈgollɪs
gloxinia, G- glɑkˈsɪnɪə, -njə; ES+glɒk-	goat got
gloze gloz |glozes ˈglozɪz |glozed glozd	goatee goˈti
glucinum, -nium gluˈsaɪnəm, -ˈsɪnɪəm, glɪu-	goatherd ˈgotˌhɝd; ES -ˌhɜd, -ˌhɝd
Gluck glʊk	goatsbeard ˈgotsˌbɪrd; ES -ˌbɪəd, S+-ˌbɛəd
glucose ˈglukos, ˈglɪu- |-coside -kəˌsaɪd	goatsucker ˈgotˌsʌkɚ; ES -ˌsʌkə(r
glue glu, glɪu |-d -d	gob, G- gɑb; ES+gɒb
Glueck glʊk	gobbet ˈgɑbɪt; ES+ˈgɒbɪt
glum glʌm	gobble ˈgɑbl̩; ES+ˈgɒbl̩; |-d -d |-ling -blɪŋ, bl̩ɪŋ
glume glum, glɪum	gobbler ˈgɑblɚ; ES ˈgɑblə(r, ˈgɒb-
glut glʌt |glutted ˈglʌtɪd	Gobbo ˈgɑbo; ES+ˈgɒbo
gluten ˈglutn̩, ˈglɪutn̩ |-ous -əs	Gobelin ˈgɑbəlɪn, ˈgob-; ES+ˈgɒb-; (*Fr* gɔˈblæ̃)
glutinous ˈglutɪnəs, ˈglɪu-	go-between ˈgobəˌtwin
glutton ˈglʌtn̩ |-ous -əs |-y -ɪ	Gobi ˈgobɪ, ˈgobi
glyceric glɪˈsɛrɪk, ˈglɪsərɪk	goblet ˈgɑblɪt; ES+ˈgɒb-
glycerin ˈglɪsrɪn, -sərɪn |-ine -rɪn, -səˌrin	goblin ˈgɑblɪn; ES+ˈgɒb-; *In 'Little Orphant Annie' Riley pronounced it* ˈgɑbəˌlɪn.
glycerol ˈglɪsəˌrol, -ˌrɑl, -ˌrɒl	goby ˈgobɪ
glyceryl ˈglɪsəˌrɪl	go-by ˈgoˌbaɪ
glycine ˈglaɪsin, glaɪˈsin	gocart ˈgoˌkɑrt; ES -ˌkɑ:t, E+-ˌkɑ:t
glycogen ˈglaɪkədʒən, -dʒɪn	god gɑd, gɒd
glycol ˈglaɪkol, -kɑl, -kɒl	God gɑd, gɒd, *less freq.* gɔd
glycoprotein ˌglaɪkəˈprotiɪn	Godalming ˈgɑdl̩mɪŋ, ˈgɒd-
glyph glɪf	godchild ˈgɑdˌtʃaɪld, ˈgɒd-
glyptic ˈglɪptɪk |-al -l̩	goddaughter ˈgɑdˌdɔtɚ, ˈgɒd-; ES -tə(r
G-man ˈdʒiˌmæn |-men -ˌmɛn	goddess ˈgɑdɪs, ˈgɒd- |-es -ɪz
Gnadenhutten *O, loc.* dʒɪˈnedn̩ˌhʌtn̩ (*Ger* -hütten ˈgnɑːdənˌhytən)	godfather ˈgɑdˌfɑðɚ, ˈgɒd-; ES -ˌfɑðə(r, E+-ˌfɑðə(r
gnarl nɑrl; ES nɑ:l, E+nɑ:l; |-ed -d	god-fearing ˈgɑdˌfɪrɪŋ, ˈgɒd-; S+-ˌfɛrɪŋ, -ˌfjɪrɪŋ, -ˌfjɛrɪŋ
gnash næʃ |gnashes ˈnæʃɪz |gnashed næʃt	god-forsaken ˈgɑdfɚˈsekən, ˈgɒd-; ES -fə-; (ˈgod-forˌsaken ˈplace)
gnat næt	Godfrey ˈgɑdfrɪ, ˈgɒd-
gnaw nɔ |gnawed nɔd |-er ˈnɔɚ; ES ˈnɔ·ə(r	godhead ˈgɑdhɛd, ˈgɒd- |-hood -hʊd
gneiss naɪs	Godiva goˈdaɪvə
gnome nom	godlike ˈgɑdˌlaɪk, ˈgɒd-
gnomic ˈnomɪk |-al -l̩ |-ally -l̩ɪ, -ɪklɪ	godly ˈgɑdlɪ, ˈgɒdlɪ
gnomon ˈnomɑn, ˈnomɒn	godmother ˈgɑdˌmʌðɚ, ˈgɒd-; ES -ˌmʌðə(r
Gnossus ˈnɑsəs; ES+ˈnɒs-; |-sus' -səs	godown *'a drink'* ˈgoˌdaʊn
gnostic ˈnɑstɪk; ES+ˈnɒs-; |-al -l̩ |-ally -l̩ɪ, -ɪklɪ |-ism -təˌsɪzəm	
gnu nu, nɪu, nju	
go go |went wɛnt |gone gɔn, gɒn, *much less*	

godown *'warehouse'* go'daʊn
godparent 'gɑd‚pɛrənt, 'gɒd-, -‚pær-, -‚per-
godsend 'gɑd‚sɛnd, 'gɒd-
godson 'gɑd‚sʌn, 'gɒd-
Godspeed 'gɑd‚spid, 'gɒd-, -'spid
Godward 'gɑdwəd, 'gɒd-; ES -wəd
Goebbels *Ger* 'gœbəls
goer 'goɚ; ES 'go·ə(r
Goethals 'goθəlz |-'s -ɪz
Goethe 'getɪ, 'gɜtə (*Ger* 'gøːtə)
Goffe gɔf, gɒf
goffer 'gafɚ, 'gɒfɚ, 'gɔfɚ; ES -fə(r; |-ed -d
|-ing -fərɪŋ, -frɪŋ
Gog gag, gɒg, gɔg
go-getter 'go'gɛtɚ; ES -'gɛtə(r
goggle 'gagḷ, 'gɒgḷ |-d -d |-ling -glɪŋ, -gḷɪŋ
goggles 'gagḷz, 'gɒg-
Gogmagog 'gagmə‚gag, 'gɒgmə‚gɒg
Gogol 'gogal, 'gogɒl
Goidelic gɔɪ'dɛlɪk
goiter, -tre 'gɔɪtɚ; ES 'gɔɪtə(r; |-(e)d -d
Golconda gɑl'kɑndə; ES+gɒl'kɒndə
gold gold, *formerly* guld
goldbeater 'gold‚bitɚ; ES -‚bitə(r
golden 'goldn̩
goldenrod 'goldn̩‚rad; ES+-‚rɒd
goldfinch 'gold‚fɪntʃ |-es -ɪz
goldfish 'gold‚fɪʃ |-es -ɪz |-'s -ɪz
goldilocks, G- 'goldɪ‚laks; ES+-‚lɒks; |-'s -ɪz
gold-plate *v* 'gold'plet |-plated -'pletɪd
goldsmith, G- 'gold‚smɪθ |-ths -θs
Goldwin, Gouldin 'goldwɪn, 'goldɪn
golf galf, gɒlf, gɔlf, *much less freq.* gaf, gɒf
|-ed -t
Golgotha 'galgəθə, 'gɒl-
goliard 'goljəd; ES 'goljəd
Goliath gə'laɪəθ
Gollancz 'galənts, -ænts; ES+'gɒl-; |-'s -ɪz
golliwog 'galɪ‚wag, -‚wɒg; ES+'gɒl-
golosh gə'laʃ; ES+-'lɒʃ; |-es -ɪz
Gomorrah, -rrha gə'mɔrə, -'mɑr-, -'mɒr-
‚gonad 'gɑnæd, 'gɒn-
gondola 'gandələ, 'gɒn- |-ed -d
gondolier ‚gandə'lɪr, ‚gɒn-; ES -'lɪə(r, S+
-'lɛə(r
gone gɔn, gɒn, *much less freq.* gan
goneness 'gɔnnɪs, 'gɒn-, *much less freq.* 'gan-
Goneril 'ganərəl, 'gɒn-, -rɪl
gonfalon 'ganfələn, 'gɒn-

gonfalonier ‚ganfələ'nɪr, ‚gɒn-; ES -'nɪə(r,
S+-'nɛə(r
gonfanon 'ganfənən, 'gɒn-
gong gɔŋ, gɒŋ, gaŋ |-ed -d
gonococcus ‚ganə'kakəs |*pl* -cocci -'kaksaɪ;
|ES+‚gɒnə'kɒk-
gonof 'ganəf, 'gɒn-
gonorrhea ‚ganə'riə, ‚gɒn-
Gonzaga gən'zagə (*It* gon'dzɑːgɑ)
Gonzalo gən'zalo
goober 'gubɚ, 'gʊbɚ; ES -bə(r
good gʊd |goodly 'gʊdlɪ
good-by, -bye gʊd'baɪ
good deal *'good bargain'* 'gʊd'dil, *'much'*
gʊ'dil
goodhearted 'gʊd'hartɪd; ES -'haːtɪd, E+
-'haːtɪd
good-humored 'gʊd'jumɚd, -'hjumɚd; ES
-məd
goodman 'gʊdmən |-men -mən
good-natured 'gʊd'netʃɚd; ES -'netʃəd;
('good-‚natured 'dog)
goodness 'gʊdnɪs |-es -ɪz
goods gʊdz
good-tempered 'gʊd'tɛmpɚd; ES -'tɛmpəd
goodwife 'gʊd‚waɪf — *see* wife
Goodwin 'gʊdwɪn
goody 'gʊdɪ
Goodyear 'gʊdʒɪr, 'gʊdjɪr; ES -ɪə(r, S+
-ɛə(r
goof guf |-y -ɪ
googly 'guglɪ
goon gun
Goop gup
goose gus |-'s -ɪz |geese gis |geese's 'gisɪz
gooseberry 'gus‚bɛrɪ, 'guz-, -bərɪ, *rarely*
'guz-
gooseherd 'gus‚hɜd; ES -‚hɜd, -‚hɝd; *formerly* 'gazɚd, 'gɒz-
gooseneck 'gus‚nɛk |-ed -t
gopher 'gofɚ; ES -fə(r; |-ed -d |-ing 'gofərɪŋ,
'gofrɪŋ
Gordian 'gɔrdɪən, -djən; ES 'gɔəd-
gore gor, gɔr; ES goə(r, E+gɔə(r; |-d -d
gorge gɔrdʒ; ES gɔədʒ; |-s -ɪz |-d -d |-ous -əs
gorget 'gɔrdʒɪt; ES 'gɔədʒɪt; |-ed -ɪd
Gorgon 'gɔrgən; ES 'gɔəgən
Gorgonian gɔr'gonɪən, -njən; ES gɔ-
Gorgonzola ‚gɔrgən'zolə; ES ‚gɔəgən-

Gorham ˈgɔrəm, *NH* ˈgorəm, ˈgɔrəm
gorilla gəˈrɪlə
Gorky, -ki ˈgɔrkɪ; ES ˈgɔəkɪ
gormand ˈgɔrmənd; ES ˈgɔəmənd
gormandize ˈgɔrmənˌdaɪz; ES ˈgɔəm-; |-s -ɪz
|-d -d
gorse gɔrs; ES gɔəs; |-s -ɪz
gory ˈgorɪ, ˈgɔrɪ; S ˈgorɪ
goshawk ˈgasˌhɔk, ˈgɒs-
Goshen ˈgoʃən
gosling ˈgazlɪŋ, ˈgɒz-
gospel ˈgɑspl̩, ˈgɒs- |-ed -d
gossamer ˈgɑsəmɚ; ES ˈgɑsəmə(r, ˈgɒs-
Gosse gɔs, gɒs, gas
gossip ˈgɑsəp; ES+ˈgɒs-; |-ed -t
gossoon gɑˈsun; ES+gɒ-
got gɑt; ES+gɒt
Gotama ˈgɔtəmə, ˈgɒt-
Göteborg ˈjetəˌbɔrg *or* Gothenburg ˈgɑtn̩-
ˌbɝg; ES ˈjetəˌbɔəg, ˈgɑtn̩ˌbɜg, -ˌbɝg, ˈgɒt-;
(*Sw* ˌjøtəˈbɔrj)
Goth gɑθ, gɒθ, gɔθ |-ths -θs
Gotham '*New York*' ˈgɑθəm, ˈgɒθəm, ˈgoθəm,
in Notts ˈgɑtəm, ˈgɒtəm, *loc.* ˈgotəm
Gothard ˈgɑtɚd; ES ˈgɑtəd, ˈgɒt-; (*Fr*
gɔˈtaːr)
Gothic ˈgɑθɪk, ˈgɒθɪk |-ism -θəˌsɪzəm
Gotland ˈgɑtlənd, ˈgɒt-
gotten ˈgɑtn̩; ES+ˈgɒtn̩
Götterdämmerung *Ger* ˈgœtərˌdɛməˌrʊŋ
Gotthard ˈgɑtɚd; ES ˈgɑtəd, ˈgɒt-; (*Fr*
gɔˈtaːr)
Gottland ˈgɑtlənd, ˈgɒt-
gouge gaʊdʒ |gouges ˈgaʊdʒɪz |gouged gaʊdʒd
—*Brit*+gudʒ
Gough gɔf, gɒf, gaf
goulash ˈgulæʃ, -laʃ |-es -ɪz
Gouldin = Goldwin ˈgoldɪn
Gouldsboro ˈguldzˌbɝo, -ə; ES -ˌbɜr-, -ˌbʌr-,
-ˌbɝ-; *Me loc.* ˈgulzbrə
Gounod ˈguno (*Fr* guˈno)
gourd gord, gɔrd, gurd; E gɔəd, gɔəd, guəd;
S gɔəd
gourmand ˈgurmənd; ES ˈguəmənd; (*Fr*
gurˈmɑ̃)
gourmet ˈgurme; ES ˈguəme; (*Fr* gurˈmɛ)
gout gaʊt
Gouverneur *NY* ˌgʌvɚˈnʊr; ES ˌgʌvəˈnʊə(r
govern ˈgʌvɚn; ES ˈgʌvən; |-ed -d

governance ˈgʌvɚnəns; ES ˈgʌvənəns; |-s -ɪz
governess ˈgʌvɚnɪs; ES ˈgʌvənɪs; |-es -ɪz
government ˈgʌvɚmənt, ˈgʌvɚnmənt; ES
ˈgʌvəmənt, ˈgʌvənmənt, ˈgʌvm̩ənt; *No
competent observer can doubt the prevalence
of* ˈgʌvɚmənt, ˈgʌvəmənt *among the leading
statesmen of US and England, even in formal
public address.*
governor ˈgʌvɚnɚ, ˈgʌvnɚ, ˈgʌvɚnɚ; ES
ˈgʌvənə(r, ˈgʌvnə(r;—ə *for* ɚ *in* ˈgʌvənɚ
shows dissimilation (§121).
gowan ˈgaʊən
Gowanda gəˈwandə, go-, -ˈwɒndə
Gower *ME poet* ˈgoɚ, ˈgaʊɚ, *Lond street*
ˈgaʊɚ; ES ˈgo·ə(r, ˈgaʊ·ə(r
gown gaʊn |-ed -d
grab græb |grabbed græbd
grabble ˈgræbl̩ |-d -d |-ling ˈgræblɪŋ, -bl̩ɪŋ
Gracchus ˈgrækəs |-'s -ɪz |*pl* -chi ˈgrækaɪ
grace, G- gres |-'s -ɪz |-s -ɪz |-d -t
gracile ˈgræsl̩, -ɪl
gracious ˈgreʃəs
grackle ˈgrækl̩
gradate ˈgredet |-d -ɪd
gradation greˈdeʃən |-ed -d |-al -l̩ |-ally - lɪ
grade gred |graded ˈgredɪd
Gradgrind, g- ˈgrædˌgraɪnd |-ian -ɪən |-ism
-ˌɪzəm
gradient ˈgredɪənt, -djənt
gradual ˈgrædʒuəl, -dʒul |-ly -ɪ, -dʒəlɪ
graduate *n, adj* ˈgrædʒuɪt, -ˌet
graduate *v* ˈgrædʒuˌet |-d -ɪd
graduation ˌgrædʒuˈeʃən
Gradus, g- ˈgredəs |-es -ɪz
graft græft; E+graft, graft; |-ed -ɪd
graham, G- ˈgreəm
grail grel
grain gren |-ed -d
grainery, -ary ˈgrenərɪ, ˈgrenrɪ—*cf* granary.
Both grainery, -ary *and* granary *date from
the 16c. In US* ˈgrenərɪ, ˈgrenrɪ *appears to
prevail.*
gram græm
gramarye, -ry ˈgræmərɪ
gramercy grəˈmɝsɪ; ES -ˈmɜsɪ, -ˈmɝsɪ,
(ˈGramercy ˈPark)
grammar ˈgræmɚ; ES ˈgræmə(r
grammarian grəˈmɛrɪən, -ˈmær-, -ˈmer-
grammatical grəˈmætɪkl̩ |-ly -ɪ, -ɪklɪ

gramme **græm**
gramophone, G- **'græmə₁fon**
Grampian **'græmpɪən, -pjən** |-s -z
grampus **'græmpəs** |-es -ɪz
Granada grə**'nadə** (*Sp* gra**'naða**)
granary **'grænərɪ**—*cf* grainery. Granary
  'grænərɪ *comes from Latin* grānārium;
  grainery, -ary *from English* grain.
Granby **'grænbɪ**; *in Mass loc.* **'græmbɪ**
Gran Chaco **'gran'tʃako**
grand **grænd**, *before some conss.*+**græn** (*cf*
  'grænd'lek *with* **'græn'vju**)
grandad **'græn₁dæd** |-dy -ɪ
grandam **'grændəm**
grandame **'grændem, -dəm**
grandaunt **'grænd'ænt**, *much less freq.* -**'ant**;
  E -**'ant**, -**'ant**, -**'ænt**
grandchild **'græn₁tʃaɪld, 'grænd-** |-ren -₁tʃɪl-
  drən
Grand Coulee **'grænd'kulɪ, -'kuli**
granddad **'græn₁dæd** |-dy -ɪ
granddaughter **'græn₁dɔtɚ, 'grænd-**; ES
  -₁dɔtə(r
grandee græn**'di**
grandeur **'grændʒɚ, -dʒʊr**; ES **'grændʒə(r,
  -dʒʊə(r**
grandfather **'græn₁faðɚ, 'grænd-**; ES -₁faðə(r,
  E+-₁faðə(r; |-ly -lɪ
Grandgent **'grændʒənt**
grandiloquence græn**'dɪləkwəns** |-ent -ənt
grandiose **'grændɪ₁os**
grandiosity ₁grændɪ**'asətɪ**; ES+-**'ɒsətɪ**
Grandison **'grændəsn̩**
grandma **'grænma, 'græmma, 'græma,
  'græmə, 'grændma**
grandmamma **'græn₁mamə, 'grænd-, -mə₁ma**
grandmother **'græn₁mʌðɚ, 'grænd-**; ES
  -₁mʌðə(r; |-ly -lɪ
grandnephew **'græn₁nɛfju, 'grænd-**, *much less
  freq.* -**'nɛvju**
grandniece **græn'nis, 'grænd-** |-s -ɪz
grandpa **'grænpa, 'græmpa, 'græmpə, 'grænd-
  pa**
grandpapa **'græn₁papə, -pə'pa, 'grænd-**
grandparent **'græn₁pɛrənt, 'grænd-, -₁pær-,
  -₁per-**; S -₁pær-, -₁per-
Grand Pré **'græn'pre, 'grænd-** (*Fr* grɑ̃**'pre**)
Grandpré *Shak.* **'grænpre, 'grændp-**; *Fr vil.*
  grɑ̃**'pre**

grandsire **'græn₁saɪr, 'grænd-**; ES -₁saɪə(r
grandson **'græn₁sʌn, 'grænd-**
grandstand **'græn₁stænd, 'grænd-**
Grand Teton **'græn'titn̩, 'grænd-, -tan, -tɒn**
granduncle **'grænd'ʌŋkl̩**
grange, G- **grendʒ** |-s -ɪz
Granicus grə**'naɪkəs** |-'s -ɪz
granite **'grænɪt** |-tic grə**'nɪtɪk, græ-**
granny **'grænɪ**
grant **grænt**; E+**grant, grɑnt**; |-ed -ɪd
Grant **grænt**
grantee græn**'ti**; E+**gran-, grɑn-**
grantor **'græntɚ, græn'tɔr**; ES -tə(r, -'tɔə(r,
  E+**gran-, grɑn-**
granular **'grænjələ**; ES **'grænjələ(r**
granulate *adj* **'grænjəlɪt**
granulate *v* **'grænjə₁let** |-d -ɪd
granulation ₁grænjə**'leʃən**
granule **'grænjul**
Granville **'grænvɪl**
grape **grep**
grapefruit **'grep₁frut, -₁frɪut**
grapeshot **'grep₁ʃat**; ES+-₁ʃɒt
grapevine **'grep₁vaɪn** |-d -d
graph **græf**; E+**graf, grɑf**; |-ed -t
graphic **'græfɪk** |-ly -lɪ |-ally -l̩ɪ
graphite **'græfaɪt** |-d -ɪd
graphophone, G- **'græfə₁fon**
grapnel **'græpnəl** |-ed -d
grapple **'græpl̩** |-d -d |-ling **'græplɪŋ, -pl̩ɪŋ**
Grasmere **'græsmɪr**; ES -mɪə(r, E+**'gras-,
  'grɑs-**
grasp **græsp**; E+**grasp, grɑsp**; |-ed -t
grass **græs**; E+**gras, grɑs**; |-es -ɪz |-ed -t
Grasse, de də**'gras**
grasshopper **'græs₁hapɚ**; ES -₁hapə(r, -₁hɒpə(r,
  E+**'gras-, 'grɑs-**
Grassmann **'grasman**
grate **gret** |grated **'gretɪd**
grateful *'thankful'* **'gretfəl** |-ly -ɪ
grateful *'filled grate'* **'gret₁ful** |-s -z
Gratiano ₁græʃɪ**'ano, ₁graʃ-, *Brit* ₁greʃ-**
gratification ₁grætəfə**'keʃən**
gratify **'grætə₁faɪ** |-fied -₁faɪd
gratin **'grætæ̃** (*Fr* gra**'tæ̃**)
grating **'gretɪŋ**
Gratiot **'græʃɪət, 'gre-**
gratis **'gretɪs**
gratitude **'grætə₁tjud, -₁trud, -₁tud**

|full **ful** |tooth **tuθ** |further **'fɝðɚ**; ES **'fɝðə** |custom **'kʌstəm** |while **hwaɪl** |how **haʊ** |toy **tɔɪ**
|using **'juzɪŋ** |fuse **fjuz, fɪuz** |dish **dɪʃ** |vision **'vɪʒən** |Eden **'idn̩** |cradle **'kredl̩** |keep 'em **'kipm̩**

Grattan ˈgrætn̩

gratuitous grəˈtjuətəs, -ˈtɪu-, -ˈtu- |-ty -tɪ

gratulate ˈgrætʃəˌlet, -tʃu-

gravamen grəˈvemɛn |-s -z |-mina -ˈvæmɪnə

grave grev |past graved grevd |pptc graven ˈgrevən or graved grevd

gravel ˈgrævl̩ |-ed -d |-ing ˈgrævl̩ɪŋ, -vlɪŋ

gravel-blind ˈgrævl̩ˌblaɪnd

graven ˈgrevən

gravestone ˈgrevˌston

graveyard ˈgrevˌjɑrd; ES -ˌjɑːd, E+-ˌjɑːd

gravid ˈgrævɪd |-ity grəˈvɪdətɪ

gravitate ˈgrævəˌtet |-d -ɪd

gravitation ˌgrævəˈteʃən

gravity ˈgrævətɪ

gravure ˈgrevjər, -jʊr; ES ˈgrevjə(r, -jʊə(r -gravure -grəˈvjʊr; ES -ˈvjʊə(r

gravy ˈgrevɪ

gray, G- gre

graybeard ˈgreˌbɪrd; ES -ˌbɪəd, S+-ˌbɛəd

grayling ˈgrelɪŋ

graze grez |grazes ˈgrezɪz |grazed grezd

grazier ˈgreʒɚ; ES ˈgreʒə(r

grease n gris |greases ˈgrisɪz

grease v gris, griz; S griz; |-s -ɪz |-d -grist, grizd — ˈgrizɪ and tə griz are phonetically normal; ˈgrisɪ and tə gris imitate the noun grease (gris).

greasewood ˈgrisˌwʊd

greasy ˈgrisɪ, ˈgrizɪ; S ˈgrizɪ — Some distinguish ˈgrisɪ 'covered with grease' from ˈgrizɪ 'slimy'.

great gret; S occas. grɛt, a historical form, cf threat θrɛt; The pronunciation grɛt parallels that of bread, deaf, sweat, thread, tread, etc.

great-aunt ˈgretˈænt, much less freq. -ˈɑnt; E -ˈɑnt, -ˈɒnt, -ˈænt

Great Britain ˈgretˈbrɪtn̩, -tən

greatcoat ˈgretˌkot |-ed -ɪd

great deal 'important bargain' ˈgretˈdil, 'large amount' ˈgreˈdil, ˈgretˈdil

greaten ˈgretn̩ |-ed -d |-ing ˈgretn̩ɪŋ, -tnɪŋ

Greatheart ˈgretˌhɑrt; ES -ˌhɑːt, E+-ˌhɑːt

greathearted ˈgretˈhɑrtɪd; ES -ˈhɑːtɪd, E+ -ˈhɑːtɪd

great-uncle ˈgretˈʌŋkl̩

greave griv |greaved grivd

grebe grib

Grecian ˈgriʃən

gree gri

Greece gris |-'s -ɪz

greed grid |-y -ɪ |-ily ˈgridlɪ, -dɪlɪ

Greek grik

Greeley ˈgrilɪ

green grin |greened grind |-ness ˈgrinnɪs

Greenaway ˈgrinəˌwe

greenback ˈgrinˌbæk

green-backed ˈgrinˈbækt ('green-ˌbacked 'bird)

greenbrier, G- ˈgrinˌbraɪɚ; ES -ˌbraɪ·ə(r

greenery ˈgrinərɪ, ˈgrinrɪ

green-eyed ˈgrinˈaɪd ('green-ˌeyed 'Becky)

greengrocer ˈgrinˌgrosɚ; ES -ˌgrosə(r; |-y -ɪ, -srɪ

greenhorn ˈgrinˌhɔrn; ES -ˌhɔən

greenhouse ˈgrinˌhaʊs |-s -ˌhaʊzɪz

Greenland ˈgrinlənd

greensward ˈgrinˌswɔrd; ES -ˌswɔəd; |-ed -ɪd

Greenville ˈgrinvɪl; S+-vl̩

Greenwich Engd ˈgrɪnɪdʒ, ˈgrɛn-, -ɪtʃ; US places usually ˈgrinwɪtʃ. How far ˈgrɪnɪtʃ, ˈgrɛn- are traditional and prevalent for some Eastern places, or recent imitations of Brit is doubtful. ˈgrɛnɪtʃ appears to prevail for Greenwich Village, NY.

greenwood, G- ˈgrinˌwʊd

greet grit |greeted ˈgritɪd

Greet, William Cabell ˈwɪljəmˈkæblˈgrit

gregarious grɪˈgɛrɪəs, -ˈgær-, -ˈger-

Gregorian grɛˈgorɪən, -ˈgɔr-; S -ˈgorɪən

Gregory ˈgrɛgərɪ

gremial ˈgrimɪəl

Gremio ˈgrimɪˌo, ˈgrimjo

Grenada Miss grɪˈnadə, Brit colony grɪˈnedə

grenade grɪˈned

grenadier ˌgrɛnəˈdɪr; ES -ˈdɪə(r, S+-ˈdɛə(r

grenadine ˌgrɛnəˈdin, ˈgrɛnəˌdin

Grendel ˈgrɛndl̩

Gresham ˈgrɛʃəm, ˈgrɛsəm — ˈgrɛʃəm is a sp. pron.

Gretchen ˈgrɛtʃɪn

Gretel ˈgretl̩ — see Hänsel and Gretel

Gretna ˈgrɛtnə

Gretna Green ˈgrɛtnəˈgrin

Greville ˈgrɛvl̩, -ɪl

grew past of grow gru, grɪu

grewsome ˈgrusəm, ˈgrɪu-

grey, G- gre

greyhound 'gre͟ˌhaʊnd
grid grɪd |gridded 'grɪdɪd
griddle 'grɪdl̩ |-d -d |-ling 'grɪdlɪŋ, -dl̩ɪŋ
griddlecake 'grɪdl̩ˌkek
gride graɪd |grided 'graɪdɪd
gridiron 'grɪdˌaɪɚn, -ˌaɪrn; ES -ˌaɪˑən, -ˌaɪən
grief grif
Grieg grig
Grierson 'grɪrsn̩; ES 'grɪəsn̩
grievance 'grivəns |-s -ɪz
grieve griv |-d -d |-dly -ɪdly |-vous -əs
griff grɪf
griffin 'grɪfɪn |griffon 'grɪfən
Griffith 'grɪfɪθ
grifter 'grɪftɚ; ES 'grɪftə(r
grig grɪg |grigged grɪgd
grill, -e grɪl |grilled grɪld
grim grɪm
grimace grɪ'mes |-s -ɪz |-d -t
grimalkin grɪ'mælkɪn, -'mɔlkɪn, -'mɔkɪn
grime, G- graɪm |grimed graɪmd |grimy
 'graɪmɪ
Grimm grɪm
grin grɪn |grinned grɪnd
grind graɪnd |ground graʊnd
grindstone 'graɪnˌston, 'graɪnd-
gringo 'grɪŋgo
Grinnell grɪ'nɛl
grip grɪp |gripped grɪpt
gripe graɪp |griped graɪpt
grippe grɪp
gripsack 'grɪpˌsæk
Griqualand 'grikwəˌlænd, 'grɪkwə-
Griselda grɪ'zɛldə
grisly 'ghastly' 'grɪzlɪ
grisly 'gristly' 'grɪslɪ, 'grɪslɪ
grist grɪst
gristle 'grɪslɪ |-tly 'grɪslɪ, 'grɪslɪ
gristmill 'grɪstˌmɪl
Griswold 'grɪzwəld
grit grɪt |gritted 'grɪtɪd |gritty 'grɪtɪ
grith grɪθ |-ths -θs
grits grɪts |-tten 'grɪtn̩
grizzle 'grɪzl̩ |-d -d |-ling 'grɪzl̩ɪŋ, -zlɪŋ
grizzly 'grɪzlɪ
groan gron |groaned grond
groat grot
grocer 'grosɚ; ES 'grosə(r; |-y -ɪ, -srɪ
Groesbeck 'grosbɛk

grog grag, grɒg, grɔg |-ged -d |-gery -ərɪ
 |-gy -ɪ
grogram 'gragrəm, 'grɒg-, 'grɔg-
groin grɔɪn |groined grɔɪnd
grommet 'gramɪt; ES+'grɒmɪt
Groningen 'gronɪŋən
groom grum, grʊm |-ed -d
groomsman 'grumzmən, 'grʊmz- |-men -mən
groove gruv |grooved gruvd
grope grop |groped gropt
grosbeak 'grosˌbik
grosgrain 'groˌgren |-ed -d
gross gros |-es -ɪz|-ed -t
grot coin grot |pl grote 'grotə or groten 'grotən
grot 'grotto' grat; ES+grɒt
grotesque gro'tɛsk |-rie -ərɪ, -skrɪ
Grotius 'groʃɪəs |or De Groot də'grot |Gro-
 tius's -ɪz
Groton US places variously pron. 'gratn̩,
 'grɒtn̩, 'grɔtn̩, 'grotn̩ — in N Engd & NY
 usually 'gratn̩, 'grɒtn̩
grotto 'grato; ES+'grɒto
grouch graʊtʃ |-es -ɪz |-ed -t
ground graʊnd |-ed -ɪd |-ling -lɪŋ
ground-hog 'graʊndˌhag, -ˌhɔg, -ˌhɒg; S
 -ˌhɔg, -ˌhag, -ˌhɒg
groundnut 'graʊndˌnʌt, 'graʊnˌnʌt
groundsel 'graʊnsl̩, 'graʊndsl̩
groundwork 'graʊndˌwɝk; ES -ˌwɜk, -ˌwɝk
group grup |grouped grupt
grouse bird graʊs |3 sg -s -ɪz |-d -t
grousy 'having grouse' 'graʊzɪ, -sɪ
grout graʊt |grouted 'graʊtɪd
grove grov |groved grovd
grovel 'gravl̩, 'grʌvl̩; ES+'grɒvl̩; |-ed -d |-ing
 -vl̩ɪŋ, -vlɪŋ — ʌ shows the original vowel,
 a being a sp. pron.
Grover 'grovɚ; ES 'grovə(r
grow gro |grew gru, grɪu |grown gron
growl graʊl |growled graʊld
grown gron
grown-up n 'gronˌʌp
grown-up adj 'gronˌʌp ('grown-ˌup 'boys)
growth groθ |-ths -θs
grub grʌb |grubbed grʌbd
grubstake 'grʌbˌstek |-staked -ˌstekt
grudge grʌdʒ |grudges 'grʌdʒɪz |grudged
 grʌdʒd
gruel 'gruəl, 'grɪuəl |-ed -d

gruesome ˈgrusəm, ˈgrɪu-
gruff grʌf
grumble ˈgrʌmbļ |-d -d |-ling ˈgrʌmblɪŋ,
-bļɪŋ
Grumio ˈgrumɪˌo, ˈgrumjo
grumpy ˈgrʌmpɪ
Grundy ˈgrʌndɪ |-ism -ˌɪzəm |-dyist -ɪst
grunt grʌnt |grunted ˈgrʌntɪd
Gruyère gruˈjɛr, griˈjɛr; ES -ˈjɛə(r; (Fr
gryˈjɛːr)
gryphon ˈgrɪfən
Guadalquivir ˌgwadļˈkwɪvɚ, ˌgwɒd-; ES
-və(r; (Sp ˌgwaðalkiˈβir)
Guadalupe Tex ˈgɔdļˌup, ˌgɔdļˈup, ˌgwadļˈup,
ˌgwɒd- (Sp ˌgwaðaˈlupe)
Guadalupe Hidalgo Mex ˌgwadļˈup·hɪˈdælgo,
ˌgwɒd- (Sp ˌgwaðaˈlupe·iˈðalgo)
Guadeloupe WI ˌgɔdļˈup, ˌgwad-, ˌgwɒd-
Guam gwam, gwɒm
guanine ˈgwanin, ˈgwɒn-
guano ˈgwano, ˈgwɒno
guarantee ˌgærənˈti |-d -d
guarantor ˈgærəntɚ, -tɔr, in contrast -ˈtɔr; ES
-tə(r, -tɔə(r, -ˈtɔə(r
guaranty ˈgærəntɪ |-tied -tɪd
guard gard; ES gɑːd, E+gaːd; |-ed -ɪd
guardhouse ˈgardˌhaʊs |-houses -ˌhaʊzɪz; ES
see guard
guardian ˈgardɪən; ES see guard
guardroom ˈgardˌrum, -ˌrʊm; ES see guard
guardsman ˈgardzmən |-men -mən; ES see
guard
Guatemala ˌgwatəˈmalə, ˌgwɒt-, older ˌgɔtə-
ˈmɔlə |-n -n
guava ˈgwavə, ˈgwɒvə
Guayaquil ˌgwaɪəˈkil (Sp ˌgwajaˈkil)
gubernatorial ˌgjubɚnəˈtorɪəl, ˌgɪu-, -ˈtɔr-;
ES -bənə-, S -ˈtor-
gudgeon ˈgʌdʒən |-ed -d
Gudrun ˈgʊdrun
guelder-rose ˈgɛldɚˌroz; ES ˈgɛldə-
Guelph gwɛlf
guerdon ˈgɝdņ; ES ˈgɜdņ, ˈgɝdņ |-ed -d
|-ing -dņɪŋ, -dnɪŋ
Guernsey, g- ˈgɝnzɪ; ES ˈgɜnzɪ, ˈgɝnzɪ
guerrilla, gueri- gəˈrɪlə
guess gɛs |guesses ˈgɛsɪz |guessed gɛst
guesswork ˈgɛsˌwɝk; ES -ˌwɜk, -ˌwɝk
guest gɛst |guested ˈgɛstɪd

guffaw gʌˈfɔ, gəˈfɔ |-ed -d
Guiana gɪˈænə, gɪˈɑnə (Sp ˈgjana)
guidance ˈgaɪdns |-s -ɪz
guide gaɪd |guided ˈgaɪdɪd
Guiderius gwɪˈdɪrɪəs, -rjəs |-'s -ɪz
guidon ˈgaɪdņ
guild gɪld
Guildenstern ˈgɪldņˌstɝn; ES -ˌstɜn, -ˌstɝn
guilder ˈgɪldɚ; ES ˈgɪldə(r
Guildford ˈgɪlfɚd; ES ˈgɪlfəd
guildhall, G- ˈgɪldˈhɔl—cf Am ˈtown ˈhall
guile gaɪl |-ful -fəl |-fully -fəlɪ |-less ˈgaɪllɪs
Guilford ˈgɪlfɚd; ES ˈgɪlfəd
guillemot ˈgɪləˌmat; ES+-ˌmɒt
guillotine n ˈgɪləˌtin
guillotine v ˌgɪləˈtin, ˈgɪləˌtin |-d -d
guilt gɪlt |-y -ɪ |-ily ˈgɪltəlɪ, -tɪlɪ
guimpe ‘chemisette’ gæmp, gɪmp (Fr gæ̃ːp)
Guinea, g- ˈgɪnɪ
Guinevere, -ver ˈgwɪnəˌvɪr, -vɚ; ES -ˌvɪə(r,
-və(r
Guiney ˈgaɪnɪ
guise gaɪz |guises ˈgaɪzɪz |guised gaɪzd
guitar gɪˈtar; ES -ˈtaː(r, E+-ˈtaː(r
Guiterman ˈgɪtɚmən; ES ˈgɪtə-
gulch gʌltʃ |gulches ˈgʌltʃɪz |gulched gʌltʃt
gulden ˈgʊldən
gules gjulz, gɪulz
gulf gʌlf |gulfed gʌlft
gulfweed ˈgʌlfˌwid
gull gʌl |gulled gʌld
Gullah ˈgʌlə
gullet ˈgʌlɪt |-ed -ɪd
gullibility ˌgʌləˈbɪlətɪ
gullible ˈgʌləbļ |-bly -blɪ
Gulliver ˈgʌləvɚ; ES ˈgʌləvə(r
gully ˈgʌlɪ |gullied ˈgʌlɪd
gulp gʌlp |gulped gʌlpt
gum gʌm |gummed gʌmd
gum arabic ˌgʌmˈærəbɪk, now rare ˌgʌmə-
ˈrebɪk
gumbo ˈgʌmbo
gumdrop ˈgʌmˌdrap; ES+-ˌdrɒp
gumption ˈgʌmpʃən |-tious -ʃəs
gums ‘alveoli’ gʌmz, much less freq. gumz,
gumz
gumshoe ˈgʌmˈʃu, ˈgʌmˌʃu
gumwood ˈgʌmˌwʊd
gun gʌn |gunned gʌnd

gunboat 'gʌn₁bot
guncotton 'gʌn₁katn̩; ES+-₁kɒtn̩
gunfire 'gʌn₁faɪr; ES -₁faɪə(r
gunman 'gʌn₁mæn, -mən |-men -₁mɛn, -mən
Gunnar 'gʊnɑr, *Am pers. name* 'gʌnɚ; ES
 -ɑː(r, -ə(r
gunnel 'gʌn̩|
gunner 'gʌnɚ; ES 'gʌnə(r; |-y -ɪ
gunny 'gʌnɪ
gunpowder, G- 'gʌn₁paʊdɚ; ES -₁paʊdə(r
gunrunning 'gʌn₁rʌnɪŋ
gunshot 'gʌn₁ʃat; ES+-₁ʃɒt
gunwale 'gʌn̩|
gurge gɝdʒ; ES gɜdʒ, gɝdʒ; |-s -ɪz |-d -d
gurgitation ₁gɝdʒə'teʃən; ES ₁gɜdʒə-, ₁gɝdʒ-
gurgle 'gɝg|; ES 'gɜg|, 'gɝg|; |-d -d |-ling
 -glɪŋ, -g|ɪŋ
Gurkha 'gʊrkə; ES 'gʊəkə
gurnard 'gɝnɚd; ES 'gɜnəd, 'gɝnəd
Gurney, -nee 'gɝnɪ; ES 'gɜnɪ, 'gɝnɪ
gush gʌʃ |gushes 'gʌʃɪz |gushed gʌʃt
gusset 'gʌsɪt |gusseted 'gʌsɪtɪd
gust gʌst |gusty 'gʌstɪ
gustation gʌs'teʃən
gustatory 'gʌstə₁torɪ, -₁tɔrɪ; S -₁torɪ
Gustavus gʌs'tevəs |-'s -ɪz
gusto 'gʌsto
gut gʌt |gutted 'gʌtɪd
Gutenberg 'gutn̩₁bɝg; ES -₁bɜg, -₁bɝg; (*Ger*
 'guːtən₁bɛrk)
Guthrie 'gʌθrɪ
Guthrun 'gʊðrun
gutta 'gʌtə
gutta-percha 'gʌtə'pɝtʃə; ES -'pɜtʃə, -'pɝtʃə
Guttenberg *US* 'gʌtn̩₁bɝg; ES -₁bɜg, -₁bɝg
gutter 'gʌtɚ; ES 'gʌtə(r; |-ed -d
guttersnipe 'gʌtɚ₁snaɪp; ES 'gʌtə-

guttural 'gʌtərəl |-ly -ɪ
guy gaɪ |guyed gaɪd
Guyandot 'gaɪən₁dat; ES+-₁dɒt
guzzle 'gʌz| |-d -d |-ling 'gʌz|ɪŋ, 'gʌzlɪŋ
Gwendolen, -ine, -yn 'gwɛnd|ɪn
Gwinnett gwɪ'nɛt
gybe dʒaɪb |-d -d
gymnasium dʒɪm'nezɪəm, -zjəm |-s -z |-sia
 -zɪə
gymnast 'dʒɪmnæst
gymnastic dʒɪm'næstɪk |-al -| |-ally -|ɪ, -ɪklɪ
gynae- *see* gyne-
gynarchy 'dʒaɪnarkɪ; ES -ɑːkɪ, E+-ɑːkɪ
gynecologic ₁dʒaɪnɪkə'ladʒɪk, ₁gaɪn-; ES+
 -'lɒdʒ-; |-al -|
gynecologist ₁dʒaɪnɪ'kalədʒɪst, ₁gaɪnɪ-; ES+
 -'kɒl-
gynecology ₁dʒaɪnɪ'kalədʒɪ, ₁gaɪnɪ-; ES+
 -'kɒl-;—*One form is as 'correct' as the
 other. The first is more Englished.*
gyp dʒɪp |gypped dʒɪpt
gypsum 'dʒɪpsəm
gypsy 'dʒɪpsɪ
gyral 'dʒaɪrəl |-ly -ɪ
gyrate 'dʒaɪret |-d -ɪd |-tion dʒaɪ'reʃən
gyrator dʒaɪ'retɚ, 'dʒaɪretɚ; ES -tə(r
gyratory 'dʒaɪrə₁torɪ, -₁tɔrɪ; S -₁torɪ
gyre dʒaɪr; ES dʒaɪə(r; |-d -d
gyrfalcon 'dʒɝ₁fɔlkən, -₁fɔkən; ES 'dʒɜ-,
 'dʒɝ-
gyro 'dʒaɪro
gyrocompass 'dʒaɪro₁kʌmpəs |-es -ɪz
gyroscope 'dʒaɪrə₁skop
gyroscopic ₁dʒaɪrə'skapɪk; ES+-'skɒp-; |-ally
 -|ɪ, -ɪklɪ
gyrostatic ₁dʒaɪrə'stætɪk |-ally -|ɪ, -ɪklɪ
gyve dʒaɪv |gyved dʒaɪvd

H

H, h *letter* etʃ |*pl* H's, Hs, *poss* H's 'etʃɪz
ha *intj, n* ha |*pl* has, ha's haz
ha *v* ha |haes haz |haed had |haing 'ha·ɪŋ
Haarlem 'harləm; ES 'haːləm, E+'haːləm
Habakkuk hə'bækək, 'hæbə₁kʌk
Habana '*Havana' Sp* a'βana
habeas corpus 'hebɪəs'kɔrpəs; ES -'kɔəpəs

haberdasher 'hæbɚ₁dæʃɚ; ES 'hæbə₁dæʃə(r;
 |-y -ɪ, -ʃrɪ
habergeon 'hæbɚdʒən; ES 'hæbədʒən
habiliment hə'bɪləmənt
habilitate hə'bɪlə₁tet |-tated -₁tetɪd
habit 'hæbɪt |-ed -ɪd |-able -əb| |-bly -blɪ
habitant 'hæbətənt

|full fʊl |tooth tuθ |further 'fɝðɚ; ES 'fɝðə |custom 'kʌstəm |while hwaɪl |how haʊ |toy tɔɪ
|using 'juzɪŋ |fuse fjuz, fɪuz |dish dɪʃ |vision 'vɪʒən |Eden 'idn̩ |cradle 'kredl̩ |keep 'em 'kipm̩

habitat 'hæbə₁tæt |-tation ₁hæbə'teʃən
habitual hə'bɪtʃuəl, -tʃul |-ly -ɪ
habituate hə'bɪtʃu₁et |-ated -₁etɪd
habitude 'hæbə₁tjud, -₁tɪud, -₁tud
habitué hə'bɪtʃu₁e, hə₁bɪtʃu'e (*Fr* abi'tqe)
Habsburg 'hæpsbɝg; ES -bɜg, -bɝg; (*Ger*
  'hɑ:psbʊrk)—*see* Hapsburg
hacienda ₁hɑsɪ'ɛndə (*Sp* a'sjenda)
hack hæk |hacked hækt
hackamore 'hækə₁mor, -₁mɔr; ES -₁moə(r,
  E+-₁mɔə(r
hackberry 'hæk₁bɛrɪ, -bərɪ
hackbut 'hækbʌt—*see* hagbut
hackle 'hækḷ |-d -d |-ling 'hæklɪŋ, 'hækḷɪŋ
hackman 'hækmən, -₁mæn |hackmen 'hæk-
  mən, -₁mɛn
hackney 'hæknɪ |hackneyed 'hæknɪd
had *stressed* 'hæd, ₁hæd; *unstr.* həd, hɛd, əd,
  ɛd, ɪd |'d d
Haddington 'hædɪŋtən
haddock 'hædək
Hades 'hediz |Hades' 'hediz
hadj hædʒ |hadjes 'hædʒɪz |hadji 'hædʒi
hadn't 'hædṇt, *before some conss.*+'hædṇ
  ('hædṇ 'sɪnɪm)
Hadrian 'hedrɪən
hadst *stressed* 'hædst, ₁hædst; *unstr.* hədst,
  ədst, dst
haem- *see* hem-
haemo- *see* hemo-
Haensel 'hɛnsḷ=Hänsel
haft hæft |hafted 'hæftɪd
hag hæg
Hagar 'hegɚ, 'hegɑr; ES 'hegə(r, 'hegɑ:(r
hagbut 'hægbʌt
Hagen 'hagən
Hagerstown 'hegɚz₁taʊn; ES 'hegəz-
haggada hə'gadə, -da |*pl* haggadoth hə'gadoθ
Haggai 'hægɪ₁aɪ, 'hægaɪ
haggard, H- 'hægɚd; ES 'hægəd
haggis 'hægɪs |-es -ɪz
haggle 'hægḷ |-d -d |-ling 'hæglɪŋ, 'hægḷɪŋ
hagiography ₁hægɪ'agrəfɪ, ₁hedʒɪ-, -'ɒg-
hagiolatry ₁hægɪ'alətrɪ, ₁hedʒɪ-; ES+-'ɒl-
hagiology ₁hægɪ'alədʒɪ, ₁hedʒɪ-; ES+-'ɒl-
Hague heg
Hahnemann 'hanəmən (*Ger* 'hɑ:nə₁man)
Haidarabad 'haɪdərə₁bæd, ₁haɪdərə'bad
haikwan 'haɪ'kwan

hail hel |hailed held |hailstone 'hel₁ston
Haile Selassie 'haɪlɪsə'lasɪ, -sə'læsɪ
hailstorm 'hel₁stɔrm; ES 'hel₁stɔəm
hair hɛr, hær; E hɛə(r, ES hæə(r; |-ed -d |-y -ɪ
hairbreadth 'hɛr₁brɛdθ, 'hær-; ES *see* hair
hairbrush 'hɛr₁brʌʃ, 'hær-; ES *see* hair
haircloth 'hɛr₁klɔθ, 'hær-, -₁klɒθ; ES *see* hair;
  pl see cloth
haircut 'hɛr₁kʌt, 'hær-; ES *see* hair
hair-do 'hɛr₁du, 'hær-; ES *see* hair
hairdresser 'hɛr₁drɛsɚ, 'hær-; ES -ə(r, *see*
  hair
hairline 'hɛr₁laɪn, 'hær-; ES *see* hair
hair's-breadth 'hɛrz'brɛdθ, 'hærz-, -₁brɛdθ;
  E 'hɛəz-, ES 'hæəz-
hairsplitter 'hɛr₁splɪtɚ, 'hær-; ES -₁splɪtə(r,
  see hair
hairspring 'hɛr₁sprɪŋ, 'hær-; ES *see* hair
Haiti 'hetɪ |Haitian 'hetɪən
hake hek
Hakluyt 'hæklut, 'hæklaɪt, 'hæklɪt
halation he'leʃən, hæ'leʃən
halberd 'hælbɚd; ES 'hælbəd; |-rt -t—*for-
  merly* 'hɔlb-, 'hɒb-, *spelt* haubert, holberd
halcyon 'hælsɪən
Haldane 'hɔlden
hale hel |haled held
half hæf; E haf, hæf, haf; |-'s -s |-lves -vz
half-and-half 'hæfṇ'hæf; E *see* half
halfback 'hæf₁bæk; E *see* half
half-baked 'hæf'bekt; E *see* half; ('half-₁baked
  'scheme)
half-blooded 'hæf'blʌdɪd; E *see* half; ('half-
  ₁blooded 'Indian)
half-breed 'hæf₁brid; E *see* half
half-caste 'hæf₁kæst; E+'haf₁kast, 'haf₁kast
half-full 'hæf'ful; E *see* half
halfhearted 'hæf'hartɪd; ES -'hɑ:tɪd, E+
  -'ha:tɪd—*see* half; ('half₁hearted 'effort)
half-hour 'hæf'aʊr; ES -'aʊə(r, E *see* half
half-length 'hæf'lɛŋkθ, -'lɛŋθ; E *see* half
half-mast 'hæf'mæst; E+'haf'mast, 'haf-
  'mast
half-moon 'hæf'mun; E *see* half
halfpenny *Brit* 'hepnɪ, 'hepənɪ |*pl* halfpence
  'hepəns, halfpennies 'hepnɪz, 'hepənɪz
half-timbered 'hæf'tɪmbɚd; ES -'tɪmbəd, E
  see half
half-tone 'hæf₁ton; E *see* half

Key: See in full §§3–47. bee bi |pity 'pɪtɪ (§6) |rate ret |yet jɛt |sang sæŋ |angry 'æŋ·grɪ
|bath bæθ; E baθ (§10) |ah ɑ |far fɑr |watch watʃ, wɒtʃ (§12) |jaw dʒɔ |gorge gɔrdʒ |go go

half-truth 'hæf₁truθ; E *see* half
halfway 'hæf'we; E *see* half; ('half₁way 'up)
half-witted 'hæf'wɪtɪd; E *see* half
Haliburton 'hælə₁bɜtn̩; ES -₁bɜtn̩, -₁bɜtn̩
halibut 'hæləbət, 'haləbət; ES+'hɒl-
Halicarnassus ₁hælɪkar'næsəs; ES -ka:'n-; |-sus' -səs
halide 'hælaɪd, 'helaɪd
halidom 'hælɪdəm |halidome 'hælɪ₁dom
Halifax 'hælə₁fæks |Halifax's 'hælə₁fæksɪz
Haligonian ₁hælə'gonɪən, ₁hælɪ-
halitosis ₁hælə'tosɪs
Haliver 'hæləvɚ, 'hæ₁lɪvɚ; ES -və(r
hall, H- hɔl
Hallam 'hæləm
Halle *Am name* 'hælɪ; *Ger city* 'halə
Halleck 'hælɪk, 'hælək
hallelujah, -iah ₁hælə'lujə, -'lɪujə
Halley 'hælɪ
Halliburton 'hælə₁bɜtn̩; ES -₁bɜtn̩, -₁bɜtn̩
Halliday 'hælə₁de
Halliwell 'hælə₁wɛl, 'hæləwəl
hallmark 'hɔl₁mark; ES 'hɔl₁ma:k, E+ -₁ma:k; |-ed -t
hallo, -loa hə'lo
halloo hə'lu |hallooed hə'lud
hallow 'hælo, -ə |-ed -d, *worship* 'hæləwɪd |-ing 'hæləwɪŋ
Halloween ₁hælo'in, ₁halo'in ('Hallow₁een 'joke)
Hallowmas 'hælo₁mæs, -məs |-es -ɪz
hallucinate hə'lusn̩₁et, -'lɪu- |-d -ɪd
hallucination hə₁lusn̩'eʃən, -₁lɪu-
hallucinatory hə'lusn̩ə₁torɪ, -'lɪu-, -₁tɔrɪ; S -₁torɪ
hallway 'hɔl₁we
halo 'helo |haloed 'helod
halogen 'hælədʒən, -dʒɪn
haloid 'hæloɪd, 'heloɪd
Halpin, -ine 'hælpɪn
Hals, Frans 'frans'hals, 'fræns'hæls |-'s -ɪz
Halstead 'holstɛd, 'holstɪd, 'hæl-
halt holt |halted 'holtɪd
halter 'holtɚ; ES 'holtə(r
halve hæv; E hav, hæv, hav |-d -d
halyard 'hæljɚd; ES 'hæljəd
ham, H- hæm
hamadryad ₁hæmə'draɪəd, -'draɪæd
Haman 'hemən

Hamburg 'hæmbɜg; ES 'hæmbɜg, -bɜg; (*Ger* 'hamburk)
hamburger 'hæmbɜgɚ; ES 'hæmbɜgə(r, -bɜgə(r
hame hem
Hamilcar hə'mɪlkar, 'hæml-; ES -ka:(r, E+-ka:(r
Hamilton 'hæml̩tən |Hamiltonian ₁hæml̩-'tonɪən
Hamite 'hæmaɪt |-tic hæm'ɪtɪk, hə'mɪtɪk
hamlet, H- 'hæmlɪt
hammer 'hæmɚ; ES 'hæmə(r; |-ed -d |-ing 'hæmərɪŋ, 'hæmrɪŋ
hammerhead 'hæmɚ₁hɛd; ES 'hæmə₁hɛd; |-ed -ɪd
hammock 'hæmək
Hammurabi ₁hamə'rabɪ, ₁hamu'rabɪ
Hampden 'hæmpdən, 'hæmdən
hamper 'hæmpɚ; ES 'hæmpə(r; |-ed -d |-ing 'hæmpərɪŋ, 'hæmprɪŋ
Hampshire 'hæmpʃɪr, 'hæmpʃɚ; ES -ʃɪə(r, -ʃə(r
Hampstead 'hæmpstɛd, 'hæmpstɪd
Hampton 'hæmptən
hamstring 'hæm₁strɪŋ |-strung -₁strʌŋ *or* -stringed -₁strɪŋd
Hamsun, Knut 'knut'hæmsən, -'hamsun
Hamtramck *Mich* hæm'træmɪk
Han han
hanaper 'hænəpɚ; ES 'hænəpə(r
Hancock 'hænkak; ES+'hænkɒk
hand hænd |handed 'hændɪd
handbag 'hænd₁bæg, 'hæn₁bæg
handball 'hænd₁bɔl, 'hæn₁bɔl
handbarrow 'hænd₁bæro, 'hæn₁bæro, -ə
handbill 'hænd₁bɪl, 'hæn₁bɪl
handbook 'hænd₁buk, 'hæn₁buk
handbreadth 'hænd₁brɛdθ, 'hæn₁brɛdθ |-ths -θs
handcar 'hænd₁kar, 'hæn-; ES -₁ka:(r, E+ -₁ka:(r
handcart 'hænd₁kart, 'hæn-; ES -₁ka:t, E+-₁ka:t
Handcock 'hænkak; ES+-kɒk
handcuff 'hænd₁kʌf, 'hæn₁kʌf |-cuffed -₁kʌft
Handel 'hændl̩ (*Ger* Händel 'hɛndəl)
Handelian hæn'dilɪən, -'dɪljən
handfast 'hænd₁fæst, 'hæn-; E+-₁fast, -₁fast
handful 'hænd₁ful, 'hæn₁ful |-s -z

|full ful |tooth tuθ |further 'fɜðɚ; ES 'fɜðə, |custom 'kʌstəm |while hwaɪl |how hau |toy tɔɪ
|using 'juzɪŋ |fuse fjuz, fɪuz |dish dɪʃ |vision 'vɪʒən |Eden 'idn̩ |cradle 'kredl̩ |keep 'em 'kipm̩

Words below in which a *before* r (farm) *is sounded* ɑ *are often pronounced in E with* a (faːm)

handgrip 'hænd‚grıp, 'hæn‚grıp

handicap 'hændı‚kæp |handicapped 'hændı‚kæpt

handicraft 'hændı‚kræft; E+-‚kraft, -‚krɑft

handicraftsman 'hændı‚kræftsmən; E+ -‚krafts-, -‚krɑfts-; |-men -mən

handiwork 'hændı‚wɝk; ES -‚wɜk, -‚wɝk

handkerchief 'hæŋkɚtʃıf, -‚tʃif; ES -kə-; |-s -tʃıvz, -tʃıfs, -‚tʃıvz, -‚tʃifs

hand-knit 'hænd'nıt, 'hæn'nıt |-ted -ıd

handle 'hændḷ |-d -d |-ling 'hændlıŋ, -dḷıŋ

handleless 'hændḷlıs

handmade 'hænd'med, 'hæn- ('hand‚made 'shoe)

handmaid 'hænd‚med, 'hæn- |-en -‚medn̩

hand-me-down 'hænmı‚daun

handout 'hænd‚aut

handrail 'hænd‚rel

handsaw 'hænd‚sɔ, 'hæn-

handsel 'hænsḷ |-ed -d

handset 'hænd'sɛt, 'hæn- ('hand‚set 'type)

handsome 'hænsəm

handspike 'hæn‚spaık, 'hænd-

handspring 'hæn‚sprıŋ, 'hænd-

hand-to-mouth 'hændtə'mauθ, 'hæn:tə-

handwork 'hænd‚wɝk; ES -‚wɜk, -‚wɝk

handwriting 'hænd‚raıtıŋ

handy 'hændı

hang hæŋ |hung hʌŋ *or* hanged hæŋd |-ing 'hæŋıŋ

hangar 'hæŋɚ, 'hæŋgar; ES 'hæŋə(r, 'hæŋgɑː(r

Hangchow 'hæŋ'tʃau (*Chin* 'xaŋ'dʒo)

hangdog 'hæŋ‚dɔg, 'hæŋ‚dɒg

hanger 'hæŋɚ; ES 'hæŋə(r

hanger-on 'hæŋɚ'an, -'ɒn, -'ɔn

hangers-on 'hæŋɚz'an, -'ɒn, -'ɔn; ES 'hæŋəz-

hangman 'hæŋmən |hangmen 'hæŋmən

hangnail 'hæŋ‚nel

hank hæŋk |hanked hæŋkt

hanker 'hæŋkɚ; ES 'hæŋkə(r; |-ed -d |-ing 'hæŋkərıŋ, 'hæŋkrıŋ

Hankow 'hæn'kau, 'hæŋ'kau (*Chinese* 'xan'ko)

hanky-panky 'hæŋkı'pæŋkı

Hanley 'hænlı

Hannah 'hænə

Hannibal 'hænəbḷ

Hanover 'hænovɚ; ES 'hænovə(r; (*Ger* Hannover ha'noːvər, *loc.* ha'noːfər)

Hanoverian ‚hæno'vırıən

Hans hæns, -z (*Ger* hans)

Hansard 'hænsɚd, 'hænsard; ES 'hænsəd, -saːd

hanse hæns |hanses 'hænsız

Hanseatic ‚hænsı'ætık, ‚hænzı'ætık

hansel 'hænsḷ |hanseled 'hænsḷd

Hänsel and Gretel 'hɛnsḷən'gretḷ

hansom 'hænsəm

Hants *short for* Hampshire hænts

hap hæp |happed hæpt |haply 'hæplı

haphazard ‚hæp'hæzɚd; ES -'hæzəd

haploid 'hæplɔıd |-loidic hæp'lɔıdık

haplosis hæp'losıs

happen 'hæpən, -pn̩ |-ed -d |-ing -pənıŋ, -pnıŋ

happy 'hæpı |-pily -pḷı, -pılı

happy-go-lucky 'hæpı‚go'lʌkı

Hapsburg 'hæpsbɝg; ES -bɜg, -bɝg; (*Ger* 'haːpsburk)

hara-kiri 'harə'kırı, 'hærə-

harangue hə'ræŋ |-d -d |-guing -'ræŋıŋ

harass 'hærəs, hə'ræs; S+'hærıs; |-es -ız |-ed -t—*The pronunciation* hə'ræs *instead of the older* 'hærəs *appears to be on the increase.*

Harbin 'har'bın; ES 'haː'bın

harbinger 'harbındʒɚ; ES 'haːbındʒə(r; |-ed -d

harbor 'harbɚ; ES 'haːbə(r; |-ed -d |-ing -bərıŋ, -brıŋ |-age -bərıdʒ, -brıdʒ

Harcourt 'harkort, -kɔrt, -kɚt; ES -koət, -kət, E+-kɔət

hard hard; ES haːd

hard-bitted 'hard'bıtıd; ES 'haːd-; ('hard‚bitted 'horse)

hard-bitten 'hard'bıtn̩; ES 'haːd-

hard-boiled 'hard'bɔıld; ES 'haːd-

harden 'hardn̩; ES 'haːdn̩; |-ed -d |-ing -dn̩ıŋ, -dnıŋ

hard-featured 'hard'fitʃɚd; ES 'haːd'fitʃəd

hard-fisted 'hard'fıstıd; ES 'haːd-

hardhack 'hard‚hæk; ES 'haːd‚hæk

hardhanded 'hard'hændıd; ES 'haːd-

hardhead 'hard‚hed; ES 'haːd-

hardheaded 'hard'hedıd; ES 'haːd-

Key: *See in full* §§3-47. bee bi |pity 'pıtı (§6) |rate ret |yet jɛt |sang sæŋ |angry 'æŋ·grı |bath bæθ; E baθ (§10) |ah ɑ |far far |watch watʃ, wɒtʃ (§12) |jaw dʒɔ |gorge gɔrdʒ |go go

Words below in which a *before* r (farm) *is sounded* ɑ *are often pronounced in* E *with* a (faːm)
Words below that have æ *before* r (carry ˈkærɪ) *are often pronounced in* N *with* ɛ (ˈkɛrɪ, §94)

hardhearted ˈhɑrdˈhɑrtɪd; ES ˈhɑːdˈhɑːtɪd
hardihood ˈhɑrdɪˌhʊd; ES ˈhɑːdɪ-
hardly ˈhɑrdlɪ; ES ˈhɑːdlɪ
hardmouthed ˈhɑrdˈmaʊˑ ð d, -θt; ES ˈhɑːd-;
 (ˈhɑrdˌmouthed ˈhorse)
hardpan ˈhɑrdˌpæn; ES ˈhɑːd-
hard-shell ˈhɑrdˌʃɛl; ES ˈhɑːd-; |-ed -d
hardship ˈhɑrdʃɪp; ES ˈhɑːd-
hardtack ˈhɑrdˌtæk; ES ˈhɑːd-
hardware ˈhɑrdˌwɛr, -ˌwær; E ˈhɑːdˌwɛə(r,
 ES -ˌwæə(r
hardwood ˈhɑrdˌwʊd; ES ˈhɑːd-
hardy, H- ˈhɑrdɪ; ES ˈhɑːdɪ; |-dily -dǀɪ, -dɪlɪ
hare hɛr, hær; E hɛə(r, ES hæə(r; |-d -d
harebell ˈhɛrˌbɛl, ˈhær-; ES *see* hare
harebrained ˈhɛrˈbrend, ˈhær-; ES *see* hare
harelip ˈhɛrˈlɪp, ˈhær-, -ˌlɪp; ES *see* hare
harelipped ˈhɛrˈlɪpt, ˈhær-; ES *see* hare;
 (ˈhareˌlipped ˈboy)
harem ˈhɛrəm, ˈhær-, ˈher-; S ˈhærəm, ˈher-
Harfleur ˈhɑrflɜ; ES ˈhɑːflɜ(r, ˈhɑːflɜ; (*Fr*
 arˈflœːr)—*in Shak* Harflew ˈhɑrflu, -flɪu;
 ES ˈhɑːf-
haricot ˈhærɪˌko |-coed -ˌkod
hark hɑrk; ES hɑːk; |-ed -t
harken ˈhɑrkən; ES ˈhɑːk-; |-ed -d |-ing
 -kənɪŋ, -knɪŋ
Harleian ˈhɑrlɪən, hɑrˈliən; ES ˈhɑːl-, hɑːˈl-
Harlem ˈhɑrləm; ES ˈhɑːləm
harlequin, H- ˈhɑrləkwɪn, -kɪn; ES ˈhɑːl-
harlequinade ˌhɑrləkwɪnˈed, -kɪn-; ES ˌhɑːl-
Harley ˈhɑrlɪ; ES ˈhɑːlɪ
harlot ˈhɑrlət; ES ˈhɑːlət; |-ry -rɪ
harm hɑrm; ES hɑːm; |-ed -d |-ful -fəl |-fully
 -fəlɪ
harmonic hɑrˈmɑnɪk; ES hɑːˈmɑnɪk, -ˈmɒn-;
 |-a -ə |-ally -ǀɪ, -ɪklɪ
harmonious hɑrˈmonɪəs; ES hɑːˈmon-; |-nium
 -nɪəm
harmonize ˈhɑrməˌnaɪz; ES ˈhɑːm-; |-s -ɪz
 |-d -d
harmony ˈhɑrmənɪ; ES ˈhɑːm-; |-nied -nɪd
harness ˈhɑrnɪs; ES ˈhɑːnɪs; |-es -ɪz |-ed -t
Harold ˈhærəld
harp hɑrp; ES hɑːp; |-ed -t
harpoon hɑrˈpun; ES hɑːˈpun; |-ed -d
harpsichord ˈhɑrpsɪˌkɔrd; ES ˈhɑːpsɪˌkɔəd

Harpy ˈhɑrpɪ; ES ˈhɑːpɪ
harquebus ˈhɑrkwɪbəs; ES ˈhɑːkwɪbəs; |-es
 -ɪz
harquebusier ˌhɑrkwɪbəsˈɪr; ES ˌhɑːkwɪbəs-
 ˈɪə(r, S+-ˈɛə(r
harridan ˈhærədən
harrier ˈhærɪɚ; ES ˈhærɪˑə(r
Harriet ˈhærɪət, ˈhærɪt
Harrison ˈhærəsṇ
Harrisburg ˈhærɪsˌbɜɡ; ES -ˌbɜɡ, -ˌbɜɡ
harrow, H- ˈhæro, -ə |-ed -d |-ing ˈhærəwɪŋ
harry, H- ˈhærɪ |harried ˈhærɪd
harsh hɑrʃ; ES hɑːʃ
hart hɑrt; ES hɑːt
Harte hɑrt; ES hɑːt
hartebeest ˈhɑrtəˌbist; ES ˈhɑːtəˌbist
Hartford ˈhɑrtfɚd; ES ˈhɑːtfəd
hartshorn ˈhɑrtsˌhɔrn; ES ˈhɑːtsˌhɔən
Harum ˈhɛrəm, ˈhærəm; S ˈhærəm
harum-scarum ˈhɛrəmˈskɛrəm, ˈhærəm-
 ˈskærəm; S ˈhærəmˈskærəm; (ˈharum-
 ˌscarum ˈmanners)
Harun-al-Raschid ˈhærunælˈræʃɪd, hɑˈrun-
 ˌɑrrɑˈʃɪd
haruspex həˈrʌspeks, ˈhærəs- |-pexes -ˌpɛksɪz
 |haruspices həˈrʌspɪˌsiz
Harvard ˈhɑrvɚd; ES ˈhɑːvəd
harvest ˈhɑrvɪst, -vəst; ES ˈhɑːvɪst; |-ed -ɪd
Harvey ˈhɑrvɪ; ES ˈhɑːvɪ
Harwich *Engd* ˈhærɪdʒ, ˈhærɪtʃ; *Mass* ˈhɑr-
 wɪtʃ; ES ˈhɑːˌwɪtʃ; |-ˈs -ɪz
Harz hɑrts; ES hɑːts
has *stressed* ˈhæz, ˌhæz; *unstr.* həz, əz |ˈs z, s
has-been ˈhæzˌbɪn
Hasbrouck ˈhæzbrʊk
Hasdrubal ˈhæzdrubḷ, ˈhæzdruˌbæl
hash hæʃ |hashes ˈhæʃɪz |hashed hæʃt
hashish, -eesh ˈhæʃɪʃ
hasn't ˈhæznt, *bef. some conss.*+ˈhæzn (ˈhæzn
 ˈgɑn)
hasp hæsp; E+hɑsp, hɑsp; |-ed -t
hassock ˈhæsək |-ed -t
hast *stressed* ˈhæst, ˌhæst; *unstr.* həst, əst, st
haste hest |hasted ˈhestɪd
hasten ˈhesṇ |-ed -d |-ing ˈhesṇɪŋ, ˈhesnɪŋ
Hastings ˈhestɪŋz |-ˈs -ɪz
hasty ˈhestɪ |hastily ˈhestǀɪ, -tɪlɪ

|full fʊl |tooth tuθ |further ˈfɜˑ ð ɚ; ES ˈfɜˑ ð ə |custom ˈkʌstəm |while hwaɪl |how haʊ |toy tɔɪ
|using ˈjuzɪŋ |fuse fjuz, fɪuz |dish dɪʃ |vision ˈvɪʒən |Eden ˈidṇ |cradle ˈkredḷ |keep 'em ˈkipm̩

hat **hæt** |hatted **'hætɪd**
hatband **'hæt₁bænd**
hatbox **'hæt₁baks; ES+-₁bɒks; |-es -z**
hatch **hætʃ** |hatches **'hætʃɪz** |hatched **hætʃt**
hatchel **'hætʃəl** |hatcheled **'hætʃəld**
hatchery **'hætʃərɪ, 'hætʃrɪ**
hatchet **'hætʃɪt** |-ed -ɪd
hatchway **'hætʃ₁we**
hate **het** |hated **'hetɪd** |hateful **'hetfəl** |-fully
-fəlɪ
hath *stressed* **'hæθ, ₁hæθ;** *unstr.* **həθ, əθ**
Hathaway **'hæθə₁we**
Hathorn(e) **'hɔθɔrn; ES 'hɔθɔən;**—*The BBC
recommends* **'hæθɔrn** *for the British name.*
hatred **'hetrɪd**
hatter **'hætɚ; ES 'hætə(r**
Hatteras **'hætərəs** |Hatteras's **'hætərəsɪz**
hauberk **'hɔbɝk; ES 'hɔbɜk, 'hɔbɝk**
Haugen **'haʊgən**
haughty **'hɔtɪ** |-tily -t|ɪ, -tɪlɪ
haul **hɔl** |hauled **hɔld** |haulage **'hɔlɪdʒ**
haunch **hɔntʃ, hɒntʃ, hantʃ** |-es -ɪz |-ed -t
haunt **hɔnt, hɒnt, hant** |-ed -ɪd
Hauptmann **'haʊptmən, 'haʊpm-** (*Ger* **'haʊpt-
man)**
hautboy **'hobɔɪ, 'obɔɪ** (*Fr* o**'bwa**)
hauteur **ho'tɝ, o'tɝ; ES -'tɜ(r -'tɝ;** (*Fr*
o'tœ:r)
Havana **hə'vænə** (*Sp* Habana a'βana)
have *stressed* **'hæv, ₁hæv;** *unstr.* **həv, əv** |'ve v
|have to *bef. conss.* **'hæftə,** *bef. vow.* **'hæftʊ,
'hæftə**—*In* "I could of done it," of *is
merely a misspelling for* have. *Their pronunciation is identical. The pron.* **'hæftə,
'hæftʊ** *is universal in unaffected familiar
speech in US and England.*
Havelock, -lok, h- **'hævlak; ES+-lɒk**
haven **'hevən** |havened **'hevənd**
haven't **'hævṇt,** *bef. some conss.+***'hævṇ**
(**'hævṇ 'sɪnɪm)**
Haverford **'hævɚfɚd; ES 'hævəfəd**
Haverhill **'hevərɪl, 'hevrɪl, -rəl**
haversack **'hævɚ₁sæk; ES 'hævə₁sæk**
Haverstraw **'hævɚ₁strɔ; ES 'hævə₁strɔ**
havior **'hevjɚ; ES 'hevjə(r**
havoc **'hævək**
Havre *US* **'hævɚ; ES 'hævə(r**
Havre *France* **'havɚ, 'havrə; ES 'havə(r,
'havrə;** (*Fr* lə'a:vr)

Havre de Grace **'hævɚdə'græs, -'gres; ES
'hævə-**
haw **hɔ** |hawed **hɔd**
Hawaii **hə'waɪjə, hə'wajə, hə'wɒjə, hə-
'waɪ·i, hə'wa·i**
Hawarden *US* **'hewɚdṇ; ES -wa:dṇ;** *Wales*
'hɔ·ɚdṇ, 'hardṇ; ES 'hɔ·ədṇ, 'ha:dṇ
hawk **hɔk** |hawked **hɔkt**
hawk-eyed **'hɔk₁aɪd**
Hawkins **'hɔkɪnz** |Hawkins's **'hɔkɪnzɪz**
hawse **hɔz** |hawses **'hɔzɪz**
hawsehole **'hɔz₁hol, 'hɔs-**
hawser **'hɔzɚ; ES 'hɔzə(r**
hawthorn, Hawthorn(e) **'hɔ₁θɔrn; ES -₁θɔən**
hay **he** |hayed **hed** |haying **'he·ɪŋ**
Hayakawa **₁haɪə'kawə**
haycock **'he₁kak; ES+'he₁kɒk**
Hayden **'hedṇ**
Haydn **'haɪdṇ, 'hedṇ**
Haydon **'hedṇ**
Hayes **hez** |Hayes's **'hezɪz**
hayfork **'he₁fɔrk; ES 'he₁fɔək**
hayloft **'he₁lɔft, 'he₁lɒft**
haymarket **'he₁markɪt; ES 'he₁ma:kɪt**
haymow **'he₁maʊ**
hayrack **'he₁ræk** |-rick -₁rɪk
hayseed **'he₁sid** |-stack -₁stæk
Hayti **'hetɪ,** *US places+***'hetaɪ**
Hayward **'hewɚd; ES 'hewəd**
hayward **'he₁wɔrd, -wɚd; ES 'he₁wɔəd, -wəd**
hazard **'hæzɚd; ES 'hæzəd;** |-ed -ɪd |-ous -əs
haze **hez** |hazes **'hezɪz** |hazed **hezd**
hazel, H- **'hezḷ** |-nut -nət, -₁nʌt
Hazledean **'hezḷ₁din**
Hazleton **'hezḷtən**
Hazlitt **'hæzlɪt**
hazy **'hezɪ** |-zily -z|ɪ, -zɪlɪ
he *stressed* **'hi, ₁hi;** *unstr.* **i, ɪ, hɪ**
head **hɛd** |headed **'hɛdɪd**
headache **'hɛd₁ek**
headband **'hɛd₁bænd**
headboard **'hɛd₁bord, -₁bɔrd; ES -₁boəd,
E+-₁bɔəd**
headcheese **'hɛd₁tʃiz** |-s -ɪz
headdress **'hɛd₁drɛs** |-es -ɪz
headfirst **'hɛd'fɝst; ES -'fɜst, -'fɝst**
headforemost **'hɛd'for₁most, -'fɔr-, -məst; ES
-'foə-, E+-'fɔə-**
headgear **'hɛd₁gɪr; ES -₁gɪə(r, S+-₁gɛə(r**

Key: See in full §§3–47. bee **bi** |pity **'pɪtɪ** (§6) |rate **ret** |yet **jɛt** |sang **sæŋ** |angry **'æŋ·grɪ**
|bath **bæθ;** E **baθ** (§10) |ah **a** |far **far** |watch **watʃ, wɒtʃ** (§12) |jaw **dʒɔ** |gorge **gɔrdʒ** |go **go**

Words below in which ea *before* r (heart) *is sounded* ɑ *are often pronounced in* E *with* a (ha:t)

heading 'hɛdɪŋ

headland *unplowed land* 'hɛdˌlænd, '*promontory*' 'hɛdlənd

headlight 'hɛdˌlaɪt

headline 'hɛdˌlaɪn |-d -d

headlock 'hɛdˌlɑk; ES+-ˌlɒk

headlong 'hɛd'lɔŋ, -ˌlɔŋ, -ɒŋ; S+-ɑŋ

headman 'hɛdmən |-men -mən

headmaster 'hɛd'mæstɚ; ES -tə(r, E+-'mas-, -'mɑs-

head-on 'hɛd'ɑn, -'ɒn, -'ɔn ('head-ˌon 'crash)

headphone 'hɛdˌfon

headpiece 'hɛdˌpis |-s -ɪz

headquarters 'hɛd'kwɔrtɚz, -ˌkw-; ES -'kwɔə-təz, -ˌkw-

headrest 'hɛdˌrɛst

headsman 'hɛdzmən |-men -mən

headspring 'hɛdˌsprɪŋ

headstock 'hɛdˌstɑk; ES+-ˌstɒk

headstone 'hɛdˌston

headstrong 'hɛdˌstrɔŋ, -ˌstrɒŋ; S+-ˌstrɑŋ

headwater 'hɛdˌwɔtɚ, -ˌwɑtɚ, -ˌwɒtɚ; ES -tə(r

headway 'hɛdˌwe

headwork 'hɛdˌwɝk; ES -ˌwɜk, -ˌwɝk

heal hil |healed hild

health hɛlθ |-ths -θs |-ful -fəl |-fully -fəlɪ

healthy 'hɛlθɪ |-thily -θəlɪ, -θɪlɪ

heap hip |heaped hipt

hear hɪr; ES hɪə(r, S+hjɛə(r, hjɪə(r, hɛə(r; |heard hɝd; ES hɜd, hɝd

hearken 'harkən; ES 'ha:kən; |-ed -d |-ing -kənɪŋ, -knɪŋ

hearsay 'hɪrˌse; ES 'hɪə-, S+'hjɛə-, 'hjɪə-, 'hɛə-

hearse hɝs; ES hɜs, hɝs; |-d -t

heart hart; ES ha:t

heartache 'hartˌek; ES 'ha:t-

heartbreak 'hartˌbrek; ES 'ha:t-

heartbroken 'hartˌbrokən, -'brokən; ES 'ha:t-

heartburn 'hartˌbɝn; ES 'ha:tˌbɜn, 'ha:tˌbɝn; |-ed -d

hearten 'hartṇ; ES 'ha:tṇ; |-ed -d |-ing -tṇɪŋ, -tnɪŋ

heartfelt 'hartˌfɛlt, -'fɛlt; ES 'ha:t-

hearth harθ; ES ha:θ; |-ths -θs—*Poetic* hɝθ, hɝθ *is still occas. heard.*

hearthstone 'harθˌston; ES 'ha:θ-;—*see* hearth

heartily 'hartḷɪ, -ɪlɪ; ES 'ha:t-

heartsease 'hartsˌiz; ES 'ha:ts-

heartsick 'hartˌsɪk, -'sɪk; ES 'ha:t-

heartsore 'hartˌsor, -ˌsɔr; ES -ˌsoə(r, E+-ˌsɔə(r; *acct*+'heart'sore

heartstring 'hartˌstrɪŋ; ES 'ha:t-

heart-to-heart 'harttə'hart; ES 'ha:ttə'ha:t

heart-whole 'hart'hol; ES 'ha:t-; ('heart-ˌwhole 'maid)

heartwood 'hartˌwʊd; ES 'ha:t-

heat hit |heated 'hitɪd

heath hiθ |-ths -θs

heathen 'hiðən |-ism -ˌɪzəm |-ness -ðənnɪs

heathenesse *arch.* 'hiðənˌɛs

heather 'hɛðɚ; ES 'hɛðə(r; |-ed -d

heatstroke 'hitˌstrok

heaume hom

heave hiv |heaved hivd *or* hove hov

heaven 'hɛvən, 'hɛvṃ |-ward -wɚd; ES -wəd

Heavener 'hivnɚ; ES 'hivnə(r

heavily 'hɛvḷɪ, -ɪlɪ

Heaviside 'hɛvɪˌsaɪd

heavy '*weighty*' 'hɛvɪ

heavy '*broken-winded*' 'hɪvɪ

heavy-hearted 'hɛvɪ'hartɪd; ES -'ha:tɪd

heavyweight 'hɛvɪˌwet

hebdomad 'hɛbdəˌmæd

hebdomadal hɛb'damədḷ; ES+-'dɒm-; |-ly -ɪ

Hebe 'hibɪ

Hebraic hi'bre·ɪk |-al -ḷ |-ally -ḷɪ

Hebraism 'hibrɪˌɪzəm |-ist -ɪst

Hebraistic ˌhibrɪ'ɪstɪk |-al -ḷ |-ally -ḷɪ, -ɪklɪ

Hebrew 'hibru, 'hibrɪu

Hebrides 'hɛbrəˌdiz

Hebron 'hibrən

Hecate 'hɛkətɪ, *in Shak.* 'hɛkɪt

hecatomb 'hɛkəˌtom, -ˌtum

Hecht hɛkt

heckle 'hɛkḷ |-d -d |-ling 'hɛklɪŋ, 'hɛkḷɪŋ

hectare 'hɛktɛr, -tær; E -tɛə(r, ES -tæə(r

hectic 'hɛktɪk |-ly -lɪ |-al -ḷ |-ally -ḷɪ

hectograph 'hɛktəˌgræf; E+-ˌgraf, -ˌgraf

Hector 'hɛktɚ; ES 'hɛktə(r

hector 'hɛktɚ; ES 'hɛktə(r; |-ed -d |-ing 'hɛktərɪŋ, 'hɛktrɪŋ

Hecuba 'hɛkjubə

he'd *abbr. spelling of* he had, he would, *stressed*
'hid, ˌhid; *unstr.* id, ɪd, hɪd

heddle 'hɛdḷ |-d -d |-ling -dḷɪŋ, -dlɪŋ

hedge hɛdʒ |hedges 'hɛdʒɪz |hedged hɛdʒd

hedgehog 'hɛdʒˌhɑg, -ˌhɔg, -ˌhɒg; S -ˌhɔg,
-ˌhɑg, -ˌhɒg

hedgerow 'hɛdʒˌro

Hedjaz hɛ'dʒaz

hedonic hi'dɑnɪk; ES+-'dɒn-; |-al -ḷ |-ally -ḷɪ

hedonism 'hidn̩ˌɪzəm |-ist -ɪst

Hedwig 'hɛdwɪg

heed hid |heeded 'hidɪd |-ful -fəl |-fully -fəlɪ

heedless 'hidlɪs

heehaw 'hiˌhɔ, 'iˌhɔ̃ (*nasal* i) |-ed -d

heel hil |heeled hild |-less 'hillɪs

heelpiece 'hilˌpis |-s -ɪz |-d -t

heeltap 'hilˌtæp |-tapped -ˌtæpt

Heep, Uriah jʊ'raɪə'hip

heft hɛft |hefted 'hɛftɪd |-y -ɪ

Hegel 'hegḷ

Hegelian he'gelɪən, hi'dʒilɪən

hegemony hi'dʒɛmənɪ, 'hɛdʒəˌmonɪ

hegira, H- hi'dʒaɪrə, 'hɛdʒərə

Heidelberg 'haɪdḷˌbɝg; ES -ˌbɝg, -ˌbɝg; (*Ger*
'haɪdəlˌbɛrk)

heifer 'hɛfɚ; ES 'hɛfə(r

Heifetz 'haɪfɪts |-'s -ɪz

heigh *intj* he, haɪ

heigh-ho *intj, n, v* 'he'ho, 'haɪ'ho |-ed -d

height haɪt—*cf* highth

heighten 'haɪtn̩ |-ed -d |-ing 'haɪtn̩ɪŋ, -tnɪŋ

Heine 'haɪnə

Heinie, -ne *nickname* 'haɪnɪ

heinous 'henəs

Heinz haɪnts, haɪnz |-'s -ɪz

heir ɛr, ær; E ɛə(r, ES æə(r; |-ess -ɪs |-esses
-ɪsɪz

heirloom 'ɛr'lum, 'ær-, -ˌlum; E 'ɛə-, ES 'æə-

Hejaz hɛ'dʒaz

hejira, H- hi'dʒaɪrə, 'hɛdʒərə

Hekate 'hɛkətɪ, *in Shak.* 'hɛkɪt

held hɛld

Helen 'hɛlɪn, -ən

Helena 'hɛlɪnə, hɛ'linə; *cf* Saint H. & Lena

Helgoland 'hɛlgoˌlænd (*Ger* -ˌlant)

heliacal hɪ'laɪəkḷ |-ly -ɪ, -əklɪ

helical 'hɛlɪkḷ |-ly -ɪ

Helicanus ˌhɛlɪ'kenəs |-'s -ɪz

helicline 'hɛlɪˌklaɪn

helicoid 'hɛlɪˌkɔɪd

helicoidal ˌhɛlɪ'kɔɪdḷ |-ly -ɪ

Helicon, h- 'hɛlɪˌkɑn, -kən; ES+-ˌkɒn

helicopter 'hɛlɪˌkɑptɚ, 'hi-; ES -tə(r, -ˌkɒp-

Heligoland 'hɛlɪgoˌlænd

heliocentric ˌhilɪo'sɛntrɪk |-al -ḷ |-ally -ḷɪ
-ɪklɪ

Heliogabalus ˌhilɪə'gæbələs |-'s -ɪz

heliograph 'hilɪəˌgræf; E+-ˌgraf, -ˌgraf

heliometer ˌhilɪ'ɑmətɚ; ES -'ɑmətə(r, -'ɒm-

Heliopolis ˌhilɪ'ɑpəlɪs; ES+-'ɒp-; |-'s -ɪz

Helios 'hilɪˌɑs; ES+-ˌɒs

helioscope 'hilɪəˌskop, 'hiljə-

heliotherapy ˌhilɪo'θɛrəpɪ

heliotrope 'hiljəˌtrop, 'hilɪə-

helium 'hilɪəm

helix 'hilɪks |-es -ɪz |helices 'hɛlɪˌsiz

hell hɛl

he'll *abbr. spelling of* he will, *stressed* 'hil, ˌhil;
unstr. il, ɪl, hɪl

hellbender 'hɛlˌbɛndɚ; ES -ˌbɛndə(r

hellbroth 'hɛlˌbrɔθ, -ˌbrɒθ |-ths -θs

hellcat 'hɛlˌkæt

hell-diver 'hɛlˌdaɪvɚ; ES -ˌdaɪvə(r

hellebore 'hɛləˌbor, -ˌbɔr; ES -ˌboə(r, E+
-ˌbɔə(r

Hellen 'hɛlɪn, -ən, -ɛn

Hellene 'hɛlin |Hellenes 'hɛlinz

Hellenic hɛ'lɛnɪk, -'lin- |-ally -ḷɪ, -ɪklɪ

Hellenism 'hɛlɪnˌɪzəm, -lən- |-ist -ɪst

Hellenistic ˌhɛlɪn'ɪstɪk, -lən- |-al -ḷ |-ally -ḷɪ,
-ɪklɪ

Hellenize 'hɛlɪnˌaɪz, -lən- |-s -ɪz |-d -d

Hellespont 'hɛləˌspɑnt, -ˌspɒnt

hell-fire, H- 'hɛl'faɪr, -ˌfaɪr; ES -aɪə(r

hellgrammite 'hɛlgrəˌmaɪt

hellhound 'hɛlˌhaʊnd

hellion 'hɛljən

hellkite 'hɛlˌkaɪt

hello hɛ'lo, hə'lo, 'hɛlo, 'hʌlo, *emph.* 'hɛl'lo,
'hʌl'lo

helm hɛlm |helmed hɛlmd

helmet 'hɛlmɪt |helmeted 'hɛlmɪtɪd

Helmholtz 'hɛlmˌholts |-'s -ɪz

helmsman 'hɛlmzmən |-men -mən

Heloise *Eng name* ˌhɛlo'iz |-'s -ɪz

Héloïse *wife of Abélard* ˌelo'iz |-'s -ɪz (*Fr*
elɔˈiːz

Helot, h- 'hɛlət, 'hilət |-ism -ˌɪzəm |-ry -rɪ

Key: See in full §§3–47. bee bi |pity 'pɪtɪ (§6) |rate ret |yet jɛt |sang sæŋ |angry 'æŋ·grɪ
|bath bæθ; E baθ (§10) |ah ɑ |far fɑr |watch wɑtʃ, wɒtʃ (§12) |jaw dʒɔ |gorge gɔrdʒ |go go

help hɛlp |helped hɛlpt |holp *arch. past &*
pptc holp |holpen *arch. pptc* 'holpən
helpful 'hɛlpfəl |-ly -ɪ
helpmate 'hɛlp‚met |helpmeet 'hɛlp‚mit
Helsingfors 'hɛlsɪŋ‚fɔrz, -‚fɔrs; ES -‚fɔəz,
-‚fɔəs
Helsinki 'hɛlsɪŋkɪ
helter-skelter 'hɛltɚ'skɛltɚ; ES 'hɛltə'skɛl-
tə(r
helve hɛlv |helved hɛlvd
Helvetia hɛl'viʃə, -ʃɪə |-n -n
Helvetii hɛl'viʃɪ‚aɪ
hem hɛm |hemmed hɛmd
Hemans 'hɛmənz, 'hɪmənz |-'s -ɪz
hematic, hae- hi'mætɪk
hematite, haem- 'hɛmə‚taɪt
hemicycle 'hɛmə‚saɪkḷ
hemicyclic ‚hɛmə'saɪklɪk, -'sɪk-
hemidemisemiquaver‚hɛmɪ‚dɛmɪ'sɛmə‚kwevɚ;
ES -‚kwevə(r
hemin, hae- 'hɪmɪn
Hemingway 'hɛmɪŋ‚we
hemiplegy 'hɛmɪ‚plidʒɪ |-gia ‚hɛmɪ'plidʒɪə
hemisphere 'hɛməs‚fɪr; ES -‚fɪə(r, S+-‚fɛə(r
hemispheric ‚hɛmə'sfɛrɪk |-al -ḷ |-ally -ḷɪ
hemispheroid ‚hɛmə'sfɪrɔɪd
hemistich 'hɛmə‚stɪk
hemlock 'hɛmlɑk; ES+-lɒk
hemoglobin, haem- ‚himə'globɪn, ‚hɛmə-
hemophilia, haem- ‚himə'fɪlɪə, ‚hɛmə-
hemorrhage, haem- 'hɛmərɪdʒ, 'hɛmrɪdʒ |-s
-ɪz
hemorrhoid, haem- 'hɛmə‚rɔɪd, 'hɛm‚rɔɪd
hemp hɛmp |hempen 'hɛmpən |-seed -‚sid
Hempl, *George, Am scholar* 'hɛmpḷ
hemstitch 'hɛm‚stɪtʃ |-es -ɪz |-ed -t
hen hɛn |henbane 'hɛn‚ben
hence hɛns
henceforth ‚hɛns'forθ, -'fɔrθ; ES -'foəθ,
E+-'fɔəθ
henceforward ‚hɛns'fɔrwəd; ES -'fɔəwəd
henchman 'hɛntʃmən |-men -mən
hencoop 'hɛn‚kup, -‚kʊp—*see* coop
hendiadys hɛn'daɪədɪs
henequen, -quin 'hɛnəkɪn
Hengist 'hɛŋgɪst, 'hɛndʒɪst
Henley 'hɛnlɪ
henna 'hɛnə |hennaed 'hɛnəd
Hennepin 'hɛnəpɪn (*Fr* ɛn'pɛ̃)

hennery 'hɛnərɪ
henpeck 'hɛn‚pɛk |-pecked -‚pɛkt
Henrietta ‚hɛnrɪ'ɛtə
henry, H- 'hɛnrɪ
hepatic hɪ'pætɪk |-a -ə |-al -ḷ
Hephaestus hi'fɛstəs |-'s -ɪz
Hephzibah 'hɛfzɪbə
Hepplewhite 'hɛpḷ‚hwaɪt
heptagon 'hɛptə‚gɑn; ES+-‚gɒn
heptagonal hɛp'tægənḷ
heptameter hɛp'tæmətɚ; ES -'tæmətə(r
heptarchy, H- 'hɛptɑrkɪ; ES -tɑ:kɪ, E+-tɑ:kɪ
Heptateuch 'hɛptə‚tjuk, -‚tɪuk, -‚tuk
Hepzibah Pyncheon 'hɛpzɪbə'pɪntʃən
her *stressed* 'hɝ, ‚hɝ; ES 'hɜ(r, ‚hɜ(r, 'hɝ, ‚hɝ;
unstr. ɚ, hɚ; ES ə(r, hə(r
Hera 'hirə, 'hɪrə
Heracles 'hɛrə‚kliz |-'s -ɪz
Heraclitus ‚hɛrə'klaɪtəs |-'s -ɪz
Herakles 'hɛrə‚kliz |-'s -ɪz
herald 'hɛrəld, hɛrld |-ed -ɪd |-ry -rɪ
heraldic hɛ'rældɪk |-al -ḷ |-ally -ḷɪ, -ɪklɪ
herb ɝb, hɝb; ES ɜb, hɜb, ɝb, hɝb
herbaceous hɝ'beʃəs; ES hɜ-, hɝ-
herbage 'ɝbɪdʒ, 'hɝb-; ES 'ɜb-, 'hɜb-, 'ɝb-,
'hɝb-
herbal 'hɝbḷ, 'ɝbḷ; ES 'hɜbḷ, 'ɜbḷ, 'hɝbḷ, 'ɝbḷ;
|-ism -‚ɪzəm |-ist -ɪst
herbarium hɝ'bɛrɪəm, -'bær-, -'ber-; ES hɜ-,
hɝ-; |-s -z |-ia -ɪə
Herbert 'hɝbɚt; ES 'hɜbət, 'hɝbət
herbiferous hɝ'bɪfərəs; ES hɜ-, hɝ-
herbivorous hɝ'bɪvərəs; ES hɜ-, hɝ-
Herculaneum ‚hɝkjə'lenɪəm; ES ‚hɜ-, ‚hɝ-
herculean, H- hɝ'kjulɪən, -'krul-, ‚hɝkjə'liən;
ES -ɜ-, -ɝ-
Hercules 'hɝkjə‚liz; ES 'hɜ-, 'hɝ-; |-'s -ɪz
herd hɝd; ES hɜd, hɝd; |-ed -ɪd
Herder *Ger poet* 'hɛrdɚ; ES 'hɛədə(r
herdsman 'hɝdzmən; ES 'hɜdz-, 'hɝdz-;
|-men -mən
here hɪr; ES hɪə(r, S+hjɛə(r, hjɪə(r, jɛə(r,
hɛə(r
Here 'hiri=Hera
hereabout ‚hɪrə'baʊt, 'hɪrə‚baʊt; S+*see* here
hereafter hɪr'æftɚ; ES hɪr'æftə(r, E+-'af-,
-'ɑf-, S+*see* here
hereat hɪr'æt; S+*see* here
hereby hɪr'baɪ; ES hɪə'baɪ, S+*see* here

hereditable hə'rɛdətəb| |-bly -blɪ
hereditament ˌhɛrə'dɪtəmənt
hereditary hə'rɛdəˌtɛrɪ |-dity -dətɪ
herefor hɪr'fɔr; ES hɪə'fɔə(r, S+see here
Hereford 'hɛrəfəd, by Am stockmen usually
'hɝfəd; ES 'hɛrəfəd, 'hɜf-, 'hɝfəd; |-shire
-ˌʃɪr, -ˌʃɚ; ES -ˌʃɪə(r, -ʃə(r
herefrom hɪr'frɑm, -'frɒm; ES hɪə-, S+see
here
herein hɪr'ɪn; S+see here
hereinafter ˌhɪrɪn'æftɚ; ES -'æftə(r, E+-'af-,
-'ɑf-, S+see here
hereinbefore ˌhɪrɪnbɪ'for, -'fɔr; ES -'foə(r,
E+-'fɔə(r, S+see here
hereinto hɪr'ɪntu, -tʊ; S+see here—acct+
ˌherein'to
hereof hɪr'ʌv, -'ɑf, -'ɒ-; S+see here
hereon hɪr'ɑn, -'ɒn, -'ɔn; S+see here
heresy 'hɛrəsɪ |heretic 'hɛrətɪk
heretical hə'rɛtɪk| |-ly -ɪ, -ɪklɪ
hereto hɪr'tu; ES hɪə'tu, S+see here
heretofore ˌhɪrtə'for, -'fɔr; ES ˌhɪətə'foə(r,
E+-'fɔə(r, S+see here
hereunder hɪr'ʌndɚ; ES -'ʌndə(r, S+see here
hereunto hɪr'ʌntu, -tʊ; S+see here—acct+
ˌhereun'to
hereupon ˌhɪrə'pɑn, -'pɒn, -'pɔn; S+see here
Hereward 'hɛrəwəd; ES 'hɛrəwəd
herewith hɪr'wɪθ, -'wɪð; ES hɪə-, S+see here;
cf wherewith
Herford 'hɝfəd; ES 'hɝfəd, 'hɝfəd
Hergesheimer 'hɝgəsˌhaɪmɚ; ES 'hɝgəs-
ˌhaɪmə(r, 'hɝgəsˌhaɪmə(r
Herington 'hɛrɪŋtən
heriot, H- 'hɛrɪət
heritable 'hɛrətəb| |-bly -blɪ
heritage 'hɛrətɪdʒ |-tance -təns |-s -ɪz
heritor 'hɛrətɚ; ES 'hɛrətə(r
Herkimer 'hɝkəmɚ; ES 'hɝkəmə(r, 'hɝkə-
mə(r
herl hɝl; ES hɜl, hɝl
Herman 'hɝmən; ES 'hɝm-, 'hɝm-
hermaphrodite hɝ'mæfrəˌdaɪt; ES hɜ-, hɝ-
hermaphroditic hɝˌmæfrə'dɪtɪk; ES hɜ-, hɝ-;
|-al -| |-ally -|ɪ, -ɪklɪ
hermeneutic ˌhɝmən'jutɪk, -mə'nɪutɪk, -'nu-;
ES ˌhɜ-, ˌhɝ-; |-al -| |-ally -|ɪ, -ɪklɪ
Hermes 'hɝmiz; ES 'hɝmiz, 'hɝmiz; |-mes'
-miz

hermetic hɝ'mɛtɪk; ES hɜ-, hɝ-; |-al -|
|-ally -|ɪ, -ɪklɪ
Hermia 'hɝmɪə, -mjə; ES 'hɝm-, 'hɝm-
Hermione hɝ'maɪənɪ; ES hɜ-, hɝ-
hermit 'hɝmɪt; ES 'hɝm-, 'hɝm-; |-age -ɪdʒ
|-ages -ɪdʒɪz
Hermon 'hɝmən; ES 'hɝm-, 'hɝm-
hernia 'hɝnɪə, -njə; ES 'hɜn-, 'hɝn-; |-s -z
|-niae -nɪˌi
hero, H- 'hɪro, 'hiro
Herod 'hɛrəd |-rodian hɛ'rodɪən
Herodias hə'rodɪəs, hɛ- |-'s -ɪz
Herodotus hə'radətəs; ES+-'rɒd-; |-'s -ɪz
heroic hɪ'ro·ɪk, hə-, hɛ- |-al -| |-ally -|ɪ |-icly
-ɪklɪ
heroin, H- drug 'hɛro·ɪn
heroine 'heroic woman' 'hɛro·ɪn
heroism 'hɛroˌɪzəm
heron 'hɛrən |-ry -rɪ
heronsew, -sewe arch. 'hɛrənˌsju, -ˌsɪu, -ˌsu
|-shaw -ˌʃɔ
herpes 'hɝpiz; ES 'hɜ-, 'hɝ-
herpetology ˌhɝpə'talədʒɪ; ES ˌhɜp-, ˌhɝp-,
-'tɒl-
Herr Ger title hɛr; ES hɛə(r
Herrick 'hɛrɪk
herring 'hɛrɪŋ |-bone -ˌbon
Herriot Am pers. name 'hɛrɪət, Fr statesman
ɛr'jo
hers hɝz; ES hɜz, hɝz
Herschel 'hɝʃəl; ES 'hɝʃ-, 'hɝʃ-
herself hɚ'sɛlf,+if not initial or after a pause
ɚ'sɛlf; ES hə-, ə-
Hertford US 'hɝtfəd; ES 'hɝtfəd, 'hɝtfəd,
Engd 'harfəd, 'hartfəd; ES 'ha:fəd,
'ha:tfəd, E+'ha:-; |-shire -ˌʃɪr, -ʃɚ; ES
-ˌʃɪə(r, -ʃə(r
Herts short for Hertfordshire harts, hɝts; ES
ha:ts, hɜts, hɝts, E+ha:ts
Hertz hɛrts, hɝts; ES hɛəts, hɜts, hɝts; |-'s
-ɪz |-ian -ɪən
he's abbr. spelling of he has, he is, stressed 'hiz,
ˌhiz; unstr. iz, ɪz, hiz, hɪz
Hesiod 'hisɪəd, 'hɛs-
Hesione hɪ'saɪənɪ, hɛ-
hesitance 'hɛzətəns |-cy -ɪ |-tant -tənt
hesitate 'hɛzəˌtet |-d -ɪd |-tion ˌhɛzə'teʃən
Hesper 'hɛspɚ; ES 'hɛspə(r
Hesperia hɛs'pɪrɪə |-n -n

Key: See in full §§3-47. bee bi |pity 'pɪtɪ (§6) |rate ret |yet jɛt |sang sæŋ |angry 'æŋ·grɪ
|bath bæθ; E baθ (§10) |ah ɑ |far fɑr |watch watʃ, wɒtʃ (§12) |jaw dʒɔ |gorge gɔrdʒ |go go

Hesperides hɛsˈpɛrəˌdiz
Hesperus ˈhɛspərəs |-'s -ɪz
Hesse *Ger region* hɛs, ˈhɛsɪ (*Ger* Hessen
ˈhɛsən)—*The Ger word* Hesse ˈhɛsə *means
'resident of Hesse'* (*Ger* Hessen).
Hessian ˈhɛʃən
hest hɛst
Hester ˈhɛstɚ; ES ˈhɛstə(r
Hestia ˈhɛstɪə
hetaera hɪˈtɪrə |hetaira hɪˈtaɪrə
Hetch Hetchy Valley ˈhɛtʃˈhɛtʃɪˈvælɪ
heterodox ˈhɛtərəˌdɑks, ˈhɛtrə-; ES+ˌdɒks;
|-y -ɪ
heterodyne ˈhɛtərəˌdaɪn
heterogeneity ˌhɛtərədʒəˈniətɪ, ˌhɛtəro-
heterogeneous ˌhɛtərəˈdʒɪnɪəs, -njəs
heteronym ˈhɛtərəˌnɪm
heterosyllabic ˌhɛtəˌroˈsɪˈlæbɪk
hetman ˈhɛtmən |*pl* hetmans ˈhɛtmənz
hew hju, hɪu |*past* -ed -d |*pptc* -ed -d *or* -n -n
hex hɛks |hexes ˈhɛksɪz |hexed hɛkst
hexachord ˈhɛksəˌkɔrd; ES -ˌkɔəd
hexa·emeron ˌhɛksəˈɛməˌrɑn, ES+-ˌrɒn
hexagon ˈhɛksəˌgɑn, -gən; ES+-ˌgɒn
hexagonal hɛksˈægən| |-ly -ɪ
hexagram ˈhɛksəˌgræm
hexahedral ˌhɛksəˈhidrəl
hexahedron ˌhɛksəˈhidrən |-s -z |-dra -drə
hexahemeron ˌhɛksəˈhɛməˌrɑn; ES+-ˌrɒn
hexameter hɛksˈæmətɚ; ES -ˈæmətə(r; |-ed -d
hexane ˈhɛksen
hexangular hɛksˈæŋgjəlɚ; ES -ˈæŋgjələ(r
hexapla ˈhɛksəplə
hexapod ˈhɛksəˌpɑd; ES+-ˌpɒd
hexarchy ˈhɛksɑrkɪ; ES ˈhɛksɑ:kɪ, E+-ɑ:kɪ
Hexateuch ˈhɛksəˌtjuk, -ˌtɪuk, -ˌtuk
hey he |heyday ˈheˌde
Heyne ˈhaɪnə
Heywood ˈhewʊd
Hezekiah ˌhɛzəˈkaɪə
hiatus haɪˈetəs |-es -ɪz
Hiawatha ˌhaɪəˈwɑθə, -ˈwɒθə
hibernal haɪˈbɝn|; ES -ˈbɜn|, -ˈbɝn|
hibernate ˈhaɪbɚˌnet; ES -bəˌnet; |-d -ɪd
hibernation ˌhaɪbɚˈneʃən; ES ˌhaɪbə-
Hibernia haɪˈbɝnɪə; ES -ˈbɜn-, -ˈbɝn-; |-n -n
|-nicism -nəˌsɪzəm
hibiscus, H- haɪˈbɪskəs, hɪ- |-es -ɪz
hiccough *erroneous sp. for* hiccup

hiccup ˈhɪkʌp, ˈhɪkəp |-ed -t
hickory, H- ˈhɪkrɪ, ˈhɪkərɪ
hickory-nut ˈhɪkrɪnət, ˈhɪkərɪ-, -ˌnʌt, *dial.*
ˈhɪkɚnət
hid hɪd
hidalgo, H- hɪˈdælgo (*Sp* iˈðalgo)
hide *'conceal'* haɪd |hid hɪd |hidden ˈhɪdn̩,
hid hɪd
hide *'skin'* haɪd |hided ˈhaɪdɪd
hide-and-seek ˈhaɪdn̩ˈsik
hidebound ˈhaɪdˌbaʊnd
hideous ˈhɪdɪəs
hie haɪ |hied haɪd
Hiems, h- ˈhaɪəmz |-'s -ɪz
hierarch ˈhaɪəˌrɑrk; ES -ˌrɑ:k, E+-ˌrɑ:k;
|-y -ɪ
hieratic ˌhaɪəˈrætɪk |-al -| |-ally -|ɪ, -ɪklɪ
hieroglyph ˈhaɪərəˌglɪf, ˈhaɪrə-
hieroglyphic ˌhaɪərəˈglɪfɪk, ˌhaɪrə- |-al -|
|-ally -|ɪ, -ɪklɪ
Hieronymus ˌhaɪəˈrɑnəməs, -ˈrɒn-
higgle ˈhɪg| |-d -d |-ling ˈhɪglɪŋ, ˈhɪg|ɪŋ
higgledy-piggledy ˈhɪg|dɪˈpɪg|dɪ
high haɪ |-er ˈhaɪɚ; ES ˈhaɪ·ə(r; |-est -ɪst
Higham ˈhaɪəm
highball ˈhaɪˌbɔl
highbinder ˈhaɪˌbaɪndɚ; ES -ˌbaɪndə(r
highborn ˈhaɪˈbɔrn; ES -ˈbɔən; (ˈhighˌborn
ˈlass)
highboy ˈhaɪˌbɔɪ
highbred ˈhaɪˈbrɛd
high-brow ˈhaɪˌbraʊ
highfalutin, -ting, -ten ˌhaɪfəˈlutn̩, -ˈlɪutn̩
highflier ˈhaɪˌflaɪɚ; ES -ˌflaɪ·ə(r
high-flown ˈhaɪˈflon (ˈhigh-ˌflown ˈspeech)
Highgate *US* ˈhaɪˌget, *Engd* ˈhaɪgɪt
highhanded ˈhaɪˈhændɪd
highjacker ˈhaɪˌdʒækɚ; ES -ˌdʒækə(r
highland, H- ˈhaɪlənd |-er -ɚ; ES -ə(r
highlight *v* ˈhaɪˌlaɪt |-ed -ɪd
highminded ˈhaɪˈmaɪndɪd
high-pitched ˈhaɪˈpɪtʃt (ˈhigh-ˌpitched ˈnote)
high-pressure ˈhaɪˈprɛʃɚ; ES -ˈprɛʃə(r
highroad ˈhaɪˌrod, -ˈrod
high-spirited ˈhaɪˈspɪrɪtɪd
high-strung ˈhaɪˈstrʌŋ (ˈhigh-ˌstrung ˈnerves)
hight *arch. v* 'call,' 'called' haɪt
hight *var. sp. of* height haɪt
high-test ˈhaɪˈtɛst

---

highth *doublet of* height **haɪtθ**, *Brit*+**haɪθ**—
  Highth *is not an error for* height, *but a pho-*
  netically normal historical variant, found
  e.g. in Milton.
high-toned **'haɪ'tond**
highty-tighty **'haɪtɪ'taɪtɪ**
highway **'haɪˌwe**
highwayman *'robber'* **'haɪˌwemən, haɪ'we-**
highwayman *'road overseer'* **'haɪweˌmæn**
  |-men -ˌmɛn
hike **haɪk** |hiked **haɪkt**
Hilaire **hɪ'lɛr, -'lær**; E **-'lɛə(r, ES -'læə(r**
hilarious **hə'lɛrɪəs, hɪ-, haɪ-, -'lær-, -'ler-**
hilarity **hə'lærətɪ, hɪ-, haɪ-**
Hilda **'hɪldə**
Hildebrand **'hɪldəˌbrænd** (*Ger* **'hɪldəˌbrant**)
Hildegarde **'hɪldəˌgard**; ES **-ˌga:d, E+-ˌga:d**
hilding **'hɪldɪŋ**
hill **hɪl** |hilled **hɪld**
hillbilly **'hɪlˌbɪlɪ**
Hillis **'hɪlɪs** |-'s **-ɪz**
hill-less **'hɪllɪs**
hillock **'hɪlək** |hillocked **'hɪləkt**
hillside **'hɪlˌsaɪd**
hilt **hɪlt** |hilted **'hɪltɪd**
hilum **'haɪləm** |-s -z |-la -lə
him *stressed* **'hɪm, ˌhɪm**; *unstr.* ɪm, hɪm
Himalaya **hɪ'maljə, -'maləjə, ˌhɪmə'leə** |-n -n
  |-s -z—*In Engd the traditional Anglicized*
  pron. still prevails (*Jones says* **hɪ'maləjə** *is*
  rare), *as it once did in America, but the pron.*
  more like the native one has recently become
  frequent here.
himself **hɪm'sɛlf**,+*if not initial or after a*
  pause ɪm'sɛlf
hind **haɪnd**
hindbrain **'haɪndˌbren, 'haɪn-**
hinder *'back'* **'haɪndɚ**; ES **'haɪndə(r**
hinder *'obstruct'* **'hɪndɚ**; ES **'hɪndə(r**; |-ed -d
  |-ing **'hɪndrɪŋ, 'hɪndərɪŋ**
hindermost **'haɪndɚˌmost**; ES **'haɪndə-**
Hindi **'hɪndi, 'hɪn'di**
hindmost **'haɪndˌmost, 'haɪn-**
Hindoo **'hɪndu, 'hɪn'du** |-ism **'hɪnduˌɪzəm**
  |-stani **ˌhɪndu'stænɪ, -'stanɪ**
Hindostan **ˌhɪndu'stæn, -'stan** |-i -ɪ
hindquarter **'haɪnd'kwɔrtɚ, 'haɪn-**; ES
  -'kwɔətə(r
hindrance **'hɪndrəns** |-s -ɪz

hindside **'haɪndˌsaɪd, 'haɪn-**
hind-side-foremost **'haɪndˌsaɪd'forˌmost,'haɪn-,**
  -'fɔr-; ES **-'foə-, E+-'fɔə-**
hindsight **'haɪndˌsaɪt, 'haɪn-**
Hindu **'hɪndu, 'hɪn'du** (**'Hinˌdu 'races**)
Hinduism **'hɪnduˌɪzəm**
Hindu Kush **'hɪndu'kuʃ, -du-**
Hindustan **ˌhɪndu'stæn, -'stan** |-i -ɪ
hinge **hɪndʒ** |hinges **'hɪndʒɪz** |hinged **hɪndʒd**
Hingham **'hɪŋəm**
hinny **'hɪnɪ**
Hinsdale **'hɪnzdel**
hint **hɪnt** |hinted **'hɪntɪd**
hinterland **'hɪntɚˌlænd**; ES **'hɪntə-**; (*Ger*
  -ˌlant)
hip **hɪp** |hipped **hɪpt** |-bone -'bon -ˌbon
hippocampus **ˌhɪpə'kæmpəs** |-es -ɪz |-pi -paɪ
hippocras **'hɪpəˌkræs**
Hippocrates **hɪ'pakrəˌtiz**; ES+-'pɒk-; |-'s -ɪz
Hippocratic **ˌhɪpə'krætɪk**
Hippocrene **'hɪpəˌkrin, ˌhɪpə'krini**
hippodrome **'hɪpəˌdrom**
hippogriff, -gryff **'hɪpəˌgrɪf**
Hippolyta **hɪ'palɪtə**; ES+-'pɒl-; |-tus -təs
  |-tus's -təsɪz
hippopotamus **ˌhɪpə'patəməs**; ES+-'pɒt-;
  |-es -ɪz |-mi -ˌmaɪ
Hiram **'haɪrəm**
hircine **'hɝsaɪn, -sɪn**; ES **'hɜ-, 'hɝ-**
hire **haɪr**; ES **haɪə(r**; |-d -d |-ling -lɪŋ
Hirohito **ˌhiro'hito**
Hirsch **hɝʃ**; ES **hɜʃ, hɝʃ**; |-'s -ɪz
hirsute **'hɝsut, -sɪut, -sjut**; ES **'hɜ-, 'hɝ-**
his *stressed* **'hɪz, ˌhɪz**; *unstr.* ɪz, hɪz—*When*
  entirely unstressed, his *has no* h, *just like he,*
  her, him, 'em, it.
Hispania **hɪs'penɪə, -njə** |-nic **hɪs'pænɪk**
Hispaniola **ˌhɪspən'jolə**
hispid **'hɪspɪd** |hispidity **hɪs'pɪdətɪ**
hiss **hɪs** |hisses **'hɪsɪz** |hissed **hɪst**
hist **hɪst** |histed **'hɪstɪd**
histology **hɪs'talədʒɪ**; ES+-'tɒl-
historian **hɪs'torɪən, -'tɔr-**; S **-'tor-**
historic **hɪs'tɔrɪk, -'tarɪk, -'tɒrɪk** |-al -l̩ |-ally
  -lɪ, -ɪklɪ
historicity **ˌhɪstə'rɪsətɪ**
historiographer **ˌhɪstorɪ'agrəfɚ, hɪsˌtorɪ-, -ɔrɪ-,**
  -ɒg-; S **-orɪ-**, ES **-fə(r**
history **'hɪstrɪ, 'hɪstərɪ** |-ried -rɪd

---

histrionic ˌhɪstrɪˈanɪk; ES+-ˈɒn-; |-al -|
|-ally -|ɪ, -ɪklɪ
hit hɪt
hit-and-miss ˈhɪtn̩ˈmɪs
hit-and-run ˈhɪtn̩ˈrʌn (ˈhit-and-ˌrun ˈdriver)
hitch hɪtʃ |hitches ˈhɪtʃɪz |hitched hɪtʃt
hitchhike ˈhɪtʃˌhaɪk |-hiked -ˌhaɪkt
hithe, H- haɪð
hither ˈhɪðɚ; ES ˈhɪðə(r; |-most -ˌmost
hitherto ˌhɪðɚˈtu; ES ˌhɪðə-; (ˈhitherˌto
ˈcame)
hitherward ˈhɪðɚwɚd; ES ˈhɪðəwəd; |-s -z
Hitler ˈhɪtlɚ; ES ˈhɪtlə(r; |-ism -ˌɪzəm |-ite
-ˌaɪt
Hitlerian hɪtˈlɪrɪən
hit-or-miss ˈhɪtɚˈmɪs; ES ˈhɪtə-ˈmɪs
hit-skip ˈhɪtˈskɪp |-ped -t (ˈhit-ˌskip ˈdriver)
Hittite ˈhɪtaɪt
hive haɪv |hived haɪvd
h'm, hm hm—*the* h *nasal, with closed lips*
ho ho
hoar, H- hor, hɔr; ES hoə(r, E+hɔə(r
hoard hord, hɔrd; ES hoəd, E+hɔəd; |-ed -ɪd
hoarfrost ˈhorˌfrɔst, ˈhɔr-, -ˌfrɒst; ES ˈhoə-,
E+ˈhɔə-
hoarhound ˈhorˌhaʊnd, ˈhɔr-; ES ˈhoə-,
E+ˈhɔə-
hoarse hors, hɔrs; ES hoəs, E+hɔəs
hoary ˈhorɪ, ˈhɔrɪ; S ˈhorɪ
hoaryheaded ˈhorɪˈhɛdɪd, ˈhɔrɪ-; S ˈhorɪ-;
(ˈhoaryˌheaded ˈjoke)
hoax hoks |hoaxes ˈhoksɪz |hoaxed hokst;
|*N Engd*+hŏks (§46)
hob hab; ES+hɒb; |-bed -d
hob-and-nob ˈhabənˈnab; ES+ˈhɒbənˈnɒb
Hobart *Tasm* ˈhobɚt, -bart, *US pers. name*
ˈhobɚt; ES -bət, -ba:t
Hobbes habz; ES+hɒbz; |-'s -ɪz
hobble ˈhab|; ES+ˈhɒb|; |-d -d |-ling -blɪŋ,
-b|ɪŋ
hobbledehoy ˈhab|dɪˌhɔɪ; ES+ˈhɒb-
hobby ˈhabɪ; ES+ˈhɒbɪ; |-horse -ˌhɔrs; ES
-ˌhɔəs
hobgoblin ˈhabˌgablɪn; ES+ˈhɒbˌgɒblɪn
hobman-blind ˈhabmənˈblaɪnd; ES+ˈhɒb-;
see hodman-blind
hobnail ˈhabˌnel; ES+ˈhɒb-; |-ed -d
hobnob ˈhabˌnab; ES+ˈhɒbˌnɒb; |-bed -d
hobo ˈhobo

Hoboken ˈhobokən
Hobson ˈhabsn̩; ES+ˈhɒbsn̩
hock hak; ES+hɒk; |-ed -t
hockey ˈhakɪ; ES+ˈhɒkɪ
hocus ˈhokəs |hocuses ˈhokəsɪz |hocused
ˈhokəst
hocus-pocus ˈhokəsˈpokəs |-ed -t
hod had; ES+hɒd
Hodgenville ˈhadʒənˌvɪl; ES+ˈhɒdʒ-, S+-v|
hodgepodge ˈhadʒˌpadʒ; ES+ˈhɒdʒˌpɒdʒ;
|-s -ɪz |-d -d
hodman-blind ˈhadmənˈblaɪnd; ES+ˈhɒd-;
see hoodman-blind
hoe ho |hoed hod |-cake -ˌkek
hog hag, hɔg, hɒg; S hɒg, hag, hɒg; |-ged -d
Hogarth ˈhogarθ; ES -ga:θ, E+-ga:θ
Hogarthian hoˈgarθɪən; ES -ˈga:θ-, E+
-ˈga:θ-
hogback ˈhagˌbæk, ˈhɔg-, ˈhɒg- |-ed -t—*cf* hog
hogmanay ˌhagməˈne, ˌhɔg-
hognose ˈhagˌnoz, ˈhɔg-, ˈhɒg- |-d -d—*cf* hog
hognut ˈhagˌnʌt, ˈhɔg-, ˈhɒg-, -nət—*cf* hog
hogshead ˈhagzˌhɛd, ˈhɔgz-, ˈhɒgz-, -zɪd—*cf*
hog
hogwash ˈhagˌwaʃ, ˈhɔg-, ˈhɒg-, -ˌwɔʃ, -ˌwɒʃ
—*cf* hog
Hohenlinden ˈhoənˌlɪndən
Hohenstaufen *Ger* ˌho:ənˈʃtaʊfən
Hohenzollern ˈhoənˌzalɚn; ES -ˌzalən, -ˌzɒl-:
(*Ger* ˌho:ənˈtsɔlərn)
hoicks hɔɪks
hoiden ˈhɔɪdn̩ |-ed -d |-ing -dn̩ɪŋ, -dnɪŋ
hoi polloi ˈhɔɪpəˈlɔɪ
hoise *arch.* hɔɪz |hoised hɔɪzd *or* hoist hɔɪst
hoist *v pres* hɔɪst |-ed -ɪd
hokeypokey ˈhokɪˈpokɪ
Hokkaido haˈkaɪdo, hɒ-
hokum ˈhokəm
Holbein ˈholbaɪn, ˈhal-, ˈhɒl-
Holborn *Lond* ˈhobɚn, ˈhol-; ES -bən; *Scotl*
holˈborn, -ˈbɔrn; ES -ˈboən, E+-ˈbɔən
hold hold |held hɛld |*arch. pptc* holden ˈholdən
holdall ˈholdˌɔl
holdback ˈholdˌbæk
Holden ˈholdən, -dɪn
holder ˈholdɚ; ES ˈholdə(r
holdfast ˈholdˌfæst; E+-ˌfast, -ˌfast
holdup ˈholdˌʌp
hole hol |holed hold

---

holiday 'halə‚de; ES+'hɒl-
holiness, H- 'holɪnɪs |-'s -ɪz
Holinshed 'halɪnz‚hɛd, 'halɪn‚ʃɛd; ES+
'hɒl-; -‚ʃɛd *is a sp. pron.; the second part=
'head.'*
holla 'halə, hə'la—*see* hollo
Holland 'haland; ES+'hɒl-
hollandaise ‚halən'dez; ES+‚hɒl-; ('hollan-
‚daise 'sauce)
hollo 'halo, hə'lo—*This word & hollaare hardly
in current use. The living word is* holler
'halə; ES 'halə(r, 'hɒl-, *shunned by many.*
hollow 'halo, 'halə; ES+'hɒl-; |-ed -d |-ing
-ləwɪŋ |-er -ləwɚ; ES -wə(r; |-est -ləwɪst
holly 'halɪ; ES+'hɒlɪ
hollyhock 'halɪ‚hak, -‚hɔk; ES+'hɒlɪ‚hɒk;
The pronunciation 'halɪ‚hɔk *is evidenced
from all parts of US and from Canada.*
Hollywood 'halɪ‚wʊd; ES+'hɒlɪ-
holm hom
Holmes homz; NEngd+hõmz (§46) |-'s -ɪz
holmia 'holmɪə |holmium 'holmɪəm |-mic
-mɪk
holocaust 'halə‚kɔst; ES+'hɒl-
Holofernes, -pher- ‚halə'fɝniz; ES ‚halə-
'fɝniz, ‚hɒl-, -'fɝniz; |-nes' -niz
holograph 'halə‚græf; ES+'hɒl-, E+-‚graf, ‚
-‚graf
holophote 'halə‚fot; ES+'hɒl-
holp *arch. past & pptc of* help holp
holpen *arch. pptc of* help 'holpən
Holstein 'holstaɪn, *with US farmers usually*
'holstin (Ger 'hɔlʃtaɪn)
Holstein-Friesian 'holstaɪn'friʒən, -stin-
holster 'holstɚ; ES -stə(r; |-ed -d |-ing 'hol-
stərɪŋ, 'holstrɪŋ
holt, H- holt; NEngd+hõlt (§46)
holy 'holɪ |holily 'holəlɪ, -lɪlɪ
holyday 'holɪ‚de
Holyhead *Wales* 'halɪ‚hɛd, -'hɛd; ES+'hɒlɪ-
Holyoke 'holɪ‚ok, *Mass city & college* 'holjok
Holyrood *Scotl* 'halɪ‚rud; ES+'hɒlɪ-
holystone 'holɪ‚ston |-d -d
holytide 'holɪ‚taɪd
Holywell 'halɪ‚wɛl, -wəl; ES+'hɒlɪ-
homage 'hamɪdʒ, 'am-; ES+hɒm-, 'ɒm-;
|-s -ɪz |-d -d
hombre *Sp 'man'* 'ɔmbre |*pl* -bres -bres
hombre '*omber'* 'ambɚ; ES 'ambə(r, 'ɒm-

home hom |homed homd; |NEngd+hõm
(§46)
homebred 'hom'brɛd ('home‚bred 'mink)
homeland 'hom‚lænd
homelike 'hom‚laɪk
homely 'homlɪ; NEngd+'hõmlɪ (§46)
homemade 'hom'med
homemaker 'hom‚mekɚ; ES -‚mekə(r
homeopath 'homɪə‚pæθ |-ths -θs
homeopathic ‚homɪə'pæθɪk |-ally -lɪ, -ɪklɪ
homeopathist ‚homɪ'apəθɪst; ES+-'ɒp-; |-thy
-θɪ
homer 'homɚ; ES 'homə(r
Homer 'homɚ; ES 'homə(r
Homeric ho'mɛrɪk |-al -l |-ally -lɪ, -ɪklɪ
homesick 'hom‚sɪk
homespun 'hom‚spʌn
homestead, H- 'hom‚stɛd, 'homstɪd
homestretch 'hom'strɛtʃ |-es -ɪz
homeward 'homwɚd; ES 'homwəd
homework 'hom‚wɝk; ES -‚wɜk, -‚wɝk
homey 'homɪ
homicidal ‚hamə'saɪdl; ES+-‚hɒm-; |-ly -ɪ
homicide 'hamə‚saɪd; ES+'hɒm-
homiletic ‚hamə'lɛtɪk; ES+‚hɒm-; |-al -l
|-ally -lɪ, -ɪklɪ
homily 'hamlɪ; ES+'hɒm-
hominy 'hamənɪ; ES+'hɒm-
homo, H- 'homo |*pl* homines 'hamə‚niz;
ES+'hɒm-
homogamic ‚homə'gæmɪk, ‚ham-; ES+‚hɒm-
homogamy ho'magəmɪ, -'mɒg-
homogeneity ‚homədʒə'niətɪ, ‚ham-; ES+
‚hɒm-
homogeneous ‚homə'dʒinɪəs, ‚ham-; ES+
‚hɒm-
homogenesis ‚homə'dʒɛnəsɪs, ‚ham-; ES+
‚hɒm-
homogenize ho'madʒə‚naɪz; ES+ -'mɒdʒ-
homologous ho'maləgəs; ES+-'mɒl-
homologue 'hamə‚lɔg, -‚lag, -‚lɒg; ES+'hɒm-
homology ho'malədʒɪ; ES+-'mɒl-
homonym 'hamə‚nɪm; ES+'hɒm-
homonymous ho'manəməs; ES+-'mɒn-;
|-my -mɪ
homophone 'hamə‚fon; ES+'hɒm-
homophonic ‚hamə'fanɪk; ES+‚hɒmə'fɒnɪk
homophonous ho'mafənəs; ES+-'mɒf-; |-ny
-nɪ

homorganic ˌhɔmɔr'gænɪk, ˌhɑm-; ES ˌhɔmɔə-'gænɪk, ˌhɑm-, ˌhɒm-
Homo sapiens 'homo'sepɪˌɛnz
homunculus ho'mʌŋkjələs |-li -ˌlaɪ
Honan 'ho'næn, -'nɑn (Chin 'xʌ'nɑn)
Honduran hɑn'dʊrən, -'dɪʊr-, -'djʊr-; ES+ hɒn-; |-ras -rəs |-ras's -rəsɪz
hone hon |honed hond
honest 'ɑnɪst; ES+'ɒn-; |-y -ɪ
honey 'hʌnɪ |honeyed 'hʌnɪd |-bee -ˌbi
honeycomb 'hʌnɪˌkom |-ed -d
honeydew 'hʌnɪˌdju, -ˌdɪu, -ˌdu
honeymoon 'hʌnɪˌmun |-ed -d
honeysuckle 'hʌnɪˌsʌkl̩ |-d -d
honey-tongued 'hʌnɪ'tʌŋd ('honey-ˌtongued 'Ann)
Hong Kong 'haŋ'kaŋ, 'hɒn'kɒŋ
Honiton 'hɑnɪtn̩, loc. 'hʌnɪtn̩; ES+'hɒn-
honk 'haŋk, 'haŋk, 'hɒŋk |-ed -t
Honolulu ˌhɑnə'lulə, -lu; ES+ˌhɒn-; native 'ho'no'lu'lu (even stress)
honor 'anɚ; ES 'anə(r, 'ɒnə(r; |-ed -d |-ing -nərɪŋ, -nrɪŋ |-able -əbl̩, -nrəbl̩ |-bly -blɪ
honorarium ˌanə'rɛrɪəm, -'rær-, -'rer-; ES+ˌɒn-; |-s -z |-ria -rɪə
honorary 'anəˌrɛrɪ; ES+'ɒn-
honorific ˌanə'rɪfɪk; ES+ˌɒn-; |-al -l̩ |-ally -l̩ɪ, -ɪklɪ
Honshu 'hɑnʃu, 'hɒn-
hooch hutʃ
hood, H- hʊd |hooded 'hʊdɪd
-hood ending, pron. -hʊd, -ˌhʊd according to number of syllables; as 'mænhʊd, 'laɪklɪˌhʊd. The pron. of all such words omitted from the vocab. can be found by adding -hʊd or -ˌhʊd directly to the main word.
hoodlum 'hʊdləm
hoodman 'hʊdmən |-men -mən
hoodman-blind 'hʊdmən'blaɪnd
hoodoo 'hudu |hoodooed 'hudud
hoodwink 'hʊdˌwɪŋk |-ed -t
hooey 'huɪ
hoof hʊf, huf |-s -s |rarely hooves -vz |-ed -t—
The pronunciation hʊf clearly prevails in the N, E, and S, and probably in Canada.
Hooghly, -gly 'huglɪ
hook hʊk |hooked hʊkt
hookah, -ka 'hʊkə
hooked adj 'hʊkɪd, hʊkt |-ness 'hʊkɪdnɪs

Hooker 'hʊkɚ; ES 'hʊkə(r
hookup 'hʊkˌʌp
hookworm 'hʊkˌwɝm; ES -ˌwɜm, -ˌwɝm
hooky 'hʊkɪ
hooligan 'hulɪgən |-ism -ˌɪzəm
hoop hʊp, hup |-ed -t
hooping-cough 'hupɪŋˌkɔf, 'hʊpɪŋ-, -ˌkɒf
hoopoe 'hupu
hooray hu're, hu-
Hoosac 'husək, -sæk
hoosegow, hoosg- 'husgau
Hoosic, -sick 'husɪk
Hoosier 'huʒɚ; ES 'huʒə(r
hoot hut |hooted 'hutɪd
Hoover 'huvɚ; ES 'huvə(r
hooves pl of hoof hʊvz, huvz
hop hap; ES+hɒp; |-ped -t
Hopatcong ho'pætkaŋ, hə-, -kɒŋ
hope, H- hop |hoped hopt; [N Engd+hɔp (§46)
Hopeh, -pei 'ho'pe
hoplite 'haplaɪt; ES+'hɒp-
hop-o'-my-thumb 'hapəmaɪ'θʌm; ES+'hɒp-
hopper 'hapɚ; ES 'hapə(r, 'hɒp-
hopscotch 'hapˌskatʃ; ES+'hɒpˌskɒtʃ; |-ed -t
Horace 'hɔrɪs, 'har-, 'hɒr-, -əs |-'s -ɪz
Horatian hə'reʃən, ho-, -ʃɪən
Horatio hə'reʃo, ho-, -ʃɪo
Horatius hə'reʃəs, ho-, -ʃɪəs |-'s -ɪz
horde hord, hɔrd; ES hoəd, E+hɔəd; |-d -ɪd
Horeb 'horəb, 'hɔr-, -ɛb; S 'hor-
Hore-Belisha 'horbə'liʃə, 'hɔr-; ES 'hoə-, E+-'hɔə-
horehound 'horˌhaund, 'hɔr-; ES 'hoə-, E+'hɔə-
horizon hə'raɪzn̩ |-ed -d |-ing -'raɪzn̩ɪŋ, -znɪŋ
horizontal ˌhɔrə'zantl̩, ˌhar-, ˌhɒr-; ES+ -'zɒn-; |-ly -ɪ
hormone 'hɔrmon; ES 'hɔəmon
Hormuz 'hɔrmʌz; ES 'hɔəmʌz; |-'s -ɪz
horn, H- hɔrn; ES hɔən; |-ed -d
hornblende 'hɔrnˌblɛnd; ES 'hɔən-
hornbook 'hɔrnˌbʊk; ES 'hɔən-
Hornell hɔr'nɛl; ES hɔə'nɛl
Horner 'hɔrnɚ; ES 'hɔənə(r
hornet 'hɔrnɪt; ES 'hɔənɪt
Hornie 'hɔrnɪ; ES 'hɔənɪ
horn-mad 'hɔrn'mæd; ES 'hɔən-
hornpipe 'hɔrnˌpaɪp; ES 'hɔən-

|full fʊl |tooth tuθ |further 'fɝðɚ; ES 'fɝðə |custom 'kʌstəm |while hwaɪl |how hau |toy tɔɪ |using 'juzɪŋ |fuse fjuz, fɪuz |dish dɪʃ |vision 'vɪʒən |Eden 'idn̩ |cradle 'kredl̩ |keep 'em 'kipm̩

horologe ˈhɒrəˌlodʒ, ˈhar-, ˈhɒr-, -ˌladʒ; ES+-ˌlɒdʒ; |-s -ız

horologer hoˈralədʒɚ, hɔ-; ES -ˈralədʒə(r, -ˈrɒl-; |-gist -dʒɪst |-gy -dʒɪ

horoscope ˈhɒrəˌskop, ˈharə-, ˈhɒrə-

horoscopy hoˈraskəpɪ, hɔ-; ES+-ˈrɒs-

horrendous hɔˈrɛndəs, ha-, hɒ-

horrent ˈhɒrənt, ˈhar-, ˈhɒr-

horrible ˈhɒrəbļ, ˈhar-, ˈhɒr- |-bly -blı

horrid ˈhɒrɪd, ˈhar-, ˈhɒr-

horrific hɔˈrɪfɪk, ha-, hɒ-

horrification ˌhɒrəfəˈkeʃən, ˌhar-, ˌhɒr-

horrify ˈhɒrəˌfaɪ, ˈhar-, ˈhɒr- |-fied -ˌfaɪd

Horrocks ˈhɒrəks, ˈhar-, ˈhɒr- |-ʼs -ız

horror ˈhɒrɚ, ˈhar-, ˈhɒr-; ES -rə(r

Horsa ˈhɒrsə; ES ˈhɔəsə

hors de combat ˌɔrdəˈkamba; ES ˈɔədə-, -ˈkɒm-; (Fr ɔrdəkõˈba)

hors d'oeuvre ɔrˈdœvrə, -ˈdʌv; ES ɔə-; (Fr ɔrˈdœːvr)

horse hɒrs; ES hɔəs; |-s -ız |-d -t

horse-and-buggy adj ˈhɒrsņˈbʌgɪ; ES ˈhɔəs-

horseback ˈhɒrsˌbæk; ES ˈhɔəs-

horsecar ˈhɒrsˌkar; ES ˈhɔəsˌkaː(r, E+-ˌkaː(r

horsecloth ˈhɒrsˌklɒθ, -ˌklɒθ |-ths -θs, -ðz—see cloth

horseflesh ˈhɒrsˌflɛʃ; ES ˈhɔəs-

horsefly ˈhɒrsˌflaɪ; ES ˈhɔəs-

horsehair ˈhɒrsˌhɛr, -ˌhær; E ˈhɔəsˌhɛə(r, ES ˈhɔəsˌhæə(r

horsehide ˈhɒrsˌhaɪd; ES ˈhɔəs-

horsejockey ˈhɒrsˌdʒakɪ; ES ˈhɔəs-, -ˌdʒɒkɪ

horselaugh ˈhɒrsˌlæf; ES ˈhɔəs-, E+-ˌlaf, -ˌlaf; |-ed -t

horseleech ˈhɒrsˌlitʃ; ES ˈhɔəs-; |-es -ız

horseman rider, manager ˈhɒrsmən; ES ˈhɔəs-; |-men -mən

horseman racing sport, expert ˈhɒrsˌmæn; ES ˈhɔəs-; |-men -ˌmɛn

horseplay ˈhɒrsˌple; ES ˈhɔəs-

horsepower ˈhɒrsˌpauɚ; ES ˈhɔəsˌpau·ə(r

horse-radish ˈhɒrsˈrædɪʃ; ES ˈhɔəs-; |-es -ız

horseshoe ˈhɒrʃˌʃu, ˈhɒrsˌʃu, -ˌʃɪu; ES ˈhɔəʃ-, ˈhɔəs-; |-d -d

horsetail ˈhɒrsˌtel; ES ˈhɔəs-

horsewhip ˈhɒrsˌhwɪp; ES ˈhɔəs-; |-ped -t

horsewoman ˈhɒrsˌwumən, -ˌwum-; ES ˈhɔəs-; |-women -ˌwɪmɪn—see woman

Horsham ˈhɒrʃəm; ES ˈhɔəʃəm; sp. pron.

Horst Wessel ˈhɒrstˈvɛs]; ES ˈhɔəst-

horsy ˈhɒrsɪ; ES ˈhɔəsɪ

hortative ˈhɒrtətɪv; ES ˈhɔətə-

hortatory ˈhɒrtəˌtorɪ, -ˌtɔrɪ: ES ˈhɔətəˌtorɪ, E+-ˌtɔrɪ

Hortense hɔrˈtɛns; ES nɔə-; |-ʼs -ız (Fr ɔrˈtãːs)

Hortensia hɔrˈtɛnsɪə, -ʃɪə; ES hɔ- |-ius -s |-ius's -sız

Hortensio hɔrˈtɛnsɪˌo, -ˈtɛnʃjo; ES hɔ-

horticulture ˈhɒrtɪˌkʌltʃɚ; ES ˈhɔətɪˌkʌltʃɔ(r

hosanna, H- hoˈzænə

hose hoz |hoses ˈhozɪz |hosed hozd

Hosea prophet hoˈziə, pers. name hoˈziə, ˈhozɪə (ˈHoˌsea ˈBiglow)

hosier ˈhoʒɚ; ES ˈhoʒə(r; |-y -ɪ, -ʒrɪ

Hosmer ˈhazmɚ; ES ˈhazmə(r, ˈhɒz-

hospice ˈhaspɪs, ˈhɒs- |-s -ız

hospitable ˈhaspɪtəbļ, ˈhɒs-, much less freq. hasˈpɪtəbļ, hɒs- |-bly -blı

hospital ˈhaspɪt], ˈhasˌpɪt], ˈhɒs-

hospitality ˌhaspɪˈtælətɪ, ˌhɒs-

hospitalization ˌhaspɪtḷəˈzeʃən, ˌhɒs-, -aɪˈz-

hospitalize ˈhaspɪtḷˌaɪz, ˈhɒs- |-s -ız |-d -d

host host |hosted ˈhostɪd

hostage ˈhastɪdʒ; ES+ˈhɒs-; |-s -ız |-d -d

hostel ˈhast]; ES+ˈhɒs-; |-ry -rɪ

hosteler ˈhast]ɚ; ES ˈhast]ə(r, ˈhɒs-

hostess ˈhostɪs |hostesses ˈhostɪsɪz

hostile ˈhast], -tɪl; ES+ˈhɒs-

hostility hasˈtɪlətɪ; ES+ˈhɒs-

hostler ˈhaslɚ, ˈaslɚ; ES ˈhaslə(r, ˈaslə(r ˈhɒs-, ˈɒs-

hot hat; ES+hɒt

hotbed ˈhatˌbɛd; ES+ˈhɒt-

hot-blooded ˈhatˈblʌdɪd; ES+ˈhɒt-

hotbox ˈhatˌbaks; ES+ˈhɒtˌbɒks; |-es -ız

hot-breathed ˈhatˈbrɛθt; ES+ˈhɒt-

hotchpot ˈhatʃˌpat; ES+ˈhɒtʃˌpɒt

hotchpotch ˈhatʃˌpatʃ; ES+ˈhɒtʃˌpɒtʃ; |-es -ız |-ed -t

hotel hoˈtɛl (ˈHoˌtel ˈCleveland)

hotfoot ˈhatˌfut; ES+ˈhɒt-; |-ed -ɪd

hothead ˈhatˌhɛd; ES+ˈhɒt-

hotheaded ˈhatˈhɛdɪd; ES+ˈhɒt-

hothouse ˈhatˌhaus; ES+ˈhɒt-; |-ses -zɪz

hotspur, H- ˈhatˌspɝ; ES ˈhatˌspɝ(r, -ˌspɝ, ˈhɒt-

Hottentot ˈhatņˌtat; ES+ˈhɒtņˌtɒt

Key: See in full §§3–47. bee bi |pity ˈpɪtɪ (§6) |rate ret |yet jet |sang sæŋ |angry ˈæŋ·grɪ |bath bæθ; E baθ (§10) |ah ɑ |far far |watch watʃ, wɒtʃ (§12) |jaw dʒɔ |gorge gɔrdʒ |go go

Houdini hu'dını
hough hɑk; ES+hɒk; |-ed -t (Sc hɒx)
Hough hʌf, hɔf, hɑf, hɒf
Houghton 'hotn̩, 'hɑutn̩, 'hɔtn̩
Houlton 'holtn̩
hound haʊnd |hounded 'haʊndɪd
Hounslow 'haʊnzlo
hour aʊr; ES aʊə(r
hourglass 'aʊr͵glæs; ES 'aʊə-, E+-͵glas,
 -͵glɑs; |-es -ɪz
houri 'hʊrɪ, 'haʊrɪ
Housatonic ͵husə'tɑnɪk; ES+-'tɒn-; loc.+
 ͵huzə-
house n haʊs |house's 'haʊsɪz |houses 'haʊzɪz
house v haʊz |houses 'haʊzɪz |housed haʊzd
houseboat 'haʊs͵bot |-ed -ɪd
housebreaking 'haʊs͵brekɪŋ
housebroken 'haʊs͵brokən
housecarl 'haʊs͵kɑrl; ES -͵kɑ:l, E+-͵kɑ:l
housefly 'haʊs͵flaɪ
houseful 'haʊs͵fʊl |fuls -͵fʊlz
household 'haʊs͵hold, -͵old
housekeeper 'haʊs͵kipɚ; ES -͵kipə(r
housel 'haʊzl̩ |houseled 'haʊzl̩d
houseless 'haʊslɪs
housemaid 'haʊs͵med
house-raising 'haʊs͵rezɪŋ
housetop 'haʊs͵tɑp; ES+-͵tɒp
housewarming 'haʊs͵wɔrmɪŋ; ES -͵wɔəmɪŋ
housewife 'woman' 'haʊs͵waɪf |-ves -vz
housewife 'sewing-kit' 'hʌzɪf, 'haʊs͵waɪf |-fes
 -fs |-ves -vz
housewife v 'haʊs͵waɪf |-s -s |-d -t
housewifery 'haʊs͵waɪfrɪ, -fərɪ, 'hʌzɪfrɪ
housework 'haʊs͵wɝk; ES -͵wɜk, -͵wɝk
housing 'haʊzɪŋ
Housman 'haʊsmən
Houston Tex soldier & city 'hjustən, 'hrus-;
 Eng botanist 'hustən, NYC street, Ga co.
 'haʊstən, Scotl 'hustən
Houyhnhnm hu'ɪnəm, 'hwɪnəm, 'hwɪn-
 ?m?m?m---
hove n & past of heave hov
hovel 'hʌvl̩, much less freq. 'hɑvl̩; ES+'hɒvl̩;
 |-ed -d |-ing -vl̩ɪŋ, -vlɪŋ
hover 'hʌvɚ, much less freq. 'hɑvɚ; ES -və(r,
 'hɒv-; |-ed -d |-ing -vərɪŋ, -vrɪŋ
how haʊ
How(e) haʊ

Howard 'haʊɚd; ES 'haʊ·əd
howbeit haʊ'biɪt
howdah 'haʊdə
how-do-you-do 'haʊdəjə'du, 'haʊdəju'du,
 'haʊdəjɪ'du, 'haʊdjə'du, 'haʊdju'du, 'haʊdɪ'du, 'haʊd'du
how-dy-do 'haʊdɪ'du
howe'er haʊ'ɛr; ES haʊ'ɛə(r
Howells 'haʊəlz |-'s -ɪz
however haʊ'ɛvɚ; ES haʊ'ɛvə(r
howitzer 'haʊɪtsɚ; ES 'haʊɪtsə(r
howl haʊl |howled haʊld |-er -ɚ; ES -ə(r
howlet 'haʊlɪt
howsoever ͵haʊso'ɛvɚ; ES -'ɛvə(r
hoy hɔɪ |hoyed hɔɪd
hoyden 'hɔɪdn̩ |-ed -d |-ing -dn̩ɪŋ, -dnɪŋ
hub hʌb |hubbed hʌbd
Hubbell 'hʌbl̩
hubbub 'hʌbʌb
Hubert 'hjubɚt, 'hɪu-; ES -bət
huckaback 'hʌkə͵bæk
huckle 'hʌkl̩ |-back -͵bæk |-backed -͵bækt
huckleberry, H- 'hʌkl̩͵bɛrɪ, -bərɪ
huckster 'hʌkstɚ; ES 'hʌkstə(r
hucksterer 'hʌkstərɚ; ES 'hʌkstərə(r
huddle 'hʌdl̩ |-d -d |-ling 'hʌdlɪŋ, 'hʌdl̩ɪŋ
Hudibras 'hjudɪ͵bræs, 'hɪu- |-'s -ɪz
Hudibrastic ͵hjudɪ'bræstɪk, ͵hɪu-
Hudson 'hʌdsn̩
hue hju, hɪu |hued hjud, hɪud
Huebner 'hjubnɚ, 'hɪub-, 'hib-; ES -nə(r;
 (Ger 'hy:bnər)
Huerta 'wɛrtə (Sp 'wɛrta)
huff hʌf |huffed hʌft
hug hʌg |hugged hʌgd
huge hjudʒ, hɪudʒ, judʒ
huggermugger 'hʌgɚ͵mʌgɚ; ES 'hʌgə͵mʌgə(r
Hugh hju, hɪu
Hughes hjuz, hɪuz |-'s -ɪz
Hugli 'huglɪ
Hugo 'hjugo, 'hɪugo
Huguenot 'hjugə͵nɑt, 'hɪu-; ES+-͵nɒt
huh hʌ (nasal ʌ) & various other grunts
Huidekoper 'haɪdɪ͵kopɚ; ES -͵kopə(r
hula or hula-hula 'hulə, 'hulə'hulə
hulk hʌlk |hulked hʌlkt
hull hʌl |hulled hʌld
hullabaloo 'hʌləbə͵lu, 'hʌləbə'lu

|full fʊl |tooth tuθ |further 'fɝðɚ; ES 'fɜðə |custom 'kʌstəm |while hwaɪl |how haʊ |toy tɔɪ
|using 'juzɪŋ |fuse fjuz, fɪuz |dish dɪʃ |vision 'vɪʒən |Eden 'idn̩ |cradle 'kredl̩ |keep 'em 'kipm̩

hullo hə'lo |hulloed hə'lod
Hulme hjum, hɪum, hʌlm
Hultzén hʊl'tsen
hum hʌm |hummed hʌmd
human 'hjumən, 'hɪumən, 'jumən |-ness
-mənnɪs
humane hju'men, hɪu'men, ju'men |-ness
-'mennɪs
humanism 'hjumən͵ɪzəm, 'hɪu- |-ist -ɪst
humanitarian hju͵mænə'tɛrɪən, hɪu-, -'ter-,
͵hjumænə-, ͵hɪu-
humanity hju'mænətɪ, hɪu-
Humber 'hʌmbɚ; ES 'hʌmbə(r
Humbert 'hʌmbɚt; ES 'hʌmbət
humble 'hʌmb|, 'ʌmb| |-d -d—The historical
'ʌmb| is well preserved in the S.
humblebee 'hʌmb|͵bi
humbler 'hʌmblɚ, 'ʌm-; ES -blə(r; |-blest
-blɪst |-bly -blɪ
Humboldt 'hʌmbolt (Ger 'hʊmbɔlt)
humbug 'hʌm͵bʌg |humbugged 'hʌm͵bʌgd
humdrum 'hʌm͵drʌm |humdrummed 'hʌm-
͵drʌmd
Hume hjum, hɪum
humerus 'hjumərəs, 'hɪu- |-es -ɪz |-ri -͵raɪ
humid 'hjumɪd, 'hɪumɪd
humidify hju'mɪdə͵faɪ, hɪu- |-fied -͵faɪd
humidity hju'mɪdətɪ, hɪu-
humidor 'hjumɪ͵dɔr, 'hɪu-; ES -͵dɔə(r
humiliate hju'mɪlɪ͵et, hɪu- |-ated -͵etɪd
humiliation hju͵mɪlɪ'eʃən, hɪu-, ͵hjumɪlɪ-,
͵hɪu-
humiliatory hju'mɪlɪə͵torɪ, hɪu-, -͵tɔrɪ; S
-͵torɪ
humility hju'mɪlətɪ, hɪu-
hummer 'hʌmɚ; ES 'hʌmə(r
hummingbird 'hʌmɪŋ͵bɚd; ES -͵bɜd, -͵bɚd
hummock 'hʌmək |hummocked 'hʌməkt
humor 'hjumɚ, 'hɪu-, 'ju-; ES -mə(r; |-ed -d
|-ing -mərɪŋ, -mrɪŋ—The pron. 'jumɚ,
'jumə(r is most likely to occur in 'sense of
humor,' 'mood,' and in the verb.
humoresque ͵hjumə'rɛsk, ͵hɪu-
humorist 'hjumərɪst, 'hɪu-, 'ju-
humoristic ͵hjumə'rɪstɪk, ͵hɪu-, ͵ju- |-al -|
humorous 'hjumərəs, 'hɪu-, 'ju-
hump hʌmp |humped hʌmpt
humpback 'hʌmp͵bæk |-backed -͵bækt
Humperdinck 'hʊmpɚ͵dɪŋk; ES 'hʊmpə-

humph hm̩m̩m̩ & various other grunts & nasal
puffs
Humphrey, -ry 'hʌmfrɪ, 'ʌm-, -pfrɪ |-s -z
|-s' -z
humus 'hjuməs, 'hɪu-
Hun hʌn
hunch hʌntʃ |hunches 'hʌntʃɪz |hunched
hʌntʃt
hunchback 'hʌntʃ͵bæk |-backed -͵bækt
hundred 'hʌndrəd, -drɪd, -dɚd; ES -drəd,
-drɪd, -dəd; |-th -θ |-fold -'fold, -͵fold
|-weight -'wet, -͵wet —'hʌndɚd, -dəd has
been current from the 14c to Tennyson and
King George V.
hung hʌŋ
Hungary 'hʌŋgərɪ |-rian hʌŋ'gɛrɪən, -'ger-
hunger 'hʌŋgɚ; ES 'hʌŋgə(r; |-ed -d |-ing
'hʌŋgərɪŋ, 'hʌŋgrɪŋ |-gry -grɪ
hunh hʌ (nasal ʌ) & other similar sounds
hunk hʌŋk
hunky 'hʌŋkɪ
hunky-dory ͵hʌŋkɪ'dorɪ, -'dɔrɪ; S -'dorɪ
Hunnish 'hʌnɪʃ
hunt hʌnt |hunted 'hʌntɪd
hunter, H- 'hʌntɚ; ES 'hʌntə(r
Hunterian hʌn'tɪrɪən
Huntingdon 'hʌntɪŋdən |-shire -͵ʃɪr, -ʃɚ; ES
-͵ʃɪə(r, -ʃə(r
Huntington 'hʌntɪŋtən
Hunts short for Huntingdonshire hʌnts
huntsman 'hʌntsmən |-men -mən
hurdle 'hɚd|; ES 'hɜd|, 'hɚd|; |-d -d |-ling
-d|ɪŋ, -dlɪŋ
hurdy-gurdy 'hɚdɪ͵gɚdɪ; ES 'hɜdɪ͵gɜdɪ,
'hɚdɪ͵gɚdɪ
hurl hɚl; ES hɜl, hɚl; |-ed -d
hurly-burly 'hɚlɪ͵bɚlɪ; ES 'hɜlɪ͵bɜlɪ, 'hɚlɪ-
͵bɚlɪ
Huron 'hjʊrən, 'hɪu-
hurrah hə'rɔ, hə'rɑ, hʊ-
hurray hə're, hʊ-
hurricane 'hɚɪ͵ken; ES 'hɜrɪ-, 'hʌrɪ-, 'hɚɪ-
hurry 'hɚɪ; ES 'hɜrɪ, 'hʌrɪ, 'hɚɪ; |-ried -d
hurry-scurry, -sk- 'hɚɪ'skɚɪ; ES 'hɜrɪ'skɜrɪ,
'hʌrɪ'skʌrɪ, 'hɚɪ'skɚɪ |-ried -d
hurt hɚt; ES hɜt, hɚt; |-ful -fəl |-fully -fəlɪ
hurtle 'hɚt|; ES 'hɜt|, 'hɚt|; |-d -d |-ling
-tlɪŋ, -t|ɪŋ
husband 'hʌzbənd |husbanded 'hʌzbəndɪd

husbandman 'hʌzbəndmən, -bənmən |-men
-mən
husbandry 'hʌzbəndrɪ
hush hʌʃ |hushed hʌʃt |-edly -ɪdlɪ
hushaby 'hʌʃəˌbaɪ
Hushai 'hjuʃɪˌaɪ, 'hɪu-, -ʃaɪ
husk hʌsk |husked hʌskt
husky 'hʌskɪ |Husky 'hʌskɪ
Huss hʌs |Huss's 'hʌsɪz |-ite -aɪt
hussar hʊ'zɑr; ES hʊ'za:(r, E+-'za:(r
hussy 'hʌsɪ, 'hʌzɪ
hustings 'hʌstɪŋz
hustle 'hʌs| |-d -d |-ling 'hʌslɪŋ, 'hʌs|ɪŋ
huswife 'hʌzɪf
hut hʌt |hutted 'hʌtɪd
hutch hʌtʃ |hutches 'hʌtʃɪz |hutched hʌtʃt
Hutten, von fən'hʊtn̩
Huxley 'hʌkslɪ
Huygens 'haɪgənz
huzza hə'za, hʊ'za
Hwang-ho 'hwæŋ'ho, 'hwaŋ-
hyacinth, H- 'haɪəˌsɪnθ |-ths -θs
Hyads 'haɪədz |Hyades 'haɪəˌdiz
hyaena haɪ'inə
hyaline 'haɪəlɪn
hyalogen haɪ'ælədʒən, -dʒɪn
Hyannis haɪ'ænɪs |-'s -ɪz
Hybla 'haɪblə
hybrid 'haɪbrɪd |-ity haɪ'brɪdətɪ
hybridization ˌhaɪbrɪdə'zeʃən, -aɪ'z-
hybridize 'haɪbrɪdˌaɪz |-s -ɪz |-d -d
Hydaspes haɪ'dæspiz |-pes' -piz
Hyderabad, Hydra- 'haɪdərəˌbæd, ˌhaɪdərə-
'bad, 'haɪdrə-, ˌhaɪdrə-
Hydra 'haɪdrə |-s -z |-drae -dri
hydracid haɪ'dræsɪd
hydrangea, H- haɪ'drendʒə, -'drændʒɪə, -dʒə
hydrant 'haɪdrənt
hydrate n 'haɪdret, -drɪt
hydrate v 'haɪdret |hydrated 'haɪdretɪd
hydraulic haɪ'drɔlɪk |-al -| |-ally -|ɪ, -ɪklɪ
hydride 'haɪdraɪd, -drɪd |drid -drɪd
hydrocarbon ˌhaɪdro'karbən, -ban; ES 'ka:b-,
-bɒn, E+'ka:b-
hydrocephaly ˌhaɪdro'sɛfəlɪ |-lic -sə'fælɪk
hydrochloric ˌhaɪdrə'klorɪk, -'klɔr-; S -'klor-
hydrochloride ˌhaɪdrə'kloraɪd, -'klɔr-, -ɪd; S
-'klor-; |-rid -ɪd
hydrocyanic ˌhaɪdrosaɪ'ænɪk

hydrodynamics ˌhaɪdrodaɪ'næmɪks
hydroelectric ˌhaɪdro·ɪ'lɛktrɪk
hydrogen 'haɪdrədʒən, -dʒɪn |-ate -ˌet |-ated
-ˌetɪd
hydrogenize 'haɪdrədʒənˌaɪz |-s -ɪz |-d -d
hydrogenous haɪ'drodʒənəs; ES+-'drɒdʒ-
hydrographer haɪ'drɑgrəfɚ, -'drɒg-; ES
-fə(r; |-phy -fɪ
hydroid 'haɪdrɔɪd
hydrolysis haɪ'drɑləsɪs; ES+-'drɒl-; |-yses
-ˌsiz
hydromechanics ˌhaɪdromɪ'kænɪks
hydromel 'haɪdrəˌmɛl
hydrometer haɪ'drɑmətɚ; ES -'drɑmətə(r,
-'drɒm-
hydropathic ˌhaɪdrə'pæθɪk |-al -|
hydropathy haɪ'drɑpəθɪ; ES+-'drɒp-
hydrophobia ˌhaɪdrə'fobɪə
hydroplane 'haɪdrəˌplen
hydroponics ˌhaɪdrə'panɪks; ES+-'pɒn-
hydroponist haɪ'drɑpənɪst; ES+-'drɒp-
hydropsy 'haɪdrapsɪ; ES+-drɒp-
hydroquinone ˌhaɪdrokwɪ'non
hydrosphere 'haɪdrəˌsfɪr; ES -ˌsfɪə(r, S+
-'sfɛə(r
hydrostatic ˌhaɪdrə'stætɪk |-s -s |-al -| |-ally
-|ɪ, -ɪklɪ
hydrosulphide, -fide, ˌhaɪdro'sʌlfaɪd, -fɪd
|-phid, -fid -fɪd
hydrosulphite ˌhaɪdro'sʌlfaɪt
hydrotherapeutics ˌhaɪdroˌθɛrə'pjutɪks, -'pɪu-
hydrous 'haɪdrəs
hydroxide haɪ'drɑksaɪd, -ɪd; ES+-'drɒks-;
|-id -ɪd
hydroxyl haɪ'drɑksɪl; ES+-'drɒk-
hydrozoan, H- ˌhaɪdrə'zoən
hyena haɪ'inə
Hygeia haɪ'dʒiə
hygiene 'haɪdʒin, 'haɪdʒɪˌin
hygienic ˌhaɪdʒɪ'ɛnɪk |-s -s |-al -| |-ally -|ɪ,
-ɪklɪ
hygienist 'haɪdʒɪənɪst
hygrometer haɪ'grɑmətɚ; ES -'grɑmətə(r,
-'grɒm-
hygrometric ˌhaɪgrə'mɛtrɪk |-al -| |-ally -|ɪ,
-ɪklɪ
hygroscope 'haɪgrəˌskop
hying ptc of hie 'haɪɪŋ
Hyksos 'hɪksos, -sas; ES+-sɒs

Hymen, h- 'haɪmən
hymeneal ˌhaɪmə'niəl |-ly -ɪ |-nean -'niən
hymenopterous ˌhaɪmə'nɑptərəs, -trəs; ES+
-'nɒp-
Hymettus haɪ'mɛtəs |-'s -ɪz
hymn hɪm |hymned hɪmd |hymning 'hɪmɪŋ
hymnal 'hɪmnəl |-nist -nɪst |-nody -nədɪ
hymnbook 'hɪmˌbʊk
hymnology hɪm'nɑlədʒɪ; ES+-'nɒl-
hyoid 'haɪɔɪd
Hypatia haɪ'peʃɪə, -ʃə
hyperacid ˌhaɪpə'æsɪd
hyperacidity ˌhaɪpərə'sɪdətɪ, -æ'sɪdətɪ
hyperbola haɪ'pɝbələ; ES -'pɜ-, -'pɝ-; |-s -z
hyperbole haɪ'pɝbəˌli, -lɪ; ES -'pɜ-, -'pɝ-;
|-s -z
hyperbolic ˌhaɪpɚ'bɑlɪk; ES ˌhaɪpə'bɑlɪk,
-'bɒl-; |-ally -ļɪ |-icly -ɪklɪ
hyperbolize haɪ'pɝbəˌlaɪz; ES -'pɜ-, -'pɝ-;
|-s -ɪz |-d -d
hyperborean, H- ˌhaɪpɚ'borɪən, -'bɔr-; ES
ˌhaɪpə'bor-, E+-'bɔr-
hypercivilized ˌhaɪpɚ'sɪvˌļaɪzd; ES ˌhaɪpə-
hypercritic ˌhaɪpɚ'krɪtɪk; ES ˌhaɪpə-; |-al -ļ
|-ally -ļɪ, -ɪklɪ |-ticism -təˌsɪzəm
hyperfunction ˌhaɪpɚ'fʌŋkʃən; ES ˌhaɪpə-
Hyperion haɪ'pɪrɪən
hyperopia ˌhaɪpɚ'opɪə
hypersensitive ˌhaɪpɚ'sɛnsətɪv; ES ˌhaɪpə-;
|-vity -ˌsɛnsə'tɪvətɪ
hyperthyroidism ˌhaɪpɚ'θaɪrɔɪdˌɪzəm; ES
ˌhaɪpə-
hypertrophy haɪ'pɝtrəfɪ; ES -'pɜ-, -'pɝ-;
|-phied -fɪd
hyphen 'haɪfən |-ed -d |-ate -ˌet |-ated -ˌetɪd
hyphenize 'haɪfənˌaɪz |-s -ɪz |-d -d
hypnosis hɪp'nosɪs |-noses -'nosiz

hypnotic hɪp'nɑtɪk; ES+-'nɒt-; |-ally -ļɪ,
-ɪklɪ
hypnotism 'hɪpnəˌtɪzəm |-tist -tɪst
hypnotize 'hɪpnəˌtaɪz |-s -ɪz |-d -d
hypo 'haɪpo
hypochondria ˌhaɪpə'kɑndrɪə, ˌhɪp-; ES+
-'kɒn-; |-driac -drɪˌæk
hypocrisy hɪ'pɑkrəsɪ; ES+-'pɒk-
hypocrite 'hɪpəˌkrɪt
hypocritical ˌhɪpə'krɪtɪk‖ |-ly -ɪ, -ɪklɪ
hypodermic ˌhaɪpə'dɝmɪk; ES -'dɝm-,
-'dɜm-; |-ally -ļɪ, -ɪklɪ
hypogene 'hɪpəˌdʒin, 'haɪpə-
hypophosphate ˌhaɪpə'fɑsfet; ES+-'fɒs-;
|-phite -faɪt
hypophosphorous ˌhaɪpə'fɑsfərəs; ES+-'fɒs-
hyposulphite ˌhaɪpə'sʌlfaɪt
hyposulphurous ˌhaɪpə'sʌlfərəs, -sʌl'fju-,
-'frʊ-
hypotenuse, -poth- haɪ'pɑtņˌus, -ˌɪus, -ˌjus,
-z; ES+-'pɒt-; |-s -ɪz
hypothecate haɪ'pɑθəˌket; ES+-'pɒθ-; |-d -ɪd
hypothecation haɪˌpɑθə'keʃən; ES+-ˌpɒθ-
hypothesis haɪ'pɑθəsɪs; ES+-'pɒθ-; |-ses
-ˌsiz
hypothesize haɪ'pɑθəˌsaɪz; ES+-'pɒθ-; |-s -ɪz
|-d -d
hypothetic ˌhaɪpə'θɛtɪk |-al -ļ |-ally -ļɪ, -ɪklɪ
hyrax, H- 'haɪræks |-es -ɪz |-races -rəˌsiz
Hyrcania hɝ'kenɪə; ES hɜ-, hɝ-; |-n -n
hyson 'haɪsņ
hyssop 'hɪsəp
hysteresis ˌhɪstə'risɪs
hysteretic ˌhɪstə'rɛtɪk |-ally -ļɪ, -ɪklɪ
hysteria hɪs'tɪrɪə, less freq. hɪs'tɛrɪə
hysteric hɪs'tɛrɪk |-s -s |-al -ļ |-ally -ļɪ, -ɪklɪ
hythe, H- haɪð

I

I, i letter aɪ |pl I's, Is, poss I's aɪz
I pro stressed 'aɪ, ˌaɪ; unstr. aɪ, əɪ, familiar ə
i-, -i- ɪ, ə—The nonfinal unaccented vowel
spelt i and originally pron. ɪ shows a tendency
in innumerable words of normal conversation
to be obscured in the direction of the sound ə,
as in possible 'pɑsəbļ, divide də'vaɪd. As a

rule only one pronunciation (ə or ɪ) is shown
in the vocab. The alternative pron. with ɪ is
permissible if it does not sound artificial (as
it would in possible), or with ə if it does not
sound slovenly (as it would in sluggish).
But such judgments depend somewhat on
habit, and as regional practice varies con-

Key: See in full §§3–47. bee bi |pity 'pɪtɪ (§6) |rate ret |yet jɛt |sang sæŋ |angry 'æŋ·grɪ
|bath bæθ; E baθ (§10) |ah ɑ |far fɑr |watch watʃ, wɒtʃ (§12) |jaw dʒɔ |gorge gɔrdʒ |go go

siderably, only an enlightened judgment and observation can decide.

-ia *ending* (mania), -ia- *plus consonant* (trivial, ruffian), -ie- *plus cons.* (alien), -io (Bassanio), -io- *plus cons.* (scorpion), -ious (tedious), -ius (radius). *These and similar combinations of unstressed* i *plus vowel regularly have double prons.* ɪə *&* jə. *In the vocab. usually the one believed to be most common in ordinary speech is given, with the understanding that the other pron. is also more or less common.*

Iachimo ˈjɑkɪˌmo; *so Shak.; mod.*+aɪˈækəˌmo

Iago ɪˈɑgo

-ial *see* -ia

iamb ˈaɪæmb |-ic aɪˈæmbɪk

iambus aɪˈæmbəs |-es -ɪz |-bi aɪˈæmbaɪ

-ian *see* -ia

iarovize ˈjɑrəˌvaɪz |-s -ɪz |-d -d

Iberia aɪˈbɪrɪə |-ian -ɪən

ibex, I- ˈaɪbɛks |-es -ɪz |ibices ˈɪbɪˌsiz, ˈaɪ-

ibidem *abbr.* ibid. ɪˈbaɪdɛm, ˈɪbɪd, ˈaɪbɪd

ibis ˈaɪbɪs |-es -ɪz

-ible *see* -able

Ibsen ˈɪbsn̩

-ically *ending of advs to words in* -ic (comic) *or in* -ical (radical), *pron.* -ɪk·ḷ·ɪ (ˈrædɪk·ḷ·ɪ) *or* -ɪk·lɪ (ˈrædɪk·lɪ). *The pron. with* -ɪk·lɪ *is very common colloquially, and in a good many words is recognized by the spelling, which usually lags behind pronunciation; as in* authentically, -thenticly, cubically, -icly, heroically, -icly, rustically, -icly, specifically, -icly, symbolically, -icly, tyrannically, -icly, *etc.*

Icarian ɪˈkɛrɪən, ɪˈker-

Icarus ˈɪkərəs, ˈaɪ- |-ˈs -ɪz

ice aɪs |ices ˈaɪsɪz |iced aɪst

iceberg ˈaɪsˌbɝg; ES -ˌbɜg, -ˌbɝg

iceboat ˈaɪsˌbot

icebound ˈaɪsˌbaʊnd

icebox ˈaɪsˌbɑks; ES+-ˌbɒks; |-es -ɪz

ice cream ˈaɪsˈkrim

ice-cream ˈaɪsˈkrim (ˈice-ˈcream ˌcone, ˈice-ˌcream ˈsoda)

icehouse ˈaɪsˌhaʊs |-ses -zɪz

Iceland ˈaɪslənd |-ic aɪsˈlændɪk

iceman ˈaɪsˌmæn, -mən |-men -ˌmɛn, -mən

Ichabod ˈɪkəˌbɑd, -ˌbɒd

ichneumon ɪkˈnjumən, -ˈnɪu-, -ˈnu-

ichor ˈaɪkɔr, -kɚ; ES ˈaɪkɔə(r, ˈaɪkə(r

ichthyologic ˌɪkθɪəˈlɑdʒɪk; ES+-ˈlɒdʒ-; |-al -ḷ |-ally -ḷɪ, -ɪklɪ

ichthyologist ˌɪkθɪˈɑlədʒɪst; ES+-ˈɒl-; |-gy -dʒɪ

ichthyosaur ˈɪkθɪəˌsɔr; ES -ˌsɔə(r

ichthyosaurus, I- ˌɪkθɪəˈsɔrəs |-es -ɪz |-ri -raɪ

icicle ˈaɪˌsɪkḷ, ˈaɪsɪkḷ |-d -d

icily ˈaɪsḷɪ, ˈaɪsɪlɪ

icing ˈaɪsɪŋ

Ickes ˈɪkɪs, -əs, -ɪz |-ˈs -ɪz

icon ˈaɪkɑn, -kɒn |-s -z |-es ˈaɪkəˌniz

iconoclasm aɪˈkɑnəˌklæzəm; ES+-ˈkɒn-; |-clast -ˌklæst

iconoclastic aɪˌkɑnəˈklæstɪk, ˌaɪkɑnə-; ES+-ɒn-; |-ally -ḷɪ, -ɪklɪ

iconography ˌaɪkənˈɑgrəfɪ, -ˈɒg-

icosahedron ˌaɪkosəˈhidrən |-dra -drə

ictus ˈɪktəs |-es -ɪz

icy ˈaɪsɪ

I'd *abbr. spelling of* I had, I would, *stressed* ˈaɪd, ˌaɪd; *unstr.* aɪd, əɪd, *occas.* əd

Idaho ˈaɪdəˌho, ˈaɪdɪˌho |-an -ən

idea aɪˈdiə, aɪˈdɪə, *occas. by sentence rhythm* ˈaɪdɪə

ideal aɪˈdiəl, aɪˈdil, aɪˈdɪəl |-ism -ˌɪzəm |-ist -ɪst

idealistic ˌaɪdiəlˈɪstɪk, -dɪəl-, aɪˌd- |-al -ḷ |-ally -ḷɪ, -ɪklɪ

ideality ˌaɪdɪˈælətɪ

idealization aɪˌdiələˈzeʃən, -ˌdɪəl-, -aɪˈz-

idealize aɪˈdiəlˌaɪz, aɪˈdɪəl- |-s -ɪz |-d -d

ideate *n* aɪˈdiɪt, -et

ideate *v* aɪˈdiet, -ˈdɪet |-d -ɪd

ideation ˌaɪdɪˈeʃən

ideatum ˌaɪdɪˈetəm |-ta -tə

idem ˈaɪdɛm

idempotent aɪˈdɛmpətənt

Iden ˈaɪdn̩

identic aɪˈdɛntɪk |-al -ḷ |-ally -ḷɪ, -ɪklɪ

identification aɪˌdɛntəfəˈkeʃən

identify aɪˈdɛntəˌfaɪ |-fied -ˌfaɪd

identity aɪˈdɛntətɪ

ideogram ˈɪdɪəˌgræm, ˈaɪdɪə-

ideograph ˈɪdɪəˌgræf, ˈaɪdɪə-; E+-ˌgraf, -ˌgraf

ideographic ˌɪdɪəˈgræfɪk, ˌaɪdɪə-

ideography ˌɪdɪˈɑgrəfɪ, ˌaɪdɪ-, -ˈɒg-

|full fʊl |tooth tuθ |further ˈfɝðɚ; ES ˈfɜðə |custom ˈkʌstəm |while hwaɪl |how haʊ |toy tɔɪ
|using ˈjuzɪŋ |fuse fjuz, fɪuz |dish dɪʃ |vision ˈvɪʒən |Eden ˈidn̩ |cradle ˈkredḷ |keep 'em ˈkipm̩

ideology ˌaɪdɪˈɑlədʒɪ, ˌɪd-; ES+-ˈɒl-	ileum ˈɪlɪəm |ileac, iliac ˈɪlɪˌæk
ides aɪdz	ilex, I- ˈaɪlɛks |-es -ɪz
id est 'that is' ˌɪdˈɛst	Ilfracombe ˈɪlfrəˌkum, ˌɪlfrəˈkum
idiocy ˈɪdɪəsɪ	iliac ˈɪlɪˌæk=ileac
idiom ˈɪdɪəm	Iliac 'of Ilium' ˈɪlɪˌæk
idiomatic ˌɪdɪəˈmætɪk |-al -ļ |-ally -ļɪ, -ɪklɪ	Iliad ˈɪlɪəd
idiosyncrasy ˌɪdɪəˈsɪnkrəsɪ, -ˈsɪŋ-	Ilion ˈɪlɪən |Ilium ˈɪlɪəm
idiosyncratic ˌɪdɪosɪnˈkrætɪk |-al -ļ |-ally -ļɪ, -ɪklɪ	ilium ˈɪlɪəm
idiot ˈɪdɪət |-ism -ˌɪzəm	ilk ɪlk
idiotic ˌɪdɪˈɑtɪk; ES+-ˈɒtɪk; |-al -ļ |-ally -ļɪ, -ɪklɪ	ill ɪl
idle ˈaɪdļ |-d -d |-ling ˈaɪdlɪŋ, -dļɪŋ |-r -dlɚ; ES -dlə(r; |-st -dlɪst	I'll abbr. spelling of I will aɪl—not a contraction of I shall (=ˈaɪʃļ) but often substituted for it
idly ˈaɪdlɪ	ill-advised ˈɪlədˈvaɪzd |-sedly -zɪdlɪ
idol ˈaɪdļ |-ed -d |-ing ˈaɪdļɪŋ	illation ɪˈleʃən |illative ˈɪlətɪv
idolater aɪˈdɑlətɚ; ES aɪˈdɑlətə(r, -ˈdɒl-; |-tress -trɪs |-try -trɪ	ill-boding ˈɪlˈbodɪŋ
idolization ˌaɪdļəˈzeʃən, -aɪˈz-	ill-bred ˈɪlˈbrɛd
idolize ˈaɪdļˌaɪz |-s -ɪz |-d -d	illegal ɪˈligļ, ɪlˈligļ |-ly -ɪ
Idomeneus aɪˈdɑmənˌjus, -məˌnɪus, -məˌnus; ES+-ˈdɒm-; |-'s -ɪz	illegality ˌɪliˈgælətɪ
Idumaea, -mea ˌɪdjuˈmiə, ˌaɪd-, -dʊ- |-n -n	illegibility ˌɪlɛdʒəˈbɪlətɪ, ˌɪllɛdʒ-, ɪˌlɛdʒ-
Idun ˈɪdʊn=Ithunn	illegible ɪˈlɛdʒəbļ, ɪlˈlɛdʒ- |-bly -blɪ
idyl, -ll ˈaɪdļ	illegitimacy ˌɪlɪˈdʒɪtəməsɪ, ˌɪllɪ- |-mate -mɪt
idyllic aɪˈdɪlɪk |-al -ļ |-ally -ļɪ, -ɪklɪ	ill-fated ˈɪlˈfetɪd ('ill-ˌfated 'project)
-ie ending see -y	ill-favored ˈɪlˈfevɚd; ES -ˈfevəd
-iel ending see -ia	ill-gotten ˈɪlˈgɑtn̩; ES+-ˈgɒtn̩
-ien ending see -ia	ill-humor ˈɪlˈjumɚ, -ˈhjumɚ, -ˈhɪu-; ES -mə(r; |-ed -d
if ɪf, f	
igloo ˈɪglu	illiberal ɪˈlɪbərəl, ɪˈlɪbrəl, ɪlˈl- |-ly -ɪ
Ignatius Loyola ɪgˈneʃəs lɔɪˈolə, lɔˈjolə	illiberality ˌɪlɪbəˈrælətɪ, ˌɪllɪb-
igneous ˈɪgnɪəs	illicit ɪˈlɪsɪt, ɪlˈlɪs-
ignescent ɪgˈnɛsn̩t	illimitable ɪˈlɪmɪtəbļ, ɪlˈlɪm- |-bly -blɪ
ignis fatuus ˈɪgnɪsˈfætʃuəs |ignes fatui ˈɪgnizˈfætʃuˌaɪ	Illini ɪˈlaɪnaɪ
	illinium ɪˈlɪnɪəm
ignite ɪgˈnaɪt |-d -ɪd |-nition ɪgˈnɪʃən	Illinoian ˌɪləˈnɔɪən
ignoble ɪgˈnobļ |-bly -blɪ	Illinois ˌɪləˈnɔɪ, -ˈnɔɪz |-nois's -ˈnɔɪz, -ˈnɔɪzɪz —ˌɪləˈnɔɪz is esp. common in the S.
ignominious ˌɪgnəˈmɪnɪəs	
ignominy ˈɪgnəˌmɪnɪ	Illinoisan ˌɪləˈnɔɪən, -ˈnɔɪzən
ignoramus ˌɪgnəˈreməs |-es -ɪz	illiteracy ɪˈlɪtərəsɪ, ɪlˈlɪt- |-rate -rɪt, -trɪt
ignorance ˈɪgnərəns |-rant -rənt	ill-looking ˈɪlˈlʊkɪŋ
ignore ɪgˈnor, -ˈnɔr; ES ɪgˈnoə(r, E+-ˈnɔə(r; |-d -d	ill-mannered ˈɪlˈmænɚd; ES -ˈmænəd
	ill-natured ˈɪlˈnetʃɚd; ES -ˈnetʃəd
Igorot ˌɪgəˈrot, ˌi- (Sp ˌigəˈrrote)	illness ˈɪlnɪs |-es -ɪz
Igraine ɪˈgren	illogical ɪˈlɑdʒɪkļ, ɪlˈl-; ES+-ˈlɒdʒ-; |-ly -ɪ, -ɪklɪ
iguana ɪˈgwɑnə	
il- 'not' see in- prefix	ill-omened ˈɪlˈomɪnd, -mənd
Il Duce ɪlˈdutʃɪ (It ilˈduːtʃe)	ill-starred ˈɪlˈstɑrd; ES -ˈstɑːd, E+-ˈstɑːd
	ill-tempered ˈɪlˈtɛmpɚd; ES -ˈtɛmpəd
	ill-timed ˈɪlˈtaɪmd ('ill-ˌtimed 'start)
	ill-treat ɪlˈtrit |-ed -ɪd
	illume ɪˈlum, ɪˈlɪum |-d -d

illuminant ɪˈlumənənt, ɪˈlɪum-
illuminate ɪˈlumə͵net, ɪˈlɪum- |-d -ɪd
illuminati, I- ɪ͵lumə'netaɪ, ɪ͵lumɪ'nati, ɪ͵lɪum-
illumination ɪ͵lumə'neʃən, ɪ͵lɪum-
illuminative ɪˈlumə͵netɪv, ɪˈlɪum-
illuminator ɪˈlumə͵netɚ, ɪˈlɪum-; ES -tə(r
illumine ɪˈlumɪn, ɪˈlɪumɪn |-d -d
ill-usage ˈɪlˈjusɪdʒ, -ˈjuz- |-s -ɪz
ill-use n ˈɪlˈjus |-s -ɪz
ill-use v ɪlˈjuz |-s -ɪz |-d -d
illusion ɪˈluʒən, ɪˈlɪuʒən |-ed -d
illusive ɪˈlusɪv, ɪˈlɪusɪv |-sory -sərɪ
illustrate ˈɪləstret, ɪˈlʌstret |-d -ɪd
illustration ͵ɪləsˈtreʃən, ɪ͵lʌsˈtreʃən
illustrative ɪˈlʌstrətɪv, ˈɪləs͵tretɪv, ɪˈlʌs͵tretɪv
illustrator ˈɪləs͵tretɚ, ɪˈlʌs͵tretɚ; ES -tə(r
illustrious ɪˈlʌstrɪəs
illy substandard for adv ill ˈɪlɪ
Illyria ɪˈlɪrɪə |-n -n
Ilokano ͵iloˈkano
Il Penseroso ͵ɪlpɛnsəˈroso (It il͵pense'ro:so)
I'm abbr. spelling of I am, stressed ˈaɪm, ͵aɪm;
    unstr. aɪm, occas. əm
im- 'not' see in- prefix
image ˈɪmɪdʒ |-s -ɪz |-d -d
imagery ˈɪmɪdʒrɪ, -dʒərɪ
imaginable ɪˈmædʒɪnəbḷ, ɪˈmædʒnəbḷ |-bly
    -blɪ
imaginary ɪˈmædʒə͵nɛrɪ
imagination ɪ͵mædʒə'neʃən |-tive ɪˈmædʒə-
    ͵netɪv
imagine ɪˈmædʒɪn |-d -d
imagist ˈɪmədʒɪst |-gism -͵dʒɪzəm
imago ɪˈmego |pl -s -z |imagines ɪˈmædʒɪ͵niz
imam ɪˈmam |imaum ɪˈmam, ɪˈmɔm
imbalm ɪmˈbam; E+-ˈbam; |-ed -d
imbark ɪmˈbark; ES -ˈba:k, E+-ˈba:k; |-ed -t
imbecile ˈɪmbəsḷ, -͵sɪl |-lity ͵ɪmbəˈsɪlətɪ
imbed ɪmˈbɛd |-bedded -ˈbɛdɪd
imbibe ɪmˈbaɪb |-bibed -ˈbaɪbd
imbitter ɪmˈbɪtɚ; ES -ˈbɪtə(r; |-ed -d
imbody ɪmˈbadɪ; ES+-ˈbɒdɪ; |-died -dɪd
imbolden ɪmˈboldṇ |-ed -d |-ing -ˈboldṇɪŋ,
    -ˈboldnɪŋ
imbosom ɪmˈbuzəm, -ˈbuzəm |-ed -d
imbower ͵ɪmˈbauɚ; ES -ˈbau·ə(r
imbricate adj ˈɪmbrɪkɪt, -͵ket
imbricate v ˈɪmbrɪ͵ket |- d -ɪd
imbrication ͵ɪmbrɪˈkeʃən

imbroglio ɪmˈbroljo (It im'brɔʎʎo)
imbrue ɪmˈbru, -ˈbrɪu |-b| -d
imbrute ɪmˈbrut, -ˈbrɪut |-d -ɪd
imbue ɪmˈbju, -ˈbɪu |-d -d
imid ˈɪmɪd |imide ˈɪmaɪd, ˈɪmɪd
imidogen ɪˈmɪdədʒən, ɪˈmɪdə-, -dʒɪn
imine ɪˈmin
imitable ˈɪmɪtəbḷ
imitate ˈɪmə͵tet |-tated -͵tetɪd |-tive -ɪv
imitation ͵ɪməˈteʃən
imitator ˈɪmə͵tetɚ; ES -͵tetə(r
immaculate ɪˈmækjəlɪt
immane ɪˈmen
immanence ˈɪmənəns |-nent -nənt
Immanuel ɪˈmænjʊəl
immaterial ͵ɪməˈtɪrɪəl |-ly -ɪ |-ism -͵ɪzəm
immateriality ͵ɪmə͵tɪrɪˈælətɪ
immature ͵ɪməˈtur, -ˈtɪur, -ˈtjur; ES -ə(r;
    |-rity -ətɪ
immeasurable ɪˈmɛʒrəbḷ, ɪmˈm-, -ˈmɛʒərə-
    |-bly -blɪ
immediacy ɪˈmidɪəsɪ
immediate ɪˈmidɪt, esp. C ɪˈmidʒət
immemorial ͵ɪməˈmorɪəl, ͵ɪmmə-, -ˈmɔr-; S
    -ˈmor-; |-ly -ɪ
immense ɪˈmɛns |-sity -ətɪ
immerse ɪˈmɝs; ES ɪˈmɜs, ɪˈmɝs; |-s -ɪz |-d -t
immersion ɪˈmɝʃən; ES ɪˈmɜʃ-, ɪˈmɝʃ-
immigrant ˈɪməgrənt, -͵grænt
immigrate ˈɪmə͵gret |-d -ɪd |-tion ͵ɪməˈgreʃən
imminence ˈɪmənəns |-nent -nənt
immiscible ɪˈmɪsəbḷ |-bly -blɪ
immitigable ɪˈmɪtəgəbḷ |-bly -blɪ
immix ɪmˈmɪks |-es -ɪz |-ed -t
immixture ɪmˈmɪkstʃɚ; ES -ˈmɪkstʃə(r
immobile ɪˈmobḷ, ɪmˈm-, -bɪl, -bɪl
immobility ͵ɪmoˈbɪlətɪ, ͵ɪmmo-
immobilization ɪ͵mobḷəˈzeʃən, ɪm͵mo-, ͵ɪmob-,
    ͵ɪmmob-, -aɪˈz-
immobilize ɪˈmobḷ͵aɪz, ɪmˈmo- |-s -ɪz |-d -d
immoderate ɪˈmadərɪt, ɪmˈmad-, -drɪt; ES+
    -ˈmɒd-
immodest ɪˈmadɪst, ɪmˈmad-; ES+-ˈmɒd-;
    |-y -ɪ
immolate ˈɪmə͵let |-d -ɪd |-tion ͵ɪməˈleʃən
immolator ˈɪmə͵letɚ; ES -͵letə(r
immoral ɪˈmɔrəl, ɪmˈm-, -ˈmar-, -ˈmɒr- |-ly -ɪ
immorality ͵ɪməˈrælətɪ, -mɔ-, -ma-, -mɒ-,
    -mo-

|full fʊl |tooth tuθ |further ˈfɝðɚ; ES ˈfɜðə |custom ˈkʌstəm |while hwaɪl |how hau |toy tɔɪ
|using ˈjuzɪŋ |fuse fjuz, fɪuz |dish dɪʃ |vision ˈvɪʒən |Eden ˈidṇ |cradle ˈkredḷ |keep 'em ˈkipm̩

immortal ɪ'mɔrtļ; ES ɪ'mɔətļ
immortality ˌɪmɔr'tælətɪ; ES ˌɪmɔ'tælətɪ
immortalize ɪ'mɔrtļˌaɪz; ES ɪ'mɔətļ-; |-s -ɪz
|-d -d
immortelle ˌɪmɔr'tɛl; ES ˌɪmɔə'tɛl
immovability ɪˌmuvə'bɪlətɪ, ɪmˌmuv-, ˌɪmuv-,
ˌɪmmuvə-
immovable ɪ'muvəbļ, ɪm'muv- |-bly -blɪ
immune ɪ'mjun, ɪ'mɪun |-nity -ətɪ
immunization ˌɪmjʊnə'zeʃən, -aɪ'z-
immunize 'ɪmjəˌnaɪz, -ju- |-s -ɪz |-d -d
immunology ˌɪmjə'nalədʒɪ, -ju-; ES+-'nɒl-
immure ɪ'mjʊr, ɪ'mɪʊr; ES -ə(r; |-d -d
immutability ɪˌmjutə'bɪlətɪ, -ˌmɪut-, ˌɪmjut-,
ˌɪmɪut-, ˌɪmm-
immutable ɪ'mjutəbļ, ɪ'mɪut- |-bly -blɪ
Imogen 'ɪmədʒɪn, -ən |-gene -ˌdʒin
imp ɪmp |imped ɪmpt
impact n 'ɪmpækt
impact v ɪm'pækt |-pacted -'pæktɪd
impair ɪm'pɛr, -'pær; E -'pɛə(r, ES -'pæə(r;
|-ed -d
impale ɪm'pel |-d -d
impalpability ˌɪmpælpə'bɪlətɪ, ɪmˌpæl-
impalpable ɪm'pælpəbļ |-bly -blɪ
impanel ɪm'pænļ |-ed -d
imparadise ɪm'pærəˌdaɪs |-s -ɪz |-d -t
impark ɪm'park; ES ɪm'pɑːk, E+-'pɑːk;
|-ed -t
impart ɪm'part; ES -'pɑːt, E+-'pɑːt; |-ed -ɪd
impartation ˌɪmpar'teʃən; ES -pɑː-, E+-pɑː-
impartial ɪm'parʃəl; ES -'pɑːʃəl, E+-'pɑːʃəl;
|-ly -ɪ
impartiality ˌɪmparʃ'ælətɪ, -ʃɪ'æl-; ES -pɑ-,
E+-pɑ-
impassability ˌɪmpæsə'bɪlətɪ, ɪmˌpæs-; E+
-pas-, -ˌpas-, -pɑs-, -ˌpɑs-
impassable ɪm'pæsəbļ; E+-'pas-, -'pɑs-;
|-bly -blɪ
impasse ɪm'pæs, 'ɪmpæs; E+-a-, -ɑ- |-s -ɪz
(Fr æ̃'pɑːs)
impassible ɪm'pæsəbļ |-bly -blɪ
impassionate adj ɪm'pæʃənɪt
impassionate v ɪm'pæʃənˌet |-d -ɪd
impassioned ɪm'pæʃənd
impassive ɪm'pæsɪv |-sivity ˌɪmpæ'sɪvətɪ
impaste ɪm'pest |-d -ɪd
impatience ɪm'peʃəns |-tient -ʃənt
impavid ɪm'pævɪd

impeach ɪm'pitʃ |-es -ɪz |-ed -t
impeachability ˌɪmpitʃə'bɪlətɪ, ɪmˌpitʃə-
impeachable ɪm'pitʃəbļ
impearl ɪm'pɝl; ES ɪm'pɜl, -'pɝl; |-ed -d
impeccability ˌɪmpɛkə'bɪlətɪ, ɪmˌpɛk-
impeccable ɪm'pɛkəbļ |-bly -blɪ
impecuniosity ˌɪmpɪˌkjunɪ'asətɪ, -ˌkɪunɪ-;
ES+-'ɒs-
impecunious ˌɪmpɪ'kjunɪəs, -'kɪun-
impede ɪm'pid |-d -ɪd |-dance -'pidņs
impediment ɪm'pɛdəmənt
impedimenta ˌɪmpɛdə'mɛntə, ɪmˌpɛd-
impedimentary ɪmˌpɛdə'mɛntərɪ, -trɪ
impel ɪm'pɛl |-pelled -'pɛld
impend ɪm'pɛnd |-ed -ɪd
impenetrability ˌɪmpɛnətrə'bɪlətɪ, ɪmˌpɛn-
impenetrable ɪm'pɛnətrəbļ |-bly -blɪ
impenitence ɪm'pɛnətəns |-tent -tənt
imperative ɪm'pɛrətɪv
imperator ˌɪmpə'retɚ; ES -'retə(r
imperatorial ˌɪmpɛrə'torɪəl, ɪmˌpɛrə-, -'tɔr-;
S -'tor-
imperceptibility ˌɪmpɚˌsɛptə'bɪlətɪ; ES ˌɪmpə-
imperceptible ˌɪmpɚ'sɛptəbļ; ES ˌɪmpə-;
|-bly -blɪ
imperceptive ˌɪmpɚ'sɛptɪv; ES ˌɪmpə-
imperfect ɪm'pɝfɪkt; ES -'pɜf-, -'pɝf-
imperfection ˌɪmpɚ'fɛkʃən; ES ˌɪmpə-
imperforate adj, n ɪm'pɝfərɪt; ES -'pɜf-,
-'pɝf-
imperforated ɪm'pɝfəˌretɪd; ES -'pɜf-, -'pɝf-
imperial ɪm'pɪrɪəl |-ly -ɪ
imperialism ɪm'pɪrɪəlˌɪzəm |-ist -ɪst
imperialistic ɪmˌpɪrɪəl'ɪstɪk |-ally -ļɪ, -ɪklɪ
imperil ɪm'pɛrəl, -ɪl |-ed -d
imperious ɪm'pɪrɪəs
imperishability ˌɪmpɛrɪʃə'bɪlətɪ, ɪmˌpɛr-
imperishable ɪm'pɛrɪʃəbļ, |-bly -blɪ
imperium ɪm'pɪrɪəm |-ria -rɪə
impermanent ɪm'pɝmənənt; ES -'pɜm-,
-'pɝm-
impermeability ˌɪmpɝmɪə'bɪlətɪ, ɪmˌpɝm-;
ES -ɜ-, -ɝ-
impermeable ɪm'pɝmɪəbļ; ES -'pɜm-,-'pɝm-;
|-bly -blɪ
impersonal ɪm'pɝsņļ, -'pɝsnəl; ES -'pɜs-,
-'pɝs-; |-ly -ɪ
impersonality ˌɪmpɝsņ'ælətɪ, ɪmˌpɝs-; ES
-ɜ-, -ɝ-

Key: See in full §§3–47. bee bi |pity 'pɪtɪ (§6) |rate ret |yet jɛt |sang sæŋ |angry 'æŋ·grɪ
|bath bæθ; E baθ (§10) |ah ɑ |far fɑr |watch watʃ, wɒtʃ (§12) |jaw dʒɔ |gorge gɔrdʒ |go go

impersonate ɪmˈpɝ·sn̩ˌet; ES -ˈpɝs-, -ˈpɝˑs-; |-d -ɪd

impersonation ˌɪmpɝ·sn̩ˈeʃən, ɪmˌpɝˑs-; ES -ɜ-, -ɜˑ-

impertinence ɪmˈpɝˑtn̩əns; ES -ˈpɝt-, -ˈpɝˑt-; |-s -ɪz |-tinent -tn̩ənt

imperturbability ˌɪmpɝˌtɝbəˈbɪlətɪ; ES -pə-, ˌtɝb-, -pəˌtɝˑb-

imperturbable ˌɪmpɝˈtɝbəb|; ES -pəˈtɝb-, -pəˈtɝˑb-; |-bly -blɪ

imperturbation ˌɪmpɝˑtɝˈbeʃən; ES -pɝtə-, -pɝˑtə-

impervious ɪmˈpɝˑvɪəs; ES -ˈpɝv-, -ˈpɝˑv-

impetigo ˌɪmpɪˈtaɪgo

impetuosity ˌɪmpɛtʃʊˈɑsətɪ, ɪmˌpɛt-; ES+ -ˈɒs-

impetuous ɪmˈpɛtʃʊəs

impetus ˈɪmpətəs |-es -ɪz

Impey ˈɪmpɪ |-an -ən

impiety ɪmˈpaɪətɪ |impious ˈɪmpɪəs

impinge ɪmˈpɪndʒ |-s -ɪz |-d -d

impish ˈɪmpɪʃ

implacability ˌɪmplekəˈbɪlətɪ, ɪmˌplek-, -læk-

implacable ɪmˈplekəb|, -ˈplæk- |-bly -blɪ

implant ɪmˈplænt; E+-ˈplant, -ˈplant; |-ed -ɪd

implausible ɪmˈplɔzəb| |-bly -blɪ

implead ɪmˈplid |-ed -ɪd

implement n ˈɪmpləmənt

implement v ˈɪmpləˌmɛnt |-ed -ɪd

implemental ˌɪmpləˈmɛnt|

implementation ˌɪmpləmɛnˈteʃən

implicate adj ˈɪmplɪkɪt

implicate v ˈɪmplɪˌket |-d -ɪd

implication ˌɪmplɪˈkeʃən |-tive ˈɪmplɪˌketɪv

implicit ɪmˈplɪsɪt

implore ɪmˈplor, -ˈplɔr; ES -ˈploə(r, E+ -ˈplɔə(r; |-d -d

imply ɪmˈplaɪ |-plied -ˈplaɪd |-pliedly -ˈplaɪ-ɪdlɪ

impolite ˌɪmpəˈlaɪt

impolitic ɪmˈpɑləˌtɪk; ES+-ˈpɒl-

imponderability ˌɪmpɑndərəˈbɪlətɪ, ɪmˌpɑn-; ES+ -ɒn-

imponderable ɪmˈpɑndərəb|; ES+-ˈpɒn-; |-bly -blɪ

import n ˈɪmport, -pɔrt; ES -poət, E+-pɔət

import v ɪmˈport, -ˈpɔrt; ES -ˈpoət, E+-ˈpɔət; |-ed -ɪd—acct+ˈimport, esp. in contrast to export, v.

importance ɪmˈpɔrtn̩s; ES -ˈpoətn̩s; |-tant -tn̩t

importation ˌɪmporˈteʃən, -pɔr-; ES -poə-, E+-pɔə-

importunate adj ɪmˈpɔrtʃənɪt; ES -ˈpɔə-

importunate v ɪmˈpɔrtʃəˌnet; ES -ˈpɔə-; |-d -ɪd

importune adj, v ˌɪmpɝˈtjun, -ˈtɪun, -ˈtun, ɪmˈpɔrtʃən; ES ˌɪmpə-, ɪmˈpɔətʃ-; |-d -d

importunity ˌɪmpɝˈtjunətɪ, -ˈtɪun-, -ˈtun-; ES ˌɪmpə-

impose ɪmˈpoz |-s -ɪz |-d -d |-sing -ɪŋ

imposition ˌɪmpəˈzɪʃən

impossibility ˌɪmpɑsəˈbɪlətɪ, ɪmˌpɑs-; ES+ -ɒs-

impossible ɪmˈpɑsəb|; ES+-ˈpɒs-; |-bly -blɪ

impost ˈɪmpost |-ed -ɪd

impostor ɪmˈpɑstɝ; ES -ˈpɑstə(r, -ˈpɒs-

impostume ɪmˈpɑstʃum; ES+-ˈpɒs-

imposture ɪmˈpɑstʃɝ; ES -ˈpɑstʃə(r, -ˈpɒs-

impotence ˈɪmpətəns |-tent -tənt

impound ɪmˈpaʊnd |-ed -ɪd |-age -ɪdʒ

impoverish ɪmˈpɑvərɪʃ, -vrɪʃ; ES+-ˈpɒv-; |-es -ɪz |-ed -t

impracticability ˌɪmpræktɪkəˈbɪlətɪ, ɪmˌpræk-

impracticable ɪmˈpræktɪkəb| |-bly -blɪ

impractical ɪmˈpræktɪk|

impracticality ˌɪmpræktɪˈkælətɪ, ɪmˌpræk-

imprecate ˈɪmprɪˌket |- d -ɪd

imprecation ˌɪmprɪˈkeʃən

imprecatory ˈɪmprɪkəˌtorɪ, -ˌtɔrɪ; S -ˌtɔrɪ

impregnability ˌɪmprɛgnəˈbɪlətɪ, ɪmˌprɛg-

impregnable ɪmˈprɛgnəb| |-bly -blɪ

impregnate adj ɪmˈprɛgnɪt

impregnate v ɪmˈprɛgnet |-d -ɪd

impregnation ˌɪmprɛgˈneʃən

impresario ˌɪmprɪˈsɑrɪˌo

imprescriptible ˌɪmprɪˈskrɪptəb| |-bly -blɪ

impress n ˈɪmprɛs |-es -ɪz

impress v ɪmˈprɛs |-es -ɪz |-ed -t |-edly -ɪdlɪ

impressibility ˌɪmprɛsəˈbɪlətɪ, ɪmˌprɛs-

impressible ɪmˈprɛsəb| |-bly -blɪ

impression ɪmˈprɛʃən |-al -| |-ally -ļɪ

impressionability ɪmˌprɛʃənəˈbɪlətɪ, -ʃnə-

impressionable ɪmˈprɛʃənəb|, -ʃnə- |-bly -blɪ

impressionism ɪmˈprɛʃənˌɪzəm |-ist -ɪst

impressionistic ɪmˌprɛʃənˈɪstɪk |-ally -ļɪ, -ɪklɪ

impressive ɪmˈprɛsɪv

|full fʊl |tooth tuθ |further ˈfɝˑðɝ; ES ˈfɝˑðə |custom ˈkʌstəm |while hwaɪl |how haʊ |toy tɔɪ |using ˈjuzɪŋ |fuse fjuz, fɪuz |dish dɪʃ |vision ˈvɪʒən |Eden ˈidn̩ |cradle ˈkred| |keep 'em ˈkipm̩

imprest *adj, n* 'ımprɛst
imprest *v* ım'prɛst |-prested -'prɛstɪd
imprimatur ˌımprɪ'metɚ; ES -'metə(r
imprimis ım'praımıs
imprint *n* 'ımprınt
imprint *v* ım'prınt |-ed -ɪd
imprison ım'prızn̩ |-ed -d |-ing -'prızn̩ıŋ,
-znıŋ
improbability ˌımprɑbə'bılətı, ım‚pr-; ES+
-rɒb-
improbable ım'prɑbəb|; ES+-'prɒb-; |-bly
-blı
improbity ım'probətı, -'prɑbətı; ES+-'prɒb-
impromptu ım'prɑmptu, -tru, -tju; ES+
-'prɒmp-
improper ım'prɑpɚ; ES -'prɑpə(r, -'prɒp-
impropriety ˌımprə'praıətı, ˌımpə'praıətı—*In*
ˌımpə'praıətı r *is lost by dissimilation*
(§121).
improvability ım‚pruvə'bılətı
improvable ım'pruvəb| |-bly -blı
improve ım'pruv |-d -d
improvidence ım'prɑvədəns; ES+-'prɒv-;
|-nt -nt
improvisation ˌımprəvaı'zeʃən, -prɑvə'ze-;
ES+-prɒv-
improvise 'ımprə‚vaız, ˌımprə'vaız |-s -ız |-d
-d |-visedly -'vaızıdlı
imprudence ım'prudn̩s, -'prıud- |-dent -dn̩t
impudence 'ımpjədəns, -pju- |-dent -dənt
impugn ım'pjun, -'prun |-ed -d |-er -ɚ; ES
-ə(r; |-able -əb| |-bly -blı
impugnable '*unconquerable*' ım'pʌgnəb|
impuissance ım'pjuısn̩s, -'pıu- |-sant -sn̩t
impulse *n* 'ımpʌls |-s -ız
impulse *v* ım'pʌls |-s -ız |-d -t
impulsion ım'pʌlʃən |-sive -sıv
impunity ım'pjunətı, -'prun-
impure ım'pjur, -'pıur; ES -ə(r; |-rity -ətı
imputability ım‚pjutə'bılətı, -‚prut-, ‚ımp-
imputable ım'pjutəb|, -'prut- |-bly -blı
imputation ˌımpju'teʃən
impute ım'pjut, -'prut |-d -ıd
in *adj, adv* ın
in *prep stressed* 'ın, ‚ın; *unstr.* ın, n̩ (cut in two
'kʌtn̩'tu), *occas. nonsyllabic* n *before the
article* a ə (I'm in a hurry ‚aımnə'hɝı,
He'll go in a minute hil'gonə'mınıt)
in- *prefix. In words like* inactive, *where* in-

*means 'not,' and the second part clearly has
its separate meaning, the* in- *just before the
main accent has a slight stress that could be
marked thus:* ‚ın'æktıv, *or under emphasis
even* 'ın'æktıv. *But if the second part does
not show a clear meaning, being fused with
the* in- *into a simple word, as* insipid ın-
'sıpıd, *then the* in- *is quite stressless. Since
with different speakers and styles of speech
there are all grades between no stress and full
stress, it is not feasible to mark this accent,
though it often exists in speech. The same
statements apply to the variants* il- *and* im-.

inability ˌınə'bılətı
in absentia ˌınəb'sɛnʃıə
inaccessibility ˌınək‚sɛsə'bılətı, ˌınæk-
inaccessible ˌınək'sɛsəb|, ˌınæk- |-bly -blı
inaccuracy ın'ækjərəsı |-rate -rıt
inaction ın'ækʃən |-active -'æktıv
inactivity ˌınæk'tıvətı
inadequacy ın'ædəkwəsı |-quate -kwıt
inadmissibility ˌınəd‚mısə'bılətı
inadmissible ˌınəd'mısəb| |-bly -blı
inadvertence ˌınəd'vɝtn̩s; ES -'vɝt-, -'vɝt-;
|-cy -ı |-ent -tn̩t
inadvisability ˌınəd‚vaızə'bılətı
inadvisable ˌınəd'vaızəb| |-bly -blı
inalienability ˌıneljənə'bılətı, ın‚eljən-, -lıən-
inalienable ın'eljənəb|, -'elıən- |-bly -blı
inalterable ın'ɔltərəb| |-bly -blı
inamorata ın‚æmə'rɑtə, ‚ınæm-
inane ın'en
inanimate ın'ænəmıt
inanity ın'ænətı |inanition ˌınə'nıʃən
inappeasable ˌınə'pizəb|
inapplicability ˌınæplıkə'bılətı, ın‚æp-
inapplicable ın'æplıkəb| |-bly -blı
inapposite ın'æpəzıt
inappreciable ˌınə'priʃıəb| |-bly -blı
inappreciative ˌınə'priʃɪ‚etıv
inapproachability ˌınə‚protʃə'bılətı
inapproachable ˌınə'protʃəb| |-bly -blı
inappropriate ˌınə'proprıt
inapt ın'æpt
inaptitude ın'æptə‚tjud, -‚trud, -‚tud
inarm ın'arm; ES -'ɑːm, E+-'aːm; |-ed -d
inarticulate ˌınar'tıkjəlıt; ES -ɑ-, E+-ɑ-
inartistic ˌınar'tıstık; ES -ɑː'tıs-, E+-aː'tıs-;
|-al -| |-ally -ı, -ıklı

Key: *See in full* §§3–47. bee bi |pity 'pıtı (§6) |rate ret |yet jɛt |sang sæŋ |angry 'æŋ·grı
|bath bæθ; E baθ (§10) |ah ɑ |far fɑr |watch wɑtʃ, wɒtʃ (§12) |jaw dʒɔ |gorge gɔrdʒ |go go

inasmuch ˌɪnəz'mʌtʃ
inattention ˌɪnə'tɛnʃən |-tive -tɪv
inaudibility ˌɪnɔdə'bɪlətɪ, ɪnˌɔd-
inaudible ɪn'ɔdəbḷ |-bly -blɪ
inaugural ɪn'ɔgjərəl, ɪn'ɔgərəl
inaugurate ɪn'ɔgjəˌret, -'ɔgə- |-d -ɪd
inauguration ɪnˌɔgjə'reʃən, -ˌɔgə-
inauspicious ˌɪnɔ'spɪʃəs
inboard 'ɪnˌbord, -ˌbɔrd; ES -ˌboəd, E+ -ˌbɔəd
inborn ɪn'bɔrn; ES -'bɔən; ('ɪnˌborn 'grace)
inbound 'ɪn'baʊnd ('ɪnˌbound 'ship)
inbreathe ɪn'bri'ð |-d -d
inbred adj ɪn'brɛd ('ɪnˌbred 'tact)
inbreed ɪn'brid |-bred -'brɛd
Inca 'ɪŋkə
incalculability ˌɪnkælkjələ'bɪlətɪ, ɪnˌkæl-
incalculable ɪn'kælkjələbḷ |-bly -blɪ
incandesce ˌɪnkən'dɛs, -kæn- |-s -ɪz |-d -t
incandescence ˌɪnkən'dɛsṇs |-cy -ɪ |-nt -ṇt
incantation ˌɪnkæn'teʃən
incapability ˌɪnkepə'bɪlətɪ, ɪnˌkep-
incapable ɪn'kepəbḷ |-bly -blɪ
incapacitate ˌɪnkə'pæsəˌtet |-d -ɪd |-ity -tɪ
incarcerate ɪn'kɑrsəˌret; ES -'kɑːs-, E+ -'kɑːs-; |-d -ɪd
incarceration ɪnˌkɑrsə'reʃən; ES -ˌkɑːs-, E+-ˌkɑːs-; ˌɪnk-
incarnadine ɪn'kɑrnəˌdaɪn, -dɪn; ES -'kɑː-, E+-'kɑː-; |-d -d
incarnate adj ɪn'kɑrnɪt, -net; ES -'kɑː-, E+-'kɑː-
incarnate v ɪn'kɑrnet; ES -'kɑː-, E+-'kɑː-; |-d -ɪd
incarnation, I- ˌɪnkɑr'neʃən; ES -kɑː-, E+-kɑː-
incase ɪn'kes |-cases -'kesɪz |-cased -'kest
incaution ɪn'kɔʃən |-tious -ʃəs
incendiary ɪn'sɛndɪˌɛrɪ |-arism -əˌrɪzəm
incense n 'ɪnsɛns |adj - d -t
incense v ɪn'sɛns |-s -ɪz |-d -t
incentive ɪn'sɛntɪv
incept ɪn'sɛpt |-ed -ɪd
inception ɪn'sɛpʃən |-tive -tɪv
inceration ˌɪnsə'reʃən
incertitude ɪn'sɝtəˌtjud, -ˌtrud, -ˌtud; ES -'sɝt-, -'sɝt-
incessancy ɪn'sɛsṇsɪ |-sant -sṇt
incest 'ɪnsɛst |-uous ɪn'sɛstʃʊəs

inch ɪntʃ |inches 'ɪntʃɪz |inched ɪntʃt
Inchbald 'ɪntʃbɔld
inchoate adj ɪn'ko·ɪt
inchoate v 'ɪnkoˌet |-d -ɪd
inchworm 'ɪntʃˌwɝm; ES -ˌwɝm, -ˌwɝm
incidence 'ɪnsədəns |-dent -dənt
incidental ˌɪnsə'dɛntḷ |-ly -ɪ
incinerate ɪn'sɪnəˌret |-d -ɪd |-tor -ɚ; ES -ə(r
incipience ɪn'sɪpɪəns |-cy -ɪ |-ent -ənt
incipit 'here begins' 'ɪnsɪpɪt
incise ɪn'saɪz |-s -ɪz |-d -d
incision ɪn'sɪʒən
incisive ɪn'saɪsɪv, -zɪv
incisor ɪn'saɪzɚ; ES -'saɪzə(r
incite ɪn'saɪt |-d -ɪd |-tation ˌɪnsaɪ'teʃən
incivility ˌɪnsə'vɪlətɪ
inclemency ɪn'klɛmənsɪ |-clement -'klɛmənt
inclinable ɪn'klaɪnəbḷ
inclination ˌɪnklə'neʃən
incline n 'ɪnklaɪn, ɪn'klaɪn
incline v ɪn'klaɪn |-d -d
inclinometer ˌɪnklɪ'nɑmətɚ; ES -'nɑmətə(r, -'nɒm-
inclose ɪn'kloz |-s -ɪz |-d -d
inclosure ɪn'kloʒɚ; ES -ʒə(r
include ɪn'klud, -'klɪud |-d -ɪd
inclusion ɪn'kluʒən, -'klɪu-
inclusive ɪn'klusɪv, -'klɪu-, -zɪv
incog ɪn'kɑg, -'kɒg
incognito ɪn'kɑgnɪˌto, -'kɒg-
incoherence ˌɪnko'hɪrəns |-cy -ɪ |-ent -ənt
incombustibility ˌɪnkəmˌbʌstə'bɪlətɪ
incombustible ˌɪnkəm'bʌstəbḷ |-bly -blɪ
income 'ɪnˌkʌm, 'ɪŋˌkʌm
incoming 'ɪnˌkʌmɪŋ
incommensurability ˌɪnkəˌmɛnʃərə'bɪlətɪ, -sərə-
incommensurable ˌɪnkə'mɛnʃərəbḷ, -sərə- |-bly -blɪ
incommensurate ˌɪnkə'mɛnʃərɪt, -sərɪt
incommode ˌɪnkə'mod |-d -ɪd |-dious -ɪəs
incommodity ˌɪnkə'mɑdətɪ; ES+-'mɒd-
incommunicability ˌɪnkəˌmjunɪkə'bɪlətɪ, -ˌmɪun-
incommunicable ˌɪnkə'mjunɪkəbḷ, -'mɪun- |-bly -blɪ
incommunicado ˌɪnkəˌmjunɪ'kado, -ˌmɪun-
incommunicative ˌɪnkə'mjunəˌketɪv, -'mɪun-
incompact ˌɪnkəm'pækt

|full fʊl |tooth tuθ |further 'fɝðɚ; ES 'fɝðə |custom 'kʌstəm |while hwaɪl |how haʊ |toy tɔ.
|using 'juzɪŋ |fuse fjuz, fɪuz |dish dɪʃ |vision 'vɪʒən |Eden 'idṇ |cradle 'kredḷ |keep 'em 'kipṃ

Those words below in which the ɑ sound is spelt o are often pronounced with ɒ in E and S

incomparability ˌɪnkʌmpərə'bɪlətɪ, -prə-, ɪn-ˌkʌm-

incomparable ɪn'kʌmpərəb], -prə- |-bly -blɪ

incompatibility ˌɪnkəmˌpætə'bɪlətɪ

incompatible ˌɪnkəm'pætəb] |-bly -blɪ

incompetence ɪn'kʌmpətəns |-cy -ɪ |-tent tənt

incomplete ˌɪnkəm'plit |-pletion -'pliʃən

incompliance ˌɪnkəm'plaɪəns |-cy -ɪ |-nt -nt

incomprehensibility ˌɪnkʌmprɪˌhɛnsə'bɪlətɪ, ɪnˌkʌm-

incomprehensible ˌɪnkʌmprɪ'hɛnsəb], ɪnˌkʌm-|-bly -blɪ |-sive -sɪv

incompressible ˌɪnkəm'prɛsəb] |-bly -blɪ

incomputable ˌɪnkəm'pjutəb], -'pɪut-

inconceivability ˌɪnkənˌsivə'bɪlətɪ

inconceivable ˌɪnkən'sivəb] |-bly -blɪ

inconclusive ˌɪnkən'klusɪv, -'klɪu-

inconformity ˌɪnkən'fɔrmətɪ; ES -'fɔəmətɪ

incongruence ɪn'kʌŋgruəns |-ent -ənt

incongruity ˌɪnkʌŋ'gruətɪ, -kəŋ-, -n'gru-, -'grɪu-

incongruous ɪn'kʌŋgruəs

inconsecutive ˌɪnkən'sɛkjətɪv

inconsequence ɪn'kʌnsəˌkwɛns |-quent -ˌkwɛnt

inconsequential ˌɪnkʌnsə'kwɛnʃəl |-ly -ɪ

inconsequentiality ˌɪnkʌnsəˌkwɛnʃɪ'ælətɪ, ɪn-ˌkʌn-

inconsiderable ˌɪnkən'sɪdərəb], -'sɪdrə- |-bly -blɪ

inconsiderate ˌɪnkən'sɪdərɪt, -'sɪdrɪt

inconsideration ˌɪnkənˌsɪdə'reʃən

inconsistence ˌɪnkən'sɪstəns |-cy -ɪ |-nt -nt

inconsolability ˌɪnkənˌsolə'bɪlətɪ

inconsolable ˌɪnkən'soləb] |-bly -blɪ

inconsonance ɪn'kʌnsənəns |-nant -nənt

inconspicuous ˌɪnkən'spɪkjuəs

inconstancy ɪn'kʌnstənsɪ |-tant -tənt

incontestable ˌɪnkən'tɛstəb] |-bly -blɪ

incontinence ɪn'kʌntənəns |-cy -ɪ |-nt -nt

incontrollable ˌɪnkən'troləb] |-bly -blɪ

incontrovertability ˌɪnkʌntrəˌvɜtə'bɪlətɪ, ɪn-ˌkʌn-; ES -ˌvɜt-, -ˌvɝt-

incontrovertible ˌɪnkʌntrə'vɜtəb], ɪnˌkʌn-; ES -'vɜt-, -'vɝt-; `acct+ɪn'controˌvertible |-bly -blɪ

inconvenience ˌɪnkən'vinjəns |-s -ɪz |-d -t |-nt -nt

inconvertibility ˌɪnkənˌvɜtə'bɪlətɪ; ES -ˌvɜt-, -ˌvɝt-

inconvertible ˌɪnkən'vɜtəb]; ES -'vɜt-, -'vɝt-; |-bly -blɪ

inconvincibility ˌɪnkənˌvɪnsə'bɪlətɪ

inconvincible ˌɪnkən'vɪnsəb] |-bly -blɪ

in-co-ordinate ˌɪnko'ɔrdn̩ɪt; ES -'ɔədn̩ɪt; |-nated -dn̩ˌetɪd

in-co-ordination ˌɪnkoˌɔrdn̩'eʃən; ES -ˌɔədn̩-'eʃən

incorporable ɪn'kɔrpərəb]; ES -'kɔəp-

incorporate adj ɪn'kɔrpərɪt, -prɪt; ES -'kɔəp-

incorporate v ɪn'kɔrpəˌret; ES -'kɔəp-; |-d -ɪd |-rative -ˌretɪv

incorporation ɪnˌkɔrpə'reʃən; ES -ˌkɔəp-; ˌɪnk-

incorporeal ˌɪnkɔr'porɪəl, -'pɔr-; ES ˌɪnkɔ-'porɪəl, E+-'pɔrɪəl

incorporeity ˌɪnkɔrpə'riətɪ; ES -kəp-; ɪnˌk-

incorrect ˌɪnkə'rɛkt ('incorˌrect 'answer)

incorrigibility ˌɪnkɔrɪdʒə'bɪlətɪ, ɪnˌkɔr-, -ɑr-, -ɒr-

incorrigible ɪn'kɔrɪdʒəb], -'kɑr-, -'kɒr- |-bly -blɪ

incorrupt ˌɪnkə'rʌpt |-ed -ɪd

incorruptibility ˌɪnkəˌrʌptə'bɪlətɪ

incorruptible ˌɪnkə'rʌptəb] |-bly -blɪ

incorruption ˌɪnkə'rʌpʃən

increase n 'ɪnkris, 'ɪŋk- |-s -ɪz

increase v ɪn'kris |-s -ɪz |-d -t |-dly -ɪdlɪ

increasingly ɪn'krisɪŋlɪ

incredibility ˌɪnkrɛdə'bɪlətɪ, ɪnˌkrɛdə-

incredible ɪn'krɛdəb] |-bly -blɪ

incredulity ˌɪnkrə'dulətɪ, -'drul-, -'djul-

incredulous ɪn'krɛdʒələs

increment 'ɪnkrəmənt, 'ɪŋk- |-al ˌɪnkrə'mɛnt]

incriminate ɪn'krɪməˌnet |-d -ɪd

incrimination ɪnˌkrɪmə'neʃən, ˌɪnkrɪmə-

incriminator ɪn'krɪməˌnetɚ; ES -ˌnetə(r

incriminatory ɪn'krɪmənəˌtorɪ, -ˌtɔrɪ; S -ˌtorɪ

incrust ɪn'krʌst |-ed -ɪd

incrustation ˌɪnkrʌs'teʃən

incubate 'ɪnkjəˌbet, 'ɪŋk- |-d -ɪd

incubation ˌɪnkjə'beʃən, ˌɪŋk-

incubator 'ɪnkjəˌbetɚ, 'ɪŋk-; ES -tə(r

incubus 'ɪnkjəbəs, 'ɪŋk- |-es -ɪz |-bi -ˌbaɪ

inculcate ɪn'kʌlket, 'ɪnkʌlˌket |-d -ɪd

inculcation ˌɪnkʌl'keʃən

Key: *See in full §§3–47.* bee bi |pity 'pɪtɪ (§6) |rate ret |yet jɛt |sang sæŋ |angry 'æŋ·grɪ |bath bæθ; E baθ (§10) |ah ɑ |far fɑr |watch wɑtʃ, wɒtʃ (§12) |jaw dʒɔ |gorge gɔrdʒ |go go

inculpate ɪnˈkʌlpet, ˈɪnkʌlˌpet |-d -ɪd
inculpation ˌɪnkʌlˈpeʃən
inculpatory ɪnˈkʌlpəˌtorɪ, -ˌtɔrɪ; S -ˌtorɪ
incult ɪnˈkʌlt (ˈɪnˌcult ˈbeard)
incumbency ɪnˈkʌmbənsɪ |-bent -bənt
incumber ɪnˈkʌmbɚ; ES -ˈkʌmbə(r; |-ed -d
|-ing -ˈkʌmbrɪŋ, -bərɪŋ
incumbrance ɪnˈkʌmbrəns |-s -ɪz
incunabula ˌɪnkjʊˈnæbjələ |sg -lum -ləm
incur ɪnˈkɝ; ES -ˈkɝ(r, -ˈkɝ; |-red -d
incurability ˌɪnkjʊrəˈbɪlətɪ, -kɪʊr-, ɪnˌk-
incurable ɪnˈkjʊrəbļ, -ˈkɪʊr- |-bly -blɪ
incuriosity ˌɪnkjʊrɪˈɑsətɪ, -kɪʊr-; ES+-ˈɒs-
incurious ɪnˈkjʊrɪəs, -ˈkɪʊr-
incurrence ɪnˈkɝəns; ES -ˈkɝəns, -ˈkʌrəns,
-ˈkɝəns; |-s -ɪz
incursion ɪnˈkɝʒən, -ˈkɝʃ-; ES -ˈkɝ-, -ˈkɝ-
incursive ɪnˈkɝsɪv; ES -ˈkɝs-, -ˈkɝs-
incurvate adj ɪnˈkɝvɪt, -vet; ES -ˈkɝv-, -ˈkɝv-
incurvate ɪnˈkɝvet; ES -ˈkɝv-, -ˈkɝv-; |-d -ɪd
incurvation ˌɪnkɝˈveʃən; ES -kɝˈv-, -kɝˈv-
incurve n ˈɪnˌkɝv; ES -ˌkɝv, -ˌkɝv
incurve v ɪnˈkɝv; ES -ˈkɝv, -ˈkɝv; |-d -d
incus ˈɪŋkəs |-es -ɪz |-cudes ɪnˈkjudiz, -ˈkɪu-
Ind ˈIndia' ɪnd, aɪnd—The historical pron. is
aɪnd, as in Chauc. and Shak.
indamin ˈɪndəmɪn |-mine -ˌmin, -mɪn
indebt ɪnˈdɛt |-ed -ɪd |-edness -ɪdnɪs
indecency ɪnˈdisņsɪ |-cent -sņt
indecipherability ˌɪndɪˌsaɪfrəˈbɪlətɪ, -fərə-
indecipherable ˌɪndɪˈsaɪfrəbļ, -fərə- |-bly -blɪ
indecision ˌɪndɪˈsɪʒən |-cisive -ˈsaɪsɪv
indeclinable ˌɪndɪˈklaɪnəbļ |-bly -blɪ
indecorous ɪnˈdɛkərəs, ˌɪndɪˈkorəs; EN+
-ˈkɔr-
indecorum ˌɪndɪˈkorəm, -ˈkɔr-; S -ˈkorəm
indeed ɪnˈdid, ņˈdid, emph.+ˈɪnˈdid (ˈjɛsņ-
ˈdid)
indefatigability ˌɪndɪˌfætɪgəˈbɪlətɪ
indefatigable ˌɪndɪˈfætɪgəbļ |-bly -blɪ
indefeasible ˌɪndɪˈfizəbļ |-bly -blɪ
indefensible ˌɪndɪˈfɛnsəbļ |-bly -blɪ
indefinable ˌɪndɪˈfaɪnəbļ |-bly -blɪ
indefinite ɪnˈdɛfənɪt
indehiscence ˌɪndiˈhɪsņs |-scent -sņt
indelibility ˌɪndɛləˈbɪlətɪ, ɪnˌdɛl-
indelible ɪnˈdɛləbļ |-bly -blɪ
indelicate ɪnˈdɛləkət, -kɪt |-cacy -kəsɪ
indemnification ɪnˌdɛmnəfəˈkeʃən

indemnify ɪnˈdɛmnəˌfaɪ |-fied -ˌfaɪd |-ity -tɪ
indemonstrable ɪnˈdɛmənstrəbļ, ˌɪndɪˈmon-
strəbļ; ES+-ˈmɒn-; |-bly -blɪ
indene ˈɪndin
indent n ɪnˈdɛnt, ˈɪndɛnt
indent v ɪnˈdɛnt |-ed -ɪd |-ation ˌɪndɛnˈteʃən
indention ɪnˈdɛnʃən
indenture ɪnˈdɛntʃɚ; ES -ˈdɛntʃə(r; |-d -d
independence ˌɪndɪˈpɛndəns |-cy -ɪ |-nt -nt
indescribable ˌɪndɪˈskraɪbəbļ |-bly -blɪ
indestructibility ˌɪndɪˌstrʌktəˈbɪlətɪ
indestructible ˌɪndɪˈstrʌktəbļ |-bly -blɪ
indeterminable ˌɪndɪˈtɝmɪnəbļ; ES -ˈtɝm-,
-ˈtɝm-; |-bly -blɪ
indeterminate ˌɪndɪˈtɝmənɪt; ES -ˈtɝm-,
-ˈtɝm-
indetermination ˌɪndɪˌtɝməˈneʃən; ES -ˌtɝm-,
-ˌtɝm-
indeterminism ˌɪndɪˈtɝmənˌɪzəm; ES -ˈtɝm-,
-ˈtɝm-; |-ist -ɪst
index ˈɪndɛks |-es -ɪz |indices ˈɪndəˌsiz |-ed -t
India ˈɪndɪə, ˈɪndjə |-n -n |-man -mən |-men
-mən
Indiana ˌɪndɪˈænə—BBC ɪndɪˈɑːnə is not Am.
Indianapolis ˌɪndɪənˈæpļɪs, -ˈæplɪs, -əs |-'s -ɪz
Indianian ˌɪndɪˈænɪən, -njən
Indic ˈɪndɪk
indic ˈɪndɪk |indican ˈɪndɪkən
indicant ˈɪndɪkənt
indicate ˈɪndəˌket |-d -ɪd |-tion ˌɪndəˈkeʃən
indicative ɪnˈdɪkətɪv, -ˈdɪkɪtɪv
indicator ˈɪndəˌketɚ; ES -ˌketə(r
indices pl of index ˈɪndəˌsiz
indict ɪnˈdaɪt |-ed -ɪd |-er, -or -ɚ; ES -ə(r
indictable ɪnˈdaɪtəbļ |-bly -blɪ
indictee ˌɪndaɪtˈi
indiction ɪnˈdɪkʃən
indictment ɪnˈdaɪtmənt
Indies ˈɪndɪz, ˈɪndiz
indifference ɪnˈdɪfrəns, -ˈdɪfərəns |-nt -nt
indigence ˈɪndədʒəns |-gent -dʒənt
indigene ˈɪndəˌdʒin
indigenous ɪnˈdɪdʒənəs
indigestibility ˌɪndəˌdʒɛstəˈbɪlətɪ
indigestible ˌɪndəˈdʒɛstəbļ |-bly -blɪ
indigestion ˌɪndəˈdʒɛstʃən
indign ɪnˈdaɪn
indignant ɪnˈdɪgnənt |-gnation ˌɪndɪgˈneʃən
indignity ɪnˈdɪgnətɪ

|full fʊl |tooth tuθ |further ˈfɝðɚ; ES ˈfɝðə |custom ˈkʌstəm |while hwaɪl |how haʊ |toy tɔɪ
|using ˈjuzɪŋ |fuse fjuz, fɪuz |dish dɪʃ |vision ˈvɪʒən |Eden ˈidņ |cradle ˈkredļ |keep 'em ˈkipm̩

indigo 'ındı͜go |-digoid -dı͜gɔɪd
indigotin ın'dıgətın, ͜ındı'gotın
Indio 'ındı͜o
indirect ͜ındə'rɛkt |-rection -'rɛkʃən
indiscernible ͜ındı'zɝnəb|, -'sɝn-; ES -ɜn-, -ɝn-; |-bly -blı
indiscreet ͜ındı'skrit |-scretion -'skrɛʃən
indiscriminate ͜ındı'skrımənıt
indiscrimination ͜ındı͜skrımə'neʃən
indispensability ͜ındı͜spɛnsə'bılətı
indispensable ͜ındı'spɛnsəb| |-bly -blı
indispose ͜ındı'spoz |-s -ız |-d -d
indisposition ͜ındıspə'zıʃən
indisputability ͜ındı͜spjutə'bılətı, -͜sprut-, ın͜dıspjutə'bılətı
indisputable ͜ındı'spjutəb|, -'sprut-, ın'dıspjutəb| |-bly -blı—Usage appears to be sensibly following the analogy of dispute.
indissolubility ͜ındı͜saljə'bılətı, ın͜dısljυ-'bılətı; ES+-͜sɒl-
indissoluble ͜ındı'saljəb|, ın'dısljυb|; ES+-'sɒl-; |-bly -blı
indistinct ͜ındı'stıŋkt
indistinguishability ͜ındı͜stıŋgwıʃə'bılətı
indistinguishable ͜ındı'stıŋgwıʃəb| |-bly -blı
indite ın'daıt |-d -ıd
indium 'ındıəm
individual ͜ındə'vıdʒυəl, -dʒυl |-ly -ı |-ism -͜ızəm |-ist -ıst
individualistic ͜ındə͜vıdʒυəl'ıstık, -dʒυl- |-ally -|ı, -ıklı
individuality ͜ındə͜vıdʒυ'ælətı
individualization ͜ındə͜vıdʒυələ'zeʃən, -dʒυl-, -aı'z-
individualize ͜ındə'vıdʒυəl͜aız, -dʒυl- |-s -ız |-d -d
indivisibility ͜ındə͜vızə'bılətı
indivisible ͜ındə'vızəb| |-bly -blı
Indo-Aryan 'ındo'ɛrıən, -'ær-, -'ɑr-, -rjən; S -'ær-, -'er-, -'ɑr-
Indo-British 'ındo'brıtıʃ
Indo-Chinese 'ındotʃaı'niz
indocile ın'das|, -sıl; ES+-'dɒs-
indocility ͜ındo'sılətı
indoctrinate ın'daktrın͜et; ES+-'dɒk-; |-d -ıd
indoctrination ın͜daktrı'neʃən, ͜ındak-; ES+-ɒ-
Indo-European ͜ındə͜jυrə'pıən, ͜ındo-

Indo-Germanic ͜ındodʒɝ'mænık, -dʒɝ-; ES -dʒə-, -dʒɝ-, -dʒɝ-
indol 'ındol, -dal, -dɒl |-dole -dol
indolence 'ındələns |-lent -lənt
indomitable ın'damətəb|; ES+-'dɒm-; |-bly -blı
Indonesian ͜ındo'niʃən, -ɜən
indoor 'ın͜dor, -͜dɔr; ES -͜doə(r, E+-͜dɔə(r
indoors n ın'dorz, -'dɔrz; ES -'doəz, E+-'dɔəz
indoors adj 'ın͜dorz, -͜dɔrz; ES -͜doəz, E+-͜dɔəz
indoors adv 'ın'dorz, -'dɔrz; ES -'doəz, E+-'dɔəz
indophenol ͜ındo'finol, -nal, -nɒl
indorse ın'dɔrs; ES -'dɔəs; |-s -ız |-d -t
indoxyl ın'daksıl; ES+-'dɒk-
Indra 'ındrə
indraft, -draught 'ın͜dræft; E+-͜draft, -͜drɑft
indrawn 'ın'drɔn ('in͜drawn 'breath)
indubitable ın'djubıtəb|, -'dıu-, -'du- |-bly -blı
induce ın'djus, -'dıus, -'dus |-s -ız |-d -t |-cible -əb| |-dly -ıdlı
induct ın'dʌkt |-ed -ıd |-ance -əns
inductile ın'dʌkt|, -tıl
inductility ͜ındʌk'tılətı
induction ın'dʌkʃən |-tive -tıv
inductivity ͜ındʌk'tıvətı
inductor ın'dʌktɚ; ES -'dʌktə(r
indue ın'dju, -'dıu, -'du |-d -d
indulge ın'dʌldʒ |-s -ız |-d -d
indulgence ın'dʌldʒəns |-s -ız |-d -t |-nt -nt
indulin 'ındjυlın |-line -͜lin, -lın
indurate adj 'ındjυrıt, -dυrıt
indurate v 'ındjυ͜ret, -dυ͜ret |-d -ıd
induration ͜ındjυ'reʃən, -dυ-
Indus 'ındəs |-'s -ız
industrial ın'dʌstrıəl |-ly -ı |-ism -͜ızəm |-ist -ıst
industrialization ın͜dʌstrıələ'zeʃən, -aı'z-
industrialize ın'dʌstrıəl͜aız |-s -ız |-d -d
industrious ın'dʌstrıəs
industry 'ındəstrı, 'ın͜dʌstrı
indwell ın'dwɛl |-dwelt -'dwɛlt
indweller 'ın͜dwɛlɚ; ES -͜dwɛlə(r
indwelling n 'ın͜dwɛlıŋ
inearth ın'ɝθ; ES -'ɝθ, -'ɝθ; |-ed -t
inebriacy ın'ibrıəsı |-briant -brıənt

---

inebriate *adj* ɪnˈibrɪɪt
inebriate *n* ɪnˈibrɪɪt, -ɪˌet
inebriate *v* ɪnˈibrɪˌet |-d -ɪd
inebriation ɪnˌibrɪˈeʃən
inebriety ˌɪnɪˈbraɪətɪ
inedibility ˌɪnɛdəˈbɪlətɪ, ɪnˌɛdə-
inedible ɪnˈɛdəb|
inedited ɪnˈɛdɪtɪd
ineducability ˌɪnɛdʒəkəˈbɪlətɪ, -dʒʊ-
ineducable ɪnˈɛdʒəkəb|, -dʒʊ-
ineffability ˌɪnɛfəˈbɪlətɪ, ɪnˌɛfə-
ineffable ɪnˈɛfəb| |-bly -blɪ
ineffaceable ˌɪnəˈfesəb| |-bly -blɪ
ineffective ˌɪnəˈfɛktɪv
ineffectual ˌɪnəˈfɛktʃʊəl, -tʃʊl |-ly -ɪ
ineffectuality ˌɪnəˌfɛktʃʊˈælətɪ
inefficacious ˌɪnɛfəˈkeʃəs |-cacy ɪnˈɛfəkəsɪ
inefficience ˌɪnəˈfɪʃəns |-cy -ɪ |-nt -nt
inelastic ˌɪnɪˈlæstɪk
inelasticity ˌɪnɪlæsˈtɪsətɪ
inelegance ɪnˈɛləgəns |-s -ɪz |-cy -ɪ |-nt -nt
ineligibility ˌɪnɛlɪdʒəˈbɪlətɪ, ɪnˌɛlɪdʒə-
ineligible ɪnˈɛlɪdʒəb| |-bly -blɪ
ineluctable ˌɪnɪˈlʌktəb| |-bly -blɪ
inept ɪnˈɛpt
ineptitude ɪnˈɛptəˌtjud, -ˌtrud, -ˌtud
inequality ˌɪnɪˈkwalətɪ, -ˈkwɒl-
inequitable ɪnˈɛkwɪtəb| |-bly -blɪ |-ty -tɪ
ineradicable ˌɪnɪˈrædɪkəb| |-bly -blɪ
inerrancy ɪnˈɛrənsɪ |-rant -rənt
inert ɪnˈɝt; ES ɪnˈɜt, -ˈɝt
inertia ɪnˈɝʃə; ES -ˈɜʃə, -ˈɝʃə
inescapable ˌɪnəˈskepəb| |-bly -blɪ
in esse ɪnˈɛsɪ
inessential ˌɪnəˈsɛnʃəl
inestimable ɪnˈɛstəməb| |-bly -blɪ
inevitability ˌɪnɛvətəˈbɪlətɪ, ɪnˌɛv-
inevitable ɪnˈɛvətəb| |-bly -blɪ
inexact ˌɪnɪgˈzækt
inexactitude ˌɪnɪgˈzæktəˌtjud, -ˌtrud, -ˌtud
inexcusable ˌɪnɪkˈskjuzəb|, -ˈskɪuz- |-bly -blɪ
inexhaustibility ˌɪnɪgˌzɔstəˈbɪlətɪ
inexhaustible ˌɪnɪgˈzɔstəb| |-bly -blɪ
inexorable ɪnˈɛksərəb| |-bly -blɪ
inexpedience ˌɪnɪkˈspidɪəns |-cy -ɪ |-nt -nt
inexpensive ˌɪnɪkˈspɛnsɪv
inexperience ˌɪnɪkˈspɪrɪəns |-d -t
inexpert ˌɪnɪkˈspɝt; ES -ˈspɜt, -ˈspɝt; (ˈinexˌpert ˈhelp)

inexpiable ɪnˈɛkspɪəb| |-bly -blɪ
inexplainable ˌɪnɪkˈsplenəb|
inexplicability ɪnˌɛksplɪkəˈbɪlətɪ, ˌɪnɛks-
inexplicable ɪnˈɛksplɪkəb| |-bly -blɪ—*Brit occasional* ˌɪnɪkˈsplɪkəb| *seems to be gaining ground here.*
inexpressible ˌɪnɪkˈsprɛsəb| |-bly -blɪ
inexpressive ˌɪnɪkˈsprɛsɪv
inexpugnable ˌɪnɪkˈspʌgnəb| |-bly -blɪ
in extenso ˌɪnɪkˈstɛnso
inextinguishable ˌɪnɪkˈstɪŋgwɪʃəb| |-bly -blɪ
in extremis ˌɪnɪkˈstrimɪs
inextricable ɪnˈɛkstrɪkəb| |-bly -blɪ
infallibility ˌɪnfæləˈbɪlətɪ, ɪnˌfælə-
infallible ɪnˈfæləb| |-bly -blɪ
infamous ˈɪnfəməs |infamy ˈɪnfəmɪ
infancy ˈɪnfənsɪ |-fant -fənt
infanta ɪnˈfæntə |infante ɪnˈfænte
infanticide ɪnˈfæntəˌsaɪd
infantile ˈɪnfənˌtaɪl, -təl, -tɪl
infantine ˈɪnfənˌtaɪn, -tɪn
infantry ˈɪnfəntrɪ |-man -mən |-men -mən
infatuate ɪnˈfætʃʊˌet |-d -ɪd
infatuation ɪnˌfætʃʊˈeʃən
infeasible ɪnˈfizəb|
infect ɪnˈfɛkt |-ed -ɪd
infection ɪnˈfɛkʃən |-tious -ʃəs |-tive -tɪv
infelicitous ˌɪnfəˈlɪsətəs |-ty -tɪ
infelt ˈɪnˌfɛlt
infer ɪnˈfɝ; ES -ˈfɜ(r, -ˈfɝ; |-red -d
inferable ɪnˈfɝəb|, ˈɪnfərəb|; ES+-ˈfɝəb|
inference ˈɪnfərəns |-s -ɪz
inferential ˌɪnfəˈrɛnʃəl |-ly -ɪ
inferior ɪnˈfɪrɪɚ; ES -ˈfɪrɪ·ə(r
inferiority ɪnˌfɪrɪˈɔrətɪ, -ˈar-, -ˈɒr-, ˌɪnfɪr-
infernal ɪnˈfɝn|; ES -ˈfɜn|, -ˈfɝn|; |-ly -ɪ
inferno, I- ɪnˈfɝno; ES -ˈfɜno, -ˈfɝno
inferrible ɪnˈfɝəb|; ES+-ˈfɝəb|
infertile ɪnˈfɝt|, -tɪl; ES -ˈfɜ-, -ˈfɝ-; |-ly -ɪ
infertility ˌɪnfɚˈtɪlətɪ; ES ˌɪnfə-
infest ɪnˈfɛst |-ed -ɪd |-ation ˌɪnfɛsˈteʃən
infidel ˈɪnfəd| |-delity ˌɪnfəˈdɛlətɪ
infield ˈɪnˌfild
infiltrate ɪnˈfɪltret |-d -ɪd
infiltration ˌɪnfɪlˈtreʃən
infinite, I- ˈɪnfənɪt, *worship occas.* -ˌnaɪt
infinitesimal ˌɪnfɪnəˈtɛsəm| |-ly -ɪ
infinitival ɪnˌfɪnəˈtaɪv|, ɪnˌfɪnə- |-ly -ɪ
infinitive ɪnˈfɪnətɪv

|full fʊl |tooth tuθ |further ˈfɝðɚ; ES ˈfɝðə |custom ˈkʌstəm |while hwaɪl |how haʊ |toy tɔɪ |using ˈjuzɪŋ |fuse fjuz, fɪuz |dish dɪʃ |vision ˈvɪʒən |Eden ˈidn̩ |cradle ˈkredl̩ |keep 'em ˈkipm̩

infinitude ɪnˈfɪnəˌtjud, -ˌtɪud, -ˌtud
infinity ɪnˈfɪnətɪ
infirm ɪnˈfɝm; ES -ˈfɝm, -ˈfɝm; |-ary -ərɪ, -rɪ
|-ity -ətɪ
infix *n* ˈɪnˌfɪks |-es -ɪz
infix *v* ɪnˈfɪks |-es -ɪz |-ed -t
inflame ɪnˈflem |-d -d |-dly -ɪdlɪ
inflammability ɪnˌflæməˈbɪlətɪ, ˌɪnflæmə-
inflammable ɪnˈflæməbl̩ |-bly -blɪ
inflammation ˌɪnfləˈmeʃən
inflammatory ɪnˈflæməˌtorɪ, -ˌtɔrɪ; S -ˌtorɪ
inflate ɪnˈflet |-d -ɪd
inflation ɪnˈfleʃən |-ary -ˌɛrɪ |-ism -ˌɪzəm |-ist
-ɪst
inflect ɪnˈflɛkt |-ed -ɪd
inflection ɪnˈflɛkʃən |-al -l̩ |-ally -l̩ɪ
inflexibility ɪnˌflɛksəˈbɪlətɪ, ˌɪnflɛksə-
inflexible ɪnˈflɛksəbl̩ |-bly -blɪ
inflexion ɪnˈflɛkʃən
inflict ɪnˈflɪkt |-ed -ɪd |-ction -kʃən
inflorescence ˌɪnfloˈrɛsn̩s, -flo-; S -flo-; |-s -ɪz
|-cent -sn̩t
inflow *n* ˈɪnˌflo
influence ˈɪnfluəns, -flɪuəns |-s -ɪz |-d -t
influential ˌɪnfluˈɛnʃəl, -flɪu- |-ly -ɪ
influenza ˌɪnfluˈɛnzə, -flɪu-
influx ˈɪnˌflʌks |-es -ɪz
infold ɪnˈfold |-ed -ɪd
inform ɪnˈfɔrm; ES -ˈfɔəm; |-ed -d |-edly -ɪdlɪ
informal ɪnˈfɔrml̩; ES -ˈfɔəml̩; |-ly -ɪ
informality ˌɪnfɔrˈmælətɪ; ES -fɔˈmælətɪ
informant ɪnˈfɔrmənt; ES -ˈfɔəmənt
information ˌɪnfɚˈmeʃən; ES ˌɪnfə-
informative ɪnˈfɔrmətɪv; ES -ˈfɔəmətɪv
infra ˈɪnfrə
infract ɪnˈfrækt |-ed -ɪd
infra dig *short for* infra dignitatem ˈɪnfrə-
ˈdɪg(nɪˈtetɛm)
infrangible ɪnˈfrændʒəbl̩ |-bly -blɪ
infrared ˌɪnfrəˈrɛd
infrequence ɪnˈfrikwəns |-cy -ɪ |-nt -nt
infringe ɪnˈfrɪndʒ |-s -ɪz |-d -d
infundibulum ˌɪnfʌnˈdɪbjələm |-la -lə
infuriate *adj* ɪnˈfjurɪt, -ˈfɪur-
infuriate *v* ɪnˈfjurɪˌet, -ˈfɪur- |-d -ɪd
infuse ɪnˈfjuz, -ˈfɪuz |-s -ɪz |-d -d |-dly -ɪdlɪ
infusible ɪnˈfjuzəbl̩, -ˈfɪuz-
infusion ɪnˈfjuʒən, -ˈfɪuʒən
infusive ɪnˈfjusɪv, -ˈfɪus-

infusoria, I- ˌɪnfjuˈsorɪə, -fɪu-, -ˈsɔrɪə; S
-ˈsorɪə; |-l -l |-n -n
-ing *ending of pres ptc & verbal n, pronounced*
-ɪŋ, -ŋ, -ɪn, -ən, n̩. *Syllabic* -ŋ *frequently*
replaces -ɪŋ *after a* k *or* g *sound, as making*
ˈmekɪŋ, ˈmekŋ, *or dragging* ˈdrægɪŋ,
ˈdrægŋ. *The pronunciation with* -ɪn, -ən
(running ˈrʌnɪn, ˈrʌnən) *or with* -n̩ (getting
ˈgetn̩) *is occasionally heard in the informal*
speech of the cultivated in all parts of the
US & C. It is more frequent in the S, where
it is not infrequently heard also on formal
occasions. In this vocabulary only -ɪŋ *is*
given, and this is usually omitted if the pro-
nunciation can be inferred by adding the
sounds -ɪŋ *directly to the head pronunciation.*
Ingaevones ˌɪndʒɪˈvoniz
ingather ɪnˈgæðɚ; ES -ˈgæðə(r; |-ed -d |-ing
-ˈgæðrɪŋ, -ˈgæðərɪŋ
ingathering *n* ˈɪnˌgæðrɪŋ, -ˌgæðərɪŋ
Inge *Dean of St. Paul's* ɪŋ
Ingelow ˈɪndʒəˌlo
ingeminate ɪnˈdʒɛməˌnet |-d -ɪd
ingenerate *adj* ɪnˈdʒɛnərɪt
ingenerate *v* ɪnˈdʒɛnəˌret |-d -ɪd
ingenious ɪnˈdʒinjəs
ingénue *Fr* æ̃ʒeˈny
ingenuity ˌɪndʒəˈnuətɪ, -ˈnɪu-, -ˈnju-
ingenuous ɪnˈdʒɛnjuəs
Ingersoll ˈɪŋgɚsəl, -ˌsal, -ˌsɒl, -ˌsɔl; ES ˈɪŋgə-
ingest ɪnˈdʒɛst |-ed -ɪd |-gestion -ˈdʒɛstʃən
Ingham ˈɪŋəm
ingle ˈɪŋgl̩ |-nook -ˌnuk
inglobe ɪnˈglob |-d -d
inglorious ɪnˈglorɪəs, -ˈglɔr-; S -ˈglor-
ingoing ˈɪnˌgoɪŋ
Ingold ˈɪŋgold, ˈɪŋgold
Ingoldsby ˈɪŋglzbɪ, ˈɪŋgəldzbɪ
ingot ˈɪŋgət |-ed -ɪd
ingraft ɪnˈgræft; E+-ˈgraft, -ˈgrɑft; |-ed -ɪd
Ingraham ˈɪŋgrɪəm, ˈɪŋgrəhəm
ingrain *n* ˈɪnˌgren
ingrain *adj, v* ɪnˈgren |-ed -d (ˈɪnˌgrein ˈrug)
ingrained *adj* ɪnˈgrend |-nedly -nɪdlɪ, -ndlɪ
Ingram ˈɪŋgrəm
ingrate *n* ˈɪngret
ingratiate ɪnˈgreʃɪˌet |-d -ɪd
ingratiatory ɪnˈgreʃɪəˌtorɪ, -ˌtɔrɪ; S -ˌtorɪ
ingratitude ɪnˈgrætəˌtjud, -ˌtɪud, -ˌtud

Key: See in full §§3–47. bee bi |pity ˈpɪtɪ (§6) |rate ret |yet jɛt |sang sæŋ |angry ˈæŋ·grɪ
|bath bæθ; E baθ (§10) |ah ɑ |far fɑr |watch wɑtʃ, wɒtʃ (§12) |jaw dʒɔ |gorge gɔrdʒ |go go

ingredient ɪnˈgridɪənt
ingress *n* ˈɪngrɛs |-es -ɪz
ingress *v* ɪnˈgrɛs |-es -ɪz |-ed -t
ingression ɪnˈgrɛʃən |-sive -ˈgrɛsɪv
ingrow ˈɪnˌgro |-grew -ˌgru, -ˌgrɪu |-grown
　-ˌgron
ingrown *adj* ˈɪnˈgron (ˈɪnˌgrown ˈhabit)
ingrowth ˈɪnˌgroθ |-ths -θs
inguinal ˈɪŋgwɪnǀ
ingulf ɪnˈgʌlf |-ed -t
ingurgitate ɪnˈgɜˑdʒəˌtet; ES -ˈgɜdʒ-, -ˈgɜˑdʒ-;
　|d -ɪd
inhabit ɪnˈhæbɪt |-ed -ɪd
inhabitability *'habitability'* ɪnˌhæbɪtəˈbɪlətɪ
inhabitability *'nonhabitability'* ˌɪnhæbɪtə-
　ˈbɪlətɪ
inhabitable *'habitable'* ɪnˈhæbɪtəbǀ
inhabitable *'not habitable'* ˈɪnˈhæbɪtəbǀ
inhabitancy ɪnˈhæbətənsɪ |-tant -tənt
inhabitation ɪnˌhæbəˈteʃən
inhalant ɪnˈhelənt
inhale ɪnˈhel |-d -d |-lation ˌɪnhəˈleʃən
inharmonic ˌɪnharˈmɑnɪk; ES -hɑːˈmɑnɪk,
　-ˈmɒn-, E+-hɑː-
inharmonious ˌɪnharˈmonɪəs; ES -hɑˈmon-,
　E+-ha-
inhere ɪnˈhɪr; ES -ˈhɪə(r, S+-ˈhɛə(r; |-d -d
inherence ɪnˈhɪrəns |-cy -ɪ |-nt -nt
inheritable ɪnˈhɛrətəbǀ |-bly -blɪ
inheritance ɪnˈhɛrətəns |-s -ɪz
inheritor ɪnˈhɛrətəˠ; ES -ˈhɛrətə(r; |-tress
　-trɪs |-tress's -trɪsɪz
inheritrix ɪnˈhɛrətrɪks |-es -ɪz
inhibit ɪnˈhɪbɪt |-ed -ɪd
inhibition ˌɪnɪˈbɪʃən, ˌɪnhɪ-
inhibitive ɪnˈhɪbɪtɪv
inhibitory ɪnˈhɪbəˌtorɪ, -ˌtɔrɪ; S -ˌtorɪ
inhospitable ɪnˈhɑspɪtəbǀ; ES+-ˈhɒs-; *much*
　less freq. ˌɪnhosˈpitable |-bly -blɪ
inhospitality ˌɪnhɑspəˈtælətɪ; ES+-hɒs-
inhuman ɪnˈhjumən, -ˈhɪumən, -ˈjumən
inhumane ˌɪnhjuˈmen, -hɪuˈmen, -juˈmen
inhumanity ˌɪnhjuˈmænətɪ, -hɪu-, -juˈmæn-
inhumation ˌɪnhjuˈmeʃən, -hɪu- |-tionist -ɪst
inhume ɪnˈhjum, -ˈhɪum |-d -d
Inigo ˈɪnɪˌgo
inimical ɪnˈɪmɪkǀ |-ly -ɪ, -ɪklɪ
inimitability ɪˌnɪmɪtəˈbɪlətɪ
inimitable ɪnˈɪmətəbǀ |-bly -blɪ

inion ˈɪnɪən
iniquitous ɪˈnɪkwətəs |-ty -tɪ
initial ɪˈnɪʃəl |-ly -ɪ
initiate *n, adj* ɪˈnɪʃɪɪt, -ˌet
initiate *v* ɪˈnɪʃɪˌet |-d -ɪd
initiation ɪˌnɪʃɪˈeʃən
initiative ɪˈnɪʃɪˌetɪv, ɪˈnɪʃɪətɪv
initiatory ɪˈnɪʃɪəˌtorɪ, -ˌtɔrɪ; S -ˌtorɪ
inject ɪnˈdʒɛkt |-ed -ɪd |-ction -kʃən
injector ɪnˈdʒɛktəˠ; ES -ˈdʒɛktə(r
injudicious ˌɪndʒuˈdɪʃəs, -dʒɪu-
injunction ɪnˈdʒʌŋkʃən |tive -tɪv
injure ˈɪndʒəˠ; ES -dʒə(r; |-d -d |-ry -ɪ
injurious ɪnˈdʒurɪəs, -ˈdʒɪu-
injustice ɪnˈdʒʌstɪs |-s -ɪz
ink ɪŋk |-ed -t |-horn -ˌhorn; ES -ˌhɔən
inkling ˈɪŋklɪŋ
inkstand ˈɪŋkˌstænd
inkwell ˈɪŋkˌwɛl
inland *adj* ˈɪnlənd
inland *n, adv* ˈɪnˌlænd, ˈɪnlənd
inlander ˈɪnləndəˠ; ES -də(r
inlaw *n* ˈɪnˌlɔ, *v* ɪnˈlɔ |-ed ɪnˈlɔd
inlay *n* ˈɪnˌle, *v* ɪnˈle |-laid ɪnˈled
inlet *n* ˈɪnˌlɛt, *v* ɪnˈlɛt
inly ˈɪnlɪ
inmate ˈɪnmet
in medias res ɪn ˈmidɪˌæs ˈriz
in memoriam ˌɪnməˈmorɪˌæm, -ˈmɔrɪ-, -ˌɑn.
　S -ˈmorɪ-
inmost ˈɪnˌmost, -məst
inn ɪn |inned ɪnd
innate ɪˈnet, ɪnˈnet (ˈɪnˌnate ˈpoise)
inner ˈɪnəˠ; ES ˈɪnə(r; |-most -ˌmost, -məst
innervate ɪˈnɜˑvet, ˈɪnəˠˌvet; ES ɪˈnɜv-, ɪˈnɜˑv-,
　ˈɪnə-; |-d -d
innervation ˌɪnəˠˈveʃən; ES ˌɪnə-
innerve ɪˈnɜˑv, ɪnˈnɜˑv; ES -ˈnɜv, -ˈnɜˑv;
　|-d -d
Innes, Inness ˈɪnɪs |-'s -ɪz
innholder ˈɪnˌholdəˠ; ES -ˌholdə(r
inning ˈɪnɪŋ
innkeeper ˈɪnˌkipəˠ; ES -ˌkipə(r
innocence ˈɪnəsn̩s |-cy -ɪ |-cent -sn̩t
innocuous ɪˈnɑkjuəs; ES+-ˈnɒk-
innominate *adj* ɪˈnɑmənɪt, ɪnˈn-; ES+-ˈnɒm-
innovate ˈɪnəˌvet |-d -ɪd |-tion ˌɪnəˈveʃən
innoxious ɪˈnɑkʃəs, ɪnˈn-; ES+-ˈnɒk-
Innsbruck ˈɪnzbruk (*Ger* ˈɪnsbruk)

ǀfull fʊl ǀtooth tuθ ǀfurther ˈfɜˑðəˠ; ES ˈfɜˑðə ǀcustom ˈkʌstəm ǀwhile hwaɪl ǀhow haʊ ǀtoy tɔɪ
ǀusing ˈjuzɪŋ ǀfuse fjuz, fɪuz ǀdish dɪʃ ǀvision ˈvɪʒən ǀEden ˈidn̩ ǀcradle ˈkredǀ ǀkeep 'em ˈkipm̩

innuendo ˌɪnjuˈɛndo

innumerable ɪˈnjumərəbl̩, ɪnˈn-, -ˈnɪum-, -ˈnum- |-bly -blɪ

innumerous ɪnˈnjumərəs, -ˈnɪum-, -ˈnum-

innutrition ˌɪnjuˈtrɪʃən, ˌɪnnju-, -nɪu-, -nu- |-tious -ʃəs

inobservance ˌɪnəbˈzɝvəns; ES -ˈzɝv-, -ˈzɝv-; |-nt -nt

inoculable ɪnˈakjələbl̩; ES+-ˈɒk-

inoculate ɪnˈakjəˌlet; ES+-ˈɒk-; |-d -ɪd

inoculation ɪnˌakjəˈleʃən; ES+-ˌɒk-

inodorous ɪnˈodərəs

inoffensive ˌɪnəˈfɛnsɪv

inofficious ˌɪnəˈfɪʃəs

inoperable ɪnˈapərəbl̩; ES+-ˈɒp-

inoperative ɪnˈapəˌretɪv, -ˈapərətɪv, -ˈaprətɪv; ES+-ˈɒp-

inopportune ˌɪnapɚˈtjun, ɪnˌap-, -ˈtɪun, -ˈtun; ES+-ɒp-, -ˌɒp-

inordinate ɪnˈɔrdn̩ɪt; ES -ˈɔədn̩ɪt

inorganic ˌɪnɔrˈgænɪk; ES -ɔəˈgæn-; |-al -l̩ |-ally -l̩ɪ, -ɪklɪ

inosculate ɪnˈaskjəˌlet; ES+-ˈɒs-; |-d -ɪd

inositol ɪˈnɒsɪˌtol

inpatient ˈɪnˌpeʃənt

inphase adj ˈɪnˌfez

inpour n ˈɪnˌpor, -ˌpɔr, -ˌpur; ES -ˌpoə(r, -ˌpuə(r, E+-ˌpɔə(r

inpour v ɪnˈpor, -ˈpɔr-, -ˈpur; ES -ˈpoə(r, -ˈpuə(r, E+-ˈpɔə(r; |-ed -d

input ˈɪnˌput

inquest ˈɪnkwɛst

inquiet ɪnˈkwaɪət

inquietude ɪnˈkwaɪəˌtjud, -ˌtɪud, -ˌtud

inquire ɪnˈkwaɪr; ES -ˈkwaɪə(r; |-d -d

inquiry ɪnˈkwaɪrɪ, ˈɪnkwərɪ

inquisition ˌɪnkwəˈzɪʃən

inquisitive ɪnˈkwɪzətɪv |-tor -tɚ; ES -tə(r

inquisitorial ɪnˌkwɪzəˈtorɪəl, ˌɪnkwɪzə-, -ˈtɔr-; S -ˈtor-

in re ɪnˈri

inroad ˈɪnˌrod

inrush n ˈɪnˌrʌʃ |-es -ɪz

inrush v ɪnˈrʌʃ |-es -ɪz |-ed -t

insalivate ɪnˈsæləˌvet |-d -ɪd

insalubrious ˌɪnsəˈlubrɪəs, -ˈlɪub- |-brity -brətɪ

insane ɪnˈsen (ˈɪnˌsane ˈroot)

insanitary ɪnˈsænəˌtɛrɪ

insanity ɪnˈsænətɪ

insatiability ɪnˌseʃɪəˈbɪlətɪ, -ˌseʃə-, ˌɪnseʃ-

insatiable ɪnˈseʃɪəbl̩, -ˈseʃə- |-bly -blɪ

insatiate ɪnˈseʃɪt |-ated -ˌetɪd

inscribe ɪnˈskraɪb |-d -d

inscription ɪnˈskrɪpʃən

inscroll ɪnˈskrol |-ed -d

inscrutability ɪnˌskrutəˈbɪlətɪ, -ˌskrɪut-, ˌɪnskr-

inscrutable ɪnˈskrutəbl̩, -ˈskrɪut- |-bly -blɪ

insculp ɪnˈskʌlp |-ed -t |-ture -tʃɚ; ES -tʃə(r

insect ˈɪnsɛkt

insectarium ˌɪnsɛkˈtɛrɪəm, -ˈter-

insectary ˈɪnsɛkˌtɛrɪ

insecticide ɪnˈsɛktəˌsaɪd |-dal -ˌsɛktəˈsaɪdl̩

insectival ˌɪnsɛkˈtaɪvl̩, ɪnˈsɛktəvl̩

insectivore ɪnˈsɛktəˌvor, -ˌvɔr; ES -ˌvoə(r, E+-ˌvɔə(r

insectivorous ˌɪnsɛkˈtɪvərəs, -ˈtɪvrəs

insecure ˌɪnsɪˈkjur, -ˈkɪur; ES -ə(r

insecurity ˌɪnsɪˈkjurətɪ, -ˈkɪurətɪ

inseminate ɪnˈsɛməˌnet |-d -ɪd

insemination ɪnˌsɛməˈneʃən, ˌɪnsɛmə-

insensate ɪnˈsɛnset, -sɪt

insensibility ˌɪnsɛnsəˈbɪlətɪ, ɪnˌsɛnsə-

insensible ɪnˈsɛnsəbl̩ |-bly -blɪ

insensitive ɪnˈsɛnsətɪv

insensitivity ˌɪnsɛnsəˈtɪvətɪ, ɪnˌsɛnsə-

insentient ɪnˈsɛnʃɪənt, -ʃənt

inseparability ˌɪnsɛpərəˈbɪlətɪ, ɪnˌsɛpərə-, -prə-

inseparable ɪnˈsɛpərəbl̩, -prə- |-bly -blɪ

insert n ˈɪnsɝt; ES -ˈsɝt, -sɝt

insert v ɪnˈsɝt; ES -ˈsɝt, -ˈsɝt; |-ed -ɪd

insertion ɪnˈsɝʃən; ES -ˈsɝʃən, -ˈsɝʃən

inset n ˈɪnˌsɛt, v ɪnˈsɛt

insheathe ɪnˈʃið |-d -d

inshore adj ˈɪnˌʃor, -ˌʃɔr; ES -ˌʃoə(r, E+-ˌʃɔə(r; adv ˈɪnˈshore

inside n, adj ˈɪnˈsaɪd (ˈɪnˌside ˈdoor)

inside adv ˈɪnˈsaɪd (ˈɪnˌside & ˈoutˌside)

inside prep ɪnˈsaɪd

insider ɪnˈsaɪdɚ; ES -ˈsaɪdə(r

insidious ɪnˈsɪdɪəs

insight ˈɪnˌsaɪt

insignia ɪnˈsɪgnɪə

insignificance ˌɪnsɪgˈnɪfəkəns |-cant -kənt

insincere ˌɪnsɪnˈsɪr; ES -ˈsɪə(r, S+-ˈsɛə(r

insincerity ˌɪnsɪnˈsɛrətɪ

Key: See in full §§3–47. bee bi |pity ˈpɪtɪ (§6) |rate ret |yet jɛt |sang sæŋ |angry ˈæŋ·grɪ |bath bæθ; E baθ (§10) |ah ɑ |far fɑr |watch watʃ, wɒtʃ (§12) |jaw dʒɔ |gorge gɔrdʒ |go go

insinuate ɪnˈsɪnjʊˌet |-d -ɪd
insinuation ɪnˌsɪnjʊˈeʃən
insipid ɪnˈsɪpɪd |-ity ˌɪnsɪˈpɪdətɪ
insipience ɪnˈsɪpɪəns |-ent -ənt
insist ɪnˈsɪst |-ed -ɪd
insistence ɪnˈsɪstəns |-cy -ɪ |-ent -ənt
in situ ɪnˈsaɪtju, -tɪu-, -tu
insnare ɪnˈsnɛr, -ˈsnær; E -ˈsnɛə(r, ES
  -ˈsnæə(r; |-d -d
insobriety ˌɪnsəˈbraɪətɪ, ˌɪnso-
insociability ˌɪnsoʃəˈbɪlətɪ, ɪnˌsoʃə-
insociable ɪnˈsoʃəb] |-bly -blɪ
insolate ˈɪnsoˌlet |-d -ɪd
insolation ˌɪnsoˈleʃən
insole ˈɪnˌsol |-d -d
insolence ˈɪnsələns |-s -ɪz |-cy -ɪ |-nt -nt
insolubility ˌɪnsaljəˈbɪlətɪ; ES+-sɒl-
insoluble ɪnˈsaljəb]; ES+-ˈsɒl-; |-bly -blɪ
insolvable ɪnˈsalvəb], -ˈsɒlv- |-bly -blɪ
insolvency ɪnˈsalvənsɪ, -ˈsɒlv- |-vent -vənt
insomnia ɪnˈsamnɪə; ES+-ˈsɒm-
insomuch ˌɪnsəˈmʌtʃ, -so-
insouciance ɪnˈsusɪəns (Fr ɛ̃suˈsjɑ̃:s)
insouciant ɪnˈsusɪənt (Fr ɛ̃suˈsjɑ̃)
inspan ɪnˈspæn |-ned -d
inspect ɪnˈspɛkt |-ed -ɪd |-ction -kʃən
inspector ɪnˈspɛktɚ; ES -ˈspɛktə(r; |-ate -ɪt
insphere ɪnˈsfɪr; ES -ˈsfɪə(r, S+-ˈsfɛə(r
inspirable ɪnˈspaɪrəb]
inspiration ˌɪnspəˈreʃən |-al -] |-ally -ļɪ
inspiratory ɪnˈspaɪrəˌtorɪ, -ˌtɔrɪ; S -ˌtorɪ
inspire ɪnˈspaɪr; ES -ˈspaɪə(r; |-d -d |-dly
  -ɪdlɪ
inspirit ɪnˈspɪrɪt |-ed -ɪd
inspissate ɪnˈspɪset |-d -ɪd
instability ˌɪnstəˈbɪlətɪ
install ɪnˈstɔl |-ed -d
installation ˌɪnstəˈleʃən
installment, -stalm- ɪnˈstɔlmənt
instance ˈɪnstəns |-s -ɪz |-d -t |-stant -stənt
instantaneous ˌɪnstənˈtenɪəs
instanter ɪnˈstæntɚ; ES -ˈstæntə(r
instar n ˈɪnstar; ES -stɑ:(r, E+-stɑ:(r
instar v ɪnˈstar; ES -ˈstɑ:(r, E+-ˈstɑ:(r;
  |-red -d
instate ɪnˈstet |-d -ɪd
in statu quo ɪnˈstetjuˈkwo, -ˈstætʃu-
instaurate ɪnˈstɔret |-d -ɪd
instauration ˌɪnstɔˈreʃən

instead ɪnˈstɛd—The historical doublet ɪnˈstɪd
  is frequently heard.
instep ˈɪnˌstɛp
instigate ˈɪnstəˌget |-d -ɪd |-tor -ɚ; ES -ə(r
instigation ˌɪnstəˈgeʃən
instill, -il ɪnˈstɪl |-ed, -led -d
instillation ˌɪnstɪˈleʃən
instinct n ˈɪnstɪŋkt
instinct adj ɪnˈstɪŋkt |-ive -ɪv
institute ˈɪnstəˌtjut, -ˌtrut-, -ˌtut |-d -ɪd
institution ˌɪnstəˈtjuʃən, -ˈtɪu-, -ˈtu- |-ary
  -ˌɛrɪ
institutionalize ˌɪnstəˈtjuʃənļˌaɪz, -ʃnəl- |-s
  -ɪz |-d -d
institutive ˈɪnstəˌtjutɪv, -ˌtɪu-, -ˌtu-
instruct ɪnˈstrʌkt |-ed -ɪd |-ction -kʃən |-ive
  -ɪv |-or -ɚ; ES -ə(r
instrument ˈɪnstrəmənt
instrumental ˌɪnstrəˈmɛntļ |-ist -ɪst |-ly -ɪ
instrumentality ˌɪnstrəmɛnˈtælətɪ
instrumentation ˌɪnstrəmɛnˈteʃən
insubordinate ˌɪnsəˈbɔrdņɪt; -dnɪt; ES -ˈbɔəd-
insubordination ˌɪnsəˌbɔrdņˈeʃən; ES -ˌbɔəd-
insubstantial ˌɪnsəbˈstænʃəl
insubstantiality ˌɪnsəbˌstænʃɪˈælətɪ
insufferable ɪnˈsʌfrəb], -fərə- |-bly -blɪ
insufficience ˌɪnsəˈfɪʃəns |-cy -ɪ |-ent -ənt
insufflate ɪnˈsʌflet, ˈɪnsəˌflet |-d -ɪd
insufflation ˌɪnsəˈfleʃən
insular ˈɪnsələ, ˈɪnsjʊ-; ES -lə(r
insularity ˌɪnsəˈlærətɪ, ˌɪnsjʊ-
insulate ˈɪnsəˌlet, ˈɪnsjʊ- |-tor -ɚ; ES -ə(r
insulation ˌɪnsəˈleʃən, -sjʊ-
insulin ˈɪnsəlɪn, -sjʊ-
insulize ˈɪnsəˌlaɪz, -sjʊ- |-s -ɪz |-d -d
insult n ˈɪnsʌlt, v ɪnˈsʌlt |-ed ɪnˈsʌltɪd
insuperability ɪnˌsupərəˈbɪlətɪ, -ˌsɪu-, -ˌsju-,
  ˌɪns-
insuperable ɪnˈsupərəb], -ˈsɪu-, -ˈsju- |-bly
  -blɪ
insupportable ˌɪnsəˈportəb], -ˈpɔrt-; ES
  -ˈpoət-, E+-ˈpɔət-; |-bly -blɪ
insuppressible ˌɪnsəˈprɛsəb] |-bly -blɪ
insurable ɪnˈʃʊrəb] |-ability ɪnˌʃʊrəˈbɪlətɪ
insurance ɪnˈʃʊrəns |-s -ɪz
insure ɪnˈʃʊr; ES -ˈʃʊə(r; |-d -d
insurer ɪnˈʃʊrɚ; ES -rə(r
insurgence ɪnˈsɝdʒəns; ES -ˈsɜdʒ-, -ˈsɝdʒ-;
  |-cy -ɪ |-ent -ənt

insurmountable ˌɪnsɚˈmaʊntəbl̩; ES -sə-;
|-bly -blɪ
insurrection ˌɪnsəˈrɛkʃən |-ary -ˌɛrɪ
insusceptibility ˌɪnsəˌsɛptəˈbɪlətɪ
insusceptible ˌɪnsəˈsɛptəbl̩ |-bly -blɪ
inswathe ɪnˈsweð |-d -d
inswept ˈɪnˌswɛpt
intact ɪnˈtækt
intaglio ɪnˈtæljo, -ˈtaljo (It inˈtaʎʎo)
intake ˈɪnˌtek
intangible ɪnˈtændʒəbl̩ |-bly -blɪ
integer ˈɪntədʒɚ; ES -dʒə(r
integral ˈɪntəgrəl |-ly -ɪ |-grable -grəbl̩
integrality ˌɪntəˈgrælətɪ
integrant ˈɪntəgrənt |-grand -ˌgrænd
integrate ˈɪntəˌgret |-grated -ˌgretɪd
integration ˌɪntəˈgreʃən
integrator ˈɪntəˌgretɚ; ES -ˌgretə(r
integrity ɪnˈtɛgrətɪ
integument n ɪnˈtɛgjəmənt
integument v ɪnˈtɛgjəˌmɛnt |-ed -ɪd
intellect ˈɪntl̩ˌɛkt
intellection ˌɪntl̩ˈɛkʃən |-tive -tɪv
intellectual ˌɪntl̩ˈɛktʃʊəl, -tʃʊl |-ly -ɪ |-ism
-ˌɪzəm |-ist -ɪst
intellectuality ˌɪntl̩ˌɛktʃʊˈælətɪ
intellectualize ˌɪntl̩ˈɛktʃʊəlˌaɪz, -tʃʊl- |-s -ɪz
|-d -d
intelligence ɪnˈtɛlədʒəns |-s -ɪz |-d -t
intelligent ɪnˈtɛlədʒənt
intelligential ɪnˌtɛləˈdʒɛnʃəl
intelligentsia ɪnˌtɛləˈdʒɛntsɪə, -ˈgɛntsɪə
intelligibility ɪnˌtɛlɪdʒəˈbɪlətɪ
intelligible ɪnˈtɛlɪdʒəbl̩ |-bly -blɪ
intemperance ɪnˈtɛmpərəns, -prəns
intemperate ɪnˈtɛmpərɪt, -prɪt
intend ɪnˈtɛnd |-ed -ɪd |-ance -əns |-ant -ənt
intense ɪnˈtɛns |-sity -ətɪ |-sive -ɪv
intensification ɪnˌtɛnsəfəˈkeʃən
intensify ɪnˈtɛnsəˌfaɪ |-fied -ˌfaɪd
intension ɪnˈtɛnʃən
intent ɪnˈtɛnt
intention ɪnˈtɛnʃən |-al -l̩, -ʃnəl |-ally -l̩ɪ,
-ʃnəlɪ
inter ɪnˈtɝ; ES -ˈtɜ(r, -ˈtɝ; |-red -d
inter- prefix ˈɪntɚ-; ES ˈɪntə(r-
interact ˌɪntɚˈækt |-ed -ɪd |-ion -kʃən |-ive -ɪv
interblend ˌɪntɚˈblɛnd; ES ˌɪntə-; |-ed -ɪd
interbreed ˌɪntɚˈbrid; ES ˌɪntə-; |-bred -ˈbrɛd

intercalary ɪnˈtɝkəˌlɛrɪ; ES -ˈtɜk-, -ˈtɝk-
intercalate ɪnˈtɝkəˌlet; ES -ˈtɜk-, -ˈtɝk-; |-d
-ɪd |-tive -ɪv
intercalation ɪnˌtɝkəˈleʃən; ES -ˌtɜk-, -ˌtɝk-
intercede ˌɪntɚˈsid; ES ˌɪntə-; |-d -ɪd
intercellular ˌɪntɚˈsɛljəlɚ; ES ˌɪntəˈsɛljələ(r
intercept n ˈɪntɚˌsɛpt; ES ˈɪntə-
intercept v ˌɪntɚˈsɛpt; ES ˌɪntə-; |-ed -ɪd
|-ption -pʃən
intercession ˌɪntɚˈsɛʃən; ES ˌɪntə-
intercessory ˌɪntɚˈsɛsərɪ; ES ˌɪntə-
interchange n ˈɪntɚˌtʃendʒ; ES ˈɪntə-; |-s -ɪz
interchange v ˌɪntɚˈtʃendʒ; ES ˌɪntə-; |-s -ɪz
|-d -d
interchangeability ˌɪntɚˌtʃendʒəˈbɪlətɪ; ES
ˌɪntə-
interchangeable ˌɪntɚˈtʃendʒəbl̩; ES ˌɪntə-;
|-bly -blɪ
interclass ˈɪntɚˈklæs; ES ˈɪntə-, E+-ˈklas,
-ˈklɑs; (ˈinterˌclass ˈgame)
intercollegiate ˌɪntɚkəˈlidʒɪɪt, -dʒɪt; ES ˌɪntə-
intercolonial ˌɪntɚkəˈlonɪəl; ES ˌɪntə-; |-ly -ɪ
intercommunicate ˌɪntɚkəˈmjunəˌket, -ˈmɪun-;
ES ˌɪntə-; |-d -ɪd
intercommunication ˌɪntɚkəˌmjunəˈkeʃən,
-ˌmɪun-; ES ˌɪntə-
intercommunion ˌɪntɚkəˈmjunjən, -ˈmɪun-;
ES ˌɪntə-
interconnect ˌɪntɚkəˈnɛkt; ES ˌɪntə-; |-ed -ɪd
interconnection ˌɪntɚkəˈnɛkʃən; ES ˌɪntə-
intercostal ˌɪntɚˈkɑstl̩, -ˈkɒs-, -ˈkɔs-; ES
ˌɪntə-; |-ly -ɪ
intercourse ˈɪntɚˌkors, -ˌkɔrs; ES ˈɪntəˌkoəs,
E+-ˌkɔəs
intercurrent ˌɪntɚˈkɝənt; ES ˌɪntəˈkɜr-,
-ˈkʌr-, -ˈkɝ-
interdenominational ˌɪntɚdɪˌnɑməˈneʃən l̩,
-ʃnəl; ES ˌɪntədɪˌnɑmə-, -ˌnɒmə-
interdental ˌɪntɚˈdɛntl̩; ES ˌɪntə-; |-ly -ɪ
interdepartmental ˌɪntɚdɪˌpɑrtˈmɛntl̩, -ˌdi-
pɑrt-; ES ˌɪntədɪˌpɑt-, -ˌdipɑt-, E+-ˌpɑt-,
-pɑːt-; |-ly -ɪ
interdependence ˌɪntɚdɪˈpɛndəns; ES ˌɪntə-;
|-ent -ənt
interdict n ˈɪntɚˌdɪkt; ES ˈɪntə-
interdict v ˌɪntɚˈdɪkt; ES ˌɪntə-; |-ed -ɪd
interdiction ˌɪntɚˈdɪkʃən; ES ˌɪntə-
interest n ˈɪntərɪst, ˈɪntrɪst
interest v ˈɪntərɪst, ˈɪntrɪst, ˈɪntəˌrɛst

interested 'ɪntərɪstɪd, -rəs-, 'ɪntrɪstɪd, -trəs-, 'ɪntəˌrɛstɪd

interesting 'ɪntərɪstɪŋ, -rəs-, 'ɪntrɪstɪŋ, -trəs-, 'ɪntəˌrɛstɪŋ—*The former pron.* ˌɪntə'rɛstɪd, -ɪŋ, *is now somewhat old-fashioned (though still heard both in America and England), but* 'ɪntəˌrɛstɪd, -ɪŋ *are still in excellent use, esp. in England.*

interfere ˌɪntə'fɪr; ES ˌɪntə'fɪə(r, S+-'fɛə(r; |-d -d |-nce -əns |-nces -ənsɪz

interferometer ˌɪntəfɪ'ramətə; ES ˌɪntəfɪ-'ramətə(r, -'rɒm-

interfuse ˌɪntə'fjuz, -'fɪuz; ES ˌɪntə-; |-s -ɪz |-d -d |-sion -ʒən

interglacial ˌɪntə'gleʃəl; ES ˌɪntə-

intergrade *n* 'ɪntəˌgred; ES 'ɪntə-

intergrade *v* ˌɪntə'gred; ES ˌɪntə-; |-d -ɪd

interim 'ɪntərɪm

interior ɪn'tɪrɪə; ES -'tɪrɪ·ə(r

interiority ɪnˌtɪrɪ'ɒrətɪ, -'ɑr-, -'ɒr-

interject ˌɪntə'dʒəkt; ES ˌɪntə-; |-ed -ɪd

interjection ˌɪntə'dʒɛkʃən; ES ˌɪntə-; |-al -ḷ |-ally -ḷɪ |-tory -tərɪ

interknit ˌɪntə'nɪt; ES ˌɪntə-; |*past & pptc* -knit -'nɪt *or* -knitted -'nɪtɪd

interlace ˌɪntə'les; ES ˌɪntə-; |-s -ɪz |-d -t

Interlaken 'ɪntəˌlakən; ES 'ɪntə-

interlard ˌɪntə'lard; ES ˌɪntə'lɑːd, E+-'lɑːd; |-ed -ɪd

interlay *n* 'ɪntəˌle; ES 'ɪntə-

interlay *v* ˌɪntə'le; ES ˌɪntə-; |-laid -'led

interleaf *n* 'ɪntəˌlif; ES 'ɪntə-; |-leaves -vz

interleaf *v* ˌɪntə'lif; ES ˌɪntə-; |-s -s |-ed -t

interleave *v* ˌɪntə'liv; ES ˌɪntə-; |-s -z |d -d

interline *n* 'ɪntəˌlaɪn; ES 'ɪntə-

interline *v* ˌɪntə'laɪn; ES ˌɪntə-; |d -d

interlineal ˌɪntə'lɪnɪəl; ES ˌɪntə-; |-ly -ɪ

interlinear ˌɪntə'lɪnɪə; ES ˌɪntə'lɪnɪ·ə(r

interlineate ˌɪntə'lɪnɪˌet; ES ˌɪntə-; |-d -ɪd

interlineation ˌɪntəˌlɪnɪ'eʃən; ES ˌɪntə-

interlink *n* 'ɪntəˌlɪŋk; ES 'ɪntə-

interlink *v* ˌɪntə'lɪŋk; ES ˌɪntə-; |-ed -t

interlocate ˌɪntə'loket; ES ˌɪntə-; |-d -ɪd

interlock *n* 'ɪntəˌlak; ES 'ɪntəˌlak, -ˌlɒk

interlock *v* ˌɪntə'lak; ES ˌɪntə'lak, -'lɒk; |-ed -t

interlocution ˌɪntələ'kjuʃən, -'kɪu-; ES ˌɪntə-

interlocutor ˌɪntə'lakjətə; ES ˌɪntə'lakjətə(r, -'lɒk-; |-tory -ˌtorɪ, -ˌtɔrɪ; S -ˌtorɪ

interlope ˌɪntə'lop; ES ˌɪntə-; |-d -t |-r -ə; ES -ə(r; *acct+*'ɪntəˌloper

interlude 'ɪntəˌlud, -ˌlɪud; ES 'ɪntə-

interlunar ˌɪntə'lunə, -'lɪunə; ES ˌɪntə-'lunə(r, -'lɪu-

intermarriage ˌɪntə'mærɪdʒ; ES ˌɪntə-; |-s -ɪz

intermarry ˌɪntə'mærɪ; ES ˌɪntə-; |-ied -d

intermeddle ˌɪntə'mɛdḷ; ES ˌɪntə-; |-d -d |-ling -'mɛdlɪŋ, -'mɛdḷɪŋ

intermediacy ˌɪntə'midɪəsɪ; ES ˌɪntə-

intermediary ˌɪntə'midɪˌɛrɪ; ES ˌɪntə-

intermediate *adj* ˌɪntə'midɪɪt; ES ˌɪntə-

intermediate *v* ˌɪntə'midɪˌet; ES ˌɪntə-; |-d -ɪd

interment ɪn'tɜmənt; ES -'tɜ-, -'tɜ-

intermezzo ˌɪntə'mɛtso, -'mɛdzo; ES ˌɪntə-; (*It* ˌɪntər'mɛddzo)

interminable ɪn'tɜmɪnəbḷ; ES -'tɜm-, -'tɜm-; |-bly -blɪ

intermingle ˌɪntə'mɪŋgḷ; ES ˌɪntə-; |-d -d |-ling -'mɪŋglɪŋ, -gḷɪŋ

intermission ˌɪntə'mɪʃən; ES ˌɪntə-

intermit ˌɪntə'mɪt; ES ˌɪntə-; |-ted -ɪd |-tent -ṇt

intermix ˌɪntə'mɪks; ES ˌɪntə-; |-es -ɪz |-ed -t |-ture -tʃə; ES -tʃə(r

intern, -e *adj* ɪn'tɜn; ES -'tɜn, -'tɜn

intern, -e *n* 'ɪntɜn; ES -tɜn, -tɜn

intern *v* 'segregate' ɪn'tɜn; ES -'tɜn, -'tɜn; |-ed -d

intern *v* 'act as intern' 'ɪntɜn; ES -tɜn, -tɜn; |-ed -d

internal ɪn'tɜnḷ; ES -'tɜnḷ, -'tɜnḷ; |-ly -ɪ

internal-combustion ɪn'tɜnḷkəm'bʌstʃən; ES -'tɜnḷ-, -'tɜnḷ-; |*acct+*'internal-

internality ˌɪntə'nælətɪ; ES ˌɪntə-

international, I- ˌɪntə'næʃənḷ, -ʃnəl; ES ˌɪntə-; |-ly -ɪ |-ism -ˌɪzəm |-ist -ɪst

internationalization ˌɪntəˌnæʃənḷə'zeʃən, -ʃnələ-, -aɪ'z-; ES ˌɪntə-

internationalize ˌɪntə'næʃənḷˌaɪz, -ʃnəl-; ES ˌɪntə-; |-s -ɪz |-d -d

internecine ˌɪntə'nisɪn, -saɪn; ES ˌɪntə-

internment ɪn'tɜnmənt; ES -'tɜn-, -'tɜn-

internship, -terne- 'ɪntɜnˌʃɪp, ɪn'tɜnʃɪp; ES -ɜn-, -ɜn-

internuncio ˌɪntə'nʌnʃɪˌo; ES ˌɪntə-

interoceanic ˌɪntəˌoʃɪ'ænɪk; ES ˌɪntə-

interpellant ˌɪntə'pɛlənt; ES ˌɪntə-

|full fʊl |tooth tuθ |further 'fɜðə; ES 'fɜðə |custom 'kʌstəm |while hwaɪl |how haʊ |toy tɔɪ |using 'juzɪŋ |fuse fjuz, fɪuz |dish dɪʃ |vision 'vɪʒən |Eden 'idṇ |cradle 'kredḷ |keep 'em 'kipṃ

interpellate ˌɪntɚˈpɛlet, ɪnˈtɝpɪˌlet; ES ˌɪntə-, -ˈtɝ-, -ˈtɝ-; |-d -ɪd
interpellation ˌɪntɚpɛˈleʃən, ɪnˌtɝpɪˈleʃən; ES ˌɪntə-, -ˌtɝ-, -ˌtɝ-
interpellator ˌɪntɚpɛˈletɚ, ɪnˈtɝpɪˌletɚ; ES ˌɪntəpɛˈletə(r, ɪnˈtɝpɪˌletə(r, -ˈtɝpɪˌletə(r
interpenetrate ˌɪntɚˈpɛnəˌtret; ES ˌɪntə-; |-d -ɪd
interpenetration ˌɪntɚˌpɛnəˈtreʃən; ES ˌɪntə-
interplanetary ˌɪntɚˈplænəˌtɛrɪ; ES ˌɪntə-
interplay n ˈɪntɚˌple; ES ˌɪntə-
interplay v ˌɪntɚˈple; ES ˌɪntə-; |-ed -d
interplead ˌɪntɚˈplid; ES ˌɪntə-; |-ed -ɪd or -plead, -pled -ˈplɛd
interpolate ɪnˈtɝpəˌlet; ES -ˈtɝ-, -ˈtɝ-; |-d -ɪd |-tor -ɚ; ES -ə(r
interpolation ɪnˌtɝpəˈleʃən; ES -ˌtɝ-, -ˌtɝ-
interposal ˌɪntɚˈpozˌ; ES ˌɪntə-
interpose ˌɪntɚˈpoz; ES ˌɪntə-; |-s -ɪz |-d -d
interposition ˌɪntɚpəˈzɪʃən; ES ˌɪntə-
interpret ɪnˈtɝprɪt; ES -ˈtɝp-, -ˈtɝp-; |-ed -ɪd
—The occasional pron. ɪnˈtɝpɪt is due to dissimilation (§121).
interpretability ɪnˌtɝprɪtəˈbɪlətɪ; ES -ˌtɝp-, -ˌtɝp-
interpretation ɪnˌtɝprɪˈteʃən; ES -ˌtɝp-, -ˌtɝp-
interpretative ɪnˈtɝprɪˌtetɪv; ES -ˈtɝp-, -ˈtɝp-
interpretive ɪnˈtɝprɪtɪv; ES -ˈtɝp-, -ˈtɝp-
interracial ˌɪntɚˈreʃəl, -ˈʃɪəl; ES ˌɪntə-
interregnum ˌɪntɚˈrɛgnəm; ES ˌɪntə-; |-s -z |-na -nə
interrelate ˌɪntɚrɪˈlet; ES ˌɪntə-; |-d -ɪd |-tion -ˈleʃən
interrenal ˌɪntɚˈrinˌ; ES ˌɪntə-
interrex ˈɪntɚˌrɛks; ES ˈɪntə-; |-reges ˌɪntɚˈridʒiz; ES ˌɪntə-
interrogate ɪnˈtɛrəˌget |-d -ɪd |-tor -ɚ; ES -ə(r
interrogation ɪnˌtɛrəˈgeʃən |-al -ˌ
interrogative ˌɪntəˈrɑgətɪv, -ˈrɒg- |-tory -ˌtorɪ, -ˌtɔrɪ; S -ˌtorɪ
interrupt ˌɪntəˈrʌpt |-ed -ɪd |-ption -pʃən
interscholastic ˌɪntɚskəˈlæstɪk, -skɒ-; ES ˌɪntə-
intersect ˌɪntɚˈsɛkt; ES ˌɪntə-; |-ed -ɪd |-ction -kʃən
interspace n ˈɪntɚˌspes; ES ˈɪntə-; |-s -ɪz
interspace v ˌɪntɚˈspes; ES ˌɪntə-; |-s -ɪz |-d -t

interspatial ˌɪntɚˈspeʃəl; ES ˌɪntə-; |-ly -ɪ
intersperse ˌɪntɚˈspɝs; ES ˌɪntəˈspɝs, -ˈspɝs; |-s -ɪz |-d -t |-dly -ɪdlɪ |-sion -ʃən, -ʒən
interstate ˌɪntɚˈstet; ES ˌɪntə-; (ˈinterˌstate ˈact)
interstellar ˌɪntɚˈstɛlɚ; ES ˌɪntəˈstɛlə(r
interstice ɪnˈtɝstɪs; ES -ˈtɝs-, -ˈtɝs-; |-s -ɪz |-d -t
interstitial ˌɪntɚˈstɪʃəl; ES ˌɪntə-; |-ly -ɪ
intertribal ˌɪntɚˈtraɪbˌ; ES ˌɪntə-
intertwine n ˈɪntɚˌtwaɪn; ES ˈɪntə-
intertwine v ˌɪntɚˈtwaɪn; ES ˌɪntə-; |-d -d
intertwist n ˈɪntɚˌtwɪst; ES ˈɪntə-
intertwist v ˌɪntɚˈtwɪst; ES ˌɪntə-; |-ed -ɪd
interurban ˌɪntɚˈɝbən; ES ˌɪntɚˈɝbən, -ˈɝb-
interval ˈɪntɚvˌ; ES ˈɪntə-; |-ed -d
intervale ˈɪntɚˌvel, attrib.+-vˌ, -vɪl; ES ˈɪntə-
intervene ˌɪntɚˈvin; ES ˌɪntə-; |-d -d
intervenience ˌɪntɚˈvinjəns; ES ˌɪntə-; |-cy -ɪ |-ient -jənt
intervention ˌɪntɚˈvɛnʃən; ES ˌɪntə-; |-al -ˌ |-ism -ˌɪzəm |-ist -ɪst
interview ˈɪntɚˌvju, -ˌvɪu; ES ˈɪntə-; |-ed -d
intervocal ˌɪntɚˈvokˌ; ES ˌɪntə-; |-ly -ɪ
intervocalic ˌɪntɚvoˈkælɪk; ES ˌɪntə-; |-ally -ˌɪ, -ɪklɪ
interweave ˌɪntɚˈwiv; ES ˌɪntə-; |-wove -ˈwov |-woven -ˈwovən or -wove -ˈwov
intestate ɪnˈtɛstet, -tɪt |-tacy -təsɪ
intestine ɪnˈtɛstɪn |-nal -ˌ |-nally -ˌɪ (BBC ˌɪntɛsˈtaɪn])
inthrall, -al ɪnˈθrɔl |-(l)ed -d
inthrone ɪnˈθron |-d -d
intimate adj ˈɪntəmɪt |-macy -məsɪ
intimate v ˈɪntəˌmet |-d -ɪd |-tion ˌɪntəˈmeʃən
intimidate ɪnˈtɪməˌdet |-d -ɪd
intimidation ɪnˌtɪməˈdeʃən
intitle ɪnˈtaɪtˌ |-d -d |-ling -tˌɪŋ, -tlɪŋ
intitule ɪnˈtɪtjul |-d -d
into before vowel ˈɪntu, ˈɪntə; before cons. ˈɪntə; before pause ˈɪntu; in poetry often ɪnˈtu
intolerability ɪnˌtɑlərəˈbɪlətɪ; ES+-ˌtɒl-
intolerable ɪnˈtɑlərəbˌ; ES+-ˈtɒl-; |-bly -blɪ
intolerance ɪnˈtɑlərəns; ES+-ˈtɒl-; |-ant -ənt
intomb ɪnˈtum |-ed -d |-ment ɪnˈtummənt
intonate ˈɪntoˌnet |-nated -ˌnetɪd
intone ɪnˈton |-d -d |-nation ˌɪntoˈneʃən
intorsion ɪnˈtɔrʃən; ES -ˈtɔəʃən
intort ɪnˈtɔrt; ES -ˈtɔət; |-ed -ɪd

Key: See in full §§3–47. bee bi |pity ˈpɪtɪ (§6) |rate ret |yet jɛt |sang sæŋ |angry ˈæŋ·grɪ |bath bæθ; E baθ (§10) |ah ɑ |far fɑr |watch wɑtʃ, wɒtʃ (§12) |jaw dʒɔ |gorge gɔrdʒ |go go

in toto ɪn'toto
intoxicant ɪn'tɑksəkənt; ES+-'tɒks-
intoxicate ɪn'tɑksə,ket; ES+-'tɒks-; |-tive
-ɪv
intoxication ɪn,tɑksə'keʃən; ES+-,tɒks-
intra 'ɪntrə
intracellular ,ɪntrə'sɛljələ; ES -lə(r
intracollegiate ,ɪntrəkə'lidʒɪɪt, -dʒɪt
intractability ,ɪntræktə'bɪlətɪ, ɪn,træktə-
intractable ɪn'træktəb| |-bly -blɪ
intractile ɪn'trækt|, -tɪl
intrados ɪn'tredɑs; ES+-dɒs; |-es -ɪz
intramolecular ,ɪntrəmə'lɛkjələ; ES -lə(r
intramural ,ɪntrə'mjʊrəl, -'mɪʊrəl
intramuscular ,ɪntrə'mʌskjələ; ES -lə(r
intransigence ɪn'trænsədʒəns |-cy -ɪ |-ent -ənt
intransitive ɪn'trænsətɪv
intrant 'ɪntrənt
intrastate ,ɪntrə'stet ('intra,state 'trade)
intravenous ,ɪntrə'vinəs
intreat ɪn'trit |-ed -ɪd
intrench ɪn'trɛntʃ |-es -ɪz |-ed -t
intrepid ɪn'trɛpɪd |-pidity ,ɪntrə'pɪdətɪ
intricate 'ɪntrəkɪt |-cacy -kəsɪ
intrigue n ɪn'trig, 'ɪntrig
intrigue v ɪn'trig |-d -d
intrinsic ɪn'trɪnsɪk |-al -| |-ally |ɪ, -ɪklɪ
intrinsicate ɪn'trɪnsɪkɪt, -,ket
introduce ,ɪntrə'djus, -'dɪus, -'dus |-s -ɪz |-d -t
introduction ,ɪntrə'dʌkʃən |-tive -tɪv |-tory
-tərɪ, -trɪ
introit ɪn'tro·ɪt
introjection ,ɪntrə'dʒɛkʃən
intromission ,ɪntrə'mɪʃən
intromit ,ɪntrə'mɪt |-ted -ɪd |-tent -ṇt
introrse ɪn'trɔrs; ES -'trɔəs
introspect ,ɪntrə'spɛkt |-ed -ɪd
introspection ,ɪntrə'spɛkʃən |-tive -tɪv
introversion ,ɪntrə'vɝʃən, -ʒən; ES -'vɝ-,
-'vɝ-; |-sive -sɪv
introvert n 'ɪntrə,vɝt; ES -,vɝt, -,vɝt
introvert v ,ɪntrə'vɝt; ES -'vɝt, -'vɝt; |-ed -ɪd
|-ive -ɪv
intrude ɪn'trud, -'trɪud |-d -ɪd
intrusion ɪn'truʒən, -'trɪuʒən |-sive -sɪv
intrust ɪn'trʌst |-ed -ɪd
intuit 'ɪntjʊɪt, -tɪu-, -tʊ-, ɪn'tjuɪt, -'trɪu-,
-'tu- |-ed -ɪd
intuition ,ɪntu'ɪʃən, -tɪu-, -tjʊ-

intuitive ɪn'tjuɪtɪv, -'tɪu-, -'tu-
intumescence ,ɪntju'mɛsṇs, -tɪu-, -tu- |-nt -ṇt
inturn 'ɪn,tɝn; ES -,tɝn, -,tɝn; |-ed -d
intussuscept ,ɪntəssə'sɛpt |-ed -ɪd |-ion -pʃən
intwine ɪn'twaɪn |-d -d
inulin 'ɪnjəlɪn
inunction ɪn'ʌŋkʃən
inundate 'ɪnən,det, -ʌn-, ɪn'ʌndet |-d -ɪd
inundation ,ɪnən'deʃən, ,ɪnʌn-
inure ɪn'jʊr; ES -'jʊə(r; |-d -d
inurn ɪn'ɝn; ES -'ɝn, -'ɝn; |-ed -d
inutile ɪn'jut|, -tɪl |-ly -ɪ
inutility ,ɪnju'tɪlətɪ
in vacuo ɪn'vækjʊ,o
invade ɪn'ved |-vaded -'vedɪd
invalid 'not valid' ɪn'vælɪd
invalid n, adj 'sick' 'ɪnvəlɪd |-ism -,ɪzəm
invalid v 'ɪnvə,lɪd |-lided -,lɪdɪd
invalidate ɪn'vælə,det |-dated -,detɪd
invalidation ɪn,vælə'deʃən, ,ɪnvælə-
invalidity ,ɪnvə'lɪdətɪ
invaluable ɪn'væljəb|, -'væljʊəb| |-bly -blɪ
invariability ,ɪnvɛrɪə'bɪlətɪ, -ver-, -vær-,
ɪn,v-
invariable ɪn'vɛrɪəb|, -'ver-, -'vær- |-bly -blɪ
invasion ɪn'veʒən |-sive -sɪv
invective ɪn'vɛktɪv
inveigh ɪn've |-ed -d
inveigle ɪn'vig|, -'veg| |-d -d |-ling -glɪŋ,
-glɪŋ
invent ɪn'vɛnt |-ed -ɪd |-ive -ɪv |-ntion -nʃən
inventory 'ɪnvən,torɪ, -,tɔrɪ; S -,torɪ
Inverness ,ɪnvə'nɛs; ES -və-; ('Inver,ness
'cape) |-ness-shire -'nɛsʃɪr, -'nɛʃʃ-, -ʃə; ES
-ʃɪə(r, -ʃə(r
inverse n, adj ɪn'vɝs; ES -'vɝs, -'vɝs; ('in-
,verse 'ratio)
inverse v ɪn'vɝs; ES -'vɝs, -'vɝs; |-s -ɪz |-d -t
|-dly -ɪdlɪ, -tlɪ
inversion ɪn'vɝʃən, -ʒən; ES -'vɝ-, -'vɝ-
invert n, adj 'ɪnvɝt; ES -vɝt, -vɝt
invert v ɪn'vɝt; ES -'vɝt, -'vɝt; |-ed -ɪd
invertebrate n, adj ɪn'vɝtəbrɪt, -,bret; ES
-'vɝt-, -'vɝt-; |-d -,bretɪd
invest ɪn'vɛst |-ed -ɪd
investigable ɪn'vɛstɪgəb| |-gatable -,getəb|
investigate ɪn'vɛstə,get |-d -ɪd |-tor -ɚ; ES
-ə(r
investigation ɪn,vɛstə'geʃən

investiture ɪn'vɛstətʃɚ; ES -tʃə(r
investment ɪn'vɛstmənt |-stor -tɚ; ES -tə(r
inveteracy ɪn'vɛtərəsɪ |-rate -rɪt
Invictus ɪn'vɪktəs
invidious ɪn'vɪdɪəs
invigorate ɪn'vɪgə,ret |-rated -,retɪd
invigoration ɪn,vɪgə'reʃən
invincibility ɪn,vɪnsə'bɪlətɪ, ,ɪnvɪnsə-
invincible ɪn'vɪnsəbḷ |-bly -blɪ
inviolability ɪn,vaɪələ'bɪlətɪ, ,ɪnvaɪələ-
inviolable ɪn'vaɪələbḷ |-bly -blɪ
inviolate ɪn'vaɪəlɪt, -,let
invisibility ,ɪnvɪzə'bɪlətɪ, ɪn,vɪzə-
invisible ɪn'vɪzəbḷ |-bly -blɪ
invitation ,ɪnvə'teʃən
invite n 'ɪnvaɪt
invite v ɪn'vaɪt |-vited -'vaɪtɪd
invocate 'ɪnvə,ket |-d -ɪd |-tion ,ɪnvə'keʃən
invoice 'ɪnvɔɪs |-s -ɪz |-d -t
invoke ɪn'vok |-voked -'vokt
involucre 'ɪnvə,lukɚ, -,ḷukɚ; ES -kə(r; |-d -d
involuntary ɪn'vɑlən,tɛrɪ; ES -'vɒl-; |-rily
-rəlɪ, esp. if emph. ,ɪnvolun'tarɪly
involute 'ɪnvə,lut, -,ḷut |-d -ɪd
involution ,ɪnvə'luʃən, -'ḷuʃən, -v|'juʃən
involve ɪn'vɑlv, -'vɒlv |-d -d |-dly -ɪdlɪ
invulnerability ,ɪnvʌlnərə'bɪlətɪ, ɪn,vʌl-, -nrə-
invulnerable ɪn'vʌlnərəbḷ, -nrə- |-bly -blɪ
inwall n 'ɪn,wɔl, v ɪn'wɔl |-ed ɪn'wɔld
inward 'ɪnwɚd; ES 'ɪnwəd; |-s -z
inweave ɪn'wiv |-wove -'wov |-woven -'wovən
    or -wove -'wov
inwind ɪn'waɪnd |-wound -'waʊnd
inwork ɪn'wɚk; ES -'wɜk, -'wɝk; |-ed -t or
    -wrought -'rɔt
inwound ɪn'waʊnd
inwove ɪn'wov |-woven -'wovən ('ɪn,woven
    'hue)
inwrap ɪn'ræp |-ped -t
inwreathe ɪn'rið |-d -d
inwrought ɪn'rɔt ('ɪn,wrought 'colors)
Io 'aɪo
-io ending see -ia
iodate 'aɪə,det |-dated -,detɪd
iodide 'aɪə,daɪd, -dɪd |iodid 'aɪədɪd
iodin 'aɪədɪn
iodine 'aɪə,daɪn, -dɪn, chem. usually -,din
iodize 'aɪə,daɪz |-s -ɪz |-d -đ
iodoform aɪ'odə,fɔrm, -'ɑd-; ES -,fɔəm, -'ɒd-

Iola aɪ'olə
Iolanthe ,aɪə'lænθɪ
-ion ending see -ia
ion 'aɪən, 'aɪɑn, -ɒn
Ion 'aɪɑn, -ɒn
Iona aɪ'onə
Ione heroine aɪ'onɪ
Ione village, geol. formation aɪ'on
Ionia aɪ'onɪə, -njə |-n -n
ionic, I- aɪ'ɑnɪk, -'ɒn-
ionium aɪ'onɪəm
ionization ,aɪənə'zeʃən, -aɪ'z-
ionize 'aɪən,aɪz |-s -ɪz |-d -d
Iosco aɪ'ɑsko; ES+-'ɒs-
iota aɪ'otə |-cism -,sɪzəm
iotize 'aɪə,taɪz |-s -ɪz |-d -d
I O U 'aɪ,o'ju
-ious ending see -ia
Iowa 'aɪəwə, loc.+'aɪə,we
I P A 'aɪ,pi'e, ,ɪntɚ'næʃənḷ fo'nɛtɪk ə,sosɪ-
    ,eʃən, ə,soʃɪ-; ES ,ɪntə-; cf A P I
ipecac 'ɪpɪ,kæk |-uanha -ju'ænə
Iphigenia ,ɪfədʒɪ'naɪə, mod. name -'dʒɪnjə
ipse dixit 'ɪpsɪ'dɪksɪt
ipso facto 'ɪpso'fækto
Ipswich 'ɪpswɪtʃ |-'s -ɪz
Iquique i'kike
iracund 'aɪrə,kʌnd
irade i'radɪ
Iran aɪ'ræn, i'rɑn |-ian aɪ'renɪən
Iraq i'rɑk |-i -ɪ
Iras 'aɪrəs |-'s -ɪz
irascibility aɪ,ræsə'bɪlətɪ, ɪ,ræsə-
irascible aɪ'ræsəbḷ, ɪ'ræsə- |-bly -blɪ
irate 'aɪret, aɪ'ret ('aɪrate 'foreman)
ire aɪr; ES aɪə(r; |-ful -fəl |-fully -fəlɪ
Iredell 'aɪrdɛl; ES 'aɪə-
Ireland 'aɪrlənd; ES 'aɪələnd
Irenaeus ,aɪrə'niəs |-'s -ɪz
Irene aɪ'rin, myth. aɪ'rini
irenic aɪ'rɛnɪk, -rinɪk |-al -ḷ |-ally -ḷɪ, -ɪklɪ
iridaceous ,aɪrɪ'deʃəs, ,ɪrɪ-
iridesce ,ɪrə'dɛs |-s -ɪz |-d -t
iridescence ,ɪrə'dɛsn̩s |-cy -ɪ |-ent -sn̩t
iridium aɪ'rɪdɪəm, ɪ-
Irion 'ɪrɪən, -ɑn, -ɒn
iris, I- 'aɪrɪs |-es -ɪz |-ed -t
Irish 'aɪrɪʃ |-man -mən |-men -mən |-woman
    -,wumən, -,wu- |-women -,wɪmɪn, -ən

iritis aɪˈraɪtɪs |-tic -ˈrɪtɪk

irk ɜ˞k; ES ɜk, ɜ˞k; |-ed -t |-some -səm

Irkutsk ɪrˈkutsk; ES ɪə-

Irma ˈɜ˞mə; ES ˈɜmə, ˈɜ˞mə

iron, I- ˈaɪ˞n; ES ˈaɪ·ən |-ed -d

ironclad ˈaɪ˞nˈklæd; ES ˈaɪ·ən-; (ˈiron‚clad ˈshoe)

iron-gray, -grey ˈaɪ˞nˈgre; ES ˈaɪ·ən-; (ˈiron‚gray ˈhair)

ironic aɪˈrɑnɪk; ES+-ˈrɒn-; |-al -ḷ |-ally -ḷɪ, -ɪklɪ

ironmonger ˈaɪ˞n‚mʌŋgɚ; ES ˈaɪ·ən‚mʌŋgə(r; |-y -gərɪ, -grɪ

ironside, I- ˈaɪ˞n‚saɪd; ES ˈaɪ·ən-; |-s -z

ironsmith ˈaɪ˞n‚smɪθ; ES ˈaɪ·ən-; |-ths -θs

ironstone ˈaɪ˞n‚ston; ES ˈaɪ·ən-

ironware ˈaɪ˞n‚wɛr, -‚wær; E ˈaɪ·ən‚wɛə(r, ES -‚wæə(r

ironwork ˈaɪ˞n‚wɜ˞k; ES ˈaɪ·ən‚wɜk, ˈaɪ·ən-‚wɜ˞k

irony ˈlike iron' ˈaɪ˞nɪ; ES ˈaɪ·ənɪ

irony kind of humor ˈaɪrənɪ

Iroquoian ‚ɪrəˈkwɔɪən

Iroquois ˈɪrə‚kwɔɪ, -‚kwɔɪz |-'s -‚kwɔɪz, -‚kwɔɪzɪz

irradiance ɪˈredɪəns |-cy -ɪ |-ant -ənt

irradiate ɪˈredɪ‚et |-ated -‚etɪd |-tive -ɪv

irradiation ‚ɪredɪˈeʃən, ɪ‚redɪ-

irrational ɪˈræʃənḷ, ɪrˈræʃ-; ES ɪˈr-, ɪəˈr-; |-ly -ɪ

irrationality ɪ‚ræʃəˈnælətɪ, ‚ɪrræʃə-; ES ɪ‚ræʃə-, ‚ɪəræʃə-

Irrawaddy ‚ɪrəˈwɑdɪ, -ˈwɒdɪ

irreclaimability ‚ɪrɪ‚kleməˈbɪlətɪ, ‚ɪrrɪ-; ES ‚ɪrɪ-, ‚ɪərɪ-

irreclaimable ‚ɪrɪˈkleməbḷ, ‚ɪrrɪ-; ES ‚ɪrɪ-, ‚ɪərɪ-; |-bly -blɪ

irreconcilability ɪ‚rɛkən‚saɪləˈbɪlətɪ, ɪr‚rɛk-; ES ɪ‚rɛk-, ɪə‚rɛk-

irreconcilable ɪˈrɛkən‚saɪləbḷ, ɪrˈrɛk-; ES ɪˈrɛk-, ɪəˈrɛk-; emph.+‚irreconˈcilable |-bly -blɪ

irrecoverable ‚ɪrɪˈkʌvərəbḷ, ‚ɪrrɪ-, -vrə-; ES ‚ɪrɪ-, ‚ɪərɪ-; |-bly -blɪ

irredeemable ‚ɪrɪˈdiməbḷ, ‚ɪrrɪ-; ES ‚ɪrɪ-, ‚ɪərɪ-; |-bly -blɪ

Irredentist ‚ɪrɪˈdɛntɪst

irreducible ‚ɪrɪˈdjusəbḷ, ‚ɪrrɪ-, -ˈdɪus-, -ˈdus-; ES ‚ɪrɪ-, ‚ɪərɪ-; |-bly -blɪ

irrefragability ɪ‚rɛfrəgəˈbɪlətɪ, ɪr‚rɛf-; ES ɪ‚rɛf-, ɪə‚rɛf-

irrefragable ɪˈrɛfrəgəbḷ, ɪrˈrɛf-; ES ɪˈrɛf-, ɪəˈrɛf-; |-bly -blɪ

irrefutability ɪ‚rɛfjutəˈbɪlətɪ, ɪr‚rɛf-, ‚ɪrɪ-‚fjutə-, ‚ɪrrɪ-, -‚frutə-; ES ɪ‚rɛf-, ɪə‚rɛf-, ‚ɪrɪ‚f-, ‚ɪərɪ‚f-

irrefutable ɪˈrɛfjutəbḷ, ɪrˈrɛf-, ‚ɪrɪˈfjutəbḷ, ‚ɪrrɪ-, -ˈfrutə-; ES ɪˈrɛf-, ɪəˈrɛf-, ‚ɪrɪˈf-, ‚ɪərɪˈf-

irregular ɪˈrɛgjələ˞, ɪrˈrɛg-; ES ɪˈrɛgjələ(r, ɪəˈrɛg-

irregularity ‚ɪrɛgjəˈlærətɪ, ‚ɪrrɛg-, ɪ‚rɛg-, ɪr‚rɛg-; ES ‚ɪrɛg-, ‚ɪərɛg-, ɪ‚rɛg-, ɪə‚rɛg-; |-lation -jəˈleʃən

irrelative ɪˈrɛlətɪv, ɪrˈrɛl-; ES ɪˈrɛl-, ɪəˈrɛl-

irrelevance ɪˈrɛləvəns, ɪrˈrɛl-; ES ɪˈrɛl-, ɪəˈrɛl-; |-cy -ɪ |-ant -ənt

irreligion ‚ɪrɪˈlɪdʒən, ‚ɪrrɪ-; ES ‚ɪrɪ-, ‚ɪərɪ-; |-gious -dʒəs

irremediable ‚ɪrɪˈmidɪəbḷ, ‚ɪrrɪ-; ES ‚ɪrɪ-, ‚ɪərɪ-; |-bly -blɪ

irremovability ‚ɪrɪ‚muvəˈbɪlətɪ, ‚ɪrrɪ-; ES ‚ɪrɪ-, ‚ɪərɪ-

irremovable ‚ɪrɪˈmuvəbḷ, ‚ɪrrɪ-; ES ‚ɪrɪ-, ‚ɪərɪ-; |-bly -blɪ

irreparability ‚ɪrɛpərəˈbɪlətɪ, ‚ɪrrɛp-, ɪ‚rɛp-, ɪr‚rɛp-; ES ‚ɪrɛp-, ‚ɪərɛp-, ɪ‚rɛp-, ɪə‚rɛp-

irreparable ɪˈrɛpərəbḷ, ɪrˈrɛp-; ES ɪˈrɛp-, ɪəˈrɛp-; |-bly -blɪ

irrepealable ‚ɪrɪˈpiləbḷ, ‚ɪrrɪ-; ES ‚ɪrɪ-, ‚ɪərɪ-; |-bly -blɪ

irreplaceable ‚ɪrɪˈplesəbḷ, ‚ɪrrɪ-; ES ‚ɪrɪ-, ‚ɪərɪ-; |-bly -blɪ

irrepressibility ‚ɪrɪ‚prɛsəˈbɪlətɪ, ‚ɪrrɪ-; ES ‚ɪrɪ-, ‚ɪərɪ-

irrepressible ‚ɪrɪˈprɛsəbḷ, ‚ɪrrɪ-; ES ‚ɪrɪ-, ‚ɪərɪ-; |-bly -blɪ

irreproachable ‚ɪrɪˈprotʃəbḷ, ‚ɪrrɪ-; ES ‚ɪrɪ-, ‚ɪərɪ-; |-bly -blɪ

irresistibility ‚ɪrɪ‚zɪstəˈbɪlətɪ, ‚ɪrrɪ-; ES ‚ɪrɪ-, ‚ɪərɪ-

irresistible ‚ɪrɪˈzɪstəbḷ, ‚ɪrrɪ-; ES ‚ɪrɪ-, ‚ɪərɪ-; |-bly -blɪ

irresolute ɪˈrɛzə‚lut, ɪrˈrɛz-, -‚lɪut, -ˈrɛzḷ‚jut; ES ɪˈrɛz-, ɪəˈrɛz-

irresolution ‚ɪrɛzəˈluʃən, ‚ɪrrɛz-, ɪ‚rɛz-, ɪr‚rɛz-, -ˈlɪu-, -zḷˈjuʃən; ES ‚ɪrɛz-, ‚ɪərɛz-, ɪ‚rɛz-, ɪə‚rɛz-

Those words below in which the ɑ *sound is spelt* o *are often pronounced with* ɒ *in E and S*

irresolvable ˌɪrɪˈzɑlvəbļ, ˌɪrrɪ-, -ˈzɒlv-; ES ˌɪrɪ-, ˌɪərɪ-

irrespective ˌɪrɪˈspɛktɪv, ˌɪrrɪ-; ES ˌɪrɪ-, ˌɪərɪ-

irresponsibility ˌɪrɪˌspɑnsəˈbɪlətɪ, ˌɪrrɪ-; ES ˌɪrɪ-, ˌɪərɪ-

irresponsible ˌɪrɪˈspɑnsəbļ, ˌɪrrɪ-; ES ˌɪrɪ-, ˌɪərɪ-; |-bly -blɪ

irresponsive ˌɪrɪˈspɑnsɪv, ˌɪrrɪ-; ES ˌɪrɪ-, ˌɪərɪ-

irretraceable ˌɪrɪˈtresəbļ, ˌɪrrɪ-; ES ˌɪrɪ-, ˌɪərɪ-; |-bly -blɪ

irretrievability ˌɪrɪˌtrivəˈbɪlətɪ, ˌɪrrɪ-; ES ˌɪrɪ-, ˌɪərɪ-

irretrievable ˌɪrɪˈtrivəbļ, ˌɪrrɪ-; ES ˌɪrɪ-, ˌɪərɪ-; |-bly -blɪ

irreverence ɪˈrɛvərəns, ɪrˈrɛv-; ES ɪˈrɛv-, ɪəˈrɛv-; |-ent -ənt

irreversibility ˌɪrɪˌvɝ·səˈbɪlətɪ, ˌɪrrɪ-; ES ˌɪrɪˌvɝ·s-, -ˌvɝ·s-, ˌɪərɪ-

irreversible ˌɪrɪˈvɝ·səbļ, ˌɪrrɪ-; ES ˌɪrɪˈvɝ·s-, -ˈvɝ·s-, ˌɪərɪ-; |-bly -blɪ

irrevocability ɪˌrɛvəkəˈbɪlətɪ, ɪrˌrɛv-; ES ɪˌrɛv-, ɪəˌrɛv-

irrevocable ɪˈrɛvəkəbļ, ɪrˈrɛv-; ES ɪˈrɛv-, ɪəˈrɛv-; |-bly -blɪ—*Cultivated speakers often pron.* ˌɪrɪˈvokəbļ, *by confusion of* revocable *with* revokable.

irrigable ˈɪrɪgəbļ |-bly -blɪ

irrigate ˈɪrəˌget |-d -ɪd |-tion ˌɪrəˈgeʃən

irritability ˌɪrətəˈbɪlətɪ

irritable ˈɪrətəbļ |-bly -blɪ

irritant ˈɪrətənt

irritate ˈɪrəˌtet |-tated -ˌtetɪd |-tive -ɪv

irritation ˌɪrəˈteʃən

irruption ɪˈrʌpʃən |-tive -tɪv

Irvine ˈɝ·vɪn; ES ˈɜ·vɪn, ˈɝ·vɪn

Irving ˈɝ·vɪŋ; ES ˈɜ·vɪŋ, ˈɝ·vɪŋ |-ton -tən

Irwin ˈɝ·wɪn; ES ˈɜ·wɪn, ˈɝ·wɪn

is *stressed* ˈɪz, ˌɪz; *unstr. & sometimes spelt* ’s: *after voiced sounds except sibilants* z; *after voiceless sounds except sibilants* s; *after the sibilants* (s, z, ʃ, ʒ, tʃ, dʒ) ɪz—*see* ’s & *§88*.

Isaac ˈaɪzək |-s -s |-s’s -sɪz

Isabel ˈɪzəˌbɛl, -bļ |-la ˌɪzəˈbɛlə

Isadora ˌɪzəˈdorə, -ˈdɔrə; S -ˈdorə

isagoge ˌaɪsəˈgodʒɪ

isagogic ˌaɪsəˈgɑdʒɪk |-al -ļ |-ally -ļɪ, -ɪklɪ

Isaiah aɪˈzeə, aɪˈzaɪə

isatin ˈaɪsətɪn

Iscariot ɪsˈkærɪət

ischium ˈɪskɪəm |-ia -ɪə

Iseult ɪˈsult

Isfahan ˌɪsfəˈhɑn, -ˈhæn

-ish *adj ending* -ɪʃ—*often omitted when the pron. can be found by adding* -ɪʃ *to the head pronunciation*

Ishbosheth ɪʃˈboʃɪθ

Ishmael ˈɪʃmɪəl |-ite -ˌaɪt

Ishtar ˈɪʃtɑr; ES -tɑːr, E+-tɑːr

Isiac ˈaɪsɪˌæk

Isidore ˈɪzəˌdor, -ˌdɔr; S -ˌdor

Isidorian ˌɪzəˈdorɪən, -ˈdɔr-; S -ˈdor-

isinglass ˈaɪzɪŋˌglæs; E+-ˌglas, -ˌglas

Isis ˈaɪsɪs |Isis’ ˈaɪsɪs

Islam ˈɪsləm, ɪsˈlɑm |-ic ɪsˈlæmɪk, -ˈlɑmɪk

Islamite ˈɪsləmˌaɪt |-tic ˌɪsləˈmɪtɪk

island ˈaɪlənd

isle aɪl |-d -d |-less ˈaɪllɪs

Isle Royale ˈaɪlˈrɔɪəl, -ˈrɔjəl

islet ˈaɪlɪt

Isleton ˈaɪltən

Isleworth ˈaɪzļwɝ·θ; ES -wɜ·θ

Islington ˈɪzlɪŋtən

Islip *Oxf, LI* ˈaɪslɪp, *Northants*+ˈaɪz-

ism *n* ˈɪzəm

-ism *ending* -ɪzəm, -ɪzm̩—*The pron.* -ɪzm̩ *is less frequent, though the vowel in* -ɪzəm *is often very brief. In the vocab. only* -ɪzəm *is given, it being understood that* -ɪzm̩ *is also a possible pron. If the syllable before has the main accent, as in* ˈtruism, -ɪz- *has slightly more stress than* -əm, *though usually the accent mark is not used. If* -ism *follows an unaccented syllable, it has a secondary accent* (ˈlɪtərəlˌɪzəm, ˈfɛməˌnɪzəm, ˈfet|ˌɪzəm).

Ismail *Rus city, Egyp viceroy* ˌɪsmɑˈil

isn’t ˈɪzn̩t, *before some conss.*+ˈɪzn̩ (There isn’t time ðɚˌɪzn̩ˈtaɪm)

isobar ˈaɪsəˌbɑr; ES -ˌbɑːr, E+-ˌbɑːr

isobaric ˌaɪsəˈbærɪk

Isobel ˈɪzəbļ, -ˌbɛl

isochromatic ˌaɪsəkroˈmætɪk

isochronal aɪˈsɑkrənļ |-ly -ɪ |-nous -nəs

isochronize aɪˈsɑkrəˌnaɪz |-s -ɪz |-d -d

isoclinal ˌaɪsəˈklaɪnļ |-clinic -ˈklɪnɪk

Key: See in full §§3–47. bee bi |pity ˈpɪtɪ (§6) |rate ret |yet jɛt |sang sæŋ |angry ˈæŋ·grɪ |bath bæθ; E baθ (§10) |ah ɑ |far fɑr |watch wɑtʃ, wɒtʃ (§12) |jaw dʒɔ |gorge gɔrdʒ |go go

Those words below in which the ɑ sound is spelt o are often pronounced with ɒ in E and S

isocline ˈaɪsəˌklaɪn
isocracy aɪˈsɑkrəsɪ
Isocrates aɪˈsɑkrəˌtiz |-ˈs -ɪz
isodynamic ˌaɪsədaɪˈnæmɪk |-al -ļ
isoelectric ˌaɪsoˌɪˈlɛktrɪk |-ally -ļɪ, -ɪklɪ
isogenous aɪˈsɑdʒənəs
isogeotherm ˌaɪsəˈdʒiəˌθɝm; ES -ˌθɝm, -ˌθɝm
isogonal aɪˈsɑgənļ |-ly -ɪ |-gonic ˌaɪsəˈgɑnɪk
isolable ˈaɪsələbļ, ˈɪs-
isolate ˈaɪsļˌet, ˈɪs- |-ated -ˌetɪd |-tive - ɪv
isolation ˌaɪsļˈeʃən, ˌɪs-
Isolda ɪˈsɑldə, ɪˈzɑl-
Isolde ɪˈsɑld, ɪˈsɑldə, ɪˈzɑl- (Ger iːˈzɔldə)
isomagnetic ˌaɪsəmægˈnɛtɪk
isomer ˈaɪsəmɚ; ES -mə(r
isomere ˈaɪsəˌmɪr; ES -ˌmɪə(r
isomeric ˌaɪsəˈmɛrɪk |-al -ļ |-ally -ļɪ, -ɪklɪ
isomerism aɪˈsɑməˌrɪzəm |-rous -rəs
isometric ˌaɪsəˈmɛtrɪk |-al -ļ |-ally -ļɪ, -ɪklɪ
isometry aɪˈsɑmətrɪ
isomorph ˈaɪsəˌmɔrf; ES -ˌmɔəf
isomorphic ˌaɪsəˈmɔrfɪk; ES -ˈmɔəfɪk; |-phism
-fɪzəm |-phous -fəs
isopiestic ˌaɪsəpaɪˈɛstɪk |-ally -ļɪ, -ɪklɪ
isopleth ˈaɪsəˌplɛθ |-ths -θs
isopod ˈaɪsəˌpɑd
isoprene ˈaɪsəˌprin
isosceles aɪˈsɑsļˌiz
isoseismal ˌaɪsəˈsaɪzmļ, -ˈsaɪs-
isoseismic ˌaɪsəˈsaɪzmɪk, -ˈsaɪs- |-al -ļ
isostasy aɪˈsɑstəsɪ
isostatic ˌaɪsəˈstætɪk |-al -ļ |-ally -ļɪ, -ɪklɪ
isothere ˈaɪsəˌθɪr; ES -ˌθɪə(r
isotherm ˈaɪsəˌθɝm; ES -ˌθɝm, -ˌθɝm
isothermal ˌaɪsəˈθɝmļ; ES -ˈθɝmļ, -ˈθɝmļ
isotonic ˌaɪsəˈtɑnɪk |-ity ˌaɪsətoˈnɪsətɪ
isotope ˈaɪsəˌtop |-pic ˌaɪsəˈtɑpɪk
isotrope ˈaɪsəˌtrop |-pic ˌaɪsəˈtrɑpɪk
isotropy aɪˈsɑtrəpɪ
Ispahan ˌɪspəˈhɑn, -ˈhæn
Israel ˈɪzrɪəl |-ite -ˌaɪt |-itish -ˌaɪtɪʃ
Issachar ˈɪsəkɚ; ES -kə(r
issuable ˈɪʃʊəbļ, ˈɪʃjʊ- |-bly -blɪ
issuance ˈɪʃʊəns, ˈɪʃjʊ- |-s -ɪz |-ant -ənt
issue ˈɪʃʊ, ˈɪʃjʊ |-d -d—ˈɪsju is mainly Brit.
Issus ˈɪsəs |Issus' ˈɪsəs
Istanbul ˌɪstɑnˈbul, ˌɪstɑm-
isthmus ˈɪsməs |-es -ɪz |-mian -mɪən

Istria ˈɪstrɪə |-n -n
it stressed ˈɪt, ˌɪt; unstr. ɪt or (spelt ˈt) t- —
see ˈtis, ˈtˈll, ˈtwas, ˈtwere, ˈtwill, ˈtwould
Italian ɪˈtæljən, ə-, now less freq. aɪˈtæljən
Italianate adj ɪˈtæljənˌet, -ɪt
Italianate v ɪˈtæljənˌet |-ated -ˌetɪd
Italianize ɪˈtæljənˌaɪz |-s -ɪz |-d -d
italic, I- ɪˈtælɪk |-ally -ļɪ, -ɪklɪ
italicize ɪˈtæləˌsaɪz |-s -ɪz |-d -d
Italy ˈɪtļɪ
Itasca aɪˈtæskə
itch ɪtʃ |itches ˈɪtʃɪz |itched ɪtʃt
Itchen ˈɪtʃɪn, -ən
it'd 'it would' ˈɪtəd
item L adv ˈaɪtɛm
item n, v ˈaɪtəm |-ed -d
itemize ˈaɪtəmˌaɪz |-s -ɪz |-d -d
iterate ˈɪtəˌret |-d -ɪd |-tive -ɪv
iteration ˌɪtəˈreʃən
Ithaca ˈɪθəkə, ˈɪθɪkə
Ithamar ˈɪθəˌmɑr; ES -ˌmɑ:(r, E+-ˌmɑ:(r
Ithunn, -un ˈɪðʊn=Idun
Ithuriel ɪˈθjurɪəl, ɪˈθɪurɪəl
itineracy aɪˈtɪnərəsɪ, ɪ- |-ancy -ənsɪ |-ant -ənt
itinerary aɪˈtɪnəˌrɛrɪ, ɪ-
itinerate aɪˈtɪnəˌret, ɪ- |-rated -ˌretɪd
it'll 'it will' ˈɪtļ
its poss ɪts |it's 'it is,' 'it has' ɪts
itself ɪtˈsɛlf
-ity word ending (fatality, familiarity, authority) -ətɪ, -ɪtɪ. It seems clear that -ətɪ is
the prevailing pron. in colloq. speech. -ɪtɪ is
probably somewhat more common in the
E & S than in the N.
-ius ending see -ia
Ivan ˈaɪvən
Ivanhoe ˈaɪvənˌho
I've 'I have' aɪv
-ive unstressed ending -ɪv—often omitted from
the vocab. when its pron. may be added directly to that of the head word
Ives aɪvz |-'s -ɪz
ivory, I- ˈaɪvrɪ, ˈaɪvərɪ
ivy ˈaɪvɪ |-ied -d
iwis, y- ɪˈwɪs |erron. I wis aɪˈwɪs
Ixion ɪksˈaɪən
izard, I- ˈɪzɚd; ES ˈɪzəd
izzard ˈɪzɚd; ES ˈɪzəd

|full fʊl |tooth tuθ |further ˈfɝðɚ; ES ˈfɝðə |custom ˈkʌstəm |while hwaɪl |how haʊ |toy tɔɪ
|using ˈjuzɪŋ |fuse fjuz, fɪuz |dish dɪʃ |vision ˈvɪʒən |Eden ˈidn̩ |cradle ˈkredļ |keep 'em ˈkipm̩

J

J, j *letter* dʒe |*pl* J's, Js, *poss* J's dʒez
jab dʒæb |jabbed dʒæbd
jabber ˈdʒæbɚ; ES -bə(r; |-ed -d |-ing
    ˈdʒæbrɪŋ, ˈdʒæbərɪŋ
Jabberwock ˈdʒæbɚˌwɑk, -ˌwɒk; ES ˈdʒæbə-
Jabesh-gilead ˈdʒebɛʃˈgɪlɪəd
Jabez ˈdʒebɪz |-'s -ɪz
jabot ʒæˈbo (*Fr* ʒaˈbo)
jacinth ˈdʒesɪnθ |-ths -θs
Jack, j- dʒæk |jacked dʒækt
jack-a-dandy ˌdʒækəˈdændɪ
jackal ˈdʒækɔl
jackanapes ˈdʒækəˌneps |-napeses -ˌnepsɪz
jackass ˈdʒækˌæs |-es -ɪz |-ed -t
jackdaw ˈdʒækˌdɔ
jacket ˈdʒækɪt |-ed -ɪd
jack-in-a-box ˈdʒækɪnəˌbɑks; ES+-ˌbɒks;
    |-es -ɪz
jack-in-the-box ˈdʒækɪnðəˌbɑks; ES+-ˌbɒks;
    |-es -ɪz
jack-in-the-pulpit ˈdʒækɪnðəˈpʊlpɪt
jackknife ˈdʒækˌnaɪf |-knives -ˌnaɪvz
Jack-of-all-trades, j- ˌdʒækəvˈɔlˌtredz
jack-o'-lantern ˈdʒækəˌlæntɚn, ˈdʒækˌl-; ES
    -tən
jack-rabbit ˈdʒækˌræbɪt
jackscrew ˈdʒækˌskru, -ˌskrɪu
Jackson ˈdʒæksn̩ |-ville -ˌvɪl; S+-vl̩
Jacksonian dʒækˈsonɪən
jackstay ˈdʒækˌste
jackstraw ˈdʒækˌstrɔ
jack-tar ˈdʒækˈtɑr; ES -ˈtɑː(r, E+-ˈtɑː(r
Jacob ˈdʒekəb, ˈdʒekəp
Jacobean ˌdʒækəˈbiən (ˈJacoˌbean ˈstyle)
Jacobi *Am* dʒəˈkobɪ, *various Germans* jə-
    ˈkobɪ (*Ger* jaˈkoːbiː)
Jacobian dʒəˈkobɪən, dʒe-
Jacobin ˈdʒækəbɪn
Jacobinic ˌdʒækəˈbɪnɪk |-al -l̩ |-ally -l̩ɪ, -ɪklɪ
Jacobite ˈdʒækəˌbaɪt
Jacobitic ˌdʒækəˈbɪtɪk |-al -l̩ |-ally -l̩ɪ, -ɪklɪ
jacobus dʒəˈkobəs |-es -ɪz
jacoby ˈdʒækəbɪ
Jacoby, *Harold* dʒəˈkobɪ, *Johann* jə-
Jacquard, j- dʒəˈkɑrd; ES -ˈkɑːd, E+-ˈkɑːd;
    (*Fr* ʒaˈkaːr)
Jacqueline ˈdʒækwəlɪn, -ˌlin

Jacquerie *Fr* ʒakˈri
jactation dʒækˈteʃən |-titation -tɪˈteʃən
jade dʒed |jaded ˈdʒedɪd
jaeger, jäg- *bird* ˈjegɚ, ˈdʒe-, *rifleman* ˈjegɚ;
    ES -gə(r; (*Ger* ˈjɛːgər)
Jael ˈdʒeəl
Jaffa ˈdʒæfə
Jaffrey ˈdʒæfrɪ
jag dʒæg |jagged dʒægd
jagged *adj* ˈdʒægɪd
jagged-toothed ˈdʒægɪdˈtuθt, -ˈðd
jaguar ˈdʒægwɑr, ˈdʒægjuˌɑr; ES -wɑː(r, -ˌɑː(r
Jahveh ˈjɑvɛ |-vism -vɪzəm |-vist -vɪst
    |-vistic jɑˈvɪstɪk
Jahweh ˈjɑwɛ |-wism -wɪzəm |-wist -wɪst
    |-wistic jɑˈwɪstɪk
jail dʒel |jailed dʒeld |-er -ɚ; ES -ə(r; *cf* gaol
jailbird ˈdʒelˌbɚd; ES -ˌbɝd, -ˌbɜd
Jain dʒaɪn |-a -ə |-ism -ɪzəm |-ist -ɪst
Jaipur dʒaɪˈpʊr; ES -ˈpʊə(r; *acct*+ˈJaipur
Jairus dʒeˈaɪrəs, ˈdʒeərəs |-'s -ɪz
jalap ˈdʒæləp
Jalna ˈdʒɑlnə
jalopy dʒəˈlɑpɪ; ES+-ˈlɒpɪ
jalousie ˌʒæluˈzi (*Fr* ʒaluˈzi)
jam dʒæm |jammed dʒæmd
Jam dʒɑm
Jamaica dʒəˈmekə |-n -n
jamb, -e dʒæm
jambeau ˈdʒæmbo |-x -z
jamboree ˌdʒæmbəˈri
James dʒemz |-ian -ɪən |-'s -ɪz
Jameson ˈdʒemsn̩
Jamestown ˈdʒemzˌtaʊn
Jamestown weed ˈdʒɪmsn̩ˌwid
Jamieson ˈdʒeməsn̩
Jamy ˈdʒemɪ
Jan dʒæn
Jane dʒen
Janeiro dʒəˈnɪro, -ˈnero (*Pg* ʒaˈnɛiru)
Janesville ˈdʒenzvɪl
Janet *fem. name* ˈdʒænɪt, dʒəˈnɛt; *Fr writer*
    ʒəˈne (*Fr* ʒaˈnɛ)
jangle ˈdʒæŋgl̩ |-d -d |-ling ˈdʒæŋglɪŋ, -gl̩ɪŋ
Janice ˈdʒænɪs |-'s -ɪz
Janicula dʒəˈnɪkjələ
Janiculum dʒəˈnɪkjələm

---

janitor ˈdʒænətɚ; ES -tə(r; |-ed -d |-ing
  ˈdʒænətərɪŋ, -trɪŋ
Janizary ˈdʒænəˌzɛrɪ
Jansen ˈdʒænsn̩ |-ism -ˌɪzəm |-ist -ɪst
January ˈdʒænjʊˌɛrɪ, ˈdʒænjʊɛrɪ
Janus ˈdʒenəs |-ʼs -ɪz
Jap dʒæp
Japan, j- dʒəˈpæn, dʒæ- |-ned -d
Japanese ˌdʒæpəˈniz (ˈJapaˌnese ˈbeetle)
jape dʒep |japed dʒept
Japhet ˈdʒefɪt
Japheth ˈdʒefɪθ, -fɪt
Japhetic dʒəˈfɛtɪk, dʒe-
Jaqueline ˈdʒækwəlɪn, -ˌlin
Jaquenetta ˌdʒækwəˈnɛtə, ˌdʒækə-
Jaques surname dʒæks, dʒeks; in Shak.
  ˈdʒekwiz, -kwɪz |-ʼs -ɪz
jar dʒɑr; ES dʒɑː(r, E+dʒɑː(r; |-red -d
jardiniere ˌdʒɑrdn̩ˈɪr; E ˌdʒɑːdn̩ˈɪə(r, ˌdʒɑːd-;
  S ˌdʒɑːdn̩ˈɪə(r, -ˈɛə(r; (Fr ʒardiˈnjɛːr)
Jared ˈdʒerɪd
jarful ˈdʒɑrˌfʊl; ES ˈdʒɑː-, E+ˈdʒɑː-; |-s -z
jargon ˈdʒɑrgən, -gɑn, -gɒn |-ed -d
jarl jɑrl; ES jɑːl, E+jɑːl; |-ess -ɪs
jarless ʻwithout jarʼ ˈdʒɑrlɪs; ES ˈdʒɑː-,
  E+ˈdʒɑː-
jarovize ˈjɑrəˌvɑɪz |-s -ɪz |-d -d
Jarrow ˈdʒæro, -ə
Jarvis ˈdʒɑrvɪs; ES ˈdʒɑː-, E+ˈdʒɑː-; |-ʼs -ɪz
jasmine, -min ˈdʒæsmɪn, ˈdʒæz-
Jason ˈdʒesn̩
jasper, J- ˈdʒæspɚ; ES ˈdʒæspə(r; |-ed -d
Jassy ˈjɑsɪ, ˈdʒæsɪ
Jastrow ˈdʒæstro
jaundice ˈdʒɔndɪs, ˈdʒɒn-, ˈdʒɑn- |-s -ɪz |-d -t
jaunt dʒɔnt, dʒɒnt, dʒɑnt |-ed -ɪd |-y -ɪ
Java ˈdʒɑvə |-n -n
Javan Bible ˈdʒevən, ˈdʒevæn
Javanese ˌdʒævəˈniz (ˈJavaˌnese ˈpeople)
javelin ˈdʒævlɪn |-ed -d
jaw dʒɔ |jawed dʒɔd
jawbone ˈdʒɔˈbon, -ˌbon
jawbreaker ˈdʒɔˌbrekɚ; ES -ˌbrekə(r
jay, J- dʒe
jayhawk ˈdʒeˌhɔk |-ed -t |-er -ɚ; ES -ə(r
jaywalk ˈdʒeˌwɔk |-ed -t |-er -ɚ; ES -ə(r
jazz dʒæz |jazzes ˈdʒæzɪz |-ed -d |-ily - ɪ, -ɪlɪ
Jeaffreson ˈdʒefəsn̩; ES ˈdʒefəsn̩
jealous ˈdʒɛləs |y -ɪ

Jeames dʒimz |-ʼs -ɪz
Jean Eng name dʒin, Fr name ʒɑ̃
jean cloth dʒin, dʒen
Jeanne Eng name dʒin, Fr name ʒɑːn
Jeanne dʼArc Fr ʒɑːnˈdɑrk
Jeannette dʒəˈnɛt
Jeans dʒinz |-ʼs -ɪz
Jebusite ˈdʒɛbjʊˌzaɪt |-sitic ˌdʒɛbjuˈzɪtɪk
Jedburgh ˈdʒɛdˌbɝo, -ə; ES -ˌbɜr, -ˌbʌr-,
  -ˌbɝ-; Brit ˈdʒɛdbərə
Jedediah ˌdʒɛdɪˈdaɪə
jeer dʒɪr; ES dʒɪə(r, S+dʒɛə(r; |-ed -d
Jefferies ˈdʒɛfrɪz |-ries' -rɪz
Jefferson ˈdʒɛfɚsn̩; ES ˈdʒɛfəsn̩
Jeffersonian ˌdʒɛfɚˈsonɪən; ES ˌdʒɛfə-
Jeffrey, -fferey ˈdʒɛfrɪ
Jeffreys ˈdʒɛfrɪz |-reys' -rɪz
Jeffries ˈdʒɛfrɪz |-ries' -rɪz
jehad dʒɪˈhɑd
Jehoiakim dʒɪˈhɔɪəˌkɪm
Jehoram dʒɪˈhorəm, -ˈhɔr-; S -ˈhorəm
Jehoshaphat dʒɪˈhɑʃəˌfæt, -ˈhɑs-; ES+-ˈhɒ-
Jehovah dʒɪˈhovə
Jehu ˈdʒihju, -hɪu
jejune dʒɪˈdʒun, -ˈdʒɪun (ˈjeˌjune ˈdiet)
jejunum dʒɪˈdʒunəm, -ˈdʒɪunəm
Jekyll ˈdʒikl̩, ˈdʒɛkl̩
jelly ˈdʒɛlɪ |-ied -d |-fish -ˌfɪʃ
Jemima dʒəˈmaɪmə
jemmy, J- ˈdʒɛmɪ
Jena ˈjenə
Jenghiz Khan, -is ˈdʒɛn·gɪzˈkɑn, ˈdʒɛŋgɪz-
Jenkins ˈdʒɛŋkɪnz |-ʼs -ɪz
Jenner ˈdʒɛnɚ; ES ˈdʒɛnə(r
jennet ˈdʒɛnɪt
Jenny, j- ˈdʒɛnɪ
jeopard ˈdʒɛpɚd; ES ˈdʒɛpəd; |-ed -ɪd |-y -ɪ
jeopardize ˈdʒɛpɚdˌaɪz; ES ˈdʒɛpəd-; |-s -ɪz
  |-d -d
Jephtha ˈdʒɛfθə, ˈdʒɛpθə
Jerauld dʒəˈrɔld
jerboa dʒɚˈboə; ES dʒəˈboə
jeremiad ˌdʒɛrəˈmaɪəd, -æd
Jeremiah ˌdʒɛrəˈmaɪə
Jeremy ˈdʒɛrəmɪ
Jericho ˈdʒɛrəˌko
Jeritza ˈjɛrɪtsə
jerk dʒɝk; ES dʒɜk, dʒɝk; |-ed -t
jerkin ˈdʒɝkɪn; ES ˈdʒɜk-, ˈdʒɝk-; |-ed -d

|full fʊl |tooth tuθ |further ˈfɝðɚ; ES ˈfɝðə |custom ˈkʌstəm |while hwaɪl |how haʊ |toy tɔɪ
|using ˈjuzɪŋ |fuse fjuz, fɪuz |dish dɪʃ |vision ˈvɪʒən |Eden ˈidn̩ |cradle ˈkredl̩ |keep ʼem ˈkipm̩

Those words below in which the ɑ sound is spelt o are often pronounced with ɒ in E and S

Jeroboam, j- ˌdʒɛrəˈboəm

Jerome dʒəˈrom, ˈdʒɛrəm

Jerrold ˈdʒɛrəld

Jerry, j- ˈdʒɛrɪ

jerry-build ˈdʒɛrɪˌbɪld |-built -ˌbɪlt

Jersey, j- ˈdʒɝ·zɪ; ES ˈdʒɜzɪ, ˈdʒɝ·zɪ; |-ed -d

Jerusalem dʒəˈrusələm, -ˈrɪu-

Jervaulx *Yks* ˈdʒɑrvɪs, ˈdʒɝ·vo; ES ˈdʒɑ:vɪs,
    ˈdʒɝvo, ˈdʒɝ·vo, E+ˈdʒɑ:vɪs; |-'s -ɪsɪz, -voz

Jervis ˈdʒɝ·vɪs, ˈdʒɑrvɪs; ES ˈdʒɜvɪs, ˈdʒɝ·v-,
    ˈdʒɑ:v-, E+ˈdʒɑ:v-; |-'s -ɪz

Jervois *Austral* ˈdʒɝ·vɪs; ES ˈdʒɜv-, ˈdʒɝ·v-

Jeshurun ˈdʒɛʃjurən, ˈdʒɛʃu-

Jespersen ˈjɛspɚsn̩; ES ˈjɛspəsn̩

jess dʒɛs |jesses ˈdʒɛsɪz |jessed dʒɛst

jessamine, J- ˈdʒɛsəmɪn

Jesse ˈdʒɛsɪ |Jessie ˈdʒɛsɪ |-sica ˈdʒɛsɪkə

Jessopp, Jessup ˈdʒɛsəp

jest dʒɛst |jested ˈdʒɛstɪd

Jesu ˈdʒizju, ˈdʒis-, -ɪu, -u

Jesuit ˈdʒɛʒuɪt, ˈdʒɛzju- |-ry -rɪ

Jesuitic, j- ˌdʒɛʒuˈɪtɪk, ˌdʒɛzju- |-al -l̩ |-ally
    -l̩ɪ, -ɪklɪ

Jesup ˈdʒɛsəp

Jesus ˈdʒizəs |-sus' -zəs

jet dʒɛt |jetted ˈdʒɛtɪd

jet-black ˈdʒɛtˈblæk (ˈjet-ˌblack ˈeyes)

Jethro ˈdʒɛθro

jetsam ˈdʒɛtsəm

jettison ˈdʒɛtəsn̩, -zn̩ |-ed -d

jetty ˈdʒɛtɪ |jettied ˈdʒɛtɪd

jeu d'esprit *Fr* ʒødɛsˈpri

Jevons ˈdʒɛvənz |-'s -ɪz

Jew dʒu, dʒɪu |-ess -ɪs |-ry -rɪ

jewel, J- ˈdʒuəl, ˈdʒɪuəl |-ry -rɪ

Jewett ˈdʒuɪt, ˈdʒɪuɪt

jew's-harp ˈdʒuzˌhɑrp, ˈdʒus-, ˈdʒɪu-; ES
    -ˌhɑ:p, E+-ˌha:p; ˈdʒusˌhɑrp *preserves a
    regular old form, dissociated from* Jew's.

Jezebel ˈdʒɛzəbl̩

Jezreel ˈdʒɛzrɪəl, dʒɛzˈril |-ite ˈdʒɛzrɪəlˌaɪt

jib dʒɪb |jibbed dʒɪbd

jibber ˈdʒɪbɚ; ES -ə(r; |-ed -d |-ing -bərɪŋ,
    -brɪŋ

jibboom ˈdʒɪbˈbum

jibe dʒaɪb |jibed dʒaɪbd

jiffy ˈdʒɪfɪ

jig dʒɪg |jigged dʒɪgd

jigger ˈdʒɪgɚ; ES -ə(r; |-ed -d |-ing -ɪŋ, -grɪŋ

jiggle ˈdʒɪgl̩ |-d -d |-ling ˈdʒɪglɪŋ, -gl̩ɪŋ

jigsaw ˈdʒɪgˌsɔ |-ed -d

jihad dʒɪˈhad

Jill dʒɪl

jilt dʒɪlt |jilted ˈdʒɪltɪd

Jim dʒɪm

jimjams ˈdʒɪmˌdʒæmz

jimmy, J- ˈdʒɪmɪ |-ied -d

Jimson weed ˈdʒɪmsn̩ˌwid

Jinghis Khan ˈdʒɪn·gɪzˈkɑn, ˈdʒɪŋgɪz-

jingle ˈdʒɪŋgl̩ |-d -d |-ling ˈdʒɪŋglɪŋ, -gl̩ɪŋ

jingo ˈdʒɪŋgo |-ed -d |-ism -ˌɪzəm

jink dʒɪŋk |jinked dʒɪŋkt

jinn *pl* dʒɪn

jinnee, -nni dʒɪˈni |*pl* jinn dʒɪn

jinniyeh dʒɪˈnijɛ |*pl* jinn dʒɪn

jinricksha, -rikisha dʒɪnˈrɪkʃə, -ʃo

jinx dʒɪŋks |jinxes ˈdʒɪŋksɪz |jinxed dʒɪŋkst

jitney ˈdʒɪtnɪ

jitters ˈdʒɪtɚz; ES ˈdʒɪtəz; |-ery -ərɪ

jiujitsu, jiujutsu dʒuˈdʒɪtsu, dʒɪu-

Joab ˈdʒoæb

Joachim, -akim *Bible* ˈdʒoəˌkɪm, *violinist*
    ˈjoəˌkɪm (*Ger* joˈɑxɪm)

Joan dʒon, ˈdʒoən, dʒoˈæn—dʒoˈæn *is a
    spelling pron., not used by those familiar
    with the traditional pron.*

Joanna dʒoˈænə

Joan of Arc ˈdʒonəvˈɑrk, dʒoˈæn-; ES -ˈɑ:k,
    E+-ˈa:k;—*see* Joan

Joaquin hwaˈkin (*Am Sp* hwa-)

job dʒɑb |-bed -d |-ber -ɚ; ES -ə(r

Job dʒob

Jobson ˈdʒɑbsn̩, ˈdʒob-

Jocasta dʒoˈkæstə

Jocelin, -ine, -lyn ˈdʒɑslɪn, ˈdʒɑsəlɪn

Jock dʒɑk

jockey ˈdʒɑkɪ |-ed -d

jocko ˈdʒɑko

jocose dʒoˈkos |-sity -ˈkɑsətɪ

jocular ˈdʒɑkjələ; ES -lə(r; |-ity ˌdʒɑkjə-
    ˈlærətɪ

jocund ˈdʒɑkənd, -ʌnd |-ity dʒoˈkʌndətɪ

jodel ˈjodl̩ |-ed -d |-ing ˈjodlɪŋ, ˈjodl̩ɪŋ

Jodhpur dʒodˈpur; ES -ˈpuə(r; *acct*+ˈJodhpur

jodhpurs ˈdʒodpɚz, ˈdʒod-; ES -pəz

Joe dʒo

Those words below in which the ɑ *sound is spelt* o *are often pronounced with* ɒ *in E and S*

Joel 'dʒoəl
Joffre *Fr* ʒɔ́fɽ
jog dʒɑg |jogged dʒɑgd
joggle 'dʒɑg| |-d -d̦ |-ling 'dʒɑglɪŋ, -g|ɪŋ
Johanna dʒo'hænə
Johannes, j- dʒo'hæniz |-es' -iz
Johannesburg dʒo'hænɪsˌbɝg, jo-; ES -ˌbɜg, -ˌbɝg
John dʒɑn, dʒɒn |-ian 'dʒonɪən
johnnycake 'dʒɑnɪˌkek
Johnny-jump-up 'dʒɑnɪ'dʒʌmpˌʌp
Johnson 'dʒɑnsn̩ |-ese ˌdʒɑnsn̩'iz
Johnsonian dʒɑn'sonɪən
Johnston 'dʒɑnstən
Johnstown 'dʒɑnzˌtaʊn
joie-de-vivre *Fr* ʒwadə'vivr
join dʒɔɪn |-ed -d
joinder 'dʒɔɪndɚ; ES 'dʒɔɪndə(r
joiner 'dʒɔɪnɚ; ES 'dʒɔɪnə(r; |-ed -d |-y -ɪ
joint dʒɔɪnt |-ɘd -ɪd |-ress -rɪs |-resses -rɪsɪz
joint-stock 'dʒɔɪnt'stɑk ('joint-ˌstock 'bank)
jointure 'dʒɔɪntʃɚ; ES 'dʒɔɪntʃə(r; |-d -d
joist dʒɔɪst, dʒɔɪs |-joists dʒɔɪsts, dʒɔɪs:
joke dʒok |joked dʒokt
Joliet *Ill* 'dʒolɪˌɛt, -ət, ˌdʒolɪ'ɛt, -al-
Jolliet, Joli- *explorer* 'dʒolɪˌɛt, -ət, ˌdʒolɪ'ɛt, -al- (*Fr* ʒɔ́'ljɛ)
jollification ˌdʒɑləfə'keʃən
jollify 'dʒɑləˌfaɪ |-fied -ˌfaɪd
jolly 'dʒɑlɪ |jollity 'dʒɑlətɪ
jolt dʒolt |jolted 'dʒoltɪd
Jon dʒɑn
Jonah 'dʒonə
Jonas 'dʒonəs |-'s -ɪz
Jonathan 'dʒɑnəθən
Jones dʒonz |-'s -ɪz
jonglery 'dʒɑŋglərɪ
jongleur 'dʒɑŋglɚ; ES 'dʒɑŋglə(r; (*Fr* ʒɔ̃-'glœ:r)
jonquil 'dʒɑŋkwɪl, 'dʒɑn-
Jonson 'dʒɑnsn̩ |-ian dʒɑn'sonɪən
Joplin 'dʒɑplɪn
Joppa 'dʒɑpə
Jordan 'dʒɔrdn̩; ES 'dʒɔədn̩
jorum 'dʒorəm, 'dʒɔr-; S 'dʒorəm
Joseph 'dʒozəf |-phine 'dʒozəˌfin
Josepha dʒo'sifə |-phus -fəs |-phus's -fəsɪz
josh dʒɑʃ |joshes 'dʒɑʃɪz |joshed dʒɑʃt

Joshua 'dʒɑʃʊə, *o.f.* 'dʒɑʃəˌwe
Josiah dʒo'saɪə
joss dʒɑs, dʒɒs |-es -ɪz
jostle 'dʒɑs| |-d -d̦ |-ling 'dʒɑslɪŋ, -s|ɪŋ
jot dʒɑt |jotted 'dʒɑtɪd
Jotunn, -un 'jɔtʊn, 'jɒt- |-heim -ˌhem
Joule dʒaʊl, dʒul, dʒol |joule dʒaʊl, dʒul
jounce dʒaʊns |jounces 'dʒaʊnsɪz |-d -t
Jourdain *Shak.* dʒʊr'den; ES dʒʊə-; *Fr name* ʒur'dæ̃
journal 'dʒɝn̩|; ES 'dʒɜn̩|, 'dʒɝn̩|; |-ed -d |-ism -ˌɪzəm |-ist -ɪst
journalese ˌdʒɝn̩|'iz, -'is; ES ˌdʒɜn̩|-, ˌdʒɝn̩|-
journalistic ˌdʒɝn̩|'ɪstɪk; ES ˌdʒɜn̩|-, ˌdʒɝn̩|-; |-ally -|ɪ, -ɪklɪ
journalize 'dʒɝn̩|ˌaɪz; ES 'dʒɜn̩|-, 'dʒɝn̩|-; |-s -ɪz |-d -d
journey 'dʒɝnɪ; ES 'dʒɜnɪ, 'dʒɝnɪ; |-ed -d |-man -mən |-men -mən
joust dʒʌst, dʒaʊst |-ed -ɪd
Jove dʒov |Jovian 'dʒovɪən
jovial 'dʒovjəl, -vɪəl |-ity ˌdʒovɪ'ælətɪ
Jovinian dʒo'vɪnɪən
Jowett 'dʒaʊɪt
jowl dʒaʊl, dʒol |-ed -d
joy dʒɔɪ |-ed -d |-ful -fəl |-fully -fəlɪ |-ous -əs
Joyce dʒɔɪs |-'s -ɪz
Juab 'dʒuæb, 'dʒɪuæb
Juan 'dʒuən, 'dʒɪuən (*Sp* xwan)
Juanita wə'nitə, wɒ-, wa- (*Sp* xwa'nita)
Juarez, Juárez 'hwares (*Am Sp* 'hwares)
Jubal 'dʒubḷ, 'dʒɪubḷ
jubilance 'dʒubḷəns, 'dʒɪu- |-cy -ɪ |-ant -ənt
jubilate 'dʒubḷˌet, 'dʒɪu- |-d -ɪd
Jubilate ˌdʒubə'leti, ˌdʒɪu-
jubilation ˌdʒubḷ'eʃən, ˌdʒɪu-
jubilee 'dʒubḷˌi, 'dʒɪu-
Judaea dʒu'diə, dʒɪu- |-n -n
Judah 'dʒudə, 'dʒɪudə
Judaic dʒu'de·ɪk, dʒɪu- |-al -| |-ally -|ɪ, -ɪklɪ
Judaism 'dʒudɪˌɪzəm, 'dʒɪu-
judaize 'dʒudɪˌaɪz, 'dʒɪu- |-s -ɪz |-d -d
Judas 'dʒudəs, 'dʒɪu- |-'s -ɪz
Judd dʒʌd
Jude dʒud, dʒɪud
Judea dʒu'diə, dʒɪu- |-n -n
judge dʒʌdʒ |judges 'dʒʌdʒɪz |-d -d
judgement 'dʒʌdʒmənt

|full fʊl |tooth tuθ |further 'fɝðɚ; ES 'fɝðə |custom 'kʌstəm |while hwaɪl |how haʊ |toy tɔɪ
|using 'juzɪŋ |fuse fjuz, fɪuz |dish dɪʃ |vision 'vɪʒən |Eden 'idn̩ |cradle 'kredḷ |keep 'em 'kipm̩

Judges 'dʒʌdʒɪz
judgeship 'dʒʌdʒʃɪp
judgmatic dʒʌdʒ'mætɪk |-al -ļ |-ally -ļɪ, -ɪklɪ
judgment 'dʒʌdʒmənt
judicable 'dʒudɪkəbļ, 'dʒɪu-
judicatory 'dʒudɪkəˌtorɪ, 'dʒɪu-, -ˌtɔrɪ; S -ˌtorɪ
judicature 'dʒudɪkətʃɚ, 'dʒɪu-; ES -tʃə(r
judiciable dʒu'dɪʃɪəbļ, dʒɪu-
judicial dʒu'dɪʃəl, dʒɪu- |-ly -ɪ
judiciary dʒu'dɪʃɪˌɛrɪ, dʒɪu-, -'dɪʃərɪ
judicious dʒu'dɪʃəs, dʒɪu-
Judith 'dʒudɪθ, 'dʒɪu-
Judson 'dʒʌdsņ
Judy 'dʒudɪ, 'dʒɪudɪ
jug dʒʌg |jugged dʒʌgd
Juggernaut, j- 'dʒʌgɚˌnɔt; ES 'dʒʌgə-; |-ed -ɪd
juggle 'dʒʌgļ |-d -d |-ling 'dʒʌglɪŋ, -gļɪŋ
jugglery 'dʒʌglərɪ
Jugoslav n 'jugoˌslav, -ˌslæv
Jugoslav adj 'jugo'slav, -'slæv ('Jugoˌslav 'state)
Jugoslavia 'jugo'slavɪə, -vjə |-n -n
Jugoslavic ˌjugo'slavɪk, -'slæv-
jugular 'dʒʌgjələ, less freq. 'dʒug-; ES -lə(r
Jugurtha dʒu'gɜθə; ES -'gɜθə, -'gɜθə
juice dʒus, dʒɪus |-s -ɪz |-d -d |-cy -ɪ
jujitsu dʒu'dʒɪtsu, dʒɪu-
juju 'dʒudʒu |-ism -ˌɪzəm |-ist -ɪst
jujube 'dʒudʒub, 'dʒɪudʒɪub (Fr ʒy'ʒyb)
jujutsu dʒu'dʒɪtsu, dʒɪu-
Jukes dʒuks, dʒɪuks |-'s -ɪz
julep 'dʒulɪp, 'dʒɪu-, -ləp
Julia 'dʒuljə, 'dʒɪul- |-n -n
Juliana ˌdʒulɪ'ænə, ˌdʒɪul-, -jɪ'ænə
Julien 'dʒuljən, 'dʒɪuljən
julienne ˌdʒulɪ'ɛn, ˌdʒɪul-
Juliet 'dʒuljət, 'dʒɪul-, -lɪət—*The frequent modern pron.* ˌdʒulɪ'ɛt *has no basis in Shakespeare's verse. Of some 47 occurrences, 43 show only two syllables and initial accent; in the 4 cases of three syllables (all highly emotional) there is no evidence that the last syllable had more than secondary accent.*
Julius 'dʒuljəs, 'dʒɪul- |-'s -ɪz
July dʒu'ļaɪ, dʒɪu- ('Juˌly 'first)
jumble 'dʒʌmbļ |-d -d |-ling 'dʒʌmblɪŋ, -bļɪŋ
Jumbo, j- 'dʒʌmbo

jump dʒʌmp |jumped dʒʌmpt
junco, J- 'dʒʌŋko
junction 'dʒʌŋkʃən |-ed -d
juncture 'dʒʌŋktʃɚ; ES 'dʒʌŋktʃə(r
June dʒun, dʒɪun
Juneau 'dʒuno, 'dʒɪu-
Jungfrau 'juŋˌfrau
jungle 'dʒʌŋgļ |-d -d
Juniata ˌdʒunɪ'ætə, ˌdʒɪu-
junior 'dʒunjɚ, 'dʒɪun-; ES -jə(r
juniority dʒun'jɔrətɪ, dʒɪun-, -'jɑr-, -'jɒr-
juniper 'dʒunəpɚ, 'dʒɪun-; ES -pə(r
Junius 'dʒunjəs, 'dʒɪun-, -nɪəs |-'s -ɪz
junk dʒʌŋk |junked dʒʌŋkt
Junker, j- 'juŋkɚ; ES 'juŋkə(r
junket 'dʒʌŋkɪt |-ed -ɪd
Juno 'dʒuno, 'dʒɪuno
junta 'dʒʌntə |junto 'dʒʌnto
Jupiter 'dʒupətɚ, 'dʒɪu-; ES -tə(r
Jura 'dʒurə, 'dʒɪurə (Fr ʒy'ra)
jural 'dʒurəl, 'dʒɪur- |-ly -ɪ
jurant 'dʒurənt, 'dʒɪur-
jurassic dʒu'ræsɪk, dʒɪu-
jurat 'dʒuræt, 'dʒɪur-
juridical dʒu'rɪdɪkļ, dʒɪu- |-ly -ɪ, -ɪklɪ
jurisconsult ˌdʒurɪskən'sʌlt, ˌdʒɪur-, -'kɑn-sʌlt; ES+-'kɒn-
jurisdiction ˌdʒurɪs'dɪkʃən, ˌdʒɪur- |-al -ļ |-ally -ļɪ
jurisprudence ˌdʒurɪs'prudņs, ˌdʒɪurɪs'prɪud- |-dent -dņt
jurist 'dʒurɪst, 'dʒɪur-
juristic dʒu'rɪstɪk, dʒɪu- |-al -ļ |-ally -ļɪ, -ɪklɪ
juror 'dʒurɚ, 'dʒɪurɚ; ES -rə(r
jury 'dʒurɪ, 'dʒɪurɪ |-man -mən |-men -mən
jury-rigged 'dʒurɪˌrɪgd, 'dʒɪurɪ-
Jusserand Fr ʒy'srɑ̃
just dʒʌst, lightly stressed adv often dʒəst, dʒɛst
justice 'dʒʌstɪs |-s -ɪz |-d -t |-ship -ˌʃɪp
justiciable dʒʌs'tɪʃɪəbļ
justiciar dʒʌs'tɪʃɪɚ; ES -'tɪʃɪ·ə(r
justiciary dʒʌs'tɪʃɪˌɛrɪ
justifiability ˌdʒʌstəˌfaɪə'bɪlətɪ
justifiable 'dʒʌstəˌfaɪəbļ |-bly -blɪ
justification ˌdʒʌstəfə'keʃən
justificatory dʒʌs'tɪfəkəˌtorɪ, 'dʒʌstəfəˌke-tərɪ; EN+-ˌtɔrɪ

Key: See in full §§3–47. bee bi |pity 'pɪtɪ (§6) |rate ret |yet jɛt |sang sæŋ |angry 'æŋ·grɪ |bath bæθ; E baθ (§10) |ah ɑ |far fɑr |watch watʃ, wɒtʃ (§12) |jaw dʒɔ |gorge gɔrdʒ |go go

justify ˈdʒʌstəˌfaɪ |-fied -ˌfaɪd
Justin ˈdʒʌstɪn |-ian dʒʌsˈtɪnɪən
Justus ˈdʒʌstəs |-ʼs -ɪz
jut dʒʌt |jutted ˈdʒʌtɪd
jute, J- dʒut, dʒɪut
Jutland ˈdʒʌtlənd

Juvenal ˈdʒuvənḷ, ˈdʒɪuv-
juvenescence ˌdʒuvəˈnɛsṇs, ˌdʒɪu- |-ent -ṇt
juvenile ˈdʒuvənḷ, ˈdʒɪu-, -nɪl, -ˌnaɪl
juvenility ˌdʒuvəˈnɪlətɪ, ˌdʒɪu-
juxtapose ˌdʒʌkstəˈpoz |-s -ɪz |-d -d
juxtaposition ˌdʒʌkstəpəˈzɪʃən |-al -ḷ

K

K, k letter ke |pl K's, Ks, poss K's kez
Kaaterskill ˈkɔtɚzˌkɪl, ˈkɑt-; ES -təz-
Kabul ˈkɑbʊl
Kadesh-Barnea ˈkedɛʃˈbɑrnɪə; ES -ˈbɑːn-,
E+-ˈbaːn-
Kaffir, Kafir ˈkæfɚ; ES ˈkæfə(r
Kahoka kəˈhokə
kaiser, K- ˈkaɪzɚ; ES ˈkaɪzə(r
Kalamazoo ˌkæləməˈzu
kale kel
kaleidoscope kəˈlaɪdəˌskop
kaleidoscopic kəˌlaɪdəˈskɑpɪk; ES+-ˈskɒp-;
|-al -ḷ |-ally -ḷɪ, -ɪklɪ
kalends ˈkælɪndz, -əndz, -nz
Kalevala ˌkɑlɪˈvɑlə
Kalkaska kælˈkæskə
Kallyope ʻcalliope' ˈkælɪˌop
Kalmuck, k-, -muk ˈkælmʌk
kalsomine ˈkælsəˌmaɪn |-d -d
Kama ˈkɑmə
Kamchatka kæmˈtʃætkə
Kamerun ˌkæməˈrun (Ger ˌkɑməˈruːn)
Kanaka kəˈnækə, ˈkænəkə
Kanawha kəˈnɔwə
Kanchenjunga ˌkʌntʃənˈdʒʌŋgə
Kandahar ˌkændəˈhɑr, ˌkʌndə-; ES -ˈhɑːr
Kandy ˈkændɪ, ˈkɑn-
Kane ken
kangaroo ˌkæŋgəˈru |-ed -d
Kankakee ˌkæŋkəˈki
Kansas ˈkænzəs, rarely -səs; S+-zɪs; |-an -ən
|-sas' -əs, -ɪs
Kant kænt (Ger kɑnt) |-ian -ɪən |-ism -ɪzəm
|-ianism -ɪənˌɪzəm
kaoliang ˌkɑolɪˈæŋ
kaolin, -ine ˈkeəlɪn
kapok ˈkepɑk, ˈkæpək; ES+-pɒk
kappa ˈkæpə

Karakoram ˌkɑrəˈkorəm, ˌkærə-; EN+
-ˈkorəm
Karelia kəˈrilɪə
Karl kɑrl; ES kɑːl, E+kɑːl
Karlsbad ˈkɑrlzbæd; ES ˈkɑːlz-, E+ˈkɑːlz-;
(Ger ˈkɑrlsbɑt)
Karlsruhe ˈkɑrlzruə; ES ˈkɑːlz-, E+ˈkɑːlz-;
(Ger ˈkɑrlsruːə, -ˈruːə)
karma ˈkɑrmə, ˈkɝmə; ES ˈkɑːmə, ˈkɝmə,
ˈkɝmə; (Hind ˈkʌrmə)
Karnak ˈkɑrnæk; ES ˈkɑː-, E+ˈkɑː-
Karroo, Karoo, k- kəˈru, kæˈru
Kashmir India kæʃˈmɪr; ES -ˈmɪə(r; |-ian
-ɪən
Kaskaskia kæsˈkæskɪə
Katahdin kəˈtɑdɪn, -dṇ
Kate, k- ket
Katharina ˌkæθəˈrinə
Katharine ˈkæθrɪn, ˈkæθərɪn
katharsis kəˈθɑrsɪs; ES -ˈθɑːs-, E+-ˈθɑːs-
Katherine ˈkæθrɪn, ˈkæθərɪn
Kathleen ˈkæθlin
kathode ˈkæθod
Kathrine ˈkæθrɪn, ˈkæθərɪn
Katrine ˈkætrɪn, ˈkætrin, Sc ˈkat-
Kattegat ˈkætɪˌgæt, ˌkætɪˈgæt
katydid ˈketɪˌdɪd |-dided -ˌdɪdɪd
Kauai ˌkɑ·uˈɑ·i
Kauffman ˈkɔfmən |Kaufman ˈkɔfmən (Ger
ˈkaufmən)
Kaukauna kɔˈkɔnə
Kavanagh ˈkævəˌnɔ, -nə
Kavanaugh ˈkævəˌnɔ, -nə
kay ke
Kay ke
kayak ˈkaɪæk
Kaye ke |Kaye-Smith ˈkeˈsmɪθ
Kazan kəˈzɑn

|full fʊl |tooth tuθ |further ˈfɝðɚ; ES ˈfɝðə |custom ˈkʌstəm |while hwaɪl |how haʊ |toy tɔɪ
|using ˈjuzɪŋ |fuse fjuz, fɪuz |dish dɪʃ |vision ˈvɪʒən |Eden ˈidṇ |cradle ˈkredḷ |keep ʼem ˈkipm̩

Kean, -e **kin**
Kearny, -ey **ˈkɑrnɪ**; ES **ˈkɑ:nɪ**, E+**ˈkɑ:nɪ**
Kearsarge **ˈkɪrsɑrdʒ**; ES **ˈkɪəsɑ:dʒ**, E+ -sɑ:dʒ; |-ˈs -ɪz
Keats kits |-ˈs -ɪz
Keble **ˈkibl̩**
Kedar **ˈkidɚ**; ES **ˈkidə(r**
kedge **kɛdʒ** |kedges **ˈkɛdʒɪz** |kedged **kɛdʒd**
kedgeree **ˈkɛdʒəˌri**, **ˌkɛdʒəˈri**
Kedron **ˈkidrən**
keel **kil** |keeled **kild** |-less **ˈkillɪs**
keelhaul **ˈkilˌhɔl** |-ed -**d**
keelson **ˈkɛlsn̩**, **ˈkil-**
keen **kin** |-ness **ˈkinnɪs**
Keene **kin**
keep **kip** |kept **kɛpt** |-sake **ˈkipˌsek**
Keewatin ki**ˈwɑtɪn**, -**ˈwɒt-**
keg **kɛg** *L.A. shows that* keg *& less freq.* **kæg** *are used by cultured informants.*
Keighly *Yks* **ˈkiθlɪ**
Keightley **ˈkitlɪ**
Keijo **ke**ˈdʒo
Keith **kiθ**
Kellar, -er **ˈkɛlɚ**; ES **ˈkɛlə(r**
Kelley, -ly, k- **ˈkɛlɪ** |kellied **ˈkɛlɪd**
Kellogg **ˈkɛləg**, -**ɑg**, -**ɒg**
Kelmscot **ˈkɛmskət** (Kelm- *1274*, Kemscott *1695*), **ˈkɛlm-**
kelp **kɛlp**
kelpie, -py **ˈkɛlpɪ**
Kelsey **ˈkɛlsɪ**
Kelso **ˈkɛlso**
kelson **ˈkɛlsn̩**
Kelt **kɛlt** |-ist -**ɪst**
kelter **ˈkɛltɚ**; ES **ˈkɛltə(r**
Keltic **ˈkɛltɪk** |-ally -**lɪ**, -**ɪklɪ**
Kelticism **ˈkɛltəˌsɪzəm** |-cist -**sɪst**
Kelvin **ˈkɛlvɪn**
Kemal kə**ˈmɑl**, **ˈkɛmɑl**
kemb **kɛm** |kembed **kɛmd** *or* kempt **kɛmpt**
Kemble **ˈkɛmbl̩**
Kemmerer **ˈkɛmərɚ**; ES **ˈkɛmərə(r**
kemp, K- **kɛmp**
Kempis **ˈkɛmpɪs** |-ˈs -**ɪz**
ken **kɛn** |kenned **kɛnd**
Kendal, -ll **ˈkɛndl̩** |-ville -**ˌvɪl**
Kenedy **ˈkɛnədɪ**
Kenelm **ˈkɛnəlm**, -**ɛlm**
Kenilworth **ˈkɛnl̩ˌwɝθ**; ES -**ˌwɜθ**, -**ˌwɝθ**

Kenmore *US* **ˈkɛnmor**, -**mɔr**; ES -**moə(r**, E+ -**mɔə(r**; *Scotl* Ken**ˈmore**
Kennan **ˈkɛnən**
Kennebec **ˌkɛnəˈbɛk** (**ˈKenneˌbec** **ˈRiver**)
Kennebunk **ˌkɛnəˈbʌŋk**
Kennebunkport **ˌkɛnəbʌŋkˈport** -**ˈpɔrt**; ES -**ˈpoət**, E+-**ˈpɔət**
Kennedy **ˈkɛnədɪ**
kennel **ˈkɛnl̩** |-ed -**d** |-ly **ˈkɛnl̩ɪ**
Kennerly **ˈkɛnɚlɪ**; ES **ˈkɛnəlɪ**
Kennesaw **ˈkɛnəˌsɔ**
Kenneth **ˈkɛnɪθ**
Kennett Square **ˈkɛnɪtˈskwɛr**, -**ˈskwær**; E -**ˈskwɛə(r**, ES -**ˈskwæə(r**
keno **ˈkino**
Kenora kə**ˈnorə**, -**ˈnɔrə**; S -**ˈnorə**
Kenosha kə**ˈnoʃə**
Kenova kə**ˈnovə**
Kensington **ˈkɛnzɪŋtən**
Kent **kɛnt** |-ish -**ɪʃ**
Kenton **ˈkɛntən**
Kentucky kən**ˈtʌkɪ**, *loc.*+kɛn**ˈtʌkɪ** |-kian -**ən**
Kenya **ˈkɛnjə**, *loc.*+**ˈkinjə**
Kenyon **ˈkɛnjən**
Keokuk **ˈkiəˌkʌk**
kepi **ˈkɛpɪ**
Kepler **ˈkɛplɚ**; ES **ˈkɛplə(r**
kept **kɛpt**, *before some conss.*+**kɛp** (**ˈkɛpˈtɔkɪŋ**)
Ker, -rr **kɝ**, **kɑr**; ES **kɜ(r**, **kɝ**, **kɑ:(r**, E+**kɑ:(r**
keratin **ˈkɛrətɪn**
kerb **kɝb**; ES **kɜb**, **kɝb**; |-stone -**ˌston**
kerchief **ˈkɝtʃɪf**; ES **ˈkɜ-**, **ˈkɝ-**; |-s -**s** |-ed -**t**
kerf **kɝf**, **kɑrf**; ES **kɜf**, **kɝf**, **kɑ:f**, E+**kɑ:f**
kermes **ˈkɝmiz**; ES **ˈkɜm-**, **ˈkɝm-**
kermis, -mess **ˈkɝmɪs**; ES **ˈkɜm-**, **ˈkɝm-**; |-es -**ɪz**
kern **kɝn**; ES **kɜn**, **kɝn**; |-ed -**d**
Kernahan, -no- **ˈkɝnəˌhæn**, **ˈkɑr-**; ES **ˈkɜ-**, **ˈkɝ-**, **ˈkɑ:-**, E+**ˈkɑ:-**
kernel **ˈkɝnl̩**; ES **ˈkɜnl̩**, **ˈkɝnl̩**; |-ed -**d**
kernelless **ˈkɝnl̩lɪs**; ES **ˈkɜn-**, **ˈkɝn-**
kerosene **ˈkɛrəˌsin**, **ˌkɛrəˈsin** |-d -**d**
Kerr **kɝ**, **kɑr**; ES **kɜ(r**, **kɝ**, **kɑ:(r**, E+**kɑ:(r**
Kerry **ˈkɛrɪ**
kersey, K- **ˈkɝzɪ**; ES **ˈkɜzɪ**, **ˈkɝzɪ**
Kershaw **kɝˈʃɔ**; ES **kɜ-**, **kɝ-**
Kesteven *Lincs* **ˈkɛstivən**, *loc.*+kɛs**ˈtivən**
kestrel **ˈkɛstrəl**
Keswick **ˈkɛzɪk**

Key: *See in full §§3–47.* bee **bi** |pity **ˈpɪtɪ** (§6) |rate **ret** |yet **jɛt** |sang **sæŋ** |angry **ˈæŋ·grɪ** |bath **bæθ**; E **bɑθ** (§10) |ah **ɑ** |far **fɑr** |watch **wɑtʃ**, **wɒtʃ** (§12) |jaw **dʒɔ** |gorge **gɔrdʒ** |go **go**

ketch, K- kɛtʃ |-es -ɪz
ketchup ˈkɛtʃəp
ketene ˈkitin
ketone ˈkiton
kettle, K- ˈkɛtļ |-drum -ˌdrʌm—ˈkɪtļ, *a historical variant, is still not infrequently heard.*
Keturah kɪˈtjʊrə, -ˈtɪʊrə
Keuka kɪˈjukə, ˈkjukə
Kew kju, kɪu
Kewanee kəˈwɑni, -ˈwɒni
Kewaunee kəˈwɔni
Keweenaw ˈkiwɪˌnɔ
key, K- ki |-ed -d |-board -ˌbord, -ˌbɔrd; ES -ˌbɔəd, E+-ˌbɔəd
Keyes kiz, kaɪz |-'s -ɪz
keyhole ˈkiˌhol
keyman ˈkiˌmæn, -ˈmæn |-men -ˌmɛn, -ˈmɛn
Keynes kenz |-'s -ɪz
keynote ˈkiˌnot, -ˈnot
Keyport ˈkiˌport, -ˌpɔrt; ES -ˌpoət, E+-ˌpɔət
Keyser ˈkaɪzɚ; ES ˈkaɪzə(r
keystone, K- ˈkiˌston |-d -d
Key West ˈkiˈwɛst
Kezia, -h kəˈzaɪə
khaddar ˈkʌdɚ; ES ˈkʌdə(r
khaki ˈkɑkɪ, ˈkækɪ |-ed -d
khan, K- kɑn, kæn
Kharkov ˈkɑrkɔf, -kɒf; ES ˈkɑː-, E+ˈkɑː-
Khartoum, -tum kɑrˈtum; ES kɑː-, E+kɑː-
Khayyám kaɪˈɑm, -ˈæm, -ˈjɑm, -ˈjæm
khedive, K- kəˈdiv |-vial -ɪəl, -jəl |-viate -ɪɪt
Khmer kmɛr; ES kmɛə(r
Khyber ˈkaɪbɚ; ES ˈkaɪbə(r
Kiangsu ˈkjæŋˈsu (*Chin* ˈdʒjɑŋˈsu)
Kiaochow ˈkjauˈtʃau (*Chin* ˈdʒjauˈdʒo)
kibe kaɪb |-bed kaɪbd
kibitzer ˈkɪbɪtsɚ, kəˈbɪt-; ES -sə(r
kibosh ˈkaɪbɑʃ, kɪˈbɑʃ; ES+-ɒʃ
kick kɪk |-ed -t |-back -ˌbæk |-off -ˌɔf, -ˌɒf
kickshaw ˈkɪkʃɔ
kickup ˈkɪkˌʌp
kid kɪd |kidded ˈkɪdɪd |-dy -ɪ
Kidd kɪd
kidnap ˈkɪdnæp |-(p)ed -t
kidney ˈkɪdnɪ
Kidron ˈkɪdrən
kidskin ˈkɪdˌskɪn
Kiel kil
Kiev kiˈɛv, -ˈɛf, ˈkiɛv, -ɛf

Kilauea ˌkilauˈeə
Kildare kɪlˈdɛr, -ˈdær; E -ˈdɛə(r, ES -ˈdæə(r
kilderkin ˈkɪldɚkɪn; ES ˈkɪldə-
kilerg ˈkɪlˌɝg; ES -ˌɜg, -ˌ3g
Kilkenny kɪlˈkɛnɪ (ˈKilˌkenny ˈcats)
kill kɪl |killed kɪld |-able -əbļ
Killarney kɪˈlɑrnɪ; ES -ˈlɑːnɪ, E+-ˈlɑːnɪ
killdeer ˈkɪlˌdɪr; ES -ˌdɪə(r, S+-ˌdɛə(r, -ˌdjɛə(r
Killiecrankie ˌkɪlɪˈkræŋkɪ
Killigrew ˈkɪləˌgru, -ˌgrɪu
killjoy ˈkɪlˌdʒɔɪ
Kilmarnock kɪlˈmɑrnək; ES -ˈmɑːn-, E+-ˈmɑːn-
Kilmer ˈkɪlmɚ; ES ˈkɪlmə(r
kiln kɪl, kɪln—*spelt kill since 1470 (so in the 1611 Bible)—The* n *sound was lost from* kiln *in the same way as it was from* ell, mill, Milne.
kiln-dry ˈkɪlˌdraɪ |-dried -ˌdraɪd
kilo ˈkɪlo, ˈki-
kilocalorie ˈkɪləˌkælərɪ
kilocycle ˈkɪləˌsaɪkļ
kilogram, -mme ˈkɪləˌgræm
kiloliter, -tre ˈkɪləˌlitɚ; ES -ˌlitə(r
kilometer, -tre ˈkɪləˌmitɚ, *much less freq.* kɪˈlɑmətɚ; ES -tə(r, -ˈlɒm-
kilowatt ˈkɪləˌwat, -ˌwɒt
kilowatt-hour ˈkɪləˌwatˈaʊr, -ˌwɒt-; ES -ˈaʊə(r
Kilpatrick kɪlˈpætrɪk
kilt kɪlt |kilted ˈkɪltɪd
kilter ˈkɪltɚ; ES ˈkɪltə(r
Kim kɪm |-ball -bļ |-berley -bɚlɪ; ES -bəlɪ
Kimbolton *O* kɪmˈboltņ, *NC* ˈkɪmbļtən, *Hunts* kɪmˈboltņ, *formerly* ˈkɪmļtən (*Shak.* Kymmalton)
kimono kəˈmonə, -no
kin kɪn
kinaesthesia ˌkɪnɪsˈθiʒə, -zɪə |-thetic -ˈθɛtɪk
Kincaid kɪnˈked, kɪŋˈked
Kincardine kɪnˈkɑrdɪn, kɪŋ-; ES -ˈkɑːd-, E+-ˈkɑːd-
Kinchinjunga ˌkɪntʃɪnˈdʒʌŋgə
kind kaɪnd
kindergarten ˈkɪndɚˌgɑrtņ; ES ˈkɪndəˌgɑːtņ; E+-ˌgɑːtņ; |-tner, -tener -tnɚ; ES -tnə(r
kindhearted ˈkaɪndˈhɑrtɪd; ES -ˈhɑːt-, E+-ˈhɑːt-; (ˈkindˌhearted ˈman)
kindle ˈkɪndļ |-d -d -d |-ling -dlɪŋ, -dļɪŋ

kindling *n* ˈkɪndlɪŋ
kindness ˈkaɪndnɪs, ˈkaɪnnɪs |-es -ɪz
kindred ˈkɪndrɪd, -əd
kine kaɪn |-pox -ˌpaks; ES+-ˌpɒks
kinema ˈkɪnəmə
kinematic ˌkɪnəˈmætɪk |-al -ḷ |-ally -ḷɪ, -ɪklɪ
kinematograph ˌkɪnəˈmætəˌgræf; E+-ˌgraf,
    -ˌgraf
kinesthesia ˌkɪnɪsˈθiʒə, -zɪə |-thetic -ˈθɛtɪk
kinetic kɪˈnɛtɪk, kaɪ- |-al -ḷ |-ally -ḷɪ, -ɪklɪ
kinfolk ˈkɪnˌfok
king, K- kɪŋ
kingbird ˈkɪŋˌbɝd; ES -ˌbɜd, -ˌbɝd
kingbolt ˈkɪŋˌbolt
kingcraft ˈkɪŋˌkræft; E+-ˌkraft, -ˌkraft
kingdom ˈkɪŋdəm
Kingdon ˈkɪŋdən
kingfisher ˈkɪŋˌfɪʃɚ; ES -ˌfɪʃə(r
kinglet ˈkɪŋlɪt
kingpin ˈkɪŋˌpɪn
Kingsbury ˈkɪŋzˌbɛrɪ, -bərɪ
kingship ˈkɪŋʃɪp
Kingsley ˈkɪŋzlɪ
Kingston, -e ˈkɪŋˌstən, ˈkɪŋzˌtən, ˈkɪŋks-
Kingstown ˈkɪŋzˌtaʊn
kink kɪŋk |kinked kɪŋkt |kinky ˈkɪŋkɪ
Kinkaid kɪnˈked, kɪŋˈked
kinkajou ˈkɪŋkəˌdʒu
kinnikinnick, -kinic ˌkɪnɪkəˈnɪk
Kinross kɪnˈrɔs, -ˈrɒs |-ross-shire -ˈrɔsʃɪr,
    -ˈrɔʃʃ-, -ˈrɒ-, -ʃɚ; ES -ʃɪə(r, -ʃə(r
Kinsey ˈkɪnsɪ, -zɪ
kinsfolk ˈkɪnzˌfok
kinship ˈkɪnʃɪp
kinsman, K- ˈkɪnzmən |-men -mən
kinswoman ˈkɪnzˌwʊmən, -ˌwu- |-women
    -ˌwɪmɪn, -ən
kiosk kɪˈask, ˈkaɪask; ES+-ˈɒsk, -ɒsk
Kioto ˈkjoto
Kiowa *US* places ˈkaɪəwə
Kiowa, -way *Indian* ˈkaɪəˌwe, -wə
Kipling ˈkɪplɪŋ
kipper ˈkɪpɚ; ES ˈkɪpə(r; |-ed -d
Kirby ˈkɝbɪ; ES ˈkɜbɪ, ˈkɝbɪ
Kirghiz kɪrˈgiz; ES kɪə-; |-'s -ɪz
kirk, K- kɝk; ES kɜk, kɝk
Kirkby ˈkɝkbɪ, ˈkɝbɪ; ES ˈkɜ-, ˈkɝ-
Kirkcaldy kɝˈkɔldɪ, -ˈkɒdɪ, -ˈkadɪ; ES kɜ-,
    kɝ-

Kirkcudbright kɝˈkubrɪ; ES kɜ-, kɝ-; |-shire
    -ˌʃɪr, -ʃɚ; ES -ˌʃɪə(r, -ʃə(r
Kirkland ˈkɝklənd; ES ˈkɜk-, ˈkɝk-
kirmess ˈkɝmɪs; ES ˈkɜm-, ˈkɝm-; |-es -ɪz
Kirtland ˈkɝtlənd; ES ˈkɜt-, ˈkɝt-
kirtle ˈkɝtḷ; ES ˈkɜtḷ, ˈkɝtḷ; |-d -d
kismet ˈkɪzmɛt, ˈkɪs-
kiss kɪs |kisses ˈkɪsɪz |kissed kɪst
kist kɪst
kit, K- kɪt |-ty -ɪ
kitcat ˈkɪtˌkæt
kitchen, K- ˈkɪtʃɪn, -ən
Kitchener, k- ˈkɪtʃɪnɚ, -ənɚ, -tʃnɚ; ES -nə(r
kitchenette ˌkɪtʃɪnˈɛt, -ən-
kitchenware ˈkɪtʃɪnˌwɛr, -ən-, -ˌwær; E
    -ˌwɛə(r, ES -ˌwæə(r
Kitchin ˈkɪtʃɪn
kite kaɪt |kited ˈkaɪtɪd
kith kɪθ
Kittanning kɪˈtænɪŋ
Kittatinny ˌkɪtəˈtɪnɪ
kitten ˈkɪtṇ—*The pron.* ˈkɪtən *is substandard.*
Kittery ˈkɪtərɪ
Kittitas ˈkɪtɪˌtæs |-'s -ɪz
kittiwake ˈkɪtɪˌwek
kittle ˈkɪtḷ
Kittredge ˈkɪtrɪdʒ |-'s -ɪz
kitty, K- ˈkɪtɪ
Kitty Hawk ˈkɪtɪˈhɔk |Kittyhawk ˈkɪtɪˌhɔk
kiva ˈkivə
Kiwanian kəˈwanɪən, -ˈwɒn- |-wanis -nɪs
kiwi ˈkiwɪ
Klaeber ˈklɛbɚ; ES ˈklɛbə(r
Klamath ˈklæməθ
KleinSmid, von fənˈklaɪnˌsmɪd
kleptomania ˌklɛptəˈmenɪə |-niac -ˈmenɪˌæk
klieg klig
Klingsor ˈklɪŋzor, -zɔr; ES -zoə(r, E+-zɔə(r
Klondike ˈklandaɪk; ES+ˈklɒn-
Klopstock ˈklapstak; ES+ˈklɒpstɒk; (*Ger*
    ˈklɔpʃtɔk)
Kluge *Ger scholar* ˈklugə; *Eng name* kludʒ,
    klɪudʒ
knack næk |knacked nækt
knag næg |knagged ˈnægɪd |-gy -ɪ
knap næp |knapped næpt |-sack -ˌsæk
knar nar; ES nɑ:(r, E+nɑ:(r; |-red -d |-ry -ɪ
knave nev |-d -d |-ry -ərɪ, -rɪ |-ship -ʃɪp
knead nid |kneaded ˈnidɪd

knee **ni** |kneed **nid** |-cap -ˌkæp
knee-deep **ˈniˈdip** (ˈknee-ˌdeep ˈclover)
knee-high **ˈniˈhaɪ**
kneel **nil** |knelt **nɛlt** or kneeled **nild**
kneepad **ˈniˌpæd** |-pan -ˌpæn
knell **nɛl** |knelled **nɛld**
Kneller **ˈnɛlɚ**; ES **ˈnɛlə(r**
knelt **nɛlt**
knew **nju, nɪu, nu**
knicker **ˈnɪkɚ**; ES **ˈnɪkə(r**; |-ed -d
Knickerbocker, k- **ˈnɪkɚˌbɑkɚ**; ES **ˈnɪkə-ˌbɑkə(r, -ˌbɒk-**; |-ed -d
knickknack **ˈnɪkˌnæk** |-ery -ərɪ, -rɪ
knife n **naɪf** |knife's **naɪfs** (in Shak. knives **naɪvz**) |pl knives **naɪvz**—The pronunciation **naɪvz** for knife's is the older possessive singular.
knife v **naɪf** |knifes **naɪfs** |knifed **naɪft**
knifeful **ˈnaɪfˌful** |-s -z
knight **naɪt** |knighted **ˈnaɪtɪd** |-age -ɪdʒ
knight-errant **ˈnaɪtˈɛrənt** |-ry -rɪ
knighthood **ˈnaɪt·hud**
knit **nɪt** |knit **nɪt** or knitted **ˈnɪtɪd**
knives **naɪvz** |knive's **naɪvz**—see knife n
knob **nɑb**; ES+**nɒb**; |-bed -d, -id |-by -ɪ
knobble **ˈnɑbl̩**; ES+**ˈnɒbl̩**; |-d -d |-ling -blɪŋ, -bl̩ɪŋ |-bly -bl̩ɪ, -blɪ
Knoblock **ˈnɑblɑk**; ES+**ˈnɒblɒk**
knock **nɑk**; ES+**nɒk**; |-ed -t |-about -əˌbaut
knockdown **ˈnɑkˌdaun**; ES+**ˈnɒk-**
knock-knee **ˈnɑkˌni**; ES+**ˈnɒk-**; |-d -ˈnid
knockout **ˈnɑkˌaut**; ES+**ˈnɒk-**
knoll **nol** |-ed -d |-y -ɪ
knop **nɑp**; ES+**nɒp**; |-ped -t |-py -ɪ
Knossus **ˈnɑsəs**; ES+**ˈnɒs-**; |-sus' -səs
knot **nɑt**; ES+**nɒt**; |-ted -ɪd |-ty -ɪ
knothole **ˈnɑtˌhol**; ES+**ˈnɒt-**
Knott **nɑt**; ES+**nɒt**
knout **naut** |knouted **ˈnautɪd**
know **no** |knew **nju, nɪu, nu** |known **non**
knowledge **ˈnɑlɪdʒ**; ES+**ˈnɒl-**; |-s -ɪz |-d -d |-able -əbl̩ |-bly -blɪ
Knowles **nolz** |-'s -ɪz
know-nothing, K-N- **ˈnoˌnʌθɪŋ**
Knox **nɑks**; ES+**nɒks**; |-'s -ɪz |-ville -vɪl; S+-vl̩
knuckle **ˈnʌkl̩** |-d -d |-ling -klɪŋ, -kl̩ɪŋ
knucklebone **ˈnʌkl̩ˌbon**
Knudsen **ˈnudsn̩, ˈnɪudsn̩, ˈnjudsn̩**

knur, -rr **nɝ**; ES **nɜ(r, nɝ**; |-(r)ed -d
knurl **nɝl**; ES **nɜl, nɝl**; |-ed -d
Knut **kəˈnut**, -ˈnɪut, -ˈnjut=Canute
knut 'nut' humorous **kəˈnʌt**
Knutsford **ˈnʌtsfɚd**; ES **ˈnʌtsfəd**
Kobe **ˈkobɪ**
Koblenz **ˈkoblɛnts** |-'s -ɪz
kobold **ˈkobɑld, -bʊld, -bold** (Ger **ˈkoːbɔlt**)
Kobuk **koˈbʊk**
Koch Ger **kɔx**; 'Assamese' **kotʃ** |-es **ˈkotʃɪz**
Kodak **ˈkodæk** |kodaked **ˈkodækt**
Kodiak **ˈkodɪˌæk**
Koekeritz **ˈkɛkərɪts** |-'s -ɪz
Koheleth **koˈhɛlɪθ**
Koh-i-noor, Kohinoor, -nur ˌko·ɪˈnur; ES -ˈnuə(r
kohl, K- **kol** |Kohlan **ˈkolən**
Kohler **ˈkolɚ**; ES **ˈkolə(r**
kohlrabi **ˈkolˌrɑbɪ, ˈkolˈrɑbɪ**
koine **ˈkɔɪnɪ, -ni**
Kokomo **ˈkokəˌmo**
kola **ˈkolə**
Komintern ˌkɑmɪnˈtɝn, ˈkɑmɪnˌtɝn; ES -ɝn, -ɜn, -ɒm-
Kongo **ˈkɑŋgo**; ES+**ˈkɒŋ-**
Königsberg **ˈkenɪgzˌbɝg**; ES -ˌbɜg, -ˌbɝg; (Ger **ˈkøːnɪksˌbɛrk**)
koodoo **ˈkudu**
Kootenay, -nai **ˈkutn̩ˌe**
kopeck, -pek **ˈkopɛk**
kopje **ˈkɑpɪ**; ES+**ˈkɒpɪ**
kor **kor, kɔr**; ES **koə(r, E+kɔə(r
Koran **koˈrɑn, -ˈræn**
Korea India **ˈkorɪˌɑ, ˈkɔr-**; S **ˈkor-**
Korea Japan **koˈriə, kɔ-**; S **ko-**; |-n -n
Korzybski **kɔrˈzɪbskɪ**; ES **kɔə-**
Kosciusko ˌkɑsɪˈʌsko; ES+**kɒs-**; mt. -zɪ-
kosher **ˈkoʃɚ**; ES **ˈkoʃə(r**
Kossuth **kɑˈsuθ, kɒ-** (Hung **ˈkɒʃut**)
kotow **koˈtau** |-ed -d
koumis, -ss, -yss **ˈkumɪs**
Koussevitzky ˌkusəˈvɪtskɪ
kowtow **kauˈtau, ko-** |-ed -d
Koyukuk **kəˈjukʊk, ko-**
kraal **krɑl** |kraaled **krɑld**
kraft **kræft**; E+**krɑft, krɑft**
Kraft, -fft **krɑft, kræft**
Krag **krɑg, kræg**
Krakatao ˌkrɑkəˈtao

|full **ful** |tooth **tuθ** |further **ˈfɝðɚ**; ES **ˈfɝðə** |custom **ˈkʌstəm** |while **hwaɪl** |how **hau** |toy **tɔɪ** |using **ˈjuzɪŋ** |fuse **fjuz, fɪuz** |dish **dɪʃ** |vision **ˈvɪʒən** |Eden **ˈidn̩** |cradle **ˈkredl̩** |keep 'em **ˈkipm̩**

Kraków ˈkreko, ˈkrækaʊ (*Pol* ˈkrakʊf)
Krapotkin *city* krəˈpɑtkɪn, -ˈpɒt-
kraut kraʊt
Kreisler ˈkraɪslɚ; ES ˈkraɪslə(r
kremlin, K- ˈkrɛmlɪn
Kresge ˈkrɛsgɪ, ˈkrɛskɪ
kreutzer, K-, kreuz- ˈkrɔɪtsɚ; ES ˈkrɔɪtsə(r
Kreymborg ˈkrɛmbɔrg; ES -bɔəg
kriegspiel ˈkrigˌspil
Kriemhild ˈkrimhɪld (*Ger* ˈkriːmhɪlt)
Krimhild ˈkrɪmhɪld
kris kris |krises ˈkrisɪz
Krishna ˈkrɪʃnə |-ism -ˌɪzəm |-ist -ɪst
Kriss Kringle ˈkrɪsˈkrɪŋgḷ
krona ˈkronə (*Sw* ˈkruːnə) |*pl* -nor -nɔr
krone ˈkronə |*Ger pl* kronen ˈkronən
krone ˈkronɛ |*Dan pl* kroner ˈkronɛr
Kropotkin *anarchist* krəˈpɑtkɪn, -ˈpɒt-
Kruger ˈkrugɚ; ES ˈkrugə(r
Krupp krʌp, krʊp (*Ger* krʊp)
Krutch krʌtʃ |-ˈs -ɪz
krypton ˈkrɪptɑn, -tɒn
Kshatriya ˈkʃætrɪjə
Kubelik ˈkubəlɪk
Kublai Khan *Chin ruler* ˈkublaɪˈkɑn
Kubla Kahn *poem* ˈkubləˈkɑn
kudos ˈkjudɑs, -dɒs, ˈkɪu- |-ed -t
kudu ˈkudu

Kufic ˈkjufɪk, ˈkɪu-
Ku-Klux, Kuklux ˈkjuˌklʌks, ˈkɪu- |-es -ɪz
|-ed -t
kulak kuˈlɑk |-ism -ɪzəm
kultur ˈkʊltʊr; ES -tʊə(r; (*Ger* kʊlˈtuːr)
kumiss ˈkumɪs
kümmel ˈkɪmḷ (*Ger* ˈkyməl)
kumquat ˈkʌmkwɑt, -kwɒt
Kundry ˈkʊndrɪ
Kuomintang ˈkwomɪnˈtæŋ, ˈgwo-, -ˈtɑŋ
Kurath, Hans ˈhænsˈkjuræθ, -ˈkɪu-, ˈhɑns-
ˈkurɑt
Kurd kɝd, kʊrd; ES kɝd, kɝd, kʊəd
Kurdistan ˌkɝdɪˈstæn, ˌkʊr-, -ˈstɑn; ES
ˌkɝd-, ˌkɝd-, ˌkʊəd-
Kure ˈkure
Kuril ˈkurɪl |-ian kuˈrɪlɪən, -ljən
Kurland ˈkʊrlənd; ES ˈkʊə-
Kutztown ˈkʊtsˌtaʊn
Kwangsi ˈkwæŋˈsi, ˈgwɑŋ-
Kwangtung *China* ˈkwæŋˈtʌŋ, ˈgwɑŋˈdʊŋ
Kwantung *Manchuria* ˈkwænˈtʌŋ, ˈgwɑn-
ˈdʊŋ
Kweichow ˈkweˈtʃaʊ, ˈgweˈdʒo
Kyd kɪd
Kyoto, Kio- ˈkjoto
Kyrie eleison ˈkɪrɪˌi əˈleəsṇ
Kythera ˈkɪθərə

L

L, l *letter* ɛl |*pl* L's, Ls, *poss* L's ɛlz
la *intj* lɔ, lɑ; *music* lɑ; *Fr article* la
laager '*camp*' ˈlagɚ; ES ˈlagə(r; |-ed -d
Laban ˈlebən
label ˈlebḷ |-ed -d |-ing ˈleblɪŋ, ˈlebḷɪŋ
labellum ləˈbɛləm |-la -ˈbɛlə
labial ˈlebɪəl |-ly -ɪ
labialize ˈlebɪəlˌaɪz |-s -ɪz |-d -d
labiate *adj* ˈlebɪˌet, -bɪɪt
labile ˈlebḷ, -bɪl
labium ˈlebɪəm |-bia -bɪə
labor ˈlebɚ; ES -bə(r; |-ed -d |-ing -brɪŋ,
-bərɪŋ
laboratory ˈlæbrəˌtorɪ, ˈlæbərə-, -brɪ-, -ˌtɔrɪ;
S -ˌtorɪ
laborer ˈlebərɚ; ES ˈlebərə(r

laborious ləˈborɪəs, -ˈbɔr-; S -ˈbor-
laborite, L- ˈlebəˌraɪt
labor-saving ˈlebɚˌsevɪŋ; ES ˈlebɚ-
Labrador ˈlæbrəˌdɔr; ES -ˌdɔə(r
laburnum ləˈbɝnəm; ES -ˈbɝn-, -ˈbɝn-
labyrinth ˈlæbəˌrɪnθ |-ths -θs
labyrinthian ˌlæbəˈrɪnθɪən
labyrinthine ˌlæbəˈrɪnθɪn, -θin, -θin
lac læk
lace les |laces ˈlesɪz |laced lest
Lacedaemon ˌlæsəˈdimən
Lacedaemonian ˌlæsədɪˈmonɪən, -njən
lacerate ˈlæsəˌret |-d -ɪd |-tion ˌlæsəˈreʃən
laches ˈlætʃɪz
Lachesis ˈlækəsɪs |-sis' -sɪs
lachrymal ˈlækrəmḷ

lachrymatory 'lækrəmə͵torɪ, -͵tɔrɪ; S -͵torɪ
lachrymose 'lækrə͵mos
laciniate lə'sɪnɪ͵et, -ɪt |-ated -͵etɪd
lack læk |lacked lækt
lackadaisical ͵lækə'dezɪk| |-ly -ɪ, -ɪklɪ
lackaday 'lækə͵de
Lackawanna ͵lækə'wɑnə, -'wɒnə
lackey 'lækɪ |-ed -d
lackluster, -tre 'læk͵lʌstɚ; ES -tə(r
Laconia lə'konɪə |-n -n
laconic, L- lə'kɑnɪk; ES+-'kɒn-; |-ally -|ɪ, -ɪklɪ
lacquer 'lækɚ; ES -ə(r; |-ed -d |-ing 'lækərɪŋ, 'lækrɪŋ
lacrosse, L- lə'krɔs, -'krɒs |-'s -ɪz
lactate 'læktet |-d -ɪd |-tation læk'teʃən
lacteal 'læktɪəl |lactic 'læktɪk
lactometer læk'tɑmətɚ; ES -'tɑmətə(r, -'tɒm-
lactone 'lækton |-tose -tos
lacuna lə'kjunə, -'kɪu- |-s -z |-nae -ni
lacustrine lə'kʌstrɪn
lacy 'lesɪ
lad læd |laddie 'lædɪ
ladder 'lædɚ; ES -də(r; |-ed -d |-ing -dərɪŋ, -drɪŋ
lade led |past -d -ɪd |pptc -d -ɪd or laden 'ledn̩
laden v 'ledn̩ |-ed -d |-ing 'ledn̩ɪŋ, 'lednɪŋ
ladle 'led| |-d -d |-ling 'led|ɪŋ, 'ledlɪŋ
Ladoga Finl 'ladogə, US places lə'dogə
ladrone lə'dron, Sc 'lædrən
lady 'ledɪ |ladies, ladies', lady's 'ledɪz
ladybird 'ledɪ͵bɝd; ES -͵bɜd, -͵bɝd
ladybug 'ledɪ͵bʌg
ladyfinger 'ledɪ͵fɪŋgɚ; ES -gə(r
lady-killer 'ledɪ͵kɪlɚ; ES -lə(r
ladylike 'ledɪ͵laɪk
ladylove 'ledɪ͵lʌv
ladyship 'ledɪ͵ʃɪp
lady-slipper 'ledɪ͵slɪpɚ; ES -pə(r
lady's-slipper 'ledɪz͵slɪpɚ; ES -pə(r
Laertes lɪ'ɝtiz, le-; ES -'ɜtiz, -'ɝtiz; |-tes' -tiz
La Farge lə'fɑrʒ, commonly Anglic. lə'fɑrdʒ; ES -'fɑ:-, E+-'fɑ:-; |-'s -ɪz
Lafayette Fr general ͵lafɪ'ɛt (Fr lafa'jɛt), US places pron. variously ͵læfɪ'(j)ɛt, ͵lefɪ'(j)ɛt, lə'fe(j)ɪt
Lafeu, Shak. Lafew lə'fju, -'fɪu
La Follette lə'fɑlɪt; ES+-'fɒl-
La Fontaine ləfɑn'ten, -fɒn- (Fr lafõ'tɛn)

lag læg |lagged lægd
lager 'camp' 'lagɚ; ES -gə(r; |-ed -d
lager beer 'lagɚ, 'lɔgɚ; ES -gə(r
Lagerlöf Sw 'lɑ:gər͵lø:v
laggard 'lægɚd; ES 'lægəd
lagniappe, -gnap- læn'jæp, 'lænjæp
lagoon lə'gun
La Guardia lə'gwɑrdɪə, -'gɑr-; ES -ɑ:d-, E+-ɑ:d-; (It lɑ'gwɑrdjɑ)
Lahore lə'hor, -'hɔr; ES -'hoə(r, E+-'hɔə(r
laic 'le·ɪk |-al -| |-ally -|ɪ, -ɪklɪ
laid past & pptc of lay led
lain pptc of lie len
lair lɛr, lær; E lɛə(r, ES læə(r; |-ed -d
laird lɛrd, lærd, Sc lerd; E lɛəd, ES læəd
laissez faire, laisser ͵lɛse'fɛr, -'fær; E -'fɛə(r, ES -'fæə(r; (Fr lɛse'fɛ:r)
laity 'leətɪ, 'le·ɪtɪ
La Junta lə'hʌntə (Am Sp lɑ'huntɑ)
lake lek
Lalla Rookh 'lɑlə'ruk, Brit 'lælə'rʊk
L'Allegro lɑ'legro (It lɑl'le:gro)
lam læm |-med -d
lama 'lɑmə
Lamar lə'mɑr; ES lə'mɑ:(r, E+-'mɑ:(r
Lamarck lə'mɑrk; ES -'mɑ:k, E+-'mɑ:k; |-ian -ɪən (Fr lɑ'mɑrk)
lamasery 'lɑmə͵sɛrɪ
lamb læm |lambed læmd |lambing 'læmɪŋ
lambaste læm'best |-d -ɪd
lambda 'læmdə
lambency 'læmbənsɪ |-bent -bənt
Lambeth 'læmbɪθ, -bəθ, -bɛθ
lambkin 'læmkɪn
lamblike 'læm͵laɪk
lambrekin 'læmbɚ͵kɪn, 'læmbrə-; ES 'læmbə-, -brə-
lambskin 'læm͵skɪn
lame lem |lamed lemd
Lamech 'lemək, -mɛk
lamella lə'mɛlə |-s -z |-lae -'mɛli
lament lə'mɛnt |-ed -ɪd
lamentable 'læməntəb| |-bly -blɪ
lamentation ͵læmən'teʃən
La Mesa lə'mesə |Lamesa lə'misə
Lamia poem 'lemɪə; Gk town lə'mɪə, 'lemɪə
lamina 'læmənə |-s -z |-nae -͵ni |-nar -nɚ; ES -nə(r
laminate adj 'læmənɪt, -͵net

|full fʊl |tooth tuθ |further 'fɝðɚ; ES 'fɝðə |custom 'kʌstəm |while hwaɪl |how haʊ |toy tɔɪ
|using 'juzɪŋ |fuse fjuz, fɪuz |dish dɪʃ |vision 'vɪʒən |Eden 'idn̩ |cradle 'kredl̩ |keep 'em 'kipm̩

laminate *v* 'læmə,net |-d -ıd |-tion ,læmə-
'neʃən
Lammas 'læməs |-tide -,taıd
Lammermoor 'læmɚ,mʊr; ES 'læmə,mʊə(r;
(*Sc* ,lamər'mu:r)
Lammermuir 'læmɚ,mjʊr, -,mıʊr; ES 'læmə-
,mjʊə(r, -,mıʊə(r; (*Sc* ,lamər'mju:r)
Lamont lə'mɑnt; ES+-'mɒnt
lamp læmp |lamped læmpt
lampad 'læmpæd
lampblack 'læmp,blæk |-ed -t
lamplight 'læmp,laıt |-er -ɚ; ES -ə(r
Lampman 'læmpmən
lampoon læm'pun |-ed -d
lamppost 'læmp,post
Lamprecht 'læmprɛkt (*Ger* 'lɑmprɛxt)
lamprey 'læmprı
Lanark 'lænɚk; ES 'lænək; |-shire -,ʃır, -ʃɚ;
ES -,ʃıə(r, -ʃə(r
Lancashire 'læŋkə,ʃır, -ʃɚ; ES -,ʃıə(r, -ʃə(r
Lancaster *Engd* 'læŋkəstɚ; ES -tə(r; *US*
places variously 'læŋkəstɚ, 'læŋ,kæstɚ,
'læn,kæstɚ; ES -tə(r
Lancastrian læŋ'kæstrıən
lance læns; E+lans, lɑns; |-s -ız |-d -t
Lancelot 'lænsələt, 'lɑn-, -,lat; ES+-'lɒt
lanceolate 'lænsıəlıt, -,let
Lancs *short for* Lancashire læŋks
land lænd |landed 'lændıd
landau 'lændɔ
landfall 'lænd,fɔl, 'læn-
land-grant 'lænd,grænt, 'læn-; E+-,grant,
-,grɑnt
landgrave 'lænd,grev, 'læn-
landgravine 'lændgrə,vin, 'læn-
landholder 'lænd,holdɚ; ES -,holdə(r
landlady 'lænd,ledı, 'læn-
landless 'lændlıs
landlocked 'lænd,lakt; ES+-,lɒkt
landlord 'lænd,lɔrd, 'læn-; ES -,lɔəd
landlubber 'lænd,lʌbɚ; ES -,lʌbə(r
landmark 'lænd,mark, 'læn-; ES -,maːk,
E+-,maːk
land-office 'lænd,ɔfıs, -,ɒfıs, -,afıs |-s -ız
Landor 'lændɚ, -dɔr; ES -də(r, -dɔə(r
landowner 'lænd,onɚ; ES -,onə(r
land-poor 'lænd'pʊr, 'læn-; ES -'pʊə(r,
-'poə(r, -'pɔə(r
landscape 'lænskep, 'lænd- |-d -t

Landseer 'lændsır, 'læn-; ES -sıə(r
Land's End 'lændz'ɛnd, 'lænz-
landskip *arch.* '*landscape*' 'lændskıp
landslide 'lænd,slaıd, 'læn-
landslip 'lænd,slıp, 'læn-
landsman 'lændzmən, 'lænz- |-men -mən
landward 'lændwɚd; ES 'lændwəd; |-s -z
lane len
Lanett lə'nɛt
Lanfranc 'lænfræŋk
Langlade 'læŋled (*Fr* lɑ̃'glad)
Langland 'læŋlənd
Langley 'læŋlı
Langmuir 'læŋmjʊr, -mıʊr; ES -ə(r
langsyne 'læŋ'saın, *in the song often* -'zaın
Langtree, -try 'læŋtrı
language 'læŋgwıdʒ |-s -ız |-d -d
langue d'oc, L- *Fr* lɑ̃g'dɔ̃k
langue d'oil *Fr* lɑ̃g'dɔ̃il, -'dɔː:j
languid 'læŋgwıd
languish 'læŋgwıʃ |-es -ız |-ed -t
languor 'læŋgɚ; ES 'læŋgə(r; |-ous -əs, -grəs
laniard 'lænjɚd; ES 'lænjəd
Lanier lə'nır; ES -'nıə(r
lank læŋk |-ily 'læŋk|ı, -ılı
lanolin 'lænəlın |-line -lın, -,lin
Lansdowne 'lænzdaʊn
Lansing 'lænsıŋ
lantern 'læntɚn; ES 'læntən
lanthanum 'lænθənəm
lanthorn *arch. sp. of* lantern 'læntɚn; ES -tən
lanyard 'lænjɚd; ES 'lænjəd
Laocoön le'akə,wan, -,wɒn, -ko,an, -,ɒn;
ES+-'ɒk-
Laodamia ,leodə'maıə
Laodicea ,leodə'sıə, ,leo-, le,adə'sıə; ES+
-,ɒd-; |-n -n
Laomedon le'amə,dan, -'ɒmə,dɒn, -dən
lap læp |lapped læpt
La Paz lə'pas (*Am Sp* la'pas)
lapboard 'læp,bord, -,bɔrd; ES -,boəd,
E+-,bɔəd
lapel lə'pɛl |lapelled lə'pɛld
lapful 'læp,fʊl |-s -z
lapidary 'læpə,dɛrı
lapin 'læpın (*Fr* la'pɛ̃)
lapis lazuli 'læpıs'læzjə,laı, -ju-
Lapithe 'læpı,θi
Laplace lə'plæs, læ- |-'s -ız (*Fr* la'plas)

Words below in which a *before* r (farm) *is sounded* ɑ *are often pronounced in* E *with* a (fa:m)
Words below that have æ *before* r (carry) **'kærɪ**) *are often pronounced in* N *with* ɛ (**'kɛɪɪ**, *§94*)

La Place lə'ples |-'s -ɪz
Lapland 'læp,lænd
Laplander 'læp,lændɚ, -ləndɚ; ES -də(r
La Plata lə'plɑtə (*Sp* la'plata)
Lapp læp
lappet 'læpɪt |-ed -ɪd
lapse læps |lapses 'læpsɪz |lapsed læpst
lapsus linguae 'læpsəs'lɪŋgwi
Laputa lə'pjutə, -'pɪu- |-tan -tn̩
lapwing 'læp,wɪŋ
lar lɑr; ES lɑ:(r; |*Latin pl* lares 'leriz |*Eng pl*
    lars -z
Laramie 'lærəmɪ
larboard 'lɑrbɚd, -,bord, -,bɔrd; ES 'lɑ:bəd,
    -,boəd, E+-,bɔəd
larcener 'lɑrsn̩ɚ; ES 'lɑ:sn̩ə(r; |-cenous -sn̩əs
    |-ceny -sn̩ɪ
larch lɑrtʃ; ES lɑ:tʃ; |-es -ɪz
lard lɑrd; ES lɑ:d; |-ed -ɪd
larder 'lɑrdɚ; ES 'lɑ:də(r
Lardner 'lɑrdnɚ; ES 'lɑ:dnə(r
Laredo lə'redo, lɑ-, -'ri-
lares *L pl of* lar 'leriz
large lɑrdʒ; ES lɑ:dʒ
large-hearted 'lɑrdʒ'hɑrtɪd; ES 'lɑ:dʒ'hɑ:tɪd
large-scale 'lɑrdʒ'skel; ES 'lɑ:dʒ-; ('large-
    ,scale 'buying)
largess, -sse 'lɑrdʒɪs; ES 'lɑ:dʒɪs; |-es, -s -ɪz
larghetto lɑr'gɛto; ES lɑ:-; (*It* lar'getto)
largo 'lɑrgo; ES 'lɑ:go
lariat *n* 'lærɪət
lariat *v* 'lærɪ,æt |-ed -ɪd
lark lɑrk; ES lɑ:k; |-ed -t
larkspur 'lɑrk,spɚ; ES 'lɑ:k,spɜ(r, -,spɝ
Larned 'lɑrnɪd; ES 'lɑ:nɪd
larrikin 'lærə,kɪn
larrup 'lærəp |larruped 'lærəpt
Lars Porsena 'lɑrz'pɔrsɪnə; ES 'lɑ:z'pɔəsɪnə
larum 'lærəm, 'lɛrəm; S 'lærəm
larva 'lɑrvə; ES 'lɑ:və; |-vae -vi |-val -vl̩
laryngal lə'rɪŋgl̩
laryngeal lə'rɪndʒɪəl |-gitis ,lærɪn'dʒaɪtɪs
laryngology ,lærɪŋ'gɑlədʒɪ; ES+-'gɒl-
laryngoscope lə'rɪŋgə,skop
larynx 'lærɪŋks |-es -ɪz |larynges lə'rɪndʒiz
La Salle lə'sæl (*Fr* la'sal)
lascar, L- 'læskɚ; ES 'læskə(r

Las Casas lɑs'kɑsəs (*Sp* las'kasas)
Lascelles 'læs|z, lə'sɛlz |-'s -ɪz (Lassells *1574*)
lascivious lə'sɪvɪəs, læ-
Las Cruces lɑs'krusɪs (*Am Sp* las'kruses)
lash læʃ |lashes 'læʃɪz |lashed læʃt
lass læs |lasses 'læsɪz |lassie 'læsɪ
lassitude 'læsə,tjud, -,tɪud, -,tud
lasso 'læso, *older* læ'su |-ed -d
last *n, adj, v* læst; E+last, lɑst; |-ed -ɪd—*bef.*
    conss. often læs ('læs'naɪt)
Las Vegas lɑs'vegəs |-'s -ɪz
latch lætʃ |latches 'lætʃɪz |latched lætʃt
latchet 'lætʃɪt
latchkey 'lætʃ,ki
latchstring 'lætʃ,strɪŋ, -,ʃtrɪŋ
late let
lateen læ'tin
latency 'letn̩sɪ |-tent -tn̩t
lateral 'lætərəl |-ly -ɪ
Lateran 'lætərən
latex 'letɛks |-es -ɪz |latices 'lætə,siz
lath *n* læθ; E+laθ, lɑθ; |-ths -ðz, -θs
lath *v* læθ; E+laθ, lɑθ; |-ths -θs |-ed -t
Lathbury 'læθ,bɛrɪ, -bərɪ
lathe leð |-thes -ðz
lather '*one who laths*' 'læðɚ; ES 'læðə(r,
    E+'laθ-, 'lɑθ-
lather '*lathe-worker*' 'leðɚ; ES 'leðə(r
lather '*foam*' 'læðɚ; ES 'læðə(r; |-ed -d |-ing
    'læðərɪŋ, 'læðrɪŋ
Lathrop 'leθrəp
lathwork 'læθ,wɚk; ES -,wɝk, -,wɝk, E+
    'laθ-, 'lɑθ-
lathy '*like a lath*' 'læθɪ; E+'laθɪ, 'lɑθɪ
Latimer 'lætəmɚ; ES 'lætəmə(r
Latin 'lætn̩, 'lætɪn |-ed -d |-ism -,ɪzəm |-ist
    -ɪst
Latinity læ'tɪnətɪ
Latinize 'lætn̩,aɪz, -tɪn,aɪz |-s -ɪz |-d -d
latish 'letɪʃ
latitude 'lætə,tjud, -,trud, -,tud
latitudinarian ,lætə,tjudn̩'ɛrɪən, -,trud-,
    -,tud-, -'er-
Latium 'leʃɪəm
Latona lə'tonə, le-
latrine lə'trin
Latrobe lə'trob

---

latron 'letrən

latten 'lætn̩

latter 'lætɚ; ES 'lætə(r; |-ly -lɪ

lattice 'lætɪs |-s -ɪz |-d -t

latticework 'lætɪsˌwɝk; ES -ˌwɜk, -ˌwɝk

Latvia 'lætvɪə |-n -n

laud, L- lɔd |lauded 'lɔdɪd

laudability ˌlɔdə'bɪlətɪ

laudable 'lɔdəbl̩ |-bly -blɪ

laudanum 'lɔdn̩əm, 'lɔdnəm

laudation lɔ'deʃən

laudatory 'lɔdəˌtorɪ, -ˌtɔrɪ; S -ˌtorɪ

Lauder 'lɔdɚ; ES 'lɔdə(r; |-derdale -ˌdel

laugh læf; E laf, læf, lɑf; |-ed -t

laughable 'læfəbl̩ |-bly -blɪ; E see laugh

laughingstock 'læfɪŋˌstak; ES+-ˌstɒk, E see
    laugh

Laughlin 'læflɪn, 'laf-, 'lak-, 'lax-; ES+'lɒ-,
    E+'la-

laughter 'læftɚ; ES -tə(r, E see laugh

Launce lɔns, lɒns, lans |-'s -ɪz

Launcelot 'lɔnsələt, 'lɒn-, 'lan-, -ˌlat; ES+
    -ˌlɒt

Launceston Tasm 'lɒnˌsestən, 'lan-; Cornw
    'lɒnstən, loc. 'lan-, 'lɒn-, -sn̩

launch lɔntʃ, lɒntʃ, lantʃ |-es -ɪz |-ed -t

launder 'lɔndɚ, 'lɒn-, 'lan-; ES -də(r; |-ed -d
    |-ing -drɪŋ, -dərɪŋ

laundress 'lɔndrɪs, 'lɒn-, 'lan- |-es -ɪz

laundry 'lɔndrɪ, 'lɒn-, 'lan-; N Engd+'lan-;
    |-dried -drɪd

Laura 'lɔrə

laureate n 'lɔrɪɪt |-ship -ˌʃɪp

laureate v 'lɔrɪˌet |-d -ɪd

laurel 'lɔrəl, 'lar-, 'lɒr- |-ed -d

Laurence 'lɔrəns, 'lar-, 'lɒr- |-'s -ɪz

Laurens 'lɔrəns, 'lar-, 'lɒr-, -ənz |-'s -ɪz

Laurentian lɔ'rɛnʃɪən, -ʃən, la-, lɒ-

Laurie 'lɔrɪ, 'lɒr-

Laurier 'lɔrɪɚ, 'lar-, 'lɒr-; ES -ɪ·ə(r; C states-
    man 'lɔrɪˌe, 'lar-, 'lɒr-

Lausanne lo'zæn (Fr lo'zan)

lava 'lavə, 'lævə

lavabo, L- lə'vebo

Lavache lə'vætʃ |-'s -ɪz, in Shak. Lavatch

lavaliere, -ier ˌlævə'lɪr; ES -'lɪə(r; (Fr lava-
    'lje:r)

lavatory 'lævəˌtorɪ, -ˌtɔrɪ; S -ˌtorɪ

lave lev |laved levd

lavender 'lævəndɚ; ES -də(r

Lavengro lə'vɛŋgro, læ-

laver 'levɚ; ES 'levə(r

Lavinia lə'vɪnɪə, -njə

lavish 'lævɪʃ |-es -ɪz |-ed -t

law lɔ |lawed lɔd |-ful -fəl |-fully -fəlɪ

law-abiding 'lɔəˌbaɪdɪŋ

lawbreaker 'lɔˌbrekɚ; ES -ˌbrekə(r

lawgiver 'lɔˌgɪvɚ; ES -ˌgɪvə(r

lawmaker 'lɔˌmekɚ; ES -ˌmekə(r

lawmaking 'lɔˌmekɪŋ

lawn lɔn |lawned lɔnd

Lawrence, -ance 'lɔrəns, 'lar-, 'lɒr- |-'s -ɪz

lawsuit 'lɔˌsut, -ˌsɪut, -ˌsjut

lawyer 'lɔjɚ; ES 'lɔjə(r

lax læks |laxes 'læksɪz

laxative 'læksətɪv |laxity 'læksətɪ

lay past of lie le

lay v le |laid led

lay n, adj le

Layamon 'leəmən, 'lajəmən

layer 'leɚ, lɛr; ES 'le·ə(r, lɛə(r; |-ed -d

layette le'ɛt

layman, L- 'lemən |laymen -mən

layoff 'leˌɔf, -ˌɒf

layout 'leˌaʊt

layover 'leˌovɚ; ES -ˌovə(r

lazar 'lezɚ; ES -zə(r;—The a in lazar was
    lengthened after the word was shortened from
    Lazarus.

lazaret, -tte ˌlæzə'rɛt |-retto -'rɛto

Lazarus 'læzərəs, -zrəs |-'s -ɪz

laze lez |lazes 'lezɪz |lazed lezd

lazy 'lezɪ |-bones -ˌbonz

lazzarone ˌlæzə'rone |pl -ni -ni (It ˌladdza-
    'ro:ne)

lea, L- li

leach, L- litʃ |leaches 'litʃɪz |leached litʃt

Leacock 'liˌkak, 'le-; ES+-ˌkɒk

lead n, v lid |led lɛd

lead metal lɛd |leaded 'lɛdɪd

Lead lid

leaden v, adj 'lɛdn̩ |-ed -d |-ing 'lɛdn̩ɪŋ,
    'lɛdnɪŋ

leader 'guide' 'lidɚ; ES 'lidə(r

leader 'lead-worker' 'lɛdɚ; ES 'lɛdə(r

leadoff 'lidˌɔf, -ˌɒf

lead-pencil 'lɛd'pɛnsl̩, -ˌpɛnsl̩

leadsman 'lɛdzmən |-men -mən

Leadville 'lɛdvɪl
leaf *n* lif |leaf's lifs |leaves livz
leaf *v* lif |leafs lifs |-ed -t—*cf* leave *v*
leafage 'lifɪdʒ |-s -ɪz
leaflet 'liflɪt
leafy 'lifɪ—*cf* leavy
league lig |leagued ligd
leaguer 'ligɚ; ES -gə(r; |-ed -d |-ing -gərɪŋ, -grɪŋ
Leah 'liə
Leahy *Am diplomat* 'le·ɪ, 'lehɪ
leak lik |leaked likt |leaky 'likɪ |-age -ɪdʒ
leal lil
Leamington 'lɛmɪŋtən, *cf* Lemington
lean lin |leaned lind *or* leant lɛnt
Leander lɪ'ændɚ; ES -'ændə(r
leanness 'linnɪs
leant *past & pptc of* lean lɛnt
lean-to 'lin‚tu
leap lip |leaped lipt, lɛpt *or* leapt lɛpt, lipt
leapfrog 'lip‚frɑg, -‚frɔg, -‚frɒg; S -‚frɔg, -‚frɑg, -‚frɒg; |-ged -d
leapt *past & pptc of* leap lɛpt, lipt
Lear lɪr; ES lɪə(r, S+lɛə(r
learn lɜn; ES lɜn, lɜn; |-ed -d, -t *or* -t -t
learned *past & pptc* lɜnd, lɜnt; ES lɜn-, lɜn-; *adj* -ned -nɪd
learnt *past & pptc of* learn lɜnt; ES lɜnt, lɜnt
lease *'rent'* lis |-s -ɪz |-d -t
lease *'tell a lie'* 'liz |-s -ɪz |-d -d
leasehold 'lis‚hold
leash liʃ |leashes 'liʃɪz |leashed liʃt
leasing *'falsehood'* 'lizɪŋ
least list
leastways 'list‚wez |leastwise 'list‚waɪz
leather 'lɛðɚ; ES 'lɛðə(r; |-n -n |-y -ɪ, -ðrɪ
leatherette, L- ‚lɛðə'rɛt |-roid 'lɛðə‚rɔɪd
leave *n* liv, *dial. & Brit army*+lif
leave *'to leaf'* liv |leaved livd
leave *'depart'* liv |left lɛft
leaved *adj* livd
leaven 'lɛvən |-ed -d |-ing 'lɛvənɪŋ, -vnɪŋ
Leavenworth 'lɛvənwɚθ, -‚wɜθ; ES -wəθ, -‚wɜθ, -‚wɜθ
leaves *pl of* leaf *& leave n, 3 sg of* leave *v* livz
leave-taking 'liv‚tekɪŋ
Leavit, -tt 'lɛvɪt
leavy 'livɪ
leaze *'tell a lie'* liz |-s -ɪz |-d -d

leazing *'falsehood'* 'lizɪŋ
Lebanon 'lɛbənən
Le Beau lə'bo, *in Shakespeare's day* lə'bɪu
Lebrun *Fr* lə'brœ̃
lecher, L- 'lɛtʃɚ; ES 'lɛtʃə(r; |-ous -əs, -tʃrəs |-y -ɪ, -tʃrɪ
lecithin 'lɛsəθɪn
Lecky 'lɛkɪ
Le Conte lɪ'kɑnt; ES+-'kɒnt
lectern 'lɛktən; ES 'lɛktən
lection 'lɛkʃən |-ary -‚ɛrɪ
lector 'lɛktɚ; ES 'lɛktə(r
lecture 'lɛktʃɚ; ES -tʃə(r; |-d -d |-ring 'lɛk-tʃərɪŋ, 'lɛktʃrɪŋ
lectureship 'lɛktʃɚ‚ʃɪp; ES 'lɛktʃə-
led *past & pptc of* lead lɛd
Leda 'lidə
ledger 'lɛdʒɚ; ES -dʒə(r; |-ed -d |-ing 'lɛdʒərɪŋ, 'lɛdʒrɪŋ
Ledyard 'lɛdjɚd; ES 'lɛdjəd
lee, L- li
leeboard 'li‚bord, -‚bɔrd; ES -‚boəd, E+-‚bɔəd
leech 'litʃ |leeches 'litʃɪz |leeched litʃt
Leeds lidz |Leeds's 'lidzɪz
leek, L- lik
leer lɪr; ES lɪə(r, S+lɛə(r; |-ed -d
lees liz
leese *'lose'* (*1611 Bible*) liz
leet lit
leeward 'liwɚd, *naut.* 'luɚd, 'lɪuɚd; ES 'liwəd, 'lu·əd, 'lɪu·əd
Leeward Islands 'liwɚd'aɪləndz, -lənz; ES 'liwəd-
leeway 'li‚we
leeze *'lose'* liz=leese
Lefevre lə'fivɚ; ES -'fivə(r
left lɛft
left-hand 'lɛft'hænd ('left-‚hand 'turn)
left-handed 'lɛft'hændɪd
leg lɛg |legged *v* lɛgd
legacy 'lɛgəsɪ
legal 'ligḷ |-ly -ɪ |-ism -‚ɪzəm |-ist -ɪst
legalistic ‚ligḷ'ɪstɪk |-ally -ḷɪ, -ɪklɪ
legality lɪ'gælətɪ
legalization ‚ligḷə'zeʃən, -aɪ'z-
legalize 'ligḷ‚aɪz |-s -ɪz |-d -d
legate 'lɛgɪt
legatee ‚lɛgə'ti

|full fʊl |tooth tuθ |further 'fɜðɚ; ES 'fɜðə |custom 'kʌstəm |while hwaɪl |how haʊ |toy tɔɪ
|using 'juzɪŋ |fuse fjuz, fɪuz |dish dɪʃ |vision 'vɪʒən |Eden 'idn̩ |cradle 'kredḷ |keep 'em 'kipm̩

legatine ˈlɛgətɪn, -ˌtaɪn

legation lɪˈgeʃən

legato lɪˈgato (It leˈgɑːto)

legend ˈlɛdʒənd |-ary -ˌɛrɪ

Leger ˈlɛdʒɚ; ES ˈlɛdʒə(r

legerdemain ˌlɛdʒɚdɪˈmen; ES ˌlɛdʒə-

legged past of leg v lɛgd, adj ˈlɛgɪd, lɛgd

leggings ˈlɛgɪŋz |leggins ˈlɛgɪnz

leghorn ˈlɛgɚn, ˈlɛgˌhɔrn; ES ˈlɛgən, -ˌhɔən

Leghorn Italy ˈlɛgˌhɔrn; ES -ˌhɔən; fowl ˈlɛgɚn, -ˌhɔrn; ES ˈlɛgən, -ˌhɔən

legibility ˌlɛdʒəˈbɪlətɪ

legible ˈlɛdʒəbl̩ |-bly -blɪ

legion ˈlidʒən |-ary -ˌɛrɪ

legionnaire ˌlidʒənˈer, -ˈær; E -ˈɛə(r, ES -ˈæə(r

legislate ˈlɛdʒɪsˌlet |-d -ɪd |-lative -ˌletɪv

legislation ˌlɛdʒɪsˈleʃən

legislator ˈlɛdʒɪsˌletɚ; ES -ˌletə(r

legislature ˈlɛdʒɪsˌletʃɚ; ES -ˌletʃə(r

legist ˈlidʒɪst

legitimate adj lɪˈdʒɪtəmɪt |-macy -məsɪ

legitimate v lɪˈdʒɪtəˌmet |-d -ɪd

legitimist lɪˈdʒɪtəmɪst |-matist -ˈdʒɪtəmətɪst

legitimize lɪˈdʒɪtəˌmaɪz |-s -ɪz |-d -d

leg-of-mutton adj ˈlɛgəˈmʌtn̩, ˈlɛgəv-

Legree lɪˈgri

legume ˈlɛgjum, lɪˈgjum, -ˈgrum

legumen lɪˈgjumən, lɛ-, -ˈgru- |-s -z |-mina -mɪnə

legumin lɪˈgjumɪn, lɛ-, -ˈgrumɪn |-ous -əs

Le Havre France ləˈhavɚ, -ˈhavrə; ES -ˈhavə(r, -ˈhavrə; (Fr ləˈɑːvr)

Lehigh ˈlihaɪ

Lehman ˈlimən, ˈlemən

lehua lɪˈhua

lei le, ˈle·ɪ

Leibnitz ˈlaɪbnɪts |-'s -ɪz (Ger Leibniz ˈlaɪpnɪts)

Leica ˈlaɪkə

Leicester ˈlɛstɚ; ES ˈlɛstə(r; |-shire -ˌʃɪr, -ʃɚ; ES -ˌʃɪə(r, -ʃə(r

Leiden ˈlaɪdn̩

Leif Ericson ˈlifˈɛrɪksn̩

Leigh pers. name li; places li, laɪ

Leila ˈlilə

Leinster ˈlɛnstɚ; ES ˈlɛnstə(r

Leipsic ˈlaɪpsɪk, O ˈlɪpsɪk

Leipzig ˈlaɪpsɪg, -sɪk (Ger ˈlaɪptsɪx)

leisure ˈliʒɚ, now less freq. ˈlɛʒɚ; ES -ʒə(r; |-d -d

Leitch litʃ |-'s -ɪz

Leith liθ

leitmotiv, -tif ˈlaɪtmoˌtif

Leland ˈlilənd

Lelia ˈlilɪə, -ljə

leman ˈlemən

Leman lake ˈlimən

Lemington ˈlɛmɪŋtən, cf Leamington

lemma ˈlɛmə |-s -z |-mata -tə

lemming ˈlɛmɪŋ

lemon ˈlɛmən |-ade ˌlɛmənˈed

Lemuel ˈlɛmjuəl

lemur ˈlimɚ; ES ˈlimə(r

Lena ˈlinə

Lenawee ˈlɛnəwɪ, -ˌwi

lend lɛnd |lent lɛnt

L'Enfant ˈlanfant (Fr lãˈfã)

length lɛŋkθ, lɛŋθ |-ths -θs |-thy -ɪ

lengthen ˈlɛŋkθən, ˈlɛŋθən |-ed -d |-ing -θənɪŋ, -θnɪŋ

lengthways ˈlɛŋkθˌwez, ˈlɛŋθ- |-wise -ˌwaɪz

lenience ˈlinɪəns, -njəns |-cy -ɪ |-ent -ənt

Lenin ˈlɛnɪn |-grad -ˌgræd, -ˌgrad

lenitive ˈlɛnətɪv |-ty ˈlɛnətɪ

Lennox ˈlɛnəks |-'s -ɪz

Lenoir US places ləˈnɔr, -ˈnɔr; ES -ˈnoə(r, E+-ˈnɔə(r

Lenoir, Étienne Fr eˈtjen ləˈnwaːr

Lenore ləˈnɔr, -ˈnɔr; ES -ˈnoə(r, E+-ˈnɔə(r

lens lɛnz |lenses ˈlɛnzɪz |lensed lɛnzd

lent lɛnt

Lent lɛnt |Lenten ˈlɛntən

lenticular lɛnˈtɪkjələ; ES -lə(r

lentigo lɛnˈtaɪgo |lentigines lɛnˈtɪdʒəˌniz

lentil ˈlɛntl̩, -tɪl

lento It ˈlɛnto

l'envoi, -voy ˈlɛnvɔɪ, lɛnˈvɔɪ (Fr lãˈvwa)

Leo ˈlio

Leominster Mass ˈlɛmɪnstɚ, Engd ˈlɛmstɚ, ˈlɛmɪn-; ES -stə(r

Leon US places ˈliən, PI leˈon

Leonard ˈlɛnɚd; ES ˈlɛnəd

Leonardo ˌliəˈnardo; ES -ˈnɑːdo

Leonardo da Vinci ˌliəˈnardo dəˈvɪntʃɪ; ES -ˈnɑːdo; (It ˌleoˈnardo daˈvintʃi)

Leonato ˌliəˈnato

Leonatus ˌliəˈnetəs |-'s -ɪz

Key: See in full §§3–47. bee bi |pity ˈpɪtɪ (§6) |rate ret |yet jɛt |sang sæŋ |angry ˈæŋ·grɪ |bath bæθ; E baθ (§10) |ah ɑ |far fɑr |watch watʃ, wɒtʃ (§12) |jaw dʒɔ |gorge gɔrdʒ |go go

Leonid 'liənɪd
Leonidas lɪ'anədəs; ES+-'ɒn-; |-'s -ɪz
leonine, L- 'liə,naɪn
Leonora ,liə'norə, -'nɔrə; S -'norə
Leontes lɪ'antiz, -'ɒntiz
leopard 'lɛpəd; ES 'lɛpəd; |-ess -ɪs
Leopold 'liə,pold, older 'lɛp|d
Lepanto lɪ'pænto
leper 'lɛpə; ES 'lɛpə(r; |-ed -d
lepidopterous ,lɛpə'dɑptərəs, -trəs; ES+
-'dɒp-
Lepidus 'lɛpɪdəs |-'s -ɪz
leprechaun 'lɛprə,kɒn
leprosy 'lɛprəsɪ |leprous 'lɛprəs
Lesbian 'lɛzbɪən
Lesbos 'lɛzbəs, -bas; ES+-bɒs
lese majesty 'liz'mædʒɪstɪ
lesion 'liʒən
Leslie 'lɛslɪ
less lɛs |lesser 'lɛsə; ES 'lɛsə(r
-less unstressed suffix -lɪs, -ləs. The pronunciation -lɛs is not normal to conversational
style, but occurs occasionally in deliberate
reading style, especially in rime. In the
vocab. only the pron. -lɪs is given, but it is
to be understood that many speakers (fewer
in the E and S) also pronounce -ləs as in
stylus 'staɪləs. In the vocabulary the ending
-less is usually not given. When -less is
added to words ending in -l or -|, two l
sounds are pronounced, as in soulless 'sollɪs,
bridleless 'braɪd|lɪs. Cf -ness.
lessee lɛs'i
lessen 'lɛsn̩ |-ed -d |-ing 'lɛsn̩ɪŋ, 'lɛsnɪŋ
Lesseps 'lɛsəps |-'s -ɪz (Fr lɛ'sɛps)
Lessing 'lɛsɪŋ
lesson 'lɛsn̩ |-ed -d |-ing 'lɛsn̩ɪŋ, 'lɛsnɪŋ
lessor 'lɛsɔr; ES 'lɛsɔə(r; (les'see & les'sor)
lest lɛst
Lester 'lɛstə; ES 'lɛstə(r
L'Estrange lɛ'strendʒ |-'s -ɪz
Le Sueur lə'sur; ES -'suə(r; (Fr Lesueur
lə'sɥœ:r)
let lɛt |-down 'lɛt,daʊn
Letcher 'lɛtʃə; ES 'lɛtʃə(r
lethal 'liθəl |-ly -ɪ
lethargic lɪ'θardʒɪk, lɛ-; ES -'θɑ:dʒ-; |-al -|
|-ally -|ɪ, -ɪklɪ
lethargy 'lɛθədʒɪ; ES 'lɛθədʒɪ

Lethe 'liθɪ, 'liθi |-d -d |-thied -θɪd
Lethean li'θiən
Letitia lɪ'tɪʃɪə, -ʃə
Leto 'lito
let's lɛts, lɛs
let's see lɛts'si, lɛt'si (originally let see)
Lett lɛt
letter 'lɛtə; ES 'lɛtə(r; |-ed -d
letterhead 'lɛtə,hɛd; ES 'lɛtə-
letter-perfect 'lɛtə'pɝfɪkt; ES 'lɛtə'pɝf-,
-'pɝf-
letterpress 'lɛtə,prɛs; ES 'lɛtə-
Lettice 'lɛtɪs |-'s -ɪz
Lettish 'lɛtɪʃ
lettuce 'lɛtɪs, -əs |-s -ɪz
letup 'lɛt,ʌp
leucocyte 'lukə,saɪt, 'lɪukə-
leucorrhea, -rhoea ,lukə'riə, ,lɪukə-
leud lud, lɪud |-s -z |-es -ɪz
Leutner 'lɔɪtnə; ES 'lɔɪtnə(r
Levant lə'vænt
Levantine lə'væntɪn, 'lɛvən,taɪn
levator lə'vetə; ES -'vetə(r; |-tores ,lɛvə-
'toriz
levee 'bank' 'lɛvɪ |-d -d, 'reception'+lə'vi
level 'lɛv|, older & still occas. 'lɛvɪl |-ly -ɪ
|-ed -d |-ing 'lɛvlɪŋ, -v|ɪŋ
levelheaded 'lɛv|'hɛdɪd ('level,headed 'move)
lever 'lɛvə, 'livə; E -və(r; S 'livə(r, 'lɛvə(r;
|-ed -d |-ing -vərɪŋ, -vrɪŋ |-age -ɪdʒ, -vrɪdʒ
Levi 'livaɪ
leviable 'lɛvɪəb|
leviathan, L- lə'vaɪəθən
levigate 'lɛvə,get |-d -ɪd
levin 'lɛvɪn
Levis 'livɪs (Fr lɛ'vi)
levitate 'lɛvə,tet |-d -ɪd |-tion ,lɛvə'teʃən
Levite 'livaɪt
Levitic lə'vɪtɪk |-al -| |-ally -|ɪ |-us -əs
levity 'lɛvətɪ
levulose 'lɛvjə,los
levy 'lɛvɪ |levied 'lɛvɪd
lewd lud, lɪud
Lewes, -is 'luɪs, 'lɪuɪs |-'s -ɪz
lewisite 'luɪs,aɪt, 'lɪuɪs-
Lewisohn 'luɪ,zon, 'lɪuɪ-, -,son
Lewiston 'luɪstən, 'lɪuɪs-
lex lɛks |leges 'lidʒɪz
lexical 'lɛksɪk|

lexicographer ˌlɛksə'kɑgrəfɚ, -'kɒg-; ES -fə(r; |-phy -fɪ

lexicon 'lɛksɪkən

Lexington 'lɛksɪŋtən

Leyden 'laɪdn̩

Lhasa 'lɑsə

liable 'laɪəbl̩ |liability ˌlaɪə'bɪlətɪ

liaison ˌlie'zɔ̃ (Fr ljɛ'zõ)

liar 'laɪɚ; ES 'laɪ·ə(r

libation laɪ'beʃən

Libby 'lɪbɪ

libel 'laɪbl̩ |-ed -d |-ing 'laɪblɪŋ, 'laɪblɪŋ

libelant, -llant 'laɪblənt

libelee, -llee ˌlaɪbl̩'i

libelous, -llous 'laɪbləs

liberal 'lɪbərəl, 'lɪbrəl |-ly -ɪ |-ism -ˌɪzəm

liberality ˌlɪbə'rælətɪ

liberalize 'lɪbərəlˌaɪz, -brəl- |-s -ɪz |-d -d

liberate 'lɪbəˌret

liberation ˌlɪbə'reʃən

liberator 'lɪbəˌretɚ; ES -ˌretə(r

Liberia laɪ'bɪrɪə |-n -n

libertarian ˌlɪbɚ'tɛrɪən, -'ter-; ES ˌlɪbə-

liberticide lɪ'bɝtəˌsaɪd; ES -'bɝt-, -'bɝt-

libertinage 'lɪbɚtɪnɪdʒ; ES 'lɪbə-

libertine 'lɪbɚˌtin; ES 'lɪbəˌtin; |-nism -tin-ˌɪzəm, -tɪnˌɪzəm

liberty 'lɪbɚtɪ; ES 'lɪbətɪ

libidinous lɪ'bɪdn̩əs

libido lɪ'baɪdo

Libra 'laɪbrə |-brae -bri

librarian laɪ'brɛrɪən, -'brer- |-ship -ˌʃɪp

library 'laɪˌbrɛrɪ, -brɪ, -brərɪ—In the occas. prons. 'laɪˌbɛrɪ, 'laɪbərɪ r is lost by dissimilation (§121), and 'laɪbrɪ is due to contraction.

librate 'laɪbret |-d -ɪd |-tion laɪ'breʃən

librettist lɪ'brɛtɪst

libretto lɪ'brɛto |-s -z |-ti -ti

Libya 'lɪbɪə |-n -n

lice laɪs |lice's 'laɪsɪz

license, -nce 'laɪsn̩s |-s -ɪz |-d -t

licensee, -cee ˌlaɪsn̩'si

licensor 'laɪsn̩sɚ; ES -sə(r; (ˌlaɪsn̩'si ən ˌlaɪsn̩'sɔr)

licentiate n, adj laɪ'sɛnʃɪt, -ˌet

licentious laɪ'sɛnʃəs

Lichas 'laɪkəs |-'s -ɪz

lichen 'laɪkɪn, -kən |-ed -d |-ous -əs

Lichfield Engd 'lɪtʃfild

lich-gate 'lɪtʃˌget

licit 'lɪsɪt

lick lɪk |licked lɪkt

lickerish adj 'lɪkərɪʃ

Licking 'lɪkɪŋ

lickspittle 'lɪkˌspɪtl̩ |-d -d |-ling -ˌspɪtlɪŋ, -ˌspɪtlɪŋ

licorice 'lɪkərɪs, 'lɪkərɪʃ, -krɪ-

lictor 'lɪktɚ; ES 'lɪktə(r

lid lɪd |lidded 'lɪdɪd

Liddell 'lɪdl̩

Liddesdale 'lɪdzˌdel

Lidice 'lidɪtsɪ, -tse (Czech li·dji·tsɛ)

lie n laɪ

lie 'falsify' laɪ |lied laɪd |lying 'laɪɪŋ

lie 'recline' laɪ |lay le |lain len |lying -ɪŋ

Liebig 'libɪg (Ger 'li:brx)

Liechtenstein 'lɪktənˌstaɪn (Ger 'lɪxtənˌʃtaɪn)

lied past of lie laɪd

lied 'song' lid |pl lieder 'lidɚ; ES 'lidə(r; (Ger li:t, 'li:dər)

lief lif |liefer 'livɚ, 'lifɚ; ES -ə(r; |liefest 'livɪst, 'lifɪst—see lieve

liege lidʒ |-s -ɪz

Liége lɪ'eʒ, -'ɛʒ (Fr ljɛ:ʒ)

lien lin, 'liən

lieu lu, lɪu

lieutenancy lu'tɛnənsɪ, lɪu-

lieutenant lu'tɛnənt, lɪu-; Brit army lɛf-, Brit navy lu- (Jones)

lieve liv |liever 'livɚ; ES -və(r; |-est -ɪst

life laɪf |life's laɪfs (in Shak. lives laɪvz) |pl lives laɪvz—The pronunciation laɪvz for life's is the older possessive singular.

lifeblood 'laɪfˌblʌd, emph.+-'blʌd

lifeboat 'laɪfˌbot

lifeguard 'laɪfˌgɑrd; ES -ˌgɑ:d, E+-ˌgɑ:d

lifelike 'laɪfˌlaɪk

lifelong 'laɪf'lɒŋ, -'lɒŋ; S+-'lɑŋ; ('lifeˌlong 'friend)

lifesaver 'laɪfˌsevɚ; ES -ˌsevə(r

life-size 'laɪf'saɪz |-d -d

lifetime 'laɪfˌtaɪm

lifework 'laɪfˌwɝk, -'wɝk; ES -ɝk, -ɝk

lift lɪft |-ed -ɪd or arch. lift lɪft

ligament 'lɪgəmənt |-al ˌlɪgə'mɛntl̩

Ligarius lɪ'gɛrɪəs, -'ger- |-s -ɪz

ligate 'laɪget |-d -ɪd |-tion laɪ'geʃən

ligature 'lɪgəˌtʃʊr, -tʃɚ; ES -ˌtʃʊə(r, -tʃə(r; |-d -d

ligeance 'laɪdʒəns, 'lidʒ- |-s -ɪz

light laɪt |lighted 'laɪtɪd or lit lɪt

lighten 'laɪtn̩ |-ed -d |-ing 'laɪtn̩ɪŋ, -tnɪŋ

lighter 'laɪtɚ; ES 'laɪtə(r; |-ed -d

lighterage 'laɪtərɪdʒ |-s -ɪz

light-fingered 'laɪt'fɪŋgɚd; ES -'fɪŋgəd

Lightfoot 'laɪtˌfʊt

light-footed 'laɪt'fʊtɪd

lighthead 'laɪtˌhɛd

lightheaded 'laɪt'hɛdɪd ('lightˌheaded 'youth)

lighthearted 'laɪt'hɑrtɪd; ES -'hɑːtɪd, E+ -'hɑːt-

lighthouse 'laɪtˌhaʊs |-ses -zɪz

lightning 'laɪtnɪŋ |lightninged 'laɪtnɪŋd

light-o'-love 'laɪtə'lʌv

lightship 'laɪtˌʃɪp

lightsome 'laɪtsəm

light-struck 'laɪtˌstrʌk

lightweight 'laɪt'wet ('lightˌweight 'coin)

lightwood 'laɪtˌwʊd, loc. S 'laɪtəd

light-year 'laɪt'jɪr, -ˌjɪr; ES -ɪə(r; cf year

ligneous 'lɪgnɪəs

lignify 'lɪgnəˌfaɪ |-fied -ˌfaɪd

lignin 'lɪgnɪn

lignite 'lɪgnaɪt

lignose 'lɪgnos |-nous -nəs

lignum vitae 'lɪgnəm'vaɪtɪ, -ti

Ligonier ˌlɪgə'nɪr; ES -'nɪə(r

ligule 'lɪgjul

ligure 'lɪgjʊr; ES 'lɪgjʊə(r

Liguria lɪ'gjʊrɪə, -'gɪʊrɪə |-n -n

Li Hung Chang 'li'hʊŋ'tʃæŋ, -'hʌŋ-, -'tʃɑŋ

likable, likeable 'laɪkəbl̩

like laɪk |liked laɪkt

-like suffix -ˌlaɪk—Words in -like are usually omitted from the vocab., since the pron. can always be found by adding -ˌlaɪk to the sound of the head word (manlike 'mænˌlaɪk). When the head word ends in a l sound, two l sounds are heard (taillike 'telˌlaɪk, eaglelike 'iglˌlaɪk, bell-like 'bɛlˌlaɪk).

likelihood 'laɪklɪˌhʊd

likely 'laɪklɪ

liken 'laɪkən |-ed -d |-ing 'laɪkənɪŋ, -knɪŋ

likeness 'laɪknɪs |-es -ɪz

likewise 'laɪkˌwaɪz

likin 'li'kin

liking 'laɪkɪŋ

lilac 'laɪlək, older 'laɪlæk

Lilian 'lɪlɪən, -ljən

lilied 'lɪlɪd

Lilith 'lɪlɪθ

Lille lil

lillibullero ˌlɪlɪbə'liro

Lilliput 'lɪləˌpʌt, -pət

Lilliputian ˌlɪlə'pjuʃən, -'prʊ-

Lilly 'lɪlɪ

lilt lɪlt |lilted 'lɪltɪd

lily 'lɪlɪ |lilied 'lɪlɪd

lily-livered 'lɪlɪ'lɪvɚd; ES -'lɪvəd

Lima US 'laɪmə, Peru 'limə, bean 'laɪmə

limb lɪm |limbed lɪmd

limbeck, -bec 'lɪmbɛk

limber 'tree trimmer' 'lɪmɚ; ES 'lɪmə(r

limber 'flex,' 'flexible' 'lɪmbɚ; ES 'lɪmbə(r; |-ed -d |-ing 'lɪmbərɪŋ, 'lɪmbrɪŋ

limbo 'lɪmbo

Limburg, -bourg Belg 'lɪmbɝg; ES 'lɪmbɜg, -bɝg; (Fr læ̃'buːr)

Limburger 'lɪmbɝgɚ; ES 'lɪmbɜgə(r, -bɝgə(r

lime laɪm |limed laɪmd

Limehouse Lond 'laɪmˌhaʊs, loc. 'lɪməs (Les Lymostes 1367, Lymost 1496, Lymehurst 1535, Lymehouse 1547—a triumph of literate ignorance)

limekiln 'laɪmˌkɪl, -ˌkɪln—see kiln

limelight 'laɪmˌlaɪt

limen 'laɪmɛn

limerick, L- 'lɪmərɪk, 'lɪmrɪk

limestone 'laɪmˌston

limewater 'laɪmˌwɔtɚ, -ˌwɑtɚ, -ˌwɒtɚ; ES -tə(r

limit 'lɪmɪt |limited 'lɪmɪtɪd

limn lɪm |limned lɪmd |-ing 'lɪmɪŋ, 'lɪmnɪŋ

limner 'lɪmɚ, 'lɪmnɚ; ES -ə(r

Limoges lɪ'moʒ |-'s -ɪz

limonene 'lɪməˌnin

limonite 'laɪməˌnaɪt

limousine 'lɪməˌzin, ˌlɪmə'zin

limp lɪmp |limped lɪmpt

limpet 'lɪmpɪt

limpid 'lɪmpɪd |-pidity lɪm'pɪdətɪ

limy 'laɪmɪ

linage 'laɪnɪdʒ |-s -ɪz

linchpin 'lɪntʃˌpɪn |-pinned -ˌpɪnd

Lincoln 'lɪŋkən

|full fʊl |tooth tuθ |further 'fɝðɚ; ES 'fɝðə |custom 'kʌstəm |while hwaɪl |how haʊ |toy tɔɪ |using 'juzɪŋ |fuse fjuz, fɪʊz |dish dɪʃ |vision 'vɪʒən |Eden 'idn̩ |cradle 'kredl̩ |keep 'em 'kipm̩

Lincolnian lɪŋ'konɪən
Lincolniana ˌlɪŋkənɪ'enə, -ko-, -'ænə, -'ɑnə
Lincolnshire 'lɪŋkənˌʃɪr, -ʃɚ; ES -ˌʃɪə(r, -ʃə(r
Lincs *short for* Lincolnshire lɪŋks
Lind lɪnd
Lindbergh 'lɪnbɝg, 'lɪnd-; ES -bɝg, -bɝg
linden, L- 'lɪndən
Lindisfarne 'lɪndɪsˌfɑrn; ES -ˌfɑːn, E+-ˌfɑːn
Lindley 'lɪndlɪ, 'lɪnlɪ
Lindsay 'lɪnzɪ, 'lɪndzɪ |Vachel 'vetʃəl
Lindsey 'lɪnzɪ, 'lɪndzɪ
line laɪn |lined laɪnd
lineage '*alignment*' 'laɪnɪdʒ |-s -ɪz
lineage '*family*' 'lɪnɪɪdʒ |-s -ɪz |-d -d
lineal 'lɪnɪəl |-ly -ɪ |-neament 'lɪnɪəmənt
linear 'lɪnɪɚ; ES 'lɪnɪ·ə(r
lineate *adj* 'lɪnɪɪt, -ˌet |-ated -ˌetɪd
lineman 'laɪnmən |-men -mən
linen 'lɪnɪn, -ən
liner 'laɪnɚ; ES 'laɪnə(r
linesman 'laɪnzmən |-men -mən
line-up 'laɪnˌʌp
ling lɪŋ
linger 'lɪŋgɚ; ES 'lɪŋgə(r; |-ed -d |-ing 'lɪŋgərɪŋ, 'lɪŋgrɪŋ
lingerie 'lænʒəˌri (*Fr* lɛ̃ʒ'ri)
lingo 'lɪŋgo
lingua franca 'lɪŋgwə'fræŋkə
lingual 'lɪŋgwəl
linguaphone, L- 'lɪŋgwəˌfon
linguiform 'lɪŋgwɪˌfɔrm; ES -ˌfɔəm
linguist 'lɪŋgwɪst
linguistic lɪŋ'gwɪstɪk |-s -s |-al -l̩ |-ally -l̩ɪ, -ɪklɪ
liniment 'lɪnəmənt
lining 'laɪnɪŋ
link lɪŋk |links lɪŋks |linked lɪŋkt
linkage 'lɪŋkɪdʒ |-s -ɪz
linkboy 'lɪŋkˌbɔɪ
linked 'lɪŋkt, *poet.* 'lɪŋkɪd
Linklater 'lɪŋkˌletɚ; ES -ˌletə(r
linkwork 'lɪŋkˌwɝk; ES -ˌwɜk, -ˌwɝk
Linley 'lɪnlɪ—*see* Lindley
Linlithgow lɪn'lɪθgo
Linnaeus lɪ'niəs |-'s -ɪz |-aean, -ean -'niən
linnet 'lɪnɪt
linoleum lɪ'nolɪəm, -ljəm
Linotype 'laɪnəˌtaɪp |-d -t
linseed 'lɪnˌsid

linsey-woolsey 'lɪnzɪ'wʊlzɪ
linstock 'lɪnˌstɑk; ES+-ˌstɒk
lint lɪnt
lintel 'lɪntl̩ |-ed -d
linter 'lɪntɚ; ES 'lɪntə(r
Lin Yutang 'lɪnju'tæŋ
lion, L- 'laɪən |-ess -ɪs |-ess's -ɪsɪz
Lionel 'laɪənl̩, 'laɪəˌnɛl
lionheart 'laɪənˌhɑrt; ES -ˌhɑːt, E+-ˌhɑːt
lion-hearted 'laɪən'hɑrtɪd; ES -'hɑːt-, E+-'hɑːt-
lionize 'laɪənˌaɪz |-s -ɪz |-d -d
lip lɪp |lipped lɪpt
lipase 'laɪpes
lipide 'laɪpaɪd, 'lɪpɪd |-pid -pɪd
Lippi 'lɪpɪ (*It* 'lippi)
Lippmann 'lɪpmən
lipstick 'lɪpˌstɪk |-sticked -ˌstɪkt
liquefaction ˌlɪkwɪ'fækʃən
liquefy 'lɪkwəˌfaɪ |-fied -ˌfaɪd
liquescence lɪ'kwɛsn̩s |-cy -ɪ |-scent -sn̩t
liqueur lɪ'kɝ; ES -'kɜ(r, -'kɝ; *Brit* lɪ'kjʊə(r; (*Fr* li'kœːr)
liquid 'lɪkwɪd
liquidambar, -ber, L- 'lɪkwɪdˌæmbɚ; ES -ˌæmbə(r
liquidate 'lɪkwɪˌdet |-d -ɪd
liquidation ˌlɪkwɪ'deʃən
liquidator 'lɪkwɪˌdetɚ; ES -ˌdetə(r
liquidity lɪ'kwɪdətɪ
liquor 'lɪkɚ; ES 'lɪkə(r; |-ed -d
liquorice 'lɪkərɪs, -krɪs, -rɪʃ
liquorish '*lickerish*' 'lɪkərɪʃ
liquorish '*licorice*' 'lɪkərɪʃ, -krɪʃ
lira 'lɪrə |-s -z |lire 'lɪre (*It* 'liːrɑ, -re)
liripipe 'lɪrɪˌpaɪp |-poop -ˌpup
Lisa *Eng name* 'laɪzə, 'lisə, *It name* 'lizɑ
Lisbon 'lɪzbən
lisle, L- laɪl (*Fr* lil)
lisp lɪsp |lisped lɪspt
lissome, -som 'lɪsəm
list lɪst |-ed -ɪd
list '*please*' lɪst |*past* listed 'lɪstɪd *or arch.* list lɪst |*pptc* listed 'lɪstɪd
listel 'lɪstl̩
listen 'lɪsn̩ |-ed -d |-ing 'lɪsn̩ɪŋ, 'lɪsnɪŋ
listener 'lɪsn̩ɚ, 'lɪsnɚ; ES -nə(r
lister, L- 'lɪstɚ; ES 'lɪstə(r
Listerine, l- 'lɪstəˌrin

Key: See in full §§3–47. bee bi |pity 'pɪtɪ (§6) |rate ret |yet jet |sang sæŋ |angry 'æŋ·grɪ |bath bæθ; E baθ (§10) |ah ɑ |far fɑr |watch wɑtʃ, wɒtʃ (§12) |jaw dʒɔ |gorge gɔrdʒ |go go

listless ˈlɪstlɪs
Liszt lɪst
lit lɪt
litany, L- ˈlɪtṇɪ
Litchfield US ˈlɪtʃfild
lɪ̈er, -tre ˈlitɚ; ES ˈlitə(r
literacy ˈlɪtərəsɪ
literal ˈlɪtərəl |-ly -ɪ |-ism -ˌɪzəm |-ist -ɪst
literary ˈlɪtəˌrɛrɪ
literate ˈlɪtərɪt
literati ˌlɪtəˈretaɪ, ˌlɪtəˈratɪ
literatim ˌlɪtəˈretɪm
literature ˈlɪtərəˌtʃʊr, -tʃɚ, ˈlɪtrə-, -ˌtjʊr; ES
  -ˌtʃʊə(r, -tʃə(r, -ˌtjʊə(r
litharge ˈlɪθɑrdʒ; ES -θɑ:dʒ, E+-θɑ:dʒ
lithe ˈlaɪð |-some -səm
lither 'more lithe' ˈlaɪðɚ; ES ˈlaɪðə(r
lither 'bad,' 'agile' ˈlɪðɚ; ES ˈlɪðə(r
lithia ˈlɪθɪə, -θjə |-ium -ɪəm |-ic -ɪk
lithograph ˈlɪθəˌgræf; E+-ˌgraf, -ˌgrɑf; |-ed -t
lithographer lɪˈθɑgrəfɚ, -ˈθɒg-; ES -fə(r;
  |-phy -fɪ
lithographic ˌlɪθəˈgræfɪk |-al -ļ |-ally -ļɪ, -ɪklɪ
lithosphere ˈlɪθəˌsfɪr; ES -ˌsfɪə(r, S+-ˌsfɛə(r
Lithuania ˌlɪθjuˈenɪə, ˌlɪθuˈenɪə |-n -n
litigable ˈlɪtɪgəbḷ |-gant ˈlɪtəgənt
litigate ˈlɪtəˌget |-d -ɪd |-tion ˌlɪtəˈgeʃən
litigious lɪˈtɪdʒɪəs
litmus ˈlɪtməs
litotes ˈlaɪtəˌtiz, ˈlaɪto-
litro ˈlitro
Littell ˈlɪtḷ, lɪˈtɛl
litten ˈlɪtṇ
litter ˈlɪtɚ; ES ˈlɪtə(r; |-ed -d
littérateur ˌlɪtərəˈtɝ; ES -ˈtɜ(r, -ˈtɝ; (Fr
  literaˈtœ:r)
little ˈlɪtḷ |-r ˈlɪtļɚ, ˈlɪtlɚ; ES -ə(r; |-st ˈlɪtļɪst,
  ˈlɪtlɪst
Littlejohn ˈlɪtḷˌdʒɑn, -ˌdʒɒn
littleneck ˈlɪtḷˌnɛk
Littleton ˈlɪtḷtən
littoral ˈlɪtərəl
liturgical lɪˈtɝdʒɪkḷ; ES -ˈtɝdʒ-, -ˈtɜdʒ-; |-ly
  -ɪ, -ɪklɪ |-gics -dʒɪks
liturgism ˈlɪtɚˌdʒɪzəm; ES ˈlɪtə-; |-gist -dʒɪst
liturgy ˈlɪtɚdʒɪ; ES ˈlɪtədʒɪ
Litvinov lɪtˈvinɔf, -ɒf
livable, liveable ˈlɪvəbḷ
live adj laɪv

live 'lief' Shak. lɪv
live v lɪv |lived lɪvd
lived 'having life' laɪvd—cf long-lived
livelihood ˈlaɪvlɪˌhʊd
livelong n, adj ˈlɪvˌlɔŋ, -ˌlɒŋ; S+-ˌlɑŋ
lively ˈlaɪvlɪ
liven ˈlaɪvən |-ed -d |-ing ˈlaɪvənɪŋ, -vnɪŋ
liver ˈlɪvɚ; ES -və(r; |-ed -d |-ing -vərɪŋ,
  -vrɪŋ
liver Liverpool arms ˈlaɪvɚ; ES ˈlaɪvə(r
liveried ˈlɪvərɪd, ˈlɪvrɪd
liverish ˈlɪvərɪʃ, ˈlɪvrɪʃ
Livermore ˈlɪvɚˌmor, -ˌmɔr; ES ˈlɪvəˌmoə(r,
  E+-ˌmɔə(r
Liverpool ˈlɪvɚˌpul; ES ˈlɪvəˌpul
Liverpudlian ˌlɪvɚˈpʌdlɪən; ES ˌlɪvə-
liverwort ˈlɪvɚˌwɝt; ES ˈlɪvəˌwɜt, ˈlɪvəˌwɝt
liverwurst ˈlɪvɚˌwɝst, -ˌwʊrst; ES ˈlɪvə-
  ˌwɜst, ˈlɪvəˌwɝst, -ˌwʊəst
livery ˈlɪvərɪ, -vrɪ |-ied -d |-man -mən |-men
  -mən
lives pl of life laɪvz |live's laɪvz—see life
lives 3 sg of live v lɪvz
lives 'lief' dial. lɪvz
livestock ˈlaɪvˌstɑk; ES+-ˌstɒk
Livia ˈlɪvɪə
livid ˈlɪvɪd |-vidity lɪˈvɪdətɪ
living ˈlɪvɪŋ |-s -z
Livingston, -e ˈlɪvɪŋstən
Livonia lɪˈvonɪə, -njə
Livy ˈlɪvɪ
lizard, L- ˈlɪzɚd; ES ˈlɪzəd
-'ll abbr. spelling of unstressed will in I'll aɪl,
  you'll jul, he'll hil, she'll ʃil, we'll wil,
  they'll ðel, it'll ˈɪtḷ; after nouns rarely abbreviated in spelling but often in pronunciation, as father will go ˈfɑðɚ əlˌgo, George
  will go ˈdʒɔrdʒ əlˌgo, that will do ˈðætḷˈdu,
  Lucy will go ˈlusɪ əlˌgo, Joe will go ˈdʒolˌgo.
  See will
llama ˈlɑmə
Llanarmon læˈnɑrmən, θlæ-; ES -ˈnɑːm-;
  (Welsh ɬaˈnarmon)
Llanberis lænˈbɛrɪs, θlæn- (Welsh ɬanˈberis)
Llandudno lænˈdʌdno, θlæn- (Welsh ɬan-
  ˈdidno)
Llanelly læˈnɛlɪ, θlæˈnɛθlɪ (S. Welsh ɬaˈneɬi)
Llangollen lænˈgɑlɪn, θlænˈgɑθl-, -ˈgɒ-, -ən
  (Welsh ɬanˈgoɬen)

|full fʊl |tooth tuθ |further ˈfɝðɚ; ES ˈfɜðə |custom ˈkʌstəm |while hwaɪl |how haʊ |toy tɔɪ
|using ˈjuzɪŋ |fuse fjuz, fruz |dish dɪʃ |vision ˈvɪʒən |Eden ˈidṇ |cradle ˈkredḷ |keep 'em ˈkipm̩

Those words below in which the ɑ *sound is spelt* o *are often pronounced with* ɒ *in E and S*

llano, L- 'lɑno, 'læno

Llano Estacado 'lɑno͵ɛstə'kɑdo, 'leno͵ɛstə-
'kedo

Llewellyn, -elyn lu'ɛlɪn, lɪu- (*Welsh* ɬə-
'welin)

Lloyd lɔɪd

Lloyd George 'lɔɪd'dʒɔrdʒ; ES -'dʒɔədʒ; |-'s
-ɪz

Llywelyn lu'ɛlɪn, lɪu- (*Welsh* ɬə'welin)

lo lo

loach lotʃ |loaches 'lotʃɪz

load lod |loaded 'lodɪd

loadstar 'lod͵stɑr; ES -͵stɑ:(r, E+-͵stɑ:(r

loadstone 'lod͵ston

loaf *n* lof |loaf's lofs |loaves lovz

loaf *v* lof |loafs lofs |loafed loft

loam lom |loamed lomd

loan lon |loaned lond

loan *Phil measure* lo'ɑn |loanes lo'ɑnes

loath loθ

loathe loð |loathed loðd

loathful 'loðfəl |-ly -ɪ

loathly *adj* 'loðlɪ

loathly *adv* 'loθlɪ, 'loðlɪ (*older form*)

loathsome 'loðsəm

lob, L- lab |lobbed labd

lobar 'lobɚ; ES 'lobə(r

lobby 'labɪ |lobbied 'labɪd |lobbyist 'labɪɪst

lobe lob |lobed lobd

lobelia, L- lo'bɪljə

loblolly 'lablalɪ

lobo 'lobo

Lobos 'lobos |-'s -ɪz

lobster 'labstɚ; ES 'labstə(r

local 'lok| |-ed -d |-ly -ɪ

locale, -al lo'kæl, -'kɑl (*Fr* lɔ'kal)

localism 'lok|͵ɪzəm |-istic ͵lok|'ɪstɪk

locality lo'kælətɪ

localization ͵lok|ə'zeʃən, -aɪ'z-

localize 'lok|͵aɪz |-s -ɪz |-d -d

Locarno lo'kɑrno; ES -'kɑ:no, E+-'kɑ:no

locate 'loket, lo'ket |-d -ɪd

location lo'keʃən |-al -|

locative 'lakətɪv, 'lakɪtɪv

loch, L- lak, lax (*Sc* lɒx, lox)

Lochaber lɑ'kæbɚ, lɒ-, -'xæb-, -abɚ; ES
-bə(r

Lochiel lɑ'kil, lɒ-, -'xil

Lochinvar ͵lakɪn'vɑr, ͵lɒ-, -xɪn-; ES -'vɑ:(r,
E+-'vɑ:(r

loci *pl of* locus 'losaɪ

lock lak |locked lakt |-age -ɪdʒ |-et -ɪt

Locke lak

Lockerbie 'lakɚbɪ; ES 'lakəbɪ

Lockhart 'lakhɑrt, -kɚt; ES -hɑ:t, -kət,
E+-hɑ:t

lockjaw 'lak͵dʒɔ

lockout 'lak͵aʊt

Lockport 'lak͵port, -͵pɔrt; ES -͵poət, E+
-͵pɔət

Locksley 'lakslɪ

locksmith 'lak͵smɪθ |-ths -θs

lockup 'lak͵ʌp

Lockyer 'lakjɚ; ES 'lakjə(r

loco 'loko |locoed 'lokod

locomotion ͵lokə'moʃən |-motive -'motɪv

locomotor ͵lokə'motɚ; ES -'motə(r

Locrine lo'kraɪn, -'krin

Locris 'lokrɪs |-'s -ɪz

loculus 'lakjələs |-es -ɪz |-li -͵laɪ

locum tenens 'lokəm'tinɪnz, -ənz

locus 'lokəs |loci 'losaɪ

locust 'lokəst

locution lo'kjuʃən, -'krɪu-

locutory 'lakjə͵torɪ, -͵tɔrɪ; S -͵torɪ

lode lod |-star -͵stɑr; ES -͵stɑ:(r, E+-͵stɑ:(r;
|-stone -͵ston

lodge ladʒ |lodges 'ladʒɪz |lodged ladʒd

Lodge ladʒ |-'s -ɪz

lodgment, -dge- 'ladʒmənt

Lodi *US* 'lodaɪ; *Italy* 'lodi (*It* 'lɔ:di)

Lodore lo'dor, -'dɔr; ES -'doə(r, E+-'dɔə(r

Lodovico ͵lodə'viko

Lodowic, -ick 'lodəwɪk, 'lad-

Loeb leb, lɛb, lob (*Ger* lø:p)

loess 'lo·ɪs (*Ger* löss lœs)

loft lɔft, lɒft

Lofthouse 'lɔftəs, 'lɒft-, -͵haʊs |-'s -ɪz

Loftus 'lɔftəs, 'lɒf- |-'s -ɪz

lofty 'lɔftɪ, 'lɒf- |-tily -t|ɪ, -tɪlɪ

log lɔg, lag, lɒg |-ged -d

Logan 'logən |-sport -z͵port, -z͵pɔrt; ES
-z͵poət, E+-z͵pɔət

logarithm 'lɔgə͵rɪðəm, 'lag-, 'lɒg-, -θəm

logarithmic ͵lɔgə'rɪðmɪk, ͵lag-, ͵lɒg-, -θmɪk
|-al -| |-ally -|ɪ, -ɪklɪ

Key: *See in full* §§3–47. bee bi |pity 'pɪtɪ (§6) |rate ret |yet jɛt |sang sæŋ |angry 'æŋ·grɪ
|bath bæθ; E bɑθ (§10) |ah ɑ |far fɑr |watch watʃ, wɒtʃ (§12) |jaw dʒɔ |gorge gɔrdʒ |go go

Those words below in which the ɑ sound is spelt o are often pronounced with ɒ in E and S

logbook 'lɔg‚bʊk, 'lɑg-, 'lɒg-
loge loʒ (*Fr* lɔ̄:ʒ)
loggerhead 'lɔgɚ‚hɛd, 'lɑg-, 'lɒg-; ES -gɚ-; |-ed -ɪd
loggia 'lɑdʒɪə, -dʒə, 'lɒdʒ-, 'lɔdʒ- |-s -z (*It* 'lɔddʒɑ |*pl* loggie 'lɔddʒe)
logic 'lɑdʒɪk |-al -əl -| |-ally -ļɪ, -ɪklɪ
logicality ‚lɑdʒɪ'kælətɪ
logician lo'dʒɪʃən
logos, L- 'lɑgɑs, 'lɒg-
logroll 'lɔg‚rol, 'lɑg-, 'lɒg- |-ed -d
logwood 'lɔg‚wʊd, 'lɑg-, 'lɒg-
logy 'logɪ
Lohengrin 'loən‚grɪn, -‚grin
loin lɔɪn |loined lɔɪnd
Loire lwar; ES lwa:(r, E+lwa:(r; (*Fr* lwa:r)
Lois 'lo·ɪs |-'s -ɪz
loiter 'lɔɪtɚ; ES -tə(r; |-ed -d |-ing -tərɪŋ, -trɪŋ
Loki 'lokɪ (*Ice* 'lɔkɪ)
Lola 'lolə
loll lɑl |lolled lɑld
Lollard 'lɑlɚd; ES 'lɑləd; |-ry -rɪ |-y -ɪ
lollipop 'lɑlɪ‚pɑp
Lomax 'lomæks |-'s -ɪz
Lombard 'lɑmbɚd, 'lʌm-, -bɑrd; ES -bəd, -bɑ:d, E+-ba:d
Lombardic lam'bɑrdɪk, lʌm-; ES -'bɑ:d-, E+-'ba:d-
Lombardy 'lɑmbɚdɪ, 'lʌm-; ES -bədɪ
Lomond 'lomənd
London 'lʌndən
Londonderry 'lʌndən‚dɛrɪ, *Irel* ‚lʌndən'dɛrɪ
Londres, l- *cigar* 'lɑndrɛs (*Fr* lɔ̄'drɛ:s)
lone lon |lonely 'lonlɪ |-some -səm; *N Engd*+ lȫn(-) (*§46*)
long lɔŋ, lɒŋ; S+lɑŋ; |-er -gɚ; ES -gə(r; |-est -gɪst
long-and-short 'lɔŋən'ʃɔrt, 'lɒŋ-; ES -'ʃɔət, S+'lɑŋ-
Longaville 'lɔŋgə‚vɪl, 'lɒŋgə-; S+'lɑŋ-
longboat 'lɔŋ‚bot, 'lɒŋ-; S+'lɑŋ-
longbow 'lɔŋ‚bo, 'lɒŋ-; S+'lɑŋ-
long-distance 'lɔŋ'dɪstəns, 'lɒŋ-; S+'lɑŋ-; ('long-‚distance 'call)
longeron 'lɑndʒərən (*Fr* lɔ̄ʒe'rɔ̄)
longevity lan'dʒɛvətɪ
Longfellow 'lɔŋ‚fɛlo, 'lɒŋ-; S+'lɑŋ-

longhand 'lɔŋ‚hænd, 'lɒŋ-; S+'lɑŋ-
longhorn 'lɔŋ‚hɔrn, 'lɒŋ-; ES -‚hɔən, S+'lɑŋ-
Longinus lan'dʒaɪnəs |-'s -ɪz
longish 'lɔŋɪʃ, 'lɒŋ-; S+'lɑŋ-
longitude 'lɑndʒə‚tjud, -‚tɪud, -‚tud
longitudinal ‚lɑndʒə'tjudņ‚l, -'tɪud-, -'tud-, -dənəl |-ly -ɪ
long-legged 'lɔŋ'lɛgɪd, 'lɒŋ-, -'lɛgd; S+'lɑŋ-
long-lived 'lɔŋ'laɪvd, 'lɒŋ-, *by false etym.*+ -'lɪvd; S+'lɑŋ-
longshoreman 'lɔŋ‚ʃormən, 'lɒŋ-, -‚ʃɔr-; E -‚ʃoə-, -‚ʃɔə-; S -‚ʃoə-,+'lɑŋ-; |-men -mən
Longstreet 'lɔŋ‚strit, 'lɒŋ-; S+'lɑŋ-
longsuffering 'lɔŋ'sʌfrɪŋ, 'lɒŋ-, -fərɪŋ; S+'lɑŋ·
Longsword 'lɔŋ‚sord, 'lɒŋ-, -‚sɔrd; E -‚soəd, -‚sɔəd; S -‚soəd, +'lɑŋ-
longways 'lɔŋ‚wez, 'lɒŋ-; S+'lɑŋ-; |-wise -‚waɪz
long-winded 'lɔŋ'wɪndɪd, 'lɒŋ-; S+'lɑŋ-
loo lu |looed lud
looby 'lubɪ
look lʊk |looked lʊkt
looker-on ‚lʊkɚ'an, -'ɒn, -ˈɒn |lookers- ‚lʊkɚz-; ES ‚lʊkəz-
lookout, L- 'lʊk‚aʊt
loom lum |loomed lumd
loon lun |loonery 'lunərɪ
Loon, van væn'lon
loony, -ey 'lunɪ
loop lup |looped lupt |-hole -‚hol
loose lus |looses 'lusɪz |loosed lust
loosen 'lusņ |-ed -d |-ing 'lusņɪŋ, -snɪŋ
loosestrife 'lus‚straɪf
loot lut |looted 'lutɪd
lop lap |lopped lapt
lope lop |loped lopt
López 'lopez (*Am Sp* 'lopes)
lop-sided 'lap'saɪdɪd ('lop-‚sided 'mind)
loquacious lo'kweʃəs |-quacity -'kwæsətɪ
Lora 'lorə, 'lɔrə; S 'lorə
Lorain, -e lo'ren
lord, L- lɔrd; ES lɔəd; |-ed -ɪd |-ling -lɪŋ |-ship -ʃɪp
lord-and-lady 'lɔrdņ'ledɪ; ES 'lɔəd-
lore lor, lɔr; ES loə(r, E+lɔə(r
Lorelei 'lorə‚laɪ, 'lɒr- (*Ger* 'lo:rə‚laɪ)
Lorenzo lo'rɛnzo, lə-

|full fʊl |tooth tuθ |further 'fɝðɚ; ES 'fɝ̄ðə |custom 'kʌstəm |while hwaɪl |how haʊ |toy tɔɪ |using 'juzɪŋ |fuse fjuz, fɪuz |dish dɪʃ |vision 'vɪʒən |Eden 'idņ |cradle 'kredļ |keep 'em 'kipm̩

Those words below in which the ɑ sound is spelt o are often pronounced with ɒ in E and S

lorgnette lɔrn'jet; ES lɔən-; (*Fr* lɔ̃r'jɛt)

lorimer, L- 'lɔrəmɚ, 'lɑr-, 'lɒr-; ES -mə(r

lorn lɔrn; ES lɔən

Lorna 'lɔrnə; ES 'lɔənə

Lorrain lo'ren (*Fr* lɔ̃'ræ̃)

Lorraine lo'ren (*Fr* lɔ̃'rɛn)

Lorris, Guillaume de *Fr* gijomdəlɔ̃'ris

lorry 'lɔrɪ, 'lɑrɪ, 'lɒrɪ |-ied -d

lory 'lorɪ, 'lɔrɪ; S 'lorɪ

losable, loseable 'luzəbl̩

Los Angeles *Cal* lɔs'æŋgələs, lɒs-, -'ændʒələs, -lɪs, -ndʒə‚liz |-'s -ɪz—*Other pronunciations exist. A resident phonetician writes, "The only one I've never heard is* los'aŋheles."

Los Angeles *Chile, Am Sp* los'aŋheles

Los Angelean lɔs‚æŋgə'liən, lɒs-, -ndʒə'liən

lose luz |loses 'luzɪz |lost lɔst, lɒst

Los Gatos lɔs'gatos, *loc.* -'gætəs |-'s -ɪz

loss lɔs, lɒs |-es -ɪz

lost lɔst, lɒst

lot lɑt |lotted 'lɑtɪd

Lot *Eng name* lɑt; *Fr riv.* lo, *loc.* lɔ̃t

loth loθ |-ful 'loðfəl |-fully 'loðfəlɪ

Lothaire, -thair lo'θer, -'θær; E -'θɛə(r, ES -'θɛə(r; (*Fr* lɔ̃'tɛ:r)

Lothario lo'θerɪ‚o, -'θær-, -'θer-

Lothian 'loðɪən

lothly *adj* 'loðlɪ, *adv* 'loθ-, 'loð-

lothsome 'loðsəm

lotion 'loʃən

lotos 'lotəs |-es -ɪz

Lotos-Eaters 'lotəs‚itɚz; ES -‚itəz

Lotta 'lɑtə, 'lɑtɪ

lottery 'lɑtərɪ

Lottie 'lɑtɪ

lotto 'lɑto

lotus, L- 'lotəs |-es -ɪz |-eater -‚itɚ; ES -ə(r

Lou lu, lɪu

loud laud

louden 'laudn̩ |-ed -d |-ing 'laudnɪŋ, -dnɪŋ

loudmouthed 'laud'mauðd, -θt

Loudon 'laudn̩ |-ville -‚vɪl |-doun -dn̩

loud-speaker 'laud'spikɚ; ES -'spikə(r

lough lɑx, lɒx

Loughborough 'lʌf‚bɝo, -ə; ES -‚bɜr-, -‚bʌr-, -‚bɝ-

Loughrig 'lʌfrɪg

Louis *Fr name* 'luɪ (*Fr* lwi)

Louis *Eng name* 'luɪs, 'lɪuɪs, 'luɪ, 'lɪuɪ |-'s -ɪz, -z

Louisa lu'izə |-'s lu'izəz

Louisburg 'luɪs‚bɝg, 'lɪuɪs-; ES -‚bɜg, -‚bɝg

louis d'or ‚luɪ'dɔr, ‚lɪuɪ-; ES -'dɔə(r

Louise lu'iz, |Louise's lu'izɪz

Louisiana ‚luɪzɪ'ænə, lu‚izɪ'ænə |-nian -nɪən —*Competent observers also report* lu‚izɪ'ænə, ‚luizɪ'ænə, ‚luɪzɪ'ænə, lə‚wizɪ'ænə, *and the accentuations* 'Louisi‚ana, Lou'isi‚ana.

Louisville 'luɪs‚vɪl, 'lɪuɪs-; *Ky* 'luɪ‚vɪl, 'lɪuɪ-, *less freq.* -ɪs‚vɪl; S+'luɪvl̩, 'luəvl̩

lounge laundʒ |-s -ɪz |-d -d

Lounsbury 'launz‚berɪ, -bərɪ

loup-garou *Fr* luga'ru |*pl* loups- lu-

lour laur; ES lauə(r; |-ed -d |-y -ɪ |-ing 'laurɪŋ

Lourdes lurd; ES luəd; (*Fr* lurd)

louse *n* laus |-'s -ɪz |lice laɪs |lice's 'laɪsɪz

louse, *v* lauz |-s -ɪz |-d -d |lousy 'lauzɪ

lout laut |-ed -ɪd

Louth *Irel* lauð, *Lincs* lauθ

Louvain lu'ven (*Fr* lu'vɛ̃)

louver 'luvɚ; ES 'luvə(r; |-ed -d

L'Ouverture, Toussaint *Fr* tusælu'ver'ty:r

Louvre 'luvrə, 'luvɚ, luv; ES 'luvrə, 'luvə(r luv; (*Fr* lu:vr)

lovability, loveab- ‚lʌvə'bɪlətɪ

lovable, loveable 'lʌvəbl̩ |-bly -blɪ

lovat, L- 'lʌvət

love lʌv |loved lʌvd

love-in-idleness 'lʌvɪn'aɪdl̩nɪs |-es -ɪz

Lovel, -ll 'lʌvl̩

Lovelace 'lʌvles, 'lʌvlɪs |-'s -ɪz

lovelock 'lʌv‚lɑk

lovelorn 'lʌv‚lɔrn; ES -‚lɔən

lovesick 'lʌv‚sɪk

Lovett 'lʌvɪt

loving-kindness 'lʌvɪŋ'kaɪndnɪs, -'kaɪnnɪs

low lo |lowed lod

Low, -e lo

lowborn 'lo'bɔrn; ES -'bɔən; ('low‚born 'lass)

lowboy 'lo‚bɔɪ

lowbred 'lo'bred ('low‚bred 'horse)

low-brow 'lo‚brau

low-browed 'lo'braud ('low‚browed 'taste)

low-down *n* 'lo‚daun

low-down *adj* 'lo'daun ('low-‚down 'trick)

Lowell 'loəl, 'lo·ıl

lower *'frown'* 'lauɚ; ES 'lau·ə(r; |-ed -d |-ing 'laurıŋ, 'lauərıŋ

lower *adj 'less high'* 'loɚ; ES 'lo·ə(r

lower *'let down'* 'loɚ; ES 'lo·ə(r; |-ed -d |-ing 'loərıŋ, 'lorıŋ

lowermost 'loɚˌmost; ES 'lo·əˌmost

lowery 'laurı, 'lauərı

Lowes loz |Lowes's 'loziz

Lowestoft 'lostəft, -tɒft, *loc.* + 'lostəf

lowland 'loˌlænd, -lənd, *adj* -lənd

lowlander 'loləndɚ; ES 'loləndə(r

low-lifed 'lo'laivd ('low-'lifed ˌfellow)

lowlihead 'lolɪˌhɛd

low-lived 'lo'laivd ('low-ˌlived 'face)

lowly 'lolɪ

Lowman 'lomən

Lowndes laundz, launz |-'s -ız

low-pressure 'lo'prɛʃɚ; ES -'prɛʃə(r

lowrie, L- *'fox'* 'laurı

lowrie *'lory'* 'lorɪ, 'lɔrɪ; S 'lorɪ

low-test 'lo'tɛst ('low-ˌtest 'gas)

Lowth lauθ

Lowville 'lauvɪl

loyal 'lɔıəl, 'lɔjəl |-ly -ı |-ty -tı |-ism -ˌızəm |-ist -ıst

Loyd lɔıd

Loyola lɔı'olə, lə'jolə

Loyolite 'lɔıoˌlait, 'lɔjəˌlait |-lism -ˌlızəm

lozenge 'lazındʒ; ES+'lɒz-; |-s -ız |-d -d

lubber 'lʌbɚ; ES 'lʌbə(r; |-ed -d |-ly -lı

Lubbock 'lʌbək

Lubec 'lubɛk, 'lıubɛk

Lübeck 'lubɛk, 'lıu- (*Ger* 'ly:bɛk)

Lubeck 'lubɛk, 'lıu- |-bish -bıʃ |-bs -bz

lubric 'lubrık, 'lıu- |-al -ļ

lubricant 'lubrıkənt, 'lıu-

lubricate 'lubrıˌket, 'lıu- |-d -ıd |-tor -ɚ; ES -ə(r

lubrication ˌlubrı'keʃən, ˌlıu-

lubricious lu'brıʃəs, lıu- |-city -'brısətı

lubricous 'lubrıkəs, 'lıu-

Lucan 'lukən, 'lıu-

Lucas 'lukəs, 'lıu- |-'s -ız

Lucasta lu'kæstə, lıu-

luce, L- lus, lıus |-s -ız |-'s -ız

lucence 'lusņs, 'lıu- |-cy -ı |-cent -sņt

Lucentio lu'sɛnʃıˌo, lıu-, -ʃjo

lucerne, -rn lu'sɜn, lıu-; ES -'sɜn, -'sɜn

Lucerne lu'sɜn, lıu-; ES -'sɜn, -'sɜn; (*Ger* Luzern lu'tsɛrn)

Lucetta lu'sɛtə, lıu-

Lucia 'luʃə, 'lıu-, -ʃıə |-n -n

Lucia di Lammermoor lu'tʃiədı'læmɚˌmur; ES -'læməˌmuə(r; (*It* lu'tʃi:adiˌlammer-'mu:r)

Luciana ˌluʃı'ænə, ˌlıu-, -'anə |-nus -nəs

lucid 'lusıd, 'lıusıd |-ity lu'sıdətı, lıu-

Lucifer, l- 'lusəfɚ, 'lıu-; ES -fə(r

Lucile, -lle lu'sil, lıu-

Lucilius lu'sılıəs, lıu-, -ljəs |-'s -ız

Lucina lu'sainə, lıu-

Lucinda lu'sındə, lıu-

Lucio 'luʃıˌo, 'lıu-, -ʃjo

lucite 'lusait, 'lıu-

Lucius 'luʃəs, 'lıu-, -ʃıəs |-'s -ız

luck lʌk |-y -ı |-ily 'lʌkļı, 'lʌkılı

Lucknow 'lʌknau

lucrative 'lukrətıv, 'lıu-

lucre 'lukɚ, 'lıu-; ES -kə(r

Lucrece lu'kris, lıu- |-'s -ız

Lucretia lu'kriʃə, lıu-, -ʃıə

Lucretius lu'kriʃəs, lıu-, -ʃıəs |-'s -ız

lucubrate 'lukjuˌbret, 'lıu-, -ku- |-brated -ˌbretıd

lucubration ˌlukju'breʃən, ˌlıu-, -ku-

Lucullus lu'kʌləs, lıu- |-'s -ız |-lan -lən |-lian -lıən

Lucy 'lusı, 'lıusı

Lud lʌd |Luddite 'lʌdait

Ludendorf 'ludņˌdɔrf; ES -ˌdɔəf

Ludgate 'lʌdˌget, 'lʌdgıt

ludicrous 'ludıkrəs, 'lıu-

Ludington 'lʌdıŋtən

Ludlow 'lʌdlo |-lovian lʌd'lovıən

Ludovic 'ludəvık |-wick -wık

Ludwig 'lʌdwıg, -wık (*Ger* 'lu:tvıx, 'lu:d-)

Luella lu'ɛlə, lıu-

lues 'luiz, 'lıu-

luff lʌf |luffed lʌft

lug lʌg |lugged lʌgd |luggage 'lʌgıdʒ

lugger 'lʌgɚ; ES 'lʌgə(r

lugsail 'lʌgˌsel, 'lʌgsļ

lugubrious lu'gjubrıəs, lıu'gıu-, lu'gub-

Luke luk, lıuk |-kan, -can -kən

lukewarm 'luk'wɔrm, 'lıuk-; ES -'wɔəm ('lukeˌwarm 'zeal)

lull, L- lʌl |-ed -d |-aby -əˌbaı

lumbago lʌmˈbego
lumbar ˈlʌmbɚ; ES ˈlʌmbə(r
lumber ˈlʌmbɚ; ES -bə(r; |-ed -d |-ing
  ˈlʌmbrɪŋ, -bərɪŋ
lumberjack ˈlʌmbɚˌdʒæk; ES ˈlʌmbə-
lumber-room ˈlʌmbɚˌrum, -ˌrʊm; ES ˈlʌmbə-
lumen ˈlumɪn, ˈlɪu-, -mən |-s -z |-mina -mɪnə
luminary ˈlumənɛrɪ, ˈlɪu-
lumine ˈlumɪn, ˈlɪu- |-d -d
luminesce ˌlumeˈnɛs, ˌlɪu- |-s -ɪz |-d -t
luminescence ˌlumeˈnɛsn̩s, ˌlɪu- |-scent -sn̩t
luminosity ˌlumeˈnɑsətɪ, ˌlɪu-; ES+-ˈnɒs-
luminous ˈlumənəs, ˈlɪu-
Lumley, -ly ˈlʌmlɪ
Lummis ˈlʌmɪs |-'s -ɪz
lummox ˈlʌməks |-es -ɪz
lump lʌmp |lumped lʌmpt
Lumpkin ˈlʌmpkɪn
Luna, l- ˈlunə, ˈlɪunə
lunacy ˈlunəsɪ, ˈlɪu-
lunar ˈlunɚ, ˈlɪunɚ; ES -nə(r; |-y -ɪ
lunate ˈlunet, ˈlɪu-, -nɪt |-tion luˈneʃən, lɪu-
lunatic ˈlunəˌtɪk, ˈlɪu-
lunatical luˈnætɪk|, lɪu- |-ly -ɪ, -ɪklɪ
lunch lʌntʃ |lunches ˈlʌntʃɪz |lunched lʌntʃt
luncheon ˈlʌntʃən |-ed -d
lunchroom ˈlʌntʃˌrum, -ˌrʊm
lune lun, lɪun
Lunenburg ˈlunənˌbɝg; ES -ˌbɜg, -ˌbɝg
lunette luˈnɛt, lɪu-
lung lʌŋ |lunged lʌŋd
lunge lʌndʒ |lunges ˈlʌndʒɪz |lunged lʌndʒd
lunger *from* lung ˈlʌŋɚ; ES ˈlʌŋə(r
Lunger *surname* ˈlʌŋɚ; ES ˈlʌŋə(r
lunger *from* lunge ˈlʌndʒɚ; ES ˈlʌndʒə(r
lunkhead ˈlʌŋkˌhɛd
lunn, L- lʌn
luny ˈlunɪ, ˈlɪunɪ
Lupercal ˈlupɚˌk|, ˈlɪu-, -ˌkæl
Lupercalia ˌlupɚˈkelɪə, ˌlɪu-, -ˈkeljə
lupine *'wolfish'* ˈlupaɪn, ˈlɪu-
lupine, -in *plant* ˈlupɪn, ˈlɪu-
lupus, L- ˈlupəs, ˈlɪu- |-pi -paɪ
Luquiens luˈkæn, lɪu- (*Fr* lyˈkjæ̃)
Luray lʊˈre, lɪu- (ˈLuˌray ˈCaverns)
lurch lɝtʃ; ES lɜtʃ, lɝtʃ; |-es -ɪz |-ed -t
lurdan, -e ˈlɝdn̩; ES ˈlɜdn̩, ˈlɝdn̩
lure lʊr, lɪʊr |-d -d
lure *'trumpet'* ˈlʊrə |*pl* luren ˈlʊrən

lurid ˈlʊrɪd, ˈlɪʊ-
lurk lɝk; ES lɜk, lɝk; |-ed -t
Lurlei ˈlʊrlaɪ; ES ˈlʊə-; (*Ger* ˈlʊrlaɪ)
luscious ˈlʌʃəs
lush lʌʃ
Lusiad ˈlusɪˌæd, ˈlɪu- |-s -z
Lusitania ˌlusəˈtenɪə, ˌlɪu-
lust lʌst |lusted ˈlʌstɪd |-ful -fəl |-fully -fəlɪ
luster, -tre ˈlʌstɚ; ES -tə(r; |-(e)d -d |lust(e)-
  ring ˈlʌstərɪŋ, ˈlʌstrɪŋ
lusterer ˈlʌstərɚ; ES ˈlʌstərə(r
lusterware, lustre- ˈlʌstɚˌwɛr, -ˌwær; E
  ˈlʌstəˌwɛə(r, ES -ˌwææ(r
lustihead ˈlʌstɪˌhɛd |lustihood ˈlʌstɪˌhʊd
lustral ˈlʌstrəl
lustrate ˈlʌstret |-d -ɪd |-tion lʌsˈtreʃən
lustrous ˈlʌstrəs
lustrum ˈlʌstrəm |-s -z |-tra -trə
lutanist ˈlutn̩ɪst, ˈlɪut-
lute lut, lɪut |-d -ɪd
lutecium luˈtiʃɪəm, lɪu-
Luther ˈluθɚ, ˈlɪu-; ES -θə(r; |-an -ən, -θrən
Lutterworth ˈlʌtɚˌwɝθ; ES ˈlʌtəwəθ
Luttrell ˈlʌtrəl
Lutz luts, lʌts |-'s -ɪz
lux lʌks |-es -ɪz |*L pl* luces ˈlusiz, ˈlɪu-
luxe lʊks, lʌks (*Fr* lyks)
Luxembourg ˈlʌksəmˌbɝg; ES -ˌbɜg, -ˌbɝg;
  (*Fr* lyksɑ̃ˈbuːr)
Luxemburg ˈlʌksəmˌbɝg; ES -ˌbɜg, -ˌbɝg;
  (*Ger* ˈlʊksəmˌbʊrk)
Luxor ˈlʌksɔr; ES ˈlʌksɔə(r
luxuriance lʌgˈʒʊrɪəns, lʌkˈʃʊr- |-cy -ɪ |-ant
  -ənt—*see* luxurious
luxuriate lʌgˈʒʊrɪˌet, lʌkˈʃʊr- |-d -ɪd—*see*
  luxurious
luxurious lʌgˈʒʊrɪəs, lʌkˈʃʊr-—*The pron.
  with* -gʒ- *is phonetically normal; that with*
  -kʃ- *is due to the analogy of* ˈlʌkʃərɪ, *q.v.*
luxury ˈlʌkʃərɪ, *much less freq.* ˈlʌgʒ-—*The
  pron. with* -kʃ- *is phonetically normal (owing
  to accent); that with* -gʒ- *is due to analogy of*
  lʌgˈʒʊrɪəs.
Luzerne *Pa* luˈzɝn, lɪu-; ES -ˈzɜn, -ˈzɝn
Luzon luˈzɑn, -ˈzɒn
-ly *ending of adjs* (timely) *& advs* (boldly) -lɪ,
  -lɪ—*Very many words in* -ly (*esp. advs*) *are
  omitted from the vocab. when the pron. can
  be found by adding the sounds* -lɪ *directly to*

the corresponding head pron., *as* slow **slo**, slowly **ˈslo-lɪ**. *But if some question of pronunciation is involved, the -ly form is entered, as in* real **ˈrɪəl** |-ly **-ɪ** *or* full **fʊl** |-ly **-ɪ**, *where only a single l is sounded, or in* sole **sol** |-ly **ˈsollɪ**, *where both are sounded, or in* wholly **ˈholɪ**, **ˈhollɪ**, *which varies. For variation between ɪ & i see -y in the vocab.*

Lyall **ˈlaɪəl**
lycanthropy **laɪˈkænθrəpɪ**
lyceum **laɪˈsiəm**, **ˈlaɪsɪəm** |L- **laɪˈsiəm**
Lychorida **laɪˈkɔrɪdə**, -ˈkɑr-, -ˈkɒr-
Lycia **ˈlɪʃɪə** |Lycian **ˈlɪʃɪən**
Lycidas **ˈlɪsədəs** |-'s **-ɪz**
Lycoming **laɪˈkʌmɪŋ**; ES+-ˈkɒm-
Lycurgus **laɪˈkɝgəs**; ES -ˈkɝg-, -ˈkɜ́g-; |-'s **-ɪz**
lyddite **ˈlɪdaɪt**
Lydekker **laɪˈdɛkɚ**, **lɪ-**; ES **-dɛkə(r**
Lydenberg **ˈlaɪdn̩ˌbɝg**; ES -ˌbɝg, -ˌbɜ́g
Lydgate **ˈlɪdget**, **-gɪt**
Lydia **ˈlɪdɪə** |-n **-n**
lye *'alkali'* **laɪ** |lyed **laɪd** |lying **ˈlaɪɪŋ**
Lyell **ˈlaɪəl**
lying *'deceiving,' 'reclining,' 'treating with lye'* **ˈlaɪɪŋ**
Lykens **ˈlaɪkɪnz**, **-kənz** |-'s **-ɪz**
Lyly **ˈlɪlɪ**
Lyme Regis **ˌlaɪmˈridʒɪs** |-'s **-ɪz**
lymph **lɪmf**, **lɪmpf** |-atic **lɪmˈfætɪk**
lymphocyte **ˈlɪmfəˌsaɪt** |-tic **ˌlɪmfəˈsɪtɪk**
lymphoid **ˈlɪmfɔɪd**
Lympne **lɪm**
lyncean **lɪnˈsiən**
lynch, L- **lɪntʃ** |lynches **ˈlɪntʃɪz** |-ed **-t**

Lynchburg **ˈlɪntʃbɝg**; ES **-bɝg**, **-bɜ́g**
Lyndhurst **ˈlɪndhɝst**; ES **-hɝst**, **-hɜ́st**
Lyndsay **ˈlɪnzɪ**, **ˈlɪndzɪ**
Lynmouth **ˈlɪnməθ**
Lynn **lɪn**
lynx **lɪŋks** |lynxes **ˈlɪŋksɪz**
lynx-eyed **ˈlɪŋksˈaɪd** ('lynx-ˌeyed 'scout)
Lyon *Eng name* **ˈlaɪən**; *Fr city see* Lyons
lyonnaise **ˌlaɪəˈnez** (*Fr* ljɔ̃ˈnɛːz)
Lyonness, -sse **ˌlaɪəˈnɛs** |-'s **-ɪz**
Lyons *Eng name* **ˈlaɪənz**, *Fr city* **ˈlaɪənz** |-'s **-ɪz** (*Fr* Lyon ljɔ̃)
Lyra, l- **ˈlaɪrə** |*gen* Lyrae **ˈlaɪri**
lyrate **ˈlaɪret**, **-rɪt**
lyre **laɪr**; ES **laɪə(r**; |-d **-d**
lyrebird **ˈlaɪrˌbɝd**; ES **ˈlaɪəˌbɝd**, **ˈlaɪəˌbɜ́d**
lyric **ˈlɪrɪk** |-al **-l̩** |-ally **-lɪ**, **-ɪklɪ**
lyricism **ˈlɪrəˌsɪzəm** |-cist **-sɪst**
lyricize **ˈlɪrəˌsaɪz** |-s **-ɪz** |-d **-d**
lyrist *lyre-player* **ˈlaɪrɪst**, **ˈlɪr-**
lyrist *lyric poet* **ˈlɪrɪst**
Lysander **laɪˈsændɚ**; ES **-ˈsændə(r**
lyse **laɪs** |lyses **ˈlaɪsɪz** |lysed **laɪst**
Lysias **ˈlɪsɪəs** |-'s **-ɪz**
Lysimachus **laɪˈsɪməkəs** |-'s **-ɪz**
lysimeter **laɪˈsɪmətɚ**; ES **-tə(r**
lysin **ˈlaɪsɪn** |-sine **ˈlaɪsin**, **-sɪn**
Lysippus **laɪˈsɪpəs** |-'s **-ɪz**
lysis **ˈlaɪsɪs**
lysol **ˈlaɪsɑl**, **-sɒl**, **-sɔl**
Lyte **laɪt**
Lytell **ˈlaɪtl̩**, **ˈlɪtl̩**, **lɪˈtɛl**
Lytle **ˈlaɪtl̩**, **ˈlɪtl̩**
Lyttleton **ˈlɪtl̩tən**
Lytton **ˈlɪtn̩**

M

M, m *letter* **ɛm** |*pl* M's, Ms, *poss* M's **ɛmz**
'm *unstressed form of* am *after* I, m
ma'am **mæm**, **mɑm**, **-m̩**, **-m**
Mab **mæb**
Mabel **ˈmebl̩**
Mabinogion **ˌmæbəˈnogɪən**
Mac-, Mc-, M'- *pron.* **mə-**, **mɪ-**, **mək-**, **mɪk-**
—*alphabetically* M' & Mc *are placed with* Mac

macabre **məˈkɑbrə**, **məˈkɑbɚ**; ES **-ˈkɑbrə**, **-ˈkɑbə(r**
macadam, **məˈkædəm** |-ize **-ˌaɪz** |-izes **-ˌaɪzɪz** |-ized **-ˌaɪzd**
MacAdam **məkˈædəm**, **mækˈædəm** |-s **-z** |-s's **-zɪz**
macadamization **məˌkædəməˈzeʃən**, **-maɪˈzeʃən**
McAdoo **ˈmækəˌdu**

|full **fʊl** |tooth **tuθ** |further **ˈfɝðɚ**; ES **ˈfɜ́ðə** |custom **ˈkʌstəm** |while **hwaɪl** |how **haʊ** |toy **tɔɪ** |using **ˈjuzɪŋ** |fuse **fjuz**, **frʊz** |dish **dɪʃ** |vision **ˈvɪʒən** |Eden **ˈidn̩** |cradle **ˈkredl̩** |keep 'em **ˈkipm̩**

McAllister, Macalister məˈkæləstə; ES -tə(r
macaroni ˌmækəˈronɪ
macaronic ˌmækəˈrɑnɪk; ES+-ˈrɒnɪk
macaroon ˌmækəˈrun (ˈmacaˌroon ˈtart)
MacArthur məkˈɑrθə; ES məkˈɑːθə(r, E+
 -ˈɑːθ-
Macassar məˈkæsə; ES məˈkæsə(r
Macaulay məˈkɔlɪ
Macbeth mækˈbɛθ, məkˈbɛθ
Maccabees ˈmækəˌbiz |-bean ˌmækəˈbiən
Maccabeus ˌmækəˈbiəs |Maccabeus's -ˈbiəsɪz
M'Carthy məˈkɑrθɪ; ES məˈkɑːθɪ, E+-ˈkɑːθɪ
McClellan məˈklɛlən
Macclesfield ˈmæk|zˌfild
McColl məˈkɔl
McCormack məˈkɔrmək; ES məˈkɔəmək
McCormick məˈkɔrmɪk; ES məˈkɔəmɪk
MacCracken məˈkrækən
McCrae məˈkre
McCrea məˈkre
McCulloch, -ough məˈkʌləx, -ˈkʌlək, -lə, -lɪ
McDougal, -ll məkˈdugl, mæk-
MacDowell *composer* məkˈdauəl
McDowell *Am general* məkˈdauəl
Macduff mækˈdʌf, məkˈdʌf
mace mes |maces ˈmesɪz |maced mest
Macedon ˈmæsəˌdɑn; ES+ˈmæsəˌdɒn
Macedonia ˌmæsəˈdonɪə, -ˈdonjə |-n -n
macerate ˈmæsəˌret |macerated ˈmæsəˌretɪd
McFarland məkˈfɑrlənd, -lən; ES -ˈfɑːl-,
 E+-ˈfɑːl-
MacFarlane məkˈfɑrlɪn, -lən; ES -ˈfɑːl-,
 E+-ˈfɑːl-
MacFlecknoe məkˈflɛkno, mæk-
McGehee məˈgihi
McGill *university* məˈgɪl, mɪˈgɪl
Macgillicuddy məˈgɪləˌkʌdɪ, ˈmægˌk-, ˈmæ-
 gˌˌk-
MacGillivray məˈgɪləvrɪ, məˈgɪləvərɪ
Machen *Arthur* ˈmækən
McHenry məkˈhɛnrɪ, məˈkɛnrɪ
machete mɑˈtʃete, məˈʃɛt, məˈʃɛtɪ (*Sp* ma-
 ˈtʃete)
Machias məˈtʃaɪəs |-'s -ɪz
Machiavelli ˌmækɪəˈvɛlɪ, -kjə- (*It* ˌmakja-
 ˈvɛlli)
Machiavellian ˌmækɪəˈvɛlɪən, -kjə-, -ljən
machinate ˈmækəˌnet |-d -ɪd |-tion ˌmækə-
 ˈneʃən

machine məˈʃin |-d -d |-ry -ərɪ, -rɪ |-ist -ɪst
McIlrath ˈmækǀˌræθ, ˈmækǀˌrɑθ
McIntosh ˈmækɪnˌtɑʃ; ES+-ˌtɒʃ; |-'s -ɪz
MacIvor, *Flora* məkˈaɪvə, -ˈivə; ES -və(r
mackerel ˈmækərəl, ˈmækrəl
Mackinac *co., isl., and strait* ˈmækəˌnɔ
Mackinaw ˈmækəˌnɔ
McKinley məˈkɪnlɪ
mackintosh ˈmækɪnˌtɑʃ; ES+-ˌtɒʃ; |-es -ɪz
McLaughlin məˈklɑklɪn, -ˈgl-, -ɑx-, -ɑf-;
 ES+-ɒ-
McLean məˈklen, məkˈlen
MacLeish məkˈliʃ |MacLeish's məkˈliʃɪz
McLeod məˈklaud
McLoughlin məˈklɑklɪn; ES+-ɒk-
MacManus məkˈmænəs, -ˈmanəs, -ˈmenəs
 |-'s -ɪz
McMechan, -en məkˈmɛkən
MacMillan mækˈmɪlən, məkˈmɪlən
MacMonnies məkˈmʌnɪz |-Monnies' -ˈmʌnɪz
Macomb məˈkom, *Mich* məˈkum, -ˈkom
Macon ˈmekən, ˈmekan, ˈmekɒn
MacReady məˈkrɛdɪ, məˈkrɪdɪ
Macrobius məˈkrobɪəs |-crobius's -ˈkrobɪəsɪz
macrocosm ˈmækrəˌkazəm; ES+-ˌkɒzəm
macron ˈmekrən, ˈmekran, ˈmekrɒn, ˈmæk-
McShea məkˈʃe
MacTavish məkˈtævɪʃ, mækˈtævɪʃ
maculate *adj* ˈmækjəlɪt, ˈmækjulɪt
maculate *v* ˈmækjəˌlet, ˈmækjuˌlet |-d -ɪd
maculation ˌmækjəˈleʃən, ˌmækjuˈleʃən
MacVeagh məkˈve
mad mæd |madded ˈmædɪd
Madagascar ˌmædəˈgæskə; ES -kə(r; |-can
 -kən
madam ˈmædəm
madame ˈmædəm (*Fr* maˈdam, *pl* mesdames
 meˈdam)
madcap ˈmædˌkæp
madden, M- ˈmædn̩ |-ed -d |-ing ˈmædnɪŋ,
 ˈmædn̩ɪŋ
madder ˈmædə; ES ˈmædə(r
made med
Madeira məˈdɪrə
Madeleine ˈmædǀˌen
Madeline ˈmædǀˌaɪn, ˈmædǀɪn
mademoiselle ˌmædəməˈzɛl (*Fr* madmwaˈzɛl,
 mamˈzɛl)
made-up ˈmedˈʌp (ˈmade-ˌup ˈstory)

Madge **mædʒ** |Madge's **'mædʒɪz**—*cf* Margery *and see §121*

madhouse **'mæd͵haʊs** |-houses -͵haʊzɪz

Madison **'mædəsṇ**

madman **'mæd͵mæn, 'mædmən** |-men -mən

Madonna **mə'dɑnə; ES+mə'dɒnə**

madras **mə'dræs, 'mædrəs, mə'drɑs**

Madras **mə'dræs, mə'drɑs** |-'s -ɪz

Madrid *US* **'mædrɪd,** *Spain* **mə'drɪd** (*Sp* **ma'ðrɪð, ma'ðri**)

madrigal **'mædrɪgḷ**

Madura *Brit India* **'mædʒʊrə, -djʊ-;** *Du E. Indies* **ma'dura**

maduro **mə'dʊro** (*Sp* **ma'ðuro**)

Mae **me**

Maeander **mɪ'ændɚ; ES mɪ'ændə(r**

Maecenas **mɪ'sinəs, mi-** |Maecenases -'sinəsɪz

maelstrom, M- **'melstrəm**

maenad **'minæd** |-s -z |maenades **'mɛnə͵diz**

maestro **'maɪstro** (*It* ma'ɛstro)

Maeterlinck **'metɚ͵lɪŋk, 'mɛtɚ-; ES 'metə-, 'mɛtə-;** (*Du* **'matər͵lɪŋk,** *Fr* matɛr'lɛ̃)

magazine *'storehouse'* **͵mægə'zin,** *'periodical'* **͵mægə'zin, 'mægə͵zin**

Magdalen *Bible* **'mægdəlɪn, -lən,** *Oxf college* **'mɔdlɪn**

Magdalene *Bible* **'mægdə͵lin, ͵mægdə'lini,** *Camb college* **'mɔdlɪn**

Magdeburg **'mægdə͵bɝg; ES 'mægdə͵bɜg, -͵bɜg;** (*Ger* **'makdə͵bʊrk**)

Magellan **mə'dʒɛlən** |Magellanic ͵mædʒə-'lænɪk

magenta, M- **mə'dʒɛntə**

Maggiore **mə'dʒorɪ, mə'dʒɔrɪ; S mə'dʒɔrɪ;** (*It* mad'dʒoːre)

maggot **'mægət** |maggoty **'mægətɪ**

Maggy **'mægɪ**—*cf* Margaret *and see §121*

Magi **'medʒaɪ**

magic **'mædʒɪk** |-al -ḷ |-ally -ḷɪ, -ɪklɪ

magician **mə'dʒɪʃən**

Maginot **'mæʒə͵no, 'mɑʒ-** (*Fr* maʒi'no)

magisterial **͵mædʒɪs'tɪrɪəl** |-ly -ɪ

magistery **'mædʒɪs͵tɛrɪ**

magistral **'mædʒɪstrəl** |-ly -ɪ |-stracy -strəsɪ

magistrate **'mædʒɪs͵tret, 'mædʒɪstrɪt**

magma **'mægmə** |magmas **'mægməz** |magmata **'mægmətə**

Magna Charta, Carta **'mægnə'kɑrtə; ES -'kɑːtə, E+-'kɑːtə**

magnanimous **mæg'nænəməs** |-mity ͵mægnə-'nɪmətɪ

magnate **'mægnet**

magnesia **mæg'niʃə, -ʒə** |-sium -ʃɪəm, -ʒɪəm

magnesite **'mægnɪ͵saɪt**

magnet **'mægnɪt**

magnetic **mæg'nɛtɪk** |-al -ḷ |-ally -ḷɪ, -ɪklɪ

magnetism **'mægnə͵tɪzəm**

magnetite **'mægnə͵taɪt**

magnetize **'mægnə͵taɪz** |-tizes -͵taɪzɪz |-d -d

magneto **mæg'nito**

magnetogenerator **mæg͵nito'dʒɛnə͵retɚ; ES -tə(r**

magnetometer **͵mægnə'tɑmətɚ; ES -tə(r, -'tɒm-**

magnetoscope **mæg'nitə͵skop, mæg'nɛtə-**

magnific **mæg'nɪfɪk** |-al -ḷ |-ally -ḷɪ, -ɪklɪ

Magnificat **mæg'nɪfɪ͵kæt**

magnification **͵mægnəfə'keʃən**

magnificence **mæg'nɪfəsṇs** |-cent -sṇt

magnifico **mæg'nɪfə͵ko**

magnify **'mægnə͵faɪ** |-fied -͵faɪd

magniloquence **mæg'nɪləkwəns** |-quent -kwənt

magnitude **'mægnə͵tjud, -͵tɪud, -͵tud**

magnolia **mæg'nolɪə, -'noljə**

magnum **'mægnəm**

Magog **'megɑg, 'megɒg**

Magoun **mə'gun**

magpie **'mæg͵paɪ**

maguey **'mægwe** (*Sp* ma'ge·i)

Magus **'megəs** |Magi **'medʒaɪ**

Magyar **'mægjɑr; ES 'mægjɑː(r, E+-gjɑː(r;** (*Hung* **'mɒdjɒr**)

Mahan **mə'hæn, 'me·ən**

Mahanoy **͵mahə'nɔɪ**

maharaja, -h **͵mahə'radʒə** (*Hind* mə'ha-'radʒə)

maharani, -nee **͵mahə'rani** (*Hind* mə'ha'rani)

mahatma **mə'hætmə, mə'hɑtmə**

Mahdi **'madi**

mah-jongg, -ng **ma'dʒɔŋ, -'dʒɒŋ, -'dʒɑŋ**

mahogany **mə'hagənɪ, mə'hɒgənɪ**

Mahometan **mə'hamətən, -'hɒm-**

Mahommed **mə'hamɪd, mə'hɒmɪd** |-an -ən

Mahon *Am name* **'mean, mə'hun, -'hɒn**

Mahoning **mə'honɪŋ**

Mahound **mə'haʊnd, mə'hund**

mahout **mə'haʊt**

---

maid **med** |maiden **'medn̩**

maidenhair **'medn̩ˌhɛr, -ˌhær; E -ˌhɛə(r, ES -ˌhæə(r**

maidenhead **'medn̩ˌhɛd** |maidenhood **'medn̩ˌhʊd**

maidservant **'medˌsɝvənt; -ˌsɝvənt, -ˌsɝvənt**

Maidstone *Engd* **'medstən, 'medˌston**

mail **mel** |mailed **meld** |mailable **'meləbl̩**

mailbag **'melˌbæg**

mailbox **'melˌbɑks; ES+'melˌbɒks; |-es -ɪz**

mailman **'melˌmæn** |mailmen **'melˌmɛn, 'melmən**

maim **mem** |maimed **memd** |-edly **-ɪdlɪ**

main **men**

Maine **men**

mainland **'menˌlænd, 'menlənd**

mainmast **'menˌmæst, -məst; E+-ˌmast, -ˌmɑst**

mainsail **'menˌsel,** *naut.* **'mensl̩**

mainsheet **'menˌʃit**

mainspring **'menˌsprɪŋ**

mainstay **'menˌste** |mainstayed **'menˌsted**

maintain **menˈten, mənˈten** |-tained **-ˈtend**

maintenance **'mentənəns, -tɪn- |-s -ɪz**

Mainwaring **'mænərɪŋ, 'menwɔrɪŋ, -wɑr-, -wɒr-**

maître d'hôtel *Fr* **mɛtrədöˈtɛl, mɛtdöˈtɛl**

maize **mez** |maizes **'mezɪz**

majestic **məˈdʒɛstɪk |-al -l̩ |-ally -lɪ, -ɪklɪ**

majesty **'mædʒɪstɪ, 'mædʒəstɪ**

majolica **məˈdʒɑlɪkə, məˈjɑl-; ES+-ɒl-**

major **'medʒɚ; ES 'medʒə(r; |-ed -d**

Majorca **məˈdʒɔrkə; ES məˈdʒɔəkə**

major-domo **'medʒɚˈdomo; ES 'medʒəˈdomo**

majority **məˈdʒɔrətɪ, -ˈdʒɑr-, -ˈdʒɒr-**

majuscule **məˈdʒʌskjul, -kɪul**

make **mek** |made **med**

makebate **'mekˌbet**

make-believe **'mekbəˌliv**

makeshift **'mekˌʃɪft**

make-up **'mekˌʌp**

makeweight **'mekˌwet**

Malabar **'mæləˌbɑr, ˌmæləˈbɑr; ES -ɑː(r, E+-ɑː(r; ('Malaˌbar 'Coast)**

Malacca **məˈlækə**

Malachi **'mæləˌkaɪ**

malachite **'mæləˌkaɪt**

maladaptation **ˌmælədæpˈteʃən, ˌmælædəpˈteʃən**

maladjusted **ˌmæləˈdʒʌstɪd |-justment -ˈdʒʌstmənt**

maladminister **ˌmælədˈmɪnəstɚ; ES -ˈmɪnəstə(r**

maladministration **ˌmælədˌmɪnəˈstreʃən**

maladroit **ˌmæləˈdrɔɪt ('malaˌdroit 'move)**

malady **'mælədɪ**

Malaga **'mæləgə**

malaise **mæˈlez (*Fr* maˈlɛːz)**

malapert **'mæləˌpɝt; ES -ˌpɝt, -ˌpɝt**

Malaprop **'mæləˌprɑp; ES+-ˌprɒp**

malapropism **'mæləprɑpˌɪzəm; ES+-prɒp-**

malapropos **ˌmælæprəˈpo**

malaria **məˈlɛrɪə, məˈlerɪə, məˈlærɪə |-l -l**

malassimilation **'mæləˌsɪməˈleʃən**

Malay **məˈle, 'mele |-an məˈleən**

Malaysian **məˈleʃən, məˈleʒən**

Malchus **'mælkəs** |Malchus's **'mælkəsɪz**

Malcolm **'mælkəm,** *formerly* **'mɔkəm**

malcontent **'mælkənˌtɛnt |-ed ˌmælkənˈtɛntɪd**

mal de mer *Fr* **maldəˈmɛːr**

Malden **'mɔldən, 'mɔldɪn** |Maldon **'mɔldən**

male **mel**

maledict **'mæləˌdɪkt |-ed -ɪd |-ion ˌmæləˈdɪkʃən**

maledictory **ˌmæləˈdɪktərɪ, -trɪ**

malefaction **ˌmæləˈfækʃən |-tor -tɚ; ES -tə(r**

malefic **məˈlɛfɪk |-al -l̩ |-ally -lɪ, -ɪklɪ**

maleficence **məˈlɛfəsn̩s |-cent -sn̩t**

malevolence **məˈlɛvələns |-lent -lənt**

malfeasance **ˌmælˈfizn̩s |-feasances -ˈfizn̩sɪz**

malformation **ˌmælfɔrˈmeʃən; ES -fɔəˈmeʃən**

malformed **mælˈfɔrmd; ES -ˈfɔəmd**

malic **'mælɪk, 'melɪk**

malice **'mælɪs |-licious məˈlɪʃəs**

malign **məˈlaɪn**

malignance **məˈlɪgnəns |-cy -ɪ |-nant -nənt**

malignity **məˈlɪgnətɪ**

malines, -line **məˈlin (*Fr* maˈlin)**

malinger **məˈlɪŋgɚ; ES -gə(r; |-ed -d |-ing -gərɪŋ, -grɪŋ**

malingerer **məˈlɪŋgərɚ; ES -ˈlɪŋgərə(r**

malison **'mæləzn̩, -sn̩**

malkin **'mɔkɪn** |Malkin **'mælkɪn, 'mɔkɪn**

mall *'maul'* **mɔl |-ed -d**

Mall **mæl, mɔl**—see Pall Mall

mallard **'mælɚd; ES 'mæləd**

malleable **'mælɪəbl̩ |-bility ˌmælɪəˈbɪlətɪ**

mallet, M- **'mælɪt**

---

mallow 'mælo, -ə
Malmesbury 'mɑmz₁bɛrɪ, 'mɑmzbərɪ
malmsey, M- 'mɑmzɪ
malnutrition ₁mælnju'trɪʃən, -nɪu-, -nu-
malodor mæl'odɚ; ES mæl'odə(r; |-ous
 -'odərəs
Malone mə'lon
malonic mə'lɑnɪk, mə'lonɪk; ES+-'lɒnɪk
Malory 'mælərɪ
malpractice mæl'præktɪs |-tices -tɪsɪz
malt mɔlt |malted 'mɔltɪd
Malta 'mɔltə
Maltese mɔl'tiz |-s -ɪz ('Mal₁tese 'cat)
Malthus 'mælθəs |Malthus's 'mælθəsɪz
Malthusian mæl'θjuzɪən, -'θɪuz-, -'θuz-, -jən
maltose 'mɔltos
maltreat mæl'trit |-ed -ɪd |-ment -mənt
Malvern US 'mælvɚn, mæl'vɝn, Engd, Aus-
 tralia 'mɔlvɝn, 'mɔlvɚn; ES -ən, -ɜn, -ɜ·n
malversation ₁mælvɚ'seʃən; ES ₁mælvə-
 'seʃən
Malvolio mæl'volɪ₁o, mæl'voljo
mama 'mɑmə, now rare mə'mɑ
Mamaroneck mə'mærə₁nɛk
mamba 'mɑmbə
Mameluke, m- 'mæmə₁luk, 'mæmə₁lɪuk
Mamilius mə'mɪlɪəs, -'mɪljəs |-'s -ɪz
mamma 'mother' 'mɑmə, now rare mə'mɑ
mamma 'milk gland' 'mæmə |mammae
 'mæmi
mammal 'mæml̩ |mammalia mæ'melɪə, -ljə
mammalogy mæ'mælədʒɪ |-gist -dʒɪst
mammary 'mæmərɪ |mammilary 'mæmə₁lɛrɪ
mammon, M- 'mæmən
mammoth 'mæməθ |-ths -θs
mammy 'mæmɪ
man, M- mæn |men mɛn |manned mænd
-man, -men second element of compound nouns
 (policeman). In most popular words pronounced in sg & pl -mən. In deliberate
 speech or sometimes with special meaning,
 the sg & pl -mən often becomes sg -₁mæn,
 pl -₁mɛn (horsemen 'cavalry' 'hɔrsmən;
 'racing sports' 'hɔrs₁mɛn). In the vocab.
 usually only the popular and colloquial forms
 are given.
manacle 'mænəkl̩, -ɪkl̩ |-d -d |-ling -kl̩ɪŋ,
 -klɪŋ
manage 'mænɪdʒ |-s -ɪz |-d -d |-ment -mənt

manageability ₁mænɪdʒə'bɪlətɪ
manageable 'mænɪdʒəbl̩ |-bly -blɪ
manageress 'mænɪdʒɚɪs, -dʒɝɪs |-esses -ɪsɪz
managerial ₁mænə'dʒɪrɪəl |-ly -ɪ
mañana mɑ'njɑnɑ (Sp mɑ'ɲɑnɑ)
Manasquan 'mænə₁skwɑn, -₁skwɒn
Manassas mə'næsəs |-nassas' -'næsəs
Manasseh mə'næsə, -sɪ
man-at-arms 'mænət'ɑrmz; ES -'ɑ:mz, E+
 -'ɑ:mz
manatee, M- ₁mænə'ti
Manchester 'mæn₁tʃɛstɚ, 'mæntʃɪstɚ; ES
 -tə(r
Manchu mæn'tʃu ('Man₁chu 'language)
Manchukuo ₁mæntʃu'kwo, ₁mæntʃuku'o,
 mæn'tʃuko
Manchukuoan ₁mæntʃu'kwoən, -ku'oən,
 mæn'tʃukəwən
Manchuria mæn'tʃʊrɪə
manciple 'mænsəpl̩
Mandalay 'mændə₁le, ₁mændə'le
mandamus mæn'deməs |-damuses -'deməsɪz
 |-ed -t
mandarin n 'mændərɪn, v ₁mændə'rin |-d -d
mandatary 'mændə₁tɛrɪ
mandate n 'mændet, -dɪt, v -det |-d -ɪd
mandator mæn'detɚ; ES mæn'detə(r
mandatory 'mændə₁torɪ, -₁tɔrɪ; S -₁torɪ
Mandeville 'mændə₁vɪl
mandible 'mændəbl̩
mandolin 'mændl̩₁ɪn, ₁mændl̩'ɪn
mandragora mæn'drægərə
mandrake 'mændrɪk, 'mændrek
mandrel, -il 'mændrəl, 'mændrɪl
mandrill 'mændrɪl
mane men |maned mend
man-eater 'mæn₁itɚ; ES 'mæn₁itə(r
manege mæ'neʒ, mæ'neʒ |-s -ɪz (Fr ma'nɛ:ʒ)
manes 'meniz
Manet mə'ne (Fr ma'nɛ)
maneuver mə'nuvɚ; ES -'nuvə(r; |-ed -d |-ing
 -'nuvərɪŋ, -'nuvrɪŋ
maneuverability mə₁nuvərə'bɪlətɪ
Manfred 'mænfrɪd, 'mænfrɛd
manful 'mænfəl |-ly -ɪ
manganese 'mæŋɡə₁nis, 'mæn-, ₁mæŋɡə'nis,
 ₁mæn-, -₁niz, -'niz
manganic mæn'ɡænɪk, mæŋ'ɡænɪk
manganite 'mæŋɡə₁naɪt, 'mæŋɡə₁naɪt

mange **mendʒ** |manged **mendʒd** |mangy
  'mendʒɪ
mangel-wurzel **'mæŋg|'wɜ·z|**, -**'wɜ·ts|**; ES
  -**'wɜ-**, -**'wɜ·-**; *acct*+-ˌwurzel
manger **'mendʒɚ**; ES **'mendʒə(r**
mangle **'mæŋg|** |-d -d |-ling **'mæŋglɪŋ, -g|ɪŋ**
mango **'mæŋgo**
mangonel **'mæŋgəˌnɛl**
mangosteen **'mæŋgəˌstin**
mangrove **'mæŋgrov, 'mæn-**
manhandle **'mænˌhænd|, ˌmæn'hænd|** |-d -d
  |-ling -dlɪŋ, -d|ɪŋ
Manhattan **mæn'hætn̩** (**'Manˌhattan 'Bor-**
  ough)
Manheim *US* **'mænhaɪm**
manhole **'mænˌhol**
manhood **'mænhʊd**
man-hour **'mæn'aʊr**; ES **'mæn'aʊə(r**
mania **'menɪə** |-niac **'menɪˌæk**
maniacal **mə'naɪək|** |-ly -ɪ
manic **'menɪk, 'mænɪk**
Manichean ˌmænə'kiən
manicure **'mænɪˌkjʊr, -ˌkɪʊr**; ES -ˌkjʊə(r,
  -ˌkɪʊ-
manifest **'mænəˌfɛst** |-fested -ˌfɛstɪd
manifestation ˌmænəfɛs'teʃən, -fəs'teʃən
manifesto ˌmænə'fɛsto
manifold **'mænəˌfold** |-folded -ˌfoldɪd
manikin **'mænəkɪn**
Manila, -lla, m- mə'nɪlə
manioc **'mænɪˌak, 'menɪˌak**; ES+-ˌɒk
maniple **'mænəp|** |manipled **'mænəp|d**
manipulate mə'nɪpjəˌlet |-lated -ˌletɪd |-lator
  -ˌletɚ; ES -ˌletə(r
manipulation məˌnɪpjə'leʃən
Manistee ˌmænə'sti
Manistique ˌmænə'stik
manito **'mænəˌto** |manitou, -tu **'mænəˌtu**
Manitoba ˌmænə'tobə, ˌmænəto'ba |-ban
  -'tobən
Manitou **'mænəˌtu**
Manitoulin ˌmænə'tulɪn
Manitowoc ˌmænətə'wak, -'wɒk
Mankato mæn'keto
mankind mæn'kaɪnd (**'manˌkind & 'woman-**
  ˌkind)
Manley **'mænlɪ**
manlike **'mænˌlaɪk**
Manlius **'mænlɪəs** |-'s -ɪz

manly, M- **'mænlɪ**
Mann, Horace **'hɔrɪs'mæn, 'harɪs, 'hɒrɪs, -əs**
Mann, Thomas **'taməs'mæn, 'man**; ES+
  'tɒməs; (*Ger* **'to:mas'man**)
manna **'mænə**
mannequin **'mænəkɪn**
manner **'mænɚ**; ES **'mænə(r**; |-s -z |-ed -d
mannerism **'mænəˌrɪzəm**
Mannheim **'mænhaɪm** (*Ger* **'manhaɪm**)
mannish **'mænɪʃ**
mannitol **'mænəˌtol, 'mænəˌtal, -ˌtɒl**
Manoah mə'noə
manoeuvre mə'nuvɚ; ES -'nuvə(r; |- d -d
  |-ring -'nuvərɪŋ, -'nuvrɪŋ
man-of-war **'mænəv'wɔr, 'mænə'wɔr**; ES
  -'wɔə(r
manometer mə'namətɚ; ES -'namətə(r,
  -'nɒm-
manor **'mænɚ**; ES **'mænə(r**
manorial mə'norɪəl, mæ-, -'nɔr-; S -'nor-
mansard **'mænsard**; ES **'mænsa:d, E+-sa:d**
manse mæns |manses **'mænsɪz**
manservant **'mænˌsɝvənt** |menservants **'mɛn-**
  ˌsɝvənts; |ES -ˌsɝv-, -ˌsɝv-
Mansfield **'mænz,fild, 'mæns,fild**
mansion **'mænʃən** |mansioned **'mænʃənd** |-ry
  -rɪ
manslaughter **'mænˌslɔtɚ**; ES -tə(r
manslayer **'mænˌsleɚ**; ES **'mænˌsle·ə(r**
mansuetude **'mænswɪˌtjud, -ˌtɪud, -ˌtud**
manteau **'mænto** (*Fr* mã'to)
Manteca mæn'tikə
mantel **'mænt|** |manteled **'mænt|d**
Mantell mæn'tɛl, **'mæntɛl**
mantelpiece **'mænt|ˌpis** |-pieces -ˌpisɪz
Manti **'mæntaɪ**
mantic **'mæntɪk**
mantilla mæn'tɪlə
mantis **'mæntɪs** |-es -ɪz |mantes **'mæntiz**
mantissa mæn'tɪsə
mantle **'mænt|** |-d -d |-ling **'mænt|ɪŋ, -tlɪŋ**
mantrap **'mænˌtræp**
mantua **'mæntʃʊə, 'mæntʊə**
Mantua **'mæntʃʊə, 'mæntʊə**, *O* **'mæntəˌwe**
manual **'mænjʊəl** |-ly -ɪ
Manuel **'mænjʊəl, 'mænjʊˌɛl**
manufactory ˌmænjə'fæktərɪ, -'fæktrɪ
manufacture ˌmænjə'fæktʃɚ, ˌmænə'fæktʃɚ;
  ES -tʃə(r; |-d -d |-ring -tʃərɪŋ, -tʃrɪŋ

Key: See in full §§3–47. bee **bi** |pity **'pɪtɪ** (§6) |rate **ret** |yet **jɛt** |sang **sæŋ** |angry **'æŋ·grɪ**
|bath **bæθ**; E ba**θ** (§10) |ah **a** |far **far** |watch **watʃ, wɒtʃ** (§12) |jaw **dʒɔ** |gorge **gɔrdʒ** |go **go**

Words below in which a *before* r (farm) *is sounded* ɑ *are often pronounced in* E *with* a (fɑ:m)
Words below that have æ *before* r (carry 'kærɪ) *are often pronounced in* N *with* ɛ ('kɛrɪ, §94)

manumission ˌmænjə'mɪʃən, ˌmænjʊ-
manumit ˌmænjə'mɪt, ˌmænjʊ- |-ted -ɪd
manure mə'njʊr, mə'nɪʊr, mə'nʊr; ES -ə(r;
|-d -d
manuscript 'mænjəˌskrɪpt
manward 'mænwəd; ES 'mænwəd; |-s -z
Manwaring 'mænərɪŋ, 'mænwɔrɪŋ, -wɑr-,
-wɒr-
manwise 'mænˌwaɪz
Manx mæŋks
Manxman 'mæŋksmən, -ˌmæn |-men -mən,
-ˌmɛn
many 'mɛnɪ |many's 'mɛnɪz |*occas. unstressed*
mənɪ (how many men 'hɑʊmənɪ'mɛn)
manysided 'mɛnɪ'saɪdɪd ('manyˌsided 'man)
Maori 'mɑʊrɪ, 'mɑrɪ
map mæp |mapped mæpt
maple, M- 'mepl̩ |mapled 'mepl̩d
Mapleton 'mepl̩tən, 'mæpl̩-
Mappleton 'mæpl̩tən
Maquoketa mə'kokɪtə
mar mɑr; ES mɑ:(r; |-red -d
Maracaibo ˌmærə'kaɪbo, ˌmɑrə-
maraschino, M- ˌmærə'skino
marathon, M- 'mærəˌθɑn, -ˌθɒn, -θən
maraud mə'rɔd |marauded mə'rɔdɪd
Marazion ˌmærə'zaɪən
marble 'mɑrbl̩; ES 'mɑ:bl̩; |-d -d |-ling -blɪŋ,
-bl̩ɪŋ
Marblehead 'mɑrbl̩ˌhɛd, 'mɑrbl̩'hɛd; ES
'mɑ:bl̩-
Marburg 'mɑrbɝg; ES 'mɑ:bɝg, 'mɑ:bɝg;
(*Ger* 'mɑrburk)
Marcade 'mɑrkəˌdi; ES 'mɑ:k-
marcasite 'mɑrkəˌsaɪt; ES 'mɑ:kəˌsaɪt
marcel mɑr'sɛl; ES mɑ:'sɛl; ('mɑrˌcel 'wave)
Marceline ˌmɑrsl̩'in; ES 'mɑ:s-
Marcella mɑr'sɛlə; ES mɑ:'sɛlə
Marcellus mɑr'sɛləs; ES mɑ:-; |-'s -ɪz
march, M- mɑrtʃ; ES mɑ:tʃ; |-es -ɪz |-ed -t
marchesa mɑr'kezə; ES mɑ:'kezə; (*It*
mɑr'ke:zɑ)
marchese mɑr'keze; ES mɑ:'keze; (*It* mɑr-
'ke:ze)
marchioness 'mɑrʃənɪs, ˌmɑrʃə'nɛs; ES
'mɑ:ʃənɪs, ˌmɑ:ʃə'nɛs; |-es -ɪz
marchpane 'mɑrtʃˌpen; ES 'mɑ:tʃˌpen

Marcius 'mɑrʃɪəs, -ʃəs; ES 'mɑ:ʃ-; |-'s -ɪz
Marco 'mɑrko; ES 'mɑ:ko
Marconi mɑr'konɪ; ES mɑ:'konɪ
marconigram mɑr'konɪˌgræm; ES mɑ'konɪ-
ˌgræm
Marcus 'mɑrkəs; ES 'mɑ:kəs; |-'s -ɪz
Mardian 'mɑrdɪən, -djən; ES 'mɑ:d-
Mardi gras 'mɑrdɪ'grɑ, -'grɔ; ES 'mɑ:dɪ-
mare mɛr, mær; E mɛə(r, ES mæə(r
Marengo, m- mə'rɛngo
mares-nest 'mɛrzˌnɛst, 'mærz-; E 'mɛəz-, ES
'mæəz-
mare's-tail 'mɛrzˌtel, 'mærz-; E 'mɛəz-, ES
'mæəz-
Margaret 'mɑrgrɪt, 'mɑrgərɪt; ES 'mɑ:g-
margaric mɑr'gærɪk, -'gɑrɪk; ES mɑ:'g-
margarine 'mɑrdʒəˌrin, -rɪn, *much less freq.*
'mɑrgə-; ES 'mɑ:dʒ-, 'mɑ:g-; *acct*+
ˌmargə'rine
Margarita ˌmɑrgə'ritə; ES ˌmɑ:gə'ritɑ
Margate *Engd* 'mɑrgɪt, *NJ* 'mɑrget, -gɪt; ES
'mɑ:g-
marge mɑrdʒ; ES mɑ:dʒ; |-s -ɪz |-d -d
margent 'mɑrdʒənt; ES 'mɑ:dʒənt
Margery 'mɑrdʒərɪ, -dʒrɪ; ES 'mɑ:dʒ-
margin 'mɑrdʒɪn; ES 'mɑ:dʒɪn; |-ed -d
marginal 'mɑrdʒɪnl̩; ES 'mɑ:dʒ-; |-ly -ɪ
marginalia ˌmɑrdʒə'nelɪə, -ljə; ES ˌmɑ:dʒ-
Margot *Eng name* (*from* Margaret) 'mɑrgət,
Fr name 'mɑrgo; ES 'mɑ:g-
margrave 'mɑrgrev; ES 'mɑ:grev
margravine 'mɑrgrəˌvin; ES 'mɑ:grəˌvin
marguerite, M- ˌmɑrgə'rit; ES ˌmɑ:gə'rit
Maria mə'raɪə, mə'riə
Marian 'mɛrɪən, 'mærɪən, 'merɪən
Mariana ˌmɛrɪ'ænə, ˌmær-, ˌmer-, *Sp schol.*
ˌmɑrɪ'ɑnə (*Sp* ˌmɑri'ɑnɑ)
Marianne ˌmɛrɪ'æn, ˌmerɪ'æn
Maria Theresa mə'raɪətə'rizə, -tə'rɛsə (*It*
mɑ'ri:ɑte'rɛ:zɑ)
Marie mə'ri, 'mɑrɪ, 'mærɪ
Marietta ˌmɛrɪ'ɛtə, ˌmerɪ-
marigold 'mærəˌgold
marijuana ˌmɑrɪ'hwɑnə (*Sp* ˌmɑri'xwɑnɑ)
marimba mə'rɪmbə
Marina mə'rinə, -'raɪnə
marine mə'rin

|full fʊl |tooth tuθ |further 'fɝðɚ; ES 'fɝðə |custom 'kʌstəm |while hwaɪl |how hɑʊ |toy tɔɪ
|using 'juzɪŋ |fuse fjuz, fɪuz |dish dɪʃ |vision 'vɪʒən |Eden 'idn̩ |cradle 'kredl̩ |keep 'em 'kipm̩

Words below in which a *before* r (farm) *is sounded* ɑ *are often pronounced in E with* a (fɑːm)
Words below that have æ *before* r (carry 'kærɪ) *are often pronounced in N with* ɛ ('kɛrɪ, §94)

mariner 'mærənɚ; ES 'mærənə(r
Mariolatry ˌmɛrɪ'alətrɪ, ˌmɛrɪ-; ES+-'ɒl-
Marion 'mɛrɪən, 'mæ-, 'me-, NC 'me-, SC 'mæ-
marionette ˌmærɪə'nɛt
Mariposa ˌmærə'posə, -'pozə
marish '*marsh*' 'mærɪʃ |marishes 'mærɪʃɪz
marish '*like a mare*' 'mɛrɪʃ, 'mærɪʃ; S 'mær-
Marissa mə'rɪsə
marital 'mærətl̩ |-ly -ɪ; (*Brit* mə'raɪtl̩)
maritime 'mærəˌtaɪm
Marius 'mɛrɪəs, 'mærɪəs, 'mɛrɪəs |-'s -ɪz
marjoram 'mardʒərəm; ES 'mɑːdʒərəm
Marjoribanks 'martʃˌbæŋks, 'marʃ-; ES 'mɑːtʃ-, 'mɑːʃ-
Marjorie, -ry 'mardʒərɪ, -dʒrɪ; ES 'mɑːdʒ-
mark, M- mark; ES mɑːk; |-ed -t |-edly -ɪdlɪ
Mark Antony 'mark'æntənɪ; ES 'mɑːk-
market 'markɪt; ES 'mɑːkɪt; |-ed -ɪd |-able -əbl̩ |-bly -blɪ
marketability ˌmarkɪtə'bɪlətɪ; ES ˌmɑːk-
Markham 'markəm; ES 'mɑːkəm
marksman 'marksmən; ES 'mɑːks-; |-men -mən
marl marl; ES mɑːl; |-ed -d
Marlborough, -ro US 'marlˌbɝˑo, -ə; ES 'mɑːl-, ˌbɝ-, -ˌbʌr-, -ˌbɝ-; Mass+'mɒlbrə; Engd 'mɒlbərə, -brə
Marlin 'marlɪn; ES 'mɑːlɪn
marline 'marlɪn; ES 'mɑːlɪn; |-spike -ˌspaɪk
Marlow, -lowe 'marlo; ES 'mɑːlo
Marmaduke 'marməˌdjuk, -ˌdɪuk, -ˌduk; ES 'mɑːmə-
marmalade 'marml̩ˌed, ˌmarml̩'ed; ES 'mɑː-mə-, ˌmɑːmə-
Marmara 'marmərə; ES 'mɑːmərə
Marmion 'marmɪən, 'marmjən; ES 'mɑːm-
Marmora 'marmərə, mar'morə, -'mɔrə; ES 'mɑːmərə, mɑː'morə, E+mɑː'mɔrə
marmoreal mar'morɪəl, -'mɔr-; ES mɑː'morɪəl, E+-'mɔr-
marmoset 'marməˌzɛt; ES 'mɑːməˌzɛt
marmot 'marmət; ES 'mɑːmət
Marne marn; ES mɑːn; (Fr marn)
maroon mə'run |marooned mə'rund
marplot 'marˌplat; ES 'mɑːˌplat, -ˌplɒt
Marprelate 'marˌprɛlɪt; ES 'mɑːˌprɛlɪt

Marquand mar'kwand, -'kwɒnd; ES mɑː-; ('Marˌquand 'Hall)
marque mark; ES mɑːk
marquee mar'ki; ES mɑː'ki
Marquesas mar'kesəs, mar'kesæs; ES mɑː-'kes-
marquetry 'markətrɪ; ES 'mɑːkətrɪ
Marquette mar'kɛt; ES mɑː'kɛt
marquis, -ess 'markwɪs; ES 'mɑːkwɪs; |-'s -ɪz (Fr mar'ki)
marquisette ˌmarkɪ'zɛt, -kwɪ'zɛt; ES ˌmɑːk-
marriage 'mærɪdʒ |-s -ɪz |-able -əbl̩
marriageability ˌmærɪdʒə'bɪlətɪ
marrow 'mæro, 'mærə |-ed -d |-ing 'mærəwɪŋ
marrowbone 'mæroˌbon, 'mærə-
marrowfat 'mærəˌfæt, 'mæro-
marrowy 'mærəwɪ
marry 'mærɪ |married 'mærɪd
Marryat 'mærɪət, 'mærɪˌæt
Mars marz; ES mɑːz; |-'s -ɪz
Marseillaise ˌmarsl̩'ez; ES ˌmɑːsl̩'ez; (Fr marsɛ'jɛːz)
Marseilles, m- mar'selz; ES mɑː'selz; |-'s -ɪz (Fr Marseille mar'sɛːj)
marsh, M- marʃ; ES mɑːʃ; |-es -ɪz |-y -ɪ
marshal, M- 'marʃəl; ES 'mɑːʃəl; |-ed -d
Marshalsea 'marʃl̩ˌsi; ES 'mɑːʃl̩ˌsi
marshmallow 'marʃˌmælo, -ˌmælə; ES 'mɑːʃ-
marsupial mar'supɪəl, -'sɪu-, -'sju-; ES mɑː-
mart, M- mart; ES mɑːt
Martel mar'tɛl; ES mɑː'tɛl
marten 'martɪn, 'martn̩; ES 'mɑːt-
Martha 'marθə; ES 'mɑːθə
martial, M- 'marʃəl; ES 'mɑːʃəl; |-ly -ɪ
Martian 'marʃɪən, 'marʃjən; ES 'mɑːʃ-
martin, M- 'martɪn, 'martn̩; ES 'mɑːt-
Martineau ˌmartɪ'no, ˌmartn̩'o; ES ˌmɑːt-
martinet ˌmartn̩'ɛt, 'martn̩ˌɛt; ES ˌmɑːt-, 'mɑːt-
Martinez mar'tinɪz; ES mɑː-; |-nez' -nɪz
martingale 'martn̩ˌgel; ES 'mɑːtn̩ˌgel
Martinique ˌmartn̩'ik; ES ˌmɑːtn̩'ik
Martinmas 'martɪnməs; ES 'mɑːtɪnməs; |-es -ɪz
martlet 'martlɪt; ES 'mɑːtlɪt
martyr 'martɚ; ES 'mɑːtə(r; |-ed -d |-dom -dəm

Words below in which a *before* r (farm) *is sounded* ɑ *are often pronounced in* E *with* a **(faːm)**

martyrological ˌmɑrtərəˈlɑdʒɪk|; ES ˌmɑːtə-, -ˈlɒdʒ-

martyrologist ˌmɑrtəˈrɑlədʒɪst; ES ˌmɑːtə-, -ˈrɒl-; |-gy -dʒɪ

Marullus məˈrʌləs |-'s -ɪz

marvel ˈmɑrv|; ES ˈmɑːv|; |-ed -d |-ing -v|ɪŋ, -v|ɪŋ |-ous -v|əs, -vləs

Marvel, -ll ˈmɑrv|; ES ˈmɑːv|

Marx mɑrks; ES mɑːks; |-ian -ɪən, -jən |-'s -ɪz

Mary ˈmɛrɪ, ˈmɛːrɪ, ˈmerɪ, ˈmærɪ—*Some speakers distinguish* Mary *from* merry *by a longer* ɛ (§55).

Maryland ˈmɛrələnd, ˈmɛrɪlənd

Marylebone *Lond road* ˈmærələbən, -ˌbon, ˈmærəbən—*see* St. Mary-le-Bone. ˈmærəbən *came from the original* Maryburn *by r-dissimilation* (§121).

Masaryk ˈmɑsəˌrik

Mascagni mɑsˈkɑnjɪ, mæs- (*It* mɑsˈkɑɲɲi)

mascara mæsˈkærə, mɑsˈkɑrə (*It* mɑsˈkɑːrɑ)

mascot ˈmæskət, -kɑt; ES+-kɒt

masculine ˈmæskjəlɪn |-linity ˌmæskjə-ˈlɪnətɪ

Masefield ˈmesˌfild, ˈmez-

mash mæʃ |mashes ˈmæʃɪz |mashed mæʃt

mashie, -y ˈmæʃɪ |mashies ˈmæʃɪz

mask mæsk; E+mask, mɑsk |-ed -t

masochism ˈmæzəˌkɪzəm

mason, M- ˈmesn̩ |masonry ˈmesn̩rɪ

masonic məˈsɑnɪk; ES+məˈsɒnɪk

Masora, -h məˈsorə, məˈsɔrə; S məˈsorə

masque mæsk; E+mask, mɑsk

masquerade ˌmæskəˈred |-raded -ˈredɪd

mass mæs |masses ˈmæsɪz |massed mæst

Mass mæs |Masses ˈmæsɪz

Massac ˈmæsək, -æk

Massachusetts ˌmæsəˈtʃusɪts, -ˈtʃuz-, -əts *L.A. of N Engd shows that about 28 per cent of the cultured informants pronounce* z.

massacre ˈmæsəkə; ES -kə(r; |-d -d |-ring -krɪŋ, -kərɪŋ

massage məˈsɑʒ |-sages -ˈsɑʒɪz |-saged -ˈsɑʒd

Massasoit ˈmæsəˌsɔɪt

Massena məˈsinə

Massenet ˌmæsəˈne (*Fr* masˈnɛ)

masseur mæˈsɝ; ES mæˈsɜ(r, -ˈsɜ·; (*Fr* maˈsœːr)

masseuse mæˈsɝz |-s -ɪz |-'s -ɪz (*Fr* maˈsøːz)

massicot ˈmæsɪˌkɑt; ES+-ˌkɒt

massif ˈmæsɪf (*Fr* maˈsif)

Massillon ˈmæslən, ˈmæsələn

Massinger ˈmæsn̩dʒɚ; ES -dʒə(r

massive ˈmæsɪv |massey ˈmæsɪ

Masson ˈmæsn̩

mast 'pole,' 'nuts' mæst; E+mast, mɑst; |-ed -ɪd

master ˈmæstɚ; ES -tə(r, E+ˈmɑs-, ˈmɑs-; |-ed -d |-ing -tərɪŋ, -trɪŋ |-ful -fəl |-fully -fəlɪ |-ly -lɪ |-y -tərɪ, -trɪ

master-at-arms ˈmæstərətˈɑrmz; ES -ˈɑːmz, E+ˈmɑs-, ˈmɑs- |-'s -ɪz

masterpiece ˈmæstɚˌpis; ES ˈmæstə-, E+ˈmɑs-, ˈmɑs-; |-s -ɪz

masterwork ˈmæstɚˌwɝk; ES ˈmæstəˌwɜk, ˈmæstəˌwɜ·k, E+ˈmɑs-, ˈmɑs-

masthead ˈmæstˌhɛd; E+ˈmɑst-, ˈmɑst-

mastic ˈmæstɪk

masticate ˈmæstəˌket |-d -ɪd |-tion ˌmæstə-ˈkeʃən

masticatory ˈmæstəkəˌtorɪ, -ˌtɔrɪ; S -ˌtorɪ

mastiff ˈmæstɪf; E+ˈmɑstɪf, ˈmɑstɪf

mastitis mæsˈtaɪtɪs

mastodon ˈmæstəˌdɑn; ES+ˈmæstəˌdɒn

mastoid ˈmæstɔɪd |mastoiditis ˌmæstɔɪdˈaɪtɪs

masturbation ˌmæstɚˈbeʃən; ES ˌmæstə-ˈbeʃən

masurium məˈsjʊrɪəm, məˈsɪʊrɪəm, mə-ˈsʊrɪəm

mat mæt |matted ˈmætɪd |matting ˈmætɪŋ

Matabele ˌmætəˈbilɪ |-leland -ˌlænd

matador ˈmætəˌdɔr; ES ˈmætəˌdɔə(r; (*Sp* ˌmataˈðɔr)

Matamoras ˌmætəˈmorəs, -ˈmɔr-; S -ˈmor-; |-'s -ɪz

Matanzas məˈtænzəs |-zas' -zəs (*Am Sp* maˈtansas)

Matawan ˌmætəˈwɑn, -ˈwɒn

match mætʃ |matches ˈmætʃɪz |matched mætʃt

matchlock ˈmætʃˌlɑk; ES+ˈmætʃˌlɒk

matchmaker ˈmætʃˌmekɚ; ES ˈmætʃˌmekə(r

matchwood ˈmætʃˌwʊd

mate met |mated ˈmetɪd

maté, -te ˈmate, ˈmæte

mater 'mother' ˈmetɚ, ˈmɑtɚ; ES -tə(r

|full fʊl |tooth tuθ |further ˈfɝðɚ; ES ˈfɜðə |custom ˈkʌstəm |while hwaɪl |how haʊ |toy tɔɪ
|using ˈjuzɪŋ |fuse fjuz, fɪuz |dish dɪʃ |vision ˈvɪʒən |Eden ˈidn̩ |cradle ˈkredl̩ |keep 'em ˈkipm̩

materfamilias ˌmetɚfə'mɪlɪˌæs; ES ˌmetə-
material mə'tɪrɪəl |-ism -ˌɪzəm |-ist -ɪst |-ly -ɪ
materiality məˌtɪrɪ'ælətɪ
materialize mə'tɪrɪəlˌaɪz |-s -ɪz |-d -d
materia medica mə'tɪrɪə'mɛdɪkə
matériel məˌtɪrɪ'ɛl (Fr mate'rjɛl)
maternal mə'tɜ·n̩|; ES mə'tɜn|, -'tɜ·n|; |-ly -ɪ
maternity mə'tɜ·nətɪ; ES -'tɜnətɪ, -'tɜ·n-
mathematic ˌmæθə'mætɪk |-s -s |-al -| |-ally
-|ɪ, -ɪklɪ
mathematician ˌmæθəmə'tɪʃən
Mather 'mæðɚ; ES 'mæðə(r
Mathew 'mæθju
Mathias mə'θaɪəs |Mathias's mə'θaɪəsɪz
Mathilda, -tilda mə'tɪldə
matin 'mætɪn
matinee ˌmætn̩'e ('matiˌnee 'seat)
matrass, -ttrass chem. 'mætrəs |-es -ɪz
matriarch 'metrɪˌɑrk; ES -ˌɑːk; |-ate -ɪt |-y -ɪ
matrices pl of matrix 'metrɪˌsiz, 'mæt-
matricide 'metrəˌsaɪd, 'mætrəˌsaɪd
matriculate mə'trɪkjəˌlet |-d -ɪd
matriculation məˌtrɪkjə'leʃən
matrimonial ˌmætrə'monɪəl, -'monjəl |-ly -ɪ
matrimony 'mætrəˌmonɪ
matrix 'metrɪks, 'mætrɪks |-es -ɪz |matrices
'metrɪˌsiz, 'mætrɪˌsiz
matron 'metrən
matronymic ˌmætrə'nɪmɪk
Mattaponi ˌmætəpə'naɪ
matte mæt |matted 'mætɪd
Matteawan ˌmætə'wan, ˌmætə'wɒn
matter 'mætɚ; ES 'mætə(r; |-ed -d
matterate 'mætəˌret |-d -ɪd |-tion ˌmætə-
'reʃən
Matterhorn 'mætɚˌhɔrn; ES 'mætəˌhɔən
matter-of-course 'mætərəv'kors, -'kɔrs; ES
-'koəs, E+-'kɔəs
matter-of-fact 'mætərəv'fækt, 'mætərə'fækt
('matter-of-ˌfact 'style)
Matthew 'mæθju |-s -z |-s's -zɪz
Matthias mə'θaɪəs |Matthias's mə'θaɪəsɪz
mattock 'mætək |-ed -t
Mattoon mæ'tun, mə-
mattress 'mætrɪs, 'mætrəs |-es -ɪz |-ed -t
maturate 'mætʃuˌret, 'mætjuˌret |-d -ɪd
maturation ˌmætʃu'reʃən, ˌmætju'reʃən
mature mə'tjur, -'tɪur, -'tur |-d -d |-rity -ətɪ
matutinal mə'tjutn̩|, mə'tɪu-, mə'tu-

matzoth 'mætsoθ, 'mɑtsoθ
Mauch Chunk 'mɔk'tʃʌŋk
Maud, -e mɔd
maudlin 'mɔdlɪn
mauger, -gre 'mɔgɚ; ES 'mɔgə(r
Maugham mɔm
maul mɔl |-ed -d
Maulmein maʊl'men, mɔl-, mol-
maulstick 'mɔlˌstɪk
Maumee mɔ'mi ('Mauˌmee 'River)
maumet 'mɔmɪt |maumetry 'mɔmɪtrɪ
Mauna Kea 'maʊnə'keə, 'mɔnə'kiə
Mauna Loa 'maʊnə'loə, 'mɔnə'loə
maunder 'mɔndɚ; ES -də(r; |-ed -d |-ing
'mɔndərɪŋ, 'mɔndrɪŋ
Maundy Thursday 'mɔndɪ'θɜ·zdɪ; ES -'θɜz-,
-'θɜ·z-
Maupassant, de də'mopəˌsant (Fr dəmopa-
'sã)
Mauretania, -ri- ˌmɔrə'tenɪə, ˌmar-, ˌmɒr-,
-njə
Maurice 'mɔrɪs, 'marɪs, 'mɒrɪs |-'s -ɪz
Maurois Fr 'morwa, mo'rwa
mausoleum, M- ˌmɔsə'liəm |-s -z |-lea -'liə
mauve mov
maverick, M- 'mævrɪk, 'mævərɪk
mavis, M- 'mevɪs |-es -ɪz
mavourneen, -nin, M- mə'vurnin, -'vor-,
-'vɔr-; ES -'vuə-, -'voə-, E+-'vɔə-
maw mɔ
Mawer 'mɔɚ; ES 'mɔ·ə(r
mawkin 'mɔkɪn = malkin
mawkish 'mɔkɪʃ
maxilla mæks'ɪlə |-lae -li
maxillary 'mæksəˌlɛrɪ, mæks'ɪlərɪ
maxim, M- 'mæksɪm
Maximilian ˌmæksə'mɪlɪən, -'mɪljən
maximite 'mæksəˌmaɪt
maximize 'mæksəˌmaɪz |-s -ɪz |-d -d
maximum 'mæksəməm |-s -z |-ma -mə
maxwell, M- 'mækswɛl, 'mækswəl
may stressed 'me, ˌme; unstr. mɪ, mə
May me
Maya 'majə |Mayan 'majən
maybe 'mebi, 'mebi, 'mɛbɪ—'mɛbɪ, occasionally heard, is phonetically normal, being
parallel to 'brɛkfəst for breakfast.
mayest 'me·ɪst
Mayfair 'meˌfɛr, -ˌfær; E -ˌfɛə(r, ES -ˌfæə(r

Mayflower, m- 'me͵flauͻ, -͵flaur; ES 'me-͵flauə(r, -͵flauə(r
mayhap 'me͵hæp, me'hæp |-s -s
mayhem 'mehɛm, 'meəm
Mayhew 'mehju, 'mehɪu
mayn't mɛnt
Maynwaring 'mænərɪŋ, 'menwɔrɪŋ, -wɑr-, -wɔr-
Mayo surname 'meo, Am Indian 'majo
mayonnaise ͵meə'nez ('mayon͵naise 'dressing)
mayor, M- 'meͻ, mɛr; ES 'me·ə(r, mɛə(r; |-alty -əltɪ
Maypole, m- 'me͵pol
maypop 'mepɑp; ES+'mepɒp
mayst mɛst
Maytide 'me͵taɪd
mazard 'mæzͻd; ES 'mæzəd
Mazatlán ͵mɑzə'tlɑn (Am Sp ͵masa'tlɑn)
mazda, M- 'mæzdə
Mazdaism, Mazde- 'mæzdə͵ɪzəm
maze mez |mazes 'mezɪz |mazed mezd |-dly -ɪdlɪ
mazer 'mezͻ; ES 'mezə(r
mazurka mə'zͻkə, -'zurkə; ES -'zͻkə, -'zͻkə, -'zuəkə
mazzard 'mæzͻd; ES 'mæzəd
Mazzini mæt'sinɪ, mɑt'sinɪ (It mɑt'tsi:ni, mɑd'dz-)
Mc- alphabetized under Mac-
me stressed 'mi, ͵mi; unstr. mɪ
mead mid |Mead, -e mid
meadow 'mɛdo, 'mɛdə |-ed -d |-ing 'mɛdəwɪŋ
Meadville 'midvɪl; S+-v͵l
meager, -gre 'migͻ; ES 'migə(r; |-(e)d -d
Meagher mɑr; ES mɑ:(r, E+mɑ:(r
meal mil |-ed -d |-less 'millɪs
mealie, -y 'corn' 'milɪ |-lies -z
mealtime 'mil͵taɪm
mealy adj 'milɪ
mealymouthed 'milɪ'mauͣ̌d, -θt |-thedly -ͣ̌ɪdlɪ, -ͣ̌dlɪ, -θtlɪ
mean min |meant mɛnt |-ness 'minnɪs
meander, M- mɪ'ændͻ; ES -'ændə(r; |-ed -d |-ing -'ændrɪŋ, -'ændərɪŋ
meant mɛnt
meantime 'min͵taɪm |meanwhile 'min͵hwaɪl
measles 'mizlz |measly 'mizlɪ
measurability ͵mɛʒərə'bɪlətɪ

measurable 'mɛʒrəb͵l, 'mɛʒərəb͵l |-bly -blɪ
measure 'mɛʒͻ; ES 'mɛʒə(r; |-d -d |-ring 'mɛʒrɪŋ, 'mɛʒərɪŋ
meat mit |meated 'mitɪd
Meath Ir co. miθ
meatman 'mit͵mæn |-men -͵mɛn
meatus mɪ'etəs |-es -ɪz |L pl -tus -təs
Mecca 'mɛkə
mechanic mə'kænɪk |-al -͵l |-ally -͵ɪ, -ɪklɪ
mechanician ͵mɛkə'nɪʃən
mechanism 'mɛkə͵nɪzəm |-nist -nɪst
mechanistic ͵mɛkə'nɪstɪk |-ally -͵ɪ, -ɪklɪ
mechanization ͵mɛkənə'zeʃən, -aɪ'z-
mechanize 'mɛkə͵naɪz |-s -ɪz |-d -d
Mechlin 'mɛklɪn
Mecklenburg US, Germany 'mɛklɪn͵bͻg, -lən-; ES -͵bͻg, -͵bͻg; (Ger 'me:klən͵burk, 'mɛk-)
medal 'mɛd͵l |-ed -d |-ist -ɪst
medallic mə'dælɪk, mɪ- |-ally -͵ɪ, -ɪklɪ
medallion mə'dæljən, mɪ- |-ist -ɪst
meddle 'mɛd͵l |-d -d |-ling 'mɛdlɪŋ, 'mɛd͵ɪŋ
meddlesome 'mɛd͵səm
Mede mid
Medea mɪ'diə
Medford 'mɛdfͻd; ES 'mɛdfəd
media, M- 'midɪə |pl mediae 'midɪ͵i
media pl of medium 'midɪə
mediacy 'midɪəsɪ
mediaeval ͵midɪ'iv͵l, ͵mɛd- |-ly -ɪ |-ism -͵ɪzəm |-ist -ɪst
medial 'midɪəl |-ly -ɪ
median, M- 'midɪən
mediate adj 'midɪɪt
mediate v 'midɪ͵et |-d -ɪd |-tion ͵midɪ'eʃən
mediatize 'midɪə͵taɪz |-s -ɪz |-d -d
mediator 'midɪ͵etͻ; ES -͵etə(r
mediatory 'midɪə͵torɪ, -͵tɔrɪ; S -͵torɪ
medic 'mɛdɪk |Medic 'midɪk
medical 'mɛdɪk͵l |-ly -ɪ, -ɪklɪ |-cable -kəb͵l
medicament n mə'dɪkəmənt, 'mɛdɪkə-
medicament v mə'dɪkə͵mɛnt |-ed -ɪd
medicamental ͵mɛdɪkə'mɛnt͵l |-ly -ɪ
medicate 'mɛdɪ͵ket |-d -ɪd |-tion ͵mɛdɪ'keʃən
Medicean ͵mɛdə'siən
Medici 'mɛdə͵tʃi (It 'mɛ:di͵tʃi)
medicinable mə'dɪsnəb͵l, in Shak. 'mɛdsɪnəb͵l
medicinal mə'dɪsn͵l |-ly -ɪ
medicine 'mɛdəsn̩ |-cined -sn̩d

medico 'mɛdɪ,ko
medicodental ,mɛdɪko'dɛntļ
medicolegal ,mɛdɪko'ligļ |-ly -ɪ
medieval ,midɪ'iv], ,mɛd- |-ly -ɪ |-ism -,ɪzəm
|-ist -ɪst
Medina *NY, O, Spenser's F.Q.* mə'daɪnə, mɪ-;
Tex co., Arab city, Belg painter, IW river
mə'dinə, me-, mɪ-; *Sp & SAm persons &*
places me'ðina
mediocre 'midɪ,okə, ,midɪ'okə; ES -kə(r
mediocrity ,midɪ'akrətɪ; ES+-'ɒk-
meditate 'mɛdə,tet |-d -ɪd |-tive -ɪv
meditation ,mɛdə'teʃən
Mediterranean, m- ,mɛdətə'renɪən |-neous
-nɪəs
medium 'midɪəm |-s -z |-dia -dɪə
medlar 'mɛdlə; ES 'mɛdlə(r
medley 'mɛdlɪ |-ed, -lied -d
Medoc, Mé- 'medak, mɪ'dak; ES+-ɒk; (*Fr*
me'dɔk)
medulla mɪ'dʌlə |-s -z |-lae -li
medullary 'mɛdļ,ɛrɪ, mɪ'dʌlərɪ
Medusa mə'djusə, -'dɪu-, -'du-, -zə
Medway 'mɛd,we
meed mid
meek, M- mik
meerschaum 'mɪrʃəm, -ʃəm; ES 'mɪə-
meet mit |met mɛt
meetinghouse 'mitɪŋ,haʊs |-houses -,haʊzɪz
Meg mɛg
megacephalic ,mɛgəsə'fælɪk |-lous -'sɛfələs
megafarad ,mɛgə'færəd, -'færæd
megalith 'mɛgə,lɪθ |-ths -θs |-ic ,mɛgə'lɪθɪk
megalomania ,mɛgələ'menɪə |-iac -ɪ,æk
megalophonous ,mɛgə'lafənəs; ES+-'lɒf-
megameter *instrument* mɛ'gæmətə; ES
-'gæmətə(r
megameter '*million meters*' 'mɛgə,mitə; ES
-tə(r
megaphone 'mɛgə,fon |-d -d |-ist -ɪst
Megara 'mɛgərə |-rian mɛ'gɛrɪən, -'gær-,
-'ger-
megatherium ,mɛgə'θɪrɪəm
Megiddo mə'gɪdo
megohm 'mɛg,om
megrim 'migrɪm
Mehetabel mə'hɛtəb] |Mehitable mə'hɪtəb]
Meier 'maɪə; ES 'maɪ·ə(r
Meighen 'miən

Meigs mɛgz |-'s -ɪz
Meikle 'mikļ
Meiklejohn 'mɪkļ,dʒɑn, -,dʒɒn, 'mikļ-
mein men
meiosis maɪ'osɪs
Meistersinger 'maɪstə,sɪŋə; ES 'maɪstə-
,sɪŋə(r
melancholia ,mɛlən'kolɪə |-lic -'kɑlɪk; ES+
-'kɒlɪk
melancholy 'mɛlən,kɑlɪ; ES+-,kɒlɪ
Melanchthon mə'læŋkθən |-ian ,mɛlæŋk-
'θonɪən
Melanesia ,mɛlə'niʃə, -ʃɪə, -'niʒ- |-n -n
mélange me'lãʒ |-s -ɪz |-d -d (*Fr* me'lã:ʒ)
melanic mə'lænɪk |-niferous ,mɛlə'nɪfərəs
melanin 'mɛlənɪn |melanism 'mɛlə,nɪzəm
melanotic ,mɛlə'natɪk; ES+-'nɒt-
Melba 'mɛlbə
Melbourne 'mɛlbən; ES 'mɛlbən
Melcher 'mɛltʃə; ES 'mɛltʃə(r
Melchers 'mɛltʃəz; ES 'mɛltʃəz; |-'s -ɪz
Melchizedek mɛl'kɪzədɪk, -,dɛk
meld mɛld |melded 'mɛldɪd
Meleager ,mɛlɪ'edʒə; ES -'edʒə(r
melee '*fray*' me'le, 'mele, 'mɛle (*Fr* mɛ'le)
melee '*diamond*' 'mɛli
Melibeus, -boeus ,mɛlə'biəs |-'s -ɪz
Melicent 'mɛləsṇt
melinite 'mɛlɪ,naɪt
meliorate 'miljə,ret |-d -ɪd |-tive -ɪv
melioration ,miljə'reʃən
Melissa mə'lɪsə
Mellen 'mɛlɪn, -ən
mellifluence mə'lɪfluəns |-nt -nt |-uous -ʊəs
Mellon 'mɛlən
mellow 'mɛlo, -ə |-ed -d |-ing 'mɛləwɪŋ |-er
'mɛləwə; ES -wə(r; |-est 'mɛləwɪst
melodic mə'lɑdɪk; ES+-'lɒd-; |-al -ļ |-ally
-ḷɪ, -ɪklɪ
melodion mə'lodɪən |-dious -dɪəs
melodist 'mɛlədɪst
melodrama 'mɛlə,drɑmə, -,dræmə
melodramatic ,mɛlədrə'mætɪk |-al -ļ |-ally
-ḷɪ, -ɪklɪ
melody 'mɛlədɪ |-ied -d
melon 'mɛlən
Melos, m- 'milas, -lɒs
Melpomene mɛl'pamənɪ, -,ni; ES+-'pɒm-
Melrose 'mɛlroz |-'s -ɪz

melt mɛlt |-ed -ɪd |*arch. pptc* molten 'moltn̩
melton, M- 'mɛltn̩
Melton Mowbray |'mɛltn̩'mobrɪ
Melun mə'lʌn (*Fr* mə'lœ̃)
Melville 'mɛlvɪl; S+'mɛlvl̩|
member 'mɛmbɚ; ES 'mɛmbə(r; |-ed -d
|-ship -ˌʃɪp
membrane 'mɛmbren |-d -d
membranous 'mɛmbrənəs, mɛm'brenəs
('mɛmˌbranous 'croup) |-neous mɛm'brenɪəs
memento mɪ'mɛnto
memento mori mɪ'mɛnto'moraɪ, -'mɔ-; S
-'mo-
Memnon 'mɛmnɑn, -nɒn
memoir 'mɛmwɑr, -wɔr; ES -wɑː(r, -wɔə(r
memorabilia, M- ˌmɛmərə'bɪlɪə
memorable 'mɛmərəbl̩, 'mɛmrə- |-bly -blɪ
memorandum ˌmɛmə'rændəm |-s -z |-da -də
memorial mə'morɪəl, -'mɔr-; S -'mor-; |-ly -ɪ
memorialize mə'morɪəlˌaɪz, -'mɔr-; S -'mor-;
|-s -ɪz |-d -d
memorization ˌmɛmərə'zeʃən, -aɪ'z-
memorize 'mɛməˌraɪz |-s -ɪz |-d -d
memory 'mɛmərɪ, -mrɪ |-ied -d
Memphis 'mɛmfɪs |-'s -ɪz
Memphremagog ˌmɛmfrɪ'megɑg, -gɒg
mem-sahib 'mɛmˌsɑ·ɪb, -ˌsɑhɪb
men mɛn |men's mɛnz
menace 'mɛnɪs, -əs |-s -ɪz |-d -t
menad 'minæd |menades 'mɛnəˌdiz
ménage, me- mə'nɑʒ, me- |-s -ɪz (*Fr* me'naːʒ)
menagerie mə'nædʒərɪ, -'næʒ- (*Fr* menaʒ'ri)
Menander mɪ'nændɚ; ES -'nændə(r
Menands mə'nændz, -'nænz |-'s -ɪz
Menard mə'nɑrd; ES -'nɑːd, E+-'nɑːd
Menas 'minəs |-'s -ɪz
Menasha mə'næʃə
Mencken 'mɛŋkɪn, -ən
mend mɛnd |mended 'mɛndɪd
mendacious mɛn'deʃəs |-dacity -'dæsətɪ
Mendel 'mɛndl̩ |-ian mɛn'dilɪən
Mendelssohn 'mɛndl̩sn̩, -ˌson
Mendelyeev ˌmɛndə'leɛf, ˌmɛndjɛ'ljeɛf
mendicancy 'mɛndɪkənsɪ |-cant -kənt
mendicity mɛn'dɪsətɪ
Mendota mɛn'dotə
Mendoza mɛn'dozə (*Am Sp* men'ðosa)
Menecrates mə'nɛkrəˌtiz |-'s -ɪz
Menelaus ˌmɛnə'leəs |-'s -ɪz

mene, mene, tekel, upharsin 'minɪ'minɪ-
'tikǀju'fɑrsɪn, -'tɛkǀ-; ES -'fɑːs-, E+-'fɑːs-
menfolk 'mɛnˌfok |-s -s
menhaden mɛn'hedn̩
menhir 'mɛnhɪr; ES -hɪə(r
menial 'minɪəl, -njəl |-ly -ɪ |-ism -ˌɪzəm
Menifee 'mɛnəˌfi
meninges mə'nɪndʒiz |-ningeal -'nɪndʒɪəl
meningitis ˌmɛnɪn'dʒaɪtɪs |*L pl* -gitides
-'dʒɪtɪˌdiz
meninx 'minɪŋks |meninges mə'nɪndʒiz
Mennonite 'mɛnənˌaɪt
Menominee, -nie mə'nɑməˌni; ES+-'nɒm-
menopause 'mɛnəˌpɔz |-s -ɪz
menservants 'mɛnˌsɝvənts; ES -ˌsɝv-, -ˌsɜv-
menses 'mɛnsiz |mensal 'mɛnsl̩
menstruate 'mɛnstruˌet |-d -ɪd |-al -struəl
menstruation ˌmɛnstru'eʃən
mensuration ˌmɛnʃə'reʃən, -sə'reʃən, -sju-
-ment *unstressed ending of nouns* -mənt, *older
& less freq.* -mɪnt. *The pronunciation* -mɛnt
for unstressed -ment (*as in* judgment) *is
artificial.   Words in* -ment *are usually
omitted from the vocab. if the pron. can be
found by adding* -mənt *to the head pron.
Verbs in* -ment (*with secondary accent*) *are
usually given, as also a few nouns like*
'augment, 'comment, 'ferment, 'torment,
in which -ment *has an* (*unmarked*) *subordinate accent.*
mental 'mɛntl̩ |-ly -ɪ |-ity mɛn'tælətɪ
Menteith mɛn'tiθ
menthol 'mɛnθol, -θɑl, -θɒl, -θɔl
mentholated 'mɛnθəˌletɪd
mention 'mɛnʃən |-ed -d |-ing -ʃənɪŋ, -ʃnɪŋ
mentor, M- 'mɛntɚ; ES 'mɛntə(r
menu 'mɛnju, 'menju, 'mɛnu, 'menu (*Fr*
mə'ny)
Menuhin 'mɛnjʊɪn
Menzies 'mɛnzɪz (*Sc* 'miŋɪz, *orig.* 'miʝɪz)
Mephibosheth mɪ'fɪbəˌʃɛθ
Mephistophelean ˌmɛfɪstə'filɪən, ˌmɛfəˌstɑfə-
'liən, -ˌstɒf-
Mephistopheles ˌmɛfə'stɑfəˌliz, -'stɒf- |-'s -ɪz
Mephistophelian ˌmɛfɪstə'filɪən
mephitic mɛ'fɪtɪk |-al -l̩ |-tis -'faɪtɪs
Meramec 'mɛrəˌmɛk
mercantile 'mɝkəntɪl, -ˌtaɪl; ES 'mɜ-, 'mɝ-;
|-ly -lɪ |+-ˌtil

|full fʊl |tooth tuθ |further 'fɝðɚ; ES 'fɝðə |custom 'kʌstəm |while hwaɪl |how haʊ |toy tɔɪ
|using 'juzɪŋ |fuse fjuz, frʊz |dish dɪʃ |vision 'vɪʒən |Eden 'idn̩ |cradle 'kredl̩ |keep 'em 'kipm̩

mercaptan mə'kæptæn; ES mə-
Mercator mɜ'keta; ES mɜ'keta(r, mɜ'keta(r
Merced mə'sɛd; ES mə-
Mercedes mɜ'sidiz; ES mɜ-, mɜ-; |-des' -diz
mercenary 'mɜsn̩ɛrɪ; ES 'mɜs-, 'mɜs-
mercer, M- 'mɜsə; ES 'mɜsə(r, 'mɜsə(r
mercerize 'mɜsəˌraɪz; ES 'mɜs-, 'mɜs-; |-s
   -ɪz |-d -d
merchandise n 'mɜtʃənˌdaɪz, -ˌdaɪs; ES
   'mɜtʃ-, 'mɜtʃ-
merchandise v 'mɜtʃənˌdaɪz; ES 'mɜtʃ-,
   'mɜtʃ-; |-s -ɪz |-d -d
merchant 'mɜtʃənt; ES 'mɜtʃ-, 'mɜtʃ-; |-man
   -mən |-men -mən
Mercia 'mɜʃɪə, -ʃə |-cian -ʃɪən, -ʃən, -sɪən
Mercier 'mɜsɪə; ES 'mɜsɪ·ə(r, 'mɜsɪ·ə(r; (Fr
   mɛr'sje)
merciful 'mɜsɪfəl; ES 'mɜs-, 'mɜs-; |-ly -ɪ
mercurate 'mɜkjəˌret; ES 'mɜk-, 'mɜk-; |-d
   -ɪd
mercurial mɜ'kjʊrɪəl, -'kɪʊ-; ES mɜ-, mɜ-;
   |-ly -ɪ
mercuric mɜ'kjʊrɪk, -'kɪʊ-; ES mɜ-, mɜ-
mercurous mɜ'kjʊrəs, 'mɜkjə-, -'kɪʊ-; ES
   -ɜ-, -ɜ-
Mercury 'mɜkjərɪ, 'mɜkərɪ, -krɪ; ES 'mɜk-,
   'mɜk-
Mercutio mɜ'kjuʃɪˌo, -'kɪʊ-, -ʃjo; ES mɜ-,
   mɜ-
mercy, M- 'mɜsɪ; ES 'mɜsɪ, 'mɜsɪ
mere mɪr; ES mɪə(r, S+ mɛə(r
Meredith 'mɛrədɪθ
Meres mɪrz; ES mɪəz; |-'s -ɪz
meretricious ˌmɛrə'trɪʃəs
merganser mə'gænsə; ES mə'gænsə(r
merge mɜdʒ; ES mɜdʒ, mɜdʒ; |-s -ɪz |-d -d
merger 'mɜdʒə; ES 'mɜdʒə(r, 'mɜdʒə(r
mergence 'mɜdʒəns; ES 'mɜdʒ-, 'mɜdʒ-
Mergenthaler 'mɜgənˌθɑlə; ES 'mɜgən-
   ˌθɑlə(r, 'mɜg-; (Ger 'mɛrgənˌtɑːlər)
Meriden 'mɛrədn̩, -dɪn
meridian, M- mə'rɪdɪən |-al -l̩ |-ally -lɪ
meringue mə'ræŋ |-d -d (Fr mə'rɛ̃:g)
Merino, m- mə'rino
Merionethshire ˌmɛrɪ'ɑnɪθˌʃɪr, -ʃə; ES -'ɑnɪθ-
   ˌʃɪə(r, -'ɒn-, -ʃə(r
merit 'mɛrɪt |-ed -ɪd
meritorious ˌmɛrə'torɪəs, -'tɔr-; S -'tor-
Merivale 'mɛrəˌvɛl

merl, -e mɜl; ES mɜl, mɜl
merlin, M- 'mɜlɪn; ES 'mɜl-, 'mɜl-
merlon 'mɜlən; ES 'mɜl-, 'mɜl-
mermaid 'mɜˌmed; ES 'mɜ-, 'mɜ-
merman 'mɜˌmæn; ES 'mɜ-, 'mɜ-; |-men
   -ˌmɛn
Merope 'mɛrəpɪ, -ˌpi
Merovingian ˌmɛrə'vɪndʒɪən, -dʒən
Merriam 'mɛrɪəm
Merrick 'mɛrɪk
Merrilies 'mɛrəˌliz |-'s -ɪz
Merrill 'mɛrəl
Merrimack, -mac 'mɛrəˌmæk
merriment 'mɛrɪmənt
merry 'mɛrɪ |-rily 'mɛrəlɪ, -rɪlɪ
merry-andrew 'mɛrɪ'ændru, -drɪu
merry-go-round 'mɛrɪgəˌraʊnd, -go-
Mersey 'mɜzɪ; ES 'mɜzɪ, 'mɜzɪ
Merton 'mɜtn̩; ES 'mɜtn̩, 'mɜtn̩
mesa, M- 'mesə (Am Sp 'mɛsa)
Mesaba mə'sabə |-bi -bɪ
mésalliance me'zælɪəns |-s -ɪz (Fr meza'ljɑ̃:s)
Mesa Verde ˌmesə'vɜd; ES -'vɜd, -'vɜd;
   (Am Sp ˌmɛsa'βɛrðe)
mescal mɛs'kæl |-ism -ɪzəm
mesdames me'dam (Fr me'dam)
meseems mi'simz
mesencephalon ˌmɛsɛn'sɛfəˌlan, -ˌlɒn
mesentery 'mɛsn̩ˌtɛrɪ |-ric ˌmɛsn̩'tɛrɪk
mesh mɛʃ |meshes 'mɛʃɪz |meshed mɛʃt
Meshach 'miʃæk
Meshek 'miʃɛk
Mesmer 'mɛsmə, 'mɛz-; ES -mə(r; (Ger
   'mɛsmər, Fr mɛz'mɛːr)
mesmeric mɛs'mɛrɪk, mɛz- |-al -l̩ |-ally -lɪ,
   -ɪklɪ—see mesmerism
mesmerism 'mɛsməˌrɪzəm, 'mɛz- (Ger
   ˌmɛsmə'rɪsmʊs, Fr mɛzme'rɪsm̩)
mesmerize 'mɛsməˌraɪz, 'mɛz- |-s -ɪz |-d -d
mesne min
Meso-Gothic, Mesog- ˌmiso'gɑθɪk, -'gɒθɪk
Mesopotamia ˌmɛsəpə'temɪə |-n -n
mesothorium ˌmɛsə'θorɪəm, ˌmɛz-, -'θɔr-; S
   -'θor-
Mesozoic ˌmɛsə'zo·ɪk
mesquite 'mɛskit, mɛs'kit
mess mɛs |messes 'mɛsɪz |messed mɛst
message 'mɛsɪdʒ |-s -ɪz |-d -d
Messala mɛ'selə |-lian -lɪən

Key: See in full §§3–47. bee bi |pity 'pɪtɪ (§6) |rate ret |yet jɛt |sang sæŋ |angry 'æŋ·grɪ
|bath bæθ; E baθ (§10) |ah ɑ |far fɑr |watch wɑtʃ, wɒtʃ (§12) |jaw dʒɔ |gorge gɔrdʒ |go go

Messeigneurs, m- ˌmɛsen'ʒɝz; ES -'ʒɜz, -'ʒɝz;
  (*Fr* mɛsɛ'ɲœːr)
messenger 'mɛsn̩dʒɚ; ES 'mɛsn̩dʒə(r
Messiah mə'saɪə |Messias mə'saɪəs |-s's -sɪz
messianic, M- ˌmɛsɪ'ænɪk |-al -l̩ |-ally -l̩ɪ,
  -ɪklɪ
Messieurs, m- 'mɛsɚz; ES 'mɛsəz (*Fr* me'sjø)
Messina mə'sinə, mɛ-
messmate 'mɛsˌmet
Messrs. 'mɛsɚz; ES 'mɛsəz (*Fr* me'sjø)
messuage 'mɛswɪdʒ |-s -ɪz
mestizo mɛs'tizo
met mɛt
meta 'mitə |-s -z |-tae -ti
metabolic ˌmɛtə'balɪk; ES+-'bɒl-; |-al -l̩
metabolism mə'tæbl̩ˌɪzəm, mɛ-
metabolize mə'tæbl̩ˌaɪz, mɛ- |-s -ɪz |-d -d
metacarpal ˌmɛtə'karpl̩; ES -'kɑːpl̩
metacarpus ˌmɛtə'karpəs; ES -'kɑːpəs; |-es
  -ɪz |-pi -paɪ
metacenter, -tre 'mɛtəˌsɛntɚ; ES -ˌsɛntə(r
metacentral ˌmɛtə'sɛntrəl |-tric -trɪk
metagalaxy ˌmɛtə'gæləksɪ |-lactic -gə'læktɪk
metage 'mitɪdʒ |-s -ɪz
metal 'mɛtl̩ |-ed -d
metallic mə'tælɪk |-al -l̩ |-ally -l̩ɪ, -ɪklɪ
metalliferous ˌmɛtl̩'ɪfərəs
metallurgic ˌmɛtl̩'ɝdʒɪk; ES -'ɝdʒ-, -'ɝdʒ-;
  |-al -l̩ |-ally -l̩ɪ, -ɪklɪ
metallurgy 'mɛtl̩ˌɝdʒɪ, mɛ'tælɚdʒɪ; ES
  -ˌɝdʒɪ, -ˌɝdʒɪ, -'tælədʒɪ
metamorphic ˌmɛtə'mɔrfɪk; ES -'mɔəfɪk
metamorphize ˌmɛtə'mɔrfaɪz; ES -'mɔə-; |-s
  -ɪz |-d -d
metamorphose ˌmɛtə'mɔrfoz, -fos; ES -'mɔə-;
  |-s -ɪz |-d -d, -t
metamorphosis ˌmɛtə'mɔrfəsɪs; ES -'mɔə-;
  |-ses -ˌsiz
metaphor 'mɛtəfɚ; ES 'mɛtəfə(r
metaphoric ˌmɛtə'fɔrɪk, -'far-, -'fɒr- |-al -l̩
  |-ally -l̩ɪ, -ɪklɪ
metaphysic ˌmɛtə'fɪzɪk |-al -l̩ |-ally -l̩ɪ, -ɪklɪ
metaphysician ˌmɛtəfə'zɪʃən
metapsychosis ˌmɛtəsaɪ'kosɪs, *less sensibly*
  mɪˌtæpsɪ'kosɪs
metastasis mə'tæstəsɪs |-ses -ˌsiz
metatarsal ˌmɛtə'tarsl̩; ES -'tɑːsl̩; |-sus -səs
  |-si -saɪ
metathesis mə'tæθəsɪs |-ses -ˌsiz

Metazoa ˌmɛtə'zoə
Metcalf, -e 'mɛtkæf; E+-kaf, -kɑf
Metchnikoff 'mɛtʃnɪˌkɔf, -ˌkɒf, -ˌkɑf
mete mit |meted 'mitɪd
Metellus mɪ'tɛləs |-'s -ɪz
metempsychosis mɛtəmsaɪ'kosɪs, məˌtɛmp-
  sɪ'kosɪs |-ses -siz
meteor 'mitɪɚ; ES 'mitɪ·ə(r; |-ite -ˌaɪt
meteoric ˌmitɪ'ɔrɪk, -'ar-, -'ɒr- |-al -l̩ |-ally
  -l̩ɪ, -ɪklɪ
meteorologic ˌmitɪərə'ladʒɪk, -ˌɔrə-, -ˌɑrə-,
  -ˌɒrə-; ES+-'lɒdʒɪk; |-al -l̩ |-ally -l̩ɪ, -ɪklɪ
meteorologist ˌmitɪə'ralədʒɪst; ES+-'rɒl-;
  |-gy -dʒɪ
meter, -tre 'mitɚ; ES 'mitə(r; |-(e)d -d
methane 'mɛθen |-nol 'mɛθəˌnol
metheglin mə'θɛglɪn
methinks mɪ'θɪŋks |methought mɪ'θɔt
method 'mɛθəd
methodic mə'θadɪk; ES+-'θɒd-; |-al -l̩ |-ally
  -l̩ɪ, -ɪklɪ
Methodism 'mɛθədˌɪzəm |-ist -ɪst
methodology ˌmɛθəd'alədʒɪ; ES+-'ɒl-
methought mɪ'θɔt
Methow 'mɛt·hau, mɛt'hau ('Metˌhow 'River)
Methuen *Mass* mɪ'θjuɪn, -'θɪu-, -ən; *surname*
  'mɛθjuɪn, -ən
Methuselah mə'θjuzlə, -'θɪuz-, -z|ə
methyl 'mɛθəl, -ɪl
methylamene ˌmɛθələ'min
methylate 'mɛθəˌlet |-lated -ˌletɪd
methylene 'mɛθəˌlin
meticulous mə'tɪkjələs
métier *Fr* me'tje
métis, métisse *Fr* me'tiːs
metonymy mə'tanəmɪ; ES -'tɒn-
metope 'mɛtəˌpi
metric 'mɛtrɪk |-al -l̩ |-ally -l̩ɪ, -ɪklɪ
metrician mɛ'trɪʃən, mə-
metrics 'mɛtrɪks |-trist -trɪst
metrology mɪ'tralədʒɪ; ES+-'trɒl-
metronome 'mɛtrəˌnom
metronomic ˌmɛtrə'namɪk; ES+-'nɒm-; |-al
  -l̩ |-ally -l̩ɪ, -ɪklɪ
metronymic ˌmitrə'nɪmɪk
metropolis mə'traplɪs, -plɪs; ES+-'trɒp-; |-es
  -ɪz
metropolitan ˌmɛtrə'palətn̩; ES+-'pɒl-

|full fʊl |tooth tuθ |further 'fɝðɚ; ES 'fɝðə |custom 'kʌstəm |while hwaɪl |how haʊ |toy tɔɪ
|using 'juzɪŋ |fuse fjuz, fɪuz |dish dɪʃ |vision 'vɪʒən |Eden 'idn̩ |cradle 'kredl̩ |keep 'em 'kipm̩

Metternich 'mɛtənɪk ES 'mɛtənɪk
mettle 'mɛtl̩ |-d -d |-some -səm
Metuchen mə'tʌtʃɪn, -ən
Metz mɛts |-'s -ɪz
Meung Fr mœ̃
Meuse mjuz, mɪuz |-'s -ɪz (Fr mø:z)
mew mju, mɪu |-ed -d
mewl mjul, mɪul |-ed -d
Mexia Tex mə'hiə, loc.+-'heə
Mexicali ˌmɛksɪ'kalɪ, -'kælɪ
Mexico 'mɛksɪˌko |-can -kən
Meyer 'maɪɚ; ES 'maɪ·ə(r; |-s -z
Meyerbeer 'maɪɚˌbɪr; ES 'maɪ·əˌbɪə(r; (Ger
  'maɪərˌbe:r)
Meynell 'mɛnl̩, 'mɛnl̩
Meyrick 'mɛrɪk, 'me-
mezzanine 'mɛzəˌnin, -nɪn
mezzo 'mɛtso, 'mɛzo, 'mɛdzo (It 'mɛddzo)
mezzo-soprano 'mɛtsosəˈprɑno, 'mɛzo-,
  'mɛdzo-, -'prɑno
mezzotint 'mɛtsəˌtɪnt, 'mɛzə-, 'mɛdzə- |-ed
  -ɪd
mho mo
mi mi
Miami maɪ'æmə, -'æmɪ
miaow, -ou mɪ'aʊ, mjaʊ |-ed -d
miasma maɪ'æzmə, mɪ- |-s -z |-mata -mətə
  |-l -ml̩
miasmatic ˌmaɪəz'mætɪk |-al -l̩ |-ally -l̩ɪ,
  -ɪklɪ
miaul mɪ'aʊl, mjaʊl |-ed -d
mib mɪb
mica 'maɪkə |-caceous, -cacious maɪ'keʃəs
Micah 'maɪkə |Micaiah maɪ'keə
Micawber mə'kɔbɚ; ES -'kɔbə(r
mice maɪs |mice's 'maɪsɪz
Michael 'maɪkl̩
Michaelmas 'mɪkl̩məs |-es -ɪz
Michaud, -chault, -chaut mɪ'ʃo (Fr mi'ʃo)
Michelangelo ˌmaɪkl̩'ændʒəˌlo, ˌmɪkl̩- (It
  ˌmiːkel'ɑndʒeˌlo)
Michelson 'maɪkl̩sn̩
Michigan 'mɪʃəgən |-der ˌmɪʃə'gændɚ; ES
  -də(r; Brit 'mɪtʃɪgən is not current in
  America.
Michiganite 'mɪʃəgənˌaɪt
mickle, M- 'mɪkl̩
Micmac 'mɪkmæk
microampere ˌmaɪkro'æmpɪr; ES -'æmpɪə(r

microanalysis ˌmaɪkroə'næləsɪs |-ses -ˌsiz
microbe 'maɪkrob
microbiology ˌmaɪkrobaɪ'alədʒɪ; ES+-'ɒl-
microcephalic ˌmaɪkrosə'fælɪk |-lous -'sɛfələs
microchemistry ˌmaɪkro'kɛmɪstrɪ
microcosm 'maɪkrəˌkazəm; ES+-ˌkɒz-
microfarad ˌmaɪkro'færəd, -'færæd
microfilm 'maɪkrəˌfɪlm |-ed -d
microgram 'maɪkroˌgræm
micrography maɪ'krɑgrəfɪ, -'krɒg-
micrometer tool maɪ'krɑmətɚ; ES -'krɑmə-
  tə(r, -'krɒm-
micrometer 'millionth of a meter' 'maɪkro-
  ˌmitɚ; ES -ˌmitə(r
micrometry maɪ'krɑmətrɪ; ES+-'krɒm-
micron 'maɪkrɑn; ES+-krɒn; |-s -z |-cra -krə
Micronesia ˌmaɪkrə'niʒə, -ʃə |-n -n
microorganism ˌmaɪkro'ɔrgənˌɪzəm; ES -'ɔə-
  gən-
microphone 'maɪkrəˌfon |-d -d
microphysics ˌmaɪkro'fɪzɪks
microscope 'maɪkrəˌskop |-d -t
microscopic ˌmaɪkrə'skɑpɪk; ES+-'skɒp-;
  |-al -l̩ |-ally -l̩ɪ, -ɪklɪ
microscopy maɪ'krɑskəpɪ, 'maɪkrəˌskopɪ; ES
  +-'krɒs-; |-pist -pɪst
microtomy maɪ'krɑtəmɪ; ES+'krɒt-
microvolt 'maɪkrəˌvolt
microwatt 'maɪkrəˌwat -ˌwɒt
micturate 'mɪktʃəˌret |-rated -ˌretɪd
micturition ˌmɪktʃə'rɪʃən
mid mɪd |-most -ˌmost |'mid mɪd
Midas 'maɪdəs |-'s -ɪz
midbrain 'mɪdˌbren
midday 'mɪdˌde, -'de
midden 'mɪdn̩
middle 'mɪdl̩ |-d -d |-ling 'mɪdl̩ɪŋ, 'mɪdlɪŋ
middle-aged 'mɪdl̩'edʒd ('middle-ˌaged 'man)
Middleboro 'mɪdl̩ˌbɝo, -ə; ES -ˌbɜr-, -ˌbʌr-,
  -ˌbɜ-
Middlebury 'mɪdl̩ˌbɛrɪ, -bərɪ
middleman 'mɪdl̩ˌmæn |-men -ˌmɛn
Middlemarch 'mɪdl̩ˌmartʃ; ES -ˌmɑːtʃ, E+
  -ˌmɑːtʃ
middler 'mɪdlɚ; ES 'mɪdlə(r
Middlesex 'mɪdl̩ˌsɛks |-'s -ɪz
Middleton 'mɪdl̩tən |-town -ˌtaʊn
middleweight 'mɪdl̩ˌwet
middling adj, adv, n 'mɪdlɪŋ

Midgard 'mɪd₁gɑrd; ES -₁gɑ:d, E+-₁gɑ:d
midge mɪdʒ |midges 'mɪdʒɪz
midget 'mɪdʒɪt
Midi *Fr* mi'di
Midian 'mɪdɪən |-ite -₁aɪt
midiron 'mɪd₁aɪɚn, -₁aɪrn; ES -₁aɪ·ən, -₁aɪən
midland, M- 'mɪdlənd
Midlothian mɪd'loðɪən
midmost 'mɪd₁most
midnight 'mɪd₁naɪt
midnoon 'mɪd'nun ('mid₁noon 'heat)
midrash, M- 'mɪdræʃ |-es -ɪz |*Heb pl* -im
  mɪd'rɑʃim |-oth -'rɑʃoθ
midrib 'mɪd₁rɪb |-bed -d
midriff 'mɪdrɪf
midship 'mɪd₁ʃɪp |-man -mən |-men -mən
midst mɪdst, mɪtst
midsummer, M- 'mɪd'sʌmɚ; ES -'sʌmə(r
midway, M- *n* 'mɪd₁we
midway *adv, adj* 'mɪd'we ('mid₁way 'out,
  'mid₁way 'air)
midweek 'mɪd'wik ('mid₁week 'meeting)
Midwest 'mɪd'wɛst ('Mid₁west 'custom)
Midwestern mɪd'wɛstɚn; ES -tən; |-er -ɚ;
  ES -ə(r
midwife 'mɪd₁waɪf |-wives -₁waɪvz |-wife's
  -waɪfs |-ry -ərɪ, -rɪ
midwinter 'mɪd'wɪntɚ; ES -'wɪntə(r
midyear 'mɪd₁jɪr; ES -₁jɪə(r, S+-₁jɛə(r
mien min
miff mɪf |miffed mɪft
might maɪt |-y -ɪ |-ily 'maɪt|ɪ, -ɪlɪ
mightest 'maɪtɪst
might-have-been *n* 'maɪtəv₁bɪn, 'maɪtə₁bɪn
mightn't 'maɪtn̩t, *before some conss.*+'maɪtn̩
  (mightn't go 'maɪtn̩'go)
mignon *'minion'* 'mɪnjən
mignon *'small'* 'mɪnjən, -jɒn (*Fr* mi'nõ)·
Mignon *Ala* 'mɪnjən; *in Goethe Fr* mi'nõ
mignonette ₁mɪnjən'ɛt
mignonne 'mɪnjən (*Fr* mi'nɔ̃n)
migraine 'maɪgren, mɪ'gren
migrant 'maɪgrənt
migrate 'maɪgret |-d -ɪd |-tion maɪ'greʃən
migratory 'maɪgrə₁torɪ, -₁tɔrɪ; S -₁torɪ
mikado, M- mə'kɑdo
mike, M- maɪk
mil mɪl
mil *Scand measure* mil

milady mɪ'ledɪ—*not current in America*
Milan *US* 'maɪlən; *Italy* mɪ'læn, 'mɪlən (*It*
  Milano mi'lɑ:no)
Milanese ₁mɪlən'iz
Milburn 'mɪlbɚn; ES 'mɪlbən
milch mɪltʃ
mild maɪld |-en -n̩ |-ened -n̩d |-ening -dn̩ɪŋ,
  -dnɪŋ
mildew 'mɪl₁dju, -₁dɪu, -₁du |-ed -d
Mildred 'mɪldrɪd
mile maɪl |-age -ɪdʒ |-ages -ɪdʒɪz
milepost 'maɪl₁post
Miles maɪlz |Miles's 'maɪlzɪz
Milesian mə'liʒən, -ʃən
milestone 'maɪl₁ston
Miletus maɪ'litəs |-'s -ɪz
milfoil 'mɪl₁fɔɪl
Milford 'mɪlfɚd; ES 'mɪlfəd
miliary 'mɪlɪ₁ɛrɪ, 'mɪljərɪ
Milicent 'mɪləsn̩t
milieu *Fr* mi'ljø
militant 'mɪlətənt |-tancy -tənsɪ
militarism 'mɪlətə₁rɪzəm |-rist -rɪst
militaristic ₁mɪlətə'rɪstɪk |-ally -[ɪ, -ɪklɪ
militarization ₁mɪlətərə'zeʃən, -trə-, -aɪ'z-
militarize 'mɪlətə₁raɪz |-s -ɪz |-d -d
military 'mɪlə₁tɛrɪ |-tate -₁tet |-tated -₁tetɪd
militia mə'lɪʃə |-man -mən |-men -mən
milk mɪlk |milked mɪlkt |-maid -₁med
milkman *retailer* 'mɪlk₁mæn |-men -₁mɛn
milkman *producer* 'mɪlkmən |-men -mən,
  -₁mɛn
milksop 'mɪlk₁sɑp; ES+-₁sɒp
milkweed 'mɪlk₁wid
mill, M- mɪl |-ed -d—*The* n *sound was lost
  from* mill (*OE* myln *'gristmill'*) *in the same
  way as from* ell, kiln, Milne.
Millais mɪ'le |-lais's -'lez |*pl* Millais mɪ'lez
Millard 'mɪlɚd; ES 'mɪləd
Millay mɪ'le
Millbourne 'mɪlbɚn; ES 'mɪlbən
Millburn 'mɪlbɚn; ES 'mɪlbən
Millbury 'mɪl₁bɛrɪ, -bərɪ
milldam 'mɪl₁dæm
Milledgeville 'mɪlɪdʒ₁vɪl; S+-v]̩
millenarian ₁mɪlə'nɛrɪən, -'ner- |-anism
  -₁ɪzəm
millenary 'mɪlə₁nɛrɪ
millennial mə'lɛnɪəl |-ly -ɪ |-alism -₁ɪzəm

---

millennium mə'lɛnɪəm |-s -z |-nia -nɪə

millepede 'mɪlə‚pid

miller, M- 'mɪlɚ; ES 'mɪlə(r; |-ite -‚aɪt

millet 'grass' 'mɪlɪt; relig. group+mɪ'lɛt

Millet Am painter 'mɪlɪt, Fr sculp., painter mɪ'le (Fr mi'lɛ, mi'jɛ)

milliampere ‚mɪlɪ'æmpɪr; ES -pɪə(r

milliard 'mɪljɚd, -jɑrd; ES -jəd, -jɑːd

Millicent 'mɪləsn̩t

Milligan 'mɪləgən

milligram 'mɪlə‚græm

Millikan 'mɪləkən

milliliter, -tre 'mɪlə‚litɚ; ES -‚litə(r

millimeter, -tre 'mɪlə‚mitɚ; ES -‚mitə(r

millimicron ‚mɪlə'maɪkrɑn; ES+-krɒn

milliner 'mɪlənɚ; ES 'mɪlənə(r; |-y -‚nɛrɪ, -nərɪ

million 'mɪljən |-th -θ |-ths -θs

millionaire ‚mɪljən'ɛr, -'ær; E -'ɛə(r, ES -'æə(r

millipede 'mɪlə‚pid

millpond 'mɪl‚pɑnd, -‚pɒnd, -‚pɔnd

millrace 'mɪl‚res |-s -ɪz

millstone 'mɪl‚ston

millstream 'mɪl‚strim

millwright 'mɪl‚raɪt

Miln, -e mɪl, mɪln—When the n sound is heard, it is a spelling pronunciation; see mill.

Milner 'mɪlnɚ; ES 'mɪlnə(r

Milnes mɪlz, mɪlnz |-'s -ɪz

Milo US name and places 'maɪlo; 'Melos' 'milo

milord mɪ'lɔrd; ES -'lɔəd;—not current in America

milreis coin 'mɪl‚res |pl same

milt, M- mɪlt |-ed -ɪd

Miltiades mɪl'taɪə‚diz |-'s -ɪz

Milton 'mɪltn̩ |-tonian mɪl'tonɪən

Miltonic mɪl'tɑnɪk; ES+-'tɒn-; |-ally -l̩ɪ

Milwaukee mɪl'wɔkɪ ('Mil‚waukee 'Road)

mime maɪm |mimed maɪmd

mimeograph, M- 'mɪmɪə‚græf; E+-‚graf, -‚grɑf; |-ed -t

mimeographic ‚mɪmɪə'græfɪk |-ally -l̩ɪ, -ɪklɪ

mimetic mɪ'mɛtɪk, maɪ- |-al -l̩ |-ally -l̩ɪ, -ɪklɪ

mimic 'mɪmɪk |-ked -t |-ally -l̩ɪ |-ry -rɪ

mimosa, M- mɪ'mosə, -zə

mina 'maɪnə |-s -z |-nae -ni

Mina 'maɪnə

minaret ‚mɪnə'rɛt, 'mɪnə‚rɛt |-ed -ɪd

minatorial ‚mɪnə'torɪəl, -'tɔr-; S -'tor-; |-ly -ɪ

minatory 'mɪnə‚torɪ, -‚tɔrɪ; S -‚torɪ

mince mɪns |minces 'mɪnsɪz |-d -t |-meat -‚mit

mind maɪnd |minded 'maɪndɪd |-ful -fəl |-fully -fəlɪ

mine n, v maɪn |mined maɪnd |pro maɪn

Mineola ‚mɪnɪ'olə

miner, M- 'maɪnɚ; ES 'maɪnə(r

mineral, M- 'mɪnərəl, 'mɪnrəl

mineralogic ‚mɪnərə'lɑdʒɪk; ES+-'lɒdʒ-; |-al -l̩ |-ally -l̩ɪ, -ɪklɪ

mineralogist ‚mɪnɚ'ælədʒɪst, -'al-; ES+-'ɒl-; |-gy -dʒɪ

Minerva mə'nɝvə; ES -'nɜvə, -'nɝvə

Ming mɪŋ

mingle 'mɪŋgl̩ |-d -d |-ling 'mɪŋglɪŋ, -gl̩ɪŋ

Mingo 'mɪŋgo

miniature 'mɪnɪtʃɚ, 'mɪnɪə-; ES -tʃə(r; |-d -d

Minie ball 'mɪnɪ‚bɔl (Fr mi'nje)

minify 'mɪnə‚faɪ |-fied -‚faɪd

minikin 'mɪnɪkɪn

minim 'mɪnɪm

minimal 'mɪnɪml̩ |-ly -ɪ

minimize 'mɪnə‚maɪz |-s -ɪz |-d -d

minimum 'mɪnəməm |-s -z |-ma -mə

minion, M- 'mɪnjən

minish 'mɪnɪʃ |-es -ɪz |-ed -t

minister 'mɪnɪstɚ; ES -tə(r; |-ed -d |-ing 'mɪnɪstərɪŋ, 'mɪnɪstrɪŋ

ministerial ‚mɪnəs'tɪrɪəl |-ly -ɪ

ministrant 'mɪnɪstrənt |-stry -strɪ

ministration ‚mɪnə'streʃən

miniver, M- 'mɪnəvɚ; ES 'mɪnəvə(r

mink mɪŋk

Minneapolis ‚mɪnɪ'æpl̩ɪs, -'æplɪs, -əs |-'s -ɪz

Minnehaha ‚mɪnɪ'hɑhɑ

minnesinger, M- 'mɪnɪ‚sɪŋɚ; ES -‚sɪŋə(r

Minnesota ‚mɪnɪ'sotə |-tan -tn̩

Minnewit 'mɪnjʊɪt, 'mɪnəwɪt=Minuit

Minnie 'mɪnɪ

minnow 'mɪno, -ə |minny 'mɪnɪ

minny-bass 'mɪnɪ‚bæs |-'s -ɪz

Minoan mɪ'noən

Minola 'mɪnələ

minor, M- 'maɪnɚ; ES 'maɪnə(r

Minorca mə'nɔrkə; ES -'nɔəkə; |-n -n

Minorite, m- 'mamə,raɪt
minority mə'nɔrətɪ, maɪ-, -'nɑr-, -'nɒr-
Minos 'mamɒs, -nɑs; ES+-nɒs; |-'s -ɪz
Minot 'maɪnət
Minotaur 'mɪnə,tɔr; ES -,tɔə(r
minster 'mɪnstɚ; ES 'mɪnstə(r
minstrel 'mɪnstrəl |-ed -d |-sy -sɪ
mint mɪnt |minted 'mɪntɪd |-age -ɪdʒ
minuend 'mɪnjʊ,ɛnd
minuet ,mɪnjʊ'ɛt |-ed -ɪd
Minuit 'mɪnjʊɪt, 'mɪnəwɪt=Minnewit
minus 'mamɒs |-es -ɪz
minuscule mɪ'nʌskjul, -kɪul
minute n, v 'mɪnɪt |-d -ɪd
minute 'small' mə'njut, maɪ-, -'nɪut, -'nut
minuteman 'mɪnɪt,mæn |-men -,mɛn
minutia mɪ'njuʃɪə, -'nɪu-, -'nu- |-tiae -ʃɪ,i
minx mɪŋks |minxes 'mɪŋksɪz
Miocene 'maɪə,sin |-cenic ,maɪə'sɛnɪk
Miquelon ,mɪkə'lɑn, -'lɒn (Fr mi'klõ)
Mirabeau 'mɪrə,bo (Fr mira'bo)
miracle 'mɪrəkḷ, 'mɪrɪ- |-d -d |-ling -klɪŋ,
   -kḷɪŋ
miraculous mə'rækjələs
Miraflores ,mɪrə'flores |-'s -ɪz
mirage mə'rɑʒ |-s -ɪz |-d -d
Miranda mə'rændə
mire maɪr; ES maɪə(r; |-d -d
Miriam 'mɪrɪəm, 'mɛrɪəm—cf Syracuse
mirk mɝk; ES mɝk, mɝk; |-some -səm |-y -ɪ
mirror 'mɪrɚ; ES 'mɪrə(r; |-ed -d
mirth mɝθ; ES mɝθ, mɝθ; |-ful -fəl |-fully
   -fəlɪ
miry 'maɪrɪ
Mirza 'mɝzə; ES 'mɝzə, 'mɝzə; (Pers
   'mirza)
misadventure ,mɪsəd'vɛntʃɚ; ES -tʃə(r; |-d -d
misalliance ,mɪsə'laɪəns |-s -ɪz
misanthrope 'mɪsən,θrop, 'mɪz-
misanthropic ,mɪsən'θrɑpɪk; ES+-'θrɒp-; |-al
   -ḷ |-ally -ḷɪ, -ɪklɪ
misanthropism mɪs'ænθrə,pɪzəm |-pist -pɪst
misanthropy mɪs'ænθrəpɪ
misapplication ,mɪsæplə'keʃən
misapply ,mɪsə'plaɪ |-ied -d
misapprehend ,mɪsæprɪ'hɛnd |-ed -ɪd
misapprehension ,mɪsæprɪ'hɛnʃən
misappropriate adj ,mɪsə'proprɪɪt
misappropriate v ,mɪsə'proprɪ,et |-d -ɪd

misappropriation ,mɪsə,proprɪ'eʃən
misbecoming ,mɪsbɪ'kʌmɪŋ
misbegotten ,mɪsbɪ'gɑtn̩; ES+-'gɒtn̩
misbehave ,mɪsbɪ'hev |-d -d |-vior -jɚ; ES
   -jə(r
misbelieve ,mɪsbə'liv, -bḷ'iv |-d -d |-r -ɚ; ES
   -ə(r
miscalculate mɪs'kælkjə,let |-d -ɪd
miscalculation ,mɪskælkjə'leʃən
miscall mɪs'kɔl |-ed -d
miscarriage mɪs'kærɪdʒ |-s -ɪz; in sense 'fail-
   ure'+-'kærɪdʒ
miscarry mɪs'kærɪ |-ied -d
miscegenation ,mɪsɪdʒə'neʃən
miscellaneous ,mɪsḷ'enɪəs, -njəs
miscellany 'mɪsḷ,enɪ
mischance mɪs'tʃæns; E+-'tʃɑns, -'tʃɑns; |-s
   -ɪz |-d -t
mischief 'mɪstʃɪf |-chievous -tʃɪvəs
miscolor mɪs'kʌlɚ; ES -'kʌlə(r; |-ed -d
misconceive ,mɪskən'siv |-d -d
misconception ,mɪskən'sɛpʃən
misconduct n mɪs'kɑndʌkt; ES+-'kɒn-
misconduct v ,mɪskən'dʌkt |-ed -ɪd
misconster 'misconstrue' Shak. mɪs'kɑnstɚ;
   ES -'kɑnstə(r, -'kɒn- |-ed -d
misconstruct ,mɪskən'strʌkt |-ed -ɪd
misconstruction ,mɪskən'strʌkʃən
misconstrue ,mɪskən'stru, -'strɪu, mɪs'kɑn-
   stru, -strɪu, ES+-'kɒn-; |-d -d
miscount mɪs'kaunt |-ed -ɪd
miscreance 'mɪskrɪəns |-cy -ɪ |-ant -ənt
miscreate ,mɪskrɪ'et |-d -ɪd |-tion -'eʃən
miscue mɪs'kju, -'kɪu |-d -d
misdate mɪs'det |-dated -'detɪd
misdeal mɪs'dil |-dealt -'dɛlt
misdeed mɪs'did
misdemean ,mɪsdɪ'min |-ed -d |-ant -ənt
misdemeanor ,mɪsdɪ'minɚ; ES -'minə(r
misdirect ,mɪsdə'rɛkt |-ed -ɪd |-ction -kʃən
misdo mɪs'du |-did -'dɪd |-done -'dʌn
misdoubt mɪs'daut |-ed -ɪd
mise miz, maɪz |-s -ɪz
misease mɪs'iz |-d -d
miser, M- 'maɪzɚ; ES 'maɪzə(r; |-ly -lɪ
miserable 'mɪzrəbḷ, -zərə- |-bly -blɪ
Miserere ,mɪzə'rɛrɪ, -'rɪrɪ
misericord, -e ,mɪzərɪ'kɔrd, mɪ'zɛrɪ,kɔrd; ES
   -ɔəd

---

misery ˈmɪzrɪ, ˈmɪzərɪ
misestimate mɪsˈɛstəˌmet |-mated -ˌmetɪd
misestimation ˌmɪsɛstəˈmeʃən, mɪsˌɛstə-
misfeasance mɪsˈfizns |-s -ɪz
misfire mɪsˈfaɪr; ES -ˈfaɪə(r; |-d -d
misfit mɪsˈfɪt |-ted -ɪd (ˈmisˌfit ˈsuit)
misfortune mɪsˈfɔrtʃən; ES -ˈfɔətʃ-; |-d -d
misgive mɪsˈgɪv |-gave -ˈgev |-given -ˈgɪvən
misgiving mɪsˈgɪvɪŋ
misgovern mɪsˈgʌvɚn; ES -ˈgʌvən; |-ed -d
misguide mɪsˈgaɪd |-d -ɪd |-dance -ns
mishandle mɪsˈhændl̩ |-d -d |-ling -dlɪŋ, -dl̩ɪŋ
mishap ˈmɪsˌhæp, mɪsˈhæp
Mishawaka ˌmɪʃəˈwɔkə
Mishnah, -na ˈmɪʃnə |Heb pl -nayoth ˌmɪʃna-
ˈjoθ
misinform ˌmɪsɪnˈfɔrm, ˌmɪsn̩-; ES -ˈfɔəm;
|-ed -d
misinformation ˌmɪsɪnfɚˈmeʃən; ES -fəˈme-
misinterpret ˌmɪsɪnˈtɚprɪt, ˌmɪsn̩-; ES -ˈtɜp-,
-ˈtɝp-; |-ed -ɪd
misinterpretation ˌmɪsɪnˌtɚprɪˈteʃən, ˌmɪsn̩-;
ES -ˌtɜp-, -ˌtɝp-
misjudge mɪsˈdʒʌdʒ |-s -ɪz |-d -d
mislabel mɪsˈlebl̩ |-ed -d |-ing -blɪŋ, -bl̩ɪŋ
mislay mɪsˈle |-laid -ˈled
mislead mɪsˈlid |-led -ˈlɛd
mismanage mɪsˈmænɪdʒ |-s -ɪz |-d -d
mismatch mɪsˈmætʃ |-es -ɪz |-ed -t
mismate mɪsˈmet |-mated -ˈmetɪd
misname mɪsˈnem |-named -ˈnemd
misnomer mɪsˈnomɚ; ES -ˈnomə(r; |-ed -d
|-ing -ˈnomərɪŋ, -ˈnomrɪŋ
misogamist mɪˈsagəmɪst; ES+-ˈsɒg-; |-my
-mɪ
misogynist mɪˈsadʒənɪst; ES+-ˈsɒdʒ-; |-ny
-nɪ
misplace mɪsˈples |-s -ɪz |-d -t
misplay mɪsˈple |-ed -d
misprint n mɪsˈprɪnt, ˈmɪsˌprɪnt
misprint v mɪsˈprɪnt |-ed -ɪd
misprision mɪsˈprɪʒən
misprize mɪsˈpraɪz |-s -ɪz |-d -d
mispronounce ˌmɪsprəˈnaʊns, -pɚ- |-s -ɪz
|-d -t
mispronunciation ˌmɪsprəˌnʌnsɪˈeʃən, -pɚ-,
-ʃɪ-
misquotation ˌmɪskwoˈteʃən
misquote mɪsˈkwot |-d -ɪd

misread mɪsˈrid |-read -ˈrɛd
misreport ˌmɪsrɪˈport, -ˈpɔrt; ES -ˈpoət,
E+-ˈpɔət; |-ed -ɪd
misrepresent ˌmɪsrɛprɪˈzɛnt |-ed -ɪd
misrepresentation ˌmɪsrɛprɪzɛnˈteʃən
misrule mɪsˈrul, -ˈrɪul |-d -d (ˈrule or ˈmis-
ˌrule)
miss, M- mɪs |misses ˈmɪsɪz |missed mɪst
missal ˈmɪsl̩
Missaukee mɪˈsɔkɪ
missay mɪsˈse |-said -ˈsɛd
misseem mɪsˈsim |-ed -d
misshape mɪsˈʃep, mɪʃˈʃep |-d -t |-n -ən
missile ˈmɪsl̩, -ɪl
mission ˈmɪʃən |-ed -d |-ary -ˌɛrɪ
Missisquoi mɪˈsɪskwɔɪ
Mississippi ˌmɪsəˈsɪpɪ, ˌmɪsːˈsɪpɪ (ˈMissis-
ˌsippi ˈRiver) |-an -ən
missive ˈmɪsɪv
Missoula mɪˈzulə
Missouri məˈzʊrɪ, -ˈzʊrə |-rian -rɪən
misspeak mɪsˈspik |-spoke -ˈspok |-spoken
-ˈspokən
misspell mɪsˈspɛl |-ed -d or -spelt -ˈspɛlt
misspend mɪsˈspɛnd |-spent -ˈspɛnt
misstate mɪsˈstet |-d -ɪd
misstep mɪsˈstɛp |-ped -t
mist mɪst |misted ˈmɪstɪd
mistakable məˈstekəbl̩ |-bly -blɪ
mistake məˈstek |-took mɪsˈtʊk |-n mə-
ˈstekən—mistook is less familiar than
mistake & was (were) mistaken; hence the
difference in syllable division.
mistaught mɪsˈtɔt
misteach mɪsˈtitʃ |-es -ɪz |-taught -ˈtɔt
mistell mɪsˈtɛl |-told -ˈtold
Mister, m- ˈmɪstɚ; ES ˈmɪstə(r; |-ed -d
misthink mɪsˈθɪŋk |-thought -ˈθɔt
mistime mɪsˈtaɪm |-d -d
mistletoe ˈmɪsl̩ˌto
mistook mɪsˈtʊk—see mistake
mistral wind ˈmɪstrəl, mɪsˈtral (Fr misˈtral)
Mistral poet, Fr misˈtral
mistranslate ˌmɪstrænsˈlet, -trænz- |-d -ɪd
mistreat mɪsˈtrit |-ed -ɪd
mistress ˈmɪstrɪs |-es -ɪz |-'s -ɪz
mistrial mɪsˈtraɪəl
mistrust mɪsˈtrʌst |-ed -ɪd; dial. in sense
'expect,' 'think' mɪˈstrʌst

Key: See in full §§3–47. bee bi |pity ˈpɪtɪ (§6) |rate ret |yet jɛt |sang sæŋ |angry ˈæŋ·grɪ
|bath bæθ; E baθ (§10) |ah ɑ |far fɑr |watch watʃ, wɒtʃ (§12) |jaw dʒɔ |gorge gɔrdʒ |go go

Those words below in which the ɑ sound is spelt o are often pronounced with ɒ in E and S

misunderstand ˌmɪsʌndɚˈstænd; ES -ʌndə-; |-stood -ˈstʊd

misusage mɪsˈjusɪdʒ, -zɪdʒ

misuse *n* mɪsˈjus |-uses -ˈjusɪz

misuse *v* mɪsˈjuz |-uses -ˈjuzɪz |-used -ˈjuzd

misword mɪsˈwɝd; ES -ˈwɜd, -ˈwɝd; |-ed -ɪd

miswrite mɪsˈraɪt |-wrote -ˈrot |-written -ˈrɪtn̩

Mitchell ˈmɪtʃəl

mite maɪt

miter, -tre ˈmaɪtɚ; ES ˈmaɪtə(r; |-(e)d -d

Mithras ˈmɪθræs |-ˈs -ɪz

Mithridates ˌmɪθrəˈdetiz |-tes' -tiz

mitigable ˈmɪtəgəbl̩

mitigate ˈmɪtəˌget |-d -ɪd |-tion ˌmɪtəˈgeʃən

mitosis mɪˈtosɪs |-toses -ˈtosiz

mitrailleur ˌmitreˈjɝ; ES -ˈjɜ(r, -ˈjɝ; (*Fr* miˈtraˈjœ:r)

mitrailleuse ˌmitreˈjɝz |-s -ɪz (*Fr* mitraˈjø:z)

mitral ˈmaɪtrəl

mitt mɪt |-en -ˈmɪtn̩ |-ened ˈmɪtn̩d

mittimus ˈmɪtəməs |-es -ɪz |-ed -t

mitzvah, mits- ˈmɪtsvɑ |*Heb pl* -voth -voθ

mix, M- mɪks |-es -ɪz |-ed -t |-edly -ɪdlɪ, -tlɪ

mixture ˈmɪkstʃɚ ES ˈmɪkstʃə(r

Mizpah, -peh ˈmɪzpə

mizzen ˈmɪzn̩ |-mast -məst, -ˌmæst; E+ -ˌmast, -ˌmɑst

mizzle ˈmɪzl̩ |-d -d |-ling ˈmɪzlɪŋ, -zlɪŋ

mnemonic niˈmɑnɪk |-al -ˈmɑnɪkl̩ |-ally -l̩ɪ, -ɪklɪ

Mnemosyne niˈmɑsn̩ˌi, -ˈmɑz-, -ˈmɒ-

Moab ˈmoæb |-ite ˈmoəbˌaɪt

moan mon |moaned mond |-ful -fəl |-fully -fəlɪ

moat mot |moated ˈmotɪd

mob mɑb |-bed -d

mobble '*muffle*' ˈmɑbl̩ |-d -d

Moberly ˈmobɚlɪ; ES ˈmobəlɪ

Mobile moˈbil (ˈMoˌbile ˈBay)

mobile ˈmobl̩, ˈmobil, -bɪl |-bility moˈbɪlətɪ

mobilization ˌmoblə̩ˈzeʃən, -aɪˈz-

mobilize ˈmoblˌ̩aɪz |-s -ɪz |-d -d

moble '*muffle*' ˈmɑbl̩ |-d -d

moble '*movable*' ˈmobl̩

Mobridge ˈmobrɪdʒ |-ˈs -ɪz

Moby Dick ˈmobɪˈdɪk

moccasin ˈmɑkəsn̩, -zn̩ |-ed -d

Mocha ˈmokə

mock mɑk, mɒk, mɔk |-ed -t |-ery -ərɪ—mɔk is widespread in the N and C, and not infrequent in the E and S.

mock-heroic ˈmɑkhɪˈroˌɪk, ˈmɒk-, ˈmɔk- |-al -l̩ |-ally -l̩ɪ, -ɪklɪ

mockingbird ˈmɑkɪŋˌbɝd, ˈmɒk-, ˈmɔk-; ES -ˌbɜd, -ˌbɝd

modal ˈmodl̩ |-ly -ɪ |-ity moˈdælətɪ

mode mod

model ˈmɑdl̩ |-ed -d |-ing ˈmɑdl̩ɪŋ, ˈmɑdlɪŋ

moderate *n, adj* ˈmɑdərɪt, ˈmɑdrɪt

moderate *v* ˈmɑdəˌret |-d -ɪd |-tor -ɚ; ES -ə(r

moderation ˌmɑdəˈreʃən

modern ˈmɑdɚn; ES ˈmɑdən, *esp. attrib.* ˈmɑdn̩

modernism ˈmɑdɚnˌɪzəm; ES ˈmɑdən-, -dn̩-

modernity mɑˈdɝnətɪ, mo-; ES -ˈdɜn-, -ˈdɝn-

modernization ˌmɑdɚnəˈzeʃən, -aɪˈz-; ES ˌmɑdən-, -dn̩-

modernize ˈmɑdɚnˌaɪz; ES ˈmɑdən-, -dn̩-; |-s -ɪz |-d -d

modernness ˈmɑdɚnnɪs; ES ˈmɑdənnɪs, ˈmɑdn̩nɪs

modest ˈmɑdɪst |modesty ˈmɑdəstɪ

Modesto moˈdɛsto

modicum ˈmɑdɪkəm |-s -z

modifiable ˈmɑdəˌfaɪəbl̩ |-bly -blɪ

modification ˌmɑdəfəˈkeʃən

modify ˈmɑdəˌfaɪ |-fied -ˌfaɪd

modish ˈmodɪʃ

modiste moˈdist (*Fr* mɔˈdist)

Modjeska məˈdʒɛskə

Modoc ˈmodɑk

Modred ˈmodrɪd

modulate ˈmɑdʒəˌlet |-d -ɪd |-tor -ɚ; ES -ə(r

modulation ˌmɑdʒəˈleʃən

module ˈmɑdʒul, -dʒɪul

modulus ˈmɑdʒələs |-es -ɪz |-li -ˌlaɪ

modus operandi ˈmodəsˌɑpəˈrændaɪ

modus vivendi ˈmodəsvɪˈvɛndaɪ

Moeso-Gothic, Moesog- ˌmisoˈgɑθɪk, -ˈgɒθɪk

Moffat, -et, -tt ˈmɑfɪt, -ət

Mogador ˌmɑgəˈdor, -ˈdɔr; ES -ˈdoə(r, E+-ˈdɔə(r; *Ohio* ˈMogaˌdore

Mogul ˈmogʌl, moˈgʌl (ˈGreat ˈMoˈgul)

mohair ˈmoˌhɛr, -ˌhær; E -ˌhɛə(r, ES -ˌhæə(r

Mohammed moˈhæmɪd |-an -ˈhæmədən

Mohave, -jave moˈhɑvɪ (*Am Sp* moˈhaβe)

Those words below in which the ɑ *sound is spelt* ɔ *are often pronounced with* ɒ *in E and S*

Mohawk ˈmohɔk
Mohican moˈhikən
Mohock ˈmohak, -hɔk
Mohonk moˈhɑŋk, -ˈhɒŋk
moidore ˈmɔɪdor, -dɔr; ES -doə(r, E+-dɔə(r
moiety ˈmɔɪətɪ, ˈmɔjətɪ
moil mɔɪl |moiled mɔɪld
Moira ˈmɔɪrə
moire mwɑr, mwɔr, mor, mɔr; ES mwɑ:(r, mwɔə(r, moə(r, E+mɔə(r
moist mɔɪst
moisten ˈmɔɪsn̩ |-ed -d |-ing ˈmɔɪsn̩ɪŋ, -snɪŋ
moisture ˈmɔɪstʃɚ; ES ˈmɔɪstʃə(r
Mojave moˈhɑvɪ (*Am Sp* moˈhɑβe)
molar ˈmolɚ; ES ˈmolə(r
molasses məˈlæsɪz
mold mold |-ed -ɪd |-y -ɪ
Moldavia malˈdevɪə, -vjə |-n -n
moldboard ˈmoldˌbord, ˈmol-, -ˌbɔrd, *dial.* ˈmʌl-; ES -ˌboəd, E+-ˌbɔəd
molder ˈmoldɚ; ES ˈmoldə(r; |-ed -d |-ing ˈmoldrɪŋ, ˈmoldərɪŋ
moldwarp ˈmoldˌwɔrp; ES -ˌwɔəp
mole mol |moled mold
Mole ˈmole
molecular məˈlɛkjələ; ES -ˈlɛkjələ(r
molecule ˈmɑləˌkjul, -ˌkɪul
molehill ˈmolˌhɪl |moleskin -ˌskɪn
molest məˈlɛst |-ed -ɪd
molestation ˌmɑləsˈteʃən, ˌmɑl-
Moliére ˌmolɪˈɛr, -lˈjɛr; ES -ɛə(r; (*Fr* mȯ-ˈljɛːr)
Moline moˈlin
Moll mɑl, mɒl, mɔl |-y -ɪ
mollification ˌmɑləfəˈkeʃən
mollify ˈmɑləˌfaɪ |-fied -ˌfaɪd
mollusk, -sc ˈmɑləsk |-ed -t |-scan məˈlʌskən
mollycoddle ˈmɑlɪˌkɑdl̩ |-d -d |-ling -ˌkɑdlɪŋ, -ˌkɑdl̩ɪŋ
Moloch ˈmolɑk
Moloney, -ny məˈlonɪ
molt molt |molted ˈmoltɪd; |*N Engd*+mɔlt (*§46*)
molten ˈmoltn̩
Moltke ˈmoltkə (*Ger* ˈmɔltkə)
Molucca məˈlʌkə |-n -n |-s -z
moly ˈmolɪ
molybdenum məˈlɪbdənəm, ˌmɑlɪbˈdinəm

molybdic məˈlɪbdɪk |-dite -daɪt
Molyneux ˈmɑlɪˌnuks, -ˌnju, -ˌnɪu, -ˌnu |-x's -ˌnuksɪz, -ˌnjuz, -ˌnɪuz, -ˌnuz
Mombasa mɑmˈbæsə, -ˈbɑsə
Momence moˈmɛns |-'s -ɪz
moment ˈmomənt |-mentary -mənˌtɛrɪ
momentaneous ˌmomənˈtenɪəs
momentarily ˈmomənˌtɛrəlɪ, *esp. if emph.* ˌmomənˈtɛrəlɪ
momentous moˈmɛntəs |-tum -təm |-tums -təmz |-ta -tə
Mommsen ˈmɑmsn̩, -zn̩ (*Ger* ˈmɔmzən)
Momus ˈmoməs |-'s -ɪz
Monaca ˈmɑnəkə
monachal ˈmɑnəkl̩ |-chism -ˌkɪzəm
monacid mɑnˈæsɪd
Monaco ˈmɑnəˌko
monad ˈmɑnæd, ˈmonæd
Monadnoc *poem* məˈnædnɑk |*mt.* -nock -nɑk
Monaghan ˈmɑnəgən, ˈmɑnəhən, -xən
Mona Lisa ˈmonəˈlizə, ˈmɑnə- (*It* ˈmonaˈliːza)
monandric məˈnændrɪk |-drous -drəs |-dry -drɪ
monarch ˈmɑnɚk; ES ˈmɑnək; |-ed -t
monarchal məˈnɑrkl̩; ES -ˈnɑːkl̩, E+-ˈnɑːkl̩; |-ly -ɪ |-chial -kɪəl
monarchic məˈnɑrkɪk; ES -ˈnɑːk-, E+-ˈnɑːk-; |-al -l̩ |-ally -l̩ɪ, -ɪklɪ
monarchy ˈmɑnɚkɪ; ES ˈmɑnəkɪ; |-chism -ˌkɪzəm |-chist -kɪst
monastery ˈmɑnəsˌtɛrɪ |-rial ˌmɑnəˈstɪrɪəl
monastic məˈnæstɪk |-al -l̩ |-ally -l̩ɪ, -ɪklɪ
monasticism məˈnæstəˌsɪzəm
Monboddo mɑnˈbado
Monckton ˈmʌŋktən
Monday ˈmʌndɪ—*spelt* Mundy *in 1647, cf* Friday
Monel, m- moˈnɛl
Monet moˈne (*Fr* mȯˈnɛ)
monetary ˈmʌnəˌtɛrɪ, ˈmɑnə-
monetize ˈmʌnəˌtaɪz, ˈmɑnə- |-s -ɪz |-d -d
money ˈmʌnɪ |-s -nies -z |-ed, -nied -d
moneybag ˈmʌnɪˌbæg
monger ˈmʌŋgɚ; ES ˈmʌŋgə(r; |-ing -grɪŋ, -gərɪŋ
Mongol ˈmɑŋgəl, -gal, -gol
Mongolia mɑŋˈgolɪə, man-, -ljə |-n -n

Key: *See in full §§3–47.* bee bi |pity ˈpɪtɪ (§6) |rate ret |yet jɛt |sang sæŋ |angry ˈæŋ·grɪ |bath bæθ; E baθ (§10) |ah ɑ |far fɑr |watch wɑtʃ, wɒtʃ (§12) |jaw dʒɔ |gorge gɔrdʒ |go go

Those words below in which the ɑ sound is spelt o are often pronounced with ɒ in E and S

mongoose, -goos 'maŋgus, 'mʌŋ-, 'man-
|-(e)s -ɪz
mongrel 'mʌŋgrəl, 'maŋ-, 'man-, -grɪl
'mongst mʌŋst, mʌŋkst
Monhegan man'higən
Monica, m- 'manɪkə
monied 'mʌnɪd |monies 'mʌnɪz
moniker, -icker 'manɪkɚ; ES 'manɪkə(r
monish 'manɪʃ |-es -ɪz |-ed -t
monism 'manɪzəm, 'mon- |-ist -ɪst
monistic mo'nɪstɪk |-al -ļ |-ally -ļɪ, -ɪklɪ
monition mo'nɪʃən
monitor 'manətɚ; ES 'manətə(r; |-ed -d |-ing
-tərɪŋ, -trɪŋ
monitory 'manəˌtorɪ, -ˌtɔrɪ; S -ˌtorɪ
monk mʌŋk |-craft -ˌkræft; E+-ˌkraft,
-ˌkraft
monkey 'mʌŋkɪ |-ed -d |-shine -ˌʃaɪn
Monkwearmouth 'mʌŋk'wɪrməθ; ES -'wɪə-
məθ
Monmouth 'manməθ |-shire -ˌʃɪr, -ʃɚ; ES
-ˌʃɪə(r, -ʃə(r
Monna Lisa 'manə'lizə (It 'mɔna'li:za)
monniker 'manɪkɚ; ES 'manɪkə(r
monoacid ˌmano'æsɪd
monobasic ˌmanə'besɪk
Monocacy mə'nakəsɪ
monocarpous ˌmanə'karpəs; ES -'ka:pəs,
E+-'ka:p-
monochord 'manəˌkɔrd; ES -ˌkɔəd
monochrome 'manəˌkrom
monocle 'manəkļ |-d -d
monoclinal ˌmanə'klaɪnļ |-ly -ɪ |-nous -nəs
monocline 'manəˌklaɪn
monoclinic ˌmanə'klɪnɪk
monocotyledon ˌmanəˌkatļ'idn̩ |-ous -'idn̩əs,
-'ɛdn̩əs
monocracy mo'nakrəsɪ
monody 'manədɪ
monogamist mə'nagəmɪst |-mous -məs |-my
-mɪ
monogram 'manəˌgræm |-med -d
monograph 'manəˌgræf; E+-ˌgraf, -ˌgraf;
|-ed -t
monolith 'manļˌɪθ |-ths -θs |-ic ˌmanļ'ɪθɪk
monologue, -log 'manļˌɔg, -ˌag, -ˌɒg |-d,
-ged -d
monomania ˌmanə'menɪə, -njə |-iac -ɪˌæk

monometallic ˌmanəmə'tælɪk
monometallism ˌmanə'mɛtļˌɪzəm |-ist -ɪst
monomial mo'nomɪəl
Monona mə'nonə
Monongahela məˌnaŋgə'hilə, -ˌnan-
Monongalia ˌmonən'gelɪə
monophthong 'manəfˌθɔŋ, 'manəˌθ-, -ˌθɒŋ
monophthongal ˌmanəf'θɔŋgļ, -ə'θ-, -ɒŋ-, -ŋļ
monophthongize 'manəfθɔŋˌaɪz, 'manəθ-,
-θɒŋˌgaɪz, -θɒŋ- |-s -ɪz |-d -d
monoplane 'manəˌplen
monopolism mə'napļˌɪzəm |-ist -ɪst
monopolization məˌnapļə'zeʃən, -aɪ'z-
monopolize mə'napļˌaɪz |-s -ɪz |-d -d
monopoly mə'napļɪ, -'naplɪ
monorail 'manəˌrel
monorailroad 'manəˌrelrod |-railway -ˌrelwe
monosyllabic ˌmanəsɪ'læbɪk |-al -ļ |-ally -ļɪ,
-ɪklɪ
monosyllabism ˌmanə'sɪləˌbɪzəm
monosyllable 'manəˌsɪləbļ
monotheism 'manəθiˌɪzəm |-ist -ˌθiɪst
monotheistic ˌmanəθi'ɪstɪk |-al -ļ |-ally -ļɪ,
-ɪklɪ
monotone 'manəˌton
monotonous mə'natņəs |-tony -tņɪ
monotype 'manəˌtaɪp
Monroe mən'ro |-rovia -'rovɪə
Monseigneur, m- ˌmansen'jɚ; ES -'jɜ(r, -'jɝ;
(Fr mõsɛ'ɲœ:r)
Monsieur, m- mə'sjɚ; ES -'sjɜ(r; (Fr mə'sjø)
Monsignor, m- man'sinjɚ; ES -jə(r; (It
monsiɲ'ɲo:re)
Monson 'mʌnsṇ
monsoon man'sun |-al -ļ
monster 'manstɚ; ES 'manstə(r; |-ed -d
monstrance 'manstrəns |-s -ɪz
monstrous 'manstrəs |-strosity man'strasətɪ
Montagu, -e 'mantəˌgju, -ˌgɪu
Montaigne man'ten
Montana man'tænə |-n -n
Montano man'tæno
Montauk man'tɔk ('Monˌtauk 'Point)
Mont Blanc mant'blæŋk, mɒnt- (Fr mõ'blã)
Montcalm mant'kam
Montclair mant'klɛr, -'klær; E -'klɛə(r, ES
-'klæə(r
Montebello ˌmantə'bɛlo

Those words below in which the ɑ sound is spelt o are often pronounced with ɒ in E and S

Monte Carlo ˌmantɪˈkarlo; ES -ˈkaː-, E+ -ˈkaː-

Monte Cristo, Montecristo ˌmantɪˈkrɪsto

Montenegro ˌmantəˈnigro |-grin -ˈnigrɪn

Monterey, -rrey ˌmantəˈre (*Am Sp* ˌmontɛ-ˈrrɛi)

Montesquieu ˌmantəˈskju, -ˈskɪu (*Fr* mõtɛs-ˈkjø)

Montessori ˌmantəˈsorɪ, -ˈsɔrɪ; S -ˈsorɪ (*It* ˌmontesˈsoːri)

Montevideo *US* ˌmantəˈvɪdɪˌo; *Uru*+ˌmantəvɪˈdeo (*Am Sp* ˌmonteβiˈðeo)

Montezuma ˌmantəˈzumə

Montferrat ˌmantfəˈræt (*It* ˌmonferˈraːto, *Fr* mõfɛˈra)

Montgomery mantˈgʌmrɪ, -ˈgʌmərɪ |-shire -ˌʃɪr, -ʃɚ; ES -ˌʃɪə(r, -ʃə(r

month mʌnθ |months mʌnθs, mʌnts

Monticello ˌmantəˈsɛlo, -ə (*It* ˌmontiˈtʃɛllo)

Montmorency *US, Can, France* ˌmantmə-ˈrɛnsɪ (*Fr* mõmõrã̃ˈsi)

Montour manˈtur; ES -ˈtuə(r

Montpelier mantˈpiljɚ; ES -ˈpiljə(r

Montpellier *France* mantˈpɛlɪˌe (*Fr* mõpəˈlje, -pɛ-)

Montreal ˌmantrɪˈɔl, ˌmʌnt-

Montrose mantˈroz |-'s -ɪz

Mont-Saint-Michel *Fr* mõsæ̃miˈʃɛl

Montserrat ˌmantsəˈræt (*Sp* ˌmontsɛˈrrat)

monument *n* ˈmanjəmənt

monument *v* ˈmanjəˌmɛnt |-mented -ˌmɛntɪd

monumental ˌmanjəˈmɛntl̩ |-ly -ɪ

moo mu |mooed mud

mooch mutʃ |mooches ˈmutʃɪz |mooched mutʃt

mood mud |moody, M- ˈmudɪ

moolly, mooly ˈmulɪ, ˈmulɪ

moon, M- mun |mooned mund |-beam -ˌbim

mooncalf ˈmunˌkæf; E -ˌkaf, -ˌkɑf, -ˌkæf; |-lves -vz

mooneye ˈmunˌaɪ |moon-eyed ˈmunˌaɪd

moonlight ˈmunˌlaɪt |-ed -ɪd *or* -lit -ˌlɪt

moonrise ˈmunˌraɪz |-s -ɪz

moonset ˈmunˌsɛt

moonshine ˈmunˌʃaɪn |-shined -ˌʃaɪnd

moonstone ˈmunˌston

moon-struck ˈmunˌstrʌk

moor, M- mur; ES muə(r; |-ed -d |-age -ɪdʒ

Moore mor, mɔr, mur; ES moə(r, muə(r, E+mɔə(r

Moorehead ˈmurˌhɛd, ˈmor-, ˈmɔr-; ES ˈmuə-, ˈmoə-, E+ˈmɔə-

Moorgate ˈmurˌget, ˈmor-, ˈmɔr-; ES ˈmuə-, ˈmoə-, E+ˈmɔə-; *loc.* -gɪt

Moorhead ˈmorˌhɛd, ˈmɔr-, ˈmur-; ES ˈmoə-, ˈmuə-, E+ˈmɔə-

Moorish ˈmurɪʃ

moose mus |moose's ˈmusɪz

Moosehead ˈmusˌhɛd

Moosilauke ˈmusˌl̩ˌɔk, ˌmusˈl̩ˌɔkɪ

moot mut |mooted ˈmutɪd

mop map |-ped -t

mope mop |moped mopt

moppet ˈmapɪt

Mopsa ˈmapsə

moraine moˈren |-nal -l̩ |-nic -ɪk

moral ˈmɔrəl, ˈmar-, ˈmɒr- |-ly -ɪ |-ist -ɪst

morale məˈræl, mo-, mɔ-, -ˈral (*Fr* mɔ̈ˈral)

morality mɔˈrælətɪ, ma-, mɒ-, mə-, mo-

moralize ˈmɔrəlˌaɪz, ˈmar-, ˈmɒr- |-s -ɪz |-d -d

moralless ˈmɔrəllɪs, ˈmar-, ˈmɒr-

Moran moˈræn, mɔ-, mə-, ˈmorən, ˈmɔr-; S mo-, mə-, ˈmor-

morass moˈræs, mɔ-, mə-; S mo-, mə-; |-es -ɪz

moratorium ˌmɔrəˈtorɪəm, ˌmar-, ˌmɒr-, -ˈtɔr-; S -ˈtorɪəm

Moravia moˈrevɪə, mə- |-n -n

Moray *Scotl* ˈmɜɪ (*Sc* ˈmʌre); ES ˈmɜrɪ, ˈmʌrɪ, ˈmɜɪ; *Am fem. name often* ˈmorɪ, ˈmɔrɪ

moray ˈmore, moˈre, ˈmo-, mɔ-; S ˈmo-, mo-

morbid ˈmɔrbɪd; ES ˈmɔəbɪd

morbidity mɔrˈbɪdətɪ; ES mɔˈbɪdətɪ

mordacious mɔrˈdeʃəs; ES mɔə-

mordancy ˈmɔrdn̩sɪ; ES ˈmɔədn̩sɪ; |-dant -dn̩t

Mordecai ˌmɔrdɪˈkeaɪ, ˈmɔrdɪˌkaɪ; ES -ɔədɪ-

mordent ˈmɔrdn̩t; ES ˈmɔədn̩t

more, M- mor, mɔr; ES moə(r, E+mɔə(r

morel, M- məˈrɛl, mo-, ma-, mɒ-

Moreland ˈmorlənd, ˈmɔr-; ES ˈmoə-, E+ˈmɔə-

Moreno məˈrino

more or less ˈmorəˈlɛs, ˈmorəˈlɛs, ˈmɔr-; ES ˈmorəˈlɛs, E+ˈmɔrə- —*In the 2d pron.* ɚ *becomes* ə *by dissimilation* (§121).

Key: *See in full* §§3–47. bee bi |pity ˈpɪtɪ (§6) |rate ret |yet jɛt |sang sæŋ |angry ˈæŋ·grɪ |bath bæθ; E baθ (§10) |ah ɑ |far fɑr |watch watʃ, wɒtʃ (§12) |jaw dʒɔ |gorge gɔrdʒ |go go

moreover mor'ovɚ, mɔr-; ES mor'ovə(r,
  E+mɔr-
mores 'moriz, 'mɔr-; S 'mor-
Morgan 'mɔrgən; ES 'mɔəgən
morganatic ˌmɔrgə'nætɪk; ES ˌmɔəg-; |-al -|
  |-ally -|ɪ, -ɪklɪ
Morganton 'mɔrgəntən; ES 'mɔəg-; |-town
  -ˌtaʊn
Morgenthau 'mɔrgənˌθɔ; ES 'mɔəg-; (Ger
  'mɔrgənˌtaʊ)
morgue mɔrg; ES mɔəg
Moriah mə'raɪə, mo-
Moriarty ˌmɔrɪ'artɪ, ˌmar-, ˌmɒr-; ES -'ɑːtɪ
moribund 'mɔrəˌbʌnd, 'mar-, 'mɒr-, -bənd
moribundity ˌmɔrə'bʌndətɪ, ˌmar-, ˌmɒr-
Morisco, m- mə'rɪsko
Morison 'mɔrəsn̩, 'mar-, 'mɒr-
Morland 'mɔrlənd; ES 'mɔələnd
Morley 'mɔrlɪ; ES 'mɔəlɪ
Mormon 'mɔrmən; ES 'mɔəmən; |-ism -ˌɪzəm
morn mɔrn; ES mɔən; |-ing -ɪŋ
Morocco, m- mə'rako; ES+-'rɒko; |-can -kən
moron 'moran, 'mɔr-; S 'mor-, ES+-ɒn
moronic mo'ranɪk, mɔ-; S mo-, ES+-'rɒn-
morose mo'ros, mə-
morpheme 'mɔrfim; ES 'mɔə-; |-mic mɔr-
  'fimɪk; ES mɔə-
Morpheus 'mɔrfɪəs, -fjus; ES 'mɔəf-; |-'s -ɪz
morphine 'mɔrfin; ES 'mɔəfin
morphology mɔr'falədʒɪ; ES mə'fal-, -'fɒl-
Morris, m- 'mɔrɪs, 'mar-, 'mɒr- |-'s -ɪz
Morrison 'mɔrəsn̩, 'mar-, 'mɒr-
Morristown 'mɔrɪsˌtaʊn, 'mar-, 'mɒr-
morrow, M- 'mɔro, 'mar-, 'mɒr-, -ə
Morse mɔrs; ES mɔəs; |-'s -ɪz
morsel 'mɔrsl̩; ES 'mɔəsl̩; |-ed -d
mort mɔrt; ES mɔət
mortal 'mɔrtl̩; ES 'mɔətl̩; |-ly -ɪ
mortality mɔr'tælətɪ; ES mɔ-
mortar 'mɔrtɚ; ES 'mɔətə(r; |-ed -d
mortarboard 'mɔrtɚˌbord, -ˌbɔrd; ES 'mɔətə-
  ˌboəd, E+-ˌbɔəd
Morte d'Arthur, Mort Darthur 'mɔrt'darθɚ;
  ES 'mɔət'dɑːθə(r; (Fr mɔrtdar'tyːr)
mortgage 'mɔrgɪdʒ; ES 'mɔə-; |-s -ɪz |-d -d
mortgagee ˌmɔrgɪ'dʒi; ES ˌmɔə-
mortgagor, -er 'mɔrgɪdʒɚ; ES 'mɔəgɪdʒə(r;
  (ˌmortga'gee & ˌmortga'gor -'dʒɔr)
mortice 'mɔrtɪs; ES 'mɔə-; |-s -ɪz |-d -t

mortification ˌmɔrtəfə'keʃən; ES ˌmɔətə-
mortify 'mɔrtəˌfaɪ; ES 'mɔətə-; |-fied -ˌfaɪd
Mortimer 'mɔrtəmɚ; ES 'mɔətəmə(r
mortise 'mɔrtɪs; ES 'mɔə-; |-s -ɪz |-d -t
mortmain 'mɔrtmen; ES 'mɔət-; |-ed -d
Morton 'mɔrtn̩, 'mɔrtn̩; ES 'moətn̩, E+
  'mɔətn̩
mortuary 'mɔrtʃʊˌɛrɪ; ES 'mɔətʃʊ-
Mosaic, m- mo'ze·ɪk |-al -| |-ally -|ɪ, -ɪklɪ
Mosby 'mozbɪ
Moschus 'maskəs, 'mɒs-; |-'s -ɪz
Moscow Id 'masko, 'mɒs-; Russia -kaʊ, -ko
Moseley 'mozlɪ
Moselle mo'zɛl
Moses 'mozɪz, -əz, -əs, -ɪs—'mozəz & 'mozəs
  are less freq. in the S.
Moslem 'mazləm, 'mas-; ES+'mɒ-
mosque mask, mɒsk, mɔsk
mosquito mə'skito, -ə
moss, M- mas, mɒs |-es -ɪz |-ed -t |-back -ˌbæk
most most; N Engd+mŏst (§46)
mot Fr mo
mote arch. v mot |past moste most, mod. must
mote n mot |moted 'motɪd
motet mo'tɛt
moth maθ, mɒθ |-ths -ðz, -θs |-th's -θs
mother 'mʌðɚ; ES 'mʌðə(r; |-ed -d |-ing
  'mʌðrɪŋ, 'mʌðərɪŋ
mother-in-law 'mʌðərɪnˌlɔ, 'mʌðɚnˌlɔ; ES
  'mʌðərɪn'lɔ, 'mʌðən'lɔ
motherland 'mʌðɚˌlænd; ES 'mʌðə-
mothers-in-law 'mʌðɚzɪnˌlɔ, 'mʌðɚznˌlɔ; ES
  'mʌðəzɪnˌlɔ, 'mʌðəznˌlɔ
moths maðz, mɒðz, -θs
mothy 'maθɪ, 'mɒθɪ
motif mo'tif
motile 'motl̩, 'motɪl
motion 'moʃən |-ed -d
motivate 'motəˌvet |-d -ɪd |-tion ˌmotə'veʃən
motive 'motɪv |-d -d
mot juste Fr mo'ʒyst
motley, M- 'matlɪ; ES+'mɒt-
motor 'motɚ; ES 'motə(r; |-ed -d |-y -ɪ
motorboat 'motɚˌbot; ES 'motə-
motorbus 'motɚˌbʌs; ES 'motə-; |-(s)es -ɪz
motorcar 'motɚˌkar; ES 'motəˌkɑː(r, E+
  -ˌkɑː(r
motorcycle 'motɚˌsaɪkl̩; ES 'motə-; |-d -d
  |-ling -ˌsaɪklɪŋ, -ˌsaɪkl̩ɪŋ

|full fʊl |tooth tuθ |further 'fɝðɚ; ES 'fɝðə |custom 'kʌstəm |while hwaɪl |how haʊ |toy tɔɪ
|using 'juzɪŋ |fuse fjuz, fɪuz |dish dɪʃ |vision 'vɪʒən |Eden 'idn̩ |cradle 'kredl̩ |keep 'em 'kipm̩

motorman ˈmotɚmən; ES ˈmotəmən; |-men
 -mən
Motteux mɑˈtju, mɒ-, -ˈtɪu, -ˈtu (Fr mɔˈtø)
mottle ˈmɑtl̩; ES+ˈmɒtl̩; |-d -d |-ling -tl̩ɪŋ,
 -tlɪŋ
motto ˈmɑto, -ə; ES+ˈmɒt-; |-ed -d
mouch ˈmutʃ |mouches ˈmutʃɪz |mouched
 mutʃt
moue Fr mu
Moukden mukˈdɛn, ˈmukdən
mould mold |-ed -ɪd |-y -ɪ
mouldboard ˈmoldˌbord, ˈmol-, -ˌbɔrd, dial.
 ˈmʌl-; ES -ˌbo͟əd, E+-ˌbɔəd
moulder ˈmoldɚ; ES ˈmoldə(r; |-ed -d |-ing
 ˈmoldrɪŋ, ˈmoldərɪŋ
mouldwarp ˈmoldˌwɔrp; ES -ˌwɔəp
Moulmein maulˈmen, mɔl-, mol-
moult molt |moulted ˈmoltɪd; |N Engd+mɔ̈lt
 (§46)
Moulton ˈmoltn̩
Moultrie US places ˈmoltrɪ, Fort & general
 ˈmutrɪ, ˈmultrɪ (formerly spelt Moutrie)
mound, M- maund |mounded ˈmaundɪd
Mounseer 'Monsieur' arch. & humorous
 maunˈsɪr; ES -ˈsɪə(r
mount, M- maunt |mounted ˈmauntɪd
mountain ˈmauntn̩, -tɪn, -tən |-ous -əs
mountaineer ˌmauntn̩ˈɪr, -tɪn-, -tən-; ES
 -ˈɪə(r, S+-ˈɛə(r
mountainside ˈmauntn̩ˌsaɪd, -tɪn-, -tən-
Mount Desert ˌmauntdɪˈzɝt, -ˈdɛzɚt; ES
 -ˈzɝt, -ˈzɜt; (ˈMount ˌDesert ˈIsland)
mountebank ˈmauntəˌbæŋk
Mountjoy ˈmauntdʒɔɪ
mourn morn, mɔrn; ES moən, E+mɔən;
 |-ed -d
mouse n maus |-'s -ɪz |mice maɪs |mice's -ɪz
mouse v mauz |mouses ˈmauzɪz |moused
 mauzd
mousehole ˈmausˌhol |Mousehole Cornw
 ˈmauzl̩
mouser ˈmauzɚ; ES ˈmauzə(r; |-y ˈmausərɪ,
 -srɪ
mousse mus |mousses ˈmusɪz
moustache ˈmʌstæʃ, məˈstæʃ |-s -ɪz |-d -t
mousy ˈmausɪ, ˈmauzɪ
mouth n mauθ |-th's -θs |-ths -ðz
mouth v mauð |mouthed mauðd |-y ˈmauðɪ,
 -θɪ

mouthful ˈmauθˌful |-fuls -ˌfulz
mouthpiece ˈmauθˌpis |-s -ɪz
movability, movea- ˌmuvəˈbɪlətɪ
movable, movea- ˈmuvəbl̩ |-bly -blɪ
move muv |moved muvd |movie ˈmuvɪ
mow 'haymow' mau |mowed maud
mow 'reap' mo |mowed mod |mowed mod or
 mown mon
mow 'grimace' mau, mo |-ed -d
Mowbray ˈmobrɪ
mower 'mowing machine' ˈmoɚ; ES ˈmo·ə(r
Mower ˈmauɚ; ES ˈmau·ə(r
Mowgli ˈmauglɪ
mown mon
Mozambique ˌmozəmˈbik
Mozart ˈmozɑrt; ES -zɑːt; (Ger ˈmoːtsart)
Mr. ˈmɪstɚ; ES ˈmɪstə(r
Mrs. ˈmɪsɪz, -əz, ˈmɪsɪs, -əs; S ˈmɪzɪz, mɪz:
 —Some speakers say ˈmɪsɪs before voiceless
 sounds, and ˈmɪsɪz before voiced (ˈmɪsɪs
 ˈpræt, ˈmɪsɪz ˈbraun).
mu Gk letter mju, mɪu, mu; Chin meas. mu
much mʌtʃ
mucid ˈmjusɪd, ˈmɪusɪd
mucilage ˈmjusl̩ɪdʒ, ˈmɪu-, -slɪdʒ
mucilaginous ˌmjuslˈædʒənəs, ˌmɪusl̩-
muck mʌk |mucked mʌkt
muckle ˈmʌkl̩
muckrake ˈmʌkˌrek |-raked -ˌrekt
mucous ˈmjukəs, ˈmɪu- |mucus ˈmjukəs,
 ˈmɪu-
mud mʌd |mudded ˈmʌdɪd |-dy -ɪ |-died -ɪd
muddle ˈmʌdl̩ |-d -d |-ling ˈmʌdlɪŋ, -dl̩ɪŋ
muddleheaded ˈmʌdl̩ˈhɛdɪd (ˈmuddleˌheaded
 ˈJoe)
mudguard ˈmʌdˌgɑrd; ES -ˌgɑːd, E+-ˌgɑːd
mudsill ˈmʌdˌsɪl
muezzin mjuˈɛzɪn, mɪu-
muff mʌf |muffed mʌft
muffin ˈmʌfɪn
muffle ˈmʌfl̩ |-d -d |-ling ˈmʌflɪŋ, ˈmʌfl̩ɪŋ
muffler ˈmʌflɚ; ES ˈmʌflə(r
mufti ˈmʌftɪ
mug mʌg |mugged mʌgd |-gy -ɪ |-wump
 -ˌwʌmp
Muhammad muˈhæməd |-an -ən
Muhlenberg ˈmjulənˌbɝg, ˈmɪu-; ES -ˌbɝg,
 -ˌbɜg
Muir mjur, mɪur |-head -ˌhɛd

Mukden mʊk'dɛn, 'mʊkdən	multitudinous ˌmʌltə'tjudn̩əs, -'tɪud-, -'tud-
mulatto mə'læto, mju-, mɪu-, -ə	multivalence ˌmʌltə'veləns, mʌl'tɪvə- |-cy -ɪ
mulberry, M- 'mʌlˌbɛɪɪ, -bəɪɪ	|-lent -lənt
Mulcaster 'mʌlkæstɚ; ES -kæstə(r	Multnomah mʌlt'nomə
mulch mʌltʃ |mulches 'mʌltʃɪz |mulched	mum, mumm mʌm |mummed mʌmd
mʌltʃt	mumble 'mʌmbl̩ |-d -d |-ling 'mʌmblɪŋ, -b‌l̩ɪŋ
mulct mʌlkt |mulcted 'mʌlktɪd	Mumbo Jumbo 'mʌmbo'dʒʌmbo
mule mjul, mɪul |-lish -ɪʃ	mummer 'mʌmɚ; ES 'mʌmə(r; |-y -ɪ
muleteer ˌmjulə'tɪr; ES -'tɪə(r, S+-'tɛə(r	mummify 'mʌmɪˌfaɪ |-fied -ˌfaɪd
muley 'mjulɪ, 'mɪu-, 'mʊlɪ, 'mulɪ	mummy 'mʌmɪ |mummied 'mʌmɪd
mull mʌl |mulled mʌld	mumps mʌmps
mullah, M-, -la 'mʌlə, 'mʊlə	munch mʌntʃ |munches 'mʌntʃɪz |munched
mullein, -len 'mʌlɪn, -ən	mʌntʃt
Mullens, -ins 'mʌlɪnz, -ənz |-'s -ɪz	Munchausen mʌn'tʃɔzn̩ ('Munˌchausen 'tales)
Muller 'mʌlɚ; ES 'mʌlə(r	Muncie 'mʌnsɪ |Muncy 'mʌnsɪ
Müller, Max 'mæks'mɪlɚ; ES -'mɪlə(r; (Ger	mundane 'mʌnden
'maks'mylər)	Munday 'mʌndɪ
mullet 'mʌlɪt	Munhall 'mʌnhɔl
mulley 'mʊlɪ, 'mulɪ	Munich 'mjunɪk, 'mɪu- (Ger München
mulligatawny ˌmʌlɪgə'tɔnɪ	'mynxən)
mulligrubs 'mʌlɪˌgrʌbz	municipal mju'nɪsəpl̩, mɪu- |-ly -pl̩ɪ, -plɪ
mullion 'mʌljən |-ed -d	municipality ˌmjunɪsə'pælətɪ, ˌmɪu-, mju-
Mulock 'mjulək, 'mɪu-, -lak; ES+-lɒk	ˌnɪsə-, mɪu-
multicellular ˌmʌltɪ'sɛljəlɚ; ES -'sɛljələ(r	munificence mju'nɪfəsn̩s, mɪu- |-cy -ɪ |-nt
multifarious ˌmʌltɪ'fɛɪɪəs, -'fær-, -'fer-	-sn̩t
multifold 'mʌltəˌfold	muniment 'mjunəmənt, 'mɪu-
multiform 'mʌltəˌfɔrm; ES -ˌfɔəm	munition mju'nɪʃən, mɪu- |-ed -d
multigraph, M- 'mʌltəˌgræf; E+-ˌgraf, -ˌgraf	Munro, -roe mən'ro
multilateral ˌmʌltɪ'lætərəl |-ly -ɪ	Munsey 'mʌnsɪ, -zɪ
multilingual ˌmʌltɪ'lɪŋgwəl	Munson 'mʌnsn̩
multimillionaire ˌmʌltəˌmɪljən'ɛr, -'ær; E	Munster 'mʌnstɚ; ES 'mʌnstə(r
-'ɛə(r, ES -'æə(r	Münster 'mɪnstɚ; ES 'mɪnstə(r; (Ger
multinuclear ˌmʌltɪ'njuklɪɚ, -'nɪu-, -'nu-; ES	'mynstər)
-lɪ‌ə(r	Münsterberg 'mɪnstɚˌbɝg; ES 'mɪnstəˌbɜg,
multiparous mʌl'tɪpərəs	'mɪnstəˌbɝg; (Ger 'mynstərˌbɛrk)
multiped 'mʌltəˌpɛd |-pede -ˌpid	mural 'mjurəl, 'mɪurəl |-ly -ɪ
multiphase 'mʌltəˌfez	Murat Am name mju'ræt, mɪu-, Fr general
multiple 'mʌltəpl̩ |-plex -ˌplɛks	mju'ræt, mɪu-, my'ra (Fr my'ra)
multiplicand ˌmʌltəplɪ'kænd	murder 'mɝdɚ; ES 'mɜdə(r, 'mɝdə(r; |-ed -d
multiplicate 'mʌltəplɪˌket	|-ing -dərɪŋ, -drɪŋ
multiplication ˌmʌltəplə'keʃən, ˌmʌltəpə- —	murderer 'mɝdərɚ; ES 'mɜdərə(r, 'mɝdərə(r
In the 2d pron. the 2d l is lost by l-dissimila-	murderous 'mɝdərəs, -drəs; ES 'mɜd-, 'mɝd-
tion (§121).	murex, M- 'mjurɛks, 'mɪu- |-es -ɪz |-rices
multiplicity ˌmʌltə'plɪsətɪ	-rəˌsiz
multiplier 'mʌltəˌplaɪɚ; ES -ˌplaɪ‌ə(r	Murfreesboro 'mɝfrɪzˌbɚo, -ə; ES 'mɝfrɪz-
multiply v 'mʌltəˌplaɪ |-plied -ˌplaɪd	ˌbɜr-, 'mɝf-, -ˌbʌr-, -ˌbɝ-
multiply adv 'mʌltəplɪ, -plɪ	muriate 'mjurɪˌet, 'mɪu-, -ɪt |-d -ˌetɪd
multipolar ˌmʌltə'polɚ; ES -'polə(r	muriatic ˌmjurɪ'ætɪk, ˌmɪu- ('muriˌatic 'acid)
multitude 'mʌltəˌtjud, -ˌtɪud-, -ˌtud	Muriel 'mjurɪəl, 'mɪu-

\|full fʊl \|tooth tuθ \|further 'fɝðɚ; ES 'fɝðə \|custom 'kʌstəm \|while hwaɪl \|how haʊ \|toy tɔɪ
\|using 'juzɪŋ \|fuse fjuz, fɪuz \|dish dɪʃ \|vision 'vɪʒən \|Eden 'idn̩ \|cradle 'kredl̩ \|keep 'em 'kipm̩

Murillo mju'rɪlo, mɪu- (Sp mu'riʎo)

murk mɝk; ES mɜk, mɝk; |-some -səm |-y -ɪ

murmur 'mɝmɚ; ES 'mɜmə(r, 'mɝmə(r; |-ed
-d |-ing -mrɪŋ, -mərɪŋ

Murphy 'mɝfɪ; ES 'mɜfɪ, 'mɝfɪ

Murphysboro 'mɝfɪz‚bɝo, -ə; ES 'mɜfɪz-
‚bɜr-, 'mɝf-, -‚bʌr-, -‚bɝ-

murrain 'mɝɪn; ES 'mɜrɪn, 'mʌrɪn, 'mɝrɪn;
|-ed -d

Murray 'mɝɪ; ES 'mɜrɪ, 'mʌrɪ, 'mɝɪ

murrey 'mɝɪ; ES 'mɜrɪ, 'mʌrɪ, 'mɝɪ

murther 'mɝðɚ; ES 'mɜðə(r, 'mɝðə(r; |-ed -d
|-ing -ðərɪŋ, -ðrɪŋ

muscadine 'mʌskədɪn, -‚daɪn

muscat 'mʌskət, -kæt

muscatel ‚mʌskə'tɛl ('musca‚tel 'wine)

Muscatine ‚mʌskə'tin

muscle, M- 'mʌsl̩ |-d -d |-ling 'mʌslɪŋ, -sl̩ɪŋ

Muscoda ‚mʌskə'de

Muscogee mʌs'kogɪ

Muscovy 'mʌskəvɪ |-vite -‚vaɪt

muscular 'mʌskjəlɚ; ES 'mʌskjələ(r

muscularity ‚mʌskjə'lærətɪ

musculature 'mʌskjələtʃɚ; ES -tʃə(r

muse, M- mjuz, mɪuz |-s -ɪz |-d -d

museum mju'zɪəm, mɪu-, -'zɪəm, 'mjuzɪəm,
'mɪu-

mush mʌʃ |-es -ɪz |-ed -t

mushroom 'mʌʃrum, -rʊm, less freq. -run

music 'mjuzɪk, 'mɪu- |-al -l̩ |-ally -l̩ɪ, -ɪklɪ

musicale ‚mjuzɪ'kæl, ‚mɪu- (Fr myzi'kal)

musician mju'zɪʃən, mɪu-

musicologist ‚mjuzɪ'kalədʒɪst, ‚mɪu-; ES+
-'kɒl-; |-gy -dʒɪ

musk mʌsk |musked mʌskt

muskallonge 'mʌskə‚landʒ, -‚lɒndʒ |-s -ɪz

Muskegon mʌs'kigən

muskellunge, -kall- 'mʌskə‚lʌndʒ |-s -ɪz

musket 'mʌskɪt |-ry -rɪ

musketeer ‚mʌskə'tɪr; ES -'tɪə(r, S+-'tɛə(r

Muskingum mʌs'kɪŋgəm, recently+mʌs'kɪŋ-
əm

muskmelon 'mʌsk‚mɛlən

Muskogee mʌs'kogɪ

muskrat 'mʌsk‚ræt, 'mʌs‚kræt

muslin 'mʌzlɪn

musquash 'mʌskwɑʃ, -kwɒʃ |-es -ɪz

muss mʌs |musses 'mʌsɪz |mussed mʌst

mussel 'mʌsl̩ |-ed -d

Musset mə'se (Fr my'sɛ)

Mussolini ‚mus'l̩'inɪ, ‚mus- (It ‚musso'li:ni)

Mussulman 'mʌsl̩mən |-s -z or -men -mən

must stressed 'mʌst, ‚mʌst; unstr. məst, before
conss.+məs (‚wi məs 'go)

mustache 'mʌstæʃ, mə'stæʃ |-s -ɪz |-d -t

mustachio mə'stɑʃo |-ed -d

Mustafa Kemal, -pha 'mʌstəfəkə'mal, -'kemal

mustang 'mʌstæŋ

mustard 'mʌstɚd; ES 'mʌstəd

muster 'mʌstɚ; ES 'mʌstə(r; |-ed -d |-ing
'mʌstərɪŋ, 'mustrɪŋ

mustn't 'mʌsn̩t, before some conss.+'mʌsn̩
('mʌsn̩ 'du ɪt)

mutability ‚mjutə'bɪlətɪ, ‚mɪutə-

mutable 'mjutəbl̩, 'mɪut- |-bly -blɪ

mutate 'mjutet, 'mɪu- |-tated - tetɪd

mutation mju'teʃən, mɪu-

mutatis mutandis mju'tetɪs mju'tændɪs,
mɪu'tetɪs mɪu-

mute mjut, mɪut |-d -ɪd

mutilate 'mjutl̩‚et, 'mɪu- |-d -ɪd

mutilation ‚mjutl̩'eʃən, ‚mɪu-

mutineer ‚mjutn̩'ɪr, ‚mɪut-; ES -'ɪə(r, S+
-'ɛə(r, -'jɛə(r; |-ed -d

mutinous 'mjutn̩əs, 'mɪut- |-ny -n̩ɪ

Mutius 'mjuʃəs, 'mɪu-, -ʃɪəs |-'s -ɪz

mutt mʌt

mutter 'mʌtɚ; ES 'mʌtə(r; |-ed -d |-ing
'mʌtərɪŋ, 'mʌtrɪŋ

mutton, M- 'mʌtn̩—The pron. 'mʌtən is not
in general use.

mutual 'mjutʃʊəl, 'mɪu- |-ly -ɪ

mutuality ‚mjutʃu'ælətɪ, ‚mɪu-

muzhik, -zjik mu'ʒik, 'muʒik

muzzle 'mʌzl̩ |-d -d |-ling 'mʌzlɪŋ, 'mʌzl̩ɪŋ

my stressed 'maɪ, ‚maɪ; unstr. before vowels
məɪ, before conss. mə, Brit stage sometimes
mɪ

Mycenae maɪ'sini |-naean ‚maɪsɪ'niən

mycologist maɪ'kalədʒɪst; ES+-'kɒl-; |-gy
-dʒɪ

Myer 'maɪɚ; ES 'maɪ·ə(r; |-s -z |-s's -zɪz

Mynheer, m- maɪn'her, -'hɪr; ES -'hɛə(r,
-'hɪə(r; (Du mijnheer mə'ne:r)

myocardiograph ‚maɪo'kardɪə‚græf; ES -'ka:-
dɪə-, E+-‚graf, -‚grɑf, -'ka:d-

myope 'maɪop |myopia maɪ'opɪə

Key: See in full §§3–47. bee bi |pity 'pɪtɪ (§6) |rate ret |yet jɛt |sang sæŋ |angry 'æŋ·grɪ
|bath bæθ; E baθ (§10) |ah ɑ |far fɑr |watch watʃ, wɒtʃ (§12) |jaw dʒɔ |gorge gɔrdʒ |go go

myopic maɪ'apɪk; ES+-'ɒp-; |-al -| |-ally -|ɪ,
  -ɪklɪ
myosis maɪ'osɪs
myosotis ˌmaɪə'sotɪs |-es -ɪz
Myra 'maɪrə
myriad 'mɪrɪəd
myriapod 'mɪrɪəˌpad; ES+-ˌpɒd
Myrick 'maɪrɪk, 'merɪk
Myrmidon, m- 'mɝməˌdan, -dən; ES
  'mɝmə-, 'mɝmə-, -ˌdɒn
Myron 'maɪrən
myrrh mɝ; ES mɝ(r, mɝ; |-ed -d |-ic -ɪk,
  'mɪrɪk
Myrrha 'mɪrə
Myrtle, m- 'mɝt|; ES 'mɝt|, 'mɝt|
myself mə'self, maɪ'self
Mysia 'mɪʃɪə |-n -n
Mysore maɪ'sor, -'sɔr; ES -'soə(r, E+-'sɔə(r

mysterious mɪs'tɪrɪəs, mɪ'stɪrɪəs
mystery 'trade' 'mɪstərɪ
mystery 'secret' 'mɪstrɪ, 'mɪstərɪ
mystic, M- 'mɪstɪk |-al -| |-ally -|ɪ, -ɪklɪ
mysticism 'mɪstəˌsɪzəm
mystification ˌmɪstəfə'keʃən
mystify 'mɪstəˌfaɪ |-fied -ˌfaɪd
myth mɪθ |-ths -θs
mythic 'mɪθɪk |-al -| |-ally -|ɪ, -ɪklɪ
mythological ˌmɪθə'ladʒɪk|; ES+-'lɒdʒ-; |-ly
  -ɪ, -ɪklɪ
mythologist mɪ'θalədʒɪst; ES+-'θɒl-; |-gy
  -dʒɪ
mythologize mɪ'θaləˌdʒaɪz; ES+-'θɒl-; |-s -ɪz
  |-d -d
Mytilene ˌmɪt|'inɪ
myxedema, -oedema ˌmɪksɪ'dimə
myxoid 'mɪksɔɪd

N

N, n *letter* ɛn |*pl* N's, Ns, *poss* N's ɛnz
Naaman 'neəmən, 'nemən
Naamathite 'neəməˌθaɪt
nab næb |nabbed næbd
Nabal 'neb|
nabob 'nebab; ES+'nebɒb
Naboth 'nebaθ; ES+'nebɒθ
nacelle nə'sɛl
Nacogdoches ˌnækə'dotʃɪz |-es' -tʃɪz
nacre 'nekɚ; ES 'nekə(r
nadir 'nedɚ; ES 'nedə(r
nag næg |nagged nægd
Nagasaki ˌnægə'sakɪ, ˌnagə'sakɪ
Nahant nə'hænt; E+nə'hant, nə'hant
Nahuatl 'nawat| |Nahuatlan 'nawatlən
Nahum 'neəm, 'nehʌm
naiad 'neæd, 'naɪæd, -əd |-s -z |-es -əˌdiz
naïf na'if |naïfs na'ifs=naïve
nail nel |nailed neld
Nain 'ne·ɪn, nen
nainsook 'nensʊk, 'nænsʊk
Nairn nɛrn, nærn, nern; ES næən, neən,
  E+neən; |-shire -ʃɪr, -ʃɚ; ES -ʃɪə(r, -ʃə(r
Naismith 'nesmɪθ
naïve na'iv |naïveté naˌiv'te, na'ivte
naked 'nekɪd, *old fash.* 'nɛkɪd

namable, nameable 'neməb| |-bly -blɪ
namby-pamby 'næmbɪ'pæmbɪ ('namby-
  ˌpamby 'air)
name nem |named nemd |namely 'nemlɪ
Nameoki ˌnæmɪ'okɪ
namesake 'nemˌsek
Namur 'nemʊr; ES 'nemʊə(r; (*Fr* na'my:r)
Nanchang 'næn'tʃæŋ (*Chin* 'nan'tʃaŋ)
Nancy *pers. name* 'nænsɪ; *France* 'nænsɪ (*Fr*
  nã'si)
nankeen, -kin næn'kin
Nanking næn'kɪŋ |Nankin næn'kɪn
Nannette næn'ɛt
Nannie 'nænɪ |nanny-goat 'nænɪˌgot
Nansemond 'nænsɪmənd
Nansen 'nænsṇ (*Norw* 'nansən)
Nantasket næn'tæskɪt
Nantes nænts |-'s -ɪz (*Fr* nã:t)
Nanticoke 'næntɪˌkok
Nanti-Glo 'næntɪ'glo
Nantucket næn'tʌkɪt ('Nanˌtucket 'coast)
Naomi 'neəˌmaɪ, ne'omaɪ, -mɪ, -mə
nap næp |napped næpt
Napa 'næpə
Napanee 'næpəˌni
nape nep, næp

Naperville ˈnepɚˌvɪl; ES ˈnepə-
napery ˈnepərɪ, ˈneprɪ
Naphtali ˈnæftəˌlaɪ
naphtha ˈnæpθə, ˈnæfθə
naphthalene ˈnæfθəˌlin, ˈnæp-
naphthene ˈnæfθin, ˈnæp-
naphthol ˈnæfθol, ˈnæp-, -θɔl, -θɒl, -θɑl
Napier ˈnepɪɚ, ˈnepjɚ, nəˈpɪr; ES ˈnepɪ·ə(r, ˈnepjə(r, nəˈpɪə(r
Napierville ˈnepɪɚˌvɪl, -pjɚ-; ES ˈnepɪ·ə-, -pjə-
napkin ˈnæpkɪn |napkined ˈnæpkɪnd
Naples ˈnepļz |-'s -ɪz
napoleon, N- nəˈpoljən, nəˈpoliən
Napoleonic nəˌpolɪˈɑnɪk; ES+-ˈɒnɪk
Nappanee ˈnæpəˌni, ˌnæpəˈni
Narbonne narˈban; ES naːˈban, -ˈbɒn; (Fr narˈbɔ̃n)
narceine, -in ˈnarsɪˌin, -ɪn; ES ˈnaːs-
narcism ˈnarˌsɪzəm; ES ˈnaːˌsɪzəm
narcissism narˈsɪsˌɪzəm; ES naˈsɪsˌɪzəm
Narcissus narˈsɪsəs; ES naːˈs-; |-sus' -səs
narcosis narˈkosɪs; ES naːˈkosɪs
narcotic narˈkatɪk; ES naːˈkatɪk, -ˈkɒtɪk
narcoticism narˈkatəˌsɪzəm; ES naˈkat-, -ˈkɒt-
narcotism ˈnarkəˌtɪzəm; ES ˈnaːk-
nard nard; ES naːd
narghile, -gile ˈnargəlɪ, -ˌle; ES ˈnaːg-
Nares nɛrz, nærz; E nɛəz, ES næəz; |-'s -ɪz
naris ˈnerɪs |pl nares ˈneriz
Narragansett ˌnærəˈgænsɪt
narrate næˈret, ˈnæret |-d -ɪd
narration næˈreʃən |narrative ˈnærətɪv
narrow ˈnæro, ˈnærə |-ed -d |-ing ˈnærəwɪŋ |-er ˈnærəwɚ; ES -wə(r; |-est ˈnærəwɪst
narrow-gauge ˈnæroˈgedʒ, ˈnærə-
narrowish ˈnærəwɪʃ
narrow-minded ˈnæroˈmaɪndɪd, ˈnærə- (ˈnarrow-ˌminded ˈhate)
narthex ˈnarθɛks; ES ˈnaːθ-; |-es -ɪz
Narvaez Sp narˈβa·eθ
Narvik ˈnarvɪk; ES ˈnaːvɪk
narwhal, -e, -wal ˈnarhwəl, -wəl; ES ˈnaː-
nasal ˈnezļ |-ly -ɪ
nasalization ˌnezļəˈzeʃən, -aɪˈz-
nasalize ˈnezļˌaɪz |-s -ɪz |-d -d
Nasby ˈnæzbɪ
nascency ˈnæsņsɪ |nascent ˈnæsņt

Naseby ˈnezbɪ
Nash(e) næʃ |-'s ˈnæʃɪz
Nashua ˈnæʃuə, loc.+ˈnæʃəˌwe
Nashville ˈnæʃvɪl; S+ˈnæʃvļ
Nasmyth ˈnesmɪθ
Nassau US ˈnæsɔ, Germany ˈnasau
Nast næst
nasturtium næˈstɝʃəm, nə-; ES -ˈstɝʃ-, -ˈstɝʃ-
nasty ˈnæstɪ; E+ˈnastɪ, ˈnastɪ
natal ˈnetļ
Natal S Afr nəˈtæl, Braz nəˈtɑl
Natalie ˈnætlɪ, ˈnetļɪ (Fr nataˈli)
natant ˈnetṇt |natation neˈteʃən
natatorial ˌnetəˈtorɪəl, -ˈtɔr-; S -ˈtor-
natatorium ˌnetəˈtorɪəm, -ˈtɔr-; S -ˈtor-; |-s -z |-ria -rɪə
natatory ˈnetəˌtorɪ, -ˌtɔrɪ; S -ˌtorɪ
Natches ˈnætʃɪz |Natches' ˈnætʃɪz
Natchitoches ˈnækɪˌtɑʃ |-'s -ɪz
Nathan ˈneθən |-iel nəˈθænjəl
natheless, -thless arch. ˈneθlɪs, ˈnæθlɪs
Natick ˈnetɪk
nation ˈneʃən |-hood -ˌhud
national ˈnæʃənļ, ˈnæʃnəl |-ism -ˌɪzəm |-ist -ɪst |-ly -ɪ
nationalistic ˌnæʃənļˈɪstɪk, -ʃnəl- |-al -ļ |-ally -ļɪ, -ɪklɪ
nationality ˌnæʃənˈælətɪ
nationalize ˈnæʃənļˌaɪz, -ʃnəl- |-s -ɪz |-d -d
native ˈnetɪv
nativity neˈtɪvətɪ, nə-
Natrona nəˈtronə
natty ˈnætɪ
natural ˈnætʃərəl, ˈnætʃrəl |-ly -ɪ
naturalism ˈnætʃərəlˌɪzəm, ˈnætʃrəl- |-ist -ɪst
naturalize ˈnætʃərəlˌaɪz, ˈnætʃrəl- |-s -ɪz |-d -d
nature ˈnetʃɚ; ES ˈnetʃə(r
Naugatuck ˈnɔgəˌtʌk
naught nɔt |naughty ˈnɔtɪ
nausea ˈnɔʒə, ˈnɔzɪə, ˈnɔsɪə, ˈnɔʃɪə, ˈnɔʃə, ˈnɔʒɪə
nauseate ˈnɔʒɪˌet, ˈnɔzɪ-, ˈnɔsɪ-, ˈnɔʃɪ-
nauseous ˈnɔʒəs, ˈnɔzɪəs, ˈnɔsɪəs, ˈnɔʃəs
Nausicaä nɔˈsɪkɪə
nautch nɔtʃ |nautches ˈnɔtʃɪz
nautical ˈnɔtɪkļ |-ly -ɪ
nautilus ˈnɔtļəs |nautiluses ˈnɔtļəsɪz
Nauvoo nɔˈvu

Key: *See in full §§3–47.* bee bi |pity ˈpɪtɪ (§6) |rate ret |yet jɛt |sang sæŋ |angry ˈæŋ·grɪ |bath bæθ; E baθ (§10) |ah ɑ |far far |watch watʃ, wɒtʃ (§12) |jaw dʒɔ |gorge gɔrdʒ |go go

Navaho, -jo 'nævə,ho
naval 'nevḷ |-ly -ɪ
Navarino ,nævə'rino (*It* ,navaˈriːno)
Navarre nə'var; ES nə'vaː(r, E+-'vaː(r
nave nev
navel 'nevḷ
Navesink 'nævə,sɪŋk, 'nevə-, 'nɛvə-
navigability ,nævəgə'bɪlətɪ
navigable 'nævəgəbḷ |-bly -blɪ
navigate 'nævə,get |-d -ɪd |-tor -tɚ; ES -tə(r
navigation ,nævə'geʃən
navvy 'nævɪ
navy 'nevɪ
nawab nə'wab, nə'wɔb
nay ne
Nazarene ,næzə'rin ('Naza,rene 'Gospel)
Nazareth 'næzərəθ, -rɪθ, 'næzr-
Nazarite 'næzə,raɪt
Nazi 'natsɪ, 'nætsɪ |-ism -,ɪzəm (*Ger* 'naːtsiː)
Nazimova na'zimo,va
Neanderthal nɪ'ændɚ,tal; ES -'ændə-; (*Ger* ne'andər,taːl)
neap nip |neaped nipt
Neapolitan ,niə'palətṇ; ES+-'pɒl-
near nɪr; ES nɪə(r, S+njɛə(r, njɪə(r, nɛə(r
near-by 'nɪr'baɪ; ES 'nɪə-, S+'njɛə-, 'njɪə-, 'nɛə-; ('near-,by 'town)
nearsighted 'nɪr'saɪtɪd; ES 'nɪə-, S+'njɛə-, 'njɪə-, 'nɛə-
neat nit |neated 'nitɪd
'neath niθ, nið
neatherd 'nit,hɝd; ES -,hɜd, -,hɝd
neat's-foot 'nits,fut
neb nɛb |nebbed nɛbd
Nebo 'nibo
Nebraska nə'bræskə |-n -n
Nebuchadnezzar ,nɛbjəkəd'nɛzɚ, ,nɛbə-; ES -'nɛzə(r; |-drezzar -'rɛzɚ; ES -'rɛzə(r
nebula 'nɛbjələ |-s -z |-lae -,li |-lous -ləs
nebulosity ,nɛbjə'lasətɪ; ES+-'lɒs-
necessarily 'nɛsə,sɛrəlɪ, *esp. if emph.* ,nɛsə-'sɛrəlɪ
necessary 'nɛsə,sɛrɪ
necessitate nə'sɛsə,tet |-d -ɪd |-tous -təs |-ty -tɪ
neck nɛk |necked nɛkt
neckerchief 'nɛkɚtʃɪf; ES 'nɛkətʃɪf
necklace 'nɛklɪs |-s -ɪz |-d -t
necktie 'nɛk,taɪ

necrology nɛ'kralədʒɪ; ES+-'krɒl-
necromancer 'nɛkrə,mænsɚ; ES -sə(r; |-cy -sɪ
necropolis nɛ'krapəlɪs; ES+-'krɒp-; |-es -ɪz
necropsy 'nɛkrapsɪ; ES+-krɒp-
necrosis nɛ'krosɪs |-croses -'krosiz
nectar 'nɛktɚ; ES 'nɛktə(r; |-ed -d |-ous -əs
nectarine 'nɛktə,rin, ,nɛktə'rin
nee ne
need nid |-ed -ɪd |-ful -fəl |-fully -fəlɪ
needle 'nidḷ |-d -d |-ful -,ful |-fuls -,fulz
needle-point 'nidḷ,pɔɪnt |-ed -ɪd
needlewoman 'nidḷ,wumən, -,wu- |-men -,wɪmɪn, -ən
needlework 'nidḷ,wɝk; ES -,wɜk, -,wɝk
needn't 'nidṇt, *before some conns.*+'nidṇ ('nidṇ 'baðɚ)—*The pron.* 'nidənt *is not in general use.*
Neenah 'ninə
ne'er nɛr; ES nɛə(r
ne'er-do-weel 'nɛrduˌwil; ES 'nɛəduˌwil
ne'er-do-well 'nɛrduˌwɛl; ES 'nɛəduˌwɛl
nefarious nɪ'fɛrɪəs, -'fær-, -'fer-
negate 'niget, nɪ'get |-d -ɪd |-tion nɪ'geʃən
negative 'nɛgətɪv |-d -d |-vism -,ɪzəm
Negaunee nɪ'gɔnɪ
neglect nɪ'glɛkt |-ed -ɪd |-ful -fəl |-fully -fəlɪ
negligee ,nɛglɪ'ʒe (*Fr* negli'ʒe) ('negliˌgee 'wear)
negligence 'nɛglədʒəns |-cy -ɪ |-gent -dʒənt
negligible 'nɛglədʒəbḷ |-bly -blɪ
negotiability nɪ,goʃɪə'bɪlətɪ, -,goʃə-
negotiable nɪ'goʃɪəbḷ, -'goʃə-
negotiate nɪ'goʃɪ,et |-d -ɪd |-tor -ɚ; ES -ə(r
negotiation nɪ,goʃɪ'eʃən
negress 'nigrɪs |-es -ɪz
negro, N- 'nigro, *esp.* S 'nɪgro, 'nɪgrə
Negroid 'nigrɔɪd
Negros *Pl* 'negros |-'s -ɪz
Negus, n- 'nigəs |-'s -ɪz
Nehemiah ,niə'maɪə
neigh ne |neighed ned
neighbor 'nebɚ; ES 'nebə(r; |-ed -d |-ing 'nebrɪŋ, 'nebərɪŋ |-hood -,hud
Neilson 'nilsṇ
neither 'niðɚ, *much less freq.* 'naɪðɚ; ES -ðə(r
Nell nɛl |Nellie 'nɛlɪ |Nelly 'nɛlɪ
Nelson 'nɛlsṇ |-ville -,vɪl; S+-vḷ
nematode 'nɛmə,tod
Nemean nɪ'miən, 'nimɪən

|full ful |tooth tuθ |further 'fɝðɚ; ES 'fɝðə |custom 'kʌstəm |while hwaɪl |how hau |toy tɔɪ
|using 'juzɪŋ |fuse fjuz, fɪuz |dish dɪʃ |vision 'vɪʒən |Eden 'idṇ |cradle 'kredḷ |keep 'em 'kipm̩

Nemesis, n- 'nɛməsɪs |-eses -ə͵siz

Neocene 'niə͵sin

neoimpressionism ͵nio·ɪm'prɛʃən͵ɪzəm |-ist -ɪst

neolith 'niə͵lɪθ |-ths -θs |-ic ͵niə'lɪθɪk

neologism ni'alə͵dʒɪzəm; ES+-'ɒl-; |-ist -ɪst

neologistic ni͵alə'dʒɪstɪk; ES+-͵ɒl-; |-al -ḷ

neology ni'alədʒɪ; ES+-'ɒl-

neon 'nian, 'niɒn

neophyte 'niə͵faɪt

Neoplatonism ͵nio'pletn͵ɪzəm

Neozoic ͵niə'zo·ɪk

Nepal, -paul nɪ'pɔl

nepenthe nɪ'pɛnθɪ

nephew 'nɛfju, -jʊ, -ɪu, *much less freq.* 'nɛv-

nephritic nɛ'frɪtɪk |-al -ḷ |-tis -'fraɪtɪs

ne plus ultra 'niplʌs'ʌltrə

nepotism 'nɛpə͵tɪzəm

Neptune 'nɛptʃun, -tʃrun, -tjun

Nereid, n- 'nɪrɪɪd

Nerissa nə'rɪsə, nɛ-

Nero 'niro, 'nɪro

nerve nɝv; ES nɜv, nɝv; |-d -d |-vous -əs

ness nɛs |-nesses 'nɛsɪs

-ness *unstressed ending* -nɪs, -nəs. *The pron.*
-nɛs is not normal to conversation but is
occasional in reading style or rime. When
only -nɪs is given in the vocab., it is to be
understood that many speakers (fewer in the
E & S) also pron. -nəs, riming slyness *with*
sinus. *When -ness is added to words ending*
in -n or -ṇ, two n sounds are pronounced
(thinness 'θɪnnɪs, fineness 'faɪnnɪs, sudden-
ness 'sʌdṇnɪs); cf -less.

nest nɛst |nested 'nɛstɪd

nestle 'nɛsḷ |-d -d |-ling 'nɛslɪŋ, 'nɛsḷɪŋ

nestling *n* 'nɛstlɪŋ, 'nɛslɪŋ

Nestor 'nɛstɚ; ES 'nɛstə(r

Nestorian nɛs'torɪən, -'tɔr-; S -'tor-

net nɛt |netted 'nɛtɪd

nether 'nɛðɚ; ES 'nɛðə(r

Netherlander 'nɛðɚ͵lændɚ, -ləndɚ; ES
'nɛðə͵lændə(r, -ləndə(r

Netherlands 'nɛðɚləndz, -nz; ES 'nɛðə-

nethermost 'nɛðɚ͵most, -məst; ES 'nɛðə-

Nettie 'nɛtɪ

netting 'nɛtɪŋ

nettle 'nɛtḷ |-d -d |-ling 'nɛtlɪŋ, 'nɛtḷɪŋ

network 'nɛt͵wɝk; ES -͵wɜk, -͵wɝk

Neufchâtel ͵njuʃə'tɛl, ͵nɪu-, ͵nu- (*Fr* nœʃa-
'tɛl) ('Neufchâ͵tel 'cheese)

neural 'njʊrəl, 'nɪurəl, 'nurəl

neuralgia nju'rældʒə, nɪu-, nu-

neurasthenia ͵njurəs'θinɪə, ͵nɪu-, ͵nu-

neurasthenic ͵njurəs'θɛnɪk, ͵nɪu-, ͵nu- |-al -ḷ
|-ally -ḷɪ, -ɪklɪ

neuritis nju'raɪtɪs, nɪu-, nu-

neurologist nju'ralədʒɪst, nɪu-, nu-; ES+
-'rɒl-; |-gy -dʒɪ

neuron 'njʊran, 'nɪu-, 'nu-, -rɒn |-rone -ron

neuropathic ͵njurə'pæθɪk, ͵nɪu-, ͵nu- |-al -ḷ
|-ally -ḷɪ, -ɪklɪ

neuropathist nju'rapəθɪst, nɪu-, nu-; ES+
-'rɒp-; |-thy -θɪ

neuropsychosis ͵njurosaɪ'kosɪs, ͵nɪu-, ͵nu-

neurosis nju'rosɪs, nɪu-, nu- |-roses -'rosiz

neurotic nju'ratɪk, nɪu-, nu-; ES+-'rɒt-;
|-ally -ḷɪ, -ɪklɪ

Neustria 'njustrɪə, 'nɪu-, 'nu- |-n -n

neuter 'njutɚ, 'nɪu-, 'nu-; ES -tə(r

neutral 'njutrəl, 'nɪu-, 'nu- |-ly -ɪ

neutrality nju'trælətɪ, nɪu-, nu-

neutralization ͵njutrələ'zeʃən, ͵nɪu-, ͵nu-,
-aɪ'z-

neutralize 'njutrəl͵aɪz, 'nɪu-, 'nu- |-s -ɪz |-d -d

neutron 'njutran, 'nɪu-, 'nu-, -trɒn

Nevada *state* nə'vædə, nɪ-, -'vadə |-n -n; *Ia,*
Mo cities, Ark co. loc. -'vedə

never 'nɛvɚ; ES 'nɛvə(r

nevermore ͵nɛvɚ'mor, -'mɔr; ES ͵nɛvə'moə(r,
E+-'mɔə(r

nevertheless ͵nɛvɚðə'lɛs; ES ͵nɛvə-

Neville 'nɛvḷ, -vɪl

Nevin 'nɛvɪn

Nevis 'nɛvɪs, 'nivɪs |-'s -ɪz

new nju, nɪu, nu

Newark 'njuɚk, 'nɪu-, 'nu-; ES -ək; *Del*+
-ark; ES -a:k

New Bern ͵nju'bɚn, ͵nɪu-, ͵nu-; ES -bɜn

Newbern 'njubɚn, 'nɪu-, 'nu-; ES -bɜn

Newberry, -bery 'nju͵bɛrɪ, 'nɪu-, 'nu-, -bərɪ

newborn 'nju'bɔrn, 'nɪu-, 'nu-; ES -'bɔən;
('new͵born 'lamb)

Newburgh 'njubɝg, 'nɪu-, 'nu-; ES -bɜg,
-bɝg

Newbury 'nju͵bɛrɪ, 'nɪu-, 'nu-, -bərɪ |-port
-͵port, -͵pɔrt, -brɪ-; ES -͵poət, E+-͵pɔət
('Newbury & ͵Newbury'port)

Newcastle 'nju₁kæs|, 'nɪu-, 'nu-; E+-₁kas|,
-₁kas|; *Engd loc.* nju'kas|
Newcomb, -mbe, -me 'njukəm, 'nɪu-, 'nu-
newcome 'nju₁kʌm, 'nɪu-, 'nu-
newcomer 'nju₁kʌmɚ, 'nɪu-, 'nu-; ES -mə(r;
acct+new'comer
Newcomerstown 'njukʌmɚz₁taʊn, 'nɪu-, 'nu-;
ES -kʌməz-
Newdigate 'njudɪgɪt, 'nɪu-, 'nu-, -₁get
newel, Newell 'njuəl, 'nɪuəl, 'nuəl
New England nju'ɪŋglənd, nɪu-, nu-
newfangled ₁nju'fæŋg|d, ₁nɪu-, ₁nu- ('new-
₁fangled 'whims)
Newfoundland *isl.* ₁njufənd'lænd, ₁nɪu-, ₁nu-,
'njufəndlənd, 'nɪu-, 'nu-; *dog* nju'faʊnd-
lənd, nɪu-, nu-
Newfoundlander nju'faʊndləndɚ, nɪu-, nu-;
ES -də(r
Newgate 'njugɪt, -get
New Hampshire nju'hæmpʃɚ, nɪu-, nu-, -ʃɪr;
ES -ʃə(r, -ʃɪə(r
New Haven nju'hevən, nɪu-, nu-, *loc.*+
-'hevm̩
New Jersey nju'dʒɝzɪ, nɪu-, nu-; ES -'dʒɜzɪ,
-'dʒɝzɪ
new-laid 'nju'led, 'nɪu-, 'nu- ('new-₁laid 'egg)
Newman 'njumən, 'nɪu-, 'nu-
Newmarket 'nju₁markɪt, 'nɪu-, 'nu-; ES
-₁ma:kɪt, E+-₁ma:kɪt
New Mexico nju'mɛksə₁ko, nɪu-, nu-
Newnan 'njunən, 'nɪu-, 'nu-
New Orleans nju'ɔrlɪənz, nɪu-, nu-; ES
-'ɔəlɪənz;—*The older pron.* ₁njuɚ'linz *is
not uncommon, and is regular in* New
Orleans molasses. *Cf* Orleans.
Newport 'nju₁port, 'nɪu-, 'nu-, -₁pɔrt; ES
-₁poət, E+-₁pɔət
news njuz, nɪuz, nuz |-boy -₁bɔɪ
New Salem nju'seləm, nɪu-, nu-; *Mass loc.*
'New ₁Salem (*cf* Salem, *Mass*)
newspaper 'njuz₁pepɚ, 'njus-, 'nɪu-, 'nu-; ES
-₁pepə(r; |-man -₁mæn |-men -₁mɛn
newsprint 'njuz₁prɪnt, 'nɪuz-, 'nuz-
newsreel 'njuz₁ril, 'nɪuz-, 'nuz-
newssheet 'njuz₁ʃit, 'njuʒ-, 'nɪu-, 'nu-
newsstand 'njuz₁stænd, 'nɪuz-, 'nuz-
newt njut, nɪut, nut
Newton 'njutn̩, 'nɪu-, 'nu- |-town -₁taʊn
Newtonian nju'tonɪən, nɪu-, nu-

New Year's 'nju₁jɪrz, 'nɪu-, 'nu-; ES -₁jɪəz,
S+-₁jɛəz; |Day -₁de |Eve -'iv
New York nju'jɔrk, nɪu-, nu-, nʊ-; ES -'jɔək;
('New ₁York 'City)
New Zealand nju'zilənd, nɪu-, nu-
next nɛkst, *before some conss.*+nɛks ('nɛks
'de, 'nɛks 'flor)
nexus 'nɛksəs |-es -ɪz
Ney ne
Nez Perce 'nɛz'pɝs; ES -'pɜs, -'pɝs; |-s -ɪz
(*Fr* neper'se |-cés -'se)
Niagara naɪ'ægrə, -gərə ('Nɪ₁agara 'Falls)
nib nɪb |nibbed nɪbd
nibble 'nɪb| |-d -d |-ling 'nɪblɪŋ, 'nɪb|ɪŋ
Nibelung 'nib|₁ʊŋ |-enlied -ən₁lid (*Ger* -₁lit)
niblick, -ic 'nɪblɪk |-cked -t
Nicaea naɪ'siə |-n -n
Nicanor nɪ'kenɚ, naɪ-; ES -'kenə(r
Nicaragua ₁nɪkə'ragwə, -'rɔgwə |-n -n
nice naɪs |-ty 'naɪsətɪ
Nice nis |-'s -ɪz
Nicene naɪ'sin ('Nɪ₁cene 'Creed)
niche nɪtʃ |niches 'nɪtʃɪz |niched nɪtʃt
Nicholas 'nɪkləs, 'nɪkləs |-'s -ɪz
Nichols 'nɪk|z |-'s -ɪz |-lson 'nɪk|sn̩
nick, N- nɪk |nicked nɪkt
nickel 'nɪk| |-ed -d |-ing 'nɪk|ɪŋ, 'nɪklɪŋ
nickelodeon ₁nɪk|'odɪən
nickel-plate *v* 'nɪk|'plet |-d -ɪd ('Nickel-
₁plate 'Rail₁road)
Nickleby 'nɪk|bɪ
nicknack 'nɪk₁næk
nickname 'nɪk₁nem |-named -₁nemd
Nicodemus ₁nɪkə'diməs |-'s -ɪz
Nicolas 'nɪkləs, 'nɪkləs |-'s -ɪz
Nicolay 'nɪk|₁e
nicotine 'nɪkə₁tin, -tɪn |-tin -tɪn
niece nis |nieces 'nisɪz
Niemen 'nimən (*Pol* 'njɛmən)
Niemeyer 'nimaɪɚ; ES -maɪ·ə(r
Niemöller *Ger* 'nimœlər
Nietzsche 'nitʃə
nifty 'nɪftɪ
Nigel 'naɪdʒəl
Niger 'naɪdʒɚ, 'naɪgɚ; ES -dʒə(r, -gə(r
Nigeria naɪ'dʒɪrɪə |-n -n
niggard 'nɪgɚd; ES 'nɪgəd; |-ly -lɪ
nigger 'nɪgɚ; ES 'nɪgə(r; |-ed -d |-ing 'nɪgərɪŋ,
'nɪgrɪŋ

|full fʊl |tooth tuθ |further 'fɝðɚ; ES 'fɜðə |custom 'kʌstəm |while hwaɪl |how haʊ |toy tɔɪ
|using 'juzɪŋ |fuse fjuz, fɪuz |dish dɪʃ |vision 'vɪʒən |Eden 'idn̩ |cradle 'kred| |keep 'em 'kipm̩

Those words below in which the ɑ sound is spelt o are often pronounced with ɒ in E and S

niggle 'nɪg| |-d -d |-ling 'nɪglɪŋ, 'nɪg|ɪŋ
niggler 'nɪglɚ; ES 'nɪglə(r
niggling *n* 'nɪglɪŋ
nigh naɪ |nighed naɪd
night naɪt |-ed -ɪd |-cap -ˌkæp |-capped -ˌkæpt
nightdress 'naɪtˌdrɛs |-es -ɪz
nightfall 'naɪtˌfɔl
nightgown 'naɪtˌgaʊn |-ed -d
nighthawk 'naɪtˌhɔk
nightingale, N- 'naɪtn̩ˌgel, 'naɪtɪn-, 'naɪtɪŋ-
nightjar 'naɪtˌdʒɑr; ES -ˌdʒɑ:(r, E+-ˌdʒɑ:(r
nightlong 'naɪtˌlɔŋ, -ˌlɒŋ; S+-ˌlɑŋ
nightmare 'naɪtˌmɛr, -ˌmær; E -ˌmɛə(r, ES
  -ˌmæə(r; |-d -d
nightshade 'naɪtˌʃed
nightshirt 'naɪtˌʃɝt; ES -ˌʃɝt, -ˌʃɝt; |-ed -ɪd
nighttime 'naɪtˌtaɪm
nightwalker 'naɪtˌwɔkɚ; ES -ˌwɔkə(r
nightward 'naɪtwɚd; ES 'naɪtwəd
night-watch 'naɪtˌwɑtʃ, -ˌwɒtʃ, -ˌwɔtʃ |-es -ɪz
night-watchman 'naɪtˈwɑtʃmən, -ˈwɒtʃ-,
  -ˈwɔtʃ- |-men -mən ('night-ˌwatchman
  'Jones)
nihil 'naɪhɪl
nihilism 'naɪəlˌɪzəm |-ist -ɪst
Nike 'naɪki
nil nɪl
Nile naɪl |Niles naɪlz |Niles's 'naɪlzɪz
Nilotic naɪˈlɑtɪk
Nilus 'naɪləs |-'s -ɪz
nimble 'nɪmb| |-d -d |-ling 'nɪmblɪŋ, 'nɪmb|ɪŋ
nimbus 'nɪmbəs |-es -ɪz |-bi -baɪ |-ed -t
Nîmes nim
Nimrod 'nɪmrɑd
Nina *fem. name* 'naɪnə; *goddess* 'ninə
nincompoop 'nɪnkəmˌpup, ˌnɪnkəmˈpup, -ɪŋ-
  kəm-
nine naɪn
ninefold *adj, adv* 'naɪnˈfold ('nineˌfold 'gain)
ninepence 'naɪnpəns |-s -ɪz
ninepenny 'naɪnˌpɛnɪ, -pənɪ
ninepins 'naɪnˌpɪnz
nineteen naɪnˈtin, 'naɪnˈtin ('nineˌteen 'years)
ninety 'naɪntɪ |-tieth 'naɪntɪθ |-tieths -ɪθs
  |-fold -ˈfold
Nineveh 'nɪnəvə |-vite -ˌvaɪt
ninny 'nɪnɪ
ninth naɪnθ |-ths -θs

Ninus 'naɪnəs |-'s -ɪz
Niobe 'naɪəbɪ, -ˌbi
niobium naɪˈobɪəm
Niobrara ˌnaɪəˈbrɛrə, -ˈbrærə, -ˈbrerə
nip nɪp |nipped nɪpt
nip-and-tuck 'nɪpənˈtʌk, 'nɪpm̩ˈtʌk
Nipissing 'nɪpəˌsɪŋ
nipper 'nɪpɚ; ES 'nɪpə(r; |-ed -d
nipple 'nɪp| |-d -d |-ling 'nɪplɪŋ, 'nɪp|ɪŋ
Nippon nɪˈpɑn, -ˈpɒn, 'nɪpɑn, -pɒn
Nipponese ˌnɪpənˈiz
nirvana, N- nɝˈvænə, nɪr-, -ˈvɑnə; ES nɝ-,
  nɝ-, nɪə-
nisi 'naɪsaɪ |nisi prius -ˈpraɪəs
Nismes nim
nit nɪt
niter, -tre 'naɪtɚ; ES 'naɪtə(r; |-(e)d -d
niton 'naɪtɑn, -tɒn
nitrate *n* 'naɪtret, -trɪt
nitrate *v* 'naɪtret |-d -ɪd |-tion naɪˈtreʃən
nitric 'naɪtrɪk |-trid -trɪd |-tride -traɪd, -trɪd
nitrify 'naɪtrəˌfaɪ |-fied -ˌfaɪd
nitrite 'naɪtraɪt
nitrobacteria ˌnaɪtrobækˈtɪrɪə
nitrocellulose ˌnaɪtroˈsɛljəˌlos
nitrogen 'naɪtrədʒən, -dʒɪn |-ate -ˌet |-ated
  -ˌetɪd
nitrogenous naɪˈtrɑdʒənəs
nitroglycerin ˌnaɪtrəˈglɪsrɪn, -sərɪn |-ine -rɪn,
  -səˌrin
nitrous 'naɪtrəs
nitwit 'nɪtˌwɪt
nix nɪks |nixes 'nɪksɪz |-ie -ɪ
Nizam naɪˈzæm, nɪ-, -ˈzɑm
no no |noes noz |noed nod
Noah 'noə
nob nab |nobbed nabd |nobby 'nabɪ
Nobel noˈbɛl ('Noˌbel 'prize)
nobility noˈbɪlətɪ
noble 'nob| |-r 'noblɚ; ES -blə(r; |-st 'noblɪst
Nobleboro 'nob|ˌbɝo, -ə; ES -ˌbɝ-, -ˌbʌr-,
  -ˌbɝ-
nobleman 'nob|mən |-men -mən
noble-minded 'nob|ˈmaɪndɪd ('noble-ˌminded
  'man)
noblesse noˈblɛs
noblesse oblige noˈblɛsoˈbliʒ (*Fr* nɔ̈blɛsɔ̈-
  ˈbli:ʒ)

Those words below in which the ɑ *sound is spelt* o *are often pronounced with* ɒ *in E and S*

noblewoman ˈnobḷˌwʊmən, -ˌwu- |-men -ˌwɪmɪn, -ən

nobly ˈnoblɪ

nobody ˈnoˌbɑdɪ, ˈnoˌbʌdɪ, ˈnobədɪ

nociassociation ˌnosɪəˌsosɪˈeʃən, -ˌsoʃɪ-

nock nɑk |nocked nɑkt

noctambulation ˌnɑktæmbjəˈleʃən, nɑkˌtæm-

noctambulism nɑkˈtæmbjəˌlɪzəm |-list -lɪst

nocturnal nɑkˈtɝnḷ; ES -ˈtɜn-, -ˈtɝn- |-ly -ɪ

nocturne ˈnɑktɝn, nɑkˈtɝn; ES -ɜn, -ɝn

nocuous ˈnɑkjʊəs

nod nɑd |nodded ˈnɑdɪd

nodal ˈnodḷ |-dality noˈdælətɪ

noddle ˈnɑdḷ |-d -d |-ling ˈnɑdlɪŋ, ˈnɑdlɪŋ

node nod |noded ˈnodɪd

nodular ˈnɑdʒələ˞; ES ˈnɑdʒələ(r

nodule ˈnɑdʒul

Noel *pers. name* ˈnoəl; *'Christmas'* noˈɛl

nog, nogg nɑg |nogged nɑgd

noggin ˈnɑgɪn

nohow ˈnoˌhaʊ

noil nɔɪl |-age -ɪdʒ

noise nɔɪz |noises ˈnɔɪzɪz |noised nɔɪzd

noisome ˈnɔɪsəm

noisy ˈnɔɪzɪ | noisily ˈnɔɪzḷɪ, -zɪlɪ

Nokomis noˈkomɪs |-'s-ɪz

nolle prosequi ˈnɑlɪˈprɑsɪˌkwaɪ

nolo contendere ˈnolokənˈtɛndəˌri

nol-pros ˌnɑlˈprɑs |-ses -ɪz |-sed -t

nomad ˈnomæd, ˈnɑmæd |-ism -ˌɪzəm

nomadic noˈmædɪk |-al -ḷ |-ally -ḷɪ, -ɪklɪ

nombles ˈnʌmbḷz = numbles

nom de plume ˈnɑmdəˌplum, -ˌplʊm (*Fr* nõdəˈplym)

Nome nom

nomenclature ˈnomənˌkletʃ˞; ES -ˌkletʃə(r— noˈmɛnklətʃə(r *is chiefly Brit.*

nominal ˈnɑmənḷ |-ly -ɪ

nominate *adj* ˈnɑmənɪt

nominate *v* ˈnɑməˌnet |-d -ɪd |-tion ˌnɑmə-ˈneʃən

nominative ˈnɑməˌnetɪv, *gram.*+ˈnɑmənətɪv, -mnə-

nominee ˌnɑməˈni

nomology noˈmɑlədʒɪ |-gist -dʒɪst

nonacceptance ˌnɑnəkˈsɛptəns, -ɪk-

nonage ˈnɑnɪdʒ, ˈnonɪdʒ

nonagenarian ˌnɑnədʒəˈnɛrɪən, ˌnonə-, -ˈner-

nonaggression ˌnɑnəˈgrɛʃən

nonalcoholic ˌnɑnælkəˈhɑlɪk, -ˈhɒl-, -ˈhɑl-

nonappearance ˌnɑnəˈpɪrəns; S+-ˈpɛr-, -ˈpjɛr-; |-s -ɪz

nonassessable ˌnɑnəˈsɛsəbḷ

nonattendance ˌnɑnəˈtɛndəns |-s -ɪz

nonbeliever ˌnɑnbəˈliv˞; -bḷˈiv˞; ES -və(r

nonbelligerent ˌnɑnbəˈlɪdʒərənt

nonce nɑns

nonchalance ˈnɑnʃələns, ˌnɑnʃəˈlɑns (*Fr* nõʃaˈlɑ̃:s) |-nt -nt (*Fr* -ˈlɑ̃)

noncollapsible ˌnɑnkəˈlæpsəbḷ

noncom nɑnˈkɑm

nomcombatant nɑnˈkɑmbətənt, -ˈkʌm-

noncombustible ˌnɑnkəmˈbʌstəbḷ

noncommissioned ˌnɑnkəˈmɪʃənd

noncommittal ˌnɑnkəˈmɪtḷ |-ly -ɪ

noncompliance ˌnɑnkəmˈplaɪəns |-s -ɪz

non compos mentis ˈnɑnˌkɑmpəsˈmɛntɪs

nonconditioned ˌnɑnkənˈdɪʃənd

nonconductive ˌnɑnkənˈdʌktɪv |-tor -t˞; ES -tə(r

nonconformance ˌnɑnkənˈfɔrməns; ES -ˈfɔəm-

nonconformist ˌnɑnkənˈfɔrmɪst; ES -ˈfɔəm-

noncontemporary ˌnɑnkənˈtɛmpəˌrɛrɪ

noncontraband nɑnˈkɑntrəˌbænd

non-co-operation ˌnɑnkoˌɑpəˈreʃən

non-co-operative ˌnɑnkoˈɑpəˌretɪv

noncorroding ˌnɑnkəˈrodɪŋ |-rosive -ˈrosɪv

nondelivery ˌnɑndɪˈlɪvərɪ, -ˈlɪvrɪ

nondescript ˈnɑndɪˌskrɪpt

nondivisible ˌnɑndəˈvɪzəbḷ

nondramatic ˌnɑndrəˈmætɪk

none *'ninth hour'* non |nones nonz

none *'not any'* nʌn

nonentity nɑnˈɛntətɪ

nonessential ˌnɑnəˈsɛnʃəl

nonesuch ˈnʌnˌsʌtʃ |-es -ɪz

nonexistence ˌnɑnɪgˈzɪstəns |-tent -tənt

nonexplosive ˌnɑnɪkˈsplosɪv

nonfactual nɑnˈfæktʃʊəl

nonfeasance nɑnˈfizn̩s

nonfiction nɑnˈfɪkʃən

nonflammable nɑnˈflæməbḷ

nonfulfillment ˌnɑnfʊlˈfɪlmənt

nonhuman nɑnˈhjumən, -ˈhɪu-

nonillion noˈnɪljən

nonimmune ˌnɑnɪˈmjun, -ˈmɪun

Those words below in which the α sound is spelt o are often pronounced with ɒ in E and S

nonindustrial ˌnanɪn'dʌstrɪəl

noninflammable ˌnanɪn'flæməb|

noninjurious ˌnanɪn'dʒʊrɪəs

nonintercourse nan'ɪntɚˌkors, -ˌkɔrs; ES -'ɪntəˌkoəs, E+-ˌkɔəs

noninterference ˌnanɪntɚ'fɪrəns; ES -ɪntə-, S+-'fɛr-

nonintervention ˌnanɪntɚ'vɛnʃən; ES -ɪntə-

nonintoxicant ˌnanɪn'taksəkənt |-cating -ˌketɪŋ

nonjoinder nan'dʒɔɪndɚ; ES -'dʒɔɪndə(r

nonjuror nan'dʒʊrɚ, -'dʒɪʊrɚ; ES -rə(r

nonmember nan'mɛmbɚ; ES -'mɛmbə(r

nonmetal nan'mɛt| |-talic ˌnanmə'tælɪk

nonmoral nan'mɔrəl, -'mɑr-, -'mɒr-

nonnegotiable ˌnannɪ'goʃɪəb|, -'goʃə-

nonobservance ˌnanəb'zɝvəns; ES -'zɝv-, -'zɝˑv-; |-ant -ənt

nonofficial ˌnanə'fɪʃəl |-ly -ɪ

nonpareil ˌnanpə'rɛl ('nonpaˌreil 'type)

nonparticipant ˌnanpɚ'tɪsəpənt; ES -pə'tɪs-

nonparticipation ˌnanpɚˌtɪsə'peʃən; ES -pə-

nonpartisan, -zan nan'pɑrtəzn̩; ES -'pɑːt-, E+-'pɑːt-

nonpaying nan'pe·ɪŋ |-payment -'pemənt

nonperformance ˌnanpɚ'fɔrməns; ES -pə-'fɔəm-

nonperiodical ˌnanpɪrɪ'adɪk|

nonpermanent nan'pɝmənənt; ES -'pɝm-, -'pɝm-

nonperpendicular ˌnanpɚpən'dɪkjələ, -pɝpm̩-; ES -pəpən'dɪkjələ(r, -pɝpm̩-, -pɝ-

nonphysical nan'fɪzɪk|

nonplus nan'plʌs, 'nanplʌs |-es -ɪz |-ed -t

nonpoetic ˌnanpo'ɛtɪk

nonpoisonous nan'pɔɪznəs, -zn̩əs

nonpolitical ˌnanpə'lɪtɪk|

nonproducer ˌnanprə'djusɚ, -'dɪu-, -'du-; ES -sə(r

nonproductive ˌnanprə'dʌktɪv

nonprofessional ˌnanprə'fɛʃən|, -ʃnəl

nonprofit nan'prafɪt

non-Protestant nan'pratəstənt

nonreality ˌnanrɪ'ælətɪ

nonrecoverable ˌnanrɪ'kʌvrəb|, -'kʌvərəb|

nonrefillable ˌnanri'fɪləb|

nonreligious ˌnanrɪ'lɪdʒəs

nonresidence nan'rɛzədəns |-dent -dənt

nonresidential ˌnanrɛzə'dɛnʃəl

nonresistance ˌnanrɪ'zɪstəns |-tant -tənt

nonrestricted ˌnanrɪ'strɪktɪd

nonreturnable ˌnanrɪ'tɝnəb|; ES -'tɝn-, -'tɝn-

nonrigid nan'rɪdʒɪd

nonrustable nan'rʌstəb|

nonsectarian ˌnansɛk'tɛrɪən, -'tɛrɪən

nonsense 'nansɛns

nonsensical nan'sɛnsɪk| |-ally -ḷɪ, -ɪklɪ

non sequitur nan'sɛkwɪtɚ; ES -'sɛkwɪtə(r

nonsharing nan'ʃɛrɪŋ, -'ʃær-; S -'ʃær-

nonskid 'nan'skɪd ('nonˌskid 'tread)

nonsmoker nan'smokɚ; ES -'smokə(r

nonstainable nan'stenəb|

nonstarter nan'stɑrtɚ; ES -'stɑːtə(r, E+-'stɑːt-

nonstop 'nan'stap ('nonˌstop 'flight)

nonstriker nan'straɪkɚ; ES -'straɪkə(r

nonsuit nan'sut, -'sɪut, -'sjut, 'nanˌs- |-ed -ɪd

nonsupport ˌnansə'port, -'pɔrt; ES -'poət, E+-'pɔət

nonsustaining ˌnansə'stenɪŋ

nonsyllabic ˌnansɪ'læbɪk

nontaxable nan'tæksəb|

nontheatrical ˌnanθɪ'ætrɪk|

nonthinking nan'θɪŋkɪŋ

nonunion nan'junjən ('nonˌunion 'shop)

nonvoter nan'votɚ; ES -'votə(r

noodle 'nud| |-d -d -ling 'nudlɪŋ, 'nud|ɪŋ

nook nʊk |nooked nʊkt |-ery -ərɪ, -rɪ

noon nun |nooned nund |-day -ˌde |-tide -ˌtaɪd |-time -ˌtaɪm

no-one 'noˌwʌn, 'nowən

noose nus |nooses 'nusɪz |noosed nust

Nootka 'nutkə

no-par 'no'par; ES -'pɑː(r, E+-'pɑː(r; ('noˌpar 'stock)

nor *usual form* nɚ; ES nə(r; *stressed* 'nɔr, ˌnɔr; ES 'nɔə(r, ˌnɔə(r

Nora, -h 'norə, 'nɔrə; S 'norə

Nordic 'nɔrdɪk; ES 'nɔədɪk; |-icism -dəˌsɪzəm

Nordica 'nɔrdɪkə; ES 'nɔədɪkə

Norfolk 'nɔrfək; ES 'nɔəfək; *Mass loc.* 'nɔrfɔk, 'nɔəfɔk

norm nɔrm; ES nɔəm

Norma 'nɔrmə; ES 'nɔəmə

normal, N- 'nɔrm|; ES 'nɔəm|; |-ly -ɪ |-cy -sɪ

normality nɔr'mælətɪ; ES nɔ'mælətɪ

normalization ˌnɔrm|ə'zeʃən, -aɪ'z-; ES ˌnɔəm-

normalize 'nɔrm|ˌaɪz; ES 'nɔəm-; |-s -ɪz |-d -d

Norman 'nɔrmən; ES 'nɔəmən; |-dy -dɪ

Norn nɔrn; ES nɔən

Norridgewock 'nɔrɪdʒˌwɑk, 'nɑr-, 'nɒr-, -ˌwɒk

Norris 'nɔrɪs, 'nɑr-, 'nɒr- |-'s -ɪz

Norse nɔrs; ES nɔəs; |-man -mən |-men -mən

north, N- nɔrθ; ES nɔəθ; |-ed -t

Northallerton nɔrθ'ælətən; ES nɔθ'ælətən

Northampton nɔrθ'hæmptən, nɔr'θæm-; ES nɔə-; |-shire -ˌʃɪr, -ʃɚ; ES -ˌʃɪə(r, -ʃə(r

Northanger 'nɔrθəndʒɚ, nɔr'θæŋgɚ; ES -ɔə-, -ə(r

Northants *short for* Northamptonshire nɔrθ-'hænts, nɔr'θænts; ES nɔə-

North Carolina ˌnɔrθkærə'laɪnə, -kɚ'laɪnə, -kə'laɪnə; ES ˌnɔəθkærə-, -kə-; *loc.*+ -'la:nə, -kæə'la:nə—*In* ˌnɔrθkə'laɪnə kɚ *becomes* kə *by dissimilation* (§121).

Northcliffe 'nɔrθklɪf; ES 'nɔəθ-; |-cote -kət, -kot

North Dakota ˌnɔrθdə'kotə, -dɪ-; ES ˌnɔəθ-

northeast, N- ˌnɔrθ'ist; ES ˌnɔəθ-; ('north-ˌeast 'wind)—*naut.*+nɔr'ist |-er -ɚ; ES -ə(r; |-ern -ɚn; ES -ən

northeastward ˌnɔrθ'istwəd; ES ˌnɔəθ'istwəd; |-s -z

norther 'nɔrðɚ; ES 'nɔəðə(r; |-n -n |-ly -lɪ |-most -ˌmost

northerner, N- 'nɔrðɚnɚ, 'nɔrðənɚ; ES 'nɔəðənɚ(r;—*In* 'nɔrðənɚ ə *results from* ɚ *by dissimilation* (§121); *this is less freq. in* northern 'nɔrðən.

northernmost 'nɔrðɚnˌmost, -məst; ES 'nɔəðən-

Northfield 'nɔrθˌfild; ES 'nɔəθ-

northing 'nɔrθɪŋ, -ðɪŋ; ES 'nɔə-

northland, N- 'nɔrθlənd, -ˌlænd

Northman 'nɔrθmən; ES 'nɔəθ-; |-men -mən

Northop *see* Northrup

Northport 'nɔrᶜˌport, -ˌpɔrt; ES 'nɔəθˌpoət, E+-ˌpɔət

Northrup, -rop 'nɔrθrəp, -θəp; ES 'nɔəθ-; *The pron.* 'nɔrθəp *is due to r-dissimilation* (§121).

Northumberland nɔrθ'ʌmbɚlənd; ES nɔθ-'ʌmbələnd

Northumbria nɔrθ'ʌmbrɪə; ES nɔθ'ʌm-; |-n -n

Northup *see* Northrup

northward 'nɔrθwəd; ES 'nɔəθwəd; |-s -z

northwest, N- ˌnɔrθ'wɛst; ES ˌnɔəθ-; *naut.*+ nɔr'w-; ES nɔə'w-; |-er -ɚ; ES -ə(r |-ern -ɚn; ES -ən

Norton 'nɔrtn̩; ES 'nɔətn̩

Norumbega ˌnɔrəm'bigə, ˌnɑr-, ˌnɒr-

Norwalk 'nɔrwɔk; ES 'nɔəwɔk

Norway 'nɔrwe; ES 'nɔəwe

Norwegian nɔr'widʒən; ES nɔə-

Norwich *US* 'nɔrwɪtʃ; ES 'nɔə-; *Engd* 'nɔrɪdʒ, 'nɑr-, 'nɒr- |-'s -ɪz

nose noz |noses 'nozɪz |nosed nozd |-sy -ɪ

noseband 'nozˌbænd |-ed -ɪd

nosebleed 'nozˌblid

nose-dive 'nozˌdaɪv |-dived -ˌdaɪvd

nosegay 'nozˌge

nosepiece 'nozˌpis |-s -ɪz

nosology no'sɑlədʒɪ; ES+-'sɒl-; |-gist -dʒɪst

nostalgia nɑ'stældʒɪə, nɒ-, -dʒə |-gic -dʒɪk

nostril 'nɑstrəl, 'nɒs-, 'nɔs-, -trɪl

nostrum 'nɑstrəm, 'nɒs-, 'nɔs-

not *stressed* 'nɑt, ˌnɑt; ES+-ɒt; *unstressed, rarely* -nət *in* cannot |-n't *enclitic* -nt, -ṇt, -t, -ŋ—*see* aren't, doesn't, can't, *etc.*

nota bene 'notə'binɪ

notability ˌnotə'bɪlətɪ

notable 'notəb|l̩ |-bly -blɪ

notarial no'tɛrɪəl, -'tær-, -'ter- |-ly -ɪ

notary 'notərɪ |-ied -d

notation no'teʃən

notch nɑtʃ; ES+nɒtʃ; |-es -ɪz |-ed -t

note not |noted 'notɪd |-book -ˌbʊk; |*N Engd*+ nõt (§46)

noteworthy 'notˌwɝðɪ; ES -ˌwɝðɪ, -ˌwɝdɪ

nothing 'nʌθɪŋ

notice 'notɪs |-s -ɪz |-d -t

noticeable 'notɪsəb|l̩ |-bly -blɪ

notification ˌnotəfə'keʃən

notify 'notəˌfaɪ |-fied -ˌfaɪd

notion 'noʃən |-ed -d |-al -l̩ |-ally -ḷɪ

notochord 'notəˌkɔrd; ES -ˌkɔəd

notoriety ˌnotə'raɪətɪ

notorious no'torɪəs, -'tɔr-; S -'tor-

Notre Dame *US* ˌnotɚ'dem; ES ˌnotə'dem; *Paris* ˌnotrə'dam (*Fr* nõtrə'dam)

Nottaway 'nɑtəˌwe; ES+-'nɒt-

|full fʊl |tooth tuθ |further 'fɝðɚ; ES 'fɝðə |custom 'kʌstəm |while hwaɪl |how haʊ |toy tɔɪ |using 'juzɪŋ |fuse fjuz, fɪuz |dish dɪʃ |vision 'vɪʒən |Eden 'idn̩ |cradle 'kredl̩ |keep 'em 'kipm̩

Nottingham *US* 'nɑtɪŋˌhæm, *Engd* 'nɑtɪŋəm;
ES+'nɒt-; |-shire -ˌʃɪr, -ʃɚ; ES -ˌʃɪə(r,
-ʃə(r

Notts *short for* Nottinghamshire nɑts; ES+
nɒts

notwithstanding ˌnɑtwɪθ'stændɪŋ, -wɪð-;
ES+ˌnɒt-

nougat 'nugət, 'nugɑ

nought nɔt

noun nɑʊn |-al -l̩ |-ally -lɪ

nourish 'nɝɪʃ; ES 'nɜrɪʃ, 'nʌr-, 'nɜ-; |-es -ɪz
|-ed -t

nous nus, nɑʊs

nouveau riche *Fr* nuvo'riʃ

nova 'novə |novas 'novəz |novae 'novi

Nova Scotia 'novə'skoʃə |-n -n

Nova Zembla 'novə'zɛmblə

novel 'nɑvl̩ |novelly 'nɑvlɪ, 'nɑvlɪ; ES+'nɒv-;
|-ist -ɪst

novelette ˌnɑvl̩'ɛt; ES+ˌnɒv-

novelize 'nɑvl̩ˌaɪz; ES+'nɒv-; |-s -ɪz |-d -d

novelty 'nɑvltɪ; ES+'nɒv-

November no'vɛmbɚ; ES no'vɛmbə(r

novena no'vinə |-s -z |-nae -ni

Novgorod 'nɑvgəˌrɑd; ES+'nɒvgəˌrɒd

Novial 'novɪəl, ˌnovɪ'al

novice 'nɑvɪs; ES+'nɒv-; |-s -ɪz

novitiate, novici- no'vɪʃɪɪt, -ˌet

Novocain, -e 'novəˌken

now nɑʊ |-adays 'nɑʊəˌdez, 'nɑʊˌdez

noway 'noˌwe |-ways -ˌwez

nowhere 'noˌhwɛr, -ˌhwær; E -ˌhwɛə(r, ES
-ˌhwæə(r

nowhither 'noˌhwɪðɚ; ES -ˌhwɪðə(r

nowise 'noˌwaɪz

noxious 'nɑkʃəs; ES+'nɒk-

Noyes nɔɪz |-'s -ɪz

nozzle 'nɑzl̩; ES+'nɒzl̩; |-d -d |-ling -zlɪŋ,
-zl̩ɪŋ

-n't *abbrev. spelling of unstressed* not *after
auxiliaries* -nt, -n̩t, -n̩, -t, *as in* don't,
doesn't, can't; *see these and similar combinations in the vocab.*

nth ɛnθ

n-tuple 'ɛntʊpl̩, -tjʊpl̩, ɛn'tʊpl̩, -'tɪu-, -'tju-
|-d -d |-ling -plɪŋ, -pl̩ɪŋ

nu *Gk letter* nu, nju, nɪu

nuance nju'ɑns, nɪu-, nu-, 'njuɑns, 'nɪu-,
'nu- |-s -ɪz |-d -t (*Fr* nɥɑ̃:s)

nub nʌb |nubbed nʌbd |nubbin 'nʌbɪn

nubble 'nʌbl̩ |-d -d |-bly -blɪ

Nubia 'njubɪə, 'nɪu-, 'nu- |-n -n

nubile 'njubl̩, 'nɪu-, 'nu-, -bɪl

nuclear 'njuklɪɚ, 'nɪu-, 'nu-; ES -klɪˌə(r

nucleate *adj* 'njuklɪt, 'nɪu-, 'nu-, -ˌet

nucleate *v* 'njuklɪˌet, 'nɪu-, 'nu- |-d -ɪd

nuclei 'njuklɪˌaɪ, 'nɪu-, 'nu-

nucleic nju'kliɪk, nɪu-, nu-

nuclein 'njuklɪɪn, 'nɪu-, 'nu-

nucleolar nju'kliələ, nɪu-, nu-; ES -lə(r

nucleolate *adj* nju'kliəlɪt, nɪu-, nu-, -ˌlet |-d
-ˌletɪd

nucleolus nju'kliələs, nɪu-, nu- |-es -ɪz |-li
-ˌlaɪ

nucleus 'njuklɪəs, 'nɪu-, 'nu- |-es -ɪz |-lei
-lɪˌaɪ

nude njud, nɪud, nud |-d -ɪd |-ism -ɪzəm |-ist
-ɪst

nudge nʌdʒ |nudges 'nʌdʒɪz |nudged nʌdʒd

nudity 'njudətɪ, 'nɪu-, 'nu-

nugatory 'njugəˌtorɪ, 'nɪu-, 'nu-, -ˌtɔrɪ; S
-ˌtorɪ

nugget 'nʌgɪt

nuisance 'njusn̩s, 'nɪu-, 'nu- |-s -ɪz

null nʌl |nulled nʌld

null and void 'nʌlən'vɔɪd

nullification ˌnʌləfə'keʃən

nullify 'nʌləˌfaɪ |-fied -ˌfaɪd

nullity 'nʌlətɪ

numb nʌm |numbed nʌmd

number *'more numb'* 'nʌmɚ; ES 'nʌmə(r

number *'count'* 'nʌmbɚ; ES 'nʌmbə(r; |-ed -d
|-ing 'nʌmbrɪŋ, 'nʌmbərɪŋ

numbest 'nʌmɪst

numbles 'nʌmbl̩z

numbly 'nʌmlɪ

numbskull 'nʌmˌskʌl |-ed -d |-edness -ɪdnɪs
|-ery -ərɪ |-ism -skʌl̩ɪzəm

numerable 'njumərəbl̩, 'nɪu-, 'nu-, -mrə-
|-bly -blɪ

numeral 'njumrəl, 'nɪu-, 'nu-, -mərəl |-ly -ɪ

numerate *adj* 'njumərɪt, 'nɪu-, 'nu-, -ˌret

numerate *v* 'njuməˌret, 'nɪu-, 'nu- |-d -ɪd
|-tor -ɚ; ES -ə(r

numeration ˌnjumə'reʃən, ˌnɪu-, ˌnu-

numerical nju'mɛrɪkl̩, nɪu-, nu- |-ly -ɪ, -ɪklɪ

numerology ˌnjumə'rɑlədʒɪ, ˌnɪu-, ˌnu-;
ES+-'ɒl-

Those words below in which the ɑ sound is spelt o are often pronounced with ɒ in E and S

numerous 'njumrəs, 'nɪu-, 'nu-, -mərəs
Numidia nju'mɪdɪə, nɪu-, nu- |-n -n
numismatic ˌnjumɪz'mætɪk, ˌnɪu-, ˌnu-, -mɪs-
|-al -l̩ |-ally -l̩ɪ, -ɪklɪ
numskull 'nʌmˌskʌl |-ed -d |-edness -ɪdnɪs
|-ery -ərɪ |-ism -skʌlˌɪzəm
nun nʌn |nunned nʌnd
Nun *Bible* nʌn
Nunc Dimittis 'nʌŋkdɪ'mɪtɪs |-es -ɪz
nuncheon 'nʌntʃən
nuncio 'nʌnʃɪˌo
nuncle 'nʌŋkl̩
nuncupative 'nʌnkjʊˌpetɪv, nʌn'kjupətɪv,
-'kɪu-
Nuneaton nʌn'itn̩
nunnery 'nʌnərɪ
nuptial 'nʌpʃəl, 'nʌptʃəl |-s -z |-ed -d
Nuremberg 'njʊrəmˌbɝg, 'nɪu-, 'nu-; ES
-ˌbɝg, -ˌbɝg; (*Ger* Nürnberg 'nʏrnbɛrk)
nurse nɝs; ES nɜs, nɝs; |-s -ɪz |-d -t
nursegirl 'nɝsˌgɝl; ES 'nɜsˌgɜl, 'nɝsˌgɝl
nursemaid 'nɝsˌmed; ES 'nɜs-, 'nɝs-
nursery 'nɝsrɪ, 'nɝsərɪ; ES 'nɜs-, 'nɝs-;
|-ied -d |-maid -ˌmed
nurseryman 'nɝsrɪmən, 'nɝsərɪ-; ES 'nɜs-,
'nɝs-; |-men -mən

nursling, nursel- 'nɝslɪŋ; ES 'nɜs-, 'nɝs-
nurture 'nɝtʃɚ; ES 'nɜtʃə(r, 'nɝtʃə(r; |-d -d
nut nʌt |nutted 'nʌtɪd
nutant 'njutn̩t, 'nɪu-, 'nu-
nutation nju'teʃən, nɪu-, nu-
nutcracker 'nʌtˌkrækɚ; ES -ˌkrækə(r
Nuthall, Nuttall 'nʌtɔl, *Engd* 'nʌtl̩
nuthatch 'nʌtˌhætʃ |-es -ɪz
Nutley 'nʌtlɪ
nutmeg 'nʌtmɛg |-ged -d |-gy -ɪ
nutrient 'njutrɪənt, 'nɪu-, 'nu-
nutriment 'njutrəmənt, 'nɪu-, 'nu-
nutrition nju'trɪʃən, nɪu-, nu- |-tious -ʃəs
nutritive 'njutrɪtɪv, 'nɪu-, 'nu-
nutshell 'nʌtˌʃɛl |-ed -d
Nuttall 'nʌtɔl, *Engd* 'nʌtl̩
nutty 'nʌtɪ
nux vomica 'nʌks'vamɪkə
nuzzle 'nʌzl̩ |-d -d |-ling 'nʌzlɪŋ, 'nʌzl̩ɪŋ
Nyack 'naɪæk
Nyanza naɪ'ænzə, nɪ-
Nyasa naɪ'æsə, nɪ- |-land -ˌlænd
Nye naɪ
nylon 'naɪlɑn, -ɒn
Nym nɪm
nymph nɪmf, nɪmpf |-al -l̩ |-ic -ɪk |-ical -ɪkl̩

O

O, o *letter* o |*pl* O's, Os, *poss* O's oz
O *intj* o
o' *prep unstressed form of* on ə (o' nights
ə'naɪts) *or of* of (o'clock ə'klɑk)
oaf of |-'s -s |oafs ofs *or* oaves ovz
Oahu o'ɑhu
oak ok |oaken 'okən
Oakes oks |-'s -ɪz
Oakland 'oklənd
oakum 'okəm
oar or, ɔr; ES oə(r, E+ɔə(r; |-ed -d |-lock
-ˌlɑk
oarsman 'orzmən, 'ɔrz-; ES 'oəz-, E+'ɔəz-;
|-men -mən
oasis o'esɪs, 'oəsɪs |oases -siz
oast ost |-house -ˌhaʊs |-houses -ˌhaʊzɪz
oat ot |oaten 'otn̩ |-cake -ˌkek |-meal -ˌmil

oath oθ |oath's oθs |oaths oðz
Oaxaca wɑ'hɑkə (*Am Sp* wɑ'hɑkɑ)
Obadiah ˌobə'daɪə
Oban 'obən
obbligato ˌɑblɪ'gɑto
obduracy 'ɑbdjərəsɪ, -djʊ-
obdurate 'ɑbdjərɪt, -djʊ-, -də-
obeah, O- 'obɪə |obeahed 'obɪəd
Obed 'obɪd, 'obɛd
obedience ə'bidɪəns |-cy -ɪ |-ent -ənt
obeisance o'besn̩s, -'bisn̩s |-sant -sn̩t
obelisk 'ɑbl̩ˌɪsk
obelus 'ɑbləs |-es -ɪz |-li 'ɑblˌaɪ
Oberammergau ˌobɚ'æmɚˌgaʊ, -'ɑmɚ-; ES
-məˌgaʊ
Oberon 'obəˌrɑn, 'obərən
obese o'bis |-sity o'bisətɪ, o'bɛs-

|full fʊl |tooth tuθ |further 'fɝðɚ; ES 'fɝðə |custom 'kʌstəm |while hwaɪl |how haʊ |toy tɔɪ
|using 'juzɪŋ |fuse fjuz, fɪuz |dish dɪʃ |vision 'vɪʒən |Eden 'idn̩ |cradle 'kredl̩ |keep 'em 'kipm̩

Those words below in which the ɑ *sound is spelt* o *are often pronounced with* ɒ *in E and S*

obey ə'be, o'be |-ed -d
obfuscate ab'fʌsket, əb-, 'abfəsˌket |-d -ɪd
obfuscation ˌabfʌs'keʃən, ˌabfəs-
obiter dictum 'abɪtɚ'dɪktəm, 'ob-; ES -tə-
obituary ə'bɪtʃuˌɛrɪ, o-
object n 'abdʒɪkt
object v əb'dʒɛkt |-jected -'dʒɛktɪd
objectify əb'dʒɛktəˌfaɪ |-fied -ˌfaɪd
objection əb'dʒɛkʃən |-able -əb|, -ʃnəb| |-bly -blɪ
objective əb'dʒɛktɪv ('subˌjective & 'obˌjective)
objectivity ˌabdʒɛk'tɪvətɪ
objector əb'dʒɛktɚ; ES -'dʒɛktə(r
objurgate 'abdʒɚˌget, əb'dʒɝˈget; ES 'abdʒə-, əb'dʒɝg-, -'dʒɝˈg-; |-d -ɪd
oblate n, adj 'ablet, əb'let
oblate v əb'let |-lated -'letɪd
oblation əb'leʃən, ab-
oblatory 'abləˌtorɪ, -ˌtɔrɪ; S -ˌtorɪ
obligate 'abləˌget |-d -ɪd |-tion ˌablə'geʃən
obligato ˌablɪ'gato
obligatory ə'blɪgəˌtorɪ, 'ablɪgə-, -ˌtɔrɪ; S -ˌtorɪ
oblige ə'blaɪdʒ |-s -ɪz |-d -d |-dly -ɪdlɪ
obligee ˌablɪ'dʒi (ˌobli'gee & ˌobli'gor)
obligor 'ablɪˌgɔr; ES -ˌgɔə(r; see above
oblique ə'blik |obliqued ə'blikt—ə'blaɪk is o.f. or military.
obliquity ə'blɪkwətɪ
obliterate ə'blɪtəˌret |-rated -ˌretɪd
obliteration əˌblɪtə'reʃən
oblivion ə'blɪvɪən |-ous -əs
oblong 'ablɔŋ, -lɒŋ; S+-lɑŋ
obloquy 'abləkwɪ
obnoxious əb'nakʃəs, ab-
oboe 'obo, 'obɔɪ
obol 'ab|
obolus 'abləs |-es -ɪz |-li 'ab|ˌaɪ
Obrdlik Czech scholar 'ɔbɚd|lik; ES 'ɔbəd-
obscene əb'sin, ab- ('obˌscene 'mind)
obsceneness əb'sinnɪs
obscenity əb'sɛnətɪ, -'sinətɪ
obscurant əb'skjurənt, -'skɪur- |-ism -ˌɪzəm
obscuration ˌabskju'reʃən, -skɪu-
obscure əb'skjur, -'skɪur; ES -'skjuə(r, -'skɪuə(r; |-d -d |-dly -ɪdlɪ
obscurity əb'skjurətɪ, -'skɪurətɪ

obsequious əb'sikwɪəs
obsequy 'absɪkwɪ
observable əb'zɝvəb|; ES -'zɔv-, -'zɝv-; |-bly -blɪ
observance əb'zɝvəns; ES -'zɔv-, -'zɝv-; |-s -ɪz |-ant -ənt |-vation ˌabzɚ'veʃən; ES -zə-
observatory əb'zɝvəˌtorɪ, -ˌtɔrɪ; ES əb'zɝvəˌtɔrɪ, -'zɝv-, E+-ˌtɔrɪ
observe əb'zɝv; ES -'zɔv, -'zɝv; |-d -d |-dly -ɪdlɪ
obsess əb'sɛs |-es -ɪz |-ed -t |-ion -'sɛʃən
obsidian əb'sɪdɪən
obsolescence ˌabsə'lɛsn̩s |-scent -sn̩t
obsolete 'absəˌlit
obstacle 'abstək|, 'abstɪk|
obstetric əb'stɛtrɪk |-al -| |-ally -|ɪ, -ɪklɪ
obstetrician ˌabstɛ'trɪʃən
obstinacy 'abstənəsɪ |-nate -nɪt
obstreperous əb'strɛpərəs, ab-
obstruct əb'strʌkt |-ed -ɪd |-ion -'strʌkʃən
obtain əb'ten |-ed -d |-able -əb|
obtrude əb'trud, -'trɪud |-d -ɪd
obtrusion əb'truʒən, -'trɪuʒən |-sive -sɪv
obtuse əb'tus, -'trɪus, -'tjus
obverse n 'abvɝs; ES 'abvɔs, -vɝs
obverse adj əb'vɝs, 'abvɝs; ES -ɔs, -ɝs
obvert əb'vɝt; ES əb'vɔt, -'vɝt; |-ed -ɪd
obviate 'abvɪˌet |-d -ɪd |-tion ˌabvɪ'eʃən
obvious 'abvɪəs
ocarina ˌakə'rinə
Occam 'akəm
occasion ə'keʒən |-ed -d
occasional ə'keʒən|, -'keʒnəl |-ly -ɪ
occident 'aksədənt
occidental ˌaksə'dɛnt| |-ly -ɪ |-ism -ˌɪzəm
occidentalize ˌaksə'dɛnt|ˌaɪz |-s -ɪz |-d -d
occipital ak'sɪpət| |-ly -ɪ
occiput 'aksɪˌpʌt, 'aksəpət |-pita ak'sɪpɪtə
occlude ə'klud, -'klɪud |-d -ɪd |-clusion -ʒən
occult ə'kʌlt |-ed -ɪd ('ocˌcult 'science)
occultation ˌakʌl'teʃən, -kəl-
occupancy 'akjəpənsɪ |-pant -pənt
occupation ˌakjə'peʃən
occupy 'akjəˌpaɪ |-pied -ˌpaɪd
occur ə'kɝ; ES ə'kɝ(r, ə'kɝ; |-red -d
occurrence ə'kɝəns; ES ə'kɝ-, ə'kʌr-, ə'kɝ-
ocean 'oʃən |-ic ˌoʃɪ'ænɪk |Oceanica -'ænɪkə
Oceana o'sɪənə, ˌoʃɪ'enə, Mich ˌoʃɪ'ænə

Key: See in full §§3–47. bee bi |pity 'pɪtɪ (§6) |rate ret |yet jɛt |sang sæŋ |angry 'æŋ·grɪ |bath bæθ; E baθ (§10) |ah ɑ |far fɑr |watch wɑtʃ, wɒtʃ (§12) |jaw dʒɔ |gorge gɔrdʒ |go go

Those words below in which the ɑ *sound is spelt* o *are often pronounced with* ɒ *in E and S*

Oceania ˌoʃɪˈænɪə, -ˈɑn-, -ˈen-

Oceanid oˈsiənɪd |Oceano ˌoʃɪˈæno

oceanography ˌoʃɪənˈɑgrəfɪ, ˌoʃən-, -ˈɒg-

Oceanus oˈsiənəs |-'s -ɪz

ocelot ˈosəˌlɑt, ˈɑsə-, -lət

ocher, ochre ˈokɚ; ES ˈokə(r; |-(e)d -d |-ing ˈokərɪŋ, ˈokrɪŋ

ochroid ˈokrɔɪd

Ockham ˈɑkəm

o'clock əˈklɑk

Ocmulgee okˈmʌlgɪ—*traditional & loc. pron.*

octachord ˈɑktəˌkɔrd; ES -ˌkɔəd

octad ˈɑktæd

octagon ˈɑktəˌgɑn, -gən

octagonal ɑkˈtægənḷ |-ly -ɪ

octahedral ˌɑktəˈhidrəl

octameter ɑkˈtæmətɚ; ES -ˈtæmətə(r

octane ˈɑkten

octangle ˈɑktæŋgḷ |-gular ɑkˈtæŋgjəlɚ; ES -ə(r

octaroon ˌɑktəˈrun

octave ˈɑktev, ˈɑktɪv

Octavia ɑkˈtevɪə |-vius -s |-vius's -sɪz

octavo ɑkˈtevo

octennial ɑkˈtɛnɪəl |-ly -ɪ

octet, -tte ɑkˈtɛt (ˈocˌtet & ˈsesˌtet)

October ɑkˈtobɚ; ES -ˈtobə(r

octodecimo ˌɑktoˈdɛsəˌmo

octogenarian ˌɑktədʒəˈnɛrɪən, -ˈner-

octogenary ɑkˈtɑdʒəˌnɛrɪ

octopus ˈɑktəpəs |-es -ɪz |-pi -ˌpaɪ

octoroon ˌɑktəˈrun

octosyllable ˈɑktəˌsɪləbḷ |-bic ˌɑktəsɪˈlæbɪk

octroi ˈɑktrɔɪ (*Fr* ɔ̃kˈtrwɑ)

octuple *n, adj, v* ˈɑktʊpḷ, -tjʊpḷ, ɑkˈtupḷ, -ˈtɪu-, -ˈtju- |-d -d |-ling -plɪŋ, -pḷɪŋ

ocular ˈɑkjəlɚ; ES ˈɑkjələ(r; |-list -lɪst

Od, 'Od, Odd *intj* ɑd, ɒd |-'s -z

odalisque, -sk ˈodḷˌɪsk

odd ɑd, ɒd |-s -z |-ity -ətɪ |-ment -mənt

Oddfellow, Odd Fellow ˈɑdˌfɛlo, ˈɒd-, -ə

ode od

Oder ˈodɚ; ES ˈodə(r

Odessa oˈdɛsə

Odin ˈodɪn

odious ˈodɪəs |odium ˈodɪəm

Odoacer ˌodoˈesɚ; ES oˈdɑmətə(r

odometer oˈdɑmətɚ; ES oˈdɑmətə(r

odontology ˌodɑnˈtɑlədʒɪ, ˌɑd-

odor ˈodɚ; ES ˈodə(r; |-ous -əs

odoriferous ˌodəˈrɪfərəs, -frəs

'Od's bodikins, odsb- ˈɑdzˈbɑdɪkɪnz

Odysseus oˈdɪsjus, oˈdɪsɪəs |-eus' -jus, -ɪəs

Odyssey ˈɑdəsɪ

oecumenic ˌɛkjʊˈmɛnɪk |-al -ḷ |-ally -ḷɪ, -ɪklɪ

oedema iˈdimə |*pl* -mata -mətə |-tous -təs

Oedipus ˈɛdəpəs |-'s -ɪz

Oeneus ˈinjus |-'s -ɪz

Oenone iˈnonɪ

o'er or, ɔr; ES oə(r, E+ɔə(r

oersted ˈɝstɛd; ES ˈɜstɛd, ˈɝs-

oesophagus iˈsɑfəgəs |-es -ɪz |-gi -ˌdʒaɪ

oestrous ˈɛstrəs, ˈis-

oestrum ˈɛstrəm, ˈis-

oestrus ˈɛstrəs, ˈis- |-es -ɪz

of *stressed* ˈɑv, ˌɑv, ˈɒv, ˌɒv, ˈʌv, ˌʌv; *unstr.* əv, *before conss.*+ə (ðə ˈlɑd ə ˈkɒl), *or after vowels* + v (ðɪ aɪˈdiə v ˌðæt)

off ɔf, ɒf

offal ˈɔfḷ, ˈɒfḷ, ˈɑfḷ

off and on ˈɔfənˈɑn, ˈɒf-, -ˈɒn, -ˈɔn

offcast ˈɔfˈkæst, ˈɒf-; E+-ˈkɑst, -ˈkɑst; (ˈoffˌcast ˈclothes)

off-color ˈɔfˈkʌlɚ, ˈɒf-; ES -ˈkʌlə(r; (ˈoffˌcolor ˈstory)

Offenbach ˈɔfənˌbɑk, ˈɒf-, -əf- (*Ger* ˈɔfənˌbɑx)

offend əˈfɛnd |offended əˈfɛndɪd

offense, -ce əˈfɛns |-s -ɪz (ˈɔˌfɛnsṇˈdiˌfɛns)

offensive əˈfɛnsɪv

offer ˈɔfɚ, ˈɒfɚ, ˈɑfɚ; ES -fə(r; |-ed -d |-ing -fərɪŋ, -frɪŋ

offertory ˈɔfɚˌtorɪ, ˈɒf-, ˈɑf-, -ˌtɔrɪ; ES -fəˌtorɪ, E+-ˌtɔrɪ

offhand ˈɔfˈhænd, ˈɒf- (ˈoffˌhand ˈway)

office ˈɔfɪs, ˈɒfɪs, ˈɑfɪs |-s -ɪz |-d -t

officeholder ˈɔfɪsˌholdɚ, ˈɒf-, ˈɑf-; ES -ə(r

officer ˈɔfəsɚ, ˈɒf-, ˈɑf-; ES -fəsə(r

official əˈfɪʃəl |-ly -ɪ |-dom -dəm

officiant əˈfɪʃɪənt

officiary əˈfɪʃɪˌɛrɪ

officiate əˈfɪʃɪˌet |-ated -ˌetɪd

officinal əˈfɪsɪnḷ

officious əˈfɪʃəs

offing ˈɔfɪŋ, ˈɒfɪŋ

offish ˈɔfɪʃ, ˈɒfɪʃ

offprint ˈɔfˌprɪnt, ˈɒf- |-ed -ɪd

|full fʊl |tooth tuθ |further ˈfɝðɚ; ES ˈfɜðə |custom ˈkʌstəm |while hwaɪl |how haʊ |toy tɔɪ
|using ˈjuzɪŋ |fuse fjuz, fɪuz |dish dɪʃ |vision ˈvɪʒən |Eden ˈidṇ |cradle ˈkredḷ |keep 'em ˈkipm̩

offscouring 'ɔf‚skaʊrɪŋ, 'ɒf-
offset n 'ɔf‚sɛt, 'ɒf-
offset v ɔf'sɛt, ɒf- |-setting -'sɛtɪŋ
offshoot 'ɔf‚ʃut, 'ɒf-
offshore 'ɔf'ʃor, 'ɒf-, -'ʃɔr; ES -'ʃoə(r, E+
 -'ʃɔə(r
offspring 'ɔf‚sprɪŋ, 'ɒf-
oft ɔft, ɒft |-times -‚taɪmz
often 'ɔfən, 'ɔftən, 'ɒf- |-times -‚taɪmz
oftener 'ɔfənɚ, 'ɒf-, -fnɚ, -tənɚ, -tnɚ; ES
 -nə(r; |-nest -nɪst
Og ɑg, ɒg, ɔg
Ogden 'ɑgdən, 'ɒgdən, 'ɔgdən
ogee o'dʒi, 'odʒi |-d -d
Ogilby 'ogļbɪ |Ogilvy, -ie 'ogļvɪ
ogive 'odʒaɪv, o'dʒaɪv |-d -d
ogle 'ogļ |ogled 'ogļd |-ling 'oglɪŋ, 'ogļɪŋ
Ogleby 'ogļbɪ |Oglethorpe -‚θɔrp; ES -‚θoəp
Ogpu 'ɑgpu, 'ɒgpu, 'ɔgpu
ogre 'ogɚ; ES 'ogə(r; |-ish, -grish -gərɪʃ, -grɪʃ
oh o |oh's, ohs oz |ohed od |ohing 'o·ɪŋ
O'Hara o'hærə, o'hɑrə
Ohio o'haɪo |Ohioan o'haɪəwən—see -ow
ohm, O- om |-age -ɪdʒ |-ages -ɪdʒɪz
oho intj o'ho
oil ɔɪl |oiled ɔɪld |oily 'ɔɪlɪ |-less 'ɔɪllɪs
oilcloth 'ɔɪl‚klɔθ, -‚klɒθ |-ths -ðz, -θs—see
 cloth
oilproof 'ɔɪl'pruf |-ed -t ('oil‚proof 'paint)
oilskin 'ɔɪl‚skɪn
oilstone 'ɔɪl‚ston
ointment 'ɔɪntmənt
Oireachtas 'ɛrəxtəs |-'s -ɪz
Ojibway, -wa o'dʒɪbwe
O.K., OK 'o'ke |-'s -'kez |-'d -'ked|-'ing
 -'ke·ɪŋ
okapi o'kɑpɪ
Okeechobee ‚okɪ'tʃobɪ, -bi
Oklahoma ‚oklə'homə |-n -n
okra 'okrə
Olaf 'oləf, 'olɑf
old old |olden 'oldn̩ |oldened 'oldn̩d
Oldcastle 'old‚kæsļ; E+-‚kɑsļ, -‚kɑsļ
old-fashioned 'old'fæʃənd, 'ol'f- ('old-‚fash-
 ioned 'girl)
old-fogyish, -gey- 'old'fogɪʃ, 'ol'f-
Oldham 'oldəm
old-maidish 'old'medɪʃ, 'ol'm- ('old-‚maidish
 'air)

oldster 'oldstɚ, 'ols-; ES -stə(r
oldwife 'old‚waɪf |-'s -‚waɪfs |-wives -‚waɪvz
old-womanish 'old'wumənɪʃ, -'wum-
old-world 'old'wɜld; ES -'wɜld, -'wɜ·ld
oleaginous ‚olɪ'ædʒənəs
oleander ‚olɪ'ændɚ; ES -də(r; ('ole‚ander
 'leaf)
oleaster ‚olɪ'æstɚ; ES -'æstə(r
oleate 'olɪ‚et, 'olɪt
olefin 'oləfɪn |-fine -fɪn, -‚fin
oleic o'liɪk, 'olɪk |olein 'olɪɪn |oleo 'olɪ‚o
oleomargarine, -in ‚olɪə'mɑrdʒə‚rin, -rɪn,
 much less freq. -'mɑrg-; ES -'mɑ:-, E+
 -'mɑ:-
oleoresin ‚olɪo'rɛzn̩, -'rɛzɪn
olfactory ɑl'fæktərɪ, -'fæktrɪ; ES+ɒl-
Olga 'ɑlgə, 'ɒlgə
olibanum o'lɪbənəm
oligarch 'ɑlɪ‚gɑrk; ES 'ɑlɪ‚gɑ:k, 'ɒlɪ-; |-y -ɪ
oligarchic ‚ɑlɪ'gɑrkɪk; ES -'gɑ:k-, ‚ɒl-
Oligocene 'ɑlɪgo‚sin; ES+'ɒl-
olio 'olɪ‚o
olivary 'ɑlə‚vɛrɪ; ES+'ɒl-
olive, O- 'ɑlɪv; ES+'ɒlɪv
Oliver 'ɑləvɚ; ES 'ɑləvə(r, 'ɒl-
Olivet 'ɑlə‚vɛt, 'ɑləvɪt; ES+'ɒl-
Olivia o'lɪvɪə, o'lɪvjə
olla L word 'ɑlə; ES+'ɒlə; |ollae -li
olla 'ɑlə; ES+'ɒlə; |pl ollas -ləz (Sp 'oʎa,
 'oʎas)
olla-podrida 'ɑləpə'dridə; ES+'ɒl-; (Sp
 'oʎapo'ðriða)
Olmsted 'ɑmstɛd, 'ɒm-, 'ʌm-, -stɪd
Olney US 'ɑlnɪ, 'ɒlnɪ, Engd 'olnɪ, loc. 'onɪ
ology 'ɑlədʒɪ; ES+'ɒl-
Olympia o'lɪmpɪə, -pjə |-n -n |-piad -pɪ‚æd
Olympic o'lɪmpɪk |-pus -pəs |-pus's -pəsɪz
Omaha 'omə‚hɔ, 'omə‚hɑ
Omar 'omɚ, 'omɑr; ES 'omə(r, 'omɑ:(r
omber, -bre 'ɑmbɚ; ES 'ɑmbə(r, 'ɒm-
omega, O- o'mɛgə, o'migə, 'omɪgə
omelet, -tte 'ɑmlɪt, 'ɑməlɪt; ES+'ɒm-
omen 'omɪn, 'omən
omer, O- 'omɚ; ES 'omə(r
omicron 'ɑmɪ‚krɑn, 'o-; ES+'ɒmɪ‚krɒn
ominous 'ɑmənəs; ES+'ɒm-
omissible o'mɪsəbļ |-bly -blɪ
omission o'mɪʃən ('o‚mission and 'com-
 ‚mission)

omissive o'mɪsɪv
omit o'mɪt, ə'mɪt |omitted -'mɪtɪd
omnibus 'ɑmnəˌbʌs, 'ɑmnəbəs; ES+'ɒm-;
|-es -ɪz
omnifarious ˌɑmnə'fɛrɪəs, -'fær-, -'fer-;
ES+ˌɒm-
omnific ɑm'nɪfɪk; ES+ɒm-
omnipotence ɑm'nɪpətəns; ES+ɒm-; |-ent
-ənt
omnipresence ˌɑmnɪ'prɛzn̩s; ES+ˌɒm-; |-nt
-n̩t
omniscience ɑm'nɪʃəns; ES+ɒm-; |-ent -ənt
omnium gatherum 'ɑmnɪəm'gæðərəm; ES+
'ɒm-
omnivorous ɑm'nɪvərəs, -'nɪvrəs; ES+ɒm-
on ɑn, ɒn, ɔn—ɔn is commonest in S and W.
onager 'ɑnədʒɚ; ES 'ɑnədʒə(r, 'ɒn-; |pl -s -z
|-gri -ˌgraɪ
onanism 'onənˌɪzəm |-ist -ɪst
once wʌns
oncoming 'ɑnˌkʌmɪŋ, 'ɒn-, 'ɔn-
ondometer ɑn'dɑmətɚ; ES ɑn'dɑmətə(r,
ɒn'dɒm-
one stressed 'wʌn, ˌwʌn; unstr. wən |-s -z
one-horse 'wʌn'hɔrs; ES 'wʌn'hɔəs; ('one-
ˌhorse 'shay)
Oneida o'naɪdə, Ky o'nidə
O'Neill o'nil
one-legged 'wʌn'lɛgɪd, -gd ('one-ˌlegged 'man)
oneness 'wʌnnɪs
Oneonta NY ˌonɪ'ɑntə; ES+-'ɒntə
onerous 'ɑnərəs; ES+'ɒn-
oneself wʌn'sɛlf, wʌnz'sɛlf, wən-
one-sided 'wʌn'saɪdɪd ('one-ˌsided 'view)
one-step 'wʌnˌstɛp |one-stepped 'wʌnˌstɛpt
one-way 'wʌnˌwe ('one-ˌway 'traffic)
onion 'ʌnjən, 'ʌnjɪn
Onions 'ʌnjənz |-'s -ɪz
onionskin 'ʌnjənˌskɪn, 'ʌnjɪn-
onlooker 'ɑnˌlukɚ, 'ɒn-, 'ɔn-; ES -ˌlukə(r
only 'onlɪ; NEngd+'ɔnlɪ (§46)
onomatapoeia ˌɑnəˌmætə'piə, oˌnɑmətə-;
ES+ˌɒn-, oˌnɒm-; |-poeic -'piɪk
onomatapoetic ˌɑnəˌmætəpo'ɛtɪk; ES+ˌɒn-
Onondaga ˌɑnən'dɔgə, -'dɑgə; ES+ˌɒn-
onrush 'ɑnˌrʌʃ, 'ɒn-, 'ɔn- |-es -ɪz
onset 'ɑnˌsɛt, 'ɒn-, 'ɔn-
onslaught 'ɑnˌslɔt, 'ɒn-, 'ɔn-
Ontarian ɑn'tɛrɪən, -'ter-; ES+ɒn- |-io -ˌo

onto bef. pause 'ɑntu, 'ɒn-, 'ɔn-; bef. conss.
-tə; bef. vow. -tʊ, -tə
ontogeny ɑn'tɑdʒənɪ; ES+ɒn'tɒdʒ-; |-ist -ɪst
ontology ɑn'tɑlədʒɪ; ES+ɒn'tɒl-
onus 'onəs |onuses 'onəsɪz
onward 'ɑnwɚd, 'ɒn-, 'ɔn-; ES -wəd; |-s -z
onyx 'ɑnɪks, 'onɪks; ES+'ɒn-; |-es -ɪz
oögenesis ˌoə'dʒɛnəsɪs
oölite 'oəˌlaɪt |oölitic ˌoə'lɪtɪk
oölogy o'ɑlədʒɪ; ES+-'ɒl-; |-gist -dʒɪst
oolong, O- 'ulɔŋ, 'ulɒŋ, 'ulɑŋ
oomiak 'umɪˌæk
oösperm 'oəˌspɝm; ES 'oəˌspɜm, -ˌspɝm
oösphere 'oəˌsfɪr; ES 'oəˌsfɪə(r, S+-ˌsfɛə(r
oöspore 'oəˌspor, -ˌspɔr; ES 'oəˌspoə(r,
E+-ˌspɔə(r
ooze uz |oozes 'uzɪz |oozed uzd |oozy 'uzɪ
opacity o'pæsətɪ
opal 'opl̩ |opaline n 'opl̩ˌin
opalescence ˌopl̩'ɛsn̩s |opalescent ˌopl̩'ɛsn̩t
opaline adj 'opl̩ɪn, 'opl̩ˌaɪn
opaque o'pek, ə'pek
ope op |oped opt
open 'opən, 'opm̩ |-ed -d |-ing 'opənɪŋ,
'opnɪŋ; NEngd+'ɔp- (§46)
open-air 'opən'ɛr, -'ær; E -'ɛə(r, ES -'æə(r
open-eyed 'opən'aɪd |-eyedly -'aɪdlɪ, -'aɪdlɪ
openhanded 'opən'hændɪd ('opənˌhanded
'giver)
openhearted 'opən'hɑrtɪd; ES -'hɑ:tɪd, E+
'hɑ:tɪd
open-hearth 'opən'hɑrθ; ES -'hɑ:θ, E+-'hɑ:θ
open-minded 'opən'maɪndɪd ('open-ˌminded
'man)
openmouthed 'opən'maʊðd, -θt
openness 'opənnɪs
openwork 'opənˌwɝk; ES 'opənˌwɜk, -ˌwɝk
opera 'ɑpərə, 'ɑprə; ES+'ɒp-
operable 'ɑpərəbl̩, 'ɑprə-; ES+'ɒp-; |-bly
-blɪ
opéra bouffe 'ɑpərə'buf, 'ɑprə-; ES+'ɒp-;
(Fr ɔpera'buf)
opéra comique Fr ɔpera·kɔ'mik
operate 'ɑpəˌret; ES+'ɒp-; |-d -ɪd
operatic ˌɑpə'rætɪk; ES+ˌɒp-; |-ally -l̩ɪ,
-ɪklɪ
operation ˌɑpə'reʃən; ES+ˌɒp-
operative 'ɑpəˌretɪv, 'ɑpərətɪv, 'ɑprətɪv;
ES+'ɒp-

|full fʊl |tooth tuθ |further 'fɝðɚ; ES 'fɝðə |custom 'kʌstəm |while hwaɪl |how haʊ |toy tɔɪ
|using 'juzɪŋ |fuse fjuz, fɪuz |dish dɪʃ |vision 'vɪʒən |Eden 'idn̩ |cradle 'kredl̩ |keep 'em 'kipm̩

operator 'apəˌretəʰ; ES 'apəˌretə(r, 'ɒp-
opere citato, op. cit. 'apəˌri·sar'teto, 'ap'sɪt;
   ES+'ɒp-
operetta ˌapə'rɛtə; ES+ˌɒp-; |-s -z |-te -ti
Ophelia ə'filjə, o'filjə
ophidian o'fɪdɪən
Ophir 'ofəʰ; ES 'ofə(r
ophthalmia af'θælmɪə, -mjə; ES+ɒf-; |-mic
   -mɪk
ophthalmitis ˌafθæl'maɪtɪs; ES+ˌɒf-
ophthalmology ˌafθæl'malədʒɪ; ES+ˌɒfθæl-
   'mɒl-
ophthalmoscope af'θælməˌskop; ES+ɒf-
opiate 'opɪˌet, 'opɪɪt
opine o'paɪn |opined o'paɪnd
opinion ə'pɪnjən |opinioned ə'pɪnjənd
opinionated ə'pɪnjənˌetɪd |-ative -ˌetɪv
opium 'opɪəm, 'opjəm
Oporto o'porto, o'pɔrto; ES o'poəto, E+
   o'pɔəto
opossum 'pasəm, ə'pasəm; ES+'ɒs-, ə'ɒs-
Oppenheim 'apənˌhaɪm; ES+'ɒp-
opponent ə'ponənt
opportune ˌapəʰ'tjun, -'tɪun, -'tun; ES+ˌɒp-;
   |-nist -ɪst |-nity -ətɪ |-neness -nɪs
opposable ə'pozəbl̩ |-bly -blɪ
oppose ə'poz |-s -ɪz |-d -d
opposite 'apəzɪt; ES+'ɒp-
opposition ˌapə'zɪʃən; ES+ˌɒp-
oppress ə'prɛs |-es -ɪz |-ed -t
oppression ə'prɛʃən |oppressive ə'prɛsɪv
oppressor ə'prɛsəʰ; ES ə'prɛsə(r
opprobrious ə'probrɪəs |-brium -brɪəm
oppugn ə'pjun, ə'pɪun |-ed -d
oppugnant ə'pʌgnənt
opsonic ap'sanɪk; ES+ɒp'sɒnɪk
opsonin 'apsənɪn; ES+'ɒp-
opt apt; ES+ɒpt; |-ed -ɪd
optative 'aptətɪv; ES+'ɒp-
optic 'aptɪk; ES+'ɒp-; |-s -s |-al -l̩ |-ally -lɪ,
   -ɪklɪ
optician ap'tɪʃən; ES+ɒp-
optime 'aptəˌmi; ES+'ɒp-
optimism 'aptəˌmɪzəm; ES+'ɒp-; |-mist
   -mɪst
optimistic ˌaptə'mɪstɪk; ES+ˌɒp-; |-al -l̩
   |-ally -lɪ, -ɪklɪ
optimum 'aptəməm; ES+'ɒp-
option 'apʃən; ES+'ɒp-; |-d -d |-al -l̩ |-ally -lɪ

optometer ap'tamətəʰ; ES ap'tamətə(r, ɒp-
   'tɒm-; |-trist -trɪst)-try -trɪ
opulence 'apjələns; ES+'ɒp-; |-cy -ɪ |-nt -nt
opus 'opəs |-es -ɪz |opera 'apərə; ES+'ɒp-
opuscule o'pʌskjul, -krul
or conj, usual form əʰ; ES ə(r; stressed 'ɔr,
   ˌɔr; ES 'ɔə(r, ˌɔə(r
or 'ere' ɔr; ES ɔə(r
-or ending -əʰ; ES -ə(r; usually not pron. -ɔr,
   -ɔə(r unless contrast is expressed or implied,
   as 'vɛndɔr—vɛn'di
oracle 'ɔrəkl̩, 'ɒrɪkl̩, 'ar-, 'ɒr- |-d -d
oracular ə'rækjələʰ, a'r-, ɒ'r, o'r-; ES -lə(r
oral 'orəl, 'ɔrəl; S 'orəl; |-ly -ɪ
orange 'orɪndʒ, 'ar-, 'ɒr-, -əndʒ |-s -ɪz |-ade
   -'ed
orangeman 'orɪndʒmən, 'a-, 'ɒ-, -ən- |-men
   -mən
orangery 'orɪndʒrɪ, 'a-, 'ɒ-, -əndʒ-
orangutan, -outang o'ræŋuˌtæn, -ˌtæŋ (Malay
   'oraŋ'utən)
orate 'oret, 'ɔret, o'ret, ɔ-; S 'o-, o-
oration o'reʃən, ɔ'reʃən; S o'reʃən
orator 'ɔrətəʰ, 'arətəʰ, 'ɒrətəʰ; ES -tə(r
oratorical ˌɔrə'tɔrɪkl̩, ˌarə'tar-, ˌɒrə'tɒr- |-ly
   -ɪ, -ɪklɪ
oratorio ˌɔrə'torɪo, ˌar-, ˌɒr-, -'tɔr-; S -'tor-
oratory 'ɔrəˌtorɪ, 'ar-, 'ɒr-, -ˌtɔrɪ; S -ˌtorɪ
orb ɔrb; ES ɔəb; |-ed -d, adj poetic -ɪd
orbicular ɔr'bɪkjələ; ES ɔ'bɪkjələ(r
orbit 'ɔrbɪt; ES 'ɔəbɪt; |-bital -bɪtl̩
orby 'ɔrbɪ; ES 'ɔəbɪ
orc ɔrk; ES ɔək
Orcadian ɔr'kedɪən; ES ɔ'kedɪən
orcein 'ɔrsiɪn; ES 'ɔəsiɪn
orchard 'ɔrtʃəʰd; ES 'ɔətʃəd
orchestra 'ɔrkɪstrə; ES 'ɔəkɪstrə
orchestral ɔr'kɛstrəl; ES ɔə'kɛstrəl |-ly -ɪ
orchestrate 'ɔrkɪsˌtret; ES 'ɔək-; |-d -ɪd
orchestration ˌɔrkɪs'treʃən; ES ˌɔəkɪs-
orchestrion ɔr'kɛstrɪən; ES ɔ'kɛstrɪən
orchid 'ɔrkɪd; ES 'ɔəkɪd
orchis 'ɔrkɪs; ES 'ɔəkɪs; |-es -ɪz
orcinol 'ɔrsɪˌnol, -ˌnal, -ˌnɒl; ES 'ɔə-
ordain ɔr'den; ES ɔə'den; |-ed -d
ordeal ɔr'dil, -'diəl, 'ɔrd-; ES ɔə'd-, 'ɔəd-
order 'ɔrdəʰ; ES 'ɔədə(r; |-ed -d |-ing -dərɪŋ,
   -drɪŋ
ordinal 'ɔrdnəl; ES 'ɔədnəl; |-ly -ɪ

Key: See in full §§3–47. bee bi |pity 'pɪtɪ (§6) |rate ret |yet jɛt |sang sæŋ |angry 'æŋ·grɪ |bath bæθ; E baθ (§10) |ah ɑ |far fɑr |watch watʃ, wɒtʃ (§12) |jaw dʒɔ |gorge gɔrdʒ |go go

ordinance 'ɔrdn̩əns, 'ɔrdnəns; ES 'ɔəd-; |-s -ɪz

ordinary 'ɔrdn̩ˌɛrɪ, 'ɔrdnɛrɪ; ES 'ɔəd-; |-ily -rəlɪ, *esp. if emph.* ˌordi'narily

ordinate *n, adj* 'ɔrdn̩ˌet, 'ɔrdn̩ɪt; ES 'ɔəd-

ordinate *v* 'ɔrdn̩ˌet; ES 'ɔəd-; |-d -ɪd

ordination ˌɔrdn̩'eʃən; ES ˌɔədn̩'eʃən

ordnance 'ɔrdnəns; ES 'ɔədnəns

ordo 'ɔrdo; ES 'ɔədo; |-dines -dɪˌniz

ordonnance 'ɔrdənəns; ES 'ɔəd-; (*Fr* ɔrdɔ-'nã:s)

Ordovician ˌɔrdə'vɪʃən; ES ˌɔədə'vɪʃən

ordure 'ɔrdʒɚ, 'ɔrdjʊr; ES 'ɔədʒə(r, -djʊə(r

öre *Dan coin sg & pl* 'ørə

ore or, ɔr; ES oə(r, E+ɔə(r

oread 'orɪˌæd, 'ɔrɪˌæd; S 'or-

Oregon 'ɒrɪˌgan, 'ɑr-, 'ɒr-, -gən

Orestes o'rɛstiz, ɔ-; S o-; |-tes' -tiz

organ 'ɔrgən; ES 'ɔəgən

organdy 'ɔrgəndɪ; ES 'ɔəgəndɪ

organic ɔr'gænɪk; ES ɔə'gænɪk; |-ally -l̩ɪ, -ɪklɪ

organism 'ɔrgən̩ˌɪzəm; ES 'ɔəgən̩ˌɪzəm; |-ist -ɪst

organization ˌɔrgənə'zeʃən, -aɪ'z-; ES ˌɔəg-

organize 'ɔrgən̩ˌaɪz; ES 'ɔəgən-; |-s -ɪz |-d -d

organon 'ɔrgəˌnan; ES 'ɔəgəˌnan, -ˌnɒn; |-s -z |-gana -gənə

organum 'ɔrgənəm; ES 'ɔəg-; |-s -z |-gana -gənə

orgasm 'ɔrgæzəm; ES 'ɔəgæzəm

orgiastic ˌɔrdʒɪ'æstɪk; ES ˌɔədʒ-; |-al -l̩

orgy 'ɔrdʒɪ; ES 'ɔədʒɪ

oriel 'orɪəl, 'ɔrɪəl; S 'orɪəl

orient, O- *n* 'orɪˌɛnt, 'ɔr-, -ənt; S 'or-

orient *adj* 'orɪənt, 'ɔr-; S 'orɪənt

orient *v* 'orɪˌɛnt, 'ɔr-; S 'orɪˌɛnt; |-ed -ɪd

oriental ˌorɪ'ɛnt̩l, ˌɔr-; S ˌor-; |-ism -ˌɪzəm |-ist -ɪst |-ly -ɪ |-ize -ˌaɪz |-izes -ˌaɪzɪz |-ized -ˌaɪzd

orientate 'orɪɛn̩ˌtet, ˌorɪ'ɛntet, 'ɔr-, ˌɔr-; S 'or-, ˌor-; |-d -ɪd

orientation ˌorɪɛn'teʃən, ˌɔr-; S ˌor-

orifice 'ɔrəfɪs, 'ɑr-, 'ɒr-

oriflamme, -amb 'ɔrəˌflæm, 'ɑr-, 'ɒr-

Origen 'ɔrədʒɪn, 'ɔrɪˌdʒɛn, 'ɑr-, 'ɒr-

origin 'ɔrədʒɪn, 'ɑr-, 'ɒr-

original ə'rɪdʒən̩l |-ly -ɪ

originality əˌrɪdʒə'nælətɪ

originate ə'rɪdʒəˌnet |-d -ɪd |-tive -ɪv

orinasal ˌorɪ'nez|, ˌɔr-; S ˌor-; |-ly -ɪ

Orinoco ˌorə'noko, ˌɔr-; S ˌor-

oriole 'orɪˌol, 'ɔr-; S 'or-

Orion o'raɪən |-'s -z |*gen* ˌɔrɪ'onɪs, ˌɑr-, ˌɒr-

orison 'ɔrɪzn̩, 'ɑr-, 'ɒr-

Orizaba ˌorɪ'sava, ˌɔr-; S ˌor-; (*Am Sp* ˌorɪ'saβa)

Orkney 'ɔrknɪ; ES 'ɔəknɪ

Orlando ɔr'lændo; ES ɔə'lændo

Orleans *La, France* 'ɔrlɪənz; ES 'ɔəlɪənz; *most US places* ɔr'linz; ES ɔə'l-; (*Fr* ɔrle'ã), *cf* New Orleans

orlop 'ɔrlap; ES 'ɔəlap, -lɒp

Ormazd, -muzd 'ɔrməzd; ES 'ɔəməzd

ormolu 'ɔrməˌlu; ES 'ɔəməˌlu

Ormuz 'ɔrmʌz; ES 'ɔəmʌz; |-'s -ɪz

ornament *n* 'ɔrnəmənt, *v* 'ɔrnəˌmɛnt; ES 'ɔən-; |-ed -ɪd

ornamental ˌɔrnə'mɛnt̩l; ES ˌɔən-; |-ly -ɪ

ornamentation ˌɔrnəmɛn'teʃən, -mən-; ES ˌɔənə-

ornate ɔr'net; ES ɔə'net

ornery 'ɔrnərɪ; ES 'ɔənərɪ

ornithology ˌɔrnə'θalədʒɪ; ES ˌɔənə-, -'θɒl-

orogeny ə'radʒənɪ; ES+ə'rɒdʒ-

orography ə'ragrəfɪ, ə'rɒg-

oroide 'oroˌaɪd, 'ɔr-; S 'or-

orology o'ralədʒɪ, ɔ-; S o-, ES+-'rɒl-

Orono 'orəˌno, 'ɔr-; S 'or-

Orosius ə'rosɪəs, -sjəs |-us' -əs

orotund 'orəˌtʌnd, 'ɔr-, 'ɑr-, 'ɒr-

orphan 'ɔrfən; ES 'ɔəfən; |-ed -d |-age -ɪdʒ

Orpheus 'ɔrfɪəs, 'ɔrfjus; ES 'ɔəf-; |-'s -ɪz

Orphic 'ɔrfɪk; ES 'ɔəfɪk

orphrey 'ɔrfrɪ; ES 'ɔəfrɪ; |-ed -d

orpiment 'ɔrpɪmənt; ES 'ɔəp-

orpine, -pin 'ɔrpɪn; ES 'ɔəpɪn

Orpington 'ɔrpɪŋtən; ES 'ɔəp-

orrery 'ɔrərɪ, 'ɑr-, 'ɒr-

orris 'ɔrɪs, 'ɑrɪs, 'ɒrɪs

Orsino ɔr'sino; ES ɔə'sino

orthodontia ˌɔrθə'danʃə, -ʃɪə; ES ˌɔəθə-, -'dɒn-

orthodox 'ɔrθəˌdaks; ES 'ɔəθə-, -ˌdɒks; |-y -ɪ

orthoepy ɔr'θo·ɪpɪ, 'ɔrθo·ɪˌpɪ; ES ɔ'θo-, 'ɔəθo-

orthographic ˌɔrθə'græfɪk; ES ˌɔəθə-; |-al -l̩ |-ally -l̩ɪ, -ɪklɪ

orthography ɔr'θagrəfɪ, -'θɒg-; ES ɔˌθ-

|full fʊl |tooth tuθ |further 'fɝðɚ; ES 'fɝðə |custom 'kʌstəm |while hwaɪl |how haʊ |toy tɔɪ
|using 'juzɪŋ |fuse fjuz, fɪuz |dish dɪʃ |vision 'vɪʒən |Eden 'idn̩ |cradle 'kredl̩ |keep 'em 'kipm̩

orthopedic, -paed- ¡ɔrθə'pidɪk; ES ¡ɔəθə-;
 |-s -s
orthophonic ¡ɔrθə'fɑnɪk; ES ¡ɔəθə'fɑn-, -'fɒn-
orthophosphoric ¡ɔrθəfɑs'fɔrɪk, -'fɑr-, -'fɒr-;
 ES ¡ɔəθəfɑs-, -fɒs-
orthopsychiatry ¡ɔrθəsaɪ'kaɪətrɪ; ES ¡ɔəθə-
orthopter ɔr'θɑptɚ; ES ɔə'θɑptə(r, -'θɒp-
oryx, O- 'orɪks, 'ɔr-, 'ɑr-, 'ɒr- |-es -ɪz
os 'bone' as; ES+ɒs; |pl ossa -ə
os 'mouth' as; ES+ɒs; |pl ora 'orə, 'ɔrə; S
 'orə
Osage o'sedʒ, 'osedʒ |-s -ɪz ('O¡sage 'orange)
Osaka o'sɑkə (Jap 'o:saka)
Osawatomie ¡osə'wɑtəmɪ, ¡asə-, ¡ɒs-, -'wɒt-,
 loc. ¡osə-
Osborn, -e 'ɔzbɚn, 'ɒz-, 'az-; ES -bən
Oscan 'askən, 'ɒskən, 'ɔskən
Oscar 'ɔskɚ, 'ɒskɚ, 'askɚ; ES -kə(r
Osceola ¡asɪ'olə; ES+¡ɒs-
oscillate 'as¡et; ES+'ɒs-; |-d -ɪd
oscillation ¡asl'efən; ES+¡ɒs-
oscillator 'as¡etɚ; ES 'as¡etə(r, 'ɒs-
oscillograph ə'sɪlə¡græf; E+-¡graf, -¡graf
oscular 'askjəlɚ; ES 'askjələ(r, 'ɒs-
osculate 'askjə¡let; ES+'ɒs-; |-d -ɪd
osculation ¡askjə'lefən; ES+¡ɒs-
Osgood 'azgʊd, 'ɒz-, 'ɔz-
O'Shaughnessy o'fɑnəsɪ
O'Shea o'fe, o'fi
Oshkosh 'afkaf; ES+'ɒfkɒf
osier 'oʒɚ; ES 'oʒə(r; |-ed -d
Osiris o'saɪrɪs |Osiris's o'saɪrɪsɪz
Osler 'oslɚ, 'ozlɚ, 'as-, 'ɒs-; ES -lə(r
Oslo 'azlo, 'aslo, 'ɒ- (Norw 'oslo, 'ʊslʊ)
Osman 'azman, 'as-, 'ɒ-, -mən
Osmanli az'mænlɪ, as-, ɒ-
osmic 'azmɪk; ES+'ɒz-; |-mious -mɪəs
 |-mium -mɪəm
osmose 'azmos, 'as-; ES+'ɒ-
osmosis az'mosɪs, as-; ES+ɒ-
osmotic az'matɪk, as-; ES+ɒz'mɒtɪk, ɒs-
osmund, O- 'azmənd; ES+'ɒz-
osprey 'asprɪ, 'ɒsprɪ, 'ɔsprɪ
Osric 'azrɪk, 'ɒz-
Ossa 'asə; ES+'ɒsə
ossein 'asiɪn; ES+'ɒs-
osseous 'asɪəs, -jəs; ES+'ɒs-
Ossian 'afən, 'asɪən; ES+'ɒ-
Ossianic ¡asɪ'ænɪk, ¡afɪ-; ES+¡ɒ-

ossification ¡asəfə'kefən; ES+¡ɒs-
ossify 'asə¡faɪ; ES+'ɒs-; |-fied -¡faɪd
Ossining 'asɪ¡nɪŋ; ES+'ɒs-
Ossipee 'asə¡pi, -pɪ; ES+'ɒs-; loc.+'ɔspɪ
osteal 'astɪəl; ES+'ɒs-
Ostend as'tɛnd; ES+ɒs-
ostensible as'tɛnsəbl; ES+ɒs-; |-bly -blɪ
ostentation ¡astən'tefən, -tɛn-; ES+¡ɒs-
ostentatious ¡astən'tefəs, -tɛn-; ES+¡ɒs-
osteology ¡astɪ'alədʒɪ; ES+¡ɒstɪ'ɒlədʒɪ
osteopath 'astɪə¡pæθ; ES+'ɒs-
osteopathic ¡astɪə'pæθɪk; ES+¡ɒs-; |-ally -|ɪ
osteopathy ¡astɪ'apəθɪ; ES+¡ɒstɪ'ɒpəθɪ
ostiary 'astɪ¡ɛrɪ; ES+'ɒs-
ostler 'aslɚ; ES 'aslə(r, 'ɒs-
ostracism 'astrə¡sɪzəm, 'ɒs-, 'ɔs-
ostracize 'astrə¡saɪz, 'ɒs-, 'ɔs- |-s -ɪz |-d -d
ostrich 'ɔstrɪtf, 'ɒs-, 'as- |-es -ɪz
Ostrogoth 'astrə¡gaθ, 'ɒstrə¡gɒθ |-ths -θs
Oswald, -wold 'azwəld, 'azwald, 'ɒzwɒld,
 'ɒzwɔld
Oswego as'wigo; ES+ɒs-
Oswestry 'azwəstrɪ, 'ɒz-, -wɛs-
Othello o'θɛlo, ə'θɛlo
other 'ʌðɚ; ES 'ʌðə(r
otherwhile 'ʌðɚ¡hwaɪl; ES 'ʌðə¡hwaɪl
otherwise 'ʌðɚ¡waɪz; ES 'ʌðə¡waɪz
otherworldly 'ʌðɚ'wɝldlɪ; ES 'ʌðə'wɝldlɪ,
 'ʌðə'wɜldlɪ
Othin 'oðɪn
Othman 'aθman, 'ɒθ-, -mən
otiose 'ofɪ¡os, 'otɪ¡os
otology o'talədʒɪ; ES+-'tɒl-; |-gist -dʒɪst
Otranto o'trænto, a-, ɒ- (It 'ɔ:tranto)
ottava rima ə'tavə'rimə (It ot'ta:va'ri:ma)
Ottawa 'atəwə, 'atə¡wa, -¡wɒ; ES+'ɒt-
otter 'atɚ; ES 'atə(r, 'ɒtə(r
Otterburn 'atɚ¡bɝn, 'atəbɚn; ES 'atə¡bɜn,
 'ɒtə-, -tə¡bɜn, -bən; The pron. 'atəbɚn is
 due to r-dissimilation (§121).
Otto 'ato; ES+'ɒto
Ottoman 'atəmən, 'ato-; ES+'ɒt-
Ouachita 'wɑ¡fɪ¡tɔ, 'wɒf-, 'wɔf-
ouananiche ¡wɑnə'nif, ¡wɒ- (Fr wana'nif)
oubliette ¡ublɪ'ɛt
ouch aʊtf |ouches 'aʊtfɪz |ouched aʊtft
ought ɔɪ |ought to 'ɔttʊ, 'ɒttə, 'ɔtʊ, 'ɒtə, 'ɔttu
oughtn't 'ɔtn̩t, bef. some conss.+'ɔtn̩ ('ɔtn̩-
 'dʒan tə'go?)

Ouida 'widə

Ouija 'widʒə

ounce aʊns |ounces 'aʊnsɪz

Oundle 'aʊndl̩

our aʊr, ɑr; ES aʊə(r, ɑ:(r; |-s -z

ourself aʊr'sɛlf, ɑr-; ES aʊə-, ɑ:-; |-lves -vz

Oursler 'aʊrzlɚ, 'aʊz-, 'ɑz-, 'ɒz-; ES -lə(r; see §121

-ous adj ending, always unstressed -əs

Ouse uz

ousel 'uzl̩

ousia u'siə

oust aʊst |ousted 'aʊstɪd

out aʊt

out-and-out 'aʊtn̩'aʊt ('out-and-ˌout 'thief)

outargue aʊt'ɑrgju; ES -'ɑ:gju, E+-'ɑ:g-; |-d -d

outbalance aʊt'bæləns |-s -ɪz |-d -t

outbid aʊt'bɪd |past & pptc -bid -'bɪd

outboard 'aʊtˌbord, -ˌbɔrd; ES -ˌboəd, E+ -ˌbɔəd

outbound 'aʊt'baʊnd ('outˌbound 'train)

outbrag aʊt'bræg |-bragged -'brægd

outbranch aʊt'bræntʃ; E+-'brɑntʃ, -'brɒntʃ; |-es -ɪz |-ed -t

outbrave aʊt'brev |outbraved aʊt'brevd

outbuilding 'aʊtˌbɪldɪŋ

outcast n 'aʊtˌkæst; E+-ˌkast, -ˌkɑst; v out'cast

outcaste n 'aʊtˌkæst; E+-ˌkast, -ˌkɑst

outcaste v aʊt'kæst; E+-'kast, -'kɑst; |-d -ɪd

outclass aʊt'klæs; E+-'klas, -'klɑs; |-es -ɪz |-ed -t

outcome 'aʊtˌkʌm

outcrop n 'aʊtˌkrɑp; ES+-ˌkrɒp

outcrop v aʊt'krɑp; ES+-'krɒp; |-ped -t

outcry n 'aʊtˌkraɪ

outcry v aʊt'kraɪ |-cried -'kraɪd

outdare aʊt'dɛr, -'dær; E -'dɛə(r, ES -'dæə(r

outdistance aʊt'dɪstəns |-s -ɪz |-d -t

outdo aʊt'du |-does -'dʌz |-did -'dɪd |-done -'dʌn

outdoor 'aʊtˌdor, -ˌdɔr; ES -ˌdoə(r, E+-ˌdɔə(r

outdoors n aʊt'dorz -'dɔrz; ES -'doəz, E+-'dɔəz

outdoors adj 'aʊtˌdorz, -ˌdɔrz; ES -ˌdoəz, E+-ˌdɔəz

outdoors adv 'aʊt'dorz, -'dɔrz; ES -'doəz, E+-'dɔəz

outer 'aʊtɚ; ES 'aʊtə(r; |-most -ˌmost, -məst

outface aʊt'fes |-faces -'fesɪz |-faced -'fest

outfall 'aʊtˌfɔl

outfield n 'aʊt'fild, 'aʊtˌfild

outfit 'aʊtˌfɪt |outfitted 'aʊtˌfɪtɪd

outflank aʊt'flæŋk |outflanked aʊt'flæŋkt

outflow n 'aʊtˌflo

outflow v aʊt'flo |outflowed aʊt'flod

outfoot aʊt'fʊt |outfooted aʊt'fʊtɪd

outgeneral aʊt'dʒɛnərəl, -'dʒɛnrəl |-ed -d

outgo n 'aʊtˌgo

outgo v aʊt'go |-went -'wɛnt |-gone -'gɔn, -'gɒn much less freq. -'gɑn

outgoing aʊt'goɪŋ ('outˌgoɪŋ 'train)

outgrow aʊt'gro |-grew -'gru, -'grɪu |-grown -'gron

outgrowth 'aʊtˌgroθ |-growths -ˌgroθs

outguess aʊt'gɛs |-guesses -'gɛsɪz |-ed -t

out-Herod aʊt'hɛrəd ('out-ˌHerods 'Herod) |-ed -ɪd

outhouse 'aʊtˌhaʊs |-houses -ˌhaʊzɪz

outing 'aʊtɪŋ

outland n 'aʊtˌlænd

outland adj 'aʊtˌlænd, -lənd |-er -ɚ; ES -ə(r

outlandish aʊt'lændɪʃ ('outˌlandish 'hats)

outlast aʊt'læst; E+-'last, -'lɑst; |-ed -ɪd

outlaw 'aʊtˌlɔ |-lawed -ˌlɔd |-lawry -ˌlɔrɪ

outlay n 'aʊtˌle

outlay v aʊt'le |-laid -'led

outlet 'aʊtˌlɛt

outlier 'aʊtˌlaɪɚ; ES -ˌlaɪ·ə(r

outline 'aʊtˌlaɪn |-lined -ˌlaɪnd

outlive aʊt'lɪv |-lived -'lɪvd

outlook n 'aʊtˌlʊk

outlook v aʊt'lʊk |-looked -'lʊkt

outlying 'aʊtˌlaɪɪŋ

outmaneuver, -noeu- ˌaʊtmə'nuvɚ; ES -və(r; |-ed -d |-ring -vərɪŋ, -vrɪŋ

outmode aʊt'mod |-moded -'modɪd

outmost 'aʊtˌmost, -məst

outnumber aʊt'nʌmbɚ; ES -'nʌmbə(r; |-ed -d |-ing -brɪŋ, -bərɪŋ

out-of-date 'aʊtəv'det, 'aʊtə'det

out-of-door 'aʊtəv'dor, -'dɔr; ES -'doə(r, E+-'dɔə(r

out-of-the-way 'aʊtəðə'we, 'aʊtəvðə'we ('out-of-the-ˌway 'place)

outpatient 'aʊtˌpeʃənt

outplay aʊt'ple |-played -'pled

---

outpoint aʊt'pɔɪnt |-pointed -'pɔɪntɪd

outpost 'aʊt,post

outpour *n* 'aʊt,por, -,pɔr; ES -,poə(r, E+ -,pɔə(r

outpour *v* aʊt'por, -'pɔr; ES -'poə(r, E+ -'pɔə(r

output 'aʊt,pʊt

outrage 'aʊt,redʒ |-rages -,redʒɪz |-d -d

outrageous aʊt'redʒəs

outrange aʊt'rendʒ |-ranges -'rendʒɪz |-d -d

outrank aʊt'ræŋk |-ranked -'ræŋkt

outré u'tre ('ou,tré 'styles)

outreach *n* 'aʊt,ritʃ |outreaches 'aʊt,ritʃɪz

outreach *v* aʊt'ritʃ |-es -ɪz |-ed -t

outremer, Outre-Mer ,utrə'mɛr; ES -'mɛə(r

outrider 'aʊt,raɪdɚ; ES 'aʊt,raɪdə(r

outrigger 'aʊt,rɪgɚ; ES 'aʊt,rɪgə(r

outright *adj* 'aʊt,raɪt

outright *adv* 'aʊt'raɪt ('out,right 'lazy)

outrival aʊt'raɪv‖ |-ed -d |-ing -v‖ɪŋ, -v‖ɪŋ

outroot aʊt'rut, -'rʊt |-ed -ɪd

outrun aʊt'rʌn |*past* -'ræn |*pptc* -'rʌn

outrunner aʊt'rʌnɚ, 'aʊt,rʌnɚ; ES -ə(r

outsell aʊt'sɛl |-sold -'sold

outset *n* 'aʊt,sɛt, *v* aʊt'sɛt

outshine aʊt'ʃaɪn |-shone -'ʃon

outshoot *n* 'aʊt,ʃut

outshoot *v* aʊt'ʃut |-shot -'ʃat; ES+-'ʃɒt

outside *n, adj* 'aʊt'saɪd ('out,side 'door)

outside *adv* 'aʊt'saɪd ('out,side & 'in,side)

outside *prep* aʊt'saɪd

outsider aʊt'saɪdɚ; ES aʊt'saɪdə(r

outsit aʊt'sɪt |outsat aʊt'sæt

outsize *n* 'aʊt,saɪz |-sizes -,saɪzɪz

outsized *adj* 'aʊt'saɪzd ('out,sized 'pair)

outskirt 'aʊt,skɝt; ES -,skɝt, -,skɝt

outsmart aʊt'smɑrt; ES -'smɑːt, E+-'smɑːt; |-ed -ɪd

outsoar aʊt'sor, -'sɔr; ES -'soə(r, E+-'sɔə(r; |-ed -d

outspan aʊt'spæn |outspanned aʊt'spænd

outspeak aʊt'spik |-spoke -'spok |-spoken -'spokən

outspent aʊt'spɛnt

outspoken 'aʊt'spokən ('out,spoken 'leader)

outspokenness aʊt'spokənnɪs

outspread *n* 'aʊt,sprɛd

outspread *v* aʊt'sprɛd

outstand aʊt'stænd |-stood -'stʊd

outstanding *adj* 'aʊt'stændɪŋ

outstare aʊt'stɛr, -'stær; E -'stɛə(r, ES -'stæə(r; |-d -d

outstation *n* 'aʊt,steʃən

outstation *v* aʊt'steʃən |-ed -d

outstay aʊt'ste |-stayed -'sted

outstretch aʊt'strɛtʃ |-es -ɪz |-ed -t

outstrip aʊt'strɪp |-stripped -'strɪpt

outtalk aʊt'tɔk |-talked -'tɔkt

outtell aʊt'tɛl |-told -'told

outtop aʊt'tap; ES+-'tɒp; |-ped -t

outturn *n* 'aʊt,tɝn; ES -,tɝn, -,tɝn

outvote aʊt'vot |-voted -'votɪd

outward 'aʊtwɚd; ES 'aʊtwəd; |-s -z

outwatch aʊt'watʃ, -'wɒtʃ, -'wɔtʃ |-es -ɪz |-ed -t

outwear aʊt'wɛr, -'wær; E -,wɛə(r, ES -'wæə(r; |-wore -'wor, -'wɔr; ES -'woə(r, E+-'wɔə(r; |-worn -'worn, -'wɔrn; ES -'woən, E+-'wɔən

outweigh aʊt'we |-weighed -'wed

outwind *'uncoil'* aʊt'waɪnd |-wound -'waʊnd

outwind *'exhaust'* aʊt'wɪnd |-winded -'wɪndɪd

outwit aʊt'wɪt |-witted -'wɪtɪd

outwork *n* 'aʊt,wɝk; ES -,wɝk, -,wɝk

outwork *v* aʊt'wɝk; ES -'wɝk, -'wɝk; |-ed -t *or* -wrought -'rɔt

outworn *adj* 'aʊt'worn, -'wɔrn; ES -'woən, E+-'wɔən; ('out,worn 'joke)

outwrite aʊt'raɪt |-wrote -'rot |-written -'rɪtn̩

ouzel 'uz‖

ova *pl* 'ovə |*sg* ovum 'ovəm

oval 'ov‖ |-ly -ɪ

ovarian o'vɛrɪən, -'vær-, -'ver-

ovary 'ovərɪ, 'ovrɪ

ovate 'ovet, 'ovɪt

ovation o'veʃən

oven 'ʌvən |-bird -,bɝd; ES -,bɝd, -,bɝd

over 'ovɚ; ES 'ovə(r

over- *Compounds in* over- *vary in accent according to meaning, rhythm, and sense stress. In compound verbs,* over= *'excessively' is apt to have more stress than* over= *'above' (cf* 'over'do *with* ,over'flow)

overact ,ovɚ'ækt |-acted -'æktɪd

overage *'surplus'* 'ovərɪdʒ, 'ovrɪdʒ |-s -ɪz

overage *'too old'* 'ovɚ'edʒ |-d -'edʒɪd, -'edʒd

over-all *adj* 'ovɚ,ɔl ('over-,all 'width)

overall *adv* ,ovɚ'ɔl

overalls ˈovɚˌɔlz, -ˌhɔlz; ES ˈovɚˌɔlz, ˈovəˌh-

overanxious ˈovɚˈæŋkʃəs -ˈæŋʃ- |-iety -æŋ-ˈzaɪətɪ

overawe ˌovɚˈɔ |-awed -ˈɔd

overbalance ˌovɚˈbæləns; ES ˌovə-; |-s -ɪz |-d -t

overbear ˌovɚˈbɛr, -ˈbær; E ˌovəˈbɛə(r, ES -ˈbæə(r; |-bore -ˈbor, -ˈbɔr; ES -ˈboə(r, E+-ˈbɔə(r; |-borne -ˈborn, -ˈbɔrn; ES -ˈboən, E+-ˈbɔən

overbearing ˌovɚˈbɛrɪŋ, -ˈbærɪŋ; E ˌovə-ˈbɛrɪŋ, ES -ˈbærɪŋ

overbid n ˈovɚˌbɪd; ES ˈovəˌbɪd

overbid v ˌovɚˈbɪd; ES ˌovə-; |past & pptc -bid -ˈbɪd

overblow ˌovɚˈblo; ES ˌovə-; |-blew -ˈblu, -ˈblɪu |-blown -ˈblon

overboard ˈovɚˌbord, -ˌbɔrd; ES ˈovəˌboəd, E+-ˌbɔəd

overbold ˈovɚˈbold; ES ˈovə-; (ˈoverˌbold ˈact)

overbuild ˈovɚˈbɪld; ES ˈovə-; |-built -ˈbɪlt

overburden n ˈovɚˌbɝdn̩; ES ˈovəˌbɝdn̩, ˈovəˌbɝˌdn̩

overburden v ˈovɚˈbɝdn̩; ES ˈovəˈbɝdn̩, ˈovəˈbɝˌdn̩; |-ed -d |-ing -dn̩ɪŋ, -dn̩ɪŋ

Overbury ˈovɚˌbɛrɪ, -bərɪ; ES ˈovə-

overbuy ˈovɚˈbaɪ; ES ˈovə-; |-bought -ˈbɔt

overcall n ˈovɚˌkɔl; ES ˈovə-

overcall v ˈovɚˈkɔl; ES ˈovə-; |-ed -d

overcapitalize ˈovɚˈkæpətlˌaɪz; ES ˈovə-; |-s -ɪz |-d -d

overcareful ˈovɚˈkɛrfəl, -ˈkær-; E ˈovə-ˈkɛəfəl, ES -ˈkæəfəl; |-ly -ɪ

overcast n ˈovɚˌkæst; ES ˈovə-, E+-ˌkast, -ˌkɑst

overcast v ˌovɚˈkæst; ES ˌovə-, E+-ˈkast, -ˈkɑst; in sense ˈsew· acct+ˈoverˌcast, ptc adj ˌoverˈcast, ˈoverˌcast

overcharge n ˈovɚˈtʃɑrdʒ; ES ˈovəˈtʃɑːdʒ, E+-ˌtʃɑːdʒ; |-s -ɪz

overcharge v ˈovɚˈtʃɑrdʒ; ES ˈovəˈtʃɑːdʒ, E+-ˈtʃɑːdʒ; |-s -ɪz |-d -d

overcloud ˌovɚˈklaud; ES ˌovə-; |-ed -ɪd

overcoat ˈovɚˌkot; ES ˈovə-

overcome ˌovɚˈkʌm; ES ˌovə-; |past -came -ˈkem |pptc -come -ˈkʌm

overconfidence ˈovɚˈkɑnfədəns; ES ˈovə-ˈkɑn-, -ˈkɒn-; |-s -ɪz

overdevelop ˈovɚdɪˈvɛləp; ES ˈovə-; |-ed -t

overdo ˈovɚˈdu; ES ˈovə-; |-does -ˈdʌz |-did -ˈdɪd |-done -ˈdʌn

overdose n ˈovɚˌdos; ES ˈovə-; |-s -ɪz

overdose v ˈovɚˈdos; ES ˈovə-; |-s -ɪz |-d -t

overdraft, -draught ˈovɚˌdræft; ES ˈovə-, E+-ˌdraft, -ˌdrɑft

overdraw ˈovɚˈdrɔ; ES ˈovə-; |-drew -ˈdru, -ˈdrɪu |-drawn -ˈdrɔn

overdress ˈovɚˈdrɛs; ES ˈovə-; |-es -ɪz |-ed -t

overdue ˈovɚˈdju, -ˈdɪu, -ˈdu; ES ˈovə-; (ˈoverˌdue ˈnote)

overeat ˈovɚˈit |-ate -ˈet |-eaten -ˈitn̩ |-eat dial. past -ˈɛt, cf ate

overemphasis ˈovɚˈɛmfəsɪs |pl -ses -ˌsiz

overemphasize ˈovɚˈɛmfəˌsaɪz |-s -ɪz |-d -d

overestimate n ˈovɚˈɛstəmɪt, -ˌmet

overestimate v ˈovɚˈɛstəˌmet |-d -ɪd

overexcite ˈovɚrɪkˈsaɪt |-d -ɪd

overexert ˈovɚrɪgˈzɝt; ES -ˈzɝt, -ˈzɝt |-ed -ɪd

overexertion ˈovɚrɪgˈzɝʃən; ES -ˈzɝʃ-, -ˈzɝʃ-

overexpose ˈovɚrɪkˈspoz |-s -ɪz |-d -d |-sure -ʒɚ; ES -ʒə(r

overfeed n, adj ˈovɚˌfid; ES ˈovə-

overfeed v ˈovɚˈfid; ES ˈovə-; |-fed -ˈfɛd

overflow n ˈovɚˌflo; ES ˈovəˌflo

overflow v ˌovɚˈflo; ES ˌovə-; |-ed -d

overgarment ˈovɚˌgarmənt; ES ˈovəˌgɑːmənt, E+-ˌgɑːm-

overgild ˌovɚˈgɪld; ES ˌovə-; |-ed -ɪd

overglaze n ˈovɚˌglez; ES ˈovə-; |-s -ɪz

overglaze v ˌovɚˈglez; ES ˌovə-; |-s -ɪz |-d -d

overgrow ˌovɚˈgro; ES ˌovə-; |-grew -ˈgru, -ˈgrɪu |-grown -ˈgron

overhand adj, adv ˈovɚˈhænd; ES ˈovə-; |-ed -ɪd (ˈoverˌhand ˈplay)

overhand n, v ˈovɚˌhænd; ES ˈovə-; |-ed -ɪd

overhang n ˈovɚˌhæŋ; ES ˈovə-

overhang v ˌovɚˈhæŋ; ES ˌovə-; |-hung -ˈhʌŋ

overhaul n ˈoverhauling’ ˈovɚˌhɔl; ES ˈovə-

overhaul v ˌovɚˈhɔl; ES ˌovə-; |-ed -d

overhauls ˈoveralls’ ˈovɚˌhɔlz; ES ˈovə-

overhead n, adj ˈovɚˌhɛd; ES ˈovə-

overhead adv ˈovɚˈhɛd; ES ˈovə-

overhear ˌovɚˈhɪr; ES ˌovəˈhɪə(r, S+-ˈhjɛə(r, -ˈhjɪə(r, -ˈhɛə(r; |-heard -ˈhɝd; ES -ˈhɝd, -ˈhɝd

overheat ˈovɚˈhit; ES ˈovə-; |-heated -ˈhitɪd

overindulge ˈovɚrɪnˈdʌldʒ |-s -ɪz |-d -d

|full fʊl |tooth tuθ |further ˈfɝðɚ; ES ˈfɝðə |custom ˈkʌstəm |while hwaɪl |how hau |toy tɔɪ |using ˈjuzɪŋ |fuse fjuz, fɪuz |dish dɪʃ |vision ˈvɪʒən |Eden ˈidn̩ |cradle ˈkredl̩ |keep 'em ˈkipm̩

overjoy 'ovɚ'dʒɔɪ; ES 'ovə-; |-ed -d
overlaid ˌovɚ'led; ES ˌovə-; ('overˌlaid 'gold)
overland adj, adv 'ovɚˌlænd; ES 'ovə-
overland v 'ovɚˌlænd, ˌovɚ'lænd; ES -və-; |-ed -ɪd
overlap n 'ovɚˌlæp; ES 'ovə-
overlap v ˌovɚ'læp; ES ˌovə-; |-ped -t
overlay past of overlie ˌovɚ'le; ES ˌovə-
overlay n 'ovɚˌle; ES 'ovə-
overlay v ˌovɚ'le; ES ˌovə-; |-laid -'led
overleaf adv 'ovɚ'lif; ES 'ovə-; n 'overˌleaf
overleap ˌovɚ'lip; ES ˌovə-; |-leaped -'lipt, -'lɛpt or -leapt -'lɛpt, -'lipt
overlie ˌovɚ'laɪ; ES ˌovə-; |past -lay -'le |pptc -lain -'len
overlook n 'ovɚˌluk; ES 'ovə-
overlook v ˌovɚ'luk; ES ˌovə-; |-ed -t
overlord 'ovɚˌlɔrd; ES 'ovəˌlɔəd
overly 'ovɚlɪ; ES 'ovəlɪ
overman 'foreman' 'ovɚmən; ES 'ovə-; |-men -mən, 'superman' -ˌmæn |-men -ˌmɛn
overman v 'ovɚ'mæn; ES 'ovə-; |-ned -d
overmaster ˌovɚ'mæstɚ; ES ˌovə'mæstə(r, E+-'mas-, -'mɑs-
overmatch ˌovɚ'mætʃ; ES ˌovə-; |-es -ɪz |-ed -t
overmuch adj, adv 'ovɚ'mʌtʃ; ES 'ovə-; ('overˌmuch 'joy)
overnight adj, adv 'ovɚ'naɪt; ES 'ovə-; ('overˌnight 'bag)
overnight n 'ovɚˌnaɪt; ES 'ovə-
overpass n 'ovɚˌpæs; ES 'ovə-, E+-ˌpas, -ˌpɑs; |-es -ɪz
overpass v ˌovɚ'pæs; ES ˌovə'pæs, E+-'pas, -'pɑs; |-es -ɪz |-ed -t
overpay 'ovɚ'pe; ES 'ovə-; |-paid -'ped
overpersuade 'ovɚpɚ'swed; ES 'ovəpə-; |-d -ɪd
overplus 'ovɚˌplʌs; ES 'ovə-; |-es -ɪz
overpower ˌovɚ'pauɚ; ES ˌovə'pauə(r; |-ed -d |-ing -'pauərɪŋ, -'paurɪŋ
overprint n 'ovɚˌprɪnt; ES 'ovə-
overprint v ˌovɚ'prɪnt; ES ˌovə-; |-ed -ɪd
overprize 'ovɚ'praɪz; ES 'ovə-; |-s -ɪz |-d -d
overproduction 'ovɚprə'dʌkʃən; ES 'ovə-
overproportion 'ovɚprə'porʃən, -'pɔr-; ES 'ovəprə'poəʃən, E+-'pɔə-; |-ed -d
overrate 'ovɚ'ret; ES 'ovə'ret; |-rated -'retɪd
Overreach 'ovɚˌritʃ; ES 'ovə-; |-'s -ɪz

overreach ˌovɚ'ritʃ; ES ˌovə-; |-es -ɪz |-ed -t
override ˌovɚ'raɪd; ES ˌovə-; |-rode -'rod |-ridden -'rɪdn̩
overripe 'ovɚ'raɪp; ES 'ovə-
overrule ˌovɚ'rul, -'rɪul; ES ˌovə-; |-d -d
overrun n 'ovɚˌrʌn; ES 'ovə-
overrun v ˌovɚ'rʌn; ES ˌovə-; |-ran -'ræn
overscrupulous 'ovɚ'skrupjələs, -rɪu-; ES 'ovə-
oversea 'ovɚ'si; ES 'ovə-; |-s -z ('overˌsea 'voyage)
oversee ˌovɚ'si; ES ˌovə-; |-saw -'sɔ |-seen -'sin
overseer 'ovɚˌsiɚ, -ˌsɪr, ˌovɚ'sɪr; ES 'ovəˌsi·ə(r, -ˌsɪə(r, ˌovə'sɪə(r
oversell 'ovɚ'sɛl; ES 'ovə-; |-sold -'sold
overset n 'ovɚˌsɛt; ES 'ovə-
overset v ˌovɚ'sɛt; ES ˌovə-
oversew 'ovɚˌso, ˌovɚ'so; ES 'ovə-, ˌovə-; |past -ed -d |pptc -ed -d or -n -n
overshade ˌovɚ'ʃed; ES ˌovə-; |-d -ɪd
overshadow ˌovɚ'ʃædo, -də; ES ˌovə-; |-ed -d |-ing -'ʃædəwɪŋ
overshine ˌovɚ'ʃaɪn; ES ˌovə-; |-shone -'ʃon
overshoe 'ovɚˌʃu, -ˌʃɪu; ES 'ovə-
overshoot ˌovɚ'ʃut; ES ˌovə-; |-shot -'ʃat; ES+-'ʃɒt
oversight 'ovɚˌsaɪt; ES 'ovə-
oversize adj 'ovɚ'saɪz; ES 'ovə-; |-d -d ('overˌsize(d) 'bolt)
oversize n 'ovɚˌsaɪz; ES 'ovə-; |-s -ɪz
oversize v ˌovɚ'saɪz; ES ˌovə-; |-s -ɪz |-d -d
overskirt 'ovɚˌskɝt; ES 'ovəˌskɜt, 'ovəˌskɝt
oversleep 'ovɚ'slip; ES 'ovə-; |-slept -'slɛpt
oversoon 'ovɚ'sun, -'sʊn; ES 'ovə-
oversoul 'ovɚˌsol; ES 'ovə-
overspend 'ovɚ'spɛnd; ES 'ovə-; |-spent -'spɛnt
overspread ˌovɚ'sprɛd; ES ˌovə-
overstate 'ovɚ'stet; ES 'ovə-; |-d -ɪd
overstay 'ovɚ'ste; ES 'ovə-; |-stayed -'sted
overstep ˌovɚ'stɛp; ES ˌovə-; |-ped -t
overstride ˌovɚ'straɪd; ES ˌovə-; |-strode -'strod |-stridden -'strɪdn̩
overstrung 'ovɚ'strʌŋ; ES 'ovə-
overstuff 'ovɚ'stʌf; ES 'ovə-; |-ed -t
oversubscribe 'ovɚsəb'skraɪb; ES 'ovə-; |-d -d
overt o'vɝt; ES o'vɜt, o'vɝt; ('oˌvert 'act)

Key: *See in full* §§3–47. bee bi |pity 'pɪtɪ (§6) |rate ret |yet jɛt |sang sæŋ |angry 'æŋ·grɪ |bath bæθ; E baθ (§10) |ah ɑ |far fɑr |watch watʃ, wɒtʃ (§12) |jaw dʒɔ |gorge gɔrdʒ |go go

overtake ˌovɚˈtek; ES ˌovə-; |-took -ˈtʊk
|-taken -ˈtekən
overtax ˈovɚˈtæks; ES ˈovə-; |-es -ɪz |-ed -t
over-the-counter ˈovɚˈðəˈkauntɚ; ES ˈovəðə-
ˈkauntə(r
overthrow n ˈovɚˌθro; ES ˈovə-
overthrow v ˌovɚˈθro; ES ˌovə-; |-threw -ˈθru,
-ˈθrɪu |-thrown -ˈθron
overtime n ˈovɚˌtaɪm; ES ˈovə-
overtime v ˌovɚˈtaɪm; ES ˌovə-; |-d -d
overtone ˈovɚˌton; ES ˈovə-
overtop ˌovɚˈtap; ES ˌovəˈtap, -ˈtɒp; |-ped -t
overtrade ˈovɚˈtred; ES ˈovə-; |-d -ɪd
overtrick ˈovɚˌtrɪk; ES ˈovə-
overtrump ˌovɚˈtrʌmp; ES ˌovə-; |-ed -t
overture ˈovɚtʃɚ, -ˌtʃur; ES ˈovətʃə(r,
-ˌtʃuə(r
overturn n ˈovɚˌtɜn; ES ˈovəˌtɜn, ˈovəˌtɝn
overturn v ˌovɚˈtɜn; ES ˌovəˈtɜn, ˌovəˈtɝn;
|-ed -d
overvalue ˈovɚˈvælju; ES ˈovə-; |-d -d
overwatch ˈovɚˈwatʃ, -ˈwɒtʃ, -ˈwɔtʃ; ES
ˈovə-; |-es -ɪz |-ed -t
overwear ˈovɚˈwɛr, -ˈwær; E ˈovəˈwɛə(r, ES
-ˈwæə(r; |-wore -ˈwor, -ˈwɔr; ES -ˈwoə(r,
E+-ˈwɔə(r; |-worn -ˈworn, -ˈwɔrn; ES
-ˈwoən, E+-ˈwɔən
overweary ˈovɚˈwɪrɪ, -ˈwirɪ; ES ˈovə-, S+
-ˈwɛrɪ; |-ied -d
overween ˈovɚˈwin; ES ˈovə-; |-ed -d |-ing -ɪŋ
overweigh ˈovɚˈwe; ES ˈovə-; |-ed -d
overweight n ˈovɚˌwet; ES ˈovə-
overweight adj ˈovɚˈwet; ES ˈovə-; (ˈover-
ˌweight ˈparcel)
overweight v ˈovɚˈwet; ES ˈovə-; |-ed -ɪd
overwhelm ˌovɚˈhwɛlm; ES ˌovə-; |-ed -d
overwind ˈovɚˈwaɪnd; ES ˈovə-; |-wound
-ˈwaund
overwork n 'too hard w.' ˈovɚˈwɝk; ES
ˈovəˈwɝk, ˈovəˈwɜk; 'extra w.' ˈoverˌwork
overwork v ˈovɚˈwɝk; ES ˈovəˈwɜk, ˈovə-
ˈwɝk; |-ed -t or -wrought -ˈrɔt
overwrought ˈovɚˈrɔt; ES ˈovəˈrɔt; (ˈover-
ˌwrought ˈnerves)
Ovid ˈavɪd; ES+ˈɒvɪd
Ovidian oˈvɪdɪən
oviduct ˈovɪˌdʌkt
oviparous oˈvɪpərəs
oviposit ˌovɪˈpazɪt; ES+-ˈpɒz-; |-ed -ɪd

Ovoca əˈvokə
ovoid ˈovɔɪd
ovule ˈovjul
ovum ˈovəm |pl ova ˈovə
-ow suffix -o, -ö, -ə. The ending -ow is seldom
pronounced (except with artificial care) with
a full o as in elbow. The commonest prons.
are with an advanced ö, nearly like ʊ, and
with ə. ö differs from ə chiefly in its lip-
rounding. In these words the symbol ö is not
used in the vocab., the symbol o being understood to include the pron. with fronted ö.
When a vowel follows the -ə (as in -ing, -er)
a w or r intervenes; as follow ˈfalə, following
ˈfaləwɪŋ or ˈfalərɪŋ. An ö sound, nearly ʊ,
is also heard in medial syllables of such
words as whatsoever.

owe o |-d -d |owing ˈo·ɪŋ
Owego əˈwigo, o-
Owen ˈo·ɪn, -ən
owl aʊl |-et -ɪt
own on |owned ond
ownership ˈonɚˌʃɪp; ES ˈonəˌʃɪp
Owosso əˈwaso, əˈwɒso
ox aks; ES+ɒks; |-'s -ɪz |-en -n̩
oxalate ˈaksəˌlet; ES+ˈɒks-; |-d -ɪd
oxalic aksˈælɪk; ES+ɒks-
oxalis ˈaksəlɪs; ES+ˈɒks-
oxazine ˈaksəˌzin, -zɪn; ES+ˈɒks-
oxbow ˈaksˌbo; ES+ˈɒks-
oxen ˈaksn̩; ES+ˈɒksn̩
oxeye ˈaksˌaɪ; ES+ˈɒks-; |-d -d
Oxford ˈaksfɚd; ES ˈaksfəd, ˈɒks-; |-shire
-ˌʃɪr, -ʃɚ; ES -ˌʃɪə(r, -ʃə(r
oxidase ˈaksəˌdes, -ˌdez; ES+ˈɒks-
oxidate ˈaksəˌdet; ES+ˈɒks-; |-d -ɪd
oxide ˈaksaɪd, ˈaksɪd; ES+ˈɒks-
oxidize ˈaksəˌdaɪz; ES+ˈɒks-; |-s -ɪz |-d -d
oxime ˈaksim, ˈaksɪm; ES+ˈɒks-
oxlip ˈaksˌlɪp; ES+ˈɒks-;—The earlier form
was ox-slip. The present syl. division may
be due to confusion with the word lip; cf
cowslip.
Oxonian aksˈonɪən; ES+ɒks-
oxtongue ˈaksˌtʌŋ; ES+ˈɒks-; |-d -d
oxyacetylene ˌaksɪəˈsɛtl̩ˌin; ES+ˌɒks-
oxycalcium ˌaksɪˈkælsɪəm; ES+ˌɒks-
oxygen ˈaksədʒən, ˈaksɪ-, -dʒɪn; ES+ˈɒks-
oxygenate ˈaksədʒənˌet; ES+ˈɒks-; |-d -ɪd

|full fʊl |tooth tuθ |further ˈfɝðɚ; ES ˈfɝðə |custom ˈkʌstəm |while hwaɪl |how haʊ |toy tɔɪ
|using ˈjuzɪŋ |fuse fjuz, fɪuz |dish dɪʃ |vision ˈvɪʒən |Eden ˈidn̩ |cradle ˈkredl̩ |keep 'em ˈkipm̩

oxygenize 'aksədʒən͵aɪz; ES+'ɒks-; |-s -ɪz |-d -d

oxyhydrogen ͵aksɪ'haɪdrədʒən, -dʒɪn; ES+͵ɒks-

oxymoron ͵aksɪ'moran, -'mɔr-; ES ͵aksɪ-'moran, ͵ɒksɪ'morɒn, E+-'mɔr-

oxysalt 'aksɪ͵sɔlt; ES+'ɒks-

oxysulphide, -fide ͵aksɪ'sʌlfaɪd, -fɪd; ES+͵ɒks-; |-phid, -fid -fɪd

oxytocic ͵aksɪ'tosɪk, -'tasɪk; ES+͵ɒksɪ'tosɪk, ͵ɒksɪ'tɒsɪk

oxytone 'aksɪ͵ton; ES+'ɒks-

oyer 'ojɚ, 'ɔɪɚ; ES 'ojə(r, 'ɔɪ·ə(r

oyez, -yes 'ojɛs, 'ojɛz |-es -ɪz

oyster 'ɔɪstɚ; ES 'ɔɪstə(r

Ozark 'ozark; ES 'oza:k, E+'oza:k

ozone 'ozon, o'zon

ozonize 'ozə͵naɪz |-s -ɪz |-d -d |-nous -nəs

P

P, p *letter* pi |*pl* P's, Ps, *poss* P's piz

pabulum 'pæbjələm

pace pes |paces 'pesɪz |paced pest

pacemaker 'pes͵mekɚ; ES 'pes͵mekə(r

Pachaug pə'tʃɔg, *cf* Patchogue

pachisi pə'tʃizɪ, pa-—*see* parcheesi

pachyderm 'pækə͵dɚm; ES -͵dɝm, -͵dɝm

pacifiable 'pæsə͵faɪəbḷ |-bly -blɪ

pacific, P- pə'sɪfɪk |-ally -ḷɪ, -ɪklɪ

pacification ͵pæsəfə'keʃən

pacificator 'pæsəfə͵ketɚ; ES -͵ketə(r

pacificatory pə'sɪfəkə͵torɪ, -͵tɔrɪ; S -͵torɪ

pacificism pə'sɪfə͵sɪzəm

pacifism 'pæsə͵fɪzəm |-fist -fɪst

pacify 'pæsə͵faɪ |pacified 'pæsə͵faɪd

pack pæk |packed pækt |-age -ɪdʒ |-ages -ɪdʒɪz

Packard 'pækɚd; ES 'pækəd

packet 'pækɪt |packeted 'pækɪtɪd

packhorse 'pæk͵hɔrs; ES 'pæk͵hɔəs; |-s -ɪz

packsack 'pæk͵sæk

packsaddle 'pæk͵sædḷ |-d -d

packthread 'pæk͵θrɛd

pact pækt

pad pæd |padded 'pædɪd

paddle 'pædḷ |-d -d |-ling 'pædḷɪŋ, 'pædlɪŋ

paddock 'pædək |paddocked 'pædəkt

paddy, padi *'rice'* 'pædɪ

Paddy *'Irishman'* 'pædɪ

Padelford pə'dɛlfɚd; ES -fəd

Paderewski ͵pædə'rɛfskɪ, -'rɛv-, -'ruskɪ, -'rɪuskɪ

padishah 'padɪ͵ʃa

padlock 'pæd͵lak; ES+-͵lɒk; |-ed -t

padre 'padrɪ (*It* 'pa:dre, *Sp* 'paðre)

Padriac Colum 'padrɪk'kaləm, -'kɒləm

padrone pə'dronɪ |-s -z (*It* pa'dro:ne |*pl* -ni -ni)

Padua 'pædʒʊə, 'pædjʊə |-n -n (*It* 'pa:dova)

Paducah pə'djukə, -'dɪu-, -'du-

paean 'piən

paediatric ͵pidɪ'ætrɪk, ͵pɛd- |-s -s

paediatrician ͵pidɪə'trɪʃən, ͵pɛd-

pagan 'pegən |paganism 'pegən͵ɪzəm

Paganini ͵pægə'ninɪ (*It* ͵paga'ni:ni)

paganize 'pegən͵aɪz |-s -ɪz |-d -d

page pedʒ |pages 'pedʒɪz |paged pedʒd

Page pedʒ |Page's 'pedʒɪz

pageant 'pædʒənt |-ry -rɪ

Paget 'pædʒɪt

paginate 'pædʒə͵net |-nated -͵netɪd

pagination ͵pædʒə'neʃən

pagoda pə'godə

Pago Pago 'paŋo'paŋo=Pangopango

pah *int, v* pa, pa, pæ, *etc.* |-ed -d

Pahlavi, p- 'palə͵vi=Pehlevi

paid *past & pptc of* pay ped

pail pel |-ed -d |-ful -͵fʊl |-fuls -͵fʊlz

pain pen |pained pend |-ful -fəl |-fully -fəlɪ

Paine pen

painstaking 'penz͵tekɪŋ

paint pent |painted 'pentɪd

paintbrush 'pent͵brʌʃ |-es -ɪz

pair pɛr, pær; E pɛə(r, ES pæə(r; |-ed -d

Paisley 'pezlɪ

Paiute paɪ'jut ('Paɪute 'language)

pajama pə'dʒæmə, pə'dʒamə |-s -z

pal pæl |palled pæld

palace 'pælɪs, -əs |-s -ɪz

paladin 'pælədɪn

Palamon 'pæləmən, -ˌman, -ˌmɒn
palanquin, -keen ˌpælən'kin, -əŋ'k- |-ed -d
palatability ˌpælətə'bɪlətɪ
palatable 'pælətəbḷ |-bly -blɪ
palatal 'pælət|
palatalization ˌpælət|ə'zeʃən, -aɪ'z-
palatalize 'pælət|ˌaɪz |-s -ɪz |-d -d
palate 'pælɪt
palatial pə'leʃəl |-ly -ɪ
palatinate, P- pə'lætṇˌet, -ɪt
palatine, P- 'pæləˌtaɪn, -tɪn
Palatka pə'lætkə
palaver pə'lævɚ; ES pə'lævə(r; |-ed -d |-ing
    pə'lævərɪŋ, pə'lævrɪŋ
pale pel |paled peld
pale-, paleo- 'pelɪ-, 'pelɪo-, Brit usually 'pæl-
paleethnology ˌpelɪɛθ'nɑlədʒɪ; ES+-'nɒl-
paleface 'pelˌfes |-faces -ˌfesɪz
paleobotany ˌpelɪo'bɑtṇɪ; ES+-'bɒt-
paleographer ˌpelɪ'ɑgrəfɚ, -'ng-; ES -fə(r
paleographic ˌpelɪə'græfɪk |-al -] |-ally -]ɪ
paleography ˌpelɪ'ɑgrəfɪ, -'ng- |-phist -fɪst
paleolith 'pelɪəˌlɪθ |-ths -θs
paleolithic ˌpelɪə'lɪθɪk
paleontologic ˌpelɪˌɑntə'lɑdʒɪk; ES+-ˌɒntə-
    'lɒdʒɪk; |-al -] |-ally -]ɪ, -ɪklɪ
paleontology ˌpelɪɑn'tɑlədʒɪ; ES+-ɒn'tɒl-;
    |-gist -dʒɪst
Paleozoic ˌpelɪə'zo·ɪk
paleozoology 'pelɪˌo·zo'ɑlədʒɪ; ES+-'ɒl-
Palermo pə'lɝmo; ES -'lɜmo, -'lɝmo; (It
    pɑ'lɛrmo)
Palestine 'pæləsˌtaɪn
Palestinian ˌpæləs'tɪnɪən, -'tɪnjən
paletot 'pæləˌto, 'pælto
palette 'pælɪt
Paley 'pelɪ
palfrey, P- 'pɔlfrɪ
Palgrave 'pɒlgrev, 'pæl-
Pali 'pɑli
palikar 'pælɪˌkɑr; ES 'pælɪˌkɑ:(r
palimpsest 'pælɪmpˌsɛst
palindrome 'pælɪnˌdrom
paling 'pelɪŋ
palingenesis ˌpælɪn'dʒɛnəsɪs |-sist -sɪst
palinode 'pælɪˌnod |-d -ɪd
palisade ˌpælə'sed |-d -ɪd |Palisades -'sedz
pall pɔl |palled pɔld
Palladian pə'ledɪən

palladic pə'lædɪk, pə'ledɪk
palladium, P- pə'ledɪəm |-s -z |-dia -dɪə
palladous pə'ledəs, 'pælədəs
Pallas 'pæləs |Pallas's 'pæləsɪz
pallbearer 'pɔlˌbɛrɚ, -ˌbærɚ; E -ˌbɛrə(r, ES
    -ˌbærə(r
pallet 'pælɪt
palliate 'pælɪˌet |-d -ɪd |-ative -ˌetɪv
palliation ˌpælɪ'eʃən
pallid 'pælɪd
pallium 'pælɪəm |-s -z |pallia 'pælɪə
pall-mall game 'pɛl'mɛl
Pall Mall London street 'pɛl'mɛl, 'pæl'mæl
pallor 'pælɚ; ES 'pælə(r
palm pɑm |palmed pɑmd |-ist -ɪst |-istry
    -ɪstrɪ
palmate 'pælmet, 'pælmɪt |-mated -metɪd
palmer, P- 'pɑmɚ; ES 'pɑmə(r
Palmerston 'pɑmɚstən; ES 'pɑməstən
palmetto pæl'mɛto
palmitate 'pælməˌtet |-mitic pæl'mɪtɪk
palmitin 'pælmətɪn |-tine -tɪn, -ˌtin
palmy 'pɑmɪ
Palmyra, p- pæl'maɪrə
Palo Alto Cal, Pa 'pælo'ælto; Ia, Tex+
    'pɑlo'ɑlto
palpable 'pælpəbḷ |-bly -blɪ
palpitant 'pælpətənt
palpitate 'pælpəˌtet |-tated -ˌtetɪd
palpitation ˌpælpə'teʃən
palsy 'pɔlzɪ |palsied 'pɔlzɪd
palter 'pɔltɚ; ES 'pɔltə(r; |-ed -d |-ing
    'pɔltərɪŋ, 'pɔltrɪŋ |-try -trɪ
paly 'pelɪ
pam pæm
Pamela 'pæmələ
Pamlico 'pæmlɪˌko
pampas 'pæmpəz, attrib. -pəs
Pampas S Amer plains 'pæmpəz
pamper 'pæmpɚ; ES 'pæmpə(r; |-ed -d |-ing
    'pæmpərɪŋ, 'pæmprɪŋ
pamphlet 'pæmflɪt, 'pæmpflɪt |-ed -ɪd
pamphleteer ˌpæmflɪ'tɪr; ES -'tɪə(r, S+
    -'teə(r; |-ed -d
Pamunkey pə'mʌŋkɪ
pan, P- pæn |panned pænd
panacea ˌpænə'sɪə, -'sɪə
Panama, p- 'pænəˌmɑ, -ˌmɔ, ˌpænə'mɑ, -'mɔ
    (Sp ˌpɑnɑ'mɑ)

Words below that have æ before r (carry ˈkærɪ) are often pronounced in N with ɛ (ˈkɛrɪ, §94)

Panamanian ˌpænəˈmenɪən, -ˈmenjən, -ˈman-
Pan-American ˈpænəˈmɛrəkən
Panay pəˈnaɪ (*Sp* paˈnai)
pancake ˈpænˌkek, ˈpæŋ-
panchromatic ˌpænkroˈmætɪk
Pancras ˈpæŋkrəs—*see* St. Pancras
pancreas ˈpæŋkrɪəs, ˈpæŋ-
pancreatic ˌpæŋkrɪˈætɪk, ˌpæŋ-
pancreatin ˈpæŋkrɪətɪn, ˈpæŋ-
panda ˈpændə
Pandar ˈpændə; ES ˈpændə(r; *cf* pander
Pandarus ˈpændərəs |Pandarus's ˈpændərəsɪz
pandect, P- ˈpændɛkt
pandemic pænˈdɛmɪk
Pandemonium, p- ˌpændɪˈmonɪəm, -ˈmonjəm
pander, -ar ˈpændə; ES ˈpændə(r; |-ed -d
|-ing ˈpændərɪŋ, ˈpændrɪŋ
Pandora pænˈdorə, -ˈdɔrə; S -ˈdorə
pandowdy pænˈdaʊdɪ
Pandulph ˈpændʌlf
pane pen |paned pend
panegyric ˌpænəˈdʒɪrɪk |-al -ļ |-ally -ļɪ, -ɪklɪ
panegyrize ˈpænədʒəˌraɪz |-s -ɪz |-d -d
panel ˈpænļ |-ed -d
panful ˈpænˌfʊl |-s -z
pang pæŋ
pangenesis pænˈdʒɛnəsɪs
Pangopango ˈpaŋoˈpaŋo = Pago Pago
panhandle, P- ˈpænˌhændļ |-d -d |-dling
-dļɪŋ, -dlɪŋ
Panhellenic ˈpænhəˈlɛnɪk, -hɛˈlɛnɪk
panic ˈpænɪk |-icked -t |panicky ˈpænɪkɪ
panicle ˈpænɪkļ |panicled ˈpænɪkļd
Panjab pʌnˈdʒɑb |-i -ɪ
panjandrum, P- pænˈdʒændrəm
panne pæn
pannier ˈpænjə, ˈpænɪə; ES ˈpænjə(r, -nɪ·ə(r
pannikin ˈpænəkɪn
panoply ˈpænəplɪ |-plied -plɪd
panorama ˌpænəˈræmə, *less freq.* -ˈramə
panoramic ˌpænəˈræmɪk |-ally -ļɪ, -ɪklɪ
pansy ˈpænzɪ
pant pænt |panted ˈpæntɪd
Pantagruel pænˈtægruˌɛl (*Fr* pătagryˈɛl)
pantalets, -ttes ˌpæntļˈɛts
pantaloon ˌpæntļˈun |-ed -d
pantechnicon pænˈtɛknɪˌkan, -kən; ES+
-ˌkɒn

pantheism ˈpænθiˌɪzəm |-ist -ɪst
pantheistic ˌpænθiˈɪstɪk |-al -ļ |-ally -ļɪ, -ɪklɪ
pantheon, P- ˈpænθɪən, -ˌɑn, pænˈθiən;
ES+-ˌɒn
panther ˈpænθə; ES ˈpænθə(r
Panthino pænˈθino
pantofle ˈpæntəfļ, pænˈtɑfļ, -ˈtufļ; ES+-ˈtɒf-
pantomime ˈpæntəˌmaɪm |-d -d |-mimist -ɪst
pantomimic ˌpæntəˈmɪmɪk
pantry ˈpæntrɪ
pants pænts
Panurge pænˈɝdʒ; ES -ˈɜdʒ, -ˈɝdʒ; |-'s -ɪz
(*Fr* paˈnyrʒ)
panzer ˈpænzə, ˈpantsə; ES -ə(r; (*Ger* ˈpantsər)
Paola pɪˈolə, pe-, *Italy* ˈpɑ:olɑ
Paoli pɪˈolaɪ, pe- (*It* ˈpɑ:oli)
pap pæp |papped pæpt
papa ˈpapə, *now rare* pəˈpɑ
papacy ˈpepəsɪ
papain pəˈpe·ɪn
papal ˈpepļ |papally ˈpepļɪ
papaverine pəˈpævəˌrin, -rɪn, -ˈpev-
papaw ˈpɔpɔ
papaya pəˈpaɪə, pəˈpajə
Papeete ˌpapɪˈete
paper ˈpepə; ES ˈpepə(r; |-ed -d |-ing ˈpe-
pərɪŋ, ˈpeprɪŋ
paperer ˈpepərə, ˈpeprə; ES ˈpepərə(r,
ˈpeprə(r
papeterie ˈpæpətrɪ (*Fr* papˈtri)
papier-mâché ˈpepəməˈʃe, ˌpæpjemæˈʃe; ES
ˈpepəməˈʃe, ˌpæpjemæˈʃe; (*Fr* papjema-
ˈʃe)
papist ˈpepɪst
papistic peˈpɪstɪk, pə- |-al -ļ |-ally -ļɪ, -ɪklɪ
papoose pæˈpus |-s -ɪz
paprika, -ca pæˈprikə, pə-
Papua ˈpæpjʊə |Papuan ˈpæpjʊən
papyrus pəˈpaɪrəs |-es -ɪz |papyri pəˈpaɪraɪ
par pɑr; ES pɑ:(r, E+pɑ:(r; |-red -d
Pará pɑˈra (ˈPará ˈrubber)
parable ˈpærəbļ |-d -d |-ling -bļɪŋ, -blɪŋ
parabola pəˈræbələ |-loid -ˌlɔɪd
parabolic ˌpærəˈbɑlɪk; ES+-ˈbɒl-; |-ally -ļɪ,
-ɪklɪ
paraboloidal pəˌræbəˈlɔɪdļ
Paracelsus ˌpærəˈsɛlsəs |-sus' -səs

Key: *See in full §§3–47.* bee bi |pity ˈpɪtɪ (§6) |rate ret |yet jɛt |sang sæŋ |angry ˈæŋ·grɪ
|bath bæθ; E baθ (§10) |ah ɑ |far fɑr |watch watʃ, wɒtʃ (§12) |jaw dʒɔ |gorge gɔrdʒ |go go

Words below in which a *before* r (farm) *is sounded* ɑ *are often pronounced in* E *with* a (fɑːm)
Words below that have æ *before* r (carry 'kærɪ) *are often pronounced in* N *with* ɛ ('kɛrɪ, §94)

parachute 'pærəˌʃut |-chuted -ˌʃutɪd
paraclete 'pærəˌklit
parade pə'red |paraded pə'redɪd
paradigm 'pærəˌdɪm, -ˌdaɪm
paradigmatic ˌpærədɪg'mætɪk |-al -l̩ |-ally -lɪ,
  -ɪklɪ
paradisaic ˌpærədɪ'se·ɪk |-al -l̩ |-ally -lɪ, -ɪklɪ
paradise, P- 'pærəˌdaɪs |-dises -ˌdaɪsɪz
paradox 'pærəˌdɑks; ES+-ˌdɒks; |-es -ɪz
paradoxical ˌpærə'dɑksɪkl̩; ES+-'dɒks-; |-ally
  -lɪ, -ɪklɪ
paraffin 'pærəfɪn |-fine -fɪn, -ˌfin
paragenesis ˌpærə'dʒɛnəsɪs
paragon 'pærəˌgɑn, -gən; ES+-ˌgɒn
paragraph 'pærəˌgræf |-ed -t; ES+-af, -ɑf
paragraphic ˌpærə'græfɪk |-al -l̩ |-ally -lɪ,
  -ɪklɪ
Paraguay 'pærəˌgwe, -ˌgwaɪ (*Sp* ˌpara'gwai)
Paraguayan ˌpærə'gwean, -'gwaɪən
parakeet 'pærəˌkit
paraldehyde pə'rældəˌhaɪd
paralipsis, -lep-, -leip- ˌpærə'lɪpsɪs, -'lɛp-,
  -'laɪp- |-ses -siz
parallax 'pærəˌlæks |-es -ɪz |-ed -t
parallel 'pærəˌlɛl |-ed -d |-ism -lɛlˌɪzəm
parallelepiped 'pærəˌlɛlə'paɪpɪd, -'pɪpɪd
parallelogram ˌpærə'lɛləˌgræm
paralysis pə'ræləsɪs |-ses -ˌsiz
paralytic ˌpærə'lɪtɪk
paralyze 'pærəˌlaɪz |-lyzes -ˌlaɪzɪz |-d -d
paramount, P- 'pærəˌmaunt |-cy -sɪ
paramour 'pærəˌmur; ES -ˌmuə(r
Paraná ˌpærə'na, -'nɔ (*Sp* ˌpara'na)
parang pɑ'rɑŋ
paranoia ˌpærə'nɔɪə |-noiac -'nɔɪæk
parapet 'pærəpɪt, -ˌpɛt |-peted -pɪtɪd, -ˌpɛtɪd
paraphernalia ˌpærəfə'nelɪə, -fɚ-, -ljə; ES
  -fə-;—*In the first pron.* ɚ *is lost by dissimilation* (§121).
paraphrase 'pærəˌfrez |-s -ɪz |-d -d
paraphrastic ˌpærə'fræstɪk |-al -l̩ |-ally -lɪ,
  -ɪklɪ
parapsychology ˌpærəsaɪ'kɑlədʒɪ; ES+-'kɒl-
parasang 'pærəˌsæŋ
parasite 'pærəˌsaɪt |-sitism -saɪtˌɪzəm
parasitic ˌpærə'sɪtɪk |-al -l̩ |-ally -lɪ, -ɪklɪ
parasol 'pærəˌsɔl, -ˌsɒl, -ˌsɑl

parasynthesis ˌpærə'sɪnθəsɪs
parasynthetic ˌpærəsɪn'θɛtɪk |-al -l̩ |-ally -lɪ,
  -ɪklɪ
paratactic ˌpærə'tæktɪk |-al -l̩ |-ally -lɪ, -ɪklɪ
parataxis ˌpærə'tæksɪs
parathyroid ˌpærə'θaɪrɔɪd |-al -θaɪ'rɔɪd|
paratyphoid ˌpærə'taɪfɔɪd
parboil 'parˌbɔɪl; ES 'pɑːˌbɔɪl; |-ed -d
parbuckle 'parˌbʌkl̩; ES 'pɑːˌbʌkl̩; |-d -d
  |-ling -ˌbʌkl̩ɪŋ, -ˌbʌklɪŋ
parcel 'parsl̩; ES 'pɑːsl̩; |-ed -d |-ing -sl̩ɪŋ,
  -slɪŋ
parcener 'parsnɚ; ES 'pɑːsnə(r; |-nary -ˌɛrɪ
parch partʃ; ES pɑːtʃ; |-es -ɪz |-ed -t |-edly
  -ɪdlɪ
parcheesi, -chesi, -chisi pə'tʃizɪ, pɑː-; N+pɚ-,
  pɑr-
parchment 'partʃmənt; ES 'pɑːtʃ-; |-ed -ɪd
pard pard; ES pɑːd
Pardee par'di; ES pɑː'di
pardie *intj* par'di; ES pɑː'di
pardon 'pardn̩; ES 'pɑːdn̩; |-ed -d |-ing
  -dn̩ɪŋ, -dnɪŋ |-able -dnəbl̩, -dn̩əbl̩ |-bly
  -blɪ
pare pɛr, pær; E pɛə(r, ES pæə(r; |-d -d
paregoric ˌpærə'gɔrɪk, -'gɑrɪk, -'gɒrɪk
parent 'pɛrənt, 'pærənt, 'perənt |-age -ɪdʒ
parental pə'rɛntl̩ |parentally pə'rɛntl̩ɪ
parenthesis pə'rɛnθəsɪs |-theses -θəˌsiz
parenthesize pə'rɛnθəˌsaɪz |-s -ɪz |-d -d
parenthetic ˌpærɛn'θɛtɪk |-al -l̩ |-ally -lɪ, -ɪklɪ
paresis pə'risɪs, 'pærəsɪs
paretic pə'rɛtɪk, pə'ritɪk
par excellence par'ɛksəˌlɑns (*Fr* parɛksɛ-
  'lãːs)
parfait par'fe, par'fɛ; ES pɑː-; (*Fr* par'fɛ)
parhelion par'hilɪən, -ljən; ES pɑː-; |-ia -ɪə
pariah pə'raɪə, 'pærɪə, 'par-
Parian 'pɛrɪən, 'pær-, 'per-; S 'pær-, 'per-
parietal pə'raɪətl̩
pari mutuel 'pærɪ'mjutʃuəl, -'mɪu- (*Fr* pa-
  rimy'tɥɛl)
Paris 'pærɪs, *jocularly* pæ'ri |-'s -ɪz (*Fr* pa'ri)
Paris, Gaston gæs'tɔnpæ'ris |-'s -ɪz (*Fr* gas-
  tõpa'riːs)
parish 'pærɪʃ |parished 'pærɪʃt
parishioner pə'rɪʃənɚ, -'rɪʃnɚ; ES -nə(r

Words below in which a *before* r (farm) *is sounded* ɑ *are often pronounced in* E *with* a (fɑ:m)
Words below that have æ *before* r (carry 'kærɪ) *are often pronounced in* N *with* ɛ ('kɛrɪ, §94)

Parisian pə'rɪʒən, pə'rɪzɪən
parity 'pærətɪ
park park; ES pɑ:k; |-ed -t |-way -ˌwe
parka 'pɑrkə; ES 'pɑ:kə
Parker 'pɑrkɚ; ES 'pɑ:kə(r
Parkman 'pɑrkmən; ES 'pɑ:kmən
parlance 'pɑrləns; ES 'pɑ:ləns; |-s -ɪz
parlay 'pɑrlɪ; ES 'pɑ:lɪ
parle pɑrl; ES pɑ:l
parley 'pɑrlɪ; ES 'pɑ:lɪ; |-ed -d
parliament 'pɑrləmənt; ES 'pɑ:ləmənt
parliamentarian ˌpɑrləmɛn'tɛrɪən, -'ter-; ES ˌpɑ:l-
parliamentary ˌpɑrlə'mɛntərɪ, -trɪ; ES ˌpɑ:l-
parlor, P- 'pɑrlɚ; ES 'pɑ:lə(r; |-maid -ˌmed
parlous 'pɑrləs; ES 'pɑ:ləs
Parmesan ˌpɑrmə'zæn; ES ˌpɑ:m-; ('Parme-ˌsan 'Cheese)
Parnassian pɑr'næsɪən, -sjən; ES pɑ'n-
Parnassus pɑr'næsəs; ES pɑ:'n-; |-sus' -səs
Parnell pɑr'nɛl, 'pɑrn|, *Irish leader* 'pɑrn|; ES pɑ:'n-, 'pɑ:n-
parochial pə'rokɪəl, -kjəl |-ly -ɪ
parody 'pærədɪ |parodied 'pærədɪd |-dist -dɪst
parol, -e *'word'* pə'rol
parole pə'rol |-d -d |-lable -əb|
Parolles pə'rɑlɪs, -'rɒl- |-'s -ɪz
paronomasia ˌpærəno'meʒə, -ʒɪə
parotid pə'rɑtɪd; ES+-'rɒtɪd
paroxysm, P- 'pærəksˌɪzəm
paroxytone pær'ɑksəˌton; ES+-'ɒks-
parquet pɑr'ke, -'kɛt; ES pɑ:-; |-ed -'ked, -'kɛtɪd
parquetry 'pɑrkɪtrɪ; ES 'pɑ:k-
parricidal ˌpærə'saɪd| |-ly -ɪ
parricide 'pærəˌsaɪd
Parrish 'pærɪʃ |-'s -ɪz
parrot 'pærət |parroted 'pærətɪd
parry 'pærɪ |parried 'pærɪd
parse pɑrs; ES pɑ:s; |-d -t (*Brit* pɑ:z)
parsec 'pɑrˌsɛk; ES 'pɑ:ˌsɛk
Parsi, -see 'pɑrsi, pɑr'si; ES 'pɑ:si, pɑ:'si
Parsifal 'pɑrsəf|, -ˌfɑl; ES 'pɑ:s-; (*Ger* 'pɑrzi-ˌfɑl)—*see* Parzival
parsimonious ˌpɑrsə'monɪəs, -njəs; ES ˌpɑ:s-
parsimony 'pɑrsəˌmonɪ; ES 'pɑ:s-

parsley 'pɑrslɪ; ES 'pɑ:slɪ
parsnip 'pɑrsnəp, -nɪp; ES 'pɑ:s-
parson 'pɑrsn̩; ES 'pɑ:sn̩; |-age -ɪdʒ
part pɑrt; ES pɑ:t; |-ed -ɪd |-ly -lɪ
partake pɚ'tek, pɑr-; ES pə'tek, pɑ:-; |-took -'tʊk |-taken -'tekən
parterre pɑr'tɛr; ES pɑ:-; |-d -d (*Fr* pɑr'tɛ:r)
parthenogenesis ˌpɑrθəno'dʒɛnəsɪs; ES ˌpɑ:θ-
Parthenon 'pɑrθəˌnɑn, -nən; ES 'pɑ:θ-, -ˌnɒn
Parthenope pɑr'θɛnəˌpi, -pɪ; ES pɑ'θɛn-
Parthia 'pɑrθɪə, -θjə; ES 'pɑ:θ-; |-n -n
partial 'pɑrʃəl; ES 'pɑ:ʃəl; |-ly -ɪ
partiality pɑr'ʃælətɪ, ˌpɑrʃɪ'æl-; ES pɑ'ʃæl-, ˌpɑ:ʃɪ'ælətɪ
partible 'pɑrtəb|; ES 'pɑ:təb|
participant pɚ'tɪsəpənt, pɑr-; ES pə-, pɑ-
participate *adj* pɚ'tɪsəpɪt, pɑr-, -ˌpet; ES pə-, pɑ-
participate *v* pɚ'tɪsəˌpet, pɑr-; ES pə-, pɑ-; |-d -ɪd
participation pɚˌtɪsə'peʃən, pɑr-; ES pə-, pɑ-
participial ˌpɑrtə'sɪpɪəl, -pjəl; ES ˌpɑ:tə-; |-ly -ɪ
participle 'pɑrtəsəp|, 'pɑrtsəp|, 'pɑrtəˌsɪp|; ES 'pɑ:t-
particle 'pɑrtɪk|; ES 'pɑ:t-; |-d -d
parti-colored 'pɑrtɪˌkʌlɚd; ES 'pɑ:tɪˌkʌləd
particular pɚ'tɪkjəlɚ, pə-, pɑr-; ES pə-'tɪkjələ(r, pɑ-;—*In the 2d pron.* ɚ *is lost by dissimilation* (§121).
particularity pɚˌtɪkjə'lærətɪ, pə-, pɑr-; ES pə-, pɑ- —*see note above*
particularize pɚ'tɪkjələˌraɪz, pə-, pɑr-; ES pə-, pɑ-; |-s -ɪz |-d -d—*see note above*
Partington 'pɑrtɪŋtən; ES 'pɑ:tɪŋ-
partisan, -zan 'pɑrtəzn̩; ES 'pɑ:təzn̩
partition pɚ'tɪʃən, pɑr-; ES pə-, pɑ:-; |-ed -d
partitive 'pɑrtətɪv; ES 'pɑ:tətɪv
partlet, P- 'pɑrtlɪt; ES 'pɑ:tlɪt
partly 'pɑrtlɪ; ES 'pɑ:tlɪ
partner 'pɑrtnɚ; ES 'pɑ:tnə(r
partook pɚ'tʊk, pɑr-; ES pə'tʊk, pɑ:-
partridge 'pɑrtrɪdʒ; ES 'pɑ:trɪdʒ; |-s -ɪz
parturition ˌpɑrtjʊ'rɪʃən; ES ˌpɑ:t-
party 'pɑrtɪ; ES 'pɑ:tɪ
party-colored 'pɑrtɪˌkʌlɚd; ES 'pɑ:tɪˌkʌləd
parure pə'rur; ES pə'rʊə(r; (*Fr* pa'ry:r)

Key: See in full §§3–47. bee bi |pity 'pɪtɪ (§6) |rate ret |yet jɛt |sang sæŋ |angry 'æŋ·grɪ |bath bæθ; E bɑθ (§10) |ah ɑ |far fɑr |watch wɑtʃ, wɒtʃ (§12) |jaw dʒɔ |gorge gɔrdʒ |go go

Words below in which a *before* r (farm) *is sounded* ɑ *are often pronounced in* E *with* a (faːm)

parvenu ˈpɑrvəˌnju, -ˌnɪu, -ˌnu; ES ˈpɑːv-; (Fr parvəˈny)

parvoline ˈpɑrvəˌlin, -lɪn; ES ˈpɑːv-

Parzival ˈpɑrtsəvḷ, -ˌvɑl; ES ˈpɑːts-; (Ger ˈpɑrtsiˌvɑl)

pas Fr pɑ

Pascal ˈpæskḷ (Fr pasˈkal)

Pasch pæsk |Pascha ˈpæskə |paschal ˈpæskḷ

pasha ˈpæʃə, ˈpɑʃə, pəˈʃɑ

Paso Robles ˈpæsoˈrobḷz, -bləs, ˈpɑsoˈroblɛs

pasquinade ˌpæskwɪˈned |-d -ɪd

pass pæs; E+pas, pɑs; |-es -ɪz |-ed -t |-able -əbḷ |-bly -blɪ

passado pəˈsɑdo

passage ˈpæsɪdʒ |-s -ɪz |-d -d |-way -ˌwe

Passaic pəˈseˑɪk, pæ-

Passamaquoddy ˌpæsəməˈkwɑdɪ, -ˈkwɒdɪ

passbook ˈpæsˌbʊk; E+ˈpas-, ˈpas-

passé, fem. passée pæˈse (Fr paˈse) (ˈpasˌsée ˈbelle)

passementerie pæsˈmɛntrɪ (Fr pasmɑ̃ˈtri)

passenger ˈpæsn̩dʒɚ; ES ˈpæsn̩dʒə(r

passe partout n ˌpæspɚˈtu, -pɑr-; ES -pəˈtu, -pɑːˈtu; (Fr paspɑrˈtu)

passe-partout v ˌpæspɚˈtu, -pɑr-; ES -pəˈtu, -pɑːˈtu; |-ed -d

passer-by ˈpæsɚˈbaɪ; ES ˈpæsə-, E+ˈpas-, ˈpas-

passim ˈpæsɪm

passion, P- ˈpæʃən |-ed -d |-ate -ɪt, -ʃnɪt

passive ˈpæsɪv |-sivity pæˈsɪvətɪ

passkey ˈpæsˌki; E+ˈpas-, ˈpas-

passover ˈpæsˌovɚ; ES -ˌovə(r, E+ˈpas-, ˈpas-

passport ˈpæsˌport, -ˌpɔrt; ES -ˌpoət, E+ˈpas-, ˈpas-, -ˌpɔət

password ˈpæsˌwɝd; ES -ˌwɜd, -ˌwɝd, E+ˈpas-, ˈpas-

Passy pæˈsi (Fr paˈsi)

past pæst; E+past, pɑst

paste pest |pasted ˈpestɪd

pasteboard ˈpestˌbord, ˈpes-, -ˌbɔrd; ES -ˌboəd, E+-ˌbɔəd

pastel pæsˈtɛl (ˈpasˌtel ˈdrawing)

pastern ˈpæstɚn; ES ˈpæstən

Pasteur pæsˈtɝ; ES -ˈtɜ(r, -ˈtɝ; (Fr pasˈtœːr)

pasteurization ˌpæstərəˈzeʃən, ˌpæstʃə-, -aɪˈz-

pasteurize ˈpæstəˌraɪz, ˈpæstʃə- |-s -ɪz |-d -d

pastille pæsˈtil |pastil ˈpæstɪl |-tile -tɪl |-(e)d -d

pastime ˈpæsˌtaɪm; E+ˈpas-, ˈpas-

pastor ˈpæstɚ; ES ˈpæstə(r, E+ˈpas-, ˈpas-; |-ate -ɪt, -trɪt

pastoral ˈpæstərəl, -trəl; E+ˈpas-, ˈpas-; |-ly -ɪ

pastorale ˌpæstəˈralɪ (It ˌpastoˈraːle)

pastorium pæsˈtorɪəm, -ˈtɔr-; S -ˈtor-

pastry ˈpestrɪ

pasturage ˈpæstʃərɪdʒ

pasture ˈpæstʃɚ; ES ˈpæstʃə(r, E+ˈpas-, ˈpas-

pasty 'pie,' chiefly Brit ˈpæstɪ, ˈpɑstɪ

pasty 'like paste' ˈpestɪ

pat pæt |patted ˈpætɪd

pat-a-cake ˈpætɪˌkek, ˈpætə- |-d -t

Patagonia ˌpætəˈgonjə, -ˈgonɪə |-n -n

patch pætʃ |patches ˈpætʃɪz |-ed -t |-able -əbḷ

Patchogue pæˈtʃɔg, pə-, cf Pachaug

patchouli, -ly ˈpætʃʊlɪ, pəˈtʃulɪ

patchwork ˈpætʃˌwɝk; ES -ˌwɜk, -ˌwɝk

pate pet |pated ˈpetɪd

pâté Fr pɑˈte

patella pəˈtɛlə |-s -z |-lae -li

paten ˈpætn̩

patency ˈpetn̩sɪ

patent 'obvious' ˈpetn̩t, 'letters patent' ˈpætn̩t |-ed -ɪd

patentee ˌpætn̩ˈti

patentor ˈpætn̩tɚ, contrasted with patentee ˌpætn̩ˈtɔr; ES -tə(r, -ˈtɔə(r

pater, P- ˈpetɚ; ES ˈpetə(r

paterfamilias ˈpetɚfəˈmɪlɪˌæs, -əs; ES ˈpetə-; |-es -ɪz

paternal pəˈtɝnḷ; ES pəˈtɜnḷ, -ˈtɝnḷ; |-ism -ˌɪzəm |-ist -ɪst |-ly -ɪ |-ize -ˌaɪz |-izes -ˌaɪzɪz |-ized -ˌaɪzd

paternalistic pəˌtɝnḷˈɪstɪk; ES -ˌtɜnḷ-, -ˌtɝnḷ-

paternity pəˈtɝnətɪ; ES pəˈtɜnətɪ, -ˈtɝn-

paternoster ˈpetɚˈnɑstɚ, ˈpætɚ-; ES ˈpetə-ˈnɑstə(r, ˈpætə-, -ˈnɒstə(r; Lond street ˈpætɚˌnɑstɚˈro; ES ˈpætəˌnɑstə-, -ˌnɒstə-

Paterson ˈpætɚsn̩; ES ˈpætəsn̩

path pæθ; E+paθ, pɑθ; |-'s -θs |-ths -ðz |-thed -θt

Pathan pəˈtɑn, pətˈhɑn

pathetic pəˈθɛtɪk |-al -ḷ |-ally -ḷɪ, -ɪklɪ

pathfinder 'pæθ₁faɪndə; ES -də(r, E+'paθ-, 'paθ-

pathogenesis ₁pæθə'dʒɛnəsɪs |-netic -dʒə-'nɛtɪk

pathogenic ₁pæθə'dʒɛnɪk

pathologic ₁pæθə'lɑdʒɪk; ES+-'lɒdʒɪk; |-al -| |-ally -ɪ, -ɪklɪ

pathologist pæ'θɑlədʒɪst, pə-; ES+-'θɒl-; |-gy -dʒɪ

pathos 'peθɑs; ES+'peɒs

pathway 'pæθ₁we; E+'paθ-, 'paθ-; |-ed -d

patience, P- 'peʃəns |-'s -ɪz |patient 'peʃənt

patina 'pan' 'pætɪnə |-nae -₁ni

patina 'film' 'pætnə |-s -z

patio 'patɪ₁o (Sp 'patjo)

Patmore 'pætmor, -mɔr; ES -moə(r, E+ -mɔə(r

Patmos 'pætməs, 'pætmɑs; ES+-mɒs; |-'s -ɪz

patois 'pætwa, -wɒ (Fr pa'twa)

patriarch 'petrɪ₁ark; ES -₁ɑ:k, E+-₁a:k; |-ate -ɪt

patriarchal ₁petrɪ'ark|; ES -'ɑ:k|, E+-'a:k|; |-ly -ɪ

Patricia pə'trɪʃə, -ʃɪə

patrician pə'trɪʃən

Patrick 'pætrɪk

patrimonial ₁pætrə'monɪəl, -njəl |-ly -ɪ

patrimony 'pætrə₁monɪ

patriot 'petrɪət, 'petrɪ₁at; ES+-₁ɒt

patriotic ₁petrɪ'atɪk; ES+-'ɒtɪk; |-al -| |-ally -ɪ, -ɪklɪ

patristic pə'trɪstɪk

Patroclus pə'trokləs |-'s -ɪz

patrol pə'trol |-led -d |-man, -men -mən

patron 'petrən

patronage 'petrənɪdʒ, 'pæt-

patroness 'petrənɪs, 'pæt- |-es -ɪz

patronize 'petrən₁aɪz |-s -ɪz |-d -d |+'pæt-

patronymic ₁pætrə'nɪmɪk

patroon pə'trun

Pattee pæ'ti

patten 'pætn̩ |pattened 'pætn̩d

patter 'pætə; ES 'pætə(r; |-ed -d

pattern 'pætən; ES 'pætən

Patti 'pætɪ, 'pæti (It 'patti)

Pattison 'pætəsn̩

patty, P- 'pætɪ |patty-cake 'pætɪ₁kek

paucity 'pɔsətɪ

paul pɔl |-ed -d

Paul pɔl |Paula 'pɔlə |Paulist 'pɔlɪst

Paulina pə'laɪnə, pɔ'laɪnə

Pauline fem. name pɔ'lin; 'of Paul' 'pɔlaɪn

Paulinus pɔ'laɪnəs |-'s -ɪz

paunch pɔntʃ, pɒntʃ, pantʃ |-es -ɪz |-ed -t

pauper 'pɔpə; ES 'pɔpə(r; |-age -ɪdʒ |-ism -₁ɪzəm

pauperize 'pɔpə₁raɪz |-s -ɪz |-d -d

pause pɔz |pauses 'pɔzɪz |paused pɔzd

pave pev |past & pptc -d -d |rare pptc -ven -vən

pavement 'pevmənt

Pavey, -vy 'pevɪ, cf Peavey

Pavia bot. 'pevɪə; It city pə'viə (It pa'vi:a)

pavilion pə'vɪljən |pavilioned pə'vɪljənd

pavior 'pevjə; ES 'pevjə(r

paw pɔ |pawed pɔd |pawing 'pɔ·ɪŋ

pawky 'pɔkɪ

pawl pɔl |-ed -d

pawn pɔn |pawned pɔnd |-broker -₁brokə; ES -ə(r

pawnee pɔn'i |-nor 'pɔnə, -n'ɔr; ES -nə(r, -n'ɔə(r

Pawnee pɔ'ni

pawnshop 'pɔn₁ʃap; ES+-₁ʃɒp

pawpaw 'pɔpɔ=papaw

Paw Paw 'pɔpɔ

Pawtucket pɔ'tʌkɪt

pax pæks |paxes 'pæksɪz

pay pe |paid, naut. payed ped |-ing 'pe·ɪŋ

payee pe'i

paymaster 'pe₁mæstə; ES -₁mæstə(r, E+ -₁mas-, -₁mas-

payment 'pemənt

Payne pen

paynim 'penɪm

pay-roll 'pe₁rol

Paz, La lə'pas (Am Sp la'pas)

pea pi

Peabody 'pi₁badɪ, -bədɪ; ES+-₁bɒdɪ

peace pis |-s -ɪz |-d -d -t |-ful -fəl |-fully -fəlɪ

peaceable 'pisəb| |-bly -blɪ

peacemaker 'pis₁mekə; ES -₁mekə(r

peach pitʃ |peaches 'pitʃɪz |peached pitʃt

peachick 'pi₁tʃɪk

peach-tree 'pitʃ₁tri

peacock 'pi₁kak; ES+-₁kɒk; |peafowl 'pi₁faul

peag, -e pig

pea-green 'pi'grin ('pea-₁green 'dress)

peahen 'pi,hɛn
peak pik |peaked pikt
peaked adj 'pikɪd, pikt; N Engd+ 'pɪkɪd
peal pil |pealed pild
pean 'heraldic pattern,' 'peen' pin
pean 'paean' 'piən
peanut 'pinət, 'pi,nʌt
pear pɛr, pær; E pɛə(r, ES pæə(r
Pearce pɪrs; ES pɪəs, S+pɛəs; |-'s -ɪz
pearl, P- pɝl; ES pɜl, pɝl; |-ed -d |-ite -aɪt
pearmain 'pɛrmen, 'pær-; E 'pɛə-, ES 'pæə-
peart 'pert' pɝt, pɪrt; ES pɜt, pɝt, pɪət,
S+pɛət
Pears pɛrz, pærz; E pɛəz, ES pæəz; |-'s -ɪz
Pearsall 'pɪrsɔl, 'pɪrs]; ES 'pɪə-
Pearse pɪrs, pɝs; ES pɪəs, pɜs, pɝs; |-'s -ɪz
Pearson 'pɪrsṇ; ES 'pɪəsṇ
Peary 'pɪrɪ
peasant 'pɛzṇt |-ry -rɪ
pease piz |-cod -,kad; ES+-,kɒd
Peaseblossom 'piz,blɑsəm; ES+-,blɒs-
peat pit |-ery -ərɪ |-wood -,wʊd
peavey, -vy 'pivɪ
Peavey 'pevɪ, 'pivɪ, cf Pavey
pebble 'pɛb] |-d -d |-ling -blɪŋ, -b|ɪŋ
pebbly 'pɛblɪ, 'pɛb|ɪ
pecan pɪ'kan, pə-, pɪ'kæn, 'pikæn—pɪ'kan
    appears to prevail in the S, but pɪ'kæn is not
    uncommon there.
peccable 'pɛkəb] |-bility ,pɛkə'bɪlətɪ
peccadillo ,pɛkə'dɪlo
peccant 'pɛkənt |-ancy -ənsɪ
peccary 'pɛkərɪ
peccavi pɪ'kevaɪ, pɛ- |-s -z
peck pɛk |pecked pɛkt
Peckham 'pɛkəm
Pecksniff 'pɛksnɪf |-ian pɛk'snɪfɪən
Pecock 'pi,kak; ES+-,kɒk
Pecos 'pekəs, -os |-'s -ɪz
pectin 'pɛktɪn |-al -] |-ase -,es |-ate -,et
pectoral 'pɛktərəl |-ly -ɪ
peculate 'pɛkjə,let |-d -ɪd |-tor -ɚ; ES -ə(r
peculation ,pɛkjə'leʃən
peculiar pɪ'kjuljɚ, -'kɪul-; ES -jə(r
peculiarity pɪ,kjulɪ'ærətɪ, pɪ,kjuljɪ'ærətɪ, pɪ-
    ,kjul'jærətɪ, -,kɪul-
pecuniary pɪ'kjunɪ,ɛrɪ, -'kɪun-
pedagogic ,pɛdə'gadʒɪk, -'gɒdʒ-; ES+
    -'gɒdʒ-; |-al -] |-ally -|ɪ, -ɪklɪ

pedagogue, -gog 'pɛdə,gag, -,gɒg, -,gɔg |-d,
    -ged -d |-guism, -ogism -,ɪzəm
pedagogy 'pɛdə,godʒɪ, -,gadʒɪ; ES+-,gɒdʒɪ
pedal n, v 'pɛd] |-ed -d |-ing 'pɛd|ɪŋ
pedal adj 'pɛd], 'pid]
pedaler 'pɛd|ɚ; ES 'pɛd|ə(r; cf peddler
pedant 'pɛdṇt |-ry -rɪ
pedantic pɪ'dæntɪk |-al -] |-ally -|ɪ, -ɪklɪ
peddle 'pɛd] |-d -d |-ling 'pɛd|ɪŋ, 'pɛdlɪŋ
peddler 'pɛd|ɚ; ES 'pɛdlə(r
pedestal 'pɛdɪst] |-ed -d
pedestrian pə'dɛstrɪən |-ism -,ɪzəm
pediatric ,pidɪ'ætrɪk, ,pɛdɪ- |-s -s
pediatrician ,pidɪə'trɪʃən, ,pɛdɪ-
pedicel 'pɛdəs] |-ed -d
pedicle 'pɛdɪk]
pedigree 'pɛdə,gri |-d -d
pediment 'pɛdəmənt |-al ,pɛdə'mɛnt]
pedimented 'pɛdə,mɛntɪd, 'pɛdəməntɪd
pedlar 'pɛd|ɚ; ES 'pɛdlə(r
pedometer pɪ'damətɚ, pɛd'am-; ES -'damə-
    tə(r, -'am-, -'dɒm-, -'ɒm-
pedro 'pidro
Pedro 'pidro, 'ped- (Sp 'peðro)
peduncle pɪ'dʌŋk] |-d -d
pee pi
Peebles 'pib|z |-'s -ɪz |-shire -,ʃɪr, -|ʒ,ʃɪr, -ʃɚ,
    -|ʃɚ; ES -,ʃɪə(r, -ʃə(r
peek pik |peeked pikt
peel, P- pil |peeled pild
peen pin |peened pind
peep pip |peeped pipt |-hole -,hol
peer pɪr; ES pɪə(r, S+pɛə(r; |-ed -d
peerage 'pɪrɪdʒ; S+'pɛr-; |-s -ɪz
peeve piv |peeved pivd |-dly -ɪdlɪ, -dlɪ
peg, P- |pegged pɛgd |peggy, P- 'pɛgɪ
Pegasus 'pɛgəsəs |-sus' -səs
Peggotty 'pɛgətɪ
peignoir pen'war, 'penwar, -ɔr; ES -a:(r,
    -ɔə(r
Peiping 'pe'pɪŋ (Chin 'be'pɪŋ)
Peiraeus paɪ'rɪəs |-'s -ɪz
Peirce pɪrs; ES pɪəs, S+pɛəs; |-'s -ɪz
pejorative 'pidʒə,retɪv, pɪ'dʒɔrətɪv, -'dʒar-,
    -'dʒɒr-
Pekin US 'pikɪn, China 'pi'kɪn |-king 'pi'kɪŋ
Pekingese ,pikɪŋ'iz |-kinese -kɪn'iz |-'s -ɪz
pekoe 'piko, Brit+'pɛko
pelage 'pɛlɪdʒ |-s -ɪz

|full fʊl |tooth tuθ |further 'fɝðɚ; ES 'fɝðə |custom 'kʌstəm |while hwaɪl |how haʊ |toy tɔɪ
|using 'juzɪŋ |fuse fjuz, fɪuz |dish dɪʃ |vision 'vɪʒən |Eden 'idṇ |cradle 'kred] |keep 'em 'kipm̩

pelagian, P- pə'ledʒɪən |pelagic pə'lædʒɪk
Pelasgian pə'læzdʒɪən, -gɪən |-gic -dʒɪk
Pelee *isl.* 'pili |Pelée *mt.* pə'le
Peleus 'piljus |-'s -ɪz
pelf pɛlf
Pelham 'pɛləm
pelican 'pɛlɪkən |-ry -rɪ
Pelion 'pilɪən
pelisse pə'lis |-s -ɪz
pellagra pə'legrə, -'læg- |-grous -grəs
pellet 'pɛlɪt |-ed -ɪd
pellicle 'pɛlɪkḷ
pell-mell, pellmell 'pɛl'mɛl |-ed -d
pellucid pə'lusɪd, -'lɪusɪd
Peloponnese ˌpɛləpə'nis |-sos, -sus -əs
Peloponnesian ˌpɛləpə'niʃən, -ʒən
Pelops 'pilɑps; ES+-lɒps; |-'s -ɪz
pelt pɛlt |pelted 'pɛltɪd |-ry -rɪ
pelter 'pɛltɚ; ES 'pɛltə(r; |-ed -d
pelvis 'pɛlvɪs |-es -ɪz |-ves -viz |-vic -vɪk
Pembina 'pɛmbɪnə, -ˌnɔ |Pembine 'pɛmbaɪn
Pemberton 'pɛmbɚtṇ; ES 'pɛmbətṇ
Pembroke *US, C* 'pɛmbrok, *Wales, Irel* -bruk
Pembrokeshire 'pɛmbrukˌʃɪr, -ʃɚ; ES -ˌʃɪə(r,
 -ʃə(r
Pemigewasset ˌpɛmɪdʒə'wɑsɪt, -'wɒsɪt
Pemiscot 'pɛmɪˌskɑt; ES+-ˌskɒt
pemmican 'pɛmɪkən
pen *n* pɛn
pen *v 'write'* pɛn |penned pɛnd
pen *v 'shut'* pɛn |penned pɛnd
penal 'pinḷ |-ly -ɪ
penalize 'pinḷˌaɪz, 'pɛnḷ- |-s -ɪz |-d -d—*The*
 pronunciation 'pɛnḷˌaɪz *is influenced by*
 'pɛnḷtɪ, *which is heard oftener than* 'pinḷ
 (penal).
penalty 'pɛnḷtɪ
penance 'pɛnəns |-s -ɪz |-d -t
pen-and-ink 'pɛnən'ɪŋk, *less freq.* 'pɛnənd'ɪŋk
Pen Argyl pɛn'ɑrdʒɪl; ES -'ɑːdʒɪl
penates, P- pə'netiz
Penbrook 'pɛnˌbruk
pence pɛns, *in combination* -pəns, -pɛns
penchant 'pɛntʃənt (*Fr* pɑ̃'ʃɑ̃)
pencil 'pɛnsḷ |-ed -d
pend pɛnd |-ed -ɪd |-ing -ɪŋ
pendant 'pɛndənt |-ed -ɪd
pendency 'pɛndənsɪ |pendent 'pɛndənt
Pendennis pɛn'dɛnɪs |-'s -ɪz

Pendergast 'pɛndɚˌgæst; ES 'pɛndə-;—r *has*
 been lost by dissimilation (*§121)—see*
 Prendergast.
Pendleton 'pɛndḷtən
pendragon, P- pɛn'drægən
pendulous 'pɛndʒələs
pendulum 'pɛndʒələm, 'pɛndḷəm, 'pɛndjələm
Penelope pə'nɛləpɪ |-an pəˌnɛlə'piən
peneplain, -plane 'pinəˌplen, ˌpinə'plen
penetrability ˌpɛnətrə'bɪlətɪ
penetrable 'pɛnətrəbḷ |-bly -blɪ
penetrate 'pɛnəˌtret |-d -ɪd |-tion ˌpɛnə-
 'treʃən
penguin 'pɛngwɪn, 'pɛŋgwɪn |-ery -ˌɛrɪ
penholder 'pɛnˌholdɚ; ES -ˌholdə(r
penicillin ˌpɛnɪ'sɪlɪn (*cf L* ˌpeni'cillus)
peninsula, P- pə'nɪnsələ, -sjulə, -ʃulə |-r -ɚ;
 ES -ə(r
penis 'pinɪs |-es -ɪz |-nes -niz
penitence 'pɛnətəns |-tent -tənt
penitential ˌpɛnə'tɛnʃəl |-ly -ɪ
penitentiary ˌpɛnə'tɛnʃərɪ, -'tɛntʃərɪ
penknife 'pɛnˌnaɪf, 'pɛnaɪf |-knives -aɪvz
penman 'pɛnmən |-men -mən |-ship -ˌʃɪp
Penn pɛn
pen-name 'pɛnˌnem
pennant 'pɛnənt
pennate 'pɛnet |-d -ɪd
Pennell 'pɛnḷ
penniless 'pɛnḷɪs, 'pɛnɪlɪs
Pennine 'pɛnaɪn
pennon 'pɛnən |-ed -d
Pennsylvania ˌpɛnsḷ'venjə, -nɪə, -sɪl- |-n -n
penny 'pɛnɪ |-ies -z |pence pɛns
penny-a-liner ˌpɛnɪə'laɪnɚ; ES -'laɪnə(r
Penn Yan ˌpɛn'jæn
pennyroyal ˌpɛnɪ'rɔɪəl, -'rɔɪəl, -'rɔɪl
pennyweight 'pɛnɪˌwet
penny-wise 'pɛnɪˌwaɪz ('penny-ˌwise 'move)
pennyworth 'pɛnɪˌwɝθ; ES -ˌwɜθ, -ˌwɝθ;
 |-ths -θs
Penobscot pə'nɑbskɑt, -skət; ES+-'nɒbskɒt
penology pi'nɑlədʒɪ; ES+-'nɒl-; |-gist -dʒɪst
Penrith 'pɛnrɪθ, pɛn'rɪθ
Penrod 'pɛnrɑd; ES+-rɒd
Pensacola ˌpɛnsə'kolə
Pensauken pɛn'sɔkən
penseroso, P- ˌpɛnsə'roso
pensile 'pɛnsḷ, 'pɛnsɪl

pension *'payment'* **'pɛnʃən** |-ed -d
pension *'lodging'* **'pɑnsɪˌɑn, -ˌɒn** (*Fr* pãˈsjõ)
pensionary **'pɛnʃənˌɛrɪ**
pensive **'pɛnsɪv** |-d -d
penstock **'pɛnˌstak; ES +-ˌstɒk**
pent **pɛnt**
pentagon **'pɛntəˌgɑn; ES +-ˌgɒn**
pentagonal **pɛnˈtægənɪ** |-ly -ɪ
pentahedron **ˌpɛntəˈhidrən** |-dral -drəl
pentameter **pɛnˈtæmətɚ; ES -ˈtæmətə(r**
pentane **'pɛnten**
Pentateuch **'pɛntəˌtjuk, -ˌtɪuk, -ˌtuk**
pentathlon **pɛnˈtæθlən, -lɑn, -lɒn**
Pentecost **'pɛntɪˌkɔst, -ˌkɒst, -ˌkɑst**
Penthesilea **ˌpɛnθɛsɪˈliə**
penthouse **'pɛntˌhaʊs** |-ses -zɪz |-d -ˌhaʊst
pentice **'pɛntɪs** |-s -ɪz |-d -t=penthouse
pentose **'pɛntos**
pent-up **'pɛntˈʌp** (**'pɛnt-ˌup 'wrath**)
penult **'pinʌlt, pɪˈnʌlt**
penultima **pɪˈnʌltəmə** |-mate -mɪt
penumbra **pɪˈnʌmbrə** |-s -z |-brae -bri
penurious **pəˈnʊrɪəs, -ˈnɪu-, -ˈnju-**
penury **'pɛnjərɪ**
Penzance **pɛnˈzæns** |-'s -ɪz
peon **'piən** |-age -ɪdʒ |-ism -ˌɪzəm
peony **'piənɪ**—*The well-known popular* **'paɪnɪ**
represents piony, *in literary use 15–19 cc*
(*Cowper has* pioney). Peony *dates from the*
16c.
people **'pipɪ** |-d -d |-ling **'piplɪŋ, 'pipļɪŋ**
peopleless **'pipļɪs**
Peoria **pɪˈorɪə, -ˈɔrɪə; S -ˈorɪə**
pep **pɛp** |-ped -t |-py -ɪ |-pily -ˌɪ, -ɪlɪ
Pepin *lake, Wis co.* **'pɛpɪn;** *Franks king* **'pɛpɪn**
(*Fr* peˈpæ̃)
pepper **'pɛpɚ; ES 'pɛpə(r;** |-ed -d |-ing
'pɛpərɪŋ, 'pɛprɪŋ |-box -ˌbɑks; ES +-ˌbɒks
pepper-and-salt **'pɛpɚnˈsɔlt, 'pɛpərən-; ES**
'pɛpən-, 'pɛpərən-
peppercorn **'pɛpɚˌkɔrn; ES 'pɛpəˌkɔən**
Pepperell **'pɛpərəl, 'pɛprəl**
pepperidge **'pɛpərɪdʒ, 'pɛprɪdʒ** |-s -ɪz
peppermint **'pɛpɚˌmɪnt; ES 'pɛpə-, 'pɛpm̩ˌɪnt**
Pepperrell **'pɛpərəl, 'pɛprəl**
pepperwort **'pɛpɚˌwɝt; ES 'pɛpəˌwɜt, 'pɛpə-
ˌwɜt**
pepsin, -e **'pɛpsɪn** |-ate -ˌet |-ated -ˌetɪd
peptic **'pɛptɪk** |-al -ļ

peptone **'pɛpton**
Pepys *diarist &* *Ir family* pips; *Eng family*
'pɛpɪs |-'s -ɪz
Pequawket **pɪˈkwɔkɪt, -ˈkwɒkɪt**
Pequot **'pikwɑt, -kwɒt**
per *prep w. object* **pɚ; ES pə(r;** *without obj.*
pɝ; ES pɜ(r, pɝ
peradventure **ˌpɝədˈvɛntʃɚ; ES ˌpɜrəd-
ˈvɛntʃə(r, ˌpɝədˈvɛntʃə(r**
perambulate **pɚˈæmbjəˌlet** |-d -ɪd |-tor -ɚ;
ES -ə(r
perambulation **pɚˌæmbjəˈleʃən**
per annum **pɚˈænəm**
percale **pɚˈkel; ES pəˈkel;** (*Fr* pɛrˈkal)
per capita **pɚˈkæpɪtə; ES pəˈkæp-**
perceive **pɚˈsiv; ES pəˈsiv;** |-d -d
per cent, percent **pɚˈsɛnt; ES pə-;** |-s -s
percentage **pɚˈsɛntɪdʒ; ES pə-;** |-s -ɪz
percentile **pɚˈsɛntaɪl, -tļ, -tɪl; ES pə-**
percept **'pɝsɛpt; ES 'pɜ-, 'pɝ-**
perceptible **pɚˈsɛptəbļ; ES pə-;** |-bly -blɪ
perception **pɚˈsɛpʃən; ES pə-;** |-tive -tɪv
perceptual **pɚˈsɛptʃʊəl; ES pə-;** |-ly -ɪ
Percival, -ce-, -e **'pɝsəvļ; ES 'pɜs-, 'pɝs-**
perch **pɝtʃ; ES pɜtʃ, pɝtʃ;** |-es -ɪz |-ed -t
perchance **pɚˈtʃæns; ES pə-, E+-ˈtʃɑns,
-ˈtʃans**
Percheron **'pɝtʃərən, -ˌɑn; ES 'pɜtʃ-, 'pɝtʃ-,
-ˌɒn**
perchlorate **pɝˈkloret, -ˈklɔr-; ES pɜˈklor-,
pɝ-, E+-ˈklɔr-;** |-ric -rɪk |-rid -rɪd |-ride
-raɪd, -rɪd
percipience **pɚˈsɪpɪəns; ES pə-;** |-ent -ənt
percolate *n* **'pɝkəlɪt, -ˌlet; ES 'pɜk-, 'pɝk-**
percolate *v* **'pɝkəˌlet; ES 'pɜk-, 'pɝk-;** |-d -ɪd
|-tor -ɚ; ES -ə(r
percuss **pɚˈkʌs; ES pə-;** |-es -ɪz |-ed -t |-ion
-ˈkʌʃən
Percy **'pɝsɪ; ES 'pɜsɪ, 'pɝsɪ**
perdie **pɚˈdi; ES pəˈdi**
per diem **pɚˈdaɪəm, -ɛm; ES pə-**
Perdita **'pɝdɪtə; ES 'pɜd-, 'pɝd-**
perdition **pɚˈdɪʃən; ES pəˈdɪʃən**
perdu, -due **pɚˈdju, -ˈdɪu, -ˈdu; ES pə-**
perdurable **pɚˈdjʊrəbļ, -ˈdɪur-, -ˈdur-; ES
pə-;** |-bly -blɪ
peregrin **'pɛrəgrɪn** |-grine -grɪn, -ˌgrin
peregrinate **'pɛrəgrɪˌnet** |-nated -ˌnetɪd
peregrination **ˌpɛrəgrɪˈneʃən**

|full **fʊl** |tooth **tuθ** |further **'fɝðɚ; ES 'fɜðə** |custom **'kʌstəm** |while **hwaɪl** |how **haʊ** |toy **tɔɪ**
|using **'juzɪŋ** |fuse **fjuz, fɪuz** |dish **dɪʃ** |vision **'vɪʒən** |Eden **'idn̩** |cradle **'kredļ** |keep 'em **'kipm̩**

peremptory pə'rɛmptərɪ, -trɪ, 'pɛrəmp͵torɪ,
-͵tɔrɪ; S -͵tɔrɪ; |-rily -rəlɪ, -rɪlɪ
perennial pə'rɛnɪəl |-ly -ɪ
perfect *adj* 'pɝfɪkt; ES 'pɝf-, 'pɝf-
perfect *v* pɚ'fɛkt, *now less freq.* 'pɝfɪkt; ES
pə'fɛkt, 'pɝf-, 'pɝf-; |-ed -ɪd
perfection pɚ'fɛkʃən; ES pə'fɛkʃən
perfervid pɝ'fɝvɪd; ES pɝ'fɝvɪd, pɝ'fɝvɪd
perfidious pɚ'fɪdɪəs; ES pɚ'fɪdɪəs
perfidy 'pɝfədɪ; ES 'pɝfədɪ, 'pɝfədɪ
perforate *adj* 'pɝfərɪt, -͵ret; ES 'pɝf-, 'pɝf-
perforate *v* 'pɝfə͵ret; ES 'pɝf-, 'pɝf-; |-d -ɪd
perforation ͵pɝfə'reʃən; ES ͵pɝfə-, ͵pɝfə-
perforce pɚ'fors, -'fɔrs; ES pə'foəs, E+-'fɔəs
perform pɚ'fɔrm; ES pə'fɔəm; |-ed -d |-ance
-əns—*A dissimilated pron.* pə'fɔrm(əns) *is
sometimes heard (§121).*
perfume *n* 'pɝfjum, -fɪum, pɚ'fjum, -'fɪum;
ES 'pɝ-, 'pɝ-, pə-
perfume *v* pɚ'fjum, -'fɪum; ES pə-; |-d -d
perfumery pɚ'fjumərɪ, -mrɪ, -'fɪum-; ES pə-;
—*A dissimilated pron.* pə'fjumərɪ *is often
heard (§121).*
perfunctory pɚ'fʌŋktərɪ; ES pə-; |-rily -rəlɪ,
-rɪlɪ
perfuse pɚ'fjuz, -'fɪuz; ES pə-; |-s -ɪz |-d -d
Pergamum 'pɝgəməm; ES 'pɝg-, 'pɝg-;
|-amus -məs |-amus's -məsɪz
pergola 'pɝgələ; ES 'pɝg-, 'pɝg-
perhaps pɚ'hæps, pɚ'æps, præps; ES pə-
'hæps, pə'ræps, præps
peri 'pɪrɪ, 'pɪrɪ
pericarditis ͵perɪkɑr'daɪtɪs; ES -kɑ:-
pericardium ͵perɪ'kɑrdɪəm; ES -'kɑ:d-; |-dia
-dɪə
Pericles 'pɛrə͵kliz |-'s -ɪz |-ean ͵pɛrə'kliən
perigee 'pɛrə͵dʒi
perihelion ͵pɛrɪ'hiliən
peril 'pɛrəl |-ed -d |-ous -əs
perimeter pə'rɪmətɚ; ES -'rɪmətə(r
perimetric *geom.* ͵pɛrə'mɛtrɪk |-al -l̩ |-ally -l̩ɪ,
-ɪklɪ
perimetric *anat.* ͵pɛrə'mitrɪk |-trium -trɪəm
perineum ͵pɛrə'niəm |-nea -'niə
period 'pɪrɪəd, 'pir-, -rɪɪd
periodic ͵pɪrɪ'ɑdɪk, ͵pir-; ES+-'ɒd-; |-al -l̩
|-ally -l̩ɪ, -ɪklɪ
periodicity ͵pɪrɪə'dɪsətɪ, ͵pir-
periosteum ͵pɛrɪ'ɑstɪəm; ES+-'ɒs-; |-tea -tɪə

periostitis ͵pɛrɪɑs'taɪtɪs; ES+-ɒs-
peripatetic ͵pɛrəpə'tɛtɪk |-al -l̩ |-ally -l̩ɪ, -ɪklɪ
peripheral pə'rɪfərəl |-ly -ɪ |-ry -rɪ
periphrase 'pɛrə͵frez |-s -ɪz |-d -d
periphrasis pə'rɪfrəsɪs |-rases -rə͵siz
periphrastic ͵pɛrə'fræstɪk |-al -l̩ |-ally -l̩ɪ,
-ɪklɪ
peripteral pə'rɪptərəl |-ry -rɪ
perique pə'rik
periscope 'pɛrə͵skop
periscopic ͵pɛrə'skɑpɪk; ES+-'skɒp-; |-al -l̩
perish 'pɛrɪʃ |-es -ɪz |-ed -t
perishability ͵pɛrɪʃə'bɪlətɪ
perishable 'pɛrɪʃəbl̩ |-bly -blɪ
peristalsis ͵pɛrə'stælsɪs |-stalses -'stælsiz
peristaltic ͵pɛrə'stæltɪk |-ally -l̩ɪ, -ɪklɪ
peristyle 'pɛrə͵staɪl
peritoneum, -nae- ͵pɛrətə'niəm |-nea, -naea
-'niə |-neal, -naeal -'niəl |-neally, -naeally
-'niəlɪ
peritonitis ͵pɛrətə'naɪtɪs
periwig 'pɛrə͵wɪg |-ged -d
periwinkle 'pɛrə͵wɪŋkl̩ |-d -d
Perizzite 'pɛrə͵zaɪt
perjure 'pɝdʒɚ; ES 'pɝdʒə(r, 'pɝdʒə(r; |-d -d
|-ring -dʒərɪŋ, -dʒrɪŋ |-ry -ɪ, -dʒrɪ
perjurer 'pɝdʒərɚ; ES 'pɝdʒərə(r, 'pɝdʒərə(r
perk pɝk; ES pɝk, pɝk; |-ed -t
Perkin, p- 'pɝkɪn; ES 'pɝk-, 'pɝk-
Perkins 'pɝkɪnz; ES 'pɝk-, 'pɝk-; |-'s -ɪz
perlite 'pɝlaɪt; ES 'pɝl-, 'pɝl-
permanence 'pɝmənəns; ES 'pɝm-, 'pɝm-;
|-cy -ɪ |-nent -nənt
permanganate pɝ'mæŋgə͵net; ES pɝ-, pɝ-
permeability ͵pɝmɪə'bɪlətɪ; ES ͵pɝ-, ͵pɝ-
permeable 'pɝmɪəbl̩; ES 'pɝ-, 'pɝ-; |-bly -blɪ
permeance 'pɝmɪəns; ES 'pɝ-, 'pɝ-; |-ant
-ənt
permeate 'pɝmɪ͵et; ES 'pɝ-, 'pɝ-; |-d -ɪd
Permiak 'pɝmɪ͵æk; ES 'pɝ-, 'pɝ-; |-ian -ɪən
permissibility pɚ͵mɪsə'bɪlətɪ; ES pə-
permissible pɚ'mɪsəbl̩; ES pə-; |-bly -blɪ
permission pɚ'mɪʃən; ES pə-; |-sive -'mɪsɪv
permit *n* 'leave' 'pɝmɪt, pɚ'mɪt; ES 'pɝ-, 'pɝ-,
pə-
permit *v* pɚ'mɪt; ES pə-; |-ted -ɪd
permit *n* 'pompano' pɚ'mɪt; ES pə-
permutation ͵pɝmjə'teʃən; ES ͵pɝ-, ͵pɝ-
permute pɚ'mjut, -'mɪut; ES pə-; |-d -ɪd

Key: *See in full §§3–47.* bee bi |pity 'pɪtɪ (§6) |rate ret |yet jɛt |sang sæŋ |angry 'æŋ·grɪ
|bath bæθ; E baθ (§10) |ah ɑ |far fɑr |watch wɑtʃ, wɒtʃ (§12) |jaw dʒɔ |gorge gɔrdʒ |go go

Pernambuco ˌpɜ˞nəm'bjuko, -'bɪu-; ES ˌpɜ-,
ˌpɜ˞-

pernicious pə˞'nɪʃəs; ES pə-
pernickety pə˞'nɪkɪtɪ; ES pə-
perorate 'pɛrəˌret |-d -ɪd |-tion ˌpɛro'reʃən
peroxid pə'rɑksɪd; ES+-'rɒks-; |-ide -aɪd
perpend n 'pɜ˞pənd; ES 'pɜ-, 'pɜ˞-
perpend v pə˞'pɛnd; ES pə-; |-ed -ɪd
perpendicular ˌpɜ˞pən'dɪkjələ˞, ˌpɜ˞pm̩-; ES
ˌpɜ˞pən'dɪkjələ(r, ˌpɜ˞pm̩-, ˌpɜ˞-
perpendicularity ˌpɜ˞pənˌdɪkjə'lærətɪ, ˌpɜ˞pm̩-;
ES ˌpɜ-, ˌpɜ˞-
perpetrate 'pɜ˞pəˌtret; ES 'pɜ-, 'pɜ˞-; |-d -ɪd
perpetration ˌpɜ˞pə'treʃən; ES ˌpɜ-, ˌpɜ˞-
perpetual pə˞'pɛtʃʊəl; ES pə-; |-ly -ɪ
perpetuate pə˞'pɛtʃʊˌet; ES pə-; |-d -ɪd
perpetuation pə˞ˌpɛtʃʊ'eʃən; ES pə-
perpetuity ˌpɜ˞pə'tjuətɪ, -'tɪu-, -'tu-; ES ˌpɜ-,
ˌpɜ˞-
perplex pə˞'plɛks; ES pə-; |-es -ɪz |-ed -t
|-edly -ɪdlɪ |-ity -ətɪ
perquisite 'pɜ˞kwəzɪt; ES 'pɜ-, 'pɜ˞-
Perrault pɛ'ro
Perry, p- 'pɛrɪ
persalt 'pɜ˞ˌsɔlt; ES 'pɜ-, 'pɜ˞-
Perse, p- pɜ˞s; ES pɜs, pɜ˞s; |-s -ɪz
per se 'pɜ˞'si; ES 'pɜ-, 'pɜ˞-
persecute 'pɜ˞sɪˌkjut, -ˌkɪut; ES 'pɜ-, 'pɜ˞-;
|-d -ɪd
persecution ˌpɜ˞sɪ'kjuʃən, -'kɪu-; ES ˌpɜ-, ˌpɜ˞-
Perseid 'pɜ˞sɪɪd; ES 'pɜ-, 'pɜ˞-
Persephone pə˞'sɛfənɪ; ES pə-
Persepolis pə˞'sɛpəlɪs; ES pə-; |-'s -ɪz
Perseus 'pɜ˞sjus, 'pɜ˞sɪəs; ES 'pɜs-, 'pɜ˞s-;
|-seus' -sjus, -ɪəs
perseverance ˌpɜ˞sə'vɪrəns; ES ˌpɜ-, ˌpɜ˞-
persevere ˌpɜ˞sə'vɪr; ES ˌpɜsə'vɪə(r, ˌpɜ˞sə-
'vɪə(r; |-d -d
Pershing 'pɜ˞ʃɪŋ; ES 'pɜ-, 'pɜ˞-
Persia 'pɜ˞ʒə, 'pɜ˞ʃə; ES 'pɜ-, 'pɜ˞-; |-n -n
persiflage 'pɜ˞sɪˌflɑʒ; ES 'pɜ-, 'pɜ˞-; (Fr
pɛrsi'flɑ:ʒ)
persimmon pə˞'sɪmən; ES pə-
persist pə˞'zɪst, -'sɪst; ES pə-; |-ed -ɪd
persistence pə˞'zɪstəns, -'sɪst-; ES pə-; |-nt
-nt
persnickety pə˞'snɪkɪtɪ; ES pə-
person, P- 'pɜ˞sn̩; ES 'pɜ-, 'pɜ˞-
persona pə˞'sonə; ES pə-; |-nae -ni

personable 'pɜ˞snəb!, 'pɜ˞snə-; ES 'pɜ-, 'pɜ˞-;
|-bly -blɪ
personage 'pɜ˞sn̩ɪdʒ, 'pɜ˞snɪdʒ; ES 'pɜ-, 'pɜ˞-;
|-s -ɪz
persona grata pə˞'sonə'gretə, -'grɑtə; ES pə-
personal 'pɜ˞sn̩!, 'pɜ˞snəl; ES 'pɜ-, 'pɜ˞-; |-ly -ɪ
personality ˌpɜ˞sn̩'ælətɪ; ES ˌpɜ-, ˌpɜ˞-
personalty 'pɜ˞sn̩!tɪ; ES 'pɜ-, 'pɜ˞-
persona non grata pə˞'sonəˌnan'gretə, -'grɑtə;
ES pə-, -ˌnɒn-
personate 'pɜ˞sn̩ˌet; ES 'pɜ-, 'pɜ˞-; |-d -ɪd
personation ˌpɜ˞sn̩'eʃən; ES ˌpɜ-, ˌpɜ˞-
personification pə˞ˌsanəfə'keʃən; ES pə-
ˌsɑnə-, -ˌsɒnə-
personify pə˞'sanəˌfaɪ; ES pə'sɑn-, -'sɒn-;
|-fied -ˌfaɪd
personnel ˌpɜ˞sn̩'ɛl; ES ˌpɜ-, ˌpɜ˞-
perspective pə˞'spɛktɪv; ES pə-; |-d -d
perspicacious ˌpɜ˞spɪ'keʃəs; ES ˌpɜ-, ˌpɜ˞-;
|-cacity -'kæsətɪ
perspicuity ˌpɜ˞spɪ'kjuətɪ, -'kɪu-; ES ˌpɜ-,
ˌpɜ˞-
perspicuous pə˞'spɪkjʊəs; ES pə-
perspiration ˌpɜ˞spə'reʃən; ES ˌpɜ-, ˌpɜ˞-
perspiratory pə˞'spaɪrəˌtorɪ, -ˌtɔrɪ; ES pə-
'spaɪrəˌtorɪ, E+-ˌtɔrɪ
perspire pə˞'spaɪr; ES pə'spaɪə(r; |-d -d
persuadable pə˞'swedəb!; ES pə-; |-bly -blɪ
persuade pə˞'swed; ES pə-; |-d -ɪd
persuasible pə˞'swesəb!; ES pə-; |-bly -blɪ
persuasion pə˞'sweʒən; ES pə-; |-sive -sɪv
pert pɜ˞t; ES pɜt, pɜ˞t
pertain pə˞'ten; ES pə-; |-ed -d
Perth pɜ˞θ; ES pɜθ, pɜ˞θ; |-shire -ʃɪr, -ʃə˞; ES
-ʃɪə(r, -ʃə˞(r
Perth Amboy 'pɜ˞θ'æmbɔɪ; ES 'pɜθ-, 'pɜ˞θ-
pertinacious ˌpɜ˞tn̩'eʃəs; ES ˌpɜt-, ˌpɜ˞t-;
|-acity -'æsətɪ
pertinence 'pɜ˞tn̩əns; ES 'pɜt-, 'pɜ˞t-; |-cy -ɪ
|-ent -ənt
perturb pə˞'tɜ˞b; ES pə'tɜb, pə'tɜ˞b; |-ed -d
|-edly -ɪdlɪ
perturbation ˌpɜ˞tə˞'beʃən; ES ˌpɜtə-, ˌpɜ˞tə-
Peru pə'ru, pə'rɪu
Perugino ˌpɛru'dʒino, ˌpɛrju- (It ˌperu'dʒi:no)
peruke pə'ruk, pə'rɪuk
peruse pə'ruz, -'rɪuz; |-s -ɪz |-d -d |-sal -!
Peruvian pə'ruvɪən, -'rɪu-
pervade pə˞'ved; ES pə'ved; |-d -ɪd

|full fʊl |tooth tuθ |further 'fɜ˞ðə˞; ES 'fɜðə |custom 'kʌstəm |while hwaɪl |how haʊ |toy tɔɪ
|using 'juzɪŋ |fuse fjuz, fɪuz |dish dɪʃ |vision 'vɪʒən |Eden 'idn̩ |cradle 'kred! |keep 'em 'kipm̩

pervasion pə'veʒən; ES pə-; |-sive -sɪv
perverse pə'vɝs; ES pə'vɜs, pə'vɝs; |-sion
    -ʒən, -ʃən
perversity pə'vɝsətɪ; ES pə'vɜs-, pə'vɝs-;
    |-ive -ɪv
pervert n 'pɝvɝt; ES 'pɝvɜt, 'pɝvɝt
pervert v pə'vɝt; ES pə'vɜt, pə'vɝt; |-ed -ɪd
pervious 'pɝvɪəs; ES 'pɝ-, 'pɝ-
peseta pə'setə, -'setə (Sp pe'seta)
pesky 'peskɪ
peso 'peso
pessimism 'pesə͵mɪzəm |-mist -mɪst
pessimistic ͵pesə'mɪstɪk |-al -| |-ally -ļɪ, -ɪklɪ
pest pest
Pestalozzi ͵pestə'latsɪ; ES+-'lɒtsɪ
pester 'pestə; ES 'pestə(r; |-ed -d |-ing
    'pestrɪŋ, 'pestərɪŋ
pesthole 'pest͵hol
pesthouse 'pest͵haus |-ses -zɪz
pestiferous pes'tɪfərəs, -frəs
pestilence 'pest|əns |-s -ɪz |-ent -ənt
pestilential ͵pest|'enʃəl |-ly -ɪ
pestle 'pes|, 'pest| |-d -d |-ling -ɪŋ, -slɪŋ,
    -stlɪŋ
pet pet |petted 'petɪd
Pétain Fr pe'tæ̃
petal 'pet| |-ed -d |-less 'pet|ɪs
Petaluma ͵pet|'umə
petard pɪ'tard; ES -'tɑːd, E+-'taːd
petcock 'pet͵kak; ES+-͵kɒk
peter, P- 'pitə; ES 'pitə(r; |-ed -d
Peterboro, -borough 'pitə͵bɝo, -ə; ES 'pitə-
    ͵bɜr-, -͵bʌr-, -͵bɝ-
Petersburg 'pitəz͵bɝg; ES 'pitəz͵bɜg, -təz-
    ͵bɝg
Petersen, -son 'pitəsn̩; ES 'pitəsn̩
Petersham Mass 'pitəz͵hæm, Engd, Austral
    'pitəʃəm; ES 'pitə-; Both 'pitəz͵hæm and
    'pitəʃəm are spelling pronunciations. The
    traditional pron. is 'pitəzəm.
petiolate 'petɪə͵let |-lated -͵letɪd
petiole 'petɪ͵ol |-d -d
petit 'petɪ |petite pə'tit
petition pə'tɪʃən |-ed -d |-ing -'tɪʃənɪŋ, -ʃnɪŋ
    |-ary -ʃə͵nerɪ
Peto 'pito
Petoskey pə'taskɪ, -'tɒs-
Petrarch 'pitrark; ES -trɑːk, E+-traːk; |-ism
    -͵ɪzəm |-ist -ɪst

Petrarchal pɪ'trark|; ES -'trɑːk|, E+-'traːk|;
    |-chan -kən |-chian -kɪən |-chianism -kɪən-
    ͵ɪzəm
petrel 'petrəl
petrifaction ͵petrə'fækʃən
petrification ͵petrəfə'keʃən
petrify 'petrə͵faɪ |-fied -͵faɪd
Petrograd 'petrə͵græd
petrography pi'tragrəfɪ, -'trɒg-
petrol 'petrəl |-ed -d
petrolatum ͵petrə'letəm
petroleum, P- pə'trolɪəm
petrologic ͵petrə'ladʒɪk; ES+-'lɒdʒ-; |-al -|
    |-ally -ļɪ, -ɪklɪ
petrology pi'tralədʒɪ; ES+-'trɒl-; |-gist
    -dʒɪst
petronel 'petrənəl
Petronius pɪ'tronɪəs |-'s -ɪz
Petroskey pɪ'traskɪ, -'trɒs-
petrous 'petrəs, 'pitrəs
Petruchio pə'trukɪ͵o, -'trɪuk-, -kjo
petticoat 'petɪ͵kot |-ed -ɪd |-ism -kot͵ɪzəm
pettifog 'petɪ͵fag, -͵fɒg, -͵fɔg |-ged -d |-gery
    -ərɪ, -rɪ
pettish 'petɪʃ
pettitoes 'petɪ͵toz
petty 'petɪ |-ily -ļɪ, -ɪlɪ
petulance 'petʃələns |-cy -ɪ |-lant -lənt
petunia pə'tjunjə, -'trun-, -'tun-, -nɪə
Petworth 'petwəθ, 'petəθ; ES -wəθ, 'petəθ
pew pju, pɪu |-ed -d
pewee 'piwi
pewit 'piwɪt, 'pjuɪt, 'pruɪt
pewter 'pjutə, 'pru-; ES -tə(r
pewterer 'pjutərə, 'pru-; ES -tərə(r
pfennig 'pfenɪg, 'fenɪg |-s -z (Ger 'pfenɪx
    |-e -nɪgə, -nɪjə)
Phaedo 'fido
Phaedra 'fidrə |Phaedrus 'fidrəs |-s's -drəsɪz
Phaëthon 'feəθən, 'feətn̩
phaeton, P- 'feətn̩
phagocyte 'fægə͵saɪt
phalange 'fæləndʒ, fə'lændʒ |-s -ɪz
phalanx, P- 'felæŋks |-es -ɪz |-nges fə'lændʒiz
phallic 'fælɪk |-al -| |-ism 'fælə͵sɪzəm
phanerogam 'fænərə͵gæm |-ic ͵fænərə'gæmɪk
phantasm 'fæntæzəm
phantasma fæn'tæzmə |-s -z |-mata -mətə

phantasmagoria ˌfæntæzmə'gorɪə, -'gɔr-; S -'gor-; |-l -l |-lly -lɪ

phantasmic fæn'tæzmɪk |-al -] |-ally -]ɪ, -ɪklɪ

phantasy 'fæntəsɪ, -zɪ |-ied -d

phantom 'fæntəm

Pharaoh 'fɛro, 'fe-, -rɪˌo

Pharisaic, p- ˌfærə'se·ɪk |-al -] |-ally -]ɪ, -ɪklɪ

Pharisaism 'færəseˌɪzəm |-ist -ˌse·ɪst

Pharisee 'færəˌsi |-ism -siˌɪzəm

pharmaceutic ˌfarmə'sjutɪk, -'sɪu-, -'su-; ES ˌfa:mə-, E+ˌfa:mə-; |-al -] |-ally -]ɪ, -ɪklɪ

pharmacist 'farməsɪst; ES 'fa:mə-, E+ 'fa:mə-

pharmacology ˌfarmə'kalədʒɪ; ES ˌfa:mə-'kal-, -'kɒl-, E+ˌfa:mə-

pharmacopoea ˌfarməkə'piə; ES ˌfa:m-, E+ˌfa:m-

pharmacy 'farməsɪ; ES 'fa:m-, E+'fa:m-

Pharpar, -phar 'farpar, -far; ES 'fa:pa:(r, -fa:(r, E+-a:-

Pharsala 'farsələ; ES 'fa:sə-, E+'fa:sə-

Pharsalia far'selɪə; ES fa-, E+fa-; |-n -n

pharyngal fə'rɪŋg]

pharyngeal fə'rɪndʒɪəl, ˌfærɪn'dʒiəl

pharynges fə'rɪndʒiz

pharyngitis ˌfærɪn'dʒaɪtɪs

pharyngoscope fə'rɪŋgəˌskop

pharynx 'færɪŋks |-es -ɪz |-rynges fə'rɪndʒiz

phase fez |phases 'fezɪz |phased fezd

phasis 'fesɪs |phases 'fesiz

pheasant 'fɛzn̩t

Phebe, p- 'fibɪ

Phelps fɛlps |-'s -ɪz

phenacetin, -e fə'næsətɪn

phenazin 'fɛnəzɪn |-zine -ˌzin, -zɪn

Phenicia fə'nɪʃɪə, -ʃə

Phenician fə'nɪʃən, fə'niʃən |-s -z

phenix, 'finɪks |-es -ɪz

phenol 'finɔl, -nɒl, -nal, -nol |-phthælein -'θælin

phenomenal fə'namən]; ES+-'nɒm-; |-ly -ɪ

phenomenon fə'naməˌnan; ES+-'nɒməˌnɒn; |-mena -mənə

phew fju, fɪu, pfju & various other puffs

phi Gk letter faɪ

phial faɪl, 'faɪəl |-ed -d

Phi Beta Kappa 'faɪˌbetə'kæpə, -ˌbitə-

Phidias 'fɪdɪəs |-'s -ɪz |-an -ən

Philadelphia ˌfɪlə'dɛlfjə, -fɪə |-n -n

philander, P- fə'lændɚ; ES -'lændə(r; |-ed -d |-ing -'lændrɪŋ, -'lændərɪŋ

philanthropic ˌfɪlən'θrapɪk; ES+-'θrɒp-; |-al -] |-ally -]ɪ, -ɪklɪ

philanthropist fə'lænθrəpɪst |-py -pɪ

Philario fɪ'larɪˌo, -rjo

philatelist fə'læt]ɪst |-ly -t]ɪ

Philemon fə'limən, faɪ-

philharmonic, P- ˌfɪlə'manɪk, ˌfɪlhar-; ES ˌfɪlə-, ˌfɪlha:-, -'mɒn-, E+-ha:-

Philip 'fɪləp |Philippa fə'lɪpə |-pan fə'lɪpən

Philippi fə'lɪpaɪ, 'fɪləˌpaɪ; WVa -'lɪpɪ, 'fɪləpɪ

Philippians fə'lɪpɪənz |-pic fə'lɪpɪk

Philippine 'fɪləˌpin

Philippsburg 'fɪləpsˌbɝg; ES -ˌbɜg, -ˌbɝg; (Ger 'fi:lɪpsˌburk)

Philips, -pps 'fɪləps |-'s -ɪz

Philipsburg 'fɪləpsˌbɝg; ES -ˌbɜg, -ˌbɝg

Philistia fə'lɪstɪə

Philistine, p- fə'lɪstɪn, 'fɪləsˌtin, 'fɪləsˌtaɪn

philistinism, P- fə'lɪstɪnˌɪzəm, 'fɪləstɪnˌɪzəm

Phillips, -pps 'fɪləps |-'s -ɪz

Phillipsburg 'fɪləpsˌbɝg; ES -ˌbɜg, -ˌbɝg

Phillis 'fɪlɪs |-'s -ɪz

Phillpot 'fɪlpət

Philo 'faɪlo

philogynist fɪ'ladʒənɪst; ES+-'lɒdʒ-; |-ny -nɪ

philologer fɪ'laladʒɚ; ES -'laladʒə(r, -'lɒl-; |-gist -dʒɪst |-gy -dʒɪ

philologic ˌfɪlə'ladʒɪk; ES+-'lɒdʒ-; |-al -] |-ally -]ɪ, -ɪklɪ

philomel, P- 'fɪləˌmɛl |Philomela ˌfɪlə'milə

philopena ˌfɪlə'pinə

philosopher fə'lasəfɚ; ES -'lasəfə(r, -'lɒs-; |-phy -fɪ

philosophical ˌfɪlə'safɪk]; ES+-'sɒf-; |-ly -ɪ, -ɪklɪ

philosophize fə'lasəˌfaɪz; ES+-'lɒs-; |-s -ɪz |-d -d

Philostrate 'fɪləˌstret

Philostratus fɪ'lastrətəs; ES+-'lɒs-; |-'s -ɪz

Philotus fɪ'lotəs |-'s -ɪz

Philpot, -pott, -putt 'fɪlpət

philter, -tre 'fɪltɚ; ES 'fɪltə(r; |-(e)d -d |-(r)ing -tərɪŋ, -trɪŋ

Phineas 'fɪnɪəs |-'s -ɪz

phlebitis flɪ'baɪtɪs, flɛ-

phlebotomy flɪ'batəmɪ, flɛ-; ES+-'bɒt-

Phlegethon 'flɛgəˌθan, -ˌθɒn

Those words below in which the ɑ sound is spelt o are often pronounced with ɒ in E and S

phlegm flɛm

phlegmatic flɛgˈmætɪk |-al -l̩ |-ally -lɪ |-icly -ɪklɪ

phloem ˈfloɛm

phlogistic floˈdʒɪstɪk |-al -l̩ |-ton -tən

phlox flɑks |-es -ɪz

phobia ˈfobɪə |-ic -ɪk |-ism -ɪzəm |-ist -ɪst

Phocian ˈfoʃən |Phocis ˈfosɪs |Phocis' -sɪs

Phoebe, p- ˈfibɪ |Phoebus ˈfibəs |-bus's -bəsɪz

Phoenicia fəˈnɪʃɪə, -ʃə

Phoenician fəˈnɪʃən, fəˈniʃən |-s -z

phoenix, P- ˈfinɪks |-es -ɪz

phonation foˈneʃən

phone fon |phoned fond

phoneme ˈfonim

phonemic foˈnimɪk |-ly -lɪ

phonetic foˈnɛtɪk, fə- |-al -l̩ |-ally -lɪ, -ɪklɪ

phonetician ˌfonəˈtɪʃən

phoneticist foˈnɛtəsɪst, fə-

phonetism ˈfonəˌtɪzəm |-tist -tɪst

phonic ˈfɑnɪk, ˈfon-

phonodeik ˈfonəˌdaɪk

phonogram ˈfonəˌgræm

phonograph ˈfonəˌgræf; E+-ˌgraf, -ˌgrɑf

phonographic ˌfonəˈgræfɪk |-ally -lɪ, -ɪklɪ

phonography foˈnɑgrəfɪ, -ˈnɒg-

phonological ˌfonəˈlɑdʒɪkl̩ |-ly -ɪ, -ɪklɪ

phonologist foˈnɑlədʒɪst |-gy -dʒɪ

phosgene ˈfɑsdʒin

phosphate ˈfɑsfet |-d -ɪd |-tic fɑsˈfætɪk

phosphid ˈfɑsfɪd |-fide -faɪd, -fɪd

phosphin ˈfɑsfɪn |-fine -fin, -fɪn

phosphite ˈfɑsfaɪt

phosphor ˈfɑsfɚ; ES ˈfɑsfə(r

phosphore ˈfɑsfor, -fɔr; ES -foə(r, E+-fɔə(r

phosphoresce ˌfɑsfəˈrɛs |-s -ɪz |-d -d

phosphorescence ˌfɑsfəˈrɛsn̩s |-scent -sn̩t

phosphoric fɑsˈfɔrɪk, -ˈfɑr-, -ˈfɒr-, -ˈfor-

phosphorous ˈfɑsfərəs, fɑsˈforəs, EN+-ˈfɔr-

phosphorus, P- ˈfɑsfərəs |Phosphori ˈfɑsfəˌraɪ

phot fɑt, fot

photic ˈfotɪk |-tism -tɪzəm

photo ˈfoto |-ed -d |-ing ˈfotəwɪŋ

photochemist ˌfotəˈkɛmɪst |-ry -rɪ

photodrama ˌfotəˈdrɑmə, -ˈdræmə

photodynamics ˌfotədaɪˈnæmɪks

photoelectric ˌfoto·ɪˈlɛktrɪk |-al -l̩ |-ally -lɪ, -ɪklɪ

photoengrave ˌfoto·ɪnˈgrev |-d -d

photogenic ˌfotoˈdʒɛnɪk |-ally -lɪ, -ɪklɪ

photograph ˈfotəˌgræf; E+-ˌgraf, -ˌgrɑf; |-ed -t

photographer fəˈtɑgrəfɚ, fo-, -ˈtɒg-; ES -fə(r; |-phy -fɪ

photographic ˌfotəˈgræfɪk |-al -l̩ |-ally -lɪ, -ɪklɪ

photogravure ˌfotəgrəˈvjʊr, -ˈgrevjɚ; ES -ˈvjʊə(r, -ˈgrevjə(r

photolithograph ˌfotəˈlɪθəˌgræf; E+-ˌgraf, -ˌgrɑf; |-ed -t

photolithographer ˌfotəlɪˈθɑgrəfɚ, -ˈθɒg-; ES -fə(r

photometer foˈtɑmətɚ; ES -ˈtɑmətə(r; |-try -trɪ

photometric ˌfotəˈmɛtrɪk |-al -l̩ |-ally -lɪ, -ɪklɪ

photon ˈfotɑn

photoplay ˈfotəˌple

photosensitive ˌfotəˈsɛnsətɪv

photospectroscope ˌfotəˈspɛktrəˌskop

photosphere ˈfotəˌsfɪr; ES -ˌsfɪə(r, S+-ˌsfɛə(r

photostat, P- ˈfotəˌstæt |-ed -ɪd

photostatic ˌfotəˈstætɪk |-ally -lɪ, -ɪklɪ

photosynthesis ˌfotəˈsɪnθəsɪs

phototropism foˈtɑtrəˌpɪzəm

phototype ˈfotəˌtaɪp

phrasal ˈfrezl̩ |-ly -ɪ

phrase frez |phrases ˈfrezɪz |phrased frezd

phraseological ˌfrezɪəˈlɑdʒɪkl̩ |-ly -ɪ, -ɪklɪ

phraseologist ˌfrezɪˈɑlədʒɪst |-gy -dʒɪ

phrenetic frɪˈnɛtɪk |-al -l̩ |-ally -lɪ, -ɪklɪ

phrenologist frɛˈnɑlədʒɪst, frɪ- |-gy -dʒɪ

phrensy ˈfrɛnzɪ |-ied -d

Phrygia ˈfrɪdʒɪə |-n -n

Phrynia ˈfrɪnɪə

phthisic ˈtɪzɪk |-al -l̩|—Phthisic *is a 16c pedantic spelling of ME tisik that little affected the pronunciation.* Phthisis *is learned Latin.*

phthisis ˈθaɪsɪs

phut *intj* ft, fʌt, fət, *etc.*

Phut fʌt

Phyfe faɪf

phylactery fəˈlæktərɪ, -trɪ

Phyle ˈfaɪli

Phyllis ˈfɪlɪs |-'s -ɪz

phylloxera fɪˈlɑksərə, ˌfɪləkˈsɪrə

Those words below in which the ɑ sound is spelt o are often pronounced with ɒ in E and S

phylon 'faɪlɑn |phylum 'faɪləm |phyla 'faɪlə
physic 'fɪzɪk |-icked -t |-al -| |-ally -|ɪ, -ɪklɪ
 |-s -s
physician fə'zɪʃən |-ed -d
physicist 'fɪzəsɪst
physiocrat 'fɪzɪə,kræt |-ic ,fɪzɪə'krætɪk
physiogenesis ,fɪzɪo'dʒɛnəsɪs
physiogenetic ,fɪzɪ,odʒə'nɛtɪk
physiogeny ,fɪzɪ'adʒənɪ |-genic -o'dʒɛnɪk
physiognomy ,fɪzɪ'agnəmɪ, -'anəmɪ
physiographer ,fɪzɪ'agrəfɚ, -'ɒg-; ES -fə(r;
 |-phy -fɪ
physiographic ,fɪzɪə'græfɪk |-al -| |-ally -|ɪ,
 -ɪklɪ
physiologic ,fɪzɪə'ladʒɪk |-al -| |-ally -|ɪ, -ɪklɪ
physiologist ,fɪzɪ'alədʒɪst |-gy -dʒɪ
physiotherapist ,fɪzɪo'θɛrəpɪst |-py -pɪ
physique fɪ'zik |-d -t
phytogenesis ,faɪto'dʒɛnəsɪs
phytogenetic ,faɪtodʒə'nɛtɪk |-al -| |-ally -|ɪ,
 -ɪklɪ
phytogenic ,faɪto'dʒɛnɪk
phytology faɪ'talədʒɪ |-gist -dʒɪst
pi paɪ
pia mater 'paɪə'metɚ; ES -'metə(r
pianissimo ,pɪə'nɪsə,mo (It pja'nissi,mo)
pianist pɪ'ænɪst, 'pɪənɪst
piano n pɪ'æno, -ə, less freq. pɪ'ano
piano 'soft,' 'softly' pɪ'ano (It 'pja:no)
pianoforte pɪ'ænə,fort, -,fortɪ, -,fɔr-; ES
 -,foə-, E+-,fɔə-
pianola ,pɪə'nolə
piaster, -tre pɪ'æstɚ; ES -'æstə(r
Piatt 'paɪət
piazza pɪ'æzə (It 'pjattsa)
pibroch 'pibrɑk (Sc -brɒx)
pica, P- 'paɪkə
picador 'pɪkə,dɔr; ES -,dɔə(r
Picardy 'pɪkɚdɪ; ES 'pɪkədɪ
picaresque ,pɪkə'rɛsk
picaroon ,pɪkə'run
picayune ,pɪkɪ'jun, ,pɪkɪ'un, ,pɪkə'jun
Piccadilly ,pɪkə'dɪlɪ ('Picca,dilly 'Circus)
piccalilli ,pɪkə'lɪlɪ
piccaninny 'pɪkə,nɪnɪ
piccolo 'pɪkə,lo
Piccolomini ,pɪkə'lomənɪ (It ,pikko'lɔ:mini)
pice paɪs

Pichon pɪ'ʃɑn, -'ʃɒn
pick pɪk |picked pɪkt |-edly -ɪdlɪ
pickaback 'pɪkə,bæk
pickaninny 'pɪkə,nɪnɪ
Pickaway 'pɪkə,we
pickax, -e 'pɪk,æks |-(e)s -ɪz |-(e)d -t
picked adj 'pointed' 'pɪkɪd, pɪkt
Pickens 'pɪkɪnz |-'s -ɪz
pickerel 'pɪkərəl, 'pɪkrəl
Pickering 'pɪkərɪŋ, 'pɪkrɪŋ
picket 'pɪkɪt |-ed -ɪd |Pickett 'pɪkɪt
pickle, P- 'pɪk| |-d -d |-ling 'pɪklɪŋ, -k|ɪŋ
picklock 'pɪk,lak
pickpocket 'pɪk,pakɪt |-ed -ɪd
pickthank 'pɪk,θæŋk
pickup 'pɪk,ʌp
Pickwick 'pɪkwɪk |-ian pɪk'wɪkɪən
picnic, P- 'pɪknɪk |-icked -t
Pico isl., volc., It count 'piko; Vt mt. 'paɪko
picot 'piko
picric 'pɪkrɪk
picrite 'pɪkraɪt
Pict pɪkt
pictograph 'pɪktə,græf; E+-,graf, -,grɑf
pictorial pɪk'torɪəl, -'tɔr-; S -'tor-; |-ly -ɪ
picture 'pɪktʃɚ; ES -tʃə(r; |-d -d |-ring 'pɪk-
 tʃərɪŋ, 'pɪktʃrɪŋ
picturesque ,pɪktʃə'rɛsk
picul 'pɪkʌl
piddle 'pɪd| |-d -d |-ling 'pɪdlɪŋ, 'pɪd|ɪŋ
piddling adj 'pɪdlɪŋ
pidgin English, pigeon 'pɪdʒɪn'ɪŋglɪʃ
pie paɪ |pied paɪd; Sp meas. pje, Sp pl pjes
piè It meas. pjɛ, It pl 'pjɛ:·i
piebald 'paɪ,bɔld
piece pis |pieces 'pisɪz |-d -t |-meal -,mil
pièce de résistance Fr pjɛsdərezis'tã:s
piecework 'pis,wɝk; ES -,wɜk, -,wɝk
pied paɪd
piedmont, P- 'pidmant
piedmontese, P- ,pidman'tiz
pieplant 'paɪ,plænt
pier pɪr; ES pɪə(r, S+pɛə(r; |-ed -d
pierce, P- pɪrs; ES pɪəs, S+pɛəs; |-s -ɪz |-d -t
Pierian paɪ'ɪrɪən
Pierpont 'pɪrpant; ES 'pɪəpant
Pierre SD pɪr; ES pɪə(r, S+pɛə(r; 'Peter'
 pɪ'ɛr, pjɛr; ES -ɛə(r

|full fʊl |tooth tuθ |further 'fɝðɚ; ES 'fɜðə |custom 'kʌstəm |while hwaɪl |how haʊ |toy tɔɪ
|using 'juzɪŋ |fuse fjuz, frʊz |dish dɪʃ |vision 'vɪʒən |Eden 'idn̩ |cradle 'kredl̩ |keep 'em 'kipm̩

Pierrot ˌpiə¹ro (*Fr* pjɛ¹ro)

Piers Plowman ¹pırz¹plaumən; ES ¹pıəz-, S+¹peəz-

Pierson ¹pırsn̩; ES ¹pıəsn̩, S+¹peəsn̩

pietism, P- ¹paıəˌtızəm |-tist -tıst |-ty -tı

pietistic ˌpaıə¹tıstık |-al -| |-ally -ı, -ıklı

piezoelectricity paıˌizo·ıˌlek¹trısətı

piffle ¹pıf| |-d -d |-ling ¹pıflıŋ, ¹pıf|ıŋ

piffling *adj* ¹pıflıŋ

pig pıg |pigged pıgd |-pen -ˌpɛn |-skin -ˌskın |-sty -ˌstaı |-tail -ˌtel

pigeon ¹pıdʒən, ¹pıdʒın—*cf* pidgin

pigeonhearted ¹pıdʒən¹hartıd, -dʒın-; ES -¹haːt-, E+-¹haːt-

pigeonhole ¹pıdʒənˌhol, ¹pıdʒın- |-holed -ˌhold

pigeon-livered ¹pıdʒən¹lıvəd, -dʒın-; ES -¹lıvəd

pigeon-toed ¹pıdʒənˌtod, ¹pıdʒın-

piggery ¹pıgərı

piggin ¹pıgın, -ən

piggy ¹pıgı |-back -ˌbæk

pigheaded ¹pıg¹hɛdıd (¹pıgˌheaded ¹lout)

pigment ¹pıgmənt |-ed -ıd |-ary ¹pıgmənˌtɛrı

pigmentation ˌpıgmən¹teʃən

Pigmy, p- ¹pıgmı |-ied -d

pignut ¹pıgˌnʌt, ¹pıgnət

pike, P- paık |piked paıkt

piked *adj* ¹paıkıd, paıkt

Pikes Peak ¹paıks¹pik

pikestaff ¹paıkˌstæf; ES+-ˌstaf, -ˌstaf

pilaster pə¹læstə; ES -¹læstə(r; |-ed -d |-ing -tərıŋ, -trıŋ

Pilate ¹paılət

pilchard ¹pıltʃəd; ES ¹pıltʃəd

pile paıl |piled paıld

pilfer ¹pılfə; ES -fə(r; |-ed -d |-ing -fərıŋ, -frıŋ

pilgrim ¹pılgrım, -əm |-ed -d

pilgrimage ¹pılgrəmıdʒ |-s -ız

pill pıl |pilled pıld

pillage ¹pılıdʒ |-s -ız |-d -d

pillar ¹pılə; ES ¹pılə(r; |-ed -d

pillbox ¹pılˌbaks; ES+-ˌbɒks; |-es -ız

pilledness ¹pılıdnıs, ¹pıldnıs

pillion ¹pıljən |-ed -d

pillory ¹pılərı |-ied -d

pillow ¹pılo, -ə |-ed -d |-ing ¹pıləwıŋ

pillowcase ¹pıloˌkes, ¹pılə- |-s -ız

pillowy ¹pıləwı

Pillsbury ¹pılzˌbɛrı, -bərı

pilose ¹paılos

pilot ¹paılət |-ed -ıd

pilothouse ¹paılətˌhaus |-houses -ˌhauzız

Pilsen ¹pılzn̩ |-er -znə, -snə, -ŋə; ES -ə(r

Pilsudski pıl¹sutskı, -¹sʌdskı

Piltdown ¹pıltˌdaun

pimento pı¹mɛnto |pimiento pım¹jɛnto

pimola pı¹molə

pimp pımp |pimped pımpt |-ery -ərı, -rı

pimple ¹pımp| |-d -d |-ply -plı, -p|ı

pin pın |pinned pınd

pinafore, P- ¹pınəˌfor, -ˌfɔr; ES -ˌfoə(r, E+-ˌfɔə(r

pince-nez ¹pænsˌne, ¹pıns- |*pl* -nez -ˌnez (*Fr* pæs¹ne)

pincers ¹pınsəz; ES ¹pınsəz; *cf* pinchers. ¹pınsəz *is from ME* pynsours *and is rare in Am use. The usual word* ¹pıntʃəz *is from* pinch, *and is not a mistake for* pincers.

pinch pıntʃ |pinches ¹pıntʃız |pinched pıntʃt

pinchbeck ¹pıntʃbɛk

pinchers ¹pıntʃəz; ES ¹pıntʃəz; *see* pincers

pinch-hit *n* ¹pıntʃˌhıt

pinch-hit *v* ¹pıntʃ¹hıt, -ˌhıt

Pinchot ¹pınʃo, ¹pıntʃo

Pinckney ¹pıŋknı |-ville -ˌvıl; S+-v|

pincushion ¹pınˌkuʃən, -ın

Pindar ¹pındə; ES ¹pındə(r

pindaric, P- pın¹dærık |-al -| |-ally -ı, -ıklı

Pindarus ¹pındərəs |-'s -ız

pindling ¹pındlıŋ

Pindus ¹pındəs |-'s -ız

pine, P- paın |pined paınd |-ny -ı |-ville -vıl; S+-v|

pineal ¹pınıəl |-ism -ˌızəm

pineapple ¹paınˌæp|

Pinero pə¹nıro, -¹niro, -¹nɛro

pinetum paı¹nitəm |-s -z |-ta -tə

pinfeather ¹pınˌfɛðə; ES -ˌfɛðə(r; |-ed -d

pinfold ¹pınˌfold |-folded -ˌfoldıd

ping pıŋ |pinged pıŋd

pinge pındʒ |pinges ¹pındʒız |pinged pındʒd

ping-pong, P- ¹pıŋˌpaŋ, -ˌpɒŋ, -ˌpɔŋ |-ed -d

pinhead ¹pınˌhɛd |-ed -ıd

pinhole ¹pınˌhol |-holed -ˌhold

pinion ¹pınjən |-ed -d

pink pıŋk |pinked pıŋkt

Pinkerton ¹pıŋkətn̩; ES ¹pıŋkətn̩

Pinkney 'pɪŋknɪ
pinnace 'pɪnɪs, -əs |-s -ɪz
pinnacle 'pɪnək|, -ɪk| |-d -d |-ling -k|ɪŋ, -klɪŋ
pinnate 'pɪnet, 'pɪnɪt
pinochle, -cle 'pi,nʌk|
piñon 'pɪnjən, 'pinjon (Am Sp pi'non)
pint paɪnt
pintail 'pɪn,tel |-tailed -,teld
pintle 'pɪnt|
pinto, P- 'pɪnto
pioneer ,paɪə'nɪr; ES ,paɪə'nɪə(r, S+-'nɛə(r; |-ed -d
pious 'paɪəs
pip pɪp |pipped pɪpt
pipage 'paɪpɪdʒ
pipe paɪp |piped paɪpt |-ful -,fʊl
pipestem 'paɪp,stɛm
pipestone, P- 'paɪp,ston
pipette, -pet pɪ'pɛt |-(te)d -ɪd
pipit 'pɪpɪt
Pippa 'pɪpə
pippin 'pɪpɪn
pipsissewa pɪp'sɪsəwə
Piqua 'pɪkwə
piquancy 'pikənsɪ |-quant -kənt
pique 'anger' pik |piqued pikt
pique insect pik, 'pike
piqué pɪ'ke
piquet pɪ'kɛt
piracy 'paɪrəsɪ
Piraeus paɪ'riəs |-'s -ɪz
Pirandello ,pɪrən'dɛlo (It ,piran'dɛllo)
pirate 'paɪrət, -rɪt |-d -ɪd
piratic paɪ'rætɪk |-al -| |-ally -|ɪ, -ɪklɪ
Pirithous paɪ'rɪθʊəs, Shak.+'paɪrɪ,θʊs |-'s -ɪz
pirogue pə'rog, pɪ-
pirouette ,pɪrʊ'ɛt |-d -ɪd
Pisa 'pizə (It 'pi:sa)
Pisanio pɪ'zɑnɪ,o, -njo
Piscataqua pɪs'kætəkwə, loc.+,kwe |-quis -kwɪs |-quog -,kwɑg, -,kwɒg
piscatology ,pɪskə'tɑlədʒɪ; ES+-'tɒl-
piscatorial ,pɪskə'torɪəl, -'tɔr-; S -'tor-
Pisces 'pɪsiz |gen Piscium 'pɪʃɪəm
piscina pɪ'saɪnə |piscinal 'pɪsɪn|
Pisgah 'pɪzgə
pish n, v pɪʃ |pishes 'pɪʃɪz |pished pɪʃt
pish intj pʃ, pɪʃ
Pisistratus pɪ'sɪstrətəs, paɪ- |-'s -ɪz

pismire 'pɪs,maɪr; ES -,maɪə(r; |-ism -maɪ-,rɪzəm
pistachio pɪs'tɑʃɪ,o, -'tæʃ-
pistareen ,pɪstə'rin
pistil 'pɪst|, -tɪl |-late -ɪt, -,et
pistol, P- 'pɪst| |-ed -d
pistole pɪs'tol
piston 'pɪstn̩, -tən
pit pɪt |pitted 'pɪtɪd
pitapat 'pɪtə,pæt, 'pɪtɪ-
Pitcairn 'pɪtkɛrn, -kærn; E -kɛən, ES -kæən
pitch pɪtʃ |pitches 'pɪtʃɪz |pitched pɪtʃt
pitchblende 'pɪtʃ,blɛnd
pitch-dark 'pɪtʃ'dɑrk; ES -'dɑ:k, E+-'dɑ:k
pitcher 'pɪtʃɚ; ES 'pɪtʃə(r; |-ful -,fʊl
pitchfork 'pɪtʃ,fɔrk; ES -,fɔək
piteous 'pɪtɪəs
pitfall 'pɪt,fɔl |-ed -d
pith pɪθ |piths pɪθs |pithed pɪθt
Pithecanthropus ,pɪθɪkæn'θropəs, -'kænθrə-pəs |-'s -ɪz
pitiable 'pɪtɪəb| |-bly -blɪ
pitiful 'pɪtɪfəl |-ly -ɪ
Pitkin 'pɪtkɪn |-s -z |-s's -zɪz
pitman, P- 'pɪtmən |pitmen 'pɪtmən
pittance 'pɪtn̩s |-s -ɪz
pitter-patter 'pɪtɚ,pætɚ; ES 'pɪtə,pætə(r
Pittsboro 'pɪts,bɝo, -ə; ES -,bɝ-, -,bʌr-, -,bɝ-
Pittsburg, -gh 'pɪtsbɝg; ES -bɝg, -bɝg
Pittsylvania ,pɪts|'venjə, -nɪə, -sɪl-
pituitary pɪ'tjuə,tɛrɪ, -'tɪu-, -'tu-
pity 'pɪtɪ |pitied 'pɪtɪd
Pius 'paɪəs |-'s -ɪz
Piute paɪ'jut ('Pi,ute 'language)
pivot 'pɪvət, 'pɪvɪt |-ed -ɪd |-al -| |-ally -|ɪ (pevet 1763)
pix pɪks |pixes 'pɪksɪz |pixed pɪkst
pixilate 'pɪks|,et |-ed -ɪd
pixy, -ie 'pɪksɪ
Pizarro pɪ'zɑro (Sp pi'θarro)
placable 'plekəb|, 'plæk- |-bly -blɪ
placard n 'plækɑrd; ES -ɑ:d, E+-ɑ:d
placard v 'plækɑrd, plæ'kɑrd; ES -ɑ:d, E+-ɑ:d; |-ed -ɪd
placate 'pleket, 'plæk- |-d -ɪd
placatory 'plekə,torɪ, 'plæk-, -,tɔrɪ; S -,torɪ
place ples |places 'plesɪz |placed plest
placebo plə'sibo

---

placenta plə'sɛntə |-s -z |-tae -ti
placer *'disposer'* 'plesɚ; ES 'plesə(r
placer *mining* 'plæsɚ; ES 'plæsə(r
Placer 'plæsɚ; ES 'plæsə(r; -ville -ˌvɪl
placid, P- 'plæsɪd |-ity plə'sɪdətɪ, plæ-
placket 'plækɪt
plagiarism 'pledʒəˌrɪzəm
plagiarize 'pledʒəˌraɪz |-s -ɪz |-d -d
plague pleg, plɛg |-d -d |-guy -ɪ
plagued *adj* 'plegɪd, 'plɛg-
plaice ples |plaices 'plesɪz
plaid plæd |plaided 'plædɪd
plain plen |plained plend |-ness 'plennɪs
plainsman 'plenzmən |-men -mən
plainsong 'plenˌsɔŋ, -ˌsɒŋ
plain-spoken 'plen'spokən ('plain-ˌspoken
'man)
plaint plent
plaintiff 'plentɪf |plaintive 'plentɪv
Plaisance plə'zɑns (*Fr* plɛ'zɑ̃:s)
plaister 'plestɚ; ES 'plestə(r
plait plet |-ed -ɪd—*see* plat, pleat. *The words*
plit, plæt, *and* plet *are sometimes spelt*
plait, *but there is a proper spelling for each.*
plan plæn |planned plænd
planchet 'plæntʃɪt
planchette plæn'ʃɛt (*Fr* plɑ̃'ʃɛt)
Planck plɑŋk
plane plen |planed plend
planet 'plænɪt |-ary 'plænəˌtɛrɪ
planetarium ˌplænə'tɛrɪəm -'tær-, -'ter- |-s
-z |-ria -rɪə
planetesimal ˌplænə'tɛsəml̩
plangency 'plændʒənsɪ |-gent -dʒənt
plank plæŋk |planked plæŋkt
plankton 'plæŋktən
Plano 'pleno
plant plænt; E+plant, plɑnt; |-ed -ɪd
Plantagenet plæn'tædʒənɪt
plantain 'plæntɪn
plantation plæn'teʃən; S+plænt'eʃən
plantigrade 'plæntəˌgred
plaque plæk
plash plæʃ |plashes 'plæʃɪz |plashed plæʃt
plasm 'plæzəm |plasma 'plæzmə
plaster 'plæstɚ; ES 'plæstə(r, E+'plas-,
'plɑs-; |-ed -d |-ing -trɪŋ, -tərɪŋ
plastic 'plæstɪk |-ally -l̩ɪ, -ɪklɪ
plasticine, P- 'plæstəˌsin

plasticity plæs'tɪsətɪ
plat plæt |platted 'plætɪd—*see* plait, pleat
Plata 'plɑtə (*Sp* 'plata)
plate plet |plated 'pletɪd |-ful -ˌfʊl
plateau plæ'to
platen 'plætn̩
plater 'pletɚ; ES 'pletə(r
platform 'plætˌfɔrm; ES -ˌfɔəm; |-ed -d
platinum 'plætnəm |-tinous -tn̩əs
platitude 'plætəˌtjud, -ˌtɪud, -ˌtud
platitudinous ˌplætə'tjudnəs, -'tɪud-, -'tud-
Plato 'pleto |-nism 'pletn̩ˌɪzəm |-nist -tn̩ɪst
Platonic ple'tɑnɪk, plə-; ES+-'tɒn-; |-al -l̩
|-ally -l̩ɪ, -ɪklɪ
platoon plæ'tun, plə'tun
Platte plæt
platter 'plætɚ; ES 'plætə(r
Plattsburg 'plætsbɝg; ES -bɝg, -bɝg
Plattsmouth 'plætsməθ
platypus 'plætəpəs |-es -ɪz |-pi -ˌpaɪ
plaudit 'plɔdɪt
plausibility ˌplɔzə'bɪlətɪ
plausible 'plɔzəbl̩ |-bly -blɪ
Plautus 'plɔtəs |-'s -ɪz |-tine -taɪn, -tɪn
play ple |played pled |-boy -ˌbɔɪ |-day -ˌde
|-fellow 'pleˌfɛlo, -ə |-ground -ˌgraʊnd
playful 'plefəl |-ly -ɪ
playhouse 'pleˌhaʊs |-s -zɪz |-mate 'pleˌmet
plaything 'pleˌθɪŋ |-time 'pleˌtaɪm
playwright 'pleˌraɪt
plaza 'plæzə, 'plɑzə (*Sp* 'plaθa)
plea pli
pleach plitʃ |pleaches 'plitʃɪz |-ed -t
plead plid |pleaded 'plidɪd *or* plead, pled plɛd
pleasance 'plɛzn̩s |-sant -zn̩t |-santry -zn̩trɪ
please pliz |pleases 'plizɪz |pleased plizd
pleasurable 'plɛʒrəbl̩, -ʒərəbl̩ |-bly -blɪ
pleasure 'plɛʒɚ; ES 'plɛʒə(r; |-d -d
pleat plit |-ed -ɪd—*see* plat, plait
pleb plɛb |plebe plib
plebeian plɪ'biən |-ism -ˌɪzəm
plebiscite 'plɛbəˌsaɪt, 'plɛbəsɪt
plebs plɛbz |plebes 'plibiz
plectrum 'plɛktrəm |-s -z |-tra -trə
pled plɛd
pledge plɛdʒ |pledges 'plɛdʒɪz |pledged plɛdʒd
pledget 'plɛdʒɪt
pledgee plɛdʒ'i
Pleiad 'pliəd, 'plaɪəd |-s -z |-ades -əˌdiz

Key: *See in full* §§3-47. bee bi |pity 'pɪtɪ (§6) |rate ret |yet jɛt |sang sæŋ |angry 'æŋ·grɪ
|bath bæθ; E baθ (§10) |ah ɑ |far fɑr |watch watʃ, wɒtʃ (§12) |jaw dʒɔ |gorge gɔrdʒ |go go

pleiosyllabic ˌplaɪəsɪˈlæbɪk

pleiosyllable *'plurisyllable'* ˈplaɪəˌsɪləbḷ

Pleistocene ˈplaɪstəˌsin

plenary ˈplinərɪ, ˈplɛn-

plenipotentiary ˌplɛnəpəˈtɛnʃərɪ, -ʃɪˌɛrɪ

plenitude ˈplɛnəˌtjud, -ˌtɪud, -ˌtud

plenteous ˈplɛntɪəs

plentiful ˈplɛntɪfəl |-ly -ɪ

plenty ˈplɛntɪ

plenum ˈplinəm |-s -z |-na -nə

pleonasm ˈpliəˌnæzəm

pleonastic ˌpliəˈnæstɪk |-al -ḷ |-ally -ḷɪ, -ɪklɪ

plethora ˈplɛθərə

plethoric ˈplɛθərɪk, plɛˈθɔrɪk, -ˈθɑr-, -ˈθɒr-

plethorical plɛˈθɔrɪkḷ, -ˈθɑr-, -ˈθɒr- |-ly -ɪ

pleura ˈplʊrə, ˈplɪʊrə |-l -l |-risy -rəsɪ

plexus ˈplɛksəs |-es -ɪz |*L pl* -xus -ksəs

pliability ˌplaɪəˈbɪlətɪ

pliable ˈplaɪəbḷ |-bly -blɪ

pliancy ˈplaɪənsɪ |pliant ˈplaɪənt

plicate ˈplaɪket |-d -ɪd

plied plaɪd

pliers ˈplaɪɚz; ES ˈplaɪ·əz

plies plaɪz

plight plaɪt |plighted ˈplaɪtɪd

Plinlimmon plɪnˈlɪmən

plinth plɪnθ |-ths -θs

Pliny ˈplɪnɪ |Plinian ˈplɪnɪən

Pliocene ˈplaɪəˌsin

plod plɑd; ES+plɒd; |-ded -ɪd

plop plɑp; ES+plɒp; |-ped -t

plosion ˈploʒən |-sive -sɪv

plot plɑt; ES+plɒt; |-ted -ɪd

plover ˈplʌvɚ; ES ˈplʌvə(r

plow, -ough plau |-ed -d |-share -ˌʃɛr, -ˌʃær;
   E -ˌʃɛə(r, ES -ˌʃæə(r

ploy plɔɪ |ployed plɔɪd

pluck plʌk |plucked plʌkt

plug plʌg |plugged plʌgd

plugugly ˈplʌgˌʌglɪ

plum, P- plʌm

plumage ˈplumɪdʒ, ˈplɪum- |-s -ɪz |-d -d

Plumas ˈpluməs, ˈplɪuməs |-'s -ɪz

plumb plʌm |plumbed plʌmd |-er -ɚ; ES -ə(r

plumbago plʌmˈbego

plume plum, plɪum |-d -d |-d *adj* -d, -ɪd

plumelet ˈplumlɪt, ˈplɪum-

plummet ˈplʌmɪt |-ed -ɪd

plump plʌmp |plumped plʌmpt

Plumptre ˈplʌmptrɪ

plumule ˈplumjul, ˈplɪum-

plumy ˈplumɪ, ˈplɪumɪ

plunder ˈplʌndɚ; ES -də(r; |-ed -d |-ing
   ˈplʌndrɪŋ, ˈplʌndərɪŋ

plunge plʌndʒ |plunges ˈplʌndʒɪz |-d -d

plunk plʌŋk |plunked plʌŋkt

Plunkett ˈplʌŋkɪt

pluperfect pluˈpɝfɪkt, plɪu-; ES -ˈpɝf-, -ˈpɝf-;
   (ˈpluˌperfect ˈtense)

plural ˈplʊrəl, ˈplɪʊ- |-ly -ɪ

plurality plʊˈrælətɪ, plɪʊ-

plurisyllabic ˌplʊrəsɪˈlæbɪk, ˌplɪʊ-

plurisyllable ˈplʊrəˌsɪləbḷ, ˈplɪʊ-

plus plʌs |plusses ˈplʌsɪz |plussed plʌst

plush plʌʃ |plushes ˈplʌʃɪz |plushed plʌʃt

Plutarch ˈplutɑrk, ˈplɪu-; ES -tɑːk, E+-tɑːk

Pluto ˈpluto, ˈplɪu-

plutocracy pluˈtɑkrəsɪ, plɪu-; ES+-ˈtɒk-

plutocrat ˈplutəˌkræt, ˈplɪu-

plutocratic ˌplutəˈkrætɪk, ˌplɪu- |-al -ḷ |-ally
   -ḷɪ, -ɪklɪ

Plutonian pluˈtonɪən, plɪu-

plutonic pluˈtɑnɪk; ES+-ˈtɒn-

Plutus ˈplutəs, ˈplɪu- |-'s -ɪz

pluvial ˈpluvɪəl, ˈplɪu-

pluviometer ˌpluvɪˈɑmətɚ, ˌplɪu-; ES -ˈɑmə-
   tə(r, -ˈɒm-

ply plaɪ |plied plaɪd |-ers -ɚz; ES -əz

Plymouth ˈplɪməθ

Plynlimon plɪnˈlɪmən

P.M., p.m. ˈpiˈɛm

pneumatic njuˈmætɪk, nɪu-, nu- |-ally -ḷɪ,
   -ɪklɪ

pneumococcus ˌnjuməˈkɑkəs, ˌnɪu-, ˌnu-;
   ES+-ˈkɒk-; |-cci -ksaɪ

pneumogastric ˌnjuməˈgæstrɪk, ˌnɪu-, ˌnu-

pneumonia njuˈmonjə, nɪu-, nu-, -nɪə

Po po

poach potʃ |poaches ˈpotʃɪz |poached potʃt

Pocahontas ˌpokəˈhɑntəs, -ˈhɒn- |-'s -ɪz

Pocatello ˌpokəˈtɛlo

pock pɑk; ES+pɒk; |-ed -t

pocket ˈpɑkɪt; ES+ˈpɒk-; |-ed -ɪd |-book
   -ˌbʊk |-knife -ˌnaɪf |-ful -ˌfʊl

pockmark ˈpɑkˌmɑrk; ES ˈpɑkˌmɑːk, ˈpɒk-,
   E+-ˌmɑːk

Pocomoke ˈpokəˌmok

Pocono ˈpokəˌno

|full fʊl |tooth tuθ |further ˈfɝðɚ; ES ˈfɝðə |custom ˈkʌstəm |while hwaɪl |how hau |toy tɔɪ
|using ˈjuzɪŋ |fuse fjuz, fɪuz |dish dɪʃ |vision ˈvɪʒən |Eden ˈidn̩ |cradle ˈkredḷ |keep 'em ˈkipm̩

Those words below in which the a *sound is spelt* o *are often pronounced with* ɒ *in E and S*

pod pad |-ded -ɪd

podgy ˈpadʒɪ

podiatry poˈdaɪətrɪ

podium ˈpodɪəm |-dia -dɪə

Poe po

poem ˈpo·ɪm, -əm

poesy ˈpo·ɪsɪ, -əsɪ, -zɪ

poet ˈpo·ɪt, -ət |-ry -rɪ

poetaster ˈpo·ɪtˌæstɚ, -ət-; ES -ˌæstə(r

poetic poˈɛtɪk |-al -l̩ |-ally -l̩ɪ, -ɪklɪ

poetize ˈpo·ɪtˌaɪz |-s -ɪz |-d -d

Pogram ˈpogrəm

pogrom ˈpogrəm, ˈpag-, ˈpɒg-, poˈgram, -ˈgrɒm

poh po

poi pɔɪ, ˈpo·ɪ

poignancy ˈpɔɪnənsɪ, -njənsɪ |-ant -ənt

poilu ˈpwalu, pɔɪˈlu (*Fr* pwaˈly)

Poincaré *Fr* pwæ̃kaˈre

Poins pɔɪnz |-ʼs -ɪz; *in Shak prob.* pɔɪnts (*spelt* Pointz)

poinsettia, P- pɔɪnˈsɛtɪə

point pɔɪnt |pointed ˈpɔɪntɪd

point-blank ˈpɔɪntˈblæŋk (ˈpoint-ˌblank ˈaim)

Point Pelee ˈpɔɪntˈpili

poise pɔɪz |poises ˈpɔɪzɪz |poised pɔɪzd

poison ˈpɔɪzn̩ |-ed -d |-ing ˈpɔɪznɪŋ, -zn̩ɪŋ

poisonous ˈpɔɪznəs, ˈpɔɪzn̩əs

Poitiers pɔɪˈtɪrz; ES -ˈtɪəz; |-ʼs -ɪz (*Fr* pwaˈtje)

Poitou pɔɪˈtu (*Fr* pwaˈtu)

poke pok |poked pokt |poky, -key ˈpokɪ; |*N Engd*+pōk (*§46*)

pokeberry ˈpokˌbɛrɪ, -bərɪ; *N Engd*+ˈpōk- (*§46*)

poker ˈpokɚ; ES -kə(r; |-ing ˈpokərɪŋ, -krɪŋ; *N Engd*+ˈpōk- (*§46*)

Polack ˈpolæk, -lak

polack, -lak ʻ*balsa*ʼ poˈlak

Poland ˈpolənd |-er -ləndɚ, -læn-; ES -ə(r

polar ˈpolɚ; ES ˈpolə(r; |-ity poˈlærətɪ

Polaris poˈlɛrɪs, -ˈlær-, -ˈler-

polariscope poˈlærəˌskop

polarization ˌpolərəˈzeʃən, -aɪˈz-

polarize ˈpoləˌraɪz |-s -ɪz |-d -d

Pole *surname* pol, pul; ʻ*Polander*ʼ pol

pole pol |-d -d |-ax(e) -ˌæks -axes -ˌæksɪz

polecat ˈpolˌkæt

polemic poˈlɛmɪk |-al -l̩ |-ally -l̩ɪ, -ɪklɪ

polenta poˈlɛntə

polestar ˈpolˌstar; ES -ˌstɑː(r, E+-ˌstɑː(r

police pəˈlis |-s -ɪz |-d -t |-man, -men -mən

policy ˈpaləsɪ |-cied -sɪd

poliomyelitis ˌpolɪoˌmaɪəˈlaɪtɪs

polish ˈpalɪʃ |-es -ɪz |-ed -t

Polish ˈpolɪʃ

polite pəˈlaɪt

politic ˈpaləˌtɪk |-s -s |-ian ˌpaləˈtɪʃən

political pəˈlɪtɪkl̩ |-ly -ɪ, -ɪklɪ

politico pəˈlɪtɪˌko

polity ˈpalətɪ

Polixenes pəˈlɪksəˌniz |-ʼs -ɪz

Polk pok; *N Engd*+pōk (*§46*)

polka ˈpolkə, ˈpokə; *N Engd*+ˈpō- (*§46*); |-ed -d

polkadot ˈpokəˌdat

Poll, p- ʻ*Polly*ʼ pal

poll *adj* ʻ*polled*ʼ pol

poll ʻ*head*,ʼ ʻ*cut*,ʼ ʻ*vote*ʼ pol |-ed -d

pollack ˈpalək

pollard, P- ˈpalɚd; ES ˈpaləd; |-ed -ɪd

pollen ˈpalən |-ed -d

pollinate ˈpaləˌnet |-d -ɪd |-tion ˌpaləˈneʃən

polliwog ˈpalɪˌwag, -ˌwɒg

pollock, P- ˈpalək

pollute pəˈlut, -ˈlɪut |-d -ɪd

pollution pəˈluʃən, -ˈlɪuʃən

Pollux ˈpaləks |-ʼs -ɪz

Polly ˈpalɪ |-anna ˌpalɪˈænə

pollywog ˈpalɪˌwag, -ˌwɒg

polo, P- ˈpolo

polonaise ˌpoləˈnez, ˌpalə- |-s -ɪz |-d -d

polonium pəˈlonɪəm

Polonius pəˈlonɪəs, -njəs |-ʼs -ɪz

poltroon palˈtrun |-ery -ərɪ, -rɪ

polyandrous ˌpalɪˈændrəs |-dry -drɪ, ˈpalɪˌæn-

Polybius pəˈlɪbɪəs |-ʼs -ɪz

Polycarp ˈpalɪˌkarp; ES -ˌkɑːp, E+-ˌkɑːp

polychromatic ˌpalɪkroˈmætɪk

polychrome ˈpalɪˌkrom |-d -d

Polycrates pəˈlɪkrəˌtiz |-ʼs -ɪz

Polydore ˈpalɪˌdor, -ˌdɔr; ES -ˌdoə(r, E+ -ˌdɔə(r

Polydorus ˌpalɪˈdorəs, -ˈdɔr-; S -ˈdor-; |-ʼs -ɪz

polygamy pəˈlɪgəmɪ |-mous -məs |-mist -mɪst

Key: See in full §§3–47. bee bi |pity ˈpɪtɪ (§6) |rate ret |yet jɛt |sang sæŋ |angry ˈæŋ·grɪ |bath bæθ; E baθ (§10) |ah ɑ |far fɑr |watch watʃ, wɒtʃ (§12) |jaw dʒɔ |gorge gɔrdʒ |go go

Those words below in which the ɑ *sound is spelt* o *are often pronounced with* ɒ *in E and S*

polyglot ˈpɑlɪˌglɑt
polygon ˈpɑlɪˌgɑn |-al pəˈlɪgən|
polygyny pəˈlɪdʒənɪ
polyhedron ˌpɑlɪˈhidrən |-dral -drəl
Polyhymnia ˌpɑlɪˈhɪmnɪə
polymer ˈpɑlɪmɚ; ES -mə(r; |-e -ˌmɪr; ES -ˌmɪə(r
polymeric ˌpɑlɪˈmɛrɪk
polymerize ˈpɑlɪməˌraɪz, pəˈlɪmə- |-s -ɪz |-d -d
Polynesia ˌpɑləˈniʃə, -ʒə |-n -n
polynomial ˌpɑlɪˈnomɪəl
polyp ˈpɑlɪp
polyped ˈpɑlɪˌpɛd
polyphase ˈpɑlɪˌfez |-sal ˌpɑlɪˈfez|
Polyphemus ˌpɑlɪˈfiməs |-ʼs -ɪz
polyphonic ˌpɑlɪˈfɑnɪk |-ny pəˈlɪfənɪ
polypus ˈpɑləpəs |-pi -ˌpaɪ |-ʼs -ɪz
polysyllabic ˌpɑləsɪˈlæbɪk |-al -| |-ally -|ɪ, -ɪklɪ
polysyllabism ˌpɑləˈsɪləˌbɪzəm
polysyllable ˈpɑləˌsɪləb|
polytechnic, P- ˌpɑləˈtɛknɪk |-al -|
polytheism ˈpɑləθiˌɪzəm
polytheistic ˌpɑləθiˈɪstɪk |-al -| |-ally -|ɪ, -ɪklɪ
Polyxena pəˈlɪksɪnə
pomace ˈpʌmɪs, -əs |-ous poˈmeʃəs
pomade poˈmed, -ˈmɑd
pome pom
pomegranite ˈpʌmˌgrænɪt, ˈpɑm-, pʌmˈgræn-, pɑm-
Pomerania ˌpɑməˈrenɪə |-n -n
Pomerene ˈpɑməˌrin
Pomeroy ˈpɑməˌrɔɪ, ˈpʌmə-, -mrɔɪ
Pomfret ˈpʌmfrɪt, ˈpɑm-
pommel n ˈpʌm|, ˈpɑm| |-ed -d
pommel v ˈpʌm| |-ed -d |-ing ˈpʌm|ɪŋ, ˈpʌmlɪŋ
pomology poˈmɑlədʒɪ
Pomona pəˈmonə
pomp pɑmp |pomped pɑmpt
pompadour, P- ˈpɑmpəˌdor, -ˌdɔr-, -ˌdʊr; ES -ˌdoə(r, -ˌdʊə(r, E+-ˌdɔə(r
pompano, P- ˈpɑmpəˌno
Pompei *It province* pɑmˈpe·i (*It* pomˈpɛːi)
Pompeian pɑmˈpeən, -ˈpiən
Pompeii *anc. city* pɑmˈpe·i, -ˈpe, ˈpɑmpɪˌaɪ
Pompeius pɑmˈpiəs |-ʼs -ɪz
Pompey ˈpɑmpɪ
pompon ˈpɑmpɑn (*Fr* põˈpõ)

pompous ˈpɑmpəs |pomposity pɑmˈpɑsətɪ
Ponce ˈponse
Ponce de Leon ˈpɑnsdəˈliən (*Sp* ˈpɔnθeˈðeleˈɔn)
poncho ˈpɑntʃo
pond pɑnd, pɒnd, pɔnd
ponder ˈpɑndɚ; ES -də(r; |-ed -d |-ing ˈpɑndrɪŋ, ˈpɑndərɪŋ
ponderable ˈpɑndərəb|, ˈpɑndrə- |-rous -rəs
Pondicherry ˌpɑndɪˈtʃɛrɪ (*Fr* Pondichéry põdiʃeˈri)
pone '*corn bread*' pon
pone *L v* ˈponi
pongee pɑnˈdʒi (ˈpɑnˌgee ˈsilk)
poniard ˈpɑnjɚd; ES ˈpɑnjəd; |-ed -ɪd
pons asinorum ˈpɑnzˌæsɪˈnorəm, -ˈnɔr-; S -ˈnor-
Pons, Lily ˈlɪlɪˈpɑnz (*S Fr* liliˈpõːns) |-ʼs -ɪz
Pontchartrain ˈpɑntʃɚˌtren; ES ˈpɑntʃə-
Pontefract ˈpʌmfrɪt, ˈpɑm-, ˈpɑntɪˌfrækt
Pontiac ˈpɑntɪˌæk
pontifex, P- ˈpɑntəˌfɛks |-fices pɑnˈtɪfəˌsiz
pontiff ˈpɑntɪf
pontifical pɑnˈtɪfɪk| |-ly -ɪ |-cate -kɪt, -ˌket
pontifices pɑnˈtɪfəˌsiz
Pontius ˈpɑntʃəs, -nʃəs, -ntɪəs |-ʼs -ɪz
pontoon pɑnˈtun |-ed -d (ˈpɑnˌtoon ˈbridge)
Pontotoc ˌpɑntəˈtɑk
Pontus ˈpɑntəs |-ʼs -ɪz
pony ˈponɪ |ponied ˈponɪd
poodle ˈpud| |-d -d |-ling ˈpudlɪŋ, ˈpud|ɪŋ
pooh pu, pʊ & *various other breath puffs*
Pooh-Bah ˌpuˈbɑ
pooh-pooh ˈpuˈpu, ˈpuˌpu |-ed -d
pool pul |-ed -d |-room ˈpulˌrum, -ˌrʊm
poop pup |pooped pupt
poor pʊr; ES pʊə(r, poə(r, pɔə(r
poor-farm '*poorhouse*' ˈpʊrˌfɑrm; ES ˈpʊə-ˌfɑːm, ˈpoə-, ˈpɔə-, E+-ˌfɑːm
poor farm '*bad farm*' *acct* ˈpoorˈfɑrm
poorhouse ˈpʊrˌhaʊs; ES ˈpʊə-, ˈpoə-, ˈpɔə-|-ses -zɪz
pop pɑp |popped pɑpt |-corn -ˌkɔrn; ES -ˌkɔən
pope, P- pop |-ry -ərɪ, -rɪ |-pish -ɪʃ
popgun ˈpɑpˌgʌn |-gunned -ˌgʌnd
Popilius poˈpɪlɪəs, -ljəs |-ʼs -ɪz
popinjay ˈpɑpɪnˌdʒe
poplar ˈpɑplɚ; ES ˈpɑplə(r
poplin ˈpɑplɪn |-ette ˌpɑplɪnˈɛt

|full fʊl |tooth tuθ |further ˈfɝðɚ; ES ˈfɝðə |custom ˈkʌstəm |while hwaɪl |how haʊ |toy tɔɪ |using ˈjuzɪŋ |fuse fjuz, fɪuz |dish dɪʃ |vision ˈvɪʒən |Eden ˈidn̩ |cradle ˈkred| |keep ʼem ˈkipm̩

Those words below in which the ɑ sound is spelt o are often pronounced with ɒ in E and S

Popocatepetl ˌpopəˈkætəˌpɛtḷ, poˌpokəˈtepətḷ
—*Whatever the Aztec, the first pron. is well
established. A learned colleague once rimed:
—'What is home without a kettle?
Popocat- without a -petl.'*
popover ˈpɑpˌovɚ; ES -ˌovə(r
popper ˈpɑpɚ; ES ˈpɑpə(r
poppet ˈpɑpɪt |-ed -ɪd
popple, P- ˈpɑpḷ
poppy ˈpɑpɪ |poppied ˈpɑpɪd
poppycock ˈpɑpɪˌkɑk
populace ˈpɑpjəlɪs, -ləs |-'s -ɪz
popular ˈpɑpjələ; ES -lə(r; |-ity ˌpɑpjə-
ˈlærətɪ
popularize ˈpɑpjələˌraɪz |-s -ɪz |-d -d
populate ˈpɑpjəˌlet |-lated -ˌletɪd |-lous -ləs
population ˌpɑpjəˈleʃən
Populist ˈpɑpjəlɪst
porcelain ˈpɔrslɪn, ˈpɔr-, -sḷɪn, -ən, -sḷˌen; ES
-ˈpɔə-, ˈpɔə-
porch pɔrtʃ, pɔrtʃ; ES pɔətʃ, E+pɔətʃ; |-es -ɪz
|-ed -t
porcine ˈpɔrsaɪn, -sɪn; ES ˈpɔə-
porcupine, P- ˈpɔrkjəˌpaɪn; ES ˈpɔək-; |-d -d
pore por, pɔr; ES poə(r, E+pɔə(r; |-d -d
porgy ˈpɔrgɪ; ES ˈpɔəgɪ
pork pork, pɔrk; ES poək, E+pɔək
pornographic ˌpɔrnəˈgræfɪk; ES ˌpɔənə-
pornography pɔrˈnɑgrəfɪ, -ˈnɒg-; ES pɔˈn-
porosity poˈrɑsətɪ, pɔ-; S po-
porous ˈporəs, ˈpɔrəs; S ˈporəs
porphyry, P- ˈpɔrfərɪ; ES ˈpɔə-
porpoise ˈpɔrpəs; ES ˈpɔəpəs; |-s -ɪz
porridge ˈpɔrɪdʒ, ˈpɑr-, ˈpɒr- |-s -ɪz |-d -d
porringer ˈpɔrɪndʒɚ, ˈpɑr-, ˈpɒr-; ES -dʒə(r
Porsena ˈpɔrsɪnə; ES ˈpɔə-
port port, pɔrt; ES poət, E+pɔət; |-ed -ɪd
|-able -əbḷ |-bly -blɪ
portability ˌpɔrtəˈbɪlətɪ, ˌpɔr-; ES ˌpoətə-,
E+ˌpɔətə-
portage, P- ˈpɔrtɪdʒ, ˈpɔr-; ES ˈpoə-, E+
ˈpɔə-; |-s -ɪz |-d -d
portal ˈpɔrtḷ, ˈpɔrtḷ; ES ˈpoətḷ, E+ˈpɔə-;
|-ed -d
Port Angeles portˈændʒələs, pɔrt-, -ˌliz; ES
poət, E+pɔt-
Port-au-Prince ˌportoˈprɪns, ˌpɔrt-; ES ˌpoət-,
E+ˌpɔət-; (*Fr* pɔrtoˈprɛ̃:s)

portcullis portˈkʌlɪs, pɔrt-; ES poət-, E+
pɔət-; |-es -ɪz |-ed -t
Porte port, pɔrt; ES poət, E+pɔət
portend porˈtɛnd, pɔr-; ES poə-, E+pɔə-;
|-ed -ɪd
portent ˈpɔrtɛnt, ˈpɔr-; ES ˈpoə-, E+ˈpɔə-
portentous porˈtɛntəs, pɔr-; ES poə-, E+pɔə-
porter, P- ˈpɔrtɚ, ˈpɔr-; ES ˈpoətə(r, E+
ˈpɔətə(r; |-ed -d
porterhouse ˈpɔrtɚˌhaus, ˈpɔr-; ES ˈpoətə-, E+
ˈpɔətə-; |*pl* -houses 'liquor-house' -ˌhauzɪz,
'steak' -ˌhausɪz
portfolio portˈfolɪˌo, pɔrt-, -ljo; ES poət-,
E+pɔət-
porthole ˈpɔrtˌhol, ˈpɔrt-; ES ˈpoət-, E+ˈpɔət-
Port Huron portˈhjurən, pɔrt-, -ˈhɪu-; ES
poət-, E+pɔət-
Portia ˈpɔrʃə, ˈpɔr-, -ʃɪə; ES ˈpoə-, E+ˈpɔə-
portico ˈpɔrtɪˌko, ˈpɔr-; ES ˈpoə-, E+ˈpɔə-;
|-ed -d
portiere ˌpɔrtɪˈɛr, ˌpɔr-; ES ˌpoə-, E+ˌpɔə-;
(*Fr* pɔrˈtjɛ:r)
portion ˈpɔrʃən, ˈpɔr-; ES ˈpoə-, E+ˈpɔə-;
|-ed -d |-ing -ʃənɪŋ, -ʃnɪŋ
Port Jervis portˈdʒɝvɪs, pɔrt-; ES poət-
ˈdʒɝvɪs, -ˈdʒɝv-, E+pɔət-; |-'s -ɪz
Portland ˈpɔrtlənd, ˈpɔrt-; ES ˈpoət-, E+
ˈpɔət-
portmanteau portˈmænto, pɔrt-; ES poət-,
E+pɔət-
Portobello ˌpɔrtəˈbɛlo, ˌpɔrtə-; ES ˌpoətə-,
E+ˌpɔətə-
Porto Bello ˌpɔrtəˈbɛlo, ˌpɔrtə-; ES ˈpoətə-,
E+ˌpɔətə-; (*Am Sp* ˌpɔrtoˈβejo)
Porto Rico ˌpɔrtəˈriko, ˌpɔrtə-; ES ˌpoətə-,
E+ˌpɔətə-; |-can -kən
portrait ˈpɔrtret, ˈpɔr-, -trɪt; ES ˈpoə-, E+
ˈpɔə-
portraiture ˈpɔrtrɪtʃɚ, ˈpɔr-; ES ˈpoətrɪtʃə(r,
E+ˈpɔə-
portray porˈtre, pɔr-; ES poə-, E+pɔə-; |-ed
-d |-al -əl
Port Said portˈsed, pɔrt-, -ˈsaɪd, -saˈid; ES
poət-, E+pɔət-
Portsmouth ˈpɔrtsməθ, ˈpɔrts-; ES ˈpoəts-;
E+ˈpɔəts-
Portugal ˈpɔrtʃəgḷ, ˈpɔr-; ES ˈpoə-, E+ˈpɔə-;
|-guese -ˌgiz

Key: *See in full §§3–47.* bee bi |pity ˈpɪtɪ (§6) |rate ret |yet jɛt |sang sæŋ |angry ˈæŋ·grɪ
|bath bæθ; E baθ (§10) |ah ɑ |far fɑr |watch watʃ, wɒtʃ (§12) |jaw dʒɔ |gorge gɔrdʒ |go go

Those words below in which the ɑ sound is spelt o are often pronounced with ɒ in E and S

portulaca ˌpɔrtʃə'lækə, ˌpɔr-; ES ˌpoə-,
E+ˌpɔə-; |P- -'lekə
pose poz |poses 'poziz |posed pozd
Poseidon po'saɪdn̩, pə-
Posey 'pozɪ
poseur po'zɝ; ES -'zɜ(r, -'zɝ; (*Fr* po'zœːr)
posit 'pazɪt |-ed -ɪd
position pə'zɪʃən |-ed -d |-al -], '*placing*' po-
positive 'pazətɪv, -ztɪv |-d -d |-vism -ˌɪzəm
positively 'pazətɪvlɪ, -ztɪv-, *emph. occas.*
    ˌpazə'tɪvlɪ
posse 'pasɪ |-man -mən |-men -mən
posse comitatus 'pasɪˌkamɪ'tetəs
possess pə'zɛs |-es -ɪz |-ed -t |-edly -ɪdlɪ
possession pə'zɛʃən |-ed -d |-ive -sɪv |-al -]
possessor pə'zɛsɚ; ES -'zɛsə(r; |-y -ɪ
posset 'pasɪt |-ed -ɪd
possibility ˌpasə'bɪlətɪ
possible 'pasəb] |-bly -blɪ
possum 'pasəm |-ed -d
post post |posted 'postɪd |-age -ɪdʒ |-al -]
post-chaise *n* 'post̩ʃez |-s -ɪz
post-chaise *v* ˌpost'ʃez |-s -ɪz |-d -d
postdate ˌpost'det |-dated -'detɪd
posterior pas'tɪrɪɚ; ES -'tɪrɪ·ə(r
posterity pas'tɛrətɪ
postern 'postɚn, 'pas-; ES -tən
postgraduate post'grædʒuɪt, pos'g-, -ˌet
posthaste 'post'hest ('post̩haste 'journey)
posthumous 'pastʃuməs
Posthumus post'hjuməs, -'hɪu- |-'s -ɪz
postilion, -ll- po'stɪljən, pa- |-ed -d
postlude 'post̩lud, -ˌlɪud
postman 'postmən |-men -mən
postmark 'post̩mark; ES -ˌmaːk, E+-ˌmaːk;
    |-ed -t
postmaster 'post̩mæstɚ, 'pos̩m-; ES -ˌmæs-
    tə(r, E+-ˌmas-, -ˌmas-
post meridiem ˌpostmə'rɪdɪˌɛm, -'rɪdɪəm
postmistress 'post̩mɪstrɪs, 'pos̩m- |-es -ɪz
post-mortem post'mɔrtəm; ES -'mɔətəm;
    |-ed -d
postnatal post'net]
post-obit post'obɪt, -'ab-
post-office 'post̩ɔfɪs, -ˌɒf-, -ˌaf- |-s -ɪz
postpaid 'post'ped, 'pos'p- ('post̩paid 'parcel)
postpone post'pon, pos'p- |-poned -'pond
postprandial post'prændɪəl |-ly -ɪ

postscript 'pos·skrɪpt, 'post- |-ed -ɪd
postulant 'pastʃələnt
postulate *n* 'pastʃəlɪt, -ˌlet
postulate *v* 'pastʃəˌlet |-lated -ˌletɪd
postulation ˌpastʃə'leʃən
posture 'pastʃɚ; ES -tʃə(r; |-d -d
posy 'pozɪ
pot pat |potted 'patɪd
potable 'potəb]
potash 'pat̩æʃ |-es -ɪz |-ed -t
potassium pə'tæsɪəm
potation po'teʃən
potato pə'teto, -ə
Potawatomi, -ami ˌpatə'watəmɪ, -'wɒt-
potbelly 'pat̩bɛlɪ |-ied -d
potboiler 'pat̩bɔɪlɚ; ES -ˌbɔɪlə(r
potboy 'pat̩bɔɪ
Poteat po'tit
poteen po'tin, pə-
potence 'potn̩s |-cy -ɪ |-tent -tn̩t
potentate 'potn̩ˌtet
potential pə'tɛnʃəl |-ly -ɪ |-ity -ˌtɛnʃɪ'ælətɪ
potentiometer pəˌtɛnʃɪ'amətɚ; ES -'amətə(r
potheen po'tin, pə-
pother 'paðɚ; ES 'paðə(r; |-ed -d
potherb 'pat̩ɝb, -ˌhɝb; ES -ˌɝb, -ˌɝb, -ˌhɝb,
    -ˌhɝb
potholder 'pat̩holdɚ; ES -ˌholdə(r
pothole 'pat̩hol |-hook -ˌhʊk
pothouse 'pat̩haʊs |-ses -zɪz
pothunter 'pat̩hʌntɚ; ES -ˌhʌntə(r
potion 'poʃən |-ed -d
Potiphar 'patəfɚ; ES 'patəfə(r
potlatch, P- 'pat̩lætʃ |-es -ɪz |-ed -t
potlicker, -likk- 'pat̩lɪkɚ; ES -ˌlɪkə(r
pot-liquor 'pat̩lɪkɚ; ES -ˌlɪkə(r
potluck 'pat̩lʌk, 'pat'lʌk
Potomac pə'tomək
Potosi *Bol* ˌpoto'si; *US* pə'tosɪ
potpie 'pat̩paɪ
potpourri pat'pʊrɪ (*Fr* popu'ri)
Potsdam 'pats̩dæm
potsherd 'pat̩ʃɝd; ES -ˌʃɝd, -ˌʃɝd
pottage 'patɪdʒ
Pottawattamie, -wato- ˌpatə'watəmɪ, -'wɒt-
potter 'patɚ; ES 'patə(r; |-ed -d |-y -ɪ
pottle 'pat] |-d -d
Pottstown 'pats̩taʊn |-ville -vɪl; S+-v]

pouch pautʃ |pouches ˈpautʃɪz |pouched
 pautʃt
pouf puf
Poughkeepsie pəˈkɪpsɪ
poult polt
poulterer ˈpoltərɚ; ES ˈpoltərə(r
poultice ˈpoltɪs |-s -ɪz |- d -t
Poultney ˈpoltnɪ
poultry ˈpoltrɪ
pounce paʊns |-s -ɪz |-d -t
pound paʊnd |pounded ˈpaʊndɪd |-cake -ˌkek
pound-foolish ˈpaʊndˈfulɪʃ (ˈpound-ˌfoolish
 ˈact)
Pounds paʊndz, paʊnz |-ʼs -ɪz
pour por, pɔr, pur; ES poə(r, puə(r, E+pɔə(r;
 |-ed -d
pourboire ˈpurˌbwɑr; ES ˈpuəˌbwɑː(r; (Fr
 purˈbwaːr)
pourparler, -ley purˈpɑrlɪ; ES puəˈpɑːlɪ; |-ed
 -d (Fr purparˈle)
pou sto ˈpuˈsto
pout paʊt |pouted ˈpaʊtɪd
poverty ˈpɑvɚtɪ; ES ˈpɑvətɪ, ˈpɒv-
Pow paʊ
powder ˈpaʊdɚ; ES -də(r; |-ed -d |-ing
 ˈpaʊdrɪŋ, ˈpaʊdərɪŋ
Powell ˈpaʊəl |Baden-P-, F. York P- ˈpoəl
power, P- ˈpaʊɚ; ES ˈpaʊ·ə(r; |-ed -d |-ful
 -fəl |-fully -fəlɪ, -flɪ
Poweshiek ˌpaʊəˈʃik
Powhatan ˌpaʊəˈtæn
Pownal, -ll ˈpaʊnl̩
powwow ˈpaʊˌwaʊ |-ed -d
Powys ˈpo·ɪs |-ʼs -ɪz
pox pɑks; ES+pɒks
praam prɑm
practicability ˌpræktɪkəˈbɪlətɪ
practicable ˈpræktɪkəbl̩ |-bly -blɪ
practical ˈpræktɪkl̩ |-ly -ɪ, ˈvirtually' -ɪklɪ
practicality ˌpræktɪˈkælətɪ
practice, v+-tise ˈpræktɪs |-s -ɪz |-d -t
practitioner prækˈtɪʃənɚ, -ʃnɚ; ES -nə(r
Praed pred
praedial ˈpridɪəl |-ity ˌpridɪˈælətɪ
praefect ˈprifɛkt
praetor ˈpritɚ; ES ˈpritə(r
praetorian prɪˈtorɪən, -ˈtɔr-; S -ˈtor-
pragmatic prægˈmætɪk |-al -l̩ |-ally -l̩ɪ, -ɪklɪ
pragmatism ˈprægməˌtɪzəm |-tist -tɪst

Prague preg, prɑg (Czech ˈprɑhɑ, Ger prɑk)—
 The hybrid pronunciation prɑg is now accepted beside preg.
prairie ˈprɛrɪ, ˈprerɪ
Prairie du Chien ˌprerɪdəˈʃin, ˌprerɪ-
praise prez |praises ˈprezɪz |praised prezd
praiseworthy ˈprezˌwɝðɪ; ES -ˌwɜðɪ, -ˌwʌðɪ
Prakrit ˈprɑkrɪt
praline ˈprɑlin; S+ˈprɔ-
pram præm, ʻpraam' prɑm
prance præns; E+prɑns, prɒns; |-s -ɪz |-d -t
prandial ˈprændɪəl |-ly -ɪ
prank præŋk |pranked, prankt præŋkt
prate pret |prated ˈpretɪd
pratique præˈtik, ˈprætɪk (Fr praˈtik)
Pratt præt
prattle ˈprætl̩ |-d -d |-ling ˈprætlɪŋ, -tl̩ɪŋ
prawn prɔn
Praxiteles præksˈɪtl̩ˌiz |-ʼs -ɪz
pray pre |prayed pred
prayer ʻpetition' prɛr, prær; E prɛə(r, ES
 ˈpræə(r
prayer ʻsupplicant' ˈpre-ɚ; ES ˈpre-ə(r
prayer-rug ˈprɛrˌrʌg, ˈprær-; E ˈprɛəˌrʌg, ES
 ˈpræə-
pre- prefix, stressed ˈpri-, ˌpri-, ˈprɛ-, ˌprɛ-;
 unstr. prɪ-, prə-, pri-. For the unstr., when
 only prɪ- is given in the vocab., it is to be
 understood that many speakers, both British
 and American, use prə- as in propose
 prəˈpoz, or pri- as in precede priˈsid. The
 pron. pɚ- is also not infrequently heard from
 speakers of unquestioned cultivation.
preach pritʃ |-es -ɪz |-ed -t |-er -ɚ; ES -ə(r
preachify ˈpritʃəˌfaɪ |-fied -ˌfaɪd
preamble ˈpriæmbl̩, prɪˈæmbl̩ |-d -d |-ling
 -blɪŋ, -bl̩ɪŋ
prearrange ˌpriəˈrendʒ |-s -ɪz |-d -d
prebend ˈprɛbənd |-ary -ˌɛrɪ |-al prɪˈbɛndl̩
Preble ˈprɛbl̩
precarious prɪˈkɛrɪəs, -ˈkær-, -ˈker-
precaution prɪˈkɔʃən |-al -l̩ |-ary -ˌɛrɪ |-tious
 -ʃəs
precede priˈsid, prɪ- |-d -ɪd
precedence prɪˈsidn̩s, ˈprɛsədəns |-s -ɪz |-cy -ɪ
precedent n ˈprɛsədənt
precedent adj prɪˈsidn̩t
precedent v ˈprɛsəˌdɛnt |-ed -ɪd
precentor prɪˈsɛntɚ; ES -ˈsɛntə(r

Key: See in full §§3–47. bee bi |pity ˈpɪtɪ (§6) |rate ret |yet jɛt |sang sæŋ |angry ˈæŋ·grɪ
|bath bæθ; E baθ (§10) |ah ɑ |far fɑr |watch watʃ, wɒtʃ (§12) |jaw dʒɔ |gorge gɔrdʒ |go go

precept 'prisept |-ed -ɪd
preceptive prɪ'sɛptɪv |-tor -tɚ; ES -tə(r
preceptress prɪ'sɛptrɪs |-es -ɪz
preceptual prɪ'sɛptʃʊəl |-ly -ɪ
precession pri'sɛʃən, prɪ- |-al -ļ
precinct 'prisɪŋkt
preciosity ˌprɛʃɪ'asətɪ, ˌprɛsɪ-; ES+-'ɒs-
precious 'prɛʃəs
precipice 'prɛsəpɪs |-s -ɪz |-d -t
precipitance prɪ'sɪpətəns |-cy -ɪ |-tant -tənt
precipitate n, adj prɪ'sɪpəˌtet, -tɪt
precipitate v prɪ'sɪpəˌtet |-tated -ˌtetɪd
precipitation prɪˌsɪpə'teʃən
precipitous prɪ'sɪpətəs
précis n pre'si, 'presi (Fr pre'si) |pl précis -z
précis v pre'si |précises pre'siz |précised
    pre'sid—acct+'précis
precise prɪ'saɪs |-s -ɪz |-d -t
precisian prɪ'sɪʒən |-ism -ˌɪzəm |-ist -ɪst
precision prɪ'sɪʒən
preclinical pri'klɪnɪkļ
preclude prɪ'klud, -'klɪud |-d -ɪd
preclusion prɪ'kluʒən, -'klɪu- |-sive -sɪv
precocious prɪ'koʃəs
precocity prɪ'kasətɪ; ES+-'kɒs-
preconceive ˌprikən'siv |-d -d
preconception ˌprikən'sɛpʃən
preconcert n pri'kansɝt, -sɚt; ES -'kansɝt,
    -'kɒn-, -sɝt, -sət
preconcert v ˌprikən'sɝt; ES -'sɝt, -'sɝt; |-ed
    -ɪd
precontract n pri'kantrækt; ES+-'kɒn-
precontract v ˌprikən'trækt, pri'kantrækt;
    ES+-'kɒn-; |-ed -ɪd
precook pri'kʊk |-ed -t
precool pri'kul |-ed -d
precursor prɪ'kɝsɚ; ES -'kɝsə(r, -'kɝsə(r
precursory prɪ'kɝsərɪ; ES -'kɝs-, -'kɝs-
predaceous, -cious prɪ'deʃəs |-city -'dæsətɪ
predate pri'det |-dated -'detɪd
predatory 'prɛdəˌtorɪ, -ˌtɔrɪ; S -ˌtorɪ; |-rily
    -rəlɪ, -rɪlɪ, emph+ˌpreda'torily
predecessor ˌprɛdɪ'sɛsɚ, 'prɛdɪˌsɛsɚ; ES -sə(r
predestinarian prɪˌdɛstə'nɛrɪən, -'ner- |-ism
    -ˌɪzəm
predestinate adj prɪ'dɛstənɪt
predestinate v prɪ'dɛstəˌnet |-nated -ˌnetɪd
predestination prɪˌdɛstə'neʃən, ˌpridɛstə-
predestine prɪ'dɛstɪn |-d -d

predetermine ˌpridɪ'tɝmɪn; ES -'tɝm-, -'tɝm-;
    |-d -d
predial 'pridɪəl |-ity ˌpridɪ'ælətɪ
predicable 'prɛdɪkəbļ |-bly -blɪ
predicament prɪ'dɪkəmənt |-al prɪˌdɪkə-
    'mɛntļ
predicate n, adj 'prɛdɪkɪt, -ət
predicate v 'prɛdɪˌket |-d -ɪd
predication ˌprɛdɪ'keʃən |-tive 'prɛdɪˌketɪv
predict prɪ'dɪkt |-ed -ɪd |-ction -kʃən
predigest ˌpridə'dʒɛst, -daɪ- |-ed -ɪd
predilection ˌprɪdļ'ɛkʃən, ˌprɛd-
predispose ˌpridɪs'poz |-s -ɪz |-d -d |- dly -ɪdlɪ
predisposition ˌpridɪspə'zɪʃən
predominance prɪ'damənəns; ES+-'dɒm-;
    |-cy -ɪ |-nant -nənt
predominate prɪ'daməˌnet; ES+-'dɒm-; |-d
    -ɪd
predomination prɪˌdamə'neʃən; ES+-ˌdɒm-
pre-eminence prɪ'ɛmənəns |-cy -ɪ |-nent -nənt
pre-empt prɪ'ɛmpt |-ed -ɪd |-ption -pʃən
preen prin |preened prind
pre-exist ˌprɪɪg'zɪst |-ed -ɪd |-ence -əns
preface 'prɛfɪs, -əs |-s -ɪz |-d -t
prefatorial ˌprɛfə'torɪəl, -'tɔr-; S -'tor-
prefatory 'prɛfəˌtorɪ, -ˌtɔrɪ; S -ˌtorɪ
prefect 'prifɛkt
prefecture 'prifɛktʃɚ; ES -fɛktʃə(r
prefer prɪ'fɝ; ES -'fɝ(r, -'fɝ; |-red -d
preferability ˌprɛfərə'bɪlətɪ
preferable 'prɛfrəbļ, 'prɛfərə- |-bly -blɪ
preference 'prɛfrəns, 'prɛfərəns |-s -ɪz
preferential ˌprɛfə'rɛnʃəl |-ly -ɪ
preferment prɪ'fɝmənt; ES -'fɝ-, -'fɝ-
prefiguration prɪˌfɪgjə'reʃən, -fɪgə-, prɪˌfɪg-
prefigure pri'fɪgɚ, -'fɪgɚ; ES -ə(r; |-d -d
prefix n 'priˌfɪks |-es -ɪz
prefix v pri'fɪks |-es -ɪz |-ed -t
pregnable 'prɛgnəbļ
pregnance 'prɛgnəns |-cy -ɪ |-nant -nənt
preheat pri'hit |-heated -'hitɪd
prehensile prɪ'hɛnsļ, -sɪl
prehistoric ˌprɪɪs'torɪk, ˌprihɪs-, -'tar-, -'tɒr-
    |-al -ļ |-ally -ļɪ, -ɪklɪ
preignition ˌprɪɪg'nɪʃən
prejudge pri'dʒʌdʒ |-s -ɪz |-d -d
prejudice 'prɛdʒədɪs |-s -ɪz |-d -t
prejudicial ˌprɛdʒə'dɪʃəl |-ly -ɪ
pre-judicial ˌpridʒu'dɪʃəl, -dʒɪu-

|full fʊl |tooth tuθ |further 'fɝðɚ; ES 'fɝðə |custom 'kʌstəm |while hwaɪl |how haʊ |toy tɔɪ
|using 'juzɪŋ |fuse fjuz, fɪuz |dish dɪʃ |vision 'vɪʒən |Eden 'idn̩ |cradle 'kredļ |keep 'em 'kipm̩

prelacy 'prɛləsɪ
prelate 'prɛlɪt |-tism -ˌɪzəm
preliminary prɪ'lɪməˌnɛrɪ
prelude 'prɛljud, 'pri-, 'prɪlud, 'prɪlɪud |-d -ɪd
premarital pri'mærət|
premature ˌprimə'tjʊr, -'tɪʊr, -'tʊr, 'priməˌt-,
   -ˌtʃʊr; ES -ə(r; ('premaˌture 'death)
premedical pri'mɛdɪk|
premeditate prɪ'mɛdəˌtet |-tated -ˌtetɪd
premeditation ˌprimɛdə'teʃən, prɪˌmɛdə-
premier n 'primɪɚ, prɪ'mɪr; ES 'primɪ·ə(r,
   prɪ'mɪə(r; Brit+'prɛmɪ·ə(r, -mjə(r
premier adj 'primɪɚ; ES 'primɪ·ə(r; Brit+
   'prɛmɪ·ə(r, -mjə(r
première prɪ'mɪr; ES -'mɪə(r; (Fr prə'mjɛːr)
premise, -iss n 'prɛmɪs |-s -ɪz
premise v prɪ'maɪz, 'prɛmɪs |-s -ɪz |-d -d, -t
premium 'primɪəm
premolar pri'molɚ; ES -'molə(r
premonition ˌprimə'nɪʃən
premonitory prɪ'mɑnəˌtorɪ, -ˌtɔrɪ; S -ˌtorɪ,
   ES+-'mɒn-
prenatal pri'net| |-ly -ɪ
Prendergast 'prɛndɚˌgæst; ES 'prɛndə-
prentice, 'p-, P- 'prɛntɪs |-s -ɪz |-d -t
preoccupation priˌɑkjə'peʃən, ˌpriɑkjə-; ES+
   -ˌɒk-, -ɒk-
preoccupy pri'ɑkjəˌpaɪ; ES+-'ɒk-; |-pied
   -ˌpaɪd
preordain ˌpriɔr'den; ES -ɔə'den; |-ed -d
preordination ˌpriɔrdn̩'eʃən; ES -ɔdn̩'eʃən
prepaid pri'ped ('preˌpaid 'charges)
preparation ˌprɛpə'reʃən
preparative prɪ'pærətɪv
preparatory prɪ'pærəˌtorɪ, -ˌtɔrɪ; S -ˌtorɪ
prepare prɪ'pɛr, -'pær; E -'pɛə(r, ES -'pæə(r;
   |-d -d |-dness -ɪdnɪs, -dnɪs
prepay pri'pe |-paid -'ped ('preˌpay 'rent)
prepense prɪ'pɛns |-s -ɪz |-d -t
preponderance prɪ'pɑndrəns, -dərəns; ES+
   -'pɒn-; |-cy -ɪ |-ant -ənt
preponderate prɪ'pɑndəˌret; ES+-'pɒn-; |-d
   -ɪd
preposition gram. ˌprɛpə'zɪʃən |-al -| |-ally -ɪ
preposition 'position before' ˌpripə'zɪʃən
prepossess ˌpripə'zɛs |-es -ɪz |-ed -t
prepossessing ˌpripə'zɛsɪŋ ('prepos̩sessing
   'eye)
prepossession ˌpripə'zɛʃən

preposterous prɪ'pɑstrəs, -tərəs; ES+-'pɒs-
prepotence prɪ'potn̩s |-cy -ɪ |-tent -tn̩t
preprint pri'prɪnt, 'priˌprɪnt
preprofessional ˌpriprə'fɛʃən|, ˌpripə-, -'fɛʃnəl
   —In the 2d pron. r is lost by dissimilation
   (§121).
prepuce 'pripjus, -pɪus |-s -ɪz
Pre-Raphaelite, pre-R- prɪ'ræfɪəˌlaɪt, -'ræfjə-,
   -'ræfə-
prerequisite pri'rɛkwəzɪt
prerogative prɪ'rɑgətɪv, -'rɒg- |-d -d
presage n 'prɛsɪdʒ |-s -ɪz, in Shak. prɪ'sɛdʒ
presage v prɪ'sɛdʒ |-s -ɪz |-d -d |- r -ɚ; ES -ə(r
presbyopia ˌprɛzbɪ'opɪə
presbyter 'prɛzbɪtɚ; ES -tə(r; |-y -bɪˌtɛrɪ
Presbyterian ˌprɛzbə'tɪrɪən |-ism -ˌɪzəm
preschool pri'skul ('preˌschool 'training)
prescience 'prɛʃɪəns, 'pri- |-ent -ənt
pre-science pri'saɪəns
prescind prɪ'sɪnd |-ed -ɪd
prescission prɪ'sɪʒən, -'sɪʃən
Prescot, -tt 'prɛskət
prescribe prɪ'skraɪb |-d -d
prescript adj prɪ'skrɪpt ('preˌscript 'rule)
prescript n 'priskrɪpt
prescription prɪ'skrɪpʃən, pɚ'skrɪpʃən
prescriptive prɪ'skrɪptɪv
presence 'prɛzn̩s |-s -ɪz |-d -t
present n 'prɛzn̩t; mil. prɪ'zɛnt
present v prɪ'zɛnt |-ed -ɪd
presentable prɪ'zɛntəb| |-bly -blɪ
presentation ˌprɛzn̩'teʃən, ˌprizɛn'teʃən
presentative prɪ'zɛntətɪv
present-day 'prɛzn̩t'de ('present-ˌday 'laws)
presentiment prɪ'zɛntəmənt
presentment prɪ'zɛntmənt
preservation ˌprɛzɚ'veʃən; ES ˌprɛzə-
preservative prɪ'zɝvətɪv; ES -'zɜv-, -'zɝv-
preserve prɪ'zɝv; ES -'zɜv, -'zɝv; |-d -d
preshow pri'ʃo |-ed -'ʃod |-n -'ʃon or -ed -'ʃod
preside prɪ'zaɪd |-d -ɪd
presidency 'prɛzədənsɪ, 'prɛzdən- |-dent
   -dənt
presidential ˌprɛzə'dɛnʃəl |-ly -ɪ
presidio prɪ'sɪdɪˌo (Sp pre'siðjo)
Presque Isle Me, Pa ˌprɛsk'aɪl, Mich -'il
press prɛs |presses 'prɛsɪz |pressed prɛst
pressmark 'prɛsˌmark; ES -ˌmaːk, E+
   -ˌmaːk; |-ed -t

pressroom 'prɛsˌrum, -ˌrʊm

pressure 'prɛʃɚ; ES 'prɛʃə(r

presswork 'prɛsˌwɜˑk; ES -ˌwɜk, -ˌwɜˑk

Prester John 'prɛstɚ'dʒan, -'dʒɒn; ES -tə-

prestidigitation ˌprɛstɪˌdɪdʒɪ'teʃən

prestidigitate ˌprɛstɪ'dɪdʒɪˌtet |-d -ɪd

prestidigitator ˌprɛstɪ'dɪdʒɪˌtetɚ; ES -tə(r

prestige 'prɛstɪdʒ, prɛs'tiʒ (Fr prɛs'ti:ʒ)

prestissimo prɛs'tɪsəˌmo (It pres'tissiˌmo)

presto 'prɛsto

Preston 'prɛstən

Prestwich 'prɛstwɪtʃ, loc.+-tɪdʒ |-'s -ɪz

Prestwick 'prɛstwɪk, 'prɛstɪk

presumable prɪ'zuməb|, -'zɪum-, -zjum- |-bly -blɪ

presume prɪ'zum, -'zɪum, -'zjum |-d -d |-dly -ɪdlɪ

presumption prɪ'zʌmpʃən |-tive -tɪv |-tuous -tʃuəs

presuppose ˌprisə'poz |-s -ɪz |-d -d

presupposition ˌprisʌpə'zɪʃən

pretence prɪ'tɛns |-s -ɪz

pretend prɪ'tɛnd |-ed -ɪd |-ant -ənt

pretender, P- prɪ'tɛndɚ; ES -'tɛndə(r

pretense prɪ'tɛns |-s -ɪz

pretension prɪ'tɛnʃən |-tentious -'tɛnʃəs

preterit, -ite 'prɛtərɪt |-ive prɪ'tɛrətɪv

pretermission ˌpritɚ'mɪʃən; ES ˌpritə-

pretermit ˌpritɚ'mɪt; ES ˌpritə-; |-ted -ɪd

preternatural ˌpritɚ'nætʃərəl, -tʃrəl; ES ˌpritə-; |-ly -ɪ

pretext n 'pritɛkst |adj -ed 'pritɛkstɪd

pretext v prɪ'tɛkst |-ed -ɪd

pretor 'pritɚ; ES 'pritə(r

Pretoria prɪ'torɪə, -'tɔr-; S -'tor-

pretorian prɪ'torɪən, -'tɔr-; S -'tor-

prettify 'prɪtɪˌfaɪ -fied -ˌfaɪd

pretty stressed 'prɪtɪ, unstr. pɚtɪ['gʊd], prɪtɪ-, prətɪ-, prʊtɪ-, pʊrtɪ-; ES+pətɪ-, pʊtɪ-; the unstressed form pɚtɪ can be heard as the last two syllables of property ['prɑ]pɚtɪ. Another common unstr. form is pɪtɪ-, in which ɪ represents an ɪ with simultaneous retroflexion of the tongue.

pretzel 'prɛtsl̩

prevail prɪ'vel |-ed -d

prevalence 'prɛvələns |-cy -ɪ |-lent -lənt

prevaricate prɪ'værəˌket |-d -ɪd |-tor -ɚ; ES -ə(r

prevarication prɪˌværə'keʃən

prevent prɪ'vɛnt |-ed -ɪd |-able, -ible -əb|

preventability prɪˌvɛntə'bɪlətɪ

preventative prɪ'vɛntətɪv

prevention prɪ'vɛnʃən |-tive -'vɛntɪv

preview n 'priˌvju, -ˌvɪu

preview v prɪ'vju, -'vɪu |-ed -d

previous 'privɪəs, 'privjəs

previse prɪ'vaɪz |-s -ɪz |-d -d

prevision prɪ'vɪʒən |-ed -d |-ing -ʒənɪŋ, -ʒnɪŋ

prevocal pri'vok| |-ly -ɪ

prevocational ˌprivo'keʃən|

prewar prɪ'wɔr; ES -'wɔə(r; ('preˌwar 'price)

prey pre |preyed pred

Priam 'praɪəm

Pribilof 'prɪbəˌlɒf, -ˌlɒf, -ˌlɔf ('Pribiˌlof 'Isls.)

price praɪs |prices 'praɪsɪz |priced praɪst

Prichard 'prɪtʃɚd; ES 'prɪtʃəd

prick prɪk |pricked prɪkt

prickle 'prɪk| |-d -d |-ling 'prɪklɪŋ, -k|ɪŋ

prickly 'prɪklɪ

pride praɪd |prided 'praɪdɪd

pried praɪd

prie-dieu Fr pri'djø

prier from pry 'praɪɚ; ES 'praɪ·ə(r

pries praɪz

priest, P- prist |-ed -ɪd

priestcraft 'prist,kræft; E+-ˌkraft, -ˌkrɑft

priesthood 'prist·hʊd

Priestley 'pristlɪ

prig prɪg |-ged -d |-gery -ərɪ |-gish -ɪʃ

prim prɪm |primmed prɪmd

primacy 'praɪməsɪ

prima donna ˌprimə'dɑnə; ES+-'dɒnə; (It ˌprima'dɔnna)

prima facie 'praɪmə'feʃɪˌi, -'feʃɪ

primage 'praɪmɪdʒ |-s -ɪz

primal 'praɪm|

primarily 'praɪˌmɛrəlɪ, -ɪlɪ, 'praɪmər-, esp. if emph. praɪ'mɛr-, -'mer-

primary 'praɪˌmɛrɪ, -mərɪ

primate 'praɪmɪt, -met

prime praɪm |primed praɪmd

primer 'what primes' 'praɪmɚ; ES -mə(r

primer 'first book,' type 'prɪmɚ; ES 'prɪmə(r

primeval praɪ'miv| |-ly -ɪ |-ism -ˌɪzəm

primitive 'prɪmətɪv |-vism -ˌɪzəm

primogenitor ˌpraɪmə'dʒɛnətɚ; ES -tə(r

primogeniture ˌpraɪmə'dʒɛnətʃɚ; ES -tʃə(r

|full fʊl |tooth tuθ |further 'fɝðɚ; ES 'fɜðə |custom 'kʌstəm |while hwaɪl |how haʊ |toy tɔɪ |using 'juzɪŋ |fuse fjuz, fɪuz |dish dɪʃ |vision 'vɪʒən |Eden 'idn̩ |cradle 'kred| |keep 'em 'kipm̩

Those words below in which the a sound is spelt o are often pronounced with ɒ in E and S

primordial praɪˈmɔrdɪəl; ES -ˈmɔəd-; |-ly -ɪ
primp prɪmp |primped prɪmpt
primrose ˈprɪmˌroz |-s -ɪz -ɪd -d
primula, P- ˈprɪmjʊlə
primus ˈpraɪməs
prince prɪns |-s -ɪz |-d -t
princess ˈprɪnsɪs |-es -ɪz |-cess' -sɪs
princesse prɪnˈsɛs, ˈprɪnsɪs |-(e)s -ɪz
Princeton ˈprɪnstən
principal ˈprɪnsəp| |-ly -p|ɪ, -plɪ
principality ˌprɪnsəˈpælətɪ
principle ˈprɪnsəp| |-d -d |-ling -plɪŋ, -p|ɪŋ
pringle, P- ˈprɪŋg| |-d -d |-ling -glɪŋ, -g|ɪŋ
prink prɪŋk |prinked prɪŋkt
print prɪnt |printed ˈprɪntɪd |-able -əb|
prior, P- ˈpraɪɚ; ES ˈpraɪ·ə(r; |-y -ɪ
prioress ˈpraɪərɪs |-'s -ɪz
priority praɪˈɔrətɪ, -ˈɑr-, -ˈɒr-
Priscian ˈprɪʃɪən, ˈprɪʃən
Priscilla prɪˈsɪlə
prise praɪz |prises ˈpraɪzɪz |prised praɪzd
prism ˈprɪzəm |-ed ˈprɪzəmd
prismatic prɪzˈmætɪk |-al -| |-ally -|ɪ, -ɪklɪ
prison ˈprɪzn̩ |-ed -d |-ing ˈprɪznɪŋ, -zn̩ɪŋ
prisoner ˈprɪznɚ, ˈprɪzn̩ɚ; ES -ə(r
prissy ˈprɪsɪ |prissily ˈprɪs|ɪ, -sɪlɪ
pristine ˈprɪstin, -tɪn, -taɪn
Pritchard ˈprɪtʃɚd; ES ˈprɪtʃəd; |-chett -tʃɪt
prithee ˈprɪðɪ
privacy ˈpraɪvəsɪ |-vate -vɪt
privateer ˌpraɪvəˈtɪr, -vɪ-; ES -ˈtɪə(r, S+
   -ˈtɛə(r
privation praɪˈveʃən
privative ˈprɪvətɪv
privet ˈprɪvɪt
privilege ˈprɪvlɪdʒ, ˈprɪvˌlɪdʒ |-s -ɪz |-d -d
privity ˈprɪvətɪ
privy n, adj ˈprɪvɪ |-vily ˈprɪv|ɪ, -vɪlɪ
prize praɪz |prizes ˈpraɪzɪz |prized praɪzd
pro pro
pro- *unstressed prefix* prə-, pro-. *When wholly
   unstressed in familiar words, the usual pron.
   is* prə-. *It varies from this through* pru-
   to pro- *(with brief* o) *in less familiar words
   or more deliberate style. The pron.* pɒ-, pə-
   is also often heard from cultivated speakers.
proa ˈproə
pro-Ally proˈælaɪ, ˌproəˈlaɪ

probability ˌprɑbəˈbɪlətɪ
probable ˈprɑbəb| |-bly -blɪ
probate ˈprobet |-bated -betɪd
probation proˈbeʃən |-al -| |-ary -ˌɛrɪ
probative ˈprobətɪv, ˈprɑb-
probatory ˈprobəˌtorɪ, -ˌtɔrɪ; S -ˌtorɪ
probe prob |probed probd |-able -əb|
probity ˈprobətɪ, ˈprɑb-
problem ˈprɑbləm, -lɪm, -lɛm
problematic ˌprɑbləˈmætɪk |-al -| |-ally -|ɪ,
   -ɪklɪ
pro bono publico ˈproˈbonoˈpʌblɪˌko
proboscis proˈbɑsɪs |-es -ɪz |L pl -scides
   -ˈbɑsəˌdiz
procedural proˈsidʒərəl
procedure prəˈsidʒɚ; ES -ˈsidʒə(r
proceed prəˈsid |-s -ˈsidz |-ed -ɪd
proceeds n ˈprosidz
process ˈprasɛs, *mainly Brit* ˈprosɛs |-es -ɪz
   |-ed -t
process 'march in procession' proˈsɛs, -ˈsɛʃ
   |-es -ɪz |-ed -t
procession prəˈsɛʃən, pro- |-al -| |-ally -|ɪ
proclaim proˈklem |-claimed -ˈklemd
proclamation ˌprɑkləˈmeʃən
proclitic proˈklɪtɪk
proclivity proˈklɪvətɪ |-tous -təs
proconsul proˈkɑns| |-ar -s|ɚ, -sjələ; ES -lə(r
proconsulate proˈkɑns|ɪt, -ˈkɑnsjəlɪt
procrastinate proˈkræstəˌnet |-nated -ˌnetɪd
procrastination proˌkræstəˈneʃən
procreant ˈprokrɪənt
procreate ˈprokrɪˌet |-d -ɪd |-tive -tɪv
procreation ˌprokrɪˈeʃən
Procrustes proˈkrʌstiz |-tes' -tiz |-tean -tɪən
Procter, proctor, P- ˈprɑktɚ; ES ˈprɑktə(r
Proctorknott ˈprɑktɚˌnɑt; ES ˈprɑktə-
Proculeius ˌprɑkjuˈliəs |-'s -ɪz
procumbent proˈkʌmbənt
procurable proˈkjurəb|, -ˈkɪur-
procuracy ˈprɑkjərəsɪ
procurance proˈkjurəns, -ˈkɪu-
procurator ˈprɑkjəˌretɚ; ES -ˌretə(r
procure proˈkjur, -ˈkɪur |-d -d
Procyon ˈprosɪˌɑn, -sɪən
prod prɑd |prodded ˈprɑdɪd
prodigal ˈprɑdɪg| |-ly -ɪ, -ɪglɪ
prodigality ˌprɑdɪˈgælətɪ

Those words below in which the a *sound is spelt* o *are often pronounced with* ɒ *in E and S*

prodigy 'pradədʒɪ |-digious prə'dɪdʒəs

produce *n* 'pradjus, 'pro-, -dɪus, -dus

produce *v* prə'djus, -'dɪus, -'dus |-s -ɪz |-d -t

producible prə'djusəbļ, -'dɪus-, -'dus-

product 'pradəkt, -dʌkt

production prə'dʌkʃən |-tive -tɪv

productivity ˌprodʌk'tɪvətɪ

proem 'proɛm, -ɪm

profanation ˌprafə'neʃən

profane prə'fen |-faned -'fend |-nity -'fænətɪ

profaneness prə'fennɪs

profess prə'fɛs |-es -ɪz |-ed -t |-edly -ɪdlɪ

profession prə'fɛʃən |-al -ļ, -ʃnəl |-ly -ɪ

professor prə'fɛsɚ; ES -'fɛsə(r; |-ate -ɪt

professorial ˌprofə'sorɪəl, ˌprafə-, -'sɔr-; S -'sor-; |-ly -ɪ

professorship prə'fɛsɚˌʃɪp; ES -'fɛsə-

proffer 'prafɚ; ES 'prafə(r; |-ed -d |-ing 'prafrɪŋ, 'prafərɪŋ

proficiency prə'fɪʃənsɪ |-cient -ʃənt

profile 'profaɪl |-filed -faɪld

profit 'prafɪt |-ed -ɪd

profitable 'prafɪtəbļ, 'praftə- |-bly -blɪ

profiteer ˌprafə'tɪr; ES -'tɪə(r, S+-'tɛə(r; |-ed -d

profligacy 'praflɪgəsɪ |-gate -gɪt, -ˌget

pro forma pro'fɔrmə; ES -'fɔəmə

profound prə'faund |-ness -nɪs, -'faunnɪs

profundity prə'fʌndətɪ

profuse prə'fjus, -'fɪus |-sive -ɪv

profusion prə'fjuʒən, -'fɪu-

progenitor pro'dʒɛnətɚ; ES -'dʒɛnətə(r

progeniture pro'dʒɛnətʃɚ; ES -'dʒɛnətʃə(r

progeny 'pradʒənɪ

prognathic prag'næθɪk

prognathous 'pragnəθəs, prag'neθəs

prognosis prag'nosɪs |-noses -'nosiz

prognostic prag'nastɪk |-al -ļ |-ally -ļɪ, -ɪklɪ

prognosticate prag'nastɪˌket |-cated -ˌketɪd

prognostication pragˌnastɪ'keʃən, ˌpragnastɪ-

program, -mme 'progræm, -grəm |-(me)d -d

progress *n* 'pragrɛs, 'pro-, -grɪs |-es -ɪz

progress *v* prə'grɛs |-es -ɪz |-ed -t

progression prə'grɛʃən |-sive -'grɛsɪv

prohibit pro'hɪbɪt |-ed -ɪd |-ive -ɪv

prohibition ˌproə'bɪʃən

project *n* 'pradʒɛkt, -dʒɪkt

project *v* prə'dʒɛkt |-ed -ɪd |-ction -kʃən

projectile prə'dʒɛktļ, -tɪl

projective prə'dʒɛktɪv |-tor -tɚ; ES -tə(r

Prokosch 'prokaʃ |-'s -ɪz

prolate 'prolet, pro'let

proletarian ˌprolə'tɛrɪən, -'tær-, -'ter- |-iat -ɪət

proliferate pro'lɪfəˌret |-d -ɪd |-rous -rəs

proliferation proˌlɪfə'reʃən

prolific prə'lɪfɪk |-al -ļ |-ally -ļɪ |-ly -lɪ

prolix pro'lɪks |-ity -ətɪ ('proˌlɪx 'style)

prologue, -log 'prolɔg, -lag, -lɒg |-d, -ged -d

prolong prə'lɔŋ, -'lɒŋ; S+-'laŋ; |-ed -d

prolongate prə'lɔŋget, -'lɒŋ-; S+-'laŋ-; |-d -ɪd

prolongation ˌprolɔŋ'geʃən, -lɒŋ-; S+-laŋ-

promenade ˌpramə'ned, -'nad |-d -ɪd

Promethean prə'miθɪən, -θjən

Prometheus prə'miθjəs, -jus, -ɪəs |-'s -ɪz

prominence 'pramənəns |-s -ɪz |-cy -ɪ |-nt -nt

promiscuity ˌpramɪs'kjuətɪ, ˌpro-, -'kɪu-

promiscuous prə'mɪskjuəs

promise 'pramɪs |-s -ɪz |-d -t

promisee ˌpramɪs'i

promisor 'pramɪsˌɔr; ES -ˌɔə(r; (ˌpromɪs'ee & ˌpromɪs'or)

promissory 'praməˌsorɪ, -ˌsɔrɪ; S -ˌsorɪ

promontory 'pramənˌtorɪ, -ˌtɔrɪ; S -ˌtorɪ

promote prə'mot |-d -ɪd |-tion prə'moʃən

prompt prampt |prompted 'pramptɪd

promptitude 'pramptəˌtjud, -ˌtɪud, -ˌtud

promulgate prə'mʌlget |-d -ɪd—'praməlˌget *is mainly Brit.*

promulgation ˌpramʌl'geʃən—ˌpraməl- *is mainly Brit.*

prone pron |proned prond |proneness 'pronnɪs

prong prɔŋ, prɒŋ; S+praŋ; |-ed -d

pronominal prə'namənļ, pro- |-ly -ɪ

pronoun 'pronaun

pronounce prə'nauns, pɚ- |-s -ɪz |-d -t |-dly -ɪdlɪ

pronto 'pranto (*Sp* 'pronto)

pronunciamento prəˌnʌnsɪə'mɛnto, -ˌnʌnʃ-

pronunciation prəˌnʌnsɪ'eʃən, pɚ-, -ˌnʌnʃɪ-

proof pruf |-ed -t—pruf *is often heard, esp. in compounds.*

proofread *v* 'prufˌrid |-read -ˌrɛd

prop prap |propped prapt

propaganda *sg* ˌprapə'gændə |-ed -d

Those words below in which the ɑ sound is spelt o are often pronounced with ɒ in E and S

propagandism ˌprɑpəˈgændɪzəm |-ist -ɪst

propagandum *false sg* ˌprɑpəˈgændəm

propagate ˈprɑpəˌget |-d -ɪd |-tion ˌprɑpə-ˈgeʃən

pro patria proˈpetrɪə

propel prəˈpɛl |-led -d |-lant, -lent -ənt

propensity prəˈpɛnsətɪ

proper ˈprɑpɚ; ES ˈprɑpə(r

property ˈprɑpɚtɪ; ES ˈprɑpətɪ; |-ied -d

prophecy ˈprɑfəsɪ

prophesy ˈprɑfəˌsaɪ |-sied -ˌsaɪd

prophet ˈprɑfɪt |-ess -ɪs |-esses -ɪsɪz

prophetic prəˈfɛtɪk |-al -ḷ |-ally -ḷɪ, -ɪklɪ

prophylactic ˌprofəˈlæktɪk, ˌprɑfə- |-al -ḷ |-ally -ḷɪ, -ɪklɪ |-laxis -ˈlæksɪs

propinquity proˈpɪŋkwətɪ, -ˈpɪŋ-

propitiate *adj* prəˈpɪʃɪɪt, -ɪˌet

propitiate *v* prəˈpɪʃɪˌet |-ated -ˌetɪd

propitiatory prəˈpɪʃɪəˌtorɪ, -ˌtɔrɪ; S -ˌtorɪ

propitious prəˈpɪʃəs

proponent prəˈponənt

Propontic proˈpɑntɪk

proportion prəˈporʃən, -ˈpɔr-; ES -ˈpoə-, E+-ˈpɔə-; |-ed -d |-able -əbḷ, -ʃnəbḷ |-bly -blɪ |-al -ḷ, -ʃnəl |-ally -ḷɪ, -ʃnəlɪ |-ate -ɪt, -ʃnɪt—*A dissimilated form* pəˈporʃən *is sometimes heard* (§121).

propose prəˈpoz |-s -ɪz |-d -d |-sal -zḷ

proposition ˌprɑpəˈzɪʃən |-al -ḷ |-ally -ḷɪ

propound prəˈpaʊnd |-ed -ɪd

propraetor, -pret- proˈpritɚ; ES -ˈpritə(r

proprietary prəˈpraɪəˌtɛrɪ

proprietor prəˈpraɪətɚ, pəˈpraɪ-; ES -tə(r; |-tress -trɪs—*The 2d pron. is due to r-dissimilation* (§121).

propriety prəˈpraɪətɪ—*A dissimilated pron.* pəˈpraɪətɪ *is probably less freq. than* ˌɪmpə-ˈpraɪətɪ *and* pəˈpraɪətɚ (§121).

propulsion prəˈpʌlʃən |-sive -sɪv

propylaeum ˌprɑpəˈliəm |-laea -ˈliə

pro rata proˈretə

prorate *n* ˈproret, *v* proˈret |-rated -ˈretɪd

prorogue proˈrog |-d -d |-gation ˌprorəˈgeʃən

prosaic proˈze·ɪk |-al -ḷ |-ally -ḷɪ, -ɪklɪ

prosateur ˌprozəˈtɜ; ES -ˈtɜ(r, -ˈtɜ; (*Fr* prozaˈtœːr)

proscenium proˈsinɪəm

proscribe proˈskraɪb |-d -d

proscription proˈskrɪpʃən |-tive -tɪv

prose proz |proses ˈprozɪz |prosed prozd

prosecute ˈprɑsɪˌkjut, -ˌkɪut |-d -ɪd

prosecution ˌprɑsɪˈkjuʃən, -ˈkɪu-

prosecutor ˈprɑsɪˌkjutɚ, -ˌkɪu-; ES -tə(r

proselyte ˈprɑsḷˌaɪt |-d -ɪd |-tism -aɪtˌɪzəm |-tist -ˌaɪtɪst

Proserpina proˈsɝpɪnə; ES -ˈsɜp-, -ˈsɝp-; |-ne -ˌni, ˈprɑsɚˌpaɪn; ES -sə-

prosit ˈprosɪt (*Ger* ˈproːzɪt)

proslavery proˈslevrɪ, -vərɪ |-ryism -ˌɪzəm

prosodist ˈprɑsədɪst |-dy -dɪ

prospect ˈprɑspɛkt |-ed -ɪd |-ive prəˈspɛktɪv

prospector ˈprɑspɛktɚ, prəˈspɛk-; ES -tə(r

prospectus prəˈspɛktəs, prɑ- |-es -ɪz

prosper ˈprɑspɚ; ES -pə(r; |-ed -d |-ing ˈprɑspərɪŋ, ˈprɑsprɪŋ |-ous -prəs, -pərəs

prosperity prɑsˈpɛrətɪ

Prospero ˈprɑspəˌro

Prospice ˈprɑspɪˌsi

prostate ˈprɑstet |-tic proˈstætɪk

prostitute ˈprɑstəˌtjut, -ˌtrut, -ˌtut |-d -ɪd

prostitution ˌprɑstəˈtjuʃən, -ˈtɪu-, -ˈtu-

prostrate ˈprɑstret |-d -ɪd |-tion prɑˈstreʃən

prosy ˈprozɪ

protagonist proˈtægənɪst |-nism -ˌɪzəm

Protagoras proˈtægərəs |-'s -ɪz

protean *adj* ˈprotɪən, proˈtiən

protean *n chem.* ˈprotɪən

protect prəˈtɛkt |-ed -ɪd |-ion -kʃən |-ive -ɪv

protector prəˈtɛktɚ; ES -tə(r; |-ate -ɪt, -trɪt

protégé, -ée ˈprotəˌʒe, ˌprotəˈʒe (*Fr* prŏteˈʒe)

proteid ˈprotiɪd |-ide -ˌaɪd, -ɪd

protein ˈprotiɪn

pro tem proˈtɛm |pro tempore proˈtɛmpəˌri

Proterozoic ˌprɑtərəˈzo·ɪk

protest *n* ˈprotɛst

protest *v* prəˈtɛst |-ed -ɪd

protestant, P- ˈprɑtɪstənt |-ism -ˌɪzəm

protestation ˌprɑtəsˈteʃən

Proteus ˈprotjus, ˈprotɪəs |-'s -ɪz

prothalamion, P- ˌproθəˈlemɪˌan, -ən

Prothero ˈprɑðəˌro

prothonotary proˈθɑnəˌtɛrɪ, ˌproθəˈnotərɪ

protocol ˈprotəˌkal, -ˌkɒl

proton ˈprotan

protoplasm ˈprotəˌplæzəm |-ic ˌprotəˈplæzmɪk

prototype ˈprotəˌtaɪp

Key: *See in full §§3–47.* bee bi |pity ˈpɪtɪ (§6) |rate ret |yet jɛt |sang sæŋ |angry ˈæŋ·grɪ |bath bæθ; E baθ (§10) |ah ɑ |far fɑr |watch watʃ, wɒtʃ (§12) |jaw dʒɔ |gorge gɔrdʒ |go go

Those words below in which the ɑ sound is spelt o are often pronounced with ɒ in E and S

prototypic ˌprotəˈtɪpɪk |-al -] |-ally -|ɪ, -ɪklɪ
Protozoa, p- ˌprotəˈzoə |-n -n |-zoic -ˈzo·ɪk
protract proˈtrækt |-ed -ɪd |-ile -], -ɪl
protraction proˈtrækʃən |-tor -tɚ; ES -tə(r
protrude proˈtrud, -ˈtrɪʊd |-d -ɪd
protrusion proˈtruʒən, -ˈtrɪʊ- |-sive -sɪv
protuberance proˈtjubərəns, -ˈtɪʊ-, -ˈtu- |-s
  -ɪz |-ant -ənt
proud praʊd
Proust prust
prove pruv |-d -d |-d -d *or* -n -ən
provenance ˈpravənəns
Provençal ˌprovənˈsal, ˌprav- (*Fr* prɔ̃vãˈsal)
Provence ˈpravɛns, proˈvans |-'s -ɪz (*Fr*
  prɔ̃vã:s)
provender ˈpravəndɚ; ES ˈpravəndə(r; |-ed -d
provenience proˈvinɪəns, -njəns |-ent -ənt
proverb ˈpravɝb, -ɚb; ES -3b, -ɝb, -əb |-ed -d
proverbial prəˈvɝbɪəl; ES -ˈvɝb-, -ˈvɝb-;
  |-ly -ɪ
provide prəˈvaɪd |-vided -ˈvaɪdɪd
providence, P- ˈpravədəns |-'s -ɪz |-nt -nt
providential ˌpravəˈdɛnʃəl |-ly -ɪ
province ˈpravɪns |-s -ɪz
Provincetown ˈpravɪnsˌtaʊn
provincial prəˈvɪnʃəl |-ly -ɪ |-ism -ˌɪzəm
provinciality prəˌvɪnʃɪˈælətɪ
provision prəˈvɪʒən |-ed -d |-al -] |-ally -|ɪ
proviso prəˈvaɪzo |-r prəˈvaɪzɚ; ES -zə(r
provocation ˌpravəˈkeʃən |-tive prəˈvakətɪv
provoke prəˈvok |-d -t
provost ˈpravəst |p- marshal ˈprovoˈmarʃəl;
  ES -ˈmɑːʃ-, E+-ˈmɑːʃ-
prow praʊ |prowed praʊd
Prowers ˈproɚz; ES ˈpro·əz; |-'s -ɪz |-ite -ˌaɪt
prowess ˈpraʊɪs |-ed -t
prowl praʊl |prowled praʊld |-er -ɚ; ES -ə(r
proximal ˈpraksəm] |-ly -ɪ |-mate *adj* -mɪt
proximate *v* ˈpraksəˌmet |-d -ɪd
proximity prakˈsɪmətɪ
proxy ˈpraksɪ |proxied ˈpraksɪd
prude prud, prɪʊd |-ry -ərɪ |-dish -ɪʃ
prudence, P- ˈprudn̩s, ˈprɪʊdn̩s |-'s -ɪz |-nt -n̩t
prudential, P- pruˈdɛnʃəl, prɪʊ- |-ly -ɪ
prune prun, prɪʊn |-d -d
prunella, P- pruˈnɛlə, prɪʊ-
prunes and prism ˈprunzn̩ˈprɪzəm, ˈprɪʊnz-
prurience ˈprurɪəns, ˈprɪʊ- |-cy -ɪ |-ent -ənt

Prussia ˈprʌʃə |-n -n
prussic ˈprʌsɪk
pry, P- praɪ |pried praɪd
Prynne prɪn
Pryor ˈpraɪɚ; ES ˈpraɪ·ə(r
prythee ˈprɪðɪ
Przemyśl ˈpʃɛmɪʃ], -s]
psalm sɑm |psalmed sɑmd |-ist -ɪst
psalmody ˈsɑmədɪ, ˈsælmədɪ
Psalter, p- ˈsɔltɚ; ES ˈsɔltə(r
psaltery ˈsɔltrɪ, ˈsɔltərɪ
pseudo ˈsjudo, ˈsɪʊ-, ˈsu- |-nym -dn̩ˌɪm
pseudonymous sjuˈdanəməs, sɪʊ-, su-
pshaw ʃɔ |pshawed ʃɔd
psi saɪ (*Gk* psi)
psoriasis səˈraɪəsɪs
Psyche ˈsaɪkɪ
psychiatric ˌsaɪkɪˈætrɪk |-al -] |-ally -|ɪ, -ɪklɪ
psychiatry saɪˈkaɪətrɪ |-trist -trɪst
psychic ˈsaɪkɪk |-al -] |-ally -|ɪ, -ɪklɪ
psychoanalysis ˌsaɪkoəˈnæləsɪs
psychoanalyst ˌsaɪkoˈæn]ɪst
psychoanalytic ˌsaɪkoˌæn]ˈɪtɪk |-al -] |-ally
  -|ɪ, -ɪklɪ
psychoanalyze ˌsaɪkoˈæn]ˌaɪz |-s -ɪz |-d -d
psychological ˌsaɪkəˈladʒɪk] |-ly -ɪ, ɪklɪ
psychologism saɪˈkaləˌdʒɪzəm
psychologize saɪˈkaləˌdʒaɪz |-s -ɪz |-d -d |-gy
  -dʒɪ
psychometry saɪˈkamətrɪ
psychoneurosis ˌsaɪko·njʊˈrosɪs, -nɪʊ-, -nʊ-
  |-roses -ˈrosiz
psychopath ˈsaɪkəˌpæθ |-ths -θs
psychopathic ˌsaɪkəˈpæθɪk
psychopathology ˌsaɪkopəˈθalədʒɪ
psychopathy saɪˈkapəθɪ
psychosis saɪˈkosɪs |-choses -ˈkosiz
psychotherapy ˌsaɪkoˈθɛrəpɪ
ptarmigan ˈtarməgən; ES ˈtɑːm-, E+ˈtɑːm-
pteridophyte ˈtɛrədoˌfaɪt
pterodactyl ˌtɛrəˈdæktɪl, -t]
Ptolemaic ˌtaləˈme·ɪk |-al -]
Ptolemy ˈtaləmɪ
ptomaine, -ain ˈtomen, toˈmen
ptosis ˈtosɪs
ptyalin ˈtaɪəlɪn
pub pʌb
puberty ˈpjubɚtɪ, ˈpɪʊ-; ES -bətɪ

|full fʊl |tooth tuθ |further ˈfɝðɚ; ES ˈfɝðə |custom ˈkʌstəm |while hwaɪl |how haʊ |toy tɔɪ
|using ˈjuzɪŋ |fuse fjuz, fɪʊz |dish dɪʃ |vision ˈvɪʒən |Eden ˈidn̩ |cradle ˈkred] |keep 'em ˈkipm̩

pubescence pju'bɛsn̩s, pɪu- |-cy -ɪ |-nt -n̩t
pubic 'pjubɪk, 'pɪu-
pubis 'pjubɪs, 'pɪu- |-bes -biz
public 'pʌblɪk
publican 'pʌblɪkən
publication ˌpʌblɪ'keʃən
publicist 'pʌblɪsɪst
publicity pʌb'lɪsətɪ, pə'blɪs-
publicize 'pʌblɪˌsaɪz |-s -ɪz |-d -d
publish 'pʌblɪʃ |-es -ɪz |-ed -t
Publius 'pʌblɪəs |-'s -ɪz
Puccini pu'tʃinɪ (It put'tʃi:ni)
Puccinia pʌk'sɪnɪə
puce pjus, pɪus
Pucelle, La læpju'sɛl, -pɪu- (Fr lapy'sɛl)
puck, P- pʌk |-ish -ɪʃ
pucka 'pʌkə
pucker 'pʌkɚ; ES 'pʌkə(r; |-ed -d |-ing
    'pʌkrɪŋ, 'pʌkərɪŋ
pudding 'pʊdɪŋ, humorous 'pʊdn̩
puddle 'pʌdl̩ |-d -d |-ling 'pʌdlɪŋ, 'pʌdl̩ɪŋ
puddly 'pʌdlɪ, 'pʌdl̩ɪ
pudd'nhead, P- 'pʌdn̩ˌhɛd
pudency 'pjudn̩sɪ, 'pɪu- |-dent -dn̩t
pudendum pju'dɛndəm, pɪu- |-da -də
pudgy 'pʌdʒɪ
Pueblo, p- 'pwɛblo, loc. pju'ɛblo, pɪu-
puerile 'pjuəˌrɪl, 'pɪu-, -rəl
puerility ˌpjuə'rɪlətɪ, ˌpɪuə-
puerperal pju'ɝpərəl, pɪu-; ES -'ɜp-, -'ɜˑp-
Puerto Rico ˌpwɛrtə'riko |-can -kən
puff, P- pʌf |-ed -t |-ball -ˌbɔl
puffin 'pʌfɪn
pug pʌg |pugged pʌgd
Puget 'pjudʒɪt, 'pɪu-
Pugh(e) pju, pɪu
pugilism 'pjudʒəˌlɪzəm, 'pɪu- |-list -lɪst
pugilistic ˌpjudʒə'lɪstɪk, ˌpɪu- |-al -l̩ |-ally -l̩ɪ,
    -ɪklɪ
pugnacious pʌg'neʃəs |-nacity -'næsətɪ
pug-nosed 'pʌg'nozd ('pug-ˌnosed 'lassie)
puisne 'pjunɪ, 'pɪunɪ
puissance 'pjuɪsn̩s, 'pɪu-, pju'ɪsn̩s, pɪu-,
    'pwɪsn̩s |-sant -sn̩t
puke pjuk, pɪuk |-d -t
pukka 'pʌkə
Pulaski Count pu'læskaɪ, -kɪ; US pə'læskaɪ
pulchritude 'pʌlkrɪˌtjud, -ˌtɪud, -ˌtud
pulchritudinous ˌpʌlkrɪ'tjudn̩əs, -'tɪud-, -'tud-

pule pjul, pɪul |-d -d
Pulitzer 'pjulɪtsɚ, 'pɪu-, formerly 'pʊl-; ES
    -sə(r
pull pʊl |pulled pʊld
pullet 'pʊlɪt
pulley 'pʊlɪ
Pullman 'pʊlmən |-s -z
pull-over n 'pʊlˌovɚ; ES -ˌovə(r
pullulate 'pʌljəˌlet |-d -ɪd |-tion ˌpʌljə'leʃən
pulmonary 'pʌlməˌnɛrɪ
Pulmotor, p- 'pʌlˌmotɚ, 'pʊl-; ES -ˌmotə(r
pulp pʌlp |pulped pʌlpt
pulpit 'pʊlpɪt |-ed -ɪd |-er -ɚ; ES -ə(r
pulpiteer ˌpʊlpɪt'ɪr; ES -'ɪə(r, S+-'ɛə(r
pulpwood 'pʌlpˌwʊd
pulque 'pʊlkɪ, 'pulke
pulsate 'pʌlset |-d -ɪd |-tion pʌl'seʃən
pulsatile 'pʌlsətl̩, -tɪl
pulse pʌls |pulses 'pʌlsɪz |pulsed pʌlst
Pulteney 'pʌltnɪ, 'pɒlt-
pulverization ˌpʌlvərə'zeʃən, -aɪ'z-
pulverize 'pʌlvəˌraɪz |-s -ɪz |-d -d
puma 'pjumə, 'pɪu-
pumice 'pʌmɪs |-s -ɪz |-d -t
pumice-stone 'pʌmɪsˌston, 'pʌmɪˌston
pummel 'pʌml̩ |-ed -d
pummice 'pʌmɪs |-s -ɪz
pump pʌmp |pumped pʌmpt
pumpernickel 'pʌmpɚˌnɪkl̩; ES 'pʌmpə-
pumpkin 'pʌmpkɪn, 'pʌŋkɪn—A L.A. in-
    formant said, "We were drilled in school not
    to say 'pʌŋkɪn," eloquent testimony to its
    prevalence. The two prons. are almost
    equally common. Both are phonetically
    normal. 'pʌŋkɪn is historically parallel to
    'pʌmpkɪn, both being normal phonetic de-
    velopments from earlier 'pʌmkɪn (pumkin).
    Cf §124.11.
pumpkin-headed 'pʌŋkɪn'hɛdɪd
pun pʌn |punned pʌnd
punch, P- pʌntʃ |-es -ɪz |-ed -t
Punch-and-Judy 'pʌntʃən'dʒudɪ, -'dʒɪu-
puncheon 'pʌntʃən
punchinello ˌpʌntʃə'nɛlo
punctilio pʌŋk'tɪlɪˌo |-tilious -'tɪlɪəs, -ljəs
punctual 'pʌŋktʃuəl, -tʃʊl |-ly -ɪ |-ity
    ˌpʌŋktʃu'ælətɪ
punctuate 'pʌŋktʃuˌet |-d -ɪd
punctuation ˌpʌŋktʃu'eʃən

Key: See in full §§3–47. bee bi |pity 'pɪtɪ (§6) |rate ret |yet jɛt |sang sæŋ |angry 'æŋ·gɪɪ
|bath bæθ; E baθ (§10) |ah ɑ |far fɑr |watch wɑtʃ, wɒtʃ (§12) |jaw dʒɔ |gorge gɔrdʒ |go go

puncture 'pʌŋktʃɚ; ES 'pʌŋktʃə(r; |-d -d
|-ring 'pʌŋktʃərɪŋ, 'pʌŋktʃrɪŋ
pundit 'pʌndɪt |-ical pʌn'dɪtɪk|
pung pʌŋ |punged pʌŋd
pungence 'pʌndʒəns |-cy -ɪ |-gent -dʒənt
Punic 'pjunɪk, 'pɪu-
punish 'pʌnɪʃ |-es -ɪz |-ed -t |-able -əb|
punitive 'pjunətɪv, 'pɪu-
Punjab pʌn'dʒɑb |-i -ɪ
punk pʌŋk
punkah, -ka 'pʌŋkə
punkin 'pʌŋkɪn
punster 'pʌnstɚ; ES 'pʌnstə(r
punt pʌnt |punted 'pʌntɪd
Punxsutawney ˌpʌŋksə'tɔnɪ
puny 'pjunɪ, 'pɪu-
pup pʌp |pupped pʌpt |-py -ɪ
pupa 'pjupə, 'pɪu- |-l -p|
pupil 'pjup|, 'pɪu- |-ed -d |-age -ɪdʒ
Pupin pju'pin, pɪu-
puppet 'pʌpɪt
pur pɝ; ES pɜ(r, pɝ; |-red -d
Purbeck 'pɝbɛk; ES 'pɜ-, 'pɝ-
purblind 'pɝˌblaɪnd; ES 'pɜ-, 'pɝ-
Purcell *composer* 'pɝs|; ES 'pɜ-, 'pɝ-
Purcell *Okla* pɚ'sɛl; ES pə'sɛl; *Can* 'pɝs|; ES
  'pɜs|, 'pɝs|
Purchas 'pɝtʃəs; ES 'pɜ-, 'pɝ-; |-'s -ɪz
purchasability ˌpɝtʃəsə'bɪlətɪ; ES ˌpɜ-, ˌpɝ-
purchasable 'pɝtʃəsəb|; ES 'pɜ-, 'pɝ-
purchase 'pɝtʃəs, -ɪs; ES 'pɜ-, 'pɝ-; |-s -ɪz
  |-d -t
purdah 'pɝdə; ES 'pɜ-, 'pɝ-
Purdue pɚ'dju, -'dɪu, -'du; ES pə-
pure pjur, pɪur; ES pjuə(r, pɪuə(r; |-d -d
purebred 'pjur'brɛd, 'pɪur-; ES 'pjuə-,
  'pɪuə-; ('pure,bred 'horse)
purée pju're, pɪu-, 'pjure, 'pɪure (*Fr* py're)
purfle 'pɝf|; ES 'pɜ-, 'pɝ-; |-d -d |-ling -f|ɪŋ,
  -flɪŋ |*n* -flɪŋ
purgation pɝ'geʃən; ES pɜ-, pɝ-
purgatory, P- 'pɝgəˌtorɪ, -ˌtɔrɪ; ES 'pɜgə-
  ˌtorɪ, 'pɝ-, E+-ˌtɔrɪ
purge pɝdʒ; ES pɜdʒ, pɝdʒ; |-s -ɪz |-d -d
purgery 'pɝdʒərɪ; ES 'pɜdʒ-, 'pɝdʒ-
purification ˌpjurəfə'keʃən, ˌpɪurə-
purify 'pjurəˌfaɪ, 'pɪurə- |-fied -ˌfaɪd
Purim 'pjurɪm, 'pɪu-, 'pu- (*Heb* pu'rim)
purism 'pjurɪzəm, 'pɪur- |-ist -ɪst

puristic pju'rɪstɪk, pɪu- |-al -| |-ally -|ɪ, -ɪklɪ
Puritan, p- 'pjurətṇ, 'pɪurə- |-ism -ˌɪzəm
puritanic ˌpjurə'tænɪk, ˌpɪurə- |-al -| |-ally
  -|ɪ, -ɪklɪ
purity 'pjurətɪ, 'pɪurətɪ
purl pɝl; ES pɜl, pɝl; |-ed -d
purlieu 'pɝlu, -lɪu; ES 'pɜ-, 'pɝ-
purloin pɝ'lɔɪn, pɚ-; ES pɜ-, pɝ-, pə-; |-ed -d
purple 'pɝp|; ES 'pɜp-, 'pɝp-; |-d -d |-ling
  -p|ɪŋ, -plɪŋ |-lish -p|ɪʃ, -p|ɪʃ
purport *n* 'pɝport, -pɔrt; ES 'pɜport, 'pɝport,
  E+-pɔət
purport *v* pɚ'port, 'pɝport, -ɔrt; ES pə'poət,
  'pɝport, 'pɝport, E+-ɔət; |-ed -ɪd
purpose 'pɝpəs; ES 'pɜ-, 'pɝ-; |-s -ɪz |-d -t
  |-dly -tlɪ |-sive -ɪv
purr pɝ; ES pɜ(r, pɝ; |-ed -d
purse pɝs; ES pɜs, pɝs; |-s -ɪz |-d -t
purse-proud 'pɝsˌpraud; ES 'pɜs-, 'pɝs-
purser 'pɝsɚ; ES 'pɜsə(r, 'pɝsə(r
purslane 'pɝslɪn, -len; ES 'pɜs-, 'pɝs-
pursuance pɚ'suəns, -'sɪu-, -'sju-; ES pə-;
  |-s -ɪz |-ant -ənt
pursue pɚ'su, -'sɪu, -'sju; ES pə-; |-d -d
  |-suit -t
pursuivant 'pɝswɪvənt; ES 'pɜs-, 'pɝs-
pursy 'pɝsɪ; ES 'pɜsɪ, 'pɝsɪ; *substandard*
  'pʌsɪ
purulence 'pjurələns, 'pɪurə-, -rjələns |-cy -ɪ
  |-lent -lənt
Purvey 'pɝvɪ; ES 'pɜvɪ, 'pɝvɪ
purvey pɚ've; ES pə've; |-ed -d |-ance -əns
purveyor pɚ'veɚ; ES pə've·ə(r
purview 'pɝvju, -vɪu; ES 'pɜ-, 'pɝ-
pus pʌs |*pl* puses 'pʌsɪz
Pusey 'pjuzɪ, 'pɪu- |-ism -ˌɪzəm
push *n, v* puʃ |pushes 'puʃɪz |pushed puʃt
push *intj* puʃ, pʃ & *various other puffs*
pushball 'puʃˌbɔl
pushcart 'puʃˌkɑrt; ES -ˌkɑ:t, E+-ˌkɑ:t
Pushkin 'puʃkɪn
pusillanimity ˌpjusjə'nɪmətɪ, ˌpɪu-
pusillanimous ˌpjusjl'ænəməs, ˌpɪu-
puss pus
pussy '*cat*' 'pusɪ
pussy '*like pus*' 'pʌsɪ
pussy '*pursy*' 'pʌsɪ
pussyfoot 'pusɪˌfut |-ed -ɪd
pustular 'pʌstʃələ; ES -lə(r

|full ful |tooth tuθ |further 'fɝðɚ; ES 'fɝðə |custom 'kʌstəm |while hwaɪl |how hau |toy tɔɪ
|using 'juzɪŋ |fuse fjuz, fruz |dish dɪʃ |vision 'vɪʒən |Eden 'idṇ |cradle 'kred| |keep 'em 'kipm

pustulation ˌpʌstʃəˈleʃən
pustule ˈpʌstʃʊl |-d -d
put n 'throw,' v 'place' pʊt
put n 'rustic' pʌt
put 'putt' pʌt |putted ˈpʌtɪd
Put pʌt
putative ˈpjutətɪv, ˈpɪu-
Put in Bay ˌpʊtɪnˈbe
Putman ˈpʌtmən
Putnam ˈpʌtnəm |-ney ˈpʌtnɪ
putrefaction ˌpjutrəˈfækʃən, ˌpɪu-
putrefy, -ri- ˈpjutrəˌfaɪ, ˈpɪu- |-fied -ˌfaɪd
putrescence pjuˈtresn̩s, pɪu- |-cy -ɪ |-nt -sn̩t
putrid ˈpjutrɪd, ˈpɪu-
Putsch Ger pʊtʃ
putt pʌt |putted ˈpʌtɪd
puttee ˈpʌtɪ |-d -d
Puttenham ˈpʌtn̩əm, ˈpʌtnəm—see Putnam
putter 'who putts' ˈpʌtɚ; ES ˈpʌtə(r
putter 'who puts' ˈpʊtɚ; ES ˈpʊtə(r
putter v ˈpʌtɚ; ES ˈpʌtə(r; |-ed -d
putty ˈpʌtɪ |puttied ˈpʌtɪd
Puvis de Chavannes pjuˈvisdəʃəˈvæn, pɪu-
   (Fr pyviːsdəʃaˈvan, pyvidʃaˈvan)
puzzle ˈpʌzl̩ |-d -d |-ling ˈpʌzlɪŋ, ˈpʌzl̩ɪŋ
pyemia, -aemia paɪˈimɪə
Pygmalion pɪgˈmeljən, -lɪən
Pygmy, p- ˈpɪgmɪ |-ied -d
pyjama pəˈdʒæmə, pəˈdʒɑmə |-s -z
pylon ˈpaɪlɑn; ES+-lɒn
pyloric pəˈlɔrɪk, paɪ-, -ˈlɑr-, -ˈlɒr-
pylorus pəˈlorəs, paɪ-, -ˈlɔr-; S -ˈlor-

Pym pɪm
Pynchon, -cheon ˈpɪntʃən
pyorrhea, -rhoea ˌpaɪəˈriə, paɪˈriə
pyramid, P- ˈpɪrəmɪd |-mided -ˌmɪdɪd
pyramidal pɪˈræmədl̩ |-ly -ɪ
Pyramus ˈpɪrəməs |-'s -ɪz
pyre paɪr; ES paɪə(r
Pyrenees ˈpɪrəˌniz |-nean ˌpɪrəˈniən
pyrethrum, P- paɪˈrɛθrəm, -ˈriθ-
pyretic paɪˈrɛtɪk
Pyrex, p- ˈpaɪrɛks
pyridin ˈpɪrədɪn |-dine -ˌdin, -dɪn
pyriform ˈpɪrəˌfɔrm; ES -ˌfɔəm
pyrites pəˈraɪtiz, paɪ-, ˈpaɪraɪts
pyrography paɪˈrɑgrəfɪ, -ˈrɒg-
pyromancy ˈpaɪrəˌmænsɪ
pyromania ˌpaɪrəˈmenɪə
pyrotechnic ˌpaɪrəˈtɛknɪk |-al -l̩ |-ally -lɪ,
   -ɪklɪ |-s -s
Pyrrha ˈpɪrə
pyrrhic, P- ˈpɪrɪk
Pyrrhus ˈpɪrəs |-'s -ɪz
Pythagoras pɪˈθægərəs |-'s -ɪz
Pythagorean pɪˌθægəˈriən
Pythian ˈpɪθɪən
Pythias ˈpɪθɪəs |-'s -ɪz
Pythius ˈpɪθɪəs |-'s -ɪz
Python, p- ˈpaɪθɑn, -θən; ES+-θɒn
pythoness ˈpaɪθənɪs |-'s -ɪz
pyx pɪks |pyxes ˈpɪksɪz |pyxed pɪkst
pyxidium pɪksˈɪdɪəm |-dia -dɪə
pyxie ˈpɪksɪ

Q

Q, q letter kju, kɪu |pl Q's, Qs, poss Q's kjuz,
   kɪuz
Qirghiz kɪrˈgiz; ES kɪə-; |-'s -ɪz
quack kwæk |-ed -t |quackery ˈkwækərɪ, -rɪ
quad kwɑd, kwɒd |-rat -rət
Quadragesima ˌkwɑdrəˈdʒɛsəmə, ˌkwɒd-
quadragesimal ˌkwɑdrəˈdʒɛsəml̩, ˌkwɒd- |-ly -ɪ
quadrangle ˈkwɑdræŋgl̩, ˈkwɒd- |-d -d
quadrant ˈkwɑdrənt, ˈkwɒd- |-al kwɑdˈrænt l̩
quadrate adj, n ˈkwɑdrɪt, ˈkwɒd-, -ret
quadrate v ˈkwɑdret, ˈkwɒd- |-d -ɪd
quadratic kwɑdˈrætɪk, kwɒd-

quadrature ˈkwɑdrətʃɚ, ˈkwɒd-, -ˌtʃʊr; ES
   -tʃə(r, -ˌtʃʊə(r
quadrennial kwɑdˈrɛnɪəl, kwɒd-, -njəl |-ly -ɪ
quadrennium kwɑdˈrɛnɪəm, kwɒd-
quadricentennial ˌkwɑdrɪsɛnˈtɛnɪəl, ˌkwɒd-,
   -njəl |-ly -ɪ
quadrilateral ˌkwɑdrəˈlætərəl, -trəl, ˌkwɒd-
   |-ly -ɪ
quadrille kwəˈdrɪl, kəˈdrɪl |-d -d
quadripartite ˌkwɑdrɪˈpɑrtaɪt, ˌkwɒd-; ES
   -ˈpɑːt-, E+-ˈpɑːt-
quadrisyllabic ˌkwɑdrəsɪˈlæbɪk, ˌkwɒd-

quadrisyllable ˈkwɑdrəˌsɪləbḷ, ˈkwɒd-
quadrivalent ˌkwɑdrəˈvelənt, ˌkwɒd-, kwɑd-
ˈrɪvələnt, kwɒd-
quadrivial kwɑdˈrɪvɪəl, kwɒd- |-vium -vɪəm
quadroon kwɑdˈrun, kwɒd-
quadruped ˈkwɑdrəˌpɛd, ˈkwɒd-
quadruple n, adj, v ˈkwɑdrʊpḷ, ˈkwɒd-,
kwɑdˈrupḷ, kwɒd-, -ˈrɪu- |-d -d |-ling -plɪŋ,
-pḷɪŋ
quadruplets ˈkwɑdrʊˌplɪts, ˈkwɒd-, kwɑd-
ˈrʊplɪts, kwɒd-, -ˈrɪu-
quadruplicate adj kwɑdˈrʊplɪkɪt, kwɒd-,
-ˈrɪu-, -ˌket
quadruplicate v kwɑdˈrʊplɪˌket, kwɒd-, -ˈrɪu-
|-d -ɪd
quaestor ˈkwɛstɚ; ES ˈkwɛstə(r
quaff kwæf, kwɑf, kwɒf, kwɔf; E+kwaf;
|-ed -t
quaggy ˈkwægɪ, ˈkwɑgɪ, ˈkwɒgɪ
quagmire ˈkwægˌmaɪr, ˈkwɑg-, ˈkwɒg-; ES
-ˌmaɪə(r
quahog, -haug ˈkwɔhɒg, ˈko-, -hɒg, kwəˈhɔg,
-ˈhɒg
quail kwel |quailed kweld
quaint kwent
quait kwet |quaits kwets=quoit—Quaits is
not a corruption of quoits, but is probably
the earlier spoken form, still used by players.
Quaitso ˈkwetso
quake kwek |quaked kwekt
Quaker ˈkwekɚ; ES ˈkwekə(r; |-ism -ˌɪzəm
qualification ˌkwɑləfəˈkeʃən, ˌkwɒl-
qualify ˈkwɑləˌfaɪ, ˈkwɒl- |-fied -ˌfaɪd
qualitative ˈkwɑləˌtetɪv, ˈkwɒlə-
quality ˈkwɑlətɪ, ˈkwɒl- |-ied -d
qualm kwɑm, kwɒm, kwɔm
Quanah ˈkwɑnə, ˈkwɒnə
quandary ˈkwɑndrɪ, ˈkwɒn-, -dərɪ
quantify ˈkwɑntəˌfaɪ, ˈkwɒn- |-fied -ˌfaɪd
quantitative ˈkwɑntəˌtetɪv, ˈkwɒn-
quantity ˈkwɑntətɪ, ˈkwɒn-
quantum ˈkwɑntəm, ˈkwɒn- |-ta -tə
quarantine ˈkwɔrənˌtin, ˈkwɑr-, ˈkwɒr- |-d -d
Quarles kwɔrlz, kwɑrlz; ES kwɔəlz, kwɑːlz;
|-'s -ɪz
quarrel ˈkwɔrəl, ˈkwɑr-, ˈkwɒr-, -rl |-ed -d
quarry ˈkwɔrɪ, ˈkwɑrɪ, ˈkwɒrɪ |-ied -d
quart kwɔrt; ES kwɔət
quartan ˈkwɔrtṇ; ES ˈkwɔətṇ

quarter ˈkwɔrtɚ; ES ˈkwɔətə(r; |-ed -d—A
dissimilated form ˈkwɒtɚ is sometimes heard
(§121).
quarterback ˈkwɔrtɚˌbæk; ES ˈkwɔətə-
quarter-deck ˈkwɔrtɚˌdɛk; ES ˈkwɔətə-
quartermaster ˈkwɔrtɚˌmæstɚ; ES ˈkwɔətə-
ˌmæstə(r, E+-ˌmas-, -ˌmɑs-
quarterstaff ˈkwɔrtɚˌstæf; ES ˈkwɔətə-,
E+-ˌstaf, -ˌstɑf; |pl -s -s or -staves -ˌstevz,
-ˌstævz; E+-ˌstavz, -ˌstɑvz
quartet, -tte kwɔrˈtɛt; ES kwɔəˈtɛt
quartile ˈkwɔrtaɪl, -tḷ, -tɪl; ES ˈkwɔət-
quarto ˈkwɔrto; ES ˈkwɔəto
quartz kwɔrts; ES kwɔəts; |-ite -aɪt
quash kwɑʃ, kwɒʃ |-es -ɪz |-ed -t
quasi ˈkwesaɪ, ˈkwezaɪ, ˈkwɑsɪ
Quassia, q- ˈkwɑʃɪə, ˈkwɒʃ-, -ʃə
quaternary kwəˈtɜnərɪ; ES -ˈtɜn-, -ˈtɜn-
quaternion kwəˈtɜnɪən, -njən; ES -ˈtɜn-,
-ˈtɜn-
quatorze kæˈtɔrz, kə-; ES -ˈtɔəz
quatrain ˈkwɑtren, ˈkwɒt-
Quatre Bras Fr katrəˈbra
quatrefoil ˈkætɚˌfɔɪl, ˈkætrə-; ES ˈkætə-,
ˈkætrə-; |-ed -d
quaver ˈkwevɚ; ES ˈkwevə(r; |-ed -d |-ing
ˈkwevərɪŋ, ˈkwevrɪŋ
quay ki |-ed kid |-age ˈkiɪdʒ
quean kwin
queasy ˈkwizɪ
Quebec kwɪˈbɛk
quebracho keˈbratʃo
queen kwin |queened kwind
Queens kwinz |-'s -ɪz |-land -ˌlænd, -lənd
|-town -ˌtaʊn |-ton -tən
queer kwɪr; ES kwɪə(r, S+kwɛə(r; |-ed -d
quell kwɛl |quelled kwɛld
quench kwɛntʃ |quenches ˈkwɛntʃɪz |-ed -t
|-able -əbḷ |-bly -blɪ
quercetin ˈkwɜsɪtɪn; ES ˈkwɜs-, ˈkwɜs-
quercine ˈkwɜsɪn, -aɪn; ES ˈkwɜs-, ˈkwɜs-
Quercus ˈkwɜkəs; ES ˈkwɜkəs, ˈkwɜk-
quern kwɜn; ES kwɜn, kwɜn
querulous ˈkwɛrələs, ˈkwɛrjələs, -rʊləs
query ˈkwɪrɪ |queried ˈkwɪrɪd
Quesnay keˈne (Fr kɛˈnɛ)
quest kwɛst |quested ˈkwɛstɪd
question ˈkwɛstʃən |-ed -d |-able -əbḷ |-bly
-blɪ |-ary -ˌɛrɪ

|full fʊl |tooth tuθ |further ˈfɜðɚ; ES ˈfɜðə |custom ˈkʌstəm |while hwaɪl |how haʊ |toy tɔɪ
|using ˈjuzɪŋ |fuse fjuz, fɪuz |dish dɪʃ |vision ˈvɪʒən |Eden ˈidṇ |cradle ˈkredḷ |keep 'em ˈkipm̩

questionnaire ˌkwɛstʃənˈɛr, -ˈær; E -ˈɛə(r,
ES -ˈæə(r

questor ˈkwɛstɚ; ES ˈkwɛstə(r

queue kju, kɪu |queued kjud, kɪud

Quezon ˈkezɑn, -zɒn (*Am Sp* ˈkeson)

quibble ˈkwɪb| |-d -d |-ling ˈkwɪblɪŋ, -b|ɪŋ

quick kwɪk |-ed -t |-en -ən |-ened -ənd |-ening
ˈkwɪkənɪŋ, ˈkwɪknɪŋ

quicklime ˈkwɪkˌlaɪm

Quickly ˈkwɪklɪ

quicksand ˈkwɪkˌsænd

quickstep ˈkwɪkˌstɛp |-stepped -ˌstɛpt

quick-witted ˈkwɪkˈwɪtɪd (ˈquick-ˌwitted ˈman)

quid kwɪd

quiddity ˈkwɪdətɪ

quidnunc ˈkwɪdˌnʌŋk

quiescence kwaɪˈɛsn̩s |-scent -sn̩t

quiet ˈkwaɪət |quieted ˈkwaɪətɪd

quietude ˈkwaɪəˌtjud, -ˌtɪud, -ˌtud

quietus kwaɪˈitəs |quietuses kwaɪˈitəsɪz

quill kwɪl |quilled kwɪld

quillet ˈkwɪlɪt

Quiller-Couch ˈkwɪlɚˈkutʃ; ES ˈkwɪlə-; |-ʼs
-ɪz

quilt kwɪlt |quilted ˈkwɪltɪd

quinary ˈkwaɪnərɪ

quinazoline kwɪnˈæzəˌlin, -lɪn

quince kwɪns |quinces ˈkwɪnsɪz

quincunx ˈkwɪnkʌŋks, ˈkwɪŋ- |-cunxes
-kʌŋksɪz

Quincy ˈkwɪnsɪ; *Mass city & family* ˈkwɪnzɪ

quindecennial ˌkwɪndɪˈsɛnɪəl, -njəl |-ly -ɪ

quinine ˈkwaɪnaɪn

quinnat ˈkwɪnæt

quinoidine kwɪˈnɔɪdin, -dɪn |-din -dɪn

quinoline ˈkwɪn|ˌin, -ɪn |-lin -ɪn

quinone kwɪˈnon (ˈquinˌone ˈcompound)

Quinquagesima ˌkwɪnkwəˈdʒɛsəmə, ˌkwɪŋ-

quinquennial kwɪnˈkwɛnɪəl, kwɪŋ-, -njəl |-ly
-ɪ |-nium -nɪəm, -njəm

quinsy ˈkwɪnzɪ

quint *cards* kwɪnt, kɪnt

quintain ˈkwɪntɪn

quintal ˈkwɪnt|

quintan ˈkwɪntən

quintessence kwɪnˈtɛsn̩s |-s -ɪz

quintessential ˌkwɪntəˈsɛnʃəl |-ly -ɪ

quintet, -tte kwɪnˈtɛt

Quintilian kwɪnˈtɪljən, -lɪən

quintillion kwɪnˈtɪljən

Quints, q- kwɪnts

quintuple *n, adj, v* ˈkwɪntʊp|, -tjʊp|, kwɪn-
ˈtʊp|, -ˈtɪu-, -ˈtju- |-d -d |-ling -plɪŋ, -p|ɪŋ

quintuplets ˈkwɪntəplɪts, -tʊ-, kwɪnˈtuplɪts,
-ˈtɪu-, -ˈtju-, -ˈtʌp-

quip kwɪp |-ped -t |-ster -stɚ; ES -stə(r

quire kwaɪr; ES kwaɪə(r; |-d -d

Quirinal ˈkwɪrən|

quirk kwɝk; ES kwɜk, kwɜ·k; |-ed -t

quirt kwɝt; ES kwɜt, kwɜ·t; |-ed -ɪd

Quisling ˈkwɪzlɪŋ

quit kwɪt |-ted -ɪd *or* quit kwɪt

quitclaim ˈkwɪtˌklem |-claimed -ˌklemd

quite kwaɪt

Quito ˈkito

quitrent ˈkwɪtˌrɛnt

quittance ˈkwɪtn̩s |-s -ɪz

quiver ˈkwɪvɚ; ES ˈkwɪvə(r; |-ed -d |-ing
ˈkwɪvrɪŋ, ˈkwɪvərɪŋ

Quixote, Don ˌdɑnkɪˈhotɪ, -ˈkwɪksət; ES+
ˌdɒn-; (*Sp* -kiˈxote)

quixotic kwɪksˈɑtɪk; ES+-ˈɒt-; |-al -| |-ally
-|ɪ, -ɪklɪ

quiz kwɪz |quizzes ˈkwɪzɪz |quizzed kwɪzd

quizzical ˈkwɪzɪk| |-ly -ɪ, -ɪklɪ

quohog, -haug ˈkwɔhɔg, ˈko-, -hɒg, kwəˈhɔg,
-ˈhɒg=quahog

quoin kɔɪn, kwɔɪn |-ed -d

quoit kwɔɪt |quoits kwɔɪts, *less freq.* kɔɪt(s)--
see quait

quondam ˈkwɑndəm, ˈkwɒndəm

quorum ˈkworəm, ˈkwɔrəm; S ˈkworəm

quota ˈkwotə |quotaed ˈkwotəd

quotation kwoˈteʃən, *less freq* koˈteʃən

quote kwot, *less freq.* kot |-d -ɪd |-table -əb|
|-bly -blɪ

quoth kwoθ |quotha ˈkwoθə

quotidian kwoˈtɪdɪən, -ˈtɪdjən

quotient ˈkwoʃənt

quo warranto ˈkwo wɔˈrænto, wɑ-, wɒ-, wə-

Key: *See in full §§3-47.* bee bi |pity ˈpɪtɪ (§6) |rate ret |yet jɛt |sang sæŋ |angry ˈæŋ·grɪ
|bath bæθ; E baθ (§10) |ah ɑ |far fɑr |watch wɑtʃ, wɒtʃ (§12) |jaw dʒɔ |gorge gɔrdʒ |go go

R

R, r *letter* ɑr; ES ɑː(r; |*pl* R's, Rs, *poss* R's
   ɑrz; ES ɑːz, E+aː(r, aːz
rabbet 'ræbɪt |rabbeted 'ræbɪtɪd
rabbi 'ræbaɪ
rabbinical ræ'bɪnɪk|, rə- |-ly -ɪ
rabbit 'ræbɪt |rabbited 'ræbɪtɪd
rabble 'ræb|
Rabelais ˌræb|'e, 'ræb|ˌe (*Fr* ra'blɛ)
Rabelaisian ˌræb|'ezɪən, -ʒən
rabid 'ræbɪd
rabies 'rebiz, 'rebɪˌiz, 'ræb-
Rabindranath Tagore rə'bɪndrəˌnɑttə'gor,
   -'gɔr; ES -'goə(r, E+-'gɔə(r
raccoon ræ'kun
race res |races 'resɪz |raced rest
racecourse 'resˌkors, -ˌkɔrs; ES -ˌkoəs, E+
   -ˌkɔəs; |-s -ɪz
raceme re'sim, rə'sim |-d -d
Rachel *name* 'retʃəl, *powder Fr* ra'ʃɛl
rachitis rə'kaɪtɪs |-chitic -'kɪtɪk
Rachmaninov, -off rɑk'mɑnɪˌnɔf, ræk-, -ˌnɒf
racial 'reʃəl, 'reʃɪəl |-ly -ɪ
Racine rə'sin, (*Fr* ra'sin)
rack ræk |racked rækt
racket 'rækɪt |racketed 'rækɪtɪd
racketeer ˌrækɪt'ɪr; ES -'ɪə(r; S+-'ɛə(r |-ed -d
raconteur ˌrækɑn'tɝ; ES -kɑn'tɜ(r, -kɒn-,
   -'tɝ
racquet 'rækɪt
racy 'resɪ |racily 'res|ɪ, -ɪlɪ
Radcliff(e), -clyffe 'rædklɪf
raddle 'ræd| |-d -d |-ling 'rædlɪŋ, 'rædlɪŋ
raddleman 'ræd|mən |-men -mən
radial 'redɪəl |-ly -ɪ
radiance 'redɪəns, 'redjəns |-s -ɪz |-ant -ənt
radiate 'redɪˌet |-d -ɪd |-tion ˌredɪ'eʃən
radiator 'redɪˌetɚ; ES 'redɪˌetə(r
radical 'rædɪk| |-ly -ɪ, -ɪklɪ
radio 'redɪˌo |-ed -d |-active ˌredɪo'æktɪv
radioactivity 'redɪˌoæk'tɪvətɪ
radiobroadcast 'redɪo'brɔdˌkæst; E+-ˌkast,
   -ˌkɑst
radiogram 'redɪəˌgræm
radiograph 'redɪəˌgræf; ES+-ˌgraf, -ˌgrɑf;
   |-ed -t
radiographer ˌredɪ'ɑgrəfɚ, -'ɒg-; ES -fə(r;
   |-phy -fɪ

radiolarian ˌredɪo'lerɪən, -'le-
radiology ˌredɪ'ɑlədʒɪ; ES+-'ɒl-
radiometer ˌredɪ'ɑmətɚ; ES -'ɑmətə(r, -'ɒm-
radiophone 'redɪəˌfon
radioscope 'redɪəˌskop
radioscopy ˌredɪ'ɑskəpɪ; ES+-'ɒs-
radiotelegram 'redɪo'teləˌgræm
radiotelegraphy 'redɪˌotə'legrəfɪ
radiotelephony 'redɪˌotə'lɛfənɪ
radiotherapy 'redɪo'θerəpɪ
radiothorium ˌredɪo'θorɪəm, -'θɔr-; S -'θor-
radish 'rædɪʃ |radishes 'rædɪʃɪz
radium 'redɪəm
radiumtherapy 'redɪəm'θerəpɪ
radius 'redɪəs |-es -ɪz |radii 'redɪˌaɪ
Radnor 'rædnɚ; ES -nə(r; |-shire -ˌʃɪr, -ʃɚ;
   ES -ˌʃɪə(r, -ʃə(r
radon 'redɑn; ES+-dɒn
Raeburn 'rebɝn; ES 'rebən
Raemaekers 'rɑmɑkɚz; ES 'rɑmɑkəz; |-'s -ɪz
Rafael 'ræfɪəl, 'refɪəl
raff ræf |raffish 'ræfɪʃ
raffia 'ræfɪə, -fjə
raffle 'ræf| |-d -d |-ling 'ræf|ɪŋ, 'ræflɪŋ
raft ræft; E+raft, rɑft; |-ed -ɪd
rafter 'ræftɚ; ES 'ræftə(r, E+'raf-, 'rɑf-
rag ræg |ragged rægd
ragamuffin 'rægəˌmʌfɪn, 'rægˌmʌfɪn
rage redʒ |rages 'redʒɪz |raged redʒd
ragged *adj* 'rægɪd
raglan 'ræglən
ragman 'rægˌmæn, -mən |-men -mən
ragman *document* 'rægmən
ragout ræ'gu |-s -z |-ed -d |-ing -ɪŋ
ragpicker 'rægˌpɪkɚ; ES -ˌpɪkə(r
ragtime 'rægˌtaɪm
ragweed 'rægˌwid
raid red |raided 'redɪd
rail rel |railed reld
railhead 'relˌhed
raillery 'relərɪ—rallery 'rælərɪ, *an old variant,*
   is said to be still heard.
railroad 'relˌrod |railroaded 'relˌrodɪd
railway 'relˌwe
raiment 'remənt |-ed -ɪd
rain ren |rained rend
rainbow 'renˌbo |-bowed -ˌbod

|full fʊl |tooth tuθ |further 'fɝðɚ; ES 'fɝðə |custom 'kʌstəm |while hwaɪl |how haʊ |toy tɔɪ
|using 'juzɪŋ |fuse fjuz, fɪuz |dish dɪʃ |vision 'vɪʒən |Eden 'idn̩ |cradle 'kred| |keep 'em 'kipm̩

raincoat 'ren₁kot |-ed -ɪd
raindrop 'ren₁drɑp; ES+-₁drɒp
rainfall 'ren₁fɔl
Rainier, *Mount* re'nɪr; ES re'nɪə(r
rainier *'wetter'* 'renɪɚ; ES 'renɪ·ə(r
rainproof *adj* 'ren'pruf ('rain₁proof 'hat)
rainproof *v* 'ren₁pruf |-proofed -₁pruft
rainstorm 'ren₁stɔrm; ES 'ren₁stɔəm
raintight 'ren'taɪt ('rain₁tight 'roof)
rainwater 'ren₁wɔtɚ, -₁wɑtɚ, -₁wɒtɚ; ES -tə(r
rainworm 'ren₁wɝm; ES -₁wɜm, -₁wɝm
raise rez |raises 'rezɪz |raised rezd
raisin 'rezn̩
raison d'être 'rezɔn'dɛt (*Fr* rɛzõ'dɛːtṛ)
raj rɑdʒ |raja, -jah 'rɑdʒə
Rajput 'rɑdʒput
rake rek |raked rekt
Raleigh 'rɔlɪ
rally 'rælɪ |rallied 'rælɪd
Ralph rælf—ref *is chiefly British*
ram ræm |rammed ræmd
Ramadan ₁ræmə'dɑn
ramble 'ræmbl̩ |-d -d |-ling 'ræmblɪŋ, -bl̩ɪŋ
ramekin 'ræməkɪn
Rameses 'ræmə₁siz |-'s -ɪz |+rə'misiz
ramie 'ræmɪ
ramification ₁ræməfə'keʃən
ramiform 'ræmə₁fɔrm; ES 'ræmə₁fɔəm
ramify 'ræmə₁faɪ |ramified 'ræmə₁faɪd
ramp ræmp |ramped ræmpt
rampage *n* 'ræmpedʒ |-geous ræm'pedʒəs
rampage *v* ræm'pedʒ |-s -ɪz |-d -d
rampant 'ræmpənt |-pancy -pənsɪ
rampart 'ræmpɑrt, 'ræmpɚt; ES -pɑːt, -pət,
E+-pɑːt
ramrod 'ræm₁rɑd; ES+-₁rɒd
Ramsay, -sey 'ræmzɪ
Ramses 'ræmsiz |-ses' -siz
Ramsgate 'ræmz₁get, *Brit* 'ræmzgɪt
ramshackle 'ræmʃækl̩ |-d -d
ramson 'ræmznn̩, -sn̩
ramtil 'ræmtɪl
ran ræn
ranch ræntʃ |ranches 'ræntʃɪz |ranched
ræntʃt
ranchero ræn'tʃero (*Sp* ran-)
ranchman 'ræntʃmən |-men -mən
rancho 'ræntʃo, 'rɑn-
rancid 'rænsɪd |rancidity ræn'sɪdətɪ

rancor 'ræŋkɚ; ES 'ræŋkə(r; |-ous -əs, -krəs
Randolph 'rændɑlf, -dɒlf
random 'rændəm
rang ræŋ
range rendʒ |ranges 'rendʒɪz |ranged rendʒd
Rangely 'rendʒlɪ
Rangoon ræŋ'gun
rangy, -gey 'rendʒɪ
Ranier re'nɪr; ES -'nɪə(r
rank ræŋk |ranked ræŋkt
rankle 'ræŋkl̩ |-d -d |-ling 'ræŋklɪŋ, -kl̩ɪŋ
ransack 'rænsæk |ransacked 'rænsækt
ransom 'rænsəm |ransomed 'rænsəmd
rant rænt |ranted 'ræntɪd
rap ræp |rapped ræpt
rapacious rə'peʃəs |-pacity -'pæsətɪ
rape rep |raped rept
rapeseed 'rep₁sid
Raphael *painter* 'ræfɪəl, *pers. name* 'ræf-,
'ref-
rapid 'ræpɪd
Rapidan ₁ræpə'dæn
rapid-fire 'ræpɪd'faɪr; ES -'faɪə(r; ('rapid-₁fire
'gun)
rapidity rə'pɪdətɪ
rapier 'repɪɚ, 'repjɚ; ES 'repɪ·ə(r, -pjə(r
rapine 'ræpɪn
Rappahannock ₁ræpə'hænək
rapparee ₁ræpə'ri
rapport ræ'port, -'pɔrt; ES -'pɔət, E+-'pɔət;
(*Fr* ra'pɔːr)
rapprochement *Fr* raprɔʃ'mã
rapscallion ræp'skæljən
rapt ræpt
rapture 'ræptʃɚ; ES 'ræptʃə(r; |-rous -əs
rara avis 'rerə'evɪs |rarae aves 'reri'eviz
rare rɛr, rær; E rɛə(r, ES ræə(r; |rarer -rɚ;
ES -rə(r
rarebit *erron. for* (Welsh) rabbit 'rɛr₁bɪt,
'rær-; ES *see* rare; rarebit *is unknown
apart from* Welsh rarebit.
rarefaction ₁rɛrə'fækʃən, ₁rær-; S ₁rær-;
|-tive -tɪv
rarefy 'rɛrə₁faɪ, 'rær-; S 'rær-; |-fied -₁faɪd
Raritan 'rærətn̩
rarity 'rɛrətɪ, 'rær-; S 'rær-
rascal 'ræskl̩ |rascally 'ræskl̩ɪ
rascality ræs'kælətɪ
rase rez |rases 'rezɪz |rased rezd

Key: See in full §§3–47. bee bi |pity 'pɪtɪ (§6) |rate ret |yet jɛt |sang sæŋ |angry 'æŋ·grɪ
|bath bæθ; E baθ (§10) |ah ɑ |far fɑr |watch wɑtʃ, wɒtʃ (§12) |jaw dʒɔ |gorge gɔrdʒ |go go

rash ræʃ |rashes 'ræʃɪz
rasher 'ræʃɚ; ES 'ræʃə(r
Rask rɑsk
Rasmussen 'rɑsmʌsn̩
rasp ræsp; E+rasp, rɑsp; |-ed -t
raspberry 'ræz͕bɛrɪ, -bərɪ; E+'raz-, 'rɑz-
Rasputin ræs'pjutɪn, -'pɪu-, rɑs'putɪn
Rasselas 'ræsə͕læs, -ləs |-'s -ɪz
rasure 'reʒɚ; ES 'reʒə(r
rat ræt |ratted 'rætɪd
ratable, ratea- 'retəb͔l |-bly -blɪ
ratafia ͕rætə'fiə
ratan ræ'tæn |-ned -d
rataplan ͕rætə'plæn |-ned -d
ratch rætʃ |ratches 'rætʃɪz |ratched rætʃt
ratchet 'rætʃɪt |racheted 'rætʃɪtɪd
Ratcliff, -e 'rætklɪf
rate ret |rated 'retɪd
Rathbone 'ræθ͕bon, -bən
rathe reð
rather 'ræðɚ; ES 'ræðə(r, 'rɑð-, 'rɑð-;—*In
N Engd the* Linguistic Atlas *shows that*
'ræðə(r, 'rɛð-, 'rʌð-, 'rɑð- *among cultivated
informants are more frequent than* 'rɑðə(r,
and that 'ræðə(r *is more frequent than*
'rɑðə(r. *In the US as a whole* 'ræðɚ,
'ræðə(r *overwhelmingly prevails,* 'rɑð-,
'rɑð-, 'rɛð-, 'rʌð- *being only sporadic. The
most regular form, historically, is* 'ræðɚ,
'ræðə(r, *like* gather, lather, Cather,
Mather, blather, slather, fathom. *The
Brit form is* 'rɑðə(r.
rathskeller 'rɑts͕kɛlɚ; ES -͕kɛlə(r
ratification ͕rætəfə'keʃən
ratify 'rætə͕faɪ |ratified 'rætə͕faɪd
ratio 'reʃo (*as L* 'reʃɪ͕o)
ratiocinate *v* ͕ræʃɪ'ɑsn̩͕et; ES+-'ɒs-; |-d -d
ratiocinate *adj* ͕ræʃɪ'ɑsn̩ɪt; ES+-'ɒs-
ratiocination ͕ræʃɪ͕ɑsn̩'eʃən; ES+-͕ɒs-
ration 'ræʃən, 'reʃən; *mil.* 'ræʃən |-ed -d
|-ing -ʃənɪŋ, -ʃnɪŋ
rational 'ræʃən͔l |-ly -ɪ |-ism -͕ɪzəm |-ist -ɪst
rationale ͕ræʃə'næl, -'nɑlɪ, -'nelɪ
rationalistic ͕ræʃən͔l'ɪstɪk |-al -͔l |-ally -͔ɪ,
-ɪklɪ
rationality ͕ræʃə'nælətɪ
rationalize 'ræʃən͔l͕aɪz, -ʃnəl- |-s -ɪz |-d -d
Ratisbon 'rætɪz͕ban, 'rætɪs-; ES+-͕bɒn
ratline, -lin 'rætlɪn |-lined -lɪnd

Raton ræ'tun ('Ra͕ton 'Pass)
ratoon ræ'tun |-ed -d
ratsbane 'ræts͕ben
rattail 'ræt͕tel
rattan ræ'tæn |-ned -d
rattle 'ræt͔l |-d -d |-ling 'ræt͔lɪŋ, 'rætlɪŋ
rattlebrain 'ræt͔l͕bren |-ed -d
rattlehead 'ræt͔l͕hɛd |-headed -'hɛdɪd ('rattle-
͕headed 'notion)
rattler 'rætlɚ, 'ræt͔lɚ; ES 'rætlə(r, 'ræt͔lə(r
rattlesnake 'ræt͔l͕snek
rattletrap 'ræt͔l͕træp
rattly 'rætlɪ, 'ræt͔lɪ
rattrap 'ræt͕træp
raucous 'rɔkəs
ravage 'rævɪdʒ |-s -ɪz |-d -d
rave rev |raved revd
ravel 'ræv͔l |-ed -d |-ing 'rævlɪŋ, 'ræv͔lɪŋ
raven *bird* 'revən
raven *v* 'rævɪn, -ən |-ed -d
Ravena rə'vinə
Ravenna rə'vɛnə, *in Ohio*+rɪ'vænə
ravenous 'rævənəs
ravin, -ine '*rapine*' 'rævɪn |-ed -d
ravine '*gorge*' rə'vin
ravish 'rævɪʃ |-es -ɪz |-ed -t
raw rɔ
rawboned 'rɔ'bond ('raw͕boned 'horse)
Rawdon 'rɔdn̩
rawhide 'rɔ͕haɪd |rawhided 'rɔ͕haɪdɪd
ray, R- re |rayed red
Rayleigh 'relɪ
Raymond 'remənd
Raynham 'renəm, *Mass loc.*+'renhæm
rayon 'rean, -ɒn
raze rez |razes 'rezɪz |razed rezd
razor 'rezɚ; ES 'rezə(r
razorback 'rezɚ͕bæk; ES 'rezə-; |-ed -t
razz ræz |razzes 'ræzɪz |razzed ræzd
razzle-dazzle *n* 'ræz͔l͕dæz͔l
razzle-dazzle *v* ͕ræz͔l'dæz͔l, 'ræz͔l͕dæz͔l |-d -d
|-ling -zlɪŋ, -z͔lɪŋ
r-colored 'ɑr͕kʌlɚd; ES 'ɑ:͕kʌləd, E+'ɑ:-
re *music* re, *prep* ri
re- *prefix: stressed* 'ri-, ͕ri-, 'rɛ-, ͕rɛ-; *unstr.*
rɪ-, ri-, rə-; *for the unstr. form when only* rɪ-
*is given in the vocabulary, it is to be under-
stood that many speakers (both British and
American) also pronounce* ri- (*esp. in more*

careful speech or when a vowel follows), *or*
rə- *as in* Ramona rə'monə.

're *abbr. sp. of unstressed* are *in* you're, we're,
they're -r; ES -ə(r

Rea re, 'riə, ri
reabsorb ˌriəb'sɔrb, -'zɔrb; ES -ɔəb; |-ed -d
reabsorption ˌriəb'sɔrpʃən; ES -'sɔəpʃən
reach ritʃ |reaches 'ritʃɪz |reached ritʃt
react rɪ'ækt |-ed -ɪd |-ction -kʃən
re-act ˌri'ækt |-ed -ɪd
reactionary rɪ'ækʃənˌɛrɪ
read *n, v* rid |*past* read rɛd |*pptc* read rɛd
Read rid
readability ˌridə'bɪlətɪ
readable 'ridəb| |-bly -blɪ
readily 'rɛd|ɪ, -ɪlɪ |-iness -ɪnɪs
Reading 'rɛdɪŋ
readjust ˌriə'dʒʌst |-ed -ɪd |-able -əb|
readmit ˌriəd'mɪt |-ted -ɪd |-mission -'mɪʃən
ready 'rɛdɪ
ready-made 'rɛdɪ'med ('ready-ˌmade 'clothes)
reaffirm ˌriə'fɝm; ES -'fɝm, -'fɝm; |-ed -d
reaffirmation ˌriæfɚ'meʃən; ES ˌriæfə-
Reagan 'regən
reagent ri'edʒənt |-gency -dʒənsɪ
real 'riəl, ril, 'rɪəl
real *coin* 'riəl, ril (*Sp* re'al)
Real 'riəl
real estate 'riləˌstet, 'riəl-, 'rɪəl-
realism 'riəlˌɪzəm, 'rɪəl- |-ist -ɪst
realistic ˌriə'lɪstɪk, ˌrɪə- |-ally -|ɪ, -ɪklɪ
reality rɪ'ælətɪ
realization ˌriələ'zeʃən, ˌrɪəl-, -aɪ'z-
realize 'riəˌlaɪz, 'rɪə- |-s -ɪz |-d -d
really 'riəlɪ, 'rilɪ, 'rɪəlɪ, 'rɪlɪ
realm rɛlm
realtor 'riəltɚ, -tɔr; ES -tə(r, -tɔə(r
realty 'riəltɪ
ream rim |reamed rimd
reanimate ri'ænəˌmet |-d -ɪd
reanimation ˌriænə'meʃən
reap rip |reaped ript |-er -ɚ; ES -ə(r
reappear ˌriə'pɪr; ES -'pɪə(r, S+-'pɛə(r,
-'pjɛə(r; |-ed -d
reappoint ˌriə'pɔɪnt |-ed -ɪd
rear rɪr; ES rɪə(r, S+rɛə(r; |-ed -d
rearm ri'ɑrm; ES -'ɑːm, E+'ɑːm; |-ed -d
rearmament ri'ɑrməmənt; ES -'ɑːm-, E+
-'ɑːm-

rearmost 'rɪrˌmost; ES 'rɪə-, S+'rɛə-
rearrange ˌriə'rendʒ |-s -ɪz |-d -d
rearward '*backward*' 'rɪrwəd; ES 'rɪəwəd,
S+'rɛə-
rearward '*rear guard*' 'rɪrˌwɔrd; ES 'rɪəˌwɔəd,
S+'rɛə-
reason 'rizn̩ |-ed -d |-ing 'riznɪŋ, 'rɪznɪŋ
reasonable 'riznəb|, 'rɪznə- |-bly -blɪ
reassemble ˌriə'sɛmb| |-d -d |-ling -'sɛmblɪŋ,
-'sɛmb|ɪŋ
reassert ˌriə'sɝt; ES -'sɝt, -'sɝt; |-ed -ɪd
reassign ˌriə'saɪn |-ed -d
reassure ˌriə'ʃʊr; ES -'ʃʊə(r; |-d -d |-dly -ɪdlɪ
|-rance -əns |-rances -ənsɪz
Reaumur, Ré- 'reəˌmjʊr, -ˌmɪʊr; ES -ə(r;
(*Fr* reo'myːr)
reave riv |reaved rivd *or* reft rɛft
reawaken ˌriə'wekən |-ed -d
rebate '*rabbet*' 'ræbɪt, 'ribet |-d -ɪd
rebate '*discount*' 'ribet, rɪ'bet; |-d -ɪd
rebec, -eck 'ribɛk
Rebecca, -bekah rɪ'bɛkə
rebel *n, adj* 'rɛb|
rebel *v* rɪ'bɛl |-led -d |-lion -jən |-lious -jəs
rebirth rɪ'bɝθ; ES -'bɝθ, -'bɝθ ('birth &
're,birth)
reborn ri'bɔrn; ES -'bɔən; ('re,born 'soul)
rebound *n* 'ri,baʊnd, rɪ'baʊnd
rebound *v* '*recoil*' rɪ'baʊnd |-ed -ɪd
rebound *pptc of* rebind ˌri'baʊnd
rebroadcast ri'brɔdˌkæst; E+-ˌkast, -ˌkast;
|*past & pptc* -cast, *radio*+-casted -ɪd
rebuff rɪ'bʌf |-ed -t
rebuild ri'bɪld |-built -'bɪlt *or arch.* -builded
-'bɪldɪd
rebuke rɪ'bjuk, -'bɪuk |-d -t
rebus 'ribəs |-es -ɪz |-ed -t
rebut rɪ'bʌt |-ted -ɪd |-tal -|
rebutter '*who rebuts*' rɪ'bʌtɚ; ES -tə(r
re-butter '*butter again*' ˌri'bʌtɚ; ES -tə(r
recalcitrance rɪ'kælsɪtrəns |-cy -ɪ |-nt -nt
recall *n* 'ri,kɔl, rɪ'kɔl
recall *v* rɪ'kɔl |-ed -d
recant rɪ'kænt |-ed -ɪd |-ation ˌrikæn'teʃən
recapitulate ˌrikə'pɪtʃəˌlet |-d -ɪd
recapitulation ˌrikəˌpɪtʃə'leʃən
recapture ri'kæptʃɚ; ES -tʃə(r; |-d -d
recast *n* 'ri,kæst; E+-ˌkast, -ˌkast
recast *v* ri'kæst; E+-'kast, -'kast

---

recede *'go back'* rɪ'sid |-d -ɪd
re-cede *'cede back'* ˌri'sid |-d -ɪd
receipt rɪ'sit |-ed -ɪd
receivable rɪ'sivəb| |-s -z
receive rɪ'siv |-d -d |-r -ɚ; ES -ə(r
receivership rɪ'sivɚˌʃɪp; ES -'sivə-
recency 'risn̩sɪ |recent 'risn̩t
recension rɪ'sɛnʃən
receptacle rɪ'sɛptək|, -tɪk|
reception rɪ'sɛpʃən |-tive -tɪv
receptivity rɪˌsɛp'tɪvətɪ, ˌrisɛp'tɪv-
recess *n* rɪ'sɛs, 'risɛs |-es -ɪz
recess *v* rɪ'sɛs |-es -ɪz |-ed -t
recession *'going back'* rɪ'sɛʃən |-sive -sɪv
recession *'ceding back'* ˌri'sɛʃən
recharge ri'tʃɑrdʒ; ES -'tʃɑ:dʒ, E+-'tʃɑ:dʒ;
|-s -ɪz |-d -d
rechate rɪ'tʃet=recheat
recheat rɪ'tʃit
recherché rəˈʃɛrʃe; ES -ˈʃɛəʃe; (*Fr* rəʃɛr'ʃe)
recidivous rɪ'sɪdəvəs |-vism -ˌvɪzəm
Recife re'sifə
recipe 'rɛsəpɪ, -ˌpi
recipient rɪ'sɪpɪənt
reciprocal rɪ'sɪprək| |-ly -ɪ
reciprocate rɪ'sɪprəˌket |-d -ɪd
reciprocation rɪˌsɪprə'keʃən
reciprocity ˌrɛsə'prɑsətɪ; ES+-'prɒs-
recital rɪ'saɪt| |-ist -ɪst
recitation ˌrɛsə'teʃən
recitative *n* ˌrɛsətə'tiv
recitative *adj* 'rɛsəˌtetɪv, rɪ'saɪtətɪv
recite rɪ'saɪt |-d -ɪd
reck rɛk |recked rɛkt |-less -lɪs
reckon 'rɛkən |-ed -d |-ing 'rɛkənɪŋ, -knɪŋ
reclaim rɪ'klem |-ed -d
reclamation ˌrɛklə'meʃən
recline *n* rɪ'klaɪn, 'riklaɪn
recline *v* rɪ'klaɪn |-d -d
recluse *n* 'rɛklus, -lɪus, rɪ'klus, -'klɪus |-s -ɪz
recluse *adj* rɪ'klus, -'klɪus
recognition ˌrɛkəg'nɪʃən
recognizable 'rɛkəgˌnaɪzəb| |-bly -blɪ
recognizance rɪ'kɑgnɪzəns, -'kɑnɪ-, -'kɒ- |-s
-ɪz
recognize 'rɛkəgˌnaɪz, -ɪg- |-s -ɪz |-d -d
re-cognize *'cognize again'* ˌri'kɑgnaɪz, -'kɒg-
|-s -ɪz |-d -d
recoil rɪ'kɔɪl |-ed -d

re-coil *'coil again'* ˌri'kɔɪl |-ed -d
recollect *'remember'* ˌrɛkə'lɛkt |-ed -ɪd |-ction
-kʃən
re-collect *'collect again'* ˌrikə'lɛkt |-ed -ɪd
|-ction -kʃən
recombine ˌrikəm'baɪn |-d -d
recommence ˌrikə'mɛns |-s -ɪz |-d -t
recommend ˌrɛkə'mɛnd |-ed -ɪd
re-commend *'c. again'* ˌrikə'mɛnd |-ed -ɪd
recommendation ˌrɛkəmɛn'deʃən
recommit ˌrikə'mɪt |-ted -ɪd |-tal -|
recompense 'rɛkəmˌpɛns |-s -ɪz |-d -t
reconcilable 'rɛkənˌsaɪləb|, *emph.*+ˌrɛkən-
'saɪl- |-bly -blɪ
reconcile 'rɛkənˌsaɪl |-d -d |-less -ˌsaɪllɪs
reconciliation ˌrɛkənˌsɪlɪ'eʃən
recondite 'rɛkənˌdaɪt, rɪ'kɑndaɪt; ES+-'kɒn-
reconnaissance rɪ'kɑnəsəns; ES+-'kɒn-; |-s
-ɪz
reconnoissance rɪ'kɑnəsəns; ES+-'kɒn-; |-s
-ɪz
reconnoiter, -tre ˌrikə'nɔɪtɚ, ˌrɛkə-; ES -tə(r;
|-(e)d -d |-ing -tərɪŋ, -trɪŋ
reconquer ri'kɑŋkɚ, -'kɒŋ-, -'kɑŋ-; ES -kə(r;
|-ed -d |-ing -kərɪŋ, -krɪŋ
reconsider ˌrikən'sɪdɚ; ES -də(r; |-ed -d
|-ing -dərɪŋ, -drɪŋ
reconsideration ˌrikənˌsɪdə'reʃən
reconstitute ri'kɑnstəˌtjut, -ˌtɪut, -ˌtut |-d -ɪd
reconstruct ˌrikən'strʌkt |-ed -ɪd |-ion -kʃən
record *n* 'rɛkɚd; ES 'rɛkəd;—'rɛkɔrd *is
mainly Brit.*
record *v* rɪ'kɔrd; ES -'kɔəd; |-ed -ɪd
recorder rɪ'kɔrdɚ; ES -'kɔədə(r
recount *n* 'riˌkaʊnt, ri'kaʊnt
recount *v* *'tell'* rɪ'kaʊnt |-ed -ɪd
re-count *'c. again'* ˌri'kaʊnt |-ed -ɪd
recoup rɪ'kup |-ed -t
recourse 'rikors, rɪ'kors, -ɔrs; ES -oəs,
E+-ɔəs
recover *'get back'* rɪ'kʌvɚ; ES -'kʌvə(r; |-ed
-d |-ing -'kʌvrɪŋ, -'kʌvərɪŋ |-y -'kʌvrɪ,
-'kʌvərɪ
re-cover *'c. again'* ˌri'kʌvɚ; ES -'kʌvə(r; |-ed
-d |-ing -vrɪŋ, -vərɪŋ
recreance 'rɛkrɪəns |-cy -ɪ |-ant -ənt
recreate *'refresh'* 'rɛkrɪˌet |-d -ɪd
re-create *'c. anew'* ˌrikrɪ'et |-d -ɪd
recreation *'play'* ˌrɛkrɪ'eʃən |-al -|

re-creation *'c. anew'* ˌrikrɪ'eʃən
recreative 'rɛkrɪˌetɪv
recriminate rɪ'krɪməˌnet |-d -ɪd
recrimination rɪˌkrɪmə'neʃən
recriminatory rɪ'krɪmənəˌtorɪ, -ˌtɔrɪ; S -ˌtorɪ
recross ri'krɒs, -'krɒs |-es -ɪz |-ed -t
recrudesce ˌrikru'dɛs, -krɪu- |-s -ɪz |-d -t
recrudescence ˌrikru'dɛsn̩s |-cy -ɪ |-nt -sn̩t
recruit rɪ'krut, -'krɪut |-ed -ɪd
rectangle 'rɛktæŋɡl̩ |-d -d
rectangular rɛk'tæŋɡjələ; ES -lə(r
rectification ˌrɛktəfə'keʃən
rectify 'rɛktəˌfaɪ |-fied -ˌfaɪd
rectilinear ˌrɛktə'lɪnɪə; ES -'lɪnɪ·ə(r
rectitude 'rɛktəˌtjud, -ˌtɪud, -ˌtud
recto 'rɛkto
rector 'rɛktə; ES -tə(r; |-ate -ɪt |-y -ɪ, -trɪ
rectum 'rɛktəm |-ta -tə |-tal -tl̩
recumbency rɪ'kʌmbənsɪ |-bent -bənt
recuperate rɪ'kjupəˌret, -'kɪu-, -'ku- |-d -ɪd
recuperation rɪˌkjupə'reʃən, -ˌkɪu-, -ˌku-
recur rɪ'kɝ; ES -'kɝ(r, -'kɝ; |-red -d
recurrence rɪ'kɝəns; ES -'kɝ-, -'kʌr-, -'kɝ-;
|-s -ɪz |-ent -ənt
recurve rɪ'kɝv; ES -'kɝv, -'kɝv; |-d -d
recusancy 'rɛkjuzn̩sɪ, rɪ'kjuz-, -'krʊz- |-nt -n̩t
red, R- red |redded 'rɛdɪd
redact rɪ'dækt |-ed -ɪd |-ction -kʃən
redan, R- rɪ'dæn
redbird 'rɛdˌbɝd; ES -ˌbɝd, -ˌbɝd
red-blooded 'rɛd'blʌdɪd ('red-ˌblooded 'worm)
redbreast 'rɛdˌbrɛst
redbud 'rɛdˌbʌd
redcap 'rɛdˌkæp
redcoat 'rɛdˌkot
red-coated 'rɛd'kotɪd ('red-ˌcoated 'glory)
Red Cross 'rɛd'krɒs, -'krɒs ('red-ˌcross 'seal)
redden 'rɛdn̩ |-ed -d |-ing 'rɛdn̩ɪŋ, 'rɛdnɪŋ
reddish 'rɛdɪʃ
Redditch 'rɛdɪtʃ |-'s -ɪz
reddle 'rɛdl̩ |-man -mən |-men -mən
rede rid |*arch. past* red rɛd
redeem rɪ'dim |-ed -d |-able -əbl̩ |-bly -blɪ
redemption rɪ'dɛmpʃən |-tive -tɪv |-tory -tərɪ
Redgauntlet 'rɛdˌɡɔntlɪt
red-handed 'rɛd'hændɪd ('red-ˌhanded 'Orchis)
redhead 'rɛdˌhɛd
redheaded 'rɛd'hɛdɪd ('red,headed 'lark)

red-hot *adj* 'rɛd'hɑt; ES+-'hɒt
red-hot *n* 'rɛdˌhɑt; ES+-ˌhɒt
redintegrate rɪ'dɪntəˌgret, rɛd'ɪn- |-d -ɪd
redintegration rɪˌdɪntə'greʃən, rɛdˌɪn-
redirect ˌridə'rɛkt, -daɪ- |-ed -ɪd
rediscount ri'dɪskaʊnt |-ed -ɪd
rediscover ˌridɪ'skʌvə; ES -'skʌvə(r; |-ed -d
|-ing -'skʌvərɪŋ, -'skʌvrɪŋ
redistribute ˌridɪ'strɪbjʊt |-d -bjətɪd
redistribution ˌridɪstrə'bjuʃən, -'brɪu-
redistrict ri'dɪstrɪkt |-ed -ɪd
Redlands 'rɛdˌlændz, -ləndz, -nz |-'s -ɪz
red-letter 'rɛd'lɛtə; ES -tə(r; |-ed -d ('red-
ˌletter 'journey)
redolence 'rɛdləns |-cy -ɪ |-lent -dl̩ənt
Redondo rɪ'dando; ES+-'dɒn-
redouble ri'dʌbl̩ |-d -d |-ling -'dʌblɪŋ, -bl̩ɪŋ
redoubt rɪ'daʊt |-ed -ɪd |-able -əbl̩ |-bly -blɪ
redound rɪ'daʊnd |-ed -ɪd
redpoll 'rɛdˌpol
redraft *n* 'riˌdræft; E+-ˌdraft, -ˌdrɑft
redraft *v* ri'dræft; E+-'draft, -'drɑft; |-ed -ɪd
redraw ri'drɔ |-drew -dru, -'drɪu |-drawn
-'drɔn
redress *n* 'ridrɛs, rɪ'drɛs
redress *v* *'repair'* rɪ'drɛs |-es -ɪz |-ed -t
re-dress *'d. again'* ˌri'drɛs |-es -ɪz |-ed -t
Redriff 'rɛdrɪf=Rotherhithe
Redruth 'rɛdruθ, rɛd'ruθ
redskin 'rɛdˌskɪn
reduce rɪ'djus, -'drus, -'dus |-s -ɪz |-d -t
reducible rɪ'djusəbl̩, -'drus-, -'dus- |-bly -blɪ
reductio ad absurdum rɪ'dʌkʃɪoˌædəb-
'sɝdəm; ES -'sɝd-, -'sɝd-
reduction rɪ'dʌkʃən |-tive -tɪv
redundance rɪ'dʌndəns |-cy -ɪ |-dant -dənt
reduplicate *n, adj* rɪ'djupləkɪt, -'drɪu-, -'du-,
-ˌket
reduplicate *v* rɪ'djupləˌket, -'drɪu-, -'du- |-d
-ɪd
reduplication rɪˌdjuplə'keʃən, -ˌdrɪu-, -ˌdu-
redwood, R- 'rɛdˌwʊd
re-echo ri'ɛko |-ed -d |-ing -'ɛkəwɪŋ
reed, R- rid |reeded 'ridɪd
re-educate ri'ɛdʒəˌket, -'ɛdʒʊ- |-d -ɪd
reef rif |reefed rift
reek rik |reeked rikt
reel ril |reeled rild
re-elect ˌriə'lɛkt |-ed -ɪd |-ction -kʃən

re-embark ˌriːmˈbɑːrk; ES -ˈbɑːk, E+-ˈbaːk;
|-ed -t
re-emphasize riˈɛmfəˌsaɪz |-s -ɪz |-d -d
re-enact ˌriːnˈækt |-acted -ˈæktɪd
re-enforce ˌriːnˈfors, -ˈfɔrs; ES -ˈfoəs, E+
-ˈfɔəs; |-s -ɪz |-d -t
re-engrave ˌriːnˈgrev |-graved -ˈgrevd
re-enter riˈɛntɚ; ES -ˈɛntə(r; |-ed -d |-ing
-ˈɛntərɪŋ, -ˈɛntrɪŋ |-try -trɪ
re-establish ˌriəˈstæblɪʃ |-es -ɪz |-ed -t
reeve n riv
reeve v riv |rove rov or reeved rivd
re-examination ˌriɪgˌzæməˈneʃən
re-examine ˌriɪgˈzæmɪn |-d -d
re-export n riˈɛksˌport, -ˌpɔrt; ES -ˌpoət,
E+-ˌpɔət
re-export v ˌriɪksˈport, -ˈpɔrt; ES -ˈpoət,
E+-ˈpɔət; |-ed -ɪd
refashion riˈfæʃən |-ed -d |-ing -ʃənɪŋ, -ʃnɪŋ
refection rɪˈfɛkʃən |-tory -tərɪ
refer rɪˈfɝ; ES -ˈfɝ(r, -ˈfɝ; |-red -d
referable ˈrɛfrəbl, ˈrɛfərə-, rɪˈfɝˈəbl; ES
ˈrɛfrə, -fərə-, -ˈfɝrə-, -ˈfɝˈə-
referee ˌrɛfəˈri |-d -d
reference ˈrɛfrəns, ˈrɛfərəns |-s -ɪz |-d -t
referendum ˌrɛfəˈrɛndəm |-s -z |-da -də
referent ˈrɛfrənt, ˈrɛfərənt
referential ˌrɛfəˈrɛnʃəl |-ly -ɪ
referrible rɪˈfɝˈəbl; ES -ˈfɝrə-, -ˈfɝˈə-
refill n ˈriˌfɪl
refill riˈfɪl |-ed -d
refine rɪˈfaɪn |-fined -ˈfaɪnd |-ry -ərɪ, -rɪ
refit n riˈfɪt, ˈriˌfɪt
refit v riˈfɪt |-ted -ɪd
reflect rɪˈflɛkt |-ed -ɪd |-ion -kʃən |-ive -ɪv
reflector rɪˈflɛktɚ; ES -ˈflɛktə(r
reflex n, adj ˈriflɛks |-es -ɪz
reflex v rɪˈflɛks |-es -ɪz |-ed -t
reflexion rɪˈflɛkʃən |-xive -ˈflɛksɪv
refloat riˈflot |-ed -ɪd
reforest riˈfɔrɪst, -ˈfɑr-, -ˈfɒr-, -əst |-ed -ɪd
reforestation ˌrifɔrɪsˈteʃən, -fɑr-, -fɒr-, -əs-
reform rɪˈfɔrm; ES -ˈfɔəm; |-ed -d
re-form 'f. anew' ˌriˈfɔrm; ES -ˈfɔəm; |-ed -d
reformation ˌrɛfɚˈmeʃən; ES ˌrɛfə-
re-formation 'f. anew' ˌrifɔrˈmeʃən; ES -fɔə-
reformatory rɪˈfɔrməˌtorɪ, -ˌtɔrɪ; ES -ˈfɔəmə-
ˌtorɪ, E+-ˌtɔrɪ
refract rɪˈfrækt |-ed -ɪd |-ction -kʃən

refractive rɪˈfræktɪv |-tory -tərɪ
refrain rɪˈfren |-frained -ˈfrend
refrangibility rɪˌfrændʒəˈbɪlətɪ
refrangible rɪˈfrændʒəbl
refresh rɪˈfrɛʃ |-es -ɪz |-ed -t
refrigerant rɪˈfrɪdʒərənt
refrigerate rɪˈfrɪdʒəˌret |-d -ɪd
refrigeration rɪˌfrɪdʒəˈreʃən
refrigerator rɪˈfrɪdʒəˌretɚ; ES -ˌretə(r
reft rɛft
refuel riˈfjuəl, -ˈfruəl |-ed -d
refuge ˈrɛfjudʒ |-s -ɪz
refugee ˌrɛfjuˈdʒi ('refuˌgee ˈfamily)
refulgence rɪˈfʌldʒəns |-cy -ɪ |-ent -ənt
refund n ˈriˌfʌnd
refund 'pay back' rɪˈfʌnd |-ed -ɪd
refund 'f. anew' ˌriˈfʌnd |-ed -ɪd
refurbish riˈfɝbɪʃ; ES -ˈfɝ-, -ˈfɝ-; |-es -ɪz
|-ed -t
refusal rɪˈfjuzl, -ˈfɪu-
refuse n, adj ˈrɛfjus, -juz
refuse 'deny' rɪˈfjuz, -ˈfɪuz |-s -ɪz |-d -d
re-fuse 'melt again,' 'replace fuse' ˌriˈfjuz,
-ˈfɪuz |-s -ɪz |-d -d
refutation ˌrɛfjuˈteʃən
refute rɪˈfjut, -ˈfɪut |-d -ɪd
regain rɪˈgen |-gained -ˈgend
regal ˈrigl |-ly -ɪ
regale 'feast' rɪˈgel |-galed -ˈgeld
regale 'prerogative' rɪˈgeli
regalia rɪˈgelɪə, -ljə
regality rɪˈgælətɪ
Regan ˈrigən
regard rɪˈgard; ES -ˈgaːd, E+-ˈgaːd; |-ed -ɪd
regatta rɪˈgætə
regency ˈridʒənsɪ
regenerate n, adj rɪˈdʒɛnərɪt
regenerate v rɪˈdʒɛnəˌret |-rated -ˌretɪd
regeneration rɪˌdʒɛnəˈreʃən, ˌridʒɛnə-
regent ˈridʒənt |-ship -ˌʃɪp
Reggie ˈrɛdʒɪ
regicidal ˌrɛdʒəˈsaɪdl ('regiˌcidal ˈprince)
regicide ˈrɛdʒəˌsaɪd
regime rɪˈʒim, re-
regimen ˈrɛdʒəˌmɛn, -mən
regiment n ˈrɛdʒəmənt
regiment v ˈrɛdʒəˌmɛnt |-ed -ɪd
regimental ˌrɛdʒəˈmɛntl |-ed -d |-ly -ɪ
regimentary ˌrɛdʒəˈmɛntərɪ

|full fʊl |tooth tuθ |further ˈfɝðɚ; ES ˈfɝðə |custom ˈkʌstəm |while hwaɪl |how haʊ |toy tɔɪ
|using ˈjuzɪŋ |fuse fjuz, fruz |dish dɪʃ |vision ˈvɪʒən |Eden ˈidn̩ |cradle ˈkredl̩ |keep 'em ˈkipm̩

regimentation ˌrɛdʒəmɛn'teʃən
Regina rɪ'dʒaɪnə |-nal -n|
Reginald 'rɛdʒɪn|d
region 'ridʒən |-ed -d |-al -| |-ally -ḷɪ
regionalism 'ridʒən|ˌɪzəm |-ist -ɪst
Regis 'ridʒɪs |-'s -ɪz
register 'rɛdʒɪstɚ; ES -tə(r; |-ed -d |-ing
  'rɛdʒɪstrɪŋ, -tərɪŋ
registrable 'rɛdʒɪstrəb| |-strant -strənt
registrar 'rɛdʒɪˌstrar, ˌrɛdʒɪ'strar; ES -ɑ:(r,
  E+-a:(r
registration ˌrɛdʒɪ'streʃən |-stry 'rɛdʒɪstrɪ
Regius, r- 'ridʒɪəs
regnal 'rɛgnəl |-nancy -nənsɪ |-nant -nənt
regrant ri'grænt; E+-'grant, -'grɑnt; |-ed -ɪd
regrate rɪ'gret |-grated -'gretɪd
regress n 'rigrɛs |-es -ɪz
regress v rɪ'grɛs |-es -ɪz |-ed -t
regression rɪ'grɛʃən |-sive -'grɛsɪv
regret rɪ'grɛt |-ted -ɪd
regrettable rɪ'grɛtəb| |-bly -blɪ
regular 'rɛgjəlɚ; ES 'rɛgjələ(r
regularity ˌrɛgjə'lærətɪ
regularize 'rɛgjələˌraɪz |-rized -ˌraɪzd
regulate 'rɛgjəˌlet |-d -ɪd |-tion ˌrɛgjə'leʃən
regulatory 'rɛgjələˌtorɪ, -ˌtɔrɪ; S -ˌtorɪ
regurgitate ri'gɝdʒəˌtet; ES -'gɝdʒ-, -'gɝˑdʒ-;
  |-tated -ˌtetɪd
regurgitation rɪˌgɝdʒə'teʃən, ˌrigɝdʒə-; ES
  -ɝdʒ, -ɝˑdʒ-
rehabilitate ˌriə'bɪləˌtet, ˌrihə- |-d -ɪd
rehabilitation ˌriəˌbɪlə'teʃən, ˌrihə-
Rehan 'riən, 'reən
rehash n 'riˌhæʃ |-es -ɪz
rehash v ri'hæʃ |-es -ɪz |-ed -t
rehearsal rɪ'hɝs|; ES -'hɝs|, -'hɝˑs|
rehearse rɪ'hɝs; ES -'hɝs, -'hɝˑs; |-s -ɪz |-d -t
Rehoboam ˌriə'boəm, ˌrihə-
Rehoboth US rɪ'hobəθ; Afr people 'reəˌboθ,
  'rehə-
Reich raɪk |-stag -sˌtag (Ger 'raɪx, -sˌtak)
reichsmark 'raɪksˌmark; ES -ˌmɑ:k, E+
  -ˌma:k; (Ger 'raɪxsˌmark)
Reid rid
reign ren |reigned rend
Reikjavik 'rekjəˌvik
Reilly 'raɪlɪ
reimburse ˌriɪm'bɝs; ES -'bɝs, -'bɝˑs; |-s -ɪz
  |-d -t

Reims rimz |-'s -ɪz (Fr ræ̃:s)
rein ren |reined rend
reincarnate ˌriɪn'karnet; ES -'ka:-, E+-'ka:-;
  |-d -ɪd
reincarnation ˌriɪnkar'neʃən; ES -kɑ:-, E+
  -ka:-
reindeer 'renˌdɪr; ES -ˌdɪə(r, S+-ˌdɛə(r,
  -ˌdjɛə(r
reinforce ˌriɪn'fors, -'fɔrs; ES -'foəs, E+
  -'fɔəs; |-s -ɪz |-d -t ('reinˌforced 'concrete)
Reinhardt, -hart 'raɪnhart; ES -hɑ:t
reinstate ˌriɪn'stet |-d -ɪd
reinsure ˌriɪn'ʃur; ES -'ʃuə(r; |-d -d |-rance
  -əns
reintegrate ri'ɪntəˌgret |-d -ɪd
reintegration ˌriɪntə'greʃən, riˌɪntə-
reintroduce ˌriɪntrə'djus, -'dɪus, -'dus |-s -ɪz
  |-d -t
reinvest ˌriɪn'vɛst |-ed -ɪd
reinvigorate ˌriɪn'vɪgəˌret |-d -ɪd
reinvigoration ˌriɪnˌvɪgə'reʃən
reissue ri'ɪʃu, -'ɪʃju |-d -d
reiterate ri'ɪtəˌret |-rated -ˌretɪd
reiteration riˌɪtə'reʃən, ˌriɪtə-
reject n 'ridʒɛkt
reject v rɪ'dʒɛkt |-ed -ɪd |-ction -kʃən
rejoice rɪ'dʒɔɪs |-s -ɪz |-d -t
rejoin 'reply' rɪ'dʒɔɪn |-ed -d |-der -dɚ; ES
  -də(r
rejoin 'j. anew' ˌri'dʒɔɪn |-ed -d
rejuvenate rɪ'dʒuvəˌnet, -'dʒɪu- |-d -ɪd |-tor
  -tɚ; ES -tə(r
rejuvenation rɪˌdʒuvə'neʃən, -ˌdʒɪu- |-nes-
  cence -'nɛsns |-nescent -'nɛsnt
rekindle ri'kɪnd| |-d -d |-ling -dlɪŋ, -d|ɪŋ
relabel ri'leb| |-ed -d |-ing -b|ɪŋ, -blɪŋ
relapse rɪ'læps |-s -ɪz |-d -t
relate rɪ'let |-lated -'letɪd
relation rɪ'leʃən |-al -| |-ally -ḷɪ
relative 'rɛlətɪv |-tivity ˌrɛlə'tɪvətɪ
relax rɪ'læks |-es -ɪz |-ed -t |-edly -ɪdlɪ
relaxation ˌrilæks'eʃən
relay n, adj 'rile, rɪ'le ('relay ˌrace)
relay v 'pass on' rɪ'le, 'rile |-ed -d
relay v 'l. anew' ˌri'le |-laid -'led
release 'free(dom)' rɪ'lis |-s -ɪz |-d -t
re-lease 'l. anew' ˌri'lis |-s -ɪz |-d -t
relegate 'rɛləˌget |-d -ɪd |-tion ˌrɛlə'geʃən
relent rɪ'lɛnt |-ed -ɪd |-less -lɪs

Key: See in full §§3–47. bee bi |pity 'pɪtɪ (§6) |rate ret |yet jɛt |sang sæŋ |angry 'æŋ·grɪ
|bath bæθ; E baθ (§10) |ah ɑ |far fɑr |watch wɑtʃ, wɒtʃ (§i2) |jaw dʒɔ |gorge gɔrdʒ |go go

relet ri'lɛt
relevance 'rɛləvəns |-cy -ɪ |-vant -vənt
reliability rɪˌlaɪə'bɪlətɪ
reliable rɪ'laɪəb| |-bly -blɪ
reliance rɪ'laɪəns |-s -ɪz |-ant -ənt
relict *n* 'rɛlɪkt
relict *adj* rɪ'lɪkt |-ed -ɪd
relied rɪ'laɪd
relief rɪ'lif
relieve rɪ'liv |-d -d |-dly -ɪdlɪ
relievo rɪ'livo (*It* rilievo ri'ljɛ:vo)
relight ri'laɪt |-ed -ɪd
religion rɪ'lɪdʒən |-gious -dʒəs
religiosity rɪˌlɪdʒɪ'asətɪ; ES+-'ɒs-
relinquish rɪ'lɪŋkwɪʃ |-es -ɪz |-ed -t
reliquary 'rɛləˌkwɛrɪ
relique 'rɛlɪk, rɪ'lik
relish 'rɛlɪʃ |-es -ɪz |-ed -t
relive ri'lɪv |-d -d
reload ri'lod |-ed -ɪd
relocate ri'loket |-d -ɪd
reluctance rɪ'lʌktəns |-cy -ɪ |-ant -ənt
relume ri'lum, -'lɪum |-d -d
rely rɪ'laɪ |-lied -'laɪd
remain rɪ'men |-ed -d |-der -dɚ; ES -də(r
remake ri'mek |-made -'med
remand rɪ'mænd; E+-'mand, -'mɑnd; |-ed
   -ɪd
remark rɪ'mark; ES -'ma:k, E+-'ma:k; |-ed
   -t |-able -əb| |-bly -blɪ
re-mark '*m. anew*' ˌri'mark; ES *see* remark
   |-ed -t
remarry ri'mærɪ |-ied -d |-iage -dʒ
Rembrandt 'rɛmbrænt (*Du* -brant)
remediable rɪ'midɪəb| |-bly -blɪ
remedial rɪ'midɪəl |-ly -ɪ
remedy 'rɛmədɪ |-ied -d |-diless -lɪs, rɪ-
   'mɛdəlɪs
remember rɪ'mɛmbɚ; ES -bə(r; |-ed -d |-ing
   -'mɛmbrɪŋ, -'mɛmbərɪŋ
remembrance rɪ'mɛmbrəns |-s -ɪz |-r -ɚ; ES
   -ə(r
Reményi 'rɛmɪnjɪ, 'rɛmɛnjɪ
remind rɪ'maɪnd |-ed -ɪd |-er -ɚ; ES -ə(r
Remington 'rɛmɪŋtən
reminisce ˌrɛmə'nɪs |-s -ɪz |-d -t
reminiscence ˌrɛmə'nɪsn̩s |-s -ɪz |-nt -sn̩t
remise rɪ'maɪz; *fencing* -'miz |-s -ɪz |-d -d
remiss rɪ'mɪs |-es -ɪz |-ed -t |-ible -əb|

remission rɪ'mɪʃən |-sive -'mɪsɪv
remit rɪ'mɪt |-ted -ɪd |-tal -| |-tance -ns
   |-tent -nt
remnant, R- 'rɛmnənt
remodel ri'mad|; ES+-'mɒd|; |-ed -d |-ing
   -dlɪŋ, -d|ɪŋ
remold ri'mold |-ed -ɪd
remonstrance rɪ'manstrəns; ES+-'mɒn-; |-s
   -ɪz |-ant -ənt
remonstrate rɪ'manstret; ES+-'mɒn-; |-d -ɪd
   |-tive -strətɪv
remonstration rɪman'streʃən, ˌrɛmən-; ES+
   -mɒn-
remora, R- 'rɛmərə
remorse rɪ'mɔrs; ES -'mɔəs; |-ful -fəl |-fully
   -fəlɪ
remote rɪ'mot |-tion -'moʃən
remould ri'mold |-ed -ɪd
remount ri'maunt |-ed -ɪd
remove rɪ'muv |-d -d |-dly -ɪdlɪ |-val -|
Remsen 'rɛmsn̩, 'rɛmzn̩
remunerate rɪ'mjunəˌret, -'mɪu- |-d -ɪd |-tive
   -ˌretɪv, -rətɪv
remuneration rɪˌmjunə'reʃən, -ˌmɪu-
Remus 'riməs |-'s -ɪz
Renaissance ˌrɛnə'zans, -'sans, rɪ'nesn̩s |-s
   -ɪz (*Fr* rənɛ'sã:s)
renal 'rin|
rename ri'nem |-d -d
Renan rɪ'næn (*Fr* rə'nã)
renascence, R- rɪ'næsn̩s |-s -ɪz |-nt -sn̩t
rencontre rɛn'kantɚ; ES -'kantə(r, -'kɒn-;
   (*Fr* rã'kõ:tr̩)
rencounter rɛn'kauntɚ; ES -tə(r; |-ed -d
   |-ing -'kauntrɪŋ, -tərɪŋ
rend rɛnd |rent rɛnt
render 'rɛndɚ; ES -də(r; |-ed -d |-ing
   'rɛndrɪŋ, -dərɪŋ
rendezvous 'randəˌvu, 'rɛn- |*pl* -vous -ˌvuz
   |-ed -d (*Fr* rãde'vu)
rendition rɛn'dɪʃən
renegade 'rɛnɪˌged |-d -ɪd
renege rɪ'nɪg, -'nig |-d -d
renew rɪ'nju, -'nɪu, -'nu |-ed -d |-edly -ɪdlɪ
Renfrew 'rɛnfru, -frɪu |-shire -ˌʃɪr, -ʃɚ; ES
   -ˌʃɪə(r, -ʃə(r
Reni 'rɛnɪ (*It* 're:ni)
reniform 'rɛnəˌfɔrm, 'rinə-; ES -ˌfɔəm
renig rɪ'nɪg -ged -d

|full fʊl |tooth tuθ |further 'fɝðɚ; ES 'fɝðə |custom 'kʌstəm |while hwaɪl |how haʊ |toy tɔɪ
|using 'juzɪŋ |fuse fjuz, fɪuz |dish dɪʃ |vision 'vɪʒən |Eden 'idn̩ |cradle 'kred| |keep 'em 'kipm̩

rennet 'rɛnɪt |rennin 'rɛnɪn
Reno *US* 'rino; *Italy* 'reno (*It* 'rɛ:no)
renominate ri'nɑmə,net; ES+-'nɒm-; |-d -ɪd
renomination ,rinɑmə'neʃən; ES+-nɒm-
renounce rɪ'naʊns |-s -ɪz |-d -t
renovate 'rɛnə,vet |-d -ɪd |-tor -ɚ; ES -ə(r
renovation ,rɛnə'veʃən
Renovo rɪ'novo
renown rɪ'naʊn |-ed -d |-edly -ɪdlɪ
Rensselaer 'rɛns|ɚ; ES 'rɛns|ə(r
rent rɛnt |rented 'rɛntɪd |rental 'rɛnt|
renumber ri'nʌmbɚ; ES -bə(r; |-ed -d |ing
    -'nʌmbrɪŋ, -'nʌmbərɪŋ
renunciation rɪ,nʌnsɪ'eʃən, -,nʌnʃɪ-
renunciative rɪ'nʌnʃɪ,etɪv, -sɪ- |-tory -,torɪ,
    -,tɔrɪ; S -,torɪ
Renwick, *James* 'rɛnwɪk, *Cumb*+'rɛnɪk
reoccupation ,riɑkjə'peʃən; ES+-ɒk-
reoccupy ri'ɑkjə,paɪ; ES+-'ɒk-; |-ied -d
reopen ri'opən, -'opm̩ |-ed -d |-ing -'opənɪŋ,
    -'opnɪŋ
reorder ri'ɔrdɚ; ES -'ɔədə(r; |-ed -d |-ing
    -drɪŋ, -dərɪŋ
reorganization ,riɔrgənə'zeʃən, -aɪ'z-; ES
    -ɔgən-
reorganize ri'ɔrgə,naɪz; ES -'ɔəgə,naɪz; |-s -ɪz
    |-d -d
rep rɛp |repped rɛpt
repack ri'pæk |-packed -'pækt
repaid '*paid back*' rɪ'ped, '*paid again*' ,ri-
repaint ri'pent |-ed -ɪd
repair rɪ'pɛr, -'pær; E -'pɛə(r, ES -'pæə(r;
    |-ed -d |-man -,mæn, -mən |-men -,mɛn,
    -mən |-able -əb|
reparable 'rɛpərəb| |-bly -blɪ
reparation ,rɛpə'reʃən
repartee ,rɛpɚ'ti; ES ,rɛpə-; |-d -d
repass ri'pæs; E+-'pas, -'pɑs; |-es -ɪz |-ed -t
repast rɪ'pæst; E+-'past, -'pɑst; |-ed -ɪd
repatriate ri'petrɪ,et |-d -ɪd
repatriation ,ripetrɪ'eʃən, ri,petrɪ-
repay '*p. back*' rɪ'pe |-paid -'ped
repay '*p. anew*' ,ri'pe |-paid -'ped
repeal rɪ'pil |-ed -d
repeat rɪ'pit |-ed -ɪd
repel rɪ'pɛl |-led -d
repellant, -ent rɪ'pɛlənt |-ance, -ence -əns
repent rɪ'pɛnt |-ed -ɪd |-ance -əns |-ant -ənt
repeople ri'pip| |-d -d |-ling -plɪŋ, -p|ɪŋ

repercussion ,ripɚ'kʌʃən; ES ,ripə-; |-ive
    -'kʌsɪv
repertoire 'rɛpɚ,twɑr, -,twɔr; ES 'rɛpə-
    ,twɑ:(r, -,twɔə(r; (*Fr* repɛr'twa:r)
repertory 'rɛpɚ,torɪ, -,tɔrɪ; ES 'rɛpə,torɪ,
    E+-,tɔrɪ
repetend 'rɛpə,tɛnd, ,rɛpə'tɛnd
repetition ,rɛpɪ'tɪʃən |-tious -ʃəs
repetitive rɪ'pɛtɪtɪv
rephrase ri'frez |-s -ɪz |-d -d
repine rɪ'paɪn |-pined -'paɪnd
replace '*restore*' rɪ'ples |-s -ɪz |-d -t
replace '*p. anew*' ,ri'ples |-s -ɪz |-d -t
replant ri'plænt; E+-'plant, -'plɑnt; |-ed -ɪd
replay ri'ple |-ed -d
replenish rɪ'plɛnɪʃ |-es -ɪz |-ed -t
replete rɪ'plit |-tion -'pliʃən
replevin rɪ'plɛvɪn |-ed -d |-vy -vɪ |-vied -vɪd
replica 'rɛplɪkə
replicate *n, adj* 'rɛplɪkɪt
replicate *v* 'rɛplɪ,ket |-cated -,ketɪd
reply rɪ'plaɪ |-plied -'plaɪd
report rɪ'port, -'pɔrt; ES -'poət, E+-'pɔət;
    |-ed -ɪd
reportorial ,rɛpɚ'torɪəl, -'tɔr-; ES ,rɛpə'tor-,
    E+-'tɔr-; |-ly -ɪ
repose rɪ'poz |-s -ɪz |-d -d |-dly -ɪdlɪ
repository rɪ'pɑzə,torɪ, -,tɔrɪ; S -,torɪ, ES+
    -'pɒz-
repossess ,ripə'zɛs |-es -ɪz |-ed -t |-ion -'zɛʃən
repousse *Fr* rəpu'se
repp rɛp |repped rɛpt
Replier 'rɛplɪr; ES -lɪə(r
reprehend ,rɛprɪ'hɛnd |-ed -ɪd
reprehensible ,rɛprɪ'hɛnsəb| |-bly -blɪ
reprehension ,rɛprɪ'hɛnʃən |-sive -sɪv
represent ,rɛprɪ'zɛnt |-ed -ɪd |-ative -ətɪv
representation ,rɛprɪzɛn'teʃən
repress rɪ'prɛs |-es -ɪz |-ed -t |-edly -ɪdlɪ
repressible rɪ'prɛsəb| |-bly -blɪ
repression rɪ'prɛʃən |-sive -'prɛsɪv
repressure ri'prɛʃɚ; ES -'prɛʃə(r; |-d -d
reprieve rɪ'priv |-d -d
reprimand *v* 'rɛprə,mænd, ,rɛprə'mænd; E+
    -and, -ɑnd; |-ed -ɪd, *n* 'rɛprɪ,mand
reprint *n* 'ri,prɪnt
reprint *v* ri'prɪnt |-ed -ɪd
reprise rɪ'praɪz |-s -ɪz |-d -d |-sal -|
reproach rɪ'protʃ |-es -ɪz |-ed -t

Key: See in full §§3–47. bee bi |pity 'pɪtɪ (§6) |rate ret |yet jɛt |sang sæŋ |angry 'æŋ·grɪ
|bath bæθ; E baθ (§10) |ah ɑ |far fɑr |watch watʃ, wɒtʃ (§12) |jaw dʒɔ |gorge gɔrdʒ |go go

reproachable rɪ'protʃəb‖ |-bly -blɪ
reprobate 'rɛprə‚bet |-d -ɪd
reprobation ‚rɛprə'beʃən
reproduce ‚riprə'djus, -'dɪus, -'dus |-s -ɪz
|-d -t
reproduction ‚riprə'dʌkʃən -tive -tɪv
reproof rɪ'pruf
re-proof 'proof again' ‚ri'pruf |-ed -t
reproval rɪ'pruv‖
reprove rɪ'pruv |-d -d |-vable -əb‖ |-bly -blɪ
reptile 'rɛpt‖, -tɪl |-lism -‚ɪzəm
reptilian rɛp'tɪlɪən
republic rɪ'pʌblɪk |-an -ən |-anism -ən‚ɪzəm
republication ‚ripʌblɪ'keʃən
republish ri'pʌblɪʃ |-es -ɪz |-ed -t
repudiate rɪ'pjudɪ‚et, -'pɪu- |-d -ɪd
repudiation rɪ‚pjudɪ'eʃən, -‚pɪu-
repugnance rɪ'pʌgnəns |-cy -ɪ |-nant -nənt
repulse rɪ'pʌls |-s -ɪz |-d -t
repulsion rɪ'pʌlʃən |-sive -sɪv
repurchase ri'pɝtʃəs, -ɪs; ES -'pɝtʃ-, -'pɝtʃ-;
|-s -ɪz |-d -t
reputability ‚rɛpjətə'bɪlətɪ
reputable 'rɛpjətəb‖ |-bly -blɪ
reputation ‚rɛpjə'teʃən
repute rɪ'pjut, -'pɪut |-d -ɪd
request rɪ'kwɛst |-ed -ɪd
requiem, R- 'rikwɪəm, 'rɛk-
requiescat ‚rɛkwɪ'ɛskæt
require rɪ'kwaɪr; ES -'kwaɪə(r; |-d -d
requisite 'rɛkwəzɪt |-tion ‚rɛkwə'zɪʃən
requite rɪ'kwaɪt |-d -ɪd |-tal -‖
reread pres ri'rid |past -read -'rɛd
re-recover ‚rirɪ'kʌvɝ; ES -'kʌvə(r
reredos 'rɪrdɑs; ES 'rɪədɑs, -dɒs; |-es -ɪz
re-refine ‚rirɪ'faɪn |-d -d
re-revise ‚rirɪ'vaɪz |-s -ɪz |-d -d
reroute ri'rut, -'raʊt |-d -ɪd
rerun ri'rʌn |-ran -'ræn |-run -'rʌn
Resaca rɪ'sakə
resale ri'sel ('re‚sale 'price)
resartus, R- rɪ'sartəs; ES -'sɑːt-, E+-'sɑːt-
rescind rɪ'sɪnd |-ed -ɪd
rescission rɪ'sɪʒən, -'sɪʃən
rescript 'riskrɪpt
rescue 'rɛskju |-d -d
reseal ri'sil |-ed -d
research n 'risɝtʃ, rɪ'sɝtʃ; ES -ɜtʃ, -ɜtʃ;
|-es -ɪz

research v rɪ'sɝtʃ, 'risɝtʃ; ES -ɜtʃ, -ɜtʃ; |-es
-ɪz |-ed -t
reseat ri'sit |-ed -ɪd
resell ri'sɛl |-sold -'sold
resemblance rɪ'zɛmbləns |-s -ɪz
resemble rɪ'zɛmb‖ |-d -d |-ling -blɪŋ, -b‖ɪŋ
resend ri'sɛnd |-sent -'sɛnt
resent 'object to' rɪ'zɛnt |-ed -ɪd
resent 'sent again' ri'sɛnt
reservation ‚rɛzɝ'veʃən; ES ‚rɛzə-
reserve rɪ'zɝv; ES -'zɜv, -'zɝv; |-d -d |-dly
-ɪdlɪ
re-serve 's. anew' ‚ri'sɝv; ES -'sɜv, -'sɝv;
|-d -d
reservoir 'rɛzɝ‚vɔr, 'rɛzə-, -‚vwɔr, -‚vwar; ES
'rɛzə‚vɔə(r, -‚vwɔə(r, -‚vwɑ:(r;—ɝ becomes
ə in 'rɛzə‚vɔr by dissimilation (§121).
reset n 'risɛt, ri'sɛt, v ri'sɛt
resettle ri'sɛt‖ |-d -d |-ling -'sɛtlɪŋ, -t‖ɪŋ
reshape ri'ʃep |-d -t |-d -t or -n -ən
reship ri'ʃɪp |-ped -t
reside rɪ'zaɪd |-d -ɪd
residence 'rɛzədəns |-cy -ɪ |-dent -dənt
residential ‚rɛzə'dɛnʃəl |-ly -ɪ
residual rɪ'zɪdʒʊəl |-duary -dʒʊ‚ɛrɪ
residue 'rɛzə‚dju, -‚dɪu, -‚du
residuum rɪ'zɪdʒʊəm |-dua -dʒʊə
resign 'give up' rɪ'zaɪn |-ed -d |-edly -ɪdlɪ
re-sign 's. again' ‚ri'saɪn |-ed -d
resignation ‚rɛzɪg'neʃən, ‚rɛs-
resilience rɪ'zɪlɪəns |-cy -ɪ |-ent -ənt
resin 'rɛzn̩, -zɪn |-ous -əs
resist rɪ'zɪst |-ed -ɪd |-ance -əns |-ant -ənt
resistible rɪ'zɪstəb‖ |-table -təb‖ |-bly -blɪ
resold ri'sold
resole ri'sol |-soled -'sold
resolute 'rɛzə‚lut, -‚lɪut, 'rɛz‖‚jut
resolution ‚rɛzə'luʃən, -'lɪu-, -z‖'juʃən
resolve rɪ'zalv, -'zɒlv |-d -d |-dly -ɪdlɪ
resolvent rɪ'zalvənt, -'zɒlv-
resonance 'rɛznəns |-s -ɪz |-cy -ɪ |-ant -ənt
resort rɪ'zɔrt; ES -'zɔət; |-ed -ɪd
re-sort 's. anew' ‚ri'sɔrt; ES -'sɔət; |-ed -ɪd
resound 'echo' rɪ'zaʊnd |-ed -ɪd
re-sound 's. anew' ‚ri'saʊnd |-ed -ɪd
resource rɪ'sors, 'risors, -ɔrs; ES -oəs, E
-ɔəs; |-s -ɪz
resourceful rɪ'sorsfəl, -'sɔrs-; ES -'soəs-,
E+-'sɔəs-; |-ly -ɪ

|full fʊl |tooth tuθ |further 'fɝðɝ; ES 'fɝðə |custom 'kʌstəm |while hwaɪl |how haʊ |toy tɔɪ
|using 'juzɪŋ |fuse fjuz, fɪuz |dish dɪʃ |vision 'vɪʒən |Eden 'idn̩ |cradle 'kred‖ |keep 'em 'kipm̩

respect rɪˈspɛkt |-ed -ɪd |-able -əbḷ |-bly -blɪ
|-ive -ɪv
respectability rɪˌspɛktəˈbɪlətɪ
respell riˈspɛl |-ed -d or -spelt -ˈspɛlt
respiration ˌrɛspəˈreʃən
respirator ˈrɛspəˌretɚ; ES -ˌretə(r
respiratory rɪˈspaɪrəˌtorɪ, -ˌtɔrɪ; S -ˌtɔrɪ
respire rɪˈspaɪr; ES -ˈspaɪə(r; |-d -d
respite ˈrɛspɪt |-d -ɪd
resplendence rɪˈsplɛndəns |-cy -ɪ |-dent -dənt
respond rɪˈspɑnd; ES+-ˈspɒnd; |-ed -ɪd |-ent
-ənt
response rɪˈspɑns; ES+-ˈspɒns; |-s -ɪz
responsibility rɪˌspɑnsəˈbɪlətɪ; ES+-ˌspɒns-
responsible rɪˈspɑnsəbḷ; ES+-ˈspɒns-; |-bly
-blɪ
responsive rɪˈspɑnsɪv; ES+-ˈspɒns-
rest rɛst |rested ˈrɛstɪd
restate riˈstet |-stated -ˈstetɪd
restaurant ˈrɛstərənt, -ˌrɑnt
restaurateur ˌrɛstərəˈtɝ; ES -ˈtɜ(r, -ˈtɝ; (Fr
rɛstöraˈtœːr)
Restigouche ˌrɛstɪˈguʃ |-ˈs -ɪz
restitution ˌrɛstəˈtjuʃən, -ˈtɪu-, -ˈtu-
restive ˈrɛstɪv
restock riˈstɑk; ES+-ˈstɒk; |-ed -t
restoration ˌrɛstəˈreʃən
restorative rɪˈstorətɪv, -ˈstɔr-; S -ˈstɔr-
restore rɪˈstor, -ˈstɔr; ES -ˈstoə(r, E+-ˈstɔə(r;
|-d -d
restrain rɪˈstren |-ed -d |-edly -ɪdlɪ, -dlɪ
restraint rɪˈstrent
restrict rɪˈstrɪkt |-ed -ɪd
restriction rɪˈstrɪkʃən |-tive -tɪv
restring riˈstrɪŋ |-strung -ˈstrʌŋ
result rɪˈzʌlt |-ed -ɪd |-ant -ˈzʌltṇt
resume rɪˈzum, -ˈzɪum, -ˈzjum |-d -d
résumé ˌrɛzuˈme, ˌrɛzjuˈme |-ed -d
resumption rɪˈzʌmpʃən |-tive -tɪv
resurface riˈsɝfɪs, -əs; ES -ˈsɝf-, -ˈsɝf-; |-s
-ɪz |-d -t
resurge rɪˈsɝdʒ; ES -ˈsɝdʒ, -ˈsɝdʒ; |-s -ɪz |-d
-d |-nce -əns |-ncy -ənsɪ |-nt -ənt
resurrect ˌrɛzəˈrɛkt |-ed -ɪd |-ction -kʃən
resurvey n riˈsɝve, ˌrisɚˈve; ES -ˈsɝ-, -ˈsɝ-,
ˌrisə-
resurvey v ˌrisɚˈve; ES -səˈve; |-ed -d
resuscitate rɪˈsʌsəˌtet |-d -ɪd
resuscitation rɪˌsʌsəˈteʃən

ret rɛt |retted ˈrɛtɪd
retail n, adj ˈritel
retail v ˈritel, ˈrepeat'+rɪˈtel |-ed -d
retain rɪˈten |-ed -d |-er -ɚ; ES -ə(r
retake n ˈriˌtek
retake v riˈtek |-took -ˈtʊk |-taken -ˈtekən
retaliate rɪˈtælɪˌet |-d -ɪd |-tive -ɪv
retaliation rɪˌtælɪˈeʃən
retaliatory rɪˈtælɪəˌtorɪ, -ˌtɔrɪ; S -ˌtɔrɪ
retard rɪˈtɑrd; ES -ˈtɑːd, E+-ˈtɑːd; |-ed -ɪd
retardation ˌritɑrˈdeʃən; ES -tɑː-, E+-tɑː-
retch rɛtʃ |retch ˈrɛtʃɪz |retched rɛtʃt
retell riˈtɛl |-told -ˈtold
retention rɪˈtɛnʃən |-tive -tɪv
retentivity ˌritɛnˈtɪvətɪ
retiarius ˌriʃɪˈɛrɪəs, -ˈɛrɪəs |-ˈs -ɪz |-rii -rɪˌaɪ
|-ary ˈriʃɪˌɛrɪ
reticence ˈrɛtəsṇs |-cy -ɪ |-cent -sṇt
reticulate adj rɪˈtɪkjəlɪt, -ˌlet
reticulate v rɪˈtɪkjəˌlet |-lated -ˌletɪd
reticulation rɪˌtɪkjəˈleʃən
reticule ˈrɛtɪˌkjul, -ˌkɪul |-d -d
reticulum rɪˈtɪkjələm |-la -lə
retina ˈrɛtṇə, -tɪnə |-s -z |-nae -tṇˌi, -tɪˌni
retinue ˈrɛtṇˌju, -ˌɪu, -ˌu, -tɪˌnju, -ˌnɪu, -ˌnu
|-d -d
retire rɪˈtaɪr; ES -ˈtaɪə(r; |-d -d
re-tire ˈchange tires' ˌriˈtaɪr; ES -ˈtaɪə(r
retold riˈtold
retook riˈtʊk
retort rɪˈtɔrt; ES -ˈtɔət; |-ed -ɪd
retouch riˈtʌtʃ |-es -ɪz |-ed -t
retrace ˈt. back' rɪˈtres |-s -ɪz |-d -t
re-trace ˈt. again' ˌriˈtres |-s -ɪz |-d -t
retract rɪˈtrækt |-ed -ɪd |-ile -ḷ, -ɪl
retractation ˌritrækˈteʃən
retraction rɪˈtrækʃən |-tive -tɪv
retread tire ˌriˈtrɛd |-ed -ɪd |n ˈriˌtrɛd
retread, re-t- ˈt. anew' riˈtrɛd |-trod -ˈtrɑd
|-trodden -ˈtrɑdṇ or -trod -ˈtrɑd; |ES+
-ˈtrɒd(ṇ
retreat rɪˈtrit |-ed -ɪd
retrench rɪˈtrɛntʃ |-es -ɪz |-ed -t
retrial riˈtraɪəl, -ˈtraɪl
retribution ˌrɛtrəˈbjuʃən, -ˈbɪu-
retributive rɪˈtrɪbjətɪv |-tory -ˌtorɪ, -ˌtɔrɪ;
S -ˌtɔrɪ
retrieve rɪˈtriv |-d -d |-al -ḷ
retroact ˌrɛtroˈækt |-ed -ɪd

Key: *See in full §§3–47.* bee bi |pity ˈpɪtɪ (§6) |rate ret |yet jɛt |sang sæŋ |angry ˈæŋ·grɪ
|bath bæθ; E baθ (§10) |ah ɑ |far fɑr |watch wɑtʃ, wɒtʃ (§12) |jaw dʒɔ |gorge gɔrdʒ |go go

retroaction ˌretro'ækʃən |-tive -tɪv
retrocede ˌretro'sid |-d -ɪd |-nce -ɲs |-nt -ɲt
retrocession ˌretro'sɛʃən |-sive -'sɛsɪv
retroflex 'retrəˌflɛks |-es -ɪz |-ed -t
retroflexion, -ction ˌretro'flɛkʃən
retrograde 'retrəˌgred |-d -ɪd
retrogress v 'retrəˌgres, ˌretrə'gres |-es -ɪz
  |-ed -t
retrogression ˌretrə'grɛʃən |-sive -'grɛsɪv
retrospect 'retrəˌspɛkt |-ed -ɪd
retrospection ˌretrə'spɛkʃən |-tive -tɪv
retry ri'traɪ |-tried -'traɪd
return rɪ'tɜn; ES -'tɜn, -'tɜn; |-ed -d
retuse rɪ'tjus, -'tɪus, -'tus
Reuben 'rubɪn, 'rɪu-, -ən
reune ri'jun |-d -d |-nion -jən |-nioned -jənd
reunite ˌriju'naɪt |-d -ɪd
Reuter 'rɔɪtɚ; ES 'rɔɪtə(r; (Ger 'rɔytər)
revalue ri'vælju |-d -d |-uation ˌrivælju'eʃən
revamp ri'væmp |-ed -t
reveal rɪ'vil |-ed -d
reveille 'rɛvlˌi, -ɪ, ˌrɛvl'i (Fr réveillez revɛ'je)
revel 'rɛvl̩ |-ed -d |-ing -vlɪŋ, -vl̩ŋ
revelation, R- ˌrɛvl̩'eʃən
reveler 'rɛvlɚ, 'rɛvlɚ; ES -ə(r; |-lry -vl̩rɪ
Revelstoke 'rɛvl̩ˌstok
revenge rɪ'vɛndʒ |-s -ɪz |-d -d
revenue 'rɛvəˌnju, -ˌnɪu, -ˌnu |-d -d
reverbatory rɪ'vɜbəˌtorɪ, -ˌtɔrɪ; ES -'vɜbə-
  ˌtorɪ, -'vɜb-, E+-ˌtɔrɪ—reduced from reverberatory by r-dissimilation (§121)
reverberate adj rɪ'vɜbərɪt, -ˌret; ES -'vɜb-,
  -'vɜb-
reverberate v rɪ'vɜbəˌret; ES -'vɜb-, -'vɜb-;
  |-d -ɪd
reverberation rɪˌvɜbə'reʃən; ES -ˌvɜb-,
  -ˌvɜb-
reverberatory rɪ'vɜbrəˌtorɪ, -bərə-, -ˌtɔrɪ; ES
  -'vɜbrəˌtorɪ, -'vɜb-, -bərə-, E+-ˌtɔrɪ
revere, R- rɪ'vɪr; ES -'vɪə(r, S+-'vɛə(r; |-d -d
reverence 'rɛvrəns, -vərəns |-s -ɪz |-d -t
reverend 'rɛvrənd, -vərənd, as a title+-rən
reverent 'rɛvrənt, 'rɛvərənt
reverential ˌrɛvə'rɛnʃəl |-ly -ɪ
reverie 'rɛvərɪ, 'rɛvrɪ
reverify ri'vɛrəˌfaɪ |-fied -ˌfaɪd
revers rə'vɪr, -'vɛr; ES -'vɪə(r, -'vɛə(r; (Fr
  rə've:r)
reversal rɪ'vɜsl̩; ES -'vɜs-, -'vɜs-

reverse rɪ'vɜs; ES -'vɜs, -'vɜs; |-s -ɪz |-d -t
  |-dly -ɪdlɪ, -tlɪ
reversible rɪ'vɜsəbl̩; ES -'vɜs-, -'vɜs-; |-bly
  -blɪ
reversion rɪ'vɜʒən, -'vɜʃ-; ES -'vɜ-, -'vɜ-;
  |-al -l̩ |-ally -lɪ |-ary -ˌɛrɪ
revert rɪ'vɜt; ES -'vɜt, -'vɜt; |-ed -ɪd
revery 'rɛvərɪ, 'rɛvrɪ
revet rɪ'vɛt |-ted -ɪd
revictual ri'vɪtl̩ |-ed -d
review rɪ'vju, -'vɪu |-ed -d
revile rɪ'vaɪl |-viled -'vaɪld
revise rɪ'vaɪz |-s -ɪz |-d -d
revision rɪ'vɪʒən |-al -l̩ |-ary -ˌɛrɪ
revisit ri'vɪzɪt |-ed -ɪd
revisory rɪ'vaɪzərɪ
revitalize ri'vaɪtl̩ˌaɪz |-s -ɪz |-d -d
revival rɪ'vaɪvl̩ |-ism -ˌɪzəm |-ist -ɪst
revive rɪ'vaɪv |-d -d
revivify ri'vɪvəˌfaɪ |-fied -ˌfaɪd
revocable 'rɛvəkəbl̩ |-bly -blɪ, cf irrevocable
revocation ˌrɛvə'keʃən
revokable rɪ'vokəbl̩, cf revocable
revoke rɪ'vok |-d -t
revolt rɪ'volt |-ed -ɪd
revolution, R- ˌrɛvə'luʃən, -'lɪu-, ˌrɛvl̩'juʃən
  |-ary -ˌɛrɪ |-ize -ˌaɪz |-izes -ˌaɪzɪz |-ized
  -ˌaɪzd
revolve rɪ'vɑlv, -'vɒlv |-d -d |-r -ɚ; ES -ə(r
revue rɪ'vju, -'vɪu (Fr rə'vy)
revulsion rɪ'vʌlʃən
reward rɪ'wɔrd; ES -'wɔəd; |-ed -ɪd
rewire ri'waɪr; ES -'waɪə(r; |-d -d
reword ri'wɜd; ES -'wɜd, -'wɜd; |-ed -ɪd
rework ri'wɜk; ES -'wɜk, -'wɜk; |-ed -t
rewrite ri'raɪt |-wrote -'rot |-written -'rɪtn̩
rex, R- rɛks |Rex's 'rɛksɪz |L pl reges 'ridʒiz
Reykjavik 'rekjəˌvik
Reynaldo rɪ'nældo
Reynard 'renɚd, 'renəd; ES -nəd
Reynolds 'renl̩dz, 'renl̩z |-'s -ɪz
rhachitis rə'kaɪtɪs |-chitic -'kɪtɪk
Rhadamanthus ˌrædə'mænθəs |-'s -ɪz
Rhaetia 'rɪʃɪə, -ʃə |-n 'riʃən
Rhaeto-Romance 'rito·ro'mæns |-manic
  -'mænɪk
rhapsodic ræp'sɑdɪk; ES+-'sɒd-; |-al -l̩
  |-ally -l̩ɪ, -ɪklɪ
rhapsodist 'ræpsədɪst |-dy -dɪ |-died -dɪd

|full fʊl |tooth tuθ |further 'fɜðɚ; ES 'fɜðə |custom 'kʌstəm |while hwaɪl |how haʊ |toy tɔɪ
|using 'juzɪŋ |fuse fjuz, fɪuz |dish dɪʃ |vision 'vɪʒən |Eden 'idn̩ |cradle 'kredl̩ |keep 'em 'kipm̩

rhapsodize 'ræpsə‚daɪz |-s -ɪz |-d -d

Rhea, r- 'riə, *Tenn co.* re

Rheims rimz |-'s -ɪz (*Fr* ræ̃:s)

Rheingold 'raɪn‚gold

Rhemish 'rimɪʃ

Rhenish 'rɛnɪʃ

rhenium 'riniəm

rheostat 'riə‚stæt |-ic ‚riə'stætɪk

Rhesus, r- 'risəs |-sus' -səs

rhetoric 'rɛtərɪk |-rician ‚rɛtə'rɪʃən

rhetorical rɪ'tɔrɪk], -'tɑr-, -'tɒr- |-ly -ɪ, -ɪklɪ

rheum rum, rɪum |-atism -ə‚tɪzəm

rheumatic ru'mætɪk, rɪu- |-al -] |-ally -]ɪ, -ɪklɪ

rhinal 'raɪn]

Rhine raɪn |-land -‚lænd

Rhinelander 'raɪnləndɚ; ES -də(r

rhinestone 'raɪn‚ston

rhinitis raɪ'naɪtɪs

rhino 'raɪno

rhinoceros raɪ'nɑsərəs, -srəs; ES+-'nɒs-; |-'s -ɪz

rhizoid 'raɪzɔɪd |-zome -zom

rho ro

Rhoades rodz |-'s -ɪz

Rhoda 'rodə

Rhode Island rod'aɪlənd, ro'daɪ-

Rhodes rodz |-'s -ɪz |-dian -dɪən

Rhodesia ro'diʒɪə, -ʒə—*see* -sia

rhodium 'rodɪəm

rhododendron ‚rodə'dɛndrən |-s -z |-dra -drə

rhodomontade ‚rɑdəman'ted, -'tad; ES+‚rɒdəmɒn-; (*Fr* rɔ̃dɔ̃mɔ̃'tad)

rhodora, R- ro'dorə, -'dɔrə; S -'dorə

Rhoecus 'rikəs |-'s -ɪz

rhomb rɑmb, rɑm, rɒ- |-bus -mbəs

Rhone ron

rhotacism 'rotə‚sɪzəm

rhubarb 'rubɑrb, 'rɪu-; ES -bɑ:b, E+-ba:b

rhumb rʌm, rʌmb

rhumba 'rʌmbə (*Sp* 'rumba)

rhyme raɪm |rhymed raɪmd |-ster -stɚ; ES -stə(r

Rhyolite 'raɪə‚laɪt

Rhys ris |Rhys's 'risɪz

rhythm 'rɪðəm, *less freq.* 'rɪðm̩

rhythmic 'rɪðmɪk |-al -] |-ally -]ɪ, -ɪklɪ

rhythmproof 'rɪðəm'pruf ('rhythm‚proof 'ear)

Rialto, r- rɪ'ælto (*It* ri'alto)

rib rɪb |ribbed rɪbd

ribald 'rɪb]d |-ry -rɪ

riband 'rɪbənd, 'rɪbən

ribband '*ribbon*' 'rɪbənd, 'rɪbən

ribband, rib-band *shipbuilding* 'rɪb‚bænd, 'rɪbənd, 'rɪbən

ribbon 'rɪbən |-ed -d

rice, R- raɪs |Rice's 'raɪsɪz

rich rɪtʃ |riches 'rɪtʃɪz |riched rɪtʃt

Richard 'rɪtʃəd; ES 'rɪtʃəd; |-son -sn̩

Richelieu ‚rɪʃə'lu, -'lɪu (*Fr* riʃə'ljə)

Richland 'rɪtʃlənd

Richmond 'rɪtʃmənd

Richter 'rɪktɚ, 'rɪx-; ES -tə(r; (*Ger* 'rɪxtər)

rick rɪk |ricked rɪkt

Rickard 'rɪkɚd; ES 'rɪkəd; |-s -z

rickets 'rɪkɪts |-ty -tɪ

rickey 'rɪkɪ

ricksha, -shaw 'rɪkʃɔ

ricochet ‚rɪkə'ʃe, -'ʃɛt |-cheted -'ʃed |-chetted -'ʃɛtɪd

rid rɪd |rid rɪd *or* ridded 'rɪdɪd

ridable 'raɪdəb] |-bly -blɪ

Ridd rɪd

riddance 'rɪdn̩s |-s -ɪz

Riddell 'rɪd], rɪ'dɛl

ridden 'rɪdn̩—'rɪdən *is seldom heard.*

riddle 'rɪd] |-d -d |-ling 'rɪdlɪŋ, 'rɪd]ɪŋ

ride raɪd |rode rod |ridden 'rɪdn̩

rideable 'raɪdəb] |-bly -blɪ

Rider, r- 'raɪdɚ; ES 'raɪdə(r

ridge rɪdʒ |ridges 'rɪdʒɪz |ridged rɪdʒd

ridgepole 'rɪdʒ‚pol |-d -d

Ridgeway, -dgway 'rɪdʒ‚we

ridicule 'rɪdɪ‚kjul, -‚kɪul |-d -d

ridiculous rɪ'dɪkjələs

Ridley 'rɪdlɪ

Rienzi rɪ'ɛnzɪ |-zo -zo (*It* ri'ɛntsi, -tso)

rifacimento rɪ‚fɑtʃɪ'mɛnto (*It* ri‚fɑtʃi'mento)

rife raɪf

riffle 'rɪf] |-d -d |-ling 'rɪflɪŋ, 'rɪf]ɪŋ

riffraff 'rɪf‚ræf

rifle 'raɪf] |-d -d |-ling 'raɪflɪŋ, 'raɪf]ɪŋ

rifleman 'raɪf]mən |-men -mən

rift rɪft |rifted 'rɪftɪd

rig rɪg |rigged rɪgd

Riga 'rigə, *NY* 'raɪgə

Rigdon 'rɪgdən

Rigel 'raɪg], 'raɪdʒəl

Key: See in full §§3–47. bee bi |pity 'pɪtɪ (§6) |rate ret |yet jɛt |sang sæŋ |angry 'æŋ‧grɪ |bath bæθ; E baθ (§10) |ah ɑ |far fɑr |watch wɑtʃ, wɒtʃ (§12) |jaw dʒɔ |gorge gɔrdʒ |go go

right **rait** |righted **'raitid**
rightabout **'raitə,baut**
right-and-left **'raitṇ'lɛft**
right-angled **'rait'æŋgḷd** ('right-,angled 'turn)
righteous **'raitʃəs**
rightful **'raitfəl** |-ly -ɪ
right-hand **'rait'hænd** ('right-,hand 'screw,
   'right-'hand ,one)
right-handed **'rait'hændid**
right-of-way ,**raitəv'we**, ,**raitə'we**
rigid **'ridʒid** |-ity ri'dʒidəti
rigmarole **'rigmə,rol** |-d -d |-lery -əri, -ri
Rigoletto ,**rigə'lɛto** (*It* ,**rigo'letto**)
rigor **'rigɚ**; ES **'rigə(r**; |-ous -əs, -grəs
rigor mortis **'raigɔr'mɔrtis**, **'rigɚ-**; ES
   'raigɔə'mɔətis, **'rigə-**
Rig-Veda **rig'vedə**, -**'vidə**
Riis **'ris** |-'s -ɪz
Rijswijk **'raiswaik**
Rikki-Tiki-Tavi ,**riki,tiki'tevi**, -**'tavi**
rile **rail** |riled **raild** |-y -ɪ
Riley **'raili**
rill **ril** |rilled **rild**
rim **rim** |rimmed **rimd**
rime **raim** |rimed **raimd** |-ster -stɚ; ES -stə(r
Rimmon **'rimən**
Rimski-Korsakov **'rimski'kɔrsə,kɔf**, -,**kɒf**;
   ES -**'kɔəsə-**
rimy **'raimi**
Rinaldo **ri'nældo**
rind **raind**, **rain**
rinderpest **'rindɚ,pɛst**; ES **'rində-**
Rinehart **'rainhart**; ES -ha:t, E+-ha:t
ring *'circle,' 'provide with a ring'* **riŋ** |ringed
   riŋd *or* rung **rʌŋ**
ring *'sound'* **riŋ** |rang **ræŋ** |rung **rʌŋ**
ringbolt **'riŋ,bolt**
ringdove **'riŋ,dʌv**
ringleader **'riŋ,lidɚ**, -**'lidɚ**; ES -də(r
ringlet **'riŋlit** |-ed -id
ringside **'riŋ,said**
ringworm **'riŋ,wɝm**; ES -,wɜm, -,wɝm
rink **riŋk** |rinked **riŋkt**
rinse **rins** |rinses **'rinsiz** |rinsed **rinst**
Rio de Janeiro **'riodədʒə'niro**, -**deʒə'nero**
   (*Pg* **'riuðəʒa'nɛiru**)
Rio Grande *US* ,**rio'grænd**, ,**rio-**, ,**raiə-**,
   ,**rio'grændi**; *Nicar, Bol* ,**rio'grande**; *Braz*
   ,**riu'grandə**

riot **'raiət** |-ed -id |-ous -əs
rip **rip** |ripped **ript**
riparian **ri'pɛriən**, **rai-**, -**'pær-**, -**'per-**
ripe **raip** |riped **raipt**
ripen **'raipən**, -**pṃ** |-ed -d |-ing **'raipniŋ**,
   -**pəniŋ**
Ripley **'ripli**
Ripman **'ripmən**
Ripon **'ripən**
riposte, -st **ri'post** |-(e)d -id
ripper **'ripɚ**; ES **'ripə(r**
ripple **'ripl** |-d -d |-ling **'ripliŋ**, **'ripḷiŋ**
riprap **'rip,ræp** |-ped -t
ripsaw **'rip,sɔ** |-ed -d
Rip van Winkle ,**ripvæn'wiŋkḷ**, -**vən-**
rise **raiz** |-s -ɪz |rose **roz** |risen **'rizṇ**—**rais** *for
   the noun* rise *once had some currency, but
   evidently never prevailed. Both meaning and
   pronunciation come from the verb.*
risibility ,**rizə'biləti**
risible **'rizəbḷ** |-bly -bḷi
risk **risk** |risked **riskt** |-y -ɪ
risqué **ris'ke** (*Fr* ris'ke)
Rita **'ritə**
ritardando ,**ritar'dændo**, -**'dan-**; ES -**ta:-**
rite **rait**
Ritson **'ritsṇ**
Rittenhouse **'ritṇ,haus** |-'s -ɪz
ritual **'ritʃuəl** |-ly -ɪ |-ism -,izəm |-ist -ist
ritualistic ,**ritʃuəl'istik** |-ally -ḷi, -ikli
ritualless **'ritʃuəllis**
rivage **'rividʒ** |-s -ɪz
rival **'raivḷ** |-ed -d |-ing **'raivliŋ**, -**vḷiŋ**
rivaless **'raivḷis** |-es -ɪz
rivalless **'raivḷlis**
rivalry **'raivḷri**
rive **raiv** |-d -d |-d -d *or* riven **'rivən**
river *'who rives'* **'raivɚ**; ES **'raivə(r**
river *'stream'* **'rivɚ**; ES **'rivə(r**; |-side -,said
Rivers **'rivɚz**; ES **'rivəz**; |-'s -ɪz
Rives **rivz** |-'s -ɪz
rivet **'rivit** |-ed -id
Rivett **'rivit**
Riviera ,**rivi'ɛrə** (*It* ri'vjɛ:ra)
rivulet **'rivjəlit**
rix-dollar **'riks,dalɚ**; ES -,**dalə(r**, -,**dɒl-**
roach **rotʃ** |-es -ɪz |-ed -t
road **rod** |-ed -id; |*N Engd*+**rɔd** (§46)
roadbed **'rod,bɛd**

Those words below in which the ɑ *sound is spelt* o *are often pronounced with* ɒ *in E and S*

roadhouse 'rod,haʊs |-houses -,haʊzɪz
roadstead 'rod,stɛd
roadster 'rodstɚ; ES 'rodstə(r
roadway 'rod,we
roam rom |roamed romd |-age -ɪdʒ
roan ron
roanoke ,roə'nok
Roanoke 'roə,nok, 'ronok
roar ror, rɔr; ES roə(r, E+rɔə(r; |-ed -d
roast rost |roasted 'rostɪd
roast beef 'rost'bif, 'ros'bif
rob, R- rab |-bed -d |-ber -ɚ; ES -ə(r
robbery 'rabrɪ, 'rabərɪ
robe rob |robed robd
Robert 'rabɚt; ES 'rabət
Roberta ro'bɝtə; ES -'bɝtə, -'bɝtə
Robeson *surname* 'robsn̩; *NC* 'rabəsn̩
Robespierre 'robzpjɛr, -pɪr; ES -pjɛə(r, -pɪə(r; (*Fr* rɔbɛs'pjɛːr)
robin, R- 'rabɪn |-son -sn̩
robot 'robət, 'rab-, -bat
Rob Roy 'rab'rɔɪ
Robsart 'rabsart; ES 'rabsaːt, E+-saːt
Robson 'rabsn̩
robust ro'bʌst |-ious -'bʌstʃəs ('ro,bust 'boy)
roc rak
Rochambeau ,roʃæm'bo (*Fr* rɔʃɑ̃'bo)
Rochdale 'ratʃdel
Rochelle ro'ʃɛl
Rochester 'ra,tʃɛstɚ, 'ratʃɪstɚ; ES -tə(r
rochet 'ratʃɪt |-ed -ɪd
rock rak |rocked rakt
rockaway, R- 'rakə,we
rock-bottom 'rak'batəm ('rock-,bottom 'price)
rock-bound 'rak,baʊnd, -'baʊnd
Rockefeller 'rakɪ,fɛlɚ, 'rakə-; ES -,fɛlə(r
rocket 'rakɪt |-ed -ɪd
Rockingham *Marquis* 'rakɪŋəm; *US* 'rakɪŋ,hæm
Rockford 'rakfɚd; ES 'rakfəd
rock-garden 'rak,gardn̩, -dɪn; ES -,gaːd-, E+-,gaːd-
Rock Island 'rak'aɪlənd
rock-ribbed 'rak'rɪbd ('rock-,ribbed 'hills)
rock salt 'rak'sɔlt
rockweed 'rak,wid
rococo rə'koko (*Fr* rɔkɔ'ko, roko-)
rod rad |rodded 'radɪd

rode rod
rodent 'rodn̩t
rodeo 'rodɪ,o, ro'deo (*Sp* ro'ðeo), *cf* roleo
Roderic, -ick 'radərɪk, 'radrɪk
Roderigo ,radə'rigo
Rodin ro'dæn |-esque ,rodæn'ɛsk (*Fr* ro'dæ̃)
rodman, R- 'radmən |-men -mən
Rodney 'radnɪ
Rodolph 'rodalf
rodomontade ,radəman'ted, -'tad (*Fr* rɔdɔmɔ̃'tad)
roe, R- ro |roed rod
roebuck, R- 'ro,bʌk
Roentgen 'rɛntgən (*Ger* 'rœntgən)
rogation ro'geʃən
rogatory 'ragə,torɪ, -,tɔrɪ; S -,tɔrɪ
Roger 'radʒɚ; ES 'radʒə(r; |-s -z |-s's -zɪz
rogerian, R- ro'dʒɪrɪən
Roget *Eng author* 'roʒe, ro'ʒe
rogue rog |rogued rogd |-ry -ərɪ |-guish -ɪʃ
roil rɔɪl, '*vex*' + rail |-ed -d |-y -ɪ
roister 'rɔɪstɚ; ES 'rɔɪstə(r; |-ed -d |-ing 'rɔɪstrɪŋ, 'rɔɪstərɪŋ
roister-doister, R-D- 'rɔɪstɚ,dɔɪstɚ; ES 'rɔɪstə,dɔɪstə(r
Roland 'rolənd
role, rôle rol
roleo 'rolɪ,o—*cf* rodeo
Rolfe ralf
roll rol |rolled rold
Rolla 'ralə
Rolle rol
rollick 'ralɪk |-ed -t
Rollin 'ralɪn |-s -z |-s's -zɪz
rolling-mill 'rolɪŋ,mɪl
rolling-pin 'rolɪŋ,pɪn
Rollo 'ralo, -ə
Rolls-Royce 'rolz'rɔɪs |-s -ɪz
Rölvaag 'rolvag, 'rɔlvɔg (*Norw* 'rœlvɔg)—*the American family prefer* 'rolvag.
roly-poly 'rolɪ,polɪ ('rolɪ'poly ,one)
Romaic ro'me·ɪk
Romain ro'men (*Fr* rɔ'mæ̃)
romaine ro'men ('ro,maine 'lettuce)
Roman 'romən |-ism -,ɪzəm |-ist -ɪst
Romance ro'mæns ('Ro,mance 'language)
romance *n* ro'mæns, rə-, 'romæns |-s -ɪz
romance *v* ro'mæns, rə- |-s -ɪz |-d -t

Those words below in which the ɑ sound is spelt o are often pronounced with ɒ in E and S

Romanes roˈmanɪz |-es' -ˈmanɪz
Romanesque ˌromənˈɛsk (ˈRomanˌesque ˈstyle)
Romanic roˈmænɪk |-ally -ḷɪ, -ɪklɪ
romanize ˈromənˌaɪz |-s -ɪz |-d -d
Romanov ˈroməˌnɔf, roˈmanɔf, -ɒf
Romansh, -sch roˈmænʃ, -ˈmanʃ
romantic roˈmæntɪk, rə- |-al -ḷ |-ally -ḷɪ, -ɪklɪ
romanticism roˈmæntəˌsɪzəm |-cist -sɪst
romanticize roˈmæntəˌsaɪz |-s -ɪz |-d -d
Romany, Romm- ˈramənɪ
ɪomaunt, R- roˈmant, -ˈmɔnt, -ˈmɒnt
Rome rom
Romeo ˈromɪˌo, ˈromjo
Romic ˈromɪk
Romney ˈramnɪ, ˈrʌmnɪ—*The historical pron. is* ˈrʌmnɪ.
Romola ˈraməlɑ
romp ramp |romped rampt |-ers -ɚz; ES -əz
Romulus ˈramjələs |-'s -ɪz
Ronald ˈranḷd
Ronan ˈronən, ˈranən, ˈrɒn-
Roncesvalles ˈransəˌvælz (*Sp* ˌrɔnθesˈβaʎes)
Roncevaux *Fr* rŏsˈvo
Ronceverte ˈransəˌvɝt; ES -ˌvɜt, -ˌvɝt
rondeau ˈrando, ranˈdo (*Fr* rŏˈdo)
rondel ˈrandḷ, -dɛl
rondelle ranˈdɛl (*Fr* rŏˈdɛl)
rondo ˈrando, ranˈdo
Rondout ˈrandaʊt
Roney ˈronɪ
Ronsard ˈransard, ranˈsard; ES -aːd (*Fr* rŏˈsaːr)
Röntgen ˈrɛntgən (*Ger* ˈrœntgən)
ronyon, runnion ˈrʌnjən
rood, R- rud
roof ruf, rʊf |-ed -t—rʊf *is less freq. in the S.*
rooftree ˈrufˌtri, ˈrʊf-
rook rʊk |-ed -t |-ery -ərɪ |-eried -ərɪd
rookie, -y ˈrʊkɪ
room rum, rʊm |-ed -d |-ful -ˌfʊl |-fuls -ˌfʊlz —rʊm *is frequent in all parts of the US, but apparently less so than* rum.
roommate ˈrumˌmet, ˈrʊm-
roorback, -ch ˈrʊrbæk; ES ˈrʊə-
Roosevelt ˈrozəˌvɛlt, ˈrozvɛlt, ˈrozəvḷt
roost rust |roosted ˈrustɪd
rooster ˈrustɚ, *less freq.* ˈrʊs-; ES -təˌr

root, R- rut, rʊt |-ed -ɪd—rʊt *is less freq. in the S.*
rootstalk ˈrutˌstɔk, ˈrʊt-
rootstock ˈrutˌstak, ˈrʊt-
Rootstown ˈrutsˌtaʊn, ˈruts-, *loc.* ˈrʊts-
rope rop |roped ropt |-walk -ˌwɔk |-py, -pey -ɪ
Roquefort ˈrokfɚt; ES -fət; (*Fr* rŏkˈfɔːr)
Rorke rork, rɔrk; ES rɔək, E+rɔək; *loc.*+ ˈrorək
rorqual ˈrɔrkwəl; ES ˈrɔək-
Rosa ˈrozə
Rosabel ˈrozəˌbɛl |-la ˌrozəˈbɛlə
rosace ˈrozes |-s -ɪz (*Fr* roˈzas)
rosacean roˈzeʃən |-ceous -ʃəs
Rosalind ˈrazˌlɪnd, ˈrazlɪnd—*in Shak.*+-aɪnd
Rosaline ˈrazḷɪn, -ˌaɪn, ˈrozḷˌin
Rosamond ˈrazəmənd, ˈrozə-
rosary ˈrozərɪ
Roscius ˈraʃɪəs |-'s -ɪz
Roscoe ˈrasko
Roscommon rasˈkamən
rose, R- roz |-s -ɪz |-d -d
roseate ˈrozɪɪt
Rosecrans ˈrozɪˌkrænz |-'s -ɪz
Roselle roˈzɛl
rosemary, R- ˈrozˌmɛrɪ, -ˈmærɪ
Rosencrantz ˈrozṇˌkrænts |-'s -ɪz
Rosenwald ˈrozṇˌwɔld
roseola roˈziələ
Roseto roˈzito
Rosetta roˈzɛtə
rosette roˈzɛt |-d -ɪd
Rosh Hashana ˈraʃhəˈʃanə, ˈroʃ-
Rosicrucian ˌrozəˈkruʃən, -ˈkrɪu- |-ism -ˌɪzəm
rosily ˈrozḷɪ, -zɪlɪ
rosin ˈrazṇ, ˈrazɪn |-ed -d
Rosinante ˌrazṇˈæntɪ
Ross, -sse rɔs, rɒs |-'s -ɪz
Rossetti roˈsɛtɪ, -ˈzɛtɪ
Rossillion roˈsɪljən, ru-, *in Shak.* Roˈsillion, Rosˈs-
Rossini roˈsinɪ (*It* rosˈsiːni)
Ross-shire ˈrɔsʃɪr, ˈrɒʃʃ-, ˈrɒ-, -ʃɚ; ES -ʃɪə(r, -ʃə(r
Rostand ˈrastænd, ˈrɒs- (*Fr* rŏsˈtã)
roster ˈrastɚ; ES ˈrastə(r; |-ed -d |-ing ˈrastərɪŋ, -strɪŋ
rostral ˈrastrəl, ˈrɒs- |-ly -ɪ

Those words below in which the ɑ sound is spelt o are often pronounced with ɒ in E and S

rostrum 'rɑstrəm, 'rɒs- |-s -z |-tra -trə
rosy 'rozɪ |rosied 'rozɪd
rot rɑt |rotted 'rɑtɪd
rota, R- 'rotə |-l -t|
rotacism 'rotə‚sɪzəm
Rotarian ro'tɛrɪən, -'tær-, -'ter-
rotary, R- 'rotərɪ
rotate 'rotet |-d -ɪd |-tion ro'teʃən
rote rot |roted 'rotɪd
rother 'rɑðɚ, 'rʌðɚ; ES -ðə(r
Rotherham 'rɑðərəm
Rotherhithe 'rɑðɚ‚haɪð; loc.+'rɛdrɪf; ES
    'rɑðə-; spelt Redriff 1595
Rothermel 'rɑðɚ‚mɛl; ES 'rɑðə-
Rothesay 'rɑθsɪ, -se
Rothley 'roθlɪ
Rothschild 'rɑθtʃaɪld, 'rɑstʃ-, 'rɑθstʃ- (Ger
    'roːt·ʃɪlt)
Rothwell 'rɑθwɛl, loc.+'roəl
rotogravure ‚rotəgrə'vjur, -'grevjɚ; ES
    -'vjʊə(r, -jə(r
rotor 'rotɚ; ES 'rotə(r
rotten 'rɑtn̩ |-ness 'rɑtn̩ɪs
rotten-egg v ‚rɑtn̩'ɛg |-ed -d
Rotterdam 'rɑtɚ‚dæm; ES 'rɑtə-
rotund ro'tʌnd |-ed -ɪd ('ro‚tund 'style)
rotunda ro'tʌndə |-dity -tɪ
rouble 'rubl̩
roué ru'e
Rouen ru'ɑn, ru'ɑ̃ (Fr rwɑ̃)
rouge ruʒ |-s -ɪz |-d -d
Rougemont 'ruʒmɑnt
rough rʌf |roughed rʌft
rough-and-ready 'rʌfn̩'rɛdɪ
rough-and-tumble 'rʌfn̩'tʌmbl̩
roughcast 'rʌf‚kæst; E+-‚kast, -‚kɑst
roughdry adj 'rʌf‚draɪ
roughdry v ‚rʌf'draɪ |-dried -'draɪd
roughen 'rʌfən |-ed -d |-ing 'rʌfənɪŋ, -fnɪŋ
roughhew ‚rʌf'hju, -'hɪu |-ed -d |-ed -d or
    -n -n
roughhouse n 'rʌf‚haus
roughhouse v 'rʌf‚haus |-s -‚hausɪz |-d -‚haust
roughneck 'rʌf‚nɛk
roughrider 'rʌf‚raɪdɚ; ES -‚raɪdə(r
roughshod 'rʌf'ʃɑd; ES+-'ʃɒd; ('rough‚shod
    'nag)
roulade ru'lɑd |-d -ɪd

roulette ru'lɛt
Roum rum
Roumania ru'menɪə |-n -n
rouncy 'raunsɪ
round raund |-ed -ɪd
roundabout n, adj 'raundə‚baut
round about adv, prep 'raundə'baut ('round
    a‚bout 'town)
roundel 'raundl̩ |-ay 'raundə‚le, -dl̩‚e
roundhead, R- 'raund‚hɛd
roundhouse 'raund‚haus |-ses -zɪz
roundness 'raundnɪs, 'raunnɪs
round-shouldered 'raund'ʃoldɚd, 'raun-; ES
    -dəd
roundup 'raund‚ʌp
roup rup
Rourke rork, rɔrk; ES roək, E+rɔək
rouse n rauz, raus spelt rouce in Shak.
rouse v rauz |rouses 'rauzɪz |roused rauzd
Rouse raus |-'s -ɪz
Rouses Point 'rausɪz'pɔɪnt
Rousillon, Rouss- ro'sɪljən, ru- (Fr rusi'jõ),
    in Shak. Ro'sillion, Ros's-
Rousseau ru'so |-ism -ɪzəm
roustabout 'raustə‚baut |-ed -ɪd
rout raut |routed ‚rautɪd
route rut, raut |-d -ɪd
routine ru'tin |-d -d ('rou‚tine 'work)
Routledge 'rʌtlɪdʒ, 'raut- |-'s -ɪz
rove past of reeve rov
rove v rov |roved rovd
row n, v 'brawl' rau |rowed raud
row n, v with oars ro |rowed rod
row n, v 'rank' ro |rowed rod
rowan tree 'roən, 'rauən
rowan 'tuft of wool' 'rauən
Rowan Stephen 'roən, Ky, NC ro'æn
rowboat 'ro‚bot
Rowe ro
rowel 'rauəl |-ed -d
rowen 'rauən
Rowena ro'inə, rə'winə
rower 'disturber,' 'napper' 'rauɚ, 'oarsman'
    'roɚ; ES -ə(r
Rowland 'rolənd
Rowlesburg 'rolzbɝg; ES -bɝg, -bɝ‧g
Rowley 'raulɪ, 'rolɪ
rowlock 'ro‚lɑk, 'rʌlək

Key: See in full §§3–47. bee bi |pity 'pɪtɪ (§6) |rate ret |yet jɛt |sang sæŋ |angry 'æŋ·grɪ
|bath bæθ; E baθ (§10) |ah ɑ |far fɑr |watch wɑtʃ, wɒtʃ (§12) |jaw dʒɔ |gorge gɔrdʒ |go go

Roxana rɑks'ænə; ES+rɒks-
Roxburgh, -ghe 'rɑks͵bɔ·o, -ə; ES -͵bɝr-,
-͵bʌr-, -͵bɔ·-, 'rɒks-, *Brit* 'rɒksbrə |-shire
-͵ʃɪr, -ʃɚ; ES -͵ʃɪə(r, -ʃə(r
Roxbury 'rɑks͵bɛrɪ, -bərɪ; ES+'rɒks-
Roy rɔɪ
royal 'rɔɪəl, 'rɔjəl |-ism -͵ɪzəm |-ist -ɪst
Royalton 'rɔɪəltən, 'rɔjəltən
royalty 'rɔɪəltɪ, 'rɔjəltɪ
Royce rɔɪs |-'s -ɪz
rub rʌb |rubbed rʌbd
rub-a-dub 'rʌbə͵dʌb, ͵rʌbə'dʌb
Rubáiyát ͵rubaɪ'jɑt, 'rubaɪ͵jɑt, ͵rubɪ'jɑt
rubato ru'bɑto
rubber 'rʌbɚ; ES -bə(r; |-ed -d |-ing
'rʌbərɪŋ, 'rʌbrɪŋ
rubberize 'rʌbə͵raɪz |-s -ɪz |-d -d
rubberneck 'rʌbɚ͵nɛk; ES 'rʌbə-; |-ed -t
rubber-stamp *adj* 'rʌbɚ'stæmp; ES 'rʌbə-;
('rubber-͵stamp 'vote)
rubber-stamp *v* ͵rʌbɚ'stæmp; ES ͵rʌbə-;
|-ed -t
rubbish 'rʌbɪʃ
rubble 'rʌbl̩ |-d -d |-ling -bl̩ɪŋ, -blɪŋ
rubbly 'rʌblɪ
Rube, r- rub, rɪub
Rubens 'rubɪnz, 'rɪu-, -ənz |-'s -ɪz
rubescence ru'bɛsn̩s, rɪu- |-scent -sn̩t
Rubicon 'rubɪ͵kɑn, 'rɪu-; ES+-͵kɒn
rubicund 'rubə͵kʌnd, 'rɪu-
rubicundity ͵rubə'kʌndətɪ, ͵rɪu-
rubidium ru'bɪdɪəm, rɪu-
rubied 'rubɪd, 'rɪu-
Rubinstein 'rubɪn͵staɪn, 'rɪu-
ruble 'rubl̩
rubric 'rubrɪk, 'rɪu- |-ked -t |-al -l̩ |-ally -l̩ɪ,
-ɪklɪ
rubricate *adj* 'rubrɪkɪt, 'rɪu-, -͵ket
rubricate *v* 'rubrɪ͵ket, 'rɪu- |-d -ɪd
ruby, R- 'rubɪ, 'rɪu- |-ied -d
ruche ruʃ, rɪuʃ |-s -ɪz |-d -t (*Fr* ryʃ)
ruck rʌk |rucked rʌkt
ruction 'rʌkʃən
Rudbeckia rʌd'bɛkɪə
rudder 'rʌdɚ; ES 'rʌdə(r; |-ed -d
Ruddigore, Ruddy- 'rʌdɪ͵gor, -͵gɔr; ES
-͵goə(r, E+-͵gɔə(r
ruddle 'rʌdl̩ |-d -d |-ling 'rʌdl̩ɪŋ, 'rʌdlɪŋ
ruddleman 'rʌdl̩mən |-men -mən

ruddy 'rʌdɪ
rude rud, rɪud
rudiment 'rudəmənt, 'rɪudə-
rudimental ͵rudə'mɛntl̩, ͵rɪu- |-tary -tərɪ, -trɪ
Rudolf, -lph 'rudalf, 'rɪu-, -dɒlf
Rudyard 'rʌdjɚd, 'rʌdʒɚd; ES -əd
rue ru, rɪu |-d -d |-ful -fəl |-fully -fəlɪ
ruff rʌf |ruffed rʌft
ruffian 'rʌfɪən, -fjən |-ism -͵ɪzəm
ruffle 'rʌfl̩ |-d -d |-ling 'rʌflɪŋ, 'rʌfl̩ɪŋ
ruffly 'rʌflɪ
rufous 'rufəs, 'rɪu-
Rufus, r- 'rufəs, 'rɪu- |-'s -ɪz
rug rʌg |rugged *'provided with rugs'* rʌgd
Rugbeian rʌg'bɪən
Rugby 'rʌgbɪ
rugged *'rough'* 'rʌgɪd
Ruhr rur; ES ruə(r; (*Ger* ruːr)
ruin 'ruɪn, 'rɪuɪn |-ed -d |-ous -əs
ruinate 'ruɪn͵et, 'rɪu- |-ated -͵etɪd
ruination ͵ruɪn'eʃən, ͵rɪu-
rule rul, rɪul |-d -d |-rship -ɚ͵ʃɪp; ES -ə͵ʃɪp
rum *liquor* rʌm, *dye* rum
Rum rum
Rumania ru'menɪə |-n -n
rumba 'rʌmbə (*Sp* 'rumba)
rumble 'rʌmbl̩ |-d -d |-ling 'rʌmblɪŋ, -bl̩ɪŋ
rumen 'rumɪn, 'rɪu-, -mən |-mina -ə
Rumford 'rʌmfɚd; ES 'rʌmfəd
Rumina ru'maɪnə, rɪu-
ruminant 'rumənənt, 'rɪu-
ruminate 'rumə͵net, 'rɪu- |-d -ɪd |-tive -ɪv
rumination ͵rumə'neʃən, ͵rɪu-
rummage 'rʌmɪdʒ |-s -ɪz |-d -d
rumor 'rumɚ, 'rɪumɚ; ES -mə(r; |-ed -d
rump rʌmp |rumped rʌmpt
rumple 'rʌmpl̩ |-d -d |-ling 'rʌmplɪŋ, -pl̩ɪŋ
rumpus 'rʌmpəs |-es -ɪz
run rʌn |ran ræn |run rʌn |running 'rʌnɪŋ
runabout 'rʌnə͵baut
runagate 'rʌnə͵get
runaway 'rʌnə͵we
runcinate *adj* 'rʌnsɪnɪt, -͵net
rundle 'rʌndl̩ |-d -d
run-down 'rʌn'daun ('run-͵down 'health)
rune run, rɪun |-d -d
rung *from* ring rʌŋ
rung *of ladder* rʌŋ |runged rʌŋd
runic 'runɪk, 'rɪu- |-ally -l̩ɪ, -ɪklɪ

|full ful |tooth tuθ |further 'fɝðɚ; ES 'fɝðə |custom 'kʌstəm |while hwaɪl |how hau |toy tɔɪ
|using 'juzɪŋ |fuse fjuz, fɪuz |dish dɪʃ |vision 'vɪʒən |Eden 'idn̩ |cradle 'kredl̩ |keep 'em 'kipm̩

runnel ˈrʌnḷ
Runnemede ˈrʌnɪˌmid
runner ˈrʌnɚ; ES ˈrʌnə(r; |-ed -d
runnion ˈrʌnjən
Runnymede ˈrʌnɪˌmid
runt rʌnt |runted ˈrʌntɪd
runway ˈrʌnˌwe
rupee ruˈpi
Rupert ˈrupɚt, ˈrɪu-; ES -pət
rupture ˈrʌptʃɚ; ES -tʃə(r; |-d -d |-ring -tʃərɪŋ, -tʃrɪŋ
rural ˈrʊrəl, ˈrɪʊrəl |-ly -ɪ |-ism -ˌɪzəm
Ruritania ˌrʊrəˈtenɪə, ˌrɪu- |-n -n
ruse ruz, rɪuz |-s -ɪz (Fr ryːz)
rush, R- rʌʃ |-es -ɪz |-ed -t |-ville -vɪl
Rushworth ˈrʌʃwɚθ; ES ˈrʌʃwəθ
rusk rʌsk |rusked rʌskt
Ruskin ˈrʌskɪn
Russ rʌs |-'s -ɪz
Russell ˈrʌsḷ |-ville -ˌvɪl; S+-vḷ
russet ˈrʌsɪt
Russia ˈrʌʃə |-n -n
Russo-Japanese ˈrʌsoˌdʒæpəˈniz
rust rʌst |rusted ˈrʌstɪd
Rustam, -tem ˈrʌstəm
rustic ˈrʌstɪk |-al -ḷ |-ally -ḷɪ |-ly -lɪ
rusticate ˈrʌstɪˌket |-cated -ˌketɪd
rustication ˌrʌstɪˈkeʃən
rusticity rʌsˈtɪsətɪ
rustle ˈrʌsḷ |-d -d |-ling ˈrʌslɪŋ, ˈrʌsḷɪŋ

rustler ˈrʌslɚ; ES ˈrʌslə(r
Rustum ˈrʌstəm
rusty ˈrʌstɪ
rut rʌt |rutted ˈrʌtɪd
rutabaga ˌrutəˈbegə, -ˈbɛgə
Rutgers ˈrʌtgɚz; ES ˈrʌtgəz; |-'s -ɪz
ruth, R- ruθ, rɪuθ
Ruthene ruˈθin, rɪu- |-nia -nɪə |-nian -nɪən
ruthenium ruˈθinɪəm, rɪu-
Rutherford ˈrʌðɚfɚd; ES ˈrʌðəfəd; |-ton -tən
Rutherfurd ˈrʌðɚfɚd; ES ˈrʌðəfəd
ruthful ˈruθfəl, ˈrɪuθ- |-ly -ɪ
ruthless ˈruθlɪs, ˈrɪuθ-
Ruthven ˈruθvən (Sc ˈrʌθvən, ˈrɪvən)
Ruthwell ˈrʌðwəl, ˈrʌθ-, Sc+ˈrɪvḷ
Rutland ˈrʌtlənd |-shire -ˌʃɪr, -ʃɚ; ES -ˌʃɪə(r, -ʃə(r
Rutledge ˈrʌtlɪdʒ |-'s -ɪz
Ruud rud
-ry unstressed ending -rɪ, -ri. For the sound of the vowel, see -y.
Ryan ˈraɪən
Rydal Mount ˈraɪdḷˈmaʊnt
Ryder ˈraɪdɚ; ES ˈraɪdə(r
rye, R- raɪ
Ryerson ˈraɪɚsṇ; ES ˈraɪ·ə-
Rylstone ˈrɪlstən, ˈrɪlz-
Rymer ˈraɪmɚ; ES ˈraɪmə(r
ryot ˈraɪət
Ryswick ˈraɪswɪk, ˈrɪz-

S

S, s letter ɛs |pl S's, Ss, poss S's ˈɛsɪz
-s pl, poss, & 3 sg ending, see -es
's abbr. spelling of has, is, us, as in he's hiz, she's ʃiz, it's ɪts, there's ðɛrz, ðɛəz, let's lɛts, this's a fine day ðɪsː ə faɪn de
-'s possessive ending, see §§87–88.
Saar sɑr; ES sɑː(r, E+saː(r; (Ger zɑːr, Fr saːr)
Saarbrücken Ger ˈzɑːrˌbrykən
Sabaoth ˈsæbɪˌɑθ, -ˌɒθ, -ˌɔθ
Sabatini ˌsæbəˈtinɪ (It ˌsabaˈtiːni)
Sabbatarian ˌsæbəˈtɛrɪən, -ˈtær-, -ˈter-
Sabbath ˈsæbəθ |Sabbaths ˈsæbəθs
sabbatical, S- səˈbætɪkḷ |-ly -ɪ, -ɪklɪ

saber, -bre ˈsebɚ; ES ˈsebə(r; |-ed, -d -d |-ing, -bring -brɪŋ, -bərɪŋ
saber-toothed ˈsebɚˌtuθt, -ˌtuðd; ES ˈsebə-
Sabine people ˈsebaɪn, places səˈbin
sable ˈsebḷ |sabled ˈsebḷd
sabot ˈsæbo, ˈsæbət (Fr saˈbo)
sabotage ˈsæbəˌtɑʒ, ˈsæbətɪdʒ (Fr sabɔˈtaːʒ)
Sabrina səˈbraɪnə
sac sæk
Sac sæk, sɔk=Sauk |Sac City Ia sɔk
saccharin ˈsækərɪn
saccharine n ˈsækərɪn, -ˌrin; adj -ˌraɪn, -rɪn
saccule ˈsækjul
sacerdotal ˌsæsɚˈdotḷ; ES ˌsæsə-; |-ly -ɪ

sachem 'setʃəm
sachet sæ'ʃe (Fr sa'ʃɛ)
Sacheverell sə'ʃɛvərəl
sack sæk |sacked sækt
sackbut 'sæk‚bʌt
sackcloth 'sæk‚klɔθ, -‚klnθ—see cloth
sackful 'sæk‚ful |-s -z
Saco 'sɔko
sacque sæk
sacral 'sekrəl
sacrament 'sækrəmənt
sacramental ‚sækrə'mɛntl̩ |-ly -ɪ |-ism ‚ɪzəm
   |-ist -ɪst
sacramentarian ‚sækrəmɛn'tɛrɪən, -'ter-
Sacramento ‚sækrə'mɛnto
sacred 'sekrɪd
sacrifice n, v 'sækrə‚faɪs, -‚faɪz |-s -ɪz |-d
   -‚faɪst, -‚faɪzd—The pron. with z is now less
   frequent.
sacrificial ‚sækrə'fɪʃəl |-ly -ɪ
sacrilege 'sækrəlɪdʒ |-s -ɪz
sacrilegious ‚sækrɪ'lɪdʒəs, -'lɪdʒ- —British
   and American ‚sækrɪ'lɪdʒəs is probably due
   to the analogy of 'sækrəlɪdʒ and the unrelated rɪ'lɪdʒəs.
sacring 'sekrɪŋ
sacristan 'sækrɪstən |sacristy 'sækrɪstɪ
sacrosanct 'sækro‚sæŋkt
sacrum 'sekrəm |-ra -rə
sad sæd
sadden 'sædn̩ |-ed -d |-ing 'sædnɪŋ, 'sædnɪŋ
saddle 'sædl̩ |-d -d |-ling 'sædlɪŋ, 'sædlɪŋ
saddlebag 'sædl̩‚bæg |-ged -d
saddlebow 'sædl̩‚bo
saddleless 'sædl̩ɪs
saddler, S- 'sædlɚ; ES 'sædlə(r
Sadducee 'sædʒə‚si, 'sædjʊ-
sadiron 'sæd‚aɪɚn; ES -‚aɪ·ən
sadism 'sædɪzəm, 'sed- |-ist -ɪst
sadistic sæ'dɪstɪk, se- |-ally -l̩ɪ, -ɪklɪ
safari sə'farɪ
safe sef
safeblower 'sef‚bloɚ; ES -‚blo·ə(r
safe-conduct 'sef'kandʌkt; ES+-'kɒn-
safeguard 'sef‚gard; ES -‚ga:d, E+-‚ga:d;
   |-ed -ɪd
safekeeping 'sef'kipɪŋ
safety 'seftɪ
safety-pin 'seftɪ‚pɪn

safety-valve 'seftɪ‚vælv
safflower 'sæf‚flauɚ, -‚flaur; ES -‚flau·ə(r,
   -‚flauə(r
saffron 'sæfrən, 'sæfɚn; ES -frən, -fən; cf
   apron
sag sæg |sagged sægd
saga 'sagə
sagacious sə'geʃəs, se- |-gacity sə'gæsətɪ
Sagadahoc 'sægədɪ‚hak, -‚hɒk
sagamore, S- 'sægə‚mor, -‚mɔr; ES -‚moə(r,
   E+-‚mɔə(r
sage sedʒ |sages 'sedʒɪz |-d -d |-brush -‚brʌʃ
Saghalien ‚sægə'lin, sə'galɪən=Sakhalin
Saginaw 'sægə‚nɔ
Sagitta, s- sə'dʒɪtə |pl & gen sg -tae -ti
Sagittarius ‚sædʒɪ'tɛrɪəs, -'ter- |gen -rii -rɪ‚aɪ
sago 'sego
Saguache sə'watʃ, -'wɒtʃ |-'s -ɪz (Am Sp
   sa'watʃe)=Sawatch
saguaro sə'gwaro, -'waro
Saguenay ‚sægə'ne
Sahara sə'hɛrə, -'herə, -'harə
sahib, S- 'sa·ɪb, 'sahɪb
said sɛd, unstressed səd (said he səd 'hi)
Saigon ‚sa·i'gon, saɪ'gon (Fr sa·i'gõ)
sail sel |sailed seld |-boat -‚bot
sailcloth 'sel‚klɔθ, -‚klnθ, see cloth
sailer 'selɚ; ES 'selə(r
sailless 'sellɪs
sailor 'selɚ; ES 'selə(r
sainfoin 'senfɔɪn
saint, S- sent—Unstressed forms sɪnt, sənt,
   sn̩t, sɪn, sən, sn̩ are chiefly British. For
   additional names in Saint-, St.- see the second part of the name.
Saint Agnes's Eve 'ægnɪsɪz (in Keats St.
   Agnes' 'ægnɪs)
Saint Albans 'ɔlbənz |-'s -ɪz
Saint Asaph 'æsəf, 'esəf, 'esæf
Saint Augustine ch. father, missionary 'ɔgəs-
   ‚tin, ə'gʌstɪn, ɔ-; Fla city 'ɔgəs‚tin
Saint Bernard La, O 'bɚnəd; ES 'bɜnəd,
   'bɝnəd; mt. pass, dog bɚ'nard, bə'nard;
   ES bə'na:d, E+-'na:d; (Fr bɛr'na:r)—In
   bə'nard ɚ became ə by dissimilation (§121).
Saint Cecilia sɪ'sɪljə, -'sɪlɪə, -'sɪljə
Saint Christopher 'krɪstəfɚ; ES 'krɪstəfə(r
Saint Clair 'kler, 'klær; E 'kleə(r, ES 'klæə(r
Saint Columb 'kaləm; ES+-'kɒləm

|full ful |tooth tuθ |further 'fɝðɚ; ES 'fɜðə |custom 'kʌstəm |while hwaɪl |how hau |toy tɔɪ
|using 'juzɪŋ |fuse fjuz, fruz |dish dɪʃ |vision 'vɪʒən |Eden 'idn̩ |cradle 'kredl̩ |keep 'em 'kipm̩

Saint Croix 'krɔɪ, Me, NB loc.+sɪŋ'-, sɪnt'-
Saint Cuthbert 'kʌθbət; ES 'kʌθbət
Sainte-Anne-de-Beaupré -'ændəbo'pre
Sainte-Beuve Fr sæt'bœːv
St. Elmo 'ɛlmo
Saint Gall 'gɔl, 'gɑl, 'gæl
Saint-Gaudens -'gɔdn̩z |-'s -ɪz
Saint Giles 'dʒaɪlz |-'s -ɪz
Saint Gotthard, Goth- 'gatəd; ES 'gatəd,
    'gɒt-; (Fr sægöꞌtaːr)
Saint Helena saint 'hɛlɪnə, -lə-, isl. & La, Cal
    places hə'linə, ˌsentꞁ'inə
St. Ives 'aɪvz, novel+'ivz |-'s -ɪz
St. John surname 'sɪndʒən, sent'dʒɑn,
    -'dʒɒn; apos. & places sent'dʒɑn, -'dʒɒn;
    in NB loc. sn̩'dʒɒn—Lowell rimed St. John
    with Mohawk Injun.
Saint Julien 'dʒuljən, 'dʒɪuljən
Saint Lawrence 'lɔrəns, 'lɑr-, 'lɒr- |-'s -ɪz
St. Leger surname, race sent'lɛdʒə, less freq.
    'sɛlɪndʒə; ES -dʒə(r
Saint Louis US places 'luɪs, 'lɪuɪs |-'s -ɪz
St. Mary-le-bone church, borough 'mɛrɪlə'bon
Saint-Mihiel Fr sæ·mi'jɛl
Saint-Moritz -'morɪts, -'mɔr-; S -'mor-; |-'s
    -ɪz
St. Pancras 'pæŋkrəs |-'s -ɪz
St. Regis 'ridʒɪs |-'s -ɪz
St. Ronan 'ronən, 'ranən, 'rɒn-
Saint-Saëns Fr sæ'sɑ̃
Saint Sophia so'faɪə, sə-
Saint Swithin 'swɪðɪn, 'swɪθɪn
Saint Valentine 'vælənˌtaɪn
Saint Vitus 'vaɪtəs |-'s -ɪz, in St. Vitus's
    dance+'vaɪtəs
saith sɛθ
sake sek
saké Jap drink 'sakɪ
Sakhalin ˌsækə'lin=Saghalien
Saki 'saki, 'sɔki
sal chem., geol. sæl; tree sal, sɔl
salaam sə'lɑm |salaamed sə'lɑmd
salability, salea- ˌselə'bɪlətɪ
salable 'seləbl̩ |-bly -blɪ
salacious sə'leʃəs
salad 'sæləd
Saladin 'sælədɪn
Salamanca ˌsælə'mæŋkə, -'mæŋkə
salamander 'sæləˌmændə; ES -ˌmændə(r

Salamis 'sæləmɪs |-'s -ɪz
sal-ammoniac ˌsælə'monɪˌæk, -njæk
Salarino ˌsælə'rino
salary 'sælərɪ |salaried 'sælərɪd
sale sel |-able -əbl̩ |-bly -blɪ
Salem 'seləm
saleratus ˌsælə'retəs
Salerio sə'lɛrɪˌo, -'lɪrɪˌo, -rjo
Salerno sə'lɝno; ES -'lɜno, -'lɝno; (It
    sa'lɛrno)
Salesbury 'selzˌbɛrɪ, -bərɪ, -brɪ—distinct from
    Salisbury
salesclerk 'selzˌklɝk; ES -ˌklɜk, -ˌklɝk
salesman 'selzmən |-men -mən
salesroom 'selzˌrum, -ˌrʊm
saleswoman 'selzˌwumən, -ˌwum- |-women
    -ˌwɪmɪn, -ən
Salian 'selɪən
Salic 'sælɪk, 'selɪk=Salique (Fr sa'lik)
salicin 'sæləsɪn
salicylate 'sæləsɪˌlet, sə'lɪsəˌlet |-lated -ˌletɪd
salicylic ˌsælə'sɪlɪk
salience 'selɪəns |salient 'selɪənt, -ljənt
salify 'sæləˌfaɪ |-fied -ˌfaɪd
saline 'selaɪn |-linity sə'lɪnətɪ
Saline sə'lin |-ville -vɪl
Salique 'sælɪk, 'selɪk=Salic (Fr sa'lik)
Salisbury 'sɔlzˌbɛrɪ, -bərɪ, -brɪ—cf §121
saliva sə'laɪvə |-vous -vəs |-ry 'sæləˌvɛrɪ
salivate 'sæləˌvet |-d -ɪd |-tion ˌsælə'veʃən
sallet 'sælɪt
sallow 'sælo, -ə |-ed -d |-ing 'sæləwɪŋ |-er
    'sæləwə; ES -wə(r; |-est 'sæləwɪst
Sallust 'sæləst
sally, S- 'sælɪ |sallied 'sælɪd
sally lunn, S- L- 'sælɪ'lʌn
salmagundi, S- ˌsælmə'gʌndɪ
salmon 'sæmən
Salmon surname 'sæmən, 'sam-; Bible
    'sælmən
Salome sə'lomɪ
salon Fr sa'lõ
Salonika, -ca, -ki ˌsælə'nikə, ˌsal-, -'naɪ-, -kɪ,
    sə'lɑnɪkə; ES+-'lɒn-
saloon sə'lun
Salop short for Shropshire 'sæləp—cf §121
Salopian sə'lopɪən
saltpiglossis, s- ˌsælpɪ'glasɪs, -'glɒs-
salpinx 'sælpɪŋks |salpinges sæl'pɪndʒiz

---

salsify ˈsælsəfɪ
sal soda ˈsælˈsodə
salt sɔlt |salted ˈsɔltɪd
salt-and-pepper ˈsɔltn̩ˈpɛpɚ; ES -ˈpɛpə(r
saltant ˈsæltənt |saltation sælˈteʃən
saltarello ˌsæltəˈrɛlo (It ˌsaltaˈrɛllo)
saltatory ˈsæltəˌtorɪ, -ˌtɔrɪ; S -ˌtorɪ
saltcellar ˈsɔltˌsɛlɚ; ES -ˌsɛlə(r
Salter ˈsɔltɚ; ES ˈsɔltə(r
Salt Lake City ˈsɔltˌlekˈsɪtɪ
saltmarsh, S- ˈsɔltˌmɑrʃ; ES -ˌmɑːʃ, E+
-ˌmɑːʃ; |-es -ɪz
Salton Sink ˈsɔltn̩ˈsɪŋk
Saltonstall ˈsɔltn̩ˌstɔl
saltpeter, -tre ˈsɔltˈpitɚ; ES -ˈpitə(r
saltworks ˈsɔltˌwɝks; ES -ˌwɜks, -ˌwɝks
salubrious səˈlubrɪəs, -ˈlɪu- |-brity -brətɪ
salutary ˈsæljəˌtɛrɪ, -jʊ-
salutation ˌsæljəˈteʃən, -jʊ-
salutatorian səˌlutəˈtorɪən, -ˌlɪu-, -ˈtɔr-; S
-ˈtor-
salutatory səˈlutəˌtorɪ, -ˈlɪu-, -ˌtɔrɪ; S -ˌtorɪ
salute səˈlut, -ˈlɪut |-d -ɪd
Saluzzo səˈlutso (It saˈluttso)
Salvador, El ɛlˈsælvəˌdɔr; ES -ˌdɔə(r; (Sp
-ˌsalβaˈðɔr)
Salvadoran, ˌsælvəˈdorən, -ˈdɔr-; S -ˈdor-;
|-dorian -rɪən
salvage ˈsælvɪdʒ |-s -ɪz |-d -d |-able -əbl̩
salvation sælˈveʃən (ˈSalˌvation ˈArmy)
salve n 'ointment,' v 'anoint' sæv; E+sav,
sav; |-d -d
salve v 'salvage' sælv |-d -d |-vable -əbl̩
Salve, s- intj ˈsælvɪ
salver 'tray' ˈsælvɚ; ES ˈsælvə(r
salvia ˈsælvɪə, ˈsælvjə
Salvini sælˈvini (It salˈviːni)
salvo ˈsælvo |-ed -d
sal volatile ˈsælvoˈlætl̩ˌi
salvor ˈsælvɚ; ES ˈsælvə(r
Sam sæm
samara ˈsæmərə
Samaria səˈmɛrɪə, səˈmerɪə |-n -n
Samaritan səˈmærətn̩, səˈmɛr- |-ism -ˌɪzəm
samarium səˈmærɪəm, səˈmɛr-, səˈmer-
Samarkand ˌsæmɚˈkænd; ES ˌsæməˈkænd
sambo, S- ˈsæmbo
sambuke ˈsæmbjuk, -bɪuk
same sem

Samian ˈsemɪən, ˈsemjən
samite ˈsæmaɪt
Samnite ˈsæmnaɪt
Samoa səˈmoə |Samoan səˈmoən
Samos ˈsemɑs, -mɒs |-'s -ɪz
Samothrace ˈsæməˌθres |-'s -ɪz |-cian ˌsæmə-
ˈθreʃən
samovar ˈsæməˌvɑr; ES -ˌvɑː(r, E+-ˌvɑː(r
samp sæmp
sampan ˈsæmpæn
samphire ˈsæmfaɪr; ES ˈsæmfaɪə(r
sample ˈsæmpl̩; E+ˈsam-, ˈsɑm-; |-d -d
|-ling -plɪŋ, -plɪŋ
sampler ˈsæmplɚ; ES ˈsæmplə(r, E+ˈsam-,
ˈsɑm-
Samson, -pson ˈsæmpsn̩, ˈsæmsn̩
Samuel ˈsæmjʊəl, ˈsæmjʊl, ˈsæmjəl
samurai ˈsæmuˌraɪ
San Antonio ˌsænənˈtonɪo, ˌsænæn-, loc.+
ˌsænənˈton
sanatorium ˌsænəˈtorɪəm, -ˈtɔr-; S -ˈtor- |-s -z
|-ria -rɪə
sanatory ˈsænəˌtorɪ, -ˌtɔrɪ; S -ˌtorɪ
San Bernardino ˈsænˌbɝnɚˈdino, -nɑr-; ES
-ˌbɝnə-, -ˌbɜnə-, -nɑ:-
Sancho Panza ˈsæŋkoˈpænzə (Sp ˈsantʃo-
ˈpanθa)
sanctification ˌsæŋktəfəˈkeʃən
sanctify ˈsæŋktəˌfaɪ |-fied -ˌfaɪd |-fiedly
-ˌfaɪdlɪ, -ˌfaɪdlɪ
sanctimonious ˌsæŋktəˈmonɪəs, -ˈmonjəs
sanctimony ˈsæŋktəˌmonɪ
sanction ˈsæŋkʃən |-ed -d
sanctity ˈsæŋktətɪ
sanctuary ˈsæŋktʃʊˌɛrɪ
sanctum ˈsæŋktəm |-s -z |rarely -ta ˈsæŋktə
Sanctus ˈsæŋktəs |-es -ɪz
sand sænd |sanded ˈsændɪd
Sand, George ˈdʒɔrdʒˈsænd; ES ˈdʒɔədʒ-;
(Fr ʒɔrʒəˈsɑ̃, -ˈsɑ̃ːd)
sandal ˈsændl̩ |-ed -d |-ing ˈsændlɪŋ, -dlɪŋ
sandalwood ˈsændl̩ˌwʊd
sandbag ˈsændˌbæg, ˈsænˌbæg |-bagged
-ˌbægd
sand-blind ˈsændˌblaɪnd, ˈsæn-
sandbur, -rr ˈsændˌbɝ, ˈsæn-; ES -ˌbɜ(r, -ˌbɝ
Sandburg ˈsændbɝg, ˈsæn-; ES -bɜg, -bɝg
Sanders ˈsændɚz, ˈsan-; ES -dəz; |-'s -ɪz
Sandford, Sanf- ˈsænfɚd; ES ˈsænfəd

Words below in which a *before* r (farm) *is sounded* ɑ *are often pronounced in* E *with* a (faːm)

sandglass ˈsændˌglæs, ˈsæn-; E+-ˌglas, -ˌglɑs; |-es -ɪz

sandhi ˈsændhi, ˈsɑn-, ˈsʌn-, -di

Sandhurst ˈsændhɜˑst; ES -hɜst, -hɜˑst

San Diego ˌsæn·diˈego

sandman ˈsændˌmæn |-men -ˌmɛn

sandpaper ˈsændˌpepɚ, ˈsæn-; ES -ˌpepə(r; |-ed -d |-ing -ˌpeprɪŋ, -ˌpepərɪŋ

sandpiper ˈsændˌpaɪpɚ, ˈsæn-; ES -ˌpaɪpə(r

Sandringham ˈsændrɪŋəm

Sandrocottus ˌsændroˈkɑtəs; ES+-ˈkɒt-; |-ˈs -ɪz

Sands sændz, sænz |-ˈs -ɪz

sandstone ˈsændˌston, ˈsæn-

Sandusky sənˈdʌskɪ, sæn-

sandwich, S- ˈsændwɪtʃ, ˈsæn- |-es -ɪz |-ed -t

Sandys ˈsændz, sænz |-ˈs -ɪz, *in Shak. spelt* Sandys, Sands

sane sen |saneness ˈsennɪs

Sanford, Sand- ˈsænfɚd; ES ˈsænfəd

San Francisco ˌsænfrənˈsɪsko

sang sæŋ

sangaree ˌsæŋgəˈri

Sanger ˈsæŋɚ, ˈsæŋgɚ; ES -ə(r

sang-froid *Fr* sãˈfrwɑ

Sangraal sæŋˈgrel

sanguine ˈsæŋgwɪn |-nary -ˌɛrɪ |-neness -gwɪnnɪs |-neous sæŋˈgwɪnɪəs

Sanhedrin, -im ˈsænɪˌdrɪn, -ˌdrɪm

sanitarian ˌsænəˈtɛrɪən, -ˈter- |-rium -rɪəm

sanitary ˈsænəˌtɛrɪ |-tation ˌsænəˈteʃən

sanity ˈsænətɪ

San Joaquin *Cal* ˌsænwɑˈkin, *PI* ˌsænhoɑˈkin

San Jose ˌsænhoˈze, -noˈze (ˈSan Joˌse ˈscale)

San Juan sænˈhwɑn, -ˈwɑn, -ɒn

sank sæŋk

San Miguel ˌsænmiˈgɛl

Sannazaro ˌsænəˈzaro (*It* ˌsannaˈdzɑːro)

sans sænz (*Fr* sã)

San Salvador sænˈsælvəˌdɔr; ES -ˌdɔə(r; (*Sp* ˌsalβaˈðɔr)

sans-culotte ˌsænzkjʊˈlɑt, -kə-, -ˈlɒt |-tism -ɪzəm |-tist -ɪst (*Fr* sãkyˈlɔt)

Sanskrit, -crit ˈsænskrɪt |-ic sænˈskrɪtɪk

sans-serif, sanserif sænˈsɛrɪf, sænzˈs-

Santa Ana, Anna ˌsæntəˈænə, ˌsæntɪˈænə

Santa Barbara ˌsæntəˈbɑrbərə, -brə; ES -ˈbɑːb-

Santa Catalina ˌsæntəˌkætlˈinə

Santa Claus ˈsæntɪˌklɔz, ˈsæntə- |-ˈs -ɪz

Santa Cruz *US, WI* ˌsæntəˈkruz; *PI* ˌsæntəˈkrus (*Am Sp* ˌsantaˈkrus); |-ˈs -ɪz |*W Pacif* ˌsæntəˈkruθ (*Sp* ˌsantaˈkruθ)

Santa Cruz de Tenerife ˌsæntəˈkruz·dɪˌtɛnəˈrif (*Sp* ˌsantaˈkruθ·ðeˌteneˈrife)

Santa Fe *NMex* ˈsæntəˌfe, ˌsæntəˈfe, *older* -ˌfi, -ˈfi

Santa Fé *Arg* ˌsantəˈfe (*Sp* ˌsantaˈfe)

Santayana ˌsæntɪˈænə, -ˈɑnə (*Sp* ˌsantaˈjana)

Santee sænˈti

Santiago ˌsæntɪˈego, -ˈɑgo (*Sp* ˌsantiˈago)

Santo Domingo ˌsæntodəˈmɪŋgo (*Sp* ˌsantoðoˈmiŋgo)

São Paulo *Pg* ˌsãuˈpaulu

Saorstat Eireann ˈsɛːrˌstɑtˈerən, -ˈɛrən

sap sæp |sapped sæpt |-head -ˌhɛd

sapheaded ˈsæpˈhɛdɪd (ˈsapˌheaded ˈlout)

sapid ˈsæpɪd |-ity sæˈpɪdətɪ, sə-

sapience ˈsepɪəns, -pjəns |-ent -ənt

sapiential ˌsepɪˈɛnʃəl |-ly -ɪ

Sapir səˈpɪr, sɑ-; ES -ˈpɪə(r

sapling ˈsæplɪŋ

sapodilla ˌsæpəˈdɪlə

saponaceous ˌsæpəˈneʃəs

saponification səˌpɑnəfəˈkeʃən; ES+-ˌpɒn-

saponine ˈsæpənɪn, -ˌnin |-nin -nɪn

saponite ˈsæpəˌnaɪt

Sapphic ˈsæfɪk

Sapphira səˈfaɪrə

sapphire ˈsæfaɪr; ES ˈsæfaɪə(r; |-d -d

sapphirine ˈsæfərɪn, -ˌrin

Sappho ˈsæfo

sappy ˈsæpɪ

saprophyte ˈsæproˌfaɪt |-tic ˌsæproˈfɪtɪk

sapsucker ˈsæpˌsʌkɚ; ES ˈsæpˌsʌkə(r

sapwood ˈsæpˌwud

Saracen ˈsærəsn̩

Saragossa ˌsærəˈgɑsə, -ˈgɒsə

Sarah, -ra ˈsɛrə, *esp.* S ˈserə

Sarajevo ˌsarəjɛˌvo, ˌsarəˈjevo

Saranac ˈsærəˌnæk

Sarasota ˌsærəˈsotə

Saratoga ˌsærəˈtogə (ˈSaraˌtoga ˈchips)

sarcasm ˈsarkæzəm; ES ˈsaːkæzəm

sarcastic sarˈkæstɪk; ES saː-; |-ally -ļɪ, -ɪklɪ

sarcoma sarˈkomə; ES saːˈkomə

Key: *See in full §§3–47.* bee bi |pity ˈpɪtɪ (§6) |rate ret |yet jɛt |sang sæŋ |angry ˈæŋ·grɪ |bath bæθ; E baθ (§10) |ah ɑ |far fɑr |watch wɑtʃ, wɒtʃ (§12) |jaw dʒɔ |gorge gɔrdʒ |go go

Words below in which a *before* r (farm) *is sounded* ɑ *are often pronounced in* E *with* a (fɑ:m)

sarcophagus sɑr'kɑfəgəs; ES sɑ'kɑf-, -'kɒf-; |-es -ɪz |-gi -ˌdʒaɪ

sard, S- sɑrd; ES sɑ:d

Sardanapalus ˌsɑrdə'næpələs; ES ˌsɑ:d-; |-'s -ɪz

sardine *stone* 'sɑrdɪn, -daɪn; ES 'sɑ:d-

sardine *fish* sɑr'din; ES sɑ:'din ('sar-ˌdine 'salad)

Sardinia sɑr'dɪnɪə, -njə; ES sɑ'd-; |-n -n

Sardis 'sɑrdɪs; ES 'sɑ:dɪs; |-'s -ɪz

sardius 'sɑrdɪəs; ES 'sɑ:dɪəs; |-es -ɪz

sardonic sɑr'dɑnɪk; ES sɑ:'dɑnɪk, -'dɒnɪk; |-ally -ļɪ, -ɪklɪ

sardonyx 'sɑrdənɪks; ES 'sɑ:d-; |-es -ɪz

sargasso, S- sɑr'gæso; ES sɑ:'gæso

Sargeant, -gent, -geaunt 'sɑrdʒənt; ES 'sɑ:dʒ-

Sargon 'sɑrgɑn; ES 'sɑ:gɑn, -gɒn

sari 'sɑri

sark sɑrk; ES sɑ:k; |-ed -t

sarong sə'rɔŋ, 'sɑrɒŋ, -ɒŋ

Saroyan sə'rojən

Sarpedon sɑr'pidņ, -dɑn; ES sɑ:'pidņ, -dɑn, -dɒn

sarsaparilla ˌsɑrspə'rɪlə, ˌsɑrsə-; ES ˌsɑ:s-

sarsenet 'sɑrsnɪt; ES 'sɑ:snɪt

Sarto, del dɛl'sɑrto; ES -'sɑ:to

sartorial sɑr'torɪəl, -rjəl, -'tɔr-; ES sɑ'tor-, E+-'tɔr-

Sartor Resartus 'sɑrtɚrɪ'sɑrtəs; ES sɑ:tərɪ-'sɑ:təs

Sarum 'sɛrəm, 'sær-, 'ser- —*cf* Salisbury

sash sæʃ |sashes 'sæʃɪz |sashed sæʃt

sashay sæ'ʃe |-ed -d

Saskatchewan sæs'kætʃəˌwɑn, səs-, -ˌwɒn, -ˌwɔn, -wən

Saskatoon ˌsæskə'tun

sassafras 'sæsəˌfræs, 'sæsf-

Sassenach 'sæsņˌæk, -əx

Sassoon sæ'sun, sə'sun

sassy 'sæsɪ

sat sæt

Satan 'setņ

satanic se'tænɪk, sə- |-al -l̩ |-ally -ļɪ, -ɪklɪ

satchel 'sætʃəl |-ed -d

sate *past of* sit set, sæt

sate '*fill*' set |sated 'setɪd

sateen sæ'tin

satellite 'sætļˌaɪt

satiability ˌseʃɪə'bɪlətɪ, ˌseʃə-

satiable 'seʃɪəbļ, 'seʃə- |-bly -blɪ

satiate 'seʃɪˌet |-d -ɪd

satiety sə'taɪətɪ, sæ't-

satin 'sætņ, 'sætɪn |-ed -d

satinette, -net ˌsætņ'ɛt, -tɪ'nɛt

satinwood 'sætņˌwʊd, 'sætɪn-

satire 'sætaɪr; ES 'sætaɪə(r

satiric sə'tɪrɪk, sæ- |-al -ļ |-ally -ļɪ, -ɪklɪ

satirist 'sætərɪst

satirize 'sætəˌraɪz |-s -ɪz |-d -d

satisfaction ˌsætɪs'fækʃən |-tory -trɪ, -tərɪ |-torily -trəlɪ, -tərəlɪ

satisfy 'sætɪsˌfaɪ |-fied -ˌfaɪd

satrap 'setræp, -trəp |-y 'setrəpɪ, 'sætrəpɪ

saturable 'sætʃərəbļ |-bly -blɪ

saturant 'sætʃərənt

saturate 'sætʃəˌret |-d -ɪd |-tion ˌsætʃə'reʃən

Saturday 'sætɚdɪ; ES 'sætə-; *see* Monday

Saturn 'sætɚn; ES 'sætən

Saturnale ˌsætɚ'neli; ES ˌsætə-; |-lia -lɪə, -ljə

Saturnian sæ'tɚnɪən; ES -'tɜn-, -'tɝn-

saturnine, S- 'sætɚˌnaɪn; ES 'sætəˌnaɪn

Saturninus ˌsætɚ'naɪnəs; ES ˌsætə-; |-'s -ɪz

satyr 'sætɚ, 'setɚ; ES 'sætə(r, 'setə(r

sauce sɔs |sauces 'sɔsɪz |sauced sɔst

saucebox 'sɔsˌbɑks; ES+-ˌbɒks; |-es -ɪz

saucepan 'sɔsˌpæn, -pən

saucer 'sɔsɚ; ES 'sɔsə(r; |-ed -d

saucy 'sɔsɪ

sauerkraut 'saʊrˌkraʊt; ES 'saʊəˌkraʊt

Sauk Center *Minn*, Sauk City *Wis* sɔk

Saul sɔl

Sault Sainte Marie 'suˌsentmə'ri

Saunders 'sɔndɚz, 'sɒn-, 'sɑn-, 'sæn- |-'s -ɪz

saunter 'sɔntɚ, 'sɒn-, 'sɑn-; ES -tə(r; |-ed -d |-ing -tərɪŋ, -trɪŋ

saurian 'sɔrɪən

sauropod 'sɔrəˌpɑd; ES+-ˌpɒd

sausage 'sɔsɪdʒ, 'sɒs-, 'sɑs- |-s -ɪz

Sausalito ˌsɔsə'lito, -ə

sauté so'te |-téed -'ted (sau te 'hash)

sauterne, S- so'tɚn; ES so'tɜn, -'tɝn

savage 'sævɪdʒ |-s -ɪz |-ry -rɪ

savanna, -ah, S- sə'vænə

savant sə'vɑnt, 'sævənt (*Fr* sa'vã)

save sev |saved sevd

|full fʊl |tooth tuθ |further 'fɝðɚ; ES 'fɝðə |custom 'kʌstəm |while hwaɪl |how haʊ |toy tɔɪ
|using 'juzɪŋ |fuse fjuz, fɪuz |dish dɪʃ |vision 'vɪʒən |Eden 'idņ |cradle 'kredļ |keep 'em 'kipm̩

save-all ˈsevˌɔl
saver ˈsevɚ; ES ˈsevə(r
savings-bank ˈsevɪŋzˌbæŋk
savior, Saviour ˈsevjɚ; ES ˈsevjə(r
savoir-faire ˈsævwarˈfɛr, -ˈfær; E ˈsævwɑ:-
ˈfɛə(r, ES -ˈfæə(r; (Fr savwarˈfɛːr)
Savonarola ˌsævənəˈrolə (It ˌsavonaˈrɔːla)
savor ˈsevɚ; ES ˈsevə(r; |-ed -d |-ing -vərɪŋ,
-vrɪŋ
savory ˈsevərɪ, ˈsevrɪ
Savoy səˈvɔɪ
Savoyard səˈvɔɪɚd, səˈvɔjɚd; ES -əd, -jəd;
(Fr savɔ̃ˈjaːr)
savvy, -ey ˈsævɪ |-ied, -eyed ˈsævɪd
saw sɔ |past sawed sɔd |pptc sawed sɔd or
sawn sɔn |-ing ˈsɔ·ɪŋ
saw past of see sɔ
Sawatch səˈwatʃ, -ˈwɒtʃ |-'s -ɪz, cf Saguache
sawbones ˈsɔˌbonz |-'s -ɪz
sawbuck ˈsɔˌbʌk
sawdust ˈsɔˌdʌst |sawdusted ˈsɔˌdʌstɪd
sawfish ˈsɔˌfɪʃ |-fish's -ˌfɪʃɪz
sawfly ˈsɔˌflaɪ
sawhorse ˈsɔˌhɔrs; ES -ˌhɔəs; |-s -ɪz
sawmill ˈsɔˌmɪl
sawn one pptc of saw sɔn
saw-toothed ˈsɔˌtuθt, -ˌtuðd
sawyer, S- ˈsɔjɚ; ES ˈsɔjə(r
Saxe sæks |-'s -ɪz
saxhorn ˈsæksˌhɔrn; ES -ˌhɔən
saxifrage ˈsæksəfrɪdʒ |-gous sæksˈɪfrəgəs
Saxon ˈsæksn̩ |Saxony ˈsæksənɪ, ˈsæksn̩ɪ
saxophone ˈsæksəˌfon |-d -d |-nist -ɪst
say se |says sɛz |saith sɛθ |said sɛd; unstressed
səz (səz ˈhi), səd (səd ˈhi)
Sayce ses |-'s -ɪz
say-so ˈseˌso
'sblood zblʌd
scab skæb |scabbed skæbd
scabbard ˈskæbɚd; ES ˈskæbəd; |-ed -ɪd
scabbed adj ˈskæbɪd, skæbd |-ness -ɪdnɪs
scabies ˈskebɪˌiz, ˈskebiz
Scabiosa ˌskebɪˈosə |scabious ˈskebɪəs
scabrous ˈskebrəs
Scafell ˈskɔˈfɛl |S- Pike ˈskɔˌfɛlˈpaɪk
scaffold ˈskæfl̩d, ˈskæfold |-ed -ɪd
scaffoldage ˈskæfl̩dɪdʒ |-ding -dɪŋ
scalawag, -ll- ˈskæləˌwæg |-ery -ərɪ, -rɪ
scald skɔld |scalded ˈskɔldɪd

scale skel |scaled skeld
scalene skeˈlin (ˈscaˌlene ˈtriangle)
Scaliger ˈskælɪdʒɚ; ES ˈskælɪdʒə(r
scallion ˈskæljən
scallop ˈskaləp, ˈskæl-; ES+ˈskɒl-; |-ed -t
Scalopus skəˈlopəs
scalp skælp |scalped skælpt
scalpel ˈskælpɛl |scalpeled ˈskælpɛld
scaly ˈskelɪ
Scamander, s- skəˈmændɚ; ES -ˈmændə(r;
|-ed -d |-ing -dərɪŋ, -drɪŋ
scamp skæmp |scamped skæmpt
scamper ˈskæmpɚ; ES -pə(r; |-ed -d |-ing
-pərɪŋ, -prɪŋ
scan skæn |scanned skænd
scandal ˈskændl̩ |-ed -d |-ing -dl̩ɪŋ, -dlɪŋ
scandalize ˈskændl̩ˌaɪz |-s -ɪz |-d -d
scandalous ˈskændl̩əs, -dləs
Scanderbeg ˈskændɚˌbɛg; ES ˈskændə-
Scandinavia ˌskændəˈnevɪə, -vjə |-n -n
scandium ˈskændɪəm
scansion ˈskænʃən
scant skænt |scanted ˈskæntɪd
scantling ˈskæntlɪŋ |-ed -d
scanty ˈskæntɪ |-tily -tl̩ɪ, -tɪlɪ
Scapa Flow ˈskæpəˈflo, ˈskapə-
'scape, scape skep |-ed -t |-goat -ˌgot
scapegrace ˈskepˌgres |-graces -ˌgresɪz
scapula ˈskæpjələ |-s -z |-lae -ˌli
scar skar; ES skɑ:(r, E+skɑ:(r; |-red -d
scarab ˈskærəb |-oid -ˌɔɪd
scarabaeus ˌskærəˈbiəs |-es -ɪz |-baei -ˈbiaɪ
Scaramouch, s- ˈskærəˌmautʃ, -ˌmuʃ |-es -ɪz
Scarboro, -rough ˈskarˌbɝo, -ə; ES ˈskɑːˌbɝ-,
-ˌbʌr-, -ˌbɝ-, E+ˈskɑː-
scarce skɛrs, skærs; E skɛəs, ES skæəs;
|-city -ətɪ
scare skɛr, skær; E skɛə(r, ES skæə(r; |-d -d
|-crow -ˌkro
scarf skarf; ES skɑːf, E+skɑːf; |-rves -vz or
-rfs -s |-ed -t |-rved -vd
scarification ˌskærəfəˈkeʃən
scarify ˈskærəˌfaɪ |-fied -ˌfaɪd
scarlatina ˌskarləˈtinə; ES ˌskɑːl-, E+ˌskɑːl-
Scarlatti skarˈlatɪ, -ˈlætɪ; ES skɑːl-; (It
skarˈlatti)
scarlet ˈskarlɪt; ES ˈskɑːlɪt, E+ˈskɑːl-
scarp skarp; ES skɑːp, E+skɑːp; |-ed -t
Scarsdale ˈskarzˌdel; ES ˈskɑːz-, E+ˈskɑːz-

Key: See in full §§3–47. bee bi |pity ˈpɪtɪ (§6) |rate ret |yet jɛt |sang sæŋ |angry ˈæŋˌgrɪ
|bath bæθ; E baθ (§10) |ah ɑ |far fɑr |watch watʃ, wɒtʃ (§12) |jaw dʒɔ |gorge gɔrdʒ |go go

scarved **skɑrvd**; ES **skɑ:vd,** E+**skɑ:vd**
scarves **skɑrvz**; ES **skɑ:vz,** E+**skɑ:vz**
scary **'skɛrɪ, 'skɛːrɪ, 'skærɪ;** S **'skærɪ**—*Some*
speakers distinguish scary *from* skerry *by a*
longer ɛ.
scat *card game* **skɑt**
scat *'git!'* **skæt** |-ted **-ɪd**
scathe **skeð**|scathed **skeðd** |-thing-**ɪŋ** |-less-**lɪs**
scatter **'skætɚ;** ES **'skætə(r;** |-ed **-d**
scatterbrain **'skætɚˌbren** |-s **-z** |-ed **-d**
scaup **skɔp**
scavenge **'skævɪndʒ** |-s **-ɪz** |-d **-d** |-r **-ɚ**; ES
-ə(r
scenario **sɪ'nɛrɪˌo, -'nær-, -'nɑr-** (*It* **ʃe'nɑːrjo**)
|-rist **-rɪst**
scene **sin** |scened **sind** |-ry **-ərɪ, -rɪ**
scenic **'sinɪk, 'sɛn-** |-al **-ļ** |-ally **-ļɪ, -ɪklɪ**
scenography **si'nɑgrəfɪ, -'nɒg-**
scent **sɛnt** |scented **'sɛntɪd**
scepter, -tre **'sɛptɚ;** ES **'sɛptə(r;** |-(e)d **-d**
|-(r)ing **'sɛptərɪŋ, -ptrɪŋ**
sceptic **'skɛptɪk** |-al **-ļ** |-ally **-ļɪ, -ɪklɪ**
scepticism **'skɛptəˌsɪzəm**
Schacht *Ger* **ʃɑxt**
schedule **'skɛdʒʊl** |-d **-d,** *Brit* **'ʃɛdjul**
scheelite **'ʃilaɪt**
Scheherazade **ʃəˌhɛrə'zɑdə, -ˌhærə-, -ˌhɪrə-**
Scheldt **skɛlt**
schematic **ski'mætɪk** |-ally **-ļɪ, -ɪklɪ**
schematism **'skiməˌtɪzəm**
schematize **'skiməˌtaɪz** |-s **-ɪz** |-d **-d**
scheme **skim** |schemed **skimd**
Schenectady **skə'nɛktədɪ**
scherzando **skɛr'tsɑndo, -'tsændo** (*It* **sker-
'tsɑndo**)
scherzo **'skɛrtso** |-s **-z** |-zi **-tsi** (*It* **'skertso**)
Schiaparelli **skɪˌɑpə'rɛlɪ, ˌskjɑp-** (*It* ˌ**skjɑpɑ-
'rɛlli**)
Schick **ʃɪk** |S- test **'ʃɪkˌtɛst**
Schiller **'ʃɪlɚ;** ES **'ʃɪlə(r;** (*Ger* **'ʃɪlər**)
schism **'sɪzəm** |-atism **-'sɪzməˌtɪzəm**
schismatic **sɪz'mætɪk** |-al **-ļ** |-ally **-ļɪ, -ɪklɪ**
schist **ʃɪst** |-ic **-ɪk** |-ose **-os** |-ous **-əs**
schizocarp **'skɪzəˌkɑrp;** ES **-ˌkɑ:p,** E+**-ˌkɑ:p**
schizophrenia **ˌskɪzə'frɪnɪə** |-ic **-'frɛnɪk**
Schlegel **'ʃlegļ** (*Ger* **'ʃle:gəl**)
Schleswig **'ʃlɛswɪg, 'ʃlɛs-** (*Ger* **'ʃle:svɪx, 'ʃlɛs-**)
|S- -Holstein **-'holstaɪn**
Schley *Am admiral,* **Ga co. slaɪ** (*Ger* **ʃlaɪ**)

Schliemann **'ʃlimən** (*Ger* **'ʃliːmɑn**)
Schmidt **ʃmɪt**
schnapps **ʃnæps, ʃnɑps** (*Ger* schnaps **ʃnɑps**)
schnauzer **'ʃnaʊzɚ;** ES **'ʃnaʊzə(r;** (*Ger*
'ʃnautsər)
Schoenbrunn *O* **'ʃenbrən, -brʊn** (*Ger* **ʃøːn-
'brʊn**)
Schofield **'skofild**
Schoharie **sko'hærɪ**
scholar **'skɑlɚ;** ES **'skɑlə(r, 'skɒl-;** |-ship **-ˌʃɪp**
scholastic **sko'læstɪk** |-al **-ļ** |-ally **-ļɪ** |-ly **-lɪ**
|-ism **-təˌsɪzəm**
Scholes **skolz** |-'s **-ɪz**
scholiast **'skolɪˌæst** |-ic **ˌskolɪ'æstɪk**
scholium **'skolɪəm** |-lia **-lɪə**
Schönbrunn **'ʃenbrʊn** (*Ger* ʃøːn'brʊn**)
school **skul** |-ed **-d** |-book **-ˌbʊk** |-boy **-ˌbɔɪ**
schoolfellow **'skulˌfɛlo, -ə**
schoolgirl **'skulˌgɝl;** ES **-ˌgɜl, -ˌgɝl**
schoolhouse **'skulˌhaʊs** |-ses **-zɪz**
schoolma'am **'skulˌmɑm, -ˌmæm**
schoolman *'scholastic'* **'skulmən** |-men **-mən**
schoolman *'schoolteacher'* **'skulˌmæn** |-men
-ˌmɛn
schoolmarm **'skulˌmɑm, -ˌmɑrm;** ES **-ˌmɑ:m,**
E+**-ˌmɑ:m**
schoolmaster **'skulˌmæstɚ;** ES **-ˌmæstə(r,**
E+**-ˌmas-, -ˌmɑs-;** |-ed **-d** |-ing **-tərɪŋ, -trɪŋ**
schoolmate **'skulˌmet**
schoolmistress **'skulˌmɪstrɪs** |-es **-ɪz**
schoolroom **'skulˌrum, -ˌrʊm**
schoolteacher **'skulˌtitʃɚ;** ES **-ˌtitʃə(r**
schoolyard **'skulˌjɑrd;** ES **-ˌjɑːd,** E+**-ˌjɑːd**
schooner **'skunɚ;** ES **'skunə(r**
schooner-rigged **'skunɚˌrɪgd;** ES **'skunə-**
Schopenhauer **'ʃopənˌhaʊɚ;** ES **-ˌhaʊ·ə(r**
schottische, -sch **'ʃɑtɪʃ;** ES+**'ʃɒt-;** |-(e)s **-ɪz**
|-(e)d **-t**
Schroon **skrun**
Schubert **'ʃubɚt, 'ʃu-;** ES **-bət;** (*Ger* **'ʃuːbərt**)
Schulenburg **'ʃulənˌbɝg;** ES **-ˌbɜg, -ˌbɝg**
Schumann **'ʃumən, 'ʃu-** |S- -Heink **-'haɪŋk**
Schurman **'ʃurmən;** ES **'ʃuəmən**
Schurz **ʃurts;** ES **ʃuəts;** |-'s **-ɪz**
Schuyler **'skaɪlɚ;** ES **'skaɪlə(r;** |-ville **-ˌvɪl**
Schuylkill **'skulkɪl**
schwa **ʃwɑ** (*Ger* **ʃvɑː**)
Schwab **ʃwɑb, ʃwɒb, ʃwɔb**
Schwartz **swɔrts;** ES **swɔəts;** |-'s **-ɪz**

|full **fʊl** |tooth **tuθ** |further **'fɝðɚ;** ES **'fɝðə** |custom **'kʌstəm** |while **hwaɪl** |how **haʊ** |toy **tɔɪ**
|using **'juzɪŋ** |fuse **fjuz, fɪuz** |dish **dɪʃ** |vision **'vɪʒən** |Eden **'idn̩** |cradle **'kredļ** |keep 'em **'kipm̩**

schweizerkäse 'swaɪtsɚˌkezə; ES -tsə-; (Ger
 'ʃvaɪtsərˌke:zə)
sciagram 'saɪəˌgræm |-graph -ˌgræf; E+
 -ˌgraf -ˌgraf
sciagraphy saɪ'ægrəfɪ
sciatic saɪ'ætɪk |-al -] |-ally -]ɪ, -ɪklɪ
sciatica saɪ'ætɪkə
science 'saɪəns |-s -ɪz |-d -t
scientific ˌsaɪən'tɪfɪk |-al -] |-ally -]ɪ, -ɪklɪ
scientist, S- 'saɪəntɪst
scientistic ˌsaɪən'tɪstɪk |-ally -]ɪ, -ɪklɪ
scilicet 'sɪlɪˌset
Scilla 'Scylla' 'sɪlə (It 'ʃilla)
Scilla 'squill' 'sɪlə
Scilly Isles 'sɪlɪ'aɪlz
scimitar, -ter 'sɪmətɚ; ES 'sɪmətə(r; |-ed -d
scintilla sɪn'tɪlə
scintillate 'sɪnt]ˌet |-d -ɪd |-tor -ɚ; ES -ə(r
scintillation ˌsɪnt]'eʃən
sciolism 'saɪəˌlɪzəm |-list -lɪst
scion 'saɪən
Scioto saɪ'otə, -to
Scipio 'sɪpɪˌo
scire facias 'saɪrɪ'feʃɪˌæs
scirrhus 'sɪrəs, 'skɪr- |-rhous -əs
scission 'sɪʒən, 'sɪʃən
scissor 'sɪzɚ; ES 'sɪzə(r; |-s -z |-ed -d
Scituate 'sɪtʃuˌet, 'sɪtʃəˌwet
sclaff sklæf |sclaffed sklæft
scleriasis sklɪ'raɪəsɪs
sclerometer sklɪ'ramətɚ; ES -'ramətə(r,
 -'rɒm-
sclerosis sklɪ'rosɪs |-roses -'rosiz
sclerotic sklɪ'ratɪk; ES+-'rɒt-; |-al -]
sclerous 'sklɪrəs
scoff skɔf, skɒf |-ed -t
scold skold |scolded 'skoldɪd
Scollard 'skalɚd; ES 'skaləd, 'skɒl-
Scollay 'skʌlɪ, sp. pron. 'skalɪ, ES+'skɒlɪ
scollop 'skaləp; ES+'skɒl-; |-ed -t
sconce skans; ES+skɒns; |-s -ɪz |-d -t
scone skon, skɒn
Scone skun, skon
scoop skup |scooped skupt |-ful 'skupˌful
scoot skut |scooted 'skutɪd
scop skap, skop; ES+skɒp
scope skop
scopolamin skoˈpaləmɪn, -'pɒl-, ˌskopə-
 'læmɪn |-ine -in, -ɪn

scorbutic skɔr'bjutɪk, -'bɪu-; ES skɔə-; |-al -]
 |-ally -]ɪ, -ɪklɪ
scorch skɔrtʃ; ES skɔətʃ; |-es -ɪz |-ed -t
score skor, skɔr; ES skoə(r, E+skɔə(r; |-d -d
scoria 'skorɪə, 'skɔr-; S 'skor-; |-riae -rɪˌi
scoriaceous ˌskorɪ'eʃəs, ˌskɔr-; S ˌskor-
scorify 'skorəˌfaɪ, 'skɔr-; S 'skor-; |-fied -ˌfaɪd
scorn skɔrn; ES skɔən; |-ed -d |-ful -fəl
 |-fully -fəlɪ
Scorpio 'skɔrpɪˌo; ES 'skɔəpɪˌo
scorpion 'skɔrpɪən; ES 'skɔəpɪən
Scot, s- skat; ES+skɒt
Scotch skatʃ; ES+skɒtʃ; |-man -mən |-men
 -mən
scotch skatʃ; ES+skɒtʃ; |-es -ɪz |-ed -t
Scotch-Irish 'skatʃ'aɪrɪʃ; ES+'skɒtʃ-
scoter 'skotɚ; ES 'skotə(r
scot-free 'skat'fri; ES+'skɒt-; ('scot-ˌfree
 'trip)
Scotia 'skoʃə, -ʃɪə
Scotland 'skatlənd; ES+'skɒt-
Scots skats; ES+skɒts; |-man -mən |-men
 -mən
Scotswoman 'skatsˌwumən, -ˌwu-; ES+
 'skɒts-; |-women -ˌwɪmɪn, -ən
Scott skat; ES+skɒt; |-dale -ˌdel
Scotticism 'skatəˌsɪzəm; ES+'skɒtə-
Scottish 'skatɪʃ; ES+'skɒt-
Scottsbluff 'skatsˌblʌf; ES+'skɒts-
Scotts Bluff 'skats'blʌf; ES+'skɒts-
Scotus 'skotəs |-'s -ɪz
scoundrel 'skaundrəl |-ly -ɪ
scour skaur; ES skauə(r; |-ed -d |-ing
 'skaurɪŋ
scourge skɝdʒ; ES skɝdʒ, skɜdʒ; |-s -ɪz |-d -d
scouse skaus |-s -ɪz
scout skaut |scouted 'skautɪd
scoutmaster 'skautˌmæstɚ; ES -ˌmæstə(r,
 E+-ˌmas-, -ˌmas-
scow skau |scowed skaud
scowl skaul |scowled skauld
scrabble 'skræb] |-d -d |-ling -blɪŋ, -b]ɪŋ
scrag skræg |scragged skrægd
scragged adj 'skrægɪd |-gled -]d |-gling -lɪŋ
 |-gly -lɪ |-gy -ɪ |-gily -]ɪ, -ɪlɪ
scram skræm |scrammed skræmd
scramble 'skræmb] |-d -d |-ling -blɪŋ, -b]ɪŋ
scrannel 'skræn]
Scranton 'skræntən

Key: See in full §§3–47. bee bi |pity 'pɪtɪ (§6) |rate ret |yet jet |sang sæŋ |angry 'æŋ·grɪ
|bath bæθ; E baθ (§10) |ah a |far far |watch watʃ, wɒtʃ (§12) |jaw dʒɔ |gorge gɔrdʒ |go go

scrap skræp |scrapped skræpt |-book -ˌbʊk
scrape skrep |scraped skrept
scraper ˈskrepɚ; ES ˈskrepə(r
scrapper ˈskræpɚ; ES ˈskræpə(r
scrapple ˈskræpl̩
scrappy ˈskræpɪ |-ily -ḷɪ, -ɪlɪ
scratch skrætʃ |scratches ˈskrætʃɪz |-ed -t
scratch-awl ˈskrætʃˌɔl
scrawl skrɔl |scrawled skrɔld
scrawny ˈskrɔnɪ
screak skrik |screaked skrikt
scream skrim |screamed skrimd
scree skri
screech skritʃ |screeches ˈskritʃɪz |-ed -t
screech-owl ˈskritʃˌaʊl
screed skrid |screeded ˈskridɪd
screen skrin |screened skrind
Screven ˈskrɪvɪn, -ən
screw skru, skrɪu |-ed -d |-driver -ˌdraɪvɚ; ES
-ˌdraɪvə(r
Scriabin skriˈɑbɪn, ˈskriəbɪn
scribble ˈskrɪbl̩ |-d -d |-ling ˈskrɪblɪŋ, -bl̩ɪŋ
scribbler ˈskrɪblɚ; ES ˈskrɪblə(r
scribe skraɪb |scribed skraɪbd
Scribner ˈskrɪbnɚ; ES ˈskrɪbnə(r
scrim skrɪm
scrimmage ˈskrɪmɪdʒ |-s -ɪz |-d -d
scrimp skrɪmp |scrimped skrɪmpt
scrimshaw ˈskrɪmʃɔ |-ed -d
scrip skrɪp |-page ˈskrɪpɪdʒ
script skrɪpt
scriptorium skrɪpˈtorɪəm, -ˈtɔr-; S -ˈtor-; |-ria
-rɪə
scriptural, S- ˈskrɪptʃərəl |-ly -ɪ |-ism -ˌɪzəm
scripture, S- ˈskrɪptʃɚ; ES ˈskrɪptʃə(r; |-d -d
Scriven ˈskrɪvən
scrivener, S- ˈskrɪvnɚ, -vənɚ; ES -nə(r
scrod skrɑd; ES+skrɒd
scrofula ˈskrɔfjələ, ˈskrɒf-, ˈskrɑf- |-lous -ləs
scroll skrol |scrolled skrold
scrooch skrutʃ |-es -ɪz |-ed -t
Scrooge skrudʒ |-'s -ɪz
Scroop skrup
scrotum ˈskrotəm |-tal -tl̩
scrouge skrudʒ, skraʊdʒ |-s -ɪz |-d -d
scrounge skraʊndʒ |-s -ɪz |-d -d
scrub skrʌb |scrubbed skrʌbd
scrubbed adj ˈskrʌbɪd
scrub-brush ˈskrʌbˌbrʌʃ |-es -ɪz

scrubby ˈskrʌbɪ
scruff skrʌf
scrummage ˈskrʌmɪdʒ |-s -ɪz |-d -d
scrumptious ˈskrʌmpʃəs
scrunch skrʌntʃ |-es -ɪz |-ed -t
scruple ˈskrupl̩, ˈskrɪu- |-d -d |-ling -plɪŋ,
-pl̩ɪŋ, |-pulous -pjələs
scrupulosity ˌskrupjəˈlɑsətɪ, ˌskrɪu-; ES+
-ˈlɒs-
scrutinize ˈskrutn̩ˌaɪz, ˈskrɪu- |-s -ɪz |-d -d
|-ny -ɪ
Scrymgeour, -e, -miger, -migar ˈskrɪmdʒɚ;
ES -dʒə(r
scud skʌd |scudded ˈskʌdɪd |-der, S- -ɚ; ES
-ə(r
Scudéry Fr skydeˈri
scudo It ˈsku:do |-di -di
scuff skʌf |scuffed skʌft
scuffle ˈskʌfl̩ |-d -d |-ling ˈskʌflɪŋ, -fl̩ɪŋ
sculduddery skʌlˈdʌdərɪ, -drɪ |-duggery
-ˈdʌgərɪ, -grɪ
sculk skʌlk |sculked skʌlkt
scull skʌl |sculled skʌld
scullduddery, -dugg- see sculduddery
scullery ˈskʌlərɪ
scullion ˈskʌljən
sculp skʌlp |-ed -t
sculpin ˈskʌlpɪn
sculptor ˈskʌlptɚ; ES ˈskʌlptə(r
sculptress ˈskʌlptrɪs |-es -ɪz
sculptural ˈskʌlptʃərəl |-ly -ɪ
sculpture ˈskʌlptʃɚ; ES -tʃə(r; |-d -d
sculpturesque ˌskʌlptʃəˈrɛsk
scum skʌm |scummed skʌmd |-my -ɪ
scumble ˈskʌmbl̩ |-d -d |-ling ˈskʌmblɪŋ,
-bl̩ɪŋ
scup skʌp |scupped skʌpt
scupper ˈskʌpɚ; ES -pə(r; |-ed -d |-ing
ˈskʌpərɪŋ, ˈskʌprɪŋ
scuppernong ˈskʌpɚˌnɔŋ, -ˌnɒŋ, -ˌnɑŋ; ES
ˈskʌpə-
scurf skɝf; ES skɜf, skɝf; |-ed -t |-y -ɪ
scurrile ˈskɝɪl, -əl; ES ˈskɜr-, ˈskʌr-, ˈskɝ-;
|-lous -əs
scurrility skəˈrɪlətɪ, skɝˈɪl-; ES+skɝˈɪl-,
skʌ-
scurry, S- ˈskɝɪ; ES ˈskɜrɪ, ˈskʌrɪ, ˈskɝɪ
scurvy ˈskɝvɪ; ES ˈskɜvɪ, ˈskɝvɪ
scut skʌt |scutted ˈskʌtɪd

Scutari 'skutǝrı, sku'tɑrı
scutate 'skjutet, 'skıu-
scutch skʌtʃ |scutches 'skʌtʃız |-ed -t
scutcheon 'skʌtʃǝn |-ed -d
scute skjut, skıut
scutella skju'tɛlǝ, skıu- |-lae -i
scutellate 'platterlike' 'skjut]ͺet, 'skıu-
scutellate 'scaly' skju'tɛlıt, 'skjut]ͺet, -kıu-
scutellum skju'tɛlǝm, skıu- |-la -ǝ
scutter 'skʌtɚ; ES 'skʌtǝ(r; |-ed -d
scuttle 'skʌt] |-d -d |-ling 'skʌt]ıŋ, -tlıŋ
Scylla 'sılǝ
scythe saıð |scythed saıðd
Scythia 'sıθıǝ |-n -n
'sdeath zdɛθ
se music se
se- unstressed word initial sı-, sǝ-, si- (sedate
    sı'det, sǝ'det, si'det); before 1 often s]-
    (select s]'ɛkt). In the vocab. when only one
    pron. is given (usually sı-), it is to be under-
    stood that many speakers also pronounce sǝ-,
    si-, s]- (si- esp. in deliberate speech).
sea si |-beach -ͺbitʃ |-beaches -ͺbitʃız
Seabeach 'si¸bitʃ, loc. 'sıbıdʒ |-'s -ız
seaboard 'si¸bord, -¸bɔrd; ES -¸boǝd, E+
    -¸bɔǝd
sea-born 'si¸bɔrn; ES -¸bɔǝn
sea-borne 'si¸born, -¸bɔrn; ES -¸boǝn, E+
    -¸bɔǝn
Seabright 'si¸braıt
seacoast 'si¸kost
seafarer 'si¸fɛrɚ, -¸færɚ; E -¸fɛrǝ(r, ES
    -¸færǝ(r
seafaring 'si¸fɛrıŋ, -¸fær-; S -¸fær-
Seaford 'sifɚd; ES 'sifǝd
seafowl 'si¸faʊl
Seager 'sigɚ; ES 'sigǝ(r
seagirt 'si¸gɝt; ES -¸gɜt, -¸gɝt
seagoing 'si¸go·ıŋ
seal sil |sealed sild |sealery 'silǝrı
sealless 'sıllıs
Sealyham 'sılı¸hæm, 'sılıǝm
seam sim |seamed simd
seaman 'simǝn |-men -mǝn |-like -ͺlaık |-ly -lı
    |-ship -ͺʃıp
seamark 'si¸mɑrk; ES -¸mɑ:k, E+-¸mɑ:k
seamstress 'simstrıs, older 'sɛm- |-es -ız
Seamus 'ʃemǝs |-'s -ız
Seanad Eireann 'sænad'erǝn, -'erǝn

séance 'seɑns, 'sıǝns |-s -ız (Fr se'ɑ̃:s)
seaplane 'si¸plen
seaport 'si¸port, -¸pɔrt; ES -¸poǝt, E+-¸pɔǝt
sear sır; ES sıǝ(r, S+seǝ(r; |-ed -d
search sɝtʃ; ES sɜtʃ, sɝtʃ; |-es -ız |-ed -t
    |-light -ͺlaıt
search-warrant 'sɝtʃ¸wɔrǝnt, -¸wɑr-, -¸wɒr-;
    ES 'sɜtʃ-, 'sɝtʃ-
Searcy 'sɝsı; ES 'sɜsı, 'sɝsı
Searle sɝl; ES sɜl, sɝl; |-s -z |-s's -zız
Sears sırz; ES sıǝz; |-'s -ız
seascape 'si¸skep
seascout 'si¸skaʊt
seashore, S- 'si¸ʃor, -¸ʃɔr; ES -¸ʃoǝ(r, E+
    -¸ʃɔǝ(r
seasick 'si¸sık
seaside 'si¸saıd
season 'sizn |-ed -d |-ing 'sizn̩ıŋ, 'sıznıŋ
seasonable 'siznǝb], 'sıznǝ- |-bly -blı
seasonal 'siznǝl |-ly -ı
seat sit |seated 'sitıd
Seattle si'æt], 'siæt] ('Se¸attle 'Wash.)
seaward 'siwɚd; ES 'siwǝd; |-s -z
seaway 'si¸we
seaweed 'si¸wid
seaworthy 'si¸wɝðı; ES -¸wɜðı, -¸wɝðı
sebaceous sı'beʃǝs
Sebago sı'bego
Sebastian sı'bæstʃǝn
Sebastopol sı'bæstǝp], Russia+¸sɛbǝs'top]
Sebring 'sibrıŋ
sebum 'sibǝm, 'sibm̩
sec sɛk
secant 'sikǝnt, 'sikænt
Secaucus sı'kɔkǝs |-'s -ız
secede si'sid, sı- |-d -d |-id
secession si'sɛʃǝn, sı- |-ism -¸ızǝm |-ist -ıst
Sechuana sɛ'tʃwɑnǝ
Seckel pear 'sɛk], 'sık]
seclude sı'klud, -'klıud |-d -d |-d -d
seclusion sı'kluʒǝn, -'klıuʒǝn
second n, adj, adv 'sɛkǝnd, 'sɛkǝnt, before
    some conss.+'sɛkǝn ('sɛkǝn'gɛt)
second v 'sɛkǝnd, -nt |-ed -ǝndıd
secondary 'sɛkǝn¸dɛrı
secondarily 'sɛkǝn¸dɛrǝlı, -ılı, esp. if emph.
    ¸sɛkǝn'dɛr-
second-class 'sɛkǝnd'klæs, 'sɛkǝn-, 'sɛkŋ-;
    E+-'klas, -'klɑs ('second-¸class 'fare)

Key: See in full §§3–47. bee bi |pity 'pıtı (§6) |rate ret |yet jɛt |sang sæŋ |angry 'æŋ·grı
|bath bæθ; E baθ (§10) |ah ɑ |far fɑr |watch wɑtʃ, wɒtʃ (§12) |jaw dʒɔ |gorge gɔrdʒ |go go

second-hand *adj, adv* **'sɛkənd'hænd**, -ənt-
('second-ˌhand 'book)
secondhand *n* **'sɛkəndˌhænd**, -ənt-
secondly **'sɛkəndlɪ**
second-rate **'sɛkənd'ret**
secret **'sikrɪt** |secrecy **'sikrəsɪ**
secretarial ˌsɛkrə'tɛrɪəl, -'ter-
secretariat ˌsɛkrə'tɛrɪət, -ˌæt, -'ter- |-ate -ɪt
secretary **'sɛkrəˌtɛrɪ**, **'sɛkəˌtɛrɪ**—*The first* r
is lost from **'sɛkəˌtɛrɪ** *by dissimilation*
(*§121*).
secrete sɪ'krit |-d -ɪd |-tion -'krɪʃən
secretive sɪ'kritɪv |-tory -tərɪ
sect sɛkt |-ary -ərɪ
sectarian sɛk'tɛrɪən, -'ter- |-ism -ˌɪzəm
sectile **'sɛktɪl** |-lity sɛk'tɪlətɪ
section **'sɛkʃən** |-ed -d |-ing -ʃənɪŋ, -ʃnɪŋ
sectional **'sɛkʃənļ** |-ly -ɪ |-ism -ˌɪzəm
sectionalize **'sɛkʃənļˌaɪz** |-s -ɪz |-d -d
sector **'sɛktɚ**; ES -tə(r; |-ed -d |-ing **'sɛktərɪŋ**,
'sɛktrɪŋ
secular **'sɛkjələ**; ES -lə(r; |-ism -ˌɪzəm
secularity ˌsɛkjə'lærətɪ
secularization ˌsɛkjələrə'zeʃən, -aɪ'z-
secularize **'sɛkjələˌraɪz** |-s -ɪz |-d -d
secund **'sikʌnd**
secure sɪ'kjur, -'kɪur; ES -'kjuə(r, -'kɪu-;
|-d -d |-rity -ətɪ
Sedalia sɪ'delɪə, -ljə
Sedan, s- sɪ'dæn (*Fr* sə'dɑ̃)
sedate sɪ'det
sedative **'sɛdətɪv**
sedentarily **'sɛdņˌtɛrəlɪ**, -ɪlɪ, *esp. if emph.*
ˌsɛdņ'tarɪlɪ
sedentary **'sɛdņˌtɛrɪ**
sedge sɛdʒ |sedges **'sɛdʒɪz** |sedged sɛdʒd
Sedgwick **'sɛdʒwɪk**, **'sɛdʒɪk**
sedgy **'sɛdʒɪ**
sediment **'sɛdəmənt**
sedimental ˌsɛdə'mɛntļ |-tary -tərɪ
sedimentation ˌsɛdəmən'teʃən, -mɛn-
sedition sɪ'dɪʃən |-tious -ʃəs
Sedley **'sɛdlɪ**
Sedlitz **'sɛdlɪts** |-'s -ɪz
seduce sɪ'djus, -'dɪus, -'dus |-s -ɪz |-d -t
seduction sɪ'dʌkʃən |-tive -tɪv
sedulity sɪ'djulətɪ, -'dɪu-, -'du-
sedulous **'sɛdʒələs**
Sedum, s- **'sidəm**

see si |saw sɔ |seen sin—*unstressed often* sɪ
(sɪ'hɪr!)
seed sid |seeded **'sidɪd** |-ling -lɪŋ
seedtime **'sidˌtaɪm**
seek sik |sought sɔt
Seek-No-Further *apple* **'siknəˌfɝðɚ**, **'sɪgnə-**;
ES -ˌfɝðə(r, -ˌfɝðə(r;—*The 2d pron., probably now rare, shows the normal phonetic
development of the proper name dissociated
from the meaning of* seek.
Seekonk **'sikɑŋk, -kɒŋk**
Seeley, Seelye **'silɪ**
seem sim |seemed simd |seemly **'simlɪ**
seen sin
seep sip |seeped sipt |-age -ɪdʒ
seer *'who sees'* **'siɚ**; ES **'si-ə(r**
seer *'prophet'* sɪr; ES sɪə(r, S+sɛə(r; |-ess -ɪs
seersucker **'sɪrˌsʌkɚ**; ES -ˌsʌkə(r, S+'sɛə-
seesaw **'siˌsɔ** |-sawed -ˌsɔd
seethe sið |-d -d *or arch.* sod sad; ES+sɒd;
|-d -d *or arch.* sodden **'sɑdņ**; ES+'sɒdņ
sefari sə'farɪ
segment **'sɛgmənt** |-ed -ɪd |-ary -mənˌtɛrɪ
segmental sɛg'mɛntļ |-ly -ɪ
segmentation ˌsɛgmən'teʃən
segregate *adj* **'sɛgrɪgɪt**, -ˌget
segregate *v* **'sɛgrɪˌget** |-d -ɪd |-tive -ɪv
segregation ˌsɛgrɪ'geʃən
Seguin sɪ'gin, 'sigɪn (*Fr* sə'gæ̃)
seiche seʃ (*Fr* sɛʃ)
Seidl **'saɪdļ**, **'zaɪdļ**
Seidlitz **'sɛdlɪts** |-'s -ɪz
seigneur sin'jɝ; ES -'jɝ(r, -'jɝ; (*Fr* sɛ'nœːr)
seignior **'sinjɚ**; ES **'sinjə(r**; |-age -ɪdʒ |-y -ɪ
seignorial sin'jorɪəl, -'jɔr-; S -'jor-
seine sen |seined send
Seine sen (*Fr* sɛːn)
seise siz |seises **'sizɪz** |seised sizd
seisin **'sizɪn**
seism **'saɪzəm**, **'saɪsəm**
seismic **'saɪzmɪk**, **'saɪs-** |-al -ļ |-ally -ļɪ, -ɪklɪ
seismogram **'saɪzməˌgræm**, **'saɪs-**
seismograph **'saɪzməˌgræf**, **'saɪs-**; E+-ˌgraf,
-ˌgraf
seismographic ˌsaɪzmə'græfɪk, ˌsaɪs- |-al -ļ
seismologic ˌsaɪzmə'lɑdʒɪk, ˌsaɪs-; ES+
-'lɒdʒ-; |-al -ļ |-ally -ļɪ, -ɪklɪ
seismologist saɪz'mɑlədʒɪst, saɪs-; ES+
-'mɒl-; |-gy -dʒɪ

seismometer saɪz'mɑmətɚ, saɪs-; ES -'mɑmə-
tə(r, -'mɒm-
seize siz |seizes 'sizɪz |seized sizd
seizin 'sizɪn
seizure 'siʒɚ; ES 'siʒə(r
Sejanus sɪ'dʒenəs |-'s -ɪz
selah 'silə
Selden 'sɛldɪn, -dən
seldom 'sɛldəm
select sə'lɛkt |-ed -ɪd |-ive -ɪv |-ion -kʃən
selectivity sə,lɛk'tɪvətɪ
selectman sə'lɛktmən |-men -mən, in N Engd
(1) səlɛkt'mæn, sɪ-, s|-, -k'mæn (2) sə-
'lɛktmæn, sɪ-, s|'ɛkt-, -kmæn, -mən
(3) 'silɛkt,mæn, -k,mæn |pl (1) -'mɛn
(2) -mɛn, -mən (3) -,mɛn (L.A.)
selector sə'lɛktɚ; ES -'lɛktə(r
Selene sə'lini |-na -nə
selenite 'sɛlə,naɪt
Selenite 'moon-dweller' 'sɛlə,naɪt, sə'linaɪt
selenium sə'liniəm
Seleucia sə'luʃɪə, -'lɪu- |-n -n
Seleucid sə'lusɪd, -'lɪu- |-ae -sə,di |-an -ən
Seleucus sə'lukəs, -'lɪu- |-'s -ɪz
self sɛlf |self's sɛlfs |selves sɛlvz
self-abasement ,sɛlfə'besmənt
self-abnegation ,sɛlfæbnɪ'geʃən
self-assertion ,sɛlfə'sɝʃən; ES -'sɝʃ-, -'sɝʃ-
self-assurance ,sɛlfə'ʃurəns |-s -ɪz
self-assured ,sɛlfə'ʃurd; ES -'ʃuəd
self-centered, -tred 'sɛlf'sɛntɚd; ES -təd;
('self-,centered 'hero)
self-command ,sɛlfkə'mænd; ES+-'mand,
-'mɑnd
self-complacence ,sɛlfkəm'plesņs |-cy -ɪ |-nt
-ņt
self-conceit ,sɛlfkən'sit |-ed -ɪd
self-condemned ,sɛlfkən'dɛmd |-nedly -mnɪdlɪ
self-confidence 'sɛlf'kɑnfədəns; ES+-'kɒn-;
|-dent -dənt
self-conscious 'sɛlf'kɑnʃəs; ES+-'kɒn-
self-consistency ,sɛlfkən'sɪstənsɪ |-tent -tənt
self-contained ,sɛlfkən'tend |-nedly -nɪdlɪ
self-control ,sɛlfkən'trol |-led -d
self-declared ,sɛlfdɪ'klɛrd, -'klærd; E -'klɛəd,
ES -'klæəd; |-redly -rɪdlɪ
self-defense, Brit -nce ,sɛlfdɪ'fɛns
self-denial ,sɛlfdɪ'naɪəl, -'naɪl
self-denying ,sɛlfdɪ'naɪɪŋ

self-determination ,sɛlfdɪ,tɝmə'neʃən; ES
-,tɝm-, -,tɝm-
self-esteem ,sɛlfə'stim
self-evident 'sɛlf'ɛvədənt
self-explanatory ,sɛlfɪk'splænə,torɪ, -,tɔrɪ; S
-,tɔrɪ
self-expression ,sɛlfɪk'sprɛʃən
self-governed 'sɛlf'gʌvənd; ES -'gʌvənd;
|-ning -nɪŋ
self-government 'sɛlf'gʌvɚmənt, -'gʌvən-
mənt; ES -və-, -vən-
self-help 'sɛlf'hɛlp
selfhood 'sɛlfhud
self-importance ,sɛlfɪm'portņs; ES -'poət-;
|tant -tņt
self-indulgence ,sɛlfɪn'dʌldʒəns |-ent -ənt
self-interest 'sɛlf'ɪntərɪst, -'ɪntrɪst
selfish 'sɛlfɪʃ
self-made 'sɛlf'med ('self-,made 'woman)
self-mastery 'sɛlf'mæstərɪ, -trɪ; E+-'mas-,
-'mɑs-
self-possessed ,sɛlfpə'zɛst |-sedly -sɪdlɪ
self-possession ,sɛlfpə'zɛʃən
self-preservation ,sɛlfprɛzɚ'veʃən; ES -zə-
self-realization ,sɛlfriələ'zeʃən, -aɪ'z-
self-regard ,sɛlfrɪ'gard; ES -'gaːd, E+-'gaːd
self-reliance ,sɛlfrɪ'laɪəns |-ant -ənt
self-reproach ,sɛlfrɪ'protʃ |-es -ɪz |-ed -t
self-respect ,sɛlfrɪ'spɛkt
self-restraint ,sɛlfrɪ'strent
Selfridge 'sɛlfrɪdʒ |-'s -ɪz
self-righteous 'sɛlf'raɪtʃəs
self-rising 'sɛlf'raɪzɪŋ ('self-,rising 'flour)
self-sacrifice 'sɛlf'sækrə,faɪs, -,faɪz |-s -ɪz
selfsame 'sɛlf'sem ('self,same 'hour)
self-satisfaction ,sɛlfsætɪs'fækʃən
self-satisfied 'sɛlf'sætɪs,faɪd
self-seeker 'sɛlf'sikɚ; ES -'sikə(r
self-service 'sɛlf'sɝvɪs; ES -'sɝv-, -'sɝv-
self-starter 'sɛlf'startɚ; ES -'staːtə(r, E+
-'staːt-
self-sufficiency ,sɛlfsə'fɪʃənsɪ |-ent -ənt
self-sustaining ,sɛlfsə'stenɪŋ
self-taught 'sɛlf'tɔt ('self-,taught 'sage)
self-will 'sɛlf'wɪl |-ed -d
Seligman 'sɛlɪgmən
Selim 'silɪm, sə'lim
Selinsgrove 'silɪnz,grov
Seljuk sɛl'dʒuk |-ian -ɪən

Key: See in full §§3–47. bee bi |pity 'pɪtɪ (§6) |rate ret |yet jɛt |sang sæŋ |angry 'æŋ·grɪ
|bath bæθ; E baθ (§10) |ah ɑ |far fɑr |watch wɑtʃ, wɒtʃ (§12) |jaw dʒɔ |gorge gɔrdʒ |go go

Selkirk ˈsɛlkɜˑk; ES -kɜk, -kɜˑk; |-shire -ˌʃɪr, -ʃɚ; ES -ˌʃɪə(r, -ʃə(r
sell sɛl |sold sold |-out n ˈsɛlˌaut
Seltzer, s- ˈsɛltsɚ; ES ˈsɛltsə(r
selvage, -vedge ˈsɛlvɪdʒ |-s -ɪz |-d -d
selves sɛlvz
semanteme səˈmæntim
semantic səˈmæntɪk |-ally -ḷɪ, -ɪklɪ |-s -s
semaphore ˈsɛməˌfor, -ˌfɔr; ES -ˌfoə(r, E+ -ˌfɔə(r
semasiological səˌmesɪəˈlɑdʒɪk|; ES+-ˈlɒdʒ-; |-ly -ɪ, -ɪklɪ
semasiologist səˌmesɪˈɑlədʒɪst; ES+-ˈɒl-; |-gy -dʒɪ
semblable ˈsɛmbləb| |-bly -blɪ
semblance ˈsɛmbləns |-s -ɪz |-ant -ənt
Semele ˈsɛməˌli
semen ˈsimən |semina ˈsɛmɪnə
semester səˈmɛstɚ; ES -ˈmɛstə(r
semiannual ˌsɛmɪˈænjʊəl |-ly -ɪ
semibreve ˈsɛməˌbriv
semicentennial ˌsɛməsɛnˈtɛnɪəl |-ly -ɪ
semicircle ˈsɛməˌsɜˑk|; ES -ˌsɜk|, -ˌsɜˑk|
semicircular ˌsɛməˈsɜˑkjələ; ES -ˈsɜkjələ(r, -ˈsɜˑkjələ(r
semicircumference ˌsɛməsɚˈkʌmfərəns, -frəns; ES -səˈkʌm-; |-s -ɪz
semicolon ˈsɛməˌkolən
semiconscious ˌsɛməˈkɑnʃəs; ES+-ˈkɒn-
semidarkness ˌsɛməˈdɑrknɪs; ES -ˈdɑːk-, E+-ˈdɑːk-
semidetached ˌsɛmədɪˈtætʃt
semifinal ˌsɛməˈfaɪn| (ˈsemiˌfinal ˈround)
semifluid ˌsɛməˈfluɪd, -ˈflɪu-
semimonthly ˌsɛməˈmʌnθlɪ
seminal ˈsɛmən| |-ly -ɪ
seminar ˈsɛməˌnɑr, ˌsɛməˈnɑr; ES -ɑː(r, E+-ɑː(r
seminary ˈsɛməˌnɛrɪ
Seminole ˈsɛməˌnol
semiofficial ˌsɛmɪəˈfɪʃəl |-ly -ɪ
semiprofessional ˌsɛməprəˈfɛʃən|, -ʃnəl |-ly -ɪ
semiquaver ˈsɛməˌkwevɚ; ES -ˌkwevə(r
Semiramis səˈmɪrəmɪs |-ˈs -ɪz
semirigid ˌsɛməˈrɪdʒɪd
semiskilled ˌsɛməˈskɪld
Semite ˈsɛmaɪt, ˈsi-
Semitic səˈmɪtɪk |-ticism -ˈmɪtəˌsɪzəm
Semitism ˈsɛməˌtɪzəm, ˈsimə-

semitone ˈsɛməˌton
semitropical ˌsɛməˈtrɑpɪk|; ES+-ˈtrɒp-
semivowel ˈsɛməˌvauəl, -ˌvaul, -ɪl
semiweekly ˌsɛməˈwiklɪ
semiyearly ˌsɛməˈjɪrlɪ; ES -ˈjɪəlɪ, S+-ˈjɛəlɪ
sempiternal ˌsɛmpɪˈtɜˑn|; ES -ˈtɜn|, -ˈtɜˑn|; |-ly -ɪ |-nity -nətɪ
Sempronius sɛmˈpronɪəs, -njəs |-ˈs -ɪz
sempstress ˈsɛmpstrɪs |-es -ɪz
sen sɛn
senate ˈsɛnɪt |-tor -ɚ, -nətɚ; ES -təˑ(r
senatorial ˌsɛnəˈtorɪəl, ˌsɛnɪ-, -ˈtɔr-; S -ˈtor-
send sɛnd |sent sɛnt
sendal ˈsɛnd|
send-off ˈsɛndˌɔf, -ˌɒf
Seneca ˈsɛnɪkə |-n -n
Senegal ˌsɛnɪˈɡɔl (Fr seneˈɡal)
Senegalese ˌsɛnɪɡəˈliz, -ɡəˈliz
Senegambia ˌsɛnəˈɡæmbɪə |-n -n
senescence səˈnɛsn̩s |-cy -ɪ |-scent -sn̩t
seneschal ˈsɛnəʃəl |-ed -d
senile ˈsinaɪl, -nɪl, -n| |-lity səˈnɪlətɪ, si-
senior ˈsinjɚ; ES ˈsinjə(r
seniority sinˈjɔrətɪ, -ˈjɑr-, -ˈjɒr-
Senlac ˈsɛnlæk
senna ˈsɛnə
Sennacherib səˈnækəˌrɪb
sennight ˈsɛnaɪt, -nɪt
señor sɛnˈjɔr; ES -ˈjɔə(r; (Sp seˈɲɔr)
señora sɛnˈjɔrə, -ˈjɔrə; S -ˈjorə; (Sp seˈɲora)
señorita ˌsɛnjəˈritə (Sp ˌseɲoˈrita)
sensation sɛnˈseʃən |-al | |-ally -ɪ
sensationalism sɛnˈseʃən|ˌɪzəm, -ʃnəl- |-ist -ɪst
sense sɛns |senses ˈsɛnsɪz |sensed sɛnst
sense stress ˈsɛnsˌstrɛs |-es -ɪz
sensibility ˌsɛnsəˈbɪlətɪ
sensible ˈsɛnsəb| |-bly -blɪ
sensitive ˈsɛnsətɪv |-tivity ˌsɛnsəˈtɪvətɪ
sensitization ˌsɛnsətəˈzeʃən, -aɪˈz-
sensitize ˈsɛnsəˌtaɪz |-s -ɪz |-d -d
sensorial sɛnˈsorɪəl, -ˈsɔr-; S -ˈsor-
sensory ˈsɛnsərɪ
sensual ˈsɛnʃʊəl |-ly -ɪ |-ism -ˌɪzəm |-ist -ɪst
sensuality ˌsɛnʃʊˈælətɪ
sensualize ˈsɛnʃʊəlˌaɪz |-s -ɪz |-d -d
sent sɛnt
sentence ˈsɛntəns |-s -ɪz |-d -t
sententious sɛnˈtɛnʃəs

|full fʊl |tooth tuθ |further ˈfɝðɚ; ES ˈfɜðə |custom ˈkʌstəm |while hwaɪl |how haʊ |toy tɔɪ
|using ˈjuzɪŋ |fuse fjuz, frʊz |dish dɪʃ |vision ˈvɪʒən |Eden ˈidn̩ |cradle ˈkred| |keep 'em ˈkipm̩

sentience 'sɛnʃəns, -ʃɪəns |-ent -ənt

sentiment 'sɛntəmənt

sentimental ˌsɛntə'mɛnt‖ |-ly -ɪ |-ism -ˌɪzəm

sentimentality ˌsɛntəmɛn'tælətɪ, -mən-

sentimentalize ˌsɛntə'mɛnt‖ˌaɪz |-s -ɪz |-d -d

sentinel 'sɛntən‖ |-ed -d

sentry 'sɛntrɪ

Senour 'sinjɚ; ES 'sinjə(r

Senusi, -nousi sə'nusɪ

Seoul sol, se'ol

sepal 'sip‖ |-ed -d

separability ˌsɛpərə'bɪlətɪ, ˌsɛprə-

separable 'sɛpərəb‖, 'sɛprə- |-bly -blɪ

separate adj, n 'sɛprɪt, 'sɛpərɪt

separate v 'sɛpəˌret, -pret |-d -ɪd

separation ˌsɛpə'reʃən

separatism 'sɛpərəˌtɪzəm, 'sɛprə-

separatist 'sɛpəˌretɪst

separator 'sɛpəˌretɚ; ES -ˌretə(r

Sephardi Heb sɪ'fardi; ES -'fɑ:di; |pl -dim -dɪm

sepia 'sipɪə

sepoy 'sipɔɪ

sepsis 'sɛpsɪs

sept sɛpt

September sɛp'tɛmbɚ, səp-; ES -'tɛmbə(r

septenary 'sɛptəˌnɛrɪ

septennial sɛp'tɛnɪəl |-ly -ɪ

septentrional sɛp'tɛntrɪən‖ |-ly -ɪ

septet, -tte sɛp'tɛt

septic 'sɛptɪk |-al -‖ |-ally -‖ɪ, -ɪklɪ

septicemia, -caem- ˌsɛptə'simɪə

septillion sɛp'tɪljən

septuagenarian ˌsɛptʃʊədʒə'nɛrɪən, -'ner-

septuagenary ˌsɛptʃʊ'ædʒəˌnɛrɪ, Brit -ə'dʒinərɪ

septuagesima, S- ˌsɛptʃʊə'dʒɛsəmə |-mal -m‖

Septuagint 'sɛptʊəˌdʒɪnt, 'sɛptʃʊə-

septum 'sɛptəm |-ta -tə

septuple n, adj, v 'sɛptʊp‖, -tjʊp‖, sɛp'tup‖, -'tru-, -'tju- |-d -d |-ling -plɪŋ, -p‖ɪŋ

sepulcher, -chre 'sɛp‖kɚ; ES -kə(r; |-(e)d -d

sepulchral sə'pʌlkrəl |-ly -ɪ

sepulture 'sɛp‖tʃɚ; ES 'sɛp‖tʃə(r; |-d -d

sequel 'sikwəl |-a sɪ'kwilə |-ae sɪ'kwili

sequence 'sikwəns |-cy -ɪ |-ent -ənt

sequential sɪ'kwɛnʃəl |-ly -ɪ

sequester sɪ'kwɛstɚ; ES -tə(r; |-ed -d |-ing -'kwɛstərɪŋ, -trɪŋ

sequestrate sɪ'kwɛstret |-d -ɪd

sequestration sɪˌkwɛs'treʃən, ˌsikwɛs-

sequin 'sikwɪn

sequitur 'sɛkwɪtɚ; ES 'sɛkwɪtə(r

sequoia, S- tree sɪ'kwɔɪə, -'kwɔjə

Sequoya pers. name sɪ'kwojə, -'kwɔɪə

seraglio sɪ'ræljo, -'ral- (It ser'raʎʎo)

Serajevo 'sɛrəjeˌvo, ˌsɛrə'jevo

serape sɛ'rapɪ (Sp se'rape)

seraph 'sɛrəf |-s -s |-im 'sɛrəˌfɪm

seraphic sə'ræfɪk, sɛ- |-al -‖ |-ally -‖ɪ, -ɪklɪ

Serapis sə'repɪs |-'s -ɪz

Serb sɝb; ES sɛb, sɝb |-ia -ɪə |-ian -ɪən

Serbo-Croatian 'sɝbo·kro'eʃən, -ʃɪən; ES 'sɝb-, 'sɝb-

sere sɪr; ES sɪə(r, S+sɛə(r

sere Heb grammar 'sere

Sere Negroid 'sere

Serena Chile se'renə; Am name sə'rinə

serenade ˌsɛrə'ned |-d -ɪd

serendipity ˌsɛrən'dɪpətɪ

serene sə'rin |-nity sə'rɛnətɪ

sereneness sə'rinnɪs

serf sɝf; ES sɝf, sɝf; |-dom -dəm

serge sɝdʒ; ES sɝdʒ, sɝdʒ; |-s -ɪz

sergeancy, -jean- 'sardʒənsɪ; ES 'sa:dʒ-, E+'sa:dʒ-; |-ant -ənt

Sergeant, -jeant, -gent 'sardʒənt; ES 'sa:dʒ-. E+'sa:dʒ-

serial 'sɪrɪəl |-ly -ɪ

seriate adj 'sɪrɪɪt, -ˌet

seriate v 'sɪrɪˌet |-d -ɪd

seriatim ˌsɪrɪ'etɪm, ˌsɛrɪ-

sericultural ˌsɛrɪ'kʌltʃərəl

sericulture 'sɛrɪˌkʌltʃɚ; ES -ˌkʌltʃə(r

series 'sɪrɪz, 'siriz, 'sɪriz, 'sɪrɪz

serif 'sɛrɪf

seriocomic ˌsɪrɪo'kamɪk; ES+-'kɒm-; |-al -‖

serious 'sɪrɪəs

serjeancy 'sardʒənsɪ; ES 'sa:dʒ-, E+'sa:dʒ-; |-ant -ənt

sermon 'sɝmən; ES 'sɝm-, 'sɝm-; |-ed -d |-ize -ˌaɪz |-izes -ˌaɪzɪz |-ized -ˌaɪzd

serous 'sɪrəs

serpent 'sɝpənt; ES 'sɝp-, 'sɝp-

serpentine, S- 'sɝpənˌtin, -ˌtaɪn; ES 'sɝp-, 'sɝp-; |-d -d

serrate adj 'sɛrɪt, -et

serrate v 'sɛret |-d -ɪd |-tion sɛ'reʃən

Key: See in full §§3–47. bee **bi** |pity **'pɪtɪ** (§6) |rate **ret** |yet **jɛt** |sang **sæŋ** |angry **'æŋ·grɪ** |bath **bæθ;** E **baθ** (§10) |ah **ɑ** |far **far** |watch **watʃ, wɒtʃ** (§12) |jaw **dʒɔ** |gorge **gɔrdʒ** |go **go**

serry 'sɛrɪ |serried 'sɛrɪd
serum 'sɪrəm |-s -z |-ra -rə
servant 'sɝvənt; ES 'sɜv-, 'sɝv-
serve sɝv; ES sɜv, sɝv; |-d -d
Servia 'sɝvɪə; ES 'sɜv-, 'sɝv-; |-n -n
service, S- 'sɝvɪs; ES 'sɜv-, 'sɝv-; |-s -ɪz |-d -t
serviceability ˌsɝvɪsə'bɪlətɪ; ES ˌsɜv-, ˌsɝv-
serviceable 'sɝvɪsəb|; ES 'sɜv-, 'sɝv-; |-bly
   -blɪ
serviette ˌsɝvɪ'ɛt; ES ˌsɜv-, ˌsɝv-
servile 'sɝv|, -ɪl; ES 'sɜv-, 'sɝv-; |-ly -lɪ, -ɪ
servility sɝ'vɪlətɪ, sɝ-; ES sɜ-, sɜ-, sɝ-
Servilius sɝ'vɪlɪəs, sɝ-, -ljəs; ES sɜ-, sɜ-,
   sɝ-; |-'s -ɪz
servitor 'sɝvətɚ; ES 'sɜvətə(r, 'sɝvətə(r
servitude 'sɝvəˌtjud, -ˌtɪud, -ˌtud; ES 'sɜv-,
   'sɝv-
sesame 'sɛsəmɪ
sesquicentennial ˌsɛskwɪsɛn'tɛnɪəl, -njəl
sesquipedalian ˌsɛskwɪpə'delɪən, -ljən
sessile 'sɛs|, -ɪl
session 'sɛʃən |-ed -d |-al -| |-ally -|ɪ
sesterce 'sɛstɝs; ES -tɜs, -tɝs; |-s -ɪz
sestet, -tte sɛs'tɛt ('sesˌtɛt 'rimes)
Sestos 'sɛstəs, -tɑs; ES+-tɒs; |-'s -ɪz
set sɛt |-back -ˌbæk |-ting -ɪŋ
Setebos 'sɛtəˌbʌs, -bəs; ES+-ˌbɒs; |-'s -ɪz
Seth sɛθ |Seth's sɛθs
Seton 'sitn̩, 'sitən
settee sɛ'ti
setter 'sɛtɚ; ES 'sɛtə(r
settle 'sɛt| |-d -d |-ling 'sɛt|ɪŋ, 'sɛtlɪŋ
settlings n 'sɛtlɪŋz
set-to 'sɛtˌtu, -'tu
setup 'sɛtˌʌp
Seul Choix loc. 'sɪʃəˌwe, -wə
Sevastopol sɪ'væstəp|, Russia+ˌsɛvəs'top|
seven 'sɛvən, 'sɛvm̩ |-s 'sɛvənz
sevenfold adj, adv 'sɛvən'fold, 'sɛvm̩-
   ('sevenˌfold 'loss)
sevenpenny 'sɛvənˌpɛnɪ, 'sɛvm̩-
seventeen ˌsɛvən'tin, 'sɛvən'tin ('sevenˌteen
   'years) |-th -θ |-ths -θs
seventh 'sɛvənθ |-ths -θs
seventy 'sɛvəntɪ |-tieth -tɪɪθ |-tieths -tɪɪθs
   |-fold -'fold
sever 'sɛvɚ; ES 'sɛvə(r; |-ed -d |-ing 'sɛvərɪŋ,
   'sɛvrɪŋ

several 'sɛvrəl, 'sɛvərəl |-ly -ɪ |-ty -tɪ
severance 'sɛvərəns, 'sɛvrəns |-s -ɪz
Severance 'sɛvrəns, 'sɛvərəns |-'s -ɪz
severe sə'vɪr; ES -'vɪə(r, S+-'vɛə(r
severity sə'vɛrətɪ
Severn 'sɛvɚn; ES 'sɛvən
Severus sə'vɪrəs |-'s -ɪz
Sevier sə'vɪr; ES -'vɪə(r, S+-'vɛə(r
Seville US sə'vɪl; Spain sə'vɪl, 'sɛvɪl (Sp
   Sevilla se'βiʎa)
Sèvres 'sɛvrə, 'sɛvɚ, -vəz; ES -vrə, -və(r,
   -vəz; (Fr sɛːvr)
sew so |sewed sod |sewed sod or sewn son
sewage 'sjuɪdʒ, 'sɪu-, 'su-
Sewall 'sjuəl, 'sɪu-, 'su-
Sewanee sə'wɒnɪ, 'swɒnɪ
Seward 'sjuɚd, 'sɪu-, 'su-; ES -əd
Sewell 'sjuəl, 'sɪu-, 'su-
sewer 'who sews' 'soɚ; ES 'so·ə(r
sewer 'servant,' 'drain' 'sjuɚ, 'sɪuɚ, 'suɚ; ES
   -ə(r; |-age -ɪdʒ
Sewickley sə'wɪklɪ
sewn son
sex sɛks |sexes 'sɛksɪz |sexed sɛkst
sexagenarian ˌsɛksədʒə'nɛrɪən, -'ner-
sexagenary sɛks'ædʒəˌnɛrɪ
Sexagesima ˌsɛksə'dʒɛsəmə |-mal -m|
sext sɛkst
sextant 'sɛkstənt
sextet, -tte sɛks'tɛt
sextile 'sɛkst|, -tɪl
sextillion sɛks'tɪljən
sexton 'sɛkstən
sextuple n, adj, v 'sɛkstʊp|, -tjʊp|, sɛks'tup|,
   -'tɪu-, -'tju- |-d -d |-ling -plɪŋ, -p|ɪŋ
sextuplets 'sɛkstʊˌplɪts, -tju-, sɛks'tuplɪts,
   -'tɪu-, -'tju-
Sextus 'sɛkstəs |-'s -ɪz
sexual 'sɛkʃʊəl |-ly -ɪ |-ality ˌsɛkʃu'ælətɪ
Seymour 'simor, -mɔr, -mɚ; ES -moə(r,
   -mə(r, E+-mɔə(r
Seyton 'sitn̩
shabby 'ʃæbɪ |shabbily 'ʃæb|ɪ, -ɪlɪ
shack ʃæk |shacked ʃækt
shackle 'ʃæk| |-d -d |-ling 'ʃæklɪŋ, -k|ɪŋ
Shackleton 'ʃæk|tən
shad ʃæd
shadberry 'ʃædˌbɛrɪ, -bərɪ
shadbush 'ʃædˌbuʃ |-es -ɪz

shaddock 'ʃædək
shade ʃed |shaded 'ʃedɪd |-dy -ɪ
shadow 'ʃædo, -ə |-ed -d |-ing 'ʃædəwɪŋ
shadowy 'ʃædəwɪ
Shadrach 'ʃedræk
Shadwell 'ʃædwɛl, -wəl
shaft ʃæft; E+ʃaft, ʃaft |-ed -ɪd
Shaftesbury, Shafts- 'ʃæfts,bɛrɪ, -bərɪ; E+
   'ʃafts-, 'ʃafts-
shag ʃæg |shagged ʃægd |shaggy 'ʃægɪ
shagbark 'ʃæg,bark; ES -,baːk, E+-,baːk
shagged adj 'ʃægɪd
shagreen ʃə'grin |-ed -d
shah, S- ʃɑ
Shairp ʃarp, ʃɛrp, ʃærp; ES ʃɑːp, ʃæəp,
   E+ʃɛəp, ʃɑːp
shake ʃek |shook ʃʊk |shaken 'ʃekən
shake-down 'ʃek,daʊn
shaker, S- 'ʃekɚ; ES 'ʃekə(r
Shakespeare 'ʃek,spɪr; ES -,spɪə(r, S+-,spɛə(r
Shakespearean, -ian ʃek'spɪrɪən; S+-'spɛr-
Shakespeareana, -iana ,ʃekspɪrɪ'enə, -'ænə,
   -'anə
shake-up 'ʃek,ʌp
shako 'ʃæko, 'ʃeko
Shakopee 'ʃækəpɪ
Shakspere, -speare 'ʃek,spɪr; ES -,spɪə(r,
   S+-,spɛə(r
shaky 'ʃekɪ
shale, S- ʃel |-r -ɚ; ES -ə(r
shall stressed 'ʃæl, ,ʃæl; unstr. ʃəl, ʃl
shalloon ʃə'lun, ʃæ-
shallop 'ʃæləp
shallott ʃə'lat; ES+-'lɒt
shallow, S- 'ʃælo, -ə |-er 'ʃæləwɚ; ES -wə(r;
   |-est 'ʃæləwɪst |-ed -d |-ing 'ʃæləwɪŋ
Shalmaneser ,ʃælmə'nizɚ; ES -'nizə(r
Shalott ʃə'lat; ES+-'lɒt
shalt stressed 'ʃælt, ,ʃælt; unstr. ʃəlt, ʃlt
sham ʃæm |shammed ʃæmd
shaman 'ʃamən, 'ʃæm-, 'ʃe-
shamble 'ʃæmbl̩ |-d -d |-ling 'ʃæmblɪŋ, -bl̩ɪŋ
   |-s -z
shambling n, adj 'ʃæmblɪŋ
shame ʃem |shamed ʃemd
shamefaced 'ʃem,fest |-ly -lɪ, ʃem'fesɪdlɪ
shamefacedness 'ʃem,festnɪs, ʃem'fesɪdnɪs
shammy 'ʃæmɪ=chamois
Shamokin ʃə'mokɪn

shamoy 'ʃæmɔɪ=chamois
shampoo ʃæm'pu |-pooed -'pud
shamrock, S- 'ʃæmrak; ES+-rɒk
Shandy 'ʃændɪ
Shanghai ʃæŋ'haɪ ('Shang,hai 'rooster)
shanghai n 'ʃæŋhaɪ
shanghai v 'ʃæŋhaɪ, ʃæŋ'haɪ |-ed -d
shank ʃæŋk |shanked ʃæŋkt
Shannon 'ʃænən
shan't ʃænt; E+ʃant, ʃant
shantey, -ty 'chantey' 'ʃæntɪ; E+'ʃan-, 'ʃan-
Shantung 'ʃæn'tʌŋ, 'ʃan'dʊŋ
Shantung, s- 'silk' ʃæn'tʌŋ
shanty 'shed' 'ʃæntɪ |-ied -d
shape ʃep |-d -t |-d -t or arch -n 'ʃepən
Shapley 'ʃæplɪ
shard ʃard; ES ʃɑːd, E+ʃaːd; |-ed -ɪd
share ʃɛr, ʃær; E ʃɛə(r, ES ʃæə(r; |-d -d
   |-holder -,holdɚ; ES -də(r
shark ʃark; ES ʃaːk, E+ʃaːk; |-ed -t
Sharon 'ʃɛrən, 'ʃærən; S 'ʃɛrən, 'ʃerən
sharp, S- ʃarp; ES ʃɑːp, E+ʃaːp; |-ed -t
sharpen 'ʃarpən, -pn̩; ES 'ʃaːp-, E+'ʃaːp-;
   |-ed -d |-ing -pənɪŋ, -pnɪŋ
Sharples 'ʃarp|z; ES 'ʃaːp-, E+'ʃaːp-; |-'s -ɪz
Sharpsburg 'ʃarpsbɝg; ES 'ʃaːpsbɝg, 'ʃaːps-
   bɝg, E+'ʃaːps-
sharpshooter 'ʃarp,ʃutɚ; ES 'ʃaːp,ʃutə(r,
   E+'ʃaːp-
sharp-sighted 'ʃarp'saɪtɪd; ES see sharp
sharp-witted 'ʃarp'wɪtɪd; ES see sharp
   ('sharp-,witted 'sneer)
Shasta 'ʃæstə
shatter 'ʃætɚ; ES 'ʃætə(r; |-ed -d
Shaughnessy 'ʃɔnəsɪ
shave ʃev |-d -d |-d -d or -n 'ʃevən
shaveling 'ʃevlɪŋ
Shavian 'ʃevɪən
shaw, S- ʃɔ
Shawanese ,ʃɔwə'niz ('Shawa,nese 'salad)
Shawangunk 'ʃɔŋgəm, 'ʃʊŋ-, 'ʃaŋ-
Shawano Wis 'ʃɔno, 'ʃɔwə,no
Shawinigan ʃə'wɪnəgən
shawl ʃɔl |shawled ʃɔld |-less 'ʃɔllɪs
shawm ʃɔm
Shawnee ʃɔ'ni ('Shaw,nee 'tribes)
shawneewood ʃɔ'ni,wʊd
shay ʃe
Shays ʃez |Shays's 'ʃezɪz |Shays' ʃez

she *stressed* 'ʃi, ˌʃi; *unstr.* ʃɪ

shea ʃi

Shea ʃe

sheaf *n* ʃif |sheaf's ʃifs |sheaves ʃivz

sheaf *v* ʃif |sheafed ʃift

shear ʃɪr; ES ʃɪə(r, S+ʃɛə(r; |-ed -d *or arch.*
  shore ʃor, ʃɔr; ES ʃoə(r, E+ʃɔə(r; |-ed -d *or*
  shorn ʃorn, ʃɔrn; ES ʃoən, E+ʃɔən

sheard ʃard; ES ʃɑ:d, E+ʃa:d

shearman 'ʃɪrmən; ES 'ʃɪə-, S+'ʃɛə-; |-men
  -mən

Shearman 'ʃɝmən; ES 'ʃɝm-, 'ʃɝm-

shearwater 'ʃɪrˌwɔtɚ, -ˌwatɚ, -ˌwɒtɚ; ES
  'ʃɪə-, -tə(r, S+'ʃɛə-

sheath ʃiθ |sheath's ʃiθs |sheaths ʃiðz

sheathe ʃið |sheathed ʃiðd

sheathing 'ʃiðɪŋ, 'ʃiθɪŋ

sheave ʃiv |sheaved ʃivd

Sheba 'ʃibə

she-bear 'ʃiˌbɛr, -'bɛr; E -'bɛə(r, ES -'bæə(r

Sheboygan ʃɪ'bɔɪgən

shed *'shelter'* ʃɛd |shedded 'ʃɛdɪd

shed *'cast off'* ʃɛd

she'd *abbr. spelling of* she had, she would,
  stressed 'ʃid, ˌʃid; *unstr.* ʃid, ʃɪd

she-devil 'ʃi'dɛvl̩ ('she-ˌdevil 'mood)

Shee ʃi

sheen ʃin |-ed -d

sheep ʃip |-ed -t

sheepcot 'ʃipˌkat; ES+-ˌkɒt; |-cote -ˌkot—*see*
  cote

sheepfold 'ʃipˌfold

sheepherder 'ʃipˌhɝdɚ; ES -ˌhɝdə(r, -ˌhɝdə(r

sheephook 'ʃipˌhuk

sheepman 'ʃipˌmæn, -mən |-men -ˌmɛn, -mən

sheepshank 'ʃipˌʃæŋk

sheepshead 'ʃipsˌhɛd

sheepshearing 'ʃipˌʃɪrɪŋ; S+-ˌʃɛrɪŋ

sheepshed 'ʃipˌʃɛd

sheepskin 'ʃipˌskɪn

sheer ʃɪr; ES ʃɪə(r, S+ʃɛə(r; |-ed -d

sheerness 'ʃɪrnɪs; ES 'ʃɪə-, S -'ʃɛə-

Sheerness ʃɪr'nɛs; ES ʃɪə-, S+ʃɛə-; |-'s -ɪz

sheet ʃit |sheeted 'ʃitɪd

Sheffield 'ʃɛfild

she-goat 'ʃi'got

sheik, -kh ʃik, *Brit* ʃek

Sheila 'ʃilə

shekel 'ʃɛkl̩

Shekina ʃɪ'kaɪnə

Shelburn, -e 'ʃɛlbɚn; ES 'ʃɛlbən

Shelby 'ʃɛlbɪ |-ville -ˌvɪl; S+-v|

Shelden, -on 'ʃɛldən, -ɪn—*double pron. perh.
  due to double etym.* (*OE* -dun, -denu)

sheldrake 'ʃɛlˌdrek |-duck -ˌdʌk

shelf *n* ʃɛlf |shelf's ʃɛlfs |shelves ʃɛlvz

shelf *v* ʃɛlf |shelfed ʃɛlft

shell ʃɛl |shelled ʃɛld

she'll *'she will' stressed* 'ʃil, ˌʃil; *unstr.* ʃil, ʃɪl

shellac, -ack ʃə'læk

Shelley 'ʃɛlɪ |-an, -eian 'ʃɛlɪən

shellfire 'ʃɛlˌfaɪr; ES -ˌfaɪə(r

shellfish 'ʃɛlˌfɪʃ |-'s -ɪz

shell-less 'ʃɛllɪs

shellproof 'ʃɛl'pruf ('shell ˌproof 'shelter)

shelly 'ʃɛlɪ

shelter 'ʃɛltɚ; ES -tə(r; |-ed -d |-ing 'ʃɛltərɪŋ,
  'ʃɛltrɪŋ

shelve ʃɛlv |shelves ʃɛlvz |shelved ʃɛlvd

Shem ʃɛm |-ite -aɪt

Shenandoah ˌʃɛnən'doə

Shenango ʃə'næŋgo

shenanigan ʃə'nænəˌgæn, -gən

shend ʃɛnd | shent ʃɛnt

Shenstone 'ʃɛnstən, -ˌston

Sheol, s- 'ʃiol

Shepard, Shepp-, -pherd 'ʃɛpɚd; ES 'ʃɛpəd

shepherd 'ʃɛpɚd; ES 'ʃɛpəd; |-ed -ɪd |-ess -ɪs

Sheraton 'ʃɛrətn̩

sherbet 'ʃɝbɪt; ES 'ʃɝb-, 'ʃɝb-

Sherborne, -burn(e) 'ʃɝbən; ES 'ʃɝbən,
  'ʃɝbən

Sherbrook 'ʃɝbruk; ES 'ʃɝ-, 'ʃɝ-

sherd ʃard, ʃɝd; ES ʃɑ:d, ʃɝd, ʃɝd, E+ʃa:d

Sheridan 'ʃɛrədn̩

sherif, -reef ʃə'rif

sheriff 'ʃɛrɪf

Sherlock 'ʃɝlak; ES 'ʃɝlak, 'ʃɝ-, -'lɒk

Sherman 'ʃɝmən; ES 'ʃɝm-, 'ʃɝm-

Sherrill 'ʃɛrəl

sherry 'ʃɛrɪ

Sherwood 'ʃɝwud; ES 'ʃɝ-, 'ʃɝ-

she's *'she is,' 'she has,' stressed* 'ʃiz, ˌʃiz;
  unstr. ʃiz, ʃɪz

Shetland 'ʃɛtlənd

Shetucket ʃɪ'tʌkɪt

shew ʃo |shewed ʃod |shewn ʃon *or* shewed ʃod

shewbread 'ʃoˌbrɛd

|full ful |tooth tuθ |further 'fɝðɚ; ES 'fɝðə |custom 'kʌstəm |while hwaɪl |how haʊ |toy tɔɪ
|using 'juzɪŋ |fuse fjuz, fɪuz |dish dɪʃ |vision 'vɪʒən |Eden 'idn̩ |cradle 'kredl̩ |keep 'em 'kipm̩

Shewmake 'ʃuˌmek, 'ʃiu-
she-wolf 'ʃi'wulf |-lves -lvz
Sheyenne ʃaɪ'ɛn
Shiah 'ʃiə
Shiawassee ˌʃaɪə'wɑsɪ
shibboleth 'ʃɪbəlɪθ |-ths -θs
Shickshinny 'ʃɪkˌʃɪnɪ
shied ʃaɪd
Shiel ʃil
shield ʃild |shielded 'ʃildɪd
shier 'ʃaɪɚ; ES 'ʃaɪ·ə(r
shies ʃaɪz
shift ʃɪft |shifted 'ʃɪftɪd
Shih ʃi
Shiite 'ʃiaɪt |-itic ʃi'ɪtɪk
Shikoku ʃi'koku
shillelagh, -lah, -ly, shillalah, -la, S- ʃə'lelə, -lɪ
shilling, S- 'ʃɪlɪŋ
shilly-shally 'ʃɪlɪˌʃælɪ |-ied -d
Shilo, Shiloh 'ʃaɪlo
shily 'ʃaɪlɪ
shim ʃɪm |shimmed ʃɪmd
shimmer 'ʃɪmɚ; ES 'ʃɪmə(r; |-ed -d |-ing
    'ʃɪmərɪŋ, 'ʃɪmrɪŋ
shimmy 'ʃɪmɪ |-ied -d
shin, S- ʃɪn |shinned ʃɪnd
Shinar 'ʃaɪnɑr, -nɚ; ES -nɑ:(r, -nə(r
shindig 'ʃɪndɪg |shindy 'ʃɪndɪ
shine ʃaɪn |shone ʃon, Brit ʃɒn, or arch. (except
    in sense 'polish') shined ʃaɪnd
shingle 'ʃɪŋgl̩ |-d -d |-ling 'ʃɪŋglɪŋ, -glɪŋ
shingly 'ʃɪŋglɪ
shinny 'ʃɪnɪ |-ied -d
shinplaster 'ʃɪnˌplæstɚ; ES -ˌplæstə(r, E+
    -ˌplas-, -ˌplas-
Shinto 'ʃɪnto |-ism -ˌɪzəm
shiny 'ʃaɪnɪ
ship ʃɪp |shipped ʃɪpt
-ship abstract noun ending, unstressed -ʃɪp or
    half-stressed -ˌʃɪp. Words in -ship are often
    omitted from the vocab. when their pron. is
    obvious.
shipboard 'ʃɪpˌbord, -ˌbɔrd; ES -ˌboəd,
    E+-ˌbɔəd
shipbuilder 'ʃɪpˌbɪldɚ; ES -ˌbɪldə(r
shipload 'ʃɪpˌlod
shipman 'ʃɪpmən |-men -mən
shipmaster 'ʃɪpˌmæstɚ; ES -ˌmæstə(r, E+
    -ˌmas-, -ˌmas-

shipmate 'ʃɪpˌmet
shippable 'ʃɪpəbl̩
Shippen 'ʃɪpən |-sburg -zˌbɝg; ES -zˌbɜg,
    -zˌbɝg
shipshape 'ʃɪpˌʃep
shipwreck 'ʃɪpˌrɛk |-wrecked -ˌrɛkt
shipwright 'ʃɪpˌraɪt
shipyard 'ʃɪpˌjard; ES -ˌja:d, E+-ˌja:d
Shiras 'ʃaɪrəs |-'s -ɪz
Shiraz ʃɪ'raz, 'ʃɪræz |-'s -ɪz
shire ʃaɪr; ES ʃaɪə(r
-shire -ʃɪr, -ʃɚ; ES -ʃɪə(r, -ʃə(r
shirk ʃɝk; ES ʃɝk, ʃɝk; |-ed -t
Shirley 'ʃɝlɪ; ES 'ʃɝ-, 'ʃɝ-
shirr ʃɝ; ES ʃɝ(r, ʃɝ; |-ed -d
shirt ʃɝt; ES ʃɝt, ʃɝt; |-ed -d |-tail -ˌtel
shirtwaist 'ʃɝtˌwest; ES 'ʃɝt-, 'ʃɝt-
shitta 'ʃɪtə
shittim 'ʃɪtɪm |-wood -ˌwud
Shiva 'ʃivə, 'ʃɪvə |-ism -ˌɪzəm
shivaree ˌʃɪvə'ri—see charivari |-d -d
shive ʃaɪv |shived ʃaɪvd
shiver 'ʃɪvɚ; ES 'ʃɪvə(r; |-ed -d |ing -vrɪŋ,
    -vərɪŋ
shivery 'ʃɪvrɪ, 'ʃɪvərɪ
shoal ʃol |shoaled ʃold
shoat ʃot
shock ʃak; ES+ʃɒk; |-ed -t
shockheaded 'ʃak'hɛdɪd; ES+'ʃɒk-; ('shock-
    ˌheaded 'boy)
shod ʃad; ES+ʃɒd
shoddy 'ʃadɪ; ES+'ʃɒdɪ
shoe ʃu, ʃiu (sp. shew 16–17cc.) |-horn -ˌhorn;
    ES -ˌhɔən; |-lace -ˌles |-laces -ˌlesɪz
    |-maker -ˌmekɚ; ES -ˌmekə(r; |-string
    -ˌstrɪŋ
shoer 'ʃuɚ, 'ʃiuɚ; ES 'ʃu·ə(r, 'ʃiu-
Shogun 'ʃoˌgʌn, -ˌgun |-ate -ɪt, -gʌnˌet, -gun-
shone ʃon, Brit ʃɒn
shoo ʃu |-ed -d
shook past of shake ʃuk
shook n, v ʃuk |shooked ʃukt
shoon ʃun
shoot ʃut |shot ʃat; ES+ʃɒt; |arch. pptc
    shotten 'ʃatn̩; ES+'ʃɒtn̩
shop ʃap; ES+ʃɒp; |-ped -t |-girl -ˌgɝl; ES see
    girl
shopkeeper 'ʃapˌkipɚ; ES -ˌkipə(r, 'ʃɒp-
shoplifter 'ʃapˌlɪftɚ; ES -ˌlɪftə(r, 'ʃɒp-

shopwalker 'ʃɑpˌwɔkɚ; ES -ˌwɔkə(r, 'ʃɒp-
shopwindow 'ʃɑpˈwɪndo, -ˌwɪn-, -də; ES+
'ʃɒp-
shopwoman 'ʃɑpˌwʊmən, -ˌwu-; ES+'ʃɒp-;
|-men -ˌwɪmɪn, -ən
shopworn 'ʃɑpˌworn, -ˌwɔrn; ES -ˌwoən,
'ʃɒp-, E+-ˌwɔən
shore ʃor, ʃɔr; ES ʃoə(r, E+ʃɔə(r; |-d -d
|-ward -wɚd; ES -wəd
Shorey 'ʃorɪ, 'ʃɔrɪ; S 'ʃorɪ
shorn ʃorn, ʃɔrn; ES ʃoən, E+ʃɔən
short ʃɔrt; ES ʃɔət; |-ed -ɪd |-age -ɪdʒ
short-and-long 'ʃɔrtn̩ˈlɔŋ, -ˈlɒŋ; ES 'ʃɔət-,
S+-ˈlɑŋ
shortbread 'ʃɔrtˌbrɛd; ES 'ʃɔət-
short-breathed 'ʃɔrtˈbrɛθt; ES 'ʃɔət-
shortcake 'ʃɔrtˌkek; ES 'ʃɔət-
shortchange ˌʃɔrtˈtʃendʒ; ES ˌʃɔət-; |-s -ɪz
|-d -d
short-circuit ˌʃɔrtˈsɝkɪt; ES ˌʃɔətˈsɝk-, ˌʃɔːt-
ˈsɝk-; |-ed -ɪd
shortcoming 'ʃɔrtˌkʌmɪŋ, -ˈkʌm- |-s -z
short-eared 'ʃɔrtˈɪrd; ES 'ʃɔətˈɪəd, S+-ˈɛəd;
('short-ˌeared 'owl)
shorten 'ʃɔrtn̩; ES 'ʃɔətn̩; |-ed -d |-ing -tnɪŋ,
-tn̩ɪŋ
Shorter C. K. 'ʃɔrtɚ; ES 'ʃɔətə(r; Ga college+
'ʃɑutɚ; ES -tə(r
shorthand 'ʃɔrtˌhænd; ES 'ʃɔət-; |-ed -ɪd
shorthanded 'ʃɔrtˈhændɪd; ES 'ʃɔət-; ('short-
ˌhanded 'job)
shorthorn 'ʃɔrtˌhɔrn; ES 'ʃɔətˌhɔən
Shorthouse 'ʃɔrtˌhaʊs; ES 'ʃɔət-; |-'s -ɪz
short-lived 'ʃɔrtˈlaɪvd; ES 'ʃɔət-; —The pron.
'ʃɔrtˈlɪvd is a misapprehension, now accepted in England.
shortsighted 'ʃɔrtˈsaɪtɪd; ES 'ʃɔət-
short-skirted 'ʃɔrtˈskɝtɪd; ES 'ʃɔətˈskɝt-,
'ʃɔətˈskɝt-; ('short-ˌskirted 'coat)
short-tempered 'ʃɔrtˈtɛmpɚd; ES 'ʃɔət-
ˈtɛmpəd
short-winded 'ʃɔrtˈwɪndɪd; ES 'ʃɔət-
Shoshone ʃoˈʃonɪ |-nian -nɪən |-nean -nɪən,
ˌʃoʃəˈniən
shot ʃɑt; ES+ʃɒt; |-ted -ɪd |-gun -ˌgʌn
shote ʃot
shotten 'ʃɑtn̩; ES+'ʃɒtn̩
Shottery 'ʃɑtərɪ; ES+'ʃɒt-
should stressed 'ʃʊd, ˌʃʊd; unstr. ʃəd, ʃd, ʃt

shoulder 'ʃoldɚ; ES 'ʃoldə(r; |-ed -d |-ing
-dərɪŋ, -drɪŋ
shouldest 'ʃʊdɪst
shouldn't 'should not' 'ʃʊdn̩t—The pron.
'ʃʊdənt is not in general use.
shouldst stressed 'ʃʊdst, ˌʃʊdst; unstr. ʃədst
shout ʃaʊt |shouted 'ʃaʊtɪd
shove 'shive' ʃov
shove 'push' ʃʌv |shoved ʃʌvd
shovel 'ʃʌvl̩ |-ed -d |-ing 'ʃʌvlɪŋ, 'ʃʌvl̩ɪŋ
shovelboard 'ʃʌvl̩ˌbord, -ˌbɔrd; ES -ˌboəd,
E+-ˌbɔəd
shovelful 'ʃʌvl̩ˌfʊl |-fuls -ˌfʊlz
show ʃo |-ed ʃod |-n ʃon or -ed ʃod
showboat 'ʃoˌbot
showbread 'ʃoˌbrɛd
showcase 'ʃoˌkes |-s -ɪz
showdown 'ʃoˌdaʊn
shower 'who shows' 'ʃoɚ; ES 'ʃo·ə(r
shower 'rain' 'ʃaʊɚ, ʃaʊr; ES 'ʃaʊ·ə(r,
ʃaʊə(r; |-ed -d |-ing 'ʃaʊrɪŋ, 'ʃaʊərɪŋ |-y
'ʃaʊrɪ, 'ʃaʊərɪ
showman 'ʃomən |-men -mən |-ship -ˌʃɪp
shown ʃon
show-off 'ʃoˌɔf, -ˌɒf
showroom 'ʃoˌrum, -ˌrʊm
shrank ʃræŋk
shrapnel 'ʃræpnəl |-ed -d
shrdlu ʃɚdˈlu; ES ʃədˈlu; cf etaoin
shred ʃrɛd |shred ʃrɛd or shredded 'ʃrɛdɪd
Shreveport 'ʃrivˌport, -ˌpɔrt; ES -ˌpoət,
E+-ˌpɔət
shrew ʃru, ʃrɪu, arch. ʃro (thus in Shak.)
shrewd ʃrud, ʃrɪud, arch. ʃrod |-ly -lɪ
Shrewsbury 'ʃruzˌbɛrɪ, 'ʃrɪuz-, 'ʃroz-, -bərɪ,
in Mass loc.+'ʃɪuzbərɪ, the first r being lost
by dissimilation (§121)
shriek ʃrik |shrieked ʃrikt
shrievalty 'ʃrivl̩tɪ
shrift ʃrɪft
shrike ʃraɪk |-d -t
shrill ʃrɪl |shrilled ʃrɪld
shrilly adj 'ʃrɪlɪ, adv 'ʃrɪllɪ
shrimp ʃrɪmp |shrimped ʃrɪmpt
shrine ʃraɪn |shrined ʃraɪnd |-nal -l̩
Shriner 'ʃraɪnɚ; ES 'ʃraɪnə(r
shrink ʃrɪŋk |shrank ʃræŋk or shrunk ʃrʌŋk
|shrunk ʃrʌŋk or shrunken 'ʃrʌŋkən |-able
-əbl̩ |-age -ɪdʒ

shrive ʃraɪv |shrived ʃraɪvd *or* shrove ʃrov
|shriven 'ʃrɪvən *or* shrived ʃraɪvd
shrivel 'ʃrɪv| |-ed -d |-ing 'ʃrɪvlɪŋ, -v|ɪŋ
Shropshire 'ʃrɑpʃɪr, -ʃɚ; ES -ʃɪə(r, -ʃə(r,
'ʃrɒp-
shroud ʃraʊd |shrouded 'ʃraʊdɪd
shrove, S- ʃrov |Shrovetide 'ʃrov,taɪd
shrub ʃrʌb |shrubbed ʃrʌbd |-bery -ərɪ, -rɪ
shrug ʃrʌg |shrugged ʃrʌgd
shrunk ʃrʌŋk |-en -ən
shuck ʃʌk |shucked ʃʌkt
shudder 'ʃʌdɚ; ES 'ʃʌdə(r; |-ed -d |-ing
'ʃʌdərɪŋ, 'ʃʌdrɪŋ |-y -dərɪ, -drɪ
shuffle 'ʃʌf| |-d -d |-ling 'ʃʌflɪŋ, -f|ɪŋ
shuffleboard 'ʃʌf|,bord, -,bɔrd; ES -,boəd,
E+-,bɔəd
Shuhite 'ʃuhaɪt, 'ʃɪu-
shun ʃʌn |shunned ʃʌnd
shunt ʃʌnt |shunted 'ʃʌntɪd
shush ʃʌʃ, ʃ: |-ed -t
shut ʃʌt |-down -,daʊn |shut-in 'ʃʌt,ɪn
shutter 'ʃʌtɚ; ES 'ʃʌtə(r; |-ed -d
shuttle 'ʃʌt| |-d -d |-ling 'ʃʌt|ɪŋ, 'ʃʌtlɪŋ
shuttlecock 'ʃʌt|,kak; ES+-,kɒk; |-ed -t
shy ʃaɪ |shied ʃaɪd
Shylock 'ʃaɪlak; ES+-lɒk
shyly 'ʃaɪlɪ
shyster 'ʃaɪstɚ; ES 'ʃaɪstə(r
si *music* si
-sia *unstressed ending* (magnesia) *variously
pronounced* -ʃə, -ʃɪə, -ʃjə, -ʒə, -ʒɪə, -ʒjə,
-sɪə, -sjə, -zɪə, -zjə. *Besides the pron. given
in the vocab. it is to be understood that one
or more of the other variants are often heard.*
Siam saɪ'æm, 'saɪæm
Siamese ,saɪə'miz ('Sia,mese 'pheasant)
Siamese *v* ,saɪə'miz |-s -ɪz |-d -d
Siasconset ,saɪə'skansɪt; ES+-'skɒn-; *loc.*
'skɒnsɪt, 'skɒn-
sib sɪb
sibboleth 'sɪbəlɪθ |-ths -θs
Sibelius sɪ'belɪəs, -'bi- |-'s -ɪz
Siberia saɪ'bɪrɪə, sə- |-n -n
sibilance 'sɪb|əns |-cy -ɪ |-ant -ənt
sibyl, S- 'sɪb|, -ɪl |-line 'sɪb|,ɪn, -ɪn
Sibylla, -illa, s- sɪ'bɪlə
sic sɪk |sicked sɪkt
Sicilia sɪ'sɪlɪə, -ljə |-n -n
Sicily 'sɪs|ɪ, -ɪlɪ

Sicinius sɪ'sɪnɪəs, -njəs |-'s -ɪz
sick sɪk |sicked sɪkt |-bed -,bɛd
sick-abed *adj* 'sɪkə'bɛd, *n* 'sɪkə,bɛd
sicken 'sɪkən |-ed -d |-ing 'sɪknɪŋ, -kənɪŋ
sickle 'sɪk| |sickled 'sɪk|d
Sickles 'sɪk|z |-'s -ɪz
sickly 'sɪklɪ
sic transit gloria mundi 'sɪk'trænsɪt'glorɪə-
'mʌndaɪ, -'glɔr-; S -'glor-
Siddons 'sɪdnz |-'s -ɪz
siddur 'sɪdʊr; ES -dʊə(r
side saɪd |sided 'saɪdɪd
sideboard 'saɪd,bord, -,bɔrd; ES -,boəd,
E+-,bɔəd
sideburns 'saɪd,bɝnz; ES -,bɜnz, -,bɝnz
sidecar 'saɪd,kar; ES -,ka:(r, E+-,ka:(r
sidehill 'saɪd'hɪl ('side,hill 'grove)
sideling *'moving aside'* 'saɪd|ɪŋ, -dlɪŋ
sideling *'sideways'* 'saɪdlɪŋ
sidelong 'saɪd,lɔŋ, -,lɒŋ; S+-,lɑŋ
sideral 'sɪdərəl
sidereal saɪ'dɪrɪəl |-ly -ɪ
sidesaddle 'saɪd,sæd|
sideslip 'saɪd,slɪp |-ped -t
sidesplitting 'saɪd,splɪtɪŋ
side-step 'saɪd,stɛp |-ped -t
sideswipe 'saɪd,swaɪp |- d -t
sidetrack 'saɪd,træk |-ed -t
sidewalk 'saɪd,wɔk
sideward 'saɪdwɚd; ES -wəd; |-s -z
sideways 'saɪd,wez |-wise -,waɪz
Sidgwick 'sɪdʒwɪk, 'sɪdʒɪk
siding 'saɪdɪŋ
sidle 'saɪd| |-d -d |-ling 'saɪd|ɪŋ, 'saɪdlɪŋ
sidling *'moving aside'* 'saɪd|ɪŋ, 'saɪdlɪŋ
sidling *'sideways'* 'saɪdlɪŋ
Sidney 'sɪdnɪ
Sidon 'saɪdn̩ |-donian saɪ'donɪən
siècle *Fr* sjɛk|
siege sidʒ |sieges 'sidʒɪz |sieged sidʒd
Siegfried 'sigfrid (*Ger* 'zi:kfri:t)
Siena sɪ'ɛnə (*It* 'sjɛ:nɑ)
Sienkiewicz ʃɛn'kjevɪtʃ |-'s -ɪz
sienna sɪ'ɛnə
sierra sɪ'ɛrə, 'sɪrə
Sierra Leone sɪ'ɛrəlɪ'onɪ, 'sɪrəlɪ'on
Sierra Nevada sɪ'ɛrənə'væədə, 'sɪrə-, -'vadə
siesta sɪ'ɛstə
sieve sɪv |sieved sɪvd

Key: See in full §§3–47. bee bi |pity 'pɪtɪ (§6) |rate ret |yet jɛt |sang sæŋ |angry 'æŋ·grɪ
|bath bæθ; E baθ (§10) |ah ɑ |far far |watch watʃ, wɒtʃ (§12) |jaw dʒɔ |gorge gɔrdʒ |go go

Sievers 'zivɚz, 'siv-; ES -vəz; |-'s -ız (Ger
  'zi:fərs, -vərs)
sift sıft |sifted 'sıftıd |-age -ıdʒ
sigh saı |sighed saıd
sight saıt |sighted 'saıtıd |-ly -lı
sight-seeing 'saıt,siıŋ
sight-seer 'saıt,siɚ; ES -,si·ə(r
sigil 'sıdʒəl, -ıl
sigillum sı'dʒıləm |-la -ə
Sigismond, -und 'sıdʒısmənd, 'sıgıs- (Ger
  'zi:gıs,munt)
sigma 'sıgmə |-moid -mɔıd
sigmoidal sıg'mɔıd| |-ly -ı
sign saın |signed saınd
signal 'sıgn| |-ed -d |-ly -ı
signalize 'sıgnə,laız |-s -ız |-d -d
signalman 'sıgn|,mæn, -mən |-men -,mɛn,
  -mən
signatory 'sıgnə,torı, -,tɔrı; S -,torı
signature 'sıgnətʃɚ, 'sıgnı-; ES -tʃə(r; |-d -d
signboard 'saın,bord, -,bɔrd; ES -,boəd, E+
  -,bɔəd
signet 'sıgnıt |-ed -ıd
significance sıg'nıfəkəns |-cy -ı |-ant -ənt
signification sıg,nıfə'keʃən, ,sıgnıfə-
significative sıg'nıfə,ketıv
signify 'sıgnə,faı |-fied -,faıd
signor, S- 'sinjor, -jɔr; ES -joə(r, E+-jɔə(r;
  (It siɲ'ɲor)
signora sin'jorə (It siɲ'ɲo:ra)
signore sin'jore (It siɲ'ɲo:re)
signorina ,sinjə'rinə (It ,sıɲɲo'ri:na)
signory 'sinjərı
signpost 'saın,post
Sigourney 'sıgɚnı; ES 'sıgənı
Sigurd 'sıgɚd; ES 'sıgəd; (Ger 'zi:gurt, Ice
  'sıgurður)
Sikes saıks |-'s -ız
Sikh sik
silage 'saılıdʒ |-s -ız
Silas 'saıləs |-'s -ız
silence 'saıləns |-s -ız |-d -t |-ent -ənt
Silenus saı'linəs |-'s -ız
Silesia saı'liʃıə, sə-, -ʃə |-n -n
silex 'saılɛks
silhouette, S- ,sılu'ɛt, ,sılə'wɛt |-d -ıd
silica 'sılıkə
silicate n 'sılıkıt, -,ket
silicate v 'sılı,ket |-d -ıd

silicic sə'lısık
silicon 'sılıkən
silicosis ,sılı'kosıs |-cotic -'katık; ES+-'kɒt-
Silius 'sılıəs |-'s -ız
silk sılk |silked sılkt
silken 'sılkən |-ed -d
silkworm 'sılk,wɝm; ES -,wɜm, -,wɝm
sill, S- sıl |silled sıld
sillabub, silli- 'sılə,bʌb, 'sılı-
silly 'sılı |-iness -nıs
silo 'saılo |siloed 'saılod
Siloam saı'loəm, sə-, -'lom
silt sılt |silted 'sıltıd
Silurian sə'lurıən, -'lıur-, saı-
silva 'sılvə |silvan 'sılvən
Silvanus sıl'venəs |-'s -ız
silver 'sılvɚ; ES 'sılvə(r; |-ed -d |-ing
  'sılvərıŋ, 'sılvrıŋ
silver-plate 'plate with silver' 'sılvɚ'plet; ES
  'sılvə-; |-d -ıd
silversmith 'sılvɚ,smıθ; ES 'sılvə-
silverware 'sılvɚ,wɛr, -,wær; E 'sılvə,wɛə(r,
  ES -,wæə(r
Silvester sıl'vɛstɚ; ES -'vɛstə(r
Silvia 'sılvıə
silvicultural ,sılvı'kʌltʃərəl |-ly -ı
silviculture 'sılvı,kʌltʃɚ; ES -,kʌltʃə(r
Silvius 'sılvıəs |-'s -ız
Simcoe 'sımko
Simcox 'sımkaks, 'sımp-; ES+-kɒks; |-'s -ız
Simeon 'sımıən
simian 'sımıən
similar 'sımələ; ES 'sımələ(r
similarity ,sımə'lærətı
simile 'sımə,li, -lı
similitude sə'mılə,tjud, -,tıud, -,tud
Simla 'sımlə
simmer 'sımɚ; ES 'sımə(r; |-ed -d |-ing
  'sımərıŋ, 'sımrıŋ
Simms sımz |-'s -ız
simnel, S- 'sımnəl
Simoïs 'sımo·ıs, 'sıməwıs
simoleon sə'molıən
Simon 'saımən
simoniac sə'monı,æk
simoniacal ,saımə'naıək|, ,sım- |-ly -ı, -ıklı
Simonides saı'manə,diz, -'mɒn- |-'s -ız
Simoniz 'saımən,aız |-es -ız |-ed -d
simon-pure 'saımən'pjur, -'pıur; ES -ə(r

---

simony 'saɪmənɪ, 'sɪm-
simoom sɪ'mum, saɪ- |-moon -'mun
simp sɪmp
Simpcox 'sɪmpkɑks; ES+-kɒks; |-'s -ɪz
simper 'sɪmpɚ; ES 'sɪmpə(r; |-ed -d |-ing
  'sɪmpərɪŋ, 'sɪmprɪŋ
simple, S- 'sɪmpl̩ |-d -d |-ling 'sɪmplɪŋ, -pl̩ɪŋ
  |-r -plɚ; ES -plə(r; |-st -plɪst
simple-minded 'sɪmpl̩'maɪndɪd
simpleton 'sɪmpl̩tən |-tonian ˌsɪmpl̩'tonɪən
simplex 'sɪmplɛks |-es -ɪz |-ed -t
simplicity sɪm'plɪsətɪ
simplification ˌsɪmpləfə'keʃən
simplify 'sɪmplə͵faɪ |-fied -͵faɪd
Simplon 'sɪmplɑn, -plɒn
simply 'sɪmplɪ
Simpson, Simson 'sɪmpsn̩, 'sɪmsn̩
Sims sɪmz |-'s -ɪz
simulacre 'sɪmjə͵lekɚ; ES -͵lekə(r
simulacrum ˌsɪmjə'lekrəm |-cra -krə
simulate adj 'sɪmjəlɪt, -͵let
simulate 'sɪmjə͵let |-d -ɪd |-tion ˌsɪmjə'leʃən
simultaneity ˌsaɪml̩tə'nɪətɪ, ˌsɪml̩-
simultaneous ˌsaɪml̩'tenɪəs, ˌsɪml̩-, -njəs
sin sɪn |sinned sɪnd |-ful -fəl |-fully -fəlɪ
Sinai 'saɪnaɪ, 'saɪnɪ͵aɪ
Sinaitic ˌsaɪnɪ'ɪtɪk |-us -əs
Sinbad 'sɪnbæd
since sɪns
sincere sɪn'sɪr, sn̩-; ES -'sɪə(r, S+-'sɛə(r
sincerity sɪn'sɛrətɪ, sn̩-
Sinclair Brit name 'sɪŋklɛr, 'sɪn-, -klær,
  'sɪŋklɚ; E -klɛə(r, ES -klæə(r, 'sɪŋklə(r
Sinclair Am name sɪn'klɛr, -'klær; E -'klɛə(r,
  ES -'klæə(r
Sindbad 'sɪnbæd
sine math. saɪn
sine 'without' 'saɪnɪ
sinecure 'saɪnɪ͵kjʊr, 'sɪnɪ-, -͵kɪʊr; ES -ə(r;
  |-rist -ɪst
sine die 'saɪnɪ'daɪ·i
sine qua non 'saɪnɪkwe'nɑn, -'nɒn
sinew 'sɪnju, 'sɪnɪu, 'sɪnu
sinewy 'sɪnjəwɪ, 'sɪnəwɪ
sing sɪŋ |sang sæŋ or sung sʌŋ |sung sʌŋ
Singapore 'sɪŋgə͵por, 'sɪŋə-, -͵pɔr; ES -͵poə(r,
  E+-͵pɔə(r; acct+ˌSinga'pore
singe sɪndʒ |singes 'sɪndʒɪz |singed sɪndʒd
singer 'who sings' 'sɪŋɚ; ES 'sɪŋə(r

singer 'who singes' 'sɪndʒɚ; ES 'sɪndʒə(r
singh, S- sɪŋ
Singhalese ˌsɪŋgə'liz |-'s -ɪz
single 'sɪŋgl̩ |-d -d |-ling 'sɪŋglɪŋ, -gl̩ɪŋ
singlehanded 'sɪŋgl̩'hændɪd
singlehearted 'sɪŋgl̩'hɑrtɪd; ES -'hɑ:t-, E+
  -'hɑ:t-
singlestick 'sɪŋgl̩͵stɪk
singlet 'sɪŋglɪt
Singleton, s- 'sɪŋgl̩tən
singletree 'sɪŋgl̩͵tri, -trɪ
singly 'sɪŋglɪ
Sing Sing 'sɪŋ͵sɪŋ
singsong 'sɪŋ͵sɔŋ, -͵sɒŋ; S+-͵sɑŋ
singular 'sɪŋgjələ; ES -lə(r
singularity ˌsɪŋgjə'lærətɪ
Sinhalese ˌsɪnhə'liz |-'s -ɪz
sinister 'sɪnɪstɚ; ES 'sɪnɪstə(r; |-tral -trəl
sink sɪŋk |sank sæŋk or sunk sʌŋk |sunk sʌŋk
sinkhole 'sɪŋk͵hol
sinner 'sɪnɚ; ES 'sɪnə(r
Sinn Fein 'ʃɪn'fen |-ism -ɪzəm
Sino-Japanese ˌsaɪno͵dʒæpə'niz, ˌsɪno-
Sinology saɪ'nɑlədʒɪ, sɪ-; ES+-'nɒl-
Sinon 'saɪnən
sinter 'sɪntɚ; ES 'sɪntə(r; |-ed -d
sinuate adj 'sɪnjʊɪt, -͵et
sinuate v 'sɪnju͵et |-d -ɪd
sinuosity ˌsɪnju'ɑsətɪ; ES+-'ɒs-
sinuous 'sɪnjʊəs
sinus 'saɪnəs |-es -ɪz
Sion 'Zion' 'saɪən
-sion unstressed ending -ʃən, -ʃn̩—The pron.
  -ʃn̩ is less common in America than in England.
Sioux su |pl Sioux su, suz |Siouan 'suən
sip sɪp |sipped sɪpt
siphon 'saɪfən, -fɑn, -fɒn |-ed -d |-age -fənɪdʒ
  |-al -fənl̩
sir stressed 'sɝ, ˌsɝ; ES 'sɜ(r, 'sɝ, ˌsɜ(r, ˌsɝ;
  unstr. sɚ; ES sə(r
sirdar, S- sɚ'dɑr; ES sə'dɑ:(r, E+-'dɑ:(r
sire saɪr; ES saɪə(r; |-d -d
siren 'saɪrən
sirenic saɪ'rɛnɪk |-al -l̩ |-ally -l̩ɪ, -ɪklɪ
Sirius 'sɪrɪəs |-'s -ɪz
sirloin 'sɝlɔɪn; ES 'sɜ-, 'sɝ-
sirocco sə'rɑko; ES+-'rɒko
sirrah 'sɪrə

Key: See in full §§3–47. bee bi |pity 'pɪtɪ (§6) |rate ret |yet jɛt |sang sæŋ |angry 'æŋ·grɪ |bath bæθ; E baθ (§10) |ah ɑ |far fɑr |watch wɑtʃ, wɒtʃ (§12) |jaw dʒɔ |gorge gɔrdʒ |go go

sirup 'sırəp, 'sɜˣəp; E 'sırəp, 'sɜrəp, 'sɜˣəp;
S 'sɜrəp, 'sʌrəp, 'sırəp, 'sɜˣəp, 'sɛrəp—*The
pron.* 'sɛrəp, *found also occasionally in N
& E, is a normal traditional form.* Cf
Syracuse, Miriam.
sisal 'saısļ, 'sısļ
Sisam 'saısəm
Sisera 'sısərə
sissify 'sısıˌfaı |-fied -ˌfaıd |sissy 'sısı
Sisson 'sısņ
sister 'sıstəˣ; ES -tə(r; |-ed -d |-ing -trıŋ,
-tərıŋ
sister-in-law 'sıstərınˌlɔ, 'sıstəˣnˌlɔ; ES 'sıstərınˌlɔ, 'sıstənˌlɔ
sisters-in-law 'sıstəˣzınˌlɔ, 'sıstəˣzņˌlɔ; ES
'sıstəzınˌlɔ, 'sıstəzņˌlɔ
Sistine 'sıstin, -tın
Sisyphus 'sısəfəs |-'s -ız |-phean ˌsısə'fiən
sit sıt |sat sæt, *arch.* sate set, sæt |sat sæt
sit-down 'sıtˌdaʊn
sit down sı'daʊn, sıt'daʊn—sı'daʊn *is the
usual conversational pronunciation.* Sat
down, *being less frequent, keeps the* t *sound.*
site saıt |sited 'saıtıd
sith sıθ
Sitka 'sıtkə
sitology saı'tɑlədʒı; ES+-'tɒl-
sitting 'sıtıŋ
Sittingbourne 'sıtıŋˌborn, -ˌbɔrn; ES -ˌboən,
E+-ˌbɔən
situate *adj* 'sıtʃʊıt, -ˌet
situate *v* 'sıtʃʊˌet |-d -ıd
situation ˌsıtʃʊ'eʃən, ˌsıtʃə'weʃən
situs 'saıtəs
Sitwell 'sıtwəl, -wɛl
Siva 'sivə, 'ʃivə, -ıvə |-ism -ˌızəm
Siward 'sjuˣd, 'sıu-, 'su-; ES -əd
siwash, S- 'saıwɑʃ, -wɔʃ, -wɒʃ |-es -ız |-ed -t
six sıks |sixes 'sıksız
sixes and sevens 'sıksızņ'sɛvənz
sixfold *adj, adv* 'sıks'fold ('sıxˌfold 'loss)
sixpence 'sıkspəns |-s -ız
sixpenny 'sıksˌpɛnı, -pənı
sixscore 'sıks'skor, 'sık'sk-, -'skɔr; ES
-'skoə(r, E+-'skɔə(r; ('sıxˌscore 'years)
six-shooter 'sıks'ʃutəˣ, 'sıkʃ'ʃ-; ES -'ʃutə(r
sixteen sıks'tin, 'sıks'tin ('sıxˌteen 'men)
sixteenmo sıks'tinmo
sixteenth sıks'tinθ, 'sıks'- |-ths -θs

sixth sıksθ |sixths sıksθs, sıks:
Sixtus 'sıkstəs |-'s -ız
sixty 'sıkstı |-ieth -ıθ |-ieths -ıθs |-fold -'fold
('sıxtyˌfold 'gain)
sizable 'saızəbļ |-bly -blı
sizar, -er 'saızəˣ; ES 'saızə(r
size saız |sizes 'saızız |sized saızd
sizeable 'saızəbļ |-bly -blı
sizzle 'sızļ |-d -d |-ling 'sızlıŋ, 'sızļıŋ
Skager Rack, -er-Rak, -errak 'skægəˣˌræk,
ˌskægəˣ'ræk; ES -gə-
Skagit 'skægıt
Skagway 'skægwe
skald skɔld, skɑld
Skaneateles ˌskænı'ætləs, *loc.* ˌskını'ætləs
|-'s -ız—*The loc. pron. apparently comes
from an older form* Skeneateles ˌskinı-
skat '*scat*' skæt |skatted 'skætıd
skat *game* skɑt
skate sket |skated 'sketıd
Skeat skit
skedaddle skı'dædļ |-d -d |-ling -dlıŋ, -dļıŋ
skee '*ski*' ski
skeesicks, -zix 'skizıks, -zəks |-'s -ız
skeet skit
skein sken |skeined skend
skeleton 'skɛlətņ |-ed -d |-tal -tļ
skeletonize 'skɛlətņˌaız |-s -ız |-d -d
skelp skɛlp |skelped skɛlpt
Skelton 'skɛltņ
skeptic 'skɛptık |-al -ļ |-ally -ļı, -ıklı
skepticism 'skɛptəˌsızəm
skerry 'skɛrı
sketch skɛtʃ |-es -ız |-ed -t |-book -ˌbʊk
skew skju, skıu |-ed -d |-er -əˣ; ES -ə(r
ski ski |skis skiz |skied skid (*Norw, Sw* ʃi)
skiagram 'skaıəˌgræm |-graph -ˌgræf; E+
-ˌgraf, -ˌgrɑf
skiagraphy skaı'ægrəfı
skid skıd |skidded 'skıdıd
Skiddaw 'skıdɔ
skier '*who skis*' 'skiəˣ; ES 'ski·ə(r
skier '*skyer*' 'skaıəˣ; ES 'skaı·ə(r
skies skaız
skiff skıf |skiffed skıft
skiing 'skiıŋ
skill skıl |skilled skıld
skillet 'skılıt
skillful, skilf- 'skılfəl |-ly -ı

|full fʊl |tooth tuθ |further 'fɜˣðəˣ; ES 'fɜˣðə |custom 'kʌstəm |while hwaıl |how haʊ |toy tɔı
|using 'juzıŋ |fuse fjuz, fıuz |dish dıʃ |vision 'vıʒən |Eden 'idņ |cradle 'kredļ |keep 'em 'kipm̩

skill-less |ˈskɪllɪs

skim skɪm |skimmed skɪmd |-mer -ɚ; ES -ə(r

skim milk |ˈskɪmˈmɪlk

skimp skɪmp |skimped skɪmpt |-y -ɪ

skin skɪn |skinned skɪnd |-ny -ɪ

skin-deep |ˈskɪnˈdip (ˈskin-ˌdeep ˈcut)

skinflint |ˈskɪnˌflɪnt

skinful |ˈskɪnˌfʊl |-fuls -ˌfʊlz

skinner, S- |ˈskɪnɚ; ES ˈskɪnə(r

skintight |ˈskɪnˈtaɪt (ˈskɪnˌtight ˈboots)

skip skɪp |skipped skɪpt

skipper |ˈskɪpɚ; ES ˈskɪpə(r; |-ed -d |-y -ɪ

skirl skɝl; ES skɝl, skɝ·l; |-ed -d

skirmish |ˈskɝ·mɪʃ; ES ˈskɝm-, ˈskɝ·m-; |-es -ɪz |-ed -t

skirr skɝ·; ES skɝ(r, skɝ·; |-ed -d

skirt skɝt; ES skɝt, skɝ·t; |-ed -ɪd

skit skɪt |skitted ˈskɪtɪd

skitter |ˈskɪtɚ; ES ˈskɪtə(r; |-ed -d

skittish |ˈskɪtɪʃ

skittle |ˈskɪtl̩ |-d -d |-s -z

skoal skol |skoaled skold

Skowhegan skaʊˈhigən

skua |ˈskjuə, ˈskɪuə

skulduddery skʌlˈdʌdɚɪ, -drɪ |-duggery -ˈdʌgɚɪ, -grɪ

skulk skʌlk |skulked skʌlkt

skull ʻheadʼ skʌl |skulled skʌld

skull ʻscullʼ skʌl |skulled skʌld

skullcap |ˈskʌlˌkæp, -ˈkæp

skullduddery, -dugg- see skulduddery

skull-less |ˈskʌllɪs

skunk skʌŋk |skunked skʌŋkt

sky skaɪ |skied or skyed skaɪd |-ey -ɪ

Skye skaɪ

skyer ʻhigh hitʼ |ˈskaɪɚ; ES ˈskaɪ·ə(r

skylark |ˈskaɪˌlɑrk; ES -ˌlɑːk, E+-ˌlɑːk; |-ed -t

skylight |ˈskaɪˌlaɪt |-ed -ɪd

skyrocket |ˈskaɪˌrɑkɪt; ES+-ˌrɒk-; |-ed -ɪd

skyscraper |ˈskaɪˌskrepɚ; ES -ˌskrepə(r

skyward |ˈskaɪwɚd; ES -wəd

slab slæb |slabbed slæbd

slab-sided |ˈslæbˈsaɪdɪd (ˈslab-ˌsided ˈgawk)

slack slæk |slacked slækt

slacken |ˈslækən |-ed -d |-ing -kənɪŋ, -knɪŋ

slag slæg |slagged slægd

slain slen

Slaithwaite |ˈsleθwet, loc.+ˈslɔət

slake slek |slaked slekt

slam slæm |slammed slæmd

slander |ˈslændɚ; ES ˈslændə(r; |-ed -d |-ing ˈslændrɪŋ, -dərɪŋ |-ous -drəs, -dərəs

slang slæŋ |slanged slæŋd |-y -ɪ

slant slænt; E+slant, slɑnt; |-ed -ɪd

slap slæp |slapped slæpt

slapdash |ˈslæpˌdæʃ |-es -ɪz |-ed -t |-ery -ərɪ, -rɪ

slapjack |ˈslæpˌdʒæk

slapstick |ˈslæpˌstɪk

slash slæʃ |slashes ˈslæʃɪz |slashed slæʃt

slat slæt |slatted ˈslætɪd

slate slet |slated ˈsletɪd

slate-pencil |ˈsletˌpɛnsl̩

slather |ˈslæðɚ, ˈsle-; ES -ðə(r; |-ed -d |-ing -ðrɪŋ, -ðərɪŋ

slattern |ˈslætɚn; ES ˈslætən

slaty |ˈsletɪ

slaughter, S- |ˈslɔtɚ; ES -tə(r; |-ed -d |-ing ˈslɔtərɪŋ, ˈslɔtrɪŋ |-ous -əs, -trəs

Slav slɑv, slæv

slave slev |slaved slevd |-ry -rɪ, -ərɪ

slaveholder |ˈslevˌholdɚ; ES -ˌholdə(r

slavey |ˈslevɪ

Slavic |ˈslævɪk, ˈslɑv-

Slavonia sləˈvonɪə |-n -n

Slavonic sləˈvɑnɪk; ES+-ˈvɒn-; |-ally -l̩ɪ, -ɪklɪ

slaw slɔ

slay sle |slew slu, slɪu |slain slen

slazy ʻsleazyʼ |ˈslezɪ

sleave sliv |sleaved slivd

sleazy |ˈslezɪ, ˈslizɪ

sled slɛd |sledded ˈslɛdɪd

sledge slɛdʒ |sledges ˈslɛdʒɪz |sledged slɛdʒd

sleek slik |sleeked slikt, cf slick

sleep slip |slept slɛpt |-y -ɪ

sleepwalker |ˈslipˌwɔkɚ; ES -ˌwɔkə(r

sleepyhead |ˈslipɪˌhɛd

sleet slit |sleeted ˈslitɪd

sleeve sliv |sleeved slivd

sleigh sle |sleighed sled

sleight slaɪt

slender, S- |ˈslɛndɚ; ES ˈslɛndə(r; |-er -drɚ -dərɚ; ES -rə(r

slept slɛpt

sleuth sluθ, slɪuθ |-ed -t

slew slu, slɪu |-ed -d

slice slaɪs |slices ˈslaɪsɪz |sliced slaɪst

Key: See in full §§3–47. bee bi |pity ˈpɪtɪ (§6) |rate ret |yet jɛt |sang sæŋ |angry ˈæŋ·grɪ |bath bæθ; E baθ (§10) |ah ɑ |far fɑr |watch wɑtʃ, wɒtʃ (§12) |jaw dʒɔ |gorge gɔrdʒ |go go

slick slɪk |slicked slɪkt
slicker ˈslɪkɚ; ES ˈslɪkə(r
slide slaɪd |slid slɪd |slid slɪd or slidden ˈslɪdn̩
Slidell slaɪˈdɛl, ˈslaɪd|
slier ˈslaɪɚ; ES ˈslaɪ·ə(r
slight slaɪt |slighted ˈslaɪtɪd
Sligo ˈslaɪgo
slily ˈslaɪlɪ
slim slɪm |slimmed slɪmd
slime slaɪm |slimed slaɪmd
slimish ˈslaɪmɪʃ
slimmish ˈslɪmɪʃ
slimpsy ˈslɪmpsɪ
slimsy ˈslɪmzɪ, ˈslɪmpsɪ
slimy ˈslaɪmɪ
sling slɪŋ |slung slʌŋ or arch. slang slæŋ
  |slung slʌŋ
slingshot ˈslɪŋˌʃɑt; ES+-ˌʃɒt
slink slɪŋk |slunk slʌŋk or arch. slank slæŋk
  |slunk slʌŋk
slip slɪp |slipped slɪpt |-per -ɚ; ES -ə(r
slipknot ˈslɪpˌnɑt; ES+-ˌnɒt
slippery ˈslɪprɪ, ˈslɪpərɪ |-rier ˈslɪprɪɚ; ES
  -rɪ·ə(r; |-riest ˈslɪprɪɪst
slippery elm ˈslɪprɪˈɛlm
slipshod ˈslɪpˌʃɑd; ES+-ˌʃɒd
slipslop ˈslɪpˌslɑp; ES+-ˌslɒp; |-ped -t
slit slɪt |past & pptc slit slɪt or rare slitted
  ˈslɪtɪd
slither ˈslɪðɚ; ES ˈslɪðə(r; |-ed -d |-ing
  ˈslɪðrɪŋ, ˈslɪðərɪŋ |-y -ðrɪ, -ðərɪ
slithy ˈslaɪðɪ
sliver ˈslɪvɚ; ES -və(r; |-ed -d |-ing ˈslɪvərɪŋ,
  -vrɪŋ |-y -vərɪ, -vrɪ
slob slɑb; ES+slɒb
slobber ˈslɑbɚ; ES ˈslɑbə(r, ˈslɒb-; |-y -brɪ,
  -bərɪ
slobberer ˈslɑbərɚ; ES ˈslɑbərə(r, ˈslɒb-
sloe slo
slog slɑg, slɒg |-ged -d
slogan ˈslogən
sloo ˈslough' slu
sloop slup
slop slɑp; ES+slɒp; |-ped -t |-py -ɪ
slope slop |sloped slopt
slosh slɑʃ; ES+slɒʃ; |-es -ɪz |-ed -t
Slosson ˈslɑsn̩, ˈslɒsn̩, ˈslɔsn̩
slot slɑt; ES+slɒt; |-ted -ɪd
sloth sloθ, slɔθ, slɒθ |-ful -fəl |-fully -fəlɪ

slouch slautʃ |slouches ˈslautʃɪz |-ed -t
slough ˈmudhole' slau, ˈmarsh' slu, slɪu
slough ˈshed skin' slʌf |-ed -t
Slough Engd slau
Slovak ˈslovæk, sloˈvæk
Slovakia sloˈvɑkɪə, -ˈvæk- |-n -n
sloven ˈslʌvən |-ed -d |-ly -lɪ
Slovene sloˈvin, ˈslovin
Slovenia sloˈvinɪə |-n -n
slow slo |slowed slod
slow-motion ˈsloˈmoʃən (ˈslow-ˌmotion ˈfilm)
slowworm ˈsloˌwɝm; ES -ˌwɜm, -ˌwɝm
sloyd slɔɪd
slub slʌb |slubbed slʌbd
slubber ˈslʌbɚ; ES -bə(r; |-ed -d |-ing
  ˈslʌbrɪŋ, ˈslʌbərɪŋ |-y -brɪ, -bərɪ
slubberer ˈslʌbərɚ; ES ˈslʌbərə(r
sludge, S- slʌdʒ |sludges ˈslʌdʒɪz |-d -d
slue slu, slɪu
slug slʌg |slugged slʌgd
slugabed ˈslʌgəˌbɛd
sluggard ˈslʌgɚd; ES ˈslʌgəd; |-gish ˈslʌgɪʃ
sluice slus, slɪus |-s -ɪz |-d -t
slum slʌm |slummed slʌmd
slumber ˈslʌmbɚ; ES -bə(r; |-ed -d |-ing
  -brɪŋ, -bərɪŋ |-ous -brəs, -bərəs
slumbrous ˈslʌmbrəs
slump slʌmp |slumped slʌmpt
slung slʌŋ
slunk slʌŋk
slur slɝ; ES slɜ(r, slɝ; |-red -d
slurp slɝp; ES slɜp, slɝp; |-ed -t
slurry ˈslɝɪ; ES ˈslɜrɪ, ˈslɝɪ
slush slʌʃ |slushes ˈslʌʃɪz |slushed slʌʃt
slut slʌt |sluttish ˈslʌtɪʃ
sly slaɪ |slyly ˈslaɪlɪ
slyer ˈslier' slaɪɚ; ES ˈslaɪ·ə(r
smack smæk |smacked smækt
Smackover ˈsmækovɚ; ES ˈsmækovə(r
small smɔl |smalled smɔld
smallclothes ˈsmɔlˌkloz, -ˌkloðz
smallpox ˈsmɔlˌpɑks; ES+-ˌpɒks; |-'s -ɪz
smalt smɔlt
smaragd ˈsmærægd |-ine sməˈrægdɪn
smart smart; ES smɑːt, E+smaːt; |-ed -ɪd
smarten ˈsmartn̩; ES see smart; |-ed -d |-ing
  -tn̩ɪŋ, -tnɪŋ
smash smæʃ |smashes ˈsmæʃɪz |smashed
  smæʃt

|full fʊl |tooth tuθ |further ˈfɝðɚ; ES ˈfɝðə |custom ˈkʌstəm |while hwaɪl |how hau |toy tɔɪ
|using ˈjuzɪŋ |fuse fjuz, fɪuz |dish dɪʃ |vision ˈvɪʒən |Eden ˈidn̩ |cradle ˈkredl̩ |keep 'em ˈkipm̩

smashup 'smæʃˌʌp
smatter 'smætɚ; ES -tə(r; |-ed -d |-ing -tərɪŋ,
　-trɪŋ
smear smɪr; ES smɪə(r, S+smɛə(r; |-ed -d
smearcase 'smɪrˌkes; ES see smear; (Ger
　'ʃmiːrˌkɛːzə)
smell smɛl |smelled smɛld or smelt smɛlt
smellage 'smɛlɪdʒ
smell-less 'smɛllɪs
smelt smɛlt |-ed -ɪd |-ery -ərɪ
Smetana 'smɛtnə
Smethport 'smɛθˌport, -ˌpɔrt; ES -ˌpoət,
　E+-ˌpɔət
Smethwick 'smɛðɪk
smilax 'smaɪlæks |-es -ɪz
smile smaɪl |smiled smaɪld |-less 'smaɪllɪs
Smintheus 'smɪnθjus |-'s -ɪz
smirch smɝtʃ; ES smɝtʃ, smɝtʃ; |-es -ɪz
　|-ed -t
smirk smɝk; ES smɝk, smɝk; |-ed -t
smite smaɪt |smote smot |smitten 'smɪtn̩ or
　smit smɪt or smote smot
smith, S- smɪθ |-ths -θs |-ery -ərɪ, -rɪ
smither 'smɪðɚ; ES -ðə(r; |-s -z
smithereens ˌsmɪðə'rinz
Smithers 'smɪðɚz; ES 'smɪðəz; |-'s -ɪz
Smithfield 'smɪθfild
smithier 'smɪðɪɚ, -ðjɚ; ES -ə(r
Smithson 'smɪθsən |-sonian smɪθ'sonɪən
Smithville 'smɪθvɪl; S+-vl̩
smithy 'smɪθɪ, 'smɪðɪ—'smɪðɪ is the older
　pronunciation. 'smɪθɪ imitates smith as
　'grɪsɪ imitates the noun grease (grɪs).
smitten 'smɪtn̩
smock smɑk; ES+smɒk; |-ed -t
smoke smok |smoked smokt |-ky -ɪ; |NEngd
　+smɔk (§46)
smokestack 'smokˌstæk
Smokies 'smokɪz
smolder 'smoldɚ; ES -də(r; |-ed -d |-ing
　-drɪŋ, -dərɪŋ
Smolensk smo'lɛnsk, smɔ-, -'ljɛnsk
Smollett 'smɑlɪt; ES+'smɒl-
smolt smolt
smooth smuð |smoothed smuðd
smoothbore 'smuðˌbor, -ˌbɔr; ES -ˌboə(r,
　E+-ˌbɔə(r
smoothen 'smuðən |-ed -d |-ing 'smuðnɪŋ,
　-ðənɪŋ

smooth-spoken 'smuð'spokən ('smooth-
　ˌspoken 'man)
smote smot
smother 'smʌðɚ; ES 'smʌðə(r; |-ed -d |-ing
　'smʌðrɪŋ, -ðərɪŋ
smoulder 'smoldɚ; ES -də(r; |-ed -d |-ing
　-drɪŋ, -dərɪŋ
smudge smʌdʒ |smudges 'smʌdʒɪz |smudged
　smʌdʒd
smug smʌg |smugged smʌgd
smuggle 'smʌgl̩ |-d -d |-ling 'smʌglɪŋ, -gl̩ɪŋ
smut smʌt |smutted 'smʌtɪd |-ty -ɪ
smutch smʌtʃ |smutches 'smʌtʃɪz |-smutched
　smʌtʃt
Smuts smʌts |-'s -ɪz
Smyrna 'smɝnə; ES 'smɝnə, 'smɝnə
Smyth smɪθ, smaɪθ |Smythe smaɪð, smaɪθ
snack snæk |snacked snækt
snaffle 'snæfl̩ |-d -d |-ling 'snæflɪŋ, -fl̩ɪŋ
snag snæg |snagged snægd
snaggletooth 'snægl̩ˌtuθ
snail snel |snailed sneld
snail-paced 'snelˌpest
snake, S- snek |snaked snekt |-ky -ɪ
snakeroot 'snekˌrut, -ˌrʊt
snap snæp |snapped snæpt |-per -ɚ; ES -ə(r
snapdragon 'snæpˌdrægən
snapshot 'snæpˌʃɑt; ES+-ˌʃɒt
snare snɛr, snær; E snɛə(r, ES snæə(r; |-d -d
snark snɑrk; ES snɑːk, E+snɑːk
snarl snɑrl; ES snɑːl, E+snɑːl; |-ed -d
snatch snætʃ |snatches 'snætʃɪz |-ed -t
snath snæθ |-ths -θs |snathe sneð
sneak snik |sneaked snikt
sneer snɪr; ES snɪə(r, S+snɛə(r; |-ed -d
sneeze sniz |sneezes 'snizɪz |sneezed snizd
snell, S- snɛl |snelled snɛld
Snelling 'snɛlɪŋ
snick snɪk |snicked snɪkt
snickersnee 'snɪkɚˌsni; ES 'snɪkə-; |-d -d
sniff snɪf |sniffed snɪft
sniffle 'snɪfl̩ |-d -d |-ling 'snɪflɪŋ, -fl̩ɪŋ
snigger 'snɪgɚ; ES -gə(r; |-ed -d |-ing
　'snɪgərɪŋ, 'snɪgrɪŋ
snip snɪp |snipped snɪpt |py -ɪ
snipe snaɪp |sniped snaɪpt
snippet 'snɪpɪt
snitch snɪtʃ |snitches 'snɪtʃɪz |-ed -t
snivel 'snɪvl̩ |-ed -d |-ing 'snɪvlɪŋ, -vl̩ɪŋ

Those words below in which the ɑ sound is spelt ɔ are often pronounced with ɒ in E and S

snob snab |-bery -ərı, -rı |-bish -ıʃ

Snoddy 'snadı

Snodgrass 'snad,græs; E+-,gras, -,gras; |-'s -ız

Snohomish sno'homıʃ |-'s -ız

snood snud |snooded 'snudıd

snook snuk, snuk

snoop snup |snooped snupt

snoot snut |snooty 'snutı

snooze snuz |snoozes 'snuzız |snoozed snuzd

Snoqualmie sno'kwalmı

snore snor, snɔr; ES snoə(r, E+snɔə(r; |-d -d

snort snɔrt; ES snɔət; |-ed -ıd

snout snaut |snouted 'snautıd

snow, S- sno |snowed snod |-y -ı

snowball 'sno,bɔl |-ed -d

snowbank 'sno,bæŋk

snowbird 'sno,bɝd; ES -,bɜd, -,bɝd

snow-blind 'sno,blaınd |-ed -ıd |-ness -nıs

snowbound, S- 'sno,baund

snow-capped 'sno,kæpt

Snowden, -don 'snodn̩ |-donian sno'donıən

snowdrift 'sno,drıft |-drop -,drap

snowfall 'sno,fɔl |-flake -,flek

snowplow 'sno,plau

snowshoe 'sno,ʃu |-storm -,stɔrm; ES -,stɔəm

snow-white 'sno'hwaıt ('snow-,white 'dove)

Snow White 'sno,hwaıt

snub snʌb |snubbed snʌbd |-ber -ɝ; ES -ə(r

snub-nose 'snʌb,noz |-s -ız

snub-nosed 'snʌb'nozd ('snub-,nosed 'Auk)

snuff snʌf |snuffed snʌft |-y -ı

snuffbox 'snʌf,baks |-es -ız

snuffers 'snʌfɚz; ES 'snʌfəz

snuffle 'snʌfl̩ |-d -d |-ling 'snʌflıŋ, -fl̩ıŋ

snug snʌg |snugged snʌgd |-gery -ərı

snuggle 'snʌgl̩ |-d -d |-ling 'snʌglıŋ, -gl̩ıŋ

Snyder 'snaıdɚ; ES 'snaıdə(r

so *stressed* 'so, ,so; *unstr.* so, sə, su

soak sok |soaked sokt; |*N Engd*+sɔk (§46)

soaken *adj* 'sokən

so-and-so 'soən,so

soap sop |soaped sopt |-stone -,ston |-suds -,sʌdz

soapwort 'sop,wɝt; ES -,wɜt, -,wɝt

soar sor, sɔr; ES soə(r, E+sɔə(r; |-ed -d

sob sab |sobbed sabd

sobeit so'biıt

sober 'sobɚ; ES 'sobə(r; |-ed -d |-ing 'sobərıŋ, -brıŋ

Sobieski ,sobı'ɛskı, so'bjɛskı

sobriety sə'braıətı, so-

sobriquet 'sobrı,ke (*Fr* sɔbri'kɛ)

socage, socc- 'sakıdʒ |-s -ız

so-called 'so'kɔld ('so-,called 'learning)

soccer 'sakɚ; ES 'sakə(r

sociability ,soʃə'bılətı

sociable 'soʃəbl̩ |-bly -blı

social 'soʃəl |-ly -ı |-ism -,ızəm |-ist -ıst

socialistic ,soʃə'lıstık |-ally -l̩ı, -ıklı

socialite 'soʃə,laıt

sociality ,soʃı'ælətı

socialize 'soʃə,laız |-s -ız |-d -d

societal sə'saıətl̩ |-ly -ı

society sə'saıətı

sociological ,soʃıə'ladʒık̩l, ,sosı- |-ly -ı

sociology ,soʃı'alədʒı, ,sosı- |-gist -dʒıst

sock sak |socked sakt

sockdolager sak'dalədʒɚ; ES -'dalədʒə(r

socket 'sakıt |-ed -ıd

Socrates 'sakrə,tiz |-'s -ız

Socratic so'krætık |-al -l̩ |-ally -l̩ı, -ıklı

sod sad |sodded 'sadıd

soda 'sodə

sodality so'dælətı

sodden 'sadn̩ |-ness 'sadn̩nıs

sodium 'sodıəm

Sodom 'sadəm |-ist -ıst |-ite -,aıt |-y -ı

soever so'ɛvɚ, su'ɛvɚ; ES -'ɛvə(r

sofa 'sofə

Sofia 'sofıə, so'fiə

Sofronia so'fronıə

soft sɔft, sɒft

soft-boiled 'sɔft'bɔıld, 'sɒft-

soften 'sɔfən, 'sɒf- |-ed -d |-ing -fənıŋ, -fnıŋ |-er -fənɚ, -fnɚ; ES -ə(r

softhead 'sɔft,hɛd, 'sɒft-

soft-headed 'sɔft'hɛdıd, 'sɒft-

softhearted 'sɔft'hartıd, 'sɒft-; ES -'ha:t-, E+-'ha:t-; ('soft,hearted 'judge)

soft-pedal ,sɔft'pɛdl̩, ,sɒft- |-ed -d

soft-shell *n* 'sɔft,ʃɛl, 'sɒft-

soft-shell *adj* 'sɔft'ʃɛl, 'sɒft- |-ed -d |'soft-,shell 'crab)

soft-soap 'sɔft'sop, 'sɒft- |-ed -t

soft-spoken 'sɔft'spokən, 'sɒft-

|full ful |tooth tuθ |further 'fɝðɚ; ES 'fɜðə |custom 'kʌstəm |while hwaıl |how hau |toy tɔı |using 'juzıŋ |fuse fjuz, fıuz |dish dıʃ |vision 'vıʒən |Eden 'idn̩ |cradle 'kredl̩ |keep 'em 'kipm̩

Those words below in which the ɑ sound is spelt o are often pronounced with ɒ in E and S

sogdologer sag'dalədʒɚ; ES -'dalədʒə(r

soggy 'sagɪ

soho so'ho |sohoed so'hod

Soho so'ho, 'soho ('So‚ho 'Square)

Sohrab 'soræb, 'sorəb, 'sɔr-; S 'sor-

soi-disant Fr swadi'zɑ̃

soil sɔɪl |soiled sɔɪld |-less 'sɔɪllɪs

soiree swɑ're (Fr swa're)

Soissons Fr swa'sõ

sojourn n 'sodʒɝn; ES -dʒɝn, -dʒɝn

sojourn v so'dʒɝn, 'sodʒɝn; ES -ɜn, -ɝn; |-ed -d

soke sok |soken 'sokən

sokeman 'sokmən |-men -mən

Sokoloff 'sokə‚lɔf, -‚lɒf, -ləv

Sol sal, sɒl, sɔl

sol music, coin sol

sol chem. sal, sol

solace 'salɪs, -əs |-s -ɪz |-d -t

Solanio sə'lanɪo, -njo

solar 'solɚ; ES 'solə(r

solarium so'lɛrɪəm, -'ler- |-s -z |-ia -ɪə

solarize 'solə‚raɪz |-s -ɪz |-d -d

sold sold

Soldan, s- 'saldən

solder 'sadɚ; ES 'sadə(r; |-ed -d |-ing 'sadərɪŋ, -drɪŋ

soldier 'soldʒɚ; ES -dʒə(r; |-ed -d |-y -ɪ

sole sol |soled sold |-ly 'sollɪ

solecism 'salə‚sɪzəm

soleless 'sollɪs

solemn 'saləm |-ity sə'lɛmnətɪ

solemnization ‚saləmnə'zeʃən, -naɪ'z-

solemnize 'saləm‚naɪz |-s -ɪz |-d -d

solenoid 'solə‚nɔɪd

solenoidal ‚solə'nɔɪdl̩ |-ly -ɪ

Solent 'solənt

sol-fa sol'fa |-ed -d ('sol-‚fa 'syllables)

solfeggio sal'fɛdʒo, -dʒɪ‚o (It sol'feddʒo)

solicit sə'lɪsɪt |-ed -ɪd |-ous -əs

solicitation sə‚lɪsə'teʃən

solicitor sə'lɪsətɚ; ES -'lɪsətə(r

solicitude sə'lɪsə‚tjud, -‚tɪud, -‚tud

solid 'salɪd |-arity ‚salə'dærətɪ

solidification sə‚lɪdəfə'keʃən

solidify sə'lɪdə‚faɪ |-fied -‚faɪd

solidity sə'lɪdətɪ

solidus 'salɪdəs |-di -‚daɪ

soliloquize sə'lɪlə‚kwaɪz |-s -ɪz |-d -d

soliloquy sə'lɪləkwɪ |-quist -kwɪst

Solinus sə'laɪnəs |-'s -ɪz

solitaire ‚salə'tɛr, -'tær; E -'tɛə(r, ES -'tæə(r; acct+'soli‚taire

solitary 'salə‚tɛrɪ |-tude -‚tjud, -‚tɪud, -‚tud

solo, S- 'solo |-ed -d |-ing 'so‚lo·ɪŋ, -ləwɪŋ

soloist 'so‚lo·ɪst, 'soləwɪst

Solomon 'saləmən

Solomon's-seal ‚saləmənz'sil, -mən'sil

Solon 'solən |-ian so'lonɪən |-ic so'lanɪk

solstice 'salstɪs |-s -ɪz

solstitial sal'stɪʃəl |-ly -ɪ

solubility ‚saljə'bɪlətɪ

soluble 'saljəbl̩ |-bly -blɪ

solus 'soləs |sola 'solə

solute 'saljut, 'soljut, 'solut, -lɪut

solution sə'luʃən, -'lɪu-

solvability ‚salvə'bɪlətɪ, ‚sɒlv-

solvable 'salvəbl̩, 'sɒlv-

Solvay 'salve

solve salv, sɒlv |-d -d |-ncy -ənsɪ |-nt -ənt

Solway 'salwe

Solyman 'salɪmən

Somali so'malɪ, sə- |-land -‚lænd

somatic so'mætɪk |-al -l̩ |-ally -l̩ɪ, -ɪklɪ

somber, -bre 'sambɚ; ES -bə(r; |-(e)d -d |-ing -bərɪŋ, -brɪŋ

sombrero sam'brɛro, -'brɪro, -'brero |-ed -d

some stressed 'sʌm, ‚sʌm; unstr. səm, sm̩, before more sə (sə'mor 'tɪ)

-some unstressed adj ending -səm—often omitted in the vocab.

somebody 'sʌm‚badɪ, -‚bʌdɪ, 'sʌmbədɪ

somehow 'sʌm‚hau

someone 'sʌm‚wʌn, 'sʌmwən

Somers 'sʌmɚz; ES 'sʌməz; |-'s -ɪz

somersault 'sʌmɚ‚sɔlt; ES 'sʌmə-; |-ed -ɪd

somerset 'sʌmɚ‚sɛt; ES 'sʌmə-; |-ed -ɪd

Somerset 'sʌmɚ‚sɛt, -sɪt; ES 'sʌmə-; |-shire -‚sɛt‚ʃɪr, -sɪt‚ʃɪr, -sɪtʃɚ; ES -‚ʃɪə(r, -ʃə(r

Somerville, -vile 'sʌmɚ‚vɪl; ES 'sʌmə-

something 'sʌmpθɪŋ, 'sʌmθɪŋ

sometime 'sʌm‚taɪm

sometimes 'sʌm‚taɪmz, sʌm'taɪmz, səm-'taɪmz

someway 'sʌm‚we

somewhat 'sʌm‚hwat, -‚hwɒt, 'sʌmhwət

Key: See in full §§3–47. bee bi |pity 'pɪtɪ (§6) |rate ret |yet jɛt |sang sæŋ |angry 'æŋ·grɪ |bath bæθ; E bɑθ (§10) |ah ɑ |far fɑr |watch watʃ, wɒtʃ (§12) |jaw dʒɔ |gorge gɔrdʒ |go go

Those words below in which the a sound is spelt o are often pronounced with ɒ in E and S

somewhere ˈsʌmˌhwɛr, -ˌhwær; E -ˌhwɛə(r, ES -ˌhwæə(r

somewhither ˈsʌmˌhwɪðɚ; ES -ˌhwɪðə(r

Somme sʌm, sɔm (Fr sɔ̃m)

somnambulate samˈnæmbjəˌlet |-d -ɪd

somnambulation ˌsamnæmbjəˈleʃən, sam-ˌnæmbjə-

somnambulism samˈnæmbjəˌlɪzəm |-list -lɪst

somniferous samˈnɪfərəs

somnolence ˈsamnələns |-cy -ɪ |-lent -lənt

Somnus, s- ˈsamnəs |-ʼs -ɪz

son sʌn |sonny ˈsʌnɪ

sonance ˈsonəns |-cy -ɪ |-nant -nənt

sonantal soˈnæntl̩ |-tic -tɪk

sonata səˈnatə

sonatina ˌsanəˈtinə, ˌsonə- (It ˌsonaˈtiːna)

song sɔŋ, sɒŋ; S+saŋ; |-bird -ˌbɝd; ES -ˌbɜd, -ˌbɝd

song-and-dance ˈsɔŋənˈdæns, ˈsɒŋ-; E+ -ˈdans, -ˈdɑns; S ˈsɔŋənˈdæns, ˈsɒŋ-, ˈsaŋ-

songster ˈsɔŋstɚ, ˈsɔŋkstɚ, ˈsɒŋ-; ES -stə(r, S+ˈsaŋ-

songstress ˈsɔŋstrɪs, ˈsɒŋ-; S+ˈsaŋ-; |-es -ɪz

son-in-law ˈsʌnɪnˌlɔ |sons-in-law ˈsʌnzɪnˌlɔ, ˈsʌnzn̩ˌlɔ

sonnet ˈsanɪt |-ed -ɪd

sonneteer ˌsanəˈtɪr; ES -ˈtɪə(r, S+-ˈtɛə(r

sonometer soˈnamətɚ; ES -ˈnamətə(r

Sonora soˈnorə, -ˈnɔrə; S -ˈnorə

sonorant səˈnorənt, -ˈnɔr-; S -ˈnor-

sonority səˈnorətɪ, -ˈnɑr-, -ˈnɒr-

sonorous səˈnorəs, -ˈnɔr-; S -ˈnor-

Soo su

Soochow ˈsuˈtʃau

soon sun, sʊn

Sooner, s- ˈsunɚ, ˈsʊn-; ES -nə(r

soot sʊt, sut, *less freq.* sʌt—sʌt *is better preserved in the S.*

sooth suθ |-ly -lɪ

soothe suð |soothed suðd

soothsay ˈsuθˌse |-er -ɚ; ES -ə(r

sooty ˈsutɪ, ˈsʊtɪ, *less freq.* ˈsʌtɪ

sop sap |sopped sapt

Sophia *saint* soˈfaɪə, sə-; *Am name* səˈfaɪə, ˈsofɪə; *cf* Sophy

sophism ˈsafɪzəm |-ist -ɪst |-ister -ɪstɚ; ES -tə(r

sophistic səˈfɪstɪk |-al -l̩ |-ally -l̩ɪ, -ɪklɪ

sophisticate səˈfɪstɪˌket |-d -ɪd

sophistication səˌfɪstɪˈkeʃən

sophistry ˈsafɪstrɪ

Sophocles ˈsafəˌkliz |-ʼs -ɪz |-clean ˌsafəˈkliən

sophomore ˈsafm̩ˌor, -ˌɔr; ES -ˌoə(r, E+-ˌɔə(r

sophomoric ˌsafəˈmorɪk, -ˈmɔr-, -ˈmɒr-

Sophronia soˈfronɪə, sə-

Sophy ˈsofɪ

soporiferous ˌsopəˈrɪfərəs, ˌsapə-

soporific ˌsopəˈrɪfɪk, ˌsapə- |-al -l̩ |-ally -l̩ɪ, -ɪklɪ

sopping ˈsapɪŋ

soprano səˈpræno, -ˈprano

Sorbonne sɔrˈban, -ˈbʌn (Fr sɔrˈbɔ̃n)

sorcerer ˈsɔrsərɚ; ES ˈsɔəsərə(r; |-cery -sərɪ

sorceress ˈsɔrsərɪs; ES ˈsɔəsə-; |-es -ɪz

Sordello sɔrˈdɛlo; ES sɔə-

sordid ˈsɔrdɪd; ES ˈsɔədɪd

sore sor, sɔr; ES soə(r, E+sɔə(r; |-head -ˌhɛd

soreheaded ˈsorˈhɛdɪd, ˈsɔr-; ES ˈsoə-, E+ˈsɔə-

sorghum ˈsɔrgəm; ES ˈsɔəgəm

sorority səˈrɔrətɪ, -ˈrar-, -ˈrɒr-

sorosis, S- səˈrosɪs

sorption ˈsɔrpʃən; ES ˈsɔəp-

sorrel, S- ˈsɔrəl, ˈsar-, ˈsɒr-

sorrento, S- səˈrɛnto

sorrow ˈsaro, ˈsɒro, ˈsɔro, -ə |-ed -d |-ing -rəwɪŋ

sorry ˈsɔrɪ, ˈsarɪ, ˈsɒrɪ

sort sɔrt; ES sɔət; |-ed -ɪd

sortie ˈsɔrti, -tɪ; ES ˈsɔə-; |-d -d

sortilege ˈsɔrtl̩ɪdʒ; ES ˈsɔət-

S O S *n* ˈɛsˌoˈɛs |*pl* -ʼs -ɪz

S O S *v* ˈɛsˌoˈɛs |-ʼes -ɪz |-ʼed -t

soso ˈsoˌso

sot sat |sotted ˈsatɪd |sottish ˈsatɪʃ

Sothern ˈsʌðɚn; ES ˈsʌðən

sotto voce ˈsatoˈvotʃɪ (It ˈsottoˈvoːtʃe)

sou su

soubrette suˈbrɛt |-tish -ɪʃ

soubriquet ˈsubrɪˌke

souchong, S- suˈʃɔŋ, -ˈtʃɔŋ, -ɒŋ (ˈsouˌchong ˈtea)

Soudan suˈdæn |-ese ˌsudəˈniz

soufflé suˈfle, ˈsufle |-ed -d

souffle ˈsufl̩

sough sʌf, saʊ |soughed sʌft, saʊd

sought sɔt

soul sol |souled sold |-less |'sollıs

sound saʊnd |-ed -ıd |-ness -nıs, 'saʊnnıs

soundboard 'saʊnd‚bord, 'saʊn-, -‚bɔrd; ES
-‚bɔəd, E+-‚bɔəd

sound-box 'saʊnd‚bɑks, 'saʊn-; ES+-‚bɒks;
|-es -ız

sound-wave 'saʊnd‚wev

soup sup |souped supt

soup-and-fish 'supən'fıʃ, 'supm̩'fıʃ

soupçon Fr sup'sõ

sour saʊr; ES saʊə(r; |-ed -d

source sors, sɔrs; ES soəs, E+sɔəs; |-s -ız

sourdough 'saʊr‚do; ES 'saʊə‚do

Souris 'sʊrıs |-'s -ız

Sousa 'suzə, 'susə

souse saʊs |souses 'saʊsız |soused saʊst

soutane su'tɑn

souter, -ar 'sutɚ; ES 'sutə(r

south, S- n, adj, adv saʊθ

south v saʊð, saʊθ |-ed -ðd, -θt

Southampton saʊθ'hæmptən, saʊ'θæmptən

Southbridge 'saʊθbrıdʒ |-'s -ız

South Carolina ‚saʊθkærə'laınə, -kɚ'laınə;
ES ‚saʊθkærə'laınə, -kə'laınə; loc.+‚sæʊθ-
kærə'la:nə, -kæə'la:nə, -kərə'la:nə

South Dakota ‚saʊθdə'kotə, -dı'kotə

Southdown 'saʊθ‚daʊn |S- Downs 'saʊθ-
'daʊnz

southeast, S- ‚saʊθ'ist ('south‚east 'wind)

southeaster ‚saʊθ'istɚ; ES -'istə(r; |-n -n

southeastward ‚saʊθ'istwɚd; ES -wəd; |-s -z

southerly 'sʌðɚlı; ES 'sʌðə-

southermost 'sʌðɚ‚most; ES 'sʌðə-

southern, Southerne 'sʌðɚn; ES 'sʌðən;
|-most -‚most, -məst

southerner 'sʌðɚnɚ, 'sʌðənɚ; ES 'sʌðənə(r;
—In 'sʌðənɚ ə has been changed from ɚ
by dissimilation (§121); this is less freq. in
easterner & westerner.

Southey 'saʊðı, 'sʌðı

Southgate 'saʊθ‚get, -gıt

southing 'saʊðıŋ

Southington 'sʌðıŋtən

southland 'saʊθlənd, -‚lænd

southpaw 'saʊθ‚pɔ

Southport 'saʊθ‚port, -‚pɔrt; ES -‚poət,
E+-‚pɔət

southron 'sʌðrən, 'sʌðərən

southward 'saʊθwɚd; ES -wəd; |-s -z

Southwark 'sʌðɚk, 'saʊθwɚk; ES -ək

Southwell 'saʊθ‚wɛl, -wəl; Notts 'sʌðəl

southwest ‚saʊθ'wɛst |-er -ɚ; ES -ə(r; |-n -n
—naut.+‚sau'w- ('south‚west 'wind)

Southwick 'saʊθwık, 'sʌðık

Southworth 'saʊθwɚθ; ES 'saʊθwəθ

souvenir ‚suvə'nır, 'suvə‚nır; ES -ıə(r

Souza 'sozə, 'suzə

sovereign 'sʌvrın, 'sʌv-, 'sɒv-, -rən |-ty -tı

soviet, S- 'sovııt, -ət, -vı‚ɛt, ‚sovı'ɛt

sovietism 'sovıə‚tızəm |-tize -‚taız

sovran 'sʌvrən, 'sɒv-, 'sʌv-

sow 'hog' saʊ

sow 'seed' so |sowed sod |sown son or sowed
sod

Sowerby Lancs, Yks, Cumb 'saʊɚbı; ES
'saʊ·əbı

soy sɔı |soybean 'sɔı'bin, -‚bin

sozin 'sozın

spa spɑ |Spa spɑ, spɔ

space spes |spaces 'spesız |spaced spest

spacious 'speʃəs

spade sped |spaded 'spedıd |-ful -‚fʊl

spadix 'spedıks |-es -ız |-dices spı'daısiz

Spaeth, Sigmund 'sıgmənd speθ

spaghetti spə'gɛtı

spahi, -hee 'spɑhi

Spain spen

spake spek

Spalding 'spɔldıŋ

spall spɔl |spalled spɔld

spalpeen 'spælpin, spæl'pin

span spæn |spanned spænd

spandrell 'spændrəl

spangle 'spæŋgl̩ |-d -d |-ling 'spæŋglıŋ, -gl̩ıŋ

Spangler 'spæŋglɚ; ES 'spæŋglə(r

Spaniard 'spænjɚd; ES 'spænjəd

spaniel 'spænjəl |-ed -d

Spanish 'spænıʃ

spank spæŋk |spanked spæŋkt

spanner 'spænɚ; ES 'spænə(r

span-new 'spæn'nju, -'nıu, -'nu ('span-‚new
'hat)

spar spɑr; ES spɑ:(r, E+spa:(r; |-red -d

spare spɛr, spær; E spɛə(r, ES spæə(r; |-d -d

sparerib 'spɛr‚rıb, 'spær-; E 'spɛə‚rıb, ES
'spæə-

Key: See in full §§3–47. bee bi |pity 'pıtı (§6) |rate ret |yet jɛt |sang sæŋ |angry 'æŋ·grı
|bath bæθ; E bɑθ (§10) |ah ɑ |far fɑr |watch wɑtʃ, wɒtʃ (§12) |jaw dʒɔ |gorge gɔrdʒ |go go

Spargo 'spɑrgo; ES 'spɑːgo, E+'spɑːgo

spark spɑrk; ES spɑːk, E+spɑːk; |-ed -t

sparkle 'spɑrkļ; ES 'spɑːkļ, E+'spɑːkļ; |-d -d
|-ling -klɪŋ, -kļɪŋ |-r -klɚ; ES -klə(r

sparrow 'spæro, -ə |-ish 'spærəwɪʃ |-y -rəwɪ

sparse spɑrs; ES spɑːs, E+spɑːs; |-sity -ətɪ

Sparta 'spɑrtə; ES 'spɑːtə, E+'spɑːtə; |-n -tn̩

Spartacus 'spɑrtəkəs; ES 'spɑːt-, E+'spɑːt-;
|-'s -ɪz

Spartanburg 'spɑrtn̩ˌbɝg; ES 'spɑːtn̩ˌbɜg,
'spɑːtn̩ˌbɝg, E+'spɑːtn̩-

spasm 'spæzəm

spasmodic spæz'mɑdɪk; ES+-'mɒd-; |-al -ļ
|-ally -ļɪ, -ɪklɪ

spastic 'spæstɪk |-ally -ļɪ, -ɪklɪ

spat *past of* spit spæt

spat spæt |spatted 'spætɪd

spatchcock 'spætʃˌkɑk; ES+-ˌkɒk; |-ed -t

spate spet |spated 'spetɪd

spathe speð |spathed speðd

spathic 'spæθɪk

spatial 'speʃəl |-ly -ɪ

spatialize 'speʃəlˌaɪz |-s -ɪz |-d -d

spatter 'spætɚ; ES 'spætə(r; |-ed -d

spatula 'spætʃələ

spatulate *adj* 'spætʃəlɪt, -ˌlet

spatulate *v* 'spætʃəˌlet |-d -ɪd

Spaulding 'spɔldɪŋ

spavin 'spævɪn |-ed -d

spawn spɔn |spawned spɔnd

spay spe |spayed sped

speak spik |spoke spok *or arch.* spake spek
|spoken 'spokən *or arch.* spoke spok

spear spɪr; ES spɪə(r, S+speə(r, spjɛə(r; |-ed
-d |-head -ˌhed |-man -mən |-men -mən
|-mint -ˌmɪnt

special 'speʃəl |-ly -ɪ |-ism -ˌɪzəm |-ist -ɪst

speciality ˌspeʃɪ'ælətɪ

specialize 'speʃəlˌaɪz |-s -ɪz |-d -d

specialty 'speʃəltɪ

specie 'spiʃɪ

species 'spiʃɪz, -ʃiz, *L pl* 'spiʃɪˌiz

specifiable 'spesəˌfaɪəbļ

specific spɪ'sɪfɪk |-al -ļ |-ally -ļɪ |-ly -lɪ

specification ˌspesəfə'keʃən

specify 'spesəˌfaɪ |-fied -ˌfaɪd

specimen 'spesəmən

speciosity ˌspiʃɪ'ɑsətɪ; ES+-'ɒs·

specious 'spiʃəs

speck spɛk |specked spɛkt

speckle 'spɛkļ |-d -d |-ling 'spɛklɪŋ, -kļɪŋ

spectacle 'spɛktəkļ, -tɪkļ, -ˌtɪkļ |-d -d

spectacular spɛk'tækjəlɚ; ES -'tækjələ(r

spectator 'spɛktetɚ, spɛk'tetɚ; ES -tə(r

specter, -tre 'spɛktɚ; ES -tə(r; |-(e)d -d

spectra 'spɛktrə

spectral 'spɛktrəl |-ly -ɪ

spectrochemistry ˌspɛktro'kɛmɪstrɪ

spectrometer spɛk'trɑmətɚ; ES -'trɑmətə(r,
-'trɒm-

spectrophotometer ˌspɛktrofo'tɑmətɚ; ES
-'tɑmətə(r, -'tɒm-

spectroscope 'spɛktrəˌskop

spectroscopic ˌspɛktrə'skɑpɪk; ES+-'skɒp-;
|-al -ļ |-ally -ļɪ, -ɪklɪ

spectroscopy spɛk'trɑskəpɪ, 'spɛktrəˌskopɪ;
ES+-'trɒs-; |-pist -pɪst

spectrum 'spɛktrəm |-s -z |-tra -trə

specular 'spɛkjələ; ES 'spɛkjələ(r

speculate 'spɛkjəˌlet |-d -ɪd |-tive -ɪv

speculation ˌspɛkjə'leʃən

speculum 'spɛkjələm |-s -z |-la -lə

sped spɛd

speech spitʃ |speeches 'spitʃɪz |-ed -t

speechify 'spitʃəˌfaɪ |-fied -ˌfaɪd

speed, S- spid |speeded 'spidɪd *or* sped spɛd

speedboat 'spidˌbot

speedily 'spidļɪ, -ɪlɪ

speedometer spi'dɑmətɚ; ES -'dɑmətə(r,
-'dɒm-

speed-up *n* 'spidˌʌp

speed up *v* 'spid'ʌp |speeded up 'spidɪd'ʌp

speer spɪr; ES spɪə(r, S+speə(r; |-ed -d

Speght, Speight spet

Speiser 'spaɪzɚ; ES 'spaɪzə(r

spell spɛl |spelled spɛld *or* spelt spɛlt

spellbind 'spɛlˌbaɪnd |-bound -ˌbaʊnd

spelling-bound 'spɛlɪŋˌbaʊnd

spelt spɛlt

spelter 'spɛltɚ; ES 'spɛltə(r; |-ed -d

spence, S- spɛns |Spence's 'spɛnsɪz

spencer, S- 'spɛnsɚ; ES 'spɛnsə(r

Spencerian spɛn'sɪrɪən

spend spɛnd |spent spɛnt

spendthrift 'spɛndˌθrɪft, 'spɛnˌθrɪft

Spens spɛns |-'s -ɪz

Spenser 'spɛnsɚ; ES 'spɛnsə(r

Spenserian spɛn'sɪrɪən

spent spɛnt

sperm spɝm; ES spɝm, spɜ˞m

spermaceti ˌspɝmə'sɛtɪ, -'sitɪ; ES ˌspɜm-, ˌspɝm-

spermatic spɝ'mætɪk; ES spɝ-, spɜ˞-; |-al -|| |-ally -|ɪ, -ɪklɪ

spermatophyte 'spɝmətə,faɪt; ES 'spɜm-, 'spɝm-

spermatozoon ˌspɝmətə'zoən, -ɒn, -ən; ES ˌspɜm-, ˌspɝm-; |-zoa -'zoə

spew spju, spɪu |-ed -d

Spey spe

sphagnum, S- 'sfægnəm

spheral 'sfɪrəḷ; S+'sfɛrəl

sphere sfɪr; ES sfɪə(r, S+sfɛə(r; |-d -d

spheric 'sfɛrɪk |-al -| |-ally -|ɪ, -ɪklɪ

sphericity sfɪ'rɪsətɪ

sphericle 'sfɛrɪk|

spheroid 'sfɪrɔɪd; S+'sfɛr-

spheroidal sfɪ'rɔɪd|; S+sfɛ-; |-ly -ɪ

sphery 'sfɪrɪ; S+'sfɛrɪ

sphincter 'sfɪŋktɚ; ES 'sfɪŋktə(r; |-al -əl

sphinx sfɪŋks |-es 'sfɪŋksɪz |-nges 'sfɪndʒiz

sphragistic sfrə'dʒɪstɪk |-s -s

sphygmograph 'sfɪgmə,græf; E+-,graf, -,graf

spica, S- 'spaɪkə |-cal -k|

spicate 'spaɪket |-d -ɪd

spice spaɪs |-s 'spaɪsɪz |-d -t |-ry -ərɪ, -rɪ

spicily 'spaɪs|ɪ, -ɪlɪ

spick spɪk |spicked spɪkt

spick-and-span 'spɪkən'spæn, 'spɪkŋ'spæn

spicket 'spɪkɪt

spiculate 'spɪkjə,let |-lated -,letɪd

spicule 'spɪkjul

spicy 'spaɪsɪ

spider 'spaɪdɚ; ES 'spaɪdə(r; |-ed -d

spied from spy spaɪd

spiel spil |spieled spild (Ger ʃpi:l)

spier 'speer,' 'screen' spɪr; ES spɪə(r, S+ spɛə(r; |-ed -d

spier 'who spies' 'spaɪɚ; ES 'spaɪ·ə(r

spies spaɪz

spiffy 'spɪfɪ

spigot 'spɪgət |-ed -ɪd

spike spaɪk |spiked spaɪkt

spikenard 'spaɪknɚd, -nɑrd; ES -nəd, -nɑːd, E+-naːd

spile spaɪl |spiled spaɪld

spill spɪl |spilled spɪld or spilt spɪlt

spillway 'spɪl,we

spilt spɪlt

spin spɪn |spun spʌn or arch. span spæn |spun spʌn

spinach 'spɪnɪtʃ, -ɪdʒ |-es -ɪz—'spɪnɪtʃ clearly prevails in US, though 'spɪnɪdʒ is also traditional here. Both go back to OF.

spinal 'spaɪn| |-ly -ɪ

spindle 'spɪnd| |-d -d |-ling -dlɪŋ, -d|ɪŋ

spindle-legged 'spɪnd|,lɛgɪd, -,lɛgd

spindlelegs 'spɪnd|,lɛgz

spindling adj 'spɪndlɪŋ |spindly 'spɪndlɪ

spindrift 'spɪn,drɪft

spine spaɪn |spined spaɪnd

spinet 'spɪnɪt

Spingarn 'spɪŋgɑrn; ES -gɑːn, E+-gɑːn

Spink, s- spɪŋk

spinnaker 'spɪnəkɚ, 'spɪnɪ-; ES -kə(r

spinney 'spɪnɪ

spinose 'spaɪnos |spinous 'spaɪnəs

Spinoza spɪ'nozə

spinster 'spɪnstɚ; ES -stə(r; |-hood -,hʊd

spinstress 'spɪnstrɪs |-es -ɪz

spinule 'spaɪnjul, 'spɪn-

spiny 'spaɪnɪ

spiraea, S- spaɪ'riə

spiral 'spaɪrəl |-ed -d |-ly -ɪ

spire spaɪr; ES spaɪə(r; |-d -d |-ry -ɪ

spirea, S- spaɪ'riə

spirit 'spɪrɪt |-ed -ɪd |-ous -əs

spiritual 'spɪrɪtʃʊəl, -tʃʊl, -tʃəl |-ly -ɪ |-ism -,ɪzəm |-ist -ɪst

spirituality ˌspɪrɪtʃʊ'ælətɪ

spiritualize 'spɪrɪtʃʊəl,aɪz, -tʃʊl-, -tʃəl- |-s -ɪz |-d -d

spirituel, -elle ˌspɪrɪtʃʊ'ɛl (Fr spiri'tɥɛl)

spirituous 'spɪrɪtʃʊəs

spirochete, -chaete 'spaɪrə,kit

spirogyra, S- ˌspaɪrə'dʒaɪrə

spirometer spaɪ'rɑmətɚ; ES -'rɑmətə(r, -'rɒm-

spirt spɝt; ES spɜt, spɝt; |-ed -ɪd

spit 'saliva' spɪt |spit spɪt or spat spæt

spit 'stick' spɪt |spitted 'spɪtɪd

spital 'spɪt| |Spitalfields 'spɪt|,fildz

spit and image, spit an' image 'spɪtṇ'ɪmɪdʒ (sometimes misapprehended as spittin' image 'spɪtṇ'ɪmɪdʒ)

spitchcock 'spɪtʃ,kɑk; ES+-,kɒk; |-ed -t

spite spaɪt |spited ˈspaɪtɪd |-ful -fəl |-fully
  -fəlɪ
spitfire ˈspɪtˌfaɪr; ES -ˌfaɪə(r; |-d -d
spitful ˈspɪtˌfʊl |-s -z
Spithead ˈspɪtˈhɛd (ˈSpitˌhead ˈroute)
Spitsbergen ˈspɪtsbɝgən; ES -bɝg-, -bɝg-
spittle ˈspɪtl̩
spittoon spɪˈtun
spitz spɪts |spitzes ˈspɪtsɪz
Spitzbergen ˈspɪtsbɝgən; ES -bɝg-, -bɝg-
Spitzenburg, -berg ˈspɪtsn̩ˌbɝg; ES -ˌbɝg,
  -ˌbɝg
splash splæʃ |splashes ˈsplæʃɪz |-ed -t
splatter ˈsplætɚ; ES ˈsplætə(r; |-ed -d
splay sple |splayed spled |-foot -ˌfʊt
spleen splin |spleened splind
splendent ˈsplɛndənt
splendid ˈsplɛndɪd |-diferous splɛnˈdɪfərəs,
  -frəs
splendor ˈsplɛndɚ; ES ˈsplɛndə(r; |-ed -d
splenetic splɪˈnɛtɪk |-al -l̩ |-ally -l̩ɪ, -ɪklɪ
splenetive ˈsplɛnətɪv
splenic ˈsplɛnɪk, ˈsplin- |-al -l̩
splice splaɪs |splices ˈsplaɪsɪz |-d -t
splint splɪnt |splinted ˈsplɪntɪd
splint-bottom ˈsplɪntˌbatəm; ES+-ˌbɒt-;
  |-ed -d
splinter ˈsplɪntɚ; ES -tə(r; |-ed -d |-ing
  ˈsplɪntərɪŋ, -trɪŋ |-y -ɪ, -trɪ
split splɪt |split splɪt or splitted ˈsplɪtɪd
splotch splatʃ; ES+splɒtʃ; |-es -ɪz |-ed -t
splurdge splɝdʒ; ES splɝdʒ, splɝdʒ; |-s -ɪz
  |-d -d
splutter ˈsplʌtɚ; ES ˈsplʌtə(r; |-ed -d
Spofford ˈspafɚd; ES ˈspafəd, ˈspɒf-
spoil spɔɪl |spoiled spɔɪld or spoilt spɔɪlt
spoilsman ˈspɔɪlzmən |-men -mən
Spokane spoˈkæn
spoke from speak spok
spoke of a wheel spok |spoked spokt
spokeshave ˈspokˌʃev
spokesman ˈspoksmən |-men -mən
spoliate ˈspolɪˌet |-d -ɪd |-tion ˌspolɪˈeʃən
spondaic spanˈde·ɪk; ES+spɒn-; |-al -l̩
spondee ˈspandi; ES+ˈspɒn-
sponge spʌndʒ |-s -ɪz |-d -d |-gy -ɪ
sponsion ˈspanʃən; ES+ˈspɒn-
sponson ˈspansn̩; ES+ˈspɒn-
sponsor ˈspansɚ; ES ˈspansə(r, ˈspɒn-; |-ed -d

spontaneity ˌspantəˈniətɪ; ES+ˌspɒn-
spontaneous spanˈteniəs; ES+spɒn-
spontoon spanˈtun; ES+spɒn-
spoof spuf |spoofed spuft
spook spuk, spʊk |-ed -t
spool spul |spooled spuld
spoon spun, spʊn |-ed -d—spʊn is freq. in
  compounds like teaspoon.
spoondrift ˈspunˌdrɪft
Spooner ˈspunɚ; ES ˈspunə(r
spoonerism ˈspunəˌrɪzəm
spoon-fed ˈspunˌfɛd, ˈspʊn-
spoonful ˈspunˌfʊl, ˈspʊn- |-fuls -ˌfʊlz
spoor spʊr, spor, spɔr; ES spʊə(r, spoə(r, E+
  spɔə(r; |-ed -d
sporadic spoˈrædɪk, spɔ-; S spo-; |-al -l̩ |-ally
  -l̩ɪ, -ɪklɪ
spore spor, spɔr; ES spoə(r, E+spɔə(r; |-d
  -d
sport sport, spɔrt; ES spoət, E+spɔət; |-ed
  -ɪd |-sman -smən |-smen -smən
spot spat; ES+spɒt; |-ted -ɪd |-light -ˌlaɪt
Spotswood ˈspatsˌwʊd; ES+ˈspɒts-
Spotsylvania ˌspatsl̩ˈvenjə, -sɪl-; ES+ˌspɒt-
Spottiswood, -e ˈspatɪsˌwʊd, ˈspats-; ES+
  ˈspɒt-
Spottswood ˈspatsˌwʊd; ES+ˈspɒts-
spousal ˈspaʊzl̩ |-ly -ɪ
spouse spaʊz, spaʊs |-s -ɪz |-d -d, -t
spout spaʊt |spouted ˈspaʊtɪd
Sprague spreg, sprɛg
sprain spren |sprained sprend
sprang spræŋ
sprat, S- spræt |spratted ˈsprætɪd
sprawl sprɔl |sprawled sprɔld
spray spre |sprayed spred
spread sprɛd
spread-eagle ˈsprɛdˌigl̩ |-d -d |-ling -ˌiglɪŋ,
  -ˌiglɪŋ
spree spri |spreed sprid
sprier ˈspraɪɚ; ES ˈspraɪ·ə(r; |-est -ɪst
sprig sprɪg |sprigged sprɪgd
sprightly ˈspraɪtlɪ
spring sprɪŋ |sprang spræŋ or sprung sprʌŋ
  |sprung sprʌŋ
springboard ˈsprɪŋˌbord, -ˌbɔrd; ES -ˌboəd,
  E+-ˌbɔəd
springbok ˈsprɪŋˌbak; ES+-ˌbɒk
springe sprɪndʒ |-s -ɪz |-d -d

springer, S- 'sprɪŋə; ES 'sprɪŋə(r
Springfield 'sprɪŋ,fild
springhalt 'sprɪŋ'hɔlt, -,hɔlt
springtime 'sprɪŋ,taɪm |-tide -,taɪd
springy 'sprɪŋɪ
sprinkle 'sprɪŋkl̩ |-d -d |-ling -klɪŋ, -kl̩ɪŋ
sprinkling n, adj 'sprɪŋklɪŋ
sprint sprɪnt |sprinted 'sprɪntɪd
sprit sprɪt
sprite spraɪt
sprocket 'sprakɪt; ES+'sprɒk-
Sproul spraʊl
sprout spraʊt |sprouted 'spraʊtɪd
spruce, S- sprus, sprɪus |-s -ɪz |-d -t
sprung sprʌŋ
spry spraɪ
spud spʌd |spudded 'spʌdɪd
spue spju, sprɪu |-d -d
spume spjum, sprɪum |-d -d
spun spʌn
spunk spʌŋk |-ie, y -ɪ |-ed -t
spur spɝ; ES spɜ(r, spɝ; |-red -d
spurge spɝdʒ; ES spɜdʒ, spɝdʒ; |-s -ɪz |-d -d
Spurgeon 'spɝdʒən; ES 'spɜdʒ-, 'spɝdʒ-
spurious 'spjʊrɪəs, 'spɪʊrɪəs
spurn spɝn; ES spɜn, spɝn; |-ed -d
spurt spɝt; ES spɜt, spɝt; |-ed -ɪd
sputter 'spʌtɚ; ES 'spʌtə(r; |-ed -d
sputum 'spjutəm, 'sprɪutəm |-ta -tə
Spuyten Duyvil 'spaɪtn̩'daɪvl̩
spy spaɪ |spied spaɪd |-er -ɚ; ES -ə(r
spyglass 'spaɪ,glæs; E+-,glas, -,glɑs; |-es -ɪz
squab skwab, skwɒb |-bed -d
squabble 'skwabl̩, 'skwɒbl̩ |-d -d |-ling -blɪŋ, -bl̩ɪŋ
squad skwad, skwɒd |-ded -ɪd
squadron 'skwadrən, 'skwɒd- |-ed -d
squalid 'skwalɪd, 'skwɒl-
squall skwɔl |squalled skwɔld |-y -ɪ
squalor 'skwalɚ, 'skwɒlɚ, less freq. 'skwelɚ; ES -lə(r
Squam, s- skwam, skwɒm
squama 'skwemə |-mae -mi |-mate -met |-mose -mos |-mous -məs
squander 'skwandɚ, 'skwɒn-; ES -də(r; |-ed -d |-ing -drɪŋ, -dərɪŋ
Squantum, s- 'skwantəm, 'skwɒn-
square, S- skwɛr, skwær; E skwɛə(r, ES skwæə(r; |-d -d |-head -,hɛd

square-rigged 'skwɛr'rɪgd, 'skwær-; E 'skwɛə-, ES 'skwæə-
squash skwaʃ, skwɒʃ |-es -ɪz |-ed -t
squat skwat, skwɒt |-ted -ɪd
squaw skwɔ
squawk skwɔk |squawked skwɔkt
squeak skwik |squeaked skwikt
squeal skwil |squealed skwild
squeamish 'skwimɪʃ
squeegee 'skwidʒi, skwi'dʒi |-d -d
Squeers skwɪrz; ES skwɪəz; |-'s -ɪz
squeeze skwiz |squeezes 'skwizɪz |-d -d
squelch skwɛltʃ |squelches 'skwɛltʃɪz |-ed -t
squib skwɪb |squibbed skwɪbd
squid skwɪd |squidded 'skwɪdɪd
squill skwɪl
squint skwɪnt |squinted 'skwɪntɪd
squint-eyed 'skwɪnt'aɪd ('squint-,eyed 'boy)
squire, S- skwaɪr; ES skwaɪə(r; |-d -d
squirearchy 'skwaɪ,rɑrkɪ; ES -,rɑ:kɪ, E+ -,rɑ:kɪ
Squires skwaɪrz; ES skwaɪəz; |-'s -ɪz
squirm skwɝm; ES skwɜm, skwɝm; |-ed -d
squirrel 'skwɝəl, skwɝl, less freq. 'skwɪrəl, 'skwʌrəl; ES 'skwɜrəl, 'skwʌrəl, 'skwɝəl, skwɜl, skwɝl, 'skwɛrəl, less freq. 'skwɪrəl
squirt skwɝt; ES skwɜt, skwɝt; |-ed -d
St. 'Saint' stressed 'sent, ,sent; unstr. sent, sənt, sɪnt—sənt & sɪnt are rarer in Amer than in Engd, where sṇt & sṇ are also common. Words beginning with St.=Saint are listed alphabetically with Saint words.
stab stæb |stabbed stæbd
Stabat Mater 'stabat'matɚ, Eng L 'stebæt-'metɚ; ES -tə(r
stability stə'bɪlətɪ, ste-
stabilization ,steblə'zeʃən, -aɪ'z-
stabilize 'stebl̩,aɪz |-s -ɪz |-d -d
stable 'stebl̩ |-d -d |-ling 'steblɪŋ, -bl̩ɪŋ
stableman 'stebl̩,mæn, -mən |-men -,mɛn, -mən
stablish 'stæblɪʃ |-es -ɪz |-ed -t
staccato stə'kato (It stak'kɑ:to)
stack stæk |stacked stækt
stacte 'stæktɪ
Stacy, -cey 'stesɪ
staddle 'stædl̩ |-d -d |-ling 'stædlɪŋ, -dl̩ɪŋ
stadholder 'stæd,holdɚ; ES -,holdə(r; |stadt- 'stæt-

Words below in which a *before* r (farm) *is sounded* ɑ *are often pronounced in* E *with* a (fɑ:m)

stadia 'stedɪə |-s -z
stadium 'stedɪəm |-s -z |-dia -dɪə
Staël stɑl, 'stɑɛl (*Fr* stal)
staff stæf; E+staf, stɑf; |-'s -s |-s -s |-ed -t
|staves stevz, stævz; E+stavz, stɑvz
Stafford 'stæfəd; ES 'stæfəd; |-shire -ˌʃɪr,
-ʃə; ES -ˌʃɪə(r, -ʃə(r
Staffs *short for* Staffordshire stæfs
staffs *one pl of* staff stæfs; E+stafs, stɑfs
stag stæg |stagged stægd
stage stedʒ |stages 'stedʒɪz |staged stedʒd
stagecoach 'stedʒˌkotʃ |-es -ɪz
stagecraft 'stedʒˌkræft; E+-ˌkraft, -ˌkrɑft
stager 'stedʒə; ES 'stedʒə(r
stagey 'stedʒɪ
stagger 'stægə; ES 'stægə(r; |-ed -d |-ing
'stægərɪŋ, 'stægrɪŋ
staghound 'stægˌhaʊnd
staging 'stedʒɪŋ
Stagira stə'dʒaɪrə |-rite 'stædʒəˌraɪt
stagnant 'stægnənt |-nancy -nənsɪ
stagnate 'stægnet |-d -ɪd |-tion stæg'neʃən
stagy 'stedʒɪ
Stahl *Am surname* stɔl (*Ger* ʃtɑ:l)
Stahr *Am surname* stɛr, stær; E stɛə(r, ES
stæə(r
staid sted
stain sten |stained stend
stair stɛr, stær; E stɛə(r, ES stæə(r; |-ed -d
|-case -ˌkes |-way -ˌwe
stake stek |staked stekt
stakeholder 'stekˌholdə; ES -ˌholdə(r
stalactite stə'læktaɪt |-lagmite -'lægmaɪt
stale stel |staled steld
stalemate 'stelˌmet |-d -ɪd
Stalin 'stɑlɪn, 'stalin |-grad -ˌgræd, -ˌgrad
Stalinsk stɑ'lɪnsk
stalk stɔk |stalked stɔkt |-y -ɪ
Stalky 'stɔkɪ, 'stɔlkɪ
stall stɔl |stalled stɔld
stallion 'stæljən
stalwart 'stɔlwət; ES 'stɔlwət
Stambaugh 'stæmbɔ
Stambul, -boul stɑm'bul, stæm-
stamen 'stemən |stamened 'stemənd
Stamford 'stæmfəd; ES 'stæmfəd
stamina 'stæmənə
staminate *adj* 'stæmənɪt, -ˌnet

staminate *v* 'stæməˌnet |-d -ɪd
stammer 'stæmə; ES 'stæmə(r; |-ed -d |-ing
'stæmərɪŋ, 'stæmrɪŋ
stamp stæmp |stamped stæmpt
stampede stæm'pid |-peded -'pidɪd
stance stæns |stances 'stænsɪz |-d -t
stanch '*stop*' stæntʃ, stɑntʃ |-es -ɪz |-ed -t
stanch '*firm*' stɑntʃ, *less freq.* stæntʃ
stanchion 'stænʃən, -tʃən |-ed -d
stand stænd |stood stʊd |-ard -əd; ES -əd
standardization ˌstændədə'zeʃən, -aɪ'z-; ES
ˌstændəd-
standardize 'stændədˌaɪz; ES -dəd-; |-s -ɪz
|-d -d
stand-by 'stændˌbaɪ, 'stænˌbaɪ
standee stæn'di
standfast 'stændˌfæst, 'stæn-; E+-ˌfast,
-ˌfɑst
Standish 'stændɪʃ |-'s -ɪz
standoff 'stændˌɔf, -ˌɒf
standoffish stænd'ɔfɪʃ, -'ɒfɪʃ
standpat 'stændˌpæt, 'stæn- |-ter -ə; ES -ə(r
standpipe 'stændˌpaɪp, 'stæn-
standpoint 'stændˌpɔɪnt, 'stæn-
standstill 'stændˌstɪl, 'stæn-
Stanfield 'stænˌfild |-ford -fəd; ES -fəd
Stanhope 'stænhop, 'stænəp
Stanislas 'stænɪsləs |-'s -ɪz
Stanislaus *Cal* ˌstænɪs'laʊ
stank 'stæŋk
Stanley, -ly 'stænlɪ
stannary 'stænərɪ
stannic 'stænɪk
stannum 'stænəm |-nous 'stænəs
Stanton 'stæntən
Stanwix 'stænwɪks |-'s -ɪz
stanza 'stænzə |stanzaed 'stænzəd
stapes 'stepiz
staple 'stepl̩ |-d -d |-ling 'steplɪŋ, -pl̩ɪŋ
stapler 'steplə; ES 'steplə(r
Staples 'steplz̩ |-'s -ɪz
star stɑr; ES stɑ:(r; |-red -d
starboard 'stɑrˌbord, -ˌbɔrd; ES 'stɑːˌboəd,
E+-ˌbɔəd
starch stɑrtʃ; ES stɑ:tʃ; |-es -ɪz |-ed -t
stare stɛr, stær; E stɛə(r, ES stæə(r; |-d -d
starfish 'stɑrˌfɪʃ; ES 'stɑː-; |-'s -ɪz
stargaze 'stɑrˌgez; ES 'stɑː-; |-s -ɪz |-d -d

|full fʊl |tooth tuθ |further 'fɝðə; ES 'fɝðə |custom 'kʌstəm |while hwaɪl |how haʊ |toy tɔɪ
|using 'juzɪŋ |fuse fjuz, fɪuz |dish dɪʃ |vision 'vɪʒən |Eden 'idn̩ |cradle 'kredl̩ |keep 'em 'kipm̩

Words below in which a *before* r (farm) *is sounded* ɑ *are often pronounced in* E *with* a (fɑːm)

stark stɑrk; ES stɑːk; |-ed -t

Stark, -ke stɑrk; ES stɑːk

starlet 'stɑrlɪt; ES 'stɑːlɪt

starlight 'stɑr‚laɪt; ES 'stɑː-; |-ed -ɪd

starling 'stɑrlɪŋ; ES 'stɑːlɪŋ

starlit adj 'stɑr‚lɪt; ES 'stɑː-; |-ten -‚lɪtn̩

Starr stɑr; ES stɑː(r

starry 'stɑrɪ

star-spangled 'stɑr‚spæŋg|d; ES 'stɑː-

start stɑrt; ES stɑːt; |-ed -ɪd

startle 'stɑrt|; ES 'stɑːt|; |-d -d |-ling -tlɪŋ, -t|ɪŋ

starvation stɑr'veʃən; ES stɑː-

starve stɑrv; ES stɑːv; |-d -d |-dly -ɪdlɪ

starveling 'stɑrvlɪŋ; ES 'stɑːvlɪŋ

stasis 'stesɪs |stases 'stesiz

Stassen 'stæsn̩

state stet |stated 'stetɪd |-ly -lɪ |-dly -ɪdlɪ

statecraft 'stet‚kræft; E+-‚krɑft, -‚krɑft

Statehouse 'stet‚haʊs |-ses -zɪz

Staten Island 'stætn̩ 'aɪlənd

stateroom 'stet‚rum, -‚rʊm

statesman 'stetsmən |-men -mən |-like -‚laɪk |-ly -lɪ |-ship -‚ʃɪp

state-wide 'stet'waɪd ('state-‚wide 'tour)

static 'stætɪk |-al -| |-ally -|ɪ, -ɪklɪ

station 'steʃən |-ed -d |-ing 'steʃənɪŋ, -ʃnɪŋ

stationary 'steʃən‚ɛrɪ

stationer 'steʃənɚ, 'steʃnɚ; ES -nə(r

stationery 'steʃən‚ɛrɪ

statist 'stetɪst

statistic stə'tɪstɪk |-s -s |-al -| |-ally -|ɪ, -ɪklɪ

statistician ‚stætə'stɪʃən

Statius 'steʃɪəs |-'s -ɪz

stator 'stetɚ; ES 'stetə(r

statoscope 'stætə‚skop

statuary 'stætʃʊ‚ɛrɪ

statue 'stætʃʊ |-d -d

statuesque ‚stætʃʊ'ɛsk

statuette ‚stætʃʊ'ɛt

stature 'stætʃɚ; ES 'stætʃə(r; |-d -d

status 'stetəs, 'stætəs |-es -ɪz

status quo 'stetəs'kwo, 'stætəs-

statute 'stætʃut |-d -ɪd

statutory 'stætʃʊ‚torɪ, -‚tɔrɪ; S -‚tɔrɪ

staunch stɔntʃ, stɑntʃ, stantʃ |-es -ɪz |-ed -t

Staunton Va 'stæntən; Ind, Ill, Engd 'stɔntən, 'stɑntən, 'stantən

Stavanger stə'væŋɚ, stɑ'vɑŋɚ; ES -ə(r

stave 'break' stev |staved stevd or stove stov

stave n stev

staves pl of staff, stave stevz, stævz; E+ stɑvz, stɑvz

stay ste |stayed sted or arch. staid sted

stead stɛd |steaded 'stɛdɪd

steadfast 'stɛd‚fæst, -fəst; E+-‚fast, -‚fast

steady 'stɛdɪ |steadied 'stɛdɪd

steak stek

steal stil |stole stol |stolen 'stolən or arch. stoln stoln

stealth 'stɛlθ |-y -ɪ |-ily -əlɪ, -ɪlɪ

steam stim |-ed -d |-boat -‚bot |-ship -‚ʃɪp

steam engine n 'stim'ɛndʒən

steam-engine adj 'stim‚ɛndʒən

steamer-rug 'stimɚ‚rʌg; ES 'stimə‚rʌg

steamtight 'stim'taɪt ('steam‚tight 'joint)

stearic stɪ'ærɪk, 'stɪrɪk

stearin 'stiərɪn, 'stɪrɪn

Stearn, -e stɝn; ES stɜn, stɝn; |-s -z |-s's -zɪz

stedfast 'stɛd‚fæst, -fəst; E+-‚fast, -‚fast

steed stid

steel stil |steeled stild |-less 'stillɪs

Steele stil

steelyard 'stɪljɚd, 'stil‚jɑrd; ES 'stɪljəd, 'stil‚jɑːd; |-s -z—When steelyards were in common use, the phonetically normal 'stɪljɚdz was usual; 'stil‚jɑrdz is a spelling pronunciation.

steep stip |steeped stipt

steepen 'stipən |-ed -d |-ing 'stipnɪŋ, -pənɪŋ

steeple 'stip| |-d -d |-ling -plɪŋ, -p|ɪŋ

steeplechase 'stip|‚tʃes |-s -ɪz |-d -t

steepleless 'stip|lɪs

steer stɪr; ES stɪə(r, S+steə(r; |-sman -zmən |smen -zmən

Steevens 'stivənz |-'s -ɪz

Stefansson 'stɛfənsn̩

Steffens 'stɛfənz |-'s -ɪz

Steger 'stigɚ; ES 'stigə(r

stegomya ‚stɛgə'maɪə

stein staɪn

Steinmetz 'staɪnmɛts |-'s -ɪz

stele 'arrow shaft' stil

stele 'pillar' 'stili

stella, S- 'stɛlə |-lar -lɚ; ES -lə(r

stellate 'stɛlɪt, -let

---

stem stɛm |stemmed stɛmd
stem-winder ˈstɛmˈwaɪndɚ, -ˌwaɪndɚ; ES -də(r
stench stɛntʃ |-es -ɪz |-ed -t
stencil ˈstɛnsl̩ |-ed -d |-ing -s|ɪŋ, -slɪŋ
stenograph ˈstɛnəˌɡræf; E+-ˌɡraf, -ˌɡraf; |-ed -t
stenographer stəˈnɑɡrəfɚ, -ˈnɒɡ-; ES -fə(r; |-phy -fɪ
stenographic ˌstɛnəˈɡræfɪk |-al -l̩ |-ally -l̩ɪ, -ɪklɪ
stent stɛnt |stented ˈstɛntɪd
Stentor ˈstɛntɔr; ES -tɔə(r
stentorian stɛnˈtorɪən, -ˈtɔr-; S -ˈtor-
step stɛp |stepped stɛpt
stepbrother ˈstɛpˌbrʌðɚ; ES -ˌbrʌðə(r
stepchild ˈstɛpˌtʃaɪld |-children -ˌtʃɪldrən, -drɪn, -dɚn; ES -drən, -drɪn, -dən
stepdame ˈstɛpˌdem
stepdaughter ˈstɛpˌdɔtɚ; ES -ˌdɔtə(r
stepfather ˈstɛpˌfɑðɚ; ES -ˌfɑðə(r, E+ -ˌfaðə(r
Stephano *Tempest* ˈstɛfəˌno, *M. of Ven.* stəˈfɑno
Stephen ˈstivən |-s -z |-son -sn̩
Stephenville ˈstivənˌvɪl; S+-v|
stepladder ˈstɛpˌlædɚ; ES -ˌlædə(r
stepmother ˈstɛpˌmʌðɚ; ES -ˌmʌðə(r
Stepney ˈstɛpnɪ
stepparent ˈstɛpˌpɛrənt, -ˌpær-, -ˌper-
steppe stɛp
steppingstone ˈstɛpɪŋˌston
stepsister ˈstɛpˌsɪstɚ; ES -ˌsɪstə(r
stepson ˈstɛpˌsʌn
stere stɪr; ES stɪə(r
stereopticon ˌstɛrɪˈɑptɪkən, ˌstɪrɪ-; ES+ -ˈɒp-
stereoscope ˈstɛrɪəˌskop, ˈstɪrɪə-
stereoscopic ˌstɛrɪəˈskɑpɪk, ˌstɪrɪə-; ES+ -ˈskɒp-; |-al -l̩ |-ally -l̩ɪ, -ɪklɪ
stereoscopy ˌstɛrɪˈɑskəpɪ, ˌstɪrɪ-; ES+-ˈɒs-
stereotype ˈstɛrɪəˌtaɪp, ˈstɪrɪə- |-d -t
stereotypy ˈstɛrɪəˌtaɪpɪ, ˈstɪrɪə-
sterile ˈstɛrəl, -ɪl
sterility stəˈrɪlətɪ, stɛ-
sterilization ˌstɛrələˈzeʃən, -aɪˈz-
sterilize ˈstɛrəˌlaɪz |-s -ɪz |-d -d
sterling, S- ˈstɝlɪŋ; ES ˈstɜ-, ˈstɝ-
stern, S- stɝn; ES stɜn, stɝn

Sterne stɝn; ES stɜn, stɝn
sternforemost ˌstɝnˈformost, -ˈfɔr-, -məst; ES ˌstɜnˈfoə-, ˌstɝn-, E+-ˈfɔə-
sternmost ˈstɝnˌmost, -məst; ES ˈstɜn-, ˈstɝn-
sternness ˈstɝnnɪs; ES ˈstɜn-, ˈstɝn-
sternpost ˈstɝnˌpost; ES ˈstɜn-, ˈstɝn-
sternum ˈstɝnəm; ES ˈstɜn-, ˈstɝn-; |-s -z |-na -nə
sterol ˈstɛrol, -ɑl, -ɒl
stertorous ˈstɝtərəs; ES ˈstɜ-, ˈstɝ-
stet stɛt |stetted ˈstɛtɪd
stethoscope ˈstɛθəˌskop
stethoscopic ˌstɛθəˈskɑpɪk; ES+ˈskɒp-; |-al -l̩ |-ally -l̩ɪ, -ɪklɪ
stethoscopy stɛˈθɑskəpɪ; ES+-ˈθɒs-
Stetson ˈstɛtsn̩
Steuben *Baron* ˈstjubɪn, ˈstɪu-, ˈstu- |-ville -ˌvɪl
Steuben *US places* stjuˈbɛn, stɪu-, stu-
stevedore ˈstivəˌdor, -ˌdɔr; ES -ˌdoə(r, E+ -ˌdɔə(r
Stevens ˈstivənz |-ˈs -ɪz |-on ˈstivənsn̩
stew stju, stɪu, stu |-ed -d
steward, S- ˈstjuwɚd, ˈstɪu-, ˈstu-; ES -əd
Stewart ˈstjuɚt, ˈstɪu-, ˈstu-; ES -ət
stewpan ˈstjuˌpæn, ˈstɪu-, ˈstu-
Steyn staɪn
Steyne stin
stibium ˈstɪbɪəm
stick *of wood* stɪk |sticked stɪkt
stick *'stab'* stɪk |stuck stʌk
stickit ˈstɪkɪt
stickle ˈstɪkl̩ |-d -d |-ling ˈstɪklɪŋ, -kl̩ɪŋ
stickleback ˈstɪkl̩ˌbæk
stickler ˈstɪklɚ; ES ˈstɪklə(r
Stickney ˈstɪknɪ
stickpin ˈstɪkˌpɪn
Stieglitz ˈstiglɪts |-ˈs -ɪz
sties staɪz
stiff stɪf |stiffed stɪft
stiffen ˈstɪfən |-ed -d |-ing ˈstɪfənɪŋ, -fnɪŋ
stiff-necked ˈstɪfˈnɛkt (ˈstiff-ˌnecked ˈox)
stifle ˈstaɪfl̩ |-d -d |-ling ˈstaɪflɪŋ, -fl̩ɪŋ
stigma ˈstɪɡmə |-s -z |-mata -mətə
stigmatic stɪɡˈmætɪk |-al -l̩ |-ally -l̩ɪ, -ɪklɪ
stigmatization ˌstɪɡmətəˈzeʃən, -aɪˈz-
stigmatize ˈstɪɡməˌtaɪz |-s -ɪz |-d -d
Stikine stɪˈkin

|full fʊl |tooth tuθ |further ˈfɝðɚ; ES ˈfɝðə |custom ˈkʌstəm |while hwaɪl |how haʊ |toy tɔɪ |using ˈjuzɪŋ |fuse fjuz, fɪuz |dish dɪʃ |vision ˈvɪʒən |Eden ˈidn̩ |cradle ˈkredl̩ |keep 'em ˈkipm̩

stile staɪl
Stiles staɪlz |-'s -ɪz
stiletto stɪˈlɛto |-ed -d
Stilicho ˈstɪlɪˌko
still stɪl |stilled stɪld
stillbirth ˈstɪlˌbɝθ; ES -ˌbɝθ, -ˌbɝθ; |-ths -θs
stillborn ˈstɪlˈbɔrn; ES -ˈbɔən; (ˈstillˌborn ˈhopes)
Stillson ˈstɪlsn̩
stilly adj ˈstɪlɪ
stilly adv ˈstɪllɪ
stilt stɪlt |stilted ˈstɪltɪd
Stilton ˈstɪltn̩
stimie ˈstaɪmɪ |stimied ˈstaɪmɪd
Stimson ˈstɪmsn̩, ˈstɪmpsn̩
stimulance ˈstɪmjələns |-cy -ɪ |-lant -lənt
stimulate ˈstɪmjəˌlet |-d -ɪd |-tive -ɪv
stimulation ˌstɪmjəˈleʃən
stimulus ˈstɪmjələs |-es -ɪz |-li -ˌlaɪ
stimy ˈstaɪmɪ |stimied ˈstaɪmɪd
sting stɪŋ |stung stʌŋ or arch. stang stæŋ |stung stʌŋ
stingaree ˈstɪŋəˌri, ˌstɪŋəˈri
stinge stɪndʒ |-s -ɪz |-d -d |stingeing -ɪŋ
stinger 'who stinges' ˈstɪndʒɚ; ES -dʒə(r
stinger 'what stings' ˈstɪŋɚ; ES ˈstɪŋə(r
stingy 'miserly' ˈstɪndʒɪ
stingy 'stinging' ˈstɪŋɪ
stink stɪŋk |stunk stʌŋk or stank stæŋk |stunk stʌŋk
stinkpot ˈstɪŋkˌpat; ES+-ˌpɒt
stint stɪnt |stinted ˈstɪntɪd
stipate ˈstaɪpet
stipe staɪp |stiped staɪpt
stipel ˈstaɪpl̩
stipend ˈstaɪpɛnd |-iary staɪˈpɛndɪˌɛrɪ
stipple ˈstɪpl̩ |-d -d |-ling -plɪŋ, -pl̩ɪŋ
stipulate adj ˈstɪpjəlɪt, -ˌlet
stipulate v ˈstɪpjəˌlet |-lated -ˌletɪd
stipulation ˌstɪpjəˈleʃən
stipule ˈstɪpjul |-d -d
stir stɝ; ES stɝ(r, stɝ; |-red -d
Stirling ˈstɝlɪŋ; ES ˈstɜ-, ˈstɝ-; |-shire -ˌʃɪr, -ʃɚ; ES -ˌʃɪə(r, -ʃə(r
stirps stɝps; ES stɜps, stɝps; |-pes -piz
stirrup ˈstɝəp, ˈstɪrəp, ˈstɛrəp; E ˈstɪrəp, ˈstɝəp, ˈstɝəp, ˈstɛrəp; S ˈstɜrəp, ˈstʌrəp, ˈstɪrəp, ˈstɝəp, ˈstɛrəp
stitch stɪtʃ |stitches ˈstɪtʃɪz |-ed -t

stithy ˈstɪðɪ, ˈstɪθɪ
stiver ˈstaɪvɚ; ES ˈstaɪvə(r
stoa, S- ˈstoə |-s -z |stoae ˈstoi
stoat stot
stock stak; ES+stɒk; |-ed -t
stockade stakˈed; ES+stɒk-; |-aded -ˈedɪd
Stockbridge ˈstakbrɪdʒ; ES+ˈstɒk-; |-'s -ɪz
stockbroker ˈstakˌbrokɚ; ES ˈstakˌbrokə(r, ˈstɒk-
stockholder ˈstakˌholdɚ; ES ˈstakˌholdə(r, ˈstɒk-
Stockholm ˈstakˌhom, -ˌholm; ES+ˈstɒk-
stockinet ˌstakɪnˈɛt; ES+ˌstɒk-
stocking ˈstakɪŋ; ES+ˈstɒk-; |-ed -d
stocking-feet ˈstakɪŋˌfit; ES+ˈstɒk-
stockman, ˈstakmən, -ˌmæn; ES+ˈstɒk-; |-men -mən, -ˌmɛn
Stockport ˈstakˌport, -ˌpɔrt; ES ˈstakˌpoət, ˈstɒk-, E+-ˌpɔət
stock-still ˈstakˈstɪl; ES+ˈstɒk-
Stockton ˈstaktən; ES+ˈstɒk-
stockyard ˈstakˌjard; ES ˈstakˌjɑːd, ˈstɒk-, E+-ˌjɑːd
Stoddard ˈstadɚd; ES ˈstadəd, ˈstɒd-
stodgy ˈstadʒɪ; ES+ˈstɒdʒɪ
stogie, -gy ˈstogɪ
Stoic, s- ˈsto·ɪk |-al -l̩ |-ally -lɪ, -ɪklɪ
Stoicism, s- ˈsto·ɪˌsɪzəm
stoke, S- stok |stoked stokt
Stoke Poges ˈstokˈpodʒɪs, -ɪz |-'s -ɪz |-ges' -dʒɪz
Stokes stoks |-'s -ɪz
Stokowski stoˈkɔfskɪ, -ˈkɔvskɪ, -ˈkɒ-
stole stol |stoled stold
stolen ˈstolən, stoln (nonsyllabic n)
stolid ˈstalɪd; ES+ˈstɒl-
stolidity stəˈlɪdətɪ
stoln stoln (nonsyllabic n)
stolon ˈstolan; ES+-ɒn
stoma ˈstomə |-ta ˈstomətə, ˈstam-; ES+ˈstɒm-
stomach ˈstʌmək |-ed -t |-er -ɚ; ES -ə(r
stomach-ache ˈstʌməkˌek
stomatoscope stoˈmætəˌskop, ˈstamətə-, ˈsto-; ES+ˈstɒm-
stomp stamp, stɒmp, stɔmp
stone, S- ston |-ed -d; |N Engd+stɔ̈n (§46)
stonecutter ˈstonˌkʌtɚ; ES -ˌkʌtə(r
stone-deaf ˈstonˈdɛf (ˈstone-ˌdeaf ˈadder)

Stoneham 'stonəm	stout, S- staut
Stonehenge 'stonhɛndʒ, -'hɛndʒ |-'s -ɪz	stouten 'stautn̩ |-ed -d |-ing -tn̩ɪŋ, -tnɪŋ
stonemason 'ston,mesn̩, -'mesn̩ |-ry -rɪ	stouthearted 'staut'hartɪd; ES -'hɑ:t-, E+ -'ha:t-; ('stout,hearted 'lass)
stonewall adj 'ston,wɔl	stove stov |stoved stovd |-pipe -,paɪp
Stonewall 'ston,wɔl	stow sto |stowed stod |-age -ɪdʒ
stonewall v ,ston'wɔl |-ed -d	Stow, -e sto, Scotl stau
stone wall 'ston'wɔl	stowaway 'stoə,we
stonework 'ston,wɝk; ES -,wɜk, -,wɝk	strabismal strə'bɪzml̩ |-ly -ɪ
Stonington 'stonɪŋtən	strabismic strə'bɪzmɪk |-al -l̩
stonish 'stanɪʃ; ES+'stɒn-; |-es -ɪz |-ed -t	strabismus strə'bɪzməs
stony 'stonɪ; N Engd+'stɔnɪ	Strabo 'strebo
stood stʊd	Strachan strɔn
stooge studʒ |stooges 'studʒɪz	Strachey 'stretʃɪ
stook stuk, stʊk |-ed -t	straddle 'strædl̩ |-d -d |-ling -dl̩ɪŋ, -dlɪŋ
stool stul |stooled stuld	Stradivarius ,strædə'vɛrɪəs, -'ver- |-'s -ɪz
stoop stup |stooped stupt	strafe stref, straf (Ger 'ʃtra:fə)
stop stap; ES+stɒp; |-ped -t	Strafford 'stræfɚd; ES 'stræfəd
stopcock 'stap,kak; ES+'stɒp,kɒk	straggle 'strægl̩ |-d -d |-ling -glɪŋ, -gl̩ɪŋ
stope stop |stoped stopt	straggly 'stræglɪ
stopgap 'stap,gæp; ES+'stɒp-	straight stret |straighted 'stretɪd
stopover 'stap,ovɚ; ES 'stap,ovə(r, 'stɒp-	straightaway 'stretə,we
stoppage 'stapɪdʒ; ES+'stɒp-; |-s -ɪz	straightedge 'stret,ɛdʒ |-s -ɪz |-d -d
stopple 'stapl̩; ES+'stɒpl̩; |-d -d |-ling -pl̩ɪŋ, -plɪŋ	straighten 'stretn̩ |-ed -d |-ing -tnɪŋ, -tn̩ɪŋ
storage 'storɪdʒ, 'stɔr-; S 'stor-; |-s -ɪz	straightforward ,stret'fɔrwəd; ES -'fɔəwəd; ('straight,forward 'style)
store stor, stɔr; ES stoə(r, E+stɔə(r; |-d -d	straight-grained 'stret'grend ('straight-,grained 'oak)
storehouse 'stor,haus, 'stɔr-; ES 'stoə-, E+'stɔə-; |-ses -zɪz	straight-out n 'stret,aut
storekeeper 'stor,kipɚ, 'stɔr-; ES 'stoə,kipə(r, E+'stɔə-	straight-out adj 'stret'aut
storeroom 'stor,rum, 'stɔr-, -,rʊm; ES 'stoə-, E+'stɔə-	straightway 'stret,we
storey, S- 'storɪ, 'stɔrɪ; S 'storɪ; |-ed -d	strain stren |strained strend |-edly -ɪdlɪ, -dlɪ
storied 'storɪd, 'stɔrɪd; S 'storɪd	strait stret
storiette ,storɪ'ɛt, ,stɔrɪ-; S ,storɪ-	straiten 'stretn̩ |-ed -d |-ing -tnɪŋ, -tn̩ɪŋ
stork stɔrk; ES stɔək	strait-laced 'stret'lest ('strait-,laced 'sect)
storm, S- stɔrm; ES stɔəm; |-ed -d	strake strek |straked strekt
Stormonth 'stɔrmənθ, -mʌnθ; ES 'stɔəm-	strand, S- strænd |stranded 'strændɪd
Storrs stɔrz; ES stɔəz; |-'s -ɪz	strange, S- strendʒ |Strange's 'strendʒɪz
Storthing, -ting 'stor,tɪŋ, 'stɔr-; ES 'stoə-, E+'stɔə-	stranger 'strendʒɚ; ES -dʒə(r; |-ed -d
story, S- 'storɪ, 'stɔrɪ; S 'storɪ; |-ied -d	strangle 'stræŋgl̩ |-d -d |-ling -glɪŋ, -gl̩ɪŋ
storyteller 'storɪ,tɛlɚ, 'stɔrɪ-; ES 'storɪ,tɛlə(r, E+'stɔrɪ-	strangulate 'stræŋgjə,let |-lated -,letɪd
Stoughton 'stotn̩	strangulation ,stræŋgjə'leʃən
stound staund |stounded 'staundɪd	strap stræp |strapped stræpt
stoup stup	Strasbourg 'stræsbɝg; ES -bɜg, -bɝg (Fr stras'bu:r, straz-; Ger 'ʃtra:sburk)
Stourbridge 'sturbrɪdʒ, 'staur-, 'stɜ-; ES 'stuə-, 'stauə-, 'stɜ-, 'stɝ-; |-'s -ɪz	Strasburg US 'stræsbɝg; ES -bɝg, -bɝg; O loc.+'strɔzbɝg
	strata 'stretə, 'strætə
	stratagem 'strætədʒəm

\|full fʊl \|tooth tuθ \|further 'fɝðɚ; ES 'fɜðə \|custom 'kʌstəm \|while hwaɪl \|how haʊ \|toy tɔɪ
\|using 'juzɪŋ \|fuse fjuz, fɪuz \|dish dɪʃ \|vision 'vɪʒən \|Eden 'idn̩ \|cradle 'kredl̩ \|keep 'em 'kipm̩

strategic strə'tidʒɪk |-al -ḷ |-ally -ḷɪ, -ɪklɪ
strategist 'strætədʒɪst |-gy -dʒɪ
Stratford 'strætfəd; ES 'strætfəd
Stratford-on-Avon 'strætfədan'evən, -ɒn-, -ɔn-; ES -fəd-
Strathclyde stræθ'klaɪd |-cona -'konə
Strathmore stræθ'mor, -'mɔr; ES -'moə(r, E+-'mɔə(r; US & attrib. 'Strath,more
strathspey, S- stræθ'spe, 'stræθ,spe
stratification ,strætəfə'keʃən
stratiform 'strætə,fɔrm; ES -,fɔəm
stratify 'strætə,faɪ |-fied -,faɪd
stratigraphic ,strætə'græfɪk |-al -ḷ |-ally -ḷɪ, -ɪklɪ
stratigraphy strə'tɪgrəfɪ
Stratton 'strætn̩
Strato 'streto
stratosphere 'strætə,sfɪr, 'stretə-; ES -,sfɪə(r, S+-,sfɛə(r
stratospheric ,strætə'sfɛrɪk, ,stretə-
stratum 'stretəm, 'stræt- |-ta -tə |-s -z
stratus 'stretəs |strati 'stretaɪ
straught strɔt
Straus, -ss straus |-'s -ɪz (Ger ʃtraus)
Stravinsky strə'vɪnskɪ
straw strɔ |strawed strɔd
strawberry 'strɔ,bɛrɪ, -bərɪ
strawboard 'strɔ,bord, -,bɔrd; ES -,boəd, E+-,bɔəd
strawy 'strɔ·ɪ
stray stre |strayed stred
streak strik |streaked strikt
streaked adj 'strikɪd, strikt
stream strim |streamed strimd |-let -lɪt
streamline 'strim,laɪn |-lined -,laɪnd
Streatham 'strɛtəm
Streator 'stritə; ES 'stritə(r
street, S- strit |streeted 'stritɪd
Streitberg 'straɪtbɝg; ES -bɝg, -bɝg; (Ger 'ʃtraɪtbɛrk)
strength strɛŋkθ, strɛŋθ |-ths -θs
strengthen 'strɛŋkθən, 'strɛŋθ- |-ed -d |-ing -θənɪŋ, -θnɪŋ
strenuosity ,strɛnju'ɑsətɪ; ES+-'ɒsətɪ
strenuous 'strɛnjʊəs
streptococcus ,strɛptə'kɑkəs; ES+-'kɒk-; |-cci -ksaɪ
Stresa 'strɛzə, 'strezə (It 'strɛːza)
Stresemann 'strɛzəmən (Ger 'ʃtreːzə,man)

stress strɛs |stresses 'strɛsɪz |-ed -t
stretch strɛtʃ |stretches 'strɛtʃɪz |-ed -t
Stretford 'strɛtfəd; ES 'strɛtfəd
strew stru, strɪu |-ed -d |-ed -d or -n -n
striate adj 'straɪɪt, -et
striate v 'straɪet |-d -ɪd |-tion straɪ'eʃən
stricken 'strɪkən |-ness 'strɪkənnɪs
Strickland 'strɪklənd
strickle 'strɪkḷ |-d -d |-ling -klɪŋ, -kḷɪŋ
strickler 'strɪklə; ES 'strɪklə(r
strict strɪkt |-ly -ktlɪ, -klɪ
stricture 'strɪktʃə; ES 'strɪktʃə(r; |-d -d
stride straɪd |strode strod |stridden 'strɪdn̩
stridence 'straɪdn̩s |-cy -ɪ |-dent -dn̩t
stridulate 'strɪdʒə,let |-lated -,letɪd
stridulation ,strɪdʒə'leʃən
strife straɪf
strike straɪk |struck strʌk |struck strʌk or stricken 'strɪkən
strikebreaker 'straɪk,brekə; ES -,brekə(r
Strindberg 'strɪndbɝg, 'strɪnb-; ES -bɝg, -bɝg
string strɪŋ |strung strʌŋ
stringed adj strɪŋd
stringency 'strɪndʒənsɪ |-gent -dʒənt
stringhalt 'strɪŋ'hɔlt, -,hɔlt
stringhalted 'strɪŋ'hɔltɪd ('string,halted 'nag)
stringpiece 'strɪŋ,pis |-s -ɪz
stringy 'strɪŋɪ
strip strɪp |stripped strɪpt
stripe straɪp |striped straɪpt
striped adj 'straɪpɪd, straɪpt
stripling 'strɪplɪŋ
stripper 'strɪpə; ES 'strɪpə(r
stripy 'straɪpɪ
strive straɪv |strove strov or strived straɪvd |striven 'strɪvən or strived straɪvd or rarely strove strov
stroboscope 'strobə,skop
stroboscopic ,strabə'skapɪk; ES+,strɒbə-'skɒp-; |-al -ḷ
stroboscopy stro'baskəpɪ; ES+-'bɒs-
strode, S- strod
stroke strok |stroked strokt
stroll strol |strolled strold
strong, S- strɔŋ, strɒŋ; S+strɑŋ; |-er -gə; ES -gə(r; |-est -gɪst
stronghold 'strɔŋ,hold, 'strɒŋ-; S+'strɑŋ-
strongish 'strɔŋɪʃ, 'strɒŋ-; S+'strɑŋ-

Words formed with sub- *often shift their accent for contrast* ('editor & 'sub‚editor)

strong-minded 'strɔŋ'maɪndɪd, 'strɒŋ-; S+
'straŋ-
strontia 'stranʃɪə; ES+'strɒn-; |-ium -m
strook struk
strop strap; ES+strɒp; |-ped -t
strophe 'strofɪ
strophic 'strafɪk, 'strof-; ES+'strɒf-; |-al -]
|-ally -]ɪ, -ɪklɪ
Strother 'straðɚ; ES 'straðə(r, 'strɒð-
Stroud straud |-sburg -zbɝg; ES -zbɜg, -zbɝg
strove strov
strow stro |strowed strod |strown stron *or*
strowed strod
stroy strɔɪ |stroyed strɔɪd
struck strʌk
structural 'strʌktʃərəl |-ly -ɪ
structure 'strʌktʃɚ; ES 'strʌktʃə(r; |-d -d
struggle 'strʌg] |-d -d |-ling -glɪŋ, -g]ɪŋ
struggler 'strʌglɚ; ES 'strʌglə(r
strum strʌm |strummed strʌmd
strumpet 'strʌmpɪt |-ed -ɪd
strung strʌŋ
strut strʌt |strutted 'strʌtɪd
Struthers 'strʌðɚz; ES 'strʌðəz; |-'s -ɪz
Strutt strʌt
strychnin, -e 'strɪknɪn |-nic -nɪk
Stuart 'stjuɚt, 'strɪu-, 'stu-; ES -ət
stub stʌb |stubbed stʌbd
stubbed *adj* 'stʌbɪd, stʌbd
stubble 'stʌb] |-d -d |-ling 'stʌblɪŋ, -b]ɪŋ
stubbly 'stʌblɪ, 'stʌb]ɪ
stubborn 'stʌbɚn; ES 'stʌbən; |-ness -nɪs
stubby 'stʌbɪ
stucco 'stʌko |stuccoed 'stʌkod
stuck stʌk
stuck-up 'stʌk'ʌp ('stuck-‚up 'manner)
stud stʌd |studded 'stʌdɪd
Studebaker 'stjudə‚bekɚ, 'strɪu-, 'stu-; ES
-ə(r
student 'stjudn̩t, 'strɪu-, 'stu-
studied 'stʌdɪd
studio 'stjudɪ‚o, 'strɪu-, 'stu- |-ious -ɪəs
study 'stʌdɪ |studied 'stʌdɪd
stuff stʌf |stuffed stʌft |-y -ɪ
stultification ‚stʌltəfə'keʃən
stultify 'stʌltə‚faɪ |-fied -‚faɪd
stumble 'stʌmb] |-d -d |-ling -blɪŋ, -b]ɪŋ
stump stʌmp |stumped stʌmpt

stun stʌn |stunned stʌnd
stung stʌŋ
stunk stʌŋk
stunt stʌnt |stunted 'stʌntɪd
stupe stjup, strɪup, stup |-d -t
stupefacient ‚stjupə'feʃənt, ‚strɪu-, ‚stu-
|-faction -'fækʃən
stupefy 'stjupə‚faɪ, 'strɪu-, 'stu- |-fied -‚faɪd
stupendous stju'pɛndəs, strɪu-, stu-
stupid 'stjupɪd, 'strɪu-, 'stu-
stupidity stju'pɪdətɪ, strɪu-, stu-
stupor 'stjupɚ, 'strɪu-, 'stu-; ES -pə(r
Sturbridge 'stɝ‚brɪdʒ; ES 'stɜ-, 'stɝ-; |-'s -ɪz
sturdy 'stɝdɪ; ES 'stɜ-, 'stɝ-; |-dily -d]ɪ,
-dɪlɪ
sturgeon, S- 'stɝdʒən; ES 'stɜ-, 'stɝ-
Sturgis 'stɝdʒɪs, 'stɜ-, 'stɝ-; |-'s -ɪz
stutter 'stʌtɚ; ES 'stʌtə(r
Stuttgart 'stʌtgɚt, -gart; ES -gət, -gɑ:t (*Ger*
'ʃtutgart)
Stuyvesant 'staɪvəsn̩t
sty staɪ |sties staɪz |stied staɪd
stye staɪ |sties, styes staɪz
Stygian 'stɪdʒɪən
style staɪl |styled staɪld |-list -ɪst
styleless 'staɪllɪs
stylistic staɪ'lɪstɪk |-al -] |-ally -]ɪ, -ɪklɪ
stylite 'staɪlaɪt |-tism -‚ɪzəm
Stylites staɪ'laɪtiz |-tes' -tiz
stylize 'staɪlaɪz |-s -ɪz |-d -d
stylus 'staɪləs |styluses 'staɪləsɪz
stymie 'staɪmɪ |-d -d
styptic 'stɪptɪk |-al -]
Styria 'stɪrɪə |-n -n
Styx stɪks |-'s -ɪz |-ian -ɪən
suable 'suəb], 'srɪu-, 'sju- |-bly -blɪ
suasion 'sweʒən |suasive 'swesɪv
suave swav, swev |-vity 'swævətɪ, 'swav-
sub sʌb
sub- *prefix, stressed* 'sʌb-, ‚sʌb-; *unstr.* səb-;
—*The accent mark is usually omitted from
partly accented* sʌb- *before an accented syllable.*
subacid sʌb'æsɪd ('sub‚acid 'juice)
subalpine sʌb'ælpaɪn, -pɪn
subaltern səb'ɔltən, *logic*+'sʌb]‚tɝn; ES
-'ɔltən, -‚tɝn, -‚tɝn
subalternate səb'ɔltɚnɪt, -'æl-; ES -tə-

Words formed with sub- *often shift their accent for contrast* ('editor & 'sub,editor)

subalternating sʌb'ɔltɚˌnetɪŋ, -'æl-; ES -tə-
subalternation sʌbˌɔltɚ'neʃən, ˌsʌbɔltə-, -ˌæl-, -æl-; ES -tə-
subaqueous sʌb'ekwɪəs, -'æk-
subarctic sʌb'ɑrktɪk, *now rare* -'ɑrt-; ES -'ɑː-, E+-'ɑː-
subaudible sʌb'ɔdəbḷ
subbase 'sʌbˌbes |-s -ɪz
subbass 'sʌbˌbes |-es -ɪz
subclass 'sʌbˌklæs; E+-ˌklas, -ˌklɑs; |-es -ɪz |-ed -t
subcommittee 'sʌbkəˌmɪtɪ
subconscious sʌb'kɑnʃəs; ES+-'kɒn-
subcontract *n* sʌb'kɑntrækt; ES+-'kɒn-
subcontract *v* ˌsʌbkən'trækt |-ed -ɪd
subcutaneous ˌsʌbkju'tenɪəs, -kɪu-
subdeacon sʌb'dikən |-ate -ɪt |-ess -ɪs |-ry -rɪ
subdean sʌb'din |-ery -ərɪ, -'dinrɪ
subdeb sʌb'dɛb
subdebutante sʌbˌdɛbju'tɑnt, ˌsʌbdɛb-, sʌb-'dɛbjəˌtænt
subdivide ˌsʌbdə'vaɪd |-d -ɪd (di'vide & 'subdiˌvide)
subdivision ˌsʌbdə'vɪʒən, 'sʌbdəˌvɪʒən
subduct səb'dʌkt |-ed -ɪd |-ction -kʃən
subdue səb'dju, -'dɪu, -'du |-d -d |-dly -dlɪ, -ɪdlɪ
subedit sʌb'ɛdɪt |-ed -ɪd |-or -ɚ; ES -ə(r
subgroup *n* 'sʌbˌgrup
subgroup *v* sʌb'grup |-ed -t
subhead 'sʌbˌhɛd
subjacency sʌb'dʒesn̩sɪ |-cent -sn̩t
subject *n, adj* 'sʌbdʒɪkt
subject *v* səb'dʒɛkt |-ed -ɪd |-ion -kʃən |-ive -ɪv
subjectivity ˌsʌbdʒɛk'tɪvətɪ
subjoin səb'dʒɔɪn |-ed -d
sub-jugate *adj* sʌb'dʒugɪt, -'dʒɪu-
subjugate *v* 'sʌbdʒəˌget |-gated -ˌgetɪd
subjugation ˌsʌbdʒə'geʃən
subjunct *n* 'sʌbdʒʌŋkt
subjunction səb'dʒʌŋkʃən |-tive -tɪv
subkingdom sʌb'kɪŋdəm, 'sʌbˌkɪŋdəm
sublease *n* 'sʌbˌlis |-s -ɪz
sublease *v* sʌb'lis |-s -ɪz |-d -t
sublet sʌb'lɛt ('let & 'subˌlet)
Sublette sə'blɛt
sublimate *n, adj* 'sʌbləmɪt, -ˌmet

sublimate *v* 'sʌbləˌmet |-mated -ˌmetɪd
sublimation ˌsʌblə'meʃən
sublime sə'blaɪm |-d -d
subliminal sʌb'lɪmənḷ, -'laɪm- |-ly -ɪ
sublimity sə'blɪmətɪ
sublunar sʌb'lunɚ, -'lɪu-; ES -nə(r; |-y -ɪ
submarginal sʌb'mɑrdʒɪnḷ; ES -'mɑː-; |-ly -ɪ
submarine *adj* ˌsʌbmə'rin ('submaˌrine 'life)
submarine *n, v* 'sʌbməˌrin |-d -d
submerge səb'mɝdʒ; ES -'mɜdʒ, -'mɝdʒ; |-s -ɪz |-d -d |-gence -dʒəns
submerse səb'mɝs; ES -'mɜs, -'mɝs; |-s -ɪz |-d -t |-sion -ʃən, -ʒən
submission səb'mɪʃən |-sive -'mɪsɪv
submit səb'mɪt |-ted -ɪd |-tal -ḷ
subnormal sʌb'nɔrmḷ; ES -'nɔəmḷ
suborder sʌb'ɔrdɚ, 'sʌbˌɔrdɚ; ES -'bɔdə(r, -ˌɔə-
subordinate *n, adj* sə'bɔrdn̩ɪt, -dnɪt; ES -'bɔəd-
subordinate *v* sə'bɔrdn̩ˌet; ES -'bɔəd-; |-d -ɪd
subordination səˌbɔrdn̩'eʃən; ES -ˌbɔəd-
suborn sə'bɔrn, sʌ-; ES -'bɔən; |-ed -d
subornation ˌsʌbɔr'neʃən; ES ˌsʌbɔə-
subplot 'sʌbˌplɑt; ES+-ˌplɒt
subpoena, -pena sə'pinə, səb'pinə |-ed -d
sub rosa sʌb'rozə
subscribe səb'skraɪb |-d -d
subscript 'sʌbskrɪpt
subscription səb'skrɪpʃən |-tive -tɪv
subsection sʌb'sɛkʃən, 'sʌbˌsɛkʃən
subsequence 'sʌbsɪˌkwɛns, -kwəns |-cy -ɪ |-nt -nt
subserve səb'sɝv; ES -'sɝv, -'sɝv; |-d -d
subservience səb'sɝvɪəns; ES -'sɝv-, -'sɝv-; |-cy -ɪ |-ient -ɪənt
subside səb'saɪd |-d -ɪd
subsidence səb'saɪdn̩s, 'sʌbsədəns |-s -ɪz
subsidiary səb'sɪdɪˌɛrɪ
subsidization ˌsʌbsədə'zeʃən, -aɪ'z-
subsidize 'sʌbsəˌdaɪz |-s -ɪz |-d -d |-dy -dɪ
subsist səb'sɪst |-ed -ɪd
subsistence səb'sɪstəns |-cy -ɪ |-ent -ənt
subsoil 'sʌbˌsɔɪl |-ed -d
subsolar sʌb'solɚ; ES -'solə(r
subspecies sʌb'spiʃɪz, 'sʌbˌspiʃɪz, -ʃɪz
substance 'sʌbstəns |-s -ɪz
substandard sʌb'stændɚd; ES -dəd

Key: *See in full §§3–47.* bee bi |pity 'pɪtɪ (§6) |rate ret |yet jɛt |sang sæŋ |angry 'æŋ·grɪ |bath bæθ; E baθ (§10) |ah ɑ |far fɑr |watch wɑtʃ, wɒtʃ (§12) |jaw dʒɔ |gorge gɔrdʒ |go go

Words formed with sub- *often shift their accent for contrast* ('editor & 'sub,editor)

substantial səb'stænʃəl |-ly -ɪ

substantiality səb,stænʃɪ'ælətɪ |-ation -'eʃən

substantival ,sʌbstən'taɪv| |-ly -ɪ

substantive 'sʌbstəntɪv |-ly 'sʌbstəntɪvlɪ

substitute 'sʌbstə,tjut, -,tɪut, -,tut |-d -ɪd
   |-tutive -ɪv

substitution ,sʌbstə'tjuʃən, -'tɪu-, -'tu-

substratum sʌb'stretəm, -'stræt-, 'sʌb,str-
   |-ta -tə

substructure sʌb'strʌktʃɚ, 'sʌb,str-; ES
   -tʃə(r

subsume səb'sum, -'sɪum, -'sjum |-d -d

subsumption səb'sʌmpʃən

subtangent sʌb'tændʒənt

subtenancy sʌb'tɛnənsɪ |-nant -nənt

subtend səb'tɛnd |-ed -ɪd

subterfuge 'sʌbtɚ,fjudʒ, -,fɪudʒ; ES 'sʌbtə-;
   |-s -ɪz |-d -d

subterranean ,sʌbtə'renɪən |-neous -nɪəs

subtile 'sʌt|, 'sʌbtɪl |-ly 'sʌt|ɪ, 'sʌtlɪ, 'sʌbt|ɪ

subtility sʌb'tɪlətɪ

subtilize 'sʌt|,aɪz, 'sʌbt|- |-s -ɪz |-d -d

subtilty 'sʌt|tɪ, 'sʌbt|tɪ

subtitle 'sʌb,taɪt| |-d -d |-ling -t|ɪŋ, -tlɪŋ

subtle 'sʌt| |-ty -tɪ |-r -tlɚ, -t|ɚ; ES -ə(r; |-st
   -tlɪst, -t|ɪst

subtly 'sʌtlɪ, 'sʌt|ɪ

subtonic sʌb'tɑnɪk; ES+-'tɒn-

subtract səb'trækt |-ed -ɪd

subtraction səb'trækʃən |-tive -tɪv

subtrahend 'sʌbtrə,hɛnd, 'sʌbtrɪ-

subtropical sʌb'trɑpɪk|; ES+-'trɒp-

suburb 'sʌbɝb; ES 'sʌbɜb, -ɝb

suburban sə'bɝbən; ES -'bɜb-, -'bɝb-; |-ite
   -,aɪt |-bia -bɪə

subvene səb'vin |-d -d |-ntion -'vɛnʃən

subversion səb'vɝʃən, -ʒən; ES -'vɝ-, -'vɝ-;
   |-sive -sɪv

subvert səb'vɝt; ES -'vɝt, -'vɝt; |-ed -ɪd

subway 'sʌb,we

succeed sək'sid |-ed -ɪd

success sək'sɛs |-es -ɪz |-ful -fəl |-fully -fəlɪ

succession sək'sɛʃən |-ive -'sɛsɪv |-sor -'sɛsɚ;
   ΣS -ə(r

succinct sək'sɪŋkt

succor 'sʌkɚ; ES 'sʌkə(r; |-ed -d

succory 'sʌkərɪ

succotash 'sʌkə,tæʃ |-'s -ɪz

succubus 'sʌkjəbəs |-es -ɪz |-bi -,baɪ

succulence 'sʌkjələns |-cy -ɪ |-lent -lənt

succumb sə'kʌm |-ed -d

such sʌtʃ, *unstressed sometimes* sətʃ

suck sʌk |sucked sʌkt |-er -ɚ; ES -ə(r

suckle 'sʌk| |-d -d |-ling 'sʌk|ɪŋ, -klɪŋ

suckling, S- *n* 'sʌklɪŋ

sucrose 'sukros, 'sɪu-, 'sju-

suction 'sʌkʃən |-al -|

sud sʌd |suds sʌdz |sudded 'sʌdɪd |-sy -zɪ

Sudan su'dæn |-ese ,sudə'niz

sudary 'sudərɪ, 'sɪu-, 'sju-

sudatorium ,sudə'torɪəm, ,sɪu-, ,sju-, -'tɔr-;
   S -'tor-

sudatory 'sudə,torɪ, 'sɪu-, 'sju-, -,tɔrɪ; S
   -,torɪ

Sudbury 'sʌd,bɛrɪ, -bərɪ

sudden 'sʌdn̩, *less freq.* 'sʌdɪn |-ness 'sʌdn̩nɪs,
   'sʌdɪnnɪs

Sudermann 'sudɚmən; ES 'sudə-; (Ger
   'zu:dər,man)

Sudeten su'detn̩ (Ger zu'de:tən)

Sudetes su'ditɪz |-detic -'dɛtɪk

sudorific ,sudə'rɪfɪk, ,sɪu-, ,sju-

suds sʌdz |-es -ɪz |-ed -d

sue su, sɪu, sju |-d -d

suede swed (Fr sɥɛd)

suet 'sʊɪt, 'sɪuɪt, 'sjuɪt

Suetonius swɪ'tonɪəs |-'s -ɪz

Suez 'suɛz, 'sɪu-, 'sju-, su'ɛz, sɪu-, sju- |-'s
   -ɪz

suffari sə'fɑrɪ

suffer 'sʌfɚ; ES 'sʌfə(r; |-ed -d |-ing 'sʌfrɪŋ,
   -fərɪŋ

sufferable 'sʌfrəb|, 'sʌfərə- |-bly -blɪ

sufferance 'sʌfrəns, 'sʌfərəns |-s -ɪz

Suffern 'sʌfɚn; ES 'sʌfən

suffice sə'faɪs, -'faɪz |-s -ɪz |-d -'faɪst, -'faɪzd

sufficiency sə'fɪʃənsɪ |-cient -ʃənt

Suffield 'sʌfild

suffix *n* 'sʌfɪks |-es -ɪz

suffix *v* sə'fɪks, 'sʌfɪks |-es -ɪz |-ed -t

suffocate 'sʌfə,ket |-d -ɪd |-tive -ɪv

suffocation ,sʌfə'keʃən

Suffolk 'sʌfək

suffragan 'sʌfrəgən |-ganate -,et

suffrage 'sʌfrɪdʒ |-s -ɪz |-tte ,sʌfrə'dʒɛt

suffuse sə'fjuz, -'fɪuz |-s -ɪz |-d -d

|full fʊl |tooth tuθ |further 'fɝðɚ; ES 'fɝðə |custom 'kʌstəm |while hwaɪl |how haʊ |toy tɔɪ
|using 'juzɪŋ |fuse fjuz, fɪuz |dish dɪʃ |vision 'vɪʒən |Eden 'idn̩ |cradle 'kred| |keep 'em 'kipm̩

suffusion səˈfjuʒən, -ˈfɪuʒ- |-sive -sɪv

Sufi ˈsufɪ |-sm ˈsufɪzəm

sugar ˈʃʊgɚ; ES ˈʃʊgə(r; |-ed -d |-ing ˈʃʊgrɪŋ, ˈʃʊgərɪŋ |-plum -ˌplʌm

sugary ˈʃʊgrɪ, ˈʃʊgərɪ

suggest səgˈdʒɛst, *less freq.* səˈdʒɛst |-ed -ɪd

suggestibility səgˌdʒɛstəˈbɪlətɪ, səˌdʒɛst-

suggestible səgˈdʒɛstəbḷ, səˈdʒɛst- |-bly -blɪ

suggestion səgˈdʒɛstʃən, səˈdʒɛs- |-tive -tɪv

suicidal ˌsuəˈsaɪdḷ, ˌsɪu-, ˌsju- |-ly -ɪ

suicide ˈsuəˌsaɪd, ˈsɪu-, ˈsju- |-d -ɪd

sui generis ˈsjuɪˈdʒɛnərɪs, ˈsɪu-, ˈsu-

suit sut, sɪut, sjut |-ed -ɪd

suitability ˌsutəˈbɪlətɪ, ˌsɪu-, ˌsju-

suitable ˈsutəbḷ, ˈsɪu-, ˈsju- |-bly -blɪ

suitcase ˈsutˌkes, ˈsɪut-, ˈsjut- |-s -ɪz

suite *'suit'* sut, sɪut, sjut |-d -ɪd

suite *'staff,' 'set'* swit, *'furniture'*+sut, sɪut, sjut

suitor ˈsutɚ, ˈsɪu-, ˈsju-; ES -tə(r

sulcal ˈsʌlkḷ |-ize -ˌaɪz |-izes -ˌaɪzɪz |-ized -ˌaɪzd

Suleiman ˈsulɪˌman

sulfanilamide ˌsʌlfəˈnɪləˌmaɪd

sulfate ˈsʌlfet |-d -ɪd

sulfathiazole ˌsʌlfəˈθaɪəˌzol |-zol -ˌzol, -ˌzɑl, -ˌzɒl, -ˌzɔl

sulfid ˈsʌlfɪd |-fide -faɪd, -fɪd

sulfite ˈsʌlfaɪt

sulfone ˈsʌlfon

sulfur ˈsʌlfɚ; ES ˈsʌlfə(r; |-ed -d |-ing ˈsʌlfərɪŋ, ˈsʌlfrɪŋ

sulfurate *adj* ˈsʌlfərɪt, -frɪt

sulfurate *v* ˈsʌlfəˌret |-rated -ˌretɪd

sulfureous sʌlˈfjurɪəs, -ˈfɪu-

sulfuret *n* ˈsʌlfjərɪt

sulfuret *v* ˈsʌlfjəˌret |-ed -ɪd

sulfuric sʌlˈfjurɪk, -ˈfɪu- (ˈsulˌfuric ˈacid)

sulfurous ˈsʌlfərəs, -fjərəs, *chem.*+sʌlˈfjurəs, -ˈfɪu-

sulfury ˈsʌlfərɪ, ˈsʌlfrɪ

Sulgrave ˈsʌlgrev

Suliman ˈsulɪˌman

sulk sʌlk |-ed -t |-y -ɪ |-ily -ḷɪ, -ɪlɪ

Sulla ˈsʌlə

sullen ˈsʌlɪn, -ən |-ness ˈsʌlɪnnɪs, -lənnɪs

Sullivan ˈsʌləvən |-vant -vənt

sully, S- ˈsʌlɪ |sullied ˈsʌlɪd

sulphanilamide ˌsʌlfəˈnɪləˌmaɪd

sulphate ˈsʌlfet |-d -ɪd

sulphathiazole ˌsʌlfəˈθaɪəˌzol |-zol -ˌzol, -ˌzɑl, -ˌzɒl, -ˌzɔl

sulphid ˈsʌlfɪd |-phide -faɪd, -fɪd

sulphite ˈsʌlfaɪt

sulphone ˈsʌlfon

sulphur ˈsʌlfɚ; ES ˈsʌlfə(r; |-ed -d |-ing ˈsʌlfərɪŋ, -frɪŋ

sulphurate *adj* ˈsʌlfərɪt, -frɪt

sulphurate *v* ˈsʌlfəˌret |-rated -ˌretɪd

sulphureous sʌlˈfjurɪəs, -ˈfɪu-

sulphuret *n* ˈsʌlfjərɪt

sulphuret *v* ˈsʌlfjəˌret |-ed -ɪd

sulphuric sʌlˈfjurɪk, -ˈfɪu- (ˈsulˌphuric ˈacid)

sulphurous ˈsʌlfərəs, -fjərəs, *chem.*+sʌlˈfjurəs, -ˈfɪu-

sulphury ˈsʌlfərɪ, ˈsʌlfrɪ

sultan, S- ˈsʌltn̩ |-a sʌlˈtænə, -ˈtɑnə

sultanate ˈsʌltn̩ɪt, -ˌet

sultry ˈsʌltrɪ

Sulu ˈsulu

sum sʌm |summed sʌmd

sumac, -ach ˈʃumæk, ˈʃɪu-, ˈsu-, ˈsɪu-, ˈsju-, ˈʃumek, ˈʃɪu——*The historically natural pron. (which still prevails) is* ˈʃumæk, ˈʃɪu- (*cf* sugar, sure), ˈsumæk *being clearly a spelling pron. used only by the literate. Perh. from use in tanning, it was early also called* ˈʃumek, ˈʃɪu- (shoemake 1600), *still not uncommon. A N Engd informant said,* "ˈʃumek, *used to dye shoes.*"

Sumatra suˈmɑtrə, -ˈmetrə |-n -n -n

Sumer ˈsumɚ, ˈsɪu-, ˈsju-; ES -mə(r

Sumerian suˈmɪrɪən, sɪu-, sju-

summa cum laude ˈsʌməˌkʌmˈlɔdɪ, ˈsuməˌkumˈlaʊdɪ

summarily ˈsʌmərəlɪ, *emph.*+sʌˈmɛrəlɪ

summarization ˌsʌmərəˈzeʃən, -aɪˈz-

summarize ˈsʌməˌraɪz |-s -ɪz |-d -d

summary ˈsʌmərɪ

summation sʌmˈeʃən

summer ˈsʌmɚ; ES ˈsʌmə(r; |-ed -d |-ing ˈsʌmərɪŋ, ˈsʌmrɪŋ

Summers ˈsʌmɚz; ES ˈsʌməz; |-'s -ɪz

summersault ˈsʌmɚˌsɔlt; ES ˈsʌmə-; |-ed -ɪd

summerset ˈsʌmɚˌsɛt; ES ˈsʌmə-; |-ed -ɪd

summertime ˈsʌmɚˌtaɪm; ES ˈsʌmə-

Summerville ˈsʌmɚˌvɪl; ES ˈsʌmə-, S+-vḷ

summit, S- ˈsʌmɪt

summon ˈsʌmən |-ed -d |-er -ɚ; ES -ə(r
summons ˈsʌmənz |-es ˈsʌmənzɪz |-ed
ˈsʌmənzd
summum bonum ˈsʌməmˈbonəm
Sumner ˈsʌmnɚ; ES ˈsʌmnə(r
sump sʌmp |sumped sʌmpt
sumpter ˈsʌmptɚ; ES ˈsʌmptə(r
sumptuary ˈsʌmptʃʊˌɛrɪ |-tuous -tʃʊəs
Sumter ˈsʌmptɚ, ˈsʌmtɚ; ES -tə(r
sun sʌn |sunned sʌnd
Sunapee ˈsʌnəpɪ, -ˌpi
sunbonnet ˈsʌnˌbɑnɪt; ES+-ˌbɒn-; |-ed -ɪd
sunbow ˈsʌnˌbo
sunburn ˈsʌnˌbɝn; ES -ˌbɜn, -ˌbɝn; |-ed -d
or -t -t
sunburst ˈsʌnˌbɝst; ES -ˌbɜst, -ˌbɝst
Sunbury ˈsʌnˌbɛrɪ, -bərɪ
sundae ˈsʌndɪ
Sunday ˈsʌndɪ |-ed -d—see Monday
sunder ˈsʌndɚ; ES -də(r; |-ed -d |-ing -dərɪŋ,
-drɪŋ
sunderance ˈsʌndrəns, -dərəns |-s -ɪz
Sunderland ˈsʌndɚlənd; ES ˈsʌndə-
sundew ˈsʌnˌdju, -ˌdɪu, -ˌdu
sundial ˈsʌnˌdaɪəl, -ˌdaɪl
sundog ˈsʌnˌdɔg, -ˌdɒg, much less freq. -ˌdɑg
sundown ˈsʌnˌdaun
sundry ˈsʌndrɪ |-ies -z
sun-dry ˈsʌnˌdraɪ |-ied -d
sunfast ˈsʌnˌfæst; E+-ˌfast, -ˌfɑst
sunfish ˈsʌnˌfɪʃ |-ʼs -ɪz
sunflower, S- ˈsʌnˌflauɚ, -ˌflaur; ES -ˌflau-
ə(r, -ˌflauə(r
sung sʌŋ
Sung sʊŋ
sunglass ˈsʌnˌglæs; E+-ˌglas, -ˌglas; |-es -ɪz
sunglow ˈsʌnˌglo
sunk sʌŋk |-en -ən
sunlight ˈsʌnˌlaɪt |-ed -ɪd |-lit -ˌlɪt
Sunna, -h ˈsʊnə |-nite ˈsʊnaɪt
sunny ˈsʌnɪ
sunproof ˈsʌnˈpruf (ˈsunˌproof ˈdye)
sunrise ˈsʌnˌraɪz |-s -ɪz
sunroom ˈsʌnˌrum, -ˌrʊm
sunset ˈsʌnˌsɛt
sunshade ˈsʌnˌʃed
sunshine ˈsʌnˌʃaɪn |-d -d |-ny -ɪ
sunspot ˈsʌnˌspat; ES+-ˌspɒt; |-ted -ɪd
sunstroke ˈsʌnˌstrok

sun-struck ˈsʌnˌstrʌk
sunup ˈsʌnˌʌp
sunward ˈsʌnwɚd; ES -wəd; |-s -z
Sun Yat-sen ˈsʌnˈjætˈsɛn, ˈsunˈjɑtˈsɛn
sup sʌp |supped sʌpt
super ˈsupɚ, ˈsɪu-, ˈsju-; ES -pə(r
superable ˈsupərəbḷ, ˈsuprə-, ˈsɪu-, ˈsju- |-bly
-blɪ
superabound ˌsupərəˈbaund, ˌsɪu-, ˌsju- |-ed
-ɪd
superabundance ˌsupərəˈbʌndəns, ˌsɪu-, ˌsju-
|-cy -ɪ |-dant -dənt
superadd ˌsupɚˈæd, ˌsɪu-, ˌsju- |-ed -ɪd
superannuate ˌsupɚˈænjʊˌet, ˌsɪu-, ˌsju- |-d
-ɪd
superannuation ˌsupɚˌænjuˈeʃən, ˌsɪu-, ˌsju-
superb suˈpɝb, sə-, sɪu-, sju-; ES -ˈpɜb,
-ˈpɝb
supercargo ˌsupɚˈkɑrgo, ˌsɪu-, ˌsju-; ES
-pəˈkɑːgo, E+-ˈkɑːgo; acct.+ˈsuperˌcargo
supercharge n ˈsupɚˌtʃɑrdʒ, ˈsɪu-, ˈsju-; ES
-pəˌtʃɑːdʒ, E+-ˌtʃɑːdʒ; |-s -ɪz |-r -ɚ; ES
-ə(r
supercharge v ˌsupɚˈtʃɑrdʒ, ˌsɪu-, ˌsju-; ES
-pəˈtʃɑːdʒ, E+-ˈtʃɑːdʒ; |-s -ɪz |-d -d
superciliary ˌsupɚˈsɪlɪˌɛrɪ, ˌsɪu-, ˌsju-; ES
-pəˈsɪl-; |-ious -ˈsɪlɪəs
superdreadnought ˌsupɚˈdrɛdˌnɔt, ˌsɪu-, ˌsju-;
ES -pəˈdrɛd-
superego ˌsupɚˈigo, ˌsɪu-, ˌsju-, -ˈɛgo
supereminent ˌsupɚˈɛmənənt, ˌsɪu-, ˌsju-
supererogate ˌsupɚˈɛrəˌget, ˌsɪu-, ˌsju- |-d -ɪd
|-tion -ˌɛrəˈgeʃən
supererogative ˌsupərəˈrɑgətɪv, ˌsɪu-, ˌsju-,
-ˈrɒg- |-tory -ˌtorɪ, -ˌtɔrɪ; S -ˌtorɪ
superficial ˌsupɚˈfɪʃəl, ˌsɪu-, ˌsju-; ES -pə-;
|-ly -ɪ |-ity -ˌfɪʃɪˈælətɪ
superficies ˌsupɚˈfɪʃɪˌiz, ˌsɪu-, ˌsju-, -ˈfɪʃiz;
ES -pə-
superfine ˌsupɚˈfaɪn, ˌsɪu-, ˌsju-; ES -pə-;
|-ness -ˈfaɪnnɪs (ˈsuperˌfine ˈtaste)
superfluity ˌsupɚˈfluətɪ, ˌsɪupɚˈflɪu-, ˌsjupɚ-
ˈflu-; ES -pə-
superfluous suˈpɝfluəs, sə-; ES -ˈpɜ-, -ˈpɝ-
superheat n ˈsupɚˌhit, ˈsɪu-, ˈsju-; ES -pə-
superheat v ˌsupɚˈhit, ˌsɪu-, ˌsju-; ES -pə-;
|-ed -ɪd
superheterodyne ˌsupɚˈhɛtərəˌdaɪn, ˌsɪu-,
ˌsju-; ES -pə-

|full fʊl |tooth tuθ |further ˈfɝðɚ; ES ˈfɝðə |custom ˈkʌstəm |while hwaɪl |how hau |toy tɔɪ
|using ˈjuzɪŋ |fuse fjuz, fɪuz |dish dɪʃ |vision ˈvɪʒən |Eden ˈidn̩ |cradle ˈkredl̩ |keep ʼem ˈkipm̩

superhuman ˌsupɚˈhjumən, ˌsɪupɚˈhɪu-,
ˌsjupɚˈhju-, -ˈjumən; ES -pə-

superimpose ˌsupɚɪmˈpoz, ˌsɪu-, ˌsju- |-s -ɪz
|-d -d

superimposition ˌsupɚˌɪmpəˈzɪʃən, ˌsɪu-, ˌsju-

superincumbent ˌsupərɪnˈkʌmbənt, ˌsɪu-, ˌsju-

superinduce ˌsupərɪnˈdjus, -ˈdus, ˌsɪupərɪn-
ˈdɪus, ˌsjupərɪnˈdjus |-s -ɪz |-d -t

superintend ˌsuprɪnˈtɛnd, ˌsɪu-, ˌsju-, -pərɪn-
|-ed -ɪd |-ence -əns |-ency -ənsɪ |-ent -ənt

superior, S- səˈpɪrɪɚ, su-; ES -ˈpɪrɪ·ə(r

superioress səˈpɪrɪərɪs, su- |-ˈs -ɪz

superiority səˌpɪrɪˈɔrətɪ, su-, -ˈɑr-, -ˈɒr-

superlative səˈpɝlətɪv, su-, sɪu-, sju-; ES
-ˈpɝ-, -ˈpɝ-

superman ˈsupɚˌmæn, ˈsɪu-, ˈsju-; ES -pə-;
|-men -ˌmɛn

supernal suˈpɝnḷ, sɪu-, sju-; ES -ˈpɝ-, -ˈpɝ-;
|-ly -ɪ

supernatural ˌsupɚˈnætʃrəl, ˌsɪu-, ˌsju-,
-tʃərəl |-ly -ɪ |-ism -ˌɪzəm

supernumerary ˌsupɚˈnjuməˌrɛrɪ, -ˈnu-, ˌsɪu-
pɚˈnɪu-, ˌsjupɚˈnju-; ES -pə-

superphosphate ˌsupɚˈfɑsfet, ˌsɪu-, ˌsju-; ES
-pəˈfɑs-, -ˈfɒs-

superpose ˌsupɚˈpoz, ˌsɪu-, ˌsju-; ES -pə-;
|-s -ɪz |-d -d

superposition ˌsupɚpəˈzɪʃən, ˌsɪu-, ˌsju-; ES
-pəpə-

superpower ˌsupɚˈpaʊɚ, ˌsɪu-, ˌsju-, -ˈpaʊr;
ES -pəˈpaʊ·ə(r, -ˈpaʊə(r; |-ed -d

superrealism ˌsupɚˈrɪəlˌɪzəm, ˌsɪu-, ˌsju-; ES
-pə-

supersaturate ˌsupɚˈsætʃəˌret, ˌsɪu-, ˌsju-;
ES -pə-; |-d -ɪd

superscribe ˌsupɚˈskraɪb, ˌsɪu-, ˌsju-; ES
-pə-; |-d -d

superscript ˈsupɚˌskrɪpt, ˈsɪu-, ˈsju-; ES -pə-

superscription ˌsupɚˈskrɪpʃən, ˌsɪu-, ˌsju-; ES
-pə-

supersede ˌsupɚˈsid, ˌsɪu-, ˌsju-; ES -pə-; |-d
-ɪd |-dure -dʒɚ; ES -dʒə(r

superstate ˈsupɚˌstet, ˈsɪu-, ˈsju-; ES -pə-

superstition ˌsupɚˈstɪʃən, ˌsɪu-, ˌsju-; ES
-pə-; |-tious -ʃəs

superstructure ˈsupɚˌstrʌktʃɚ, ˈsɪu-, ˈsju-;
ES -pəˌstrʌktʃə(r

supertax ˈsupɚˌtæks, ˈsɪu-, ˈsju-; ES -pə-;
|-es -ɪz

supervene ˌsupɚˈvin, ˌsɪu-, ˌsju-; ES -pə-;
|-d -d |-vention -ˈvɛnʃən

supervise n ˈsupɚˌvaɪz, ˈsɪu-, ˈsju-; ES -pə-;
|-s -ɪz

supervise v ˌsupɚˈvaɪz, ˌsɪu-, ˌsju-; ES -pə-;
|-s -ɪz |-d -d |-sion -ˈvɪʒən

supervisor ˌsupɚˈvaɪzɚ, ˌsɪu-, ˌsju-; ES
-pəˈvaɪzə(r; —acct.+ˈsuperˌvisor

supine n ˈsupaɪn, ˈsɪu-, ˈsju-

supine adj suˈpaɪn, sɪu-, sju- |-ness -ˈpaɪnnɪs

supper ˈsʌpɚ; ES ˈsʌpə(r; |-ed -d |-ing -pərɪŋ,
-prɪŋ

supplant səˈplænt; E+-ˈplant, -ˈplɑnt; |-ed
-ɪd

supple ˈsʌpḷ |-d -d |-ling ˈsʌplɪŋ, -pḷɪŋ |-r
-plɚ; ES -plə(r; |-st -plɪst

supplely ˈsʌpḷlɪ, ˈsʌpḷɪ

supplement n ˈsʌpləmənt

supplement v ˈsʌpləˌmɛnt |-mented -ˌmɛntɪd

supplementary ˌsʌpləˈmɛntrɪ, -ˈmɛntərɪ

suppliance 'entreaty' ˈsʌplɪəns |-cy -ɪ |-ant
-ənt

suppliance 'supply' səˈplaɪəns |-s -ɪz

supplicancy ˈsʌplɪkənsɪ |-cant -kənt

supplicate ˈsʌplɪˌket |-d -ɪd

supplication ˌsʌplɪˈkeʃən

supply v səˈplaɪ |-plied -ˈplaɪd

supply 'supplely' ˈsʌplɪ

support səˈport, -ˈpɔrt; ES -ˈpoət, E+-ˈpɔət;
|-ed -ɪd |-able -əbḷ |-bly -blɪ

suppose səˈpoz |-s -ɪz |-d -d |-dly -ɪdlɪ;
|N Engd+səˈpɒz (§46)

supposition ˌsʌpəˈzɪʃən

supposititious səˌpɑzəˈtɪʃəs; ES+-ˌpɒz-

suppository səˈpɑzəˌtorɪ, -ˌtɔrɪ; ES -ˈpɑzə-
ˌtorɪ, -ˈpɒz-, E+-ˌtɔrɪ

suppress səˈprɛs |-es -ɪz |-ed -t |-edly -ɪdlɪ

suppressible səˈprɛsəbḷ

suppression səˈprɛʃən |-sive -ˈprɛsɪv

suppurate ˈsʌpjəˌret |-rated -ˌretɪd |-tive -ɪv

suppuration ˌsʌpjəˈreʃən

supra ˈsuprə, ˈsɪu-, ˈsju-

supremacy səˈprɛməsɪ, su-, sɪu-, sju-

supreme səˈprim, su-, sɪu-, sju-

Surat ˈsurət, suˈræt, ˈsurʌt

Surbiton ˈsɝbɪtṇ; ES ˈsɝb-, ˈsɝb-

surcease sɝˈsis; ES sɝ-, sɝ-; |-s -ɪz |-d -t

surcharge n ˈsɝˌtʃɑrdʒ; ES ˈsɝˌtʃɑ:dʒ, ˈsɝ-
ˌtʃɑ:dʒ, E+-ˌtʃɑ:dʒ; |-s -ɪz

Key: *See in full §§3–47.* bee bi |pity ˈpɪtɪ (§6) |rate ret |yet jɛt |sang sæŋ |angry ˈæŋ·grɪ
|bath bæθ; E baθ (§10) |ah ɑ |far fɑr |watch wɑtʃ, wɒtʃ (§12) |jaw dʒɔ |gorge gɔrdʒ |go go

surcharge *v* sɜˈtʃɑrdʒ; ES sɜˈtʃɑːdʒ, sɜ-
ˈtʃɑːdʒ, E+-ˈtʃɑːdʒ; |-s -ɪz |-d -d (ˈsur-
ˌcharged ˈmind)

surcingle ˈsɜˈsɪŋgl̩; ES ˈsɜ-, ˈsɜˈ-; |-d -d

surcoat ˈsɜˈˌkot; ES ˈsɜ-, ˈsɜˈ-

surd sɜd; ES sɜd, sɜˈd

sure ʃʊr; ES ʃʊə(r, ʃɔə(r, ʃɔə(r; |-ly -lɪ

sure-footed ˈʃʊrˈfʊtɪd; ES ˈʃʊə-, ˈʃɔə-, ˈʃɔə-;
(ˈsure-ˌfooted ˈmule)

surety ˈʃʊrtɪ, ˈʃʊrətɪ; ES ˈʃʊətɪ, ˈʃɔə-, ˈʃɔə-,
ˈʃʊrətɪ

surf sɜf; ES sɜf, sɜˈf; |-ed -t

surface ˈsɜˈfɪs, -əs; ES ˈsɜf-, ˈsɜˈf-; |-s -ɪz
|-d -t

surfboat ˈsɜˈfˌbot; ES ˈsɜf-, ˈsɜˈf-

surfeit ˈsɜˈfɪt; ES ˈsɜf-, ˈsɜˈf-; |-ed -ɪd

surge sɜdʒ; ES sɜdʒ, sɜˈdʒ; |-s -ɪz |-d -d

surgeon ˈsɜˈdʒən; ES ˈsɜdʒ-, ˈsɜˈdʒ-; |-ed -d
|-ery -ərɪ, -dʒrɪ

surgical ˈsɜˈdʒɪkl̩; ES ˈsɜdʒ-, ˈsɜˈdʒ-; |-ly -ɪ,
-ɪklɪ

Surinam ˌsʊrɪˈnɑm, -ˈnæm

surly ˈsɜˈlɪ; ES ˈsɜlɪ, ˈsɜˈlɪ; |-lily -lɪlɪ

surmise *n* sɜˈmaɪz, ˈsɜˈmaɪz; ES sə-, ˈsɜ-, ˈsɜˈ-

surmise *v* sɜˈmaɪz; ES sə-; |-s -ɪz |-d -d |-dly
-ɪdlɪ

surmount sɜˈmaʊnt; ES səˈmaʊnt; |-ed -ɪd

surname ˈsɜˈˌnem; ES ˈsɜ-, ˈsɜˈ-; |-d -d

surpass sɜˈpæs; ES sə-, E+-ˈpas, -ˈpɑs; |-es
-ɪz |-ed -t

surplice ˈsɜˈplɪs; ES ˈsɜ-, ˈsɜˈ-; |-s -ɪz |-d -t

surplus ˈsɜˈplʌs, -pləs; ES ˈsɜ-, ˈsɜˈ-; |-es -ɪz

surprise səˈpraɪz, sɜ-; ES sə-; |-s -ɪz |-d -d
|-dly -ɪdlɪ—*In the first pron.* sɜˈ- *became* sə-
by dissimilation (§121).

surrealism səˈrɪəlˌɪzəm |-ist -ɪst

surrealistic səˌrɪəlˈɪstɪk |-ally -l̩ɪ, -ɪklɪ

surrebut ˌsɜˈrɪˈbʌt; ES ˌsɜˈrɪˈbʌt, ˌsɜˈrɪ-;
|-ted -ɪd |-tal -l̩

surrejoin ˌsɜˈrɪˈdʒɔɪn; ES ˌsɜˈrɪ-, ˌsɜˈrɪ-;
|-ed -d |-der -də; ES -də(r

surrender səˈrɛndə; ES -də(r; |-ed -d |-ing
-ˈrɛndrɪŋ, -ˈrɛndərɪŋ

surreptitious ˌsɜˈəpˈtɪʃəs; ES ˌsɜr-, ˌsʌr-, ˌsɜˈ-

surrey, S- ˈsɜˈɪ; ES ˈsɜrɪ, ˈsʌrɪ, ˈsɜˈɪ

surrogate ˈsɜˈəˌget; ES ˈsɜrə-, ˈsʌrə-, ˈsɜˈə-

surround səˈraʊnd |-ed -ɪd

Surry ˈsɜˈɪ; ES ˈsɜrɪ, ˈsʌrɪ, ˈsɜˈɪ

surtax ˈsɜˈˌtæks; ES ˈsɜ-, ˈsɜˈ-; |-es -ɪz |-ed -t

Surtees ˈsɜˈtiz; ES ˈsɜ-, ˈsɜˈ-; |-tees' -tiz

surtout sɜˈtut, -ˈtu; ES sə-; (*Fr* syrˈtu)

surveillance sɜˈveləns, -ˈveljəns; ES sə-; |-s
-ɪz

survey *n* ˈsɜˈve, sɜˈve; ES ˈsɜ-, ˈsɜˈ-, sə-

survey *v* sɜˈve; ES səˈve; |-ed -d

surveyor sɜˈveə, sɜˈveə; ES səˈve·ə(r;
səˈveə *is due to r-dissimilation (§121).*

survival sɜˈvaɪvl̩; ES sə-; |-ism -ˌɪzəm |-ist
-ɪst

survive sɜˈvaɪv; ES sə-; |-d -d

Susa ˈsusə

Susan ˈsuzn̩, ˈsɪuzn̩, ˈsjuzn̩

Susanna, -h suˈzænə, sɪu-, sju-

susceptibility səˌsɛptəˈbɪlətɪ

susceptible səˈsɛptəbl̩ |-bly -blɪ

suspect '*suspected person*' ˈsʌspɛkt

suspect '*suspicion*' səˈspɛkt

suspect *v* səˈspɛkt |-ed -ɪd

suspend səˈspɛnd |-ed -ɪd |-nse -ns

suspension səˈspɛnʃən |-sive -sɪv |-sory -sərɪ

suspicion səˈspɪʃən |-cious -ʃəs

suspiration ˌsʌspəˈreʃən

suspire səˈspaɪr; ES -ˈspaɪə(r; |-d -d

Susquehanna ˌsʌskwɪˈhænə

Sussex ˈsʌsɛks, -ɪks |-'s -ɪz

sustain səˈsten |-ed -d |-edly -ɪdlɪ

sustenance ˈsʌstənəns |-s -ɪz

sustentation ˌsʌstɛnˈteʃən

Sutherland ˈsʌðələnd; ES ˈsʌðə-; |-shire
-ˌʃɪr, -ʃə; ES -ˌʃɪə(r, -ʃə(r

Sutherlandia ˌsʌðəˈlændɪə; ES ˌsʌðə-

sutler ˈsʌtlə; ES ˈsʌtlə(r; |-age -ɪdʒ |-y -ɪ

sutor ˈsutə, ˈsɪu-, ˈsju-; ES -tə(r

sutra ˈsutrə

Sutro ˈsutro

suttee sʌˈti, ˈsʌti

suttle ˈsʌtl̩

Sutton ˈsʌtn̩

suture ˈsutʃə, ˈsɪu-, ˈsju-; ES -tʃə(r; |-d -d

Suwannee səˈwɔni, su-, ˈswɔni, swɔˈni

Suzanne suˈzæn, sɪu-, sju-

suzerain ˈsuzərɪn, -ˌren, ˈsɪu-, ˈsju- |-ty -tɪ

svarabhakti ˌsvarəˈbæktɪ, -ˈbak-

svelte svɛlt (*Fr* svɛlt, zvɛlt)

swab swab, swɒb |-bed -d |-ber -ə; ES -ə(r

Swabia ˈswebɪə |-n -n

swaddle ˈswadl̩, ˈswɒdl̩ |-d -d |-ling -dl̩ɪŋ,
-dlɪŋ

|full fʊl |tooth tuθ |further ˈfɜˈðə; ES ˈfɜˈðə |custom ˈkʌstəm |while hwaɪl |how haʊ |toy tɔɪ
|using ˈjuzɪŋ |fuse fjuz, fɪuz |dish dɪʃ |vision ˈvɪʒən |Eden ˈidn̩ |cradle ˈkredl̩ |keep 'em ˈkipm̩

swaddling *adj* ˈswɑdlɪŋ, ˈswɒd-
swag swæg |swagged swægd
swage swedʒ |swages ˈswedʒɪz |swaged
swedʒd
swagger ˈswægɚ; ES ˈswægə(r; |-ed -d |-ing
ˈswægərɪŋ, ˈswægrɪŋ
Swahili swɑˈhilɪ
swain, S- swen |-ed -d
swale, S- swel |swaled sweld
swallow ˈswɑlo, ˈswɒlo, -lə |-ed -d |-ing -ləwɪŋ
swam swæm
swamp swɑmp, swɒmp, swɒmp; E swɒmp,
swɔmp, swɑmp; S swɔmp, swɑmp, swɒmp
—*These orders of prevalence are based on
known collections. Fuller statistics might
change them.*
Swampscott ˈswɒmpskət, ˈswɒmp-, ˈswɑmp-
swan swɑn, swɒn, swɔn |-ned -d
Swanage ˈswɑnɪdʒ, ˈswɒn- |-ˈs -ɪz
swang swæŋ
swank swæŋk |swanked swæŋkt
swan's-down ˈswɑnzˌdaʊn, ˈswɒnz-, ˈswɔnz-
Swansea ˈswɑnsɪ, ˈswɒnsɪ, -zɪ
Swanwick ˈswɑnɪk, ˈswɒn-
Swanzey ˈswɑnzɪ, ˈswɒnzɪ
swap swɑp, swɒp, swɔp |-ped -t
Swaraj, s- swəˈrɑdʒ |-ism -ɪzəm |-ist -ɪst
sward swɔrd; ES swɔəd; |-ed -ɪd
sware swɛr, swær; E swɛə(r, ES swæə(r
swarm swɔrm; ES swɔəm; |-ed -d
swart swɔrt; ES swɔət
swarth swɔrθ; ES swɔəθ
Swarthmore ˈswɔrθmor, -mɔr; ES ˈswɔəθ-
moə(r, E+-mɔə(r; *loc.*+ˈswɑθmor—*In
ˈswɑθmor the first r is lost by dissimilation
(§121).*
Swarthout ˈswɔrθaʊt; ES ˈswɔəθ-
swarthy ˈswɔrðɪ, -θɪ; ES ˈswɔə-
swash swɑʃ, swɒʃ |-es -ɪz |-ed -t
swashbuckle ˈswɑʃˌbʌkl̩, ˈswɒʃ- |-d -d |-ling
-ˌbʌklɪŋ, -ˌbʌkl̩ɪŋ |-r -ˌbʌklɚ; ES -ˌbʌklə(r
swastika ˈswɑstɪkə, ˈswɒs-, ˈswæs-
swat swɑt, swɒt |-ted -ɪd
swath swɑθ, swɑð, swɒθ, swɒ- |-ˈs -θs, -ðz
|-ths -θs, -ðz
swathe '*swath*' sweð |-thes -ðz
swathe *v* sweð |swathed sweðd
sway swe |swayed swed
Swaziland ˈswɑzɪˌlænd

swear swɛr, swær; E swɛə(r, ES swæə(r;
|swore swor, swɔr; ES swoə(r, E+swɔə(r;
or arch. sware swɛr, swær; E swɛə(r, ES
swæə(r; |sworn sworn, swɔrn; ES swoən,
E+swɔən
sweat swɛt |*past & pptc* sweat swɛt *or* sweated
ˈswɛtɪd
sweatily ˈswɛtl̩ɪ, -ɪlɪ
Swede swid |Sweden ˈswidn̩ |-dish -ɪʃ
Swedenborg ˈswidn̩ˌbɔrg; ES -ˌbɔəg
Swedenborgian ˌswidn̩ˈbɔrdʒɪən; ES -ˈbɔədʒ-
sweep swip |swept swɛpt |-stake -ˌstek
sweet, S- swit |sweeted ˈswitɪd |-bread -ˌbrɛd
sweet-breathed ˈswitˈbrɛθt
Sweetbriar, S- Briar ˈswitˌbraɪɚ; ES -ˌbraɪ·ə(r
sweetbrier, -ar ˈswitˌbraɪɚ; ES -ˌbraɪ·ə(r
sweeten ˈswitn̩ |-ed -d |-ing ˈswitn̩ɪŋ, -tnɪŋ
sweetheart ˈswitˌhɑrt; ES -ˌhɑːt, E+-ˌhaːt
sweetmeat ˈswitˌmit
sweet-potato ˈswitpəˌteto, -ˈteto, -tə
swell swɛl |swelled swɛld |swelled swɛld *or*
swollen ˈswolən, swoln
swelp swɛlp
swelter ˈswɛltɚ; ES ˈswɛltə(r; |-ed -d |-ing
ˈswɛltərɪŋ, ˈswɛltrɪŋ |-try -trɪ
swerve swɝv; ES swɜv, swɝˑv; |-d -d
Swete swit
Sweyn swen
swift, S- swɪft |-en -ən |-ened -ənd
swift-footed ˈswɪftˈfʊtɪd (ˈswift-ˌfooted ˈdeer)
swig swɪg |swigged swɪgd
swill swɪl |swilled swɪld
swim swɪm |swam swæm |swum swʌm *or*
arch. swam swæm
Swinburne ˈswɪnbɚn; ES ˈswɪnbən
swindle ˈswɪndl̩ |-d -d |-ling -dlɪŋ, -dl̩ɪŋ
swindler ˈswɪndlɚ; ES ˈswɪndlə(r
Swindon ˈswɪndən
swine swaɪn |-herd -ˌhɝd; ES -ˌhɜd, -ˌhɝˑd
swing swɪŋ |swung swʌŋ |-er -ɚ; ES -ə(r
swinge swɪndʒ |-s -ɪz |-d -d |-r -ɚ; ES -ə(r
swingle ˈswɪŋgl̩ |-d -d |-ling -glɪŋ, -gl̩ɪŋ
swingletree ˈswɪŋgl̩ˌtri, -trɪ
swinish ˈswaɪnɪʃ
swink *arch.* swɪŋk |swank swæŋk *or* swonk
swʌŋk *or* swinked swɪŋkt |swonk swʌŋk *or*
swonken ˈswʌŋkən *or* swinked swɪŋkt
Swinnerton ˈswɪnɚtən; ES ˈswɪnə-
Swinton ˈswɪntən

swipe swaɪp |swiped swaɪpt	syllogism 'sɪlə͵dʒɪzəm |-gist -dʒɪst
swirl swɜˑl; ES swɜl, swɜˑl; |-ed -d	syllogistic ͵sɪlə'dʒɪstɪk |-al -ḷ |-ally -ḷɪ, -ɪklɪ
swish swɪʃ |swishes 'swɪʃɪz |-swished swɪʃt	sylph sɪlf |-ic -ɪk |-id -ɪd
Swiss swɪs |-'s -ɪz	sylva 'sɪlvə |sylvan 'sɪlvən
switch swɪtʃ |switches 'swɪtʃɪz |-ed -t |-board	Sylvania sɪl'venɪə, -njə
-͵bord, -͵bɔrd; ES -͵boəd, E+-͵bɔəd	Sylvester sɪl'vɛstɚ; ES -'vɛstə(r
switchel 'swɪtʃəl	Sylvia 'sɪlvɪə |Sylvian 'sɪlvɪən
swith swɪθ |swithe swaɪð	symbiosis ͵sɪmbaɪ'osɪs, ͵sɪmbɪ-
Swithin 'swɪðɪn, -θɪn	symbiotic ͵sɪmbaɪ'ɑtɪk, -bɪ-; ES+-'ɒt-; |-al
Switzer 'swɪtsɚ; ES 'swɪtsə(r; |-land -lənd	-ḷ |-ally -ḷɪ, -ɪklɪ
swivel 'swɪvḷ |-ed -d |-ing 'swɪvḷɪŋ, -vḷɪŋ	symbol 'sɪmbḷ |-ed -d |-ing 'sɪmbḷɪŋ, -blɪŋ
swizzle 'swɪzḷ |-d -d |-ling 'swɪzlɪŋ, -zḷɪŋ	symbolic sɪm'bɑlɪk; ES+-'bɒl-; |-al -ḷ |-ally
swob swɑb, swɒb |-bed -d	-ḷɪ |-ly -lɪ
swollen 'swolən, swoln |swoln swoln	symbolism 'sɪmbḷ͵ɪzəm |-ist -ɪst
swollenness 'swolənnɪs	symbolistic ͵sɪmbḷ'ɪstɪk |-al -ḷ |-ally -ḷɪ, -ɪklɪ
swoon swun |swooned swund	symbolization ͵sɪmbḷə'zeʃən, -aɪ'z-
swoop swup |swooped swupt	symbolize 'sɪmbḷ͵aɪz |-s -ɪz |-d -d
swop swɑp, swɒp |-ped -t	symmetric sɪ'mɛtrɪk |-al -ḷ |-ally -ḷɪ, -ɪklɪ
sword sord, sɔrd; ES soəd, E+sɔəd; |-fish	symmetry 'sɪmɪtrɪ
-͵fɪʃ |-play -͵ple |-sman -zmən |-smen	Symonds, -ons 'saɪməndz, 'sɪm-, -nz |-'s -ɪz
-zmən	sympathetic ͵sɪmpə'θɛtɪk |-al -ḷ |-ally -ḷɪ,
swore swor, swɔr; ES swoə(r, E+swɔə(r;	-ɪklɪ
|-rn -n	sympathize 'sɪmpə͵θaɪz |-s -ɪz |-d -d
swot swɑt, swɒt |-ted -ɪd	sympathy ͵sɪmpəθɪ
swound arch. swaund, swund, saund |-ed -ɪd	symphonic sɪm'fɑnɪk; ES+-'fɒn-; |-ally -ḷɪ,
'swounds zwaundz, zaundz, -nz	-ɪklɪ
Swoyersville 'swɔɪɚz͵vɪl; ES 'swɔɪəz-	symphony 'sɪmfənɪ
swum swʌm	symposium sɪm'pozɪəm |-s -z |-sia -zɪə
swung swʌŋ	symptom 'sɪmptəm
Sybaris 'sɪbərɪs |-'s -ɪz |-rite 'sɪbə͵raɪt	symptomatic ͵sɪmptə'mætɪk |-al -ḷ |-ally -ḷɪ,
Sybaritic ͵sɪbə'rɪtɪk |-al -ḷ |-ally -ḷɪ, -ɪklɪ	-ɪklɪ
sybil, S- 'sɪbḷ, -ɪl |-line 'sɪbḷ͵in, -ɪn	synaesthesia ͵sɪnəs'θiʒɪə, -ʒə
sycamore, S- 'sɪkə͵mor, -͵mɔr; ES -͵moə(r,	synagogue 'sɪnə͵gɔg, -͵gɑg, -͵gɒg
E+-͵mɔə(r	synapse sɪ'næps |-sis -ɪs |-ses -iz
syce saɪs |syces 'saɪsɪz	synchromesh 'sɪŋkrə͵mɛʃ, 'sɪn- |-es -ɪz
sycophancy 'sɪkəfənsɪ |-phant -fənt	synchronal 'sɪŋkrənḷ, 'sɪn-
sycophantic ͵sɪkə'fæntɪk |-al -ḷ |-ally -ḷɪ,	synchronic sɪn'krɑnɪk, sɪŋ-; ES+-'krɒn-;
-ɪklɪ	|-al -ḷ |-ally -ḷɪ, -ɪklɪ
Sydenham 'sɪdṇəm, 'sɪdnəm	synchronism 'sɪŋkrə͵nɪzəm, 'sɪn-
Sydney 'sɪdnɪ	synchronize 'sɪŋkrə͵naɪz, 'sɪn- |-s -ɪz |-d -d
Sylla 'sɪlə	synchronous 'sɪŋkrənəs, 'sɪn-
syllabi 'sɪlə͵baɪ	synclinal sɪn'klaɪnḷ, sɪŋ-, 'sɪŋklɪnḷ, 'sɪn-
syllabic sɪ'læbɪk |-al -ḷ |-ally -ḷɪ, -ɪklɪ	|-ly -ɪ
syllabicate sɪ'læbɪ͵ket |-d -ɪd	syncline 'sɪŋklaɪn, 'sɪn-
syllabication sɪ͵læbɪ'keʃən	syncopate 'sɪŋkə͵pet, 'sɪn- |-d -ɪd
syllabification sɪ͵læbəfə'keʃən	syncopation ͵sɪŋkə'peʃən, ͵sɪn-
syllabify sɪ'læbə͵faɪ |-fied -͵faɪd	syncope 'sɪŋkəpɪ, 'sɪn-, -͵pi
syllable 'sɪləbḷ |-d -d |-ling -bḷɪŋ, -blɪŋ	syncretism 'sɪŋkrɪ͵tɪzəm, 'sɪn-
syllabus 'sɪləbəs |-es -ɪz |-bi -͵baɪ	syndic 'sɪndɪk |-al -ḷ |-alism -ḷ͵ɪzəm

syndicate *n* 'sındıkıt, -ˌket
syndicate *v* 'sındıˌket |-d -ıd
syne **saın**, *in the song often* **zaın**
synecdoche sı'nɛkdəkı
synesthesia ˌsınəs'θiʒıə, -ʒə
Synge **sıŋ**
synod sınəd |-al -l̩ |-ally -lı
synodic sı'nadık; ES+-'nɒd-; |-al -l̩ |-ally -lı, -ıklı
synonym 'sınəˌnım
synonymous sı'nanəməs; ES+-'nɒn-; |-my -mı
synopsis sı'napsıs; ES+-'nɒp-; |-pses -psiz
synoptic sı'naptık; ES+-'nɒp-; |-al -l̩ |-ally -lı, -ıklı
syntactical sın'tæktık|l̩ |-ly -ı
syntax 'sıntæks |-es -ız
synthesis 'sınθəsıs |-theses -θəˌsiz
synthesize 'sınθəˌsaız |-s -ız |-d -d
synthetic sın'θɛtık |-al -l̩ |-ally -lı, -ıklı
syphilis 'sıf|lıs |-lous -ləs
syphilitic ˌsıf|'ıtık |-ally -lı, -ıklı
syphon 'saıfən, -fan, -fɒn |-ed -d |-age -fənıdʒ |-al -fən|

Syracusan ˌsırə'kjuzən, -'kıu-, -sən
Syracuse *NY* 'sırəˌkjus, 'sɛr-, -ˌkıus, ˌsırə'k-, ˌsɛr- |-'s -ız— *The traditional, phonetically regular, pron. is clearly* 'sɛr-, ˌsɛr- (*cf.* 'mɛrıəm *for* Miriam), *still in use, but largely superseded by the spelling pronunciation* 'sır-, ˌsır-. *Cf* Terrell. *In Sicily* 'sırəˌkjus, -ˌkıus, *Brit* 'saırəˌkjuz
Syria 'sırıə |Syrian 'sırıən |Syriac 'sırıˌæk
syringa sə'rıŋgə
syringe 'sırındʒ |-s -ız |-d -d
syrinx, S- 'sırıŋks |-es -ız |-nges sə'rındʒiz
syrup 'sırəp, 'sɝəp; E 'sırəp, 'sɝrəp, 'sɝəp; S 'sɝrəp, 'sʌrəp, 'sırəp, 'sɝəp, 'sɛrəp—*see* sirup
system 'sıstəm, -tım
systematic ˌsıstə'mætık |-al -l̩ |-ally -lı, -ıklı
systematism 'sıstəməˌtızəm |-tist -tıst
systematize 'sıstəməˌtaız |-s -ız |-d -d
systemic sıs'tɛmık |-ally -lı, -ıklı
systole 'sıstəˌli, -lı
systolic sıs'talık; ES+-'tɒl-
syzygy 'sızədʒı
Szechwan 'sɛ'tʃwan, 'sɝtʃwæn

T

T, t *letter* **ti** |*pl* T's, Ts, *poss* T's **tiz**
't (1) *abbr. spelling of unstressed* it *in* 'tis, 't'll, 'twas, 'twere, 'twill, 'twould **t-**
't (2) *abbr. spelling of* not *in* can't **-t**
tab **tæb** |tabbed **tæbd**
tabard, T- 'tæbəˑd; ES 'tæbəd; |-ed -ıd
tabaret 'tæbərıt
Tabasco tə'bæsko
tabby, T- 'tæbı
tabernacle, T- 'tæbəˌnæk|l̩, -ˌnɛk|; ES 'tæbə-; |-d -d |-ling -k|ıŋ, -klıŋ
tabes 'tebiz
tabetic tə'bɛtık, -'bitık
Tabitha 'tæbəθə
tablature 'tæbləˌtʃur, -tʃɚ; ES -ˌtʃuə(r, -tʃə(r
table 'teb|l̩ |-d -d |-ling -blıŋ, -b|ıŋ
tableau 'tæblo, tæb'lo |-ed -d
tablecloth 'teb|ˌklɔθ, -ˌklɒθ—*see* cloth
table d'hote 'tæb|'dot, 'tab|- (*Fr* tablə'do:t)

tableknife 'teb|ˌnaıf |-knives -ˌnaıvz
tableland 'teb|ˌlænd
tableless 'teb|lıs
tablespoon 'teb|ˌspun, -ˌspun
tablespoonful 'teb|spunˌful, -spun-, ˌteb|ˈspunˌful, -'spun-
tablet 'tæblıt |-ed -ıd
tableware 'teb|ˌwɛr, -ˌwær; E -ˌwɛə(r, ES -ˌwæə(r
tabloid, T- 'tæblɔıd
taboo tə'bu, tæ'bu |-ed -d
tabor 'tebɚ; ES 'tebə(r; |-ed -d |-ing -bərıŋ, -brıŋ
taboret ˌtæbə'rɛt, 'tæbərıt
tabret 'tæbrıt
tabu tə'bu, tæ'bu |-ed -d
tabular 'tæbjələ; ES -lə(r
tabulate 'tæbjəˌlet |-d -ıd |-tor -ɚ; ES -ə(r
tache tætʃ |taches 'tætʃız
tachiol 'tækıˌol, -ˌal; ES+-ˌɒl

Key: See in full §§3–47. bee **bi** |pity 'pıtı (§6) |rate **ret** |yet **jɛt** |sang **sæŋ** |angry 'æŋ·grı |bath **bæθ**; E **baθ** (§10) |ah **ɑ** |far **fɑr** |watch **watʃ, wɒtʃ** (§12) |jaw **dʒɔ** |gorge **gɔrdʒ** |go **go**

tachometer tə'kɑmətɚ, tæ-; ES -'kɑmətə(r,
 -'kɒm-
tachygraphy tæ'kɪgrəfɪ
tachymeter tə'kɪmətɚ, tæ-; ES -'kɪmətə(r;
 |-try -trɪ
tacit 'tæsɪt
taciturn 'tæsəˌtɝn; ES -ˌtɜn, -ˌtɝn
taciturnity ˌtæsə'tɝnətɪ; ES -'tɜn-, -'tɝn-
Tacitus 'tæsətəs |Tacitus's 'tæsətəsɪz
tack tæk |tacked tækt
tackle 'tækl̩ |-d -d |-ling -klɪŋ, -kl̩ɪŋ
Tacna 'tɑknə (Sp 'tɑknɑ)
Tacoma tə'komə
tact tækt |-ful -fəl |-fully -fəlɪ
tactic 'tæktɪk |-s -s |-al -l̩ |-ally -l̩ɪ, -ɪklɪ
tactician tæk'tɪʃən
tactile 'tæktl̩, 'tæktɪl
tactual 'tæktʃʊəl |-ly -ɪ
tad, T- tæd |-pole -ˌpol
tael tel
ta'en arch. pptc of take 'ten
taeniafuge 'tinɪəˌfjudʒ, -ˌfɪudʒ |-s -ɪz
taeniasis ti'naɪəsɪs
taffeta 'tæfɪtə |taffity 'tæfətɪ
taffrail 'tæfˌrel
taffy, T- 'tæfɪ |-fied -fɪd
tag tæg |tagged tægd
Tagalog 'tægəˌlɑg, -ˌlɒg, -ˌlɔg
Tagore tə'gor, tə'gɔr; ES tə'goə(r, E+-'gɔə(r
tagrag 'tægˌræg |-ed -d |-gery -ərɪ, -rɪ
Tagus 'tegəs |Tagus's 'tegəsɪz
Tahiti tɑ'hitɪ, -ti |-tian -tɪən
Tai, t- 'tɑ·i
tail tel |tailed teld
tailboard 'telˌbord, -ˌbɔrd; ES -ˌboəd, E+
 -ˌbɔəd
Tailefer, Taill- surname 'tɑləvɚ, 'tʌl-; ES
 -və(r, 'tɒl-
taille tel
tailless 'tellɪs
taillight 'telˌlaɪt
tailor, T- 'telɚ; ES 'telə(r; |-ed -d |-ing -ɪŋ
tailor-made 'telɚ'med; ES 'telə-; ('tailor-
 ˌmade 'suit)
tailpiece 'telˌpis |-pieces -ˌpisɪz
tailrace 'telˌres |-races -ˌresɪz
tailstock 'telˌstɑk; ES+-ˌstɒk
Taine ten (Fr tɛn)
taint tent |tainted 'tentɪd

Taiwan 'taɪ'wɑn
Taj Mahal 'tɑdʒmə'hɑl, 'tɑʒ-
take tek |took tʊk |taken 'tekən
take care te'kɛr, tek'kɛr, -'kær; E -'kɛə(r, ES
 -'kæə(r
takedown 'tekˌdaʊn
take-off 'tekˌɔf, -ˌɒf
taker 'tekɚ; ES 'tekə(r
Talbot, t- 'tɔlbət
talc tælk |-ose 'tælkos |-um 'tælkəm
tale tel
talebearer 'telˌbɛrɚ, -ˌbærɚ; E -ˌbɛrə(r, ES
 -ˌbærə(r
talecarrier 'telˌkærɪɚ; ES -ˌkærɪ·ə(r
talemonger 'telˌmʌŋgɚ; ES -ˌmʌŋgə(r
talent 'tælənt |-ed -ɪd
taler 'tɑlɚ; ES 'tɑlə(r; (Ger 'tɑ:lər)
tales 'jurymen' 'teliz
talesman 'telzmən, 'teliz- |-men -mən
taleteller 'telˌtɛlɚ; ES -ˌtɛlə(r
Taliaferro Ga 'tɑləvɚ, 'tʌl-; ES -və(r, 'tɒl-
Taliesin ˌtælɪ'ɛsɪn
talion 'tælɪən, -ljən
talisman 'tælɪsmən, 'tælɪz- |-mans -mənz
talk tɔk |talked tɔkt |-ative -ətɪv |-ie -ɪ
talking-to 'tɔkɪŋˌtu
tall tɔl
tallage 'tælɪdʒ |-s -ɪz |-d -d
Tallahassee ˌtælə'hæsɪ
Tallahatchie ˌtælə'hætʃɪ
Tallapoosa ˌtælə'pusə
tallboy 'tɔlˌbɔɪ
Talleyrand-Perigord, de 'tælɪˌrænd (Fr də
 tɑlrɑ̃·peri'gɔ:r, talrɑ̃-)
tallith 'tælɪθ
tallow 'tælo, 'tælə |-ed -d |-ing 'tæləwɪŋ
tallowy 'tæləwɪ
tally 'tælɪ |tallied 'tælɪd
tallyho intj ˌtælɪ'ho
tallyho n, v 'tælɪˌho |-hoed -ˌhod
Talmage 'tælmɪdʒ |Talmage's 'tælmɪdʒɪz
Talmud 'tælmʌd, 'tælməd |-ic tæl'mʌdɪk
talon 'tælən |taloned 'tælənd
talus 'teləs |taluses 'teləsɪz |tali 'telaɪ
tamale tə'mɑlɪ
Tamar 'temɚ; ES 'temə(r
tamarack 'tæməˌræk, 'tæmræk
tamarind 'tæməˌrɪnd
tamarisk 'tæməˌrɪsk

|full fʊl |tooth tuθ |further 'fɝðɚ; ES 'fɝðə |custom 'kʌstəm |while hwaɪl |how haʊ |toy tɔɪ
|using 'juzɪŋ |fuse fjuz, fɪuz |dish dɪʃ |vision 'vɪʒən |Eden 'idn̩ |cradle 'kredl̩ |keep 'em 'kipm̩

Words below in which a *before* r (farm) *is sounded* ɑ *are often pronounced in* E *with* a (fɑ:m)

tamasha tə'mɑʃə

tamber 'tæmbɚ; ES 'tæmbə(r = timbre

tambour 'tæmbʊr; ES 'tæmbʊə(r; |-ed -d

tambourin 'tæmbʊˌrɪn (*Fr* tăbu'ræ̃)

tambourine ˌtæmbə'rin |-d -d

tame tem |tamed temd |-mable, -meable -əb|

Tamerlane 'tæmɚˌlen; ES 'tæmə-

Tamil 'tæm|, 'tæmɪl

Tammany 'tæmənɪ

Tamora 'tæmərə, 'tæmrə

Tam o'Shanter 'tæmə'ʃæntɚ; ES -'ʃæntə(r

tam-o'shanter ˌtæmə'ʃæntɚ; ES -tə(r; |-ed -d

tamp tæmp |tamped tæmpt

Tampa 'tæmpə

tamper 'tæmpɚ; ES 'tæmpə(r; |-ed -d |-ing 'tæmpərɪŋ, 'tæmprɪŋ

Tampico tæm'piko, 'tæmpɪˌko (*Sp* tam'piko)

tampion 'tæmpɪən, -pjən |-ed -d

tampon 'tæmpɑn, -pɒn

Tamworth 'tæmwɚθ; ES 'tæmwəθ

tan tæn |tanned tænd

tanager 'tænədʒɚ, 'tænɪ-; ES -dʒə(r

Tanagra 'tænəgrə

tanbark 'tænˌbɑrk; ES -ˌbɑ:k

Tancred 'tæŋkrɪd, 'tænkrɪd

tandem 'tændəm

Taney *justice* 'tɔnɪ

tang tæŋ |tanged tæŋd |tanging 'tæŋɪŋ

Tanganyika ˌtæŋgən'jikə, ˌtæŋgæn-

tangelo 'tændʒəˌlo

tangent 'tændʒənt |tangency 'tændʒənsɪ

tangential tæn'dʒɛnʃəl |-ly -ɪ

Tangerine *'of Tangier'* ˌtændʒə'rin

tangerine *fruit* 'tændʒəˌrin, ˌtændʒə'rin

tangibility ˌtændʒə'bɪlətɪ

tangible 'tændʒəb| |-bly -blɪ

Tangier tæn'dʒɪr; ES tæn'dʒɪə(r

tangle 'tæŋg| |-d -d |-ling 'tæŋglɪŋ, -g|ɪŋ

Tanglewood 'tæŋg|ˌwʊd

tango 'tæŋgo |-ed -d

tank tæŋk |tanked tæŋkt

tankard 'tæŋkɚd; ES 'tæŋkəd

tanker 'tæŋkɚ; ES 'tæŋkə(r

tannate 'tænet

tanner, T- 'tænɚ; ES 'tænə(r; |-y 'tænərɪ

Tannhäuser 'tænˌhɔɪzɚ, 'tɑn-; ES -ˌhɔɪzə(r; (*Ger* 'tɑnˌhɔyzər)

tannic 'tænɪk |tannin 'tænɪn

tansy 'tænzɪ

tantalize 'tænt|ˌaɪz |-s -ɪz |-d -d

tantalum 'tænt|əm

Tantalus 'tænt|əs |Tantalus's 'tænt|əsɪz

tantamount 'tæntəˌmaʊnt

tantara 'tæntərə, tæn'tærə, -'tɑrə

tantivy, T- tæn'tɪvɪ |-tivied -'tɪvɪd

tantrum 'tæntrəm

Taos *NMex* taʊs, 'taʊəs, 'taɑs (*Am Sp* taus) |-'s -ɪz

Taoism 'tɑoˌɪzəm, 'tɑuɪzəm

tap tæp |tapped tæpt

tapa 'tɑpə

tape tep |taped tept |-line 'tepˌlaɪn

taper 'tepɚ; ES 'tepə(r; |-ed -d |-ing -pərɪŋ, -prɪŋ

tapestry 'tæpɪstrɪ |-tried -trɪd

tapeworm 'tepˌwɝm; ES -ˌwɜm, -ˌwɜ·m

taphouse 'tæpˌhaʊs |-houses -ˌhaʊzɪz

tapioca ˌtæpɪ'okə

tapir 'tepɚ; ES 'tepə(r

tapis tæ'pi, 'tæpi, 'tæpɪs (*Fr* ta'pi)

tappa 'tɑpə

Tappan 'tæpən

tappet 'tæpɪt

taproom 'tæpˌrum, -ˌrʊm

taproot 'tæpˌrut, -ˌrʊt |-ed -ɪd

tapster 'tæpstɚ; ES 'tæpstə(r

tar tɑr; ES tɑ:(r; |-red -d |-ring 'tɑrɪŋ

Tara *Irel* 'tærə, *goddess* 'tɑrə

taradiddle 'tærəˌdɪd| |-d -d |-ling -d|ɪŋ, -dlɪŋ

Taranto tə'rænto (*It* 'tɑ:ranto)

tarantula tə'ræntʃələ |-s -z |-lae -li

tarboosh tɑr'buʃ; ES tɑ:'buʃ; |-ed -t

Tarbox 'tɑrˌbɑks; ES 'tɑ:ˌbɑks, -ˌbɒks; |-'s -ɪz

tardigrade 'tɑrdɪˌgred; ES 'tɑ:dɪ-

tardy 'tɑrdɪ; ES 'tɑ:dɪ; |-dily -d|ɪ, -dɪlɪ

tare tɛr, tær; E tɛə(r, ES tæə(r; |-d -d

Tarentum tə'rɛntəm

targe tɑrdʒ; ES tɑ:dʒ; |-s -ɪz |-d -d

target 'tɑrgɪt; ES 'tɑ:gɪt; |-ed -ɪd

tariff 'tærɪf |tariffed 'tærɪft

Tarkington 'tɑrkɪŋtən; ES 'tɑ:k-

tarlatan, -le- 'tɑrlətn̩; ES 'tɑ:l-; |-ed -d

Tarleton 'tɑrltən; ES 'tɑ:l-

tarn tɑrn; ES tɑ:n; |-side -ˌsaɪd

Key: See in full §§3–47. bee bi |pity 'pɪtɪ (§6) |rate ret |yet jɛt |sang sæŋ |angry 'æŋ·grɪ |bath bæθ; E bɑθ (§10) |ah ɑ |far fɑr |watch wɑtʃ, wɒtʃ (§12) |jaw dʒɔ |gorge gɔrdʒ |go go

Words below in which a *before* r (farm) *is sounded* ɑ *are often pronounced in* E *with* a (fɑːm)
Words below that have æ *before* r (carry 'kærɪ) *are often pronounced in* N *with* ɛ ('kɛrɪ, §94)

tarnish 'tɑrnɪʃ; ES 'tɑːn-; |-es -ɪz |-ed -t
taro 'tɑro
tarpaulin tɑr'pɔlɪn; ES tɑːˈpɔlɪn; |-ed -d
Tarpeia tɑr'piə; ES tɑːˈpiə; |-n -n
tarpon 'tɑrpɑn; ES 'tɑːpɑn, -pɒn, S+tɑːˈpɒn
Tarquin 'tɑrkwɪn; ES 'tɑːkwɪn
tarradiddle 'tærəˌdɪd| |-d -d |-ling -d|ɪŋ, -dlɪŋ
tarragon 'tærəˌgɑn; ES+-ˌgɒn
Tarrant 'tærənt
tarriance 'tærɪəns |-s -ɪz
tarry 'like tar' 'tɑrɪ
tarry 'stay' 'tærɪ |tarried 'tærɪd
tarsal 'tɑrs|; ES 'tɑːs|
Tarshish 'tɑrʃɪʃ; ES 'tɑːʃɪʃ; |-'s -ɪz
tarsometatarsus 'tɑrsoˌmɛtə'tɑrsəs; ES 'tɑːso-ˌmɛtə'tɑːsəs; |-si -saɪ
tarsus, T- 'tɑrsəs; ES 'tɑːsəs; |tarsi -saɪ |-sus' səs
tart tɑrt; ES tɑːt; |-ed -ɪd
tartan 'tɑrtn̩; ES 'tɑːtn̩; |-ed -d
tartar, T- 'tɑrtɚ; ES 'tɑːtə(r
Tartarean, -ian tɑr'tɛrɪən, -'tær-, -'ter-; ES tɑ't-
tartare sauce 'tɑrtɚˌsɔs; ES 'tɑːtə-
tartaric tɑr'tærɪk, -'tɑrɪk; ES tɑːˈt-
Tartarus 'tɑrtərəs; ES 'tɑːtərəs; |-'s -ɪz
Tartary 'tɑrtərɪ; ES 'tɑːtərɪ; =Tatary
tartlet 'tɑrtlɪt; ES 'tɑːtlɪt
tartrate 'tɑrtret; ES 'tɑːtret; |-d -ɪd
Tartufe, -ffe tɑr'tuf; ES tɑːˈtuf; (Fr tɑr'tyf)
task tæsk; E+task, tɑsk; |-ed -t
taskmaster 'tæskˌmæstɚ; ES 'tæskˌmæstə(r, E+'taskˌmɑstə(r, 'tɑskˌmɑstə(r
Tasman 'tæzmən
Tasmania tæz'menɪə, -njə |-n -n
tasse tæs |tasses 'tæsɪz
tassel 'tæs| |-ed -d |-ing 'tæs|ɪŋ, 'tæslɪŋ—cf tossel
Tasso 'tæso (It 'tɑsso)
taste test |-d -ɪd |-ful 'testfəl |-fully -fəlɪ
tasty 'testɪ |tastily 'test|ɪ, -tɪlɪ
tat tæt |tatted 'tætɪd
ta-ta 'tɑˌtɑ accent varies
Tatar 'tɑtɚ; ES 'tɑtə(r; =Tartar
Tatarian tɑ'tɛrɪən, -'tær-, -'ter-
Tataric tɑ'tærɪk

Tatary 'tɑtɚɪ
tatler, T- 'tætlɚ; ES 'tætlə(r
tatterdemalion ˌtætɚdɪ'meljən, -lɪən; ES ˌtætə-
Tattersall 'tætɚˌsɔl, -səl; ES 'tætə-
Tattershall Lincs 'tætɚʃəl, -səl; ES 'tætə-; ʃ by sp. pron.
tattle 'tæt| |-d -d |-ling 'tæt|ɪŋ, 'tætlɪŋ
tattler 'tætlɚ, 'tætlɚ; ES -ə(r
tattoo tæ'tu |tattooed tæ'tud
tau tɔ, tau
Tauchnitz 'tauknɪts (Ger 'tauxnɪts) |-'s -ɪz
taught past pptc of teach tɔt
taunt tɔnt, tɒnt, tɑnt |-ed -ɪd
Taunton Engd, Mass 'tɔntən, 'tɒn-, loc. 'tɑntən, Mass+'tɑntn̩ (Fr to:p)
taupe top (Fr to:p)
Taurus 'tɔrəs |Taurus's 'tɔrəsɪz |gen -ri -raɪ
taut tɔt |-en -n̩ |-ened -n̩d |-ening -n̩ɪŋ, -nɪŋ
tautog 'tɔtɑg, -tɒg, -tɔg
tautological ˌtɔt|'ɑdʒɪk|; ES+-'ɒdʒ-; |-ly -ɪ, -ɪk|ɪ
tautology tɔ'tɑlədʒɪ; ES+-'tɒl-; |-gism -ˌdʒɪzəm |-gist -dʒɪst |-gous -gəs
tautosyllabic ˌtɔtəsɪ'læbɪk
tavern 'tævɚn; ES 'tævən; |-ed -d
Tavistock 'tævɪsˌtɑk; ES+-ˌtɒk
taw tɔ |tawed tɔd
Tawas 'tɔwəs |-'s -ɪz
tawdry 'tɔdrɪ
tawny 'tɔnɪ
tax tæks |taxes 'tæksɪz |taxed tækst
taxability ˌtæksə'bɪlətɪ
taxable 'tæksəb| |-bly -blɪ |-ation tæks'eʃən
tax-exempt 'tæksɪg'zɛmpt ('tax-ex‚empt 'bond)
taxi n 'tæksɪ |taxis 'tæksɪz
taxi, -y v 'tæksɪ |taxies 'tæksɪz |taxied -d
taxicab 'tæksɪˌkæb |-cabbed -ˌkæbd
taxidermal ˌtæksə'dɝm|; ES -'dɜm|, -'dɝm|; |-mic -mɪk
taxidermist 'tæksəˌdɝmɪst; ES -ˌdɜmɪst, -ˌdɝmɪst; |-my -mɪ
taximeter 'tæksɪˌmitɚ; ES -ˌmitə(r
taxiplane 'tæksɪˌplen |-ed -d
taxis 'tæksɪs
taxonomy tæks'ɑnəmɪ; ES+-'ɒn-

|full ful |tooth tuθ |further 'fɝðɚ; ES 'fɜðə |custom 'kʌstəm |while hwaɪl |how hau |toy tɔɪ
|using 'juzɪŋ |fuse fjuz, fruz |dish dɪʃ |vision 'vɪʒən |Eden 'idn̩ |cradle 'kred| |keep 'em 'kipm̩

Tay te
Tayler 'telə; ES 'telə(r
Taylor 'telə; ES 'telə(r
Tchad tʃæd, tʃad
Tchaikovsky, -wsky tʃaɪ'kɔfskɪ, -'kɒf-, -vskɪ,
   -'kauskɪ
tea ti |teaed tid
tea-ball 'ti,bɔl
teacake 'ti,kek
teach titʃ |teaches 'titʃɪz |taught tɔt
teachability ,titʃə'bɪlətɪ
teachable 'titʃəbl̩ |-bly -blɪ
teacher 'titʃə; ES 'titʃə(r
teacup 'ti,kʌp |-ful 'tikʌp,ful |-fuls -,fulz
Teagarden 'ti,gardn̩, -dɪn; ES -,ga:d-, E+
   -,ga:d-
Teague tig
teak tik |-wood -,wud
teakettle 'ti,kɛtl̩, 'tikɪtl̩
teal til
team tim |teamed timd |-ster -stə; ES -stə(r
teammate 'tim,met
teamwork 'tim,wɝk; ES -,wɜk, -,wɝ·k
teapot 'ti,pat; ES+-,pɒt
teapotful 'tipat,ful; ES+-pɒt-; |-fuls -,fulz
tear 'eyewater' tɪr; ES tɪə(r, S+tɛə(r; |-ed -d
tear 'rip' tɛr, tær; E tɛə(r, ES tæə(r; |tore
   tor, tɔr; ES toə(r, E+tɔə(r; |torn tɔrn, tɔrn;
   ES toən, E+tɔən
tearoom 'ti,rum, -,rʊm
Tearsheet 'tɛr,ʃit, 'tær-; E 'tɛə-, ES 'tæə-
Teasdale 'tizdl̩, -,del—cf Tisdall, Tees
tease tiz |teases 'tizɪz |teased tizd
teasel 'tizl̩ |-ed -d |-ing 'tizl̩ɪŋ, -zlɪŋ
teashop 'ti,ʃap; ES+-,ʃɒp
teaspoon 'ti,spun, -,spʊn, 'tis,p-
teaspoonful 'tispun,ful, -spʊn- |-fuls -,fulz
teat tit
Teaticket ,ti'tɪkɪt
teazel, -zle 'tizl̩ |-(e)d -d |-(l)ing -zl̩ɪŋ, -zlɪŋ
Teazle 'tizl̩
technic 'tɛknɪk |-al -l̩ |-ally -l̩ɪ, -ɪklɪ
technicality ,tɛknɪ'kælətɪ
technician tɛk'nɪʃən
technique tɛk'nik
technocracy tɛk'nakrəsɪ; ES+-'nɒk-
technocrat 'tɛknə,kræt |-ic ,tɛknə'krætɪk
technologic ,tɛknə'ladʒɪk; ES+-'lɒdʒ-; |-al -l̩
   |-ally -l̩ɪ, -ɪklɪ

technology tɛk'nalədʒɪ; ES+-'nɒl-
techy 'tɛtʃɪ |-chily -tʃəlɪ, -tʃɪlɪ
tectal 'tɛktl̩
tectum 'tɛktəm |-ta -tə
Tecumseh tɪ'kʌmsɪ, -'kʌmpsɪ
ted tɛd |tedded 'tɛdɪd
Teddy 'tɛdɪ
Te Deum tɪ'diəm, ti-
tedious 'tidɪəs, 'tidʒəs
tedium 'tidɪəm |-s -z
tee ti |teed tid
teem tim |teemed timd
teen tin |-s -z
teen-age 'tin,edʒ
teenage 'tinɪdʒ
teeny 'tinɪ
teepee 'tepee' 'tipi
Tees tiz |-'s -ɪz |-dale -,del, -dl̩
teeter 'titə; ES 'titə(r; |-ed -d
teeth tiθ |-less -lɪs
teethe tið |teethed tiðd |-thing 'tiðɪŋ
teethridge 'tiθ,rɪdʒ |-s -ɪz
teetotal ti'totl̩ |-ed -d |-ing -'totl̩ɪŋ, -tlɪŋ
teetotaler, -ller ti'totlə, -'totlə; ES -ə(r
teetotalism ti'totl̩,ɪzəm |-ist -ɪst
teetotally ti'totl̩ɪ, emph.+ti'totl̩ɪ
teetotum ti'totəm |-ed -d
tegument 'tɛgjəmənt |-al ,tɛgjə'mɛntl̩
tegumentary ,tɛgjə'mɛntərɪ
te-hee ti'hi |te-heed ti'hid
Teheran ,tɪə'ran, ,tɛhə'ran, tɛ'ran
Tehuantepec tə,wantə'pɛk, tə'wantə,pɛk,
   -ɒntə-
Teign tɪn, tin, ten
Teignmouth 'tɪnməθ
tekel 'tikl̩, 'tɛkl̩—cf mene
Tekoa tɪ'koə
Telamon 'tɛləmən
telautograph tɛl'ɔtə,græf; E+-,graf, -,graf
telegram 'tɛlə,græm |-med -d
telegraph 'tɛlə,græf; E+-,graf, -,graf; |-ed -t
telegrapher tə'lɛgrəfə; ES -fə(r; |-phy -fɪ
telegraphic ,tɛlə'græfɪk |-al -l̩ |-ally -l̩ɪ, -ɪklɪ
Telemachus tə'lɛməkəs |-'s -ɪz
teleological ,tɛlɪə'ladʒɪkl̩, ,tilɪ-; ES+-'lɒdʒ-;
   |-ly -ɪ
teleology ,tɛlɪ'alədʒɪ, ,tilɪ-; ES+-'ɒl-
telepathic ,tɛlə'pæθɪk |-ally -ɪ, -ɪklɪ
telepathy tə'lɛpəθɪ

telephone 'tɛlə‚fon |-d -d
telephonic ‚tɛlə'fɑnɪk; ES+-'fɒn-; |-al -|
  |-ally -ɪ, -ɪklɪ
telephony tə'lɛfənɪ
telephotography ‚tɛləfo'tɑgrəfɪ, -'tɒg-
telescope 'tɛlə‚skop |-d -t
telescopic ‚tɛlə'skɑpɪk; ES+-'skɒp-; |-al -|
  |-ally -ɪ, -ɪklɪ
telescopy tə'lɛskəpɪ
teletype, T- 'tɛlə‚taɪp |-d -t
teletypewriter ‚tɛlə'taɪp‚raɪtɚ; ES -‚raɪtə(r
television 'tɛlə‚vɪʒən |-visor -‚vaɪzɚ; ES -zə(r
tell tɛl |told told
telltale 'tɛl‚tel
tellurium tɛ'lʊrɪəm, -'lɪʊ-
Temanite 'timən‚aɪt
temblor tɛm'blɔr; ES -'blɔə(r; (Sp tem'blɔr)
temerity tə'mɛrətɪ
Temescal ‚tɛmə'skæl
Tempe 'tɛmpɪ
temper 'tɛmpɚ; ES -pə(r; |-ed -d |-ing 'tɛm-
  pərɪŋ, -prɪŋ
temperament 'tɛmprəmənt, -pərə-
temperamental ‚tɛmprə'mɛntl̩, -pərə- |-ly -ɪ
temperance 'tɛmprəns, -pərəns
temperate 'tɛmprɪt, -pərɪt
temperature 'tɛmprətʃɚ, -pərə-; ES -tʃə(r
tempest 'tɛmpɪst |-ed -ɪd
tempestuous tɛm'pɛstʃʊəs
Templar 'tɛmplɚ; ES 'tɛmplə(r
temple, T- 'tɛmpl̩ |-d -d |-ton -tən
tempo 'tɛmpo |-s -z |-pi -pi
temporal 'tɛmpərəl, -prəl |-ly -ɪ
temporarily 'tɛmpə‚rɛrəlɪ, esp. if emph.
  ‚tɛmpə'rɛrəlɪ
temporary 'tɛmpə‚rɛrɪ
temporize 'tɛmpə‚raɪz |-s -ɪz |-d -d
tempt tɛmpt |-ed -ɪd |-ation tɛmp'teʃən
tempus fugit 'tɛmpəs'fjudʒɪt, -'fɪu-
ten tɛn
tenability ‚tɛnə'bɪlətɪ
tenable 'tɛnəbl̩ |-bly -blɪ
tenacious tɪ'neʃəs |-city tɪ'næsətɪ
Tenafly 'tɛnə‚flaɪ
tenancy 'tɛnənsɪ |-ant -ənt |-anted -əntɪd
tenantry 'tɛnəntrɪ
tench tɛntʃ |tenches 'tɛntʃɪz
tend tɛnd |-ed -ɪd |-ance -əns |-ency -ənsɪ
tendencious, -tious tɛn'dɛnʃəs

tender 'tɛndɚ; ES 'tɛndə(r; |-ed -d |-ing
  'tɛndərɪŋ, -drɪŋ
tenderer 'tɛndərɚ, 'tɛndrɚ; ES -dərə(r,
  -drə(r
tenderfoot 'tɛndɚ‚fʊt; ES 'tɛndə-
tender-footed 'tɛndɚ'fʊtɪd; ES 'tɛndə-
tenderhearted 'tɛndɚ'hɑrtɪd; ES 'tɛndə-
  'hɑːtɪd, E+-'hɑːtɪd; ('tender‚hearted 'father)
tenderloin 'tɛndɚ‚lɔɪn; ES 'tɛndə-; |-ed -d;
tendinous, -donous 'tɛndənəs
tendon 'tɛndən
tendril 'tɛndrɪl, -əl |-ed -d
Tenebrae 'tɛnə‚bri
tenebrous 'tɛnəbrəs
Tenedos 'tɛnədəs, -‚dɑs; ES+-‚dɒs; |-'s -ɪz
tenement 'tɛnəmənt |-ed -ɪd
Tenerife, -ffe ‚tɛnə'rɪf, -'rif (Sp ‚tene'rife)
tenet 'tɛnɪt, 'tinɪt
tenfold adj, adv 'tɛn'fold ('ten‚fold 'loss)
teniafuge 'tinɪə‚fjudʒ, -‚fɪudʒ |-s -ɪz
teniasis ti'naɪəsɪs
Teniers 'tɛnjɚz, -ɪɚz; ES 'tɛnjəz, -ɪ·əz; |-'s
  -ɪz (Flem tɛ'nirs, Fr te'nje)
Tennessean ‚tɛnə'siən
Tennessee ‚tɛnə'si, 'tɛnə‚si ('Tennes‚see 'air)
tennis 'tɛnɪs
Tennyson 'tɛnəsn̩
tenon 'tɛnən |-ed -d
tenor 'tɛnɚ; ES 'tɛnə(r; |-ed -d
tenpenny 'tɛn‚pɛnɪ, -pənɪ
tenpins 'tɛn‚pɪnz
Tensas 'tɛnsɔ
tense tɛns |tenses 'tɛnsɪz |tensed tɛnst
tensile 'tɛnsl̩, -sɪl
tension 'tɛnʃən |-sity 'tɛnsətɪ
tensor 'tɛnsɚ, -sɔr; ES 'tɛnsə(r, -sɔə(r
ten-strike 'tɛn‚straɪk
tent tɛnt |tented 'tɛntɪd
tentacle 'tɛntəkl̩, -ɪkl̩ |-d -d
tentative 'tɛntətɪv
tenterhook 'tɛntɚ‚hʊk; ES 'tɛntə-
tenth tɛnθ |-ths -θs
tenuity tɛn'juətɪ, tɪ'nɪuətɪ, tɪ'nuətɪ
tenuous 'tɛnjʊəs
tenure 'tɛnjɚ; ES 'tɛnjə(r
tepee 'tipi
tepid 'tɛpɪd |-ity tɛ'pɪdətɪ
Terah 'tɪrə, 'tirə

|full fʊl |tooth tuθ |further 'fɝðɚ; ES 'fɝðə |custom 'kʌstəm |while hwaɪl |how haʊ |toy tɔɪ
|using 'juzɪŋ |fuse fjuz, fɪuz |dish dɪʃ |vision 'vɪʒən |Eden 'idn̩ |cradle 'kredl̩ |keep 'em 'kipm̩

teraph ˈtɛrəf |-im ˈtɛrəˌfɪm

Terbeek ˈtɝˈbɪk, təˈbik; ES ˈtɜb-, ˈtɝˈb-, təˈb-; (Du tərˈbeːk)

terbium ˈtɝˈbɪəm; ES ˈtɜb-, ˈtɝˈb-

tercel ˈtɝˈs|; ES ˈtɜs|, ˈtɝˈs|

tercentenary tɝˈsɛntəˌnɛrɪ, ˌtɝˈsɛnˈtɛnərɪ; ES -ɝ-, -ɝˈ-; mainly Brit -sɛnˈtinərɪ

terebinth ˈtɛrəˌbɪnθ |-ths -θs

Terence ˈtɛrəns |-ʼs -ɪz

Teresa təˈrisə, -ˈrizə, -ˈrɛsə (It teˈrɛːzɑ)

tergiversate ˈtɝˈdʒɪvɝˌset; ES ˈtɜdʒɪvə-, ˈtɝˈdʒɪvə-; |-d -ɪd

tergiversation ˌtɝˈdʒɪvɝˈseʃən; ES ˌtɜdʒɪvə-, ˌtɝˈdʒɪvə-

Terhune tɝˈhjun, -ˈhɪun; ES tɜ-, tɝˈ-

term tɝm; ES tɜm, tɝˈm; |-ed -d

Termagant, t- ˈtɝˈməgənt; ES ˈtɜm-, ˈtɝˈm-; |-gancy -gənsɪ

terminable ˈtɝˈmɪnəb|; ES ˈtɜm-, ˈtɝˈm-; |-bly -blɪ

terminal ˈtɝˈmən|; ES ˈtɜm-, ˈtɝˈm-; |-ly -ɪ

terminate ˈtɝˈməˌnet; ES ˈtɜm-, ˈtɝˈm-; |-d -ɪd

termination ˌtɝˈməˈneʃən; ES ˌtɜm-, ˌtɝˈm-

terminer ˈtɝˈmɪnɝ; ES ˈtɜmɪnə(r, ˈtɝˈmɪnə(r

terminology ˌtɝˈməˈnɑlədʒɪ; ES ˌtɜm-, ˌtɝˈm-, -ˈnɒl-

terminus ˈtɝˈmənəs; ES ˈtɜm-, ˈtɝˈm-; |-es -ɪz |-ni -ˌnaɪ

termite ˈtɝˈmaɪt; ES ˈtɜm-, ˈtɝˈm-

tern tɝn; ES tɜn, tɝˈn

ternary ˈtɝˈnərɪ; ES ˈtɜn-, ˈtɝˈn-

ternate ˈtɝˈnɪt, -net; ES ˈtɜn-, ˈtɝˈn-

Terpsichore tɝˈpˈsɪkərɪ, -ˌri; ES tɜp-, tɝˈp-

terpsichoreal ˌtɝˈpsɪkəˈriəl; ES ˌtɜp-, ˌtɝˈp-; |-ly -ɪ |-an -ən

terrace ˈtɛrɪs, -əs |-s -ɪz |-d -t

terra cotta, -ra-c- ˈtɛrəˈkɑtə; ES+-ˈkɒtə

Terra del Fuego ˈtɛrəˌdɛlfuˈego, -ˈfwego

terra firma ˈtɛrəˈfɝˈmə; ES -ˈfɜmə, -ˈfɝˈmə

terrain tɛˈren, ˈtɛren

terrane tɛˈren, ˈtɛren

terrapin ˈtɛrəpɪn

Terre Haute ˈtɛrəˈhot, loc.+ˈtɛrɪˈhʌt

Terrell ˈtɛrəl, cf Tyrrell, Syracuse

terrene tɛˈrin (ˈterˌrene ˈdays)

terrestrial təˈrɛstrɪəl |-ly -ɪ

terrible ˈtɛrəb| |-bly -blɪ

terrier ˈtɛrɪɝ; ES ˈtɛrɪ·ə(r; dial. ˈtærɪɝ, cf farrier

terrific təˈrɪfɪk |-al -| |-ally -|ɪ |-icly -ɪklɪ

terrify ˈtɛrəˌfaɪ |-fied -ˌfaɪd

territorial, T- ˌtɛrəˈtorɪəl, -ˈtɔr-; S -ˈtor-; |-ly -ɪ

territoriality ˌtɛrəˌtorɪˈælətɪ, -ˌtɔrɪ-; S -ˌtorɪ-

territory ˈtɛrəˌtorɪ, -ˌtɔrɪ; S -ˌtorɪ

terror ˈtɛrɝ; ES ˈtɛrə(r; |-ed -d |-some -səm

terrorism ˈtɛrəˌrɪzəm |-rist -rɪst

terrorize ˈtɛrəˌraɪz |-s -ɪz |-d -d

Terry ˈtɛrɪ

terse tɝˈs; ES tɜs, tɝˈs

tertian ˈtɝˈʃən; ES ˈtɜʃən, ˈtɝˈʃən

tertiary, T- ˈtɝˈʃɪˌɛrɪ, -ʃərɪ; ES ˈtɜʃ-, ˈtɝˈʃ-

tertium quid ˈtɝˈʃɪəmˈkwɪd; ES ˈtɜʃ-, ˈtɝˈʃ-

Tertullian tɝˈtʌlɪən, -ljən; ES tɝ-; |-ism -ˌɪzəm

terza rima ˈtɛrtsəˈrimə; ES ˈtɛətsə-; (It ˈtɛrtsɑˈriːmɑ)

Tesla ˈtɛslə

tesselate adj ˈtɛs|ɪt, -ˌet

tesselate v ˈtɛs|ˌet |-d -ɪd

test tɛst |tested ˈtɛstɪd |-acy -əsɪ

testament n ˈtɛstəmənt

testament v ˈtɛstəˌmɛnt |-ed -ɪd

testamental ˌtɛstəˈmɛnt| |-ly -ɪ |-tary -tərɪ, -trɪ

testate ˈtɛstet |-tated -tetɪd

testator ˈtɛstetɝ, tɛsˈtetɝ; ES -tə(r

testatrix tɛsˈtetrɪks |-es -ɪz |-trices -trɪˌsiz

testicle ˈtɛstɪk|

testify ˈtɛstəˌfaɪ |-fied -ˌfaɪd

testimonial ˌtɛstəˈmonɪəl, -njəl |-alist -ɪst

testimony ˈtɛstəˌmonɪ

teston ˈtɛstn̩

test-tube ˈtɛstˌtjub, -ˌtɪub, -ˌtub

testudo tɛsˈtjudo, -ˈtɪu-, -ˈtu- |-dines -dn̩ˌiz

testy ˈtɛstɪ |-tily -t|ɪ, -tɪlɪ

tetanus ˈtɛtnəs |tetany ˈtɛtn̩ɪ

tetchy ˈtɛtʃɪ

tête-à-tête ˈtetəˈtet (Fr tɛtaˈtɛːt)

tether ˈtɛðɝ; ES -ðə(r; |-ed -d |-ðərɪŋ, -ðrɪŋ

Teton ˈtitn̩, -tɑn; ES+-tɒn; |-s -z

tetotum tiˈtotəm |-ed -d

tetrachord ˈtɛtrəˌkɔrd; ES -ˌkɔəd

tetraethyl ˌtɛtrəˈɛθəl, -ɪl

tetragon ˈtɛtrəˌgɑn; ES+-ˌgɒn

tetrahedron ˌtɛtrəˈhidrən |-dral -drəl

tetralogy tɛˈtrælədʒɪ

tetrameter tɛˈtræmətɝ; ES -mətə(r

Key: See in full §§3–47. bee bi |pity ˈpɪtɪ (§6) |rate ret |yet jɛt |sang sæŋ |angry ˈæŋ·grɪ |bath bæθ; E baθ (§10) |ah ɑ |far fɑr |watch watʃ, wɒtʃ (§12) |jaw dʒɔ |gorge gɔrdʒ |go go

tetrarch 'titrɑrk, 'tɛt-; ES -ɑːk, E+-aːk
tetrasyllabic ˌtɛtrəsɪ'læbɪk
tetrasyllable 'tɛtrəˌsɪləb|
Tetrazzini ˌtɛtrə'zɪnɪ (*It* ˌtetrɑt'tsiːni)
tetter 'tɛtə; ES 'tɛtə(r; |-ed -d |-ous -əs
Tetzel 'tɛts|
Teucer 'tjusə, 'tɪu-, 'tu-; ES -sə(r
Teufelsdröckh, -droeckh 'tɔɪf|zˌdrɛk
Teuton 'tjutn̩, 'tɪu-, 'tu-
Teutonic tju'tɑnɪk, tɪu-, tu-; ES+-'tɒn-
Teviot 'tivɪət, 'tɛv-, 'tɪv-
Tewkesbury, -ksb- 'tjuksˌbɛrɪ, 'tɪu-, 'tu-, -bərɪ
Texan 'tɛksn̩, 'tɛksən
Texarkana ˌtɛksɑr'kænə; ES ˌtɛksɑː'k-
Texas 'tɛksəs; S+'tɛksɪs, -səz, -sɪz; |-as' -s, -z
text tɛkst |texted 'tɛkstɪd |-book -ˌbʊk
textile 'tɛkst|, -tɪl, -taɪl
textual 'tɛkstʃʊəl |-ly -ɪ
textural 'tɛkstʃərəl |-ly -ɪ
texture 'tɛkstʃə; ES 'tɛkstʃə(r; |-d -d
Tezel 'tɛts|
Thackeray 'θækərɪ, 'θækrɪ |-ayan -ən |-ayite -ˌaɪt
Thackerayana ˌθækərɪ'enə, -'ænə, -'ɑnə
Thackley 'θæklɪ
Thaddaeus -deus *Bib.* θæ'diəs, 'θædɪəs
Thaddeus *mod. name* 'θædɪəs |-'s -ɪz
Thai 'tɑ·i
Thailand 'taɪlənd
Thais *courtesan* 'θe·ɪs, *opera* tɑ'is |-'s -ɪz
Thaisa θe'ɪsə, 'θe·ɪsə, -zə
thaler 'tɑlə; ES 'tɑlə(r; (*Ger* 'tɑːlər)
Thaler 'θelə; ES 'θelə(r
Thales 'θeliz |-les' -liz
Thalia *Muse* θə'laɪə, *fem. name* 'θelɪə, -ljə
Thaliard 'θæljəd; ES 'θæljəd
thallium 'θælɪəm
Thames *US* θemz, tɛmz, temz; *C, Engd, NZ* tɛmz |-'s -ɪz
than *usually unstressed* ðən, ðɛn, ðn̩, n̩, n; *stressed* 'ðæn, ˌðæn
thanatopsis, T- ˌθænə'tɑpsɪs; ES+-'tɒp-
thane θen |-ess -ɪs |-esses -ɪsɪz
Thanet 'θænɪt—*a sp. pron.; OE* Tænett
thank θæŋk |-ed -t
thankful 'θæŋkfəl |-ly -ɪ |-ness -nɪs
thankless 'θæŋklɪs |-ness -nɪs

thanksgiving, T- ˌθæŋks'gɪvɪŋ ('Thanks-ˌgiving 'turkey)
Thanksgiving Day ˌθæŋks'gɪvɪŋˌde
thankworthy 'θæŋkˌwɝðɪ; ES -ˌwɜðɪ, -ˌwɝðɪ
that *demonstrative* ðæt; *conj, relative* ðət
thatch θætʃ |thatches 'θætʃɪz |-ed -t
thaumaturgic ˌθɔmə'tɝdʒɪk; ES -'tɜdʒ-, -'tɝdʒ-
thaumaturgy 'θɔməˌtɝdʒɪ; ES -ˌtɜdʒɪ, -ˌtɝdʒɪ
thaw θɔ |thawed θɔd |-y 'θɔ·ɪ
Thaxter 'θækstə; ES 'θækstə(r
Thayer θɛr, θær; E θɛə(r, ES θæə(r
the *usually unstressed: before conss.* ðə; *before vowels, & often before* j- *or* hi-, hɪ-, he-, hɛ-*pronounced* ðɪ, *in the* S+ðə; *rarely stressed* 'ði, ˌði
Thea 'θiə
thearchy 'θiɑrkɪ; ES -ɑːkɪ, E+-ɑːkɪ
theater, -tre 'θiətə, 'θɪə-; ES -tə(r
theatric θɪ'ætrɪk |-s -s |-al -| |-ally -|ɪ, -ɪklɪ
Thebes θibz |-'s -ɪz |Theban 'θibən
The Dalles ðə'dælz
thé dansant, *pl* thés dansants *Fr* tedɑ̃'sɑ̃
thee ði, *unstressed*+ðɪ
theft θɛft
thegn θen
thein 'θiɪn |-ine -in, -ɪn
their ðɛr, ðær, ðer; ES ðɛə(r, ðæə(r, ðeə(r; *unstressed*+ðə; ES ðə(r
theirs ðɛrz, ðærz, ðerz; ES ðɛəz, ðæəz, ðeəz
theism 'θiɪzəm |-ist -ɪst
theistic θi'ɪstɪk |-al -| |-ally -|ɪ, -ɪklɪ
them *stressed* 'ðɛm, ˌðɛm; *unstr.* ðəm, ðm̩
thematic θi'mætɪk |-al -| |-ally -|ɪ, -ɪklɪ
theme θim |themed θimd
Themistocles θə'mɪstəˌkliz |-'s -ɪz
themselves ðəm'sɛlvz
then ðɛn |thenness 'ðɛnnɪs
thence ðɛns, *less freq.* θɛns—*cf* thither
thenceforth ˌðɛns'fɔrθ, ˌθɛns-, -'fɔrθ; ES -'foəθ, E+-'fɔəθ, *acct*+'thence,forth
thenceforward ˌðɛns'fɔrwəd, ˌθɛns-; ES -'fɔəwəd
Theobald *Am name* 'θiəˌbɔld, *Shak. editor* 'tɪb|d |-'s 'θiəˌbɔldz, 'tɪb|dz, 'tɪb|z
theocracy θi'ɑkrəsɪ; ES+-'ɒk-; |-rasy -rəsɪ
theocrat 'θiəˌkræt
theocratic ˌθiə'krætɪk |-al -| |-ally -|ɪ, -ɪklɪ
Theocritus θi'ɑkrɪtəs; ES+-'ɒk-; |-'s -ɪz

|full fʊl |tooth tuθ |further 'fɝðə; ES 'fɝðə |custom 'kʌstəm |while hwaɪl |how haʊ |toy tɔɪ
|using 'juzɪŋ |fuse fjuz, fɪuz |dish dɪʃ |vision 'vɪʒən |Eden 'idn̩ |cradle 'kred| |keep 'em 'kipm̩

theodolite θi'ɑd|ˌaɪt; ES+-'ɒd-
Theodora ˌθiə'dorə, -'dɔrə; S -'dorə
Theodore 'θiəˌdor, -ˌdɔr; ES -ˌdoə(r, E+
-ˌdɔə(r
Theodoric θi'ɑdərɪk; ES+-'ɒd-
Theodosia ˌθiə'doʃɪə |-sian -ʃən, -ʃɪən
Theodosius ˌθiə'doʃɪəs |-'s -ɪz
theologian ˌθiə'lodʒən, -dʒɪən
theologic ˌθiə'lɑdʒɪk; ES+-'lɒdʒ-; |-al -ḷ
|-ally -ḷɪ, -ɪklɪ
theologue, -log 'θiəˌlɔg, -ˌlɑg, -ˌlɒg
theology θi'ɑlədʒɪ; ES+-'ɒl-
Theophilus θi'ɑfələs; ES+-'ɒf-; |-'s -ɪz
Theophrastus ˌθiə'fræstəs |-'s -ɪz
theorbo θi'ɔrbo; ES -'ɔəbo
theorem 'θiərəm
theoretic ˌθiə'rɛtɪk |-al -ḷ |-ally -ḷɪ, -ɪklɪ
theorism 'θiəˌrɪzəm |-ist -rɪst
theorize 'θiəˌraɪz |-s -ɪz |-d -d
theory 'θiərɪ, 'θiɛrɪ
theosophic ˌθiə'sɑfɪk; ES+-'sɒf-; |-al -ḷ |-ally
-ḷɪ, -ɪklɪ
theosophy θi'ɑsəfɪ; ES+-'ɒs-; |-phist -fɪst
therapeutic ˌθɛrə'pjutɪk, -'pɪu- |-al -ḷ |-ally
-ḷɪ, -ɪklɪ |-s -s
therapy 'θɛrəpɪ
there *'in that place'* (stressed) 'ðɛr, 'ðær, ˌðɛr,
ˌðær; E 'ðɛə(r, ˌðɛə(r, ES 'ðæə(r, ˌðæə(r
there *meaningless expletive* (unstressed) ðɚ;
ES ðə(r; (*lightly stressed*) ðɛr, ðær; E
ðɛə(r, ES ðæə(r
thereabout ˌðɛrə'baʊt, ˌðærə-; S ˌðærə-;
|-s -s
thereafter ðɛr'æftɚ, ðær-; E ðɛr'æftə(r, ES
ðær-, E+-'ɑftə(r, -'ɑftə(r
thereat ðɛr'æt, ðær-; S ðær-
thereby ðɛr'baɪ, ðær-; E ðɛə'baɪ, ES ðæə-
therefor ðɛr'fɔr, ðær-; E ðɛə'fɔə(r, ES ðæə-
therefore 'ðɛrˌfor, 'ðær-, -ˌfɔr; E 'ðɛəˌfoə(r,
'ðæə-, -ˌfɔə(r; S 'ðæəˌfoə(r; o.f. 'ðɝ-, 'ðɝ-
therefrom ðɛr'frɑm, ðær-, -'frɒm; E ðɛə-, ES
ðæə-
therein ðɛr'ɪn, ðær-; S ðær'ɪn
thereinafter ˌðɛrɪn'æftɚ, ˌðær-; E ˌðɛrɪn-
'æftə(r, ES ˌðær-, E+-'ɑftə(r, -'ɑftə(r
thereinbefore ˌðɛrɪnbɪ'for, ˌðær-, -'fɔr; E
-'foə(r, -'fɔə(r; S ˌðærɪnbɪ'foə(r
thereinto ðɛr'ɪntu, ðær-, -tʊ, ˌðɛrɪn'tu, ˌðær-;
S ðær'ɪn-, ˌðærɪn'tu

thereof ðɛr'ɑv, ðær-, ðɝ-, -'ɑf, -'ɒ-; S ðær-,
ðɚ-
thereon ðɛr'ɑn, ðær-, -'ɒn, -'ɔn; S ðær'ɒn,
-'ɒn, *less freq.* -'ɑn
there's *stressed* 'ðɛrz, 'ðærz, ˌðɛrz, ˌðærz; E
'ðɛəz, ˌðɛəz, ES 'ðæəz, ˌðæəz; *unstr.* ðɚz;
ES ðəz
Theresa tə'risə, θə-, -'rizə, -'rɛsə (*It* te'rɛːza)
therethrough ðɛr'θru, ðær-; E ðɛə-, ES ðæə-
thereto ðɛr'tu, ðær-; E ðɛə-, ES ðæə-;
('thereˌto 'added)
theretofore ˌðɛrtə'for, ˌðær-, -'fɔr; E ˌðɛətə-
'foə(r, ˌðæə-, -'fɔə(r; S ˌðæətə'foə(r
thereunder ðɛr'ʌndɚ, ðær-; E ðɛr'ʌndə(r, ES
ðær-
thereunto ðɛr'ʌntu, ðær-, -tʊ, ˌðɛrʌn'tu,
ˌðær-; S ðær'ʌn-, ˌðærʌn'tu
thereupon ˌðɛrə'pɑn, ˌðær-, -'pɒn, -'pɔn; S
ˌðær-
therewith ðɛr'wɪθ, ðær-, -'wɪð; E ðɛə-, ES
ðæə-; *cf* wherewith
therewithal ˌðɛrwɪð'ɔl, ˌðær-; E ˌðɛə-, ES
ˌðæə-
therm, -e θɝm; ES θɝm, θɝm; |-al -ḷ |-ally -ḷɪ
thermic 'θɝmɪk; ES 'θɝm-, 'θɝm-; |-al -ḷ
|-ally -ḷɪ, -ɪklɪ
thermion 'θɝmɪən; ES 'θɝm-, 'θɝm-
thermionic ˌθɝmɪ'ɑnɪk; ES ˌθɝm-, ˌθɝm-,
-'ɒn-; |-ally -ḷɪ, -ɪklɪ
thermit, T- 'θɝmɪt; ES 'θɝm-, 'θɝm-; |-mite
-maɪt
thermocouple 'θɝmoˌkʌpḷ; ES 'θɝm-, 'θɝm-
thermodynamic ˌθɝmodaɪ'næmɪk; ES ˌθɝm-,
ˌθɝm-; |-al -ḷ |-ally -ḷɪ, -ɪklɪ |-s -s
thermometer θə'mɑmətɚ, θɚ-; ES θə'mɑmə-
tə(r, -'mɒm- —*In* θə'mɑmətɚ θɚ- *has
become* θə- *by dissimilation* (§121).
thermometric ˌθɝmə'mɛtrɪk; ES ˌθɝm-,
ˌθɝm-; |-al -ḷ |-ally -ḷɪ, -ɪklɪ
Thermopylae θɚ'mɑpḷˌi; ES θə'mɑp-, -'mɒp-
thermos, T- 'θɝməs; ES 'θɝm-, 'θɝm-
thermostat 'θɝməˌstæt; ES 'θɝm-, 'θɝm-
thermostatic ˌθɝmə'stætɪk; ES ˌθɝm-, ˌθɝm-;
|-ally -ḷɪ, -ɪklɪ
Thersites θɚ'saɪtiz; ES θɚ-; |-tes' -tiz
thesaurus θɪ'sɔrəs |-es -ɪz |-ri -raɪ
these ðiz
Theseus 'θisjus, 'θisus, 'θisɪəs |-eus' -s
thesis 'θisɪs |theses 'θisiz

Key: *See in full §§3–47.* bee bi |pity 'pɪtɪ (§6) |rate ret |yet jɛt |sang sæŋ |angry 'æŋ·grɪ
|bath bæθ; E baθ (§10) |ah ɑ |far fɑr |watch wɑtʃ, wɒtʃ (§12) |jaw dʒɔ |gorge gɔrdʒ |go go

Thespis 'θεspɪs |-'s -ɪz |-pian -pɪən
Thessalónian ˌθεsə'lonɪən |-s -z
Thessalonica ˌθεsələ'naɪkə, -'lɑnɪkə; ES+
-'lɒn-
Thessalonike ˌθεsələ'nikɪ
Thessaly 'θεs|ɪ |-lian θε'selɪən
theta 'θeɪtə, 'θitə
Thetis 'θitɪs |-'s -ɪz
theurgic θi'ɝdʒɪk; ES -'ɜdʒ-, -'ɝdʒ-; |-al -|
|-ally -|ɪ, -ɪklɪ
theurgy 'θiɝdʒɪ; ES -ɜdʒɪ, -ɝdʒɪ; |-gist
-dʒɪst
thew θju, θɪu, θu |-s -z |-ed -d
they ðe; *unstressed sometimes* ðε, ðɪ
they'd *'they would,' 'they had'* ðed
they'll *'they will'* ðel—They'll *is an abbreviation of* they will, *not of* they shall ('ðeʃəl),
though it often replaces 'ðeʃəl.
they're *'they are'* ðer, ðεr; ES ðeə(r, ðεə(r
they've *'they have'* ðev; *unstressed sometimes*
ðεv, ðɪv, ðəv
thiazole 'θaɪəˌzol |-zol -ˌzol, -ˌzɑl, -ˌzɒl, -ˌzɔl
Thibet tɪ'bεt, 'tɪbɪt |-an -n̩
Thibodaux ˌtɪbə'do
thick θɪk |thicked θɪkt
thick-and-thin 'θɪkən'θɪn, 'θɪkn̩-, 'θɪkŋ-
thicken 'θɪkən |-ed -d |-ing 'θɪkənɪŋ, -knɪŋ
thicket 'θɪkɪt |-ed -ɪd
thickheaded 'θɪk'hεdɪd ('thickˌheaded 'fly)
thickset 'θɪk'sεt
thick-skinned 'θɪk'skɪnd
thick-witted 'θɪk'wɪtɪd
thief θif |thief's θifs |thieves θivz
Thiel til
thieve θiv |thieved θivd |-ry -ərɪ, -rɪ
thigh θaɪ |thighed θaɪd
thill θɪl
thimble 'θɪmb|l̩ |-d -d |-ling 'θɪmblɪŋ, -b|ɪŋ
thimbleful 'θɪmb|ˌful |-fuls -ˌfulz
thimblerig 'θɪmb|ˌrɪg |-ged -d
thin θɪn |thinned θɪnd |-ness 'θɪnnɪs
thine ðaɪn
thing θɪŋ |-umajig 'θɪŋəməˌdʒɪg
thingumbob 'θɪŋəmˌbab, 'θɪŋəˌbab; ES+
-ˌbɒb
think θɪŋk |thought θɔt |-able -əb| |-bly -blɪ
thinnish 'θɪnɪʃ
thin-skinned 'θɪn'skɪnd ('thin-ˌskinned 'face)
third θɝd; ES θɜd, θɝd

third-class 'θɝd'klæs; ES 'θɜd-, 'θɝd-, E+
-'klas, -'klɑs
Thirlmere 'θɝlmɪr; ES 'θɜlmɪə(r, 'θɝlmɪə(r
thirst θɝst; ES θɜst, θɝst; |-ed -ɪd |-y -ɪ
thirteen θɝ'tin; ES θɜ-, θɝ-; (ˌhe's 'thir'teen,
'thirˌteen 'men)
thirty 'θɝtɪ; ES 'θɜtɪ, 'θɝtɪ; |-tieth -tɪθ
|-tieths -tɪθs |-fold -'fold
this ðɪs |these ðiz
Thisbe 'θɪzbɪ
thistle 'θɪs| |-d -d |-ling 'θɪslɪŋ, -s|ɪŋ
thistledown, T- 'θɪs|ˌdaʊn
thither 'θɪðɚ, 'θɪðɚ; ES -ðə(r; |-ward -wəd;
ES -wəd; *For* thither, *now chiefly a book
word,* 'θɪðɚ *is replacing older* 'ðɪðɚ, *but for*
thence, *more often heard,* ðεns *is still usual.*
tho' ðo
thole θol |tholed θold
Thomas 'tɑməs; ES+'tɒm-; |-'s -ɪz |-a -ə
|-in, -ine -ɪn
Thomaston 'tɑməstən; ES+'tɒm-; |-town
-ˌtaʊn |-ville -ˌvɪl; S+-v|
Thomism 'tomɪzəm, 'θom- |-ist -ɪst
Thompson 'tɑmpsn̩, -msn̩; ES+'tɒm-
Thomson 'tɑmpsn̩, -msn̩; ES+'tɒm-
thong θɔŋ, θɒŋ; S+θɑŋ; |-ed -d
Thopas 'topəs |-'s -ɪz
Thor θɔr; ES θɔə(r
thoracic θo'ræsɪk |-al -|
thorax 'θoræks |-es -ɪz |-races -rəˌsiz
Thoreau 'θoro, θə'ro, 'θɔ·o; ES+'θɜro, 'θʌro
thorium 'θorɪəm |-rite 'θoraɪt
thorn θɔrn; ES θɔən; |-ed -d
Thorold 'θorold
thoron 'θoran; ES+-ɒn
thorough 'θɝ·o, -ə; ES 'θɜr-, 'θʌr-, 'θɝ-;
|-bred -ˌbrεd, -'brεd |-fare -ˌfεr, -ˌfær; E
-ˌfεə(r, ES -ˌfæə(r; |-going -'go·ɪŋ
thorp, -pe, T- θɔrp; ES θɔəp
those ðoz
thou ðaʊ
though ðo
thought θɔt |-ful -fəl |-fully -fəlɪ
thousand 'θaʊzn̩d, 'θaʊzn̩ |-th -θ |-ths -θs
|-fold -'fold
Thrace θres |-'s -ɪz |-cian 'θreʃən
Thrale θrel
thrall θrɔl |thralled θrɔld |-dom -dəm
thrall-less 'θrɔllɪs

|full ful |tooth tuθ |further 'fɝðɚ; ES 'fɝðə |custom 'kʌstəm |while hwaɪl |how haʊ |toy tɔɪ
|using 'juzɪŋ |fuse fjuz, fɪuz |dish dɪʃ |vision 'vɪʒən |Eden 'idn̩ |cradle 'kred| |keep 'em 'kipm̩

thrash θræʃ |thrashes 'θræʃɪz |-ed -t—Thrash
is not an error for thresh, *but a historical
variant in literary use since the 16c. It is the
usual word in American agriculture.*

Thraso 'θreso

thrasonical θre'sɑnɪk|; ES+-'sɒn-; |-ly -ļɪ,
-ɪklɪ

thrave θrev |thraved θrevd

thread θrɛd |threaded 'θrɛdɪd

threadbare 'θrɛdˌbɛr, -ˌbær; E -ˌbɛə(r, ES
-ˌbæə(r

Threadneedle 'θrɛdˌnidļ

threat θrɛt |threated 'θrɛtɪd

threaten 'θrɛtn̩ |-ed -d |-ing 'θrɛtnɪŋ, -tn̩ɪŋ

three θri

threefold 'θri'fold ('threeˌfold 'gain)

three-four 'θri'for, -'fɔr; ES -'foə(r, E+-'fɔə(r;
('threeˌfour 'time)

three-legged 'θri'lɛgɪd, -'lɛgd

threepence 'θrɪpəns, 'θrɛp- |-s -ɪz

threepenny 'θriˌpɛnɪ, -pənɪ, 'θrɪpənɪ

three-ply 'θri'plaɪ ('threeˌply 'tire)

threescore 'θri'skor, -'skɔr; ES -'skoə(r,
E+-'skɔə(r

threescore-and-ten 'θriˌskorən'tɛn, -ˌskɔr-; S
-ˌskor-

threesome 'θrisəm

threnody 'θrɛnədɪ

thresh θrɛʃ |threshes 'θrɛʃɪz |-ed -t—*see*
thrash

threshold 'θrɛʃold, 'θrɛʃhold

threw θru, θrɪu

thrice θraɪs

thrift θrɪft |thrifted 'θrɪftɪd

thrifty 'θrɪftɪ |-tily -tļɪ, -tɪlɪ

thrill θrɪl |thrilled θrɪld

thrips θrɪps |-es -ɪz

thrive θraɪv |throve θrov *or* thrived θraɪvd
|thrived θraɪvd *or* thriven 'θrɪvən

throat θrot |throated 'θrotɪd; |N Engd+θrɔt
(§46)

throb θrɑb; ES+θrɒb; |-bed -d

Throckmorton 'θrɑkmortn̩, -mɔrtn̩; ES
-moətn̩, -mɔətn̩, 'θrɒk-

throe θro |throed θrod

thrombosis θrɑm'bosɪs, θrɒm-

throne θron |throned θrond

throng θrɔŋ, θrɒŋ; S+θraŋ; |-ed -d

Throop trup, θrup

throstle 'θrɑsļ; ES+'θrɒsļ

throttle 'θrɑtļ |-d -d |-ling -tļɪŋ, -tlɪŋ

through θru, θrɪu |-out -'aʊt

throve θrov

throw θro |threw θru, θrɪu |thrown θron

throwback 'θroˌbæk

thrum θrʌm |thrummed θrʌmd

thrush θrʌʃ |thrushes 'θrʌʃɪz

thrust θrʌst |*arch.* thrusted 'θrʌstɪd

Thucydides θju'sɪdəˌdiz, θɪu-, θu- |-'s -ɪz

thud θʌd |thudded 'θʌdɪd

thug θʌg |thugged θʌgd

Thule 'θjulɪ, 'θɪu-, 'θu-, -li

thulia 'θjulɪə, 'θɪu-, 'θu- |-ium -ɪəm

thumb θʌm |thumbed θʌmd

thumbnail 'θʌm'nel, -ˌnel ('thumbˌnail
'sketch)

thumbscrew 'θʌmˌskru, -ˌskrɪu |-ed -d

thumbtack 'θʌmˌtæk |-ed -t

Thummim 'θʌmɪm

thump θʌmp |thumped θʌmpt

thunder 'θʌndɚ; ES 'θʌndə(r; |-ed -d |-ing
'θʌndrɪŋ, -dərɪŋ |-bolt -ˌbolt

thundercloud 'θʌndɚˌklaʊd; ES 'θʌndə-

thunderhead 'θʌndɚˌhɛd; ES 'θʌndə-

thunderous 'θʌndərəs, -drəs

thundershower 'θʌndɚˌʃaʊɚ, -ˌʃaʊr; ES
'θʌndəˌʃaʊ-ə(r, -ˌʃaʊə(r

thunderstone 'θʌndɚˌston; ES 'θʌndə-

thunderstorm 'θʌndɚˌstɔrm; ES 'θʌndə-
ˌstɔəm

thunderstruck 'θʌndɚˌstrʌk; ES 'θʌndə-

thurible 'θjʊrəbļ, 'θɪur-

Thuringia θju'rɪndʒɪə, θɪu-, θu- |-n -n

Thurio 'θjʊrɪˌo, 'θɪur-, 'θur-

Thursday 'θɝzdɪ; ES 'θɜz-, 'θɝz- —*see* Monday

Thurston 'θɝstn̩; ES 'θɜs-, 'θɝs-

thus ðʌs |thusly 'ðʌslɪ

thwack θwæk |thwacked θwækt

thwart θwɔrt; ES θwɔət; |-ed -ɪd

Thwing twɪŋ

thy ðaɪ

thyme taɪm |thymed taɪmd

thymol 'θaɪmol, -mɑl, -mɒl

thymus, T- 'θaɪməs |-es -ɪz

thyreoid 'θaɪrɪˌɔɪd

Thyreus 'θaɪrɪəs |-'s -ɪz

thyroid 'θaɪrɔɪd

Key: See in full §§3–47. bee bi |pity 'pɪtɪ (§6) |rate ret |yet jɛt |sang sæŋ |angry 'æŋ·grɪ
|bath bæθ; E baθ (§10) |ah ɑ |far fɑr |watch wɑtʃ, wɒtʃ (§12) |jaw dʒɔ |gorge gɔrdʒ |go go

Thyrsis 'θɜˑsɪs; ES 'θɜs-, 'θɜˑs-; |-sis' -sɪs
thyrsus 'θɜˑsəs; ES 'θɜs-, 'θɜˑs-; |-si -saɪ
thyself ðaɪ'sɛlf
ti ti
-tia *ending, variously pronounced* -ʃə, -ʃɪə,
  -ʃjə. *Besides the pron. given in the vocab.,*
  one or more of the variants are often heard.
tiara taɪ'erə, -'ɛrə, tɪ'arə
Tibbalds 'tɪb|dz, -b|z |-'s -ɪz
Tibbals 'tɪb|z |-'s -ɪz
Tiber 'taɪbɚ; ES 'taɪbə(r
Tiberias taɪ'bɪrɪəs |-ius -ɪəs |-'s -ɪz
Tibet tɪ'bɛt, 'tɪbɪt |-an -ṇ
tibia 'tɪbɪə |-s -z |-biae -bɪˌi
Tibullus tɪ'bʌləs |-'s -ɪz
tic tɪk
tick tɪk |ticked tɪkt
Tickell 'tɪk|
ticket 'tɪkɪt |-ed -ɪd
tickle 'tɪk| |-d -d |-ling 'tɪklɪŋ, -k|ɪŋ
ticklish 'tɪklɪʃ, 'tɪk|ɪʃ
Ticknor 'tɪknɚ; ES 'tɪknə(r
ticktacktoe ˌtɪktæk'to, ˌtɪttæt'to |-too -'tu
ticktock 'tɪk'tak, -ˌtak, tɪk'tak; ES+-ɒk;
  |-ed -t
Ticonderoga ˌtaɪkandə'rogə, taɪˌkan-; ES+
  -ɒn-
tidal 'taɪd| |-ly -ɪ
tidbit 'tɪdˌbɪt
tiddledywinks 'tɪd|dɪˌwɪŋks
tiddlywinks 'tɪd|ɪˌwɪŋks, 'tɪdlɪ-
tide taɪd |tided 'taɪdɪd |-dings -ɪŋz
tidewater 'taɪdˌwɔtɚ, -ˌwatɚ, -ˌwɒtɚ; ES
  -tə(r
tidy 'taɪdɪ |tidied 'taɪdɪd
tie taɪ |tied taɪd
Tieck tik
Tientsin 'tjɛn'tsɪn, 'tɪn-
tier *'who ties'* 'taɪɚ; ES 'taɪ·ə(r
tier *'layer'* tɪr; ES tɪə(r, S+tɛə(r
tierce tɪrs; ES tɪəs; S+tɛəs
Tierra del Fuego tɪ'ɛrəˌdɛlfu'ego, 'tjɛrə-,
  -'fwego (*Sp* 'tjɛrra·ðɛl'fwego)
tie-up 'taɪˌʌp
tiff tɪf |tiffed tɪft
Tiffany 'tɪfənɪ
tiffin, T- 'tɪfɪn |tiffined 'tɪfɪnd
Tiflis 'tɪflɪs |-'s -ɪz
tiger 'taɪgɚ; ES 'taɪgə(r; |-ed -d

tigerish 'taɪgərɪʃ, 'taɪgrɪʃ
Tigert 'taɪgɚt; ES 'taɪgət
Tighe taɪ
tight taɪt |-s -s
tighten 'taɪtṇ |-ed -d |-ing 'taɪtṇɪŋ, -tnɪŋ
tightfisted 'taɪt'fɪstɪd
tightrope 'taɪtˌrop |-roped -ˌropt
tightwad 'taɪtˌwad, -ˌwɒd
Tiglath-pileser 'tɪglæθpə'lizɚ, -paɪ-; ES -zə(r
tiglon 'taɪglan, -ɒn, -ən
tigress 'taɪgrɪs |-'s -ɪz
Tigris 'taɪgrɪs |-'s -ɪz
tigrish 'taɪgrɪʃ
tike taɪk
Tilbury, t- 'tɪlˌbɛrɪ, -bərɪ
Tilda 'tɪldə
tilde 'tɪldə, -dɪ
Tilden 'tɪldɪn, -ən
tile taɪl |tiled taɪld
till *v* tɪl |tilled tɪld
till *conj, prep* tɪl, t|; *rarely stressed* 'tɪl, ˌtɪl
tiller 'tɪlɚ; ES 'tɪlə(r; |-ed -d
Tillotson 'tɪlətsṇ
Tilsit 'tɪlzɪt
tilt tɪlt |tilted 'tɪltɪd
tilth tɪlθ
Tilton 'tɪltṇ |-ville -ˌvɪl
tiltyard 'tɪltˌjard; ES -ˌjɑːd, E+-ˌjɑːd
Timandra tɪ'mændrə
timbal 'tɪmb|
timbale 'tɪmb| (*Fr* tæ̃'bal)
timber 'tɪmbɚ; ES 'tɪmbə(r; |-ed -d |-ing
  'tɪmbərɪŋ, -brɪŋ
timbre 'tɪmbɚ, 'tæm-; ES -bə(r; (*Fr* tæ̃:mbr)
timbrel 'tɪmbrəl |-ed -d
Timbuctoo *poem* ˌtɪmbʌk'tu, tɪm'bʌktu
Timbuktu *town* tɪm'bʌktu
time taɪm |timed taɪmd |-ly -lɪ
time-honored 'taɪm'anɚd; ES -'anəd, -'ɒn-;
  ('time-ˌhonored 'custom)
timekeeper 'taɪmˌkipɚ; ES -ˌkipə(r
timepiece 'taɪmˌpis |-s -ɪz
timeserving 'taɪmˌsɝvɪŋ; ES -ˌsɜv-, -ˌsɝv-
timetable 'taɪmˌteb|
timid 'tɪmɪd |-midity tɪ'mɪdətɪ, tə-
Timnite 'tɪmnaɪt
Timon 'taɪmən
timorous 'tɪmərəs, 'tɪmrəs
Timotheus tɪ'moθɪəs, -θjəs |-'s -ɪz

|full fʊl |tooth tuθ |further 'fɝðɚ; ES 'fɜðə |custom 'kʌstəm |while hwaɪl |how haʊ |toy tɔɪ
|using 'juzɪŋ |fuse fjuz, fɪuz |dish dɪʃ |vision 'vɪʒən |Eden 'idṇ |cradle 'kred| |keep 'em 'kipm̩

Timothy, t- 'tɪməθɪ
timpanist 'tɪmpənɪst
timpano 'tɪmpə͵no |*pl* -ni -͵ni (*It* 'timpɑ͵no)
Timpanogos ͵tɪmpə'nogəs |-'s -ɪz
tin tɪn |tinned tɪnd
tinct tɪŋkt |tincted 'tɪŋktɪd
tincture 'tɪŋktʃɚ; ES -tʃə(r; |-d -d
Tindal, -dale 'tɪndl̩
tinder 'tɪndɚ; ES 'tɪndə(r; |-ed -d
tinderbox 'tɪndɚ͵bɑks; ES 'tɪndə͵bɑks,
-͵bɒks; |-es -ɪz
tine taɪn |tined taɪnd
tin-foil 'tɪn͵fɔɪl |-ed -d
ting tɪŋ |-ed -d
tinge tɪndʒ |tinges 'tɪndʒɪz |-d -d
tinged *past of* ting tɪŋd |*of* tinge tɪndʒd
tingle 'tɪŋgl̩ |-d -d |-ling 'tɪŋglɪŋ, -glɪ̩ŋ
tinhorn *adj* 'tɪn͵hɔrn; ES -͵hɔən
tinker, T- 'tɪŋkɚ; ES 'tɪŋkə(r; |-ed -d |-ing
'tɪŋkərɪŋ, -krɪŋ
tinkle 'tɪŋkl̩ |-d -d |-ling 'tɪŋklɪŋ, -kl̩ɪŋ
tinner 'tɪnɚ; ES 'tɪnə(r; |-y -ɪ
tinnitus tɪ'naɪtəs
tinny 'tɪnɪ
tinsel 'tɪnsl̩ |-ed -d
tinsmith 'tɪn͵smɪθ |-ths -θs
tint tɪnt |tinted 'tɪntɪd
Tintagel tɪn'tædʒəl
Tintern 'tɪntɚn; ES 'tɪntən
tintinnabular ͵tɪntɪ'næbjəlɚ; ES -lə(r; |-y
-͵lɛrɪ |-lous -ləs |-lum -ləm
tintinnabulation ͵tɪntɪ͵næbjə'leʃən
Tintoretto ͵tɪntə'rɛto (*It* ͵tinto'retto)
tintype 'tɪn͵taɪp
tinware 'tɪn͵wɛr, -͵wær; E -͵wɛə(r, ES
-͵wæə(r
tinwork 'tɪn͵wɝk; ES -͵wɝk, -͵wɝ·k
tiny 'taɪnɪ
Tioga taɪ'ogə
-tion *unstressed ending* -ʃən, -ʃn̩—*The pron.*
-ʃn̩ *is less common in America than in
England.*
tip tɪp |tipped tɪpt
Tippecanoe ͵tɪpəkə'nu
Tipperary ͵tɪpə'rɛrɪ
tippet 'tɪpɪt |-ed -ɪd
tipple 'tɪpl̩ |-d -d |-ling 'tɪplɪŋ, -pl̩ɪŋ
tippler 'tɪplɚ, 'tɪpl̩ɚ; ES -ə(r
Tippoo Sahib tɪ'pu'sɑ·ɪb, -'sɑhɪb

tipstaff 'tɪp͵stæf; E+-͵staf, -͵stɑf; |-s -s
|-staves -͵stevz
tipster 'tɪpstɚ; ES 'tɪpstə(r
tipsy 'tɪpsɪ
tiptoe 'tɪp͵to |-d -d
Tipton 'tɪptən
tiptop 'tɪp'tɑp; ES+-'tɒp; ('tɪp͵top 'day)
tirade 'taɪred, tə'red |-d -ɪd
tire taɪr; ES taɪə(r; |-d -d |-some -səm
Tiresias tə'rɛsɪəs, taɪ-, -'rɪs-, -ʃɪəs |-'s -ɪz
tirewoman 'taɪr͵wʊmən; ES 'taɪə-
tiro 'taɪro
Tirol 'tɪrəl, -ɑl, -ɒl, tɪ'rol
Tirolean tɪ'rolɪən, ͵tɪrə'lɪən
Tirolese ͵tɪrə'liz
Tirzah 'tɝzə; ES 'tɝzə, 'tɝ·zə
'tis *'it is'* 'tɪz, ͵tɪz (͵jɛs'tɪz, 'jɛs͵tɪz)—*when
without stress, replaced in US by* it's ɪts
(ɪts'kold).
Tisbury 'tɪz͵bɛrɪ, -bərɪ
Tischendorf 'tɪʃən͵dɔrf; ES -͵dɔəf
Tisdall, -dale 'tɪzdl̩
Tishbite 'tɪʃbaɪt
tissue 'tɪʃʊ |-d -d
tissue-paper 'tɪʃʊ͵pepɚ, 'tɪʃə-; ES -pə(r
tit tɪt |titted 'tɪtɪd
Titan, t- 'taɪtn̩
Titania tɪ'tenɪə, taɪ- |-n -n
titanic, T- taɪ'tænɪk |-al -l̩ |-ally -l̩ɪ, -ɪklɪ
titanium taɪ'tenɪəm, tɪ-
titbit 'tɪt͵bɪt, 'tɪd͵bɪt
Titchener 'tɪtʃənɚ, 'tɪtʃnɚ; ES -nə(r
Titcomb 'tɪtkəm
tit for tat 'tɪtfɚ'tæt; ES -fə-
tithe taɪð |tithed taɪðd
Tithonus tɪ'θonəs |-'s -ɪz
Titian, t- 'tɪʃən, -ʃɪən
Titicaca ͵tɪtɪ'kɑkə (*Sp* ͵titi'kɑkɑ)
titillate 'tɪtl̩͵et |-ated -͵etɪd
titillation ͵tɪtl̩'eʃən
Titinius tɪ'tɪnɪəs, taɪ- |-'s -ɪz
titivate 'tɪtə͵vet |-d -ɪd |-tion ͵tɪtə'veʃən
titlark 'tɪt͵lɑrk; ES -͵lɑ:k, E+-͵lɑ:k
title 'taɪtl̩ |-d -d |-ling 'taɪtl̩ɪŋ, -tlɪŋ
titleless 'taɪtl̩lɪs
Titmarsh 'tɪtmɑrʃ; ES -mɑ:ʃ, E+-mɑ:ʃ; |-'s
-ɪz
titmouse 'tɪt͵maʊs |-'s -ɪz |-mice -͵maɪs
titter 'tɪtɚ; ES 'tɪtə(r; |-ed -d

tittivate 'tɪtəˌvet |-d -ɪd |-tion ˌtɪtə'veʃən
tittle 'tɪtl̩
tittle-tattle 'tɪtl̩ˌtætl̩ |-d -d
titular 'tɪtʃələ, 'tɪtjə-; ES -lə(r; |-y -ˌlɛrɪ
Titus 'taɪtəs |-'s -ɪz |-ville -ˌvɪl
Tiverton 'tɪvətən; ES 'tɪvə-
Tivoli, t- 'tɪvəlɪ (It 'tiːvoli)
tivy 'tɪvɪ |tivied 'tɪvɪd
't'll 'it will' tl̩
tmesis 'tmisɪs, tə'misɪs |tmeses -siz
TNT 'tiˌɛn'ti
to stressed 'tu, ˌtu; unstr: before conss. tə;
   before vowels tʊ, tə; after -t often ə (ought to
   go 'ɔtə'go)
toad tod; N Engd+tɔ̃d (§46)
toadflax 'todˌflæks |-es -ɪz
toadstone 'todˌston
toadstool 'todˌstul
toady 'todɪ |toadied 'todɪd
to-and-fro 'tuən'fro
toast tost |toasted 'tostɪd
toastmaster 'tostˌmæstɚ; ES -ˌmæstə(r,
   E+-ˌmas-, -ˌmas-
tobacco tə'bæko, -ə |-nist tə'bækənɪst
Tobago tə'bego
Tobiah to'baɪə, tə- [-bias -'baɪəs [-as's -sɪz
Tobit 'tobɪt
toboggan tə'bagən, -'bɒg-
Tobolsk tə'balsk, -'bɒlsk
Tobruk to'bruk, 'toˌbruk ('Toˌbruk 'Harbor)
Toby 'tobɪ
toccata tə'katə (It tok'kaːta)
tocome tə'kʌm
Tocqueville 'takvɪl; ES+'tɒk-; (Fr tɔk'vil)
tocsin 'taksɪn; ES+'tɒk-
today, to-day tə'de
Todd tad; ES+tɒd
toddle 'tadl̩; ES+'tɒdl̩; |-d -d |-ling -dlɪŋ,
   -dl̩ɪŋ
toddy 'tadɪ; ES+'tɒdɪ; |-ied -d
to-do tə'du
toe to |toed tod |-nail n 'to'nel, 'toˌnel
toenail v 'toˌnel |-nailed -ˌneld
toff tɔf, tɒf
toffee, -ffy 'tɔfɪ, 'tɒfɪ, 'tafɪ
toft, T- tɔft, tɒft
tog tag, tɒg |-s -z |-ged -d |-gery -əɪ, -ɪ
toga 'togə |-ed -d
together tə'gɛðɚ; ES -'gɛðə(r

toggle 'tagl̩, 'tɒgl̩ |-d -d |-ling -glɪŋ, -gl̩ɪŋ
Togo 'togo |-land -ˌlænd
toil tɔɪl |-ed -d |-some -səm |-less 'tɔɪlɪs
toilet 'tɔɪlɪt |-ed -ɪd |-ry -rɪ
toilette tɔɪ'lɛt, twa'lɛt (Fr twa'lɛt)
toilworn 'tɔɪlˌworn, -ˌwɔrn; ES -ˌwoən, E+
   -ˌwɔən
Tokay to'ke
token 'tokən |-ed -d |-ing 'tokənɪŋ, -knɪŋ
Tokyo, -kio 'tokɪˌo, -kjo
Toland 'tolənd
tolbooth, toll- 'tolˌbuθ, 'tal-, 'tɒl-, -ˌbuð
told told
tole tol |toled told
Toledo tə'lido, tl̩'ido, -də (Sp to'leðo)
tolerable 'talərəbl̩, 'talrə-; ES+'tɒl-; |-bly
   -blɪ
tolerance 'talərəns, -lrəns; ES+'tɒl-; |-cy -ɪ
   |-nt -nt
tolerate 'taləˌret; ES+'tɒl-; |-d -ɪd
toleration ˌtalə'reʃən; ES+ˌtɒl-
toll tol |tolled told |-gate -ˌget
Tolland 'talənd; ES+'tɒlənd
tollgatherer 'tolˌgæðərɚ; ES -ˌgæðərə(r
Tolstoy 'talstɔɪ, 'tɒl-
Toluca tə'lukə
toluene 'taljʊˌin; ES+'tɒl-
Tom tam, tɒm
tomahawk 'taməˌhɔk, 'tamɪ-; ES+'tɒm-;
   |-ed -t
tomato tə'meto, -ə, much less freq. -'mat-,
   -'mat-, -'mæt-
tomb tum |tombed tumd |-stone -ˌston
Tombigbee tam'bɪgbɪ; ES+tɒm-
tomboy 'tamˌbɔɪ, 'tɒm-
tomcat 'tamˌkæt, 'tɒm-
Tom, Dick, and Harry 'tamˌdɪkn̩'hærɪ,
   'tɒm-, -ˌdɪkn̩-
tome tom
tomfool 'tam'ful, 'tɒm- |-ed -d ('tomˌfool
   'joke)
tomfoolery ˌtam'fulərɪ, ˌtɒm-, -'fulrɪ
Tomlinson 'tamlɪnsn̩, 'tɒm-
Tommy 'tamɪ, 'tɒmɪ
tomorrow, to-m- tə'mɔro, -'mar-, -'mɒr-, -ə
Tompkins, Tomk- 'tampkɪnz, 'tɒmp- |-'s -ɪz
tomtit 'tamˌtɪt, 'tɒm-
tom-tom 'tamˌtam; ES+'tɒmˌtɒm; |-ed -d
ton tʌn

|full fʊl |tooth tuθ |further 'fɝðɚ; ES 'fɝ̃ðə |custom 'kʌstəm |while hwaɪl |how haʊ |toy tɔɪ
|using 'juzɪŋ |fuse fjuz, fruz |dish dɪʃ |vision 'vɪʒən |Eden 'idn̩ |cradle 'kredl̩ |keep 'em 'kipm̩

Those words below in which the ɑ sound is spelt o are often pronounced with ɒ in E and S

ton *Fr* tõ

tonal ˈtonl̩ |-ly -ɪ |-ity toˈnælətɪ

Tonawanda ˌtɑnəˈwɑndə, -ˈwɒn-

Tonbridge ˈtʌnbrɪdʒ |-'s -ɪz

tone, t'one (*better* 'tone) *'the one'* tʌn—*see* tother

tone *v* ton |toned tond

toneme ˈtonim |-mic toˈnimɪk

tong tɔŋ, tɒŋ; S+taŋ; |-s -z

Tongaland ˈtɑŋgəˌlænd, ˈtɒŋ-

tongue tʌŋ |tongued tʌŋd |-guey, -guy -ɪ

tongue-tie ˈtʌŋˌtaɪ |-tied -ˌtaɪd

tonic ˈtɑnɪk |-ally -l̩ɪ, -ɪklɪ

tonicity toˈnɪsətɪ

tonight, to-night təˈnaɪt

tonite ˈtonaɪt

tonnage ˈtʌnɪdʒ |-s -ɪz |-d -d

tonneau təˈno, tʌ- |-s, -x -z |-ed -d

tonsil ˈtɑnsl̩, -sɪl |-lar, -ar -ɚ; ES -ə(r

tonsillectomy ˌtɑnsl̩ˈɛktəmɪ

tonsillitis ˌtɑnsl̩ˈaɪtɪs

tonsillotomy ˌtɑnsl̩ˈatəmɪ

tonsorial tɑnˈsoriəl, -ˈsɔr-; S -ˈsor-

Tonstall ˈtʌnstl̩

tonsure ˈtɑnʃɚ; ES ˈtɑnʃə(r |-d -d

tontine ˈtɑntin, tɑnˈtin

tony, T- ˈtonɪ

too tu

Tooele tuˈɛlə

took tʊk

Tooke tʊk

tool tul |tooled tuld

Toombs tumz |-'s -ɪz

toot tut |tooted ˈtutɪd

tooth *n* tuθ |teeth tiθ |*adj* toothed -θt, -ðd

tooth *v* tuθ, tuð |-ed -θt, -ðd

toothache ˈtuθˌek

toothbrush ˈtuθˌbrʌʃ |-es -ɪz

toothpick ˈtuθˌpɪk

toothsome ˈtuθsəm |toothy ˈtuθɪ

tootle ˈtutl̩ |-d -d |-ling ˈtutl̩ɪŋ, -tlɪŋ

top tɑp |topped tɑpt

topaz ˈtopæz |-es -ɪz

topcoat ˈtɑpˌkot |-ed -ɪd

tope top |toped topt |-r ˈtopɚ; ES ˈtopə(r

Topeka təˈpikə

topgallant ˌtɑpˈgælənt, *naut.* təˈgælənt

top-heavy ˈtɑpˌhɛvɪ

Tophet, -th ˈtofɪt, -ɛt

topic ˈtɑpɪk |-al -l̩ |-ally -l̩ɪ, -ɪklɪ

topknot ˈtɑpˌnɑt |-ted -ɪd

Toplady ˈtɑpˌledɪ

toplofty ˈtɑpˈlɔftɪ, -ˈlɒf- (ˈtɑpˌlofty ˈair)

topmast ˈtɑpˌmæst, *naut.* -məst; E+-ˌmast, -ˌmast

topmost ˈtɑpˌmost, -məst

top-notch ˈtɑpˈnɑtʃ (ˈtop-ˌnotch ˈstory)

topographer toˈpɑgrəfɚ, tə-, -ˈpɒg-; ES -fə(r; |-phy -fɪ

topographic ˌtɑpəˈgræfɪk |-al -l̩ |-ally -l̩ɪ, -ɪklɪ

topple ˈtɑpl̩ |-d -d |-ling ˈtɑplɪŋ, -pl̩ɪŋ

topsail ˈtɑpˌsel, *naut.* ˈtɑpsl̩

Topsham ˈtɑpsəm

topside ˈtɑpˈsaɪd (ˈtopˌside ˈcut)

topsoil ˈtɑpˌsɔɪl |-ed -d

Topsy ˈtɑpsɪ

topsy-turvy ˈtɑpsɪˈtɝvɪ; ES -ˈtɜvɪ, -ˈtɝˑvɪ; |-ied -d

toque tok

torah, -ra, T- ˈtorə, ˈtɔrə; S ˈtorə; |-s -z |-roth -roθ

torch tɔrtʃ; ES tɔətʃ; |-es -ɪz |-ed -t

torchon ˈtɔrʃɑn; ES ˈtɔəʃɑn; (*Fr* tõrˈʃõ)

tore tor, tɔr; ES toə(r, E+tɔə(r

toreador ˈtoriəˌdor, ˈtɒr-; ES -ˌdɔə(r; (*Sp* ˌtoreaˈðor)

toric ˈtorɪk, ˈtɑr-, ˈtɒr-

torment *n* ˈtɔrmɛnt; ES ˈtɔə-

torment *v* tɔrˈmɛnt; ES tɔə-; |-ed -ɪd

torn tɔrn, tɔrn; ES tɔən, E+tɔən

tornado tɔrˈnedo; ES tɔə-

Toronto təˈrɑnto

torpedo tɔrˈpido; ES tɔə-; |-ed -d |-ing -ˈpidəwɪŋ

torpid ˈtɔrpɪd; ES ˈtɔəpɪd

torpidity tɔrˈpɪdətɪ; ES tɔˈpɪdətɪ

torpor ˈtɔrpɚ; ES ˈtɔəpə(r

Torquay tɔrˈki; ES tɔəˈki

torque tɔrk; ES tɔək; |-d -t

Torquemada ˌtɔrkɪˈmadə; ES ˌtɔək-; (*Sp* ˌtɔrkeˈmaða)

Torrence, Torrens ˈtɔrəns, ˈtɑr-, ˈtɒr- |-'s -ɪz

torrent ˈtɔrənt, ˈtɑr-, ˈtɒr-

torrential tɔˈrɛnʃəl, tɑ-, tɒ- |-ly -ɪ

Torres Strait ˈtɔrɪzˈstret, ˈtɑr-, ˈtɒr-, -ɪsˈs-

Key: See in full §§3–47. bee bi |pity ˈpɪtɪ (§6) |rate ret |yet jɛt |sang sæŋ |angry ˈæg·grɪ |bath bæθ; E baθ (§10) |ah ɑ |far fɑr |watch wɑtʃ, wɒtʃ (§12) |jaw dʒɔ |gorge gɔrdʒ |go go

Torrey ˈtɔrɪ, ˈtɑrɪ, ˈtɒrɪ
Torricelli ˌtɔrɪˈtʃɛlɪ, ˌtɒr- (*It* ˌtorriˈtʃelli)
torrid ˈtɔrɪd, ˈtɑr-, ˈtɒr-
torridity tɔˈrɪdətɪ, tɑ-, tɒ-
Torrington ˈtɔrɪŋtən, ˈtɑr-, ˈtɒr-
torsion ˈtɔrʃən; ES ˈtɔəʃən; |-al -| |-ally -ḷɪ
torso ˈtɔrso; ES ˈtɔəso
tort tɔrt; ES tɔət
tortilla *Am Sp* tɔrˈtija
tortious ˈtɔrʃəs; ES ˈtɔəʃəs
tortoise ˈtɔrtəs, -tɪs; ES ˈtɔət-; |-s -ɪz
tortoise-shell ˈtɔrtəsˌʃɛl, -tɪs-, -ʃˌʃɛl
Tortuga tɔrˈtugə; ES tɔə-
tortuosity ˌtɔrtʃuˈasətɪ; ES ˌtɔətʃu-, -ˈɒs-
tortuous ˈtɔrtʃuəs; ES ˈtɔətʃuəs
torture ˈtɔrtʃɚ; ES ˈtɔətʃə(r; |-d -d |-rous -əs
torus ˈtorəs, ˈtɔr-; S ˈtor-; |-es -ɪz |-ri -raɪ
Tory ˈtorɪ, ˈtɔrɪ; S ˈtorɪ
Toscanini ˌtaskəˈninɪ, ˌtɒs-, ˌtʌs- (*It* ˌtoska-
ˈni:ni)
tosh tɑʃ; ES+tɒʃ; |-es -ɪz |-ed -t
toss tɔs, tɒs |-es -ɪz |-ed -t |-up -ˌʌp
tossel ˈtɑsḷ, ˈtɒsḷ |-ed -d |-ing -sḷɪŋ, -slɪŋ
Tosti ˈtɔstɪ, ˈtɒs-, ˈtas- (*It* ˈtɔsti)
tot tɑt; ES+tɒt; |-ted -ɪd
total ˈtotḷ |-ed -d |-ly -ɪ |-ity toˈtælətɪ
totalitarian ˌtotæləˈtɛrɪən, toˌtælə-, -ˈter-,
less freq. ˌtotḷəˈt-
totalization ˌtotḷəˈzeʃən, -aɪˈz-
totalizator ˈtotḷəˌzetɚ; ES -ˌzeta(r
totalize ˈtotḷˌaɪz |-s -ɪz |-d -d
tote tot |toted ˈtotɪd
totem ˈtotəm
tother, t'other (*better* 'tother) ˈtʌðɚ; ES -ðə(r
—*In this* t *and in* tone, '*the one,' initial* t
was final t *of the old definite article* that,
not the initial of modern the.
Tottel ˈtatḷ; ES+ˈtɒtḷ
Totten ˈtatn̩; ES+ˈtɒtn̩
Tottenham ˈtatnəm, ˈtatn̩əm; ES+ˈtɒt-
totter ˈtatɚ; ES ˈtatə(r, ˈtɒt-
toucan ˈtukæn, tuˈkan
touch tʌtʃ |touches ˈtʌtʃɪz |-ed -t |-down
-ˌdaun
touch-and-go ˈtʌtʃənˈgo
touchstone, T- ˈtʌtʃˌston, ˈtʌtʃˌʃton
tough tʌf |toughed tʌft
toughen ˈtʌfn̩ |-ed -d |-ing ˈtʌfnɪŋ, -fn̩ɪŋ
Toulon tuˈlɑn, -ˈlɒn (*Fr* tuˈlõ)

Toulouse tuˈluz |-'s -ɪz (*Fr* tuˈlu:z)
toupee tuˈpe, tuˈpi (*Fr* toupet tuˈpɛ)
tour tur; ES tuə(r; |-ed -d |-ist -ɪst
Touraine tuˈren (*Fr* tuˈrɛn)
tour de force ˌturdəˈfors, -ˈfɔrs; ES -ˈfoəs,
E+ˈfɔəs; (*Fr* turdəˈfɔrs)
tournament ˈtɝnəmənt, ˈtur-; ES ˈtɜn-, ˈtɝn-
ˈtuən-
Tourneur ˈtɝnɚ; ES ˈtɜnə(r, ˈtɝnə(r
tourney ˈtɝnɪ, ˈturnɪ; ES ˈtɜnɪ, ˈtɝnɪ, ˈtuənɪ
tourniquet ˈturnɪˌkɛt, -ˌke, ˈtɝn-; ES ˈtuən-,
ˈtɜn-, ˈtɝn-
Tours tur; ES tuə(r; (*Fr* tu:r)
tousle ˈtauzḷ |-d -d |-ling ˈtauzlɪŋ, -zḷɪŋ
Toussaint L'Ouverture *Fr* tusæ̃·luverˈty:r
tout taut |touted ˈtautɪd
tow to |towed tod |-age -ɪdʒ
Towanda toˈwandə, -ˈwɒn-
toward *adj* tord, tɔrd; ES toəd, E+tɔəd
toward *prep* tord, tɔrd, təˈword; ES toəd,
təˈwɔəd, E+tɔəd; |-s -z
towboat ˈtoˌbot
Towcester ˈtostɚ, *loc.*+ˈtaustɚ; ES -tə(r
towel taul, ˈtauəl |-ed -d
tower '*who tows*' ˈtoɚ; ES ˈto·ə(r
tower *building* ˈtauɚ, taur; ES ˈtau·ə(r,
tauə(r; |-ed -d |-ing ˈtaurɪŋ, ˈtauərɪŋ
towhead ˈtoˌhɛd
towhee ˈtauhi, ˈtohi
towline ˈtoˌlaɪn
town taun |-ed -d |-ship -ʃɪp
town hall ˈtaunˈhɔl |townhouse ˈtaunˌhaus
Townsend, -shend ˈtaunznd̩
townsfolk ˈtaunzˌfok
townspeople ˈtaunzˌpipḷ
towpath ˈtoˌpæθ; E+-ˌpaθ, -ˌpɑθ; |-ths -ðz
towrope ˈtoˌrop
toxemia, -aemia taksˈimɪə; ES+tɒks-; |-ic
-ɪk
toxic ˈtaksɪk; ES+ˈtɒks-; |-al -| |-ally -ḷɪ,
-ɪklɪ
toxicity taksˈɪsətɪ; ES+tɒks-
toxicology ˌtaksɪˈkalədʒɪ; ES+ˌtɒksɪˈkɒl-
toxin ˈtaksɪn; ES+ˈtɒks-; |-ine -ɪn, -in
toy tɔɪ |toyed tɔɪd
Toynbee ˈtɔɪnbɪ
trace tres |traces ˈtresɪz |-ed -t |-ry -ərɪ, -rɪ
traceable ˈtresəbḷ |-bly -blɪ
trachea ˈtrekɪə, trəˈkiə |-s -z |-cheae -ˈki·i

trachoma ɪrəˈkomə, tre-
track træk |tracked trækt |-age -ɪdʒ
tract trækt
tractability ˌtræktəˈbɪlətɪ
tractable ˈtræktəb|̩ |-bly -blɪ
tractarian trækˈtɛrɪən, -ˈter- |-ism -ˌɪzəm
tractate ˈtræktet
tractile ˈtræktǀ̩, -tɪl
traction ˈtrækʃən |-tive -tɪv
tractor ˈtræktɚ; ES ˈtræktə(r
Tracy ˈtresɪ
trade tred |traded ˈtredɪd |-sman -zmən
 |-smen -zmən
trade-mark ˈtredˌmɑrk; ES -ˌmɑːk, E+
 -ˌmɑːk; |-ed -t
trade-union ˈtredˈjunjən |-ism -ˌɪzəm
tradition trəˈdɪʃən |-al -ǀ̩ |-ally -ǀ̩ɪ
traduce trəˈdjus, -ˈdɪus, -ˈdus |-s -ɪz |-d -t
Trafalgar Spain, London trəˈfælgɚ; ES
 -ˈfælgə(r; (Sp trafalˈgar)
traffic ˈtræfɪk |-ked -t
Trafford ˈtræfɚd; ES ˈtræfəd
tragacanth ˈtrægəˌkænθ |-ths -θs
tragedian trəˈdʒidɪən
tragedienne trəˌdʒidɪˈen (Fr traʒeˈdjɛn)
tragedy ˈtrædʒədɪ
tragic ˈtrædʒɪk |-al -ǀ̩ |-ally -ǀ̩ɪ, -ɪklɪ
tragicomedy ˌtrædʒɪˈkɑmədɪ; ES+-ˈkɒm-
trail, T-, Traill trel |trailed treld
train tren |-ed -d |-band -ˌbænd
trainman ˈtrenmən |-men -mən, -ˌmɛn
trait tret
traitor ˈtretɚ; ES ˈtretə(r; |-ess -ɪs, -trɪs |-ous
 -əs, -trəs
traitress ˈtretrɪs |-es -ɪz
Trajan ˈtredʒən
traject n ˈtrædʒɛkt
traject v trəˈdʒɛkt |-ed -ɪd |-ction -kʃən
trajectory trəˈdʒɛktərɪ, -trɪ
tram træm |trammed træmd
trammel ˈtræmǀ̩ |-ed -d
tramp træmp |tramped træmpt
trample ˈtræmpǀ̩ |-d -d |-ling -plɪŋ, -pǀ̩ɪŋ
trance træns; E+trans, trɑns; |-s -ɪz |-d -t
Tranio ˈtrenɪˌo, ˈtrɑn-, -njo
tranquil ˈtræŋkwɪl, ˈtræŋ- |-ly -ɪ, -kwəlɪ
tranquillity trænˈkwɪlətɪ, træŋ-
transact trænsˈækt, trænz- |-ed -ɪd |-ion
 -kʃən

transalpine trænsˈælpɪn, trænz-, -paɪn
transatlantic ˌtrænsətˈlæntɪk, ˌtrænz- |-ally
 -ǀ̩ɪ, -ɪklɪ
transcend trænˈsɛnd |-ed -ɪd
transcendence trænˈsɛndəns |-cy -ɪ |-ent -ənt
transcendental ˌtrænsɛnˈdɛntǀ̩ |-ly -ɪ |-ism
 -ˌɪzəm |-ist -ɪst
transcontinental ˌtrænskɑntəˈnɛntǀ̩; ES+
 -kɒn-
transcribe trænˈskraɪb |-scribed -ˈskraɪbd
transcript ˈtrænˌskrɪpt |-ption trænˈskrɪpʃən
transept ˈtrænsɛpt |-al trænˈsɛptǀ̩
transfer n ˈtrænsfɚ; ES -fɜ(r, -fɚ
transfer v trænsˈfɚ; ES -ˈfɜ(r, -ˈfɚ; |-red -d
transferability ˌtrænsfɚˈbɪlətɪ; ES+-fɜrə-;
 acct+transˌferəˈbility
transferable trænsˈfɚəbǀ̩; ES+-ˈfɜrə-; |-bly
 -blɪ
transference trænsˈfɚəns; ES+-ˈfɜrəns
transfiguration ˌtrænsfɪgjəˈreʃən, ˌtrænsˌfɪgjə-
transfigure trænsˈfɪgjɚ; ES -ˈfɪgjə(r; |-d -d
transfix trænsˈfɪks |-es -ɪz |-ed -t |-ion -kʃən
transform trænsˈfɔrm; ES -ˈfɔəm; |-ed -d
transformation ˌtrænsfɚˈmeʃən; ES -fə-
 ˈmeʃən
transfuse trænsˈfjuz, -ˈfɪuz |-s -ɪz |-d -d
transfusion trænsˈfjuʒən, -ˈfɪu-
transgress trænsˈgrɛs, trænz- |-es -ɪz |-ed -t
transgression trænsˈgrɛʃən, trænz-
transience ˈtrænʃəns |-cy -ɪ |-ent -ənt
transigent ˈtrænsədʒənt
transit ˈtrænsɪt, -zɪt
transition trænˈzɪʃən, trænsˈɪʃən
transitive ˈtrænsətɪv
transitory ˈtrænsəˌtorɪ, ˈtrænzə-, -ˌtɔrɪ; S
 -ˌtorɪ
Trans-Jordan trænsˈdʒɔrdn̩, trænz-; ES
 -ˈdʒɔədn̩
Transjordania ˌtrænsdʒɔrˈdenɪə, ˌtrænz-,
 -njə; ES -dʒɔˈden-; |-n -n
translate trænsˈlet, trænz- |-d -ɪd |-tion
 -ˈleʃən
transliterate trænsˈlɪtəˌret, trænz- |-d -ɪd
transliteration ˌtrænslɪtəˈreʃən, ˌtrænz-
translucence trænsˈlusn̩s, trænz-, -ˈlɪu- |-cy
 -ɪ |-cent -sn̩t
transmigrate trænsˈmaɪgret, trænz- |-d -ɪd
transmigration ˌtrænsmaɪˈgreʃən, ˌtrænz-
transmissible trænsˈmɪsəbǀ̩, trænz-

transmission træns'mɪʃən, trænz-
Trans-Mississippi ˌtrænsmɪsə'sɪpɪ, ˌtrænz-
transmit træns'mɪt, trænz- |-ted -ɪd |-tal -ḷ
transmutation ˌtrænsmju'teʃən, ˌtrænz-,
-mɪu-
transmute træns'mjut, trænz-, -'mɪut |-d -ɪd
transoceanic ˌtrænsoʃɪ'ænɪk, ˌtrænz-
transom 'trænsəm |-ed -d
transpacific ˌtrænspə'sɪfɪk
transparence træns'pɛrəns, -'pær-; S -'pær-;
|-cy -ɪ |-rent -rənt
transpire træn'spaɪr; ES -'spaɪə(r; |-d -d
transplant træns'plænt; E+-'plant, -'plant;
|-ed -ɪd
transport n 'trænsport, -pɔrt; ES -poət,
E+-pɔət
transport v træns'port, -'pɔrt; ES -'poət,
E+-'pɔət; |-ed -ɪd
transportation ˌtrænspɚ'teʃən; ES -pə-
transposal træns'pozḷ
transpose træns'poz |-s -ɪz |-d -d ('trans-
ˌposed 'accent)
transposition ˌtrænspə'zɪʃən
transship træns'ʃɪp, trænʃ'ʃɪp |-ped -t
Trans-Siberian ˌtrænssaɪ'bɪrɪən, ˌtrænsaɪ-
transubstantiate ˌtrænsəb'stænʃɪˌet |-d -ɪd
transubstantiation ˌtrænsəbˌstænʃɪ'eʃən
Transvaal træns'val, trænz-
transversal træns'vɝsḷ, trænz-; ES -'vɝsḷ,
-'vɝs]; |-ly -ɪ
transverse træns'vɝs, trænz-; ES -'vɝs,
-'vɝs; ('trans,verse 'section)
Transylvania ˌtrænsḷ'venjə, -nɪə |-n -n
trap træp |trapped træpt
trapeze træ'piz, trə- |-s -ɪz
trapezium trə'pizɪəm |-s -z |-zia -zɪə
trapezoid 'træpəˌzɔɪd |-al ˌtræpə'zɔɪdḷ
Trappist, t- 'træpɪst
traprock 'træpˌrak; ES+-ˌrɒk
trapshooting 'træpˌʃutɪŋ
trash træʃ |trashes 'træʃɪz |-ed -t |-y -ɪ
trauma 'trɔmə, 'traumə |-s -z |-mata -mətə
traumatic trɔ'mætɪk |-ally -ḷɪ, -ɪklɪ
traumatism 'trɔməˌtɪzəm
travail 'trævel, -vḷ |-ed -d
travail 'trave' trə'vel (Fr tra'va:j)
travel 'trævḷ |-ed -d |-ing 'trævlɪŋ, -vḷɪŋ
traveler, -ller 'trævlɚ, 'trævḷɚ; ES -ə(r
travelogue, -log 'trævḷˌɔg, -ˌɑg, -ˌɒg

Travers 'trævɚz; ES 'trævəz; |-'s -ɪz
traverse 'trævɚs, 'trævɝs; ES -vəs, -vɝs,
-vɝs; |-s -ɪz |-d -t—acct+tra'verse
Traverse 'trævɚs; ES 'trævəs; |-'s -ɪz
travertin 'trævɚtɪn; ES 'trævə-; |-tine -tɪn,
-ˌtin
travesty 'trævɪstɪ, -vəstɪ |-tied -d
Travis 'trævɪs |-'s -ɪz
trawl trɔl |trawled trɔld
tray tre |trayed tred
treacherous 'trɛtʃərəs, 'trɛtʃrəs |-ry -rɪ
treacle 'trikḷ |-d -d |-ling 'triklɪŋ, -klɪŋ
tread trɛd |trod trad; ES+trɒd; |trodden
'tradn̩ or trod trad; ES+-ɒ-
treaded adj 'trɛdɪd
treadle 'trɛdḷ |-d -d |-ling 'trɛdlɪŋ, -dlɪŋ
treadmill 'trɛdˌmɪl |-ed -d
treason 'trizn̩ |-ed -d |-ing -zn̩ɪŋ, -znɪŋ
treasonable 'triznəbḷ, 'triznə- |-bly -blɪ
treasonous 'triznəs, 'triznəs
treasure 'trɛʒɚ; ES -ʒə(r; |-d -d |-ring
'trɛʒərɪŋ, -ʒrɪŋ |-ry -ʒərɪ, -ʒrɪ
treasurer 'trɛʒrɚ, -ʒərɚ; ES -rə(r
treasure-trove 'trɛʒɚ'trov; ES 'trɛʒə-
treat, T- trit |treated 'tritɪd
treatise 'tritɪs |-s -ɪz |treaty 'tritɪ
Trebizond 'trɛbɪˌzand; ES+-ˌzɒnd
treble 'trɛbḷ |-d -d |-bly -blɪ
Trebonius trɪ'bonɪəs, -njəs |-'s -ɪz
tree tri |treed trid
treeman 'triˌmæn |-men -ˌmɛn
treenail, tren- 'triˌnel, 'trɛnḷ, 'trʌnḷ
tree-run 'tri'rʌn ('tree,run 'apples)
tree-toad 'triˌtod
trefoil 'trifɔɪl
Treitschke 'traɪtʃkə
trek trɛk |trekked trɛkt
Trelawny trɪ'lɔnɪ
trellis 'trɛlɪs |-es -ɪz |-ed -t
tremble 'trɛmbḷ |-d -d |-ling -blɪŋ, -bḷɪŋ
trembly 'trɛmblɪ
tremendous trɪ'mɛndəs—trɪ'mɛndʒuəs, -dʒəs
is an old variant frequently heard, spelt
tremenduous in 1632, 1742 (Young's Night
Thoughts), 1796.
tremolo 'trɛmḷˌo, 'trɛməˌlo |-ed -d
Tremont US places trɪ'mant, in Me loc.
'trɪmɒnt; ES+-'mɒnt; Boston street 'trɛ-
mənt, 'trɛmant, 'trimant; ES+-mɒnt

|full fʊl |tooth tuθ |further 'fɝðɚ; ES 'fɝðə |custom 'kʌstəm |while hwaɪl |how haʊ |toy tɔɪ
|using 'juzɪŋ |fuse fjuz, fɪuz |dish dɪʃ |vision 'vɪʒən |Eden 'idn̩ |cradle 'kredḷ |keep 'em 'kipm̩

tremor 'tremɚ, 'trimɚ; ES -mə(r
tremulous 'tremjələs
trenail 'triˌnel, 'trenḷ, 'trʌnḷ
trench trentʃ |trenches 'trentʃɪz |-ed -t
trenchancy 'trentʃənsɪ |-chant -tʃənt
trencherman 'trentʃɚmən; ES -tʃə-; |-men -mən
trend trend |trended 'trendɪd
Trent trent
Trenton 'trentən
trepan trɪ'pæn |-panned -'pænd
trephine trɪ'faɪn, -'fin |-d -d
trepid 'trepɪd |-ity trə'pɪdətɪ
trepidation ˌtrepə'deʃən
trespass 'trespəs, -ˌpæs; E+-ˌpas, -ˌpas; |-es -ɪz |-ed -t
tress tres |tresses 'tresɪz |tressed trest
Tressel 'tresḷ
trestle 'tresḷ |-d -d |-ling -slɪŋ, -sḷɪŋ
Trevelyan trɪ'veljən, -'vɪl-
Treves trivz |-'s -ɪz (Fr trɛːv, Ger Trier triːr)
Trevisa trə'visə
trews truz, trɪuz |-man -mən |-men -mən
trey tre |trey-ace 'tre'es
triable 'traɪəbḷ
triad 'traɪæd, -əd
trial 'traɪəl, traɪl
triangle 'traɪˌæŋgḷ |-d -d |-ling -glɪŋ, -gḷɪŋ
triangular traɪ'æŋgjəlɚ; ES -'æŋgjələ(r
triangularity ˌtraɪæŋgjə'lærətɪ, traɪˌæŋ-
triangulate adj traɪ'æŋgjəlɪt, -ˌlet
triangulate v traɪ'æŋgjəˌlet |-lated -ˌletɪd
triangulation ˌtraɪæŋgjə'leʃən, traɪˌæŋ-
Trias 'traɪəs |-sic traɪ'æsɪk
tribal 'traɪbḷ |-ly -ɪ
tribase 'traɪˌbes |-sic traɪ'besɪk
tribe traɪb |-sman -zmən |-smen -zmən
tribrach 'traɪbræk, 'trɪb-
tribulation ˌtrɪbjə'leʃən
tribunal trɪ'bjunḷ, traɪ-, -'bɪun-
tribunate 'trɪbjənɪt, -ˌnet
tribune 'trɪbjun, newspapers often trɪ'bjun, -'bɪun
tributary 'trɪbjəˌterɪ
tribute 'trɪbjut |-buted -bjutɪd
trice traɪs |trices 'traɪsɪz |triced traɪst
tricentennial ˌtraɪsen'tenɪəl, -njəl
triceps 'traɪseps |-es -ɪz |-cipites traɪ'sɪpəˌtiz
trichina trɪ'kaɪnə |-nae -ni |-nous 'trɪkənəs

Trichinopoly, -li ˌtrɪtʃɪ'napəlɪ; ES+-'nɒp-
trichinosis ˌtrɪkə'nosɪs
trick trɪk |tricked trɪkt |-ery -ərɪ, -rɪ
trickle 'trɪkḷ |-d -d |-ling -klɪŋ, -kḷɪŋ
trickster 'trɪkstɚ; ES -stə(r; |-cksy -ksɪ |-cky -kɪ
tricolor 'traɪˌkʌlɚ; ES -ˌkʌlə(r; |-ed -d
tricot 'triko (Fr tri'ko)
tricotine ˌtrɪkə'tin (Fr trikɔ'tin)
tricuspid traɪ'kʌspɪd
tricycle 'traɪsɪkḷ |-d -d |-ling -klɪŋ, -kḷɪŋ
trident 'traɪdṇt
tridental traɪ'dentḷ |-tate -tet
tried traɪd
triennial traɪ'enɪəl |-ly -ɪ
trier 'traɪɚ; ES 'traɪ·ə(r
Trier trɪr; ES trɪə(r; (Ger triːr)
tries traɪz
Trieste trɪ'est (It tri'ɛste)
trifle 'traɪfḷ |-d -d |-ling 'traɪflɪŋ, -fḷɪŋ
trifling adj 'traɪflɪŋ |-fler -flɚ; ES -flə(r
trifoliate traɪ'folɪt, -lɪˌet
triforium traɪ'forɪəm, -'fɔr-; S -'for-; |-s -z |-ria -ɪə
trig trɪg |trigged trɪgd
trigger 'trɪgɚ; ES 'trɪgə(r; |-ed -d
triglyph 'traɪglɪf |-ed -t |-al -ḷ
triglyphic traɪ'glɪfɪk |-al -ḷ
trigonometric ˌtrɪgənə'metrɪk |-al -ḷ |-ally -ḷɪ, -ɪklɪ
trigonometry ˌtrɪgə'namətrɪ; ES+-'nɒm-
trigraph 'traɪgræf; E+-graf, -graf
trihedron traɪ'hidrən |-s -z |-dra -drə
trilateral traɪ'lætərəl |-ly -ɪ
Trilby 'trɪlbɪ
trilinear traɪ'lɪnɪɚ; ES -'lɪnɪ·ə(r
trilingual traɪ'lɪŋgwəl
triliteral traɪ'lɪtərəl |-ly -ɪ
trill trɪl |trilled trɪld
trillion 'trɪljən |-th -θ |-ths -θs
trillium 'trɪlɪəm |-s -z
trilobate traɪ'lobet |-d -ɪd |-bal -bḷ
trilobite 'traɪləˌbaɪt
trilogic trɪ'ladʒɪk, traɪ-; ES+-'lɒdʒ-
trilogy 'trɪlədʒɪ
trim trɪm |-med -d |-mer -ɚ; ES -ə(r
trimeter 'trɪmətɚ; ES 'trɪmətə(r
trimetric traɪ'metrɪk |-al -ḷ
trimonthly traɪ'mʌnθlɪ

Those words below in which the ɑ sound is spelt o are often pronounced with ɒ in E and S

Trinculo 'trɪŋkjəˌlo
trine, T- traɪn |-nal -|
Trinidad 'trɪnəˌdæd |-ian ˌtrɪnə'dædɪən
Trinitarian ˌtrɪnə'tɛrɪən, -'ter- |-ism -ˌɪzəm
trinitrotoluene traɪˌnaɪtro'taljuˌin
trinity, T- 'trɪnətɪ
trinket 'trɪŋkɪt |-ed -ɪd |-ry -rɪ
trinomial traɪ'nomɪəl |-ly -ɪ |-ism -ˌɪzəm
trio *music* 'trio, *'group of three'* 'trio, 'traɪo
Trio 'trio
triolet 'traɪəlɪt
trip trɪp |tripped trɪpt
tripartite traɪ'pɑrtaɪt, 'trɪpɚˌtaɪt; ES -'pɑːt-,
-pə-, E+-'pɑːt-
tripe traɪp
triphthong 'trɪfθɔŋ, 'trɪp-, -θɒŋ |-ed -d
triphthongal trɪf'θɔŋg|, trɪp-, -'θɒŋ|, -'θɒŋ-
|-ly -ɪ
triplane 'traɪˌplen
triple 'trɪp| |-d -d |-ling -plɪŋ, -p|ɪŋ
triplet 'trɪplɪt |-s -s
triplex 'trɪplɛks, 'traɪ-
triplicate *n, adj* 'trɪpləkɪt, -ˌket
triplicate *v* 'trɪpləˌket |-cated -ˌketɪd
triplication ˌtrɪplə'keʃən
triply 'trɪplɪ
tripod 'traɪpad
Tripoli 'trɪpəlɪ |-tan trɪ'pɑlətn̩
Tripolis 'trɪpəlɪs |-'s -ɪz
tripos 'traɪpɑs |-es -ɪz
triptych 'trɪptɪk
trireme 'traɪrim
trisect traɪ'sɛkt |-ed -ɪd |-ction -kʃən
Tristan 'trɪstən
triste *Fr* trist
Tristram 'trɪstrəm
trisyllabic ˌtrɪsɪ'læbɪk, ˌtraɪ- |-al -| |-ally -|ɪ,
-ɪklɪ
trisyllable trɪ'sɪləb|, traɪ-, 'trɪsɪl-, 'traɪ-
trite traɪt
Triton 'traɪtn̩
triturate 'trɪtʃəˌret |-d -ɪd |-tion ˌtrɪtʃə'reʃən
triumph 'traɪəmf, -mpf |-ed -t
triumphal traɪ'ʌmf|, -'ʌmpf|
triumphance traɪ'ʌmfəns, -'ʌmpf- |-cy -ɪ |-nt
-nt
triumvir traɪ'ʌmvɚ; ES -'ʌmvə(r; |-ate -ɪt
triune 'traɪjun, traɪ'jun ('triˌune 'God)

trivalence traɪ'veləns, 'trɪvələns |-cy -ɪ |-lent
-lənt
trivet 'trɪvɪt
trivia 'trɪvɪə |-l 'trɪvjəl, -vɪəl
triviality ˌtrɪvɪ'ælətɪ
trivialize 'trɪvɪəlˌaɪz, -vjəl- |-s -ɪz |-d -d
trivium 'trɪvɪəm |-via -vɪə
triweekly traɪ'wiklɪ ('triˌweekly 'news)
Trix trɪks |-'s -ɪz |-y, -ie -ɪ
Troad 'troæd
Troas 'troəs, 'troæs |-'s -ɪz
Trocadero ˌtrɑkə'dɪro (*Fr* trɔkade'ro)
trochaic tro'ke·ɪk
troche 'trokɪ
trochee 'troki
trod trɑd |trodden 'trɑdn̩
troglodyte 'trɑgləˌdaɪt, 'trɒg-
Troilus 'trɔɪləs, 'tro·ɪləs |-'s -ɪz—*in Chaucer*
usually trisyllabic; in Shak. only twice so
Trojan 'trodʒən
troll trol |trolled trold
trolley, -lly 'trɑlɪ |-ed, -ied -d
trollop 'trɑləp |-ed -t
Trollope 'trɑləp |-pian trɑ'lopɪən
trombone 'trɑmbon, trɑm'bon ('tromˌbone
'solo)
Trondheim, -hjem 'tranhɛm, 'tranjɛm
trone tron |troned trond
troop trup |trooped trupt |-er -ɚ; ES -ə(r
trope trop
trophic 'trɑfɪk |-al -| |-ally -|ɪ, -ɪklɪ
trophy 'trofɪ |-ied -d
tropic 'trɑpɪk |-al -| |-ally -|ɪ, -ɪklɪ
tropism 'tropɪzəm |-ist -ɪst |-pistic tro'pɪstɪk
troposphere 'tropəˌsfɪr; ES -ˌsfɪə(r, S+
-ˌsfɛə(r
troppo 'trapo (*It* 'ˈrɔppo)
Trossachs 'trasæks, -səks, 'trɒs-
trot trat |trotted 'tratɪd
troth trɔθ, troθ, trɒθ |-'s -θs |-ths -θs, -ðz
|-ed -t
Trotsky 'tratskɪ
trotter 'tratɚ; ES 'tratə(r
troubadour 'trubəˌdur, -ˌdor, -ˌdɔr; ES
-ˌduə(r, -ˌdoə(r, E+-ˌdɔə(r
Troubetskoy tru'bɛt'skɔɪ, -'bɛtskɔɪ
trouble 'trʌb| |-d -d |-ling 'trʌblɪŋ, -b|ɪŋ
troublesome 'trʌb|səm |-ly -lɪ

troublous ˈtrʌbləs

Troubridge ˈtrubrɪdʒ, *cf* Trowbridge

trough trɔf, trɒf, -θ |-s -fs, -vz, -θs, -ðz— -θ
is esp. freq. in N Engd.

trounce traʊns |trounces ˈtraʊnsɪz |-d -t

troupe trup |trouped trupt

trousered ˈtraʊzəˑd; ES -zəd; |-sers -z

trousseau truˈso, ˈtruso

trout traʊt |trouted ˈtraʊtɪd

trouvère truˈvɛr; ES -ˈvɛə(r

trove trov

trover ˈtrovəˑ; ES ˈtrovə(r

trow tro |trowed trod

Trowbridge ˈtrobrɪdʒ |-ʼs -ɪz, *cf* Troubridge

trowel ˈtraʊəl, traʊl |-ed -d

Troy, t- trɔɪ |-an -ən |-ans -ənz

truancy ˈtruənsɪ, ˈtrɪu- |-ant -ənt

truce trus, trɪus |-s -ɪz |-d -t

truck trʌk |trucked trʌkt

truckle ˈtrʌkl̩ |-d -d |-ling ˈtrʌklɪŋ, -kl̩ɪŋ

truculence ˈtrʌkjələns, ˈtruk- |-cy -ɪ |-nt -nt

trudge trʌdʒ |trudges ˈtrʌdʒɪz |-d -d

Trudgen, t- ˈtrʌdʒən |-ed -d

true tru, trɪu |-d -d |-love -ˌlʌv

truepenny ˈtruˌpɛnɪ, ˈtrɪu-

truffle ˈtrʌfl̩, ˈtrufl̩ |-d -d

truism ˈtruɪzəm, ˈtrɪu-

trull trʌl

truly ˈtrulɪ, ˈtrɪulɪ

Truman ˈtrumən, ˈtrɪu-

Trumbull ˈtrʌmbl̩

trump trʌmp |trumped trʌmpt |-ery -ərɪ, -rɪ

trumpet ˈtrʌmpɪt |-ed -ɪd

truncate ˈtrʌŋket |-d -ɪd |-tion trʌŋˈkeʃən

truncheon ˈtrʌntʃən |-ed -d

trundle ˈtrʌndl̩ |-d -d |-ling ˈtrʌndlɪŋ, -dl̩ɪŋ

trunk trʌŋk |trunked trʌŋkt

trunnion, T- ˈtrʌnjən |-ed -d

Truro ˈtruro, ˈtrɪuro

truss trʌs |trusses ˈtrʌsɪz |trussed trʌst

trust trʌst |trusted ˈtrʌstɪd |-ee trʌsˈti

trustful ˈtrʌstfəl |-ly -ɪ

trustworthy ˈtrʌstˌwɝˈðɪ; ES -ˌwɜˈðɪ, -ˌwɝˈðɪ

trusty ˈtrʌstɪ

truth truθ, trɪuθ |-ʼs -θs |-ths -ðz, -θs

truthful ˈtruθfəl, ˈtrɪuθ- |-ly -ɪ

try traɪ |tried traɪd

trylon ˈtraɪlɑn; ES +-lɒn

try-on ˈtraɪˌɑn, -ˌɒn, -ˌɔn

Tryon ˈtraɪən

tryout ˈtraɪˌaʊt

trypanosome ˈtrɪpənəˌsom

trysail ˈtraɪˌsel, *naut.* ˈtraɪsl̩

try-square ˈtraɪˌskwɛr, -ˌskwær; E -ˌskwɛə(r,
ES -ˌskwæə(r

tryst trɪst, traɪst |-ed -ɪd

tsar tsɑr; ES tsɑː(r, E+tsɑː(r

tsarevitch ˈtsɑrəˌvɪtʃ; E+ˈtsɑrə-; |-ʼs -ɪz

tsarevna tsɑˈrɛvnə; E+tsɑ-

tsarina tsɑˈrinə; E+tsɑ-

Tschaikovsky, -wsky tʃaɪˈkɔfskɪ, -ˈkɒf-,
-vskɪ, -ˈkaʊskɪ

tsetse ˈtsɛtsɪ

Tsingtao ˈtsɪŋˈtaʊ

T-square ˈtiˌskwɛr, -ˌskwær; E -ˌskwɛə(r, ES
-ˌskwæə(r

Tsushima tsəˈʃimə, ˈtsuʃɪˌmɑ

Tuareg ˈtwarɛg

tub tʌb |tubbed tʌbd

tuba *ʻhornʼ* ˈtjubə, ˈtɪubə, ˈtubə |-s -z |-bae -bi

tuba *mythical tree* ˈtubə

tuba *nut, liquor* ˈtubɑ

Tuba ˈtubə

Tubal ˈtjubl̩, ˈtɪubl̩, ˈtubl̩

Tubal-cain ˈtjublˌken, ˈtɪu-, ˈtu-

tube tjub, tɪub, tub |-bal -l̩ |-bar -əˑ; ES -ə(r

tuber ˈtjubəˑ, ˈtɪu-, ˈtu-; ES -bə(r

tubercle ˈtjubəˑkl̩, ˈtɪu-, ˈtu-; ES -bəkl̩

tubercular tjuˈbɝkjələˑ, tɪu-, tu-, tə-; ES -ˈbɝ-
kjələ(r, -ˈbɝkjələ(r; |-lin -lɪn |-lous -ləs

tuberculosis tjuˌbɝkjəˈlosɪs, trɪu-, tu-, tə-;
ES -ˌbɝk-, -ˌbɝk-

tuberose *ʻtuberousʼ* ˈtjubəˌros, ˈtɪu-, ˈtu-

tuberose *flower* ˈtjubˌroz, ˈtɪub-, ˈtub- |-s -ɪz

tuberous ˈtjubərəs, ˈtɪu-, ˈtu-

tubular ˈtjubjələˑ, ˈtɪu-, ˈtu-; ES -lə(r

tubule ˈtjubjul, ˈtɪubjul, ˈtubjul

tuck, T- tʌk |tucked tʌkt

tuckahoe, T- ˈtʌkəˌho

tucker, T- ˈtʌkəˑ; ES ˈtʌkə(r; |-ed -d |-ing
ˈtʌkərɪŋ, ˈtʌkrɪŋ

tucket ˈtʌkɪt

Tucson tuˈsɑn, -ˈsɒn, -ˈsɔn—*acct*+ˈTucson

Tudor ˈtjudəˑ, ˈtɪu-, ˈtu-; ES -də(r

Tuesday ˈtjuzdɪ, ˈtɪuz-, ˈtuz-—*see* Monday

tufa ˈtjufə, ˈtɪufə, ˈtufə

tuff tʌf

tuft tʌft |tufted ˈtʌftɪd

---

tug tʌg |tugged tʌgd |-boat -ˌbot
Tuileries 'twilərız (*Fr* tɥil'ri)
tuition tju'ıʃən, tɪu-, tu- |-al -ḷ |-ary -ˌɛrɪ
Tulane tju'len, tɪu-, tu-
Tulare tu'lɛrɪ, -'lærɪ; S -'lærɪ
tularemia, -raem- ˌtulə'rimɪə
tulip 'tjuləp, 'tɪu-, 'tu-, -ɪp
Tullamore ˌtʌlə'mor, -'mɔr; ES -'moə(r,
   E+-'mɔə(r; ('Tullaˌmore 'Road)
tulle tjul, tɪul, tul (*Fr* tyl)
Tullichewan ˌtʌlɪ'kjuən, -'kɪuən (*Sc* -'xjuən)
Tully 'tʌlɪ
Tulsa 'tʌlsə
tumble 'tʌmbḷ |-d -d |-ling 'tʌmblɪŋ, -bḷɪŋ
tumble-down 'tʌmbḷ'daʊn ('tumble-ˌdown
   'shed)
tumbler 'tʌmblɚ; ES 'tʌmblə(r
tumbrel, -bril 'tʌmbrəl
tumefaction ˌtjumə'fækʃən, ˌtɪu-, ˌtu-
tumefy 'tjuməˌfaɪ, 'tɪu-, 'tu- |-fied -ˌfaɪd
tumescence tju'mɛsns, tɪu-, tu- |-scent -snt
tumid 'tjumɪd, 'tɪu-, 'tu-
tumidity tju'mɪdətɪ, tɪu-, tu-
tumor 'tjumɚ, 'tɪu-, 'tu-; ES -mə(r; |-ed -d
   |-ous -əs
tumult 'tjumʌlt, 'tɪu-, 'tu- |-ed -ɪd
tumultuous tju'mʌltʃʊəs, tɪu-, tu-
tumulus 'tjumjələs, 'tɪu-, 'tu- |-es -ɪz |-li -ˌlaɪ
tun tʌn |tunned tʌnd
tuna 'tunə
Tunbridge 'tʌnbrɪdʒ |-'s -ɪz
tundra 'tʌndrə, 'tʊndrə
tune tjun, tɪun, tun |-d -d
tungsten 'tʌŋstən
tunic 'tjunɪk, 'tɪu-, 'tu- |-ked -t |-le -ḷ
Tunis 'tjunɪs, 'tɪu-, 'tu- |-'s -ɪz
Tunisia tju'nɪʃɪə, tɪu-, tu-, -ʃə |-n -n
Tunkhannock tʌŋk'hænək
tunnel 'tʌnḷ |-ed -d
tunny 'tʌnɪ
Tunstall 'tʌnstḷ
tup tʌp |tupped tʌpt
Tupelo, t- 'tjupəˌlo, 'tɪu-, 'tu-
Turania tju'renɪə, tɪu-, tu- |-n -n
turban 'tɝbən; ES 'tɜb-, 'tɝb-; |-ed -d
Turberville, -vile 'tɝbɚˌvɪl; ES 'tɜbə-, 'tɝbə-
turbid 'tɝbɪd; ES 'tɜbɪd, 'tɝbɪd
turbidity tɝ'bɪdətɪ; ES tɜ-, tɝ-
turbinate *adj* 'tɝbənɪt, -ˌnet; ES 'tɜb-, 'tɝb-

turbinate *v* 'tɝbəˌnet; ES 'tɜb-, 'tɝb-; |-d -ɪd
turbine 'tɝbaɪn, -bɪn; ES 'tɜ-, 'tɝ-
turbot 'tɝbət; ES 'tɜ-, 'tɝ-
turbulence 'tɝbjələns; ES 'tɜb-, 'tɝb-; |-cy -ɪ
   |-lent -lənt
Turco 'tɝko; ES 'tɜko, 'tɝko
Turcoman 'tɝkəmən; ES 'tɜk-, 'tɝk-; |-s -z
tureen tu'rin, tɪu'rin, tju'rin
turf *n* tɝf; ES tɜf, tɝf; |-'s -s |-s -s *or* -rves -vz
turf *v* tɝf; ES tɜf, tɝf; |-s -s |-ed -t
Turgenev tʊr'gɛnjɪf; ES tʊə-; (*Rus* tʊr-
   'gɛnjɪf)
turgent 'tɝdʒənt; ES 'tɜdʒ-, 'tɝdʒ-
turgescence tɝ'dʒɛsns; ES tɜ-, tɝ-; |-cy -ɪ
   |-scent -snt
turgid 'tɝdʒɪd; ES 'tɜdʒ-, 'tɝdʒ-
turgidity tɝ'dʒɪdətɪ; ES tɜ-, tɝ-
Turin 'tjʊrɪn, 'tɪu-, 'tu-
Turk tɝk; ES tɜk, tɝk; |-ish -ɪʃ
Turkestan ˌtɝkɪ'stæn, -'stan; ES ˌtɜkɪ-,
   ˌtɝkɪ-
Turkey, t- 'tɝkɪ; ES 'tɜkɪ, 'tɝkɪ
Turkmen 'tɝkmɛn; ES 'tɜk-, 'tɝk-
Turkmenistan ˌtɝkmɛnɪ'stæn, -'stan; ES
   ˌtɜk-, ˌtɝk-
Turkoman 'tɝkəmən; ES 'tɜk-, 'tɝk-; |-s -z
Turkomen 'tɝkəˌmɛn; ES 'tɜk-, 'tɝk-
Turlock 'tɝlak; ES 'tɜ-, 'tɝ-, -lɒk
turmoil 'tɝmɔɪl; ES 'tɜ-, 'tɝ-
turn tɝn; ES tɜn, tɝn; |-ed -d |-about
   -əˌbaʊt
turnbuckle 'tɝnˌbʌkḷ; ES 'tɜn-, 'tɝn-
Turnbull 'tɝnˌbʊl; ES 'tɜn-, 'tɝn-
turncoat 'tɝnˌkot; ES 'tɜn-, 'tɝn-; |-ed -ɪd
turndown 'tɝnˌdaʊn; ES 'tɜn-, 'tɝn-
turner, T- 'tɝnɚ; ES 'tɜnə(r, 'tɝnə(r
turnip 'tɝnəp, -ɪp; ES 'tɜn-, 'tɝn-; |-ed -t
turnkey 'tɝnˌki; ES 'tɜn-, 'tɝn-
turnout 'tɝnˌaʊt; ES 'tɜn-, 'tɝn-
turnover 'tɝnˌovɚ; ES 'tɜnˌovə(r, 'tɝnˌovə(r
turnpike 'tɝnˌpaɪk; ES 'tɜn-, 'tɝn-; |-d -t
turnspit 'tɝnˌspɪt; ES 'tɜn-, 'tɝn-
turnstile 'tɝnˌstaɪl; ES 'tɜn-, 'tɝn-
turntable 'tɝnˌtebḷ; ES 'tɜn-, 'tɝn-
turpentine 'tɝpənˌtaɪn, 'tɝpm̩-; ES 'tɜp-,
   'tɝp-; |-d -d
Turpin 'tɝpɪn; ES 'tɜpɪn, 'tɝpɪn
turpitude 'tɝpəˌtjud, -ˌtɪud, -ˌtud; ES 'tɜp-,
   'tɝp-

turquoise 'tɝˑkwɔɪz, -kɔɪz; ES 'tɜ-, 'tɝˑ-;
　|-s -ɪz
turret 'tɝˑɪt, 'tʊrɪt; ES 'tɜr-, 'tʌr-, 'tɝˑ-, 'tʊr-;
　|-ed -ɪd
turtle 'tɝˑt|; ES 'tɜt|, 'tɝˑt|; |-d -d |-ling -t|ɪŋ,
　-tlɪŋ |-dove -'dʌv, -ˌdʌv
turves tɝˑvz; ES tɜvz, tɝˑvz
Tuscaloosa ˌtʌskə'lusə
Tuscan 'tʌskən |-y -ɪ
Tuscarawas ˌtʌskə'rɔwəs |-'s -ɪz
Tuscarora ˌtʌskə'rorə, -'rɔrə; S -'rorə
Tusculum 'tʌskjələm
tush tʌʃ |tushes 'tʌʃɪz |tushed tʌʃt
tusk tʌsk |tusked tʌskt
Tuskegee tʌs'kigɪ
Tussaud tə'so, tʊ-
tussle 'tʌs| |-d -d |-ling 'tʌslɪŋ, 'tʌs|ɪŋ
tussock 'tʌsək |-ed -t
tut intj ⁊ (voiceless suction tongue-blade
　alveolar click)
tut n, v tʌt |tutted 'tʌtɪd
Tutankhamen ˌtutaŋk'amɪn, -ən
tutelage 'tut|ɪdʒ, 'tɪu-, 'tju-
tutelary 'tut|ˌɛrɪ, 'tɪu-, 'tju-
tutor 'tutɚ, 'tɪu-, 'tju-; ES -tə(r; |-ed -d
tutorial tu'torɪəl, tɪu-, tju-, -'tɔr-; S -'tor-;
　|-ly -ɪ
tutti-frutti 'tutɪ'frutɪ (It 'tutti'frutti)
Tuttle 'tʌt|
tu-whit tʊ'hwɪt |tu-whoo tʊ'hwu
Tuxedo, t- tʌk'sido, -də
Twaddell musician, linguist twa'dɛl, twɒ-,
　twə-, physicist 'twad|, 'twɒd|
twaddle 'twad|, 'twɒd| |-d -d |-ling -dlɪŋ,
　-d|ɪŋ
twain, T- twen |-ed -d
twang twæŋ |twanged twæŋd
'twas 'it was' stressed 'twaz, 'twɒz, 'twʌz,
　ˌtwaz, ˌtwɒz, ˌtwʌz; unstr. twəz
'twasn't 'it was not' 'twaznt, 'twɒznt, 'twʌznt,
　ˌtwaznt, ˌtwɒznt, ˌtwʌznt
tweak twik |tweaked twikt
Tweddell 'twɛd|—the purely phonetic form of
　Tweed-dale; 'twid̩del, 'twid|, twə'dɛl, etc.,
　are due to other influences. Cf Tweedmouth
Tweed, t- twid
Tweeddale 'twid̩del, 'twid|
Tweedle 'twid|
tweedle 'twid| |-d -d |-ling 'twidlɪŋ, -d|ɪŋ

tweedledee, T- ˌtwid|'di |-d -d |-dum -'dʌm
Tweedmouth 'twidməθ, -ˌmauθ, loc. 'twɛd-
　məθ, cf Tweddell
Tweedsmuir 'twidzˌmjʊr, -ˌmɪur; ES
　-ˌmjʊə(r, -ˌmɪuə(r
'tween twin
tweet-tweet 'twit'twit |-ed -ɪd
tweezers 'twizɚz; ES -zəz; |-zered -zɚd; ES
　-zəd
twelfth twɛlfθ |-ths -θs
Twelfth-night 'twɛlfθˌnaɪt
twelve twɛlv |-mo -mo |-month -ˌmʌnθ
twelvepenny 'twɛlvˌpɛnɪ, -pənɪ
Twemlow 'twɛmlo
twenty 'twɛntɪ |-tieth -tɪθ |-tieths -tɪθs
twentyfold 'twɛntɪ'fold ('twentyˌfold 'loss)
'twere 'it were' stressed 'twɝ, ˌtwɝ; ES -ɝ(r,
　-ɝ; unstr. twɚ; ES twə(r
twice twaɪs
twice-told 'twaɪs'told ('Twice-ˌTold 'Tales)
Twickenham 'twɪkənəm, 'twɪknəm, formerly
　+'twɪt- (17c Twittenham)
twiddle 'twɪd| |-d -d |-ling 'twɪdlɪŋ, -d|ɪŋ
twig twɪg |twigged twɪgd
twilight 'twaɪˌlaɪt
twill twɪl |twilled twɪld
'twill 'it will' stressed 'twɪl, ˌtwɪl; unstr. t|—
　Unstr. twəl, tw| are rarely used.
twin twɪn |twins twɪnz |twinned twɪnd
twine twaɪn |twined twaɪnd
twinge twɪndʒ |twinges 'twɪndʒɪz |-d -d
twinkle 'twɪŋk| |-d -d |-ling 'twɪŋklɪŋ, -k|ɪŋ
twinkling n 'twɪŋklɪŋ
twirl twɝl; ES twɜl, twɝl; |-ed -d
twist twɪst |twisted 'twɪstɪd
twit twɪt |twitted 'twɪtɪd
twitch twɪtʃ |twitches 'twɪtʃɪz |twitched
　twɪtʃt
twitter 'twɪtɚ; ES 'twɪtə(r; |-ed -d |-ing
　'twɪtərɪŋ, -trɪŋ
'twixt twɪkst
two tu
two-by-four adj 'tubə'for, -'fɔr; ES -'foə(r,
　E+-'fɔə(r
two-by-four n 'tubəˌfor, -ˌfɔr; ES -ˌfoə(r,
　E+-ˌfɔə(r
two-faced 'tu'fest ('two-ˌfaced 'Janus)
two-fisted 'tu'fɪstɪd
twofold adj, adv 'tu'fold ('twoˌfold 'gain)

two-handed 'tu'hændıd ('two-ˌhanded 'engine)

two-legged 'tu'lɛgɪd, -'lɛgd

twopence 'tʌpəns |-s -ız

twopenny 'tu‚pɛnɪ, -pənɪ, 'tʌpənɪ

twosome 'tusəm

'twould 'it would' stressed 'twʊd, ˌtwʊd; unstr. twəd

two-way 'tu'we ('two-ˌway 'bridge)

Twyford 'twaɪfəd; ES 'twaɪfəd

Tybalt 'tɪb|t

Tyburn 'taɪbən; ES 'taɪbən

Tychicus 'tɪkɪkəs |-'s -ız

Tycho 'taɪko

tycoon taɪ'kun

Tygart 'taɪgət; ES 'taɪgət

tying 'taɪɪŋ

tyke taɪk

Tyler, -lor 'taɪlə; ES 'taɪlə(r

tympan 'tɪmpən |-ic tɪm'pænɪk

tympanum 'tɪmpənəm |-s -z |-na -nə |-ny -nɪ

Tynan 'taɪnən

Tyndale 'tɪnd| |Tyndall 'tɪnd|

Tyne taɪn |-mouth 'tɪnməθ, 'taɪn-

type taɪp |typed taɪpt |-script -ˌskrɪpt

Typee 'taɪ'pi |-s -z

typesetter 'taɪpˌsɛtə; ES -ˌsɛtə(r

typewrite 'taɪpˌraɪt |-wrote -ˌrot |-written -ˌrɪtn̩ |-r -ə; ES -ə(r

typhoid 'taɪfɔɪd, taɪ'fɔɪd ('ty‚phoid 'fever)

typhoidal taɪ'fɔɪd|

typhonic taɪ'fɑnɪk; ES+-'fɒn-

typhoon taɪ'fun

typhous 'taɪfəs |typhus 'taɪfəs

typic 'tɪpɪk |-al -| |-ally -|ɪ, -ɪklɪ

typify 'tɪpəˌfaɪ |-fied -ˌfaɪd

typist 'taɪpɪst

typographer taɪ'pɑgrəfə, -'pɒg-; ES -fə(r; |-phy -fɪ

typographic ˌtaɪpə'græfɪk |-al -| |-ally -|ɪ, -ɪklɪ

typothetae taɪ'pɑθəˌti, ˌtaɪpə'θiti; ES+-'pɒθ-

tyrannic tɪ'rænɪk, taɪ- |-al -| |-ally -|ɪ |-icly -ɪklɪ

tyrannicide tɪ'rænəˌsaɪd, taɪ-

tyrannize 'tɪrəˌnaɪz |-s -ız |-d -d

tyrannous 'tɪrənəs |-ny -nɪ

tyrant 'taɪrənt |-ed -ɪd

Tyre taɪr; ES taɪə(r; |-rian 'tɪrɪən

tyre taɪr; ES taɪə(r; |-d -d

tyro 'taɪro

Tyrol 'tɪrəl, -ɑl, -ɒl, tɪ'rol

Tyrolean tɪ'rolɪən, ˌtɪrə'liən

Tyrolese ˌtɪrə'liz

Tyrone Irel tɪ'ron, US taɪ'ron, tɪ-

Tyrrell 'tɪrəl, 'tɛrəl, cf Terrell

Tyrrhenian tɪ'rinɪən

Tyrtaeus tɝ'tiəs; ES tɝ-, tɜ-; |-'s -ız

Tyrwhitt 'tɪrɪt, 'tɛrɪt, cf Tyrrell

Tyson 'taɪsn̩

Tytler 'taɪtlə; ES 'taɪtlə(r

tzar tsɑr; ES tsɑ:(r, E+tsɑ:(r

tzarina tsɑ'rinə; E+tsɑ-

tzetze 'tsɛtsɪ

U

U, u letter ju, jɪu |pl U's, Us, poss U's juz, jɪuz

ubiety ju'baɪətɪ

ubiquitary ju'bɪkwəˌtɛrɪ |-tous -təs |-ty -tɪ

U-boat 'juˌbot

Udall, Udale, Udell 'jud|, cf Yewdale

udder 'ʌdə; ES 'ʌdə(r; |-ed -d |-ful -ˌfʊl

udometer ju'dɑmətə; ES -'dɑmətə(r, -'dɒm-

udometric ˌjudə'mɛtrɪk

Uffizi Gallery u'fitsi

Uganda ju'gændə, u'gɑndɑ

ugh ux & various guttural sounds

ugly 'ʌglɪ

uh-huh 'yes' 'ʌ'hʌ, 'no' 'hʌ?ʔʌ (nasal ʌ)

uhlan 'ulən, 'ulɑn

Uhland 'ulənd (Ger 'u:lɑnt)

Uinta, -h ju'ɪntə

uitlander, U- 'aɪtˌlændə; ES -ˌlændə(r; (Du 'œytˌlɑndər)

ukase 'jukes, ju'kez

Ukraine 'jukren, ju'kren, ju'kraɪn |-nian ju'krenɪən, -'kraɪnɪən

ukulele ˌjukə'lelɪ (Hawaii ˌukʊ'lele)

ulcer 'ʌlsə; ES 'ʌlsə(r; |-ate -ˌet |-ous -əs

ulceration ˌʌlsə'reʃən

|full fʊl |tooth tuθ |further 'fɝðə; ES 'fɝðə |custom 'kʌstəm |while hwaɪl |how haʊ |toy tɔɪ
|using 'juzɪŋ |fuse fjuz, fɪuz |dish dɪʃ |vision 'vɪʒən |Eden 'idn̩ |cradle 'kred| |keep 'em 'kipm̩

Ulfilas ˈʌlfɪləs, ˈʊl- |-ˈs -ɪz
ullage ˈʌlɪdʒ |-s -ɪz |-d -d
Ullswater ˈʌlzˌwɔtɚ, -ˌwɑ-, -ˌwɒ-; ES -tə(r
Ulmus, u- ˈʌlməs
ulna ˈʌlnə |-s -z |-nae -ni
ulster, U- ˈʌlstɚ; ES ˈʌlstə(r; |-ite -ˌaɪt
ulterior ʌlˈtɪrɪɚ; ES -ˈtɪrɪ·ə(r
ultima ˈʌltəmə |-mate -mɪt
ultima Thule ˈʌltəməˈθjuli, -ˈθɪuli
ultimatum ˌʌltəˈmetəm |-s -z |-ta -tə
ultimo ˈʌltəˌmo
ultra ˈʌltrə
ultraconservative ˌʌltrəkənˈsɝvətɪv; ES -ˈsɝv-, -ˈsɝv-
ultrafashionable ˌʌltrəˈfæʃnəb|, -ˈfæʃənə-
ultramarine ˌʌltrəməˈrin
ultramicroscope ˌʌltrəˈmaɪkrəˌskop
ultramicroscopic ˌʌltrəˌmaɪkrəˈskɑpɪk; ES+ -ˈskɒpɪk; |-al -|
ultramodern ˌʌltrəˈmɑdɚn; ES -ˈmɑdən, -ˈmɒd-; |-ism -ˌɪzəm |-ist -ɪst
ultramodernistic ˌʌltrəˌmɑdɚnˈɪstɪk; ES -ˌmɑdən-, -ˌmɒdən-
ultramontane ˌʌltrəˈmɑnten; ES+-ˈmɒn-
ultramundane ˌʌltrəˈmʌnden
ultranationalism ˌʌltrəˈnæʃnəlˌɪzəm, -ʃənəl-
ultrareligious ˌʌltrərɪˈlɪdʒəs
ultraroyalist ˌʌltrəˈrɔɪəlɪst, -ˈrɔjəlɪst
ultraviolet ˌʌltrəˈvaɪəlɪt
ultra vires ˌʌltrəˈvaɪriz
ululant ˈjuljələnt |-late -ˌlet |-lated -ˌletɪd
ululation- ˌjuljəˈleʃən
Ulysses juˈlɪsiz |Ulysses' juˈlɪsiz
umbel ˈʌmb| |-ed -d |-lar -ɚ; ES -ə(r
umbellate ˈʌmb|ɪt, -ˌet |-ated -ˌetɪd
umber ˈʌmbɚ; ES ˈʌmbə(r; |-ed -d |-ing ˈʌmbərɪŋ, -brɪŋ
umbilical ʌmˈbɪlɪk| |-ly -ɪ
umbilicus ʌmˈbɪlɪkəs, ˌʌmbɪˈlaɪkəs |-es -ɪz |-ci -ˌsaɪ, -ˈlaɪsaɪ
umbles ˈʌmb|z
umbra ˈʌmbrə |-s -z |-brae -bri
umbrage ˈʌmbrɪdʒ |-s -ɪz |-d -d
umbrageous ʌmˈbredʒəs
umbrella ʌmˈbrɛlə, əm-
Umbria ˈʌmbrɪə |-n -n
umbriferous ʌmˈbrɪfərəs
umiak, oom- ˈumɪˌæk
umlaut ˈʊmlaʊt |umlauted ˈʊmlaʊtɪd

umph m̥m̥m̥ & *various other grunts and nasal puffs*
umpire ˈʌmpaɪr; ES ˈʌmpaɪə(r; |-d -d
Umpqua ˈʌmpkwə
umpteen ˈʌmpˈtin |-th -θ |-tieth -tɪθ
un- *prefix* ʌn-, ˌʌn-, ˈʌn- *according to rhythm and meaning (see §19)*
Una ˈjunə
unabashed ˌʌnəˈbæʃt |-bashedly -ˈbæʃɪdlɪ
unabated ˌʌnəˈbetɪd (ˈunaˌbated ˈzeal)
unable ʌnˈeb|
unabridged ˌʌnəˈbrɪdʒd |-bridgedly -ˈbrɪdʒɪdlɪ
unaccented ʌnˈæksɛntɪd, ˌʌnækˈsɛntɪd
unacceptable ˌʌnəkˈsɛptəb|, -ɪk- |-bly -blɪ
unaccommodating ˌʌnəˈkɑməˌdetɪŋ; ES+ -ˈkɒm-
unaccompanied ˌʌnəˈkʌmpənɪd
unaccountable ˌʌnəˈkaʊntəb| |-bly -blɪ
unaccounted-for ˌʌnəˈkaʊntɪdˌfɔr; ES -ˌfɔə(r
unaccustomed ˌʌnəˈkʌstəmd
unacquainted ˌʌnəˈkwentɪd
unaddressed ˌʌnəˈdrɛst (ˈunadˌdressed ˈnote)
unadorned ˌʌnəˈdɔrnd; ES -ˈdɔənd; |-nedly -nɪdlɪ
unadulterated ˌʌnəˈdʌltəˌretɪd
unadvisable ˌʌnədˈvaɪzəb| |-bly -blɪ
unadvised ˌʌnədˈvaɪzd |-visedly -ˈvaɪzɪdlɪ
unaffected ˌʌnəˈfɛktɪd (ˈunafˌfected ˈjoy)
unafraid ˌʌnəˈfred
unaided ʌnˈedɪd (ˈunˌaided ˈeffort)
Unaka juˈnekə
Unalaska ˌunəˈlæskə, ˌʌn-
unalienable ʌnˈeljənəb|, -ˈelɪən- |-bly -blɪ
unallotted ˌʌnəˈlɑtɪd; ES+-ˈlɒtɪd
unallowable ˌʌnəˈlaʊəb| |-bly -blɪ
unalloyed ˌʌnəˈlɔɪd (ˈunalˌloyed ˈpleasure)
unalterable ʌnˈɔltərəb|, -trə- |-bly -blɪ
unaltered ʌnˈɔltɚd; ES -ˈɔltəd
unambiguous ˌʌnæmˈbɪgjʊəs
un-American ˌʌnəˈmɛrəkən (ˈun-Aˌmerican ˈway)
unaneled *'unannointed'* ˌʌnəˈnild
unanimity ˌjunəˈnɪmətɪ
unanimous juˈnænəməs, ju-
unannealed *'unsoftened'* ˌʌnəˈnild
unannounced ˌʌnəˈnaʊnst
unanswerable ʌnˈænsərəb|, -srə-; E+-ˈan-, -ˈɑn-; |-bly -blɪ

Key: *See in full §§3–47.* bee bi |pity ˈpɪtɪ (§6) |rate ret |yet jɛt |sang sæŋ |angry ˈæŋ·grɪ |bath bæθ; E baθ (§10) |ah ɑ |far fɑr |watch wɑtʃ, wɒtʃ (§12) |jaw dʒɔ |gorge gɔrdʒ |go go

unanswered ʌn'ænsɚd; ES -'ænsəd, E+-'an-, -'ɑn-
unappeasable ˌʌnə'pizəbl̩ |-bly -blɪ
unappetizing ʌn'æpəˌtaɪzɪŋ
unappreciable ˌʌnə'priʃɪəbl̩, -ʃəbl̩ |-bly -blɪ
unappreciated ˌʌnə'priʃɪˌetɪd |-tive -tɪv
unapproachable ˌʌnə'protʃəbl̩ |-bly -blɪ
unapproached ˌʌnə'protʃt
unapproved ˌʌnə'pruvd ('unapˌproved 'act)
unapt ʌn'æpt
unargued ʌn'ɑrgjʊd; ES -'ɑ:gjʊd; E+ -'a:gjʊd
unarm ʌn'ɑrm; ES -'ɑ:m, E+-'a:m; |-ed -d |-edly -ɪdlɪ
unarmored ʌn'ɑrmɚd; ES -'ɑ:məd, E+ -'a:məd
unartistic ˌʌnɑr'tɪstɪk; ES -ɑ:'tɪstɪk, E+-a:-; |-al -l̩ |-ally -l̩ɪ, -ɪklɪ
unashamed ˌʌnə'ʃemd |-shamedly -'ʃemɪdlɪ
unasked ʌn'æskt; E -'askt, -'æskt, -'ɑskt
unassailable ˌʌnə'seləbl̩ |-bly -blɪ
unassimilated ˌʌnə'sɪməˌletɪd
unassisted ˌʌnə'sɪstɪd ('unasˌsisted 'eye)
unassuming ˌʌnə'sumɪŋ, -'sɪum-, -'sjum-
unattached ˌʌnə'tætʃt ('unatˌtached 'rope)
unattainable ˌʌnə'tenəbl̩ |-bly -blɪ
unattested ˌʌnə'tɛstɪd
unattractive ˌʌnə'træktɪv ('unatˌtractive 'air)
unauspicious ˌʌnɔ'spɪʃəs ('unauˌspicious 'day)
unauthentic ˌʌnɔ'θɛntɪk |-ally -l̩ɪ, -ɪklɪ
unauthenticated ˌʌnɔ'θɛntɪˌketɪd
unauthorized ʌn'ɔθəˌraɪzd |-zedly -zɪdlɪ
unavailable ˌʌnə'veləbl̩ |-bly -blɪ
unavailing ˌʌnə'velɪŋ ('unaˌvailing 'plea)
unavenged ˌʌnə'vɛndʒd
unavoidable ˌʌnə'vɔɪdəbl̩ |-bly -blɪ
unavowed ˌʌnə'vaʊd |-vowedly -'vaʊɪdlɪ
unaware ˌʌnə'wɛr, -'wær; E -'wɛə(r, ES -'wæə(r; |-s -z
unbaked ʌn'bekt ('unˌbaked 'dough)
unbalance ʌn'bæləns |-s -ɪz |-d -t
unbaptized ˌʌnbæp'taɪzd
unbar ʌn'bɑr; ES -'bɑ:(r, E+-'ba:(r; |-red -d
unbated ʌn'betɪd ('unˌbated 'zeal)
unbearable ʌn'bɛrəbl̩, -'bær-; S -'bær-; |-bly -blɪ
unbeaten ʌn'bitn̩ ('unˌbeaten 'team)
unbecoming ˌʌnbɪ'kʌmɪŋ
unbeknown ˌʌnbɪ'non

unbelief ˌʌnbə'lif, -bl̩'if, -bɪ'lif
unbelievable ˌʌnbə'livəbl̩, -bl̩'iv-, -bɪ'liv- |-bly -blɪ
unbeliever ˌʌnbə'livɚ, -bl̩'ivɚ, -bɪ'livɚ; ES -və(r; |-ving -vɪŋ
unbelt ʌn'bɛlt |-ed -ɪd
unbend ʌn'bɛnd |-bent -'bɛnt or -bended -'bɛndɪd |-able -əbl̩ |-bly -blɪ
unbeseeming ˌʌnbɪ'simɪŋ
unbiased ʌn'baɪəst ('unˌbiased 'view)
unbid ʌn'bɪd |-den -n̩
unbind ʌn'baɪnd |-bound -'baʊnd
unblamable ʌn'bleməbl̩ |-bly -blɪ
unbleached ʌn'blitʃt ('unˌbleached 'muslin)
unblemished ʌn'blɛmɪʃt
unblessed, -st ʌn'blɛst |-sedness -sɪdnɪs
unblushing ʌn'blʌʃɪŋ
unbodied ʌn'bɑdɪd; ES+-'bɒdɪd
unbolt ʌn'bolt |-ed -ɪd
unborn ʌn'bɔrn; ES -'bɔən
unbosom ʌn'buzəm, -'buzəm |-ed -d
unbought ʌn'bɔt
unbounded ʌn'baʊndɪd ('unˌbounded 'joy)
unbowed 'not bowed down' ʌn'baʊd
unbowed 'not bent as a bow' ʌn'bod
unbrace ʌn'bres |-s -ɪz |-d -t
unbraid ʌn'bred |-ed -ɪd ('unˌbraided 'hair)
unbreakable ʌn'brekəbl̩ |-bly -blɪ
unbreathed ʌn'briðd—cf breathed
unbridle ʌn'braɪdl̩ |-d -d |-ling -dl̩ɪŋ, -dl̩ɪŋ
unbroken ʌn'brokən ('unˌbroken 'series)
unbruised ʌn'bruzd, -'brɪuzd
unbuckle ʌn'bʌkl̩ |-d -d |-ling -kl̩ɪŋ, -kl̩ɪŋ
unburden ʌn'bɝdn̩; ES -'bɝdn̩, -'bɝdn̩; |-ed -d
unburied ʌn'bɛrɪd
unburned ʌn'bɝnd; ES -'bɝnd, -'bɝnd; |-nt -nt
unbusinesslike ʌn'bɪznɪsˌlaɪk
unbutton ʌn'bʌtn̩ |-ed -d |-ing -'bʌtnɪŋ, -tn̩ɪŋ
uncage ʌn'kedʒ |-s -ɪz |-d -d
uncalled-for ʌn'kɔldˌfɔr; ES -ˌfɔə(r
uncanny ʌn'kænɪ -nily -'kænl̩ɪ, -nɪlɪ
uncanonical ˌʌnkə'nɑnɪkl̩; ES+-'nɒn-; |-ly -ɪ, -ɪklɪ
uncap ʌn'kæp |uncapped ʌn'kæpt
uncared-for ʌn'kɛrdˌfɔr, -'kærd-; E -'kɛəd-ˌfɔə(r, ES -'kæəd-

|full fʊl |tooth tuθ |further 'fɝðɚ; ES 'fɝðə |custom 'kʌstəm |while hwaɪl |how haʊ |toy tɔɪ
|using 'juzɪŋ |fuse fjuz, fɪuz |dish dɪʃ |vision 'vɪʒən |Eden 'idn̩ |cradle 'kredl̩ |keep 'em 'kipm̩

uncatalogued, -logged ʌn'kæt|ˌɔgd, -ˌɑgd, -ˌɒgd

uncaught ʌn'kɔt

unceasing ʌn'sisɪŋ ('unˌceasing 'flow)

uncensored ʌn'sɛnsɚd; ES -'sɛnsəd

uncensured ʌn'sɛnʃɚd; ES -'sɛnʃəd

unceremonious ˌʌnsɛrə'monɪəs, -'monjəs

uncertain ʌn'sɝtn̩, -'sɝtɪn; ES -'sɝt-, -'sɝt-; |-ty -tɪ

unchain ʌn'tʃen |unchained ʌn'tʃend

unchallenged ʌn'tʃælɪndʒd, -əndʒd

unchangeable ʌn'tʃendʒəb| |-bly -blɪ

unchanged ʌn'tʃendʒd |-ness -'tʃendʒɪdnɪs

unchanging ʌn'tʃendʒɪŋ ('unˌchanging 'heat)

uncharitable ʌn'tʃærətəb| |-bly -blɪ

uncharted ʌn'tʃɑrtɪd; ES -'tʃɑːtɪd, E+-'tʃɑːt-

unchaste ʌn'tʃest

unchastened ʌn'tʃesn̩d ('unˌchastened 'heart)

unchastity ʌn'tʃæstətɪ

unchecked ʌn'tʃɛkt ('unˌchecked 'speed)

unchristian ʌn'krɪstʃən

unchurch ʌn'tʃɝtʃ; ES -'tʃɝtʃ, -'tʃɝtʃ; |-es -ɪz |-ed -t

uncial 'ʌnʃɪəl, 'ʌnʃəl, 'ʌnsɪəl |-ly -ɪ

uncircumcised ʌn'sɝkəmˌsaɪzd; ES -'sɝk-, -'sɝk-; |-sedness -zɪdnɪs

uncivil ʌn'sɪv| |-ized -ˌaɪzd |-ly -ɪ

unclad ʌn'klæd

unclaimed ʌn'klemd ('unˌclaimed 'honor)

unclasp ʌn'klæsp; E+-'klasp, -'klɑsp; |-ed -t

unclassified ʌn'klæsəˌfaɪd

uncle 'ʌŋk| |uncled 'ʌŋk|d

unclean ʌn'klin |-ed -d

uncleanly adv ʌn'klinlɪ, adj ʌn'klɛnlɪ

unclench ʌn'klɛntʃ |-es -ɪz |-ed -t

Uncle Remus 'ʌŋk|'riməs |-'s -ɪz

Uncle Sam 'ʌŋk|'sæm

Uncle Tom's Cabin 'ʌŋk|ˌtɑmz'kæbɪn, -ˌtɒmz-

uncloak ʌn'klok |uncloaked ʌn'klokt

unclose adj ʌn'klos

unclose v ʌn'kloz |-s -ɪz |-d -d

unclothe ʌn'kloð |-s -ðz |-d -d |-dly -ɪdlɪ

uncloud ʌn'klaʊd |-clouded -'klaʊdɪd

unco 'ʌŋko

uncoil ʌn'kɔɪl |-coiled -'kɔɪld

uncolored ʌn'kʌlɚd; ES -'kʌləd

uncomely ʌn'kʌmlɪ ('unˌcomely 'speech)

uncomfortable ʌn'kʌmfɚtəb|; ES -'kʌmfət-, -'kʌmftə-; |-bly -blɪ

uncommercial ˌʌnkə'mɝʃəl; ES -'mɝʃəl, -'mɝʃəl; |-ly -ɪ

uncommon ʌn'kamən; ES+-'kɒm-

uncommunicative ˌʌnkə'mjunəˌketɪv, -'mɪun-

uncomplaining ˌʌnkəm'plenɪŋ

uncompleted ˌʌnkəm'plitɪd ('uncomˌpleted 'job)

uncomplimentary ˌʌnkɑmplə'mɛntərɪ, -trɪ; ES+-kɒm-

uncomprehending ˌʌnkɑmprɪ'hɛndɪŋ; ES+-kɒm-

uncompromising ʌn'kɑmprəˌmaɪzɪŋ; ES+-'kɒm-

unconcealed ˌʌnkən'sild ('unconˌcealed 'ire)

unconcern ˌʌnkən'sɝn; ES -'sɝn, -'sɝn; |-ed -d |-edly -ɪdlɪ

unconcerted ˌʌnkən'sɝtɪd; ES -'sɝt-, -'sɝt-

unconditional ˌʌnkən'dɪʃən|, -ʃnəl |-ly -ɪ

unconditioned ˌʌnkən'dɪʃənd

unconfined ˌʌnkən'faɪnd |-finedly -'faɪnɪdlɪ

unconfirmed ˌʌnkən'fɝmd; ES -'fɝmd, -'fɝmd; |-medly -mɪdlɪ

unconformity ˌʌnkən'fɔrmətɪ; ES -'fɔəmətɪ

uncongenial ˌʌnkən'dʒinjəl |-ly -ɪ

unconnected ˌʌnkə'nɛktɪd

unconquerable ʌn'kɑŋkərəb|, -'kɒŋ-, -'kɔŋ-, -krəb| |-bly -blɪ

unconquered ʌn'kɑŋkɚd, -'kɒŋ-, -'kɔŋ-; ES -kəd

unconscious ʌn'kɑnʃəs; ES+-'kɒn-

unconsecrated ʌn'kɑnsɪˌkretɪd; ES+-'kɒn-

unconsidered ˌʌnkən'sɪdɚd; ES -'sɪdəd; ('unconˌsidered 'trifles)

unconstant ʌn'kɑnstənt; ES+-'kɒn-

unconstitutional ˌʌnkɑnstə'tjuʃən|, -'tru-, -'tu-; ES+-kɒn-; |-ly -ɪ

unconstrained ˌʌnkən'strend |-nedly -nɪdlɪ

uncontestable ˌʌnkən'tɛstəb| |-bly -blɪ

uncontrollable ˌʌnkən'troləb| |-bly -blɪ

uncontrolled ˌʌnkən'trold |-ledly -lɪdlɪ

unconventional ˌʌnkən'vɛnʃən|, -ʃnəl |-ly -ɪ

unconverted ˌʌnkən'vɝtɪd; ES -'vɝt-, -'vɝt-; |-tible -təb| |-bly -blɪ

unconvinced ˌʌnkən'vɪnst |-cedly -sɪdlɪ

uncooked ʌn'kʊkt ('unˌcooked 'food)

un-co-ordinated ˌʌnko'ɔrdn̩ˌetɪd; ES -'ɔədn̩-

uncork ʌn'kɔrk; ES ʌn'kɔək; |-ed -t

uncorrected ˌʌnkə'rɛktɪd

uncorroborated ˌʌnkə'rɑbəˌretɪd; ES+-'rɒb-

uncorrupted ˌʌnkəˈrʌptɪd	under- *Compounds in* under- *vary in accent*
uncountable ʌnˈkaʊntəbl̩ |-bly -blɪ	*according to meaning, rhythm, and sense*
uncouple ʌnˈkʌpl̩ |-d -d |-ling -plɪŋ, -plɪŋ	*stress. See note at prefix* over-
uncouth ʌnˈkuθ (ˈunˌcouth ˈaspect)	under ˈʌndɚ; ES ˈʌndə(r
uncover ʌnˈkʌvɚ; ES -ˈkʌvə(r; |-ed -d |-ing	underact ˈʌndɚˈækt |-acted -ˈæktɪd
-ˈkʌvərɪŋ, -vrɪŋ	underage *'shortage'* ˈʌndɚɪdʒ, ˈʌndrɪdʒ |-s
uncreated ˌʌnkrɪˈetɪd (ˈuncreˌated ˈworlds)	-ɪz
uncredited ʌnˈkrɛdɪtɪd |-table -təbl̩ |-bly -blɪ	underage ˈʌndɚˈedʒ (ˈunderˌage ˈpupil)
uncritical ʌnˈkrɪtɪkl̩ |-ly -ɪ, -ɪklɪ	underbid *n* ˈʌndɚˌbɪd; ES ˈʌndəˌbɪd
uncrossed ʌnˈkrɔst, -ˈkrɒst	underbid *v* ˌʌndɚˈbɪd; ES ˌʌndə-; |*past &*
uncrowned (ˈunˌcrowned ˈking)	*pptc* -bid -ˈbɪd
unction ˈʌŋkʃən |-tious -ʃəs |-tional -ʃənl̩	underbred *n* ˈʌndɚˌbrɛd; ES ˈʌndəˌbrɛd
unctuosity ˌʌŋktʃʊˈɑsətɪ; ES+-ˈɒs-	underbred *adj* ˈʌndɚˈbrɛd; ES ˈʌndə-
unctuous ˈʌŋktʃʊəs	underbrush ˈʌndɚˌbrʌʃ; ES ˈʌndə-
uncultivable ʌnˈkʌltəvəbl̩	underbuy ˈʌndɚˈbaɪ; ES ˈʌndə-; |-bought
uncultivatable ʌnˈkʌltəˌvetəbl̩ |-vated -ˌvetɪd	-ˈbɔt
uncultured ʌnˈkʌltʃɚd; ES -ˈkʌltʃəd	undercarriage ˈʌndɚˌkærɪdʒ; ES ˈʌndə-; |-s
uncurdled ʌnˈkɝdl̩d; ES -ˈkɜdl̩d, -ˈkɝdl̩d	-ɪz
uncurious ʌnˈkjʊrɪəs, -ˈkɪʊrɪəs	undercharge *n* ˈʌndɚˌtʃɑrdʒ; ES ˈʌndə-
uncurl ʌnˈkɝl; ES -ˈkɜl, -ˈkɝl; |-ed -d	ˌtʃɑːdʒ, E+-ˌtʃɑːdʒ; |-s -ɪz
uncurtained ʌnˈkɝtnd, -tɪnd; ES -ˈkɜt-,	undercharge *v* ˈʌndɚˈtʃɑrdʒ; ES ˌʌndəˈtʃɑːdʒ,
-ˈkɝt-	E+-ˈtʃɑːdʒ; |-s -ɪz |-d -d
uncut ʌnˈkʌt (ˈunˌcut ˈpages)	underclothed ˈʌndɚˈkloðd; ES ˈʌndə-
undamaged ʌnˈdæmɪdʒd	underclothes ˈʌndɚˌkloz, -ˌkloðz; ES ˈʌndə-
undated ʌnˈdetɪd	underconsumption ˈʌndɚkənˈsʌmpʃən; ES
undaunted ʌnˈdɔntɪd, -ˈdɒntɪd, -ˈdɑntɪd	ˈʌndə-
undazzled ʌnˈdæzl̩d (ˈunˌdazzled ˈeyes)	undercover ˌʌndɚˈkʌvɚ; ES ˌʌndəˈkʌvə(r
undebated ˌʌndɪˈbetɪd |-table -təbl̩	undercurrent ˈʌndɚˌkɝənt; ES ˈʌndəˌkɝrənt,
undeceive ˌʌndɪˈsiv |-d -d	-ˌkʌrənt, -ˌkɝ-
undecided ˌʌndɪˈsaɪdɪd	undercut *n* ˈʌndɚˌkʌt; ES ˈʌndə-
undecipherable ˌʌndɪˈsaɪfərəbl̩, -frəbl̩ |-bly	undercut *v* ˌʌndɚˈkʌt; ES ˌʌndə-
-blɪ	underdo ˌʌndɚˈdu; ES ˌʌndə-; |-does -ˈdʌz
undecorated ʌnˈdɛkəˌretɪd	|-did -ˈdɪd |-done -ˈdʌn
undefeated ˌʌndɪˈfitɪd	underdog ˈʌndɚˌdɔg, -ˈdɒg-, -ˌd-; ES ˈʌndə-
undefended ˌʌndɪˈfɛndɪd (ˈundeˌfended ˈisle)	underestimate *n* ˈʌndɚˈɛstəmɪt, -ˌmet
undefensible ˌʌndɪˈfɛnsəbl̩ |-bly -blɪ	underestimate *v* ˈʌndɚˈɛstəˌmet |-d -ɪd
undefiled ˌʌndɪˈfaɪld |-filedly -ˈfaɪlɪdlɪ	underestimation ˈʌndɚˌɛstəˈmeʃən
undefined ˌʌndɪˈfaɪnd |-nedly -nɪdlɪ |-nable	underexpose ˈʌndɚɪkˈspoz |-s -ɪz |-d -d |-sure
-nəbl̩ |-bly -blɪ	-ʒɚ; ES -ʒə(r
undelayed ˌʌndɪˈled (ˈundeˌlayed ˈmail)	underfeed *n* ˈʌndɚˌfid; ES ˈʌndə-
undelivered ˌʌndɪˈlɪvɚd; ES -vəd; |-rable	underfeed *v* ˈʌndɚˈfid; ES ˈʌndə-; |-fed -ˈfɛd
-vrəbl̩, -vərəbl̩	underfoot ˌʌndɚˈfʊt; ES ˌʌndə-; (ˈunderˌfoot
undemocratic ˌʌndɛməˈkrætɪk |-ally -ḷɪ, -ɪklɪ	ˈvassal)
undemonstrative ˌʌndɪˈmɑnstrətɪv; ES+	undergarment ˈʌndɚˌgɑrmənt; ES ˈʌndə-
-ˈmɒn-	ˌgɑːmənt, E+-ˌgɑːmənt
undeniable ˌʌndɪˈnaɪəbl̩ |-bly -blɪ	undergo ˌʌndɚˈgo; ES ˌʌndə-; |-went -ˈwɛnt
undenominational ˌʌndɪˌnɑməˈneʃənl̩, -ʃnəl;	|-gone -ˈgɔn, -ˈgɒn
ES+-ˌnɒm-	undergraduate ˌʌndɚˈgrædʒʊɪt, -ˌet; ES
undependable ˌʌndɪˈpɛndəbl̩ |-bly -blɪ	ˌʌndə-

underground *adj, adv* ˈʌndɚˈgraʊnd; ES ˈʌndə-; (ˈunderˌground ˈstream)
underground *n* ˈʌndɚˌgraʊnd; ES ˈʌndə-
undergrown ˈʌndɚˈgron; ES ˈʌndə-
undergrowth ˈʌndɚˌgroθ; ES ˈʌndə-; |-ths -θs
underhand ˈʌndɚˈhænd; ES ˈʌndə-; (ˈunderˌhand ˈstroke)
underhanded ˈʌndɚˈhændɪd; ES ˈʌndə-
underhung ˌʌndɚˈhʌŋ; ES ˌʌndə-
underivable ˌʌndɪˈraɪvəbl̩
underlaid ˌʌndɚˈled; ES ˌʌndə-
underlay *n* ˈʌndɚˌle; ES ˈʌndə-
underlay *past of* underlie ˌʌndɚˈle; ES ˌʌndə-
underlay *v* ˌʌndɚˈle; ES ˌʌndə-; |-laid -ˈled
underlie ˌʌndɚˈlaɪ; ES ˌʌndə-; |-lay -ˈle |-lain -ˈlen
underline *n* ˈʌndɚˌlaɪn; ES ˈʌndə-
underline *v* ˌʌndɚˈlaɪn; ES ˌʌndə-; |-d -d
underling ˈʌndɚlɪŋ; ES ˈʌndə-
underlip ˈʌndɚˈlɪp; ES ˈʌndə-; (ˈunderˌlip & ˈupper ˌlip)
underman *n* ˈʌndɚˌmæn; ES ˈʌndə-; |-men -ˌmen
underman *v* ˈʌndɚˈmæn; ES ˈʌndə-; |-ned -d
undermine ˌʌndɚˈmaɪn; ES ˌʌndə-; |-d -d
undermost ˈʌndɚˌmost; ES ˈʌndə-
underneath ˌʌndɚˈniθ, -ˈnið; ES ˌʌndə-
undernourish ˈʌndɚˈnɝɪʃ; ES ˈʌndəˈnɜrɪʃ, -ˈnʌr-, -ˈnɜ-; |-es -ɪz |-ed -t
underofficer ˈʌndɚˌɒfəsɚ, -ˌɒf-, -ˌaf-; ES -sə(r
underpass ˈʌndɚˌpæs; ES ˈʌndə-, E+-ˌpɑs, -ˌpɒs
underpay ˈʌndɚˈpe; ES ˈʌndə-; |-paid -ˈped
underpin ˌʌndɚˈpɪn; ES ˌʌndə-; |-ned -d
underpinning *n* ˈʌndɚˌpɪnɪŋ; ES ˈʌndə-
underpopulated ˈʌndɚˈpɑpjəˌletɪd; ES ˈʌndə-ˈpɑp-, -ˈpɒp-
underprivileged ˈʌndɚˈprɪvəlɪdʒd; ES ˈʌndə-
underprize ˈʌndɚˈpraɪz; ES ˈʌndə-; |-s -ɪz |-d -d
underproduction ˈʌndɚprəˈdʌkʃən; ES ˈʌndə-
underrate ˈʌndɚˈret; ES ˈʌndəˈret; |-d -ɪd
underripe ˈʌndɚˈraɪp; ES ˈʌndə-
underrun ˌʌndɚˈrʌn; ESˌʌndə-; |-ran -ˈræn |-run -ˈrʌn
underscore ˌʌndɚˈskor, -ˈskɔr; ES ˌʌndə-ˈskoə(r, E+-ˈskɔə(r; |-d -d—*acct* + ˈunderˌscore

undersea ˈʌndɚˈsi; ES ˈʌndə-; (ˈunderˌsea ˈlife)
undersecretary ˌʌndɚˈsɛkrəˌtɛrɪ; ES ˌʌndə-
undersell ˌʌndɚˈsɛl; ES ˌʌndə-; |-sold -ˈsold
undershirt ˈʌndɚˌʃɝt; ES ˈʌndəˌʃɜt, -ˌʃɝt
undershoot *v* ˌʌndɚˈʃut; ES ˌʌndə-; |-shot -ˈʃɑt; ES+-ˈʃɒt
undershot *adj* ˈʌndɚˌʃɑt; ES ˈʌndəˌʃɑt, -ˌʃɒt
underside ˈʌndɚˈsaɪd; ES ˈʌndə-; (ˈunderˌside & ˈupper ˌside)
undersign ˌʌndɚˈsaɪn; ES ˌʌndə-; |-ed -d
undersigned *n* ˌʌndɚˈsaɪnd; ES ˌʌndə-; (ˈunderˌsigned ˈagent)
undersize *adj* ˈʌndɚˈsaɪz; ES ˈʌndə-; |-d -d (ˈunderˌsize(d) ˈbolt)
undersize *n* ˈʌndɚˌsaɪz; ES ˈʌndə-; |-s -ɪz
underskirt ˈʌndɚˌskɝt; ES ˈʌndəˌskɜt, -ˌskɝt
underslung ˌʌndɚˈslʌŋ; ES ˌʌndə-
understand ˌʌndɚˈstænd; ES ˌʌndə-; |-stood -ˈstʊd
understandability ˌʌndɚˌstændəˈbɪlətɪ; ES ˌʌndə-
understandable ˌʌndɚˈstændəbl̩; ES ˌʌndə-; |-bly -blɪ
understate ˈʌndɚˈstet; ES ˈʌndə-; |-d -ɪd
understood ˌʌndɚˈstʊd; ES ˌʌndə-
understrapper ˈʌndɚˌstræpɚ; ES ˈʌndə-ˌstræpə(r
understudy ˈʌndɚˌstʌdɪ; ES ˈʌndə-
undertake ˌʌndɚˈtek; ES ˌʌndə-; |-took -ˈtʊk |-taken -ˈtekən
undertaker *'who undertakes'* ˌʌndɚˈtekɚ; ES ˌʌndəˈtekə(r; *'funeral director'* ˈunderˌtaker
undertaking *'enterprise'* ˌʌndɚˈtekɪŋ; ES ˌʌndə-; *'directing funerals'* ˈunderˌtaking
undertone ˈʌndɚˌton; ES ˈʌndə-; |-d -d
undertook ˌʌndɚˈtʊk; ES ˌʌndə-
undertow ˈʌndɚˌto; ES ˈʌndə-
undertrump ˌʌndɚˈtrʌmp; ES ˌʌndə-; |-ed -t
undervaluation ˈʌndɚˌvæljuˈeʃən; ES ˈʌndə-
undervalue ˈʌndɚˈvælju; ES ˈʌndə-; |-d -d
underwater *n* ˈʌndɚˌwɔtɚ, -ˌwatɚ, -ˌwɒtɚ; ES -tə(r; *adj cf* ˈunderˈwater ˌwork *and* ˈunderˌwater ˈmines
underwear ˈʌndɚˌwɛr, -ˌwær; E ˈʌndəˌwɛə(r, ES ˈʌndəˌwæə(r
underweight ˈʌndɚˈwet; ES ˈʌndə-; (ˈunderˌweight ˈboxer)
underwent ˌʌndɚˈwɛnt; ES ˌʌndə-

Key: *See in full §§3–47.* bee bi |pity ˈpɪtɪ (§6) |rate ret |yet jɛt |sang sæŋ |angry ˈæŋ·grɪ |bath bæθ; E baθ (§10) |ah ɑ |far fɑr |watch watʃ, wɒtʃ (§12) |jaw dʒɔ |gorge gɔrdʒ |go go

underwood, U- ˈʌndɚˌwʊd; ES ˈʌndə-; |-ed
-ɪd

underworld ˈʌndɚˌwɝld; ES ˈʌndəˌwɜld,
-ˌwɝld

underwrite ˌʌndɚˈraɪt; ES ˌʌndə-; |-wrote
-ˈrot |-written -ˈrɪtn̩

underwriter ˈʌndɚˌraɪtɚ; ES ˈʌndəˌraɪtə(r

undescribable ˌʌndɪˈskraɪbəb!| |-bly -blɪ

undeserved ˌʌndɪˈzɝvd; ES -ˈzɜvd, -ˈzɝvd;
|-vedly -vɪdlɪ

undesigning ˌʌndɪˈzaɪnɪŋ

undesirability ˌʌndɪˌzaɪrəˈbɪlətɪ

undesirable ˌʌndɪˈzaɪrəb!| |-bly -blɪ

undesired ˌʌndɪˈzaɪrd; ES -ˈzaɪəd; |-ly -rɪdlɪ

undetected ˌʌndɪˈtɛktɪd

undetermined ˌʌndɪˈtɝmɪnd; ES -ˈtɜm-,
-ˈtɝm-; |-nable -nəb!| |-bly -blɪ

undeterred ˌʌndɪˈtɝd; ES -ˈtɜd, -ˈtɝd

undeveloped ˌʌndɪˈvɛləpt

undeviating ʌnˈdivɪˌetɪŋ

undid ʌnˈdɪd

undies ˈʌndɪz

undigested ˌʌndəˈdʒɛstɪd, daɪ- |-tible -təb!|

undignified ʌnˈdɪgnəˌfaɪd

undiluted ˌʌndɪˈlutɪd, -daɪ-, -ˈlɪutɪd

undiminished ˌʌndəˈmɪnɪʃt

undimmed ʌnˈdɪmd (ˈunˌdimmed ˈlights)

Undine ˈʌndin, ˈʌndaɪn

undiplomatic ˌʌndɪpləˈmætɪk |-ally -ɪ, -ɪklɪ

undiscerned ˌʌndɪˈzɝnd, -ˈsɝnd; ES -3nd,
-3ˈnd; |-nedly -nɪdlɪ

undiscernible, -able ˌʌndɪˈzɝnəb!|, -ˈsɝn-; ES
-3n-, -3ˈn-; |-bly -blɪ

undisciplined ʌnˈdɪsəˌplɪnd

undisclosed ˌʌndɪsˈklozd

undiscouraged ˌʌndɪsˈkɝɪdʒd; ES -ˈkɜr-,
-ˈkʌr-, -ˈkɝ-

undiscovered ˌʌndɪˈskʌvɚd; ES -ˈskʌvəd;
|-verable -vərəb!|, -vrəb!| (ˈundisˌcovered
ˈcountry)

undiscriminating ˌʌndɪˈskrɪməˌnetɪŋ

undisguised ˌʌndɪsˈgaɪzd |-sedly -zɪdlɪ |-sable
-zəb!| |-bly -blɪ

undismayed ˌʌndɪsˈmed (ˈundɪsˌmayed ˈheart)

undisposed ˌʌndɪˈspozd

undisputed ˌʌndɪˈspjutɪd, -ˈspɪutɪd

undissolved ˌʌndɪˈzɑlvd, -ˈzɒlvd; |-vable
-vəb!| |-bly -blɪ

undistilled ˌʌndɪˈstɪld

undistinguished ˌʌndɪˈstɪŋgwɪʃt |-shable -ʃəb!|

undistracted ˌʌndɪˈstræktɪd

undistributed ˌʌndɪˈstrɪbjətɪd

undisturbed ˌʌndɪˈstɝbd; ES -ˈstɜbd, -ˈstɝbd
|-bedly -bɪdlɪ

undiversified ˌʌndəˈvɝsəˌfaɪd; ES -ˈvɜsə-,
-ˈvɝsə-

undivided ˌʌndəˈvaɪdɪd

undivulged ˌʌndəˈvʌldʒd (ˈundiˌvulged ˈpur-
pose)

undo ʌnˈdu |-does -ˈdʌz |-did -ˈdɪd |-done
-ˈdʌn

undomestic ˌʌndəˈmɛstɪk |-ticated -tɪˌketɪd

undone ʌnˈdʌn (ˈdone & ˈunˌdone)

undouble ʌnˈdʌb!| |-d -d |-ling -blɪŋ, -b!ɪŋ

undoubted ʌnˈdautɪd (ˈunˌdoubted ˈfact)

undrained ʌnˈdrend

undramatic ˌʌndrəˈmætɪk |-ally -!ɪ, -ɪklɪ

undrape ʌnˈdrep |-d -t

undreamed ʌnˈdrimd |-dreamt -ˈdrɛmpt

undress n ˈʌnˌdrɛs, adj ʌnˈdrɛs (ˈunˌdress
ˈgarb)

undress v ʌnˈdrɛs |-es -ɪz |-ed -t

undrilled ʌnˈdrɪld

undrinkable ʌnˈdrɪŋkəb!|

Undset ˈʊnsɛt

undue ʌnˈdju, -ˈdɪu, -ˈdu (ˈunˌdue ˈhaste)

undulant ˈʌndjələnt, ˈʌndələnt

undulate adj ˈʌndjəlɪt, ˈʌndə-, -ˌlet

undulate v ˈʌndjəˌlet, ˈʌndə- |-d -ɪd

undulation ˌʌndjəˈleʃən, ˌʌndə-

undulatory ˈʌndjələˌtorɪ, ˈʌndə-, -ˌtɔrɪ; S
-ˌtorɪ

unduly ʌnˈdjulɪ, -ˈdɪulɪ, -ˈdulɪ

undutiful ʌnˈdjutɪfəl, -ˈdɪu-, -ˈdu- |-ly -ɪ

undyed ʌnˈdaɪd (ˈunˌdyed ˈwool)

undying ʌnˈdaɪɪŋ

unearned ʌnˈɝnd; ES -ˈɜnd, -ˈɝnd

unearth ʌnˈɝθ; ES -ˈɜθ, -ˈɝθ; |-ed -t |-ly -lɪ

uneasily ʌnˈizɪ|ɪ, -ˈizɪlɪ

uneasy ʌnˈizɪ (ˈunˌeasy ˈsleep)

uneaten ʌnˈitn̩ |-table -təb!|

uneclipsed ˌʌnɪˈklɪpst

uneconomical ˌʌnikəˈnɑmɪk!|, -ɛk-; ES+
-ˈnɒm-; |-ly -ɪ, -ɪklɪ

unedifying ʌnˈɛdəˌfaɪɪŋ

uneducable ʌnˈɛdʒəkəb!|, -dʒʊ-

uneducated ʌnˈɛdʒəˌketɪd, -dʒʊ-

unembarrassed ˌʌnɪmˈbærəst, -ɪst

|full fʊl |tooth tuθ |further ˈfɝðɚ; ES ˈfɝðə |custom ˈkʌstəm |while hwaɪl |how haʊ |toy tɔɪ
|using ˈjuzɪŋ |fuse fjuz, fɪuz |dish dɪʃ |vision ˈvɪʒən |Eden ˈidn̩ |cradle ˈkred!| |keep 'em ˈkipm̩

unemotional ˌʌnɪˈmoʃən|, -ʃnəl |-ly -ɪ
unemphatic ˌʌnɪmˈfætɪk |-ally -ịɪ, -ɪklɪ
unemployable ˌʌnɪmˈplɔɪəb|
unemployed ˌʌnɪmˈplɔɪd |-ployment -ˈplɔɪmənt
unenclosed ˌʌnɪnˈklozd
unencumbered ˌʌnɪnˈkʌmbɚd; ES -ˈkʌmbəd
unending ʌnˈɛndɪŋ (ˈunˌending ˈlabor)
unendorsed ˌʌnɪnˈdɔrst; ES -ˈdɔəst
unendurable ˌʌnɪnˈdjurəb|, -ˈdɪur-, -ˈdur-
  |-bly -blɪ |-ring -ɪŋ
unenforceable ˌʌnɪnˈforsəb|, -ˈfɔrs-; ES
  -ˈfoəs-, E+-ˈfɔəs-; |-bly -blɪ
unengaged ˌʌnɪnˈgedʒd (ˈunenˌgaged ˈtime)
unenjoyable ˌʌnɪnˈdʒɔɪəb|
unenlightened ˌʌnɪnˈlaɪtn̩d |-ning -tn̩ɪŋ, -tnɪŋ
unenterprising ʌnˈɛntɚˌpraɪzɪŋ; ES -ˈɛntə-
unentertaining ˌʌnɛntɚˈtenɪŋ; ES -ɛntə-
unenthusiastic ˌʌnɪnˌθjuzɪˈæstɪk, -ˌθɪuz-,
  -ˌθuz- |-ally -ịɪ, -ɪklɪ
unenvied ʌnˈɛnvɪd |-viable -vɪəb| |-bly -blɪ
unequal ʌnˈikwəl |-ed -d |-ly -ɪ
unequipped ˌʌnɪˈkwɪpt
unequivocal ˌʌnɪˈkwɪvək| |-ly -ɪ, -əklɪ
unerring ʌnˈɝɪŋ, -ˈɛr-; ES -ˈɜrɪŋ, -ˈɝɪŋ,
  -ˈɛrɪŋ
unescapable ˌʌnəˈskepəb| |-bly -blɪ
unessential ˌʌnəˈsɛnʃəl |-ly -ɪ
unestimated ʌnˈɛstəˌmetɪd
unethical ʌnˈɛθɪk| |-ly -ɪ, -ɪklɪ
uneven ʌnˈivən (ˈunˌeven ˈground)
uneventful ˌʌnɪˈvɛntfəl |-ly -ɪ
unexaggerated ˌʌnɪgˈzædʒɚˌretɪd
unexampled ˌʌnɪgˈzæmp|d; E+-ˈzamp-,
  -ˈzɑmp-
unexceptionable ˌʌnɪkˈsɛpʃənəb|, -ʃnəb| |-bly
  -blɪ
unexceptional ˌʌnɪkˈsɛpʃən|, -ʃnəl |-ly -ɪ
unexchanged ˌʌnɪksˈtʃendʒd |-geable -dʒəb|
  |-bly -blɪ
unexciting ˌʌnɪkˈsaɪtɪŋ (ˈunexˌciting ˈlife)
unexcused ˌʌnɪkˈskjuzd, -ˈskɪuzd |-sable
  -zəb| |-bly -blɪ
unexecuted ʌnˈɛksɪˌkjutɪd, -ˌkɪutɪd
unexhausted ˌʌnɪgˈzɔstɪd |-tible -təb| |-bly
  -blɪ
unexpected ˌʌnɪkˈspɛktɪd (ˈunexˌpected ˈguest)
unexpended ˌʌnɪkˈspɛndɪd
unexperienced ˌʌnɪkˈspɪrɪənst

unexpired ˌʌnɪkˈspaɪrd; ES -ˈspaɪəd
unexplained ˌʌnɪkˈsplend |-nedly -nɪdlɪ
  |-nable -nəb| |-bly -blɪ
unexploded ˌʌnɪkˈsplodɪd (ˈunexˌploded
  ˈmyth)
unexplored ˌʌnɪkˈsplord, -ˈsplɔrd; ES -ˈsploəd,
  E+-ˈsplɔəd
unexposed ˌʌnɪkˈspozd
unexpressed ˌʌnɪkˈsprɛst |-sable, -sible, -səb|
  |-bly -blɪ
unexpressive ˌʌnɪkˈsprɛsɪv (ˈunexˌpressive
  ˈshe)
unexpurgated ʌnˈɛkspɚˌgetɪd, ˌʌnɪkˈspɝgetɪd;
  ES -ˈɛkspə-, -ɪkˈspɝ-, -ˈspɝ-
unfaded ʌnˈfedɪd |-dable -dəb| |-bly -blɪ
unfading ʌnˈfedɪŋ (ˈunˌfading ˈblue)
unfailing ʌnˈfelɪŋ
unfair ʌnˈfɛr, -ˈfær; E -ˈfɛə(r, ES -ˈfæə(r
unfaithful ʌnˈfeθfəl |-ly -ɪ
unfaltering ʌnˈfɔltrɪŋ, -ˈfɔltərɪŋ
unfamiliar ˌʌnfəˈmɪljɚ; ES -ˈmɪljə(r
unfamiliarity ˌʌnfəˌmɪlɪˈærətɪ, -ˌmɪljɪˈærətɪ,
  -ˌmɪlˈjærətɪ
unfashionable ʌnˈfæʃnəb|, -ʃənə- |-bly -blɪ
unfasten ʌnˈfæsn̩ |-ed -d |-ing -ˈfæsnɪŋ,
  -ˈfæsn̩ɪŋ; E+-ˈfɑs-, -ˈfɑs-
unfathered ʌnˈfɑðɚd; ES -ˈfɑðəd, E+-ˈfɑð-
unfathomed ʌnˈfæðəmd |-mable -əməb| |-bly
  -blɪ
unfavorable ʌnˈfevrəb|, ˈfevərə- |-bly -blɪ
unfed ʌnˈfɛd (ˈunˌfed ˈflock)
unfeeling ʌnˈfilɪŋ
unfeigned ʌnˈfend |-nedly -nɪdlɪ
unfelt ʌnˈfɛlt (ˈunˌfelt ˈsorrow)
unfenced ʌnˈfɛnst
unfermented ˌʌnfɚˈmɛntɪd; ES -fəˈmɛntɪd
unfertilized ʌnˈfɝt|ˌaɪzd; ES -ˈfɝt|-, -ˈfɝt|-
unfetter ʌnˈfɛtɚ; ES -ˈfɛtə(r; |-ed -d
unfilial ʌnˈfɪlɪəl, -ˈfɪljəl |-ly -ɪ
unfilled ʌnˈfɪld (ˈunˌfilled ˈquota)
unfinished ʌnˈfɪnɪʃt
unfired ʌnˈfaɪrd; ES -ˈfaɪəd
unfit ʌnˈfɪt |-ted -ɪd
unfix ʌnˈfɪks |-es -ɪz |-ed -t
unflagging ʌnˈflægɪŋ
unflattering ʌnˈflætərɪŋ, -ˈflætrɪŋ
unflavored ʌnˈflevɚd; ES -ˈflevəd
unfledged ʌnˈflɛdʒd (ˈunˌfledged ˈyouth)
unfold ʌnˈfold |-ed -ɪd

Key: *See in full* §§3–47. bee bi |pity ˈpɪtɪ (§6) |rate ret |yet jɛt |sang sæŋ |angry ˈæŋ·grɪ |bath bæθ; E baθ (§10) |ah ɑ |far fɑr |watch wɑtʃ, wɒtʃ (§12) |jaw dʒɔ |gorge gɔrdʒ |go go

unforbidden ˌʌnfɚ'bɪdn̩; ES -fə'bɪdn̩
unforced ʌn'forst, -'fɔrst; ES -'fɔəst, E+ -'fɔəst; |-cedly -sɪdlɪ
unforeseeable ˌʌnfor'siəbl̩, -fɔr-; ES -foə-, E+-fə-; |-bly -blɪ
unforeseen ˌʌnfor'sin, -fɔr-, -fɚ-; ES -foə-, -fə-, E+-fɔə-
unforgettable ˌʌnfɚ'gɛtəbl̩; ES -fə-; |-bly -blɪ
unforgiven ˌʌnfɚ'gɪvən; ES -fə-; |-givable -'gɪvəbl̩ |-bly -blɪ
unforgot ˌʌnfɚ'gat; ES -fə'gɑt, -'gɒt; |-ten -n̩
unformed ʌn'fɔrmd; ES -'fɔəmd
unformulated ʌn'fɔrmjəˌletɪd; ES -'fɔəm-
unfortified ʌn'fɔrtəˌfaɪd; ES -'fɔətəˌfaɪd
unfortunate ʌn'fɔrtʃənɪt; ES -'fɔətʃənɪt
unfounded ʌn'faʊndɪd ('unˌfounded 'rumor)
unframed ʌn'fremd
unfree ʌn'fri |-d -d
unfrequent ʌn'frikwənt |-ncy -nsɪ
unfrequented ˌʌnfrɪ'kwɛntɪd
unfriended ʌn'frɛndɪd
unfrock ʌn'frɑk; ES+-'frɒk; |-ed -t
unfruitful ʌn'frutfəl, -'frɪut- |-ly -ɪ
unfulfilled ˌʌnfʊl'fɪld ('unfulˌfilled 'hope)
unfunded ʌn'fʌndɪd
unfurl ʌn'fɝl; ES -'fɜl, -'fɝl; |-ed -d
unfurnished ʌn'fɝnɪʃt; ES -'fɜn-, -'fɝn-
ungainly ʌn'genlɪ
ungallant ʌn'gælənt
ungalled ʌn'gɔld ('unˌgalled 'jade)
ungarbled ʌn'gɑrbl̩d; ES -'gɑːbl̩d, E+-'gɑːb-
ungarnished ʌn'gɑrnɪʃt; ES -'gɑːn-, E+ -'gɑːn-
ungathered ʌn'gæðɚd; ES -'gæðəd
ungenerous ʌn'dʒɛnərəs, -'dʒɛnrəs
ungentle ʌn'dʒɛntl̩ |-tly -tlɪ
ungentlemanly ʌn'dʒɛntl̩mənlɪ
ungifted ʌn'gɪftɪd
ungird ʌn'gɝd; ES -'gɜd, -'gɝd; |-ed -ɪd
ungirt ʌn'gɝt; ES -'gɜt, -'gɝt
unglazed ʌn'glezd ('unˌglazed 'china)
ungloved ʌn'glʌvd
unglue ʌn'glu, -'glɪu |-d -d
ungodly ʌn'gɑdlɪ, -'gɒdlɪ, -'gɔdlɪ
ungot ʌn'gat; ES+-'gɒt; |-ten -n̩
ungoverned ʌn'gʌvɚnd; ES -'gʌvənd; |-nable -nəbl̩ |-bly -blɪ
ungraceful ʌn'gresfəl |-ly -ɪ
ungracious ʌn'greʃəs

ungraded ʌn'gredɪd
ungrammatical ˌʌngrə'mætɪkl̩ |-ly -ɪ, -ɪklɪ
ungrateful ʌn'gretfəl |-ly -ɪ
ungrounded ʌn'graʊndɪd ('unˌgrounded 'fear)
ungrudging ʌn'grʌdʒɪŋ
unguard ʌn'gɑrd; ES -'gɑːd, E+-'gɑːd; |-ed -ɪd
unguent 'ʌŋgwənt |-ed -ɪd
unguided ʌn'gaɪdɪd
ungulate 'ʌŋgjəlɪt, -ˌlet
unhackneyed ʌn'hæknɪd
unhair ʌn'hɛr, -'hær; E -'hɛə(r, ES -'hæə(r; |-ed -d
unhallowed ʌn'hælod, -'hæləd
unhampered ʌn'hæmpɚd; ES -'hæmpəd
unhand ʌn'hænd |-ed -ɪd
unhandicapped ʌn'hændɪˌkæpt
unhandsome ʌn'hænsəm ('unˌhandsome 'deed)
unhandy ʌn'hændɪ |-dily -dl̩ɪ, -dɪlɪ
unhanged ʌn'hæŋd
unhappy ʌn'hæpɪ |-pily -pl̩ɪ, -pɪlɪ
unhardened ʌn'hɑrdn̩d; ES -'hɑːdn̩d, E+ -'hɑːd-
unharmed ʌn'hɑrmd; ES -'hɑːmd, E+ -'hɑːmd
unharmonious ˌʌnhɑr'monɪəs, -njəs; ES -hɑ-, E+-hɑ-
unharness ʌn'hɑrnɪs; ES -'hɑːnɪs, E+ -'hɑːnɪs; |-es -ɪz |-ed -t
unhat ʌn'hæt |-hatted -'hætɪd
unhatched ʌn'hætʃt
unhealthful ʌn'hɛlθfəl |-ly -ɪ
unhealthily ʌn'hɛlθəlɪ, -ɪlɪ
unhealthy ʌn'hɛlθɪ ('unˌhealthy 'fogs)
unheard ʌn'hɝd; ES -'hɜd, -'hɝd
unheard-of ʌn'hɝdˌɑv, -ˌɒv, -ˌʌv; ES -'hɜd-, -'hɝd-
unheedful ʌn'hidfəl |-ly -ɪ
unhelm ʌn'hɛlm |-ed -d
unheralded ʌn'hɛrəldɪd
unheroic ˌʌnhɪ'ro·ɪk, -hi- |-al -l̩ |-ally -l̩ɪ, -ɪklɪ
unhesitating ʌn'hɛzəˌtetɪŋ
unhindered ʌn'hɪndɚd; ES -'hɪndəd
unhinge ʌn'hɪndʒ |-s -ɪz |-d -d
unhitch ʌn'hɪtʃ |-es -ɪz |-ed -t
unholy ʌn'holɪ |-holily -'holəlɪ, -lɪlɪ
unhonored ʌn'ɑnɚd; ES -'ɑnəd, -'ɒnəd
unhood ʌn'hʊd |-ed -ɪd

|full fʊl |tooth tuθ |further 'fɝðɚ; ES 'fɝðə |custom 'kʌstəm |while hwaɪl |how haʊ |toy tɔɪ
|using 'juzɪŋ |fuse fjuz, fɪuz |dish dɪʃ |vision 'vɪʒən |Eden 'idn̩ |cradle 'kredl̩ |keep 'em 'kipm̩

unhook ʌnˈhʊk |-ed -t
unhoped ʌnˈhopt
unhoped-for ʌnˈhopt͵fɔr; ES -͵fɔə(r
unhorse ʌnˈhɔrs; ES -ˈhɔəs; |-s -ɪz |-d -t
unhouse ʌnˈhaʊz |-s -ɪz |-d -d
unhung ʌnˈhʌŋ (ˈun͵hung ˈpicture)
unhurried ʌnˈhɝɪd; ES -ˈhɜrɪd, -ˈhʌrɪd, -ˈhɜɪd
unhurt ʌnˈhɝt; ES -ˈhɜt, -ˈhɜt
unhusk ʌnˈhʌsk |-ed -t
unhygienic ͵ʌnhaɪdʒɪˈɛnɪk |-ally -l̩ɪ, -ɪklɪ
unhyphenated ʌnˈhaɪfə͵netɪd
Uniat ˈjunɪ͵æt
unicameral ͵junɪˈkæmərəl
unicellular ͵junɪˈsɛljələ; ES -lə(r
Unicoi ˈjunɪ͵kɔɪ
unicorn, U- ˈjunɪ͵kɔrn; ES -͵kɔən
unidentified ͵ʌnaɪˈdɛntə͵faɪd, ͵ʌnə-
unidiomatic ͵ʌnɪdɪəˈmætɪk |-ally -l̩ɪ, -ɪklɪ
unifiable ˈjunə͵faɪəb|l |-bly -blɪ
unification ͵junəfəˈkeʃən
unifier ˈjunə͵faɪɚ; ES -͵faɪ·ə(r
uniform ˈjunə͵fɔrm; ES -͵fɔəm
uniformitarian ͵junə͵fɔrməˈtɛrɪən, -ˈter-; ES -͵fɔəmə-
uniformity ͵junəˈfɔrmətɪ; ES -ˈfɔəm-
unify ˈjunə͵faɪ |-fied -͵faɪd
unilateral ͵junɪˈlætərəl |-ly -ɪ
unilluminated ͵ʌnəˈlumə͵netɪd, -ˈlɪum-
unimaginable ͵ʌnɪˈmædʒɪnəb|l, -ˈmædʒnəb|l |-bly -blɪ
unimagined ͵ʌnɪˈmædʒɪnd (ˈuni͵magined ˈjoy)
unimpaired ͵ʌnɪmˈpɛrd, -ˈpærd; E -ˈpɛəd, ES -ˈpæəd
unimpassioned ͵ʌnɪmˈpæʃənd
unimpeachable ͵ʌnɪmˈpitʃəb|l |-bly -blɪ
unimpeded ͵ʌnɪmˈpidɪd (ˈunim͵peded ˈway)
unimportance ͵ʌnɪmˈpɔrtn̩s; ES -ˈpɔətn̩s; |-nt -n̩t
unimposing ͵ʌnɪmˈpozɪŋ
unimpressionable ͵ʌnɪmˈprɛʃnəb|l, -ʃənəb|l
unimpressive ͵ʌnɪmˈprɛsɪv
unimproved ͵ʌnɪmˈpruvd (ˈunim͵proved ˈland)
uninclosed ͵ʌnɪnˈklozd
unincorporated ͵ʌnɪnˈkɔrpə͵retɪd; ES -ˈkɔəp-
unincumbered ͵ʌnɪnˈkʌmbɚd; ES -ˈkʌmbəd
unindorsed ͵ʌnɪnˈdɔrst; ES -ˈdɔəst
uninfected ͵ʌnɪnˈfɛktɪd
uninflammable ͵ʌnɪnˈflæməb|l

uninflected ͵ʌnɪnˈflɛktɪd (ˈunin͵flected ˈstem)
uninfluenced ʌnˈɪnfluənst, -flɪuənst
uninformed ͵ʌnɪnˈfɔrmd; ES -ˈfɔəmd
uninhabitable ͵ʌnɪnˈhæbɪtəb|l |-bly -blɪ
uninhabited ͵ʌnɪnˈhæbɪtɪd
uninitiated ͵ʌnɪˈnɪʃɪ͵etɪd
uninjured ʌnˈɪndʒɚd; ES -ˈɪndʒəd
uninspired ͵ʌnɪnˈspaɪrd; ES -ˈspaɪəd
uninstructed ͵ʌnɪnˈstrʌktɪd
unintelligent ͵ʌnɪnˈtɛlədʒənt |-gence -dʒəns
unintelligibility ͵ʌnɪn͵tɛlədʒəˈbɪlətɪ
unintelligible ͵ʌnɪnˈtɛlədʒəb|l |-bly -blɪ
unintended ͵ʌnɪnˈtɛndɪd (ˈunin͵tended ˈjoke)
unintentional ͵ʌnɪnˈtɛnʃən|l, -ʃnəl |-ly -ɪ
uninterested ʌnˈɪntərɪstɪd, -ˈɪntrɪstɪd, -ˈɪntə͵rɛstɪd |-ting -tɪŋ—see interesting
unintermitting ͵ʌnɪntəˈmɪtɪŋ; ES -ɪntə-
uninterrupted ͵ʌnɪntəˈrʌptɪd
uninvited ͵ʌnɪnˈvaɪtɪd |-ting -tɪŋ
union ˈjunjən |-ize -͵aɪz |-izes -͵aɪzɪz |-ized -͵aɪzd
unipod ˈjunə͵pad; ES+-͵pɒd
unique juˈnik
unisexual ͵junɪˈsɛkʃʊəl |-ly -ɪ
unison ˈjunəzn̩, ˈjunəsn̩
unissued ʌnˈɪʃud, -ˈɪʃjud—see issue
unit ˈjunɪt |-age -ɪdʒ |-ages -ɪdʒɪz
Unitarian, u- ͵junəˈtɛrɪən, -ˈterɪən, -rjən
unitary ˈjunə͵tɛrɪ
unite juˈnaɪt |-d -ɪd
United States juˈnaɪtɪdˈstets, often ˈju͵naɪtɪdˈstets
unitive ˈjunətɪv |unity ˈjunətɪ
univalent ͵junəˈvelənt, juˈnɪvələnt
universal ͵junəˈvɝs|l; ES -ˈvɜs|l, -ˈvɝs|l; |-ly -ɪ
universality ͵junəvɝˈsælətɪ, -vɚˈsæl-; ES -vɜ-, -vɝ-, -və-
universalize ͵junəˈvɝs|l͵aɪz; ES -ˈvɜs-, -ˈvɝs-; |-s -ɪz |-d -d
universe ˈjunə͵vɝs; ES -͵vɜs, -͵vɝs; |-s -ɪz
university ͵junəˈvɝsətɪ, -ˈvɝstɪ; ES -ˈvɜs-, -ˈvɝs-; (ˈUni͵versity ˈHeights)
unjust ʌnˈdʒʌst(ˈun͵just ˈsteward)
unjustified ʌnˈdʒʌstə͵faɪd |-fiable -͵faɪəb|l |-bly -blɪ
unkempt ʌnˈkempt
unkept ʌnˈkɛpt
unkind ʌnˈkaɪnd
unknit ʌnˈnɪt |-ted -ɪd

unknowable ʌnˈnoəb| |-bly -blɪ
unknown ʌnˈnon (ˈunˌknown ˈplace)
unlabeled ʌnˈleb|d
unlabored ʌnˈlebɚd; ES -ˈlebəd
unlace ʌnˈles |-s -ɪz |-d -t
unlade ʌnˈled |-laded -ˈledɪd |-laden -ˈledn̩
unladylike ʌnˈledɪˌlaɪk
unlaid ʌnˈled (ˈunˌlaid ˈghost)
unlamented ˌʌnləˈmɛntɪd
unlash ʌnˈlæʃ |-es -ɪz |-ed -t
unlatch ʌnˈlætʃ; |-es -ɪz |-ed -t
unlawful ʌnˈlɔfəl |-ly -ɪ
unlearn ʌnˈlɜn; ES -ˈlɜn, -ˈlɜ·n; |-ed -d, -t or
   -t -t
unlearned past & pptc ʌnˈlɜnd, -ˈlɜ·nt; ES
   -ˈlɜn-, -ˈlɜ·n-; adj -nɪd
unlearnt ʌnˈlɜnt; ES -ˈlɜnt, -ˈlɜ·nt
unleash ʌnˈliʃ |-es -ɪz |-ed -t
unleavened ʌnˈlɛvənd (ˈunˌleavened ˈbread)
unled ʌnˈlɛd
unless ənˈlɛs
unlessoned ʌnˈlɛsn̩d (ˈunˌlessoned ˈgirl)
unlettered ʌnˈlɛtɚd; ES -ˈlɛtəd; (ˈunˌlettered
   ˈMuse)
unlicensed ʌnˈlaɪsənst
unlighted ʌnˈlaɪtɪd
unlike ʌnˈlaɪk |-ly -lɪ |-lihood -lɪˌhʊd
unlimber ʌnˈlɪmbɚ; ES -ˈlɪmbə(r; |-ed -d
   |-ing -brɪŋ, -bərɪŋ
unlimited ʌnˈlɪmɪtɪd
unlined ʌnˈlaɪnd (ˈunˌlined ˈfur)
unlink ʌnˈlɪŋk |-ed -t
unlisted ʌnˈlɪstɪd
unlit ʌnˈlɪt (ˈunˌlit ˈcandle)
unload ʌnˈlod |-ed -ɪd
unlock ʌnˈlak; ES+-ˈlɒk; |-ed -t
unlooked-for ʌnˈlʊktˌfɔr; ES -ˌfɔə(r
unloose ʌnˈlus |-s -ɪz |-d -t |-n -ˈlusn̩
unlovable ʌnˈlʌvəb| |-bly -blɪ
unloved ʌnˈlʌvd |-lovely -ˈlʌvlɪ
unlucky ʌnˈlʌkɪ (ˈunˌlucky ˈstrike)
unmagnetic ˌʌnmægˈnɛtɪk |-al -|
unmailed ʌnˈmeld |-lable -ləb|
unmake ʌnˈmek |-made -ˈmed
unman ʌnˈmæn |-manned -ˈmænd
unmanageable ʌnˈmænɪdʒəb| |-bly -blɪ
unmanly ʌnˈmænlɪ
unmannered ʌnˈmænɚd; ES -ˈmænəd
unmannerly ʌnˈmænɚlɪ; ES -ˈmænəlɪ

unmanufactured ˌʌnmænjəˈfæktʃɚd, -mænə-;
   ES -tʃəd
unmarked ʌnˈmarkt; ES -ˈmɑːkt, E+-ˈmɑːkt
unmarketable ʌnˈmarkɪtəb|; ES -ˈmɑːk-,
   E+-ˈmɑːk-
unmarriageable ʌnˈmærɪdʒəb|
unmarried ʌnˈmærɪd (ˈunˌmarried ˈman)
unmask ʌnˈmæsk; E+-ˈmask, -ˈmɑsk; |-ed -t
unmatched ʌnˈmætʃt |-matchable -ˈmætʃəb|
   |-bly -blɪ
unmeaning ʌnˈminɪŋ
unmeant ʌnˈmɛnt
unmeasurable ʌnˈmɛʒrəb|, -ʒərəb| |-bly -blɪ
unmechanical ˌʌnmɪˈkænɪk| |-ly -ɪ, -ɪklɪ
unmeet ʌnˈmit
unmelodious ˌʌnməˈlodɪəs
unmelted ʌnˈmɛltɪd (ˈunˌmelted ˈsnow)
unmentioned ʌnˈmɛnʃənd |-nable -ʃənəb|,
   -ʃnəb| |-bly -blɪ
unmerchantable ʌnˈmɜtʃəntəb|; ES -ˈmɜtʃ-,
   -ˈmɜ·tʃ-
unmerciful ʌnˈmɜsɪfəl; ES -ˈmɜs-, -ˈmɜ·s-;
   |-ly -ɪ, -flɪ
unmerited ʌnˈmɛrɪtɪd
unmethodical ˌʌnməˈθɑdɪk|; ES+-ˈθɒd-; |-ly
   -ɪ, -ɪklɪ
unmew ʌnˈmju, -ˈmɪu |-ed -d
unmilitary ʌnˈmɪləˌtɛrɪ
unmindful ʌnˈmaɪndfəl, -ˈmaɪnf- |-ly -ɪ
unmistakable ˌʌnməˈstekəb| |-bly -blɪ
unmistaken ˌʌnməˈstekən
unmitigable ʌnˈmɪtəgəb| |-bly -blɪ
unmitigated ʌnˈmɪtəˌgetɪd
unmixed ʌnˈmɪkst (ˈunˌmixed ˈevil)
unmodified ʌnˈmɑdəˌfaɪd; ES+-ˈmɒd-
unmolested ˌʌnməˈlɛstɪd
unmoor ʌnˈmʊr; ES -ˈmʊə(r; |-ed -d
unmoral ʌnˈmɔrəl, -ˈmarəl, -ˈmɒrəl |-ly -ɪ
unmorality ˌʌnməˈrælətɪ, -mɔ-, -ma-, -mɒ-,
   -mo-
unmortgaged ʌnˈmɔrgɪdʒd; ES -ˈmɔəgɪdʒd
unmotivated ʌnˈmotəˌvetɪd
unmounted ʌnˈmaʊntɪd (ˈunˌmounted ˈprint)
unmourned ʌnˈmornd, -ˈmɔrnd; ES -ˈmoənd,
   E+-ˈmɔənd
unmoved ʌnˈmuvd |-vable -vəb| |-bly -blɪ
   |-vedly -vɪdlɪ
unmuffle ʌnˈmʌf| |-d -d |-ling -flɪŋ, -f|ɪŋ
unmusical ʌnˈmjuzɪk|, -ˈmɪuz- |-ly -ɪ

unmuzzle ʌn'mʌz| |-d -d |-ling -zlɪŋ, -z|ɪŋ
unnail ʌn'nel |-ed -d
unnamed ʌn'nemd |-mable -məb|
unnatural ʌn'nætʃərəl, -'nætʃrəl |-ly -ɪ
unnavigable ʌn'nævəgəb| |-bly -blɪ
unnecessarily ʌn'nɛsəˌsɛrəlɪ, esp. if emph.
ˌʌnnɛsə'sɛrəlɪ
unnecessary ʌn'nɛsəˌsɛrɪ
unneedful ʌn'nidfəl |-ly -ɪ
unnegotiable ˌʌnnɪ'goʃɪəb| |-bly -blɪ
unneighborly ʌn'nebəlɪ; ES -'nebəlɪ
unnerve ʌn'nɝv; ES -'nɜv, -'nɝv; |-d -d
unnoted ʌn'notɪd ('unˌnoted 'action)
unnoticeable ʌn'notɪsəb| |-bly -blɪ
unnumbered ʌn'nʌmbəd; ES -'nʌmbəd
unobjectionable ˌʌnəb'dʒɛkʃnəb|, -ʃənə- |-bly
-blɪ
unobliging ˌʌnə'blaɪdʒɪŋ ('unoˌbliging 'boor)
unobservant ˌʌnəb'zɝvənt; ES -'zɝv-, -'zɝv-
unobstructed ˌʌnəb'strʌktɪd
unobtainable ˌʌnəb'tenəb| |-bly -blɪ
unobtrusive ˌʌnəb'trusɪv, -'trɪus-
unoccasioned ˌʌnə'keʒənd
unoccupied ʌn'ɑkjəˌpaɪd; ES+-'ɒk-
unoffending ˌʌnə'fɛndɪŋ |-fensive -'fɛnsɪv
unoffered ʌn'ɔfəd, -'ɒf-, -'af-; ES -fəd
unofficial ˌʌnə'fɪʃəl |-ly -ɪ
unopen ʌn'opən, -'opm̩ |-ed -d |-ing -pnɪŋ,
-pənɪŋ
unopposed ˌʌnə'pozd ('unopˌposed 'measure)
unorganized ʌn'ɔrgənˌaɪzd; ES -'ɔəg-
unoriginal ˌʌnə'rɪdʒən| |-ly -ɪ
unorthodox ʌn'ɔrθəˌdaks; ES -'ɔəθəˌdaks,
-ˌdɒks
unostentatious ˌʌnɑstən'teʃəs; ES+-ɒs-
unowned ʌn'ond ('unˌowned 'goods)
unpack ʌn'pæk |-ed -t
unpaid ʌn'ped
unpaired ʌn'pɛrd, -'pærd; E -'pɛəd, ES
-'pæəd
unpalatable ʌn'pælətəb|, -lɪtə- |-bly -blɪ
unparalleled ʌn'pærəˌlɛld
unpardonable ʌn'pardnəb|, -'pardn̩əb|; ES
-'pɑːd-, E+-'paːd-; |-bly -blɪ
unparliamentary ˌʌnparlə'mɛntərɪ, -trɪ; ES
-pɑl-, E+-pal-
unpartisan, -zan ʌn'partəzn̩; ES -'pɑːt-,
E+-'paːt-
unpasteurized ʌn'pæstəraɪzd, -'pæstʃə-

unpatriotic ˌʌnpetrɪ'atɪk; ES+-'ɒtɪk; |-ally
-|ɪ, -ɪklɪ
unpaved ʌn'pevd ('unˌpaved 'street)
unpeg ʌn'pɛg |-ged -d
unpeople ʌn'pip| |-d -d |-ling -plɪŋ, -p|ɪŋ
unperceivable ˌʌnpə'sivəb|; ES -pə-; |-bly
-blɪ
unperforated ʌn'pɝfəˌretɪd; ES -'pɝf-, -'pɝf-
unpersuaded ˌʌnpə'swedɪd; ES -pə'swedɪd
unpersuasive ˌʌnpə'swesɪv; ES -pə'swesɪv
unperturbed ˌʌnpə'tɝbd; ES -pə'tɝbd, -pə-
'tɝbd; |-bable -bəb| |-bly -blɪ
unperused ˌʌnpə'ruzd, -'rɪuzd
unphilosophic ˌʌnfɪlə'safɪk; ES+-'sɒf-; |-al -|
|-ally -|ɪ, -ɪklɪ
unpicked ʌn'pɪkt ('unˌpicked 'fruit)
unpierced ʌn'pɪrst; ES -'pɪəst, S+-'pɛəst
unpile ʌn'paɪl |-d -d
unpin ʌn'pɪn |-ned -d
unpitied ʌn'pɪtɪd ('unˌpitied 'grief)
unpitying ʌn'pɪtɪɪŋ
unplaced ʌn'plest
unplait ʌn'plet |-ed -ɪd—see unplat, unpleat
unplanned ʌn'plænd
unplanted ʌn'plæntɪd; E+-'plant-, -'plant-
unplat ʌn'plæt |-ted -ɪd—see unplait, unpleat
unplayable ʌn'pleəb|
unpleasant ʌn'plɛzn̩t
unpleasing ʌn'plizɪŋ
unpleat ʌn'plit |-ed -ɪd—see plait, unplat
unpledged ʌn'plɛdʒd
unplowed ʌn'plaud ('unˌplowed 'land)
unplumbed ʌn'plʌmd
unpoetic ˌʌnpo'ɛtɪk |-al -| |-ally -ɪ, -ɪklɪ
unpoised ʌn'pɔɪzd
unpolished ʌn'palɪʃt; ES+-'pɒlɪʃt
unpolitic ʌn'paləˌtɪk; ES+-'pɒl-; |-ly -lɪ
unpolitical ˌʌnpə'lɪtɪk| |-ly -ɪ, -ɪklɪ
unpolled ʌn'pold
unpolluted ˌʌnpə'lutɪd, -pə'lɪutɪd
unpopular ʌn'papjələ; ES -'papjələ(r, -'pɒp-
unpopularity ˌʌnpapjə'lærətɪ; ES+-pɒp-
unpractical ʌn'præktɪk| |-ly -ɪ, -ɪklɪ
unpracticed ʌn'præktɪst ('unˌpracticed 'art)
unprecedented ʌn'prɛsəˌdɛntɪd |-ly -lɪ, esp. if
emph. ˌunprece'dentedly
unpredictable ˌʌnprɪ'dɪktəb| |-bly -blɪ
unprejudiced ʌn'prɛdʒədɪst
unpremeditated ˌʌnprɪ'mɛdəˌtetɪd

Key: See in full §§3–47. bee bi |pity 'pɪtɪ (§6) |rate ret |yet jɛt |sang sæŋ |angry 'æŋ·grɪ
|bath bæθ; E baθ (§10) |ah ɑ |far far |watch watʃ, wɒtʃ (§12) |jaw dʒɔ |gorge gɔrdʒ |go go

unprepared ˌʌnprɪˈpɛrd, -ˈpærd; E -ˈpɛəd, ES -ˈpæəd; |-ness -nɪs, -rɪdnɪs |-redly -rɪdlɪ
unprepossessing ˌʌnpripəˈzɛsɪŋ
unpresentable ˌʌnprɪˈzɛntəbļ |-bly -blɪ
unpressed ʌnˈprɛst (ˈunˌpressed ˈcheese)
unpresuming ˌʌnprɪˈzumɪŋ, -ˈzɪum-, -ˈzjum-
unpretending ˌʌnprɪˈtɛndɪŋ |-tentious -ˈtɛnʃəs
unprevailing ˌʌnprɪˈvelɪŋ (ˈunpreˌvailing ˈwoe)
unpreventable ˌʌnprɪˈvɛntəbļ |-bly -blɪ
unpriced ʌnˈpraɪst
unprincipled ʌnˈprɪnsəpļd
unprivileged ʌnˈprɪvəlɪdʒd
unprocurable ˌʌnprəˈkjʊrəbļ, -ˈkɪur-
unproductive ˌʌnprəˈdʌktɪv
unprofessional ˌʌnprəˈfɛʃənļ, -ˈfɛʃnəl |-ly -ɪ
unprofitable ʌnˈprɑftəbļ, -ˈfɪtə-; ES+-ˈprɒf-; |-bly -blɪ
unprogressive ˌʌnprəˈgrɛsɪv, -pro-
unprohibited ˌʌnproˈhɪbɪtɪd
unpromising ʌnˈprɑmɪsɪŋ; ES+-ˈprɒm-
unprompted ʌnˈprɑmptɪd; ES+-ˈprɒmp-
unpronounceable ˌʌnprəˈnaʊnsəbļ, -pɚ- |-bly -blɪ
unpropitious ˌʌnprəˈpɪʃəs, -pro-
unproportioned ˌʌnprəˈporʃənd, -ˈpɔr-; ES -ˈpoə-, E+-ˈpɔə-
unprotected ˌʌnprəˈtɛktɪd
unproved ʌnˈpruvd (ˈunˌproved ˈthesis)
unproven ʌnˈpruvən
unprovided ˌʌnprəˈvaɪdɪd
unprovoked ˌʌnprəˈvokt |-kedly -kɪdlɪ
unpublished ʌnˈpʌblɪʃt
unpunctual ʌnˈpʌŋktʃʊəl, -tʃʊl |-ly -ɪ
unpunctuality ˌʌnpʌŋktʃʊˈælətɪ
unpunctuated ʌnˈpʌŋktʃʊˌetɪd
unpunished ʌnˈpʌnɪʃt |-shable -ʃəbļ
unpurchasable ʌnˈpɝtʃəsəbļ; ES -ˈpɜtʃ-; -ˈpɝtʃ-
unpursuing ˌʌnpɚˈsuɪŋ, -ˈsɪu-, -ˈsju-; ES -pə-
unquailing ʌnˈkwelɪŋ (ˈunˌquailing ˈspirit)
unqualified ʌnˈkwɑləˌfaɪd, -ˈkwɒl- |-ly -lɪ
unquenched ʌnˈkwɛntʃt |-chable -tʃəbļ |-bly -blɪ
unquestionable ʌnˈkwɛstʃənəbļ |-bly -blɪ
unquestioned ʌnˈkwɛstʃənd
unquiet ʌnˈkwaɪət (ˈunˌquiet ˈgrave)
unquotable ʌnˈkwotəbļ
unquote ʌnˈkwot |-d -ɪd
unraised ʌnˈrezd

unratified ʌnˈrætəˌfaɪd
unravel ʌnˈrævļ |-ed -d |-ing -ˈrævlɪŋ, -vļɪŋ
unread ʌnˈrɛd
unreadable ʌnˈridəbļ |-bly -blɪ
unready ʌnˈrɛdɪ |-readily -ˈrɛdļɪ, -dɪlɪ
unreal ʌnˈrɪəl, ʌnˈril, ʌnˈrɪəl |-ly -ɪ—see really
unreality ˌʌnrɪˈælətɪ
unrealized ʌnˈrɪəlˌaɪzd, -ˈrɪəl- |-zable -zəbļ
unreason ʌnˈrizṇ |-ed -d |-ing -ˈriznɪŋ, -zṇɪŋ
unreasonable ʌnˈriznəbļ, -zṇəbļ |-bly -blɪ
unrebuked ˌʌnrɪˈbjukt, -ˈbɪukt
unreceipted ˌʌnrɪˈsitɪd (ˈunreˌceipted ˈbill)
unreceived ˌʌnrɪˈsivd
unreciprocated ˌʌnrɪˈsɪprəˌketɪd
unreckoned ʌnˈrɛkənd
unrecognized ʌnˈrɛkəgˌnaɪzd |-zable -zəbļ |-bly -blɪ
unreconcilable ʌnˈrɛkənˌsaɪləbļ |-bly -blɪ, emph. +ˌunreconˈcilable, -bly
unrecorded ˌʌnrɪˈkɔrdɪd; ES -ˈkɔədɪd
unredeemed ˌʌnrɪˈdimd
unreel ʌnˈril |-ed -d
unreeve naut. ʌnˈriv |-rove -ˈrov or -reeved -ˈrivd
unrefined ˌʌnrɪˈfaɪnd (ˈunreˌfined ˈsugar)
unreflecting ˌʌnrɪˈflɛktɪŋ
unreformed ˌʌnrɪˈfɔrmd; ES -ˈfɔəmd; |-mable -məbļ
unrefuted ˌʌnrɪˈfjutɪd, -ˈfɪutɪd |-table -təbļ
unregarded ˌʌnrɪˈgardɪd; ES -ˈgɑːdɪd, E+-ˈgaːd-
unregenerate ˌʌnrɪˈdʒɛnərɪt |-rated -ˌretɪd
unregistered ʌnˈrɛdʒɪstɚd; ES -ˈrɛdʒɪstəd
unregulated ʌnˈrɛgjəˌletɪd
unrehearsed ˌʌnrɪˈhɝst; ES -ˈhɜst, -ˈhɝst
unrelated ˌʌnrɪˈletɪd (ˈunreˌlated ˈfacts)
unrelaxed ˌʌnrɪˈlækst
unrelenting ˌʌnrɪˈlɛntɪŋ
unreliability ˌʌnrɪˌlaɪəˈbɪlətɪ
unreliable ˌʌnrɪˈlaɪəbļ |-bly -blɪ
unrelieved ˌʌnrɪˈlivd |-vedly -vɪdlɪ
unreligious ˌʌnrɪˈlɪdʒəs
unremembered ˌʌnrɪˈmɛmbɚd; ES -ˈmɛmbəd
unremitting ˌʌnrɪˈmɪtɪŋ
unremovable ˌʌnrɪˈmuvəbļ |-bly -blɪ
unremunerative ˌʌnrɪˈmjunəˌretɪv, -ˈmɪun-, -ərətɪv
unrenowned ˌʌnrɪˈnaʊnd

|full fʊl |tooth tuθ |further ˈfɝðɚ; ES ˈfɜðə |custom ˈkʌstəm |while hwaɪl |how haʊ |toy tɔɪ
|using ˈjuzɪŋ |fuse fjuz, fɪuz |dish dɪʃ |vision ˈvɪʒən |Eden ˈidṇ |cradle ˈkredļ |keep 'em ˈkipm̩

unrented ʌnˈrɛntɪd (ˈunˌrented ˈfarm)

unrepair ˌʌnrɪˈpɛr, -ˈpær; E -ˈpɛə(r, ES -ˈpæə(r; |-ed -d

unrepealed ˌʌnrɪˈpild

unrepentant ˌʌnrɪˈpɛntənt

unreported ˌʌnrɪˈportɪd, -ˈpɔrtɪd; ES -ˈpoətɪd, E+-ˈpɔətɪd

unrepresented ˌʌnrɛprɪˈzɛntɪd |-tative -tətɪv

unrepressed ˌʌnrɪˈprɛst |-sible -səbḷ

unrequested ˌʌnrɪˈkwɛstɪd

unrequited ˌʌnrɪˈkwaɪtɪd |-table -təbḷ

unreserve ˌʌnrɪˈzɝv; ES -ˈzɜv, -ˈzɝv; |-d -d |-dly -ɪdlɪ

unresisting ˌʌnrɪˈzɪstɪŋ

unresponsive ˌʌnrɪˈspɑnsɪv; ES+-ˈspɒn-; |-sible -səbḷ

unrest ʌnˈrɛst |-ed -ɪd |-ful -fəl |-fully -fəlɪ

unrestrainable ˌʌnrɪˈstrenəbḷ |-bly -blɪ

unrestrained ˌʌnrɪˈstrend |-nt -nt |-nedly -nɪdlɪ

unrestricted ˌʌnrɪˈstrɪktɪd

unretentive ˌʌnrɪˈtɛntɪv

unretrieved ˌʌnrɪˈtrivd |-vable -vəbḷ

unrevealed ˌʌnrɪˈvild (ˈunreˌvealed ˈtruth)

unrevenged ˌʌnrɪˈvɛndʒd

unrevoked ˌʌnrɪˈvokt

unrewarded ˌʌnrɪˈwɔrdɪd; ES -ˈwɔədɪd

unrhymed ʌnˈraɪmd

unrighteous ʌnˈraɪtʃəs

unrightful ʌnˈraɪtfəl |-ly -ɪ

unrimed ʌnˈraɪmd (ˈunˌrimed ˈverse)

unrip ʌnˈrɪp |-ripped -ˈrɪpt

unripe ʌnˈraɪp |-ened -ənd, -ˈraɪpṃd

unrivaled ʌnˈraɪvḷd

unrobe ʌnˈrob |-robed -ˈrobd

unroll ʌnˈrol |-rolled -ˈrold

unromantic ˌʌnroˈmæntɪk |-al -ḷ |-ally -ḷɪ, -ɪklɪ

unroof ʌnˈruf, -ˈrʊf |-ed -t

unrove *past of* unreeve ʌnˈrov

unruled ʌnˈruld, -ˈrɪuld |-edly -ɪdlɪ

unsaddle ʌnˈsædḷ |-d -d |-ling -ˈsædḷɪŋ, -dlɪŋ

unsafe ʌnˈsef (ˈunˌsafe ˈroad)

unsaid ʌnˈsɛd

unsalable, -saleable ʌnˈseləbḷ |-bly -blɪ

unsalaried ʌnˈsælərɪd

unsalted ʌnˌsɔltɪd (ˈunˌsalted ˈbutter)

unsanctioned ʌnˈsæŋkʃənd

unsanitary ʌnˈsænəˌtɛrɪ

unsatisfactory ˌʌnsætɪsˈfæktrɪ, -tərɪ |-torily -trəlɪ, -tərəlɪ

unsatisfied ʌnˈsætɪsˌfaɪd

unsaturated ʌnˈsætʃəˌretɪd

unsavory ʌnˈsevərɪ, -ˈsevrɪ

unsay ʌnˈse |-says -ˈsɛz |-said -ˈsɛd

unscared ʌnˈskɛrd, -ˈskærd; E -ˈskɛəd, ES -ˈskæəd

unscarred ʌnˈskɑrd; ES -ˈskɑ:d, E+-ˈskɑ:d

unscathed ʌnˈskeðd

unscented ʌnˈsɛntɪd (ˈunˌscented ˈsoap)

unscholarly ʌnˈskɑləlɪ; ES -ˈskɑləlɪ, -ˈskɒl-

unschooled ʌnˈskuld

unscientific ˌʌnsaɪənˈtɪfɪk |-al -ḷ |-ally -ḷɪ, -ɪklɪ

unscramble ʌnˈskræmbḷ |-d -d |-ling -blɪŋ, -bḷɪŋ

unscreened ʌnˈskrind (ˈunˌscreened ˈcoal)

unscrew ʌnˈskru, -ˈskrɪu |-ed -d

unscriptural ʌnˈskrɪptʃərəl |-ly -ɪ

unscrupulous ʌnˈskrupjələs, -ˈskrɪup-

unseal ʌnˈsil |-ed -d

unseam ʌnˈsim |-ed -d

unsearchable ʌnˈsɝtʃəbḷ; ES -ˈsɜtʃ-, -ˈsɝtʃ-

unseasonable ʌnˈsiznəbḷ, -zṇə- |-bly -blɪ

unseasoned ʌnˈsiznd (ˈunˌseasoned ˈwit)

unseat ʌnˈsit |-seated -ˈsitɪd

unseaworthy ʌnˈsiˌwɝðɪ; ES -ˌwɜðɪ, -ˌwɝðɪ

unseconded ʌnˈsɛkəndɪd

unsectarian ˌʌnsɛkˈtɛrɪən, -ˈter- |-ism -ˌɪzəm

unsecured ˌʌnsɪˈkjurd, -ˈkɪurd; ES -əd

unseeing ʌnˈsiɪŋ

unseemly ʌnˈsimlɪ

unseen ʌnˈsin (ˈseen and ˈunˌseen)

unsegmented ʌnˈsɛgməntɪd

unselfish ʌnˈsɛlfɪʃ

unsentimental ˌʌnsɛntəˈmɛntḷ |-ly -ɪ

unserviceable ʌnˈsɝvɪsəbḷ; ES -ˈsɜvɪs-, -ˈsɝvɪs-; |-bly -blɪ

unset ʌnˈsɛt

unsettle ʌnˈsɛtḷ |-d -d |-ling -ˈsɛtḷɪŋ, -tlɪŋ

unsew ʌnˈso |*past* -sewed -ˈsod |*pptc* -sewed -ˈsod *or* -sewn -ˈson

unsex ʌnˈsɛks |-es -ɪz |-ed -t

unshackle ʌnˈʃækḷ |-d -d |-ling -klɪŋ, -kḷɪŋ

unshaded ʌnˈʃedɪd

unshaken ʌnˈʃekən |-kable -kəbḷ |-bly -blɪ

unshaped ʌnˈʃept |-pely -plɪ |-pen -pən

unshaven ʌnˈʃevən

Key: See in full §§3-47. bee bi |pity ˈpɪtɪ (§6) |rate ret |yet jɛt |sang sæŋ |angry ˈæŋ·grɪ |bath bæθ; E baθ (§10) |ah ɑ |far fɑr |watch wɑtʃ, wɒtʃ (§12) |jaw dʒɔ |gorge gɔrdʒ |go go

unsheathe ʌnˈʃið |-d -d
unshed ʌnˈʃɛd
unsheltered ʌnˈʃɛltəd; ES -ˈʃɛltəd
unship ʌnˈʃɪp |-ped -t
unshod ʌnˈʃɑd; ES+-ˈʃɒd; (ˈunˌshod ˈhorse)
unshrinkable ʌnˈʃrɪŋkəbl̩
unshrinking ʌnˈʃrɪŋkɪŋ (ˈunˌshrinking ˈstation)
unshrunk ʌnˈʃrʌŋk |-en -ən
unsifted ʌnˈsɪftɪd
unsight ʌnˈsaɪt |-ed -ɪd |-ly -lɪ
unsigned ʌnˈsaɪnd
unsinewed ʌnˈsɪnjud, -ˈsɪnɪud, -ˈsɪnud
unsingable ʌnˈsɪŋəbl̩
unsinkable ʌnˈsɪŋkəbl̩
unsisterly ʌnˈsɪstəlɪ; ES -ˈsɪstəlɪ
unskilled ʌnˈskɪld (ˈunˌskilled ˈlabor)
unskillful, -skilf- ʌnˈskɪlfəl |-ly -ɪ
unsling ʌnˈslɪŋ |-slung -ˈslʌŋ
unsnap ʌnˈsnæp |-ped -t
unsnarl ʌnˈsnɑrl; ES -ˈsnɑːl, E+-ˈsnɑːl; |-ed -d
unsociability ˌʌnsoʃəˈbɪlətɪ
unsociable ʌnˈsoʃəbl̩ |-bly -blɪ
unsocial ʌnˈsoʃəl |-ly -ɪ
unsoiled ʌnˈsɔɪld
unsold ʌnˈsold
unsolder ʌnˈsadə; ES -ˈsadə(r, -ˈsɒd-
unsoldierly ʌnˈsoldʒəlɪ; ES -ˈsoldʒəlɪ
unsolicited ˌʌnsəˈlɪsɪtɪd
unsoluble ʌnˈsaljəbl̩; ES+-ˈsɒl-
unsolvable ʌnˈsalvəbl̩, -ˈsɒlv- |-bly -blɪ
unsolved ʌnˈsalvd, -ˈsɒlvd
unsophisticated ˌʌnsəˈfɪstɪˌketɪd
unsophistication ˌʌnsəˌfɪstɪˈkeʃən
unsorted ʌnˈsɔrtɪd; ES -ˈsɔətɪd
unsought ʌnˈsɔt (ˈunˌsought ˈhelp)
unsound ʌnˈsaund |-ed -ɪd
unsowed ʌnˈsod |-sown -ˈson
unsparing ʌnˈspɛrɪŋ, -ˈspær-; S -ˈspærɪŋ
unspeakable ʌnˈspikəbl̩ |-bly -blɪ
unspecified ʌnˈspɛsəˌfaɪd
unspent ʌnˈspɛnt
unspoiled ʌnˈspɔɪld |-spoilt -ˈspɔɪlt
unspoken ʌnˈspokən
unsportsmanlike ʌnˈsportsmənˌlaɪk, -ˈsports-; ES -ˈspoəts-, E+-ˈspɔəts-
unspotted ʌnˈspatɪd; ES+-ˈspɒtɪd
unsprung ʌnˈsprʌŋ

unstable ʌnˈstebl̩ |-bly -blɪ
unstained ʌnˈstend |-nable -nəbl̩ |-nedly -nɪdlɪ
unstamped ʌnˈstæmpt
unstandardized ʌnˈstændədˌaɪzd; ES -ˈstændəd-
unstarched ʌnˈstɑrtʃt; ES -ˈstɑːtʃt, E+ -ˈstɑːtʃt
unstate ʌnˈstet |-d -ɪd
unsteady ʌnˈstɛdɪ |-dily -dl̩ɪ, -dɪlɪ
unsteel ʌnˈstil |-steeled -ˈstild
unstick ʌnˈstɪk |-stuck -ˈstʌk
unstinted ʌnˈstɪntɪd
unstitch ʌnˈstɪtʃ |-ed -t
unstop ʌnˈstap; ES+-ˈstɒp; |-ped -t
unstrained ʌnˈstrend
unstrap ʌnˈstræp |-ped -t
unstratified ʌnˈstrætəˌfaɪd
unstressed ʌnˈstrɛst (ˈunˌstressed ˈword ˈstressed & ˈunˌstressed)
unstriated ʌnˈstraɪetɪd
unstring ʌnˈstrɪŋ |-strung -ˈstrʌŋ
unstuck ʌnˈstʌk
unstudied ʌnˈstʌdɪd
unstuffed ʌnˈstʌft
unsubmissive ˌʌnsəbˈmɪsɪv
unsubstantial ˌʌnsəbˈstænʃəl |-ly -ɪ
unsubstantiality ˌʌnsəbˌstænʃɪˈælətɪ
unsubstantiated ˌʌnsəbˈstænʃɪˌetɪd
unsuccess ˌʌnsəkˈsɛs |-ful -fəl |-fully -fəlɪ
unsuggestive ˌʌnsəgˈdʒɛstɪv, -səˈdʒɛstɪv
unsuitability ˌʌnsutəˈbɪlətɪ, -sɪut-, -sjut-
unsuited ʌnˈsutɪd, -ˈsɪut-, -ˈsjut- |-table -təbl̩ |-bly -blɪ
unsullied ʌnˈsʌlɪd
unsung ʌnˈsʌŋ
unsupportable ˌʌnsəˈportəbl̩, -ˈpɔrt-; ES -ˈpoət-, E+-ˈpɔət-; |-bly -blɪ
unsuppressed ˌʌnsəˈprɛst |-sible -səbl̩ |-bly -blɪ
unsure ʌnˈʃur; ES -ˈʃuə(r; (ˈunˌsure ˈhopes)
unsurmounted ˌʌnsəˈmauntɪd; ES -sə-; |-table -təbl̩ |-bly -blɪ
unsurpassed ˌʌnsəˈpæst; ES -səˈpæst, E+ -ˈpast, -ˈpɑst
unsusceptible ˌʌnsəˈsɛptəbl̩
unsuspected ˌʌnsəˈspɛktɪd |-ting -tɪŋ
unsuspicious ˌʌnsəˈspɪʃəs
unsustained ˌʌnsəˈstend

|full fʊl |tooth tuθ |further ˈfɝðɚ; ES ˈfɝðə |custom ˈkʌstəm |while hwaɪl |how haʊ |toy tɔɪ |using ˈjuzɪŋ |fuse fjuz, fruz |dish dɪʃ |vision ˈvɪʒən |Eden ˈidn̩ |cradle ˈkredl̩ |keep 'em ˈkipm̩

unswathe ʌnˈsweð |-d -d
unswayed ʌnˈswed
unsweetened ʌnˈswitn̩d
unswept ʌnˈswɛpt
unswerving ʌnˈswɜˑvɪŋ; ES -ˈswɜv-, -ˈswɜˑv-
unsymmetrical ˌʌnsɪˈmɛtrɪkl̩ |-ly -ɪ, -ɪklɪ
unsympathetic ˌʌnsɪmpəˈθɛtɪk |-ally -l̩ɪ, -ɪklɪ
unsystematic ˌʌnsɪstəˈmætɪk |-al -l̩ |-ally -l̩ɪ, -ɪklɪ
untactful ʌnˈtæktfəl |-ly -ɪ
untainted ʌnˈtentɪd (ˈunˌtainted ˈhonor)
untaken ʌnˈtekən
untalented ʌnˈtæləntɪd
untamed ʌnˈtemd |-mable, -meable -məbl̩
untangle ʌnˈtæŋgl̩ |-d -d |-ling -glɪŋ, -gl̩ɪŋ
untanned ʌnˈtænd (ˈunˌtanned ˈhides)
untarnished ʌnˈtɑrnɪʃt; ES -ˈtɑːn-, E+-ˈtɑːn-
untasted ʌnˈtestɪd
untaught ʌnˈtɔt
untaxed ʌnˈtækst |-xable -ksəbl̩
unteachable ʌnˈtitʃəbl̩ |-bly -blɪ
untenable ʌnˈtɛnəbl̩ |-bly -blɪ
untended ʌnˈtɛndɪd
untented ʌnˈtɛntɪd
Untermeyer ˈʌntɚˌmaɪɚ; ES ˈʌntəˌmaɪ-ə(r
unterrified ʌnˈtɛrəˌfaɪd
untested ʌnˈtɛstɪd
unthanked ʌnˈθæŋkt |-kful -kfəl |-kfully -kfəlɪ
unthinkable ʌnˈθɪŋkəbl̩ |-bly -blɪ |-king -kɪŋ
unthought ʌnˈθɔt |-ful -fəl |-fully -fəlɪ
unthread ʌnˈθrɛd |-ed -ɪd
unthrifty ʌnˈθrɪftɪ (ˈunˌthrifty ˈknave)
unthrone ʌnˈθron |-d -d
untidy ʌnˈtaɪdɪ |-dily -dl̩ɪ, -dɪlɪ
untie ʌnˈtaɪ |-tied -ˈtaɪd
until ənˈtɪl
untilled ʌnˈtɪld
untimely ʌnˈtaɪmlɪ
untinged ʌnˈtɪndʒd
untired ʌnˈtaɪrd; ES -ˈtaɪəd; |-ring -rɪŋ
untitled ʌnˈtaɪtl̩d
unto not in familiar use. Before vowel ˈʌntu;
  before cons. ˈʌntə, ˈʌntu; before pause ˈʌntu;
  in poetry often ʌnˈtu
untold ʌnˈtold (ˈunˌtold ˈriches)
untouchability ˌʌntʌtʃəˈbɪlətɪ
untouched ʌnˈtʌtʃt |-chable -tʃəbl̩ |-bly -blɪ

untoward ʌnˈtord, -ˈtɔrd; ES -ˈtoəd, E+ -ˈtɔəd
untraceable ʌnˈtresəbl̩ |-bly -blɪ
untrained ʌnˈtrend
untrammeled ʌnˈtræml̩d
untransferable ˌʌntrænsˈfɝˑəbl̩; ES -ˈfɜrə-, -ˈfɝ-
untranslatable ˌʌntrænsˈletəbl̩, -trænz- |-bly -blɪ
untraveled ʌnˈtrævl̩d
untraversed ʌnˈtrævɚst, -ˈtrævɜˑst; ES -ˈtrævəst, -ˈtrævɜst, -ˈtrævɜˑst
untread ʌnˈtrɛd |past -trod -ˈtrɑd |pptc -trodden -ˈtrɑdn̩ or -trod -ˈtrɑd; ES+ -ˈtrɒd(n̩)
untrimmed ʌnˈtrɪmd
untrod ʌnˈtrɑd; ES+-ˈtrɒd; |-den -n̩
untroubled ʌnˈtrʌbl̩d
untrue ʌnˈtru, -ˈtrɪu |-ly -lɪ
untruss ʌnˈtrʌs |-es -ɪz |-ed -t
untrustful ʌnˈtrʌstfəl |-ly -ɪ
untruth ʌnˈtruθ, -ˈtrɪuθ |-ths -ðz, -θs |-ful -fəl |-fully -fəlɪ
unturned ʌnˈtɝnd; ES -ˈtɜnd, -ˈtɝˑnd
untutored ʌnˈtutɚd, -ˈtɪutɚd, -ˈtjutɚd; ES -təd
untwine ʌnˈtwaɪn |-d -d
untwist ʌnˈtwɪst |-ed -ɪd
unused ʌnˈjuzd |-sable -zəbl̩ |-bly -blɪ
unusual ʌnˈjuʒʊəl, -ˈjuʒʊl, -ˈjuʒəl |-ly -ɪ
unuttered ʌnˈʌtɚd; ES -ˈʌtəd; |-rable -tərəbl̩ |-bly -blɪ
unvaccinated ʌnˈvæksn̩ˌetɪd
unvalued ʌnˈvæljud
unvaried ʌnˈvɛrɪd, -ˈverɪd, -ˈværɪd |-rying -rɪɪŋ
unvarnished ʌnˈvɑrnɪʃt; ES -ˈvɑːn-, E+ -ˈvɑːn-
unveil ʌnˈvel |-ed -d
unventilated ʌnˈvɛntl̩ˌetɪd
unverified ʌnˈvɛrəˌfaɪd |-fiable -ˌfaɪəbl̩ |-bly -blɪ
unversed ʌnˈvɝst; ES -ˈvɜst, -ˈvɝˑst
unvexed ʌnˈvɛkst
unvisited ʌnˈvɪzɪtɪd
unvocal ʌnˈvokl̩ |-ized -ˌaɪzd
unvoiced ʌnˈvɔɪst (ˈunˌvoiced ˈthought)
unwanted ʌnˈwantɪd, -ˈwɔntɪd, -ˈwɒntɪd; S -ˈwɔntɪd, -ˈwɒntɪd, -ˈwantɪd

---

unwarily ʌnˈwɛrəlɪ, -ˈwɛrəlɪ, -ˈwærəlɪ

unwarlike ʌnˈwɔrˌlaɪk; ES -ˈwɔə-

unwarned ʌnˈwɔrnd; ES -ˈwɔənd; |-nedly -nɪdlɪ

unwarranted ʌnˈwɔrəntɪd, -ˈwɑr-, -ˈwɒr- |-table -təb| |-bly -blɪ

unwary ʌnˈwɛrɪ, -ˈwɛrɪ, -ˈwærɪ—see wary

unwashed ʌnˈwɑʃt, -ˈwɔʃt, -ˈwɒʃt

unwatched ʌnˈwɑtʃt, -ˈwɒtʃt, -ˈwɔtʃt

unwavering ʌnˈwevrɪŋ, -ˈwevərɪŋ

unwearable ʌnˈwɛrəb|, -ˈwær-; S -ˈwær-

unwearied ʌnˈwɪrɪd, -ˈwir-; S+-ˈwɛrɪd; |-rying -rɪɪŋ

unweave ʌnˈwiv |past -wove -ˈwov or -weaved -ˈwivd |pptc -woven -ˈwovən or -wove -ˈwov

unwed adj ʌnˈwɛd |-ded -ɪd

unweight ʌnˈwet |-ed -ɪd

unwelcome ʌnˈwɛlkəm (ˈunˌwelcome ˈnews)

unwell ʌnˈwɛl

unwept ʌnˈwɛpt

unwholesome ʌnˈholsəm

unwieldy ʌnˈwildɪ

unwilling ʌnˈwɪlɪŋ

unwincing ʌnˈwɪnsɪŋ

unwind ˈuncoil' ʌnˈwaɪnd |-wound -ˈwaʊnd

unwind ˈdeprive of breath' ʌnˈwɪnd |-ed -ɪd

unwinking ʌnˈwɪŋkɪŋ

unwise ʌnˈwaɪz |unwisdom ʌnˈwɪzdəm

unwished ʌnˈwɪʃt

unwitnessed ʌnˈwɪtnɪst

unwitting ʌnˈwɪtɪŋ

unwomanly ʌnˈwʊmənlɪ, -ˈwʊmənlɪ

unwonted ʌnˈwɑntɪd—see wont

unworkable ʌnˈwɝkəb|; ES -ˈwɝk-, -ˈwɝk-; |-bly -blɪ

unworldly ʌnˈwɝldlɪ; ES -ˈwɝld-, -ˈwɝld-

unworn ʌnˈworn, -ˈwɔrn; ES -ˈwoən, E+ -ˈwɔən

unworshipped ʌnˈwɝʃəpt; ES -ˈwɝʃ-, -ˈwɝʃ-

unworthy ʌnˈwɝðɪ; ES -ˈwɝðɪ, -ˈwɝðɪ

unwound ˈuncoiled' ʌnˈwaʊnd

unwounded ˈunhurt' ʌnˈwundɪd, -ˈwaʊndɪd

unwrap ʌnˈræp |-ped -t

unwrinkle ʌnˈrɪŋk| |-d -d

unwritten ʌnˈrɪtn̩ (ˈunˌwritten ˈlaw)

unwrought ʌnˈrɔt

unyielding ʌnˈjildɪŋ

unyoke ʌnˈjok |-yoked -ˈjokt

up adv, prep, stressed ˈʌp, ˌʌp; unstr. ʌp, əp

up n, adj ʌp, v ʌp |upped ʌpt

up- prefix ʌp-, ˌʌp-, ˈʌp- according to rhythm and meaning; unstr. əp-

up and down, up-and-down ˈʌpənˈdaʊn, ˈʌpm̩ˈdaʊn (ˈup-and-ˌdown ˈmotion)

up and up, up-and-up ˈʌpənˈʌp, ˈʌpəndˈʌp

Upanishad uˈpænɪˌʃæd, uˈpʌnɪˌʃad

upas ˈjupəs |upases ˈjupəsɪz

upborne ʌpˈborn, -ˈbɔrn; ES -ˈboən, E+ -ˈbɔən

upbraid ʌpˈbred |-ed -ɪd

upbringing n ˈʌpˌbrɪŋɪŋ

upbuild ʌpˈbɪld |-built -ˈbɪlt or arch. -ed -ˈbɪldɪd

upcast n, adj ˈʌpˌkæst; E+-ˌkast, -ˌkast—cf downcast

upcountry n, adj, adv ˈʌpˈkʌntrɪ (ˈupˈcountry ˌfolk, ˈupˌcountry ˈtown)

upend v ʌpˈɛnd |-ended -ˈɛndɪd

upgather ʌpˈgæðɚ; ES -ˈgæðə(r; |-ed -d |-ing -ˈgæðrɪŋ, -ˈgæðərɪŋ

upgrade adj, adv ˈʌpˈgred (ˈupˌgrade & ˈdownˌgrade)

upgrowth ˈʌpˌgroθ |-ths -θs

upharsin juˈfarsɪn; ES -ˈfɑːsɪn, E+-ˈfaːs-

upheaval ʌpˈhiv|, ˈʌpˌhiv|

upheave ʌpˈhiv |-heaved -ˈhivd

upheld ʌpˈhɛld

uphill n ˈʌpˌhɪl, ʌpˈhɪl

uphill adj ˈʌpˈhɪl (ˈupˌhill ˈwork)

uphill adv ˈʌpˈhɪl (ˈupˌhill & ˈdownˌhill)

uphold ʌpˈhold |-held -ˈhɛld |arch. pptc+ -holden -ˈholdən

upholster ʌpˈholstɚ; ES -stə(r; |-ed -d |-ing -strɪŋ, -stərɪŋ

upholsterer ʌpˈholstərɚ, -ˈholstrɚ; ES -rə(r

upholstery ʌpˈholstrɪ, -ˈholstərɪ

upkeep n ˈʌpˌkip

upkeep v ʌpˈkip |-kept -ˈkɛpt

upland n, adj, adv ˈʌplənd, ˈʌpˌlænd

uplander ˈʌpləndɚ, ˈʌpˌlændɚ; ES -də(r

uplift n ˈʌpˌlɪft

uplift v ʌpˈlɪft |-lifted -ˈlɪftɪd, arch. past & pptc+-lift -ˈlɪft

upmost ˈʌpˌmost

upon stressed əˈpɑn, əˈpɒn, əˈpɔn; unstr. occas. əpən; restressed əˈpʌn

upper ˈʌpɚ; ES ˈʌpə(r

|full fʊl |tooth tuθ |further ˈfɝðɚ; ES ˈfɝðə |custom ˈkʌstəm |while hwaɪl |how haʊ |toy tɔɪ |using ˈjuzɪŋ |fuse fjuz, fɪuz |dish dɪʃ |vision ˈvɪʒən |Eden ˈidn̩ |cradle ˈkredl̩ |keep ʼem ˈkipm̩

upper-class ˈʌpɚˈklæs; ES ˈʌpəˈklæs, E+
-ˈklɑs, -ˈklɑs
uppercut n, v ˈʌpɚˌkʌt; ES ˈʌpə-
uppermost ˈʌpɚˌmost; ES ˈʌpə-
uppers ˈʌpɚz; ES ˈʌpəz
uppish ˈʌpɪʃ
Uppsala ˈʌpˌsɑlə (Sw ˈɵpˌsɑ:lɑ)
upraise ʌpˈrez |-s -ɪz |-d -d
uprear ʌpˈrɪr; ES -ˈrɪə(r, S+-ˈrɛə(r; |-ed -d
upright n, adj, v ˈʌpˌraɪt |-ed -ɪd
upright adv ˈʌpˌraɪt, ʌpˈraɪt
uprise n ˈʌpˌraɪz |-s -ɪz
uprise v ʌpˈraɪz |-s -ɪz |-rose -ˈroz |-risen
-ˈrɪzn̩
uprising n ˈʌpˌraɪzɪŋ, ʌpˈraɪzɪŋ
uproar ˈʌpˌror, -ˌrɔr; ES -ˌroə(r, E+-ˌrɔə(r;
v upˈroar
uproarious ʌpˈrorɪəs, -ˈrɔrɪəs; S -ˈrorɪəs
uproot ʌpˈrut, -ˈrʊt |-ed -ɪd
uprouse ʌpˈraʊz |-s -ɪz |-d -d
Upsala ˈʌpˌsɑlə (Sw ˈɵpˌsɑ:lɑ)
upset n ˈʌpˌsɛt
upset adj, v ʌpˈsɛt
upshot ˈʌpˌʃɑt; ES+-ˌʃɒt
upside ˈʌpˈsaɪd, ˈʌpˌsaɪd
upside down, upside-down ˈʌpˌsaɪdˈdaʊn
upsilon ˈjupsələn, -ˌlɑn, -ˌlɒn, Brit. jup-
ˈsaɪlən
upspring n ˈʌpˌsprɪŋ
upspring v ʌpˈsprɪŋ |past -sprang -ˈspræŋ or
-sprung -ˈsprʌŋ |pptc -sprung -ˈsprʌŋ
upstage adj, adv, v ˈʌpˈstedʒ |-s -ɪz |-d -d
upstairs n, ʌpˈstɛrz, -ˈstærz; E -ˈstɛəz, ES
-ˈstæəz; acct+ˈupˌstairs, adj, adv ˈupˈstairs
upstanding ʌpˈstændɪŋ
upstart n, adj ˈʌpˌstart; ES -ˌsta:t, E+-ˌsta:t
upstart v ʌpˈstart; ES -ˈsta:t, E+-ˈsta:t; |-ed
-ɪd
upstate adj, adv ˈʌpˈstet (ˈupˌstate ˈtown)
upstream adj, adv ˈʌpˈstrim; v ʌpˈstrim |-ed -d
upstroke ˈʌpˌstrok
upsweep n ˈʌpˌswip
upsweep v ʌpˈswip |-swept -ˈswɛpt
upswing n ˈʌpˌswɪŋ
upswing v ʌpˈswɪŋ |-swung -ˈswʌŋ
uptake ˈʌpˌtek
upthrust ˈʌpˌθrʌst
up-to-date ˈʌptəˈdet (ˈup-toˌdate ˈnews)
uptown n ʌpˈtaʊn, ˈʌpˌtaʊn

uptown adj, adv ˈʌpˈtaʊn (ˈupˌtown & ˈdown-
ˌtown)
upturn n ˈʌpˌtɜ·n; ES -ˌtɜn, -ˌtɝn
upturn v ʌpˈtɜ·n; ES -ˈtɜn, -ˈtɝn; |-ed -d
upward ˈʌpwɚd; ES ˈʌpwəd; |-s -z
Ur ɜ·; ES ɜ(r, ɝ
uraemia juˈrimɪə, -mjə |-mic -mɪk
uraenite juˈrænəˌnaɪt
Ural ˈjʊrəl
Ural-Altaic ˈjʊrəlˈælˈte·ɪk
uranalysis ˌjʊrəˈnæləsɪs |-yses -əˌsiz
Urania juˈrenɪə |-n -n
uranic juˈrænɪk
uraninite juˈrænəˌnaɪt
uranite ˈjʊrəˌnaɪt
uranium juˈrenɪəm, -njəm
Uranus ˈjʊrənəs |-'s -ɪz
urban, U- ˈɜ·bən; ES ˈɜbən, ˈɝbən
Urbana ɜ·ˈbænə; ES ɜˈbænə, ɝˈbænə
urbane ɜ·ˈben; ES ɜˈben, ɝˈben; |-ness -ˈben-
nɪs
urbanite ˈɜ·bənˌaɪt; ES ˈɜb-, ˈɝb-
urbanity ɜ·ˈbænətɪ; ES ɜˈbæn-, ɝˈbæn-
urbanize ˈɜ·bənˌaɪz; ES ˈɜb-, ˈɝb-; |-s -ɪz
|-d -d
urchin ˈɜ·tʃɪn; ES ˈɜtʃɪn, ˈɝtʃɪn
Urdu ˈʊrdu, ʊrˈdu, ɜ·ˈdu; ES ˈʊədu, ʊəˈdu,
ɝˈdu, ɝˈdu
urea juˈriə, ˈjʊrɪə |-l -l
uredo juˈrido
uremia juˈrimɪə, -mjə |-mic -mɪk
urethra juˈriθrə |-s -z |-rae -ri
urethritis ˌjʊrɪˈθraɪtɪs
uretic juˈrɛtɪk
urge ɜ·dʒ; ES ɜdʒ, ɝdʒ; |-s -ɪz |-d -d |-nt -ənt
|-ncy -ənsɪ
Uriah juˈraɪə
uric ˈjʊrɪk
Uriel ˈjʊrɪəl
Urim ˈjʊrɪm
urinal ˈjʊrənl̩
urinalysis ˌjʊrəˈnæləsɪs |-yses -əˌsiz
urinary ˈjʊrəˌnɛrɪ
urinate ˈjʊrəˌnet |-d -ɪd |-tion ˌjʊrəˈneʃən
urine ˈjʊrɪn
urn ɜ·n; ES ɜn, ɝn
urology jʊrˈɑlədʒɪ; ES+-ˈɒl-
Urquhart ˈɜ·kɚt, -kɪt; ES ˈɜk-, ˈɝk-; (Sc
ˈɝxərt)
Ursa ˈɜ·sə; ES ˈɜsə, ˈɝsə

Ursa Major ˈɝsəˈmedʒɚ; ES ˈɜsəˈmedʒə(r,
ˈɝsəˈmedʒə(r; |gen Ursae Majoris ˈɝsi-,
ˈɜsiməˈdʒɔrɪs |Minor -ˈmaɪnɚ; ES -nə(r;
|gen Minoris -mɪˈnɔrɪs
ursine ˈɝsaɪn, -sɪn; ES ˈɜs-, ˈɝs-
Ursula ˈɝsjʊlə, ˈɝsələ; ES ˈɜs-, ˈɝs-; |-line
-lɪn, -ˌlaɪn (in Shak. Ursley ˈʊrslɪ, modern
ˈɝslɪ)
Ursus ˈɝsəs; ES ˈɜsəs, ˈɝsəs |-sus' -səs
Urswick ˈɝzwɪk, ˈɝzɪk; ES ˈɜz-, ˈɝz-
Uruguay ˈjʊrəˌgwe, -ˌgwaɪ (Sp ˌuruˈgwai)
Uruguayan ˌjʊrəˈgwean, -ˈgwaɪən
us stressed ˈʌs, ˌʌs; unstr. əs |-'s s (let's lɛts)
usability ˌjuzəˈbɪlətɪ
usable ˈjuzəbl̩
usage ˈjusɪdʒ, less freq. ˈjuzɪdʒ |-s -ɪz
usance ˈjuzn̩s |-s -ɪz
use n jus |uses ˈjusɪz
use v juz |uses ˈjuzɪz |used juzd |-able -əbl̩
used to adj 'accustomed to,' v 'was (were)
accustomed to': before a pause ˈjustu, before
vowels ˈjustʊ, before vowels or conss. ˈjustə
useful ˈjusfəl |-ly -ɪ
useless ˈjuslɪs
user ˈjuzɚ; ES ˈjuzə(r
usher, U- ˈʌʃɚ; ES ˈʌʃə(r; |-ed -d |-ing -ʃərɪŋ,
-ʃrɪŋ
Usk ʌsk
usquebaugh ˈʌskwɪˌbɔ
usual ˈjuʒʊəl, ˈjuʒʊl, ˈjuʒəl |-ly -ɪ
usufruct ˈjuzjuˌfrʌkt, ˈjus-
usurer ˈjuʒərɚ; ES ˈjuʒərə(r

usurious juˈʒʊrɪəs, -rjəs
usurp juˈzɝp, -ˈsɝp; ES -ʒp, -ɝp; |-ed -t
usurpation ˌjuzɚˈpeʃən, -sɚ-; ES ˌjuzə-, -sə-
usury ˈjuʒərɪ, ˈjuʒrɪ
Utah ˈjutɔ, ˈjutɑ |-an -ən
Ute jut, ˈjutɪ
utensil juˈtɛnsl̩
uterus ˈjutərəs |-es -ɪz |-ri -ˌraɪ |-rine -rɪn
Uther ˈjuθɚ; ES ˈjuθə(r
Utica ˈjutɪkə
utile ˈjutɪl
utilitarian ˌjutɪləˈtɛrɪən, juˌtɪlə-, -ˈter-
utility juˈtɪlətɪ
utilization ˌjutl̩əˈzeʃən, -aɪˈz-
utilize ˈjutl̩ˌaɪz |-s -ɪz |-d -d |-zable -əbl̩
utmost ˈʌtˌmost, ˈʌtməst
Utopia juˈtopɪə, -pjə |-n -n
Utrecht ˈjutrɛkt (Du ˈytrɛxt)
utricle ˈjutrɪkl̩
utter, U- ˈʌtɚ; ES ˈʌtə(r; |-ed -d
utterance ˈʌtərəns, ˈʌtrəns |-s -ɪz
utterer ˈʌtərɚ; ES ˈʌtərə(r
uttermost ˈʌtɚˌmost, -məst; ES ˈʌtə-
uvula ˈjuvjələ |-lar -lɚ; ES -lə(r
Uxbridge ˈʌksbrɪdʒ |-'s -ɪz
uxorial ʌkˈsorɪəl, ʌgˈz-, -ɔrɪəl; S -orɪəl; |-ious
-ɪəs
uxoricide ʌkˈsorəˌsaɪd, ʌgˈz-, -ɔr-; S -or-
Uzbek ˈʌzbɛk |Uzbeg ˈʌzbɛg
uzzard 'izzard' ˈʌzɚd; ES ˈʌzəd
Uzziah ʌˈzaɪə
Uzziel ʌˈzaɪəl

V

V, v letter vi |pl V's, Vs, poss V's viz
vacant ˈvekənt |vacancy ˈvekənsɪ
vacate ˈveket |-cated -ketɪd
vacation veˈkeʃən, və-, vɪ- |-ed -d |-ing
-ʃənɪŋ, -ʃnɪŋ
vaccinate ˈvæksn̩ˌet |-d -ɪd |-tion ˌvæksn̩ˈeʃən
vaccine ˈvæksin, -sɪn
Vachel ˈvetʃəl
vacillate ˈvæsl̩ˌet |-d -ɪd |-tion ˌvæsl̩ˈeʃən
vacillatory ˈvæsl̩əˌtorɪ, -ˌtɔrɪ; S -ˌtɔrɪ
vacuity væˈkjuətɪ, və-, -ˈkɪu-
vacuo ˈvækjuˌo |-uous -juəs

vacuum ˈvækjuəm |-s -z |vacua ˈvækjuə
vade mecum ˈvedɪˈmikəm
vagabond ˈvægəˌbɑnd, -ˌbɒnd |-age -ɪdʒ
vagary vəˈgɛrɪ, ve-, -ˈgerɪ
vagina vəˈdʒaɪnə |-nal -nl̩ ˈvædʒən̩l, vəˈdʒaɪnl̩
vagrant ˈvegrənt |-grancy -grənsɪ
vagrom malapropism ˈvegrəm
vague veg
vagus ˈvegəs |-es -ɪz |-vagi ˈvedʒaɪ
vail vel |vailed veld
Vailima vaɪˈlimə
vain ven |-ness ˈvennɪs

|full fʊl |tooth tuθ |further ˈfɝðɚ; ES ˈfɜðə |custom ˈkʌstəm |while hwaɪl |how haʊ |toy tɔɪ
|using ˈjuzɪŋ |fuse fjuz, fɪuz |dish dɪʃ |vision ˈvɪʒən |Eden ˈidn̩ |cradle ˈkredl̩ |keep 'em ˈkipm̩

vainglory ven'glorɪ, -'glɔrɪ; S -'glorɪ; |-rious
-rɪəs
vair vɛr, vær; E vɛə(r, ES væə(r
valance 'væləns |-s -ɪz |-d -t
vale 'valley' vel
vale 'farewell' 'veli
valediction ˌvælə'dɪkʃən
valedictorian ˌvælədɪk'torɪən, -'tɔr-; S -'tor-
valedictory ˌvælə'dɪktərɪ, -trɪ
valence chem. 'veləns |-cy -sɪ
Valencia və'lɛnʃɪə, -ʃə |-n -n
Valenciennes vəˌlɛnsɪ'ɛnz (Fr valɑ̃'sjɛn)
valentine, V- 'vælənˌtaɪn
Valera, de dəvə'lerə, -'lɛrə, -'lɪrə
Valeria və'lɪrɪə |-ius -s |-ius's -sɪz
valet 'vælɪt |-ed -ɪd (Fr va'lɛ)—A pseudo-
  French 'væle, væ'le is sometimes heard.
  Valet, with a t, has been English for at least
  400 years.
valetudinarian ˌvæləˌtjudn̩'ɛrɪən, -ˌtɪu-, -ˌtu-,
  -'erɪən
valetudinary ˌvælə'tjudn̩ˌɛrɪ, -'tɪu-, -'tu-
Valhalla væl'hælə
valiant 'væljənt |-nce -ns |-ncy -nsɪ
valid 'vælɪd
validate 'væləˌdet |-d -ɪd
validity və'lɪdətɪ
valise və'lis |-s -ɪz
Valkyrie væl'kɪrɪ
valley 'vælɪ |-ed -ɪd
Vallombrosa ˌvæləm'brosə (It ˌvallom'bro:sa)
valor 'vælɚ; ES 'vælə(r; |-ous -əs
valorization ˌvælərə'zeʃən, -aɪ'z-
valorize 'væləˌraɪz |-s -ɪz |-d -d
Valparaiso ˌvælpə'rezo, in SA +-'raɪso, -zo
  (Sp ˌbalpara'iso)
valuable 'væljəbl̩, 'væljʊəbl̩ |-bly -blɪ
valuation ˌvælju'eʃən
valuator 'væljuˌetɚ; ES -ˌetə(r
value 'vælju |valued 'væljud
valve vælv |-d -d
valvular 'vælvjələ; ES -lə(r
vamoose væ'mus |-s -ɪz |-d -t
vamp væmp |vamped væmpt
vampire 'væmpaɪr; ES 'væmpaɪə(r; |-ed -d
van væn |vanned vænd
vanadium və'nedɪəm, -djəm
Van Buren væn'bjurən, -'bɪurən
Vancouver væn'kuvɚ; ES -'kuvə(r

vandal, V- 'vændl̩ |-ism -ˌɪzəm
vandalize 'vændl̩ˌaɪz |-s -ɪz |-d -d
Vanderbilt 'vændɚˌbɪlt; ES 'vændə-
Van Dieman, v- væn'dimən
Van Doren væn'dorən, -'dɔr-; S -'dor-
van Dyck, Dijk væn'daɪk
Van Dyck væn'daɪk
Vandyke, Van Dyke, van D- væn'daɪk
vane ven |vaned vend
Vanessa və'nɛsə
van Eyck væn'aɪk
vanguard 'vænˌgard; ES -ˌga:d, E+-ˌga:d
vanilla və'nɪlə
vanish 'vænɪʃ |-es -ɪz |-ed -t
vanity 'vænətɪ
van Loon væn'lon
vanquish 'væŋkwɪʃ, 'væŋ-
vantage 'væntɪdʒ |-s -ɪz |-d -d
vanward 'vænwɚd; ES 'vænwəd
vapid 'væpɪd |vapidity væ'pɪdətɪ, və-
vapor 'vepɚ; ES 'vepə(r; |-ous -əs, -prəs
vaporific ˌvepə'rɪfɪk
vaporization ˌvepərə'zeʃən, -aɪ'z-
vaporize 'vepəˌraɪz |-s -ɪz |-d -d |-ry -rɪ
Vargas 'vargəs; ES 'va:g-; (Pg 'vargəʃ)
variability ˌvɛrɪə'bɪlətɪ, ˌver-, ˌvær-
variable 'vɛrɪəbl̩, 'ver-, 'vær- |-bly -blɪ
variant 'vɛrɪənt, 'ver-, 'vær- |-nce -ns
variation ˌvɛrɪ'eʃən, ˌver-, ˌvær-
varicolored 'vɛrɪˌkʌlɚd, 'ver-, 'vær-; ES
  -ˌkʌləd
varicose 'værɪˌkos, 'vɛrɪ- |-d -t
varicosis ˌværɪ'kosɪs
variegate 'vɛrɪˌget, 'ver-, 'vær- |-d -ɪd
variegation ˌvɛrɪ'geʃən, ˌver-, ˌvær-
variety və'raɪətɪ |-tal -tl̩ |-tally -tl̩ɪ
variola və'raɪələ
varioloid ˌvɛrɪə'lɔɪd, ˌver-, ˌvær-
variorum ˌvɛrɪ'orəm, ˌver-, ˌvær-, -'ɔrəm; S
  -'orəm
various 'vɛrɪəs, 'ver-, 'vær-
varlet 'varlɪt; ES 'va:lɪt, E+'va:l-; |-ry -rɪ
varment, -mint 'varmənt; ES 'va:mənt, E+
  'va:m-
Varney 'varnɪ; ES 'va:nɪ, E+'va:nɪ
varnish 'varnɪʃ; ES 'va:n-, E+'va:n-; |-es -ɪz
Varrius 'værɪəs |-'s -ɪz
Varro 'væro
varsity 'varsətɪ, 'varstɪ; ES 'va:s-, E+'va:s-

Varuna ˈværunə, ˈvʌr-

vary ˈvɛrɪ, ˈvɛːrɪ, ˈvɛrɪ, ˈværɪ |-ried -rɪd— *Some speakers distinguish* vary *from* very *by a longer* ɛ (§55).

vascular ˈvæskjələ˞; ES ˈvæskjələ(r

vase ves, *much less freq.* vez, (*Brit* vɑz) |-s -ɪz

vaseline ˈvæsḷˌin, -ɪn

vassal ˈvæsḷ |-ed -d

vast væst; E+vast, vɑst; |-ity -ətɪ

vat væt

Vatican ˈvætɪkən

vaudeville ˈvodəˌvɪl, ˈvodv-, ˈvɔdəˌvɪl (*Fr* vodˈvil)

Vaughan, -ghn vɔn

vault vɔlt |-ed -ɪd

vaunt vɔnt, vɒnt, vant |-ed -ɪd

Vaux *Eng name* vɔks |-ʾs -ɪz, *Fr vil.* vo

Vauxhall ˈvɑksˈhɔl; ES+ˈvɒks-; (ˈVauxˌhall ˈGardens)

vavasour ˈvævəˌsur; ES -ˌsuə(r

vaward ˈvɔwə˞d; ES ˈvɔwəd

ʾve *abbr. spelling of unstressed* have v, *as in* Iʾve ɑɪv, youʾve ˈjuv, juv, weʾve ˈwiv, wɪv, theyʾve ðev

veal vil |vealed vild

vector ˈvɛktə˞; ES ˈvɛktə(r

Veda ˈvedə, ˈvidə |-dic -dɪk

vedette vəˈdɛt

vee vi

veer vɪr; ES vɪə(r; |-ed -d

Vega *star* ˈvigə, *Sp poet* ˈvegə (*Sp* ˈbega)

vegetable ˈvɛdʒtəbḷ, ˈvɛdʒətəbḷ |-tal -dʒətḷ

vegetarian ˌvɛdʒəˈtɛrɪən, -ˈter-

vegetate ˈvɛdʒəˌtet |-d -ɪd |-tive -ɪv

vegetation ˌvɛdʒəˈteʃən

vehement ˈviəmənt, ˈvihɪ- |-nce -ns

vehicle ˈviɪkḷ, ˈviəkḷ, ˈvihɪkḷ

vehicular viˈhɪkjələ˞; ES -ˈhɪkjələ(r

veil vel |veiled veld

vein ven |veined vend

velar ˈvilə˞; ES ˈvilə(r

velarize ˈviləˌrɑɪz |-s -ɪz |-d -d

Velásquez, -láz- vəˈlɑskɛθ, vəˈlæskwɪz (*Sp* beˈlaskɛθ, -ˈlaθ-) |-ʾs -kɛθs, -kwɪzɪz

veld, -dt vɛlt

vellum ˈvɛləm

velocipede vəˈlɑsəˌpid; ES+-ˈlɒs-

velocity vəˈlɑsətɪ; ES+-ˈlɒs-

velours vəˈlur; ES -ˈluə(r

velum ˈviləm

velure vəˈlur, -ˈlɪur; ES -ˈluə(r, -ˈlɪuə(r

Velutus vəˈlutəs, -ˈlɪu- |-ʾs -ɪz

velvet ˈvɛlvɪt |-ed -ɪd |-y -ɪ

venal ˈvinḷ |-nality viˈnælətɪ

venation viˈneʃən

vend vɛnd |-ed -ɪd |-ee vɛnˈdi

vender ˈvɛndə˞; ES ˈvɛndə(r

vendetta vɛnˈdɛtə |-s -z

vendibility ˌvɛndəˈbɪlətɪ

vendible ˈvɛndəbḷ |-bly -blɪ

vendition vɛnˈdɪʃən

vendor ˈvɛndə˞; ES -də(r; (vɛnˈdi ən vɛnˈdɔr)

vendue vɛnˈdju, -ˈdɪu, -ˈdu

veneer vəˈnɪr; ES -ˈnɪə(r; |-ed -d

venerability ˌvɛnərəˈbɪlətɪ

venerable ˈvɛnərəbḷ, -nrə- |-bly -blɪ

venerate ˈvɛnəˌret |-d -ɪd |-tion ˌvɛnəˈreʃən

venereal vəˈnɪrɪəl

venery ˈvɛnərɪ

Venetian vəˈniʃən—*The old variant* vəˈnɪʃən *is still heard, spelt* Venicyan, Venitian *15–19cc; cf OF* Venicien, *Fr* Vénitien.

Venezuela ˌvɛnəˈzwilə |-n -n (*Am Sp* ˌbeneˈswela)

venge vɛndʒ |-s -ɪz |-d -d |-ful -fəl |-fully -fəlɪ

vengeance ˈvɛndʒəns |-s -ɪz

venial ˈvinɪəl, -njəl |-ly -ɪ

Venice ˈvɛnɪs |-ʾs -ɪz

venire facias vɪˈnɑɪriˈfeʃɪˌæs

venison ˈvɛnəzn (*Brit* ˈvɛnzn̩)

Venizelos ˌvɛnɪˈzelɑs, -lɒs, -ləs |-ʾs -ɪz

venom ˈvɛnəm |-ed -d |-ous -əs

venous ˈvinəs

vent vɛnt |-ed -ɪd

ventail ˈvɛntel

Ventidius vɛnˈtɪdɪəs, -ˈtɪdʒəs |-ʾs -ɪz

ventilate ˈvɛntḷˌet |-d -ɪd |-tor -ə˞; ES -ə(r

ventilation ˌvɛntḷˈeʃən

ventral ˈvɛntrəl |-ly -ɪ

ventricle ˈvɛntrɪkḷ

ventriloquism vɛnˈtrɪləˌkwɪzəm |-quist -kwɪst

Ventura vɛnˈturə

venture ˈvɛntʃə˞; ES -tʃə(r; |-d -d |-ring -tʃərɪŋ, -tʃrɪŋ |-rous -tʃərəs, -tʃrəs

venue ˈvɛnju, ˈvɛnɪu, ˈvɛnu

Venus ˈvinəs |-es -ɪz |-ʾs -ɪz

Vera ˈvɪrə

veracious vəˈreʃəs |-racity -ˈræsətɪ

|full fʊl |tooth tuθ |further ˈfɝðə˞; ES ˈfɝðə |custom ˈkʌstəm |while hwɑɪl |how hɑu |toy tɔɪ |using ˈjuzɪŋ |fuse fjuz, fɪuz |dish dɪʃ |vision ˈvɪʒən |Eden ˈidn̩ |cradle ˈkredḷ |keep ʾem ˈkipm̩

Veracruz, V- Cruz ˈvɛrəˈkruz |-'s -ɪz (Am Sp
ˈberaˈkrus)
veranda, -ah vəˈrændə |-daed, -dahed -dəd
verb vɝb; ES vɜb, vɝb; |-al -] |-ally -ɪ̩
verbatim vɚˈbetɪm, vɝ-; ES və-, vɜ-, vɝ-
verbena vəˈbinə; ES vəˈbinə
verbiage ˈvɝbɪɪdʒ, -bjɪdʒ; ES ˈvɜb-, ˈvɝb-
verbose ˈbos, vɝ-; ES və-, vɜ-, vɝ-;
|-bosity -ˈbɑsətɪ; ES+-ˈbɒs-
verboten fəˈbotn̩; ES fə-; (Ger fɛrˈbo:tən)
verdant ˈvɝdn̩t; ES ˈvɜd-, ˈvɝd-; |-ncy -n̩sɪ
Verde, Cape ˈkepˈvɝd; ES -ˈvɜd, -ˈvɝd
Verdi ˈvɛrdɪ; ES ˈvɛədɪ; (It ˈverdi)
verdict ˈvɝdɪkt; ES ˈvɜd-, ˈvɝd-
verdigris ˈvɝdɪˌgris; ES ˈvɜd-, ˈvɝd-
verditer ˈvɝdɪtɚ; ES ˈvɜdɪtə(r, ˈvɝdɪtə(r
Verdun vɛrˈdʌn, ˈverdən; ES vɛəˈdʌn,
ˈveədən; (Fr vɛrˈdœ̃)
verdure ˈvɝdʒɚ, -dʒur; ES ˈvɜdʒɚ(r, ˈvɝdʒə(r,
-dʒuə(r; |-rous -rəs
Vere, de dəˈvɪr; ES dəˈvɪə(r
verge vɝdʒ; ES vɜdʒ, vɝdʒ; |-s -ɪz |-d -d
verger ˈvɝdʒɚ; ES ˈvɜdʒə(r, ˈvɝdʒə(r
Verges ˈvɝdʒiz, -dʒɪz; ES ˈvɜ-, ˈvɝ-; |-ges'
-dʒiz, -dʒɪz
Vergil ˈvɝdʒəl; ES ˈvɜdʒ-, ˈvɝdʒ-
Vergilian vɚˈdʒɪlɪən, vɝ-, -ljən; ES və-, vɜ-,
vɝ-
verify ˈvɛrəˌfaɪ |-fied -ˌfaɪd |-fiable -ˌfaɪəb]
|-bly -blɪ
verily ˈvɛrəlɪ
verisimilar ˌvɛrəˈsɪmələ; ES -ˈsɪmələ(r
verisimilitude ˌvɛrəsəˈmɪləˌtjud, -ˌtɪud, -ˌtud
veritable ˈvɛrətəb] |-bly -blɪ |-ty ˈvɛrətɪ
verjuice ˈvɝˌdʒus, -ˌdʒɪus; ES ˈvɜ-, ˈvɝ-
vermeil ˈvɝm], -mɪl; ES ˈvɜ-, ˈvɝ-
vermicelli ˌvɝməˈsɛlɪ; ES ˌvɜm-, ˌvɝm-; (It
ˌvermiˈtʃɛlli)
vermiform ˈvɝməˌfɔrm; ES ˈvɜməˌfɔəm,
ˈvɝm-
vermifuge ˈvɝməˌfjudʒ, -ˌfɪudʒ; ES ˈvɜm-,
ˈvɝm-
vermilion, V- vɚˈmɪljən; ES və-
Vermillion vɚˈmɪljən; ES və-
vermin ˈvɝmɪn; ES ˈvɜmɪn, ˈvɝm-; |-ous -əs
Vermont vɚˈmɑnt, vɝ-; ES vəˈmɑnt, vɜ-,
vɝ-, -ˈmɒnt
vermouth ˈvɝmuθ, vɚˈmuθ; ES ˈvɜ-, və-,
ˈvɝ-; (Fr vɛrˈmut, Ger Wermut ˈve:rmu:t)

vernacular vɚˈnækjələ; ES vəˈnækjələ(r
vernal ˈvɝn]; ES ˈvɜn], ˈvɝ-; |-ly -ɪ
Verne vɝn; ES vɜn, vɝn; (Fr vɛrn)
Verner's law ˈvɛrnɚz ˈlɔ, ˈvɝnɚz; ES ˈvɛənəz,
ˈvɝnəz, ˈvɝnəz
vernier ˈvɝnɪɚ; ES ˈvɝnɪ·ə(r, ˈvɝnɪ·ə(r
Vernon ˈvɝnən; ES ˈvɜnən, ˈvɝnən
Verona vəˈronə (It veˈro:na)
Veronica vəˈrɑnɪkə, -ˈrɒn-
Versailles US vɚˈselz; ES və-; France vɚ-
ˈselz, vɛrˈsaɪ; ES və-, vɛə-; (Fr vɛrˈsɑ:j)
versatile ˈvɝsətɪ̩, -tɪl; ES ˈvɜs-, ˈvɝs-
versatility ˌvɝsəˈtɪlətɪ; ES ˌvɜs-, ˌvɝs-
verse vɝs; ES vɜs, vɝs; |-s -ɪz |-d -t
versicle ˈvɝsɪk]; ES ˈvɜs-, ˈvɝs-
versicolor ˈvɝsɪˌkʌlɚ; ES ˈvɜsɪˌkʌlə(r, ˈvɝs-
versification ˌvɝsəfəˈkeʃən; ES ˌvɜs-, ˌvɝs-
versify ˈvɝsəˌfaɪ; ES ˈvɜs-, ˈvɝs-; |-fied -ˌfaɪd
version ˈvɝʒən, ˈvɝʃən; ES ˈvɜ-, ˈvɝ-
verso ˈvɝso; ES ˈvɜso, ˈvɝso
verst vɝst; ES vɜst, vɝst
versus ˈvɝsəs; ES ˈvɜs-, ˈvɝs-
vertebra ˈvɝtəbrə; ES ˈvɜt-, ˈvɝt-; |-brae
-ˌbri |-bras -brəz |-brate -ˌbret
vertex ˈvɝtɛks; ES ˈvɜ-, ˈvɝ-; |-s -ɪz |-tices
-təˌsiz
vertical ˈvɝtɪk]; ES ˈvɜt-, ˈvɝt-; |-ly -ɪ, -ɪklɪ
vertiginous vɝˈtɪdʒənəs; ES vɜ-, vɝ-
vertigo ˈvɝtɪˌgo; ES ˈvɜt-, ˈvɝt-; |-s -z,
as L vɚˈtaɪgo |-tigines vɚˈtɪdʒəˌniz; ES və-
vertu vɝˈtu; ES vɜ-, vɝ-; (It verˈtu:)
Verulam ˈvɛrʊləm, ˈvɛrələm
vervain ˈvɝven; ES ˈvɜven, ˈvɝ-
verve vɝv; ES vɜv, vɝv
very ˈvɛrɪ—Some educated Americans often
pronounce very almost like ˈvɝɪ, but no one
regards it as standard.
vesicle ˈvɛsɪk]
Vespasian vɛsˈpeʒɪən, -ʒən
vesper ˈvɛspɚ; ES ˈvɛspə(r
Vespucci vɛsˈputʃɪ (It vesˈputtʃi)
vessel ˈvɛs] |vesseled ˈvɛs]d
vest vɛst |vested ˈvɛstɪd
Vesta ˈvɛstə |vestal ˈvɛst]
vestee vɛsˈti
vestibule ˈvɛstəˌbjul, -ˌbɪul |-d -d
vestige ˈvɛstɪdʒ |-s -ɪz
vestigial vɛsˈtɪdʒɪəl |-ly -ɪ
vestment ˈvɛstmənt |-ed -ɪd

vestry 'vɛstrɪ
vesture 'vɛstʃɚ; ES -tʃə(r; |-d -d
vesuvian, V- və'suvɪən, -'sɪu-, -'sju- |-ius
-ɪəs, -vjəs |-ius's -əsɪz
vet vɛt |vetted 'vɛtɪd
vetch vɛtʃ |vetches 'vɛtʃɪz
veteran 'vɛtərən, 'vɛtrən
veterinarian ˌvɛtrə'nɛrɪən, -tərə-, -'ner-
veterinary 'vɛtrəˌnɛrɪ, 'vɛtərəˌnɛrɪ
veto 'vito |vetoed 'vitod
vex vɛks |vexes 'vɛksɪz |-ed -t |-edly -ɪdlɪ
vexation vɛks'eʃən |-tious -ʃəs
via 'vaɪə
viable 'vaɪəbl̩
viaduct 'vaɪəˌdʌkt
vial 'vaɪəl, vaɪl
viand 'vaɪənd
viaticum vaɪ'ætɪkəm |-s -z |-ca -kə
vibrant 'vaɪbrənt |-ncy -nsɪ
vibrate 'vaɪbret |-d -ɪd |-tor -ɚ; ES -ə(r
vibration vaɪ'breʃən |-tive 'vaɪbrətɪv, -bre-
vibrato vi'brɑto
vibratory 'vaɪbrəˌtorɪ, -ˌtɔrɪ; S -ˌtorɪ
viburnum, V- vaɪ'bɝnəm; ES -'bɜn-, -'bɝn-
vicar 'vɪkɚ; ES 'vɪkə(r
vicarial vaɪ'kɛrɪəl, vɪ-, -'ker- |-ious -ɪəs
vice n vaɪs |vices 'vaɪsɪz
vice prep 'vaɪsɪ, -si
vice-admiral 'vaɪs'ædmərəl |-ty -tɪ
vice-chancellor 'vaɪs'tʃænsələ, -slɚ; ES -lə(r;
|-ship -ˌʃɪp
vice-consul 'vaɪs'kɑnsl̩; ES+-'kɒn-; |-ar -ɚ,
-sjələ; ES -ə(r; |-ate -ɪt |-ship -ˌʃɪp
vicegerent vaɪs'dʒɪrənt |-ncy -nsɪ |-ship -ˌʃɪp
vice-governor 'vaɪs'gʌvənɚ, -vnɚ, -'gʌvɚnɚ;
ES -'gʌvənə(r, -vnə(r; |-ship -ˌʃɪp—
'gʌvɚnɚ becomes 'gʌvənɚ by dissimilation
(§121).
vicennial vaɪ'sɛnɪəl |-ly -ɪ
vice-president 'vaɪs'prɛzədənt, -'prɛzdənt
|-ncy -nsɪ |-ship -ˌʃɪp
viceregal vaɪs'rigl̩ |-ly -ɪ
vice-regent 'vaɪs'ridʒənt |-ncy -nsɪ
viceroy 'vaɪsrɔɪ |-ship -ˌʃɪp
viceroyal vaɪs'rɔɪəl, -'rɔjəl |-ty -tɪ
vice versa 'vaɪsɪ'vɝsə; ES -'vɜsə, -'vɝsə
Vichy 'viʃɪ, 'vɪʃɪ (Fr vi'ʃi)
vicinage 'vɪsn̩ɪdʒ |-nal -sn̩əl, -sənl̩
vicinity və'sɪnətɪ

vicious 'vɪʃəs
vicissitude və'sɪsəˌtjud, -ˌtrud, -ˌtud
Vicksburg 'vɪksbɝg; ES -bɜg, -bɝg
victim 'vɪktɪm |-ize -ˌaɪz |-izes -ˌaɪzɪz |-ized
-ˌaɪzd
victor 'vɪktɚ; ES 'vɪktə(r
Victoria, v- vɪk'torɪə, -'tɔr-, -rjə; S -'tor-;
|-n -n |-ious -ɪəs, -rjəs
victory 'vɪktrɪ, 'vɪktərɪ
victress 'vɪktrɪs |-es -ɪz
Victrola vɪk'trolə
victual 'vɪtl̩ |victuals 'vɪtl̩z (vittle 1575)
vicuna vɪ'kjunə, -'kɪunə (Sp bi'kuna)
Vida first name 'vaɪdə, 'vidə; It poet 'vidə
(It 'vi:dɑ)
vide 'see' 'vaɪdɪ
videlicet, abbr. viz. vɪ'dɛləsɪt, vɪz
vie vaɪ |vied vaɪd |vying 'vaɪɪŋ
Vienna vɪ'ɛnə |-nese ˌvɪə'niz
view vju, vɪu |-ed -d |-point -ˌpɔɪnt
vigesimal vaɪ'dʒɛsəml̩
vigil 'vɪdʒəl
vigilant 'vɪdʒələnt |-lance -ləns
vigilante ˌvɪdʒə'læntɪ
vigor 'vɪgɚ; ES 'vɪgə(r; |-ous -əs
viking, V- 'vaɪkɪŋ
vile vaɪl |vilely 'vaɪllɪ
vilification ˌvɪləfə'keʃən
vilify 'vɪləˌfaɪ |-fied -ˌfaɪd
vill vɪl |villa 'vɪlə
village 'vɪlɪdʒ |-s -ɪz |-d -d
villain 'vɪlən |-ous -əs |-y -ɪ
villanage, -ain-, -en-, -ein- 'vɪlənɪdʒ
villein 'vɪlɪn
Villiers 'vɪlɚz, 'vɪljɚz; ES 'vɪləz, -ljəz
villous 'vɪləs
Vilna 'vɪlnə
vim vɪm
vinaigrette ˌvɪnə'grɛt |-d -ɪd
Vincennes US vɪn'sɛnz |-'s -ɪz |France Fr
væ̃'sɛn
Vincent 'vɪnsn̩t
Vincentio vɪn'sɛnʃɪˌo, -ʃjo
Vinci, Leonardo da ˌliə'nɑrdo də'vɪntʃɪ; ES
-'nɑ:do; (It ˌleo'nɑrdo dɑ'vɪntʃi)
vincible 'vɪnsəbl̩ |-bly -blɪ
vindicability ˌvɪndəkə'bɪlətɪ
vindicable 'vɪndəkəbl̩ |-bly -blɪ

vindicate 'vɪndəˌket |-d -ɪd |-tor -ɚ; ES -ə(r
vindication ˌvɪndə'keʃən
vindicative 'vɪndəˌketɪv, vɪn'dɪkətɪv
vindicatory 'vɪndəkəˌtorɪ, -ˌtɔrɪ; S -ˌtɔrɪ
vindictive vɪn'dɪktɪv
vine vaɪn |vined vaɪnd
vinegar 'vɪnɪgɚ; ES -gə(r; |-y -ɪ, -grɪ
vineyard 'vɪnjɚd; ES 'vɪnjəd
viniculture 'vɪnɪˌkʌltʃɚ; ES -ˌkʌltʃə(r
vinous 'vaɪnəs |-nosity vaɪ'nɑsətɪ; ES+-'nɒs-
vintage 'vɪntɪdʒ |-s -ɪz |-d -d
vintner 'vɪntnɚ; ES 'vɪntnə(r
viny 'vaɪnɪ
viol 'vaɪəl, vaɪl
viola mus. instr. vɪ'olə, 'vaɪələ (It vi'ɔːla)
viola flower 'vaɪələ
Viola name 'vaɪələ, vaɪ'olə, in Shak. 'vaɪələ
violable 'vaɪələbḷ |-bly -blɪ
violate 'vaɪəˌlet |-d -ɪd |-tion ˌvaɪə'leʃən
violent 'vaɪələnt |-nce -ns |-nces -nsɪz
Violenta ˌvaɪə'lɛntə
violet 'vaɪəlɪt
violin ˌvaɪə'lɪn |-ed -d
violine, -lin chem. 'vaɪəˌlin, -lɪn
violinist ˌvaɪə'lɪnɪst
violoncellist ˌviəlɑn'tʃɛlɪst, ˌvaɪələn'sɛlɪst;
ES+-lɒn-; |-llo -lo (It ˌviolon'tʃɛllo)
viper 'vaɪpɚ; ES 'vaɪpə(r; |-ous -əs, -prəs
virago və'rego, vaɪ'rego
virelay 'vɪrəˌle
vireo 'vɪrɪˌo
virgate n, adj 'vɚgɪt, -get; ES 'vɜ-, 'vɝ-
virgate v 'vɚget; ES 'vɜ-, 'vɝ-; |-d -ɪd
Virgil 'vɚdʒəl; ES 'vɜdʒ-, 'vɝdʒ-
Virgilia vɚ'dʒɪlɪə, vɝ-; ES və-, vɜ-, vɝ-;
|-n -n
virgin 'vɚdʒɪn; ES 'vɜ-, 'vɝ-; |-ed -d |-al -ḷ
|-ally -ḷɪ
Virginia vɚ'dʒɪnjə, esp. N Engd -'dʒɪnɪə; ES
və-; |-n -n
Virgin Islands 'vɚdʒɪn'aɪləndz; ES 'vɜdʒ-,
'vɝdʒ-
virginity vɚ'dʒɪnətɪ; ES və-
Virgo 'vɚgo, gen 'vɚdʒɪnɪs; ES 'vɜ-, 'vɝ-
virgule 'vɚgjul; ES 'vɜg- 'vɝg-
viridescent ˌvɪrə'dɛsn̩t |-nce -ns
viridity və'rɪdətɪ
virile 'vɪrəl, 'vaɪrəl |-rility və'rɪlətɪ, vɪ-
virtu vɝ'tu; ES vɜ-, vɝ-; (It vir'tu:)

virtual 'vɚtʃuəl; ES 'vɜ-, 'vɝ-; |-ly -ɪ
virtue 'vɚtʃu; ES 'vɜ-, 'vɝ-; |-tuous -tʃuəs
virtuosity ˌvɚtʃu'ɑsətɪ; ES ˌvɜtʃu'ɑsətɪ,
-'ɒs-, ˌvɝ-
virtuoso ˌvɚtʃu'oso; ES ˌvɜ-, ˌvɝ-; (It
ˌvirtu'oːso)
virulent 'vɪrjələnt, 'vɪrulənt, 'vɪrə- |-nce -ns
virus 'vaɪrəs |viruses 'vaɪrəsɪz
visa n 'vizə |pl visas 'vizəz=visé
visa v 'vizə |visas 'vizəz |visaed 'vizəd=visé
visage 'vɪzɪdʒ |-s -ɪz |-d -d
visard 'vɪzɚd; ES 'vɪzəd; |-ed -ɪd=vizard
vis-à-vis ˌvizə'vi |pl same (Fr viza'vi)
Visayan vi'sajən
viscera 'vɪsərə |rare sg viscus 'vɪskəs
viscid 'vɪsɪd |viscidity vɪ'sɪdətɪ
viscose 'vɪskos |viscous 'vɪskəs
viscosity vɪs'kɑsətɪ; ES+-'kɒs-
viscount 'vaɪkaunt |-ess -ɪs |-ess's -ɪsɪz
vise vaɪs |-s -ɪz |-d -t
visé n 'vize |pl visés 'vizez=visa
visé v 'vize |visés 'vizez |viséed 'vized=visa
visibility ˌvɪzə'bɪlətɪ
visible 'vɪzəbḷ |-bly -blɪ
Visigoth 'vɪzɪˌgɑθ, -ˌgɒθ, -ˌgɔθ
vision 'vɪʒən |-ary -ˌɛrɪ
visit 'vɪzɪt |-ed -ɪd |-or -ɚ; ES -ə(r
visitant 'vɪzətənt |-itation ˌvɪzə'teʃən
visor 'vaɪzɚ, much less freq. 'vɪzɚ; ES -zə(r;
|-ed -d
vista 'vɪstə
Vistula 'vɪstʃulə
visual 'vɪʒuəl |-ly -ɪ
visualize 'vɪʒuəlˌaɪz |-s -ɪz |-d -d
vital 'vaɪtḷ |-ly -ɪ |-tality vaɪ'tælətɪ
vitals 'vaɪtḷz
vitamin 'vaɪtəmɪn |vitamine 'vaɪtəˌmaɪn,
-mɪn
vitiate 'vɪʃɪˌet |-d -ɪd |-iable 'vɪʃɪəbḷ
viticulture 'vɪtɪˌkʌltʃɚ; ES -ˌkʌltʃə(r
vitreous 'vɪtrɪəs
vitrescent vɪ'trɛsn̩t |-nce -ns |-ncy -n̩sɪ
vitric 'vɪtrɪk
vitrify 'vɪtrəˌfaɪ |-fied -ˌfaɪd
vitriol 'vɪtrɪəl |-ed -d
vitriolic ˌvɪtrɪ'ɑlɪk; ES+-'ɒl-
vituperate vaɪ'tupəˌret, vɪ-, -'tɪu-, -'tju- |-d
-ɪd
vituperation vaɪˌtupə'reʃən, vɪ-, -ˌtɪu, -ˌtju-

Vitus ˈvaɪtəs |-ˈs -ɪz
viva *'long live!'* ˈvivə (*It* ˈviːvɑ)
vivace viˈvɑtʃɪ (*It* viˈvɑːtʃe)
vivacious vaɪˈveʃəs |-vacity -ˈvæsətɪ
vivarium vaɪˈvɛrɪəm, -ˈver- |-s -z |-ia -ɪə
viva-voce ˈvaɪvəˈvosɪ |-d -d
Vivian, -en ˈvɪvɪən, -vjən
vivid ˈvɪvɪd
vivification ˌvɪvəfəˈkeʃən
vivify ˈvɪvəˌfaɪ |-fied -ˌfaɪd
viviparous vaɪˈvɪpərəs
vivisect ˌvɪvəˈsɛkt |-ed -ɪd |-section -ˈsɛkʃən
vixen ˈvɪksn̩
viz. vɪz, vɪˈdɛləsɪt
vizard *arch. var. of* visor ˈvɪzɚd; ES ˈvɪzəd
vizier vɪˈzɪr, ˈvɪzjɚ, ˈvɪzɪɚ; ES vɪˈzɪə(r,
ˈvɪzjə(r, ˈvɪzɪ·ə(r
vizor ˈvaɪzɚ, ˈvɪz-; ES -zə(r; |-ed -d, *cf* visor
Vladivostok ˌvlædɪˈvɑstɑk; ES+-ˈvɒstɒk
vocable ˈvokəbl̩ |-bly -blɪ
vocabulary vəˈkæbjəˌlɛrɪ, vo-
vocal ˈvokl̩ |-ly -ɪ
vocalic voˈkælɪk
vocalize ˈvokl̩ˌaɪz |-s -ɪz |-d -d
vocation voˈkeʃən
vocative ˈvɑkətɪv, ˈvɑkɪ-; ES+ˈvɒk-
vociferate voˈsɪfəˌret |-d -ɪd |-rous -rəs
vodka ˈvɑdkə, ˈvɒdkə
vogue vog |vogued vogd
voice vɔɪs |-s -ɪz |-d -t
void vɔɪd |-ed -ɪd |-able -əbl̩ |-ance -n̩s
voile vɔɪl (*Fr* vwal)
volant ˈvolənt
Volapük, -puk ˌvoləˈpyk, ˈvaləˌpʊk, ˈvɒl-
|-ism -ˌɪzəm |-ist -ɪst
volatile ˈvɑlətl̩, -tɪl; ES+ˈvɒl-; |-ly -lɪ
volatility ˌvɑləˈtɪlətɪ; ES+ˌvɒl-
volcanic vɑlˈkænɪk; ES+vɒl-; |-ally -l̩ɪ, -ɪklɪ
volcano vɑlˈkeno; ES+vɒl-
volcanology ˌvɑlkənˈɑlədʒɪ; ES+ˌvɒlkən-
ˈɒlədʒɪ
vole vol |-d -d
volery ˈvɑlərɪ; ES+ˈvɒl-
Volga ˈvɑlgə, ˈvɒlgə
volition voˈlɪʃən |-al -l̩ |-ally -l̩ɪ
volitive ˈvɑlətɪv; ES+ˈvɒl-
Volkslied *Ger* ˈfɔlksˌliːt |*pl* -lieder -ˌliːdər
volley ˈvɑlɪ; ES+ˈvɒlɪ; |-ed -d |-ball -ˌbɔl
volplane ˈvɑlˌplen; ES+ˈvɒl-; |-d -d

Volpone vɑlˈponɪ, vɒl-
Volscian ˈvɑlʃən, ˈvɒl-, -ʃɪən |-s -z
Volstead ˈvɑlstɛd, -stɪd, ˈvɒl-
Volsunga Saga ˈvɑlsʊŋgəˌsɑgə, ˈvɒl-
volt volt |-age -ɪdʒ |-ages -ɪdʒɪz
voltaic vɑlˈte·ɪk; ES+vɒl-
Voltaire vɑlˈtɛr, vɒl-, -ˈtær; E -ˈtɛə(r, ES
-ˈtæə(r; (*Fr* vɔlˈtɛːr) |-rean, -rian -ɪən
voltameter vɑlˈtæmətɚ; ES -ˈtæmətə(r, vɒl-
voltammeter ˈvoltˈæmˌmitɚ; ES -ˌmitə(r
volte-face ˈvɑltˌfas, ˈvɑltə-, ˈvɒl- (*Fr* vɔltə-
ˈfas)
Voltemand, -ti- ˈvɑltəˌmænd, ˈvɒl-
voltmeter ˈvoltˌmitɚ; ES -ˌmitə(r
volubility ˌvɑljəˈbɪlətɪ; ES+ˌvɒl-
voluble ˈvɑljəbl̩; ES+ˈvɒl-; |-bly -blɪ
volume ˈvɑljəm; ES+ˈvɒl-; |-d -d
volumeter vəˈlumətɚ, -ˈlɪu-, vəlˈju-, vɑlˈju-;
ES -tə(r, vɒl-
volumetric ˌvɑljəˈmɛtrɪk; ES+ˌvɒl-; |-al -l̩
|-ally -l̩ɪ, -ɪklɪ
voluminous vəˈlumənəs, vəˈlɪu-
Volumnia vəˈlʌmnɪə, -njə |-ius -s |-ius's -sɪz
voluntary ˈvɑlənˌtɛrɪ; ES+ˈvɒl-; |-rily -rəlɪ,
esp. if emph. ˌvɑlənˈtɛrɪlɪ
volunteer ˌvɑlənˈtɪr; ES -ˈtɪə(r, ˌvɒl-, S+
-ˈtɛə(r
voluptuary vəˈlʌptʃuˌɛrɪ |-tuous -tʃuəs
volute vəˈlut, vəˈlɪut |-d -ɪd
vomit ˈvɑmɪt; ES+ˈvɒm-; |-ed -ɪd
voodoo ˈvudu |-ed -d
voracious voˈreʃəs
vortex ˈvɔrtɛks; ES ˈvɔətɛks; |-es -ɪz -tices
-tɪˌsiz
vortical ˈvɔrtɪkl̩; ES ˈvɔə-; |-ly -ɪ
vortiginous vɔrˈtɪdʒənəs; ES vɔ-
Vosges voʒ |Vosgian, -gean ˈvoʒɪən |-ˈs -ɪz
votaress, -tress ˈvotərɪs, ˈvotrɪs |-es -ɪz
votary ˈvotərɪ
vote vot |voted ˈvotɪd
votive ˈvotɪv
vouch vautʃ |-es -ɪz |-ed -t
voucher ˈvautʃɚ; ES ˈvautʃə(r
vouchsafe vautʃˈsef |-s -s |-d -t
vow vau |vowed vaud
vowel ˈvauəl, vaul, ˈvauɪl |-ed -d |-like -ˌlaɪk
vox vaks, vɒks |voces ˈvosiz
voyage ˈvɔɪ·ɪdʒ, ˈvɔjɪdʒ |-s -ɪz |-d -d
voyager ˈvɔɪ·ɪdʒɚ, ˈvɔjɪdʒɚ; ES -ə(r

---

full fʊl |tooth tuθ |further ˈfɝðɚ; ES ˈfɜðə |custom ˈkʌstəm |while hwaɪl |how hau |toy tɔɪ
|using ˈjuzɪŋ |fuse fjuz, fɪuz |dish dɪʃ |vision ˈvɪʒən |Eden ˈidn̩ |cradle ˈkredl̩ |keep 'em ˈkipm̩

voyageur *Fr* vwaja'ʒœːr
vraisemblance *Fr* vrɛsã'blãːs
Vriesland 'frizlənd, -ˌlænd
Vulcan 'vʌlkən |-canian vʌl'kenɪən
vulcanite 'vʌlkənˌaɪt
vulcanize 'vʌlkənˌaɪz |-s -ɪz |-d -d
vulcanology ˌvʌlkən'alədʒɪ; ES+-'ɒl-
vulgar 'vʌlgɚ; ES 'vʌlgə(r; |-ism -ˌɪzəm
vulgarian vʌl'gɛrɪən, -'gær-, -'ger-

vulgarity vʌl'gærətɪ
vulgarize 'vʌlgəˌraɪz |-s -ɪz |-d -d
Vulgate 'vʌlget, -gɪt
vulnerable 'vʌlnərəbļ |-bly -blɪ
Vulpecula vʌl'pɛkjʊlə |-lid -lɪd
vulpine 'vʌlpaɪn
vulture 'vʌltʃɚ; ES 'vʌltʃə(r
vulva 'vʌlvə
vying *ptc of* vie 'vaɪɪŋ

W

W, w *letter* 'dʌb·lju, 'dʌbļjʊ, 'dʌbjʊ |*pl* W's,
Ws, *poss* W's 'dʌb·ljʊz, 'dʌbļjʊz, 'dʌbjʊz
Wabash 'wɔbæʃ |-'s -ɪz
wabble 'wabļ, 'wɒb- |-d -d |-ling -blɪŋ, -bļɪŋ
|-bly -blɪ, -bļɪ
Wace *Eng dean* wes, *Norm poet* wes, wæs,
was
Waco 'weko
wad wad, wɒd |-ded -ɪd
waddle 'wadļ, 'wɒdļ |-d -d |-ling -dlɪŋ, -dļɪŋ
wade wed |waded 'wedɪd
Wadsworth 'wadzwɚθ, 'wɒd-; ES -wəθ
wafer 'wefɚ; ES 'wefə(r; |-ed -d |-ing
'wefərɪŋ, 'wefrɪŋ
waffle wafļ, 'wɒfļ, 'wɔfļ
waft wæft, waft, waft |-ed -ɪd
wafture 'wæftʃɚ, 'waf-, 'wɔf-; ES -tʃə(r
wag wæg |wagged wægd
wage wedʒ |wages 'wedʒɪz |waged wedʒd
wager 'wedʒɚ; ES 'wedʒə(r; |-ed -d |-ing
'wedʒərɪŋ, 'wedʒrɪŋ
waggery 'wægərɪ
waggle 'wægļ |-d -d |-ling 'wæglɪŋ, 'wægļɪŋ
Wagner *Eng name* 'wægnɚ, *Ger musician*
'wægnɚ, 'vagnɚ; ES -nə(r; (*Ger* 'vaːgnər)
Wagnerian wæg'nɪrɪən, vag-
wagon 'wægən, 'wægŋ |-ed -d
wagonette ˌwægən'ɛt
wagon-lit *Fr* vagõ'li
Wagram *Ger* 'vaːgram
Wagstaff 'wægˌstæf; E+-ˌstaf, -ˌstaf
wagtail 'wægˌtel
Wahabi, Wahh-, -bee wa'habɪ, wə-
Wahr, *George* wɔr; ES wɔə(r
waif wef |waifed weft

Waikiki 'waɪˌkiki
wail wel |wailed weld |-ful -fəl |-fully -fəlɪ
wain wen
wainscot 'wenskət, -ˌskat, -ˌskot; ES+-ˌskɒt;
|-ed -ɪd |-ing -ɪŋ
wainwright, W- 'wenˌraɪt
waist west |waisted 'westɪd
waistband 'westˌbænd, 'wes-, -bənd
waistcloth 'westˌklɔθ, -ˌklɒθ—*see* cloth
waistcoat 'westˌkot, 'wesˌkot, 'wɛskət |-ed -ɪd
waistline 'westˌlaɪn
wait wet |-ed -ɪd |-er -ɚ; ES -ə(r; |-ress -rɪs
waive wev |waived wevd |waiver 'wevɚ; ES
-ə(r
wake wek |*past* waked wekt *or* woke wok
|*pptc* waked wekt, *rarely* woken 'wokən
Wakefield 'wekˌfild
wakeful 'wekfəl |-ly -ɪ
Wake Island 'wek 'aɪlənd
wakeless 'weklɪs
waken wekən |-ed -d |-ing 'wekənɪŋ, 'weknɪŋ
wake-robin 'wekˌrabɪn; ES+-ˌrɒbɪn
Walden 'wɔldən, -dɪn
Waldenses wal'dɛnsiz, wɒl-
Waldo 'wɔldo
Waldoboro 'wɔldəˌbɝo, -ə; ES -ˌbɝr-, -ˌbʌr-,
-ˌbɝ-
Waldorf 'wɔldɔrf; ES -dɔəf
wale wel |waled weld
Wales welz |Wales's 'welzɪz
Walhalla wæl'hælə, væl'hælə
walk wɔk |walked wɔkt
walkaway 'wɔkəˌwe
walker, W- 'wɔkɚ; ES 'wɔkə(r
walkout 'wɔkˌaʊt

Key: See in full §§3–47. bee bi |pity 'pɪtɪ (§6) |rate ret |yet jɛt |sang sæŋ |angry 'æŋ·grɪ
|bath bæθ; E baθ (§10) |ah a |far far |watch watʃ, wɒtʃ (§12) |jaw dʒɔ |gorge gɔrdʒ |go go

walkover ˈwɔkˌovɚ; ES -ˌovə(r
walk-up ˈwɔkˌʌp
Walküre, Die Ger di valˈkyːrə
Walkyrie wælˈkırı, væl-
wall wɔl |walled wɔld
wallaby ˈwaləbı, ˈwɒl-
Wallace ˈwɔlıs, ˈwɒl-, ˈwal- |-ʼs -ız
Wallachia waˈlekıə, wɒ-
wallah, -la ˈwalə, ˈwɒlə
Walla Walla ˈwalaˈwalə, ˈwɒləˈwɒlə
Wallenstein ˈwalənˌstaın, ˈwɒl- (Ger ˈvalən-
ˌʃtaın)
Waller ˈwɔlɚ, ˈwɒlɚ, ˈwalɚ; ES -ə(r
wallet ˈwalıt, ˈwɒlıt, ˈwɔlıt
walleye ˈwɔlˌaı |-d -d
wallflower ˈwɔlˌflauɚ, -ˌflaur; ES -ˌflau·ə(r,
-ˌflauə(r
Wallingford ˈwɔlıŋfɚd, ˈwɒl-, ˈwal-; ES -fəd
Walloon waˈlun, wɒ-, wə-
wallop ˈwaləp, ˈwɒləp |-ed -t
wallow ˈwalo, ˈwɒlo, -lə |-ed -d |-ing -ləwıŋ
wallpaper ˈwɔlˌpepɚ; ES -ˌpepə(r
walnut ˈwɔlnət, ˈwɒl-, -ˌnʌt
Walpole ˈwɔlˌpol
walrus ˈwɔlrəs, ˈwal-, ˈwɒl- |-es -ız
Walsh wɔlʃ, walʃ, wɒlʃ |-ʼs -ız
Walsingham ˈwɔlsıŋəm, ˈwal-, ˈwɒl-
Walter ˈwɔltɚ; ES ˈwɔltə(r
Waltham Engd ˈwɔltəm, -lθəm; Mass
ˈwɔlθæm, -θəm—Waltham was at first
ˈwaldˌham, then ˈwaltˌham, ˈwaltəm,
ˈwɔltəm—The h sound was lost long ago, and
the letters -th- wrongly taken to represent θ.
Now the error is established, both in America
and England.
Walthamstow Engd ˈwɔlθəmˌsto, ˈwɔltəm-
Walton ˈwɔltn̩
waltz wɔlts |-es -ız |-ed -t
Walworth ˈwɔlwɚθ; ES -wɚθ
Wampanoag ˌwampəˈnoæg, ˌwɒm-
wampum ˈwampəm, ˈwɒmpəm, ˈwɔmpəm
wampus ˈwampəs, ˈwɒm-, ˈwɔm- |-es -ız
wamus, wamm- ˈwaməs, ˈwɒm-, ˈwam- |-es
-ız
wan wan, wɒn |-ned -d
Wanamaker ˈwanəˌmekɚ, ˈwɒn-; ES -ˌmekə(r
wand wand, wɒnd
wander ˈwandɚ, ˈwɒndɚ; ES -də(r; |-ed -d
|-ing -drıŋ, -dərıŋ

wanderlust ˈwandɚˌlʌst, ˈwɒn- (Ger ˈvandər-
ˌlust)
wane wen |waned wend
wangle ˈwæŋgl̩ |-d -d |-ling ˈwæŋglıŋ, -gl̩ıŋ
Wannamaker ˈwanəˌmekɚ, ˈwɒn-; ES
-ˌmekə(r
wanness ˈwannıs, ˈwɒn-
want want, wɔnt, wɒnt; S wɔnt, wɒnt, want;
|-ed -ıd |want to often ˈwantə
wantage ˈwantıdʒ etc. see want
Wantage ˈwantıdʒ, ˈwɒn-
wanton ˈwantən, ˈwɒntən |-ness -tənnıs
Wapakoneta ˌwapəkəˈnɛtə, ˌwɒpə-
Wapello wəˈpɛlo, wa-, wɒ-
wapentake ˈwapənˌtek, ˈwɒp-, ˈwæp-
wapiti ˈwapətı, ˈwɒp-
war wɔr; ES wɔə(r; |-red -d
Warbeck ˈwɔrbɛk; ES ˈwɔəbɛk
warble ˈwɔrbl̩; ES ˈwɔəbl̩; |-d -d |-ling -blıŋ,
-bl̩ıŋ |-bler -blɚ; ES -blə(r
Warburton ˈwɔrbɚtn̩; ES ˈwɔəbətn̩
ward, W- wɔrd; ES wɔəd; |-ed -ıd |-en -n̩
|-er -ɚ; ES -ə(r; |-ress -rıs |-ship -ʃıp
wardrobe ˈwɔrdˌrob; ES ˈwɔədˌrob
wardroom ˈwɔrdˌrum, -ˌrum; ES ˈwɔəd-
ware, W- wɛr, wær; E wɛə(r, ES wæə(r
Wareham ˈwɛrəm, ˈwær-; S ˈwær-; Mass
loc.+ˈwæəhæm
warehouse n ˈwɛrˌhaus, ˈwær- |-ses -zız; ES
see ware
warehouse v ˈwɛrˌhauz, ˈwær-, -ˌhaus |-s -ız
|-d -d, -t; ES see ware
wareroom ˈwɛrˌrum, ˈwær-, -ˌrum; ES see
ware
warfare ˈwɔrˌfɛr, -ˌfær; E ˈwɔəˌfɛə(r, ES
-ˌfæə(r; |-d -d
warily ˈwɛrəlı, ˈwerəlı, ˈwærəlı—The pron.
with e is esp. freq. in the S.
warison ˈwærəsn̩
warlike ˈwɔrˌlaık; ES ˈwɔə-
warlock ˈwɔrˌlak; ES ˈwɔəˌlak, -ˌlɒk
warm wɔrm; ES wɔəm; |-ed -d
warm-blooded ˈwɔrmˈblʌdıd; ES ˈwɔəm-;
(ˈwarm-ˌblooded ˈvalor)
warmhearted ˈwɔrmˈhartıd; ES ˈwɔəm-
ˈhaːtıd, E+-ˈhaːtıd
warmth wɔrmpθ, wɔrmθ; ES wɔəm-
warn wɔrn; ES wɔən; |-ed -d
warp wɔrp; ES wɔəp; |-ed -t

|full ful |tooth tuθ |further ˈfɚˈðɚ; ES ˈfɚˈðə |custom ˈkʌstəm |while hwaıl |how hau |toy tɔı
|using ˈjuzıŋ |fuse fjuz, fıuz |dish dıʃ |vision ˈvıʒən |Eden ˈidn̩ |cradle ˈkredl̩ |keep ʼem ˈkipm̩

warpath 'wɔr‚pæθ; ES 'wɔə-, E+-‚paθ, -‚pɑθ;
|-ths -ðz

warplane 'wɔr‚plen; ES 'wɔə-

warrant 'wɔrənt, 'warənt, 'wɒrənt |-ed -ɪd

warrantee ‚wɔrən'ti, ‚war-, ‚wɒr-

warrantor 'wɔrən‚tɔr, 'war-, 'wɒr-; ES -tɔə(r;
(‚warran'tee & ‚warran'tor)

warranty 'wɔrəntɪ, 'war-, 'wɒr-

warren, W- 'wɔrɪn, 'war , 'wɒr-, -ən

Warrick 'wɔrɪk, 'warɪk, 'wɒrɪk—see Warwick

warrior 'wɔrɪɚ, 'war-, 'wɒr-, -rjɚ; ES -rɪ·ə(r,
-rjə(r

Warsaw 'wɔrsɔ; ES 'wɔəsɔ

warship 'wɔr‚ʃɪp; ES 'wɔə-

warsle 'warsl̩; ES 'wɑ:sl̩; |-d -d |-ling -slɪŋ,
-sl̩ɪŋ

wart wɔrt; ES wɔət; |-ed -ɪd

Warton 'wɔrtn̩; ES 'wɔətn̩

Warwick US 'wɔrwɪk; ES 'wɔəwɪk; less freq.
'wɔrɪk, 'warɪk, 'wɒrɪk; Engd 'wɔrɪk,
'warɪk, 'wɒrɪk

Warwickshire 'wɔrɪk‚ʃɪr, 'war-, 'wɒr-, -ʃɚ;
ES -‚ʃɪə(r, -ʃə(r

warworn 'wɔr‚wɔrn, -‚wɔrn; ES 'wɔə‚wɔən,
E+-‚wɔən

wary 'wɛrɪ, 'werɪ, 'wærɪ—The pron. with e is
esp. freq. in the S.

was stressed 'waz, ‚waz, 'wɒz, ‚wɒz; unstr.
wəz; restressed 'wʌz, ‚wʌz

wash waʃ, wɔʃ, wɒʃ |-es -ɪz |-ed -t |-able -əbl̩

washboard 'waʃ‚bord, 'wɔʃ-, 'wɒʃ-, -‚bɔrd;
ES -‚boəd, E+-‚bɔəd

washed-out 'waʃt'aut, 'wɔʃt-, 'wɒʃt-

washed-up 'waʃt'ʌp, 'wɔʃt-, 'wɒʃt- ('washed-
‚up 'look)

washer 'waʃɚ, 'wɔʃɚ, 'wɒʃɚ; ES -ʃə(r; |-man,
-men -mən |-woman -‚wumən |-women
-‚wɪmɪn—see woman

Washington 'waʃɪŋtən, 'wɔʃ-, 'wɒʃ-

Washita 'waʃɪ‚tɔ, 'wɪ‚ʃ-, ' ‚ʃ-

washrag 'waʃ‚ræg, 'wɔʃ-, 'wɒʃ-

washroom 'waʃ‚rum, 'wɔʃ-, 'wɒʃ-, -‚rum

washstand 'waʃ‚stænd, 'wɔʃ-, 'wɒʃ-

washwoman 'waʃ‚wumən, 'wɔʃ-, 'wɒʃ-
|-women -‚wɪmɪn—see woman

washy 'waʃɪ, 'wɔʃɪ, 'wɒʃɪ

wasn't 'waznt, 'wɒznt, 'wʌznt, before some
conss.+-zn̩ (ɪt 'wazn̩ gud)

wasp wasp, wɔsp, wɒsp

wassail 'wasl̩, 'wɒsl̩, 'wæsl̩, -el |-ed -d

Wasserman 'wasɚmən, 'vas-; ES -sə-; (Ger
'vasər‚man)

wast 2 sg of was, stressed 'wast, 'wɒst, ‚wast,
‚wɒst; unstr. wəst

wastage 'westɪdʒ |-s -ɪz

waste west |-d -ɪd |-ful -fəl |-fully -fəlɪ

wastebasket 'west‚bæskɪt; E+-‚bas-, -‚bɑs-

wastepaper 'west'pepɚ; ES -'pepə(r

waster 'westɚ; ES 'westə(r

wastrel 'westrəl

watch watʃ, wɒtʃ, wɔtʃ |-es -ɪz |-ed -t

watchcase 'watʃ‚kes, 'wɒtʃ-, 'wɔtʃ-

watchdog 'watʃ‚dɔg, 'wɒtʃ-, 'wɔtʃ-, -‚dɒg

watchful 'watʃfəl, 'wɒtʃ-, 'wɔtʃ- |-ly -ɪ

watchmaker 'watʃ‚mekɚ, 'wɒtʃ-, 'wɔtʃ-; ES
-‚mekə(r

watchman 'watʃmən, 'wɒtʃ-, 'wɔtʃ- |-men
-mən

watchtower 'watʃ‚tauɚ, 'wɒtʃ-, 'wɔtʃ-; ES
-‚tau·ə(r

watchword 'watʃ‚wɝd, 'wɒtʃ-, 'wɔtʃ-; ES
-‚wɜd, -‚wɝd

water 'wɔtɚ, 'watɚ, 'wɒtɚ; ES -tə(r;—The
same variants of water occur in the following
compounds and derivatives.

water-borne 'wɔtɚ‚born, -‚bɔrn; ES 'wɔtə-
‚boən, E+-‚bɔən

waterbuck 'wɔtɚ‚bʌk; ES 'wɔtə-

Waterbury 'wɔtɚ‚bɛrɪ, 'wɔtə‚bɛrɪ, -bərɪ; ES
'wɔtə-; Loss of ɚ in the second pron. is due
to dissimilation (§121).

watercourse 'wɔtɚ‚kors, -‚kɔrs; ES 'wɔtə-
‚koəs, E+-‚kɔəs; |-s -ɪz

watercraft 'wɔtɚ‚kræft; ES 'wɔtə‚kræft, E+
-‚kraft, -‚krɑft

watercress 'wɔtɚ‚krɛs; ES 'wɔtə-; |-es -ɪz

Wateree ‚wɔtə'ri

waterfall 'wɔtɚ‚fɔl; ES 'wɔtə-

waterfowl 'wɔtɚ‚faul; ES 'wɔtə-

water-inch 'wɔtɚ'ɪntʃ |-es -ɪz

wateriness 'wɔtɚɪnɪs, 'wɒtrɪ-

waterlog 'wɔtɚ‚lɔg, -‚lag, -‚lɒg; ES 'wɔtə-;
|-ged -d |-gedness -ɪdnɪs

Waterloo ‚wɔtɚ'lu; ES ‚wɔtə-

waterman, W- 'wɔtɚmən; ES 'wɔtə-; |-men
-mən

watermark 'wɔtɚ‚mark; ES 'wɔtə‚ma:k,
E+-‚ma:k; |-ed -t

Key: See in full §§3–47. bee bi |pity 'pɪtɪ (§6) |rate ret |yet jɛt |sang sæŋ |angry 'æŋ·grɪ
|bath bæθ; E baθ (§10) |ah ɑ |far far |watch watʃ, wɒtʃ (§12) |jaw dʒɔ |gorge gɔrdʒ |go go

watermelon ˈwɔtɚˌmɛlən; ES ˈwɔtə-
waterproof *n, v* ˈwɔtɚˌpruf; ES ˈwɔtə-; |-ed -t
waterproof *adj* ˈwɔtɚˈpruf; ES ˈwɔtə-;
  (ˈwaterˌproof ˈpaint)
waterscape ˈwɔtɚˌskep; ES ˈwɔtə-
watershed ˈwɔtɚˌʃɛd; ES ˈwɔtə-
waterside ˈwɔtɚˌsaɪd; ES ˈwɔtə-
water-soak ˈwɔtɚˌsok; ES ˈwɔtə-; |-ed -t
water-soluble ˈwɔtɚˌsɑljəbḷ; ES ˈwɔtəˌsɑl-,
  -ˌsɒl-
waterspout ˈwɔtɚˌspaʊt; ES ˈwɔtə-
watertight ˈwɔtɚˈtaɪt; ES ˈwɔtə-; (ˈwater-
  ˌtight ˈjoint)
waterway ˈwɔtɚˌwe; ES ˈwɔtə-
waterwork ˈwɔtɚˌwɝk; ES ˈwɔtəˌwɝk, ˈwɔtə-
  ˌwɝ·k; |-s -s
waterworn ˈwɔtɚˌworn, -ˌwɔrn; ES ˈwɔtə-
  ˌwoən, E+-ˌwɔən
watery ˈwɔtərɪ, ˈwɔtrɪ
Watson ˈwɑtsn̩, ˈwɒtsn̩
watt, W- wɑt, wɒt |-age -ɪdʒ |-ages -ɪdʒɪz
Watteau wɑˈto, wɒˈto (*Fr* vaˈto)
watt-hour ˈwɑtˈaʊr, ˈwɒt-; ES -ˈaʊə(r
wattle ˈwɑtḷ, ˈwɒtḷ |-d -d |-ling -tḷɪŋ, -tlɪŋ
wattmeter ˈwɑtˌmitɚ, ˈwɒt-; ES -ˌmitə(r
Watts wɑts, wɒts |-'s -ɪz
Waukegan wɔˈkigən
Waukesha ˈwɔkɪˌʃɔ
wave wev |-d -d |-y -ɪ
Wavell ˈwevḷ
waver ˈwevɚ; ES -və(r; |-ed -d |-ing -vrɪŋ,
  -vərɪŋ
Waverly ˈwevɚlɪ; ES ˈwevəlɪ
wax wæks |waxes ˈwæksɪz |waxed wækst
  |-en -n̩
waxwing ˈwæksˌwɪŋ
waxwork ˈwæksˌwɝk; ES -ˌwɝk, -ˌwɝ·k
way, W- we
waybill ˈweˌbɪl |-ed -d
wayfarer ˈweˌfɛrɚ, ˈweˌfærɚ; E -ˌfɛrə(r, ES
  -ˌfærə(r
wayfaring ˈweˌfɛrɪŋ, -ˌfærɪŋ; S -ˌfærɪŋ
Wayland ˈwelənd
waylay ˌweˈle |-laid -ˈled (ˈwayˌlaid ˈtwice)
Wayne wen
wayside ˈweˌsaɪd
wayward ˈwewɚd; ES ˈwewəd
wayworn ˈweˌworn, -ˌwɔrn; ES ˈweˌwoən,
  E+-ˌwɔən

we *stressed* ˈwi, ˌwi, *occas.* ˌwɪ *in* we're ˌwɪr;
  unstr. wɪ, wi
weak wik
weaken ˈwikən |-ed -d |-ing ˈwikənɪŋ, -knɪŋ
weak-kneed ˈwikˈnid (ˈweak-ˌkneed ˈcoward)
weakling ˈwiklɪŋ
weal wil
weald, W- wild
wealth wɛlθ |wealthy ˈwɛlθɪ |-ily -əlɪ
wean win |weaned wind
weapon ˈwɛpən |-ed -d
wear wɛr, wær; E wɛə(r, ES wæə(r; |wore
  wor, wɔr; ES woə(r, E+wɔə(r; |worn
  worn, wɔrn; ES woən, E+wɔən
Wear *Eng riv.* wɪr; ES wɪə(r; |-mouth -məθ
Weare *US* wɛr, wær; E wɛə(r, ES wæə(r;
  Dev, Som wɪr; ES wɪə(r
wearisome ˈwɪrɪsəm
weary ˈwɪrɪ, ˈwirɪ; S+ˈwɛrɪ; |-ied -ɪd
weasand ˈwizn̩d
weasel ˈwizḷ |-ed -d |-ing ˈwizḷɪŋ, ˈwizlɪŋ
weather ˈwɛðɚ; ES ˈwɛðə(r
weather-beaten ˈwɛðɚˌbitn̩; ES ˈwɛðəˌbitn̩
weatherboard ˈwɛðɚˌbord, -ˌbɔrd; ES ˈwɛðə-
  ˌboəd, E+-ˌbɔəd; |-ed -ɪd
weather-bound ˈwɛðɚˌbaʊnd; ES ˈwɛðə-
weathercock ˈwɛðɚˌkɑk; ES ˈwɛðəˌkɑk,
  -ˌkɒk
Weatherford ˈwɛðɚfɚd; ES ˈwɛðəfəd
weatherglass ˈwɛðɚˌglæs; ES ˈwɛðəˌglæs,
  E+-ˌglas, -ˌglɑs
weatherproof ˈwɛðɚˈpruf; ES ˈwɛðə-;
  (ˈweatherˌproof ˈtop)
weather-wise ˈwɛðɚˌwaɪz; ES ˈwɛðə-
weatherworn ˈwɛðɚˌworn, -ˌwɔrn; ES ˈwɛðə-
  ˌwoən, E+-ˌwɔən
weave wiv |wove wov |woven ˈwovən *or* wove
  wov
web wɛb |webbed wɛbd
Weber *Am name* ˈwɛbɚ, ˈwibɚ, *Ger name*
  ˈvebɚ; ES -bə(r; (*Ger* ˈve:bər)
weber *elec.* ˈvebɚ, ˈwibɚ; ES -bə(r
webfoot ˈwɛbˌfʊt, -ˈfʊt |-feet -ˌfit, -ˈfit
web-footed ˈwɛbˈfʊtɪd (ˈweb-ˌfooted ˈbird)
Webster, w- ˈwɛbstɚ; ES ˈwɛbstə(r
Websterian wɛbˈstɪrɪən
webworm ˈwɛbˌwɝm; ES -ˌwɝm, -ˌwɝ·m
wed wɛd |wedded ˈwɛdɪd |wedded ˈwɛdɪd *or*
  wed wɛd

|full fʊl |tooth tuθ |further ˈfɝðɚ; ES ˈfɝðə |custom ˈkʌstəm |while hwaɪl |how haʊ |toy tɔɪ
|using ˈjuzɪŋ |fuse fjuz, fɪuz |dish dɪʃ |vision ˈvɪʒən |Eden ˈidn̩ |cradle ˈkredḷ |keep 'em ˈkipm̩

we'd *abbr. spelling of* we had, we would, *stressed* ˈwid, ˌwid, *unstr.* wɪd, wid

Weddell ˈwɛdḷ, wəˈdɛl—*cf* Weddle

wedding ˈwɛdɪŋ

Weddle ˈwɛdḷ

wedge wɛdʒ |wedges ˈwɛdʒɪz |wedged wɛdʒd

wedge-shaped ˈwɛdʒˌʃept

Wedgwood, w- ˈwɛdʒˌwʊd

wedlock ˈwɛdlɑk; ES+-ˌlɒk

Wednesday ˈwɛnzdɪ—*see* Monday, Friday

wee wi

weed wid |weeded ˈwidɪd |weedy ˈwidɪ

Weedon ˈwidṇ

week wik |weekday ˈwikˌde |weekly ˈwiklɪ

week end *n* ˈwikˈɛnd

week-end *adj* ˈwikˈɛnd (ˈweek-ˈend ˌparty, ˈweek-ˌend ˈtrip)

week-end *v* ˈwikˈɛnd |-ed -ɪd

Weems wimz |Weems's ˈwimzɪz

ween win |weened wind

weep wip |wept wɛpt

weevil ˈwivḷ |-ed -d

weft wɛft |-ed -ɪd

weigela, W- waɪˈdʒilə, -ˈgilə

weigelia, W- waɪˈdʒiljə, -ˈgil-, -lɪə

weigh we |weighed wed

weight wet |weighted ˈwetɪd

Wei-hai-wei ˈweˈhaɪˈwe

Weimar *Ger* ˈvaɪmɑr

weir wɪr; ES wɪə(r, S+wɛə(r; |-ed -d

weird wɪrd; ES wɪəd, S+wɛəd

Welch wɛltʃ, wɛlʃ |-'s -ɪz

welcome ˈwɛlkəm |welcomed ˈwɛlkəmd

weld wɛld |welded ˈwɛldɪd

Weldon ˈwɛldən

welfare ˈwɛlˌfɛr, -ˌfær; E -ˌfɛə(r, ES -ˌfæə(r

welkin ˈwɛlkɪn

well wɛl |welled wɛld

we'll *abbr. spelling of* we will, *stressed* ˈwil, ˌwil; *unstr.* wɪl, wil

Welland ˈwɛlənd

wellaway ˈwɛləˈwe

well-being ˈwɛlˈbiɪŋ

wellborn ˈwɛlˈbɔrn; ES ˈwɛlˈbɔən

well-bred ˈwɛlˈbrɛd (ˈwell-ˌbred ˈlook)

well-doer ˈwɛlˈduɚ; ES -ˈduˑə(r

Wellesley ˈwɛlzlɪ

well-favored ˈwɛlˈfevɚd; ES -ˈfevəd

well-found ˈwɛlˈfaʊnd

well-founded ˈwɛlˈfaʊndɪd (ˈwell-ˌfounded ˈact)

well-groomed ˈwɛlˈgrumd

wellhead ˈwɛlˌhɛd

Wellington ˈwɛlɪŋtən

well-known ˈwɛlˈnon (ˈwell-ˌknown ˈfact)

well-meaning ˈwɛlˈminɪŋ

well-nigh ˈwɛlˈnaɪ (ˈwell-ˌnigh ˈdead)

well-read ˈwɛlˈrɛd

well-spoken ˈwɛlˈspokən

wellspring ˈwɛlˌsprɪŋ

well-thought-of ˈwɛlˈθɔtˌɑv, -ˌɒv, -ˌʌv

well-to-do ˈwɛltəˈdu (ˈwell-to-ˌdo ˈfarmer)

Welsh wɛlʃ, wɛltʃ |-man, -men -mən

welt wɛlt |welted ˈwɛltɪd

Weltanschauung *Ger* ˈvɛltˌɑnˌʃaʊˑʊŋ

welter ˈwɛltɚ; ES ˈwɛltə(r; |-ed -d |-ing -tərɪŋ, -trɪŋ

welterweight ˈwɛltɚˌwet; ES ˈwɛltə-

Weltpolitik *Ger* ˈvɛltpoliˌtiːk

Weltschmerz *Ger* ˈvɛltˌʃmɛrts

Wembley ˈwɛmblɪ

Wemys wimz |-'s -ɪz

wen wɛn

Wenceslaus ˈwɛnsɪsˌlɔs |-'s -ɪz

wench wɛntʃ |-es -ɪz |-ed -t

wend wɛnd |*past & pptc* wended ˈwɛndɪd *or* went wɛnt—went *is now associated with* go.

went *past & pptc of* wend *&* go wɛnt

wept *past of* weep wɛpt

were *past of* be: *stressed* ˈwɝ, ˌwɝ, *o.f.* ˈwɛɪ, ˌwɛɪ, ˈwær, ˌwær; ES ˈwɝ(r, ˌwɝ(r, ˈwɝ, ˌwɝ, *o.f.* ˈwɛə(r, ˌwɛə(r, ˈwæə(r, ˌwæə(r; *unstr.* wɚ; ES wə(r

we're *abbr. spelling of* we are: *stressed* ˈwɪr, ˈwɪr, ˌwir, ˌwɪr; ES -ɪə(r, -ɪə(r; *unstr.* wɪː; ES wɪə(r

weren't wɝnt; ES wɝnt, wɝnt

werewolf, werw- ˈwɪrˌwʊlf, ˈwɝ-; ES ˈwɪə-, ˈwɝ-, ˈwɝ-, S+ˈwɛə-

wert *stressed* ˈwɝt, ˌwɝt; ES -ɝt, -ɝt; *unstr.* wɚt; ES wət

Weser *Ger riv.* ˈvezɚ; ES ˈvezə(r; *rarely* ˈwiz- (*Ger* ˈveːzər)

Wesley ˈwɛslɪ |-an -ən (ˈwɛzlɪ *is mainly Brit*)

Wessex ˈwɛsɪks, ˈwɛsɛks |-'s -ɪz

west, W- wɛst |-er -ɚ; ES -ə(r

Westbourne ˈwɛstborn, -bɔrn, -bən; ES -boən, -bən, E+-bɔən

Key: See in full §§3–47. bee bi |pity ˈpɪtɪ (§6) |rate ret |yet jɛt |sang sæŋ |angry ˈæŋ·grɪ |bath bæθ; E baθ (§10) |ah ɑ |far fɑr |watch wɑtʃ, wɒtʃ (§12) |jaw dʒɔ |gorge gɔrdʒ |go go

In the words below pronounced with **hw**, *many speakers replace* **hw** *with plain* **w**

Westcott, Wescott ˈwɛskət

westerly, W- ˈwɛstəlɪ; ES ˈwɛstəlɪ

western, W- ˈwɛstən; ES -tən; |-er -ɚ; ES -ə(r; |-most -ˌmost, -məst—*occas.* ˈwɛstənɚ *by r-dissimilation* (§121)

West Ham ˈwɛstˈhæm

Westinghouse ˈwɛstɪŋˌhaʊs |-'s -ˌhaʊsɪz

Westminster ˈwɛstˌmɪnstɚ, -ˈmɪn-; ES -stə(r

Westmoreland *Pa* wɛstˈmorlənd, -ˈmɔr-; ES -ˈmoə-, E+-ˈmɔə-; *Va* ˈwɛstmələnd; ES -mə-

Westmorland *Engd, Can* ˈwɛstmələnd; ES -mə-

west-northwest ˈwɛstˌnɔrθˈwɛst; ES -ˌnɔəθ-

Westphalia wɛstˈfelɪə, -ljə |-n -n

west-southwest ˈwɛstˌsaʊθˈwɛst

West Virginia ˈwɛstvɚˈdʒɪnjə, *less freq.* -nɪə; ES -və-; |-n -n

westward, W- ˈwɛstwəd; ES -wəd; |Ho -ˈho

wet wɛt |*past & pptc* wet wɛt *or* wetted ˈwɛtɪd

wether ˈwɛðɚ; ES ˈwɛðə(r

we've *abbr. spelling of* we have, *stressed* ˈwiv, ˌwiv; *unstr.* wɪv, wiv

Weybridge ˈwebrɪdʒ |-'s -ɪz

Weygand ˈvegənd (*Fr* veˈgã)

Weyman ˈwaɪmən

Weymouth ˈweməθ

wh- —*In the vocab. only the sound* **hw** *is given for the spelling* **wh**, *but it is to be understood that in all such cases many speakers replace* **hw** *with plain* **w**. *See* §25.

whack hwæk |whacked hwækt

whale hwel |whaled hweld |-back -ˌbæk |-boat -ˌbot |-bone -ˌbon

whang hwæŋ |whanged hwæŋd

wharf hwɔrf; ES hwɔəf; |-'s -s |-ves -vz *or* -s -s |-ed -t—*In N Engd many pronounce* w *in* wharf *who use* hw *in other words; in Delmarva the exact reverse has been reported.* wɔəf *is also common in the* S.

wharfinger ˈhwɔrfɪndʒɚ; ES ˈhwɔəfɪndʒə(r

Wharton ˈhwɔrtn̩; ES ˈhwɔətn̩

wharve, wa- hwɔrv, wɔrv; ES -ɔəv

what *stressed* ˈhwɑt, ˌhwɑt, ˈhwɒt, ˌhwɒt, ˈhwʌt, ˌhwʌt; *unstr.* hwət, wət

whate'er hwɑtˈɛr, hwɒt-, hwət-; ES -ˈɛə(r

whatever hwɑtˈɛvɚ, hwɒt-, hwət-; ES -ˈɛvə(r

Whatmough ˈhwɑtmo, ˈhwɒt-

whatnot ˈhwɑtˌnɑt, ˈhwɒt-; ES+-ˌnɒt

whatsoever ˌhwɑtsoˈɛvɚ, ˌhwɒt-; ES -ˈɛvə(r

wheat hwit |wheaten ˈhwitn̩

wheatear ˈhwitˌɪr; ES -ˌɪə(r, S+-ˌɛə(r

Wheatstone ˈhwitstən, -ˌston

wheedle hwidl̩ |-d -d |-ling ˈhwidlɪŋ, -dl̩ɪŋ

wheel hwil |wheeled hwild

wheelbarrow ˈhwilˌbæro, -rə—*The L.A. and other evidence show that* ˈhwilˌbaro *is occas. heard from cultivated speakers.*

wheel-chair ˈhwilˈtʃɛr, -ˈtʃær; E -ˈtʃɛə(r, ES -ˈtʃæə(r

Wheeler ˈhwilɚ; ES ˈhwilə(r

wheelhouse ˈhwilˌhaʊs |-houses -ˌhaʊzɪz

wheelless ˈhwillɪs

wheelman ˈhwilmən |-men -mən

wheelwright ˈhwilˌraɪt

wheeze hwiz |wheezes ˈhwizɪz |wheezed hwizd

whelk hwɛlk |whelked hwɛlkt

whelm hwɛlm |whelmed hwɛlmd

whelp hwɛlp |whelped hwɛlpt

when hwɛn |-as hwɛnˈæz

whence hwɛns

whencesoever ˌhwɛnsˌsoˈɛvɚ; ES -ˈɛvə(r

whene'er hwɛnˈɛr, hwən-; ES -ˈɛə(r

whenever hwɛnˈɛvɚ, hwən-; ES -ˈɛvə(r

whensoever ˌhwɛnsoˈɛvɚ; ES -ˈɛvə(r

where hwɛr, hwær; E hwɛə(r, ES hwæə(r

whereabout *n* ˈhwɛrəˌbaʊt, ˈhwær-; S ˈhwær-; |-s -s

whereabout *adv* ˌhwɛrəˈbaʊt, ˌhwær-; S ˌhwær-; |-s -s

whereas hwɛrˈæz, hwær-; S hwær-

whereat hwɛrˈæt, hwær-; S hwær-

whereby hwɛrˈbaɪ, hwær-; E hwɛə-, ES hwæə-

where'er hwɛrˈɛr, hwær-; E hwɛrˈɛə(r, ES hwær-

wherefor hwɛrˈfɔr, hwær-; E hwɛəˈfɔə(r, ES hwæə-

wherefore ˈhwɛrˌfor, ˈhwær-, -ˌfɔr; E ˈhwɛəˌfoə(r, ˈhwæə-, -ˌfɔə(r; S ˈhwæəˌfoə(r

wherefrom hwɛrˈfrɑm, hwær-, -ˈfrɒm; E hwɛə-, ES hwæə-

wherein hwɛrˈɪn, hwær-; S hwærˈɪn

whereinto hwɛrˈɪntu, hwær-, -tʊ, ˌhwɛrɪnˈtu, hwær-; S hwærˈɪn-, ˌhwærɪnˈtu

---

In the words below pronounced with **hw,** *many speakers replace* **hw** *with plain* **w**

whereof hwɛrˈɑv, hwær-, -ˈɒv; S hwær-
whereon hwɛrˈɑn, hwær-, -ˈɒn, -ˈɔn; S hwær-;
-ˈɔn *is esp. freq. in the S and W.*
wheresoe'er ˌhwɛrsoˈɛr, ˌhwær-; E ˌhwɛəso-
ˈɛə(r, ES ˌhwæ ə-
wheresoever ˌhwɛrsoˈɛvɚ, ˌhwær-; E ˌhwɛəso-
ˈɛvə(r, ES ˌhwæ ə-
wherethrough hwɛrˈθru, hwær-; E hwɛə-, ES
hwæ ə-
whereto hwɛrˈtu, hwær-; E hwɛə-, ES
hwæ ə-; (ˈWhereˌto ˈtends allˌthis?)
whereunder hwɛrˈʌndɚ, hwær-; E hwɛr-
ˈʌndə(r, ES hwær-
whereunto hwɛrˈʌntu, hwær-, -tʊ, ˌhwɛrʌn-
ˈtu, ˌhwær-; S hwærˈʌn-, ˌhwærʌnˈtu
whereupon ˌhwɛrəˈpɑn, ˌhwær-, -ˈpɒn, -ˈpɔn;
S ˌhwær-
wherever hwɛrˈɛvɚ, hwær-; E hwɛrˈɛvə(r, ES
hwær-
wherewith hwɛrˈwɪθ, hwær-, -ˈwɪð; E hwɛə-,
ES hwæ ə-; hwɛrˈwɪθ *has the regular voiceless* θ *of the stressed syllable, while* hwɛrˈwɪð
imitates older unstressed wɪð. *Similarly*
herewith, therewith.
wherewithal *n* ˈhwɛrwɪðˌɔl, ˈhwær-; E ˈhwɛə-,
ES ˈhwæ ə-
wherewithal *adv* ˌhwɛrwɪðˈɔl, ˌhwær-; E
ˌhwɛə-, ES ˌhwæ ə-
wherry ˈhwɛrɪ |wherried ˈhwɛrɪd
whet hwɛt |whetted ˈhwɛtɪd |-stone -ˌston
whether ˈhwɛðɚ; ES ˈhwɛðə(r
whew hwɪu, hwju, Φju, Φɪu, xju, xɪu, *etc.*
Whewell ˈhjuəl, ˈhruəl
whey hwe |wheyed hwed |-face -ˌfes |-faced
-ˌfest
which hwɪtʃ |-ever hwɪtʃˈɛvɚ; ES -ˈɛvə(r
whichsoever ˌhwɪtʃsoˈɛvɚ; ES -ˈɛvə(r
whiff hwɪf |whiffed hwɪft
whiffle ˈhwɪfl̩ |-d -d |-ling ˈhwɪflɪŋ, -fl̩ɪŋ
whiffletree ˈhwɪfl̩ˌtri, -trɪ
Whig hwɪg |Whigged hwɪgd
while hwaɪl |-d -d |-s -z |-lom -əm |-st -st
whim hwɪm |-med -d |-sey, -sy -zɪ
whimper ˈhwɪmpɚ; ES -pə(r; |-ed -d |-ing
-pərɪŋ, -prɪŋ
whimsical ˈhwɪmzɪkl̩ |-ly -ɪ, -ɪklɪ
whin hwɪn
whine hwaɪn |whined hwaɪnd

whinner ˈhwɪnɚ; ES ˈhwɪnə(r
whinny ˈhwɪnɪ |whinnied ˈhwɪnɪd
whip hwɪp |whipped hwɪpt
whipcord ˈhwɪpˌkɔrd; ES -ˌkɔəd
whiplash ˈhwɪpˌlæʃ |-es -ɪz |-ed -t
whippersnapper ˈhwɪpɚˌsnæpɚ; ES ˈhwɪpə-
ˌsnæpə(r
whippet ˈhwɪpɪt |-ed -ɪd
whippletree ˈhwɪpl̩ˌtri, -trɪ
whippoorwill ˌhwɪpɚˈwɪl; ES ˌhwɪpəˈwɪl—
acct + ˈwhippoorˌwill
whipsaw ˈhwɪpˌsɔ |-sawed -ˌsɔd
whipsocket ˈhwɪpˌsɑkɪt; ES+-ˌsɒkɪt
whipstitch ˈhwɪpˌstɪtʃ |-ed -t
whipstock ˈhwɪpˌstɑk, -ˌstɒk
whir hwɝ; ES hwɝ(r, hwɜ; |-red -d |-ring
ˈhwɝɪŋ; ES ˈhwɜrɪŋ, ˈhwɝ-
whirl hwɝl; ES hwɜl, hwɝl; |-ed -d
whirligig ˈhwɝlɪˌgɪg; ES ˈhwɜl-, ˈhwɝl-
whirlpool ˈhwɝlˌpul; ES ˈhwɜl-, ˈhwɝl-
whirlwind ˈhwɝlˌwɪnd; ES ˈhwɜl-, ˈhwɝl-
whish hwɪʃ |whishes ˈhwɪʃɪz |whished hwɪʃt
whisht *intj* hwɪʃt
whisk hwɪsk |whisked hwɪskt
whiskers ˈhwɪskɚz; ES ˈhwɪskəz
whiskey ˈhwɪskɪ |-ed -d
whisper ˈhwɪspɚ; ES ˈhwɪspə(r; |-ed -d |-ing
-prɪŋ, -pərɪŋ
whist hwɪst |-ed -ɪd
whistle ˈhwɪsl̩ |-d -d |-ling ˈhwɪslɪŋ, -sl̩ɪŋ
whistler, W- ˈhwɪslɚ; ES -lə(r
whit hwɪt
Whitby ˈhwɪtbɪ
white, W- hwaɪt |-d -ɪd
whitebeard ˈhwaɪtˌbɪrd; ES -ˌbɪəd
whitecap ˈhwaɪtˌkæp |-capped -ˌkæpt
Whitechapel ˈhwaɪtˌtʃæpl̩
white-collar ˈhwaɪtˈkɑlɚ; ES -ˈkɑlə(r, -ˈkɒl-;
(ˈwhite-ˈcollar ˌman, ˈwhite-ˌcollar ˈjob)
white-faced ˈhwaɪtˈfest (ˈwhite-ˌfaced ˈcow)
Whitefield *Method. preacher* ˈhwɪtˌfild, ˈhwaɪt-
whitefish ˈhwaɪtˌfɪʃ |-es -ɪz
Whitefriars ˈhwaɪtˌfraɪrz; ES -ˌfraɪəz
Whitehall ˈhwaɪtˈhɔl (ˈWhiteˌhall ˈPalace),
surname ˈhwaɪtˌhɔl
white-headed ˈhwaɪtˈhɛdɪd
white-hot ˈhwaɪtˈhɑt; ES+-ˈhɒt
white-livered ˈhwaɪtˈlɪvɚd; ES -ˈlɪvəd

Key: *See in full §§3–47.* **bee** bi |**pity** ˈpɪtɪ (§6) |**rate** ret |**yet** jɛt |**sang** sæŋ |**angry** ˈæŋ·grɪ
|**bath** bæθ; E baθ (§10) |**ah** ɑ |**far** fɑr |**watch** watʃ, wɒtʃ (§12) |**jaw** dʒɔ |**gorge** gɔrdʒ |**go** go

In the words below pronounced with hw, many speakers replace hw with plain w

whiten ˈhwaɪtn̩ |-ed -d |-ing ˈhwaɪtn̩ɪŋ, -tnɪŋ
whitesmith ˈhwaɪtˌsmɪθ |-ths -θs
whitewash ˈhwaɪtˌwɑʃ, -ˌwɔʃ, -ˌwɒʃ |-es -ɪz |-ed -t
whitewing ˈhwaɪtˌwɪŋ
whitewood ˈhwaɪtˌwʊd
whither ˈhwɪðɚ; ES ˈhwɪðə(r
whithersoever ˌhwɪðɚsoˈɛvɚ; ES ˌhwɪðəso-ˈɛvə(r
whitherward ˈhwɪðɚwɚd; ES ˈhwɪðəwəd
whiting, W- ˈhwaɪtɪŋ
whitlow ˈhwɪtlo
Whitman ˈhwɪtmən
Whitmonday ˈhwɪtˈmʌndɪ
Whitmore ˈhwɪtmor, -mɔr; ES -moə(r, E+-mɔə(r
Whitney ˈhwɪtnɪ
Whitsun ˈhwɪtsn̩ |-tide -ˌtaɪd
Whitsunday ˈhwɪtˈsʌndɪ, ˈhwɪtsn̩ˌde
Whittier ˈhwɪtɪɚ; ES ˈhwɪtɪ·ə(r
Whittington ˈhwɪtɪŋtən
whittle ˈhwɪtl̩ |-d -d |-ling ˈhwɪtl̩ɪŋ, -tlɪŋ
whiz, -zz hwɪz |whizzes ˈhwɪzɪz |whizzed hwɪzd
who *interrog* hu
who *rel partly stressed* ˌhu, *unstr.* hʊ
whoa hwo, wo, ho; *unstressed* hʊ:
whoe'er huˈɛr, hʊˈɛr; ES -ˈɛə(r
whoever huˈɛvɚ, hʊˈɛvɚ; ES -ˈɛvə(r
whole hol, hʊl; *N Engd*+hɔl (*§46*)
wholehearted ˈholˈhɑrtɪd; ES -ˈhɑːtɪd, E+-ˈhɑːtɪd
whole-or-none ˈholɚˈnʌn; ES ˈholəˈnʌn
wholesale ˈholˌsel
wholesome ˈholsəm
whole-souled ˈholˈsold (ˈwhole-ˌsouled ˈfriend)
wholly ˈholɪ, *esp. if emph.* ˈhollɪ; *N Engd*+ˈhɔlɪ
whom hum, *unstressed occas.* hʊm
whoop hup, hwup |-ed -t
whoopee *n* ˈhwupi, ˈhwʊpi, ˈhu-, ˈhʊ-; *intj*+ˈwhooˈpee
whooping-cough ˈhupɪŋˌkɔf, ˈhʊpɪŋ-, -ˌkɒf
whop hwɑp, hwɒp |-per -ɚ; ES -ə(r
whore hor, hɔr; ES hoə(r, E+hɔə(r; |-dom -dəm
whoremaster ˈhorˌmæstɚ, ˈhɔr-; ES ˈhoə-ˌmæstə(r, E+ˈhɔə-, -ˌmas-, -ˌmɑs-

whoremonger ˈhorˌmʌŋgɚ, ˈhɔr-; ES ˈhoə-ˌmʌŋgə(r, E+ˈhɔə-
whoreson ˈhorsn̩, ˈhɔrsn̩; ES ˈhoəsn̩, E+ˈhɔəsn̩
whorl hwɝl; ES hwɜl, hwɝl
whortleberry ˈhwɝtl̩ˌbɛrɪ, -bərɪ; ES ˈhwɜtl̩-, ˈhwɝtl̩-
whose huz, *unstressed occas.* hʊz
whoso ˈhuso
whosoever ˌhusoˈɛvɚ; ES -ˈɛvə(r
why *interrog* hwaɪ; *intj* hwaɪ, waɪ; *unstressed expletive* waɪ, hwaɪ
Wichita ˈwɪtʃəˌtɔ
wick wɪk |wicked 'having wick(s)' wɪkt
wicked 'evil' ˈwɪkɪd
wicker ˈwɪkɚ; ES ˈwɪkə(r; |-ed -d
wickerwork ˈwɪkɚˌwɝk; ES ˈwɪkəˌwɜk, ˈwɪkəˌwɝk
wicket ˈwɪkɪt |wicketed ˈwɪkɪtɪd
Wickham ˈwɪkəm
wickiup, wik- ˈwɪkɪˌʌp
Wiclif, Wy-, Wickliffe, Wy- ˈwɪklɪf
wicopy ˈwɪkəpɪ
Widdicombe ˈwɪdɪkəm
wide waɪd |-n -n̩ |-ned -n̩d |-ning -nɪŋ, -nɪŋ
wide-angle *adj* ˈwaɪdˈæŋgl̩ (ˈwide-ˌangle ˈlens)
wide-awake ˈwaɪdəˈwek
wide-open ˈwaɪdˈopən, -ˈopm̩
widespread ˈwaɪdˈsprɛd
widgeon, wig- ˈwɪdʒən
widow ˈwɪdo, -ə |-ed -d
widower ˈwɪdəwɚ; ES ˈwɪdəwə(r; |-ered -d
widowhood ˈwɪdoˌhʊd, ˈwɪdə-
width wɪdθ, wɪtθ |-ths -θs
wield wild |wielded ˈwildɪd
wienerwurst ˈwinɚˌwɝst, ˈwinɪ-; ES ˈwinə-ˌwɜst, ˈwinɪ-, -ˌwɝst
wife waɪf |wife's waɪfs, waɪvz (*in Shak.* wives waɪvz) |*pl* wives waɪvz—*The pronunciation waɪvz for wife's is not the plural, but the older possessive singular.*
wifely ˈwaɪflɪ
wig wɪg |wigged wɪgd
Wigan ˈwɪgən
wiggle ˈwɪgl̩ |-d -d |-ling ˈwɪglɪŋ, ˈwɪgl̩ɪŋ
wiggler ˈwɪglɚ; ES ˈwɪglə(r
wiggly ˈwɪglɪ, ˈwɪgl̩ɪ
wight, W- waɪt

|full fʊl |tooth tuθ |further ˈfɝðɚ; ES ˈfɝðə |custom ˈkʌstəm |while hwaɪl |how haʊ |toy tɔɪ |using ˈjuzɪŋ |fuse fjuz, fruz |dish dɪʃ |vision ˈvɪʒən |Eden ˈidn̩ |cradle ˈkredl̩ |keep 'em ˈkipm̩

Wigton ˈwɪgtən |Wigtown ˈwɪgtən, -ˌtaʊn

Wigtownshire ˈwɪgˌtaʊnˌʃɪr, -ʃə; ES -ˌʃɪə(r, -ʃə(r

wigwag ˈwɪgˌwæg |wigwagged ˈwɪgˌwægd

wigwam ˈwɪgwɑm, -wɒm, -wɔm

Wilberforce ˈwɪlbəˌfors, -ˌfɔrs; ES ˈwɪlbə-ˌfoəs, E+-ˌfɔəs

Wilbraham *Mass* ˈwɪlbrəˌhæm, *Engd* ˈwɪl-brɪəm

Wilbur ˈwɪlbə; ES ˈwɪlbə(r

wild, W- waɪld

wildcat ˈwaɪldˌkæt, ˈwaɪlˌkæt |-ed -ɪd

wildebeest ˈwɪldəˌbist

wilder, W- ˈwaɪldə; ES ˈwaɪldə(r

wilder *v* ˈwɪldə; ES ˈwɪldə(r; |-ed -d |-ing ˈwɪldərɪŋ, -drɪŋ

wilderness ˈwɪldənɪs; ES ˈwɪldənɪs; |-es -ɪz

wildfire, W- ˈwaɪldˌfaɪr; ES -ˌfaɪə(r

wilding, W- ˈwaɪldɪŋ

wildwood ˈwaɪldˌwʊd

wile waɪl |wiled waɪld

Wilfred ˈwɪlfrɪd, -frəd

Wilhelmina ˌwɪlhɛlˈminə

Wilkes wɪlks |-'s -ɪz

Wilkes-Barre ˈwɪlksˌbærɪ

Wilkinsburg ˈwɪlkɪnzˌbɝg; ES -ˌbɜg, -ˌbɝg

Wilkinson ˈwɪlkɪnsn̩

will *trans v* wɪl |willed wɪld

will *aux v stressed* ˈwɪl, ˌwɪl; *unstr.* wəl |'ll əl, *after some conss.* l̩ (ˈnɛdl̩ go), *after vowels* l, əl (wil go, ˈðeəl go)

Willa ˈwɪlə

Willamette wɪˈlæmɪt

Willard ˈwɪləd; ES ˈwɪləd

Willesden ˈwɪlzdən

willful, wilf- ˈwɪlfəl |-ly -ɪ

William ˈwɪljəm |-s -z |-s's -zɪz |-son -sn̩

Williamsburg ˈwɪljəmzˌbɝg; ES -ˌbɜg, -ˌbɝg

Willimantic ˌwɪləˈmæntɪk

willing ˈwɪlɪŋ

Willis ˈwɪlɪs |-'s -ɪz

Willkie ˈwɪlkɪ

will-less ˈwɪllɪs

will-o'-the-wisp ˌwɪləðəˈwɪsp

Willoughby ˈwɪləbɪ

willow, W- ˈwɪlo, ˈwɪlə |-y ˈwɪləwɪ

willowware ˈwɪloˌwɛr, -lə-, -ˌwær; E -ˌwɛə(r, ES -ˌwæə(r

willy, W- ˈwɪlɪ |willied ˈwɪlɪd

willy-nilly ˈwɪlɪˈnɪlɪ

Willys ˈwɪlɪs |-'s -ɪz

Wilmcote ˈwɪŋkət, ˈwɪmkət

Wilmington ˈwɪlmɪŋtən

Wilno ˈvɪlnə=Vilna

Wilson ˈwɪlsn̩

wilt *aux v stressed* ˈwɪlt, ˌwɪlt; *unstr.* wəlt, əlt, lt (ðaʊlt si)

wilt *v* wɪlt |wilted ˈwɪltɪd

Wilton ˈwɪltn̩

Wilts *short for* Wiltshire wɪlts

Wiltshire ˈwɪltˌʃɪr, -ʃə; ES -ʃɪə(r, -ʃə(r

wily ˈwaɪlɪ

wimble ˈwɪmbl̩ |-d -d |-ling ˈwɪmblɪŋ, -bl̩ɪŋ

Wimbledon ˈwɪmbl̩dən

Wimborne ˈwɪmborn, -bɔrn, -bən; ES ˈwɪmboən, -bən, E+-bɔən

wimple ˈwɪmpl̩ |-d -d |-ling ˈwɪmplɪŋ, -pl̩ɪŋ

Wimpole ˈwɪmpol

win wɪn |won wʌn

Winant ˈwaɪnənt

wince wɪns |winces ˈwɪnsɪz |winced wɪnst

winch wɪntʃ |winches ˈwɪntʃɪz |winched wɪntʃt

Winchelsea ˈwɪntʃəlsɪ

Winchester ˈwɪnˌtʃɛstə, ˈwɪntʃɪstə; ES -tə(r

wind *n* wɪnd, *older and poet.* waɪnd

wind 'to exhaust' wɪnd |winded ˈwɪndɪd

wind 'blow horn' waɪnd, wɪnd |wound waʊnd *or rarely* winded ˈwaɪndɪd, ˈwɪndɪd

wind *v* 'twist' waɪnd |wound waʊnd

windable ˈwaɪndəbl̩, ˈwɪnd-, *accord. to sense—see wind*

windage 'effect of air' ˈwɪndɪdʒ

windbag ˈwɪndˌbæg, ˈwɪn- |-ged -d |-gery -ərɪ

wind-blown ˈwɪndˌblon, ˈwɪn-

wind-borne ˈwɪndˌborn, ˈwɪn-, -ˌbɔrn; ES -ˌboən, E+-ˌbɔən

windbreak ˈwɪndˌbrek, ˈwɪn-

winder ˈwaɪndə, ˈwɪndə, *acc. to sense—see wind*; ES -də(r

Windermere ˈwɪndəˌmɪr; ES ˈwɪndəˌmɪə(r

windfall, W- ˈwɪndˌfɔl, ˈwɪn-

windflower ˈwɪndˌflaʊə, ˈwɪn-, -ˌflaʊr; ES -ˌflaʊ·ə(r, -ˌflaʊə(r

Windham ˈwɪndəm, *loc. in Vt*+ˈwɪndhæm, ˈwɪndæm

winding ˈwaɪndɪŋ, ˈwɪndɪŋ, *acc. to sense—see wind*

windjammer ˈwɪndˌdʒæmɚ, ˈwɪn-; ES -ˌdʒæmə(r

windlass ˈwɪndləs |windlasses ˈwɪndləsɪz

windmill ˈwɪnˌmɪl, ˈwɪnd-

window ˈwɪndo, -də |-ed -d |-ing ˈwɪndəwɪŋ

windowpane ˈwɪndoˌpen, -də-

windpipe ˈwɪndˌpaɪp, ˈwɪn-

windrow ˈwɪnˌro, ˈwɪndˌro

wind-shaken ˈwɪndˌʃekən, ˈwɪn-

windshield ˈwɪndˌʃild, ˈwɪn-

Windsor ˈwɪnzɚ; ES ˈwɪnzə(r

windstorm ˈwɪndˌstɔrm, ˈwɪn-; ES -ˌstɔəm

wind-swept ˈwɪndˌswɛpt, ˈwɪn-

windtight ˈwɪndˈtaɪt, ˈwɪn- (ˈwɪndˌtight ˈwall)

windup ˈwaɪndˌʌp

windward, W- ˈwɪndwɚd; ES ˈwɪndwəd

windy ˈwɪndɪ, ˈwaɪndɪ, *acc. to sense—see* wind

wine waɪn |wined waɪnd

winebibber ˈwaɪnˌbɪbɚ; ES -ˌbɪbə(r

wineglass ˈwaɪnˌglæs; E+-ˌglas, -ˌglɑs; |-ful -ˌful

winegrower ˈwaɪnˌgroɚ; ES -ˌgro·ə(r

winery ˈwaɪnərɪ

Winesap ˈwaɪnˌsæp

wineskin ˈwaɪnˌskɪn

Winfred ˈwɪnfrɪd, -frəd

wing wɪŋ |winged wɪŋd

winged *adj* wɪŋd, ˈwɪŋɪd |*adv* -ly -ɪdlɪ

wing-footed ˈwɪŋˈfʊtɪd (ˈwing-ˌfooted ˈTime)

wingspread ˈwɪŋˌsprɛd

wing-weary ˈwɪŋˌwɪrɪ, -ˌwɪrɪ; S+-ˌwɛrɪ

wingy ˈwɪŋɪ

Winifred ˈwɪnəfrɪd, -frəd

wink wɪŋk |winked wɪŋkt

winkle, W- ˈwɪŋkl̩ |-d -d |-ling ˈwɪŋklɪŋ, -kl̩ɪŋ

Winnebago ˌwɪnəˈbego

Winnepesaukee ˌwɪnəpəˈsɔkɪ

Winnipeg ˈwɪnəˌpɛg

winnow ˈwɪno, -ə |-ed -d |-ing ˈwɪnəwɪŋ

winsome ˈwɪnsəm

Winsted ˈwɪnstɛd, -stɪd

winter, W- ˈwɪntɚ; ES ˈwɪntə(r; |-ed -d |-ing ˈwɪntərɪŋ, ˈwɪntrɪŋ

Winterbourne ˈwɪntɚˌborn, -ˌbɔrn, -ˌburn; ES ˈwɪntəˌboən, -ˌbuən, E+-ˌbɔən

wintergreen ˈwɪntɚˌgrin; ES ˈwɪntə-

winterkill ˈwɪntɚˌkɪl; ES ˈwɪntə-; |-ed -d

wintertide ˈwɪntɚˌtaɪd; ES ˈwɪntə-

Winthrop ˈwɪnθrəp

wintry ˈwɪntrɪ, ˈwɪntərɪ

wipe waɪp |wiped waɪpt

wirable ˈwaɪrəbl̩

wire waɪr; ES waɪə(r; |-ed -d

wiredancer ˈwaɪrˌdænsɚ; ES ˈwaɪəˌdænsə(r, E+-ˌdans-, -ˌdɑns-

wiredraw ˈwaɪrˌdrɔ; ES ˈwaɪə-; |-drew -ˌdru, -ˌdrɪu |-drawn -ˌdrɔn

wirehair *n* ˈwaɪrˌhɛr, -ˌhær; E ˈwaɪəˌhɛə(r, ES -ˌhæə(r

wire-haired ˈwaɪrˈhɛrd, -ˈhærd; E ˈwaɪəˈhɛəd, ES -ˈhæəd; (ˈwire-ˌhaired ˈpup, a ˈwire-ˈhaired one)

wireless ˈwaɪrlɪs; ES ˈwaɪəlɪs; |-es -ɪz |-ed -t

wirepulling ˈwaɪrˌpʊlɪŋ; ES ˈwaɪə-

wirespun ˈwaɪrˌspʌn; ES ˈwaɪəˌspʌn

wirework ˈwaɪrˌwɝk; ES ˈwaɪəˌwɜk, -ˌwɝk

wireworm ˈwaɪrˌwɝm; ES ˈwaɪəˌwɜm, ˈwaɪəˌwɝm

wiring ˈwaɪrɪŋ

wirra ˈwɪrə

wiry ˈwaɪrɪ

wis *v erron. from* iwis *adv* wɪs |-ses -ɪz |-sed -t

wis *v erron. pres of* wit *v* wɪs

Wisconsin wɪsˈkɑnsn̩; ES+-ˈkɒn-

wisdom ˈwɪzdəm

wise *n, adj* waɪz

wise *v* waɪz |-s -ɪz |-d -d

wiseacre ˈwaɪzˌekɚ, ˈwaɪzəkɚ; ES -ˌekə(r, -əkə(r

wisecrack ˈwaɪzˌkræk |-ed -t

wish wɪʃ |wishes ˈwɪʃɪz |wished wɪʃt |-edly -ɪdlɪ

wishbone ˈwɪʃˌbon

wishful ˈwɪʃfəl |-ly -ɪ

wish-wash ˈwɪʃˌwɑʃ, -ˌwɔʃ, -ˌwɒʃ

wishy-washy ˈwɪʃɪˌwɑʃɪ, -ˌwɔʃɪ, -ˌwɒʃɪ

wisp wɪsp |wisped wɪspt

wist *n & past of v* wit wɪst

wistaria, W- wɪsˈtɛrɪə, -ˈterɪə

wisteria, W- wɪsˈtɪrɪə

wistful ˈwɪstfəl |-ly -ɪ

wit *arch. v: inf* wɪt |*pres sg, pl* wot wɑt, wɒt |*past & pptc* wist wɪst |*pres ptc* witting ˈwɪtɪŋ

wit *n* wɪt

witan *hist. n pl* ˈwɪtən

witch wɪtʃ |witches ˈwɪtʃɪz |witched wɪtʃt

witchcraft ˈwɪtʃˌkræft; E+-ˌkraft, -ˌkrɑft

|full fʊl |tooth tuθ |further ˈfɝðɚ; ES ˈfɜðə |custom ˈkʌstəm |while hwaɪl |how haʊ |toy tɔɪ
|using ˈjuzɪŋ |fuse fjuz, fɪuz |dish dɪʃ |vision ˈvɪʒən |Eden ˈidn̩ |cradle ˈkredl̩ |keep 'em ˈkipm̩

witchery ˈwɪtʃərɪ
witching ˈwɪtʃɪŋ
witenagemot, -te *hist. n* ˈwɪtənəgəˌmot
with *prep* wɪð, wɪθ—*The choice between* wɪð
and wɪθ *may depend partly on phonetic con-*
ditions, but there is no consistent general
practice. wɪθ *is clearly not substandard.*
with *'binder'* wɪθ, wɪð=withe |*pl* withs -θs,
-ðz
withal *adv, prep* wɪˈðɔl, wɪθˈɔl
Witham *Essex* ˈwɪtəm (*OE* wit·ham); *riv.*
ˈwɪðəm (*OE* wiðma); *surnames* ˈwɪð-, ˈwɪθ-
withdraw wɪðˈdrɔ, wɪθ- |-drew -ˈdru, -ˈdrɪu
|-drawn -ˈdrɔn
withdrawal wɪðˈdrɔəl, wɪθ-, -ˈdrɔl
withdrew wɪðˈdru, wɪθ-, -ˈdrɪu
withe *'binder'* waɪð, wɪθ, wɪð |withes waɪðz,
wɪθs, wɪðz
wither ˈwɪðɚ; ES ˈwɪðə(r; |-ed -d |-ing
ˈwɪðrɪŋ, ˈwɪðərɪŋ
withers, W- ˈwɪðɚz; ES ˈwɪðəz; |-'s -ɪz
withhold wɪθˈhold, wɪð- |*past & pptc* -held
-ˈhɛld |*arch. pptc* -holden -ˈholdən
within wɪðˈɪn, wɪθˈɪn
withindoors wɪðˈɪnˌdorz, wɪθ-, -ˌdɔrz; ES
-ˌdoəz, E+-ˌdɔəz
without wɪðˈaut, wɪθ-
withoutdoors wɪðˈautˌdorz, wɪθ-, -ˌdɔrz; ES
-ˌdoəz, E+-ˌdɔəz
withstand wɪθˈstænd, wɪð- |-stood -ˌstud
withy ˈwɪðɪ, ˈwɪθɪ
witless ˈwɪtlɪs |witling ˈwɪtlɪŋ
witness ˈwɪtnɪs |-es -ɪz |-ed -t
Wittenberg ˈwɪtn̩ˌbɝg; ES -ˌbɝg, -ˌbɝg; (*Ger*
ˈvɪtənˌbɛrk)
witticism ˈwɪtəˌsɪzəm
witting ˈwɪtɪŋ
witty ˈwɪtɪ |wittily ˈwɪtl̩ɪ, ˈwɪtɪlɪ
wive waɪv |wived waɪvd
wivern, wyv- ˈwaɪvɚn; ES ˈwaɪvən
wives, wives' waɪvz
wizard ˈwɪzɚd; ES ˈwɪzəd; |-ry -rɪ
wizen ˈwɪzn̩ |wizened ˈwɪzn̩d |-ing -zn̩ɪŋ,
-znɪŋ
wo *intj or var. of* woe wo
woad wod
wobble ˈwɑbl̩, ˈwɒbl̩ |-d -d |-ling -blɪŋ, -bl̩ɪŋ
|-ly -blɪ, -bl̩ɪ
wobegone ˈwobɪˌgɔn, -ˌgɒn

Woburn *Mass* ˈwobɚn, ˈwubɚn; ES -bən;
London ˈwo-, *Beds* ˈwu-
Wodehouse ˈwudˌhaus, -dəs |-'s -ɪz
Woden, -an ˈwodn̩
woe wo |-ful -fəl |-fully -fəlɪ
woebegone ˈwobɪˌgɔn, -ˌgɒn
woke wok |woken ˈwokən; |*NEngd*+wɔ̃k
(§46)
Woking ˈwokɪŋ
Wolcot(t) ˈwulkət
wold wold
wolf wulf |wolf's wulfs, -vz |wolves wulvz
Wolfe wulf |Wolfe's wulfs
wolfhound ˈwulfˌhaund
wolfish ˈwulfɪʃ, ˈwulvɪʃ
wolfram, W- ˈwulfrəm (*Ger* ˈvɔlfrɑm)
wolframite ˈwulfrəmˌaɪt
Wollaston ˈwuləstn̩
Wollstonecraft ˈwulstənˌkræft; E+-ˌkraft,
-ˌkrɑft
Wolseley ˈwulzlɪ
Wolsey ˈwulzɪ
wolverine, -ene ˌwulvəˈrin
wolves wulvz
woman ˈwumən, ˈwumən |women ˈwɪmɪn, -ən
—*The prons.* ˈwomən *& ˈwʌmən are re-*
ported as occas., esp. in the S.
womanhood ˈwumənˌhud, ˈwumən-
womankind ˈwumənˈkaɪnd, ˈwum-, -ˌkaɪnd
womanlike ˈwumənˌlaɪk, ˈwum- |-manly
-mənlɪ
womb wum |wombed wumd
wombat ˈwɑmbæt, ˈwɒmbæt
women ˈwɪmɪn, -ən |-folk -ˌfok
won *past & pptc of* win wʌn
won *Korean coin* wɑn, wɒn
wonder ˈwʌndɚ; ES -də(r; |-ed -d |-ing -drɪŋ,
-dərɪŋ |-ful -fəl |-fully -fəlɪ, -flɪ
wonderland, W- ˈwʌndɚˌlænd; ES ˈwʌndə-
wonder-stricken ˈwʌndɚˌstrɪkən; ES ˈwʌndə-
wonder-struck ˈwʌndɚˌstrʌk; ES ˈwʌndə-
wonderwork ˈwʌndɚˌwɝk; ES ˈwʌndəˌwɝk,
-ˌwɝk
wondrous ˈwʌndrəs
wont *'custom,'* *'accustomed'* wʌnt, wont, *less*
freq. wɔnt, want, wɒnt |-ed -ɪd—*To many*
wont *is not vernacular, & hence is subject to*
spelling pron., & perhaps to the influence of
won't.

Key: *See in full* §§3–47. bee bi |pity ˈpɪtɪ (§6) |rate ret |yet jɛt |sang sæŋ |angry ˈæŋ·grɪ
|bath bæθ; E baθ (§10) |ah ɑ |far fɑr |watch wɑtʃ, wɒtʃ (§12) |jaw dʒɔ |gorge gɔrdʒ |go go

won't wont, wʌnt, *much less freq.* wunt
woo wu |wooed wud
wood wud |-bin -ˌbɪn |-bine -ˌbaɪn |-chuck
-ˌtʃʌk |-cock -ˌkɑk; ES+-ˌkɒk
Woodbury ˈwudˌbɛrɪ, -bərɪ
woodcraft ˈwudˌkræft; E+-ˌkrɑft, -ˌkrɑft
woodcut ˈwudˌkʌt
wooden ˈwudn̩ |-head -ˌhɛd |-ness ˈwudn̩nɪs
woodenheaded ˈwudn̩ˈhɛdɪd (ˈwoodenˌheaded
ˈboy)
woodenware ˈwudn̩ˌwɛr, -ˌwær; E -ˌwɛə(r, ES
-ˌwæə(r
woodland *n* ˈwudˌlænd, -lənd; *adj* ˈwudlənd
woodlander ˈwudləndɚ; ES -ləndə(r
woodman, W- ˈwudmən |-men -mən
wood-note ˈwudˌnot
woodpecker ˈwudˌpɛkɚ; ES -ˌpɛkə(r
Woodrow ˈwudro
Woodruff ˈwudrəf, ˈwudruf
woodsman ˈwudzmən |-men -mən
Woodstock ˈwudˌstɑk; ES+-ˌstɒk
woodsy ˈwudzɪ
woodward *'forester'* ˈwudˌwɔrd, -wɚd; ES
-ˌwɔəd, -wəd
woodward *adv* ˈwudwɚd; ES ˈwudwəd; |-s -z
Woodward ˈwudwɚd, ˈwudɚd; ES ˈwudwəd,
ˈwudəd
wood-wind ˈwudˌwɪnd
woodwork ˈwudˌwɚk; ES ˈwudˌwɜk, -ˌwɝk;
|-er -ɚ; ES -ə(r
woody ˈwudɪ
wooer ˈwuɚ; ES ˈwu·ə(r
woof *n* wuf; *intj* ˈwuf
wool wul |woolen ˈwulɪn, -ən |woolly ˈwulɪ
Woolf wulf
woolfell ˈwulˌfɛl
woolgathering ˈwulˌgæðərɪŋ, -ˌgæðərɪŋ
woolgrower ˈwulˌgroɚ; ES -ˌgro·ə(r
woolpack ˈwulˌpæk
woolsack, W- ˈwulˌsæk
woolsey, W- ˈwulzɪ
Woolwich *Engd* ˈwulɪdʒ, ˈwulɪtʃ |-'s -ɪz
Wooster ˈwustɚ; ES ˈwustə(r
Wootton, Wooton, Wotton ˈwutn̩
Worcester ˈwustɚ; ES ˈwustə(r; |-shire -ˌʃɪr,
-ʃɚ; ES -ˌʃɪə(r, -ʃə(r; *loc.*+ˈustə(r, ˈustɚ—
The first r *in* Worcester *was lost by the 16c.*
word wɚd; ES wɜd, wɝd; |-ed -ɪd |-book
-ˌbuk

Wordsworth ˈwɚdzwɚθ; ES ˈwɜdzwəθ,
ˈwɝdzwɚθ
Wordsworthian wɚdzˈwɚθɪən, -ðɪən, -jən;
ES wɜdzˈwɚ-, wɝdzˈwɝ-
wore wor, wɔr; ES woə(r, E+wɔə(r
work wɚk; ES wɜk, wɝk; |-ed -t *or* wrought
rɔt
workaday ˈwɚkəˌde; ES ˈwɜk-, ˈwɝk-
workbag ˈwɚkˌbæg; ES ˈwɜk-, ˈwɝk-
workbench ˈwɚkˌbɛntʃ; ES ˈwɜk-, ˈwɝk-;
|-es -ɪz
workday ˈwɚkˌde; ES ˈwɜk-, ˈwɝk-
workhouse ˈwɚkˌhaus; ES ˈwɜk-, ˈwɝk-;
|-ses -zɪz
workingman ˈwɚkɪŋˌmæn; ES ˈwɜk-, ˈwɝk-;
|-men -ˌmɛn
workman ˈwɚkmən; ES ˈwɜk-, ˈwɝk-; |-men
-mən |-manlike -mənˌlaɪk |-manship -mən-
ˌʃɪp
workout ˈwɚkˌaut; ES ˈwɜk-, ˈwɝk-
workpeople ˈwɚkˌpipl̩; ES ˈwɜk-, ˈwɝk-
workshop ˈwɚkˌʃɑp; ES ˈwɜk-, ˈwɝk-, -ˌʃɒp
worktable ˈwɚkˌtebl̩; ES ˈwɜk-, ˈwɝk-
workwoman ˈwɚkˌwumən, -ˌwum-; ES ˈwɜk-,
ˈwɝk-; |-women -ˌwɪmɪn, -ən
world wɚld; ES wɜld, wɝld; |-ling -lɪŋ
worldly-wise ˈwɚldlɪˈwaɪz; ES ˈwɜld-, ˈwɝld-
world-wide ˈwɚldˈwaɪd; ES ˈwɜld-, ˈwɝld-
worm wɚm; ES wɜm, wɝm
worm-eaten ˈwɚmˌitn̩; ES ˈwɜm-, ˈwɝm-
wormhole ˈwɚmˌhol; ES ˈwɜm-, ˈwɝm-;
|-c̣ -d
Worms wɚmz; ES wɜmz, wɝmz; (*Ger* vɔrms)
wormseed ˈwɚmˌsid; ES ˈwɜm-, ˈwɝm-
wormwood ˈwɚmˌwud; ES ˈwɜm-, ˈwɝm-
worn worn, wɔrn; ES woən, E+wɔən; |-ness
-nɪs
worn-out ˈwornˈaut, ˈwɔrn-; ES ˈwoən-,
E+ˈwɔən-; (ˈworn-ˌout ˈshoes)
worry ˈwɚɪ; ES ˈwɜrɪ, ˈwʌrɪ, ˈwɝɪ; |-ied -d
worse wɚs; ES wɜs, wɝs; |-en -n̩ |-ened -n̩d
|-ening -n̩ɪŋ, -nɪŋ
worship ˈwɚʃəp; ES ˈwɜʃəp, ˈwɝʃ-; |-ped -t
worst wɚst; ES wɜst, wɝst; |-ed -ɪd
Worstead ˈwustɪd
worsted *yarn* ˈwustɪd
worsted *'beaten'* ˈwɚstɪd; ES ˈwɜs-, ˈwɝs-
wort wɚt; ES wɜt, wɝt
worth wɚθ; ES wɜθ, wɝθ; |-thy -ðɪ

|full ful |tooth tuθ |further ˈfɚðɚ; ES ˈfɝðə |custom ˈkʌstəm |while hwaɪl |how hau |toy tɔɪ
|using ˈjuzɪŋ |fuse fjuz, fɪuz |dish dɪʃ |vision ˈvɪʒən |Eden ˈidn̩ |cradle ˈkredl̩ |keep 'em ˈkipm̩

worth-while ˈwɝθˈhwaɪl; ES ˈwɝθ-, ˈwɝθ-
wot *pres of v* wit wɑt, wɒt
Wotton ˈwʊtn̩, ˈwɑt-, ˈwɒt-, *cf* Wootton
would *stressed* ˈwʊd, ˌwʊd; *unstr.* wəd, əd, d
wouldest ˈwʊdɪst
wouldn't ˈwʊdn̩t, *before some conss.*+ˈwʊdn̩
  (ˈwʊdn̩ du)—*The pron.* ˈwʊdənt *is substandard.*
wouldst, -d'st *stressed* ˈwʊdst, ˌwʊdst; *unstr.*
  wədst, ədst, dst
wound '*hurt*' wund, *less freq.* waʊnd |-ed -ɪd
wound *past of* wind waʊnd
wove wov |woven ˈwovən
wow waʊ
wrack ræk |wracked rækt
wraith reθ |-ths -θs
Wrangel *Russia* ˈræŋgl̩ |-ell *Alas* ˈræŋgl̩
wrangle ˈræŋgl̩ |-d -d |-ling ˈræŋglɪŋ, -glɪŋ
wrangler '*who wrangles*' ˈræŋglɚ, -glɚ; ES
  -ə(r
wrangler '*honors man*' ˈræŋglɚ; ES ˈræŋglə(r
wrastle ˈræsl̩ |-d -d |-ling ˈræslɪŋ, ˈræslɪŋ—
  ˈræsl̩ *is not a mispronunciation of* wrestle, *but
  represents the original form* wrastle, *found in
  Chauc., Shak., 1611 Bible, and still current.*
wrath ræθ; E+rɑθ, rɑθ; |-ful -fəl |-fully -fəlɪ
  (*Brit* rɔθ, rɒθ)
wreak rik |wreaked rikt
wreath *n* riθ |wreaths riðz, -θs |-ed -t
wreathe *v* rið |-s -z |-d -d
Wreay *Engd* re, *loc.* rɪə
wreck rɛk |-ed -t |-age -ɪdʒ |-ages -ɪˈʒɪz
wren, W- rɛn
wrench rɛntʃ |wrenches ˈrɛntʃɪz |-ed -t
Wrentham ˈrɛnθəm, ˈrɛntθəm
wrest rɛst |wrested ˈrɛstɪd
wrestle ˈrɛsl̩ |-d -d |-ling ˈrɛslɪŋ, ˈrɛslɪŋ—*cf*
  wrastle
wretch rɛtʃ |wretches ˈrɛtʃɪz
wretched ˈrɛtʃɪd
wriggle ˈrɪgl̩ |-d -d |-ling ˈrɪglɪŋ, ˈrɪglɪŋ
wriggler ˈrɪglɚ; ES ˈrɪglə(r

wright, W- raɪt
wring rɪŋ |wrung rʌŋ
wrinkle ˈrɪŋkl̩ |-d -d |-ling ˈrɪŋklɪŋ, -klɪŋ
wrinkleless ˈrɪŋkl̩lɪs
wrinkly ˈrɪŋklɪ
Wriothesley ˈraɪslɪ, ˈrɒtslɪ, *cf* Wrottesley
wrist rɪst |wristed ˈrɪstɪd
wristband ˈrɪstˌbænd, ˈrɪzbənd
wristlet ˈrɪstlɪt, ˈrɪslɪt
wristlock ˈrɪstˌlɑk; ES+-ˌlɒk
writ rɪt
write raɪt |wrote rot, *arch.* writ rɪt |written
  ˈrɪtn̩, *arch.* writ rɪt, wrote rot
write-up ˈraɪtˌʌp
writhe raɪð |writhed raɪðd
written *pptc of* write ˈrɪtn̩
wrong rɔŋ, rɒŋ; S+rɑŋ; |-doer -ˈduɚ; ES,
  -ˈduə(r; *acct*+ˈwrongˈdoer, ˈwrongˌdoer
wrongheaded ˈrɔŋˈhɛdɪd, ˈrɒŋ-, S+ˈrɑŋ-
wrote rot
wroth rɔθ, rɒθ
Wrottesley ˈratslɪ, ˈrɒtslɪ
wrought rɔt
wrought-iron *adj* ˈrɔtˈaɪɚn; ES -ˈaɪ·ən
wrought-up ˈrɔtˈʌp (ˈwrought-ˌup ˈtemper)
wrung rʌŋ
wry raɪ |-neck ˈraɪˌnɛk
Wulfila ˈwʊlfɪlə=Ulfilas
Wulfstan ˈwʊlfstən, -stæn, -stɑn
Wurlitzer ˈwɝlɪtsɚ; ES ˈwɝlɪtsə(r, ˈwɝ-
Würtemberg ˈwɝtəmˌbɝg; ES ˈwɝtəmˌbɝg,
  ˈwɝtəmˌbɝg; (*Ger* ˈvyrtəmˌbɛrk)
Wuthering ˈwʌðərɪŋ
Wyandot, -tte ˈwaɪənˌdɑt; ES+-ˌdɒt
Wyatt ˈwaɪət
Wycherley ˈwɪtʃɚlɪ; ES ˈwɪtʃəlɪ
Wycliffe, -clif, Wiclif ˈwɪklɪf |-ite -ˌaɪt
Wycombe ˈwɪkəm
wye, W- waɪ
Wykeham ˈwɪkəm
Wyoming waɪˈomɪŋ, ˈwaɪəmɪŋ
wyvern ˈwaɪvɚn; ES ˈwaɪvən

X

X, x *letter* ɛks |*pl* X's, Xs, *poss* X's ˈɛksɪz
Xanadu ˈzænəˌdu

Xanthippe, -ti- zænˈtɪpɪ
xanthous ˈzænθəs

Key: *See in full* §§3–47. bee bi |pity ˈpɪtɪ (§6) |rate ret |yet jɛt |sang sæŋ |angry ˈæŋ·grɪ
|bath bæθ; E baθ (§10) |ah ɑ |far fɑr |watch wɑtʃ, wɒtʃ (§12) |jaw dʒɔ |gorge gɔrdʒ |go go

Xavier ˈzævɪɚ, ˈzev-, -jɚ; ES -vɪ·ə(r, -vjə(r
xebec ˈzibɛk
Xenia *Ohio* ˈzinjə, ˈzinɪə
Xenocrates zəˈnɑkrəˌtiz; ES+-ˈnɒk-; |-'s -ɪz
xenomania ˌzɛnəˈmenɪə, -njə
Xenophanes zəˈnɑfəˌniz; ES+-ˈnɒf-; |-'s -ɪz
xenophobia ˌzɛnəˈfobɪə, -bjə
Xenophon ˈzɛnəfən

Xerxes ˈzɝˑksiz, ˈzɝˑkziz; ES ˈzɜk-, ˈzɝˑk-·
|Xerxes' -ksiz, -kziz
xi saɪ, zaɪ (*Gk* ksi)
Xmas ˈkrɪsməs |-es -ɪz
XP ˈkaɪˈro
X-ray ˈɛksˈre |-ed -d (ˈX-ˌray ˈpicture)
xylograph ˈzaɪləˌgræf; E+-ˌgraf, -ˌgraf
xylophone ˈzaɪləˌfon, ˈzɪl-

Y

Y, y *letter* waɪ |*pl* Y's, Ys, *poss* Y's waɪz
-y *ending, pron.* -ɪ *or* -i, *of ns, adjs, & advs*
(glory, glories, money, icy, fully ˈfʊlɪ, -i).
The sound varies in America from -ɪ *toward*
-i, *though the* -i *is seldom as high* (*close*) *as*
in the pl of basis (bases ˈbesiz—*cf* Macy's
ˈmesɪz, -iz) *or of* stasis (stases ˈstesiz—
cf Stacy's). *The* -i *variant is commonest in*
the N & E, but rare in the S. In America
as a whole -ɪ *appears to prevail. As it is not*
feasible in the vocabulary to give both variants
-ɪ & -i *for the numerous words in* -y, *it must*
be understood that, though only -ɪ *is given,*
very many speakers use the higher vowel
approaching -i. *The ending* -y *is often*
omitted from the vocab.
yacht jɑt; ES+jɒt; |-ed -ɪd |-sman -smən
|-smen -smən
Yadkin ˈjædkɪn
Yahoo, y- ˈjɑhu, ˈjehu, jəˈhu
Yahweh, -we ˈjɑwɛ |-wism -wɪzəm |-wist
-wɪst |-wistic jɑˈwɪstɪk
yak jæk
Yakima ˈjækəmə
Yakut jɑˈkʊt
Yakutsk jɑˈkʊtsk, jə-
Yale jel
yam jæm
yammer ˈjæmɚ; ES -mə(r; |-ed -d |-ing
ˈjæmərɪŋ, ˈjæmrɪŋ
Yancey ˈjænsɪ
Yangtze-Kiang ˈjæŋtsɪˈkjæŋ
yank jæŋk |-ed -t
Yank jæŋk |Yankee ˈjæŋkɪ |-eeism -ɪˌɪzəm
Yankee-Doodle ˈjæŋkɪˈdudl̩
yap jæp |yapped jæpt

Yap jɑp |-man -mən |-men -mən
Yaqui ˈjɑki
yard jɑrd; ES jɑːd, E+jaːd; |-ed -ɪd
yardarm ˈjɑrdˌɑrm; ES ˈjɑːdˌɑːm, E+ˈjaːd·
ˌaːm
yardstick ˈjɑrdˌstɪk; ES ˈjɑːd-, E+ˈjaːd-
yare jɛr, jær; E jɛə(r, ES jæə(r
Yarmouth ˈjɑrməθ; ES ˈjɑːməθ, E+ˈjaːməθ
yarn jɑrn; ES jɑːn, E+jaːn; |-ed -d
yarovize ˈjɑrəˌvaɪz |-s -ɪz |-d -d
yarrow, Y- ˈjæro, ˈjærə
yataghan, -gan ˈjætəˌgæn, -gən
yaw jɔ |yawed jɔd
yawl jɔl
yawn jɔn |yawned jɔnd
yawp, yaup jɔp, jɒp, jɑp |-ed -t
Yazoo ˈjæzu
y-clad ɪˈklæd
y-clept ɪˈklɛpt
ye *pro, stressed* ˈji; *unstr.* jɪ
ye *arch. spelling for the def. art.* the ðə, ðɪ, *in*
which y is not the same letter as in you, *but*
is the old th-*letter* þ. *Ignorance has well-nigh*
established the ridiculous pron. ji.
yea je
yean jin |yeaned jind |-ling ˈjinlɪŋ
year jɪr; ES jɪə(r, S+jɛə(r; |-book -ˌbʊk
yearling ˈjɪrlɪŋ; ES ˈjɪə-, S+ˈjɛə-;—ˈjɝˑlɪŋ,
ˈjɝ-, -lɪ *are old-fashioned Am prons. The*
corresponding ˈjɜlɪŋ, -lɪ *have recently come*
into standard Brit use.
yearlong ˈjɪrˈlɔŋ, -ˈlɒŋ; ES ˈjɪə-, S+ˈjɛə-,
-ˈlɒŋ
yearly ˈjɪrlɪ; ES ˈjɪəlɪ, S+ˈjɛə-
yearn jɝn; ES jɜn, jɝn; |-ed -d
yeast jist |-y ˈjistɪ, *in Shak.* ˈjɛstɪ

|full fʊl |tooth tuθ |further ˈfɝˑðɚ; ES ˈfɝˑðə |custom ˈkʌstəm |while hwaɪl |how haʊ |toy tɔɪ
|using ˈjuzɪŋ |fuse fjuz, fɪuz |dish dɪʃ |vision ˈvɪʒən |Eden ˈidn̩ |cradle ˈkredl̩ |keep 'em ˈkipm̩

Yeats jets |Yeats's 'jetsız
yegg jɛg
yelk jɛlk *doublet of* yolk |yelked jɛlkt
yell jɛl |yelled jɛld
yellow 'jɛlo, -ə |-ed -d |-ing 'jɛləwıŋ
yellowhammer 'jɛlo͵hæmɚ, 'jɛlə-; ES -͵hæmə(r
Yellowstone 'jɛlo͵ston, 'jɛlə-
yellowthroat 'jɛlo͵θrot, 'jɛlə-
yellowwood 'jɛlo͵wʊd, 'jɛlə-
yelp jɛlp |yelped jɛlpt
Yemen 'jɛmən, 'je- |-ite -͵aıt
yen jɛn
yeoman 'jomən |-men -mən |-ry -rı
Yeovil 'jovıl
Yerkes 'jɝkiz; ES 'jɝkiz, 'jɝkiz; |-es' -iz
yes jɛs |yeses 'jɛsız |yesed jɛst
yester 'jɛstɚ; ES 'jɛstə(r
yesterday 'jɛstɚdı, -͵de; ES 'jɛstə-
yesternight 'jɛstɚ'naıt; ES 'jɛstə-
yestreen jɛs'trin
yesty *'yeasty'* 'jɛstı
yet jɛt
yew ju, jıu—*Many speakers distinguish* yew *from* you.
Yewdale 'ju͵del, 'judḷ, *cf* Udall
Yggdrasill 'ıgdrə͵sıl
Yiddish 'jıdıʃ
yield jild |yielded 'jildıd
yip jıp |yipped jıpt
Ymir 'imır, 'ımır; ES -mıə(r; |Ymer -mɚ; ES -mə(r
yodel 'jodḷ |-ed -d |-ing 'jodlıŋ, 'jodḷıŋ
yoga 'jogə
yogi 'jogi |yogin 'jogın
yoick jɔık |-ed -t |yoicks *intj* jɔıks
yoke jok |yoked jokt |-fellow -͵fɛlo, -ə
yokel 'jokḷ
Yokohama ͵jokə'hamə
yolk jok, jolk |-ed -t; |*N Engd*+jɔ̃k (*§46*)
Yom Kippur 'jom'kıpɚ, -ʊr; ES -ə(r, -ʊə(r
yon jan, jɒn |-d -d |-der -dɚ; ES -də(r
Yonge jʌŋ
Yonkers 'jaŋkɚz, 'jɒŋ-; ES -kəz |-'s -ız
yore jor, jɔr; ES joə(r, E+jɔə(r
Yorick 'jorık, 'jarık, 'jɒrık
York, -ke jɔrk; ES jɔək; |Yorkist -ıst
Yorks *'Yorkshire'* jɔrks; ES jɔəks
Yorkshire 'jɔrkʃır, -ʃɚ; ES 'jɔəkʃıə(r, -ʃə(r

York State 'jɔrk͵stet; ES 'jɔək-
Yorktown 'jɔrk͵taun; ES 'jɔək-
Yosemite jo'sɛmətı
you *stressed* 'ju, ͵ju; *unstr.* jʊ, jə; *combined with final* -t -'tʃu, -tʃʊ, -tʃə (don't'ʃu? 'mɛtʃʊ); *or with final* -d -'dʒu, -dʒʊ, -dʒə (wʊ'dʒu? 'dıdʒʊ?)
you'd *abbr. spelling of* you had, you would: *stressed* 'jud, ͵jud; *unstr.* jʊd, jəd
Youghiogheny *river* jakə'gɛnı, ͵jɒk-
you'll *abbr. spelling of* you will, *stressed* 'jul, ͵jul; *unstr.* jʊl, jəl
young jʌŋ |-er 'jʌŋgɚ; ES -gə(r; |-est -gıst
youngish 'jʌŋıʃ
youngling 'jʌŋlıŋ
youngster 'jʌŋstɚ, 'jʌŋkstɚ; ES -stə(r
younker 'jʌŋkɚ; ES 'jʌŋkə(r
your *stressed* 'jur, ͵jur; ES 'juə(r, ͵juə(r, 'joə(r, ͵joə(r, E+'jɔə(r, ͵jɔə(r; *unstr.* jʊr, jɚ; ES jʊə(r, joə(r, jə(r, E+jɔə(r
you're *abbr. spelling of* you are, *stressed* 'jur, ͵jur, 'jʊr, ͵jʊr; ES 'juə(r, ͵juə(r, 'jʊə(r, ͵jʊə(r; *unstr.* jʊr, jɚ; ES juə(r, jə(r
yours jurz; ES juəz, joəz, E+jɔəz
yourself jur'sɛlf, jɚ'sɛlf; ES juə'sɛlf, joə'sɛlf, jə'sɛlf, E+jɔə'sɛlf; |-selves -'sɛlvz
youth juθ |-'s -θs |-s -ðz, -θs |-ful -fəl |-fully -fəlı
you've *abbr. of* you have, *stressed* 'juv, ͵juv; *unstr.* jʊv, jəv
yow *doublet of* ewe jo—*see* ewe
yow *intj* jau
yowl jaul |yowled jauld
Ypres 'iprə, 'iprəz (*Fr* ipʁ), *often* 'waıpɚz (ES -pəz), *cf* Yreka
Ypsilanti ͵ıpsə'læntı, -tə
Yreka waı'rikə
Yser 'aızɚ, 'izɚ; ES -zə(r; (*Fr* i'zɛːr)
yttrium 'ıtrıəm
Yucatan ͵jukə'tæn, -'tan ('Yuca͵tan 'gum)
yucca, Y- 'jʌkə
Yugoslav, J- *n* 'jugo͵slav, -͵slæv
Yugoslav, J- *adj* 'jugo'slav, -'slæv ('Yugo-͵slav 'state)
Yugoslavia, J- 'jugo'slavıə, -vjə |-n -n
Yugoslavic, J- ͵jugo'slavık, -'slæv-
Yukon 'jukan, -kɒn
yule, Y- jul, jıul |-tide -͵taıd—*Some speakers distinguish* yule *from* you'll.

Key: *See in full §§3–47.* bee bi |pity 'pıtı (§6) |rate ret |yet jɛt |sang sæŋ |angry 'æŋ·grı |bath bæθ; E baθ (§10) |ah ɑ |far fɑr |watch watʃ, wɒtʃ (§12) |jaw dʒɔ |gorge gɔrdʒ |go go

Yutang juˈtæŋ—*see* Lin Yutang
Yvonne ɪˈvɑn, ɪˈvɒn, *humorous* waɪˈvɑnɪ, *cf*
  Ypres, Yreka, Gnadenhutten

Ywain, -e ɪˈwen (ˈYˌwain & ˈGawain)
ywis *arch. adv* ɪˈwɪs
y-wrought ɪˈrɔt

Z

Z, z *letter* zi, *o.f.* ˈɪzɚd; ES ˈɪzəd; *Brit* zɛd |*pl*
  Z's, Zs, *poss* Z's ziz
Zabulon ˈzæbjələn=Zebulun
Zacchaeus, -cheus zæˈkiəs |-'s -ɪz
Zachariah, -a ˌzækəˈraɪə |-as -əs |-as's -əsɪz
Zachary ˈzækərɪ
Zambezi, -si zæmˈbizɪ
Zanesville ˈzenzvɪl
Zangwill ˈzæŋwɪl
zany ˈzenɪ
Zanzibar ˈzænzəˌbɑr; ES -ˌbɑ:(r, E+-ˌbɑ:(r
Zarathustra ˌzærəˈθustrə
zareba, -reeba zəˈribə
Zdanowicz ˈstænəˌvɪtʃ |-'s -ɪz
zeal, Z- zil
Zealand ˈzilənd
Zeal-of-the-Land Busy ˈziləvðəˌlænd ˈbɪzɪ
zealot ˈzɛlət |-ry -rɪ
zealous ˈzɛləs
Zebedee ˈzɛbəˌdi
zebra ˈzibrə
zebu ˈzibju, ˈzibɪu
Zebulun, -lon ˈzɛbjələn
Zechariah ˌzɛkəˈraɪə
zed zɛd
zee zi
Zeeland ˈzilənd (*Du* ˈze:lɑnt)
Zeitgeist ˈzaɪtˌgaɪst (*Ger* ˈtsaɪtˌgaɪst)
zenana zɛˈnɑnə
Zend zɛnd |Zend-Avesta ˈzɛndəˈvɛstə
zenith ˈzinɪθ |-ths -θs
Zeno *Gk phil.* ˈzino, *It admiral* ˈzeno (*It*
  ˈdzɛ:no)
Zenobia zəˈnobɪə, -bjə
Zephaniah ˌzɛfəˈnaɪə
zephyr ˈzɛfɚ; ES ˈzɛfə(r
Zephyrus ˈzɛfərəs |-'s -ɪz
Zeppelin, z- ˈzɛpəlɪn, ˈzɛplɪn (*Ger* ˌtsɛpəˈli:n)
zero ˈzɪro, ˈziro
Zerubbabel zəˈrʌbəbļ
zest zɛst |-ed -ɪd |-ful -fəl |-fully -fəlɪ

zeta ˈzetə, ˈzitə
zeugma ˈzjugmə, ˈzɪug-, ˈzug-
Zeus zus, zɪus, zjus |-'s -ɪz
zigzag ˈzɪgzæg |zigzagged ˈzɪgzægd
Zimbalist ˈzɪmbļɪst
zinc zɪŋk |zincked, zinced zɪŋkt
zincify ˈzɪŋkəˌfaɪ |-fied -ˌfaɪd
zincite ˈzɪŋkaɪt
zing zɪŋ |zinged zɪŋd
zinnia, Z- ˈzɪnɪə, ˈzɪnjə
Zion ˈzaɪən |-ism -ˌɪzəm |-ist -ɪst |-ite -ˌaɪt
zip zɪp |zipped zɪpt
Zipangu zɪˈpæŋgu
Zipper, z- ˈzɪpɚ; ES ˈzɪpə(r; |-ed -d
zircon ˈzɝkɑn, -kɒn; ES ˈzɝk-, ˈzɝ̈k-
zirconium zɚˈkonɪəm; ES zə-
zither ˈzɪθɚ; ES ˈzɪθə(r; |-ed -d |-n -n
zloty ˈzlɑtɪ, ˈzlɒtɪ |-ys -z
Zoar ˈzor, ˈzɔr, ˈzoɚ, ˈzɔɚ; ES zoə(r, ˈzo·ə(r,
  E+zɔə(r, ˈzɔ·ə(r; |-ite -ˌaɪt
zodiac ˈzodɪˌæk |zodiacal zoˈdaɪəkļ
Zoe ˈzo·ɪ, zo
Zola ˈzolə (*Fr* zɔˈla)
Zollverein *Ger* ˈtsɔlfɛrˌˀaɪn
zombi, -bie ˈzɑmbɪ, ˈzɒmbɪ
zone zon |-nal -ļ |-nally -ļɪ
zoo zu
zoogeographical ˌzoəˌdʒiəˈgræfɪkļ |-ly -ɪ, -ɪklɪ
zoogeography ˌzoəˈdʒiˈɑgrəfɪ, -ˈɒg-
zoological ˌzoəˈlɑdʒɪkļ; ES+-ˈlɒdʒ-; |-ly -ɪ,
  -ɪklɪ
Zoological Gardens *Lond* zuˈlɑdʒɪkļ, ˌzuə-
  ˈlɑdʒ-; ES+-ˈlɒdʒ-
zoology zoˈɑlədʒɪ; ES+-ˈɒl-; |-ist -ɪst
zoom zum |zoomed zumd
zoomorphism ˌzoəˈmɔrfɪzəm; ES -ˈmɔəf-
zoophyte ˈzoəˌfaɪt
zoosperm ˈzoəˌspɝm; ES -ˌspɝm, -ˌspɝ̈m
zoospore ˈzoəˌspor, -ˌspɔr; ES -ˌspoə(r, E+
  -ˌspɔə(r
Zophar ˈzofɚ; ES ˈzofə(r

|full fʊl |tooth tuθ |further ˈfɝðɚ; ES ˈfɝ̈ðə |custom ˈkʌstəm |while hwaɪl |how haʊ |toy tɔɪ
|using ˈjuzɪŋ |fuse fjuz, fɪuz |dish dɪʃ |vision ˈvɪʒən |Eden ˈidn̩ |cradle ˈkredļ |keep 'em ˈkipm̩

Zorn *Sw artist* sɔrn; ES sɔən

Zoroaster ˌzoro'æstɚ; ES -'æstə(r; |-trian -trɪən

Zouave, z- zu'av, zwav

zounds zaʊndz, zaʊnz

Zuider Zee, Zuy- 'zaɪdɚ'ze, -'zi; ES 'zaɪdə-; (*Du* 'zœydər'ze:)

Zulu 'zulu |-land 'zuləˌlænd, 'zulʊ-

Zuñi 'zunjɪ, 'sun- (*Am Sp* 'suɲi)

Zurich 'zʊrɪk, 'zɪʊrɪk, 'zjʊrɪk (*Ger* 'tsy:rɪx)

Zutphen 'zʌtfən, 'zʊt-

Zuyder Zee—*see* Zuider Zee

zwieback 'tswiˌbak, 'swi- (*Ger* 'tsvi:ˌbak)

Zwingli 'zwɪŋglɪ |-an -ən |-anism -ənˌɪzəm |-anist -ənɪst (*Ger* 'tsvɪŋli:)

zymase 'zaɪmes

zyme zaɪm

zymology zaɪ'malədʒɪ; ES+-'mɒl-

zymosis zaɪ'mosɪs

zymotic zaɪ'matɪk; ES+-'mɒt-; |-ally -ˌɪ, -ɪklɪ

zymurgy 'zaɪmɝˈdʒɪ; ES -mɝdʒɪ, -mɝˈdʒɪ

Key: *See in full §§3–47.* bee **bi** |pity **'pɪtɪ** (§6) |rate **ret** |yet **jɛt** |sang **sæŋ** |angry **'æŋ·grɪ** |bath **bæθ**; E **baθ** (§10) |ah **ɑ** |far **fɑr** |watch **watʃ, wɒtʃ** (§12) |jaw **dʒɔ** |gorge **gɔrdʒ** |go **go** |full **fʊl** |tooth **tuθ** |further **'fɝˈðɚ**; ES **'fɝˈðə** |custom **'kʌstəm** |while **hwaɪl** |how **haʊ** |toy **tɔɪ** |using **'juzɪŋ** |fuse **fjuz, fɪuz** |dish **dɪʃ** |vision **'vɪʒən** |Eden **'idn̩** |cradle **'kredl̩** |keep 'em **'kipm̩**